DEUTSCHES
HISTORISCHES
MUSEUM

EUROPE AND THE SEA

Edited by
Dorlis Blume, Christiana Brennecke,
Ursula Breymayer and Thomas Eisentraut
for the Deutsches Historisches Museum

HIRMER

CONTENT

ESSAYS

CATALOGUE

APPENDIX

EUROPE AND THE SEA

It is a comprehensive and important topic: At the special exhibition *Europe and the Sea*, with its focus on cultural history, the German Historical Museum explores the complex relationship between Europeans and the sea as well as the sea's strong influence on Europe. Among the continents, Europe has the highest ratio of coastline to total area, but the sea can often seem quite distant to many Central and Eastern Europeans. At first glance, the role it plays in the daily life of many nations appears important only for those living on the coast. The central theme of the exhibition *Europe and the Sea* is how the sea shaped Europe's development and continues to do so today. The exhibition spans the period from antiquity to the present and examines the importance of the sea as a space in which Europeans ruled and traded, as a connecting element and border, as a resource and an object of longing and imagination. Today, the function of the sea as a connecting element and boundary of the European continent continues to be of great relevance: millions of people are setting off to Europe to escape war, terror and poverty. But other factors are also attracting greater attention than in the past, such as the use and overuse of marine resources, and are also playing an important role for the environment and the global climate.

The idea of narrating the history of Europe from the perspective of sea is not entirely new. In 1949, Fernand Braudel presented *The Mediterranean and the Mediterranean World in the Age of Philip II*, which was based on many years of research that he completed in 1939. In this work he abandons the traditional narrative perspectives linked to national history and opens a new transnational vista. He focuses on the sea, which represents both a border and connecting element between states and countries. From today's perspective, the book is a pioneering achievement because at the time Braudel posed and answered a number of historiographical questions whose full significance for historical research and the work at historical museums is just becoming clear today. If we take the important issues of the present as the starting point of our study of history, we can no longer naively place restrictions on geographical spaces and historical periods. Is it possible to understand German history without considering the history of its neighbouring countries? And without looking at the history of the neighbours' neighbours? Which actors do we focus on if we wish to narrate history without resorting to the mythical idea that nations make their own history? The curators of the exhibition further developed the perspective outlined by Braudel. The sea, which they use as the starting point of their accounts, is no longer confined to the Mediterranean. From the vantage point of contemporary historiography, the history of Europe also includes the trade routes used by European seafarers to transport, among other things, slaves to Central America and cotton to Europe and Asia. But there is another way in which the exhibition pushes the boundaries of traditional modes of narration: namely, by making new connections between phenomena that used to be assigned to either intellectual or natural history. This approach reflects the observation in recent decades that the history of the "natural environment" – including climate history – can no longer be separated from the political and cultural history of humanity.

Professor Jürgen Elvert, holder of the Jean Monnet Chair of European History at the University of Cologne, made the suggestion that we devote a broad cultural-historical exhibition to the topic of the sea at the German Historical Museum. We are indebted to him and his wife, Martina Elvert, for this idea and for their expert input and diverse support. We would also like to thank all of our colleagues who worked with great passion and energy to organise *Europe and the Sea* at the German Historical Museum. Special thanks go to our project manager Dorlis Blume, the curators Ursula Breymayer, Dr. Christiana Brennecke and Thomas Eisentraut, the project assistant Kerstin Kemner and the registrar Nicole Schmidt. The preparations for the exhibition were supported by a committed advisory board consisting of Professor Jürgen Elvert, Professor Günther Heydemann, Professor Sunhild Kleingärtner, Professor Lisa Kosok, Dr. Michael Kraus, Professor Michael North and Professor Rudolf Schieffer. The exhibition was designed by Nadine Rasche and Werner Schulte. With the support of the Department of Education and Communication, they developed a "design for everyone" that allows visitors to actively engage with the content of the exhibition, regardless of their prior knowledge. Continuing a proven tradition, Peter Nils Dorén and Ilka Linz once again designed the catalogue. Finally, we would like to thank the lenders to the exhibition and the authors of this publication.

Professor Raphael Gross
President of the Deutsches Historisches Museum

FOREWORD

The history of the European continent has been shaped in important ways by global ties reaching across the seas. These could be established because there was ample shipbuilding and seafaring expertise in Europe. In the fifteenth century, Europeans had the necessary geographical and navigational knowledge and technical capabilities to launch overseas voyages of discovery. These voyages differed from the earlier, somewhat random contacts between individual Europeans and non-European civilisations in that they were based on a plan, even if this was relatively unsophisticated. The goal was to reap economic benefits, extend individual spheres of political influence and, finally, to continue the fight against Islam. The initial encounters with non-European phenomena were marked by a lack of comprehension on the part of the Europeans. For this reason, the development of modern European civilisation should be seen in part as an attempt to understand the information that was reaching Europe.

Over time, the Europeans covered the globe with a finely meshed network of maritime transportation and trade routes that were used to carry people, goods and information to all parts of the world. Legal and administrative norms, as well as moral values, spread in the same way. Some of these norms and values are considered unacceptable today, while others have retained their validity. All have exerted a lasting influence on the development of the affected regions. This applies not only to the spatial order of the subjugated and newly founded settlements and cities, but also to established legal systems and to the moral standards that drew on Christianity, for better or worse. Europe also changed, as the example of imported crops shows: these crops led not only to new food and consumption habits, but also to permanent changes to the cultural landscape in Europe. Port cities formed the central hubs of this global network and continue to perform this function today.

That this history can be presented to an interested public in the form of an exhibition is the result of many years of interdisciplinary collaboration between representatives of the relevant fields. I would particularly like to thank the German Historical Museum's curators Dorlis Blume, Christiana Brennecke, Ursula Breymayer, Thomas Eisentraut and Kerstin Kemner. More than forty colleagues from Germany and abroad have participated in the project in varying constellations, and I wish to extend a heart-felt thanks to all of you, especially the participants who have supported the project from the start and made a significant contribution to its success. In this connection I would like to mention Markus A. Denzel, Ulrich Fellmeth,

Gerd Hoffmann-Wieck, Michael Jeismann, Jochen Oltmer, Wolfgang Reinhard, Jens Ruppenthal, Christoph Schäfer, Wolfgang Schmale, Hasso Spode, Heinrich Walle, Reinhard Wendt and Michael Zeuske. A personal thanks goes to my wife, Martina Elvert, whose view of the world has expanded mine. It was only logical to conclude that the sea played a particularly important role in this process as a connecting element between Europe and the world.

Professor Jürgen Elvert
Professor of nineteenth and twentieth century history at the University of Cologne, holder of the Jean Monnet Chair of European History

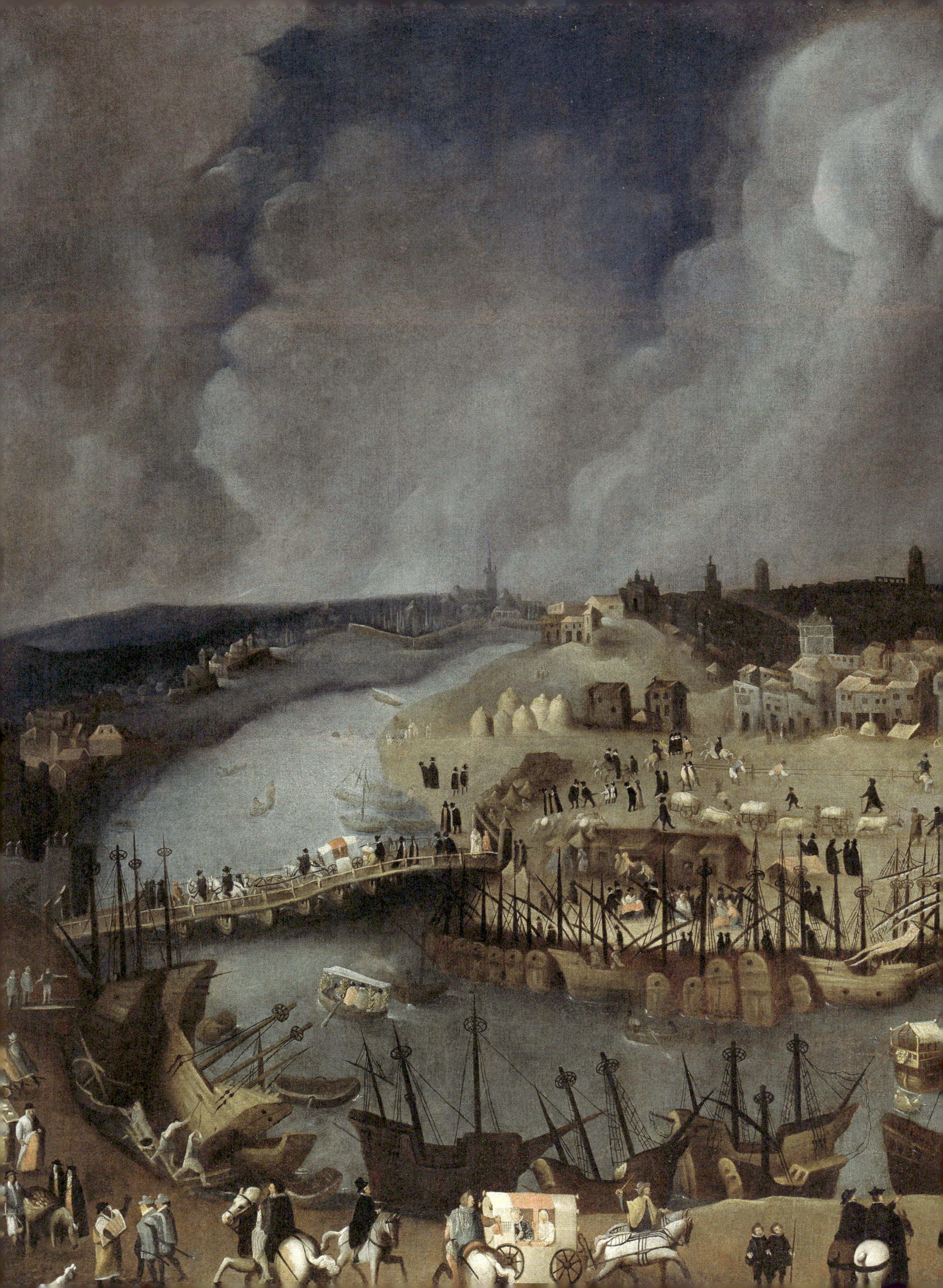

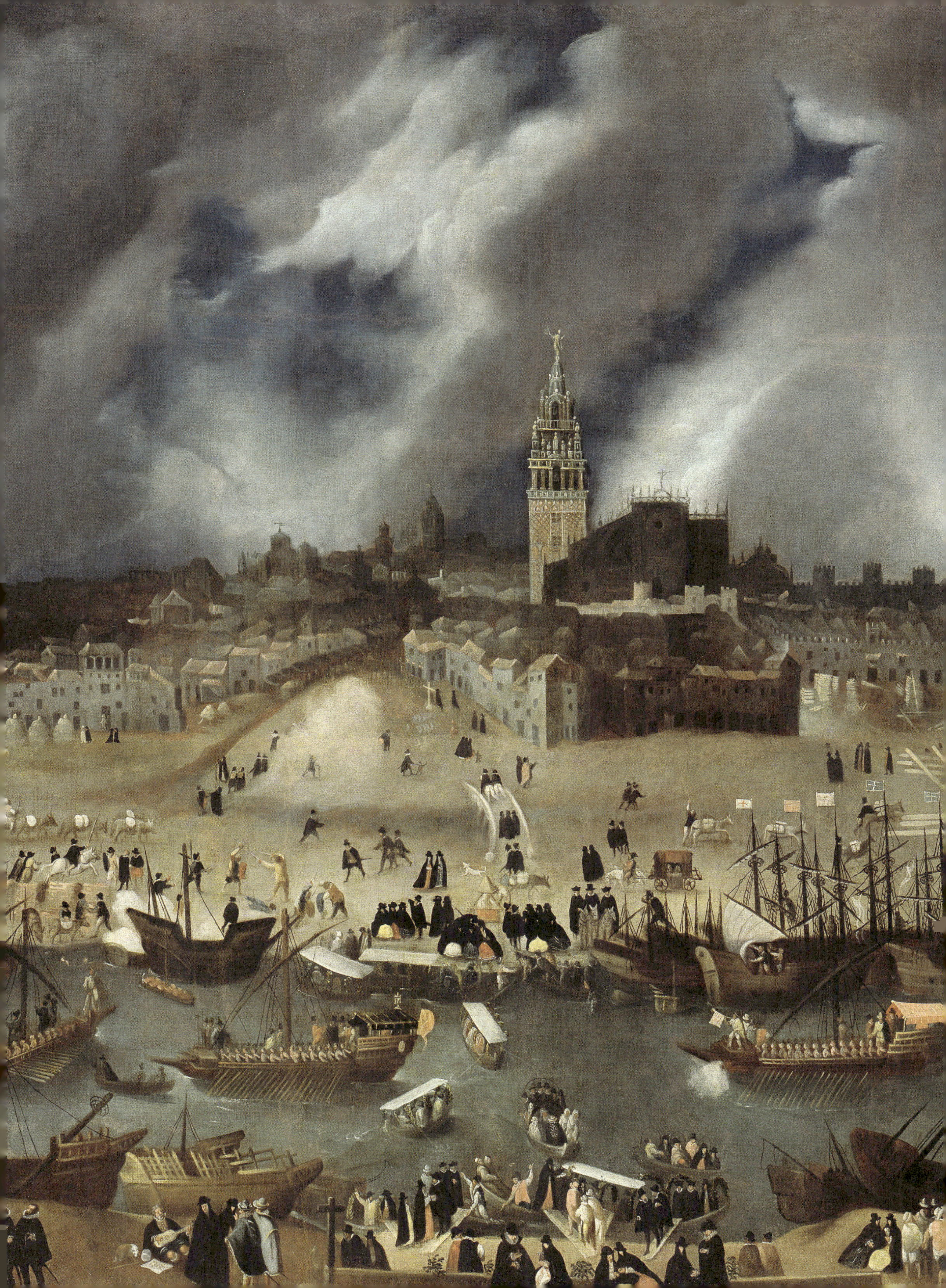

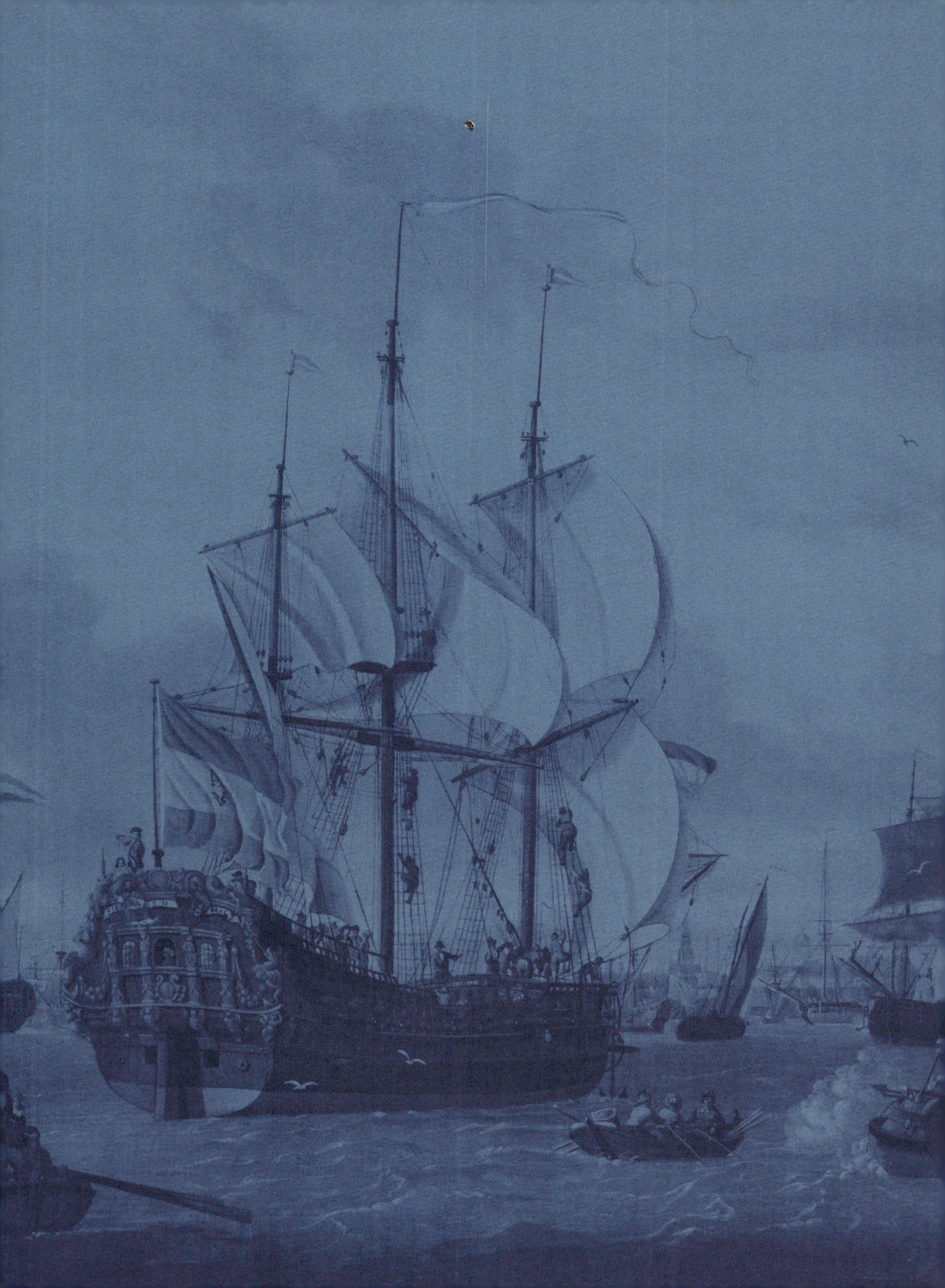

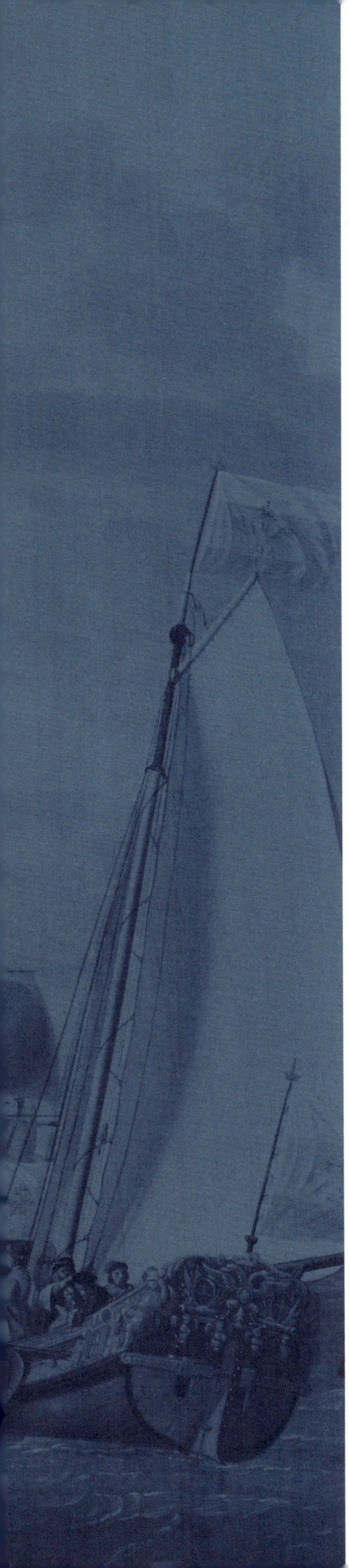

I
TERRITORY AND TRADE

Ernst Baltrusch

ANCIENT HORIZONS

Appropriating the Sea

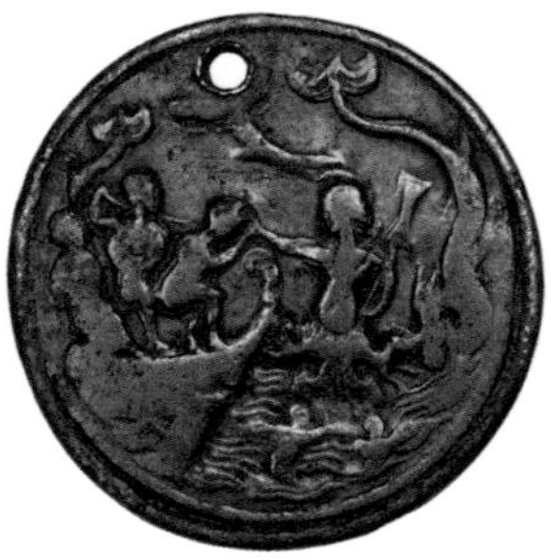

1/4
Odysseus and Scylla,
c. 355–395/423

From myth to logos?

"War, Commerce, and bold Piracy / A triad form, shall ne'er be parted"[1] – Goethe's Mephistopheles was not the first to recognise such a trinity in maritime life. It can also be found in the earliest examples of European literature, the *Iliad* and the *Odyssey* from the eighth century BC. It was linked to knowledge (*Iliad* 2.614) and was thus soon joined by a fourth companion – myth. Myth is the brother of logos, as it were, since in Homer's works both terms have the same basic meaning: "word" or "story". Later myth stood for the fabulous, which concealed the unapproachable, the unpredictable, the incomprehensible and, finally, the terrible. In the fifth century BC, for example, Thucydides wrote that the ancient and the mythical were unverifiable and implausible, because they stood in opposition to the factual, knowledge and logos (Thucydides 1.21.1).

However, the mythical and the real do not have a sequential relationship to the sea – there is no progression from myth to logos. Rather, they exist side by side. In the texts of classical antiquity that address the Mediterranean, the Aegean and the Black Sea, war is unthinkable without ships. This is why the famous Catalogue of Ships in the *Iliad* indicates the exact number of vessels available to the Greeks in the Trojan War (*Iliad* 2.484–762). In Homer's second epic poem, the *Odyssey*, which was written a little bit later and tells of Odysseus' ten-year wanderings, myth and logos are conflated – though at times also antithetical to each other.

Throughout antiquity, an irrational, emotional relationship with the sea was combined with a rational one. This ambivalence – or even dialectic – is characteristic of the ancient world's basic attitude towards the sea. Homer shows that the sea was used for war, commerce and piracy. He has his protagonist, Odysseus, tell a fabricated story about his life after returning home from his ten-year journey. Odysseus explains that he comes from a good family in Crete, but was forced to leave his homeland. He went first to Egypt and then to Phoenicia by sea. In addition, Odysseus speaks boastfully about his pirating (*Odyssey* 14.222–228): "A life of labour on the land would never have suited me, nor would a house, even if it was full of handsome children. I loved war, and the oared ships, shining spears and arrows, fateful things that make others shudder."[2] War, commerce and piracy – in the *Odyssey*, these

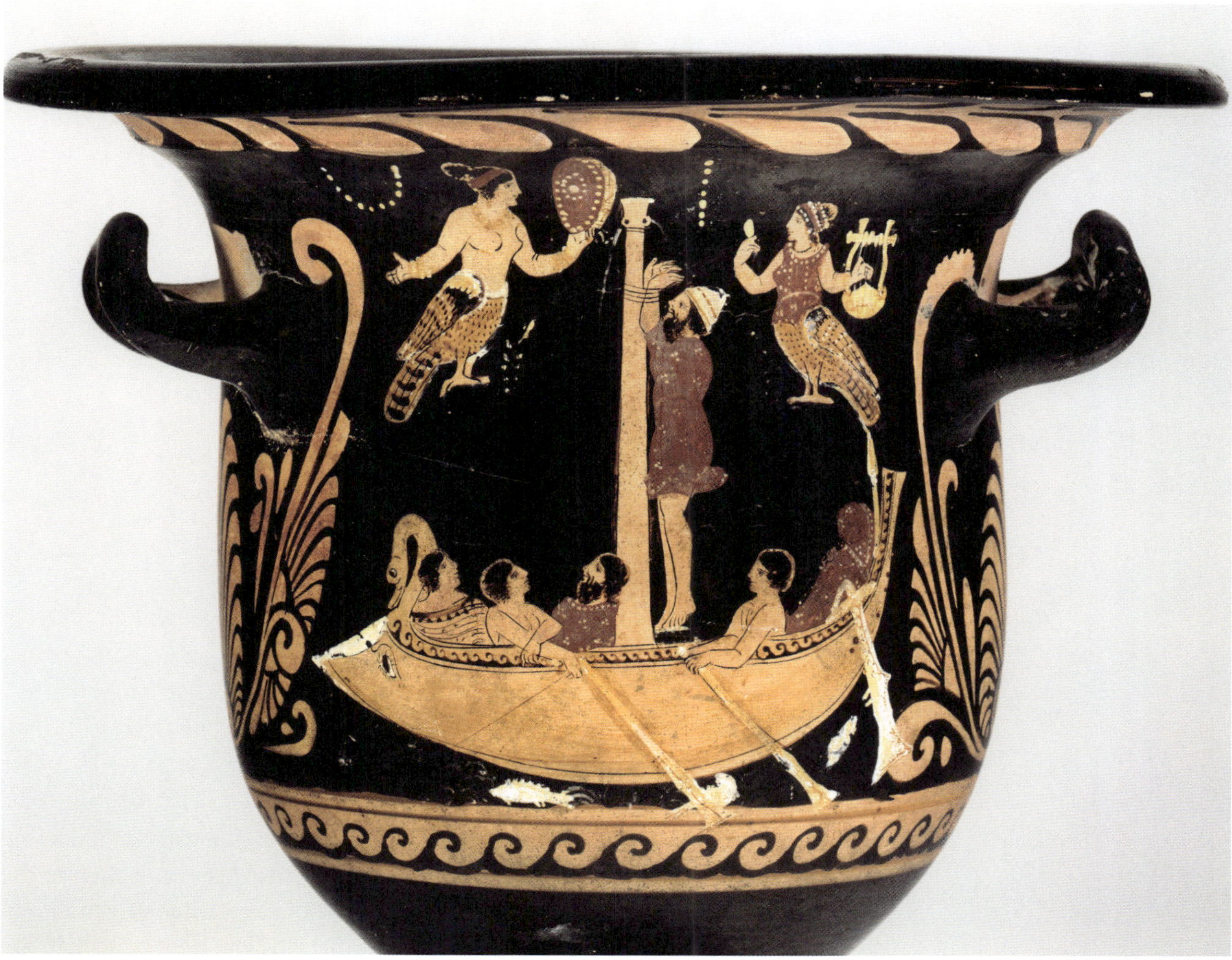

Vase by the painter Python, showing Odysseus and the Sirens, 4th cent. B.C.

are joined by the mysterious, mythical aspect of the sea, by the stories of Aeolus, the unpredictable ruler of the winds, by tales of the man-eating Laestrygonians, the sea monsters Scylla and Charybdis, and the beguiling, horrifying Sirens, in whose presence the winds die down so that these wondrous creatures can enchant seafarers with their songs and lure them to their island (*Odyssey* 12.165–200). These sailors' yarns were well received at a time when Greek colonists were leaving their homeland to explore the seas in search of new places to live. In this period or a little later, humanity gained an initial idea of what the earth actually looked like. In the earliest known descriptions of the world, the three continents are grouped around the Mediterranean: Europe in the north, Asia in the south and east, and Libya/Africa in the south. The Black Sea, the Caspian far to the east and the ocean surrounding the continents represent the earth's watery surface (ill. Map by Hecataeus, ca. 500 BC). Was the size of the oceans known at this time? Modern studies cast doubt on this idea.[3]

The ambivalence of the sea

The sea was a key reference point in the Greco-Roman period, and the most important Greek cities –Athens, Corinth, Carthage and Syracuse, to name the most influen-

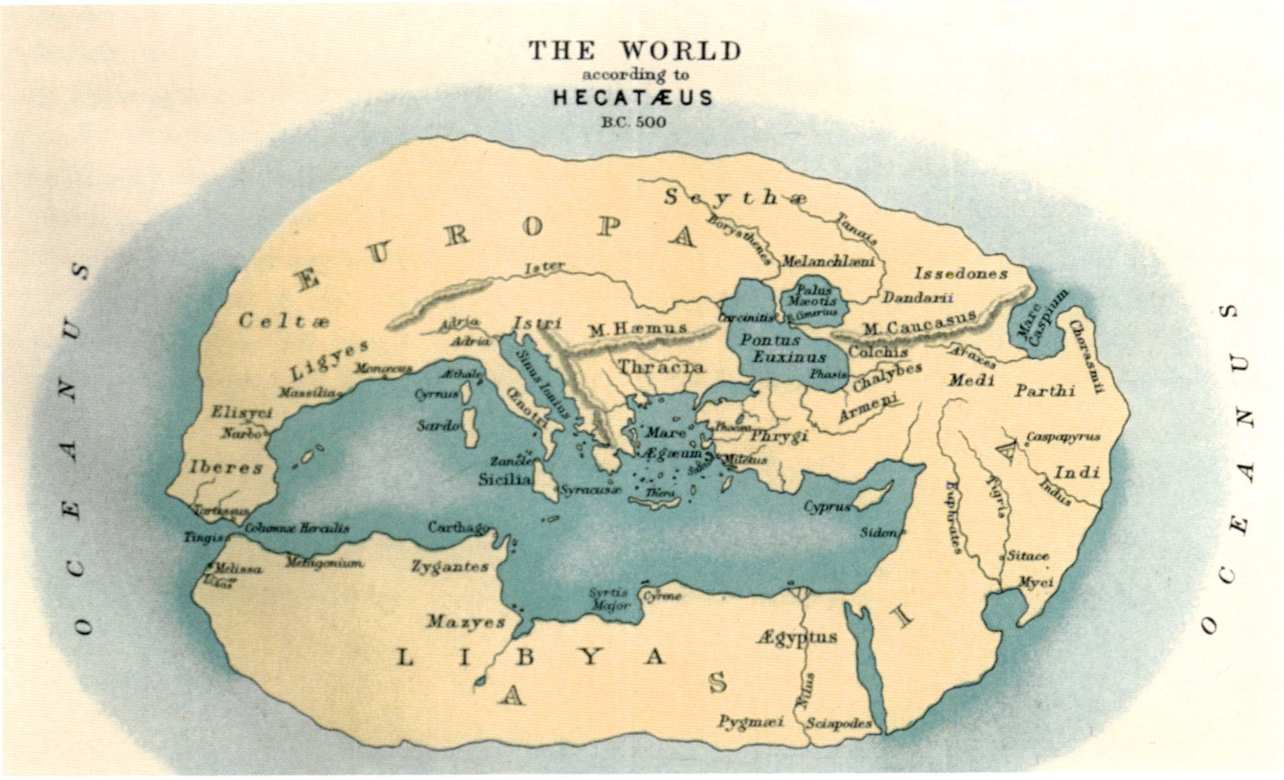

Hecataeus' map of the world, c. 500 B.C.

tial – were positioned around it like "frogs around the pond" (Plato). Nor did Rome lie far from the sea. It has justifiably been claimed that this close connection to the sea distinguished Greco-Roman antiquity from most of the earlier or simultaneously existing advanced civilisations.[4] The land-sea dialectic can even be seen in the political and cultural structures of the ancient Mediterranean world. In the Bible, for example, the maritime Philistines and the seafaring Phoenicians are contrasted by the inland Jews, just as sea-loving Homer (not just in the *Odyssey*) stands in contrast to the agrarian Hesiod, who lived around the same time. Furthermore, the liberal, democratic maritime power of Athens was the antithesis of the isolated, aristocratic land power of Sparta, just as the worldly, sea-trading power of Carthage was antithetical to Rome, which, in the early Republic, was entirely land-based and influenced by farmers. This dialectic extends to domestic politics as well: whether it was a belief in progress or criticism of civilisation, models of the future or tributes to the past, successes or failures, the sea always occupied a central position in ancient thought.

Important critical thinkers of the period, including Thucydides, Sallust and Cicero, associated the sea with negative developments. "Maritime cities are likewise exposed to corrupt influences, and revolutions of manners," observed Cicero. "There was no cause which more deeply undermined Corinth and Carthage, and at last overthrew them both, than this wandering and dispersion of their citizens, whom the passion of commerce and navigation had induced to abandon their agricultural and military interests."[5] Cicero, a conservative, republican-minded Roman, interpreted Greek and Carthaginian naval power from this negative perspective, believing that an orientation towards the sea necessarily bred greed, destabilised the political and social order and thus had an adverse effect on military strength, which in his eyes could be achieved solely through the infantry (hoplites) and the cavalry. Consequently, naval armaments are not included among the respected *cultus armorum*.

Of course, from the eighth century BC on, a coastal location was common for the archaic and classical Greek *polis*. This type of city-state was highly organised and autonomous, waged war and made alliances. But above all, the polis gave birth to politics – i.e. the participation of all citizens in city resolutions. Supplied with grain, wool and meat from the interior, these cities were connected to the outside world via the sea, which facilitated trade and brought economic prosperity. During the Second Greek Colonisation from 750 to 550 BC, settlers from cities such as Corinth, Miletus and Megara established new poleis on distant shores in an undertaking that was clearly maritime. The Mediterranean and the Black Sea were now surrounded by Greek towns. The Greeks became more familiar with the world and its seas, and the Oracle of Delphi became a kind of information centre providing details of sea routes, mooring sites and the dangers of voyages.

What did this dialectical appropriation of the sea mean for the study and knowledge of the sea in antiquity, for attempts to chart and master it? Who "owned" the sea? Was there such a thing as a *dominium maris*, an "aquitorium", as it were,[6] a surveyed and thus indivisible region of the sea comparable to a "territorium" on land? The ancient world at least made the claim that there was a *dominium maris*. Later, during the Age of Discovery in early modern times, political developments shaped the dispute between proponents of a *mare liberum* (Hugo Grotius, *Mare liberum*, 1609) and supporters of a *mare clausum* (John Selden, *Mare clausum*, 1635). The Dutch jurist Hugo Grotius emphasised the natural antagonism between land and sea as a basis for demanding "freedom of the seas". According to Grotius, the sea was indefinite, illimitable, "flowing" in a literal sense and therefore the common property of all. By contrast, the polymath John Selden from the South of England argued that the establishment of a *dominium maris* was in fact lawful. Such debates, as reflective of the times as they were, drew heavily on ancient discourses that had taken a similar direction. In the late fifth century BC, for example, sea-ruling Athens closed off the Aegean to the neighbouring rival city of Megara (Thucydides 1.67.4). Megara's ships were no longer allowed to call at any port on what was now the Athenian Sea or to engage in trade. Later, the Romans claimed the Mediterranean as their own and expressed this claim terminologically with the phrase *mare nostrum* or *mare internum*.

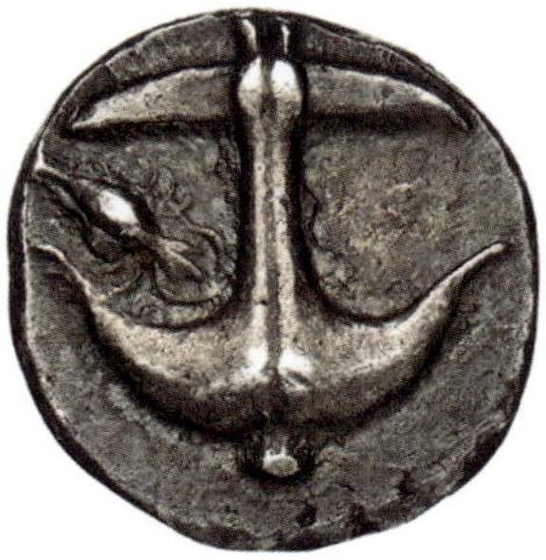

1/6
The Thracian port of Apollonia Pontika, c. 420–390 B.C.

For the ancients, the various meanings and interpretations of the sea were essentially dialectical in nature – the sea was an elementary threat and a controllable space, divisive and connective, a risk and a chance, a prison and an open, free space, and communication-enhancing and communication-inhibiting (due to pirates, foreign powers and other dangers). Depending on their perspective, people either turned away from the sea and surrendered to their fate or turned towards it and ambitiously seized the opportunities.

Command of the sea

As concerns the topic of Europe and the sea, an additional element (and by no means the least important one) is command of the sea. Scholars often use the Greek term "thalassocracy" to describe this phenomenon in all periods of history – though not quite correctly, as a new study has shown. After all, the term (which literally means "rule of the sea") is found in just three ancient texts, two of which are scholia. And the geographer Strabo probably uses it only in a "playful, creative way".[7] Its modern usage is undoubtedly a reinterpretation. Nevertheless, in antiquity, maritime power was apparently a key category in times of war and peace (as regards trade, manufacturing and shipping). This is suggested by the phrases used by the two Athenian statesmen Themistocles (Thucydides 1.93.4) and Pericles. The modern naval strategist Alfred Thayer Mahan (1840–1914) explicitly refers to the term as well. Of course, ancient and modern times differ in that modern command of the sea is oceanic, whereas ancient command of the sea was Mediterranean. However, the Roman Empire, in particular, broke free of these boundaries. In any case, command of the sea was exercised in antiquity by large powers such as Phoenicia, Athens, Carthage and Rome and by numerous smaller ones such as Rhodes, Corinth and Syracuse. The sources frequently link this political phenomenon to great figures – in the case of the Greeks, to both Themistocles, who won the Battle of Salamis against the Persians in 480 BC, and the Athenian politician Pericles; in the case of the Romans, to Pompey the Great, his son, Caesar and Augustus (and, most appropriately, to Agrippa).

Appropriating the sea

But what did people know about the sea in antiquity? In the second century AD, the famous geographer and astronomer Claudius Ptolemy discussed and compared the size of the seas that were known at the time. "Of the named seas that are surrounded by land, the Indian Ocean is the largest, the Mediterranean the second largest, the Hyrcanian or Caspian Sea is the third largest" (*Geography* 7.5.9). By using the term "our sea", Ptolemy expresses political control of the Mediterranean. In ancient literature, the Atlantic is alluded to only as the sea west of Gibraltar, and there was apparently no comprehensive picture of the Indian Ocean either. "The open sea remained foreign to the ancients," writes Michael Rathmann after examining the relevant texts.[8]

Since the sea was not really "owned" in antiquity and an "aquitorium" never became reality in the sense of a territory, what was useful, as always, was spectacles. The Roman Empire's *naumachiae* (literally "battles at sea") in the first century BC were staged battles that were held in part on manmade lakes and involved fleets of different "nationalities" competing against one another. Famous sea battles were also re-enacted. Augustus, for example, ordered a re-enactment of the Battle of Salamis, which had been fought between the Greeks and Persians in 480 BC (Cassius Dio 55.10.6–8). Nero had a wooden amphitheatre built on the Campus Martius, ordered gladiatorial games to be played there and "suddenly" (as the source says) filled the theatre with sea water and sea animals and thus transformed it into a sea. This formed the prelude to a *naumachia* (Cassius Dio 61.9.5; Sueton, *Nero* 12.4). The goal was not to realistically reconstruct a specific battle, but to establish a link to the well-known Greek sea powers long replaced by Rome – to Athens, Syracuse, Corinth and Korkyra, all fine-sounding names that were known as maritime powers from Greek history-writing. Now that Rome ruled the world, this association increased the symbolic value and splendour of the Roman spectacles.

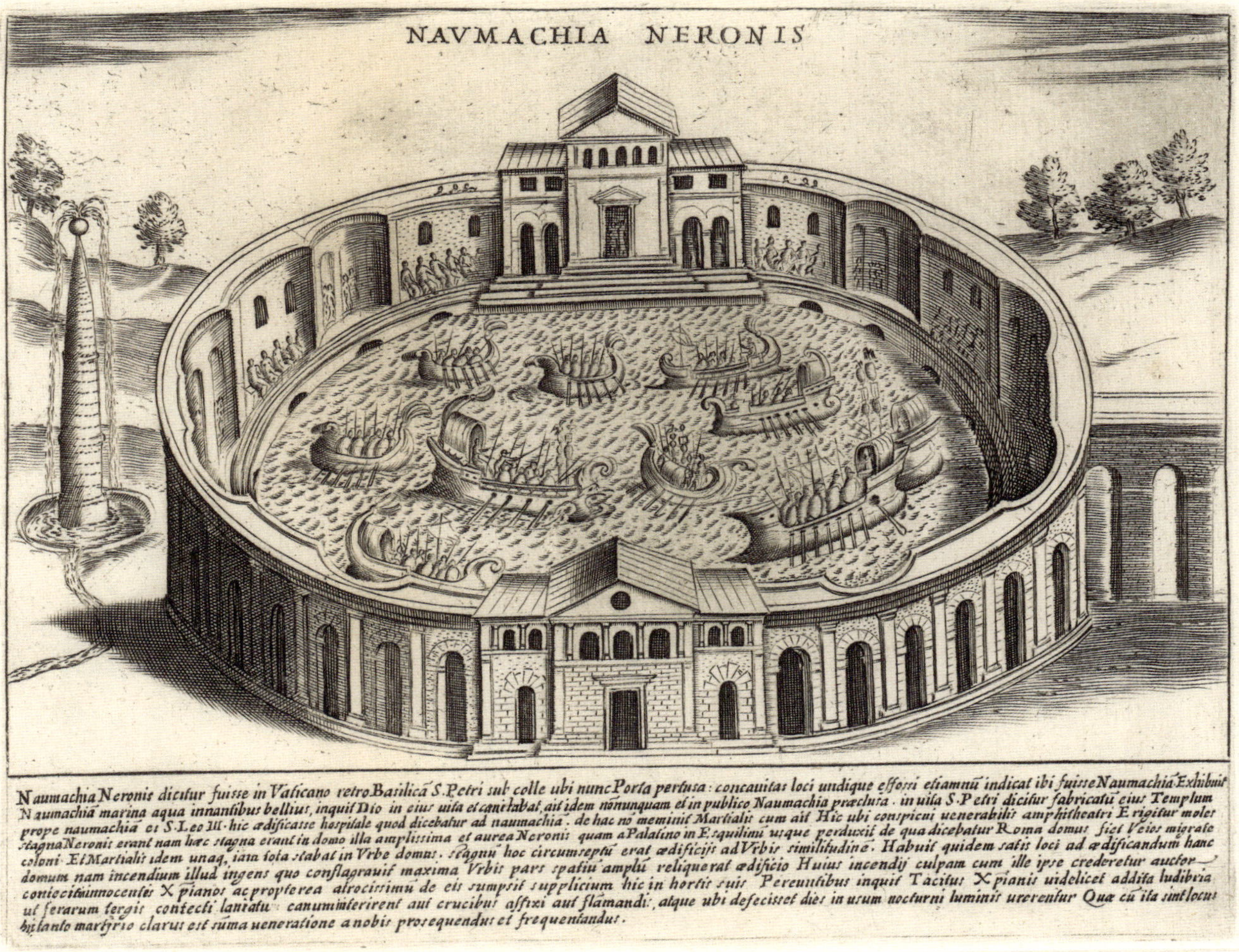

Giacomo Lauro, depiction of a *naumachia*, 1612/1628

Romans also demonstrated their appropriation of the sea through *piscinae*, or fish ponds. This expensive fashion was apparently confined to the period between the first half of the first century BC and the end of the first century AD. It was an age of imperial euphoria: Marius, Sulla, Pompey, Caesar, Antonius, Sextus Pompey and Augustus stood for a Roman elite who laid claim to world rule, whose method was war and whose objective was power and everlasting glory. Just below this upper echelon, nobles competed for fame, prestige, electoral success and close ties to those at the very top. The construction of a *piscina* near their villas was a high-profile performative act that is described in numerous anecdotes in the sources, some expressing admiration, others focusing on compromising situations. For example, Lucullus had labourers arduously drill into a mountain in order to ensure a water supply for his *piscina*, and he put more work into this project than into building his entire country estate. Nevertheless, the *piscinae* symbolised control over both nature and water and earned their builders respect and prestige. For the Flavian poet Statius, fish ponds were the symbol of Roman rule over the world and the subjugation of nature (Statius, *Silvae* 2.2.30–62). Just as Rome civilised the barbarian tribes, so too did the emperor tame and civilise the sea. And just as the generals made war under the auspices of the emperor, so too did the estate owners represent the glory of the empire and thus the emperor. The Romans' self-understanding as masters of the world was reflected in such stagings of naval supremacy. They were part of the way rule was represented.

Sea views

These practices had no impact on the negative view of the sea. Hesiod, the archaic-period poet, farmer and cattle breeder from the region of Boeotia, describes the risks and dangers of the sea and sea-related factors such as trade as more harmful for society than beneficial, a negative perspective that can be found in the portrayal of the Phaeacians in the *Odyssey* (*Odyssey* 8.136–37). Some time later, at the turn of the fourth to the third century BC, comic playwright Menander spoke of three evils in the world: "sea and fire and woman".[9] In offering this bon mot, Menander's intent is undoubtedly comic, for what (male) reader would wish to deny the indispensability and risks associated with these three world-shaping phenomena. The ancients clearly imagined the sea as being inhabited by gods and demons; however, it was precisely Lucian's "sci-fi" novel *Verae historiae* that showed its positive aspects, demonstrating that curiosity prevails over the unknown. On the one hand, the Second Greek Colonisation was marked by uncertainty and fears of what the new settlers would encounter both during their sea voyages and in the new lands, especially because the ancient world typically demonised all that was distant (numerous examples of this can be found in Tacitus' reports on Germania and Britain and in Herodotus' world history). On the other hand, the same colonisation process used the sea as an opportunity to make a new start, as the foundation of life in new settlements, as a theatre of war to assert oneself, and as a means of communication with parent cities and other towns. As mentioned above, this dialectic shaped the political structures of the Mediterranean world both externally and internally. The internal political conflicts in Athens and Rome cannot be explained without considering the influence of the sea. The sea even determined the constitution of Rome, for it was a victory at sea that led to the establishment of the Augustan monarchy – the Principate – and the end of the (inferior) agrarian-based Roman Republic. In ancient times, even the military defined itself via either the infantry or the navy, and such definitions in turn shaped political structures. This is shown quite clearly by Athenian democracy, which would have been unthinkable without a fleet as its foundation.

The Imperium Romanum

During the golden age of democracy in the fifth century BC, the city of Athens and its port of Piraeus were oriented towards the sea because economic power was based on the sea, military power on ships, and political power on the oarsmen. That said, the dialectic of the sea was an all-pervasive phenomenon in this period as well, as the late fifth-century treatise *Constitution of the Athenians* shows. Whether it was immigration, the oarsmen's dominance or democracy – the anonymous author considers all to be negative.

Of course, the Imperium Romanum is an even clearer embodiment of a dialectical relationship with the sea. Not only do Roman authors discuss the admiration for the appropriation of the sea that had its roots in the First Punic War, they also

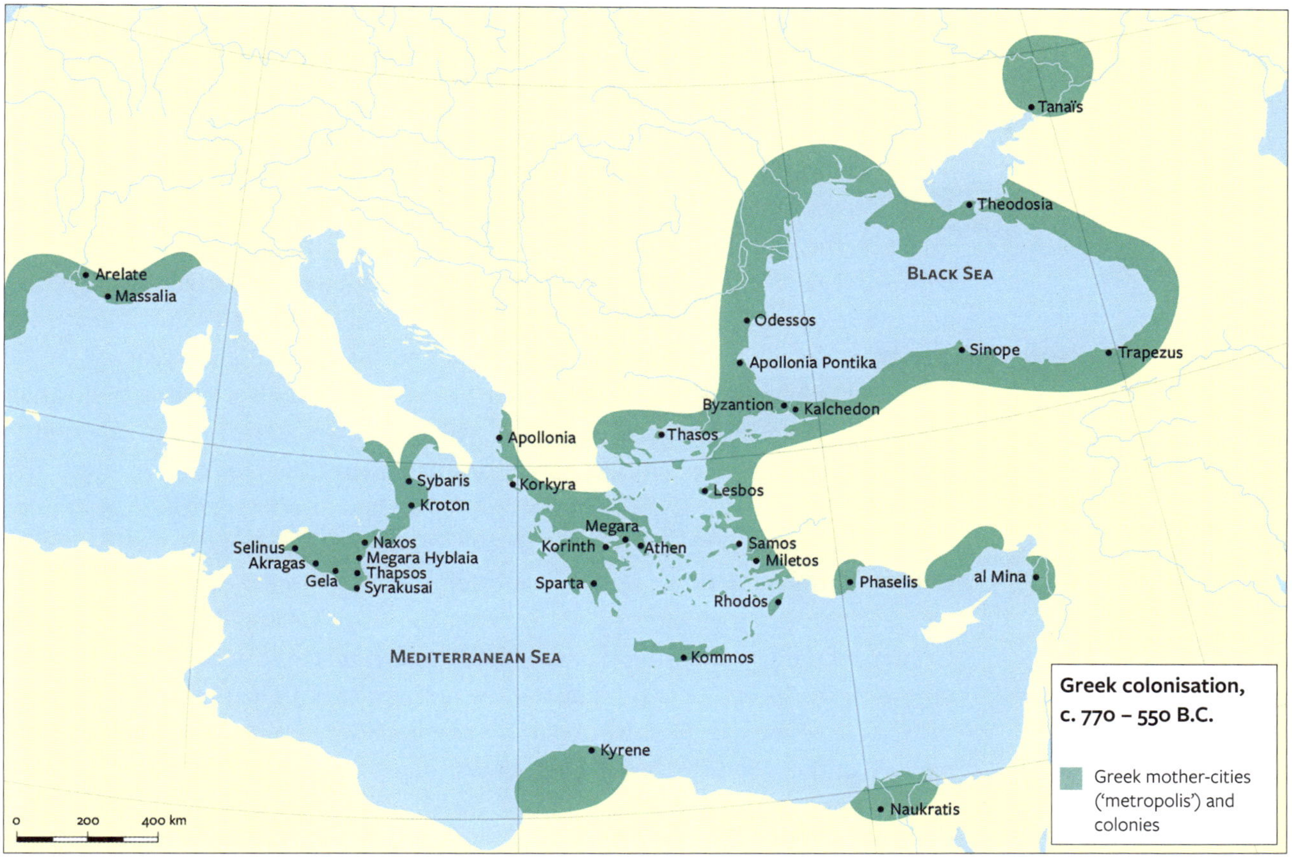

Map showing Greek colonisation in the period c. 750–550 B.C. Source: Der Neue Pauly, Supplemente Band 3, Historischer Atlas der antiken Welt, eds. Anne-Maria Wittke, Eckart Olshausen, Richard Szydlak, Stuttgart / Weimar 2007

address the negative consequences of this seaward orientation in critiques of civilisation. Cicero (*De re publica* 2.5–6), for example, emphasises the wisdom of the city's founder, Romulus, in selecting an ideal site that was both close to and distant from the sea and that could thus benefit from all the related advantages (supplies, trade, control), while avoiding the disadvantages (pirates, immigration, external influences). The Romans were aware of the dichotomies of the sea: naval armament – naval losses; security – foreign control; freedom of travel – piracy; openness – xenophobia; trading profits – trading prohibitions; strategic use of sea regions (as practised by Pompey in the 60s BC) – restriction of military action to coastal waters and regions; scant interest by ancient geographers – targeted and asserted rule over the *orbis terrarum*, including the seas; *mare liberum – mare clausum* (as in the so-called Megarian psephisma from 433/2 BC).

In the imperial period that began with Augustus' rule, the ideological integration of the sea into the empire – symbolically expressed in the elaborate *naumachia* spectacles – became part of this dialectic or ambivalence. Naval power was thus reflected not only in large fleets and sea battles, but also in the abundance of goods, the security on the seas and cultural exchange – concepts that the sophist Aelius Aristides addressed at great length in his Roman Oration from 146 AD.

Antiquity's relationship with the sea reached its zenith in Rome and was the inevitable result of the establishment of a vast empire surrounding the Mediterranean with access to the Atlantic in the west and the Indian Ocean in the east. This changed the way people viewed both the world and the sea and set the stage for global developments. Among these are phenomena that continue to have an impact today, such as Christianisation processes and standardisation trends in an empire that extended from Britain to Syria and from Germania to Egypt. Such developments would have been inconceivable without the political use of the sea as an interior space.

Because of their constant references to the sea, its mastery and control,[10] many ancient texts continue to provide a foundation for modern foreign policy today. For example, the report by Athenian historian Thucydides on the Peloponnesian War between the maritime power of Athens and the land power of Sparta is an important part of the curriculum at many military academies in the United States and even at Harvard's Kennedy School of Government. The ancient world is regarded as the "inventor" not only of military and economic power, but also, in a more abstract sense, of political command of the sea, which does not need to "pay off", but is required "ideologically" (an idea developed by Pericles in his speeches in the first and second book of Thucydides' history). Like modern international law, the ancient discourse on the sea has been transmitted to contemporary audiences and modern Europe through various sources, including the extremely important seventeenth-century debate between John Selden and Hugo Grotius on the opening and freedom of the sea, on the one hand, and its closure and control, on the other. Beginning with the legend of Odysseus, the sea first needed to secure a place in human consciousness before its horror could be overcome or minimised. The three companions of the Mephistophelian trinity – war, trade and piracy – played a key role in making this happen.

1 Johann Wolfgang von Goethe, *Faust: A Tragedy, Part Second*, translated by Arthur Gurney (1842).
2 Homer, the *Odyssey*, translated by A. S. Kline, http://www.poetryintranslation.com/PITBR/Greek/Odyssey14.php#anchor_Toc90268193
3 Michael Rathmann, "Das Meer bei den antiken Geographen", in Ernst Baltrusch et al. (eds.), *Seemacht, Seeherrschaft und die Antike* (Stuttgart, 2016), 47–77, 49.
4 Raimund Schulz, "Europa und das Meer in der Antike", in Michael Gehler et al. (eds.), *Europa-Räume: Von der Antike bis zur Gegenwart* (Hildesheim, 2016), 59–72.
5 Cicero, *On the Commonwealth*, 2.7, translated by Francis Barham, see http://oll.libertyfund.org/titles/cicero-treatise-on-the-commonwealth--5#toc_list
6 See Wolfgang Graf Vitzthum, *Der Staat der Staatengemeinschaft*, Schönburger Gespräche zu Recht und Staat, vol. 6 (Paderborn, 2006), 27ff.
7 Hans Kopp, "'Thalassokratie': Zur historischen Semantik und Wirkungsgeschichte eines Hilfsbegriffs", in Baltrusch et al (eds.), *Seemacht, Seeherrschaft und die Antike*, 27–45, 41–42.
8 Michael Rathmann, "Das Meer bei den antiken Geographen", in Baltrusch et al. (eds.), *Seemacht, Seeherrschaft und die Antike*, 47–77, here 75
9 Menander, *Monosticha* 231
10 Baltrusch et al. (eds.), *Seemacht, Seeherrschaft und die Antike*.

Roger Crowley

OWNING THE SEA

The Rise of the Maritime Powers

At the start of the fifteenth century, the Chinese Ming dynasty possessed the most advanced and powerful maritime capability in the world. Its huge junks sailed the Indian Ocean with impunity. Its navigational skills, its military resources and its ability to project power were unmatched, yet after 1433 it never put to sea again. The emperor decreed a fleet to be unnecessary: China's vast land-based empire simply needed nothing from the sea. Instead the second half of the last millennium of human history has witnessed the surprising but inexorable rise of the European maritime powers that came to connect the world's oceans and to assert a global dominance that has lasted into the twentieth century. The line of ascent has passed from the Italian city-states in the Mediterranean in the fifteenth century, through the Atlantic pioneers – Portugal and Spain – and on to the waters of Northern Europe, to the Dutch Republic, France and Britain.

Maritime capability demands particular conditions. Ships are costly to build and fleets expensive to maintain. In the age of oar and sail they consumed considerable natural resources and depended on much skilled labour. A Venetian galley, which had a service life of no more than one decade, required thirty beech trees just to fashion its oars; it took five years and 5,000 oak trees to complete the construction of Britain's most famous sail-powered warship, THE VICTORY. Navies and merchant fleets rely on considerable industrial infrastructure, in the form of dockyards and port facilities, long-term commitment and continuous investment. Unlike armies they cannot be easily disbanded and remobilized. Unmaintained ships rot. Their crews drift away.

Although autocratic kingdoms have been capable of periods of naval supremacy, the rise of European maritime hegemony, the willingness to commit to the sea and to pay for it, have generally been characterized by high levels of civic commitment. Such support came from merchant societies or those with strong relationships between merchant communities and their governing bodies, because the compulsion to the sea has been trade and the facility that water gives to the movement of goods and access to markets. In turn there has been a requirement for efficient instruments of violence to protect these assets. In the process the sea project has profoundly affected the industrial, fiscal and constitutional evolution of Europe.

The driver for maritime supremacy has been necessity. "To sail is necessary; to live is not", the Roman general Pompey once famously declared, putting to sea in a storm with a vital grain supply for the city's people. Venice, Portugal, the Dutch Republic and Britain were all polities with small populations and poor natural resources. Each was closely bound to the requirement to live by trade – at its most basic level to feed their populations – due to their geography. The European continent has a large coastline in proportion to its territory and each has had an inevitable relationship with the sea. The impulse for maritime expansion was set down in an Venetian appeal to the papacy in 1343 for permission to trade with the Muslim world, "since by the Grace of God our city has grown and increased by the labours of merchants creating traffic and profits for us in diverse parts of the world by land and sea and this is our life and that of our sons, because we cannot live otherwise and know not how except by trade".

Europe's sailing expertise was sharpened by continuous competition. The Venetians and their successors fought a series of intense trade wars for the maritime spaces that led to lucrative markets and colonial possessions: Venice and Genoa; Portugal and Spain; the Dutch Republic with Spain, France and England; Britain and France. The characteristic objective was to control sea lanes, bottlenecks and strategic ports that led to commercial opportunities, rather than the domination of large land masses that they lacked the resources to hold. All of these efforts were aimed at establishing monopolies. As the English adventurer Sir Walter Raleigh put it at the end of the sixteenth century, "He that commands the sea commands the trade, and he that is lord of the trade of the world is lord of the wealth of the world".

In the medieval and early modern world, Venice provided the prototype for European naval power. No polity in history has aligned its interests so closely with maritime success. The city was literally in the sea. With no land and no natural resources it was dependent from its birth on merchant ventures. Venice was uniquely organised to trade and sell. It was a city of merchants and sailors with no ruling feudal aristocracy. Survival depending on sailing; sailing depended on the quality of its ships,

2/2
Gaspar van Wittel, *The Piazzetta and the Doge's Palace in Venice*, 1695/1736

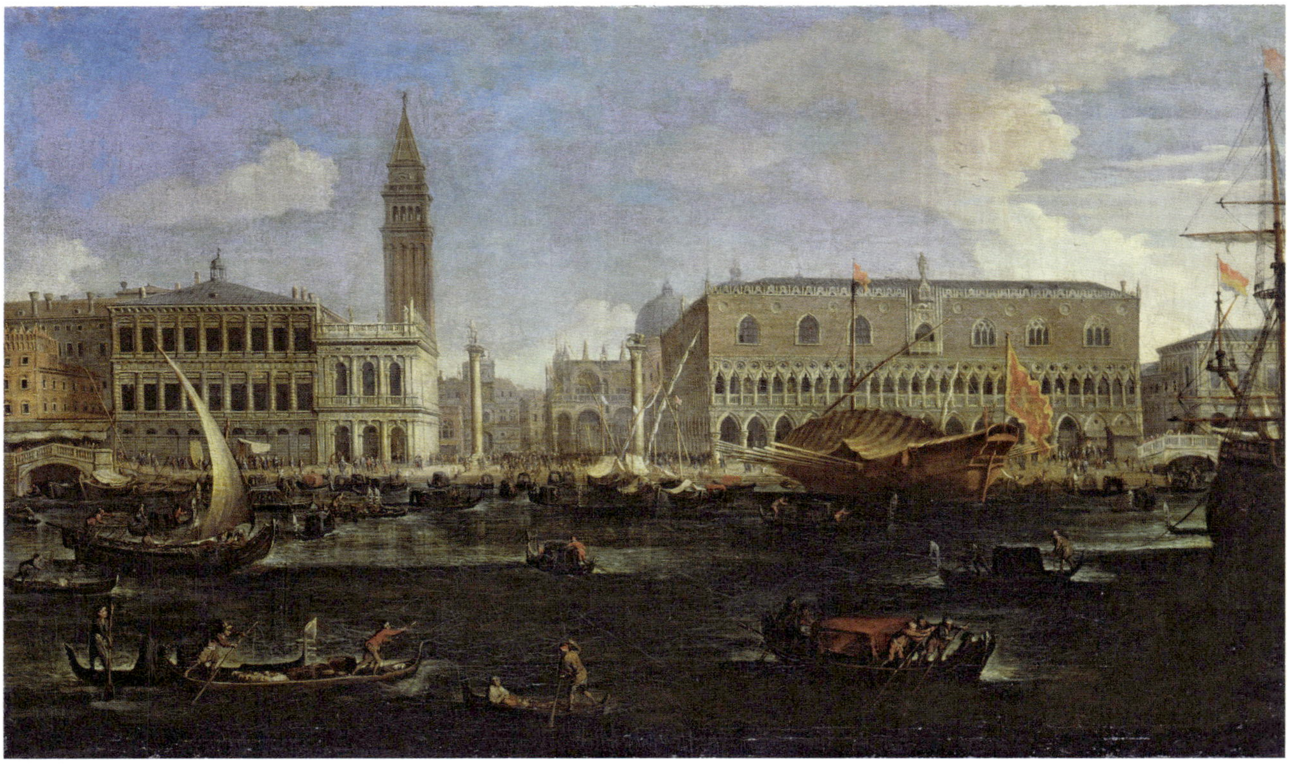

freedom from piracy and competitors, and access to markets. Over hundreds of years the Venetians cultivated a system that integrated all the component parts of maritime supremacy into the commercial, financial, industrial and constitutional management of their city. They recognized early on the absolute importance of dominating their immediate maritime space, the Adriatic, to avoid being hemmed in. From there, they moved out to create a radiating network of fortified bases that controlled the seaways to markets, particularly the spice trade to Alexandria, and they protected them with efficient violence. It was a model that successors would seek to emulate.

Venice paid obsessive attention to shipbuilding and its material infrastructure. By 1400 the state arsenal was the largest industrial complex in the world. Here the Venetians built and repaired everything necessary for maritime trade and war. In addition to merchant ships and war galleys, the arsenal turned out ropes, sails, gunpowder, oars, weapons and cannons by methods that were ahead of their time. They analysed every stage of the manufacturing process and broke it down into an early type of assembly line construction. Galleys were built in kit form by craftsmen who specialized in the individual components, so that in times of war ships could be put together at lightning speed. Their concern for quality control was similarly unique. All work was subject to rigorous inspection; ropes were colour tagged according to their intended use; every ship had a specified carrying capacity with a load line marked on its side, a forerunner of the Plimsoll mark. This care was a function of the city's deep understanding of the demands of the sea. A vessel, its crew and thousands of ducats of valuable merchandise could founder on shoddy work. Venice's survival ultimately depended on its management of practical materials and they meshed it with novel fiscal and commercial systems: marine insurance and share schemes in trading ventures, rational taxation, and a stable currency. They also forged their own narrative of maritime supremacy, as would their successors. For Venice it was the annual ceremony of marrying the sea. Later, Portuguese kings would style themselves "Lords of Navigation", and eighteenth-century Britons sang "Britannia rules the waves".

The end of the fifteenth century saw the start of resolute challenges to the Venetian spice monopoly from the Iberian Peninsula. The voyages of Christopher Columbus and Vasco da Gama inaugurated a shift to the Atlantic as the arena for European maritime expansion. Decades of stop-start exploration of the African coast by the Portuguese crystallised into a coherent national project to find a seaway to India, driven by the desire to outflank Venice's spice trade with Egypt. This long gestation led to the development of unmatched oceanic navigational skills and knowledge of the Atlantic winds, as well as fierce contests with Spain. These were resolved by papal intercession and by the concept of oceanic monopoly, dividing the maritime space beyond Europe into defined areas of exclusive exploration. The notion of a *mare clausum* granted the Portuguese a paper monopoly on the sea route to the East, and the Spanish to the Americas, but the head start that these powers had made it practically impossible for competitors to challenge their dominance. The Portuguese drew on a considerable quantity of European intellectual capital: Jewish mathematicians and astronomers, Italian commercial agents, and Flemish and German cannon founders. No other European power had the ability to quickly compete with the Iberian pioneers.

Within the Indian Ocean, strategic acumen and information gathering skills enabled Portugal to replicate the lightweight maritime networks of Venice on a vast scale. Under the visionary conquistador Afonso de Albuquerque it quickly grasped the choke points of trade – the mouths of the Red Sea and the Persian Gulf, and the straits

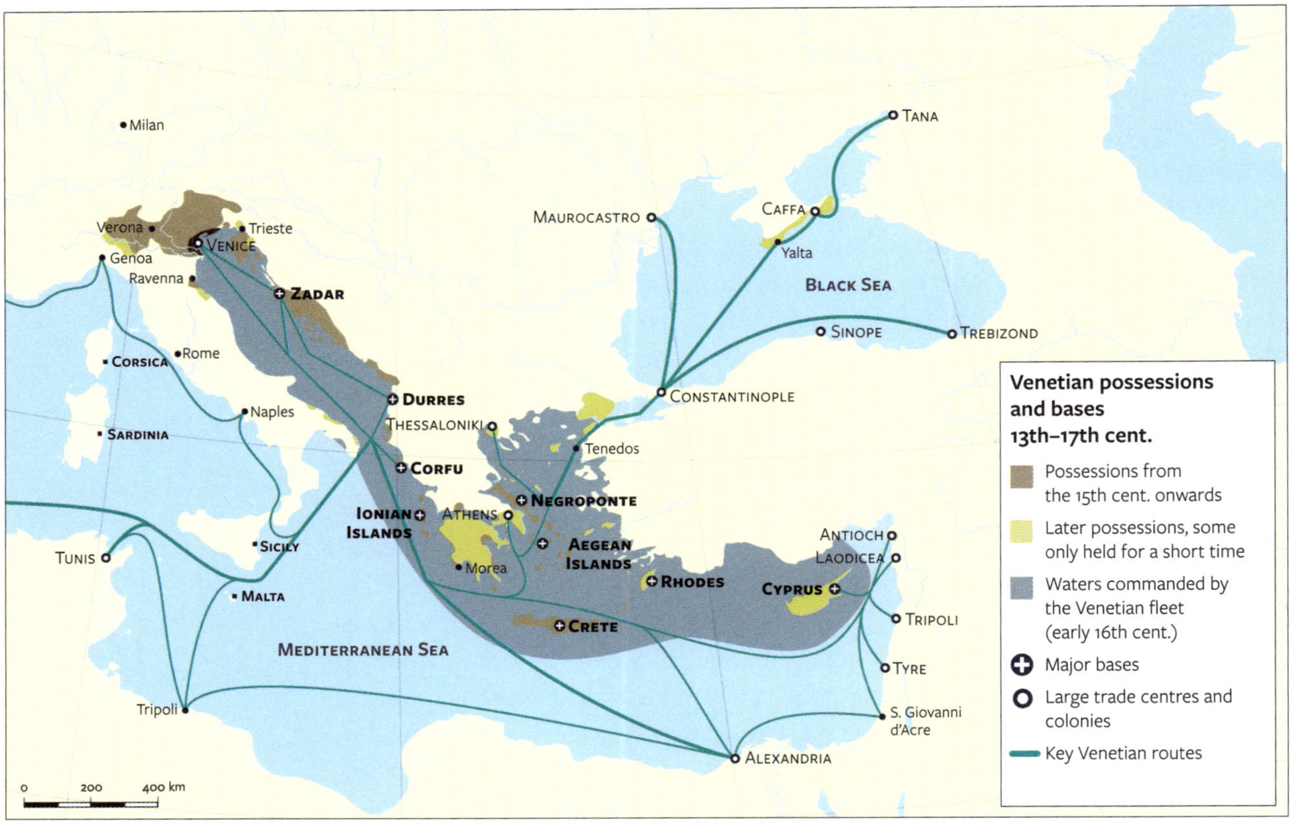

Map of Venetian possessions and bases in the period 13th–17th cent.
Source: Fondazione Musei Civici di Venezia, Ufficio Attività Educative

of Malacca, which was the crux of the sea route to China. It moved to dominate them with strategically placed forts. Portuguese ships faced no armed competition at sea. In their fast-firing bronze cannon they possessed an unmatched technological advantage, one that would allow European navies a monopoly on violence across the globe until the twentieth century. With only a few thousand men and mobile sea power, they managed for a century to maintain a commanding position in the spice trade. The trade routes that the Portuguese created forged linkages between China and Japan, the Indian Ocean, Brazil, Africa and Europe. The Iberian pioneers started Europe's expansion overseas and the development and control of long-range maritime trading networks.

Portugal attempted to reinforce its theoretical monopoly rights by imposing an embargo on their uniquely won knowledge of the winds and sea lanes to the East. Pilots' log books and sea charts were confiscated on return to Lisbon. It became a capital offence to sell maps or provide sailing information to outsiders, but the leakage of information proved impossible to stem. The kings of Portugal and Spain were attempting to run tightly controlled royal monopolies on the vast wealth pouring in from the Indies and the Americas, but the Iberian pioneers lacked the industrial maritime infrastructure or an entrepreneurial merchant class to maximise the rewards or protect their trade routes. Most of the pepper was sold on the markets of Antwerp and Bruges, and Portugal's ownership of the sea route to India – and Spain's to the Americas – would be curtailed first by enterprising pirates and then by state-sponsored navies.

The maritime competition to the Iberian monopoly came in the late sixteenth and early seventeenth century from the waters of Northern Europe, from England and most vigorously the Spanish Netherlands (the Netherlands, Belgium and Luxembourg). In the late medieval and early modern world these were the centres of dynamic capitalism.

It would be the flood regions of Holland and Zeeland in particular that emerged as the true heirs of Venice's merchant-driven hegemony, in the formation of the Dutch Republic. Like Venice, these lands, surrounded on three sides by salt and freshwater, lacked natural resources and had an intense relationship with the sea, by which they were threatened and on which they depended. Their strategic position midway between the Lisbon and the Baltic, and with access to the heart of Europe up the Rhine, made them ideally placed to dominate Europe's bulk carrying trade. They carried Portuguese pepper to the spice markets of Antwerp and grain, fish and timber back from the Baltic. With the development of superior shipbuilding skills, using wind-powered sawmills for rapid construction, they built formidable merchant fleets to standard designs that could undercut all rivals. By 1560 they had a fleet of 1,800 merchant vessels, the largest in Europe. By 1600 they had learned to cast relatively cheap cast-iron guns.

At the same time, the Dutch had developed co-operation, enterprise and a spirit of independence that accompanied the rise of Protestantism. Like Venice there was a close integration between sea power and commercial interests that saw the evolution of sophisticated investment and banking systems that allowed the loan of cheap money for the funding of trading ventures. The Federated Dutch Republic would become essentially a merchant state. When the war of independence against their Habsburg rulers broke out in 1568, the Dutch were well-placed to fight at sea, and by 1600 they were attacking Spanish and Portuguese ships and bases across the world. For the first time European fleets had the capability to compete far from their home continent. The prime instrument of Dutch sea power was the development of private merchant trade corporations, such as the Dutch East India Company, empowered by the state to make treaties and wage war. They stripped the Portuguese of their prize spice trade in the East Indies with the claim that the sea was free to all, then imposed their own monopolies and enforced them with violence. By virtue of their seafaring skills, commercial acumen, superior fiscal instruments and the enormous profits from a monopoly spice trade, they achieved a dominance far out of proportion to their population and resources, making Amsterdam the commercial capital of Europe.

These seventeenth-century contests were formative to the development of European sea power. They saw the decline of the Mediterranean as a dynamic trading hub and the eclipse of the Iberian pioneers. Maritime industrial and naval power was increasingly concentrated in the North Sea and the English Channel. The Dutch struggle against Spain was a war that integrated state building with merchant objectives. Money deployed in merchant ventures and the naval capability to defend them depended on an overlap of interests between merchants and the executive powers of the state. Above all it was an issue of money. When commercial rivalry in the Channel led to fierce Anglo-Dutch trade wars, efficient finance gave the Dutch a competitive edge. The king of England, Charles II, was unable to consistently pay his sailors and in 1667 his fleet was in disarray. The Dutch sailed up the Thames, burned the English fleet and carried off its flagship, THE ROYAL CHARLES, in triumph.

What the English learned from the fiasco of THE ROYAL CHARLES was to start building the infrastructure required for a professional navy and gradually to persuade their monarchs to find ways to pay for it. The seventeenth century saw the evolution of standing state navies in the Netherlands, England and France, paid for out of taxation, as instruments of state policy. Developments in sailing ships, gunnery and maritime tactics, in naval bureaucracies and professional officer corps, in dockyard facilities, supply, recruitment and training saw naval capability become central to state

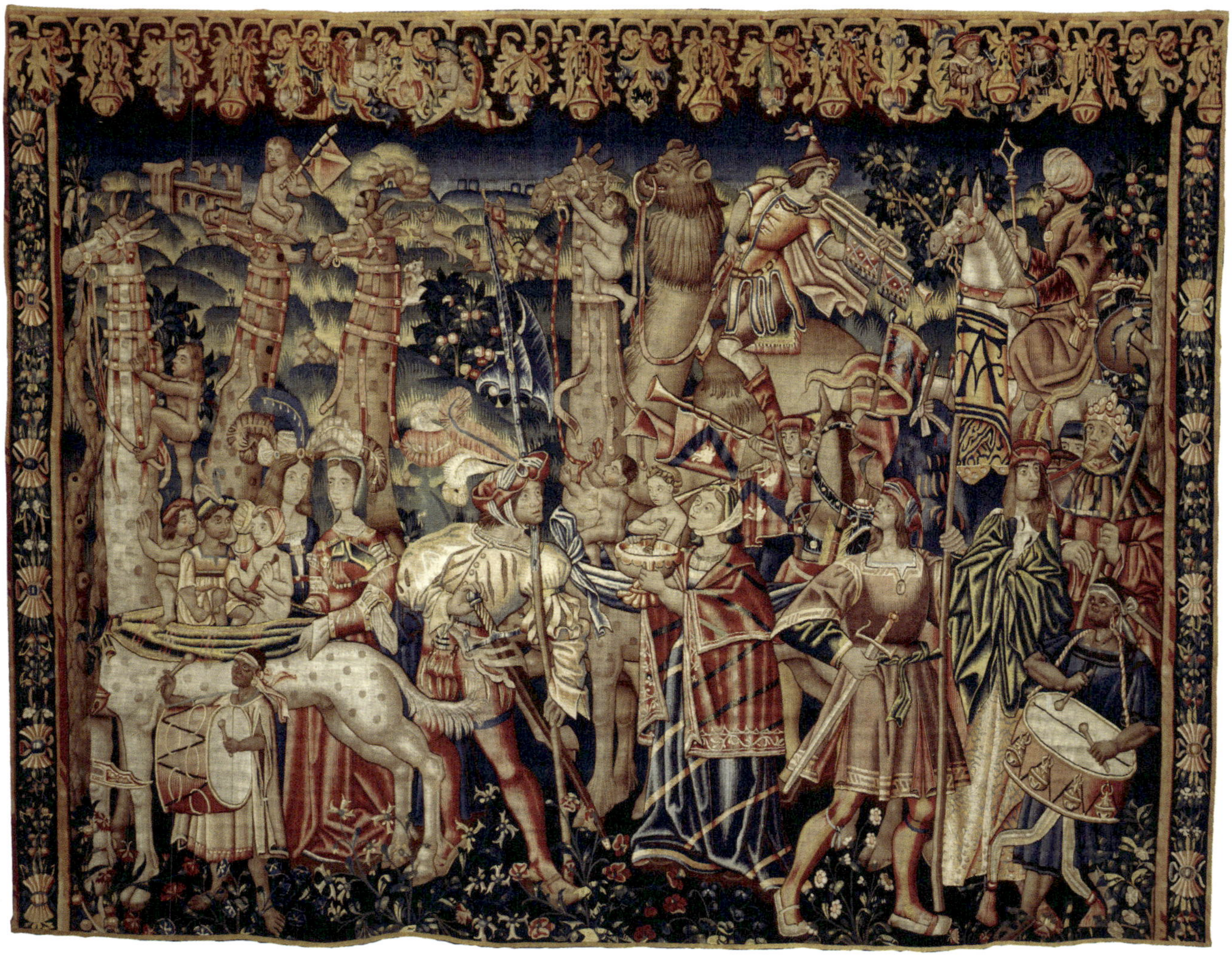

Jean Grenier, tapestry depicting the triumphal march of the Portuguese, 1504

building. It was these initiatives that would allow northern European navies to project their power across the world.

The Channel wars were a three-way fight between the emergent Northern European navies in different combinations but in time the Dutch would be eclipsed by their envious rivals. Under Louis XIV, the French built a formidable navy as a projection of the monarchy's power. From the late seventeenth century, France and a unified Britain (after 1707) began to dominate the maritime arena. By the 1690s the two countries were engaged in a long-term contest for oceanic trade and colonial empire that would last until 1815. Initially the powerful French fleet had the advantage. The French gained control of the Channel in 1693 after the defeat of a combined English and Dutch fleet. England's merchant convoys were being plundered, its business communities were in despair, and its treasury empty. By 1759 the balance of power had been largely reversed. In the meantime, Britain achieved a remarkable turnaround that would lay the foundations of an unrivalled supremacy at sea.

The traumatic French defeats and the resulting pressure of merchant interests on the British monarchy spurred the nation into a concerted effort that would make an effective navy a pillar of a prosperous state. The creation in 1694 of a Bank of England funded by interest-bearing loans provided the fiscal resources that had been enjoyed by the Dutch, and would allow Britain a continuous stream of investment denied to the French crown. Within a decade, 150 new warships had been built. It was the start of a cycle of financial investment and trading returns that were fed by and stimulated an early industrial revolution and increases in agricultural production.

The eighteenth century unleashed the full potential of sailing ships that would allow Europeans to sail, fight, explore and trade across the whole globe, to develop efficiently supplied colonies and footholds on any continent. These were the most complex machines of the time, which required enormous human, industrial, fiscal and administrative resources. In addition to 2,000 trees, the construction of an eighteenth century man-of-war involved 6,000 square metres of sail canvas, sixteen kilometres of rope and seventeen tonnes of iron fittings. It was Britain that would rise best to the challenges of the age of sail.

With the aid of its Dutch-style finance, Britain's naval spending power quickly gave it enormous advantages. Its manpower quadrupled to 44,000, a larger population than any city outside London. Its contracts for food and supplies increased agricultural input by a third. The requirement for iron for nails and anchors was met by new production techniques. The navy became an engine of economic growth that brought huge returns in traded goods. Sea power and commerce were closely linked and created a national sense of patriotic destiny. When the British acquired Gibraltar in 1713, they laid down the first in a chain of bases that would in time stretch across the world, and in fifty years they acquired resources that the combined French and Spanish navies could not match.

Britain and France were at war for sixty-three years and fought forty engagements for control of profitable markets and imperial possessions. Almost all of these

Peter van de Velde, *Burning of the English Fleet at Chatham, 20 June 1667*, 1667/1700

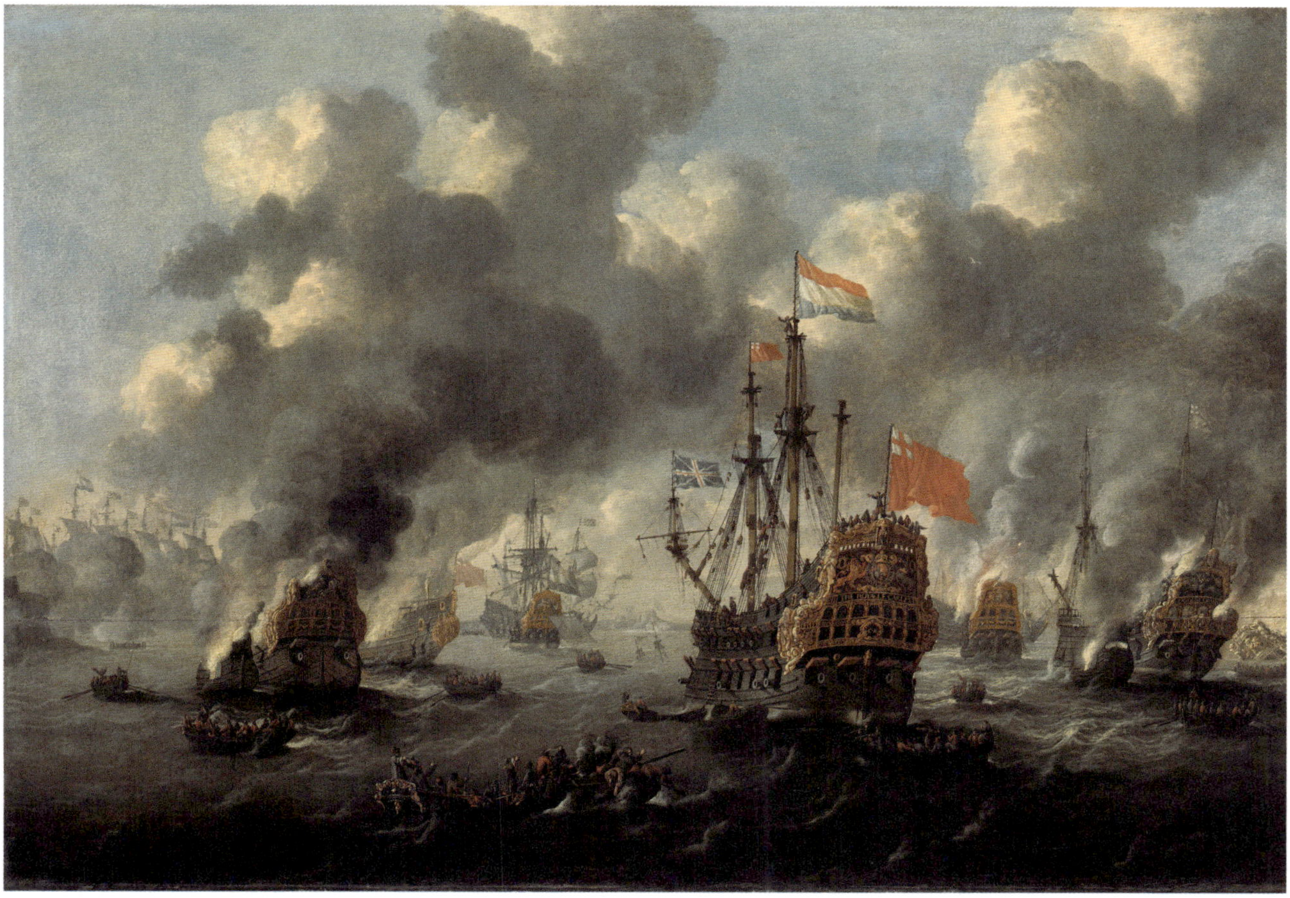

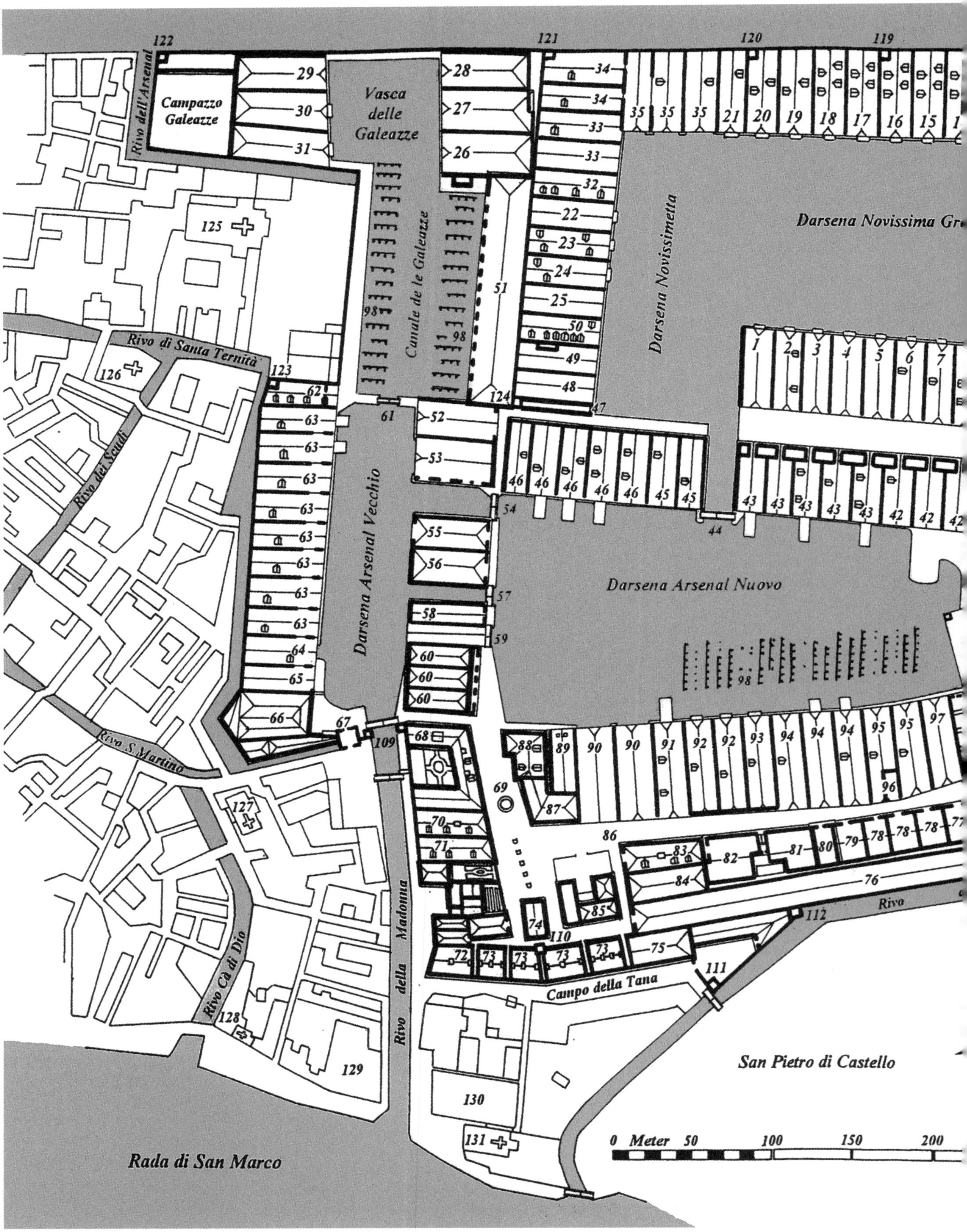
Rivo dell'Arsenal
Campazzo Galeazze
Vasca delle Galeazze
Canale de le Galeazze
Darsena Novissimetta
Darsena Novissima Gr
Rivo di Santa Ternità
Rivo dei Scudi
Darsena Arsenal Vecchio
Darsena Arsenal Nuovo
Rivo S.Martino
Rivo Cà di Dio
Rivo della Madonna
Campo della Tana
Rivo
San Pietro di Castello
Rada di San Marco
0 Meter 50 100 150 200

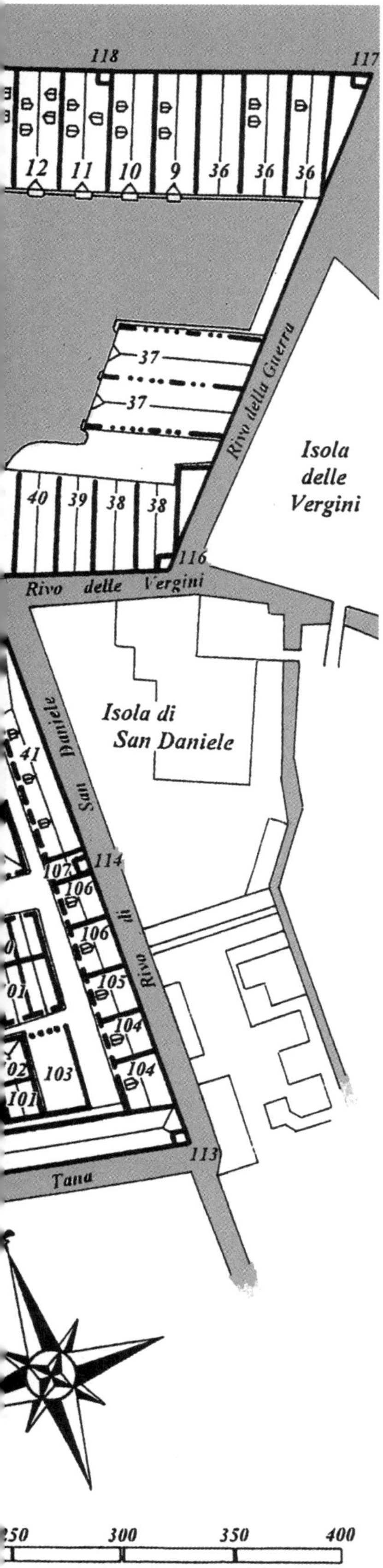

Diagram of the facilities and storehouses of the Arsenal in 1797
Source: Karl Klaus Körner, *Das Erbe der Serenissima*, publ. by Heeresgeschichtliches Museum/Militärhistorisches Institut Wien, Vienna 2010

1–8 Riparto Isolotto: shipyards no. 1 to no. 8
9–21 Riparto Novissima Grande: shipyards no. 9 to no. 21
22–25 Riparto Novissimetta: shipyards no. 22 to no. 25
26–31 Riparto Cantieri Galeazze: shipyards no. 26 to no. 31
32–34 Riparto Nappe:
32 Shipyard for small vessels
33 Storehouses for softwood
34 Storehouses for dried wood
35 Cantieri di San Cristofo-lo: covered basins
36 Riparto Loreto: shipyards for small vessels
37 Cantieri alla Canna: covered basins
38–40 Riparto Gaggiandra:
38 Storehouses for softwood
39 Sawmill
40 Storehouse for coniferous wood
41 Workshops for oars, etc. Wooden parts for rowing vessels
42–43 Cantieri bassi Rip° Isolotto:
42 Storehouses for masts and yards
43 Storehouses for bent wood
44 Ponte delle Seghe
45–46 Riparto Alberi:
45 Shipyards for galleys
46 Storehouses for prefabricated wooden parts
47 Tar storehouse
48 Ship-breaking yard
49 Shipyard for small vessels
50 Model hall and school for mathematics and shipbuilding
51 Storehouse for oak logs and sawmill for rough-cut wood
52 Storehouse for softwood
53 Covered basin
54 Ponte del Bucintoro
55 Storage site for the Bucentaur
56 Arms cleaning area
57 Ponte della Canova
58 Storehouse for pitch
59 Ponte della Valere
60 Sail-making workshops and storehouses
61 Ponte del Molo
62–64 Riparto Arsenale Vecchio:
62 Storehouses for softwood
63 Shipyards for small vessels and rowing vessels
64 Covered basin for the state barges of the doges
65 Storehouse for barrels
66 Sala d'Armi
67 Arsenal gate
68 Residence of the Patroni dell'Arsenal
69 Drinking water fountain
70 Storehouse for ironware and masonry tools
71 Storehouse for oars
72 Boring mill for cannon barrels
73 Foundries
74 Smithy
75 Storehouse for rope-making supplies
76 Corderia della Tana
77 Carpenter's workshop
78 Workshops for wooden blocks and pulleys
79 Saltpetre storehouse
80 Lead foundry
81 Armoury workshop
82 Coal storehouse
83 Oar-making workshop
84 Barrel-making workshop
85 Tar-processing facility
86 Stradale di Campagna
87 Chain and nail smithies
88 Anchor smithy
89 Storehouse for chains
90 Covered basins
91–97 Riparto Campagna:
91 Workshops for tops (platforms on the lower masts), etc. Wooden parts for square-rigged ships
92 Storehouses for new ropes
93 Storehouses for gun carriages
94 Storehouses for old ropes
95 Storehouses for masts
96 Workshop for decora-tive carving
97 Workshops for gun carriages
98 Palisades for conserving oak
99 Storehouses for cannon balls and grenades
100 Storehouses for artillery accessories
101 Storehouses for small arms
102 Storehouses for grease
103 Cannon balls stacked in pyramids
104 Storehouses for used artillery accessories
105 Wood-turning workshop
106 Storehouses for field artillery
107 Coal storehouse
108 Administrative office for artillery

109 Torri all'Ingresso Marittimo
110 Torre San Biagio
111 Torresin al Ponte della Tana
112 Torre di Mezzo
113 Torre San Pietro e Paolo
114 Torre San Daniele
115 Torre alle Vergini
116 Torre San Andrea
117 Torre San Pietro
118 Torre San Antonio
119 Torre San Michiele
120 Torre San Francesco
121 Torre San Cristofolo
122 Torre alla Celestia
123 Torre San Giovanni
124 Torre della Campanella

125 Chiesa Celestia
126 Chiesa San Ternità
127 Chiesa San Martino
128 Ospizio Casa di Dio
129 Stabilimento dei Forni
130 Granary
131 Chiesa San Biagio

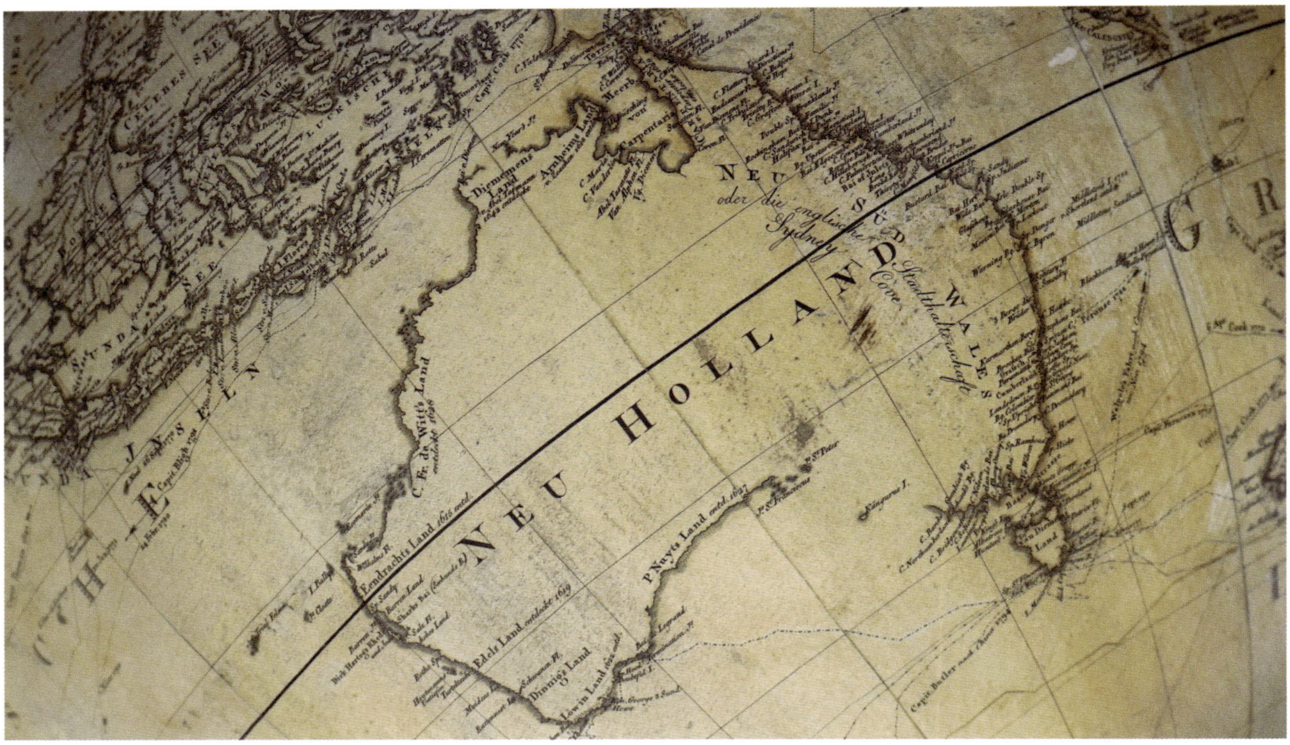

4/26
Daniel F. Sotzmann, globe of the Earth showing routes taken by geographic explorers (detail), 1808

sea battles took place beyond home waters. With the capabilities of their fleets Europeans were conducting maritime warfare on a global scale. The protagonists clashed in the Indian Ocean, in the valuable sugar islands of the Caribbean and on transoceanic shipping routes. France and Britain were evenly matched until the mid-eighteenth century but continuous funding granted Britain a brisker tempo of naval development than that available to the French kings, hampered as they were by simultaneous land wars and the stop-start financing of their fleets. In time British naval expenditure was double that of France. Increased efficiencies in naval organisation and bureaucracy, a new breed of professional officers and a willingness to pay for the navy by a nation that identified with the sea, allowed Britain to develop footholds of empire around the world, claiming land in India and North America. The British navy bred a spirit of confidence and aggression. Its commanders were expected to attack and to win and were delivered cautionary lessons for failures to do so. The Admiralty executed Admiral Byng on his own deck for failing to attack the French on Menorca in 1756, "to encourage the others", as Voltaire put it. Systematic development of core competencies, including the prevention of scurvy and other diseases, gave the British the ability to keep ships at sea for long periods. In 1759, they developed a blockade tactic and used it to bottle up the French fleet at Brest for eight months without firing a shot, thereby cutting off supplies to her colonies. The subsequent destruction of a French invasion fleet at Quiberon Bay at the year's end signalled the start of Britain's supremacy as the world's leading sea power. Keeping fleets at sea for long periods depended not just on seamanship but also on systematic improvements in supply, diet and hygiene. The difficulties and costs of manning fleets were always high. Between 1793 and 1801 alone the British lost 65,000 men, including 20,000 sailors, to disease while fighting with the French for the sugar islands of the Caribbean.

The second half of the eighteenth century also saw European ships exploring,

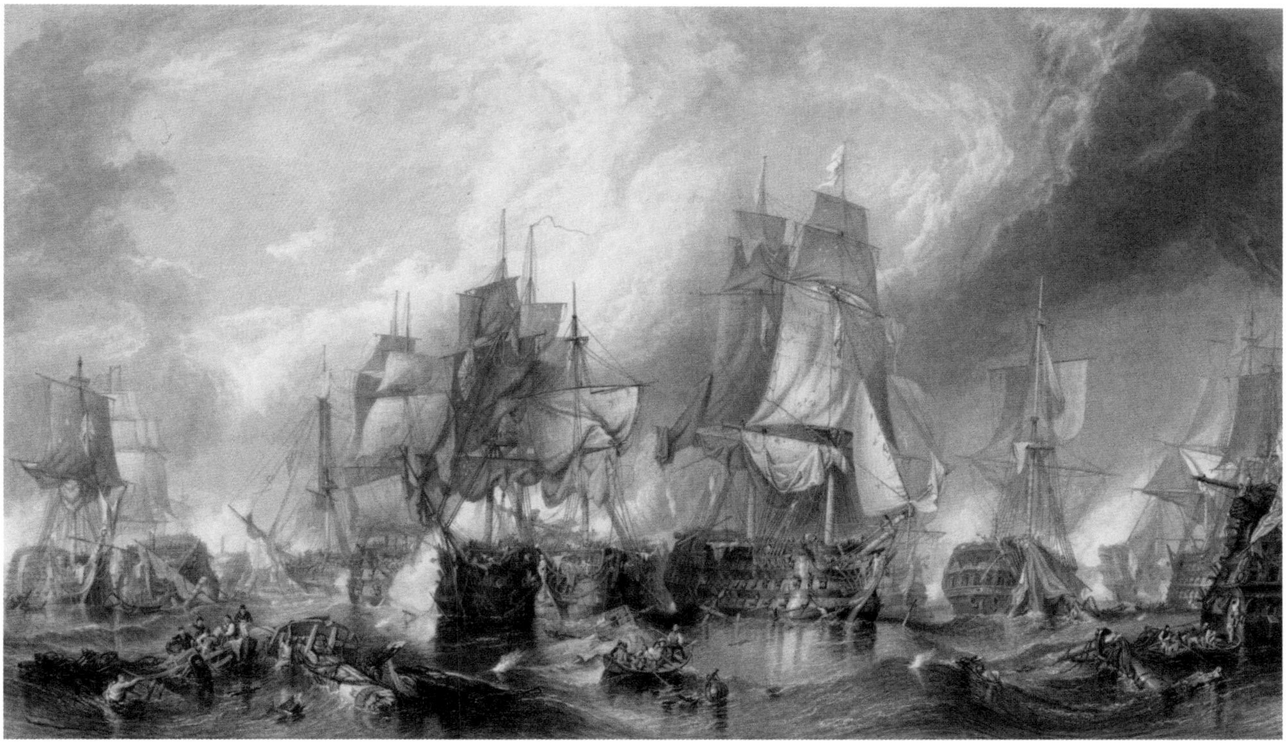

William Clarkson Stanfield, *The Battle of Trafalgar, 1805*, 1839

mapping and naming the world with increasing confidence, thanks to improvements in navigation and marine instruments, such as the ability to correct for magnetic compass variations and to precisely position longitude with maritime clocks. Cartography, hydrography and exploration became state enterprises. The voyages of Captain Cook to Australia and Louis XVI's promotion of science and exploration created new information about the world and the lands to which Europeans could lay claim.

The failure of the French to dismember Britain's overseas possessions gifted Britain huge mercantile profits, many of which were ploughed back into its navy. Its maritime supremacy was completed during the Revolutionary and Napoleonic Wars at the turn of the nineteenth century. To defeat the combined French and Spanish navies, Britain solved the two perennial problems of warfare in the age of sail: adequate manpower and plentiful finance. The navy had authorisation to conscript men for the fleet and so increased its manpower by a factor of seven, to 144,000. It funded the long struggle with a radical fiscal instrument: a ten per cent income tax. Within one year it had raised enough money for 100 warships. If neither of these strategies were popular, they were at least tolerated, providing an indication of Britain's national identity with the sea, and the revolutions in finance, industry and commerce that maritime commitment had created in the heart of a national system. The defining victory at Trafalgar in 1805, after a long blockade of Cadiz, was the result of years of continuous investment in leadership, training and group morale. Speaking after the battle, one commander, Admiral Cornwallis, pinpointed where Britain's ownership of the sea truly lay. Even allowing for Nelson's talismanic leadership, "it was the effect of system, not of chance".

Trafalgar cemented Britain's particular position as the leading sea power of the age, but in a wider sense European maritime dominance allowed the continent to buy and sell, establish colonies, run empires and monopolise the global economy into the twentieth century.

Olaf Mörke

MORE THAN WOOD FOR SALT

Economic and Cultural Contacts in the Hanseatic Region

In the late Middle Ages, coastal shipping was the norm for the nautical profession. Although it was gradually joined by overseas navigation in the sixteenth and seventeenth century, even in this period shipping on the Atlantic's marginal seas continued to account for a large share of European maritime traffic. This is true not only of the Mediterranean Sea in the south, but also of the North and Baltic Seas in the north, which in the fourteenth and fifteenth century formed the heart of the Hanseatic trading system: "The region in which the Hanseatic merchants were at home and the Hanseatic cities were located extended from the Zuiderzee in the west to Estonia and Livonia in the east, from Visby in the north (and from Stockholm in the fourteenth century) to the Cologne–Erfurt–Breslau–Krakow axis in the south."[1] Cologne, Lübeck, Braunschweig, Gotlandic Visby and Danzig (now Gdańsk) ranked among the most important cities in the late medieval Hansa. Even after the focus of northern and western European trade shifted to the Atlantic region in the sixteenth century and after the political and economic influence of the Hanseatic alliance waned, many of these former Hanseatic cities retained their importance or were able to strengthen their position as economic centres. One of them was Hamburg, which played only a marginal role in the classical Hanseatic period, but became a major beneficiary of the economic shift to the north-west because of its direct link to the Atlantic and North Sea regions. But even on the Baltic coast there was one important Hanseatic trading and port town that continued to flourish long after the Hanseatic League had passed its peak: Danzig.

The city on the mouth of the Vistula, which had been ruled by the Teutonic Order until 1454 and then become an autonomous city-state under the loose control of the Polish Crown, benefited from its favourable location. Connected to the Polish interior via the Vistula and situated at the intersection between trade on the Vistula and the Baltic, it grew from a settlement with an impressive 3,000 to 5,000 inhabitants in the thirteenth century to a city of roughly 30,000 in 1500 and 40,000 in 1600. Because of its geographical location, Danzig was predestined to become the centre of commercial contacts between western Europe – i.e. England, France and the Netherlands – and the vast economic area of Poland–Lithuania.

A diverse range of goods flowed through the Hanseatic League as a whole and the city of Danzig in particular – not only in an east-west but also in a north-south

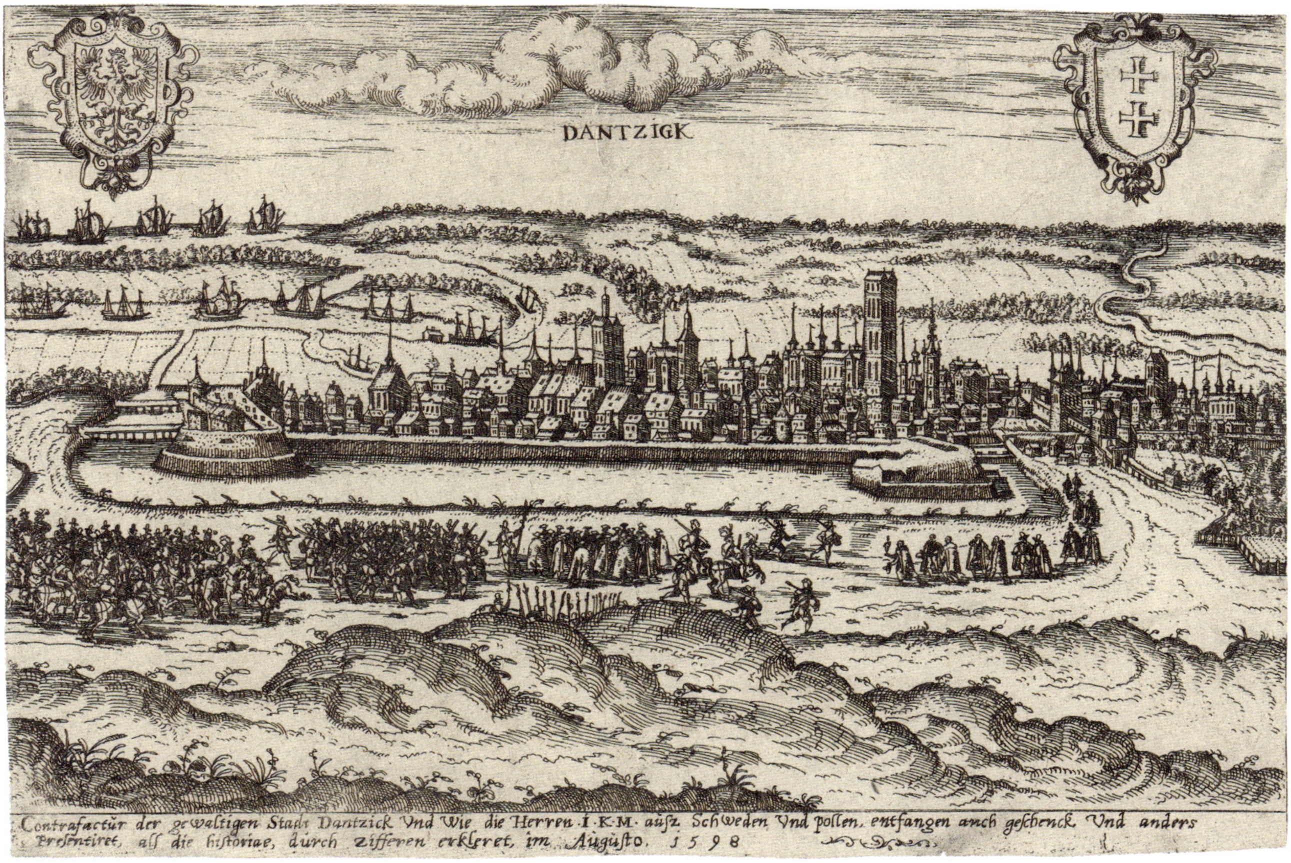

Reception of King Sigismund III in front of the gates of Danzig in August 1598, after 1598

direction. Western Europe provided cloth, salt, herring and high-quality foods such as wine. From Scandinavia came iron, copper, furs and fish. Poland–Lithuania and Russia supplied tar, potash, furs, honey, wax and forestry products such as wood, which was an important source of energy at the time and essential for Dutch and English shipbuilding. The Vistula provided access to the Slovak copper mining regions and, beyond them, to the Black Sea trade. The export of grain (the most important staple at the time) to the relatively densely populated areas of western Europe grew steadily in importance. The grain trade was highly profitable for two reasons: it was grown cost-effectively on a large-scale as part of the manorial economy in the hinterland of the Baltic coast stretching from East Elbia to Poland–Lithuania; and it met with growing demand particularly in the urban areas of north-western Europe.

These were the spatial and economic structures in which Hanseatic life played out. Popular perceptions of the Hansa have been shaped by two main phenomena: first, cities and localities such as Danzig, Lübeck, Cologne, Hamburg, Reval (Tallinn) and Deutsche Brücke in the Norwegian town of Bergen; and second, a ship called the cog. These stationary and "moving" places (cities and ships) were the external signs of the Hanseatic League's inner workings. Permanent locations and mobility existed in a dialectical relationship. Although merchant families maintained a base in an individual city for generations, their members moved to other parts of the Hanseatic region, creating far-flung networks.

In 1430, for example, Tiedemann Giese moved from the Westphalian city of Unna to the Baltic Sea region, settling in Danzig. His descendants achieved great wealth and influence there. In 1532, Georg Giese (1497–1562) had his portrait painted in London by Hans Holbein the Younger (1497–1543). This painting is probably the best-known Renaissance portrait of a merchant from north of the Alps. Georg Giese had been living in the city since 1522. Working at the Steelyard, which the Hanseatic League had established as a trading base in London in 1475, he "performed responsible administrative duties".[2] Shortly after the painting was made, Giese returned to Danzig, where he was appointed a lay judge in 1536 and a councillor in 1545 – important public offices that were typically held by members of influential merchant families. For families like the Gieses, it was common to send younger members to distant places, where they could gain business experience and make useful contacts. The selection of the Hanseatic trading base in London reflected the close ties that had existed between this western outpost of the Hanseatic League and the city of Danzig around 1,300 kilometres away since the late Middle Ages.

Goods were usually transported between the North and the Baltic Seas by water. The ship was the cheapest means of transport for bulk commodities such as wood, salt and grain. However, use of the sea route between the western and eastern halves of the Hanseatic League was a politically sensitive issue. The route led through the Øresund, known as the Sound in English, the strait that today serves more to connect Denmark and Sweden than to separate the two. From the High Middle Ages until 1658, though, both sides belonged to the Kingdom of Denmark, which thus controlled passage between the North and the Baltic Seas. From 1429 to 1857, all vessels that passed through the strait were required to pay "Sound Dues" to the Danish Crown. This toll was a constant source of conflict between Denmark, the other Baltic lands and especially the maritime users of the Sound – initially the Hanseatic League, but later also the Swedes and the Dutch.

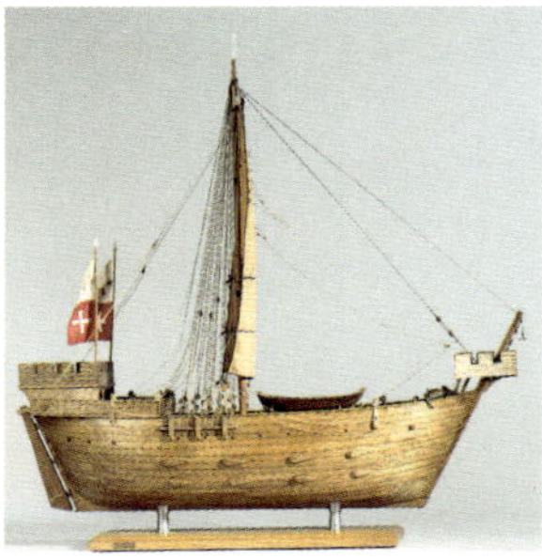

Model of a Hanseatic cog, based on the vessel in the seal of the city of Elbing (from 1350), 1972

The Hanseatic League shaped not only late medieval economic history, but also the political history of the lands on the North and Baltic Seas. The alliance of Hanseatic cities owes its existence to a conflict of political and economic interests. In 1358, German merchants – mainly the inhabitants of Lübeck – were involved in a conflict with the County of Flanders and the city of Bruges which led to a joint economic embargo of Flanders by what was henceforth known as the "steden van de dudeschen hense" (cities of the German Hansa). Not only does the Flanders blockade illustrate how the Hanseatic cities joined forces to form a close cooperative alliance in the second half of the fourteenth century; it also documents the close connection between economic ties and political power. The great variety of economic, political and cultural relations and exchange processes led to the emergence of the "sister seas"[3] region.

The cities soon began seeing themselves as members of a Hanseatic alliance. Their conflict with Flanders had first escalated in 1351, when – due to an incident at sea off the coast of Bruges – King Edward III of England ordered goods from these cities to be confiscated in England and, in addition, disrupted the wool trade. In 1360, under Lübeck's leadership, the Hanseatic cities decided to block the Danish straits in order to prevent grain from being smuggled into the Netherlands. In 1361, the tensions culminated in an open sea war with Denmark, which ended with heavy losses for the Hanseatic fleet and its withdrawal from the Sound. Amidst these political developments, which led to the Hanseatic cities' closer organisational integration, Lübeck's special position became increasingly evident. Between 1356 and 1407, a total of forty-three of the sixty-seven Hanseatic meetings – called *Tagfahrten* – took place in the city.

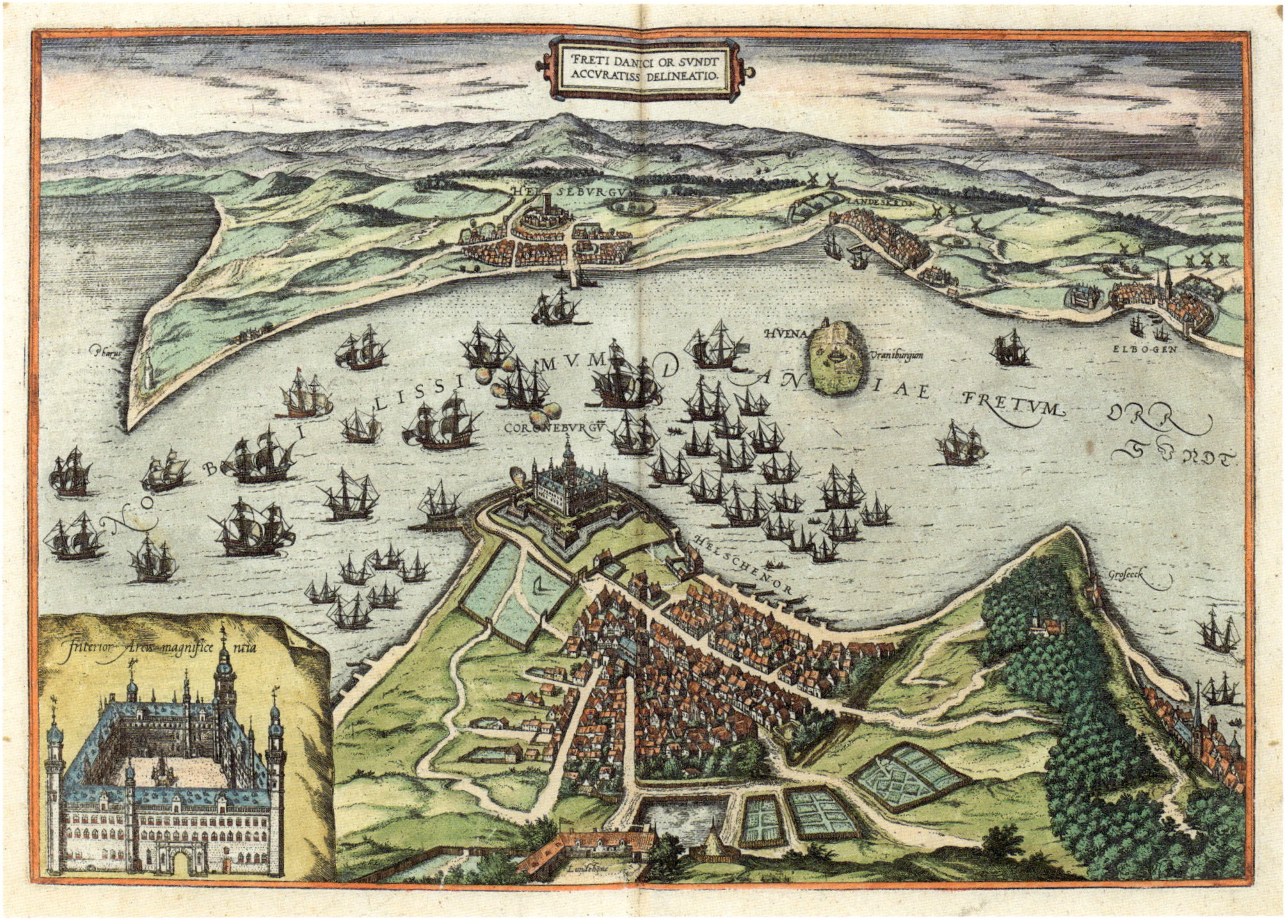

Franz Hogenberg, view of the Øresund with the Danish Kronborg Castle, after 1588

In the period following the failed naval operations of 1361/62, the Hanseatic cities, or at least those on the coast, demonstrated their ability to work together. In 1367 they succeeded in establishing a long-term city alliance in the form of the Confederation of Cologne. Of course, the inland Hanseatic cities – joined by Hamburg and Bremen – did not participate, as they had little interest in a naval war on the Baltic. However, a number of Dutch cities that are usually not considered part of the Hanseatic League were involved, including Amsterdam in Holland and Brielle in Zeeland. In addition, the confederation had the support of Sweden, Holstein and the Danish aristocrats who opposed the Danish king.

Under Hanseatic leadership, the next war ended favourably for the confederation. In 1370, the Hanseatic cities made peace with Denmark in the city of Stralsund. Under the terms of the peace treaty, Denmark was forced to guarantee restitution of the Hanseatic privileges in the territories of the Danish Crown, including complete freedom of trade on land and by sea. In addition, for a period of fifteen years, the confederation was pledged four Danish fortresses on the Sound, located in Helsingborg, Malmö, Skanör and Falsterbo. They gave it effective control of the strait for the entire period.

The introduction of Danish Sound Dues in 1429 was the sign of a fundamental transformation of the political structures in the sister seas region. The Hanseatic League remained committed to the "basic constitutional principle of a free union, under which every member has the right to make decisions [...] on affairs of funda-

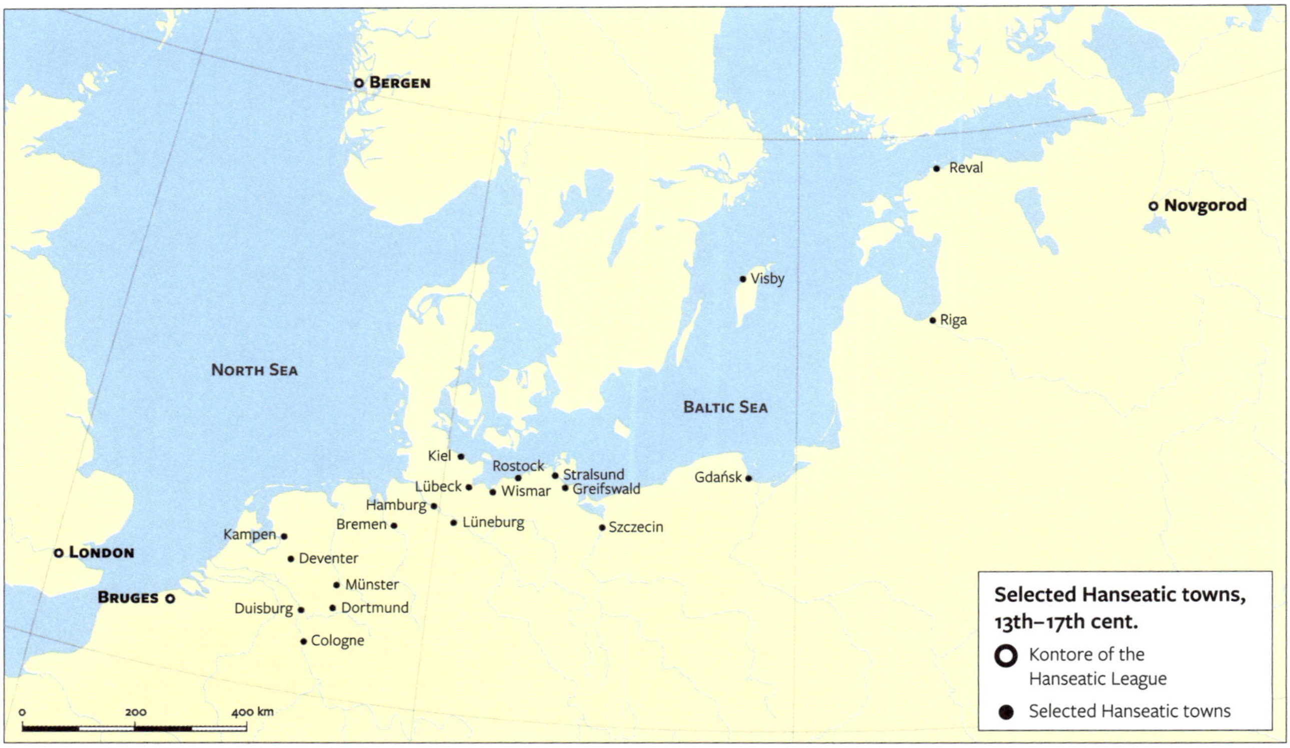

Map of Hanseatic towns in the North Sea and Baltic Sea regions, c. 1500. Source: *Die Hanse,* ed. Rolf Hammel-Kiesow, Munich 2014

mental importance".[4] A loose organisation such as this ensured a high degree of flexibility in the use of informal commercial networks. However, in view of the national consolidation process that had started in the thirteenth century, gained further momentum in the fifteenth century and ultimately gave rise to a Europe of nations and states, the principle of a free union of cities was becoming anachronistic. The loss of importance of the Hanseatic League as an organisation did not result in a general decline of the Hanseatic cities. Lübeck was no longer a dominant player and was forced to compete with equal or stronger rivals in a changed political and economic landscape, but it did so with great success. Danzig and Hamburg remained "hubs of the changing global trade" – or first assumed this role in the early modern period.[5] Their prosperity no longer depended on the Hansa. Actors with state support now shaped events on the North and Baltic Seas.

This is demonstrated by a map made and published by the Swede Olaus Magnus (1490–1557) in 1539. After 1526, Olaus, a Catholic priest, had first lived in Danzig and then in exile in Italy. His *Carta Marina et Descriptio Septentrionalium Terrarum* (Marine map and Description of the Northern Lands) describes the region around the North and Baltic Seas as a spatial unit.[6] It is a precise depiction of an area in which not only the Hanseatic cities, but also the Dutch, English, Scots, Danes and Swedes pursued their activities.

By marking a vessel off the English coast "Danzik", another one in the Skagerrak strait "Hollandi", and others off the Icelandic coast (presumably whalers and merchant vessels) "Scoti", "Angli", "Lubicenes" (residents of Lübeck) and "Hambvrgenses" (residents of Hamburg), Olaus illustrates the transformation of the region. By showing the Hamburg ship firing cannonballs at the Scots – which shatter their mainmast – he offers a sarcastic commentary on the encounter between the two vessels. According to Olaus, the scene reflects "the merchants' dispute over the best place to ply their trade. After all, a judge on land does not ask how they fight at sea, but rather, what they do on land."[7] The drawing of a Swedish warship firing a salvo north of Gotland has a similar function. The map provides an impressive view of maritime trade and demonstrations of power in a shipping and economic area riven by conflict.

An important economic factor is illustrated by the *naves frumentarie* (grain vessels) near the Lithuanian city of Vilnius in the east: "Here many ships are built to carry the grain by river [...] to Danzig in Prussia. From there it goes to Spain, France, England and Holland."[8] In this passage Olaus emphasises the economic integration of the Baltic and North Seas in one core area of trade. Grain was a staple commodity that was grown on a large scale at the time, especially in Poland, and urgently needed in western Europe. Most of all, he stresses the great importance of Danzig as a hub of the grain trade in the first half of the sixteenth century.

Everyday life in the large port cities on the North and Baltic Seas was characterised not only by economic contacts along the coasts and across the waters, but also by cultural exchange. The dissemination of the brick Gothic style continues to be a visible sign of this exchange today. The largest city churches built in this style are St. Mary's Church in Lübeck, St. Nicholas' Church in Stralsund and the St. Mary's churches in Greifswald, Stargard and Danzig. Together with the city halls in Lübeck and Stralsund, which date to the thirteenth and fourteenth centuries, and the late Gothic merchants' houses with their characteristic stepped gables, these houses of worship testify to an urban architecture that originated in Lübeck and spread along the southern Baltic coast.

The life of the Danzig native Georg Giese illustrates the close connection between economic and cultural exchange in a later period. In the post-Hanseatic age, it was also shown by the circle of people with whom Samuel Hartlib (ca. 1600–1662) corresponded. Hartlib was born in Elbing (near Danzig), the son of a wealthy German merchant and an Englishwoman whose father was also a businessman in the town. He attended several European universities, including Cambridge, and settled permanently in England in 1628. He corresponded extensively with scholars in England, the Netherlands, the Swiss Confederation, the Holy Roman Empire and the southern Baltic region stretching from Lübeck to Königsberg. The Danzig native Johannes Hevelius (1611–1687) was one of Hartlib's most important correspondents in the Baltic region. A brewer by trade, Hevelius had risen to become a lay judge and councillor in his native city and was famous across Europe as an astronomer and lunar topographer. In 1630 he moved to the Dutch city of Leiden to study law for a year. He afterwards travelled to England, where he met Hartlib, and then to France. Hevelius returned to Danzig in 1634 and from the 1640s on devoted himself primarily to his scientific studies. He corresponded with Hartlib mainly about books and optical instruments.[9]

Hevelius was part of a communication system that integrated the intellectual elites of the Baltic rim into a network of relations spanning the North and Baltic Seas. Its central reference point was the Netherlands – and, increasingly in the seventeenth century, Great Britain. Although Hevelius deliberately chose Leiden as a place to study, knowledge transfer at the time also proceeded from east to west – as his own independent astronomical research shows. But this is not to deny that the Netherlands and Great Britain played a leading role in the cultural sphere.

Over time, cultural transfer progressed in the same way as the economic ties that had integrated the Baltic lands into an Atlantic-based economic space from

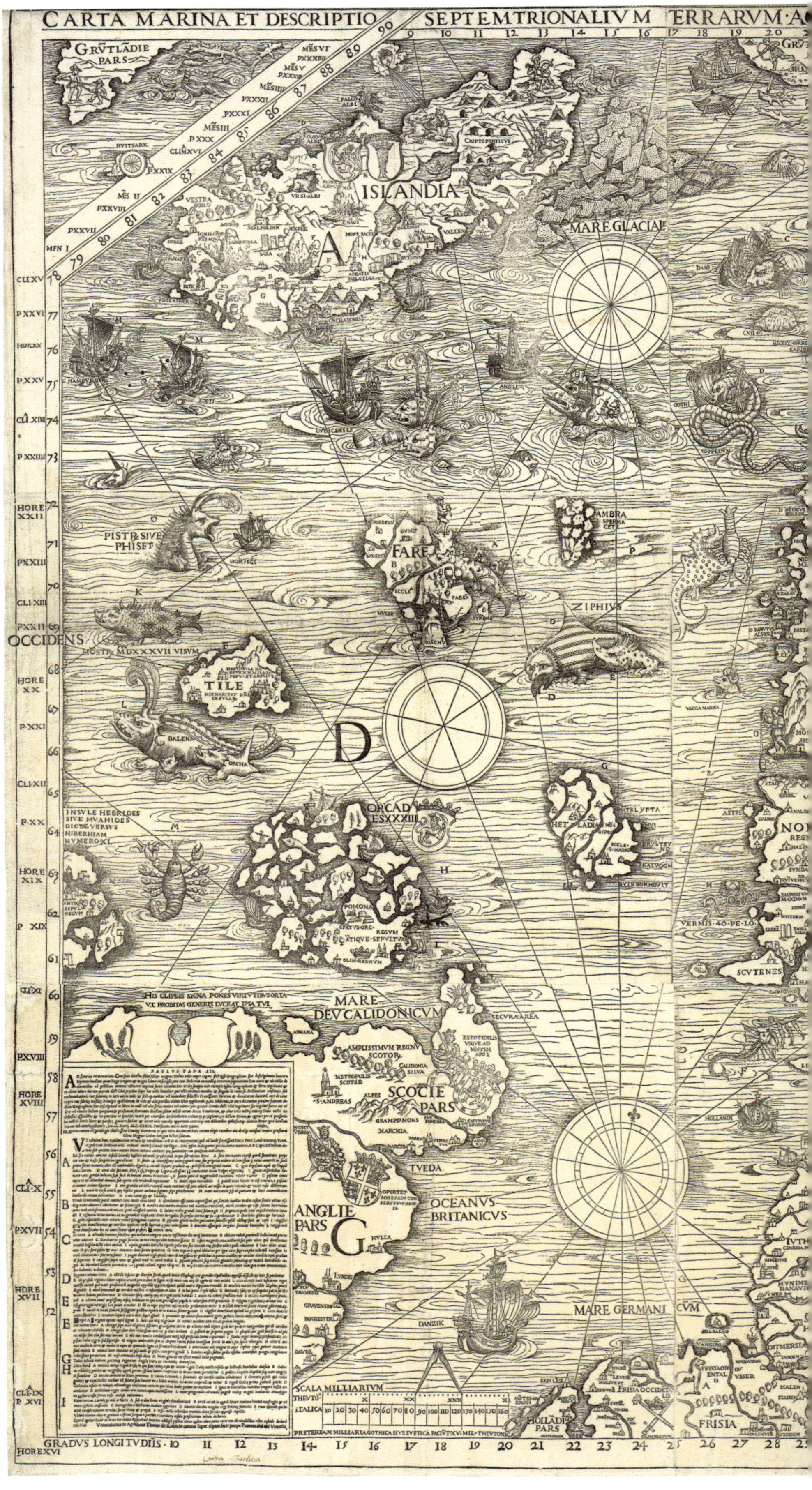

Olaus Magnus, *Carta Marina* (Marine map and Description of the Northern Lands), 1539

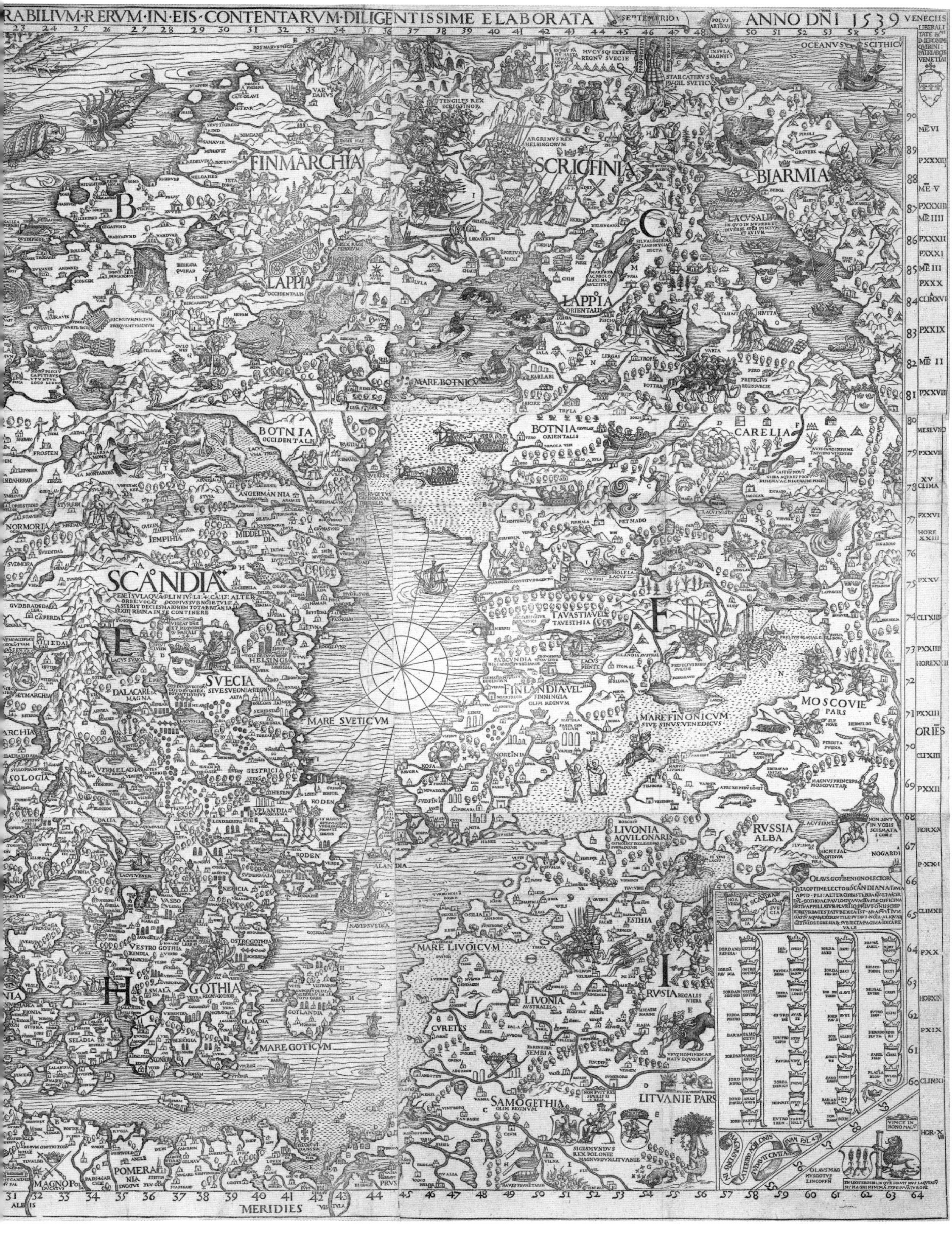
RABILIVM·RERVM·IN·EIS·CONTENTARVM·DILIGENTISSIME ELABORATA
SEPTEMTRIO
ANNO DNI 1539
OCEANVS SCITHICV
FINMARCHIA
SCRICFINIA
BIARMIA
LAPPIA
LAPPIA ORIENTALIS
MARE BOTNICV
BOTNIA OCCIDENTALIS
BOTNIA ORIENTALIS
CARELIA
SCANDIA
SVECIA
DALACARLIA MAGNA
TAVASTIA VEL TAVESTHIA
FINLANDIA VEL FINNINGIA OLIM REGNVM
MARE SVETICVM
MARE FINONICVM SIVE SINVS VENEDICVS
MOSCOVIE PARS
RVSSIA ALBA
LIVONIA AQVILONARIS
ESTHIA
MARE LIVOICVM
LIVONIA AVSTRALIS
GOTHIA
MARE GOTICVM
CVRETES
SAMOGETHIA OLIM REGNVM
LITVANIE PARS
POMERANIA
MERIDIES

the sixteenth century onwards. Within this space, the Baltic lands became the junior partners of the economic and political powers on the western edge of the North Sea, which remained focused on the Atlantic without losing sight of the Baltic region.[10]

The rise of the Netherlands to become the leading economic power in seventeenth-century Europe was ultimately based on the trade in grain from the southern Baltic region, which at the time was described as the *moedercommercie* – the "mother trade" behind the Dutch economic boom. In order to finance grain imports, the Dutch – and especially the inhabitants of Holland and Zeeland – sold products they had produced themselves and thus secured a share of the market for beer, cloth and North Sea herring in the Baltic region. "The demand for cargo space for the expanding trade provided the inhabitants of Holland and Zeeland with access to the Baltic region. In 1580, half of Danzig's imports and exports were transported by Dutch ships, and the share of Dutch boatmen in the Baltic trade increased to between 60 and 70 per cent in the seventeenth century."[11]

The Dutchman Louis De Geer (1587–1652) – who, incidentally, was also in contact with Hartlib's circle – had one of the most astonishing commercial careers of his age. As a young man, he had founded a weapons and iron business in Holland and saw demand for armaments grow during the Thirty Years' War. He built a commercial empire that encompassed the extraction of raw materials, the production and marketing of weapons, and banking and lending operations. Two main factors provided him with ideal conditions: first, the weapons that were required not only for the European powers, but also for Sweden's new "great power" politics in the Baltic rim; and second, the Swedish mining industry with its iron and copper deposits in the mining region in central Sweden. When De Geer arranged a Dutch loan for the king of Sweden in 1618, his own share as a creditor was secured by deliveries of Swedish copper. His business relations with the crown continued to expand rapidly. He acquired, modernised and expanded a range of production facilities. In the 1620s he created a tripartite system consisting of weapons production in Sweden, marketing in Amsterdam and use of the weapons in the German theatres of war.[12] In 1644, in agreement with the Netherlands, he fitted out a fleet at his own expense in order to protect Gothenburg from the Danes.

In 1641, De Geer, who had been living in Sweden since 1627, was elevated to the Swedish nobility. He had prestigious palaces built in Norrköping and Stockholm, their style based on contemporary models from the Dutch Republic. His building activities are a spectacular example of the exemplary function of Dutch architecture in the early "great power" period in Sweden. De Geer embodies the leading economic and cultural role played by the Dutch in the Baltic region. This has been described as the "Dutchification" of the area in the period spanning the second half of the sixteenth and the seventeenth century.[13]

In the late eighteenth century, it was the British who then influenced economic exchange and other relations. Britishness apparently also left its mark on the consumption and thought patterns of the urban elites. From the 1750s on, for example, the news sheet *Wöchentliche Danziger Anzeigen und dienliche Nachrichten* presented advertisements and sales offers for numerous British products, including iron and steel goods, fabrics, fashions, domestic luxury items and medicine.[14] These types of products apparently met the needs of the local upper classes, who could use them to show how modern they were.

In view of these overall developments, it is fair to say that trade on the Baltic was one of the "booming sectors of the global economy in the eighteenth century".[15] However, it is also clear that despite the actors' great diversity, there continued to be a strong focus on the Dutch and English (or British) as the leading economic powers on the North Sea. Hence, in the classical Hanseatic period of late Middle Ages, as well as in the early modern era with its many new actors, everyday life in the port and commercial cities was shaped by far-flung exchange relations that were not limited to the economic sphere. Modes of behaviour and patterns of culture that deeply affected and shaped people's experiential horizons followed on the heels of the trade along the coasts and across the Baltic and the North Seas.

1 Rolf Hammel-Kiesow, *Die Hanse*, 4th edition (Munich, 2008), 10–11.
2 Kurt Löcher, "Der Londoner Stahlhof und Hans Holbein", in Cord Meckseper (ed.), *Stadt im Wandel: Kunst und Kultur des Bürgertums in Norddeutschland 1150–1650*, vol. 3, exhibition catalogue (Stuttgart/Bad Cannstatt, 1985), 667–86, here 672.
3 The "sisters" referred to here are the North and Baltic Seas. See Olaf Mörke, *Die Geschwistermeere: Eine Geschichte des Nord- und Ostseeraumes* (Stuttgart, 2015).
4 Hammel-Kiesow, *Die Hanse*, 78.
5 Peter Moraw, *Von offener Verfassung zu gestalteter Verdichtung: Das Reich im späten Mittelalter 1250 bis 1490* (Frankfurt am Main, 1985), 316.
6 A facsimile of the *Carta Marina* can be found in Olaus Magnus, *Die Wunder des Nordens*, ed. Elena Balzamo and Reinhard Kaiser (Frankfurt a. M., 2006). This publication also contains an edition of *Beschreibung der Völker des Nordens*, which Olaus Magnus published in 1567 (Latin original: *Historia de gentibus septentrionalibus*, 1555). The English translations are based on the German text.
7 Olaus Magnus, *Die Wunder des Nordens*, 52.
8 Ibid., 81.
9 Klara Deecke and Ingrid Gabel, "Der Hartlib-Kreis im südlichen Ostseeraum", in Martin Krieger und Michael North (eds.), *Land und Meer: Kultureller Austausch zwischen Westeuropa und dem Ostseeraum in der Frühen Neuzeit* (Cologne, 2004), 221–252.
10 For both a general and more specific discussion, see Mörke 2015, 119–142.
11 Michael North, *Geschichte der Ostsee: Handel und Kulturen* (Munich, 2011), 114–15.
12 J. Thomas Lindblad, "Louis de Geer (1587–1652): Dutch Entrepreneur and the Father of the Swedish Industry", in Clé Lesger and Leo Noordegraaf (eds.), *Entrepreneurs and Entrepreneurship in Early Modern Times: Merchants and Industrialists within the Orbit of the Dutch Staple Market* (The Haag, 1995), 77–84.
13 Michael North, "Die Niederlandisierung des Ostseeraumes", in Jörg Hackmann and Robert Schweitzer (eds.), *Nordosteuropa als Geschichtsregion* (Helsinki and Lübeck, 2006), 368–377; Edmund Kizik, "Niederländische Einflüsse in Danzig, Polen und Litauen vom 16. bis zum 18. Jahrhundert", in Martin Krieger and Michael North (eds.), *Land und Meer: Kultureller Austausch zwischen Westeuropa und dem Ostseeraum in der Frühen Neuzeit* (Cologne, 2004), 51–76.
14 Almut Hillebrand, *Danzig und die Kaufmannschaft großbritannischer Nation: Rahmenbedingungen, Formen und Medien eines englischen Kulturtransfers im Ostseeraum des 18. Jahrhunderts* (Frankfurt am Main, 2009), 189–90.
15 North, 2011, 180.

Stefan Rinke

“NEW WORLDS”

Discoveries and Subjugation

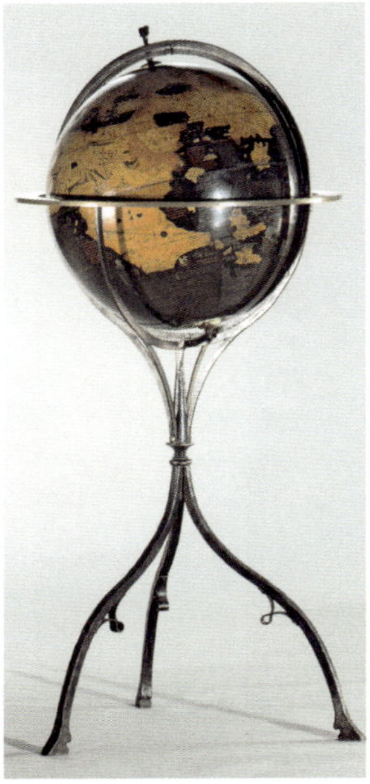

4/24
Copy of the Behaim Globe, c. 1892 (original 1492)

Human beings have embarked on journeys of discovery for different motives since time immemorial. They have scouted, explored and conquered new territories along with their inhabitants. As Europeans gained greater experience with shipbuilding and navigation, the sea became an increasingly important transit space. It extended the borders of the known world and allowed new worlds to be discovered. By the end of the Middle Ages, the oceans had considerably expanded the horizons of these journeys. Those undertaken from the fifteenth century onwards were a special characteristic of this era, which was later called the “modern period” because of the related discoveries. For centuries, European historians have regarded this process as a key element of the “Europeanisation” of the world. Only recently has there been greater interest in the “discovered” and “subjugated” peoples who did not voluntarily line the streets to applaud the Europeans upon their arrival.

From a European perspective, the discovery of America in 1492 is one of the most obvious turning points in world history. “Discovery” implies something entirely new, but in fact the Vikings had landed on the North American coast around five hundred years earlier. And thousands of years before them, the region was claimed and settled for the first time by people from other parts of the globe. The term “America” did not exist in 1492. It is based on the idea of a spatial unit, which was not recognised until Amerigo Vespucci (1454–1512) published his travelogue *Mundus Novus* or *New World*.

Ancient and medieval origins

It is no accident that the impetus to establish contact with America came from Europe. Europeans had various reasons and motives to embark on the long, uncertain voyage to the west. The idea of a realm of the dead, located in the direction of the setting sun, was known from ancient cultures. The assumption of a land of the blessed lying in the west, fueled by ancient Greek and Egyptian sources, mixed with fears stirred by other legends: of unknown sea monsters, eerie darkness, stillness and other natural barriers erected by the gods to protect their realm from intruders. As can be concluded from such imaginings, the ocean in the west was seen as the boundary of the realm reserved for human beings.

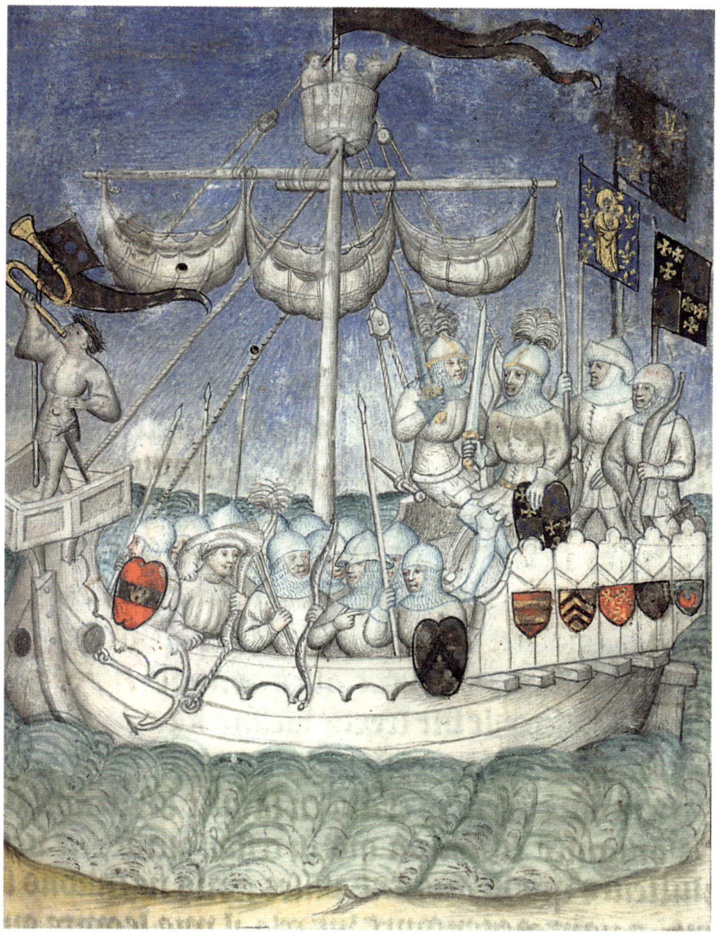

4/2
Pierre Bontier/Jean le Verrier,
The conquest and the conquerors of the Canary Islands (detail), c. 1405

These legends were known to the people who lived on this ocean's coasts – in places such as the Iberian Peninsula and Ireland and thus at the assumed *finis terrae* or end of the world. However, unfavourable winds or the search for new fish stocks often took these people into unfamiliar territory. We do not know how many mariners lost their lives in the west, but those that returned brought knowledge of the western sea and the islands they had discovered there. As the Middle Ages progressed, this knowledge slowly grew more detailed.

One legend that was widely disseminated in the Middle Ages tells of the Irish monk Brendan and his voyage westward in the sixth century. In the western sea, Brendan reportedly discovered the promised "Isle of the Blessed", which had paradisiacal features. Christopher Columbus (ca. 1451–1506) is said to have read a version of this legend titled *Navigatio Sancti Brendani* (Voyage of Saint Brendan the Abbot). In antiquity and the Middle Ages, voyagers assumed they would find wondrous islands in the West Atlantic, including not only Antillia – the "Isle of Seven Cities" – but also Brasil (Gaelic for "Isle of the Blessed") and the Isle of the Hesperides. The origins of these legends are difficult to trace, but their power lay in the fact that, according to Herodotus (fifth century BC), unexpected treasures existed there. This is why they were included in fifteenth-century maps.

Genuine discoveries were also made. A few centuries after Brendan's voyage, seafaring Irish monks discovered not only the Faroe Islands but then, around 795, Thule Island – present-day Iceland. They were later expelled from Thule by the

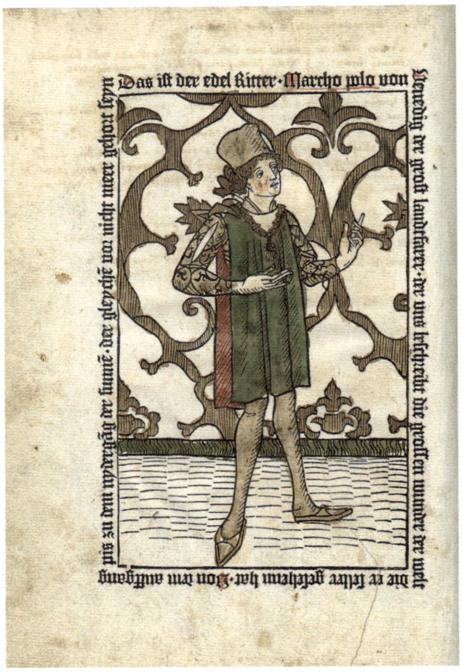

2/5
Marco Polo, *Il Milione*, German edition, 1477

Norwegians. As part of the Viking expansion, Erik the Red (ca. 950–ca. 1003) discovered Greenland in 981/82 and his son Leif Eriksson (ca. 970–ca. 1020) landed in Newfoundland ("Vinland") off the North American coast around 1000/1001. However, most of this knowledge was lost or not widely disseminated, not least because the Vikings did not recognise these lands as part of a new continent.

In the late thirteenth century, the Europeans' knowledge of the world took a crucial step forward. In this period they were primarily interested in Asia and planned a Christian-Mongol alliance against Islam. The Franciscans Giovanni da Pian del Carpine (ca. 1185–1252) and Wilhelm of Rubruk (1215/20 – ca. 1270) were despatched to make initial contact. These activities formed the backdrop to the life of Venetian explorer Marco Polo (1254–1324) and the journeys he took in the empire of Kublai Khan, the Great Khan of the Mongols (1271–1292). Showing a penchant for exaggeration, Marco Polo's travel report *Il Milione*[1] – which he dictated in Genoese captivity in 1299 – brought news of the vast riches of both Cathay (China) and Cipangu (Japan) and an overestimation of Asia's eastward expansion to Europe.

The much less reliable travel report by Sir John Mandeville (ca. 1300–1371), which emerged after 1355 and was based on a journey to the Holy Land, was every bit as influential. It combines real observations with fictitious stories about monstrous creatures and fantastical islands. It tells of one-eyed and one-footed men, Amazons, and the Isle of the Blessed, where men and women walk about stark naked, have only communal property and unfortunately indulge in cannibalism. While this travelogue still views Jerusalem as the centre of the world, it suggests the earth can be circumnavigated by ship.

Such fluid transitions between myth, speculation and knowledge, between biblical and ancient ideas about the cosmos, are reflected in the atlases and cosmographies that emerged in the late Middle Ages and that by no means present the earth as flat. The authors drew on the ancient Greek model of a globe divided into inhabitable and uninhabitable parts; the inhabitable sphere in the northern half corresponds to that of the antipodes in the southern half. In addition to these overall representations of the earth, there existed map-like depictions of the known, inhabitable world that were circular in design and showed the continents surrounded by T-shaped bodies of water with Jerusalem at the centre. One example is the well-known Ebstorf Map of the World dating to the early fourteenth century. Together with its descriptive text, it portrays important sites of biblical history based on the work of Isidore of Seville (ca. 560–636). What remains answered, though, is who exactly lived on the still unexplored continent in the south, the *terra australis*. In this part of the world, the maps often show monsters and strange creatures from the legends and myths that probably inspired works such as the *World Chronicle* by Hartmann Schedel (1440–1514).

In addition to these theologically influenced works, cartographers made maps in the thirteenth century that met the specific needs of sailors from regions along the Atlantic coast and also from Italy. A key role was played by the Arab Muhammad al-Idrīsī (1099–1165), who lived in Sicily around 1150. Working at the interface between medieval and early modern conceptions of the world, al-Idrīsī created the most important world map of the pre-modern period. These sea or portolan charts, which portray the coasts and islands of the known seas, culminated in the Catalan Atlas, produced by Abraham Cresques (1325–1387) in 1375. In the fifteenth century, a number of ancient authors were rediscovered, which laid the groundwork for additional valuable insights. The *Geographia* by the Alexandrian scholar Claudius Ptolemy (100–168) assumed considerable importance.

4/23
Claudius Ptolemy, *Oikumene* (Map of the known world), 2nd cent. A.D. (facsimile 1983)

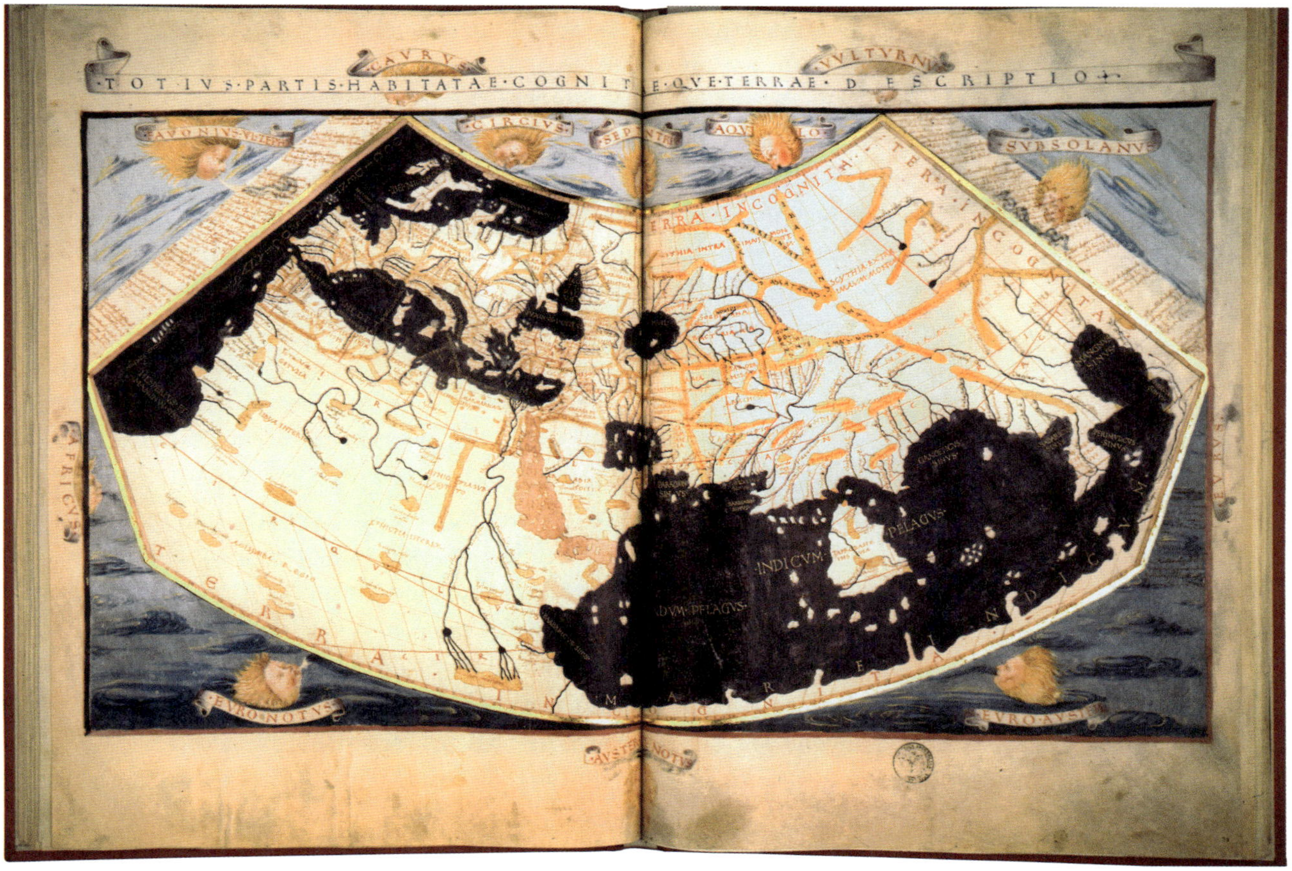

Under the title *Cosmographia*, its Latin version attracted great attention. Its insights into the spherical shape of the earth and the method of stereographic projection were disseminated by numerous maps. This revival of the ancient conception of the world extended well into the sixteenth century. In 1459, Ptolemaic ideas and newly acquired knowledge found their way into the world map of the Venetian monk Fra Mauro (ca. 1385–1459), which reflects the European understanding of the world that was rapidly expanding due to the voyages of discovery.

The Portuguese and Spanish

That this map was commissioned by Afonso V of Portugal (1432–1481) is not surprising, for Portugal played a leading role in southern European expansion in the fifteenth century, which was driven by political and commercial developments in the eastern Mediterranean region. Trade with the East was clearly the main objective of all the discoverers, but Christian missionary work in the unexplored regions became an additional motive once the Crusades began. There was also a genuine interest in foreign peoples and cultures. Motives became mixed when Islam grew into a more serious threat and the old trade routes were disrupted. When trade opportunities in the eastern Mediterranean region were further restricted in the fifteenth century – especially after the Ottoman conquest of Constantinople in 1453 – the focus of economic activities and seafaring expeditions shifted to the western Mediterranean and the Atlantic. The Iberian powers were thus able to exploit their geographical advantage and take the lead from the Italians. They drew on the knowledge and financial capital of the Genoese, Florentine and Venetian communities that could be found throughout the Mediterranean region from the twelfth century onwards.

The *Reconquista* or reconquest of the Iberian Peninsula from Arab Muslim rule ended in 1492 and unleashed tremendous expansionary forces. Portugal had completed this process in the mid-thirteenth century and thus at a much earlier date than neighbouring Castile. Portuguese expansion in the Atlantic region began in the fifteenth century, reaching an initial peak when Bartolomeu Dias (1450–1500) sailed around the Cape of Good Hope in 1487/88. Nevertheless, an additional ten years were to pass before Vasco da Gama (1469–1524) set out on a journey in 1497 that would take him to his desired destination, India, by sea. By that time, the reconquest of the territory of the Castilian Crown had also been completed, and Spain was competing with Portugal to make discoveries at sea.

By 1492, the Iberian kingdoms had gained valuable experience from the *Reconquista*, the expeditions in the Atlantic and the colonisation of the Canary Islands. They knew how to explore, conquer and rule foreign lands and seas. The Portuguese and Spanish had learned that distant journeys into the unknown were a risk worth taking because the profits from new settlements and commercial enterprises could be enormous. They did not respect what was foreign to them, but condemned it according to the categories of their time. This meant that they spared anyone who submitted to their will and was willing to accept the Christian faith, but were ruthless in dealings with those who stood in the way of their conquests. Betrayal, extortion, robbery and enslavement were the instruments of the Iberian expansion. The explorers were convinced that they were serving a noble cause. Legitimised by the Pope, they believed that they were acting on higher orders, as it were – indeed, that they were on a crusade. The men who fought these battles and survived the adventurous voyages were a special breed. They were conquerors who in the newly discovered territories fought against "pagan" peoples who were seen as existing outside the European value system. If they were only forceful enough, they stood to profit from the unforeseen opportunities for social advancement and spatial mobility. Ultimately, their goal was to acquire status symbols such as large-scale land holdings and social ranks that would have been extremely difficult for them to attain in "old" Europe.

Interpretations

Columbus had not the slightest doubt that his discoveries were of great importance and portrayed them as a God-ordained victory for all of Christianity which would bring great wealth and prosperity and whose significance would extend far beyond his age. However, in interpreting the strange things he saw with his own eyes as part of the biblical story of salvation, he remained trapped in traditional thinking. A few years later, as the dimensions of his discoveries became clear, contemporaries such as the famous Dominican friar Bartolomé de las Casas (1484–1566) spoke of a new age that was comparable to no other. As a result, in the European version of world history, the year 1492 was seen as a central turning point, a rupture that separated the allegedly dark Middle Ages from the rebirth of the human spirit in the Renaissance.

What made Columbus's journey influential was the profound transformation of communication media at the time, brought about by the invention of printing with movable type. The successes were deliberately connected to the completion

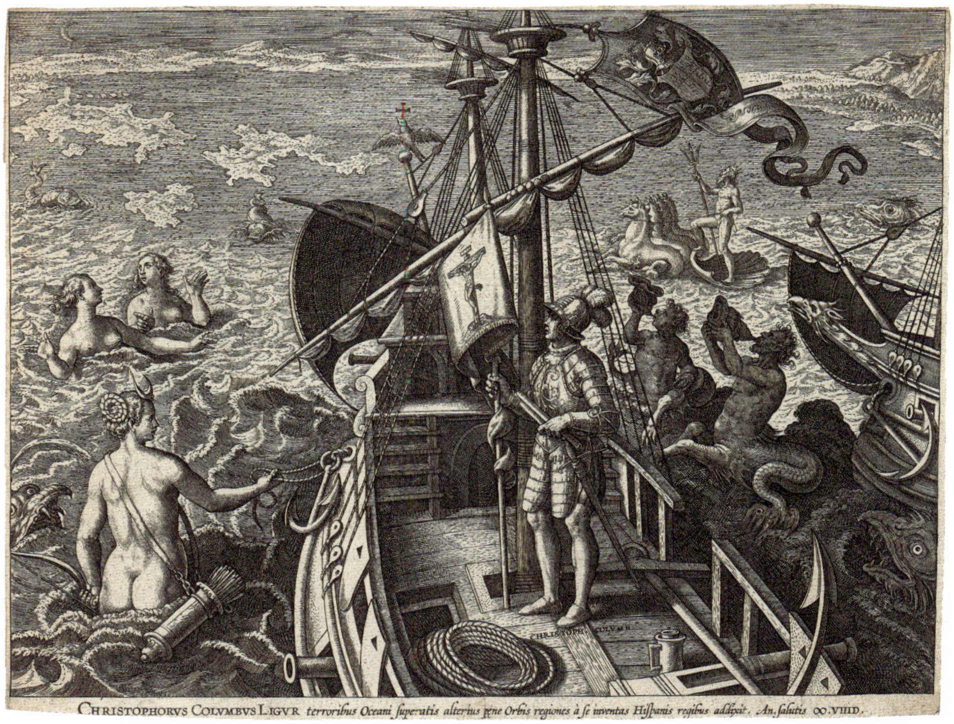

Jan van der Straet, Christopher Columbus on his ship, c. 1589

of the *Reconquista* and the expulsion of Jews from Spain. As a result, it was possible to tie the discovery of America to other important developments in 1492. Beyond Spain, these included numerous European events around 1500 – or events originating in Europe – such as the creation of Martin Behaim's terrestrial globe in Nuremberg, further expeditions and, in particular, Vasco da Gama's voyage to India along the eastern sea route. The upheaval in many areas of life and the experience of the new created the impression of a temporal break.

This idea of a transition in the temporal dimension corresponded to changing ideas about space. Nevertheless, the perception of upheaval spread only slowly. Columbus was unaware of the spatial dimension because he believed he had discovered the islands he had expected to find off the coast of Cathay (China). His error was quickly recognised by the voyagers who followed in his footsteps over the next decade. Especially after the publication of Vespucci's *Mundus Novus* in 1502/03, the continental character of the discovered region became clear, even if it took longer for this knowledge to reach a broader audience. As a result, the European conception of the world, though still drawing on medieval knowledge, changed fundamentally.

The discovery of Americas opened up entirely new possibilities. Even the feasibility of circumnavigating the earth was soon demonstrated, which provided a foundation for a new awareness of the world. After Columbus, the knowledge gained from empirical observations gradually replaced ancient myths in efforts to explain what was new. In 1492, one part of the globe – the lands discovered by Columbus – entered into a dialogue with the (suddenly) "Old World", which in turn expanded its networks at an ever greater pace as a result of the intensifying exchange processes. The resulting interactions first spanned the Atlantic and later assumed global proportions. Once a mere appendage to the Eurasian landmass, Europe rose to become the "West" that made a successful bid for power in the following period.

European kingdoms became colonial rulers over foreign peoples in distant lands, whom they violently oppressed and exploited. Economic ties facilitated the trade in exotic goods, which fundamentally changed life in many ways. The migration of people from different parts of the globe – sometimes voluntarily, but mostly forced – gave rise to new populations. Animals, plants and pathogens arrived with the people. With the European expansion to America, Christianity spread as a world religion and grew in importance as a rival to Islam. These contacts and encounters changed not only those directly touched by them. From a European perspective, the year 1492 clearly marks a historical turning point.

Other discoverers

But did this also apply to the "discovered" peoples, who, in contrast to Columbus, did not leave a written record of events? It was not only the absence of written sources that led the Europeans to regard the indigenous peoples as the passive, voiceless objects of European industriousness for centuries – and as part of the wilderness that needed to be eliminated. A key aspect of the new European view of the world, which resulted from the discovery of America, was the Europeans' self-conception as the centre and rulers of the world.

Thanks to recent research, a more nuanced understanding of the indigenous perspective is possible. The assumption by European scholars that the indigenous peoples regarded the arrival of the Europeans as a return of their gods and integrated it into their messianic prophecies was long considered valid. It is based on the idea that indigenous societies were "traditional" and hence incapable of interpreting the unknown in a rational way. What was not recognised was that a specific European understanding of rational action formed the basis of these ideas – and that Columbus did not live up to this standard in any way himself.

New interpretations of the source materials suggest that the situation is likely to have been different for many of the peoples who came into contact with Europeans for the first time. The various indigenous ethnicities responded quite pragmatically to the new and were indeed capable of understanding the arrival of the Europeans. They also had historical knowledge, even if it was passed down from one generation to the next in different ways (usually orally) than was the case in Europe. The Europeans' arrival was certainly a surprising experience for most, but encounters with culturally diverse foreigners with superior weapons was nothing new to them, particularly in the Caribbean region.

According to Columbus's report, the exchange of gifts paved the way for the first communication between Europeans and indigenous groups. As a result, the first social relations emerged between lifeworlds that were completely different. Despite the language barrier, the inhabitants of the Caribbean islands – the Taino – immediately understood the "language" of the gift and responded in a way that was comprehensible to the Europeans. However, what was incomprehensible and destined to remain so was the value that the gifts had in the other group's cultural context. The gifts the Spaniards made to the Taino were grotesquely valueless from a European perspective, and the Europeans interpreted their counterparts' excessive gratitude and counter-gifts as a sign of weakness. However, from the indigenous point of view, the bells, beads and colourful fabrics they received had a symbolic value that was linked to their belief system. This misunderstanding extended beyond the interpretation of the gift exchange. What the Europeans took to be names of places where gold had been discovered were merely the names of places central to Taino mythology. Many things seemed consistent with European knowledge and the European legends that Columbus knew from his reading. This prior knowledge turned out to be baggage that worsened the comprehension problems.

In later periods, the indigenous states on the mainland responded in different ways to the European invaders. This was due, not least, to the fact that the European invasion dragged on for many decades, if not centuries, after it began in 1492. From the indigenous perspective, there was a considerable difference between 1) witnessing the arrival of the first Europeans or encountering them soon after their arrival, and 2) experiencing the conquest of the Inca Empire forty years later, when knowledge of the newcomers had changed considerably. Even around 1570, after the consolidation of the Iberian kingdoms, the vast American territories had not yet been completely conquered. Depending on the historical context and the cultural background of these highly diverse peoples, who were first collectively referred to as "Indios" (i.e. natives of India) by Columbus, the clash with the Europeans was experienced quite differently.

However, as concerns the indigenous population and the year 1492, we can nevertheless speak of a turning point without supporting a Eurocentric line of

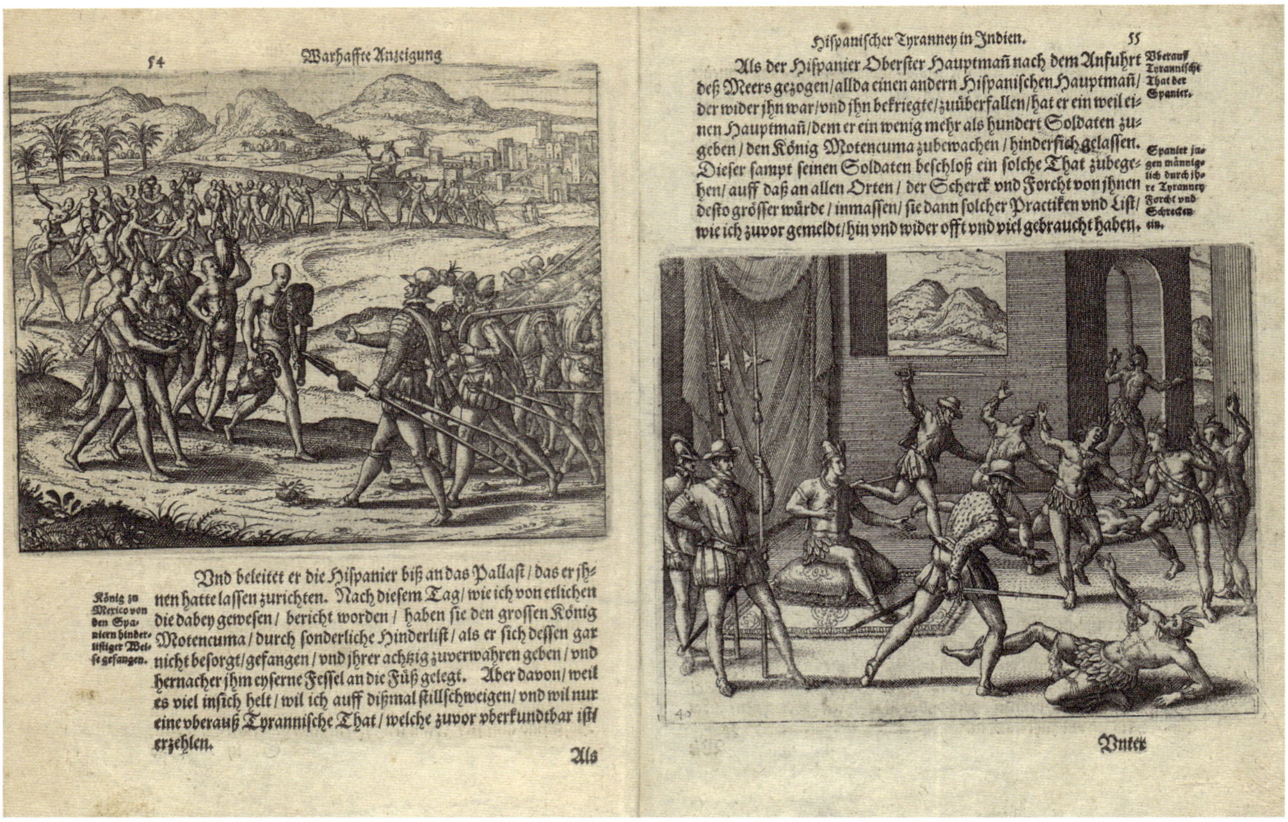
54 Warhaffte Anzeigung

Vnd beleitet er die Hispanier biß an das Pallast / das er jhnen hatte lassen zurichten. Nach diesem Tag / wie ich von etlichen die dabey gewesen / bericht worden / haben sie den grossen König Motencuma / durch sonderliche Hinderlist / als er sich dessen gar nicht besorgt / gefangen / vnd jhrer achtzig zuverwahren geben / vnd hernacher jhm eyserne Fessel an die Füß gelegt. Aber davon / weil es viel insich helt / wil ich auff dißmal stillschweigen / vnd wil nur eine vberauß Tyrannische That / welche zuvor vberkundtbar ist / erzehlen.

König in Mexico von den Spaniern hinderlistiger Weise gefangen.

Als

Hispanischer Tyranney in Indien. 55

Als der Hispanier Oberster Hauptman nach dem Anfuhrt deß Meers gezogen / allda einen andern Hispanischen Hauptman / der wider jhn war / vnd jhn bekriegte / zuüberfallen / hat er ein weil einen Hauptman / dem er ein wenig mehr als hundert Soldaten zugeben / den König Motencuma zubewachen / hinder sich gelassen. Dieser sampt seinen Soldaten beschloß ein solche That zubegehen / auff daß an allen Orten / der Schreck vnd Forcht von jhnen desto grösser würde / immassen / sie dann solcher Practiken vnd List / wie ich zuvor gemeldt / hin vnd wider offt vnd viel gebraucht haben.

Vberauß Tyrannische That der Spanier.

Spanier jagen männiglich durch jhre Tyranney Forcht vnd Schrecken ein.

Vnter

Bartolomé de Las Casas, *Kurzgefasster Bericht von der Verwüstung der Westindischen Länder (A Short Account of the Destruction of the Indies)*, 1613

argumentation. After all, the year marked the beginning of one of the greatest demographic disasters in human history. Pre-Columbian history had been characterised by invasions, foreign rule and the overlayering of cultures and empires by the newcomers, but with the arrival of the European conquerors and, soon afterwards, the African slaves, the inhabitants of Americas experienced change on a previously unknown scale. Their life was to be transformed more fundamentally than ever before.

1 The English title of the work is *The Travels of Marco Polo.*

Michael North

EUROPE MEETS ASIA

Between Missionary Work and Cultural Exchange

Since time immemorial, the seas have connected different regions of the globe by facilitating the transport of people and goods to even the most remote locations. Luxury items such as sugar became bulk commodities because it was possible to cultivate them in the New World and ship them to Europe. The new commodity cultures changed lifestyles. One example is tea consumption, which spread from China to Europe and North America via England and the Netherlands. In 1800, the English consumed an average of 2.5 pounds of tea per capita annually, sweetening it with 17 pounds of sugar. Tea, sugar and porcelain entered into a cultural symbiosis with the surrounding furnishings: tea vessels were developed with new shapes and decorations and arranged on specially designed tables or displayed in special furniture.

The exchange of goods across the seas shaped the participating societies and resulted in the emergence of new societies and commodity cultures on either shore. In Asia and Europe, cultural goods were produced that met local and global demand, which in turn influenced their artisanal production. Exports of Chinese porcelain and Japanese lacquerware not only inspired imitations in Europe, but also led to a general fondness for chinoiserie in a variety of forms. By contrast, import bans on printed Indian textiles in the eighteenth century encouraged calico printing in England and Europe, which revolutionised fashions and led to the spread of European cotton fabrics across the world.

Asian goods such as silk, spices, pearls, precious stones and essential oils were known to the Europeans even before the discovery of the sea route to India, having arrived via complex trade relations on land and by sea. Long before Europeans encountered the inhabitants of Asia, they were confronted with Asian goods. Merchants, merchandise and the occasional travel report stirred fantasies about Asia that ultimately inspired Europeans to search for direct routes to the region. After Vasco da Gama (1469–1524) discovered the sea route to India, the Portuguese learned of the famous trading centre in Malacca – a meeting place for Arab, Indian and Chinese merchants. It is not surprising that Malacca became a prized possession in campaigns of conquest and was taken by the Portuguese in 1511.

Maritime traffic was intensified on the routes from the Middle East to India and China that had been known since medieval times. Merchants, sailors, soldiers, envoys, missionaries, pilgrims and slaves travelled the world's seas. The expansion

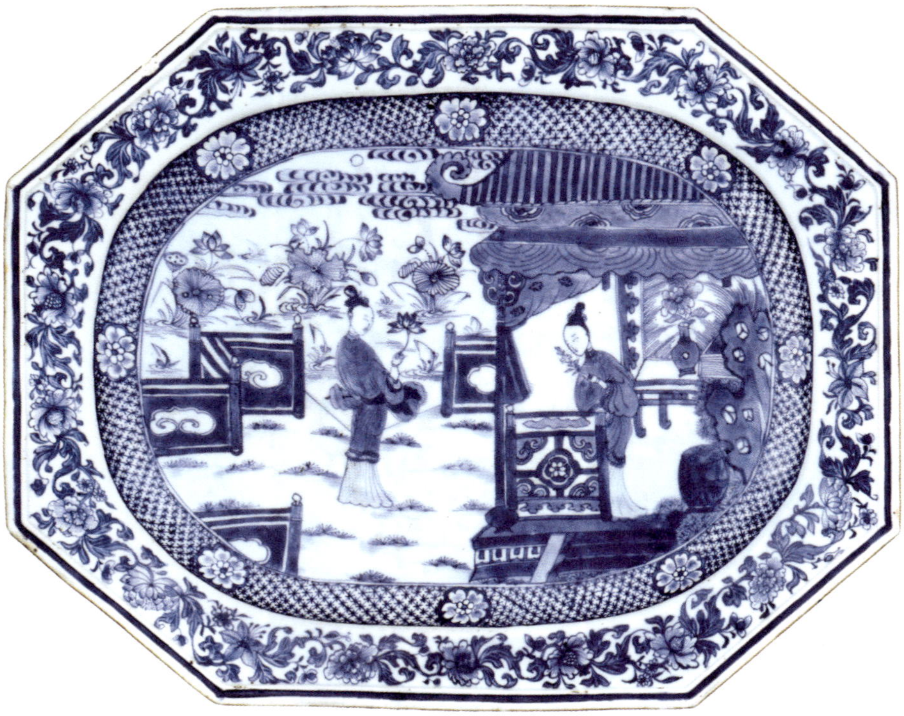

Chinese blue-and-white porcelain with architectural and landscape motifs, 1662/1722

of trade in the Indian Ocean breathed new life into old ports while promoting the establishment of new trading centres. These developments benefited coastal inhabitants and migrants from the interior, who wanted to participate in the economic boom. The Europeans who arrived in Asia moved through a network of trading stations dominated by local merchants and seafaring dynasties.

The largest group was the Chinese, who were represented everywhere. Working in the port cities, they established ties (via rivers) to producers in the interior and procured the goods that were popular overseas. They supplied the Europeans at the trading stations primarily with silk, porcelain, screens, paper and, later, tea. Afterwards, in cities such as Batavia, they loaded their junks with precious metals, sandalwood, buffalo horn, bird's nests, ivory, pepper and other spices and transported them to China. In later periods they also carried tin and cloth.

It was not only Batavia, but also Ayutthaya, Malacca and Hôi An that were home to the large Chinese communities that maintained ties to the Pacific region and Spanish America via Manila. The Japanese merchants living there arranged for the transport of the Chinese goods to Japan, where shipping to outside destinations was limited or regulated by permit.

In addition, merchants from the Middle Kingdom served as intermediaries between the global trade networks and the local producers in South-East Asia. This is illustrated by the emerging market for shellac, which was produced in South-East Asia. Natural shellac is formed when lac bugs colonise trees – in most cases, banyans – and secrete a scarlet resinous substance on their branches. At the time, this substance was dried, ground and shipped to China and Japan, where it was used as a lacquer to preserve and decorate wooden cabinets, boxes, wall screens and other furniture. Chinese and Japanese lacquerware was highly prized not only in the Indian Ocean region but above all in Europe, which led to growing demand and an enormous production boom.

In their studies of global cultural exchange, historians and art historians have focused intensely on both the role and missionary work of the Jesuits who went to southern and eastern Asia in the Portuguese-Spanish network in order to convert the upper classes in India, Japan and China. Jesuits, in particular, acquainted themselves with local customs and practices in order to gain access to the indigenous societies. They attempted to strike a balance between previous beliefs and the new teachings. However, as can be seen in early seventeenth-century Japan, missionary work soon resulted in the persecution of Christians and the expulsion of the Portuguese. The Jesuits had greater success in China, where they were valued as experts on Western technology, knowledge, art and architecture. However, even there they never established permanent structures because they were unable to convert the Mandarin. An estimated 920 Jesuits travelled to China between 1552 and 1800. That number may seem small, but the Jesuit missionaries had considerable journalistic impact in conjunction with their campaigns to secure material support for their worldwide missionary work. They appealed to the Europeans' curiosity and interest in distant lands and supplemented stories of conversion successes with observations about the lifestyles of the new or future Christians. They created an information system of letters, scholarly essays, travelogues and devout missionary reports. They also sent curiosities, plants, animals and other objects back to Europe.

Martino Martini, *Nova et Accuratissima Sinarum Imperii Tabula* (New and accurate map of the Chinese empire), 1658

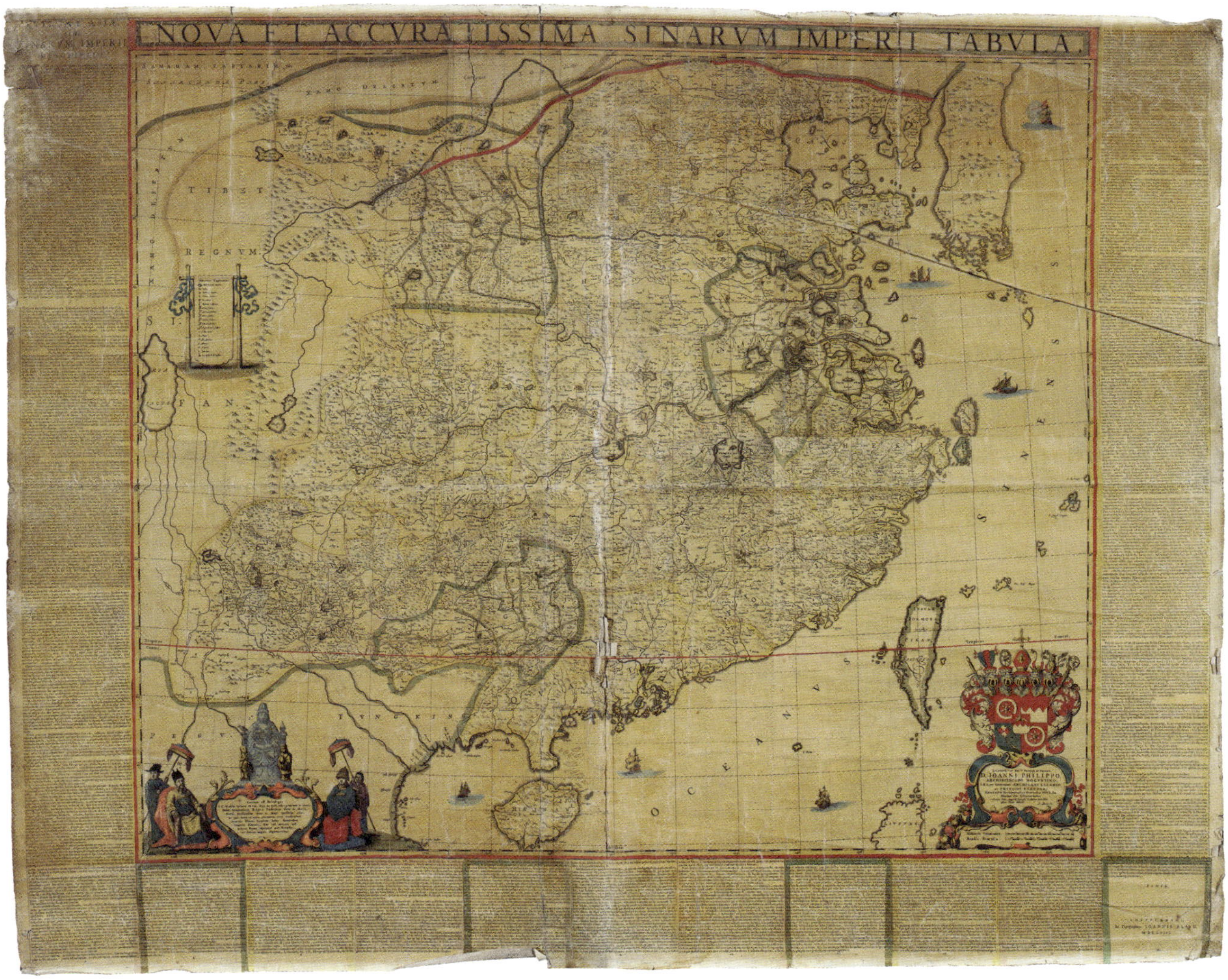

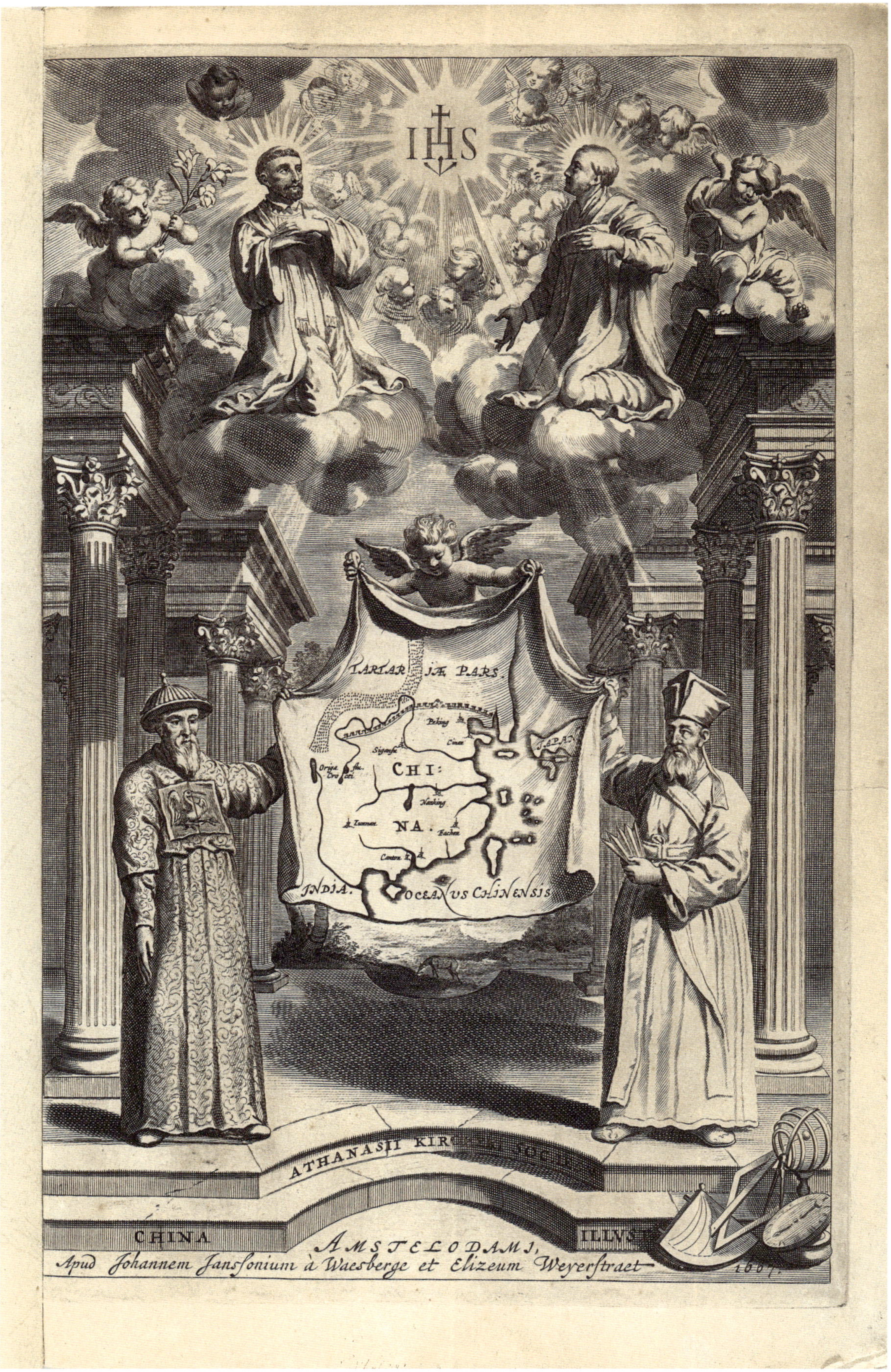
IHS
TARTAR IÆ PARS
CHI:
NA.
INDIA.
OCEANUS CHINENSIS
ATHANASII KIRC
CHINA
ILLVS
AMSTELODAMI,
Apud Johannem Jansonium à Waesberge et Elizeum Weyerstraet

If these figures are compared to those of the European merchants, other dimensions become clear. Between 1600 and 1800, around five thousand Dutch (or Europeans in Dutch service) travelled to South-East Asia on Dutch ships each year, two-thirds of whom remained in the region. Thus, both the Dutch and the Europeans in their service had a greater impact on the region and the Dutch motherland.

Through their presence, the Dutch exerted a significant influence on cultural exchange with Asia. The large number of actors involved in the transfer process connected not only maritime regions from the Arabian Sea to the East China Sea, but also the world's oceans. After all, Dutch merchants were also active in the North and South Atlantic. The success of the Dutch was also based on their great willingness to adapt. For example, they quickly learned the customs of the different Asian societies in which they lived and performed the required ceremonies in the interest of their business. They conducted correspondence in Malay, Persian (Farsi), Portuguese and Chinese; they performed the kowtow (unlike the British and Russians); and they submitted to the complex customs at the courts of the Moguls, the rulers of Kandy and Mataram, and the court of Siam. They occasionally shared European technical and scientific knowledge with the native population and were thus often the only source of knowledge about the world.

The colonial societies differed in terms of the goods they traded and the manner of collaboration between the Europeans and the native population. While the Dutch lived together with many other ethnic groups in Batavia and Cape Town, they were isolated in Dejima and were only occasionally allowed to receive visitors. Once a year, the director, along with the physician and scribe from the trading post, was required to make an official trip to Edo to pay respects to the shogun. These delegations eventually grew to include between 100 and 150 people, including Japanese interpreters and escorts. The journey took around three months and the delegations incurred substantial costs for the gifts they gave to the shogun and other dignitaries. A list of the expected gifts was usually made available to the Dutch some time in advance. The *dagregisters* (official diaries) from Dejima provide precise information on this reciprocal process and are thus an important source that illuminates cultural exchange between Japan, the Netherlands and Europe. Not only did the delegations provide the Dutch with the opportunity to leave Dejima once a year, but, conversely, they also enabled the Japanese to meet people from the West. Particularly when the Dutch made stops in Kyoto, Japanese officials came out to meet them and become acquainted with Western customs and practices. Japanese scholars specialised in Western studies (called *rangaku* or "Holland studies"), while European mediators such as Engelbert Kämpfer (1651–1716) and Carl Peter Thunberg (1743–1828) conveyed scholarly knowledge from Japan to the Netherlands and the rest of Europe. Philipp Franz Siebold (1796–1866) was able to build on both these men's research when – like his abovementioned predecessors – he worked as a physician for the Vereenigde Oostindische Compagnie (Dutch East India Company) in Dejima. Siebold brought Western medical knowledge to Japan and founded a medical school for Japanese students in Nagasaki. In addition, he gathered information about Japanese flora and fauna and the living habits of the Japanese people. To this end he compiled botanical, zoological and ethnographic collections, which for the most part still exist in Leiden and Munich today. Western medical knowledge was highly prized in Japan, but Siebold's collecting activities, which came to light when part of his collection

5/6
Athanasius Kircher, *China illustrata* (Treatise on China), 1667

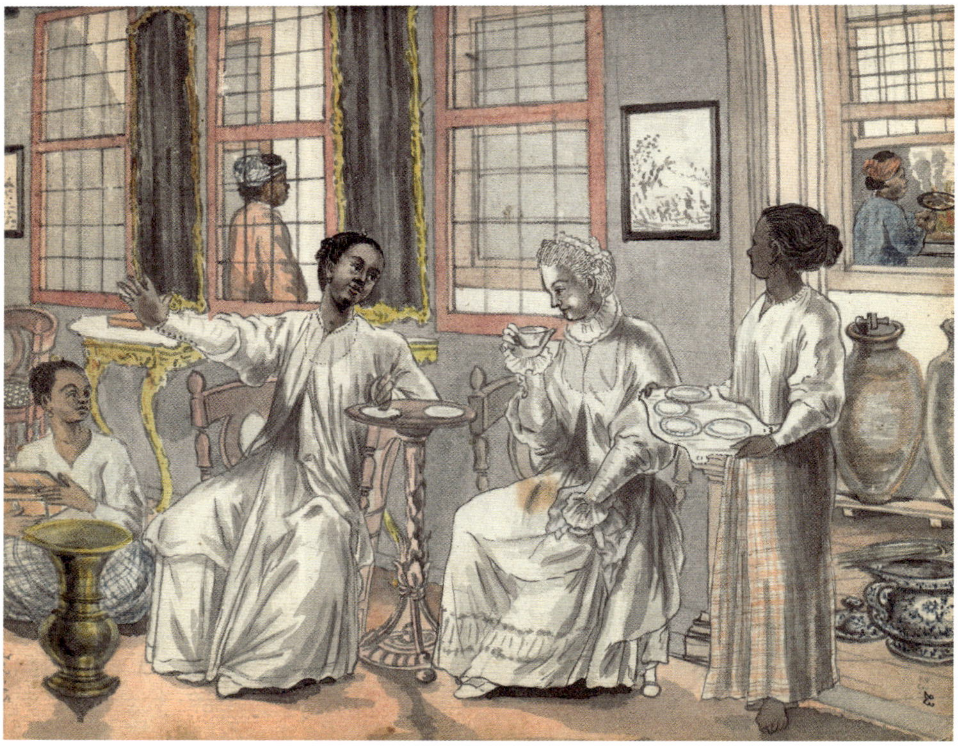

Jan Brandes, *Teatime in a European household in Batavia*, 1779/1785

went down in a ship, met with opposition and resulted in his expulsion from Japan as a spy.

In Batavia and elsewhere, Europeans attempted to adapt their practices and cultural goods to local customs and requirements. This concerned not only the construction of homes, which had to withstand the monsoon rains, but also lifestyles, which represented a symbiosis between the customs of the Europeans' home countries and the local regions. Thus, the material culture of the Dutch, Chinese and Armenians in Batavia exhibited both European and Asian elements. Households were decorated with Dutch and Chinese paintings, drawings and prints – as well as with Chinese porcelain, lanterns and bird cages. European-style Rococo seating was just as popular as "Chinese" chairs and lacquered Japanese furniture and clocks. The Chinese had a special preference for ornamented Frisian clocks.

Nothing illustrates these trends better than the famous watercolour by the pastor Jan Brandes (1743–1808), who worked in Batavia in the 1780s and painted the region and its people. His "tea visit" (ill.) shows an encounter between women of European and Eurasian descent in a luxuriously furnished reception room in Batavia. The room is filled with latest objects of European and Asian home décor. The wall between the European sash windows is hung with Chinese paintings and gilded mirrors imported from Europe. The marble tables and the modern three-legged gueridons, meant for teacups, show that this is an upper-class household. We also see Chinese porcelain, water vessels from Tonkin and a copper spittoon. Slaves in traditional sarongs serve the opulently dressed ladies.

The early scholarly study of languages, customs and practices was noteworthy. One of the earliest examples is the dictionary compiled by Frederick de Houtman (1571–1627) and titled *Spraeck ende woord-boeck, Inde Maleysche ende Madagaskarsche Talen met vele Arabische ende Turcsche woorden*. Houtman participated in the first

Dutch journeys to Asia. He was taken prisoner in Aceh in 1599 and held for twenty-six months. During his imprisonment he learned Malay so well that when he returned home in 1603, he was able to publish his dictionary. Not only did it provide Dutch words and their Malay equivalents, but it also included dialogues that travellers could use after arriving by boat or in audiences with a king. The appendix contained a number of his observations on the stars and the night skies

This work marked the start of a long tradition of knowledge transfer that had considerable impact in the eighteenth century. It included publications such as *D'Amboinsche Rariteitkamer*, a "curiosity cabinet" by Georg Eberhard Rumpf (1627–1702) that was published in 1705, and *Oud en Nieuw Oost-Indiën* by François Valentijn (1666–1727), which appeared in 1724–1726. Valentijn's influential work describes not only the geography, natural history and various ethnic groups of "East India", but also its religions. In it, the Protestant Enlightenment thinker and firm believer in progress examines "superstition" in the region and also promotes projects that aimed to translate the Bible into Malay. With these works the Dutch painted a portrait of the world of the Indian Ocean and conveyed their own ideas to the native societies.

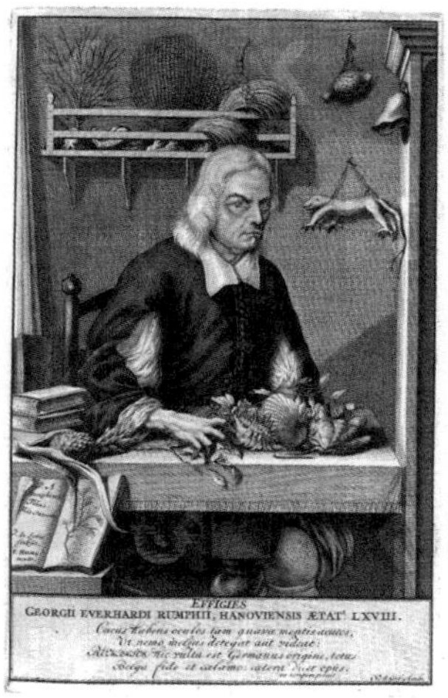

Jacob de Later, portrait of Georg Everhard Rumphius, 1705

Gift exchanges played a special role in the encounter between Europe and Asia. Without gifts, it was impossible for the Europeans to gain favour with the native princes. Vasco da Gama had learned this lesson the hard way, for his hastily gathered gifts (twelve pieces of striped cotton fabric, four scarlet-coloured caps, six hats, four branches of coral, six brass hand basins, a case of sugar, a barrel of olive oil and two barrels of honey) did little to impress the raja of Calicut, who lived in a splendid palace and was accustomed to gifts of gold and ivory. Thus, merchants and diplomats, before making contact with Asian dignitaries, had to give considerable thought to which gifts they could use to win their favour. The factors that needed to be considered including regional hierarchies and the status of the trading companies in the respective countries. At the very top of the pecking order were the Great Mogul of India, the shah of Persia, the shogun of Japan and the emperor of China, each of whom were given particular deferential treatment and gifts. Positioned beneath them were, for example, the rulers of the vassal states, who, like the king of Siam, were tributaries of the emperor of China. There were also numerous sultans and other rulers – for example, in the island kingdom of Indonesia – who had granted the Dutch trade privileges either voluntarily or under coercion. In addition, extravagant gifts were required for special occasions such as the visits paid to the Great Mogul or the shah of Persia to mark their accession to the throne. The gifts were highly diverse and included European items and Asian luxury goods that were sent from one region to the next. The luxury goods from Asia consisted mainly of textiles, but also included carpets and rose water from Persia, Japanese lacquerware and essential oils. A large number of animals were also given as gifts, including rare birds, horses and dogs. In addition to weaponry (pistols, rifles, cannons and suits of armour), the European gifts most prized by Asian rulers were scientific instruments such as compasses, telescopes, barometers, microscopes and clocks. What was also popular were globes, magnifying glasses, mirrors, spectacles and, interestingly enough, painted and unpainted window glass. Coral from the Mediterranean and amber from the Baltic Sea were just as sought after as gold jewellery and jewels. European paintings occupied a special position, and many rulers, including the moguls of India and Abbas I of Persia, even asked for painters to decorate their palaces.

Like today's state visits, the gift exchanges were negotiated long in advance by diplomats. Dutch residents or merchants in the various trading centres received lists from local officials describing the objects the rulers wanted. Often this resulted in a correspondence between the various parties that still exists today and that provides us with information about the mutual exchange process. It was not always possible to satisfy the local rulers' requests when, for example, goods ordered from the Netherlands were lost in shipwrecks or the ships were delayed. This meant that it could take several years for a ruler's request to be fulfilled. In some cases, the princes returned their gifts and asked for others. In the late seventeenth century, for example, King Phetracha of Siam returned a coach to the Dutch governor-general in Batavia because it could not be used in Siam. Nevertheless, he kept the six black horses sent as a team. Nor did the paintings always suit the tastes of their recipients. In the 1660s, for example, two Dutch battle paintings were sent to Japan because local officials had claimed that the shogun liked such scenes. After the paintings arrived, though, the local Japanese governor got cold feet because he feared the many dead sailors and the burning, sinking ships would not be to the shogun's liking. As a result, the paintings were sent back to Batavia. Meetings and gift exchanges were preceded by complex negotiations in which an important mediating role was played by the local bureaucracy serving the Asian rulers. We know, for example, that a Russian delegation was not granted trade privileges in Japan after its members refused to kowtow.

The Europeans were even given young male and female slaves as gifts. In return for their gifts, though, they mostly received silk fabrics, kimonos, ornamented daggers or horses. Back in Europe, Asian gifts (which generally did not differ from the usual range of Asian goods) entered everyday culture when, for example, the Dutch dressed in kimonos and had their portraits painted in these "japonsche rocken". At the trading centres and courts in Asia, local artisans, like the princes, took note of the European good and created imitations. One example is the gilded leather wallpaper that, while serving as a wall covering in the Netherlands, was used in Japan to make wall screens, bags and other containers, thus laying the foundation for Japanese leather production.

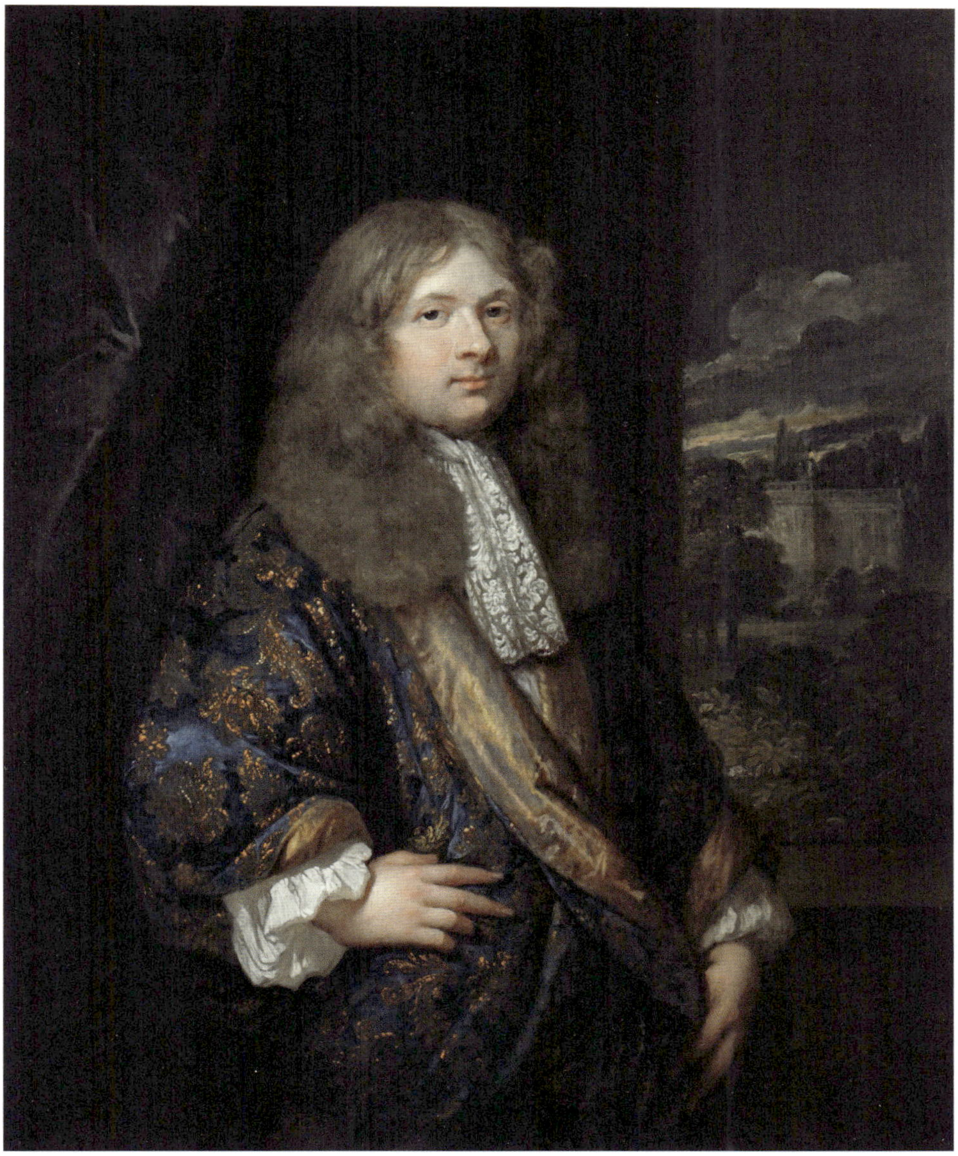

Casper Netscher, portrait of
Louis Wolters, 1682/1683

Philip de Souza

CLOSE TO THE WIND

The Age of the Sailing Ship

A keen observer of the harbours of major commercial ports such as Amsterdam, Bremen, Cadiz, Genoa, London, Marseille or Venice in the seventeenth or eighteenth century would have been impressed by the size of the sailing ships on view and the huge variety of goods they were transporting, from a vast range of origins and to equally far-flung destinations. Local ships both large and small carried basic commodities such as timber, wool and fish between Europe's many harbours. Long-distance maritime trade, through what was by 1600 a global network of commercial ports, brought exotic cargoes to Europe from the New World and the Far East such as tea, tobacco, silk and pepper. This network was created and maintained by the projection of military force using powerful fleets of warships. The story of how sailing ships came to play a key role in the development of modern European civilization is a long and complex one, and only some of the key features can be outlined here.

The most important mercantile power in Northern European waters in the medieval era was the Hanseatic League, a confederation of German trading ports which developed from relatively humble beginnings in the new Baltic port of Lübeck in the thirteenth and fourteenth centuries into a maritime trading network that reached from its Baltic homeland across the North Sea, into the Atlantic Ocean and even the Mediterranean. The impetus for the creation of the Hanseatic League came from the determination of merchants from Lübeck, and partner ports such as Hamburg, Rostock, Danzig (now Gdańsk) and Riga, to dominate trade with the Slavic and Scandinavian peoples around the Baltic Sea. The Hanseatic ports had the economic and political strength to deploy major naval forces, but their true power lay in the collective bargaining power of their merchants. The commercial gains they achieved for all parties involved by means of their excellent ships, their navigational expertise and their business skills enabled them to secure tax concessions and exclusive rights on a wide range of goods from grain, timber, wool and furs to silks and spices. They were dispersed across much of Northern Europe in enclaves that were initially organised into autonomous local associations called *Kontoren,* but around 1356 these all came under the jurisdiction of the *Hansetag*, a representative assembly whose meetings were held in Lübeck. By the late fourteenth century there were over thirty

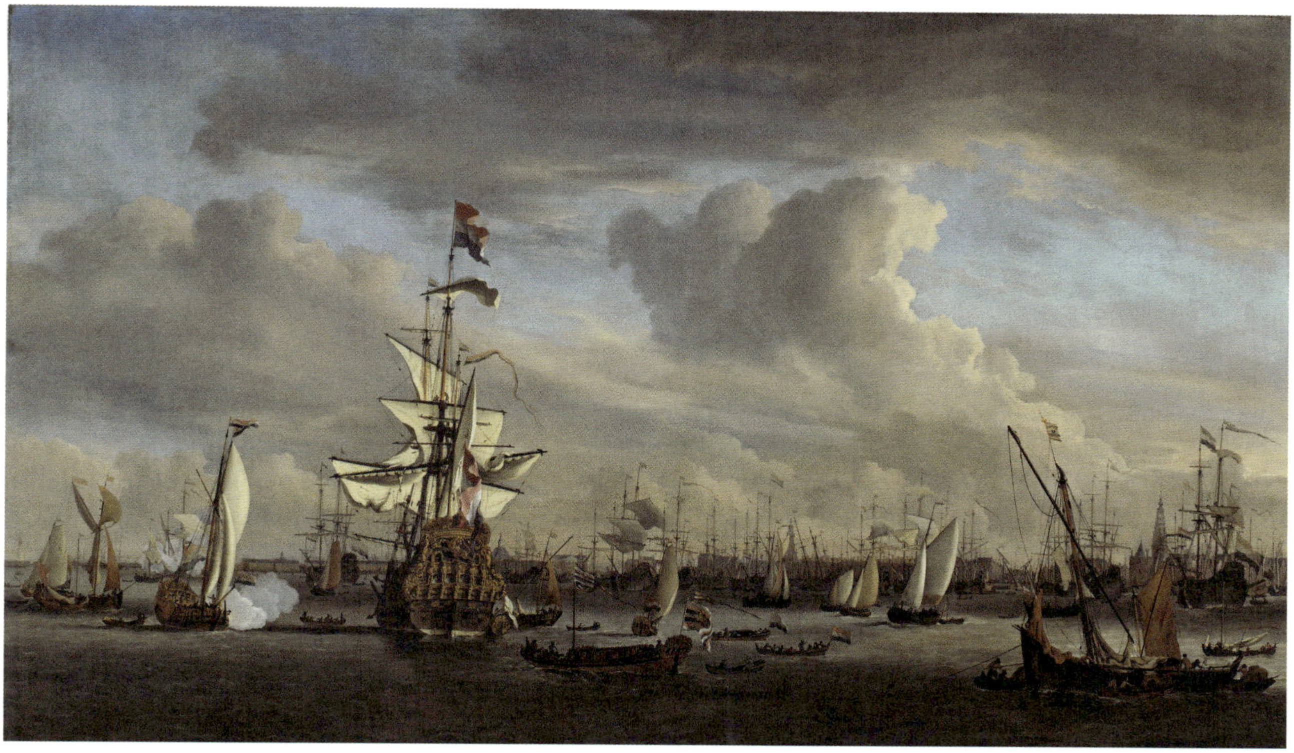

Willem van de Velde the Younger, the GOLDEN LION on the IJ by Amsterdam, 1686

German members and Hanseatic *Kontoren* could be found in major ports like Bruges, London, Bergen and Novgorod.

The second half of the fifteenth century saw the growth of mercantile associations and merchant companies in many other Northern European towns and cities, many of them modelled to a greater or lesser extent on those of the Hanseatic ports. Their challenges to Hanseatic monopolies were supported by the powerful European kingdoms, including Denmark, England, Spain and Sweden, and later by the burgeoning ports in the Netherlands. The Bruges Kontor was moved to Antwerp, but that closed in 1593, and Hanseatic merchants were expelled from London in 1597. The Swedish kings in particular were prepared to use their naval fleets to contest Hanseatic dominance, not just to wrest control of the maritime trade carried out from their own ports, such as Stockholm, but further afield, into the North Sea, the Atlantic and Mediterranean, where the demand for Swedish timber, iron and tar was growing. The members of the Hanseatic League could not stand up to such powerful opposition and many of them made local agreements acknowledging the power of these increasingly ambitious sovereigns. A final attempt was made in 1669 to revive the *Hansetag* at Lübeck, but only eight representatives attended.

Maritime trade in the Mediterranean was severely disrupted by the warfare that both accompanied and followed the collapse of the Western Roman Empire in the fifth century and the rise of Islam in the seventh century, but even in the most chaotic periods it did not cease entirely. During the Middle Ages new maritime trading networks developed as Christian and Islamic rulers created stable political conditions that promoted economic interaction. The city of Venice, founded in the sixth century in a lagoon north of the Po river delta as a refuge from war, emerged as the leading carrier of trade goods between the eastern and western halves of the Mediterranean. The Venetians obtained favoured status in the great ports of Constantinople and Alexandria and were quick to exploit the opportunities opened up for Christian merchants by the creation of Crusader states in the Levant following the fall of Jerusalem in 1099. They shipped large amounts of spices, medicines, silks and sugar back to the Adriatic and on to Central and Northern Europe, where textiles, timber and metals filled the Venetian ships returning to the East.

The Venetians built many merchant vessels and warships in their private and state-owned shipyards. Their naval forces were used to secure control of the Adriatic and to defeat those of rival Italian cities, especially Genoa, and from the ninth century onwards they assisted the Byzantine emperors and the European kings in their campaigns against the Islamic world, in return for major political and financial gains. The price of Venetian participation in the Fourth Crusade, which captured Constantinople in 1204, included territories along the major sea routes, of which the island of Crete was by far the most important. The Venetians encouraged maritime trade by supporting local merchants, suppressing piracy and improving harbour facilities. By the mid-fourteenth century their city was the richest trading emporium in Europe, but the rise of the Ottoman Turks, who conquered Constantinople in 1453, presented Venetians with a rival whose resources proved too great for them to resist. A Venetian-led naval victory at Lepanto in 1571 could not prevent the loss of Cyprus, and Crete fell to the Ottoman Empire in a war that lasted from 1645 to 1669. By the early eighteenth century, Venice's only remaining overseas possessions were the islands of Levkas and Corfu in the Ionian Sea. A lasting peace with the Turks was achieved in 1718, but Venice was taken by the forces of Napoleon in 1797, and thereafter the city became a pawn in the larger game of international rivalry between France, the Austro-Hungarian Empire and the emerging kingdom of Italy.

From the middle of the fifteenth century onwards, state sponsorship of maritime exploration, intended to achieve both commercial opportunities and territorial expansion, brought large areas of Africa, India, the Far East and the Americas under European control. The most famous of these great voyages of discovery was made in 1492 by a fleet of just three small sailing ships, commanded by Christopher Columbus (Cristobal Colón), a Genoese mariner who was based in Portugal until 1485, when he obtained the patronage of the Spanish monarchs Ferdinand of Aragon and Isabella of Castile. It was a spectacular if unanticipated success, failing in its intended aim to reach Asia by sailing westwards, but achieving landfall in the Caribbean, thereby initiating European contact with the peoples of the Americas. Columbus made three more return voyages between 1493 and 1504 that opened up a regular sea route to what became known as the New World for explorers, traders, settlers and would-be rulers. The Spanish monarchy was quick to realize the economic opportunities offered by the rich lands of Central and South America and encouraged its wealthier nobles to back ambitious adventurers like Hernan Cortés, conqueror of the Aztecs in 1521, and Francisco Pizarro, who led a series of maritime expeditions against the Inca Empire in Peru, which culminated in the capture and execution of the great Incan emperor Atahualpa in 1533. These and other Spanish victories in the sixteenth century laid the foundations for the world's first global maritime empire. Large amounts of gold and even greater quantities of silver were either sent back to Spain or carried to

Acapulco on the western coast of Mexico. From there, ships took it to Manila in the Philippines, where it was exchanged for highly valued Asian goods, such as spices and Chinese silks, which were shipped back to Mexico or Peru and eventually on to Spain.

Columbus had initially tried to interest the Portuguese king in his idea of a voyage to cross the Atlantic to China, but political issues forced Portugal's attentions eastwards. Encouraged by Prince Henry the Navigator (1394-1460), mariners based in Portugal had already discovered many of the Atlantic islands and explored the western coast of Africa, where they established trading stations. One of these stations was Elmina on the coast of Ghana, which was the most important port for the growing trade in gold, ivory and slaves. Commercial rivalry and a bitter succession quarrel led to war with Spain, culminating in a naval battle off Elmina in 1478. The 1479 Treaty of Alcáçovas-Toledo ended the war and divided the Atlantic Ocean into a western Spanish zone and an eastern Portuguese one, which meant that Columbus had to seek Spanish backing, while his Portuguese counterparts attempted to reach Asia via Africa. In a voyage lasting from 1486 to 1489, Bartolomeu Dias rounded the Cape of Good Hope and entered the Indian Ocean. In 1496 the Portuguese king Manuel I (1495-1521) commissioned Vasco da Gama to find a route to India. His small fleet set out from Elmina and arrived at the port of Calicut on the Malabar Coast of India in 1498. The local ruler was unimpressed by their royal warrant, or the textiles and ceramics they had to offer, but they returned with a small cargo of spices. This was the big prize that drew the Portuguese into the Indian Ocean, where pepper and other valuable goods were shipped by Arab merchants into the Red Sea, brought overland to Alexandria and the Levant, and carried across the Mediterranean to Europe, mostly in Muslim, Venetian and Catalan vessels. Determined to dominate this lucrative trade, the Portuguese followed up with a larger fleet in 1500, commanded by Pedro Álvares Cabral. Initially blown off course by a violent storm, Cabral's ships unexpectedly made landfall on the coast of Brazil before heading on to Calicut. After a brief attempt to establish a trading station was thwarted by hostility from Muslim merchants wary of their ambitions, the Portuguese adopted a more aggressive approach and despatched a much stronger fleet under Vasco da Gama in 1502. They quickly captured a series of entrepôts from the eastern coast of Africa, where Mombasa became their main base in 1505, across to the western coast of India and beyond, taking Cochin (1503), Goa (1510), Malacca (1511) and Calicut (1513). King Manuel I created an official state department, the Estado da Índia in 1505, which worked in parallel with a commercial organization, the Casa da Índia, to coordinate operations which soon generated impressive profits from import and export duties, harbour tolls, transhipping fees and charges for naval escorts.

Demand for the goods that the Spanish and Portuguese were bringing back by sea from Africa, Asia and the Americas encouraged Northern Europeans to venture into these regions as state-sponsored maritime traders and plunderers who aimed to gain control of these lucrative trading networks by force. The leading nations were the English and the Dutch, who had been forced to enlarge their merchant and naval fleets in the course of wars with France and Spain in the latter part of the sixteenth century. The British East India Company (EIC), established in 1600, and the Dutch Vereenigde Oostindische Companie (VOC), formed in 1602,

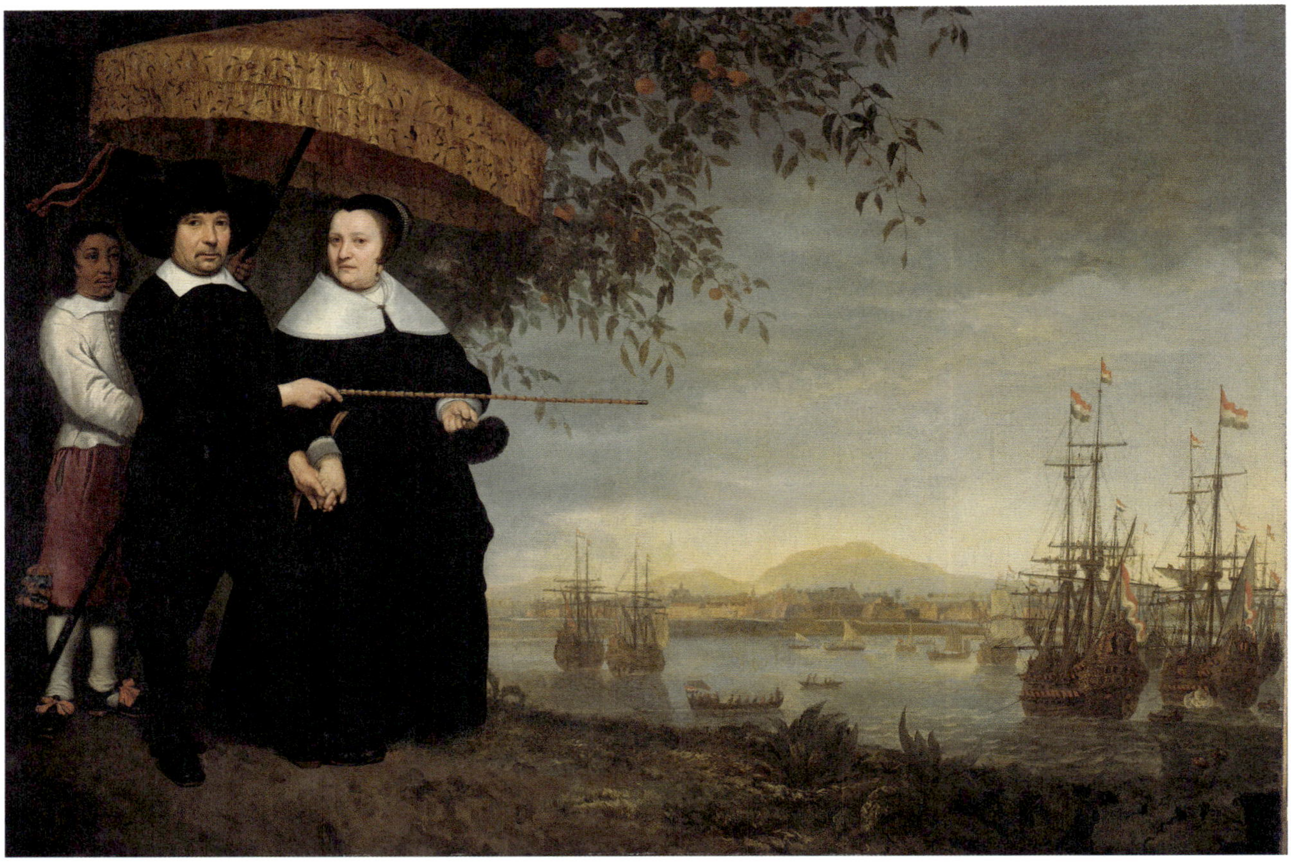

Aelbert Cuyp, *A senior merchant of the Dutch East India Company and his wife*, 1640/1660

were associations of highly ambitious merchants and colonialists that used a combination of aggressive business practices and military force to dominate seaborne commerce, seize major ports and eventually even to take control of key centres of production around the Arabian Sea, the Indian Ocean and the Far East, supplanting many long established local mariners in the process. The VOC opened up maritime trade routes to Japan and China, forced the Portuguese out of Malacca in 1641 and created a powerful base at Jakarta from which they dominated trade in pepper and other spices. In the eighteenth and nineteenth centuries, the EIC led the subjugation or replacement of the feudal rulers of India, Burma and the emirates of the Persian Gulf, forcing them to agree to political and commercial treaties on terms highly favourable to the British. These maritime empires were founded on the exploits of ambitious, often ruthless, adventurers who sailed their handfuls of ships into unknown waters, and their growth and continuation were wholly dependent on larger fleets of merchant vessels and warships that maintained their links with Europe by sea.

The sailing ship itself is one of humanity's greatest technological inventions and is found in a myriad of variations all over the world. Although sailing ships are essentially tools for achieving practical ends, they are also objects of great historical and cultural significance. The iconic shape of the Scandinavian longboat, for example, with the elegant upward curve at both prow and stern, is forever associated with the Vikings, but it served several very practical purposes. It made the ships easy to beach in an era when harbour facilities were rudimentary and rare. It allowed them to run before the wind on the open seas, and its shallow draft enabled them to be rowed considerable distances inland along rivers. The wide hull could accommodate relatively large crews for raiding expeditions, or bulky cargoes of supplies and trade goods.

By the thirteenth century, Northern European ports harboured two principal types of ship designed for trade: the cog and the hulk. The cog (*Kogge*) was a type of large, flat-bottomed sailing ship with a hull width roughly one-third of its length. Cogs carried one square-rigged sail on a tall mast, and were steered by a rudder, which, from the mid-thirteenth century onwards, was mounted at the stern. They were slow vessels, managing no more than two to three knots per hour, but they could navigate both high seas and shallow waters, particularly on tidal estuaries, and their box-like hulls provided ample cargo space. Because of their versatility, they were widely used by Northern European traders from the middle of the eleventh to the fifteenth century, especially those of the Hanseatic League, whose merchants developed the type to carry bulk cargoes like grain, timber and minerals.

The other popular trading ship in medieval Northern Europe was the hulk (*Holk*). It was also fitted with a square sail on a single mast, but, unlike the cog, its hull typically had a rounded profile, often likened to a banana or bean pod, curving upward at both prow and stern. The hulk had one major advantage over the cog: it enjoyed greater seaworthiness due to its rounded bottom. By the fourteenth century, the hull shape was adapted to include features such as a broader hull terminating in a straight sternpost with a hinged rudder, and these hybrid vessels had largely replaced cogs as the principal cargo ships in northern waters by the middle of the fifteenth century.

For much of the medieval era, the mariners of Mediterranean Europe continued to use the same types of vessels that their ancestors had developed in antiquity. Merchant vessels were sailing ships with short rounded hulls, whereas warships were longer-hulled, oared galleys. Square sails fitted to centrally located mainmasts were standard, but additional masts with fore-and-aft sails, which had been used on some Mediterranean ships since the second century AD, were common. They are generally referred to as lateen sails and there were two main versions: the large quadrilateral or "Arab" type, and the smaller triangular type. A new type of sailing ship called the caravel, which developed out of the small fishing boats that plied their trade on the Atlantic coastline of Iberia, was widely used by Portuguese, Spanish and Italian sailors for trading and exploratory voyages by the end of the fourteenth century. The larger Portuguese caravels had blunt, transom-ended sterns, carried both square and lateen sails, and were fitted with large rudders.

Northern mariners ventured into the Mediterranean with increasing frequency during the eleventh and twelfth centuries for both military and commercial purposes, but it was not until the fourteenth century that hybrid vessels combining design features and technology from both northern and southern shipbuilding traditions began to appear. In the early fifteenth century, Genoese and Venetian merchants made less use of their traditional round ships and galleys, favouring instead the carrack, which had the higher-sided, squatter hull shape typical of northern hulks and carried one or two square sails. During the fourteenth century, larger sailing ships began to be built which, in addition to a large square mainsail on their central masts, featured a smaller square topsail at the head of this mast, shorter stern, or mizzen masts fitted with lateen sails, and foremasts

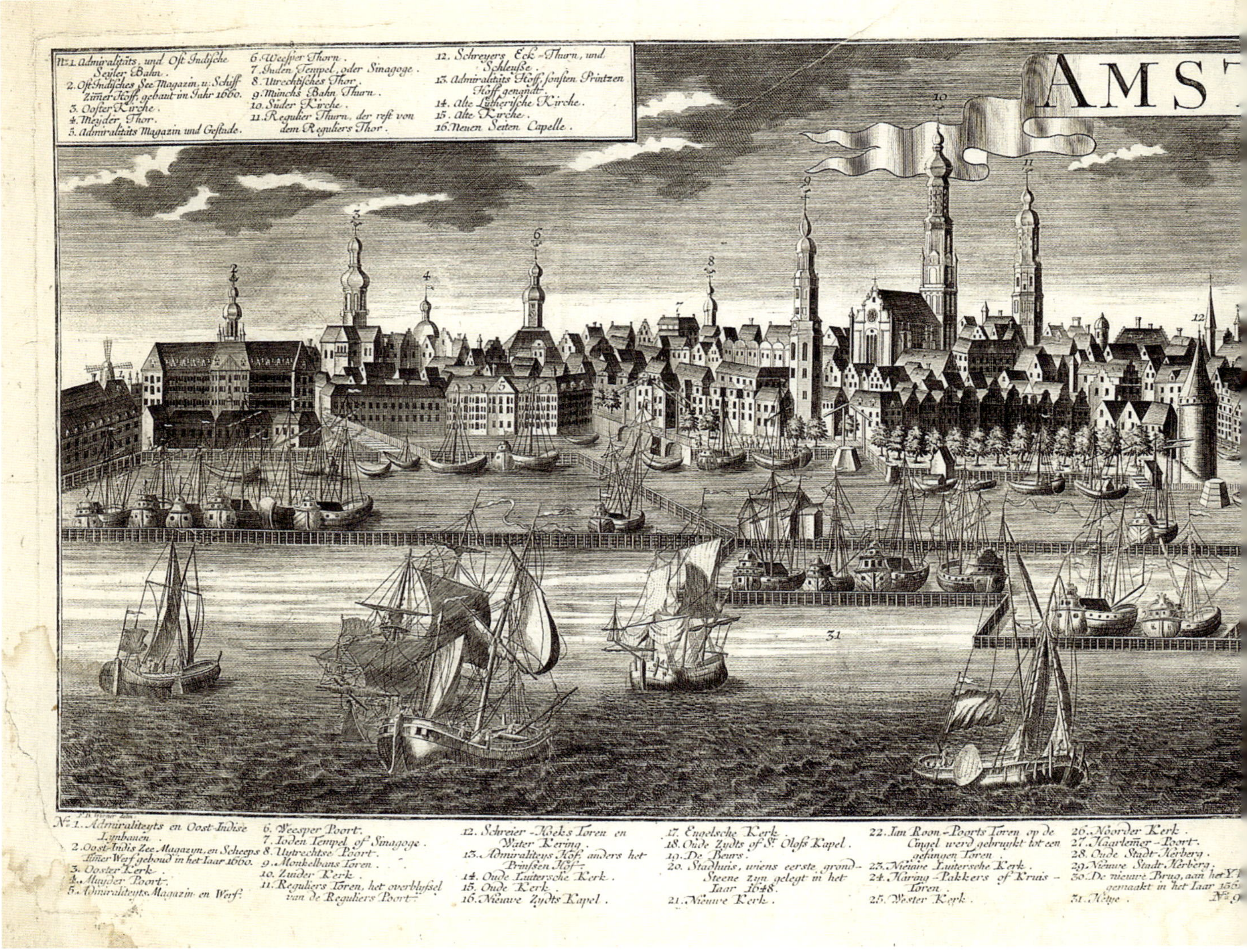

carrying small fore-and-aft sails, or spritsails attached to a bowsprit. The widespread adoption during the fifteenth century of multiple masts was an extremely important development in European ship design. It enabled vessels to set varied amounts of sail canvas, to use alternative rigs, and to trim the sails in different ways according to the sailing conditions. Vasco da Gama's ships mostly used square rigged sails along the Atlantic coast of Africa, but they converted to lateen sails for the challenging voyage across the Indian Ocean.

One rare example of the transfer of maritime technology from the Far East to Europe is the adoption of the leeboard, a pivoting drop-keel fitted to the sides of a sailing ship to temporarily increase the vessel's draft, providing greater stability and significantly reducing the leeway made by a ship when sailing close to the wind and when turning through the wind. They are very useful when sailing on inland waterways and in coastal waters where sudden, rough seas are a frequent hazard. There is evidence that Chinese ships used leeboards from as early as the eighth century, and they seem to have been copied by Dutch mariners, who introduced them to northern waters in the sixteenth century. They rapidly became a standard feature on sailing barges and fishing vessels.

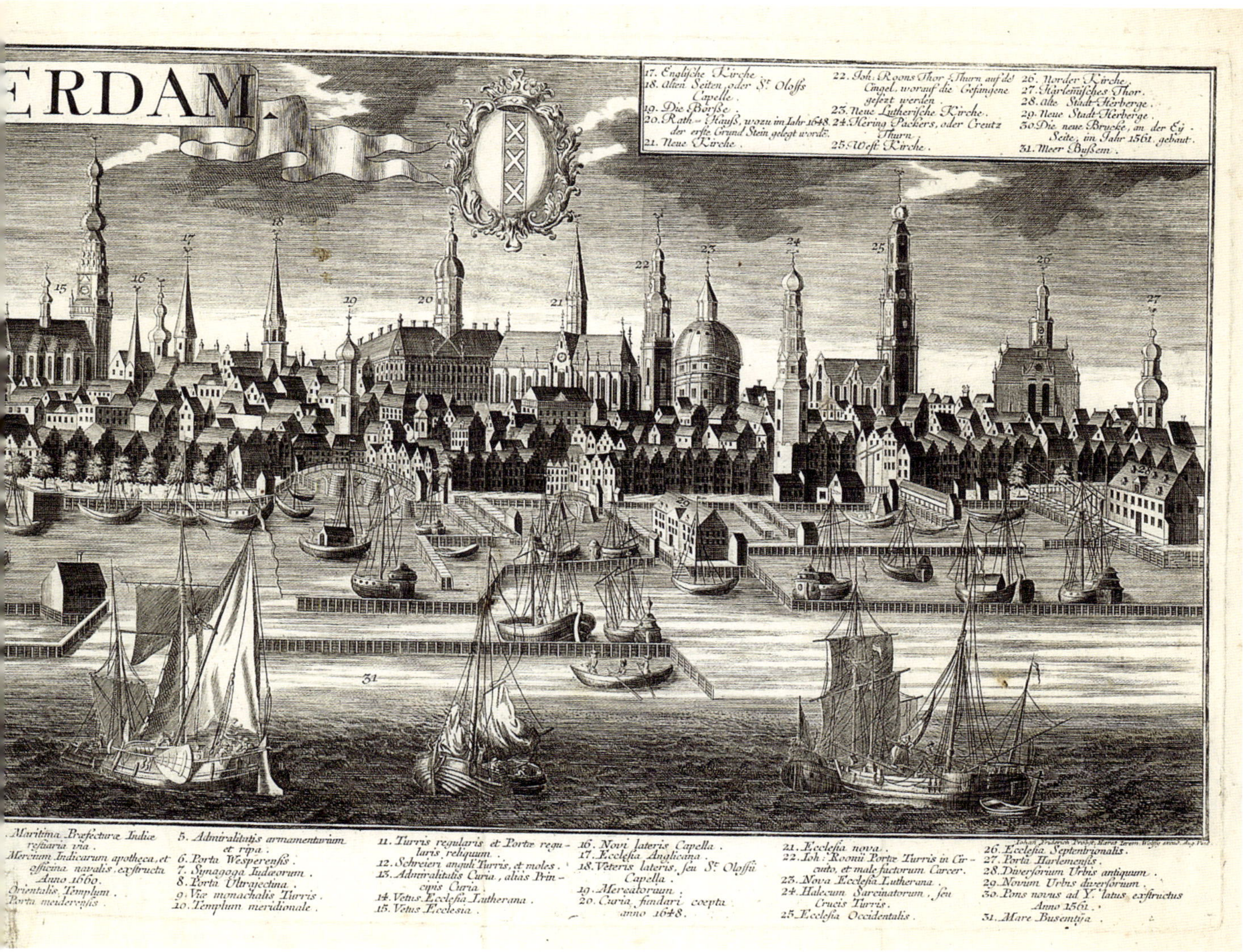

Friedrich Bernhard Werner, view of Amsterdam, c. 1720

The innovations of the fourteenth and fifteenth centuries resulted in what are known as full-rigged sailing ships, which were larger, faster and more manoeuvrable in difficult winds, and thus more reliable than those of the medieval era. Their greater range and carrying capacity enabled European mariners to explore and trade around the globe in the sixteenth and seventeenth centuries. There were many variations of the full-rigged sailing ship. One such was the *fluyt*, a full-rigged three-masted ship named for the high tapering sides of its hull, which became the principal merchant vessel of the Dutch Republic in the seventeenth century. The flat-bottomed hull of the *fluyt* typically had a length to breadth ratio of five or six to one, which made it slow but capacious, ideally suited for the carriage of bulk goods, such as grain, salt and timber between the North Sea and the Baltic. These ships carried few guns and were therefore vulnerable to purpose-built warships, as well as to more heavily-armed merchant vessels that were operated by European and North African pirates and privateers, which meant that Dutch merchant fleets frequently had to sail in escorted convoys during the seventeenth and eighteenth centuries.

The culmination of centuries of sailing ship evolution was the fast, ocean-going cargo ship known as the "clipper". This vessel typically had three very tall main masts, with four to six square sails on each, plus additional fore-and-aft sails on mizzenmasts and bowsprits. From the 1850s clippers were built to a standard American design in the USA and Northern Europe. They could average fifteen knots on long voyages and carried high-value commodities ranging from tea to gold. Their speed also made them in demand as passenger carriers, and in 1868 the British-built THERMOPYLAE sailed from London to Melbourne in just fifty-nine days. It was only the advent of powerful steamships that forced them into decline.

People were arguably the single most significant cargo to be carried by Europe's ocean-going sailing ships. The majority of a ship's crew were ordinary seamen who often began their maritime life as youths and faced the daily risk of a premature death at sea due to storms, disease or combat. More specialised members included carpenters and cooks, as well as officers trained in the science of navigation and, on the larger ships, doctors who practised medicine in the primitive conditions on board. All were subject to the orders of the vessel's captain, and their lives could well depend on his day-to-day decisions. Passengers might be merchants, soldiers or some of the thousands of Europeans who migrated from their homes across the Atlantic, Indian and Pacific Oceans to make new lives in the Americas, in Africa, in the Indian subcontinent or in Australasia. However, many people who sailed between these continents were forced to do so, some as convicts, but many more as slaves, captured in Africa and brought to the Americas. The slave ships were often designed as multi-purpose cargo vessels, carrying one form of merchandise from their home ports to African trading stations, transporting African slaves to the burgeoning estates and plantations that were appearing in the Caribbean islands, North and South America, and bringing the products of these regions back to Europe.

It was above all the capacity to project military force by means of their heavily armed fleets that enabled the European powers to dominate vast areas of the global seas in the sixteenth, seventeenth and eighteenth centuries. Their powerful cannons and aggressive raiding strategies enabled them to seize and hold vital ports and to defeat attempts by local naval powers to drive them out. The most celebrated type of warship from this period is the galleon, which evolved out of the sail and oar-powered galleys of the late medieval Mediterranean. On the Iberian peninsula, some of the features of the caravel and the *nao* were incorporated in a design which had four masts and two gun decks for the large iron cannons that replaced smaller bronze ones in the sixteenth century. Galleons of this type were among the principal vessels of the mighty Spanish Armada that attempted to invade England in 1588. England, the Dutch Republic and other Northern European states adopted variations of the four-masted galleon for war, trade and piracy. By the middle of the seventeenth century, the addition of further gun decks and wheeled cannons with greater range paved the way for the development of the ship of the line, essentially a sturdily built, mobile artillery platform suitable both for bombardment of land targets and co-ordinated, line-of-battle warfare.

Sailing ships were built all over Europe. All of the major commercial ports had shipyards that employed hundreds or even thousands of men. The sailing ships that comprised the ever-expanding mercantile and naval fleets of the European nations required enormous amounts of timber and iron for their construction, and equally impressive supplies of hemp, tar, pitch and canvas to equip and maintain them, much of which came from the Baltic region. This meant that every

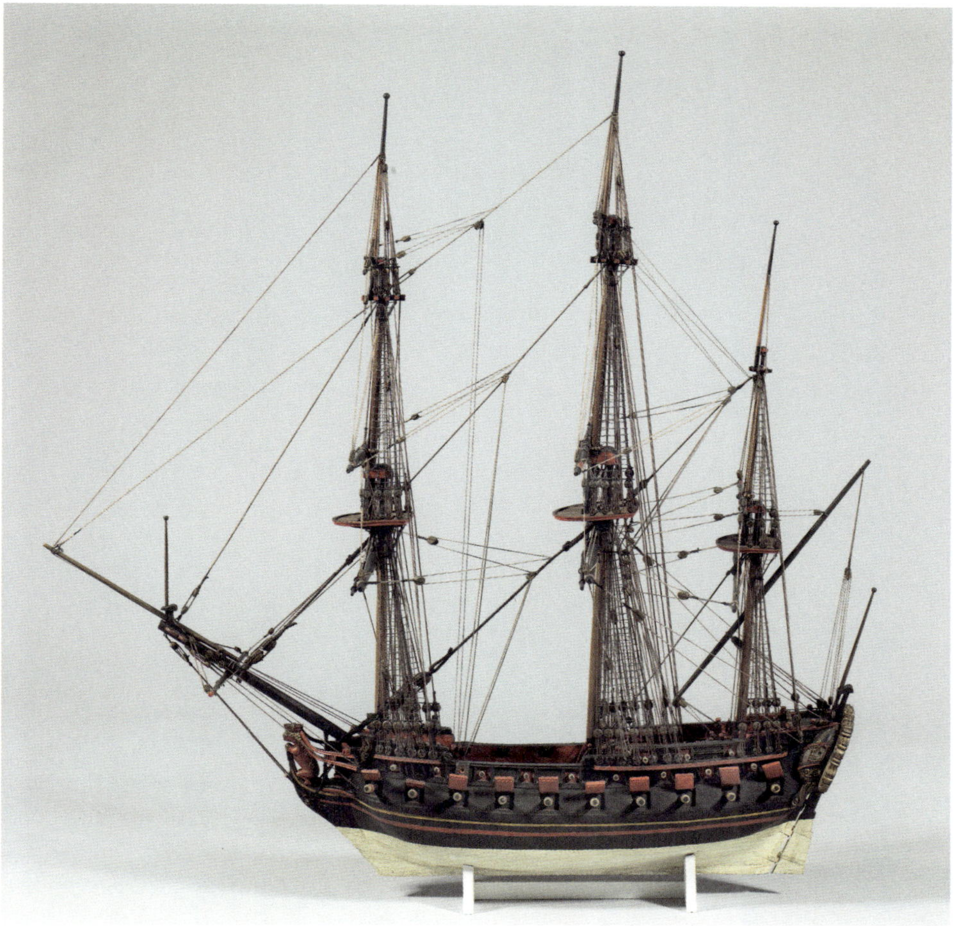

6/5
De Eendragt, model of an East Indiaman ship, 1775/1800

shipyard was also a vast storehouse of valuable materials. Large sailing ships, with multiple masts carrying numerous different sails, required vast amounts of cordage. Therefore, an essential facility in all dockyards was the rope walk, where hemp fibres were laboriously pulled and twisted into lines and ropes then coated with tar to waterproof them. Such installations were major structures, often hundreds of metres long. In seventeenth-century Amsterdam, for example, the wharfs at Oostenburg housed two ropewalks side by side, one for the Dutch Admiralty and another for the Dutch East India Company (VOC), each sporting a richly decorated façade. Here, just as in other sections of the dockyards, there was a constant worry that fire might cause catastrophic damage. Indeed, in 1673 a fire did break out in the Admiralty Ropewalk, but it was eventually extinguished. That event is memorialised in a sketch of 1690 by the artist Jan van der Heyden (1637-1712), which features the deployment of a special "hose-fire-engine" patented by van der Heyden.

The age of the sailing ships was inconceivable without the support of services provided on land. The construction of ships, the provision of their equipment and rigging, and their overhauling was done in shipyards located in the immediate proximity of larger port cities. Every shipyard was a site of innovation as well as a site for the storage and trans-shipment of valuable goods. In addition, craftsmen and engineers from various countries worked together on the construction and successful realisation of new ship designs. It was only with this confluence of dif-

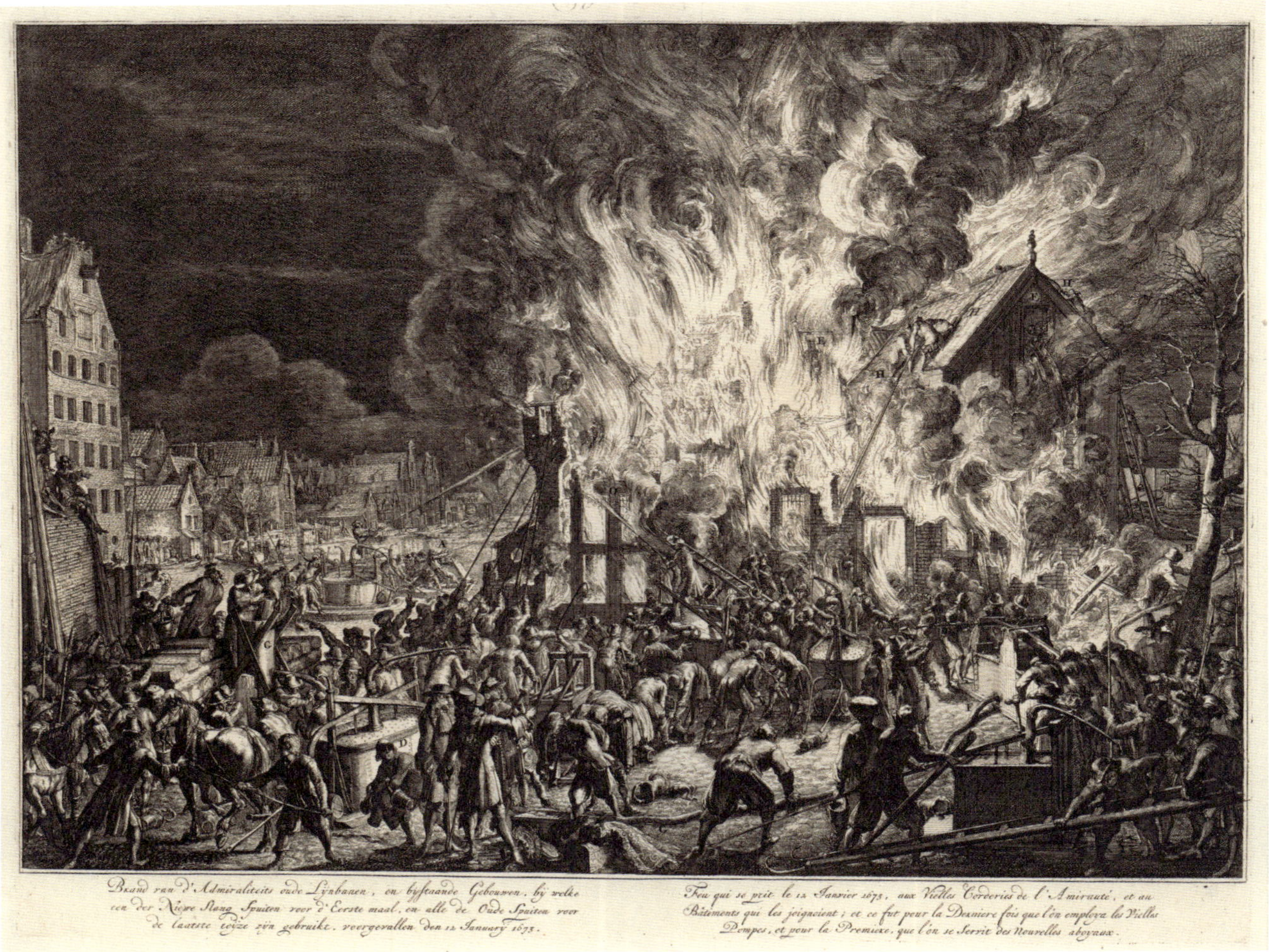

Romeyn de Hooghe (after Jan van der Heyden), *Fire in the Ropeyard of the Dutch Admiralty 1673*, 1690/1735

ferent construction methods, knowledge and skills that the development of new types of ships was possible, for example the *fluyt*, which resulted from the combination of northern and southern European ship-building techniques.

Thomas Eisentraut

SHIPS OF WOOD, MEN OF IRON

The Lives of Sailors

The seventeenth and eighteenth centuries were a maritime era for Europe. The many wars and land battles, including the Thirty Years' War (1618–1648), the War of the Spanish Succession (1701–1714), the Great Northern War (1700–1721) and Seven Years' War (1756–1763), cannot obscure this fact. The epochal change was the result of victories and defeats on the world's seas. The great nations and countries that continue to be influential maritime powers today – Portugal, Spain, the Netherlands, England and France – were opponents who fought for command of the seas and the resulting benefits. However, it was not only the kings and monarchs who fought these battles, navigated the world's seas and brought new knowledge to Europe. Ordinary men, most unknown, experienced daily life on the vessels and played a key role in Europe's development.

Sailing ships and crews in the seventeenth and eighteenth centuries

Life on board the merchant vessels and warships was extremely demanding for the sailors. The crews did not always consist of volunteers. In times of war, those on warships, in particular, were "impressed", meaning they were forced into service. While volunteers and conscripts were granted shore leave, these sailors were not allowed to leave the vessels for months or even years at a time.[1] At the turn of the century, large warships could measure 50 metres long by 10 metres wide, and the limited space on the vessels was shared by up to seven hundred men. The prevailing international makeup of crews was a special feature of maritime life: men from different parts of Europe served on board together.

Hierarchy, discipline, mutinies and punishment

Fixed rules were established early on to regulate life on the vessels.[2] This can be seen most clearly in the on-board hierarchy, which had a similar structure on merchant vessels and warships. At the very top was the captain, who was assisted by a specific number of officers depending on the vessel type. The captain had absolute authority and represented the king in his absence. In a crisis, the crew's unconditional trust often depended on whether the captain was charismatic. The crew lived in difficult conditions, and often a small spark sufficed to cause a mutiny. Many of these rebellions have remained in collective memory, including those on individual vessels such as the Dutch BATAVIA (1629) and the British BOUNTY (1789), and those affecting entire squadrons, such as the mutinies in the British Navy at Spithead and Nore (1797).[3] Mutiny represented the most serious crime and was punishable by hanging. In order to nip rebellious behaviour and violence in the bud, draconian punishments were imposed, the severity of which depended on the offender's rank. Whereas common sailors were usually flogged with a cat o' nine tails (a whip with nine knotted thongs) for most offenses, officers were often only required to pay a high fine, which was given as alms to the needy on land. A detailed code of conduct was regularly read aloud on the ship in order to ensure that the illiterate knew their rights and duties and the different punishments.

Work, "off-watch" and games

The work day on the ship was divided into four-hour shifts. Time was measured by a marine sandglass in which sand flowed from one bulb to the next every thirty min-

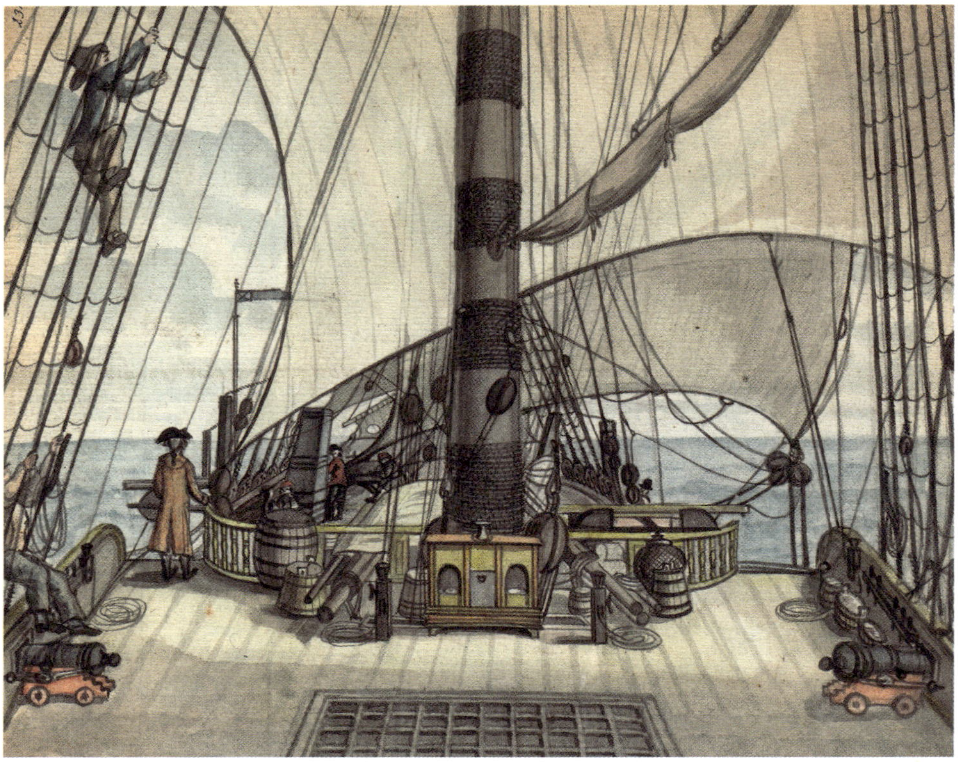

Jan Brandes, scene on the deck of a Dutch East Indiaman, 1778/1787

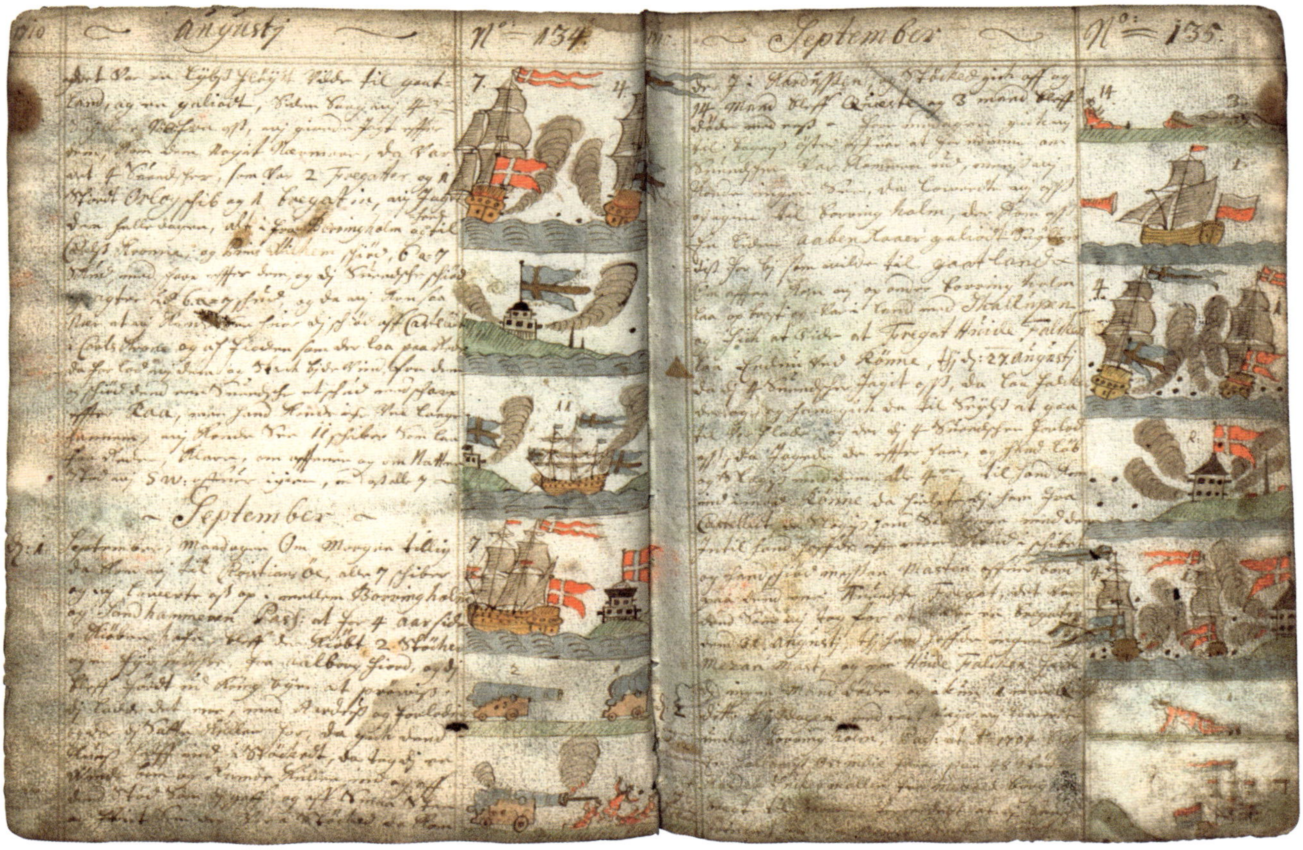

Double-page spread from the diary of Norwegian sailor Daniel Trosner, 1710

utes. The ship's bell was rung at the turning of the glass so that the crew members below deck could keep track of the time. This was called "striking the bells".

While the ships were at sea, men were constantly needed to set, adjust or take in the sails. In addition, the firing of the cannons was regularly drilled, wind and weather permitting. The crew cleaned and maintained the vessel, giving special attention to the standing and running rigging and thus to maintenance of the ropes. There was always something to repair on board the vessel. Sails needed to be mended, ropes spliced and the hull inspected for damage. While "off-watch" (off-duty), the sailors could recover from work, eat and sleep. If they were literate, they could also use this time to write letters or make entries in their diaries. Few written sources provide information about the sailors' lives that is as detailed as the diary kept by the Norwegian sailor Daniel Trosner (1685–1741) from 1710 to 1714.[4] Archaeological investigations of shipwrecks have uncovered objects that give us an idea of the sailors' private lives. Bone or wooden dice and small gaming pieces show that games of chance and board games were played on board. The top of a sailor's chest, carved or inscribed with a chequered pattern and thus suitable for chess or checkers, often served as a board.

Malnutrition, diseases and death on board

In terms of the food available on board, the sailors did not have an easy time of it. The ships carried mainly non-perishable food. Twice-baked bread, called "hardtack", was the main meal, along with salted meat and dried fish. Due to storage conditions, the quality of the food and drinking water grew steadily worse with time. Drinking water often started smelling foul after just two weeks at sea and the sailors tried mixing it with alcohol to make it potable again. This is how grog was invented. A variety of beverages were drunk on ships – in addition to water, mainly hard liquor. From the seventeenth century to 1970, a daily ration of rum was dispensed on British vessels, which sometimes resulted in drunkenness and disciplinary offenses. That most of the food was eaten cold is self-explanatory. Because the ships were made of wood, there was a great risk of fire, and meals were cooked in the galley only when seas were calm and the weather was fair. Otherwise open fires were banned in every part of the vessel. The resulting cold and damp, together with darkness below deck, weighed on the sailors' spirits.

One of the main problems on the ships was maintaining the health of the entire crew for longer periods of time. Without sufficient numbers of healthy, strong men on board, the sailing vessels were not manoeuvrable or deployable in battle and thus useless. It was therefore in the captain's best interest to keep his crew healthy. As long as the vessels sailed near the coast, they could take in fresh provisions, which made food-related illnesses rare. However, from the late fifteenth century on, the voyages of discovery resulted in long periods on the high seas. It was in this era that the sailors increasingly contracted a serious illness that broke out around two months after leaving port: scurvy.

Without sufficient intake of vitamin C, the first symptoms appear after 68 days; the first deaths occur after 84 days; after 111 days, scurvy carries off the entire crew.[5]

Roughly half of the afflicted died from the disease, which is caused by a vitamin C deficiency. In 1747, the Scottish naval physician James Lind (1716–1794) undertook the first systematic attempt to treat sailors suffering from the disease.[6] He administered different additives to their diet, such as cider, diluted sulphuric acid, vinegar, seawater, oranges and lemons. The sailors who regularly drank orange and lemon juice recovered. On the basis of this finding, Lind demanded, among other things, that British ships carry adequate amounts of fresh fruit. One of the first captains to follow his recommendations was James Cook (1728–1779), but it was not until 1795 that the British admiralty issued a binding order for a daily ration of lemon juice.[7]

6/25
Ship's biscuit, 1784

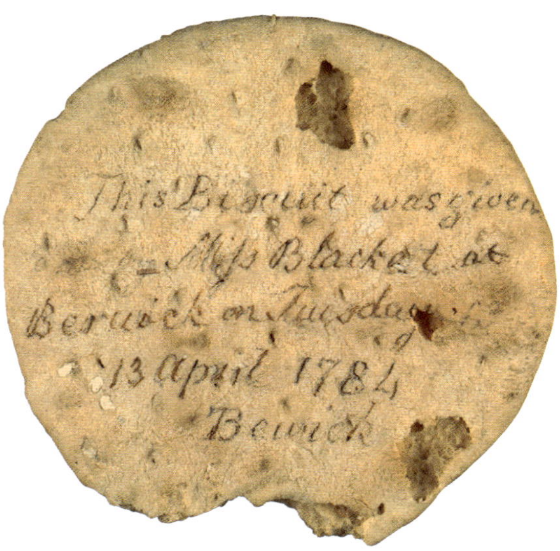

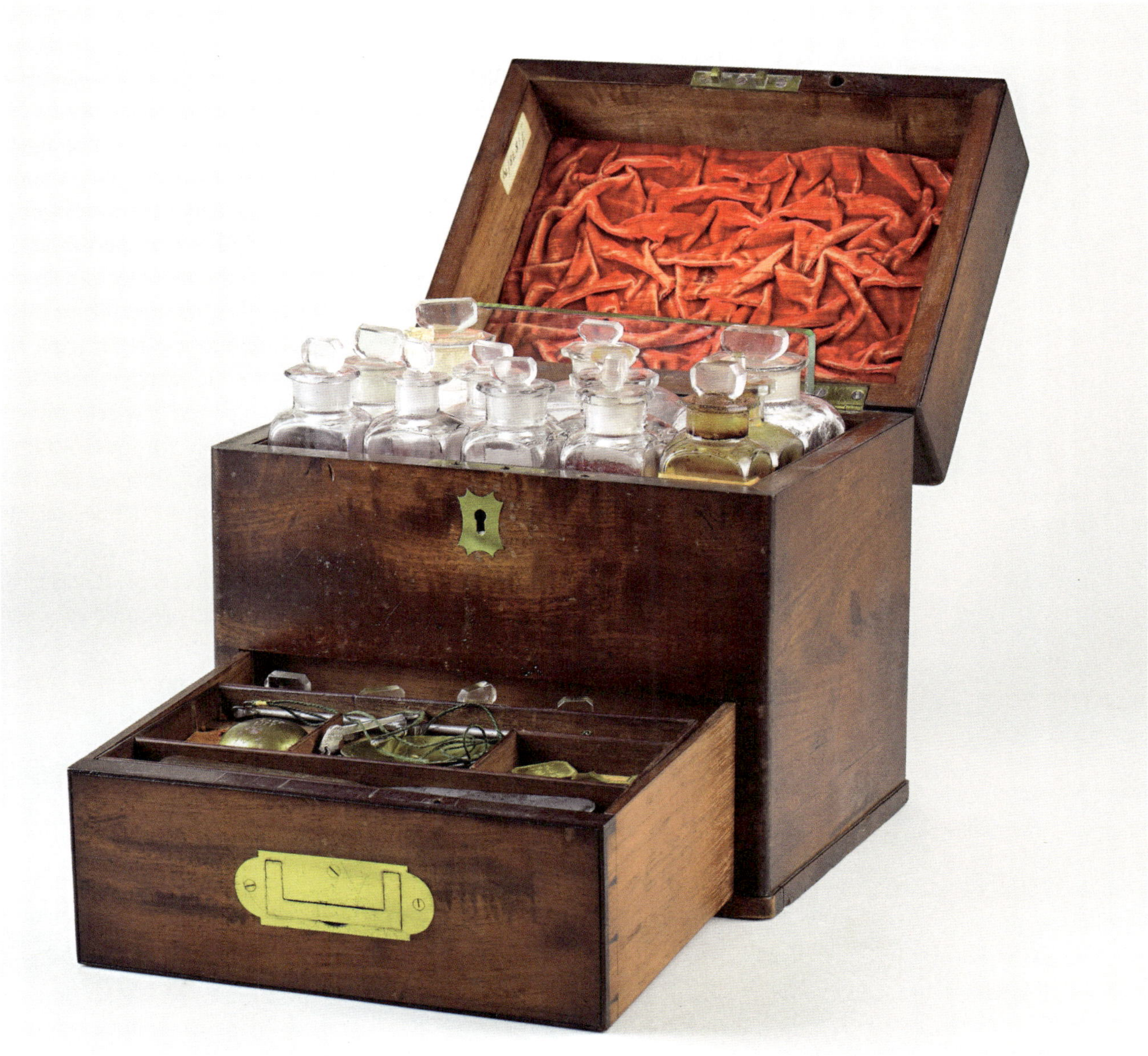

From the second half of the eighteenth century on, the British led the world in the field of maritime medicine, which is shown, among other things, by the constant expansion of on-board dispensaries. One of the reasons that so much effort was put into searching for and developing new drugs, was that qualified crew members were difficult to replace and became an increasingly valuable resource.

6/33
Ship's apothecary, c. 1880

In European waters, the captains and their crews suffered primarily from diseases long known to them. These included not only dysentery and other diarrhoeal diseases caused by contaminated water, but also smallpox, typhus and the plague, which broke out repeatedly for shorter periods of time. The plague affected Europeans from the second half of the fourteenth century onwards, on land and at sea. The disease was probably a "stowaway" that had travelled from Asia to Europe along the maritime trade routes; ship crews were among the first afflicted. Between 1708 and 1714, the plague wiped out entire communities in the Baltic region. The connection between good hygiene and the various diseases was soon recognised, and in order to reduce harmful effects for human health, various cleaning processes were introduced on board.

Today we were once again drilled and trained in the use of our guns. Under a new order, all bunks and nets need to be aired for cleanliness and health reasons on a daily basis, weather permitting. And at 8 o'clock in the evening, we once again fumigated the 'tween-deck with frankincense and other smoke-producing goods that cost 30 imperial talers a pound, all because of the plague and other illnesses.[8]

Separate hospitals were established to stop the spread of contagious diseases. The German word *Lazarett* (military hospital) derives from the name of the Venetian island of Lazzaretto Vecchio, where one of the earliest documented plague hospitals was founded in the fifteenth century. Around the same time, the principle of quarantine – temporary isolation – was developed to determine whether travellers were healthy or ill. In the fourteenth century, the ideal time period was determined to be forty days and physicians stuck to this for centuries. In non-European waters, tropical diseases were an additional problem and one of the main causes of crew attrition. They included both yellow fever (first documented on British vessels in 1553) and malaria.[9]

Most on-board injuries were caused by accidents and carelessness. It was easy to crush fingers in a block and many injuries were caused by badly secured cargo or equipment. The recoil of a fired cannon also posed risks.

We gave the signal and fired a shot. One of our gunners was supposed to reload the cannon, but it was not well cleaned and a spark got into the bore and set the gun off. He lost his right hand, which was shot off.[10]

On average, more men were killed by accidents, infections, epidemics and other illnesses on board than in combat.

If we look back at the harsh life and dangerous conditions on the ships, we gain greater respect for the work of sailors. If not for their crews, neither Columbus nor Cook would have been able to successfully complete their voyages and permanently change our vision of the world.

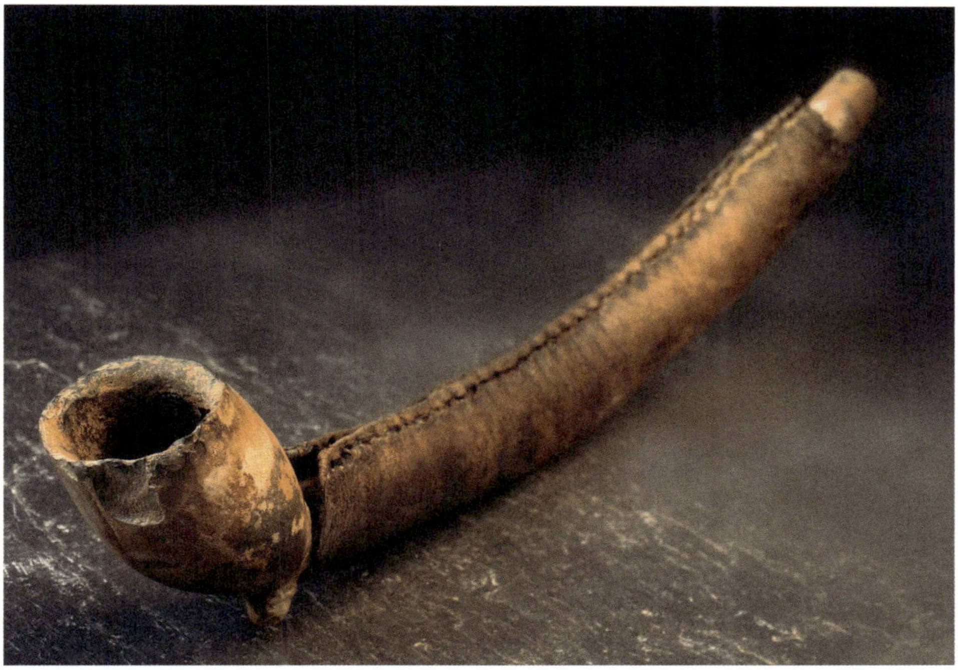

6/27
Repaired clay pipe with a leather sleeve, before 1715

1 Eberhard Schmitt (ed.), *Indienfahrer 2: Seeleute und Leben an Bord im Ersten Kolonialzeitalter (15. bis 18. Jahrhundert)*, Dokumente zur Geschichte der europäischen Expansion, vol. 7 (Wiesbaden 2008), 97–101.

2 Frederick IV, *Siøe-Artikler Og Krigsrets Instruction* [...], Copenhagen 1700, 1–144. Brian Lavery (ed.), *Shipboard Life and Organisation, 1731–1815* (Singapore/Sydney, 1998), 9–44.

3 Lavery 1998, 426–27.

4 *Nils Trosners dagbok ført på flåten 1710–1714*, 2 vols., unprinted source, National Archives of Norway, Oslo, Manuscript Collection, EA-3667/G/L0048a, EA-3667/G/L0048b. See also the extensive German-language commentary on the diary in Thomas Eisentraut, "Das Tagebuch von Nils Trosner, 1710–1714", in Robert Oldach und Thomas Wegener Friis (eds.), *Staat – Militär – Gesellschaft: Festschrift für Jens E. Olesen zum 65. Geburtstag*, Publikationen des Lehrstuhls für Nordische Geschichte, vol. 20 (Greifswald, 2015), 163–195.

5 Roger Crowley, *Die Eroberer: Portugals Kampf um ein Weltreich* (Darmstadt, 2016), 65.

6 Klaus Volbehr, *Kleine Geschichte der Hygiene und Arzneimittelversorgung auf Schiffen* (Hamburg, 1987), 69.

7 Karl-Heinz Reger, *"Dann sprang er über Bord": Alltagspsychologie und psychische Erkrankung an Bord britischer Schiffe im 19. Jahrhundert* (Göttingen, 2014), 192.

8 *Nils Trosners dagbok*, vol. 1, 372. English based on the German translation by Thomas Eisentraut, 2017.

9 Georg-Michael Fleischer, *Schiffschirurgen von Kolumbus bis Nelson: Vergessene Helden der Seefahrtgeschichte* (Heidelberg, 2017), 131.

10 *Nils Trosners dagbok*, vol. 1, 209. English based on the German translation by Thomas Eisentraut, 2017.

Krystel Gualdé

IN CHAINS

Nantes and the Transatlantic Slave Trade

"Tearing people away from their country, by treachery or violence, to sell them at public markets like ordinary cattle; drawing by habit no distinction between people and animals; forcing them to work under the pain of blows; feeding them, not out of consideration for their life, but so that they continue to yield profits; abandoning them when they are old or sick as soon as it can no longer be expected that their work will pay for their treatment; only allowing them to become fathers so that they can bring children into the world to suffer the same fate, children who become the master's property, whom he can tear away from their parents and sell; just so that they see how their women and daughters are exposed without decency, without humanity, to every abuse of these men. This is how we treat other human beings!"
Jean-Antoine-Nicolas de Caritat, Marquis de Condorcet
Notes on the Pensées *of Blaise Pascal*
1776

The discovery of the American continent by Christopher Columbus (ca. 1451–1506) in 1492 changed the face of the world for Europeans, transforming it to what now seemed to be an immeasurably large place with virginal qualities. The signing of the Treaty of Tordesillas between the significant sea powers of Spain and Portugal on 7 June 1494 set the borders of their respective territorial dominions in the new areas that were to be exploited. The Treaty divided the world along a demarcation line extending from pole to pole that ran 370 *leguas* (about 1,770 kilometres) west of the Cape Verde islands: Brazil (whose existence at that time was unknown to Europeans) thereby fell to Portugal, with the rest of South America belonging to Spain.

While the French had begun exploring the lands around the Saint Lawrence River in 1497, the Spanish and the Portuguese advanced into South America. The British found their footing in North America. In 1579, they reached the Californian coast via the Pacific, and five years later they landed on the Atlantic coast for the first time in what later became Virginia. They were confronted by the colonial ambitions of the Dutch, who had founded a small colony in the north, which is now New York. Due to their hegemony in the south, Spain and Portugal, which were ruled from 1580 to 1640 by the Iberian Union, reaped significant profits. This applied in particular to the Portuguese, who soon held a monopoly over the introduction of African slaves to the West Indies. The dominance of the two Iberian states in South America gave rise to greediness. The British, Dutch, French and Spanish waged wars against one another to secure their territorial claims in these new regions. After the line of demarcation drawn in 1494 had been questioned multiple times, it was abolished in 1588.

France founded its first colony in 1608 by laying the foundations of the city of Québec; the French territories in North America were called *la Nouvelle-France* (New France) at the time. The French also settled on the island of Saint Christopher (today St. Kitts) in 1625. Ten years later, they settled in Martinique and Guadeloupe, where the first slaves arrived as early as 1641. In 1643, the French reached Guyana, and by 1659 they were firmly established in the western part of the island of Hispaniola (one of the West Indian islands), which they named Saint-Domingue.

When Europeans founded their first trading posts in Africa, slavery and the slave trade already existed there. The character and extent of slavery, however, changed drastically with the establishment of the transatlantic slave trade, which the European powers used to develop their American colonies. The number of men, women and children who were enslaved at the time is without parallel in historical records.

In March 1685, King Louis XIV (1638–1715) signed the *Code noir* (the Black Code) in Versailles. This collection of legal texts served as the “regulations for the government and the judicial and public administration of the French islands in America, as well as for the control of the trade in blacks and slaves in the named regions”.[1] The *Code noir* defined slaves as personal chattels who were fully given over to the will of the slaveholder. The living conditions of slaves in the French colonies were very poor, consistently so, and mortality was constantly high. It was for this reason that the colonists constantly purchased new prisoners: the slaves

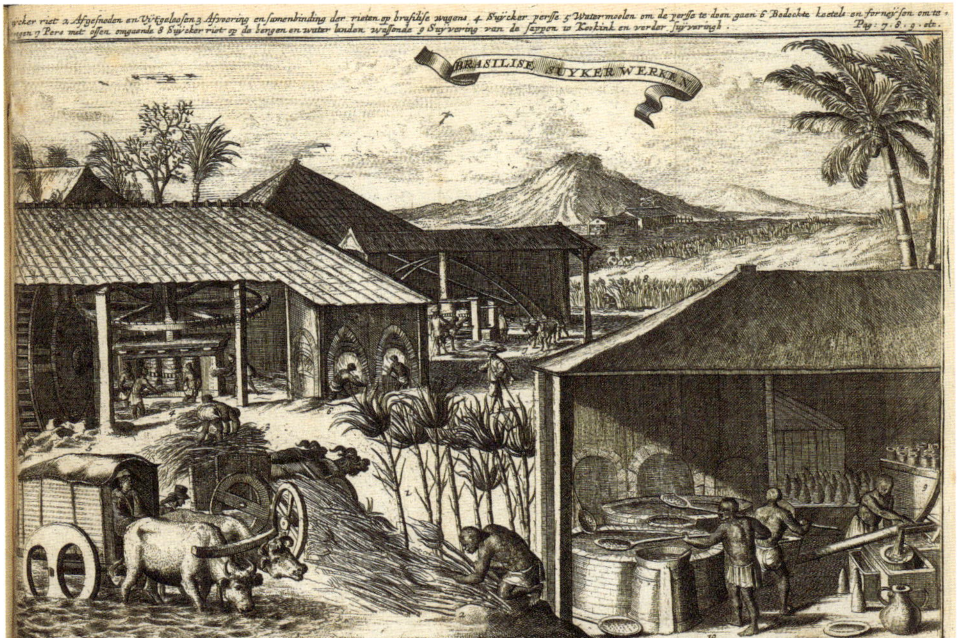

8/2
Romeyn de Hooghe, slaves in a sugar factory, 1682

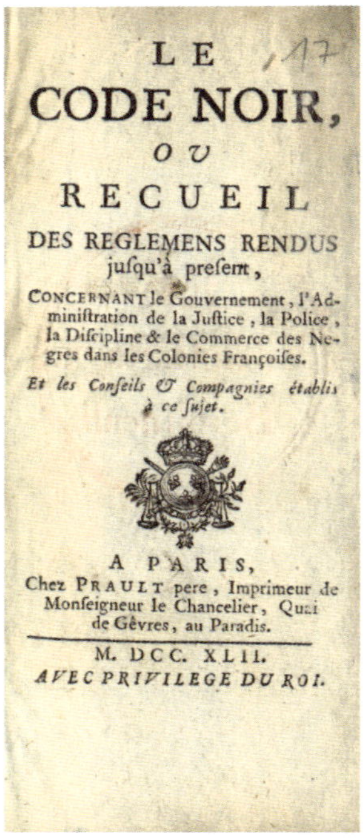

LE

CODE NOIR,

OU

RECUEIL

DES REGLEMENS RENDUS juſqu'à preſent,

CONCERNANT le Gouvernement, l'Adminiſtration de la Juſtice, la Police, la Diſcipline & le Commerce des Negres dans les Colonies Françoiſes.

Et les Conſeils & Compagnies établis à ce ſujet.

A PARIS,

Chez PRAULT pere, Imprimeur de Monſeigneur le Chancelier, Quai de Gêvres, au Paradis.

M. DCC. XLII.

AVEC PRIVILEGE DU ROI.

7/3
Jean-Baptiste Colbert, et al., The *Code Noir* (Black Code) decree, 1742

on the plantations rarely survived more than twenty years, and much less if they were used for hard labour, i.e. in the fields.

France was not the only country that imposed regulations regarding the status of blacks in the colonies, who were to be humiliated as slaves; the first regulations came into force in the 1660s in the British colonies, namely on Barbados Island and in Virginia. These laws were less comprehensive than their French counterparts and were designed primarily to define the special position of the slave. He was thought to be an inferior being over which the owner held sole discretion. The regulations also sought to prevent sexual relations between masters and slaves, because every child of a female slave was considered "naturally" to be a slave itself.

In 1697, the signing of the Treaty of Rijswijk by France and Spain stabilised the existing division of the new continent. This peace treaty ended the war that had been unleashed by the expansionary politics of Louis XIV and in which France had stood against the Grand Alliance (the European Great Powers of the League of Augsburg). Quite soon thereafter, the profiteers of the plantation system – namely the colonists – viewed the service of African slaves as the best possible solution for relieving labour shortages: there were not enough French "contract labourers" who sold their manpower to the colonies for a period of three years. In Africa, meanwhile, the intensity of wars and raids increased. The rapidly expanding demand for slaves brought long-term changes to Africa's social structures. Domestic rulers profited from European demands; they began punishing the slightest of offences with enslavement, selling their prisoners to the Europeans.

The slave trade assumed epic, unprecedented proportions. According to estimates, about 200,000 prisoners were taken from the African coast to the American colonies throughout the entire sixteenth century; by the end of the eighteenth century, however, 100,000 people suffered this fate each year. Overall, about thir-

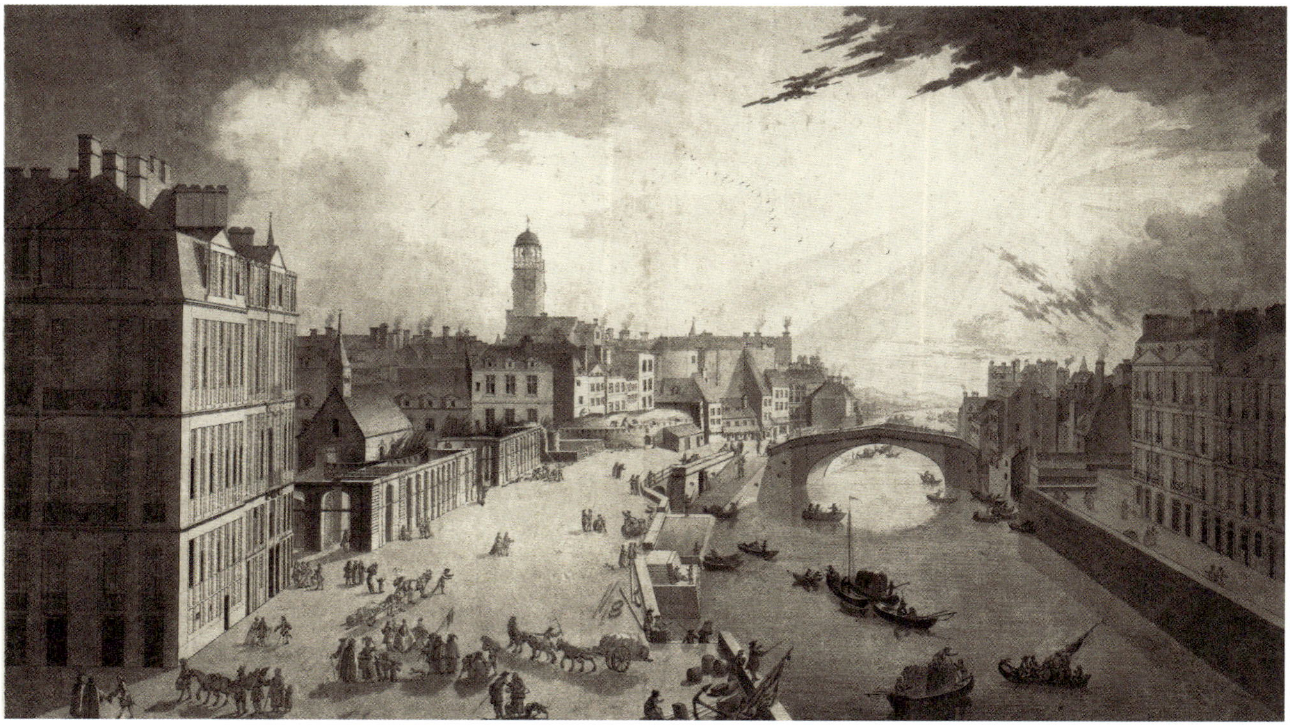

7/2
Antoine Hénon, perspective view of the city of Nantes, 1767–1771

teen million men, women and children fell victim to the slave trade between 1600 and 1867.

The Portuguese were the most important actors in the transatlantic slave trade, followed by the British. Contemporary estimates assume that almost three quarters of all prisoners completed the Atlantic passage on Portuguese, Brazilian or British ships. France and Spain, with their trading posts on the Uruguayan coast, followed closely in third and fourth place. Spain's *Código carolino* of 1784 – a "legal code governing the moral, political and economic treatment of blacks on the island of Hispaniola" (*Código de legislación para el gobierno moral, político y económico de los negros de la isla Española*) – followed the example of the *Code noir.*

The overwhelming majority of slaves came from the Central African west coast (almost 5,693,000 people), with many of them coming from the Bay of Benin (1,999,600 people), from the Bay of Biafra and the coast of Guinea.[2] A total of 140 slave trading posts have been documented along the African coast, yet eighty per cent of the slaves were shipped from a mere twenty ports. The largest of these ports was Luanda, the capital city of modern-day Angola. For 2,826,000 people, this was the beginning of a one-way journey that typically led to Brazil.

Nantes entered the slave trade at a relatively late date, yet drew significant profits from the expeditions of the French East Indies Company (*Compagnie française des Indes Orientales*) until the beginning of the eighteenth century. The first two slave expeditions set out from Nantes in 1656 and 1657. Their profits remained modest. The slave trade in Nantes intensified in the early eighteenth century, rapidly establishing itself. It profited from the dissolution of the monopoly held by the major French trading companies, which gave rise to competition between state companies and private enterprises. Although Nantes also experienced periods of relative decline – for example, because of the political situation in Europe, and competition from other French ports such as Bordeaux, La Rochelle, Lorient, Saint-Malo and Le Havre – it undeniably played a leading role in the slave trade. The growing wealth of the shipping companies and merchants involved in the slave trade was significant, even if the direct rate of profit seems modest at first, around six per cent. This relatively low number testifies to the extremely speculative nature of slave expeditions, which could turn out to be very profitable or catastrophic for the financiers involved. In Nantes, these profits ensured wealth for the port and consequently also for the city's merchant elite, who hailed from the lower middle class, the merchant bourgeoisie and the aristocracy. Profits also exercised an enormous appeal for foreign merchants who actively participated in the expansion of the slave trade and the distribution of colonial wares in Europe. By extension, the entire merchant class in Nantes soon profited from the transatlantic slave trade. Some manufacturers delivered the goods that were traded for slaves on the African coast, while others distributed the goods imported from the colonies.

In general, the slave ships from Nantes sailed to Loango, the economic centre of the eponymous kingdom. This territory lay to the north of the Kingdom of Kakongo and extended from the port of Mayumba to the port of Malembo in the eighteenth century. Estimates indicate that more than 400,000 prisoners left Loango by the beginning of the nineteenth century on board British, Dutch and French ships headed for the Caribbean colonies. Between 1697 and 1803, a total of 495,000 African men, women and children were loaded on to Nantes's slave ships.

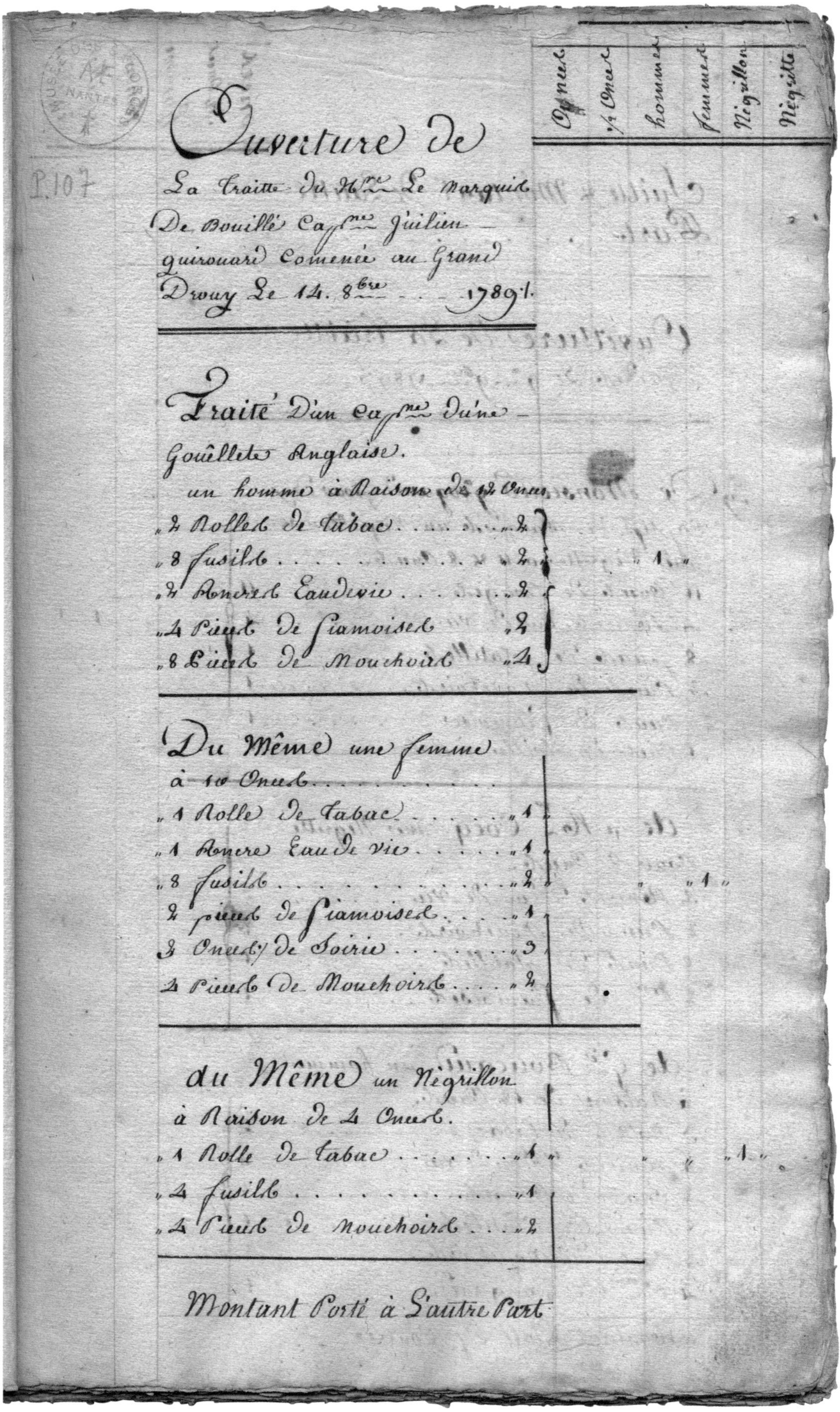

P.107

	Onces	½ Onces	hommes	femmes	Négrillon	Négritte
Ouverture de La traitte du Nre Le marquis De Bouillé Capne Juilien guirouard Comencée au Grand Drouy Le 14. 8bre 1789.						
Traité D'un Capne D'une Gouellete Anglaise. un homme à Raison de 12 Onces						
2 Rolles de tabac ... 2						
8 fusils ... 2			1			
2 Ancres Eaudevie ... 2						
4 Pieces de Siamoises ... 2						
8 Pieces de Mouchoirs ... 4						
Du Même une femme à 10 Onces						
1 Rolle de tabac ... 1						
1 Ancre Eau de vie ... 1						
8 fusils ... 2				1		
2 pieces de Siamoises ... 1						
3 Onces de Soirie ... 3						
4 Pieces de Mouchoirs ... 2						
du Même un Négrillon à Raison de 4 Onces.						
1 Rolle de tabac ... 1					1	
4 fusils ... 1						
4 Pieces de mouchoirs ... 2						

Montant Porté à L'autre Part

The Atlantic passage was marked by extreme violence, a sequel to the cruelty of the African and European slave traders on land who exercised brutality at every stage, from imprisonment to the departure of the ships. For example, prisoners were often marked with a branding iron by the ship's captain after being purchased. The ship's monogram, burned into their flesh, was meant to prevent any confusion in the office of sale or in transition camps on the way to the colonies. The Atlantic passage lasted on average two months and was an unparalleled torture for these men, women and children, which was only worsened by the fact that they were unaware of their destination. The prisoners were divided by sex, ostensibly to prevent agitation, and packed into the steerage. Brief "periods of refreshment" on deck were meant to keep them in prime physical condition so that they could be sold in the colonies at a good price. Hygiene became a true obsession for captains, who feared epidemics such as typhus or dysentery. The prisoners were washed regularly, and the men were shaved. They had to clean the decks and steerage in which they were housed, usually in cramped quarters where they had to lie down. Their provisions were supposed to be just enough to prevent scurvy, which was caused by a vitamin deficiency; but these improved shortly only before reaching the colonies.

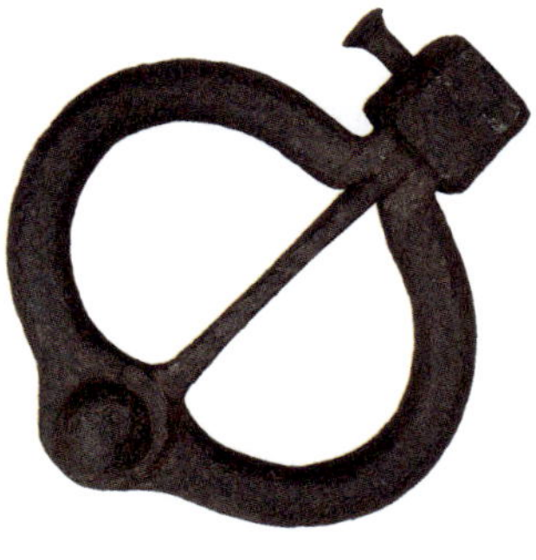

7/13
Hand shackle, probably 18th cent.

Crews were particularly afraid of revolts on board the slave ships. About three per cent of slave expeditions on ships from Nantes experienced revolts, which were put down with extremely brutal violence. Boredom and "melancholy" were thought to be the causes of such unrest. Many shipping companies therefore called upon their captains to provide entertainment for the prisoners: "A nearly infallible secret recipe for maintaining peace among the blacks until they reach their destination is to perform music for them, even if it is just with a lyre or bagpipes".[3] It was said that there was nothing better than "to hire a novice from western Brittany who knew how to play the bagpipes so that he could keep the blacks happy and in good health".[4] There was also to be as much dancing and singing as possible, because "movement makes the joints supple, keeps scurvy and sadness at bay, and singing maintains cheerfulness".[5]

The sale of the prisoners was a decisive moment, both in the Antilles and in the American colonies. For the ship's captain, it meant the end of the slave passage and a return to the home port, via the most direct way possible and loaded with colonial goods. Sales revenues determined the financial success or failure of the expedition for the shipping company and everyone who was financially involved in the expedition's organization. For the prisoners, the sale was the moment that completed their transition from free human beings into slaves. In Saint-Domingue, slaves were sold on board or at special offices on land. Such sales were advertised in newspapers and posters at the port city. In the French colonies, these transactions were concentrated in four places: Port-au-Prince, Cap Français, Saint-Marc and Jérémie. In general, the sale price was paid for by means of loans that ran for two or three years. Payment was made in natural resources: sugar, coffee, cacao, cotton and indigo. Often, three shiploads of natural resources were required to pay off one shipload of slaves.

The prisoners sold to the colonists were an indispensable labour force for the plantations. Their masters identified the slaves with their brands. The average age of prisoners was between fifteen and thirty. The majority of them had to perform work in the fields and factories. Others became house slaves, or domestic servants. A few

7/11
Balance sheet for the slave ship Marquis de Bouillé, 1789/1790

colonists preferred to buy children, who were docile and malleable and were meant to support the white overseers. The most talented among them (*nègres à talents*) worked as craftsmen or merchants, performing the same work as free people.

Slave life in the colonies was marked by labour and suppression. Because slaves were generally considered to be a type of cattle, they held slim hope for a better life, or more precisely, freedom. In actuality, it was extremely rare for a slave to be granted freedom. Those who benefited from the slave trade viewed the high mortality of enslaved peoples as a justification for a constant supply of reinforcements. Slaves who managed to escape formed groups together in secret. These groups were particularly feared in Saint-Domingue. They were hunted down, and any prisoners taken offered an occasion for brutal retribution. Terrible punishments were meant to provide an example, although mutilation was avoided because it would have rendered the slave worthless.

The American Revolution was followed by the French Revolution in 1789, which put an end to absolute monarchy in France. Monarchs elsewhere in Europe feared that this movement could spread. The notion of the equality of mankind, which originated in the philosophy of the Enlightenment, gained serious social momentum; on 26 August 1789, the principle of equality was incorporated and announced in the Declaration of the Rights of Man and of the Citizen. This had direct consequences that also divided the population of Nantes; while some accepted the principles of the revolution with enthusiasm, others did not want to lose the most important source of their wealth. Shipping companies, merchants and colonists came together with like-minded people in Bordeaux to engage in a battle against the abolitionist advances of the *Société des Amis des Noirs* ("Society of the Friends of the Blacks"). After a slave revolt broke out in 1791 on Saint-Domingue, the French National Convention abolished the slave trade on 4 February 1794; however, Napoleon reintroduced it in 1802.

The slave trade never returned to Saint-Domingue, though. The insurgent slaves – initially led by François-Dominique Toussaint-Louverture (1743–1803) and then by Jean-Jacques Dessalines (1758–1806) – had prevailed against the resistance of the colonists. On 1 January 1804, Saint-Domingue won its independence and was henceforth known as Haiti. Independence meant that 455,000 slaves won back their freedom.

The loss of Saint-Domingue meant that France had lost eighty per cent of its income from its colonies. In 1817, Louis XVIII (1755–1824) forbid the slave trade in France and declared the business illegal. Nantes followed this pronouncement less faithfully than did other cities. A second abolition law, passed on 25 April 1827, also had little success. Between 1818 and 1831, 308 ships were equipped in Nantes for the slave trade, and the city again became France's most significant slave port. Within this period of time, it is estimated that 100,000 men, women and children were carried off on board French slave ships. Only the law of 4 March 1831 truly had an effect because it levied harsh sanctions against shipping companies and financiers involved in slave expeditions.

While trading in slaves was already prohibited, France only abolished slavery itself with the law of 27 April 1848. In comparison to other countries, this step came rather late; Denmark had already prohibited the slave trade in 1803, closely followed by England in 1807, and – at least in terms of the transatlantic trade in slaves – the United States of America in 1808.[6] In the 1820s, slavery was abolished

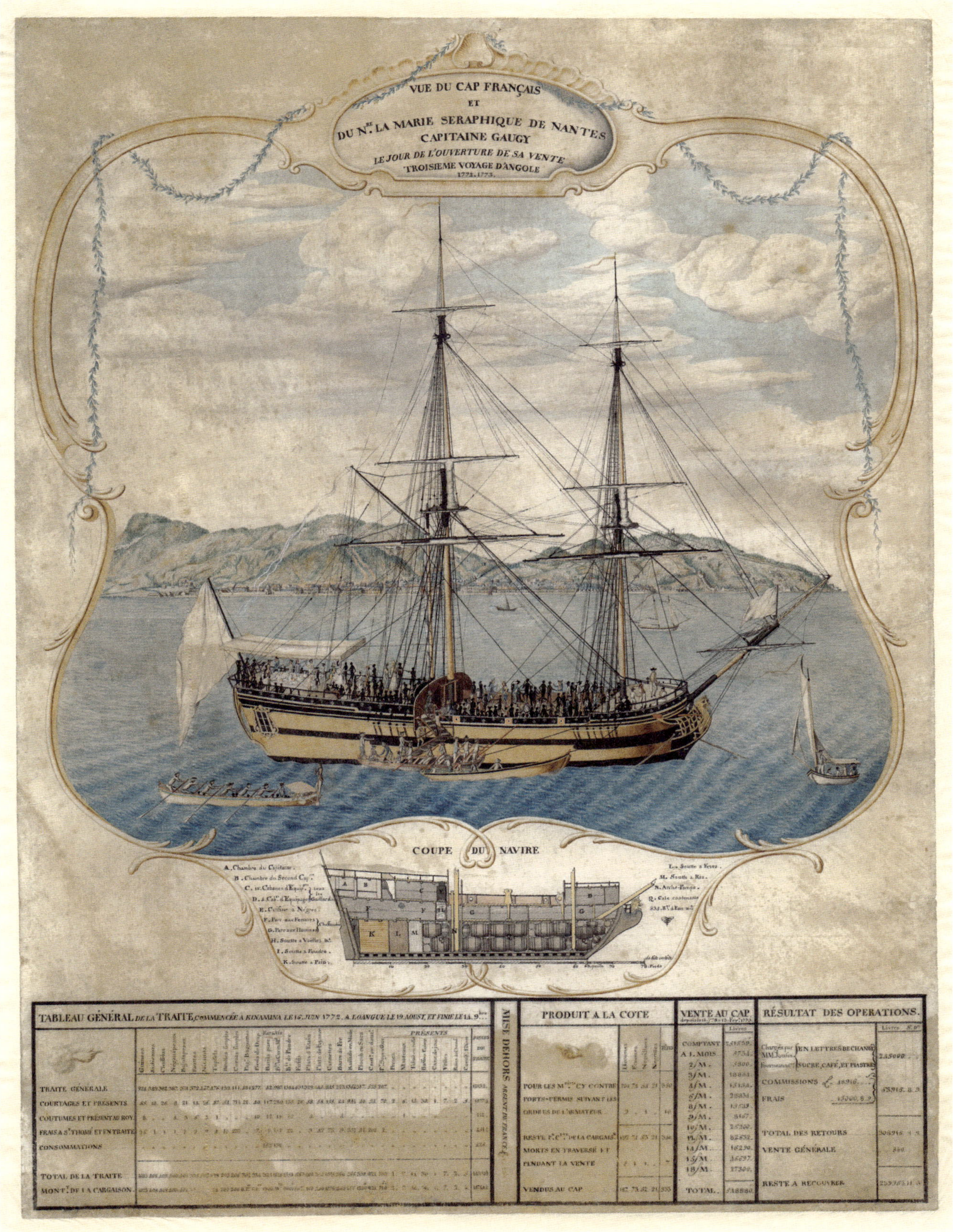

7/14
Scene depicting the sale of slaves on board the MARIE-SÉRAPHIQUE, 1775/1800

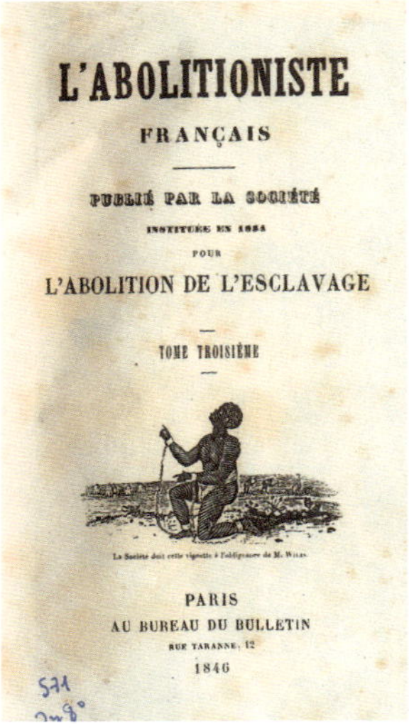
L'ABOLITIONISTE
FRANÇAIS
PUBLIÉ PAR LA SOCIÉTÉ
POUR
L'ABOLITION DE L'ESCLAVAGE
TOME TROISIÈME
PARIS
AU BUREAU DU BULLETIN
1846

7/19
Mark Wilks, *L'Abolitioniste Français* (The French abolitionist), 1846

in Peru, Chile, Costa Rica, Bolivia, Mexico and several Central American countries. The British colonies began to gradually abolish slavery in 1833 in a process that was completed in 1838. In the 1850s, slavery was abolished in Colombia (Decree of 21 May 1851), Ecuador, Argentina, Venezuela and Brazil. In Brazil, however, abolition was not complete until 1888.

In the twentieth century, additional countries abolished slavery, particularly in Africa (i.e., Kenya 1907[7], Ethiopia 1942, Mauritania 1981), the Arabian Peninsula (i.e., Kuwait 1949, Qatar 1952, Saudi Arabia 1962, Oman 1970), and in the Near East (i.e., Afghanistan 1923, Iran 1928, Pakistan 1992).

Although the transatlantic slave trade has ended, with numerous countries passing a series of laws that in various ways condemn and forbid slavery, the practice still exists. The United Nations (UN) and the International Labour Organisation (ILO) estimate that, even today, there are almost 200 million people[8], including many children, who live under the conditions of forced labour and slavery.

1 In the French original the slaves were identified as "nègres", which can be translated both as "black" ("noir") and "negro" ("nègre"), which in both cases was closely affiliated with the status of being a slave; compare "négrier" in its meaning at the time of "slave trader" or, today, "exploiter". The citations for this article were translated from the French.

2 All figures are taken from David Eltis and David Richardson, *Atlas of the Transatlantic Slave Trade* (New Haven and London: Yale UP, 2010).

3 Jacques Savary des Brulons, *Dictionnaire universel de commerce*, Vol. 3 (L–Z), ed. Philémon-Louis Savary, Paris 1741, esp. 554 f., online: http://gallica.bnf.fr/ark:/12148/bpt6k111738x (last accessed on 18 January 2018).

4 Letter to Faboulet, 28 March 1764, held in the Archives départementales de Loire-Atlantique.

5 "Observations touchant le soin des nègres dans le voyage de Guinée", manuscript from an anonymous captain from Nantes around 1777; held in the Bibliothèque municipale de Nantes, M 878.

6 In the United States, however, it was not until the South had been defeated in the Civil War and the Thirteenth Amendment to the Constitution passed in 1865 that slavery was finally abolished in all of the federal states.

7 This pertains to the abolition of traditional African slavery, meaning that Kenyan society abolished slavery there, not Kenya's British colonial rulers.

8 These are current figures from the *Organisation international du Travail*, accessed on 18 January 2018, http://www.ilo.org/global/about-the-ilo/newsroom/news/WCMS_574719/lang--fr/index.htm.

Lasse Heerten

INTEGRATING THE WORLD

Maritime Globalisation(s)

Well into the eighteenth century, coasts were considered dismal places, threatened by the nearby sea and exposed to its dangers. It was not until European modernity that coasts became the objects of romantic longing and destinations for beach holidays. "The lure of the sea"[1] – this phrase could also be used to describe current trends in historical research. To be sure, historians have long studied bodies of water of all kinds, and the Mediterranean and the Atlantic were early objects of historical enquiry, but for years the discipline has been caught up in a veritable wave of maritime historical studies.

Global historical perspectives have played a key role in the rediscovery of the seas by historians. In the container-driven globalisation of the present day, more than 90 per cent of all goods are transported by sea. However, more recent historical research has shown that the history of maritime globalisation processes extends far back in time.[2]

Periods and regions: the networks of maritime globalisation processes

The maritime integration of the world can be roughly divided into three periods: the age of sail, that of steam and that of container shipping. The heyday of sailing vessels coincided more or less with European expansion, which began in the fifteenth century. Technological innovations made it possible to build ever larger ships without increases in crew size. This resulted in space not only for more cargo, but also for additional provisions, which in turn facilitated longer voyages. The age of sail ended in the mid-nineteenth century, when steam-powered vessels demonstrated their military superiority over sailing ships and gradually began dominating commercial and passenger shipping. The increased use of containers and the extensive shift of passenger traffic to aviation from the 1960s onwards was the next major turning point in the history of maritime globality and heralded the world we know today.

In the age of sail, the rhythms of trade and transport were determined by the tides, winds and ocean currents. For example, the prevailing winds off the European coast in the Atlantic were westerlies, which made voyages to America diffi-

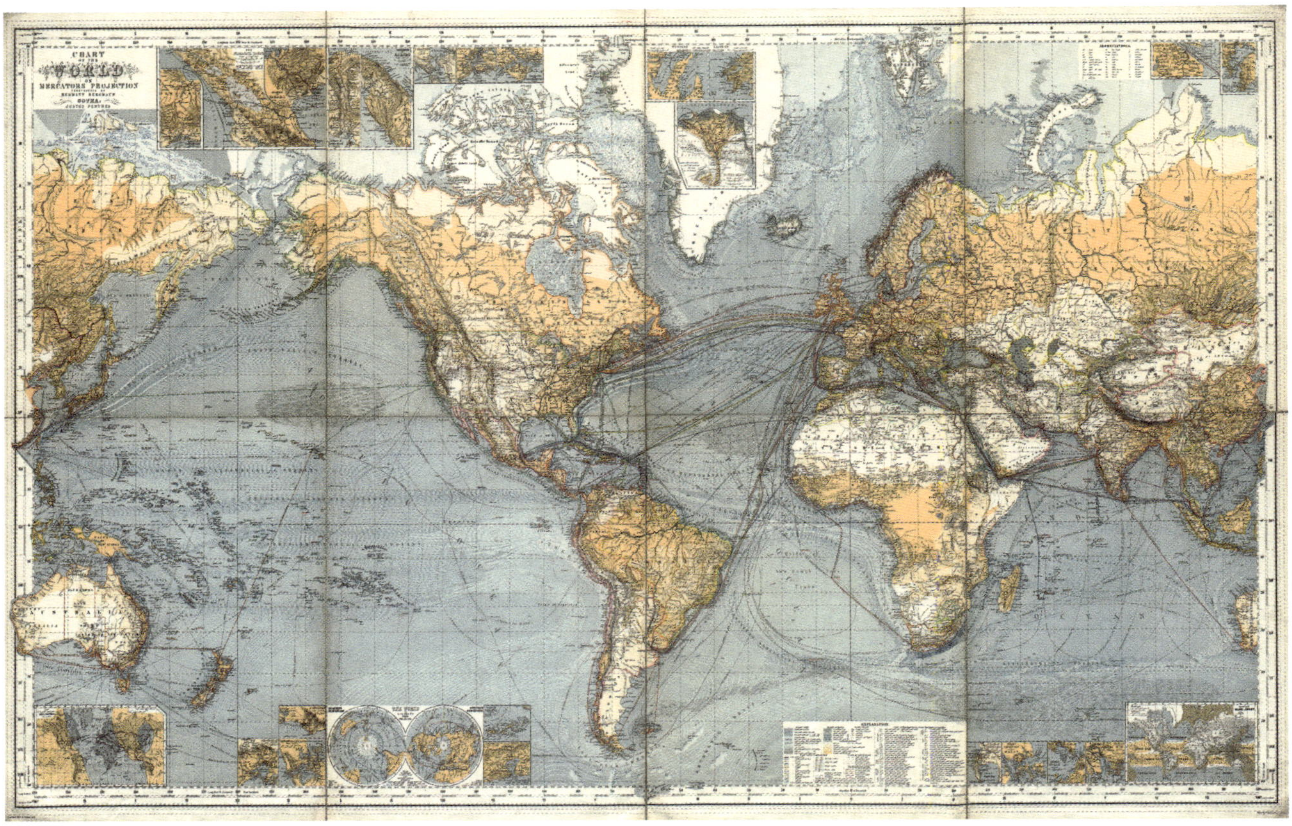

8/41
Hermann Berghaus, chart of the world on Mercator's projection, 1871

cult. Farther to the south, trade winds blew from the east. When these were discovered during the southern expansion of Spain and Portugal along the western coast of Africa in the fifteenth century, they made expeditions to the west possible. These wind and current conditions shaped the triangular transatlantic trade from the late seventeenth century to the early nineteenth century: ships carrying manufactured goods such as cloth and firearms sailed from the ports of western Europe to the slave coasts of West Africa. There, with the help of the trade winds, the human "goods" that had been loaded on board were taken to the plantations of the Americas, where local commodities – mainly sugar, tobacco and cotton – were shipped to Europe via the North Atlantic.

European expansion was not the result of Europe's technological, military or political superiority. In fact, this superiority did not exist in Arab or Asian regions. It emerged from a complex combination of other factors, particularly Europe's dominance along a variety of sea routes and shorelines. European expansion in Asia was thus linked to its expansion in America and Africa.

This process can be illustrated by the example of cotton.[3] Well into the eighteenth century, the manufacturers of cotton fabrics on the Indian subcontinent led the world in the production of printed textiles. In the seventeenth century, though, the British East India Company began edging its way into this market. One of its goals was to export Indian fabric not only to Europe, but also to Africa, where it was in great demand and used to purchase slaves. These slaves were then sold to America as plantation workers and the proceeds were used to purchase Indian textiles once again. When opposition arose in Great Britain to the import of Indian cotton goods – which in many ways were superior to local products –

British merchants took charge of fabric production themselves. American plantations now grew cotton on a massive scale for European factories. European travellers had acquired knowledge of Asian production processes through what must be called industrial espionage. Thus, the labour came from Africa, the crops were grown in North and South America, and production took place in Europe, where the profits increasingly remained as well.

In the age of steam-driven globalisation, these dominant European structures took on increasingly rigid forms. The First Opium War (1839–1842) was an important turning point in this connection. As vividly described by the Indian author Amitav Ghosh (b. 1956) in *Flood of Fire*, book three of his Ibis trilogy, it was the Nemesis – an ironclad paddle steamship – that established the British navy's military superiority over the Chinese fleet in battles in the Pearl River Delta. Steam power enabled vessels to travel upstream, which was impossible for sailing ships. Thus, even before the construction of railways, rivers that reached deep into the interior like arms of the sea could be used as "highways of imperialism".[4]

Generally speaking, in the age of steam, the world became interconnected via its seas. This is shown by the "Chart of the World" – a large English wall map published by the Leipzig-based Perthes company between 1863 and 1924. Showing a network of global transport routes, this map adorned the offices of shipping lines, trading companies and government ministries and shaped contemporary ideas and practices of maritime globalisation. The depictions of the major seas clearly influenced the options of maritime trade.

On the level of the actual routes, the network of globalisation that was made possible by steam vessels was centred on the North Atlantic, where quick crossings were now possible in both directions. The world's most frequently travelled route connected New York – the most important port in America – with north-western Europe, where the three other major steam-age ports were located: London, Liverpool and Hamburg. The global network of steamboat lines was focused on just a handful of routes, most of which originated in ports in north-west Europe. These ports were connected via the Atlantic not only to the east

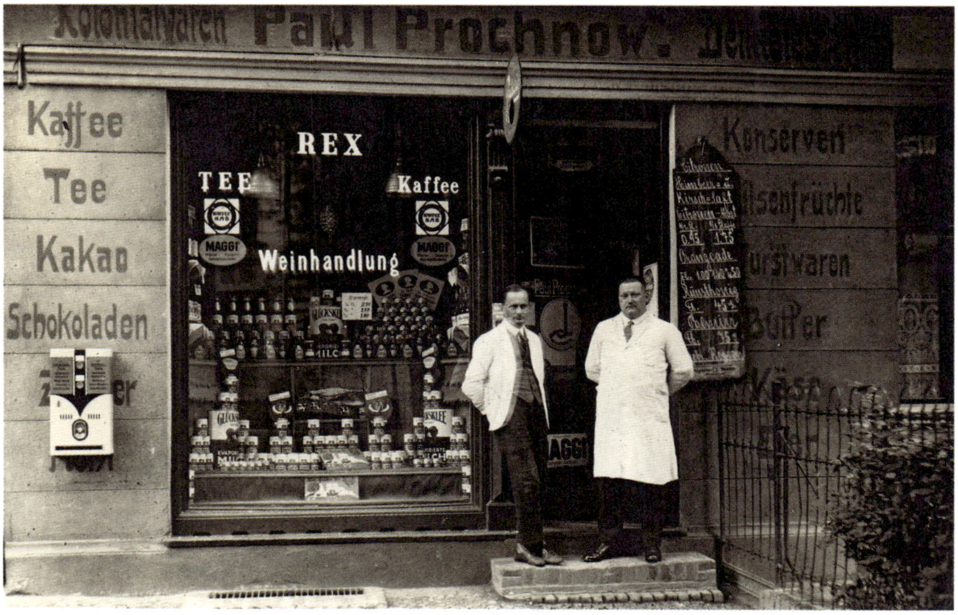

Colonial goods shop in Berlin, 1929

coast of North America, but also to the South American ports of Rio de Janeiro and Rio de La Plata. Other important routes led to Japan via the Mediterranean Sea, the Suez Canal, the Indian Ocean and the Strait of Malacca – or to Australia along the West African coast and the Cape of Good Hope. The only important line that did not originate in north-western Europe led from Hong Kong and Yokohama across the Pacific to San Francisco.[5]

Thus, the global steamship network was not equally dense in all places, nor did it expand in all places at the same speed. Some parts of the world were integrated into the network only loosely because services were not continuous, regular or quick in all places – assuming they existed at all. In addition, the global transport system remained highly diverse, and the expansion of the individual sub-networks had ambivalent effects. The Suez Canal, which opened in 1869, is one example. It accelerated certain types of traffic while inhibiting others – after all, a canal is always a boundary. It cut through a caravan route that had been the most important commercial connection between Cairo and Damascus for centuries. After it opened, a simple ferry service was introduced near El Qantara, but the caravans had to wait for ships to pass before being carried to the opposite shore.[6] For this reason, it is fitting to speak of maritime "globalisations" in the plural and to focus on the heterogeneity and ambivalence of these processes. Finally, sailing vessels did not immediately lose importance after the steamboat was introduced. The most modern and efficient sailing ships were built in the late nineteenth and early twentieth centuries and profitably used to transport a range of durable goods, including the saltpetre that was carried around Cape Horn to the ports of northern Chile.

Steam technology nevertheless marked a turning point. After all, while it was hardly possible to increase the tonnage carried by sailing vessels, there appeared to be no limits to the amount of goods that could be handled by the new steamships. The expansion of this network is partly attributable to the spread of the new technology itself, for steam shipping stoked the demand for a specific raw material: coal. Because coal supplies needed to be constantly replenished, a network of coaling stations emerged that spanned the entire globe. Like Singapore, Shanghai and Hong Kong, all of which had served as coaling stations of the British Empire, many of these developed into ports of global significance.

The steam age was also of great importance for the history of capitalism. The ever larger vessels required immense investments. As a result, shipping and trading companies were either converted into stock corporations or replaced by them, and banks played an increasingly important role in financing global transport.

When the first steamboat lines were founded in the mid-nineteenth century, the technology was not yet very efficient or profitable. Many people were afraid of the long voyages, which were uncomfortable at best and life-threatening at worst. This changed after 1850, when improved technology increased the safety of the crossings. Nevertheless, the enterprises that went bankrupt included not only the liner services of trading companies which, lacking foresight, used sailing vessels instead of steamships, such as the service run by the Hamburg "South Sea King" Johan Cesar VI. Godeffroy (1813–1885), but also numerous businesses that turned to steam technology too early. Despite their transformation into corporations, many shipping companies depended directly and indirectly on government subsidies for success. Imperial ties were essential because the shipping companies transported not only mail, but also government representatives and the European Powers' troops. However, it was above all passenger transport that enabled many of the shipping lines that had escaped insolvency to become globally operating concerns: steam vessels became a means of transport for the masses, most of whom were emigrants. Shipping lines such as the Compagnie Générale Transatlantique, Cunard, the Hamburg-Amerikanische Packetfahrt-Actien-Gesellschaft (Hapag), the Holland-Amerika Lijn, Holt, Norddeutsche Lloyd and the Peninsular & Oriental Steam Navigation Co. Ltd. (P&O) were the global players of the nineteenth and early twentieth centuries. They transformed the age of steam into the age of global migration; both facilitated and mutually influenced each other.

Places: ports as the hubs of maritime globalisation processes

On 29 October 1888, the city of Hamburg was festively decorated to celebrate its accession to the German Customs Union and the completion of the first free port facilities. The Hanseatic city had joined the German Empire when the latter had been founded on 1 January 1871, but, as a free port city, it had remained a customs-free zone on its entire territory. After abandoning the economic policy of free trade in the late 1870s, the imperial government exerted pressure on Hamburg to join the Customs Union. The Hanseatic city was able to negotiate comprehensive financial and customs benefits. Despite accession to the Customs Union, free port zones were established in which goods could still be traded duty-free. Receiving 40 million reichsmarks from the imperial government, Hamburg began building the so-called Speicherstadt in 1883, a warehouse district that became the heart of its modern port. To make room for the new buildings, an entire section of the city centre on the islands of Kehrwieder and Wandrahm was torn down and around twenty thousand people were resettled. Thus, a new nexus of economic life emerged in the direct vicinity of the city centre and within walking distance of the town hall and stock exchange.

Port expansion had in fact already begun in the 1850s and 1860s with the deepening of the Elbe and the construction of the Sandtorhafen, the first artificial

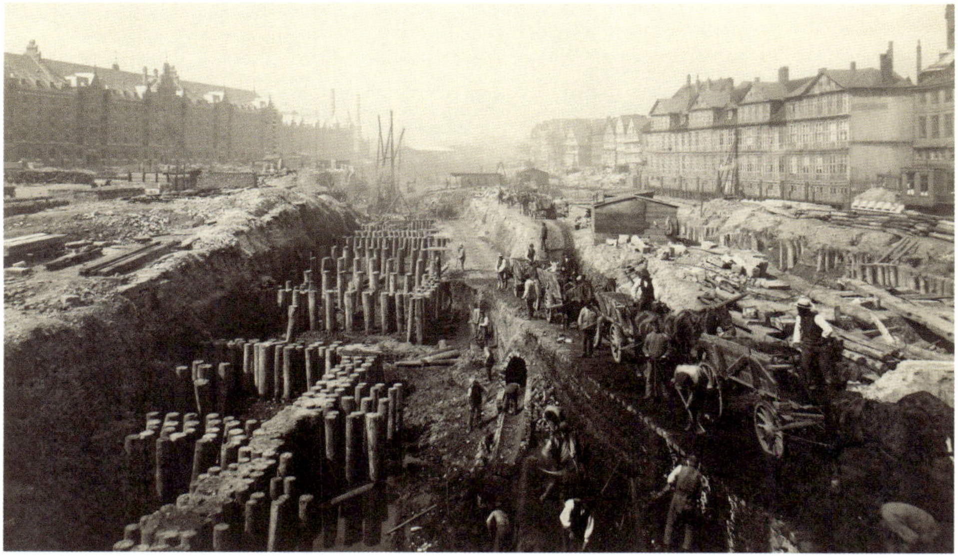

8/30
Georg Koppmann, excavations between Kannengiesser bridge and Kornhaus bridge for the construction of the free port, 20 July 1887

harbour basin in the Hanseatic city. The debate on enlarging the harbour goes back even further. In the preceding decades, the predominant view was that Hamburg should be transformed into a non-tidal port modelled on London. Ultimately, an open tidal port was built because calculations had shown that the tidal range of the Elbe was smaller than that of the Thames, which carried salty seawater up to London. Thus, even in a tidal port, loading and unloading at the wharfs in Hamburg was possible at almost all times, despite the tides.

Nevertheless, London remained an important benchmark not only for Hamburg, but also for cities across the globe that discussed port expansion projects in the age of steam. In 1800, the British capital, which had a population of around 900,000, was still smaller than Peking, the only city of a million inhabitants in the world. However, by the eve of the First World War, it had grown to more than seven million inhabitants. As the economic and political centre of the British Empire, London became the pre-eminent metropolis of the steam age, a role that was inseparably linked to the growth of its port, which was the world's largest at the time. In the second half of the eighteenth century, the tremendous growth in the volume of ships had pushed the capacity of the "Pool of London" to its limits – the natural harbour basin to which the city owed its growth. With the construction of the London Docks near the banking district between 1799 and 1815, London now had artificial harbour basins, controlled by locks. The West India Docks were opened on the Isle of Dogs in 1802, and the East India Docks, situated farther to the east, were inaugurated in 1803. Not only did these docks increase the port's capacity, but they also allowed goods from all over the world – e.g. ivory, spices, coffee, cocoa, cloth and tea – to be stored in enclosed areas behind massive warehouse walls, where they were protected from theft.

The dominance of London and the British Empire in world trade left its mark on the global network of port cities. In order to pursue imperial goals, other countries implemented massive investment programmes designed to improve

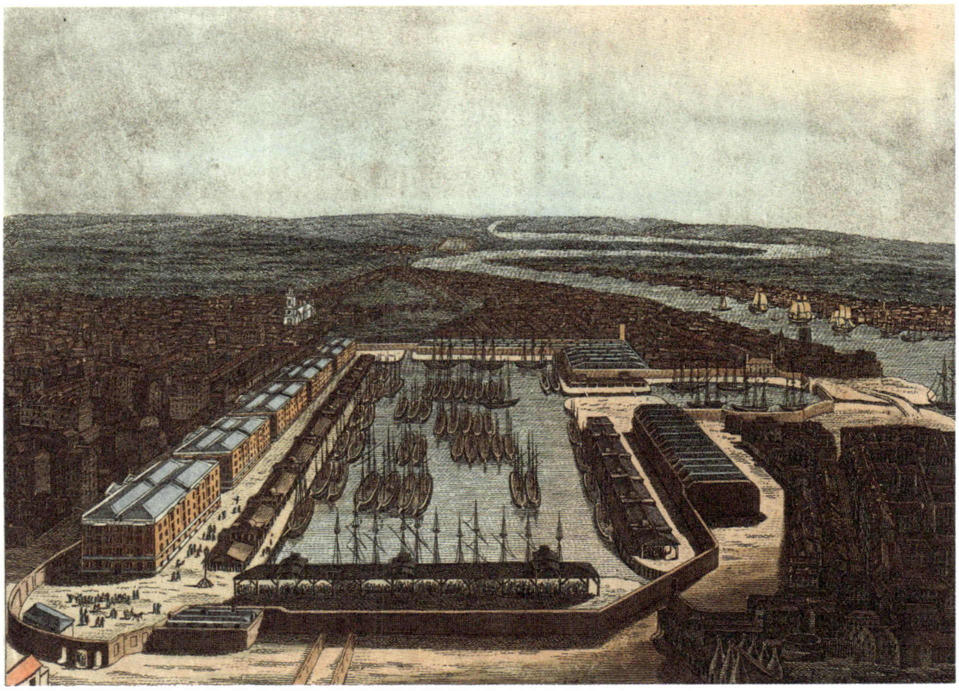

8/25
Docklands in London, c. 1813

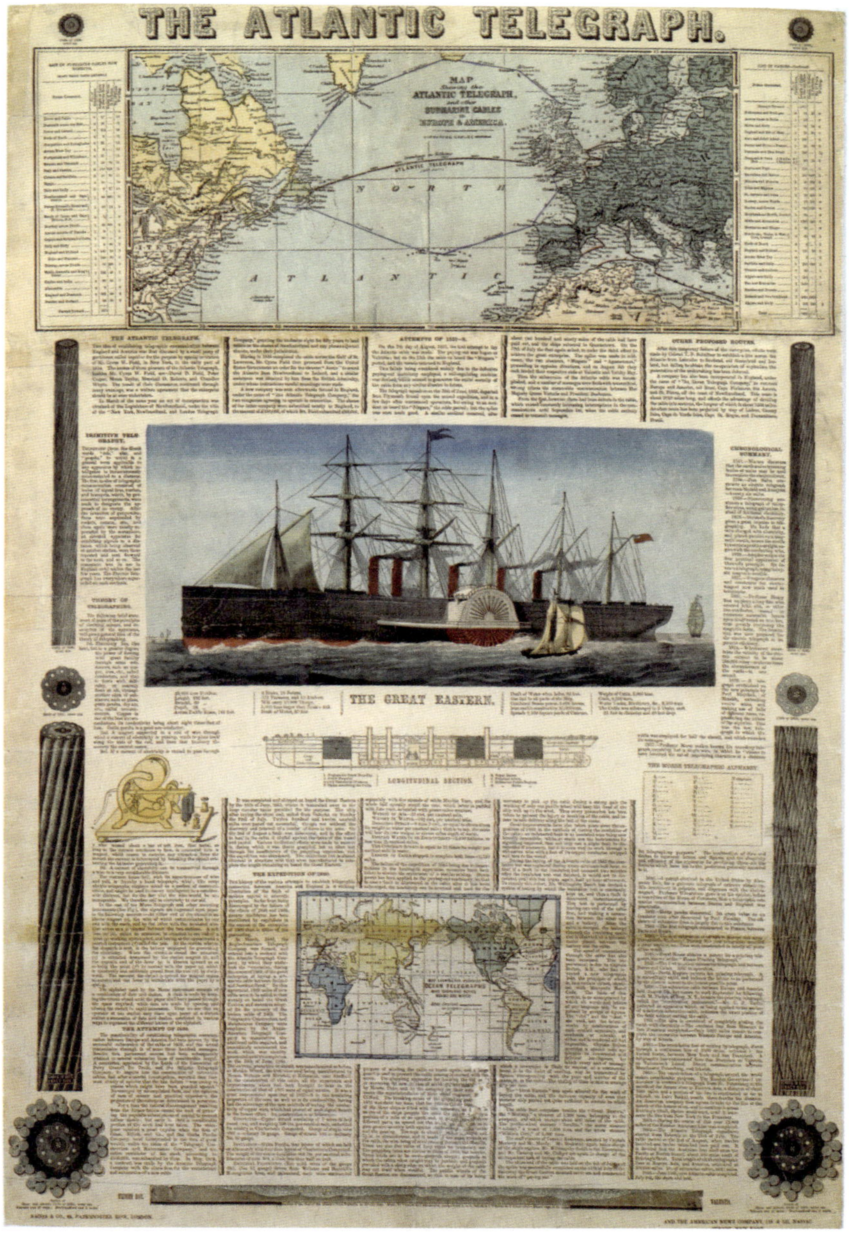

Illustrated special issue about the Great Eastern laying the transatlantic cable, 1866

their port infrastructure. The Ottoman Empire modernised its ports as part of the Tanzimat reforms, as did Japan in the Meiji Restoration. In the Habsburg Empire, plans were made to transform Trieste into a maritime base for imperial expansion, and Hamburg was to play the same role in the German Empire.

Individual port cities such as Hamburg and London expanded in conjunction with global transformation processes. Due to the new telegraph, steamship and underwater cable lines, they grew into increasingly interconnected hubs of the global economy. From 1859 on, individual ports consisted of continually expanding complexes of wharfs, cranes, warehouses and shipyards. Artificial harbours were dug and rivers were dredged to allow ever larger steamships to enter. At the same time, the port cities became more closely connected with the interior through the expansion of railways, roads and inland waterways. In short, the port cities developed into important interfaces between land and sea traffic.

In many port cities, such construction activities reached a peak in the late nineteenth century, albeit for different reasons. Political and economic considerations determined whether and in what form the projects were implemented. In colonial and quasi-colonial regions – e.g. on the Chinese coast – the responsible parties often did not build cranes due to the large supply of cheap labour. In addition, states and municipalities had to agree on whether the large port expansion investments made sense. In Buenos Aires, for example, which has no natural harbour of its own, ocean liners were loaded and unloaded offshore until the 1880s, when the local oligarchs agreed to invest in new port facilities. In Osaka in the same period, the impetus came from the private sector, and the municipality decided to assume the risk of port modernisation without the help of the government in Tokyo. In Hamburg, by contrast, financial support from the imperial government was a decisive factor. The expansion of the infrastructure in individual cities in turn affected other parts of the network. From the 1830s on, under British rule, Singapore became a hub of world trade at the intersection between various global and Asian trade routes, and the expansion of its port accelerated the marginalisation of the ports of Malacca and Penang, which had previously been more important facilities. It also caused Chinese merchants to leave these cities for Singapore. Port cities were interwoven in complex ways at various levels, and developments at one location always affected the other parts of the system.

Outlook: maritime pasts and the global present

Today, anyone who opens a newspaper, turns on the TV or unfolds a laptop in order to get business news will probably confront images of container terminals. Omnipresent in media presentations of the global economy, containers have become an icon of contemporary globalisation. Despite their symbolic significance, though, container ships and ports play only a minor role in most people's lives. Passenger traffic has shifted almost entirely to aviation. Today's container terminals are highly automated, fenced-in facilities that have few employees and have been removed from city centres. Whereas container ships have continually grown in size, smaller numbers of people are now needed to load, unload and operate them. As a result, there are now only a handful of sailors who take shore leave, a custom that for centuries dominated life in port towns. And due to the considerably shortened lay times, these sailors normally spend only a few hours onshore. The port communities typical of the steam age no longer exist.

This is precisely the reason for our interest in our maritime past today. Whether in literary portrayals, museum presentations or the redesigned waterfronts of abandoned "historic" harbours such as Hamburg's HafenCity, maritime globality – which is directly linked to steam-age workplaces and social milieus – first captured our interest when it was no longer a present we experienced ourselves but had become a vanished past. Maritime romanticism first became popular when sailors disappeared from the streets of the port cities. Evidence of this can be found in popular culture: with their sentimental portrayals of sailors, Hans Albers (1891–1960) and Freddy Quinn (b. 1931) carved out careers for themselves at that historic moment in time when this world was in decline and the steam age was ending. Since then it has been resurrected by various economic interests,

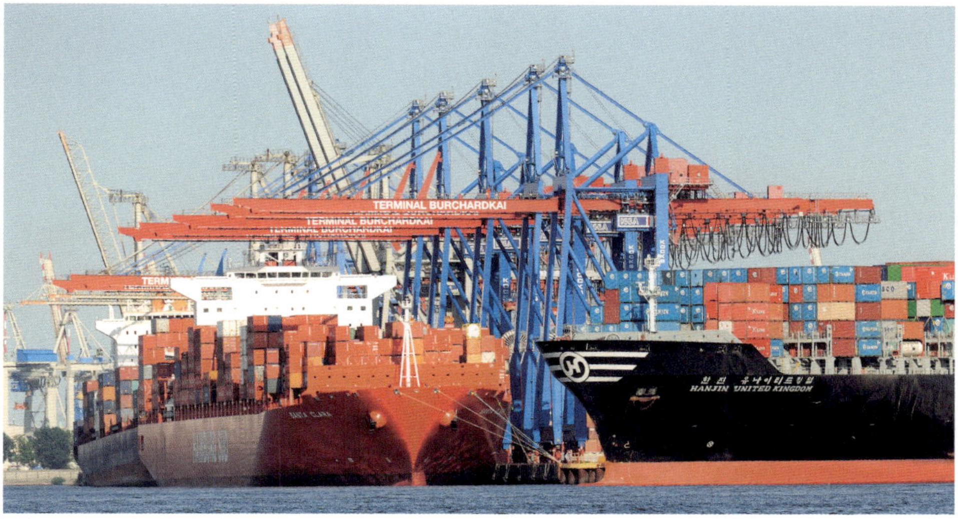

8/49
Container ships in the Port of Hamburg, c. 2016

including the sex and entertainment industry in Hamburg's red light district, St. Pauli. Historians may have rediscovered coasts, seas, rivers and oceans in our global present, but this did not happen because present-day globalisation is taking place mainly on the seas, but because this maritime globality is no longer part of our daily lives.

1 "The Lure of the Sea: Discovery of the Seaside in the Western World 1750–1840" is title of the English translation (London: Penguin, 1995) of the historian Alain Corbin's French work *Le territoire du vide: L'Occident et le plaisir du rivage 1750–1840*.

2 For a detailed discussion of what follows, see Lasse Heerten, "Ankerpunkte der Verflechtung: Hafenstädte in der neueren Globalgeschichtsschreibung", *Geschichte und Gesellschaft* 43, no. 1 (2017): 146–175, including further bibliographical references.

3 On what follows, see Sven Beckert, *King Cotton: Eine Globalgeschichte des Kapitalismus* (Munich, 2014).

4 Kenneth Onwuka Dike, *Trade and Politics in the Niger Delta, 1830–1885: An Introduction to the Economic and Political History of Nigeria* (Oxford, 1966), s. v.

5 Jürgen Osterhammel, *Die Verwandlung der Welt: Eine Geschichte des 19. Jahrhunderts* (Munich, 2009), 1016.

6 Valeska Huber, *Channelling Mobilities: Migration and Globalisation in the Suez Canal Region and Beyond, 1869–1914* (Cambridge, 2013).

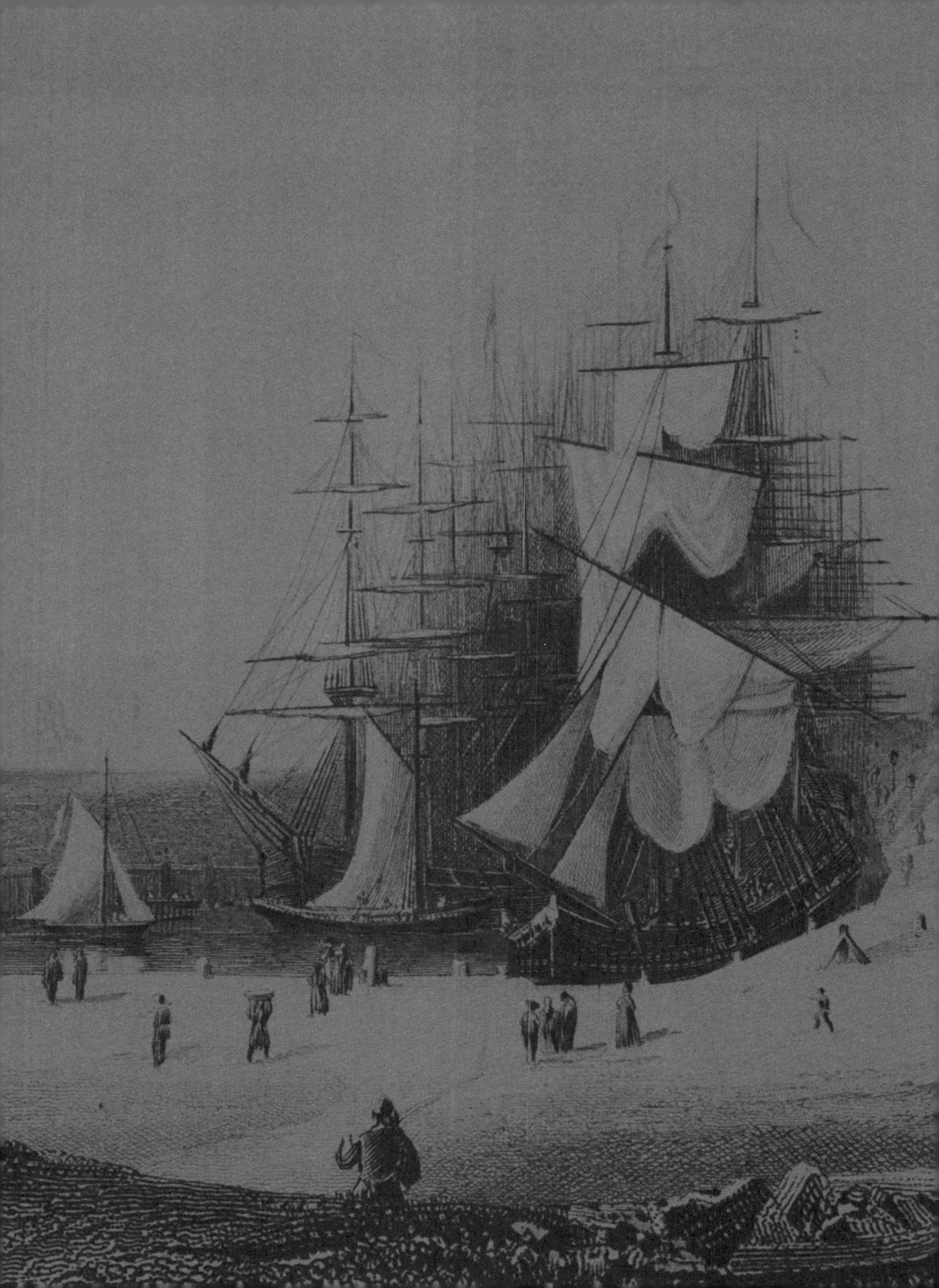

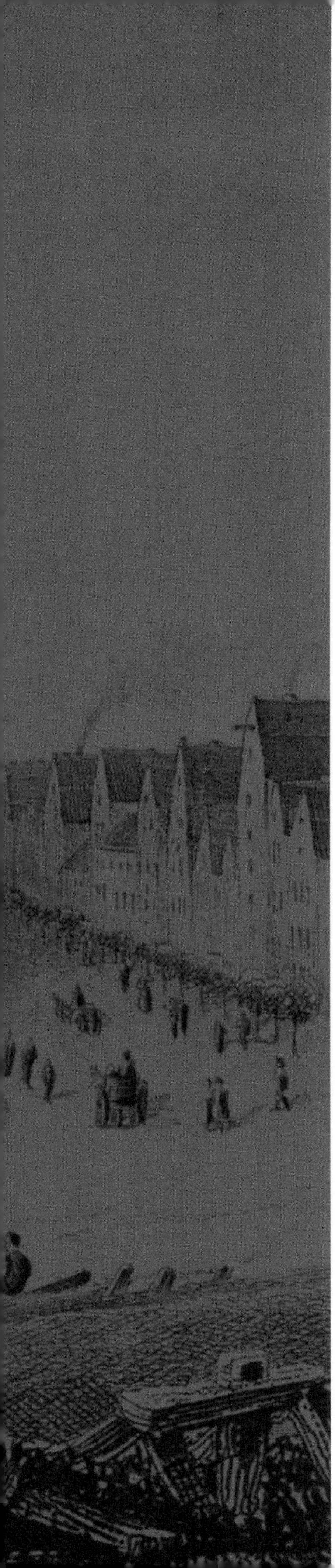

II
BRIDGE AND BARRIER

Alfred Kube

DANCING UPON THE SEA

The Age of European Mass Overseas Migration, 1815 to 1970

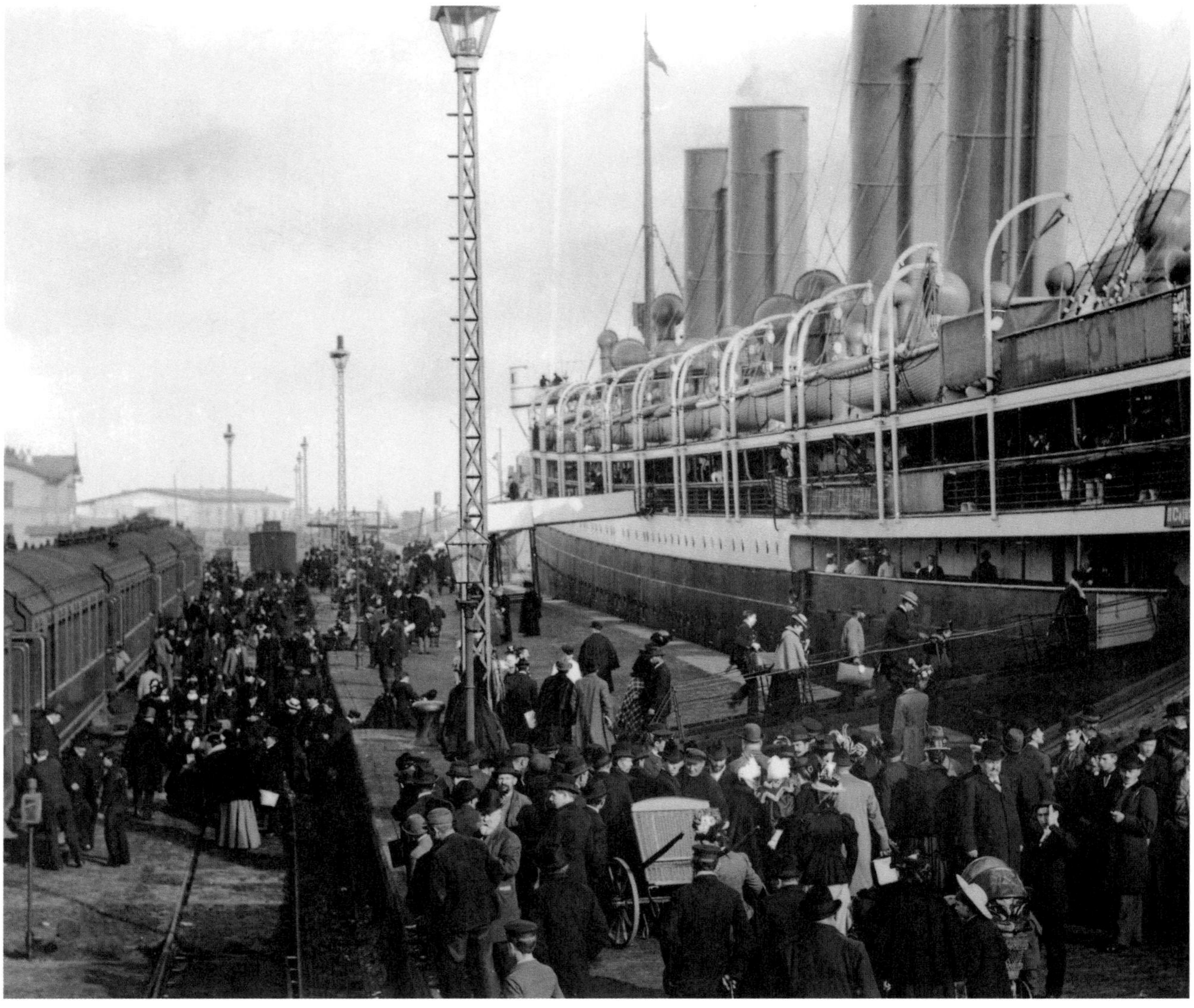

Emigration, immigration, and many forms of mobility have shaped European history.[1] One particular form of these population movements was the mass migration from Europe over the seas, which reached its climax in the period from 1815 to 1914. In the long nineteenth century, about fifty to sixty million migrants from Europe embarked upon the arduous and often dangerous journey across the ocean.[2] The most attractive destination of these intercontinental migrants was the United States of America, where thirty-two to forty million newcomers from Europe settled during this time. In the ten years before the First World War alone, approximately 800,000 to 1.2 million Europeans immigrated to the United States each year. The next most popular destination was Argentina, with 6.5 million immigrants, followed by Brazil, Australia, New Zealand and Canada.

Migrants from German-speaking countries were the most strongly represented among European immigrants to the United States, numbering 5.5 million in the long nineteenth century. At the beginning of the century, it was primarily Germans from southern and southwestern Germany who made their way overseas. Beginning in 1850, the emigration wave also enfolded the northwest, later including the northeast and the east. Immigrants came from a broad social spectrum, ranging over time from members of the peasant class to craftsmen, labourers and wealthy merchants. Emigrants were entire families and masses of individuals aged fifteen to forty. The primary reason for migrating was dissatisfaction with living conditions at their respective locations; causes could include agricultural crises, the lack of available work, a dissatisfactory inheritance or succession, and much more. At some times and in certain regions, political or religious reasons played a role. Ultimately, individual motivations for migration in the nineteenth century met with effective recruitment policies by various countries that had an urgent need for labour.

It was a favourable time for major migration waves. After the European wars reached a preliminary conclusion with the Congress of Vienna in 1815, political normality returned to Europe and made transit journeys possible. At the same time, a supply crisis stemming from the particularly cold winter of 1816/17 complicated the lives of many people. The abolition of emigration prohibitions in German countries facilitated migration movements. Research has explained the onset of mass migration overseas by means of the push-pull model: migration motives in the homeland (the "push factor") met with the temptations of the target countries (the "pull factor"). A third factor that we could call the "profit factor" also acted as a catalyst for unleashing a massive wave of overseas migration. Many shipping companies and port cities saw overseas migration as a new field of business that could generate enormous levels of income. A horde of captains, ship owners and shipping companies were determined to take advantage of the situation by contributing to the promotion of overseas migration.

Up to the beginning of the nineteenth century, the owners of ships used in transoceanic traffic earned most of their money by transporting raw materials from overseas to Europe. On the way back to pick up more cargo, ships often carried space-efficient manufactured products and handicrafts, or frequently just ballast.

Passengers boarding the Kaiser Wilhelm der Grosse in Bremerhaven, 1898

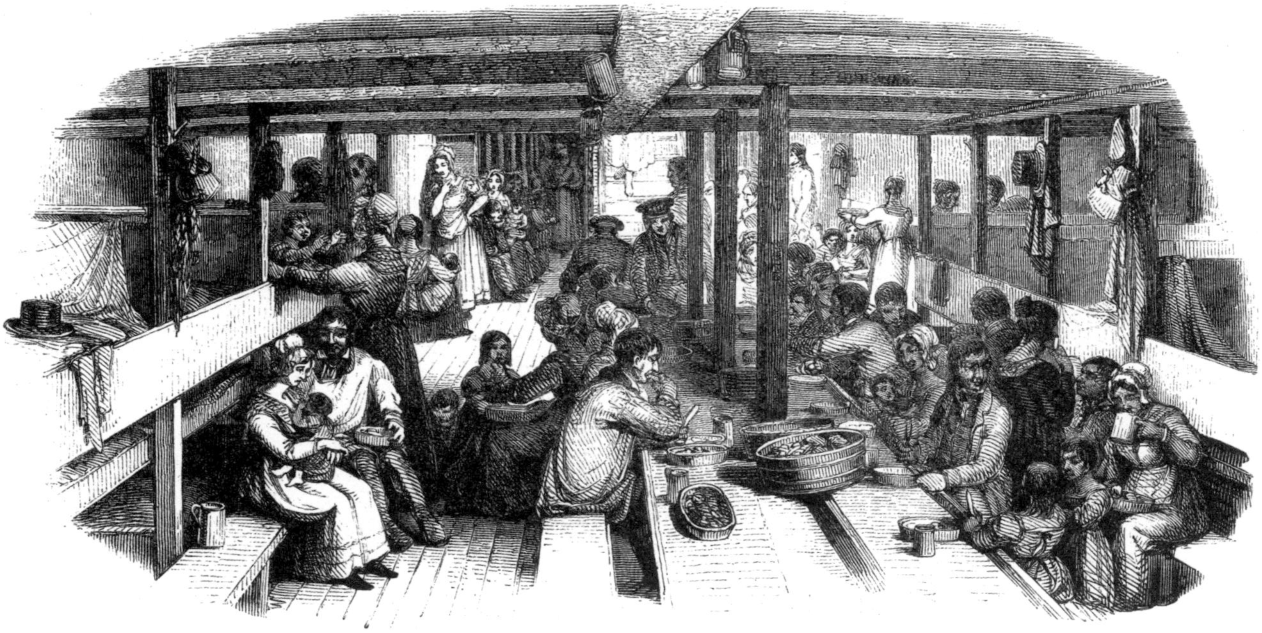

Steerage deck of an emigration ship, *Illustrirte Zeitung*, 1847

The transport of migrants from Europe to overseas destinations provided freight ships with an additional, lucrative cargo. By the mid-nineteenth century, the purchase price of a sailing vessel was already paid off after four to five overseas trips with migrants onboard. The construction of wooden sheds in the cargo spaces, the "steerage", enabled the transportation of up to 270 people on boats and full-rigged ships, which at mid-century were thirty to forty metres long. Depending on the route and the weather, sailing ships could cover the crossing from Europe to North America in forty to sixty days, under favourable conditions. Ship owners focused on profit, not the comfort of their passengers. The steerage was a space for sleeping and eating, as well as common activities. There were no tables or benches. Pressing, narrow spaces, poor provisions and unhygienic conditions often resulted in illness and even death.[3]

The first port cities to practise this business model were Liverpool and Le Havre. Liverpool was Britain's most important harbour and had been the point of departure for overseas journeys to the English colonies since the mid-seventeenth century. Although Liverpool was not centrally located in Europe, we estimate that about nine million immigrants left the western coast of England between 1830 and 1930. By the second half of the nineteenth century, Liverpool was the largest emigrant port in Europe. Le Havre, on the Atlantic coast of France, was already an important port of call for ships from the French colonies before the nineteenth century. Unlike Liverpool, Le Havre was favourably situated in geographic terms as a transit port. Migrants coming from southern Europe travelled over the Rhine River to Cologne, then hired a coach, or after 1850 took the train, to Le Havre. By the mid-nineteenth century, Le Havre had become the most important port of embarkation for migrants from German-speaking countries, eclipsing Rotterdam and Antwerp.

The waybills of the nineteenth century – which had to be submitted under the Steerage Act of 1819 in the U.S. immigration ports of New York, Boston, Baltimore, Philadelphia, New Orleans, Galveston and Charleston – list 135 European emigration ports.[4] In England and Scotland alone, there were twenty-five ports from which emigrant ships embarked. The largest port of embarkation by far was Liverpool, although the port had a bad reputation due to chronic overcrowding. The majority of the mass emigration from Ireland, triggered by the devastating potato blight of 1846/47, went through Liverpool.[5] In contrast, about three million Irish migrants – relatively few – departed from twenty-two Irish ports. Numerous Scandinavians, Russians and Poles travelled to Liverpool to embark for overseas travel. Many migrants from German countries also endured the laborious and difficult journey to Liverpool.

Liverpool's attractiveness resulted from its relatively cheap ticket prices and the large number of competing shipping lines, but the successful activity of emigration agents – who cast a broad net over all of Europe for ship owners, captains, travel agents, shipping clerks and shipping companies – played a major part in this development.[6] In the beginning, it was domestic innkeepers, grocers or teachers who worked as recruiters in the home countries. The agents negotiated transit contracts for a fee; these contracts governed the transport conditions and organisation of the journey and provided migrants with the information they needed. Despite innumerable frauds and scams, agencies formed the logistical foundation for the business of migration in Europe. Agent activity led to the organisation of these journeys becoming routine over time, which made it much easier for those considering emigration to decide to leave Europe and begin making their travel arrangements. Furthermore, many people in the home countries had received letters from those who had emigrated earlier, and these letters strengthened many potential emigrants' desire to

Passengers dancing on an emigration ship, 1887

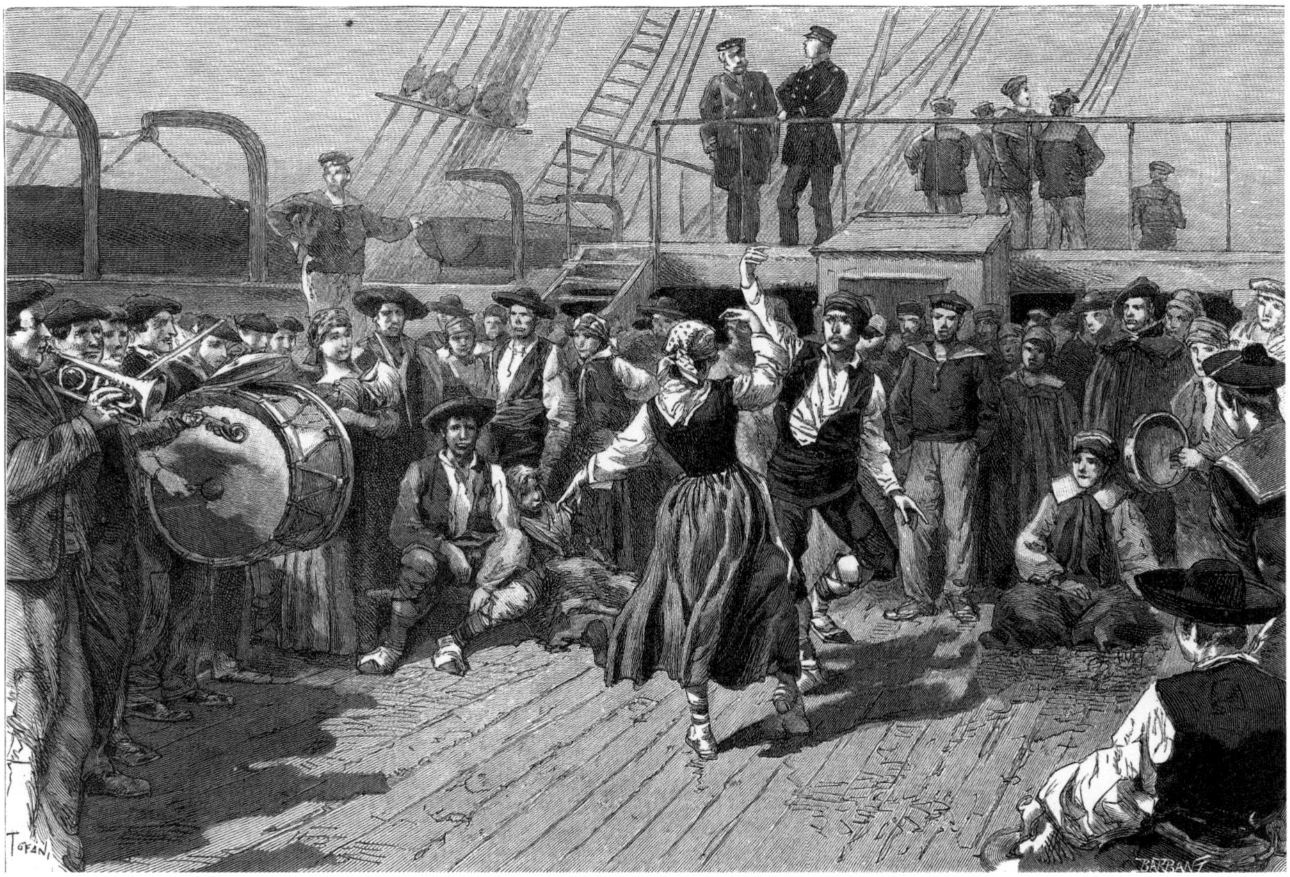

follow their lead. Various migration strategies were supported by diverse, full-fledged networks. The agency model was perfected and legally regulated over the course of the nineteenth century, which led to a reduction in the frequency of irregularities. Increasingly, full-time agencies with thousands of employees took over the business.

The shipping companies in northern Europe's most important emigration ports – Liverpool, London, Le Havre, Antwerp, Amsterdam, Rotterdam, Bremerhaven and Hamburg – also used national magazines and newspapers to advertise their services. Because they regularly purchased advertising space, these companies were also granted influence over news coverage. The Liverpool shipping companies were particularly active in this regard; they hoped by this means to push back against their port's bad reputation. For example, on 6 July 1850, *The Illustrated London News*, a weekly magazine with a high circulation in the United Kingdom since 1842, published a richly illustrated article of several pages that reported on the difficult, but otherwise exemplary, journey beginning at Liverpool. Both a chapter and a half-page woodcut bore the heading, "Dancing Between Decks". Migrants danced in the steerage to the music of a violinist and, according to the report, would continue to do so, "according to the reports of captains and others, during the whole voyage".[7] The shipping companies described emigration as an uncomplicated pleasure in the press.

Images of dancing emigrants in the steerage or on the upper deck were found throughout the entire European press over the course of the nineteenth century, including in the French magazine, *Le Tour du Monde. Nouveau Journal des Voyages*[8] as well as the Leipzig-based *Illustrirte Zeitung*, which appeared throughout Germany.[9] In October 1896, the magazine *Daheim. Ein deutsches Familienblatt mit Illustrationen* reported on an "improvised ball in the steerage".[10] The author's article and illustrator was Hans Bohrdt (1857–1945), who was a painter in the service of the shipping giants Hamburg-Amerikanischen Packetfahrt-Actien-Gesellschaft (Hapag) and the Bremer Norddeutschen Lloyd (NDL). These two shipping companies dominated the German business with migrants in the latter half of the nineteenth century. Although the German Emigrant Database lists thirteen German emigration ports, in the final analysis it was only Hamburg and Bremen/Bremerhaven that were financially successful over the long term.[11]

Bremen assumed a special role among Europe's port cities. No other city invested so extensively in the business with migrants.[12]At the beginning of the nineteenth century, Bremen saw a promising field of business in the increasing volume of overseas migration, mainly because Bremen had reached a low point in trade due to a lack of export goods. Silting in the Weser River had advanced so far that ships coming from the North Sea were only able to reach Bremen with difficulty because the city was situated about seventy kilometres up the Weser. This is why Bremen purchased a piece of land from the Kingdom of Hanover in 1827 at the mouth of the Weser to the North Sea, where they built a channel port that would allow ships to pass through during the entire year.

In order to secure competitive advantages, Bremen in 1832 passed the first law that governed the overseas passage of migrants. The law prescribed, among other things, minimum standards for space requirements in the steerage and minimum food provisions for emigration ships. The trade with migrants attracted numerous businesses, such as inns, hostels and merchants, to the "Bremer Haven". The location offered lucrative opportunities because migrants often had to wait for weeks in the ports before their ships set sail. In 1851, Bremerhaven drafted a municipal constitution and insisted on communal independence. Nevertheless, the port city remained dependent on Bremen's shipping policies, because a Bremen Senate decision determined that all of the merchants, businesses and shipping companies that earned income from the migration business had to have their offices in the city of Bremen. As a consequence, "Bremen" was entered as the port of departure on the passenger manifests, even though the ships set out from Bremerhaven.

Emigration through Bremerhaven attained a new dimension with the founding of NDL in 1857. The Bremen-based shipping company developed into one of the largest and most successful shipping companies in the world. NDL was in constant competition with Hapag, which was founded in Hamburg in 1847. Both shipping companies built increasingly larger and faster steamships. The close intermeshing of personnel between the leadership of the NDL and the Bremen Senate caused the ports in Bremerhaven to continually adapt and expand to meet the technical requirements of the shipping companies. In 1862, Bremerhaven was connected to the railway network. The Bremen Senate now ordered that migrants had to stay in Bremen until their ships left the port. Special trains brought emigrants to Bremerhaven just in time for departure. Passenger processing took place in a hall built especially for this purpose, located on the quay directly next to the railway tracks.

By the end of the 1870s, over ninety per cent of migrants chose to travel the transatlantic route by steamship. The new high-speed steamers of the 1880s crossed the Atlantic in just seven days and could hold 1,000 passengers in steerage. First- and second-class cabins were available for wealthier emigrants and business travellers. The accommodation and feeding of steerage passengers improved with the

9/13
Johann Heinrich Sander, view of the Old Port of Bremerhaven, 1841

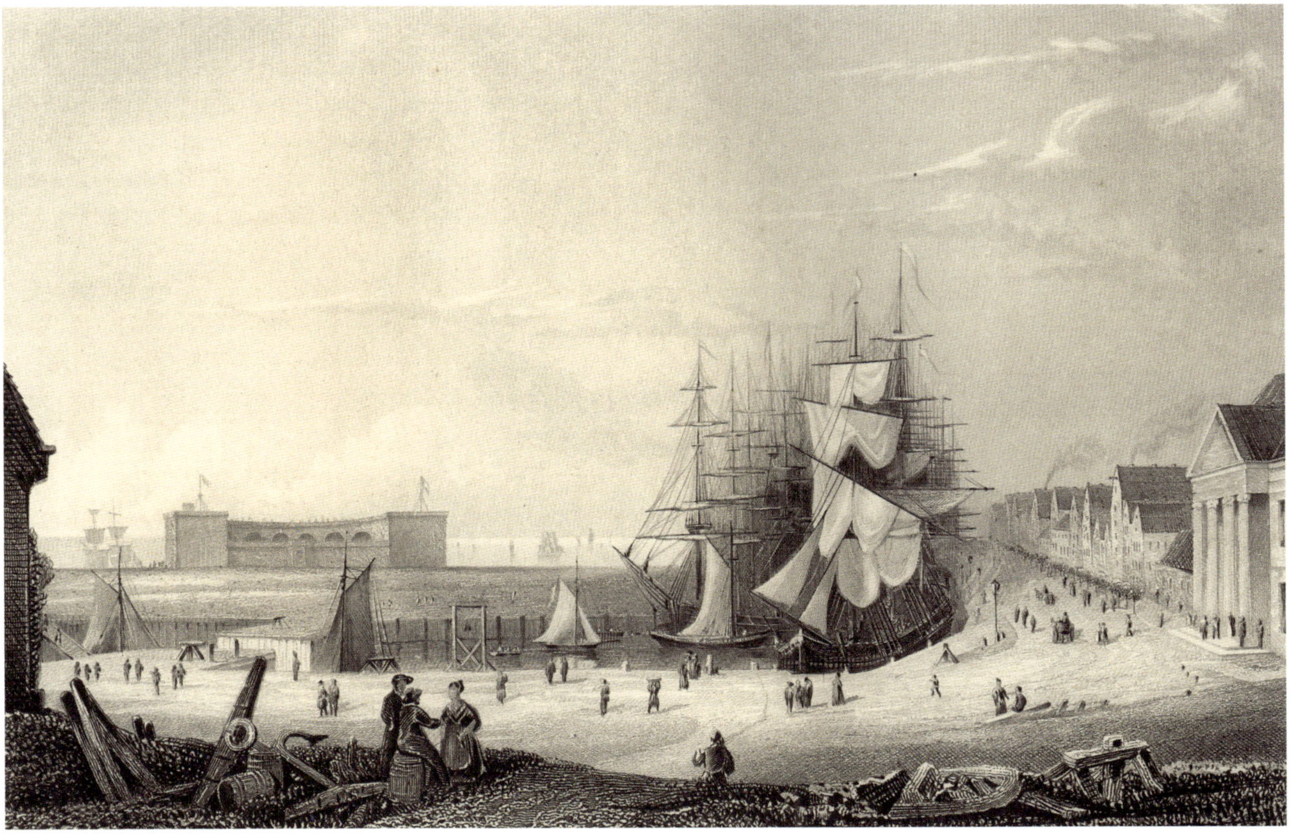

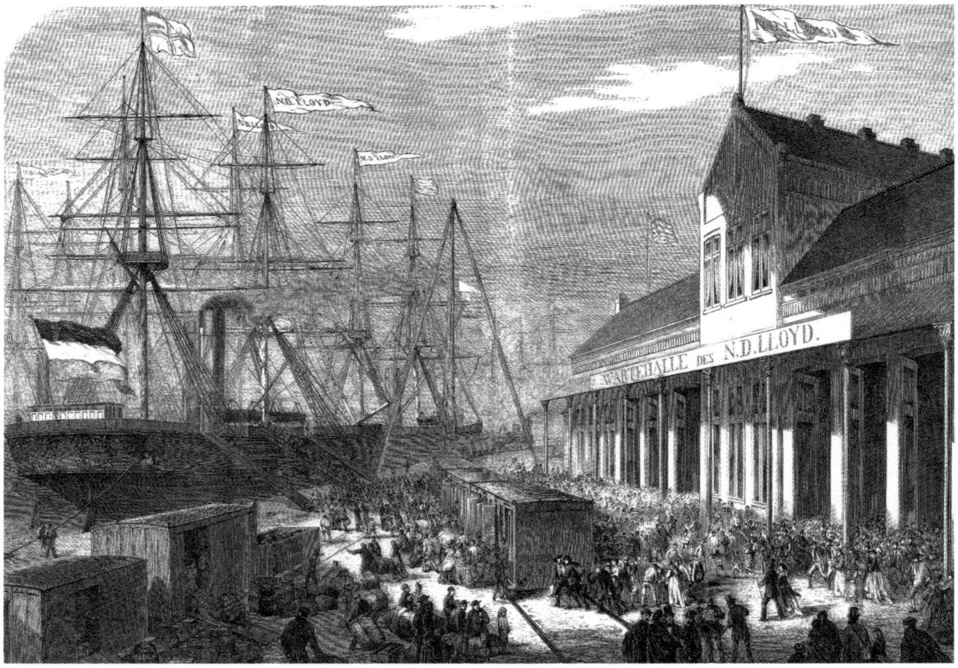

9/17
Carl Justus Fedeler, view of the Norddeutscher Lloyd waiting hall in Bremerhaven, 1871

steamships. Over ninety per cent of emigrants selected the USA as their destination beginning in the late 1870s. New York had established itself as the central immigration port. Registration facilities were Castle Garden as of 1855 and Ellis Island as of 1892, where a precisely regulated and strictly organized supervision of newcomers was assured.

Bremerhaven developed into one of Europe's largest emigration ports by the end of the nineteenth century. Overall, well over seven million emigrants departed from Bremerhaven. Since the 1880s, emigration from the German Reich had fallen due to domestic demand for labourers; this development was accompanied by a concomitant shift to areas in Eastern Europe as centres of emigration. A strong increase in population, epidemics, economic crises and political suppression were the most important causes for mass emigration from Eastern and South Eastern Europe, Russia and the Austro-Hungarian Empire in particular. Anti-Semitic pogroms in Russia also caused about 1.8 million Jews to immigrate to North America. As of 1894, Eastern European migrants had to go through registration, medical examinations and disinfection at eleven stations on the German border. Special trains brought them from the aggregation point at Ruhleben near Berlin to the ports of embarkation. NDL renewed its efforts to employ professional agents to motivate those interested in immigration to pass through Bremen and Bremerhaven. In 1907 alone, over 234,000 embarked from Bremerhaven.

At the turn of the century, Johann Friedrich Missler in Bremen directed the largest emigration agency in Europe.[13]Missler had established branch offices in the Central, Eastern and Southern European regions since 1881. Between 1885 and 1923, he brokered about 1.8 million emigrants to NDL. In 1907, Missler had massive halls built in Bremen-Findorff in which up to 3,400 emigrants could be housed. By doing this, Bremen was following Hamburg's lead after a cholera epidemic in 1892 in that city's "emigrant barracks" at the America quay, where steerage passengers had to stay before their departure. In 1901, there was an expansion of this sealed-off area on

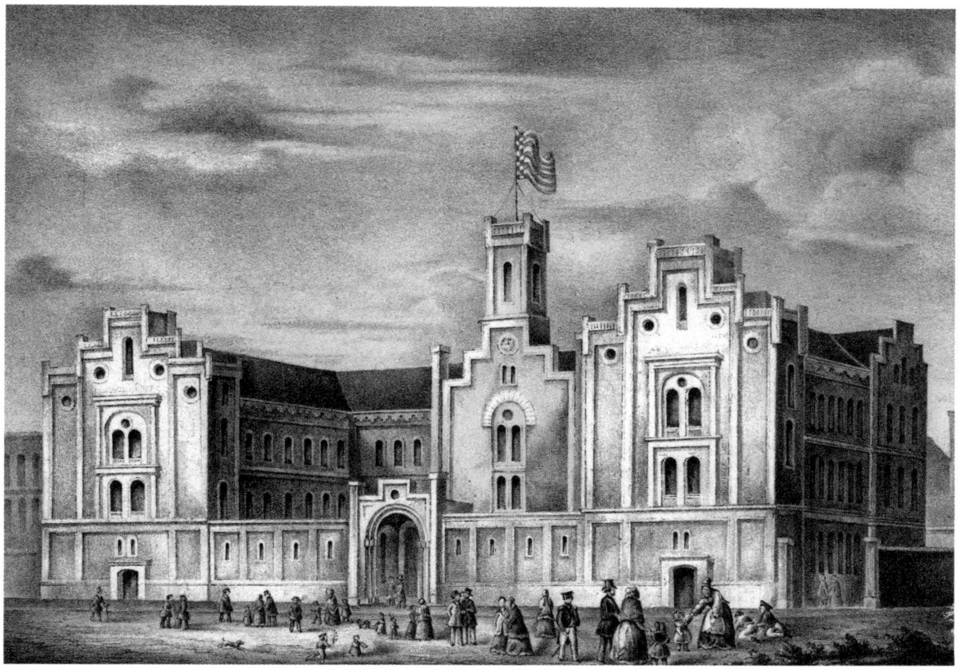

View of the emigrant hostel opened in Bremerhaven in 1850, 1853

the island of Veddel in the Elbe River, which became the direct destination of emigrant trains so that passengers could be kept at a distance from the city. Along with Bremen and Bremerhaven, Hamburg profited mightily from mass migration from Eastern Europe. With over five million emigrants, Hamburg established itself as the second-largest port of emigration after Bremerhaven.

The faster and more affordable the journeys became, the greater the number of those who returned to Europe. Before 1914, up to one third of all European immigrants to the USA returned, for various reasons, to their countries of origin. The First World War (1914–1918) put an abrupt end to mass overseas migration, as almost all of the European nations were engaged in military conflicts. After the end of the war, migration numbers climbed once again, as a large number of emigrants had piled up; they had decided before the war to leave, and now they wanted to see their decision through. Many displaced persons, along with those who had been uprooted from their homeland, saw their future in North America after the major territorial losses that followed the First World War. Nationalist reservations in the USA, however, led to a qualitatively different immigration policy in the 1920s. The immigration law of 1921 established a quota system for annual maximums of specific nationalities. The Great Depression also led to the USA becoming less attractive as an immigration destination. The beginning of the "Third Reich" caused an increase in overseas migration. The Nazi regime passed "racial laws" and persecuted their political opponents, leading about half a million people to flee from German-speaking lands beginning in 1933, among them about 278,500 people who professed the Jewish faith or who had Jewish ancestry.[14] The most important immigration destination for them was initially Palestine. Only in 1937 did the USA start to become the preferred destination for Jewish refugees. On 23 October 1941, the Nazi regime imposed an emigration prohibition that put an effective stop to people leaving the country.

After the Second World War (1939–1945), millions of people were on the move. The contemporary, vague catch-all term *displaced persons* encompassed former forced labourers, prisoners of war, Eastern Europeans and former prisoners of the concentration camps who were living in the three Western zones of occupation in Germany.[15] As of 1947, the International Refugee Organization – and as of 1952, the Intergovernmental Committee for European Migration – began organizing emigration programmes via Bremerhaven for these "persons deprived of a homeland". The recipient states were the USA, Canada, Australia, a few South American countries and South Africa. After emigration restrictions were loosened in 1948, West Germans were also able once again to emigrate. Between 1947 and 1958, a total of about 1.3 million people emigrated overseas from Bremerhaven.

In the 1960s, passenger ships provided regular service from Bremerhaven to North America and Australia. NDL advertised cut-price "emigration tickets" to New York.[16]As airline traffic increased, however, less and less people left Europe via overseas routes. The airplane reduced travel times to the USA to one day. Returning to one's homeland had now become easier, and migration became less final. Furthermore, the economic recovery in West Germany after the war caused emigration to become less attractive to West Germans, since full employment reigned and labour was in short supply. The 1970s saw the end of the age of intercontinental liner shipping, the most important economic foundation of which had been, for almost 150 years, European mass migration over the oceans.

1 See Dirk Hoerder, *Geschichte der deutschen Migration. Vom Mittelalter bis heute* (Munich, 2010), 20.

2 See Brian Lambkin, "Hallelujah, wir fahren nach Amerika! Die europäischen Ausgangskulturen in West-, Mittel- und Nordeuropa", in *Aufbruch in die Fremde. Migration gestern und heute*, ed. Diethelm Knauf and Barry Moreno (Bremen, 2009), 28; Jochen Oltmer, *Globale Migration. Geschichte und Gegenwart* (Bonn, 2016), 11.

3 See Markus Günther, *Auf dem Weg in die Neue Welt. Die Atlantiküberquerung im Zeitalter der Massenauswanderung 1818–1914* (Augsburg, 2005), 145ff.

4 See Anja Benscheidt and Alfred Kube, *Die Deutsche Auswanderer-Datenbank. Passagierlisten als Forschungsquelle* (Bremerhaven, 2006), 24ff.

5 See Gordon Read, "Transithafen Liverpool. Die europäische Auswanderung über England nach New York, 1870–1913", in *Hoffnung Amerika. Europäische Auswanderung in die Neue Welt*, ed. Karin Schulz (Bremerhaven, 1994), 151ff.

6 See Agnes Bretting, "Von der Alten in die Neue Welt", in *Aufbruch in die Fremde. Europäische Auswanderung nach Übersee*, ed. Dirk Hoerder and Diethelm Knauf (Bremen, 1992), 91ff.

7 *The Illustrated London News*, 6 July 1850, 21. Archive of the Historical Museum of Bremerhaven.

8 See *Le Tour du Monde. Nouveau Journal des Voyages*, 1887, 135. Archive of the Historical Museum of Bremerhaven.

9 See *Illustrirte Zeitung*, no. 1637, 14 November 1874, 385. Archive of the Historical Museum of Bremerhaven.

10 *Daheim. Ein deutsches Familienblatt mit Illustrationen*, no. 2, October 1896, 26. Archive of the Historical Museum of Bremerhaven.

11 See Benscheidt/Kube 2006, Deutsche Auswanderer-Datenbank, 50ff.

12 See Anja Benscheidt and Alfred Kube, *Brücke nach Übersee. Auswanderung über Bremerhaven 1830–1974* (Bremerhaven, 2006), 12ff.

13 See Dirk Hoerder, "The Traffic of Emigration via Bremen/Bremerhaven. Merchants' Interest, Protective Legislation, and Migrants' Experiences", *Journal of American Ethnic History* 13, no. 1 (1993): 85ff.

14 See Michael Grüttner, *Brandstifter und Biedermänner. Deutschland 1933–1939* (Bonn, 2015), 157.

15 See Anja Bensscheidt and Alfred Kube, *Die Nachkriegszeit auf Bremerhavener Pressefotos* (Bremerhaven, 2015), 100ff.

16 See Benscheidt and Kube, *Brücke nach Übersee*, 110.

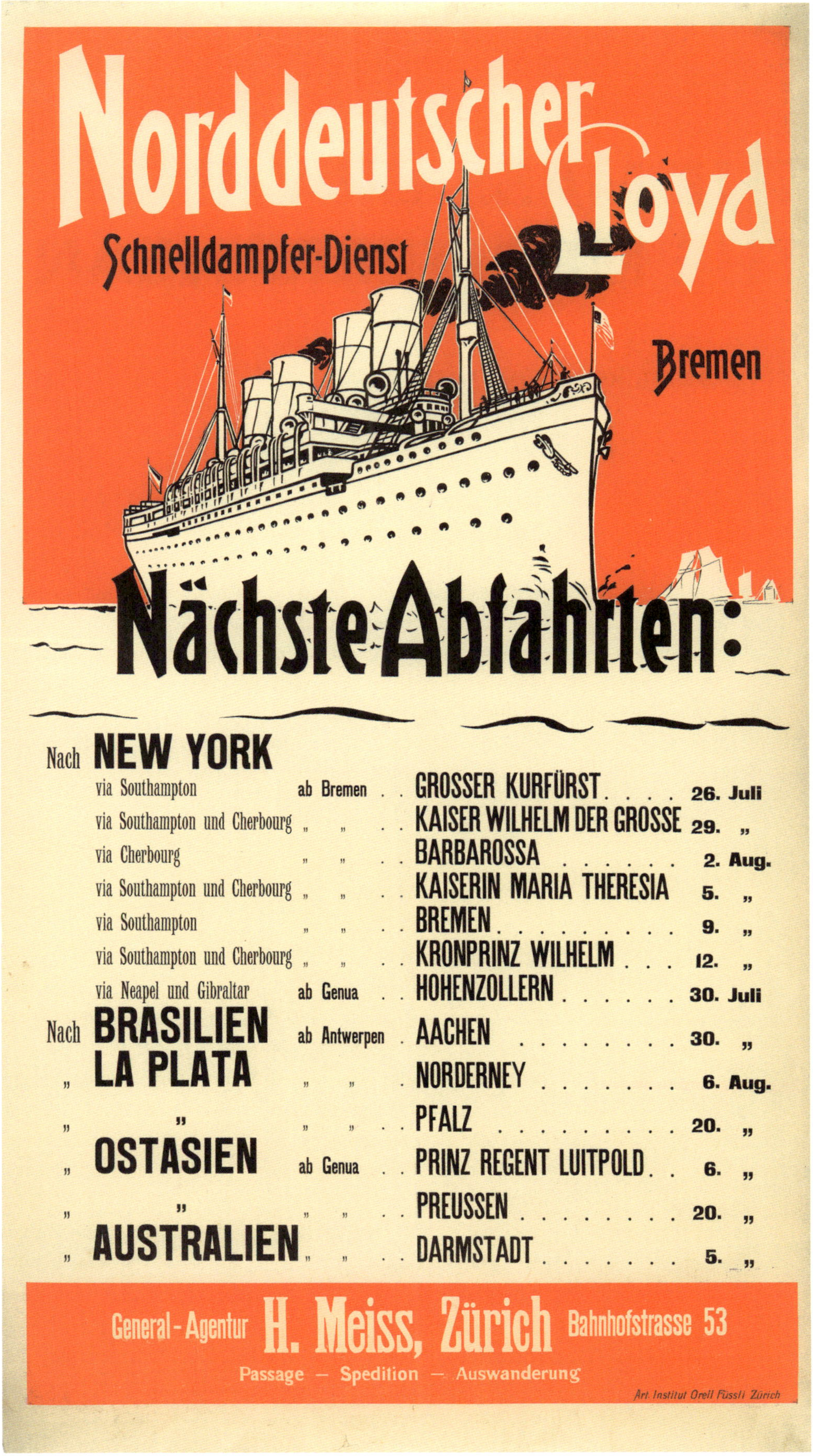

9/19
Advertising poster,
“Norddeutscher Lloyd
express steamer Bremen”,
1907

Cord Pagenstecher

THE MASS GRAVE OF THE MEDITERRANEAN

Immigration, Repulsion, Victims

In the history of European civilisation, the Mediterranean has proven over the centuries to be a space of departure and arrival, hope and danger. Immigration over the Mediterranean is certainly one of today's most pressing topics; media reports have been showing images of capsizing refugee boats for years. This essay attempts to locate trans-Mediterranean immigration, as well as the struggle against it and its victims, in a broader historical context. This essay outlines a few frameworks, dimensions and patterns of perception. The term "migrants", which includes both men and women, is used in the broadest sense, encompassing those looking for work, those fleeing political and religious persecution (under the Geneva Refugee Convention) and those seeking asylum (under national asylum laws).

Hope and threat

Beginning with the journey of the pilgrims to the New World, millions of Europeans left their continent behind, full of hope, for the overseas passage to embrace what the American Declaration of Independence called their inalienable rights: Life, freedom and the pursuit of happiness. After the Second World War, Western Europe awakened similar hopes; the former colonial powers became the destination of emigrant ships from their former overseas territories. A few people also used the sea to escape the Iron Curtain. GDR citizens, for example, fled with boats over the Baltic Sea, and Albanians swam to the Greek island of Corfu, to live in the freer and more prosperous West.

This hope lives on today, whether in Moroccan Tangier, in the prisons of Libya, the ruins of Aleppo, or the mountains of Eritrea. In his novel *Leaving Tangier*, Tahar ben Jelloun (born in 1944) describes this widely held dream of Europe, conceived in the cafés of Tangier, with a view over the Strait of Gibraltar, just fourteen kilometres distant. Many know about the dangers of the passage; they themselves have already lost relatives and friends to the ocean. And yet, this dream leads migrants over the sea, with their hope of leaving behind war and persecution, of escaping poverty and oppression, of building a life with dignity and a future for their families.

On the other shore, however, migrants are described as a threat, as a maritime catastrophe (a stream, wave, flood tide) or as a military danger (assault, invasion). Europe is imagined as a fortress, critically in such publications as Gabriele del Grande's blog, *Fortress Europe*, or affirmatively in increasing numbers of far right-wing posters. Newspaper caricatures began playing with this image in the early 1990s; in 2015, Austria's Minister of the Interior, Johanna Mikl-Leitner (ÖVP) proclaimed, "We must build a fortress Europe".

Death in the sea

The Mediterranean lies between Africa's dreams and Europe's fears; it is the cradle of Europe, yet it is becoming a mass grave, growing larger each year. In the last twenty-five years, over 25,000 people have died at Europe's maritime borders; two-thirds of the corpses still lie at the bottom of the sea.

The initiative *United Against Racism* has been documenting the victims of Europe's isolationist policy since 1993.[1] Of the 33,305 dead registered up to June 2017, about 26,595 drowned, most of them in the Mediterranean. On the way to Italy, more than 15,000 have died; to Spain, over 5,000; to Greece, more than 3,000. Other sources have arrived at similar figures, including the Italian expert Gabriele del Grande, the journalists from *The Migrants' Files*, the UN High Commissioner for Refugees (UNHCR) and the migration organisation IOM.[2]

Many shipwrecks have gone almost unnoticed; on Christmas night 1996, for example, 283 migrants drowned before the Sicilian municipality of Portopalo. Survi-

Narciso Contreras / SOS MEDITERRANEE, body bags on the rescue ship AQUARIUS – the bodies were recovered from an inflatable dinghy east of Tripoli, 1 July 2017

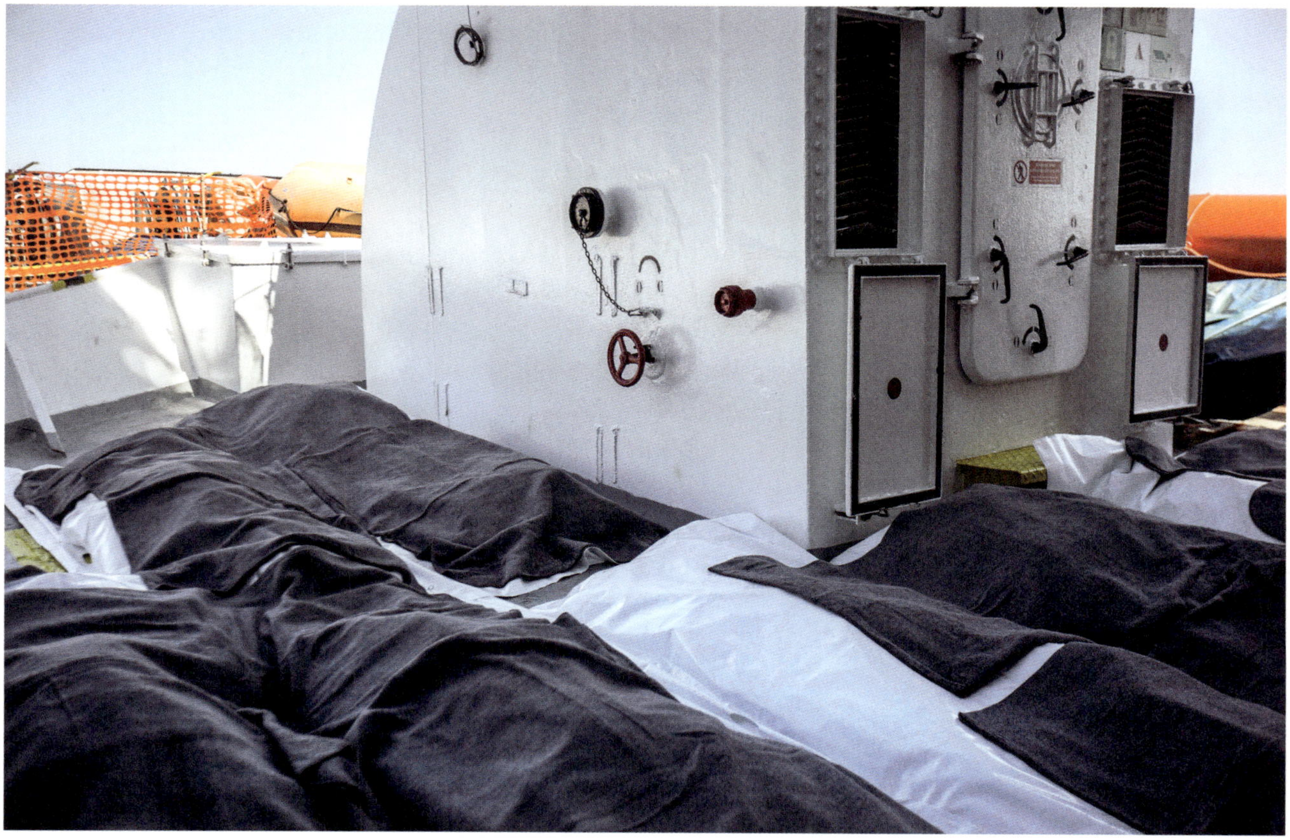

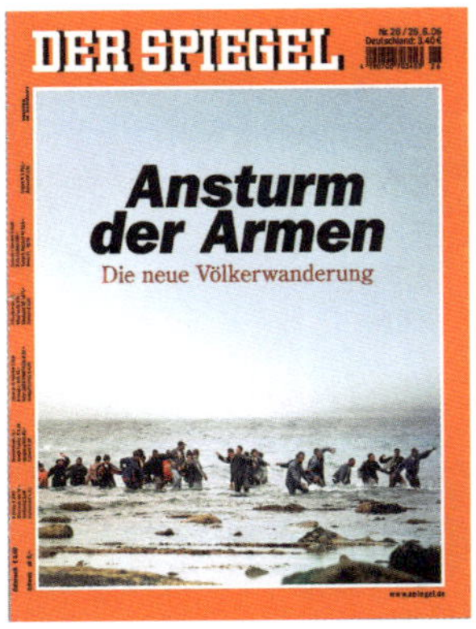

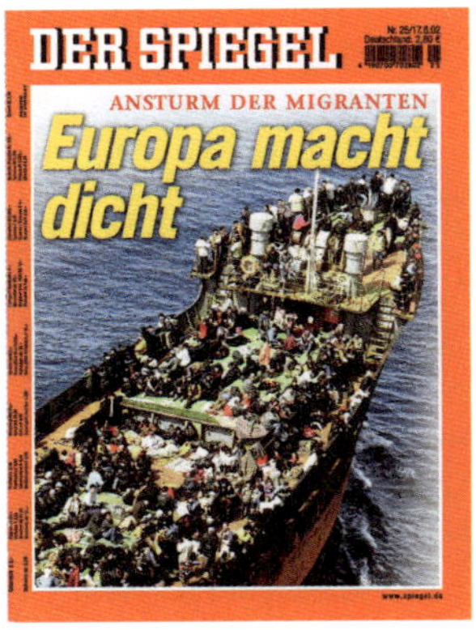

Cover page, "Ansturm der Armen" (Onslaught of the poor), *Der Spiegel*, no. 26, 2006

Cover page, "Europa macht dicht" (Europe seals itself off), *Der Spiegel*, no. 25, 2002

vors' reports were not considered credible; only five years later did a journalist investigate the story of the "ghosts of Portopalo".[3] Other catastrophes only result in brief notices in local newspapers.

Only the tragedy of Lampedusa brought the victims into the foreground of the immigration debate. On 3 October 2013, a Libyan cutter sank just a few miles from the island of Lampedusa, with 545 migrants on board. Of these, 155 people were rescued and 366 corpses were recovered. Many leading European politicians travelled to Lampedusa and voiced their concerns. The Italian navy began a campaign called "Mare Nostrum", which resulted in the rescue of over 100,000 people from the seas as well as the arrest of 728 smugglers.[4] Due to a lack of support from the European Union, however, "Mare Nostrum" was shut down after one year; the number of deaths began to increase again.

The tragedy of Lampedusa was the largest ship disaster in the Mediterranean, but it was not to be the last. Four more boats sank, each resulting in the deaths of over 400 people, on 10 September 2014, 12 April 2015, 19 April 2015 and 18 April 2016. The media now reported frequently on such events, and due to the omnipresence of smartphones, videos of these tragedies were often transmitted directly into the living rooms of Europe. Yet the occasional sympathy evinced by Europeans faded away quickly. Perhaps the images were all too monotonous in their uniformity, almost always showing groups of dark-skinned people, filmed from above; it is rare to see portrayals of individuals.

One image, however, generated major attention: on 2 September 2015, thirteen Syrians drowned near Bodrum, among them the three-year-old Aylan Kurdi. The photograph of his dead body lying on the beach went round the world. This image caused dismay and outrage, but did not result in any changes in policy. The following year, 2016, saw the highest number of deaths on Europe's seas, with over 5,000 fatalities. After the closure of the Balkan Route, many refugees were forced to attempt the long and dangerous passage from Libya to Italy.

The full boat: A prehistory

Let us take a brief look back in history. Both the term "Fortress Europe" and the metaphor, "the boat is full", arose during the time of the Holocaust. The Swiss Minister of Justice Eduard von Steiger used this argument to justify the repulsion of Jewish refugees in 1942, which all but assured their murder in Nazi camps. Six decades later, about 4,000 survivors would receive compensation payment from a fund financed by Swiss banks.

The USA and other countries denied entry visas to refugees from Nazi Germany, including the family of Anne Frank. The refugee ship St. Louis sailed in vain to the coasts of Cuba and Florida and was then sent back to Europe. The FBI investigated those who helped refugees, such as Varian Fry (1907–1967), who brought those persecuted by the Nazis onto ships in Marseille as stowaways.

It was for this reason that the right to asylum as an individually actionable basic right was included in the Basic Law of the Federal Republic of Germany in 1949. The practical impact of this law, however, remained limited during the Cold War; in the three decades since 1979, the Federal Republic has only granted asylum to 57,000 people. At the time, however, images of overcrowded refugee boats went

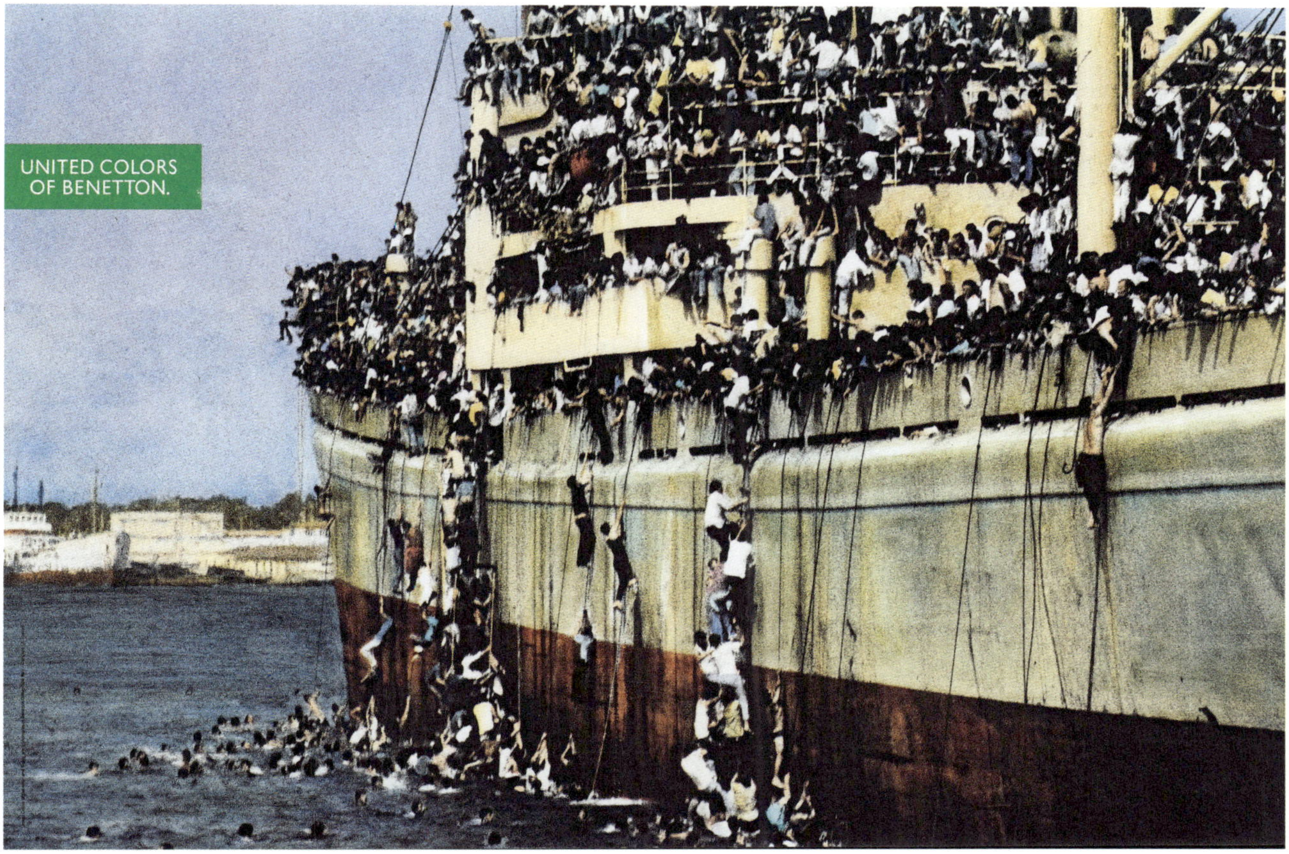

Oliviero Toscani, advertisement for United Colors of Benetton, 1991

around the world. Hundreds of thousands of Vietnamese fled the Communist regime and poverty in war-torn Vietnam. These powerful images mobilised a willingness to help in West German society. The journalist Rupert Neudeck (1939–2016) equipped the hospital ship Cap Anamur, and the Christian Democratic opposition pressed for rapid delivery of aid to those persecuted by Communism.[5] West Germany accepted about 30,000 of these Vietnamese "boat people".

Shortly thereafter, however, the mood turned; as soon as 28 May 1980, the *Frankfurter Allgemeine Zeitung* called for "dams against the flood of asylum-seekers", thereby setting the tone for many election campaigns in the 1980s. In order to establish a terminology other than the term "refugees", Christian Democratic politicians now spoke of *Asylanten*, or "asylum-seekers", a German term which called to mind associations with the German word *Simulanten*, or "malingerers".

In 1991, another photograph of an overcrowded refugee ship made its way through the media; on 8 August, a freighter with over 10,000 Albanians on board came into the Italian port of Bari.[6] The images of clusters of people on board the ship rapidly became symbols of the politics surrounding asylum, in all of the media and even as Benetton advertising. On 9 September 1991, *Spiegel* magazine illustrated its title story, "Refugees – emigrants – asylum-seekers. Invasion of the poor" with an image of an overflowing ark called Germany. The metaphor of the full boat, which had up to that point only been acceptable in private society, now became the subject of intellectual discourse. It fit in the set of images presenting "a stream of immigrants" and a "flood of asylum-seekers". And it worked: the CDU/CSU, SPD and FDP restricted the asylum law in 1993 after xenophobic election campaigns and violent clashes inspired by such rhetoric. Whoever comes from a so-called secure third country has no fundamental claim to asylum.

Schengen and Dublin: Legal frameworks

The sealing off of Europe, or to be more precise of the politically cooperating core states, only first began after the opening of their borders in Eastern Europe. West Germany, for example, had already urged the GDR in 1985 to cease issuing transit visas for Tamil refugees, who up to that point had had no problems travelling to West Berlin through Schönefeld airport.[7]

The first agreement on a European system of borders was first signed in 1985 as well. In the Luxembourgish wine village of Schengen, five Western European states agreed to a gradual dismantling of the border controls between these countries; the "Schengen II" implementation agreement of 1990 governed the details. The abolition of passport controls at internal EU borders constitutes, along with the Euro, perhaps the most significant tangible aspect of European unification. This intra-European freedom of travel, however, is associated with strict controls at Europe's external borders. In May 1991, Spain introduced visa requirements for citizens of the Maghreb states. Controls at the internal borders for Poland were only removed in 2007 after the other governments had been assured that the external borders were secure.

The EU member states agreed in Dublin in 1990 to basic rules for joint asylum policy. The core element here was the third country rule, pushed primarily by Germany, according to which the asylum application processes should be completed in the first "secure third country" that a refugee entered in the course of their flight. The "Dublin II" (2003) and "Dublin III" (2013) EU directives specified procedural rules for this process. This effectively pushed the refugee problem to the edge of Europe, where hundreds, and later thousands, died each year.

A Berlin Wall on the beach?

The expansion of the European border regime initially included technological upgrades to borders, training of border police and the establishment of Europe-wide databases. After joining the Schengen states in 1992, Spain intensified its monitoring of the Strait of Gibraltar by using night-vision equipment and machine guns. However, as one official from the Guardia Civil told the *Spiegel*, "We cannot build the Berlin Wall here on the beach".[8] Nevertheless, in 1993 Spain built its first border fences around its exclaves of Ceuta and Melila on the Moroccan coast. The fence was expanded in subsequent years to a height of six metres and equipped with barbed wire, motion detectors and cameras. Greece fortified the Evros River, on its border with Turkey, in similar ways. Entry by air also fell under strict regulations: since 2001, airlines that transport a person without a valid visa into the Schengen Area have to pay all of the costs for their accommodation and deportation.

The surveillance of the Mediterranean as an external European border, however, became increasingly important. The Strait of Gibraltar was so carefully mon-

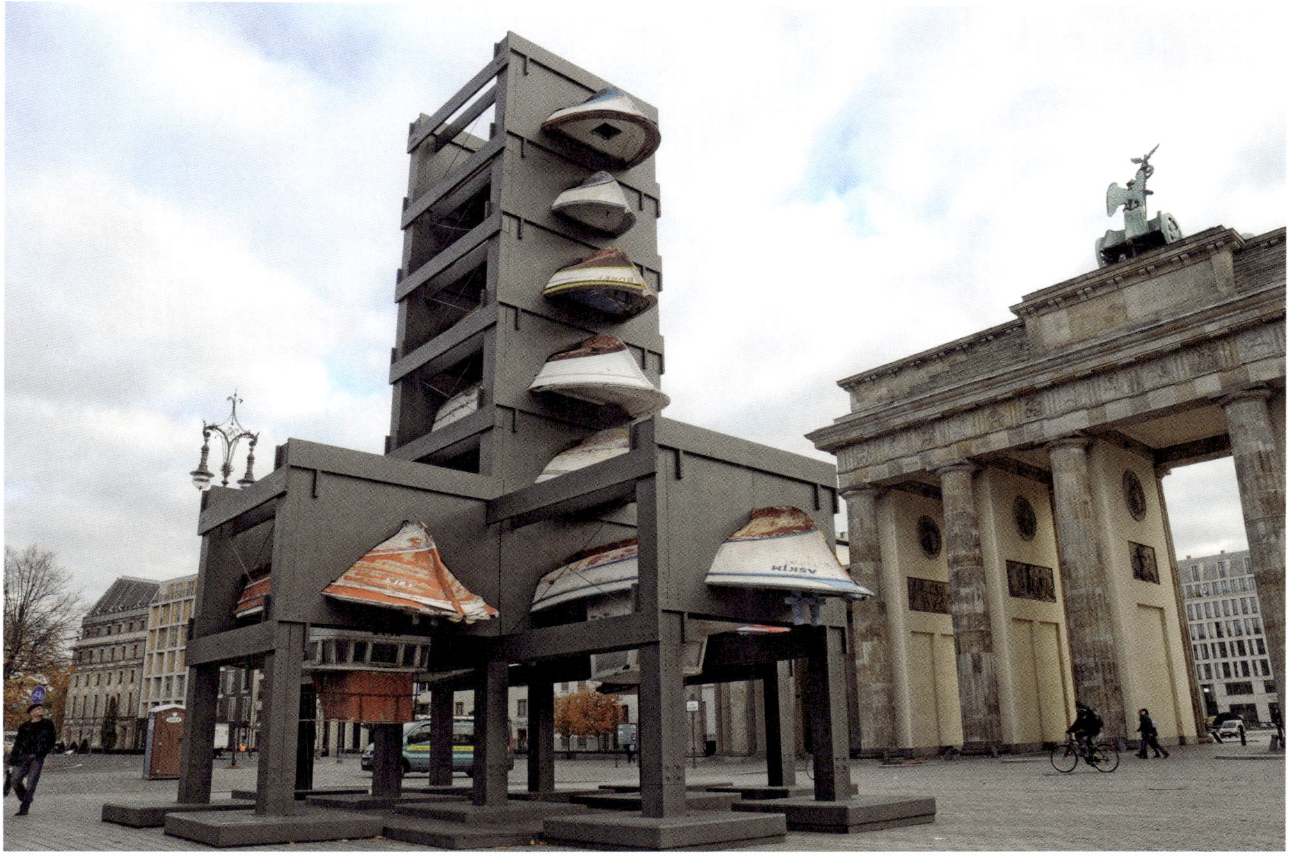

Kalliopi Lemos, *At Crossroads* (installation with refugee boats at the Brandenburg Gate in Berlin), 2009

itored that refugee boats had to take longer, more dangerous routes over the Atlantic to the Canary Islands or through the central Mediterranean to Italy. As a consequence, the numbers of the dead – and the profits of the smugglers – rose steeply.

At first, however, this all took place in the shadows of media attention. It was the name of the Cap Anamur, inextricably associated with the events of 1979 in Vietnam, that would again draw public attention to the refugee problem, although in a different context; this time, another ship named Cap Anamur that belonged to the Cap Anamur organisation was at the centre of the action in the Mediterranean. In 2004, Italy refused to grant permission for the ship to dock, even though the boat was carrying thirty-seven survivors rescued at sea. When the Cap Anamur nevertheless docked in a Sicilian port due to the medical emergencies on board, the government impounded the ship, deported the migrants and accused the crew of aiding and abetting illegal immigration. The trial ended however in 2009 in acquittal; although Silvio Berlusconi's government wanted to use the case to set an example, they only managed to do so in part.[9]

However, the accusation of criminal immigrant smuggling caught on in Europe. This legal intimidation of voluntary aid workers is broadly distributed; in the 1990s, taxi drivers were also condemned as immigrant smugglers.[10]In debates about private sea rescue campaigns in 2017, these accusations surfaced again; however, initiatives such as "SOS Méditerranée" found broad support in European civil society.

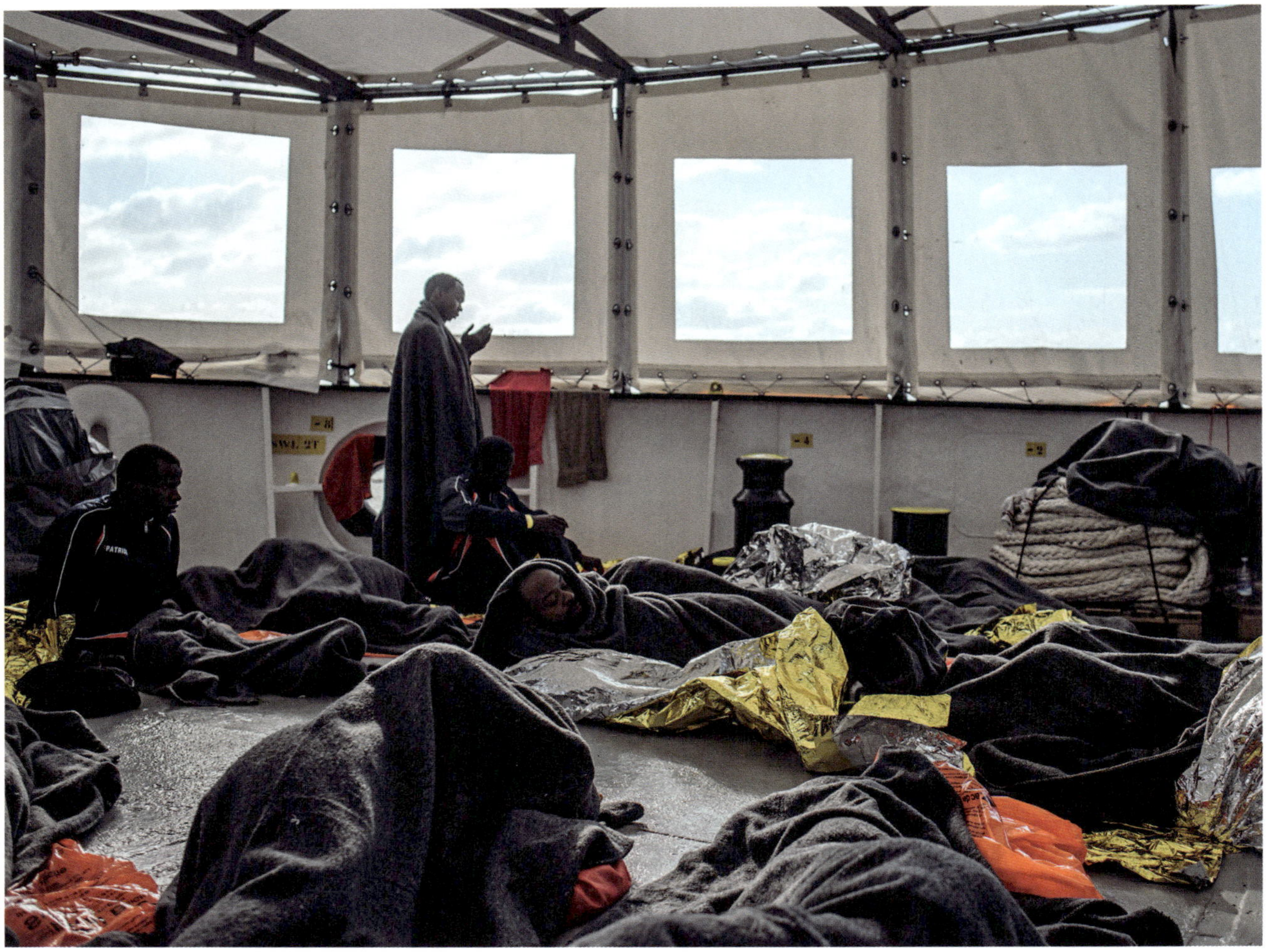

Kevin McElvaney / SOS MEDITERRANEE, people who had been picked up the night before are recovering on the rescue ship AQUARIUS, 23 December 2016

Frontex: The sea as a wall

Since 2005, the European border protection agency Frontex has coordinated the coast guards and border police of member states and conducted risk analyses and deportation flights. In late 2013, the cutting-edge satellite and drone system EUROSUR went into operation. In the Frontex centre in a Warsaw office tower, monitors show satellite images of the Mediterranean; green dots stand for boats that have been picked up. Graphic designers for the Frontex website generate the *Migratory Routes Map*, which is updated each month and presents these data points as arrows presented as threats to Europe.[11]

Frontex has participated again and again in illegal push-back operations. For example, a German police helicopter reported a boat with seventy-five migrants on board south of Lampedusa to the Italian coast guard on 18 June 2009. The coast guard then escorted the ship into international waters and handed over the ship to a Libyan patrol vessel without examining it.[12] In a similar case, the European Court for Human Rights decided in February 2012 that the Italian push-backs violated the Geneva Refugee Convention's regulations against repulsion and awarded the plaintiffs affected by this illegal collective expulsion 15,000 Euros each.[13] Nevertheless, in 2013, several refugee boats were pushed back into Turkey by the Greek coast guard, with Frontex involvement.[14]

Gaddafi and Erdoğan: The outsourcing of border controls

Efforts to repel refugees have increasingly been outsourced to countries on the other side of the ocean. In a series of treaties, the countries of North Africa, most of which are under authoritarian rule, agreed to strengthen their border controls, establish reception camps for black African migrants and accept refugees deported from Europe. The migrants sent back to Morocco or Mauritius were then confined by the local authorities in camps in the Sahara, or simply set loose in the desert.[15]

Europe has made cooperative agreements in this regard with Libya. As early as 2004, Germany's Minister of the Interior, Otto Schily (SPD), pleaded for "reception facilities" in Libya. After the treaty of friendship between Italy's Prime Minister Berlusconi and Libya's dictator Gaddafi in 2008, Italy sent several refugee boats, without any evaluation of asylum claims, back to Libya. Although arbitrary imprisonment, torture and other human rights violations were documented there, the EU Commission decided in October 2010 to make a similar agreement with Libya, a land rich in oil that has never become a signatory to the Geneva Refugee Convention.[16] The agreement was not implemented because of the civil war that erupted in Libya just four months later.

The EU treaty with Turkey under Recep Tayyip Erdoğan followed the same pattern in March 2016, although the country had never signed the convention regarding European refugees.[17] In Libya, however, where the country had fallen into chaos, the EU had to find new contacts for the outsourcing of migration repulsion. Since the summer of 2017, local militias that control smuggling of weapons, drugs and human beings, have received equipment, boats and salaries from Italy whenever they prevented migrant boats from setting out.[18]

Conclusion

Again and again, EU commissions, ministerial councils and parliaments have announced that they will combat the causes that motivate refugees to flee, as well as create "secure and legal paths" for entry in order to "undermine the business model of refugee smugglers".[19] Yet specific measures remain to be seen. The Advocate General of the European Court for Human Rights, in contrast, indicated a clear path in his plea of February 2017. On the basis of the Charter of Basic Rights, he claimed that the EU states are obligated to guarantee demonstrably persecuted asylum-seekers "a legal path of access to international protection under the supervision of member state agencies". According to his argument, the agencies must issue humanitarian visas for entry by airplane and facilitate an orderly asylum process in the target country.[20] The Court for Human Rights, however, has not followed this plea. In order to apply for an evaluation of an asylum claim, many refugees must continue to undertake the dangerous journey over the ocean.

European repulsion of migration is effective. According to information from the UN High Commissioner for Refugees, only about three per cent of an estimated sixty-five million refugees worldwide reach Europe. In 2016, 362,753 people (which constitute about 0.07 per cent of the total 512 million EU citizens) came over the Mediterranean; the year 2015 was an exception, with about 0.2 per cent. Neverthe-

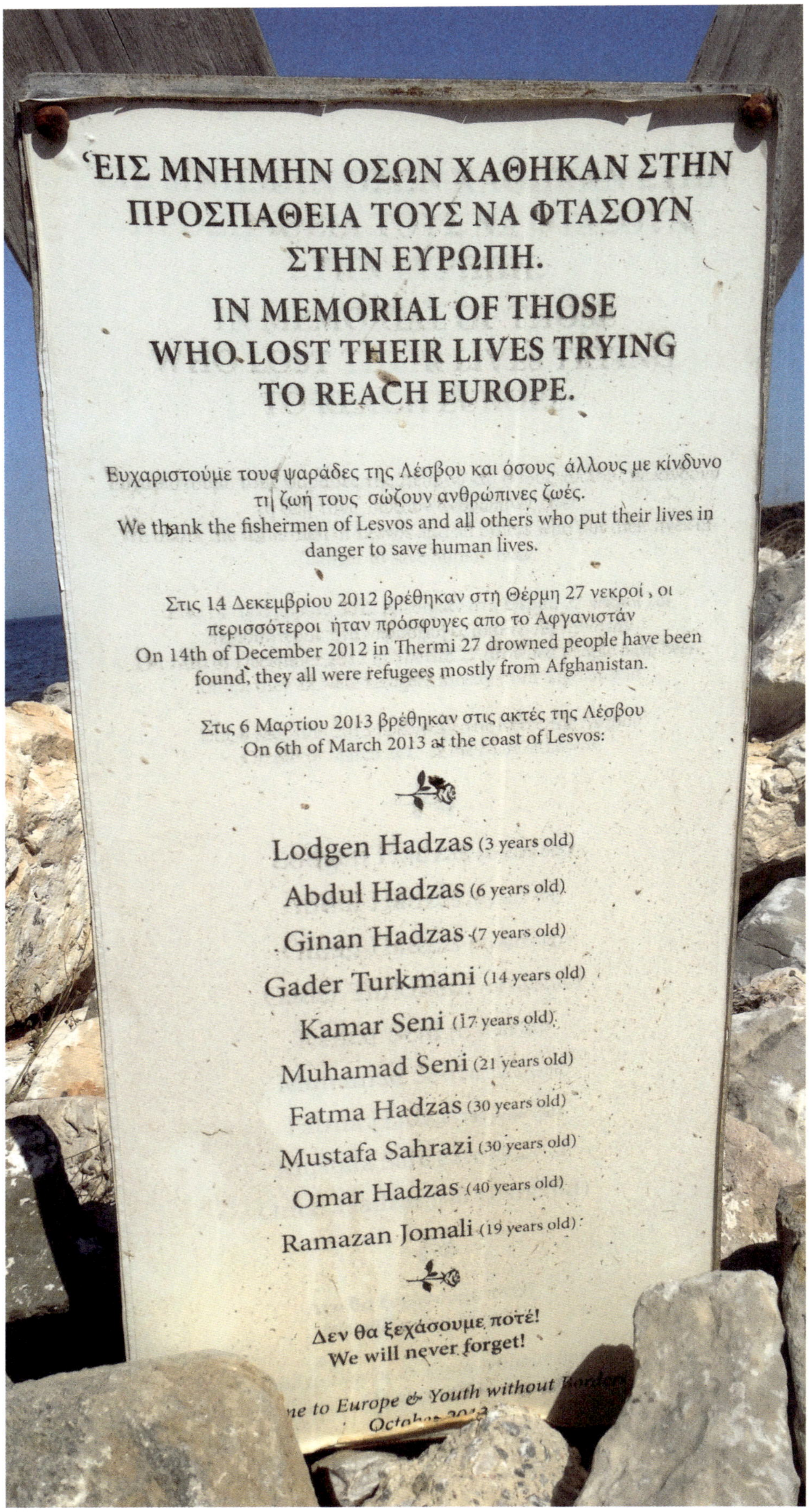

Memorial on the Greek island of Lesbos, dedicated to refugees who drowned on 14 December 2012

less, European policy seems to be overwhelmed. Racist parties have won larger shares of the vote for years now, yet not as much in Spain, which is an immigration country, as in states that have almost no immigration, such as Poland or Hungary. All the same, many Europeans approve of even more strict rejection of migrants, if we look to voting patterns. Unlike previous years, Europe's democratic public sphere now knows about the victims of such policies; yet thousands of deaths apparently meet with broad acceptance.

Over 25,000 deaths in Europe's seas, about 15,000 of them in the last four years, and every year there are more fatalities. Who remembers the dead? The families live with the memories of their relatives who have either disappeared or been buried in places that are often inaccessible to them. In some places, a few local initiatives strive for a provisional remembrance of those who die in shipwrecks; inconspicuous commemorative plaques have to be set up in such a way that they do not disturb tourism. Gabriele del Grande believes that one day memorial sites will be erected around the Mediterranean with the names of the victims: "And we will not even be able to tell our grandchildren that we did not know about it".[21]

1 United Against Refugee Deaths 2017: *List of 33,305 documented deaths of refugees and migrants due to the restrictive policies of Fortress Europe*, http://unitedagainstrefugeedeaths.eu. All of the Internet sites cited here were last accessed on 5 December 2017.

2 For 1988–2015 see Gabriele del Grande, *Fortress Europe* (blog), http://fortresseurope.blogspot.de; for 2000–2016 see *The Migrants' Files 2016*, http://www.themigrantsfiles.com; from 2014 onwards, see UNHCR 2017: http://data2.unhcr.org/en/situations/mediterranean; IOM 2017: http://migration.iom.int/europe.

3 Giovanni Maria Bellu, *I fantasmi di Portopalo. Natale 1996: la morte di 300 clandestini e il silenzio dell'Italia* (Segrate 2004); Thomas Götz, "Die verschwiegene Tragödie", *Berliner Zeitung*, 19 June 2001, http://www.berliner-zeitung.de/16210050.

4 Bernd Kasparek, "Was war Mare Nostrum? Dokumentation einer Debatte um die italienische Marineoperation", in *movements. Journal for Critical Migration and Border Regime Studies* 1 no. 1 (2015), http://movements-journal.org/issues/01.grenzregime/11.kasparek--mare-nostrum-debatte.html.

5 Frank Bösch, "Engagement für Flüchtlinge. Die Aufnahme vietnamesischer 'Boat People' in der Bundesrepublik", in the online edition of *Zeithistorische Forschungen / Studies in Contemporary History* 14 Vol. 1 (2017), http://www.zeithistorische-forschungen.de/1-2017/id=5447; Rupert und Christel Neudeck, *Was man nie vergessen kann. Erinnerungen vietnamesischer Bootsflüchtlinge* (Wuppertal 2017).

6 See the extensive discussion in Cord Pagenstecher, "'Das Boot ist voll'. Schreckensvision des vereinten Deutschland", in Gerhard Paul (ed.), *Das Jahrhundert der Bilder, Bd. II: 1949 bis heute* (Göttingen: Vandenhoeck & Ruprecht, 2008), 606–613. This was also published as Volume 734 in a series of the German Federal Agency for Civic Education, with the same pagination.

7 Heiner Busch, "Vom Einheitlichen Binnenmarkt zum Gemeinsamen Abschiebungsraum. Politische Grenzsicherung in Europa", in *Bürgerrechte & Polizei/CILIP* 45 no. 2 (1993), http://www.cilip.de/ausgabe/45/raum.htm.

8 "Spanien: Bestrafung der Armen", *Der Spiegel*, 16 November 1992, http://www.spiegel.de/spiegel/print/d-13691306.html.

9 Barbara Hans, "Urteil im Cap-Anamur-Prozess: Freispruch für den Einzelkämpfer", *Der Spiegel*, 7 October 2009, http://www.spiegel.de/panorama/gesellschaft/urteil-im-cap-anamur-prozess-freispruch-fuer-den-einzelkaempfer-a-653762.html.

10 Liane von Billerbeck and John Goetz, "Haft für Taxifahrer, weil sie Ausländer beförderten. 'So was wie Sie darf ich nicht fahren!'", *Berliner Zeitung*, 7 October 1998, http://www.berliner-zeitung.de/16749758.

11 Thomas Bärnthaler and Malte Herwig, "An ihnen führt kein Weg vorbei", *Süddeutsche Zeitung Magazin* 27 (2014), http://sz-magazin.sueddeutsche.de/texte/anzeigen/41999/; Frontex, *Migratory Routes Map*, http://frontex.europa.eu/trends-and-routes/migratory-routes-map. Compare with a very similar graph in *Der Spiegel* 37 (1991).

12 Human Rights Watch, "Pushed Back, Pushed Around. Italy's Forced Return of Boat Migrants and Asylum Seekers, Libya's Mistreatment of Migrants and Asylum Seekers", 21 September 2009, https://www.hrw.org/sites/default/files/reports/italy0909webwcover_0.pdf.

13 Hirsi Jamaa et al vs. Italy, European Court of Human Rights, judgment of 23 February 2012, application no. 27765/09, English version available at: https://hudoc.echr.coe.int/eng#{"itemid":["001-109231"]}.

14 Pro Asyl, "Pushed Back. Systematic human rights violations against refugees in the Aegean Sea and at the Greek-Turkish land border", https://www.proasyl.de/wp-content/uploads/2014/02/proasyl_pushed_back_24.01.14_a4.pdf.

15 Detailed accounts in Gabriele del Grande, *Mamadous Fahrt in den Tod. Die Tragödie der irregulären Migranten im Mittelmeer* (Karlsruhe, 2008), 41ff., 85ff.

16 Andrea Böhm, "Unser Türsteher", *ZEIT Online*, 25 November 2010, http://www.zeit.de/2010/48/Europa-Fluechtlinge-Libyen/komplettansicht.

17 Till Schwarze, "Flüchtlingsabkommen mit der Türkei. Für Merkel funktioniert der Deal", *ZEIT Online*, 2 February 2017, http://www.zeit.de/politik/ausland/2017-02/fluechtlingsabkommen-tuerkei-eu-inhalt.

18 Michael Obert, "Die Menschenfänger", *Süddeutsche Zeitung Magazin*, 9 June 2017, 22–39; Christian Unger, "Warum weniger Flüchtlinge aus Libyen in Europa ankommen", *Berliner Morgenpost*, 11 September 2017, https://www.morgenpost.de/politik/article211884685/Warum-weniger-Fluechtlinge-aus-Libyen-in-Europa-ankommen.html.

19 EU Parliament resolution, The situation in the Mediterranean and the need for a holistic EU approach to migration (12 April 2016), http://www.europarl.europa.eu/sides/getDoc.do?pubRef=-//EP//TEXT+TA+P8-TA-2016-0102+0+DOC+XML+V0//EN, under item R.

20 Final pleading of General Attorney Paolo Mengozzi on 7 February 2017, Case no. C638/16 PPU: X, X versus État belge, http://curia.europa.eu/juris/documents.jsf?num=C-638/16.

21 Gabriele del Grande, "Un cimitero chiamato Mediterraneo", *Fortress Europe* (blog), 16 February 2016, http://fortresseurope.blo.

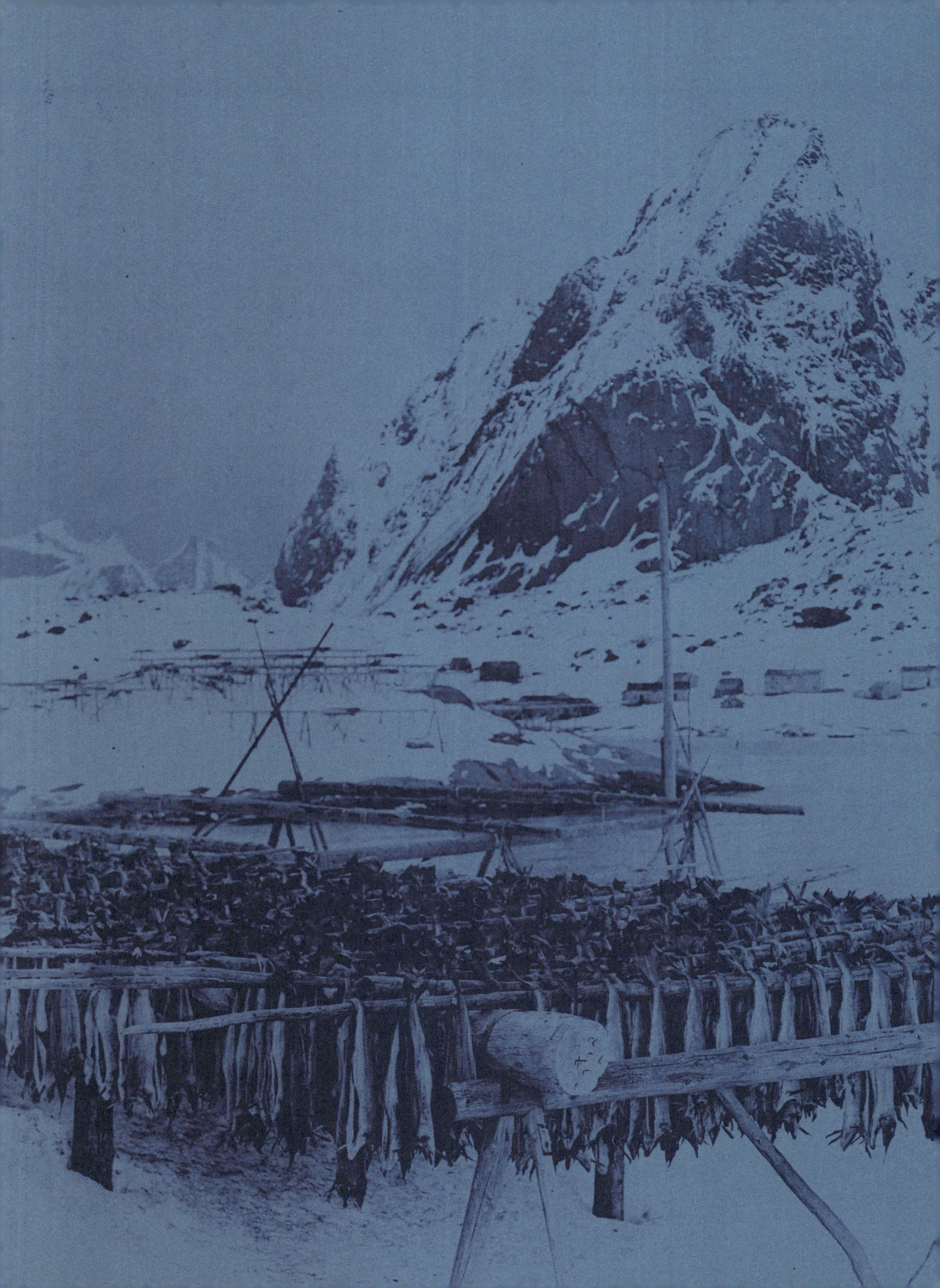

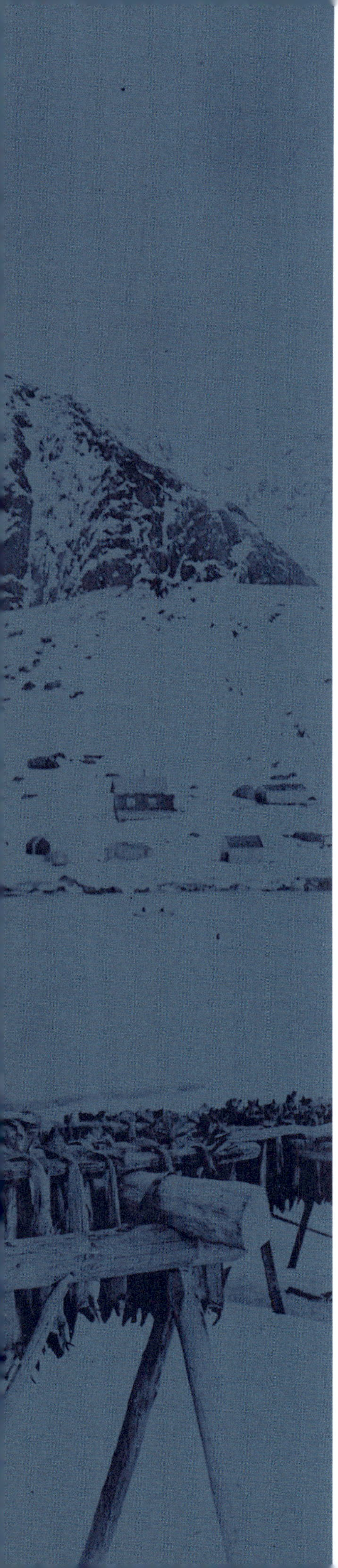

III
RESOURCES

Anders Haaland and Gunnar Ellingsen

MARINE RESOURCES

From Fish to Oil

Bergen – depending on ocean resources for 1,000 years

Bergen is the second largest city in Norway and the centre of a region of 400,000 people. Oil and gas, shipping and tourism, together with regional administration and scientific research and education, are the major industries in the region. The city has Europe's second largest milieu of fishery and ocean researchers and is the base for the two largest salmon farming concerns in the world. The harbour is one of the most important delivery points for oil and gas and for supplying offshore facilities in the North Sea.

Bergen is ideally situated between the marine resources in the north and the markets in the south. It was founded in 1070, was the largest town in Norway for 700 years, and until 1500 A.D. it was the largest city in all of Scandinavia. Bergen was Norway's most important port for the export of stockfish and cod-liver oil, products made from sea mammals, and later herring as well as imports. Stockfish from Lofoten, the first mass-produced commercial product in Norway, was exported to England from the twelfth century and later to large parts of Germany and the Netherlands.

In the history of Europe and the seas, the port of Bergen is a good example of how the abundance, unpredictable variation or shortage of resources have affected life along the coast. The influx of herring to the west coast in the 1950s was probably the largest concentrated movement of living biomass in the northern hemisphere. This essay seeks to explore how Bergen has grown as a result of resources in the ocean, international orientation and its adaptability to changing circumstances. Geography and topography – the Gulf Stream, the fjords and archipelagos along the coastline – are also parts of the picture.

A long, ragged coast filled with resources

Bergen's position in Norwegian international trade is a result of its location. The city developed at a good, natural harbour, Vågen. On a protected beach the ships of the day, with their shallow draft, could land or dock at wooden quays in front of small

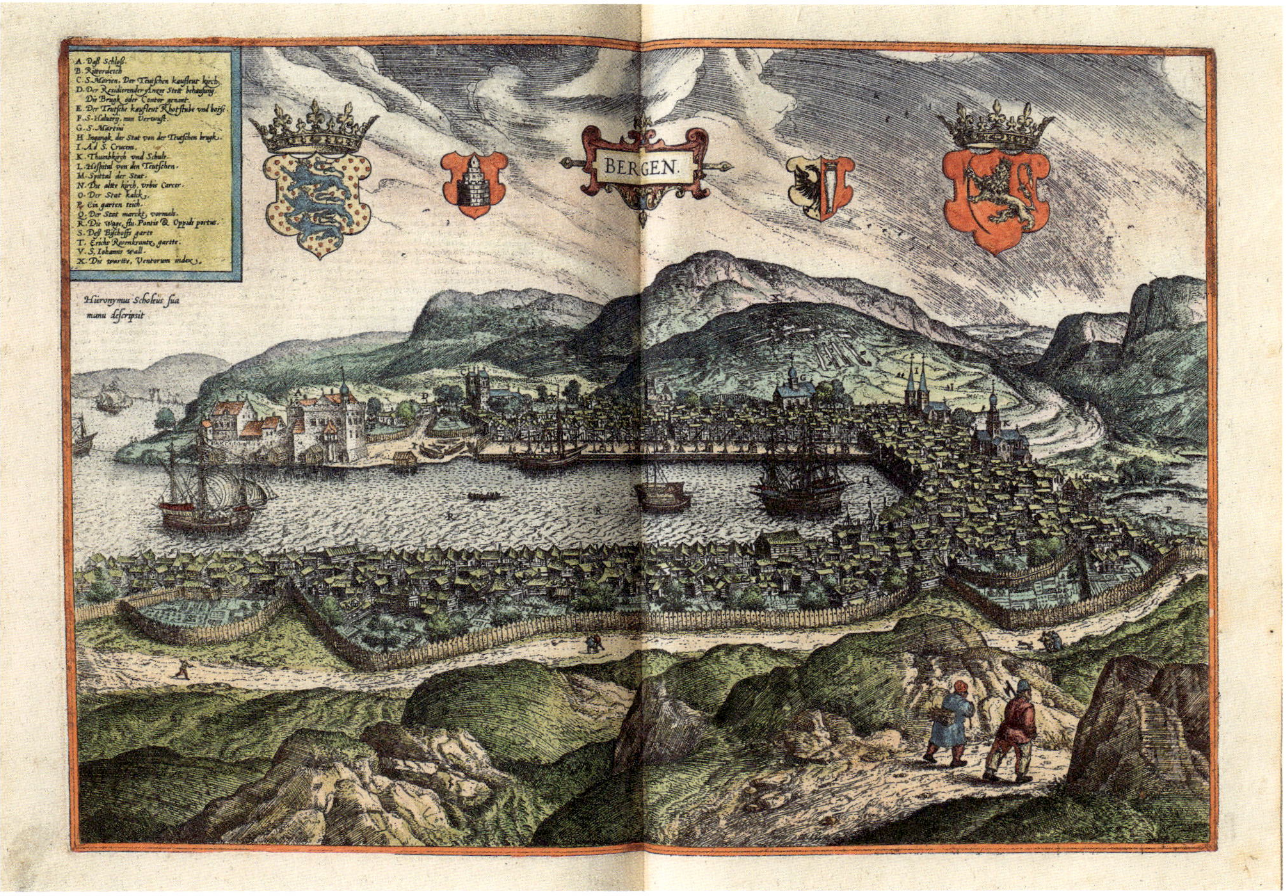

10/1
Franz Hogenberg, view of the city of Bergen, after 1588

wooden warehouses. Vågen is a tributary of the Byfjorden, and is protected from the open sea by a belt of islands along the coast. Byfjorden was centrally positioned among the four, major fjord systems of western Norway, and close to the Norse population on the Orkneys, the Shetland and Faroe Islands, Iceland and Greenland.

This coast is Europe's longest and most distinctive. It is 3,000 kilometres long and carved up by islands, inlets, sounds, bays and fjords; the longest fjords connect the sea to the high mountains. Filled with fresh, nourishing and ice-free salt water by the Gulf Stream, this coast was an excellent basis for hunting and fishing.

Bergen was an ideal loading point between foreign trading vessels and boats from production areas in the north and west. These areas were so widespread that it was nearly impossible for trade ships to sail northwards to collect goods themselves during the short summer season.

After a visit to Bergen in 1263, Cardinal William of Sabina stated that he had never seen so many ships from so many countries assembled in one single harbour. Bergen had become an international resource hub.

Stockfish

The mature Norwegian Arctic cod, called skrei, have since time immemorial migrated from the Barents Sea along the Norwegian coast, to their spawning grounds in the lee of Lofoten's chain of islands, making it the world's largest "nursery". Every female cod lays about one million eggs per kilogram of her weight, and each female weighs on average between three and four kilograms. In the Middle Ages, the influx could have numbered between sixty to eighty million fish per year.

These enormous influxes of skrei in the late winter in a large sheltered bay were a gift from nature. The location was fortuitous, as Lofoten has always been the best place to wind-dry such large fish. The fish are gutted, decapitated and hung up on wooden frames. They hang unattended until they are taken down in June, when they are dry and hard as stone. The temperature in Lofoten is high enough to prevent the fish from freezing and low enough to discourage flies and maggots. The result is stockfish: concentrated food rich in protein and preservable for four to five years without packaging.

It is believed that the Lofoten fisheries became large-scale and commercial as early as the twelfth century. At that time many new towns were being founded in Northern Europe. Their more differentiated occupational structures, with new crafts and trades independent from farming, created larger markets for food products and therefore trade: "a trade revolution". The fasting rituals of the Catholic Church, which prohibited the consumption of meat but allowed the eating of fish, further expanded the markets for stockfish.

The Hanseatic League in Bergen

The German tradesmen's guild of the twelfth century (1160-) was transformed in 1350 to the Hanseatic League, which was comprised of more than one hundred North German towns and had its headquarters in Lübeck. Starting around 1200, the export of stockfish went mainly to towns on the eastern coast of England on either

10/4
Cod being dried to make stockfish, 1924

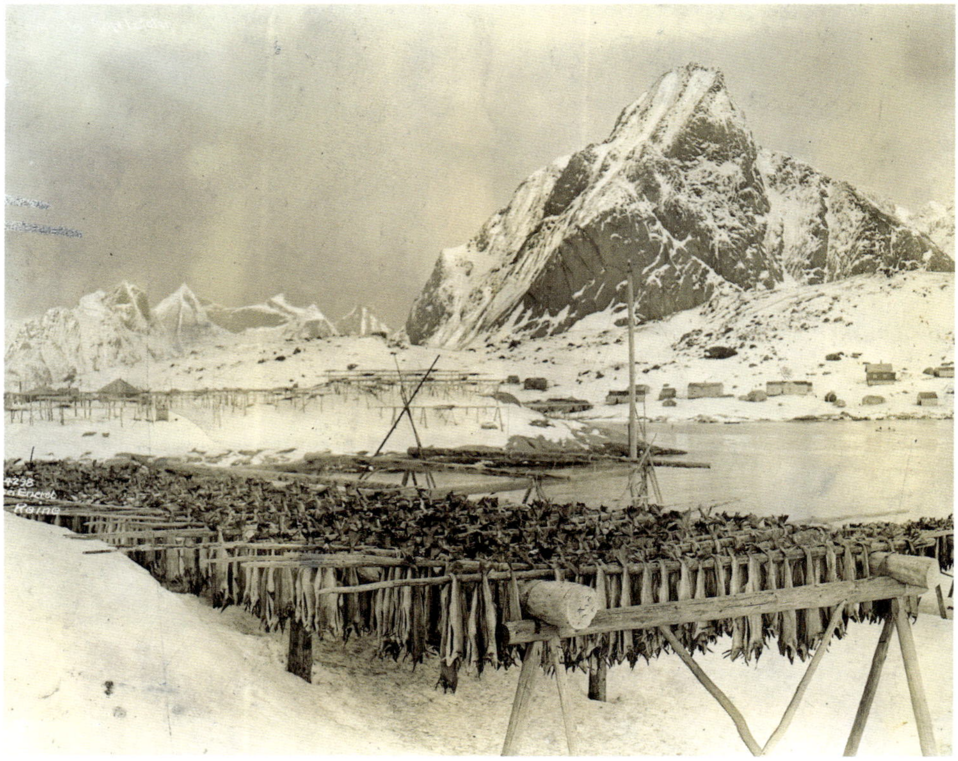

English or Norwegian ships, together with its by-product of cod liver oil. In return came corn. The Hanseatic League entered this market around 1280 and ran a three-way trade in corn from the Baltic to Bergen, stockfish to England, and from there wool to the textile towns of Flanders.

Coastal Norway was dependant on a stable supply of corn. Late in the 1290s the League consented to the Norwegian king's order not to operate actively north of Bergen. This regulation strengthened Bergen as a controlling port in the stockfish trade. During the fifteenth century there were as many as 2,000 Germans here in the summertime, of which 1,000 stayed year-round. The German presence weighed heavily on the town with its Norwegian population of between 6,000 and 7,000. The volume of trade through Bergen was considerable. Between 1300 and 1600, export averaged 3,000 to 4,000 tonnes of stockfish annually, or about seven to nine million fish.

The League maintained the important stockfish export, even during the difficult times after the Black Death. They had enough capital to finance the Lofoten fishermen for their next season; "The Nordland debt" between fishermen in the north and traders in Bergen was a bond of obligations that could last for generations, and the traders' greatest asset. Bergen did far better than most Norwegian towns during the difficult two hundred years after 1350.

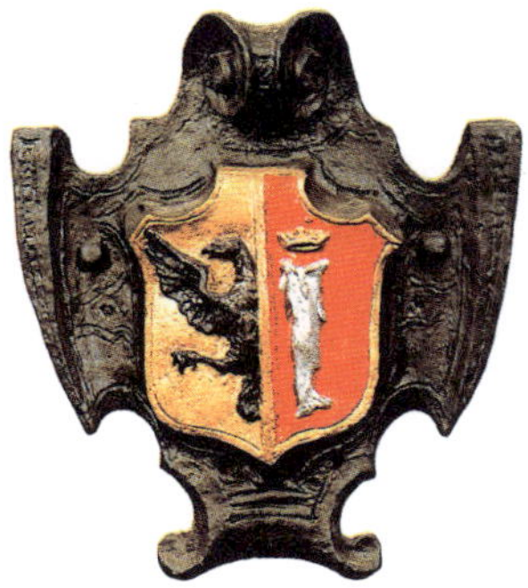

Coat of arms of the Lübeck *Bergenfahrer* with stockfish symbol, 1280

Why were there not rich herring fisheries in the Middle Ages? The importance of salt

As early as the Viking period there must have been a large influx of Norwegian spring spawning herring (NVG herring) along the coast. For centuries before 1200 A.D., herring was fished, both with seines and with nets, but mainly for local consumption. There are many reasons for its absence in trade in this period. The first is salt, which was a scarce commodity at the time. Rock salt from the Lüneburg Heath was expensive because it had to be transported overland to Lübeck and from there by boat.

Furthermore, in the latter part of the twelfth century, there were rich herring fisheries by the south-eastern coast of Skåne (Scania), and later in Bohuslän. The Hanseatic League had enough with the salt and herring trade in these closer areas.

Also, the low levels of urbanisation in Norway hampered the production of salted herring. Since the herring's geographical mobility was far greater than that of the skrei, seasonal fishing stations did not develop on the west coast. Barrels required skilled craftsmen and salt merchants, and therefore urban populations. In the Middle Ages there were only two ports worth mentioning between the Oslofjord and Russia: Bergen and Trondheim.

Finally, the amount of tasty salt herring from sixteenth-century Scottish and Dutch drift-net fishing in the North Sea closed the market for the less valuable Norwegian salt herring. Furthermore, Norwegian salt, obtained by boiling seawater, was of a low quality.

From the end of the eighteenth century, an increasing amount of skrei went to the new trade product called clipfish, or split and salted skrei dried on bare rock. Salted cod requires a great deal of salt, which was brought from France and the Iberian Peninsula by Norwegian ships. Cheap sea salt also opened up the opportunity to

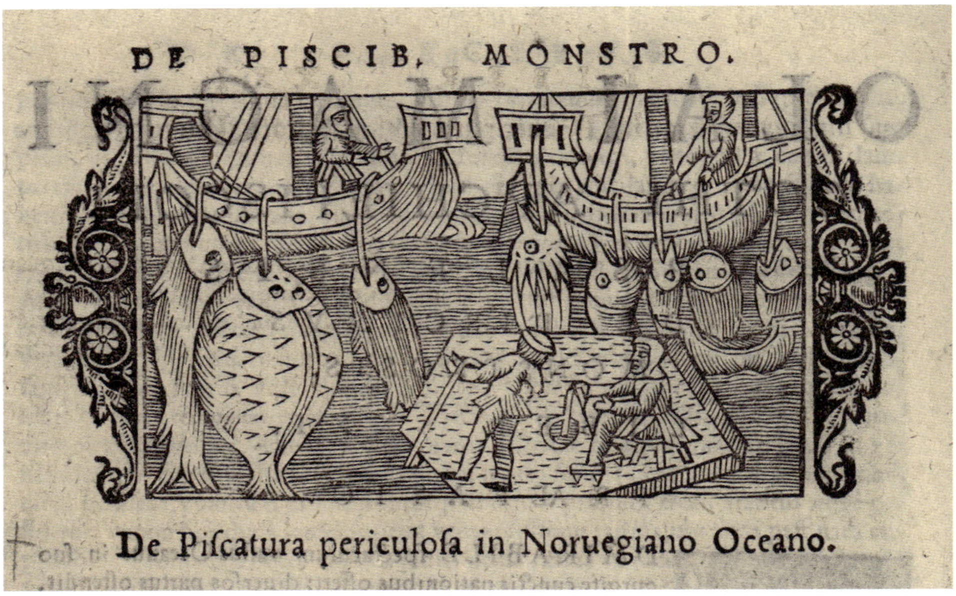

10/6
Olaus Magnus, *Of dangerous fishing in the Norwegian Sea,* 1555

process enormous hauls of NVG herring. Despite humble beginnings, the export of salted herring rose from a few thousand to 20,000 barrels a year in the sixteenth century, rising further to 200,000 barrels per year in 1740, only to disappear completely in 1784 when the herring did not show up.

150 years with periodically plentiful herring fishing (1808–1958)

As it disappeared from the Bohuslän coast, the herring suddenly returned to the west coast again. After the peace of 1814, the markets for Swedish salt herring lay open to Norwegians. Exports passed 150,000 barrels in the 1820s and reached a zenith of 745,000 in 1862. If we include domestic consumption, the total catch was probably one million barrels. Forty thousand western Norwegian farmers, working in open boats, fished the herring coming in shoals all the way into the fjords and close to the shore. Ten thousand others were employed in the salting process and in transporting the herring from the fishing grounds to the herring towns of Bergen and Stavanger, and to other new, smaller herring towns. Herring – with its availability, low economic requirements and its applicability both for sale and private consumption – made it possible for the male population on the coast to combine farming and fishing; they were called farmer-fishermen.

When the herring fisheries stagnated in the 1860s, later to disappear in 1870, Bergen resorted to shipping. By quickly converting from sail to steam, the city became the most important maritime town in a country that, in the 1880's, was the world's fourth largest maritime nation. Stavanger became an industrial town with a large-scale production of sardines made from small fish known as sprats.

The NVG herring returned to the west coast in the 1890s. Nevertheless, measured in the number of fishermen and in catch volumes, the Norwegian fishing industry was one of Europe's largest. However, it was technically and financially backward. The 100,000 farmer-fishermen utilised an equal number of boats, mainly open wooden boats with oars and sails, and 3,000 to 4,000 with decks.

There were only around 170 steam powered fishing vessels, compared to more than 2,000 in Great Britain and several hundred in France and Germany. Steam-powered fishing boats remained out of the economic reach of the farmer-fishermen, since they only fished seasonally. However, when affordable combustion engines became available around 1905, they started a revolution. They could be installed in even the smallest wooden boats and they stimulated the development of more solid, covered vessels. Within two decades Norway had, by far, the world's largest motorised fishing fleet.

The new engines, together with new gear such as drift nets and purse seines, led to a dramatic increase in the size of catch, from three to six million hectolitres (a unit of measure roughly equivalent to a barrel) between 1914 and 1940 alone. The markets could not cope with such large amounts of salt herring and the newer product, fresh herring. The solution was to process the extra herring into oil and flour for industrial fat stuffs and for agricultural uses. Consequently, prices for herring sank so low that they threatened the profitability of the whole herring industry. Herring fishermen organised themselves and obtained a state monopoly on all sales of raw herring. The new Norwegian herring sales organisation, Norges Sildesalgslag, became the world's largest cooperative organisation based on the total number of members. Their headquarters is in Bergen, centrally positioned in the fishing region.

Trawler fishing for herring, c. 1965–1970

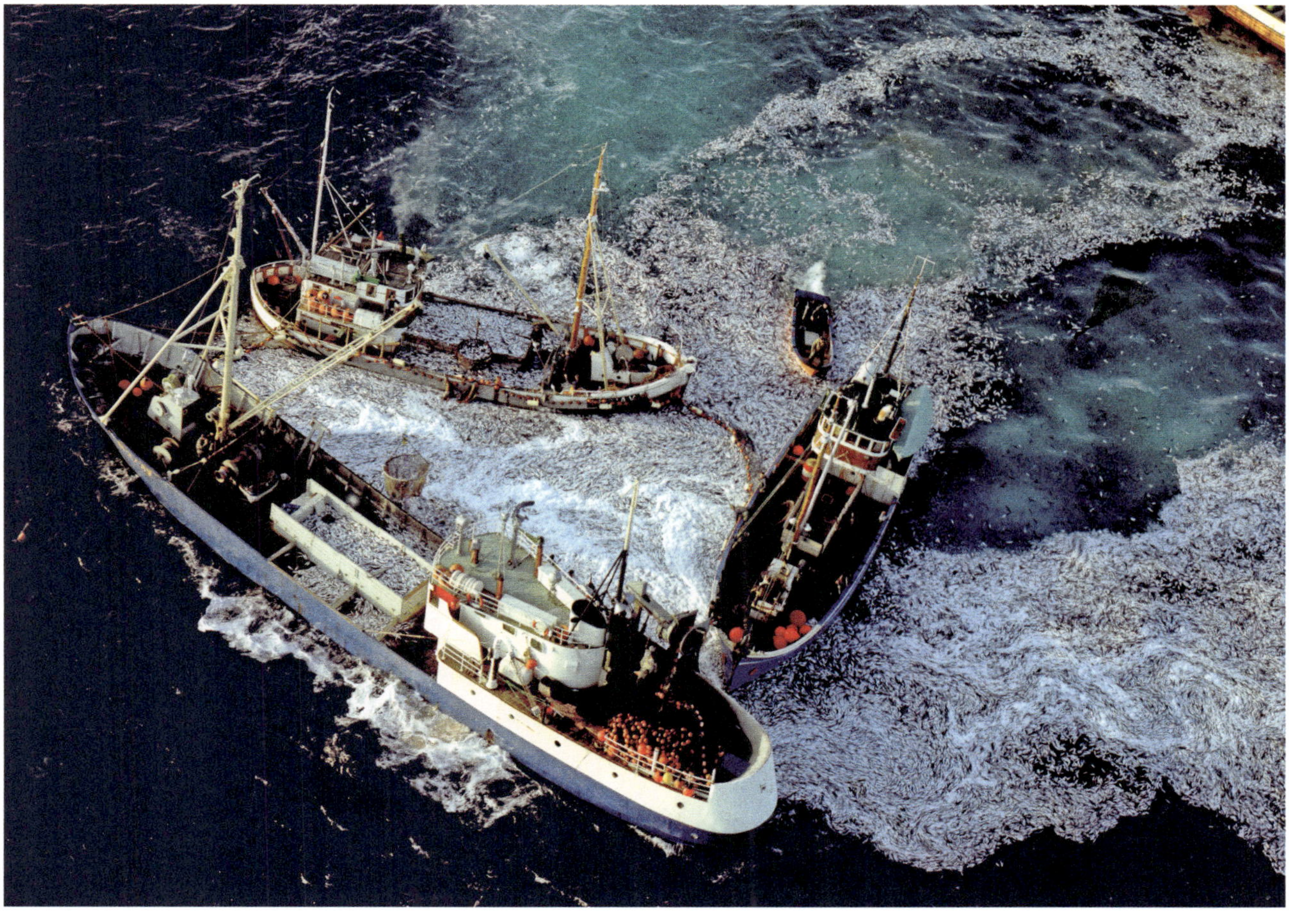

Adaptation – from coastal to ocean fishing

In the late 1950s herring fishing failed, with yield falling from 1.2 million to fifteen thousand tonnes by 1969 – an ecological catastrophe. The stock of Norwegian spring spawning herring was reduced from sixteen million tonnes in 1945 to 10,000 tonnes in 1975. It was saved by strict conservation regulations between 1972 and the 1990s, and survived as a Norwegian coastal livestock. Today the yields have returned to the levels of the golden age of the 1950s.

What was a fleet of 500 purse seiners with expensive gear to do when there was no stock? For technical reasons, they were constricted to operations in inshore waters. However, there was another population of herring, the North Sea herring, which did not enter the coast. In order to fish in the open oceans, a new type of equipment was needed: the American ring net with a powerful winch attached to the vessel. This led to one of the fastest reorganisations in Norwegian industrial history between 1963 and 1967: the fleet of boats converted into, or specially built for, ring net fishing increased from four to 500. Thanks to the use of winches and nylon, the size of the ring nets increased to 600 metres in circumference and 200 metres deep. During the 1960s and 1970s the new fleet caught large amounts of North Sea herring, mackerel, capelin and whiting. The fish were ground into oil and flour. This caused the smaller boats that fished the coast for herring to lose their livelihoods.

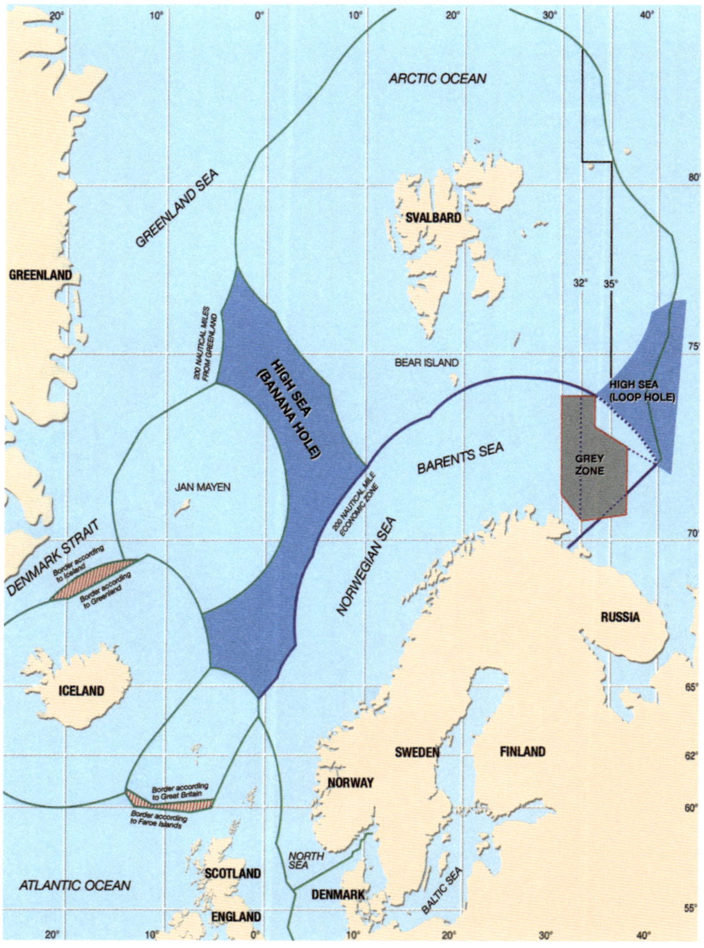

Economic zones in the North Atlantic, c. 2000

The Norwegian state tried to slow the overfishing by imposing concessions and fishing quotas and stimulating condemnations. An effective management system was made possible by a UN resolution in 1977, giving coastal states control over the fish populations inside zones of 200 nautical miles. Due to its long coastline, peripheral position, and the distant islands of Jan Mayen and Svalbard, this gave Norway responsibility for two million km^2 of sea, an area six times larger than its mainland. Sustainable taxation and national quotas were set via negotiation. The international resource management system has worked well, including for cod and other white fish.

From industrial fishing for wild fish to "farming the blue fields"

Regulation did not impede technical and economic modernisation. Ring net boats are more effective than ever, but the fleet has been reduced to sixty boats. Almost all of the packing facilities for NVG herring, barrel and motor factories and small boatyards have disappeared. Sardine canneries and almost all of the herring oil plants are closed down, with just a few remaining to supply feed to sea farms. The last load of stockfish was shipped through Bergen in 1999, and the export of fresh fish and herring from here has ended.

A positive contrast to this is the growth in aquaculture. However insignificant this may have been in 1970 (600 tonnes), today this industry produces 1.3 million tonnes of salmon at an export value far larger than the combined value of all wild fish. In 2016, aquaculture was responsible for sixty-five per cent of the seafood export value of 92 billion NOK.

Fish farming has roots in Norway that date back to river cultivation in the 1850s. The breakthrough, however, did not come until the Danish / German model of breeding rainbow trout in freshwater dams was abandoned in favour of another method. Salmon breeding first began in Norway around 1970, when breeding fish were selected from the best among the wild population and placed in sea cages in sheltered saltwater. This effectively exploited the coastline as a production element,

Salmon aquaculture in northern Norway, 2012

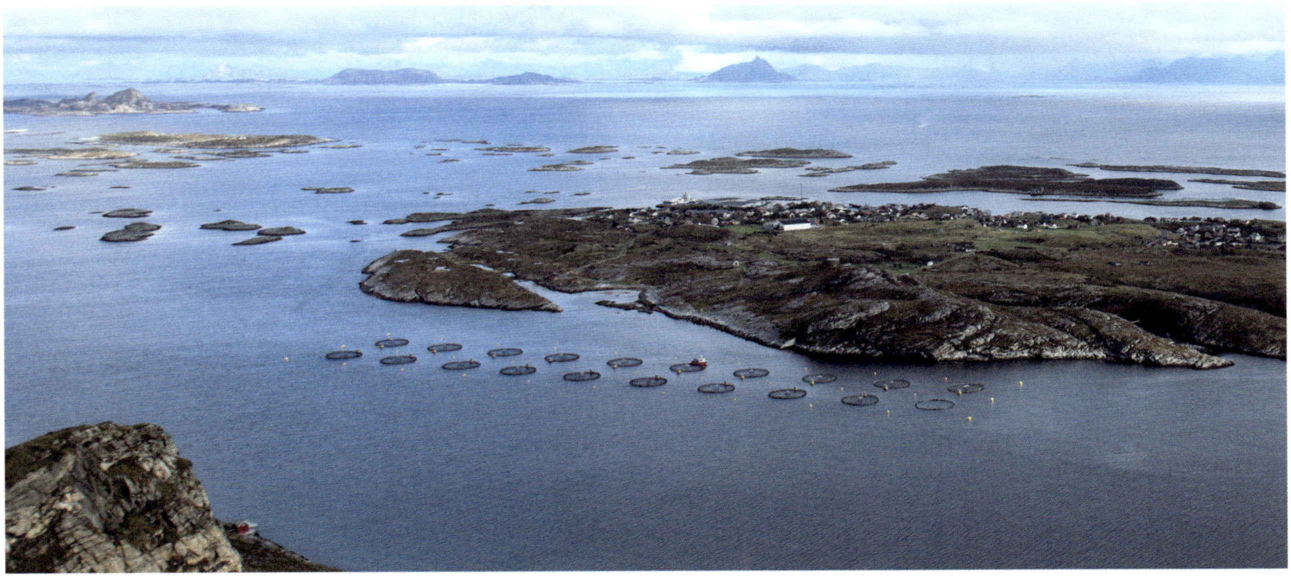

which led to the creation of its own biomass. Hatching and fostering the newly-hatched young fish, however, still takes place in freshwater. Salmon make up more than ninety per cent of overall fish farming production.

While enthusiastic amateurs started the process with small, spread-out facilities, the industry is now heavily science-based with a stronger concentration of ownership; aquaculture is big business. Fish diseases and the use of antibiotics have almost been eliminated, and production in tanks and sea cages are controlled and monitored by computers down to the smallest details. No other domestic livestock has such an effective ratio of feed to slaughter weight. The county of Hordaland, with the Bergen region at its centre, has played a crucial role in this development. The two largest salmon companies in the world have their headquarters in Bergen, and two leading research centres that are also departments of the Institute of Maritime Research are located in the region.

Aquaculture has room for further expansion, especially because salmon thrive equally well in the colder waters further north as in the old, more heavily populated areas in the south. In 2010 all 4,000 sea cages, including their safety and no-fishing zones, occupied only 0.1 per cent of the sea area inside the coastal baseline. Compared to agriculture, this is equal to 0.8 per cent of the arable soil and pasture area used by an industry that produces less than a quarter of the meat harvested from aquaculture.

Black Gold

One optimistic vision holds that "silver from the sea" will replace "black gold" by 2050; in other words, that seafood will contribute more to the gross domestic product than the petroleum sector. But there is still a long way to go. Oil and gas extraction has been the greatest growth engine of the Norwegian economy since the 1980s, and it has made Norway one of the world´s richest countries. During the last ten to fifteen years, oil and gas have made up one-fifth of the national product and forty to fifty per cent of exports. At its peak in the 1990s, Norway ranked amongst the world's largest exporters of oil and gas. In contrast, together with saltwater fishing and agriculture, aquaculture contributes one to two per cent of the GDP and between six to seven per cent of all exports.

Oil exploration began cautiously. Multinational oil companies became interested in the Norwegian ocean region after large finds of gas in Holland in 1959, but the ownership rights for the seabed were unclear. The Norwegian state declared supremacy over the continental shelf in 1963 and reached an agreement with Great Britain and Denmark, organizing territorial claims on the median line principle. In 1962 seismic surveys of the subsea geology began and in 1965 the Norwegian state advertised concessions for blocks south of the sixty-second latitude line. Exploratory drilling resulted in "world-class" finds and Norway's future as an important petroleum-producing nation became clear.

Parliament then developed a comprehensive national oil policy. "The Ten Oil Commandments" state that resources should be owned by the state and should benefit the nation as a whole. All activities on the Norwegian continental shelf should be under national supervision and control. A broad-reaching and competent oil industry was planned. Regional politics were important; the industry should be spread as much as possible along the coast and the environment should be taken into consid-

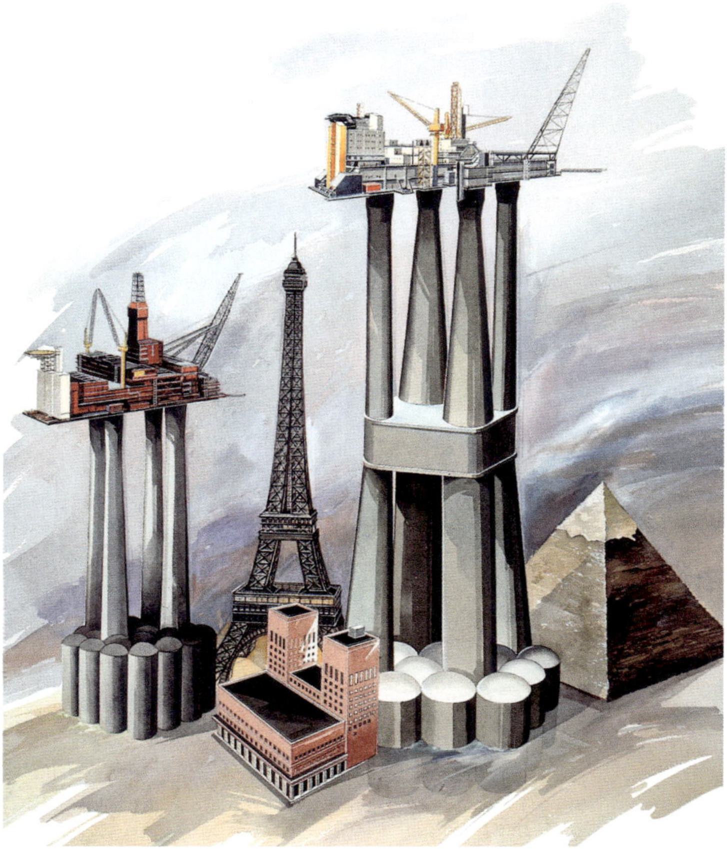

Comparison of the platforms Statfjord A and Troll A, c. 2000

eration. In 1972 the state established its own oil company, Statoil – which was instrumental in the development of most of the oil fields – and its agency, the Norwegian Petroleum Directorate, the year after. Around 1980 the state had developed a coherent model for business and management of petroleum resources. Together with taxation policies, the Norwegian state's share ownership has accumulated large amounts of profits in the state's pension fund. This fund is one of the largest in the world, presently valued at around 8,000 billion NOK.

Even though the country did not have an oil industry in 1970, competence did exist in the field of crude oil due to the ownership and operation of one of the world's largest fleets of oil tankers. Several of the shipyards participated in building super tankers and gas tankers, and the hydroelectric power nation was a leader in the building of large concrete dams in the high mountains.

In 1995 the concrete Platform Troll A was placed at a depth of 300 metres, sixty kilometres west of the mouth of Sognefjord. Its superstructure and gas flare tower rose to a height of 476 metres. It was the tallest and heaviest object nan had ever moved on Earth; the rebar alone weighed as much as five Eiffel Towers. It provides ten per cent of all natural gas to Western Europe through a pipeline that leads the gas from the rig down and up the 380-metre-deep Norwegian trench in a tunnel, to an enormous processing plant at Kollsnes, northwest of Bergen. The cleaned, dried and compressed gas is sent in another pipeline to Emden in Germany. Forty per cent of Norwegian gas exports originate in Kollsnes.

Stavanger became the oil capital, since both Statoil and the Norwegian Petroleum Directorate had their headquarters there, and most foreign operators followed suit. The first supply bases were also founded here. However, as the development of the oil fields moved northward, Bergen's importance grew accordingly. The city built its first supply base in 1974, Coast Center Base at Ågotnes, and ten years later a base at Mongstad north of Bergen. Both are among the largest in the country and service a number of oil fields in the North Sea. While all Norwegian oil fields were administrated and controlled from Stavanger up to 1984, today a majority of the North Sea oil fields are run from Bergen.

With a refinery, a CO_2 processing plant and enormous underground halls for temporary storage of crude oil, Mongstad became Europe's second largest petroleum port after Rotterdam, with a turnover in the late 1990s of seventy-six million tonnes of liquid bulk. An additional twenty million tonnes of crude oil were shipped from similar storage halls at Sture in Øygarden, where the oil came through a pipeline from the Oseberg field, the first pipeline connecting field and land. The petroleum industry in Bergen achieved international eminence in subsea technology during the change from expensive concrete platforms to remotely controlled, widespread wellheads on the seabed.

The extraction of oil and gas from sources far beneath the deep water seabed, out of range of divers and often in stormy weather, is an "extreme sport". The only major accident thus far has been the Bravo blowout in the Ekofisk field in 1977. The damage done to the environment, however, was limited because the light oil mixed with the seawater. In the following forty years of intense activity, there have been no major oil spillages. It is said that the Norwegian oil and gas industry operates under "one of the strongest environmental regimes in the world".

Perspectives

The successful utilization of marine biological and mineral resources is primarily due to the ability of private entrepreneurs to adapt to changing circumstances. The state has also played a part at crucial stages by supporting businesses, securing necessary infrastructure and imposing regulations meant for the best of both private firms and society. This applies to the fishing industry, aquaculture and not least the petroleum sector. The fear of losing national control over natural resources in distant waters explains, in part, why the Norwegians chose to stay outside the EU in 1994.

This heavy dependence on marine and maritime resources has been profitable for Norway and Bergen to the present day. The possibilities of continued expansion in aquaculture are considered great, and marine researchers are mapping the enormous stocks of "meso-fish" some hundred metres down in the sea. But this dependence also entails challenges: How will the migration patterns of important stocks of wild fish change with rising levels of temperature and acidity in the sea? Will the Gulf Stream "lose power" as the Greenland ice cap melts down? The mighty petroleum industry has already met the first impact of the green shift in production and consumption. The need for adaptability is therefore greater than ever.

Dagmar Röhrlich

BENEATH THE WAVES

Investigating the Seas

When the METEOR passed through Wilhelmshaven Lock on 16 April 1925, the weather was cold and rainy. The vessel carried the 133 members of the German Atlantic expedition, who were seen off by naval commanders, well-known German marine scientists and thousands of onlookers. This was the first research expedition that Germany had undertaken since its defeat in the First World War, an ambitious political and scientific project that was intended to restore the country to the ranks of the world's leading research nations. As part of its two-year mission, the expedition was charged with carrying out chemical and physical investigations of the Atlantic Ocean, zigzagging between North Africa and South America and travelling almost as far south as the Antarctic. Oceanographer Alfred Merz (1880–1925), who directed the Institute of Marine Science in Berlin, planned to study water circulation, heat balance and ocean chemistry at around 350 stations along fourteen east-west latitudinal routes called *Profile*, or cross-sections.

Merz's earlier proposal – centring on a research voyage in the Pacific – did not come to fruition for cost reasons. Germany, which had been hit hard by the economic crisis, did not have the funds either to finish constructing or to refit the METEOR. The keel of the gunship had been laid at the imperial shipyards in Danzig in February 1914, but the vessel was not yet finished when it was launched on 18 January 1915. After the outbreak of war in August 1914, such lightly armed ships were no longer important for Germany's naval strategy – whether for coastal defence or, as was the case with the METEOR, for foreign missions.

Because Germany was permitted to maintain only a small navy under the Treaty of Versailles, naval commanders looked for ways to retain possession of the vessel at the end of the First World War. A plan was developed to refit the unfinished ship for marine research under the navy's supervision. The vessel was currently lying at anchor in the roads and had not yet been claimed by the victorious powers. In late 1919, the admiralty of the German navy, which had been reduced in size to around ten thousand men and just a few ships, decided to finish constructing the METEOR as a survey and research vessel.[1] They had probably been swayed by the argument that, especially after the loss of the colonies, a longer research voyage abroad would provide an opportunity "to show the outside world that German sea defence and the country itself were still intact".[2] Today marine research is an inter-

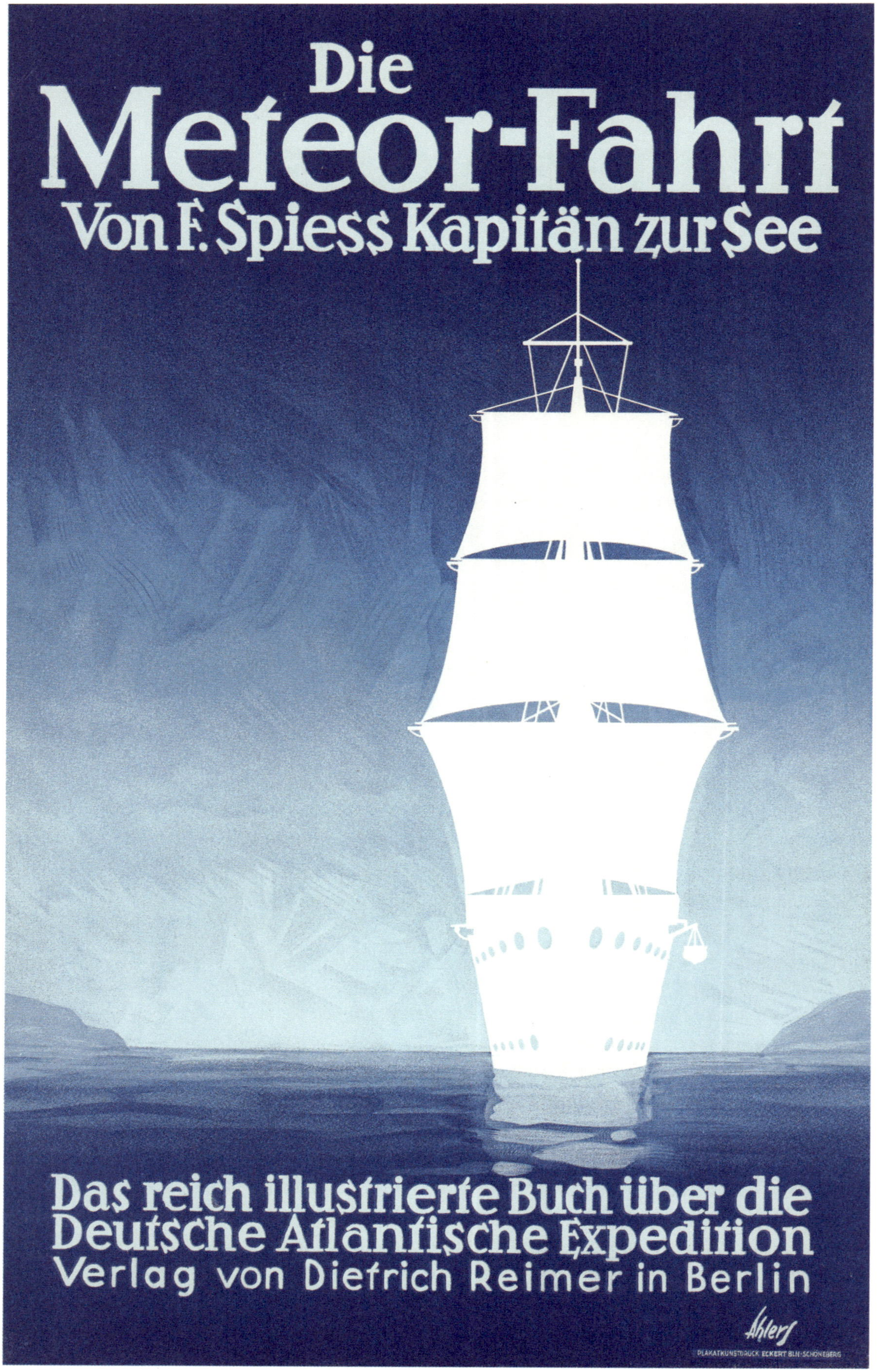
Die
Meteor-Fahrt
Von F. Spiess Kapitän zur See
Das reich illustrierte Buch über die
Deutsche Atlantische Expedition
Verlag von Dietrich Reimer in Berlin
Ahlers

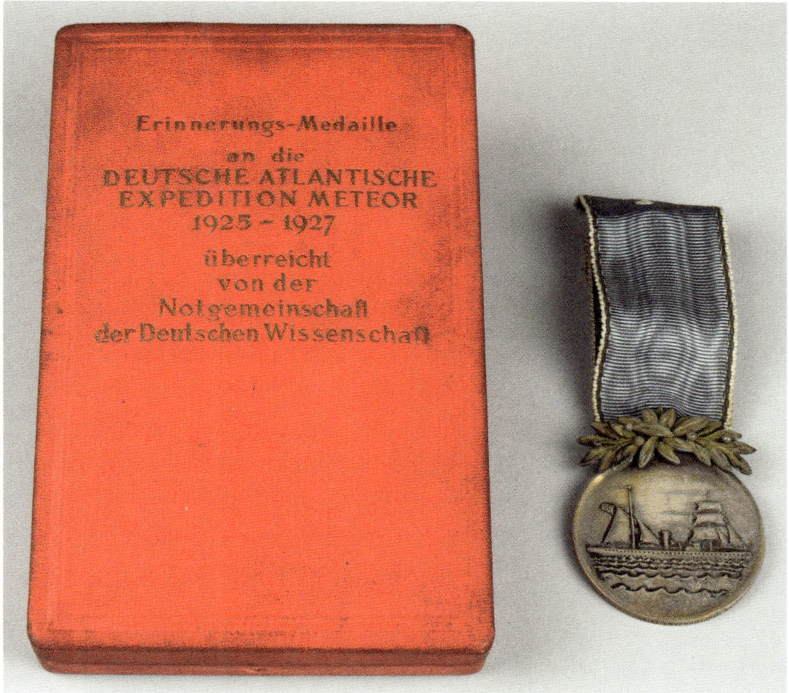

Medal issued by *Notgemeinschaft der Deutschen Wissenschaft* to mark the completion of the German Atlantic Expedition, 1927

national affair, but at the time science, national prestige and the military were closely intertwined. This was a legacy of the nineteenth century. The famous CHALLENGER expedition (1872–1876) in the United Kingdom, for example, received enormous support after the science journal *Nature* reported that Sweden, Germany and the United States were planning similar deep-sea expeditions.[3]

The navy supported the German Atlantic expedition on a massive scale. Of the 133 men on board the METEOR, a total of 118 were soldiers. They were joined by six civilian crew members and nine scientists: four oceanographers, a geologist, a chemist, two meteorologists and a biologist. Before the voyage began, the officers and several crew members had learnt to take depth measurements with newly developed "echo sounders" and to collect meteorological data with balloons and kites so that they could assist the researchers. Because one goal of the expedition was to estimate primary plankton production in the South Atlantic, the ship's physician had been taught how to identify plankton catches. Alfred Merz was the expedition's scientific director and frigate captain Fritz Spieß (1881–1959) was in command of the vessel. After Merz's untimely death in August 1925, Spieß took on the role of scientific director as well. He was promoted to the rank of full captain towards the end of the voyage.

Merz's goal was to prove that ocean currents were caused by differences in water density, which themselve result from differences in salinity and temperature. For this reason he aimed to systematically "sample" an entire ocean for the first time, measuring not only currents, the stratification of ocean water, its chemistry and temperature, but also wind conditions, sea-floor morphology and geology. It was important for Fritz Spieß that this work be carried out with military discipline, and on-board activities were thus highly regimented. All of the crew members knew exactly what they needed to do at the measurement stations and the scientists had been introduced to a "military etiquette" on the vessel that was completely foreign

11/20
Fritz Ahlers, poster advertising the publication "The METEOR voyage", 1928

to them.[4] According to Captain Spieß, it was this strict discipline that made the mission a success.

The history of marine research reaches far back in time and the German Atlantic expedition was thus part of a long tradition. Aristotle (384–322 BC) had studied the tides and questioned whether life existed in the deep sea. The first maps with sea routes and sailing instructions were made in the fourth century BC. However, centuries were to pass before the astrolabe and the Jacob's staff, which was used to measure angles, made it possible for sailors to calculate positions at sea such that they could return to their discoveries with some degree of certainty. From the eighteenth century onwards, the sextant and the ship's chronometer greatly simplified navigation and provided a foundation for studying oceanographic conditions.

Modern marine research began with a voyage by the Challenger in 1872. The four-year Challenger expedition studied the topographical, physical, chemical and biological conditions of the world's seas. This premiere was followed by several other research voyages, including the German Valdivia expedition of 1898/99. On these early expeditions, scientists acquired basic knowledge and defined standard methods for comparing results. They recognised that taking samples alone was not sufficient to understand the world's seas and that these samples needed to be systematically recorded.

Measuring ocean depths was therefore one of the German Atlantic expedition's main objectives. Depth measurements on the high seas can be tricky business because vessels tend to drift and sounding lines never hang vertically. In addition, the researchers in this period used hemp lines, which were so heavy that they continued to unwind even after their weights had hit the sea floor. Because deep water currents also catch and carry off the lines, it is no wonder that we often find references to enormous depths. It seems that some lines did not reach the sea floor even at depths of eighteen kilometres.

The first reliable method for measuring ocean depths was developed in 1853 by the American John Mercer Brooke (1826–1906). It consisted of a mechanical system in which the sinker – ideally, a drilled cannonball with a hollow metal tube through its centre – was lowered on a thin measuring wire. The device was designed such that when it reached the ocean floor, the metal tube penetrated the soil, the weight fell off and only the measuring wire and the tube were pulled up to the surface. In this way, researchers were able not only to determine water depth, but also to retrieve a sample of the ocean floor. This was the system used on the earlier Challenger expedition. It was an elaborate, time-consuming method that required a stationery vessel, but it delivered good results. For this reason, in addition to various echo sounders, the Meteor also took along two of these traditional sounding systems.

The development of echo sounding is associated with the names of three scientists who patented simple sonar systems independently of one another at roughly the same time: the German physicist Alexander Behm (1880–1952), the Canadian inventor Reginald A. Fessenden (1866–1932) and the British mathematician Lewis Fry Richardson (1881–1953). All three had been horrified by the sinking of the Titanic in 1912 and wanted to prevent such accidents in the future through the use of echo sounders, with which ships could detect icebergs. The idea is simple: a sound wave is emitted in water, spreads out in all directions and is reflected by the iceberg. The distance is calculated on the basis of the time it takes for the echo to return to the ship. Unfortunately, as it turned out, the principle did not work for icebergs because they reflect sound so poorly. However, it did work for the ocean floor, which brought an end to sounding lines. In the days of the METEOR, depths still needed to be calculated "by hand" using the measured times, but this technique was still much quicker than sounding lines.

It was in the twentieth century that studies of the ocean floor really took off, made possible by advances in technology. Sonar technology was constantly improved – primarily to detect enemy submarines. Nevertheless, the improvements benefited civilian shipping and scientific research as well. Today's multibeam sonar systems, which emit ultrasound signals and use satellite-based GPS to determine the ship's position, provide detailed views of the deep ocean floor, which is far from being charted in all places. A good example is the Southern Ocean surrounding Antarctica. It was not until 2013 that the project IBCSO (International Bathymetric Chart of the Southern Ocean) published the first digital images of the ocean floor south of the 60th parallel, parts of which were interpolated.[5] The METEOR's crew would have been excited by the data and imaging techniques, as they had measured only a few sites south of the 60th parallel. Still, with their soundings, they had discovered a depression in the ocean floor at a depth of more than five thousand metres: the South Shetland Trench. This deep-sea furrow was a product of the complex puzzle of tectonic plates existing in the region. In 1925, though, the development of plate tectonic theory was still a long way off. It was not until the 1960s that sufficient data of the ocean floor were available for this undertaking, obtained from sonar systems with the help of magnetic and seismic methods.

But back to the METEOR: before the voyage, around 3,000 depth measurements were available for the entire South Atlantic; by its completion, there were far more than 60,000, of which only 650 were from wire soundings.[6] With the help of these data, scientists recognised for the first time that the mid-ocean ridge in the South Atlantic was a continuous underwater mountain range. However, in view of the size of the South Atlantic, these measurements provided only a sketchy picture; and when he returned to Germany, Captain Fritz Spieß explained that, viewed statistically, it was as if only a single depth measurement had been taken for an area "the size of Switzerland".[7]

After Merz's death, work on the vessel was continued in his spirit. Today, the German Atlantic expedition is synonymous with the transition from descriptive marine science to oceanography. It marks the start of physical studies that are based on large quantities of data and that examine phenomena such as ocean currents, tides, turbulence and heat transport. The findings confirmed Merz's hypothesis that differences in water temperature and salinity are one cause of ocean currents. And these currents are controlled by a complex interplay of forces that result from the position of the continents, the Coriolis effect,[8] the winds and sea-floor typography. Deep-sea basins, abyssal rises and continental slopes guide these currents, as mountains do the air. Nevertheless, it was not until the early 1970s that oceanographers had collected enough data to visualise this global network of sea currents. A "global conveyor belt", it transports vast quantities of water over distances of thousands of kilometres and consists of the Gulf Stream at the ocean's surface and North Atlantic Deep Water flowing southward along the ocean floor from the Greenland Sea.

Ocean currents are enormous systems that transport heat from the tropics to the poles, carry nutrients up from the depths and oxygenate the deep sea. Particu-

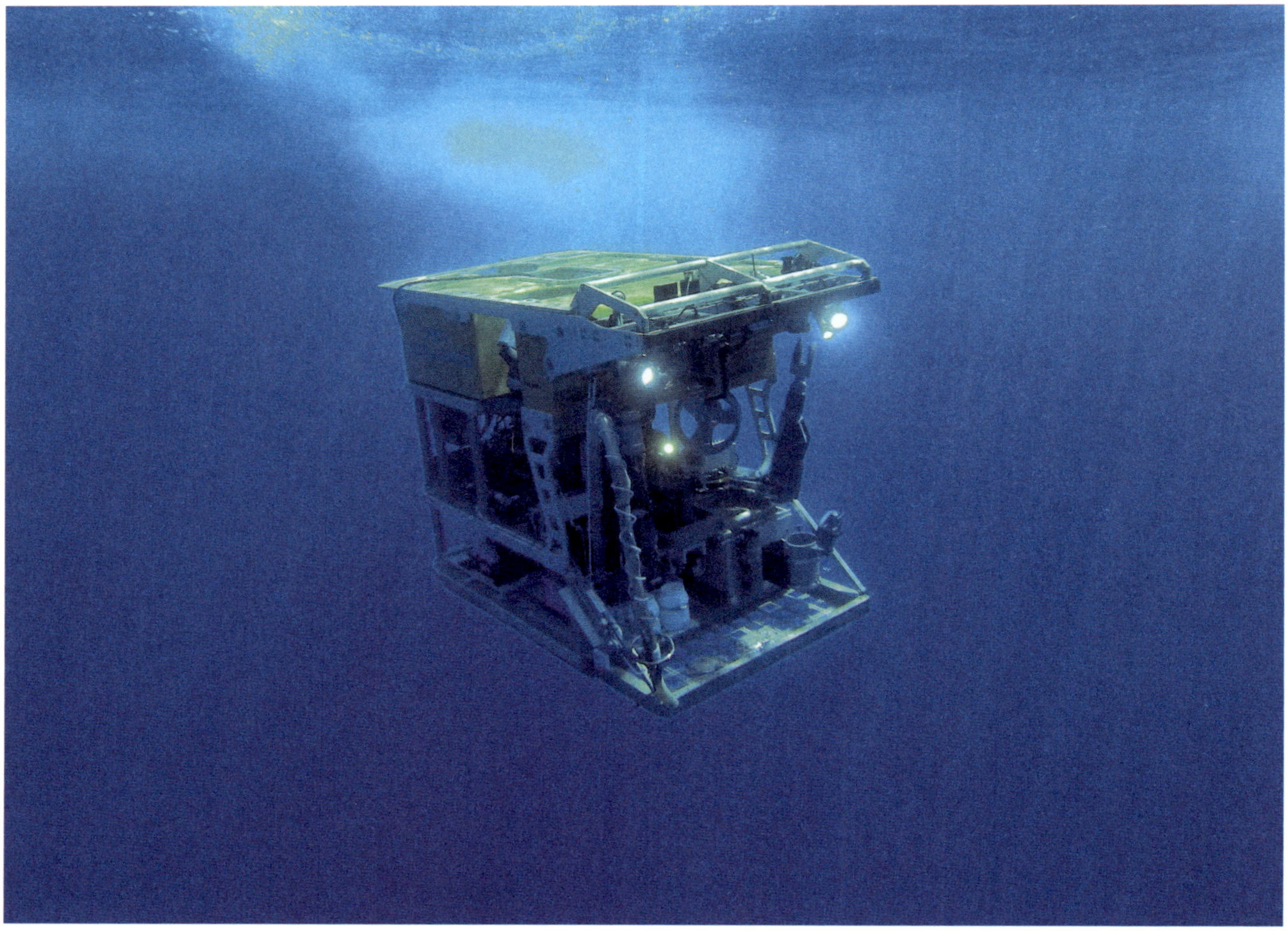

Deep-sea remote-operated vehicle ROV KIEL 6000 during the expedition of the research ship SONNE in the Indian Ocean, 13 December 2013

larly during the winter months, the deep sea absorbs vast quantities of oxygen because the gas is able to dissolve better in cold water. From measurements taken in the Atlantic, scientists know that deep currents distribute this "inhaled" oxygen throughout the ocean in a relatively short time. Observations of pollutant distribution in the deep sea – including radioactive tritium,[9] which was released in the atmospheric nuclear weapons tests of the 1950s and early 1960s, as well as artificially produced chlorofluorocarbons – show that ocean currents cover the 9,600 kilometres from the Labrador Sea to the equator in just twenty-three years. Very old deep water is known to oceanographers only from the Pacific – and even there it is just 1,600 years old. Deep currents are highly dynamic systems, for which we should be thankful: without the continual supply of oxygen from the surface, the deep sea would choke on toxic hydrogen sulphide. As in the early phase of the earth's history, it would be dominated by bacteria, which would be able to build reefs unimpeded, not consumed by any other organism.

Not only do ocean currents influence our climate, as the Gulf Stream clearly shows in Europe. They also form the basis of life in the largest ecosystem in the world: the deep sea. The intensive study of this ecosystem was first made possible by further advances in technology. Today, important insights into the alien world beneath the waves come from submarines, camera sleds, sea-floor drilling equipment, remotely operated vehicles (ROVs) and autonomous underwater vehicles (AUVs) – equipment that can be deployed at depths of thousands of metres. It was not proven that life exists in the deep sea until the nineteenth century, and the animals that live there are often quite bizarre. Viperfish are a good example: their teeth are too long to fit into their mouths, giving them the appearance of living steel-jaw traps. The purpose of their martial-looking jaws is not to miss a meal. Viperfish live at depths of 400 to 1,800 metres, in a world characterised not only by high pressure, cold temperatures and darkness, but also by scarcity. After all, (nearly) all life in the deep sea depends on the production of biomass near the water's surface. At this level, it runs at full throttle and provides food for a variety of organisms, ranging from microalgae to fast, muscular predators such as tuna. Only what dies or is excreted sinks to the dark world beyond the sunlight and becomes food for other creatures. Organisms that live in the deep sea must be able to survive on little food and seize every opportunity to eat – unless they belong to the denizens of the deep that set out each night to catch food near the water's surface, in the shelter of darkness. Every day at sunset, myriad shrimp, tiny crabs, jellyfish and fish begin their daily migration. They include the lantern fish, which measures between 2.5 and 7 centimetres and each night swims more than 500 metres to the surface and then back again.

But there are other ways to survive in the deep, as an unexpected discovery by the American research vessel Knarr demonstrated in February 1977. The ship was towing a sensor-equipped camera sled through the water off the Galápagos Islands, a dive that yielded three thousand colour images. Most showed bare rock, while others captured shredded-looking formations in a seascape of narrow canyons and towering walls. There were also images of fresh-looking lava – and, finally, thirteen photos of hundreds of white and countless brown shells. Black smokers had been discovered, the hot volcanic vents on the ocean floor with the now famous black "chimneys" and bizarre fauna. This was the first time ever that an ecosystem had come to light that ran on geochemical energy from the earth's interior and was not dependent on the sun. A dogma had fallen by the wayside.

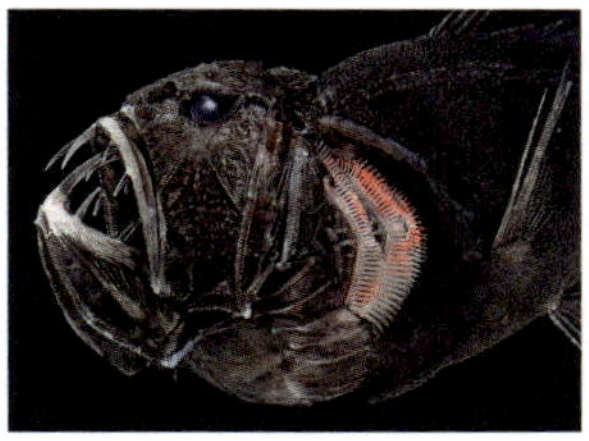

Wet specimen, *Anoplogaster cornuta* (common fangtooth), 2015

Researchers are currently studying not only the unusual ecosystem of the black smokers, including the colonies of giant tube worms that look like plastic hoses and have fiery red plumes on their heads, but also the metals they contain. These metals were dissolved out of rock by volcanically heated water and afterwards solidified upon contact with the ice-cold water in the deep sea. The ore deposits can have such a high metal content that some of the extinct systems are mineable. For this reason, the deep sea is once again being studied as a potential source of raw materials – as in the 1960s, when attention was focused on the manganese nodules in the Pacific. Now it is the metal requirements of the high-tech industry that are driving the search for deposits. In addition to black smokers, these manganese nodules – ore-rich concretions that form in the deep-sea mud of the Pacific – are once again capturing the attention of prospectors. However, there is also an interest in the manganese crusts of deep-sea mountains – underwater volcanoes, extinct for millions of years, that have become coated with valuable metals from the seawater.

The scientists on board the Meteor would probably have rubbed their eyes in wonder at such deposits in the sea. After all, one of the arguments used to drum up support for the expedition was that sufficient amounts of gold could be retrieved from the sea to ease the burden of Germany's reparation payments. Fritz Haber had supported this venture, which seems utopian from a modern perspective, and in 1920 secretly established "Working Group M" at his institute (where "M" stands for "marine gold"). Although the idea proved uneconomical in 1923, the project continued until 1927.[10] As a result, the chemistry lab on board the METEOR measured not only phosphorus, nitrogen and carbon dioxide concentrations in sea water, but also precious metal content.[11] All of these efforts were in vain, at least with respect to gold.

At this time no one could have known that a large number of metals, including gold and silver, had accumulated in the manganese nodules, manganese crusts, and colonies of black smokers. Today, in the twenty-first century, there is once again a keen interest in exploiting these resources. However, because of all the experiences with land mining, which is often destructive, top priority has been given to protecting the deep sea from the start. Researchers are thus examining the question of whether – and how – such deep-sea resources can be extracted in an environmentally friendly way. After all, human beings are already pushing the oceans to their limits. They have profoundly changed the entire system through overfishing, overfertilisation and climate change. They have caused the oceans to acidify through the carbon dioxide emitted into the air and are responsible for the growth of low-oxygen zones in the sea, which are also a product of warming and overfertilisation.

In view of the various threats to the seas, the next phase in the development of oceanographic research will be particularly important. After all, technological advances in the form of miniaturised electronics have once again made a new chapter possible: deep-sea observatories. These sensor- and camera-equipped stations are ending the researchers' dependence on ships that can only provide snapshots in time. They have set the stage for constant measurements that document change over the course of time and thus deepen our understanding of underlying processes.

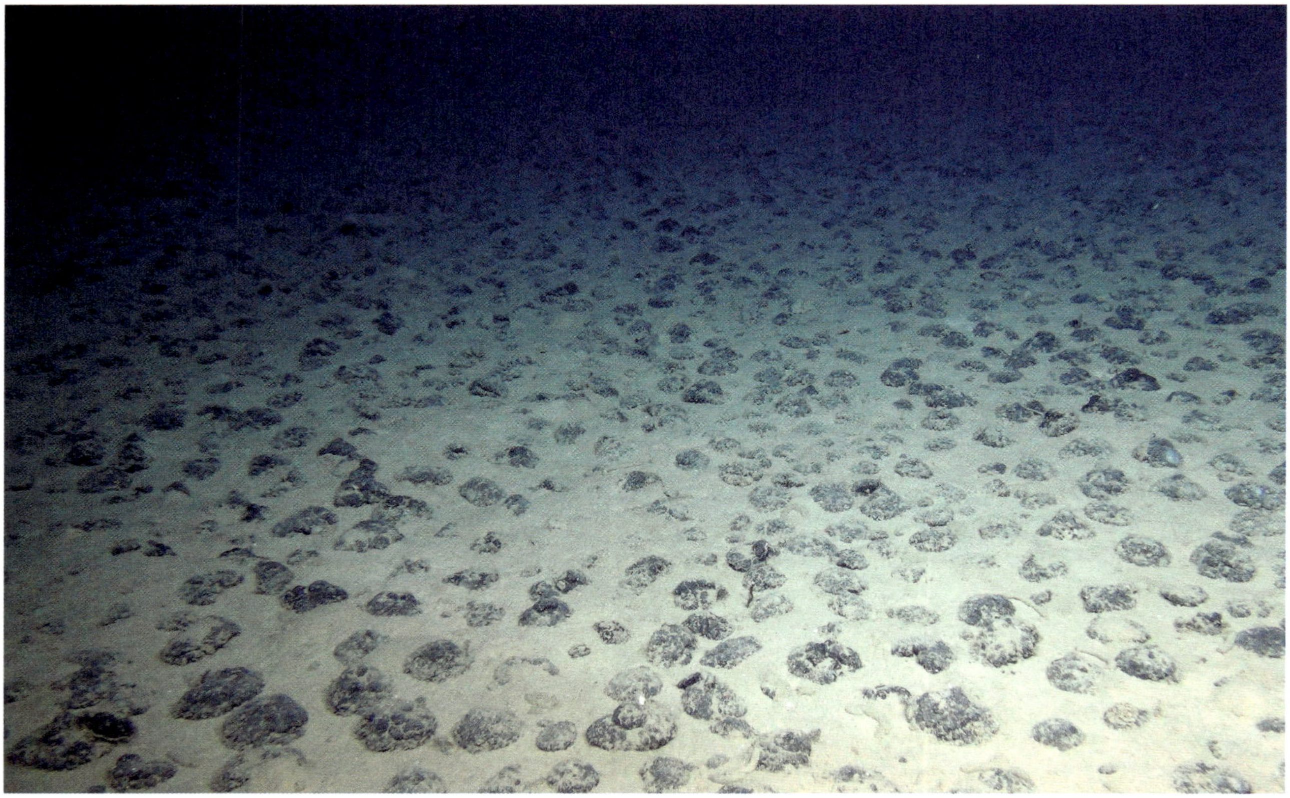

Field of manganese nodules in the Pacific, 2015

One of these new stations is the *Hausgarten* Observatory between Greenland and Svalbard in the Fram Strait, operated by the Alfred Wegener Institute, Helmholtz Centre for Polar and Marine Research. With the help of two automatic camera systems, scientists there have discovered, for example, that pollution from plastic bags, pieces of glass and fishing nets has increased more than twenty fold over a ten-year period in this remote area of the deep sea.

Plastics have been produced since the 1940s. They live on for a long time in the sea – and year for year, due to our consumption habits, an additional eight million tonnes enter the oceans.[12] From the equator to the poles, plastic bobs up and down just about everywhere, sometimes in large pieces, sometimes in the form of fine microplastic particles. As studies have shown, plastic garbage kills tortoises, which mistake plastic bags for jellyfish, and microplastic is even a burden for watt worms, which ingest the tiny plastic particles after these particles have absorbed pollutants like sponges. In this way, our garbage enters the food chain and at some point ends up on our plates.

1 Reinhard Hoheisel-Huxmann, *Die Deutsche Atlantische Expedition 1925–1927: Planung und Verlauf* (Hamburg, 2007), 7.
2 Fritz Spieß, *Die "Meteor"-Fahrt: Forschungen und Erlebnisse der Deutschen Atlantischen Expedition 1925–1927* (Berlin, 1928), 2.
3 Mary Sears and Daniel Merriman, *Oceanography: The Past* (New York, 1980), 189.
4 Hoheisel-Huxmann, 2007, 23.
5 Jan Erik Arndt et al., *The International Bathymetric Chart of the Southern Ocean (IBSCO) Version 1.0 – A New Bathymetric Compilation Covering Circum-Antarctic Waters*, 2013, Geophysical Research Letters, vol. 40, issue 12, 3111–3117, doi: 10.1002/grl.50413.
6 Hans Maurer, "Die Echolotungen der 'Meteor'", in Albert Defant (ed.), *Wissenschaftliche Ergebnisse der Deutschen Atlantischen Expedition auf dem Forschungs- und Vermessungsschiff "Meteor" 1925–1927*, vol. 2 (Berlin and Leipzig, 1933), 23ff.
7 Hoheisel-Huxmann, 2007, 106.
8 The Coriolis effect, named after the French scientist Gaspard Gustave de Coriolis (1792–1843), is a pseudo-force that is caused by the earth's rotation and that deflects bodies perpendicular to the direction of both their movement and the earth's rotation.
9 Tritium is a natural hydrogen isotope whose nucleus consists of one proton and two neutrons. It is also called "super heavy" hydrogen.
10 Thomas Steinhauser et al., *Hundert Jahre an der Schnittstelle von Chemie und Physik: Das Fritz-Haber-Institut der Max-Planck-Gesellschaft zwischen 1911 und 2011* (Berlin, 2011), 68ff.
11 Hoheisel-Huxmann, 2007, 67.
12 http://cleanseas.org (accessed on 15 december 2017

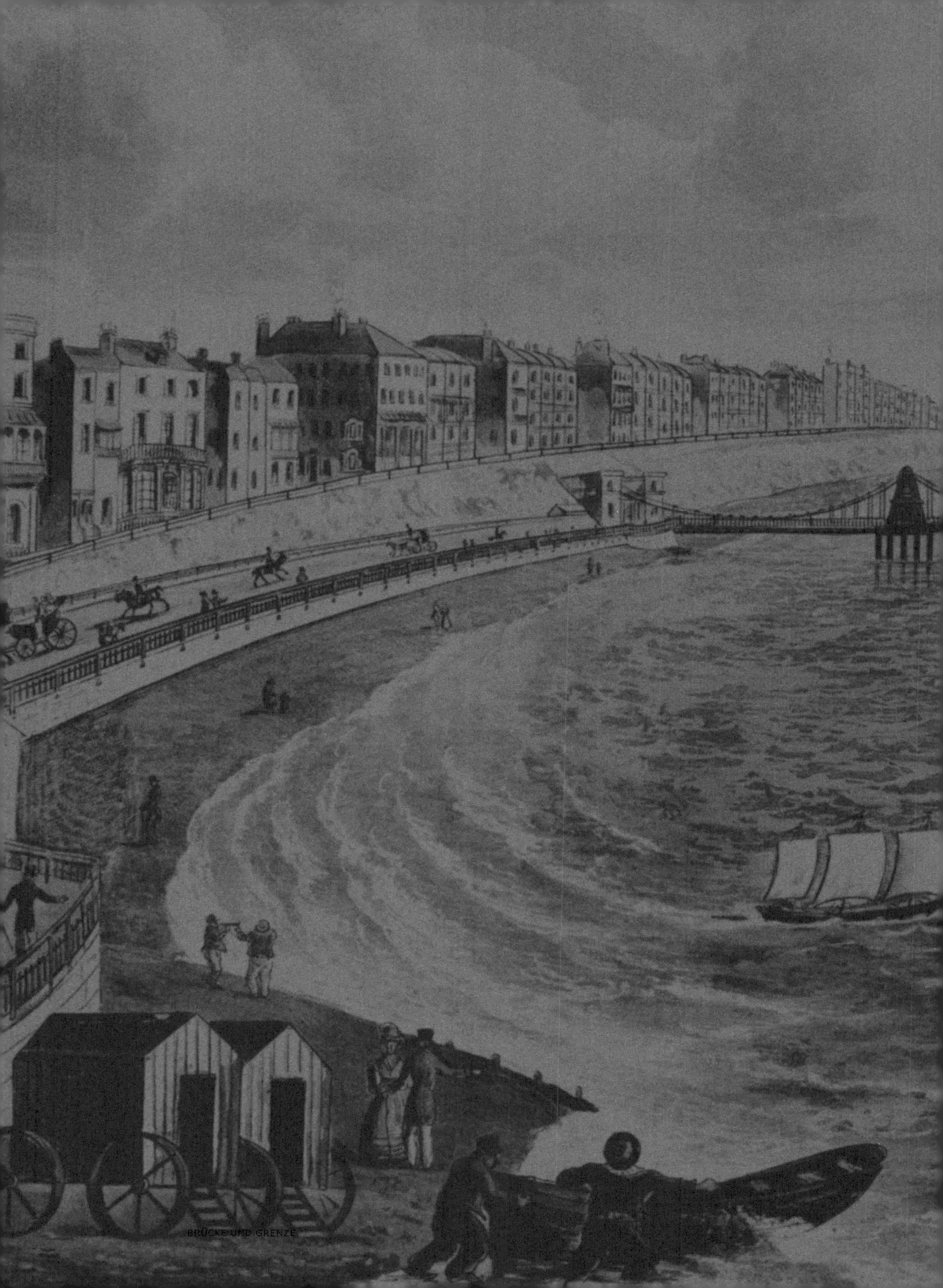

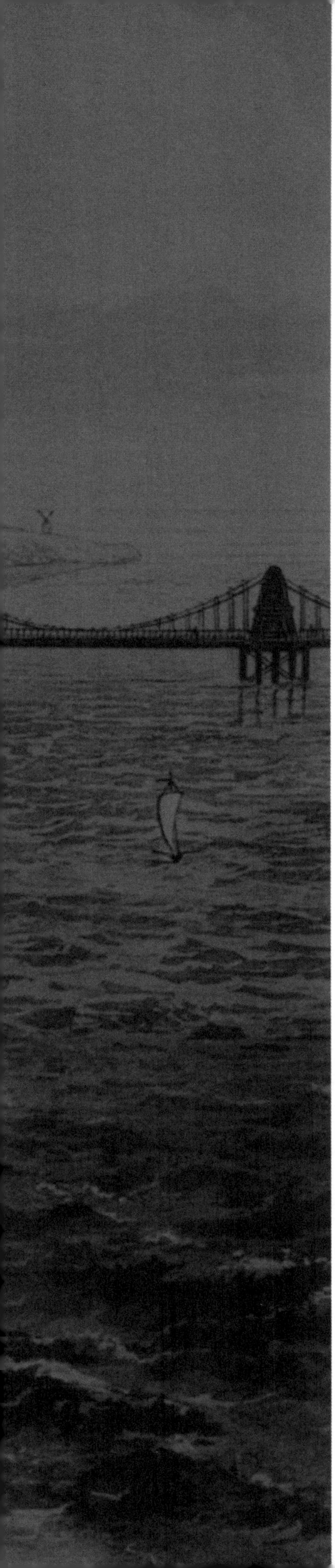

IV
FOCUS OF IMAGINATION AND YEARNING

Rüdiger Hachtmann

BEACH LIFE AND SEASIDE RESORTS, COASTAL TOURISM AND CRUISE SHIPS

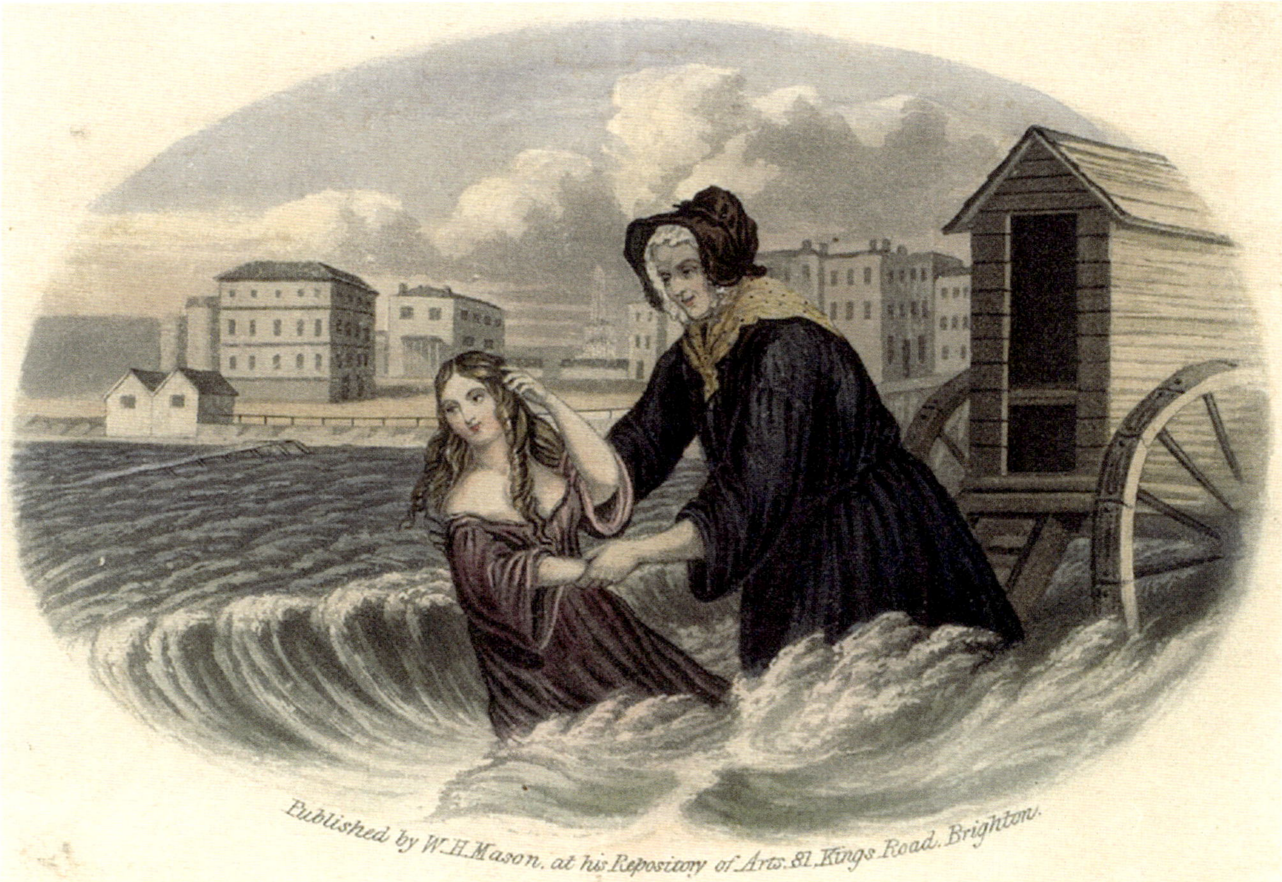

The coasts of the European seas, namely the Mediterranean coastlines, have attracted "holiday-makers" for millennia. The cool, fresh and pleasant winds made the shorelines attractive for proto-tourism in antiquity, a "tourism predating (modern) tourism". One need think only of the chains of villages that stretched from the coast of Ostia before the gates of Rome to the Gulf of Naples, opulent buildings in which wealthy Romans spent the summer to escape the hot and humid metropolis.

In the Middle Ages and the Early Modern period, however, mankind viewed the sea primarily as a threat. The sea inspired fear as an elemental power that could wash away entire coastlines. Dangers in human form were also a source of anxiety, not least among them pirates, who were later romanticised and mythologised in such figures as Klaus Störtebeker.

The sea and the shore therefore only developed into holiday regions much later, namely around the mid-eighteenth century.[1] At this time, the modern state had largely done away with pirates and thereby secured travel routes, including on the seas, and had begun to tame the sea with dike construction and to develop warning systems, for example with the drastically improved illumination power of lighthouses and weather balloons since the late eighteenth century.

Much like Alpine tourism, the seaside resorts that arose in the mid-eighteenth century on the eastern coast of Britain were an "invention" of the British. On the European continent, however, seaside resorts only came into being as the eighteenth century gave way to the nineteenth. They rapidly became sites of sophisticated sociability and secular pleasures, with spas, casinos, libraries and theatres.

People "enjoyed" the sea with ample caution, for external "application", with healing powers being attributed to seawater. Only gradually did a vibrant life develop on shore. Early on, visitors to seaside resorts changed their clothes in bathing machines, structures meant to provide privacy as one changed into swimwear, shielded from curious glances, and then they would take a few steps into the water. Sandcastles came into fashion on German beaches in the last two decades of the nineteenth century. The sea and the shore, however, had become sites of projection or the occasion for inspiring allegories long ago, and thereby a beloved landscape subject for painting. One example of this artistic trend is Caspar David Friedrich (1774–1840), particularly his Greifswald works or his *The Monk by the Sea*.

I.

Maritime tourism cannot be reduced to seaside holidays. In addition to seaside resorts and tourism in landscapes close to the ocean, there was also tourism in coastal cities, which had a longer history. Venice for example was already a centre of pilgrimage tourism in the early modern period, as a stopover on the way to Jerusalem. Yet Venice had its own power, its unique buildings exerting a powerful fascination even long ago; the city provides an exemplary instance of how coastal tourism could also be a journey of education, not just a beach holiday. Today, Venice

12/3
Alfred Crowquill/Charles J. Basebi, illustration of a dipper at work in Brighton, 1848

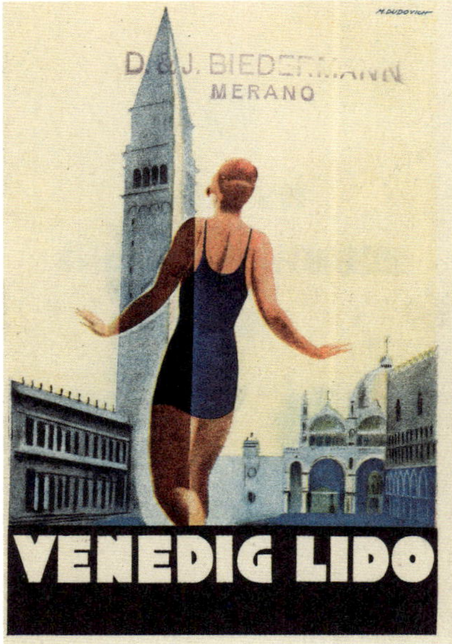

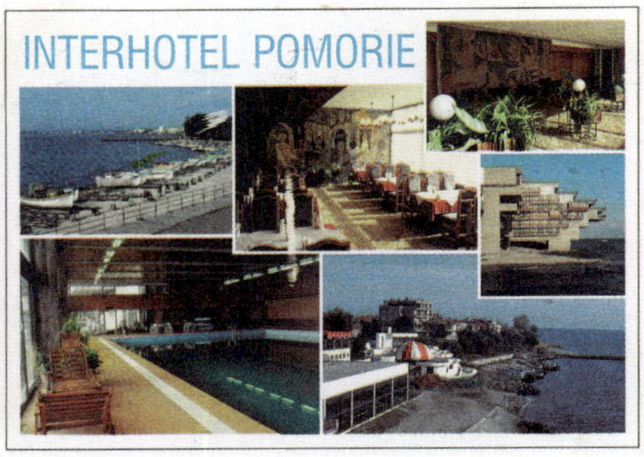

Marcello Dudovic, German-language guidebook to Venice, c. 1936

Picture postcard of the Interhotel Pomorie in Bulgaria, 1996

also stands for the problematic dimension of environmental concerns always associated with cruise ships and seaside tourism: idyllic canals, ancient palaces – and then, in the background, a ten-story-tall floating skyscraper glides into the background, reminding viewers of the massive environmental pollution caused by cruise ship tourism. The waves in the wake of these massive ships, as well as their exhaust gases, endanger the very thing that visitors have come to admire.

The railways and the steamship played a decisive role in early tourism. Both functioned as engines of the Industrial Revolution and as central elements of an infrastructural leap towards modern tourism. The steamship gave rise to a specific variant of tourism that has constantly gained significance ever since: cruises. In the German context, the Norwegian cruises of Wilhelm II popularised this form of travel. The last German emperor's northern tours, the cruises offered later by the Nazi "Strength Through Joy" organization, and the boom in cruises in Europe's northern reaches that continue to this day illustrate in an impressive way that the subject of "Europe and the sea" goes beyond the Mediterranean; in geographic terms at least, the North Sea and especially the Baltic are "more European" than the Mediterranean. The Black Sea, often overlooked as a holiday region by historians of tourism, also deserves mention in any discussion of European tourism; one need only think of the beaches of Bulgaria, which became a "Riviera" for East German tourists in the 1960s, or the Crimea, which under the Soviet Union counted ten million seasonal guests each year, or Odessa.

Cruises can also be associated in different ways with another variant of tourism, namely catastrophe tourism. This is the circumnavigation of active volcanoes, of course at a safe distance, or visits to the Costa Concordia, which ran aground on the Italian coast in 2012 and has since drawn masses of voyeuristic tourists. This accident, the sinking of the Titanic, or the tsunami of 2004 that killed more than 8,000 people in the coastal regions of Thailand alone, one-third of them tourists, makes it clear that holidays at sea, let alone on the shore, are in no way without risk.

12/45
Advertising poster for Nordic voyages, 1928

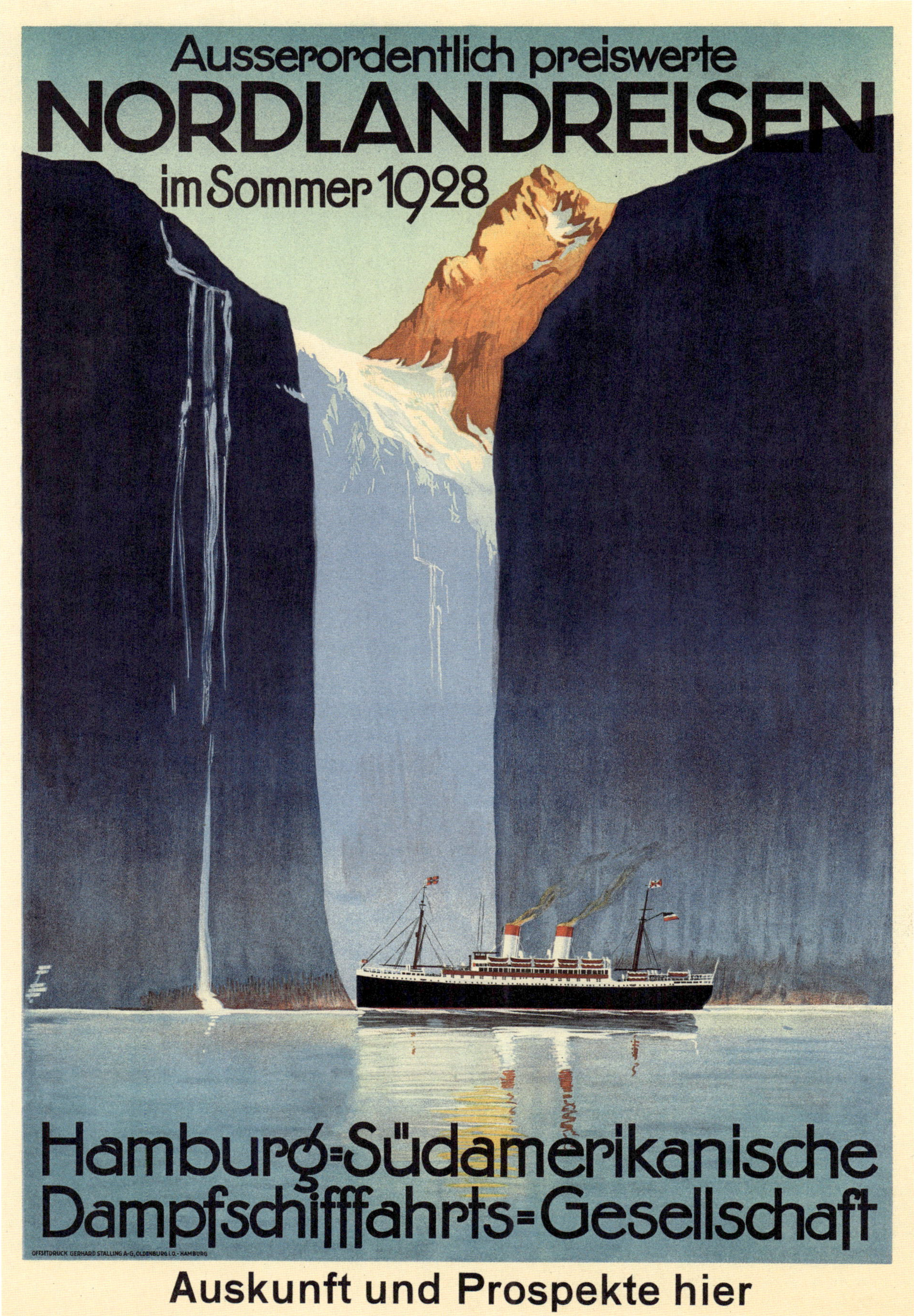
Ausserordentlich preiswerte
NORDLANDREISEN
im Sommer 1928
Hamburg-Südamerikanische
Dampfschifffahrts-Gesellschaft
OFFSETDRUCK GERHARD STALLING A-G, OLDENBURG I.O. - HAMBURG
Auskunft und Prospekte hier
P 57/1073

II.

Cruises, seaside resorts and cultural tourism in coastal cities were not designed in an egalitarian way. Even today, tourism can retain a striking element of social demarcation, yet it still testifies to the futility of social distinctions. We find evidence of this phenomenon in the nobility's disparagement of bourgeois tourists; a few decades later, the educated classes expressed irritation about the ostensibly uncultured petite bourgeois who sought rest and relaxation, about Strength Through Joy in the 1930s, and later, in the 1960s, about "Neckermann tourists" and their purportedly poor manners.

The railways in particular enabled members of the German lower class to embark upon holiday. Shorter travel times and favourably priced tickets put seaside resorts within their reach. Fixed working times and regulations governing holiday time contributed to the gradual dismantling of the idea of tourism as a social privilege. The class society of the railways mirrored the *social* class system that was taking shape. Where someone sat in the train was now determined by spending power, not by class-based prerogatives.

The tension between social distinction and increasing openness to a bourgeois public, combined with the introduction of new forms of transportation, led to the Europeanisation of tourism. The British nobility felt that they were being driven from the seaside resorts by the British bourgeoisie. They fled to France and Italy, to the Côte d'Azur and the Italian Riviera. Nice, for example, came to resemble a British colony beginning in 1830, with its "Promenade des Anglais", hotels and stores run by British owners, and Anglican churches. The situation was similar in Cannes – with horse racing, clay pigeon shooting, golf and polo – until bourgeoisie and lower-income sections of the population followed the nobility, travelling by rail and by sea.

Social exclusivity in tourism remained, and remains, temporary. Nevertheless, social, generational and gender differences continue to be upheld. These markers, however, were expressed in the manner in which people travelled.

III.

It is important to note that we are speaking here about the "equalisation", not the "democratisation", of travel. It would be a mistake to read the history of modern tourism as a linear, positive history of progress. The dark side of tourism cannot be denied. There was, for example, the anti-Semitism that took root at the seaside resorts before 1933, broadly before the twentieth century, and not just on the island of Borkum, where both residents and holiday-makers were infamous for their hostility to Jews.[2] The mass tourism organised by the Nazi Strength Through Joy organisation beginning in 1933/34 explicitly excluded German Jews. This kind of tourism was, on one hand, an integrative strategy; it was meant to make it easier for the German working class to forget the dissolution of their trade unions in May 1933, as well as the rigorous abolition of their collective and individual rights. On the other hand, the Strength Through Joy ships and their cruises to the Baltic Sea, the North Sea and the Mediterranean were a way for the Nazi regime to present a positive image to an international audience.

At the same time, the Strength Through Joy organisation became a symbol of modernity. The launching of the Strength Through Joy ships Wilhelm Gustloff and Robert Ley in 1937 and 1938, as well as six other chartered steamships, was just the beginning. Robert Ley, the head of the German Labour Front and thereby also

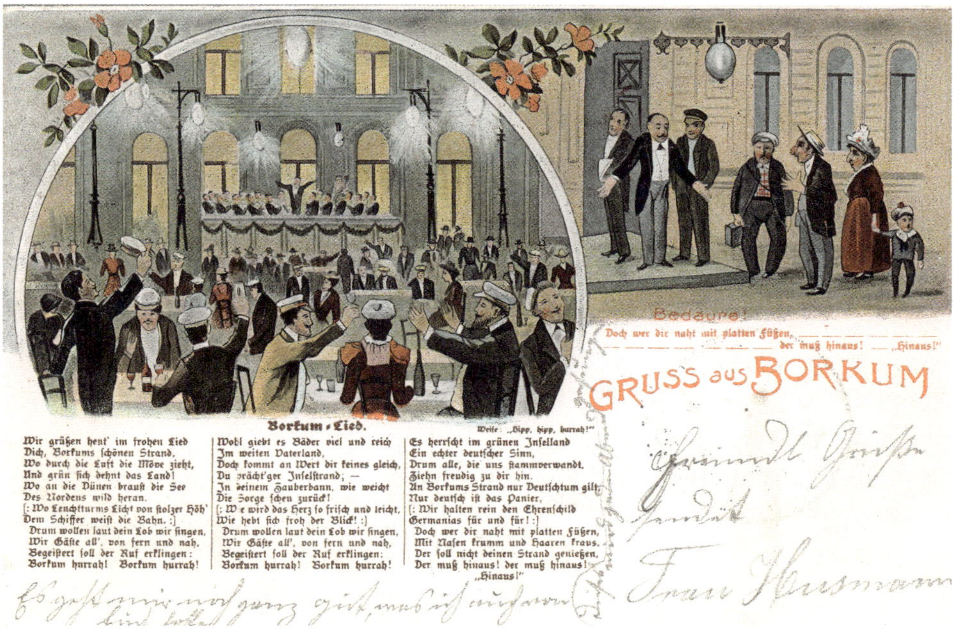

12/21
Anti-Semitic picture postcard, "Greetings from Borkum", 1905

the Strength Through Joy programme, planned the mass production of passenger liners in Germany's shipyards.[3] The megalomaniacal Prora project, a "seaside resort for twenty-thousand people" on the island of Rügen, was further evidence of these ambitions. Prora became the precursor of the gigantic hotels that arose in greater numbers on Europe's shores after 1945. In Prora, Strength Through Joy holiday-makers would join a flowing mass of thousands of people who were channelled through the facility's own train station into rooms throughout the eight-kilometre-long building complex and were fed in enormous dining halls. Then they were supposed to relax on Rügen's most beautiful beach, arrayed like sardines in a tin can.[4]

Strength Through Joy tourists were not supposed to "get any ideas" – Robert Ley feared this – or to discuss political ideas and call for democracy. This is why the Strength Through Joy Sports Office assigned hosts who offered sports and gymnas-

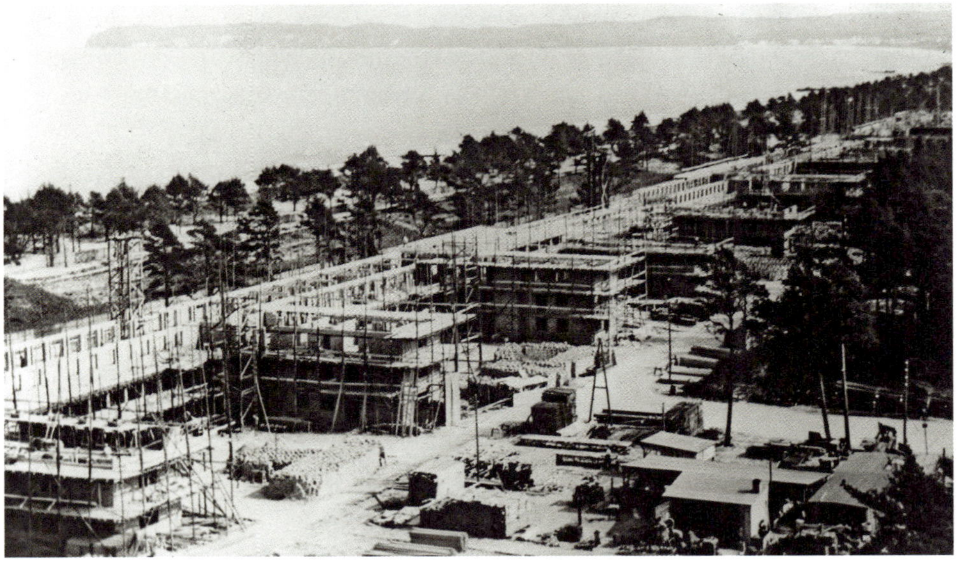

12/53
Construction work on the KdF seaside resort of Prora on Rügen, 1938

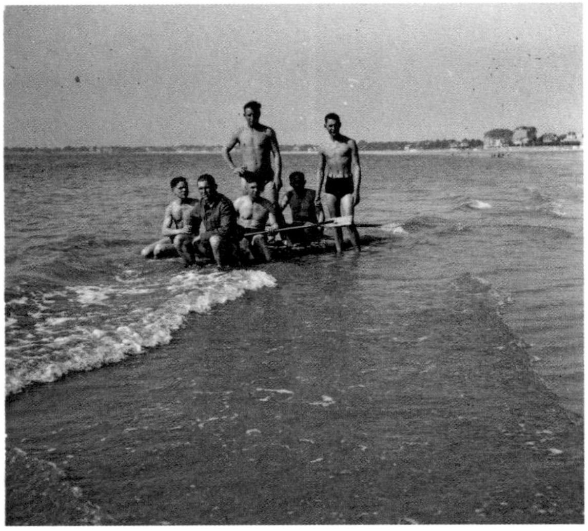

German troops on the Atlantic coast of France, 1941

tics courses at the programme's seaside resorts.[5] This started happening in 1935/36, close to the same time as similar developments on the British Isles, where in 1936 the first *Butlin's Holiday Camp* opened. Tourists looking for diversions and relaxation encountered holiday entertainers who sought to maintain a good mood by offering athletic courses, as well as beauty competitions, competitive eating of chips, and other attractions.

Above all, however, Prora and the Strength Through Joy ships were the promise of a Fordist mass consumer society, organised along racial lines. These enticements were only supposed to be enjoyed by members of the "Aryan master race". The prerequisites for mass tourism after 1945, now without explicit racial connotations, had been set down prior to 1939.

If the population of both German states after 1945 soon reclaimed the mantel of "world champion travellers", this was indirectly due to the crypto-tourism of the Second World War. For countless soldiers, war meant long years of relaxed boredom behind the frontlines or in non-combat zones. It was no accident that, leading up to 1943, Baedeker and other publishing houses brought out travel guides for metropolises such as Paris as well as for beautiful sections of the European coastline. It is often difficult to tell the difference between occasional photos taken by tourists and the snapshots found in the photo albums of Wehrmacht soldiers far away from the front. German soldiers had had a taste of the "great wide world" and didn't want to miss out after 1945.

The contradictions of modern tourism became particularly palpable during the Nazi period, but they were not limited to the period between 1933 and 1945. Post-war tourism also had strange affinities with authoritarian regimes. One example was the stream of German tourists to Spain, organised by Neckermann, which helped provide economic stability to the Franco regime into the 1970s. There was also the boom in Greek tourism, which was not interrupted by the Regime of the Colonels (1967–1974). So dictatorships are not necessarily a form of governance that frighten tourists away. It is uncertainty that causes tourists to avoid certain countries, for example if they have reason to fear for their own lives or if they have to confront the unpredictable caprices of authoritarian rulers. Turkey provides a contemporary example, with mass tourism tending to avoid a very beautiful country due to the Erdoğan regime.

IV.

The example of Turkey also demonstrates that the definition of Europe is not just a geographical question; it also has its political and economic features, and thereby historical conditions. This is not new. Well into the Early Modern period, Europe was described predominantly as the "Christian Occident", although the myth of Europa – the kidnapping of the daughter of the Phoenician King Agenor by Zeus, who transformed himself into a bull – comes from a pre-Christian pagan age and can be traced to modern-day Lebanon.

It is certainly debatable how "European" the Mediterranean was and is, with its long coastlines in North Africa and Asia Minor as well as its ancient "prehistory", the remains of which still can be marvelled at today on the coasts of the *Mare Nostrum*. In terms of tourism, we can only classify it as "European" since the 1990s, at the latest. And yet this tourism extends far beyond the narrowly drawn geographical borders of Europe, including the tourism infrastructure found in Turkey, Israel, Egypt, Tunisia and Morocco. These centres of tourism scarcely differ from the holiday residences in southern Spain, yet the countries south of the Sahara are a very different story. But perhaps this is too exaggerated a description. It may be that what we experience as the "European" development of (maritime) tourism is the globalisation of a tourism informed by capitalism and commercial interests, one that will not end in Africa or other continents.

Without a doubt, tourism broadens our horizons, in the literal and figurative sense. Yet how deeply has tourism shaped our ideas about Europe? It would be an exaggeration to claim that, without tourism, there would be no idea of Europe broadly distributed throughout society. Yet pilgrimage tourism, which as we hinted earlier may also have had secular motifs, gave those involved at least a feeling for Europe, even in the demarcation vis-à-vis others, for example against Islam, which closed the route to the Holy Land. The *Grand Tour* of young nobles, which reached its apogee in the seventeenth and eighteenth century, contributed to the formation of a European consciousness; the same applied to the bourgeois journey of education. Of course, this created *European* identities while refining a sense of what was actually or ostensibly special about their own country; this was particularly strong in the bourgeoisie, who were the central bearers of the *nation*-state movement. The expansion of tourism to the lower classes did not change this ambivalence in any major way.

Tourism is therefore no panacea for anti-foreign sentiment. Before 1933, both the Germans and the British were considered the most avid travellers in the world; yet, during the Nazi period, Germans embodied xenophobia more than any other nation. This provides a clear illustration that tourism in no way provides some inevitable protection against racism and the hatred of foreigners.

The desire to travel also has contradictory consequences at another level: on the one hand, the tourist seeks to assimilate what is specific to a culture and the allure of striking landscapes. On the other hand, the tourist contributes significantly to the cultural alignment of Europe, even of all of the world's regions, because he (even as an "alternative tourist") brings along the customs of Western urban modernity; the tourism industry seeks to carve a path and establish infrastructure everywhere for the tourist. It is the needs of Western-style tourism that, according to Hasso Spode, "de-place" holiday regions and give many of the beaches around the Mediterranean the same, monotonous look.

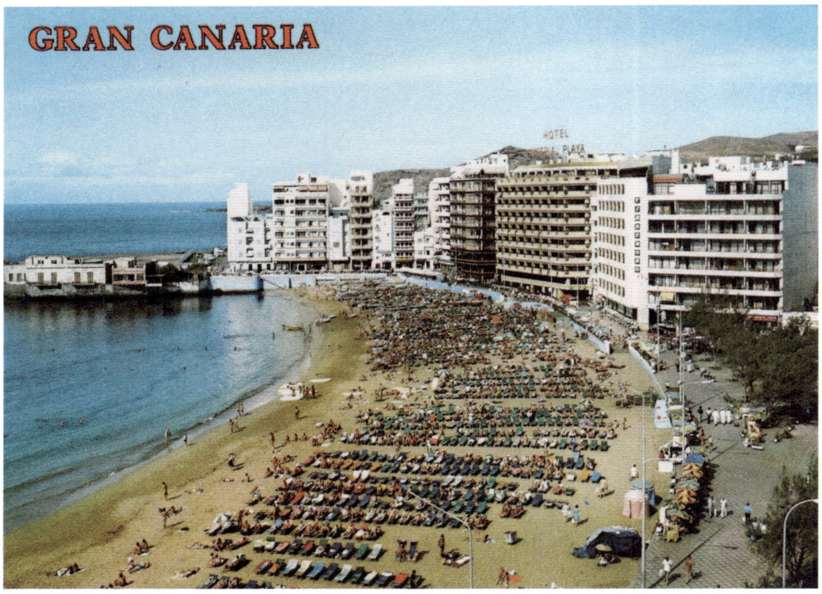

Picture postcard of Gran Canaria, c. 1975

Just as the borders between individual countries and tourism regions are becoming increasingly difficult to discern, so do the boundaries between tourism and non-tourism migration movements blur – just as when we invoke "Europe" and "the sea". All European seas were and are transit spaces; they are not a privileged space reserved only for tourists. The current refugee situation, and the often cursorily acknowledged refugee catastrophes in the Mediterranean, demonstrate that tourism in the twentieth century, and probably in the twenty-first as well, is difficult to separate clearly from such phenomena as flight from war, hardship and dictatorship. We need only recall the history of exile during the Nazi dictatorship, or how strongly GDR tourism in the west of the Rostock district was shaped by so-called border protection.[6] Even today, many of those who come to a country seeking asylum often arrive with a tourist visa in their hands.

Furthermore, European and global tourism are associated with two other phenomena of transnational migration flows – labour migration and constant relocation. Initially, the differences between labour migrants and tourists seem crystal clear: one group stays for an unlimited time abroad, the other for just a short time. One group lives in simple, often primitive living quarters, while the others enjoy comfortable, often luxurious accommodations built specifically for them. One group are often greeted by locals with open scepticism; the others are often welcomed in a fulsome, obsequious manner. The main tourism flows moved and continue to move from north to south, while labour migrants have always moved in the opposite direction, from south to north.

Nevertheless, the boundaries between tourism, labour migration and constant relocation after the end of one's working life, a kind of pensioner migration, are becoming increasingly unclear. We need only point to the many Germans and Scandinavians who change their permanent residence to the Andalusian coast or Majorca, or the numerous German citizens, not just pensioners, who have moved into charming Tuscan farms or labyrinthine Ligurian villages. An indirect, transnational form of labour migration, however, is whenever an Italian, Portuguese, Spanish, Greek or Turkish guest worker returns to his home country, where, if he has saved enough money, he opens a restaurant or small hotel on the beach. The establishment flourishes because the former guest worker speaks perfect German and knows what Germans want as tourists.

On one hand, we could say, European tourism educates the citizens of other nations on how to be European. On the other hand, tourism need not be all too wrapped up with "Europe". The extent to which the horizons of many Europeans in recent decades, above all Central Europeans, have expanded beyond the "Christian Occident" to the global can be seen in the increasingly broad array of culinary cultures that we can now enjoy in Europe. Pizza, pasta – with seafood – and souflaki started the trend; sushi, spring rolls and Thai duck followed. And today, the spectrum of ostensibly exotic dishes that are available everywhere here now, for example Nepalese or Tibetan delicacies, is nowhere near exhaustion or saturation.

Tourism in the meanwhile is pushing European boundaries, at least if we look at the destination countries. In 1971, a total of four per cent of all West German tourists travelled to holiday sites outside of Europe. In 1988, this proportion more than tripled to fourteen per cent. German tourism outside of Europe has now exceeded the twenty per cent mark.[7] As can be guessed from Germany's love of travel, Europe is only a transit station on the way to global tourism. However, this prognosis is bound up with some conditions: the worldwide political and economic constellations must remain stable and peaceful to some degree. Wars, acts of terror and tyrannies are poisonous, both for European and non-European maritime tourism.

1 Alain Corbin, *Meereslust. Das Abendland und die Entdeckung der Küste 1750-1840* (West Berlin, 1988). For an overview of the history of tourism, see Hasso Spode, *Wie die Deutschen "Reiseweltmeister" wurden* (Erfurt, 2003); Rüdiger Hachtmann, *Tourismus-Geschichte* (Göttingen, 2007); Hachtmann, *Tourismus und Tourismus-Geschichte*, in *Docupedia-Zeitgeschichte* (ed.), 22 December 2010: http://docupedia.de/zg/Tourismus und Tourismusgeschichte (accessed on 15 December 2017).

2 Frank Bajohr, *"Unser Hotel ist judenfrei". Bäder-Antisemitismus im 19. und 20. Jahrhundert* (Frankfurt, 2003).

3 Rüdiger Hachtmann, *Das Wirtschaftsimperium der Deutschen Arbeitsfront* (Göttingen, 2012), 527ff.

4 Hasso Spode, "Fordism, Mass Tourism and the Third Reich. The 'Strength through Joy' Seaside as an Index Fossil", *Journal of Social History* 38 (2004): 127–155; Hachtmann 2007, 160ff., 173ff.

5 Rüdiger Hachtmann , "'Bäuche wegmassieren' und 'überflüssiges Fett in unserem Volke beseitigen' – der kommunale Breitensport der NS-Gemeinschaft 'Kraft durch Freude'", in *Sport und Nationalsozialismus*, ed. Frank Becker and Ralf Schäfer (Göttingen, 2016), 46.

6 Christopher Görlich, *Urlaub vom Staat. Zur Geschichte des Tourismus in der DDR* (Cologne, Weimar & Vienna, 2012).

7 Sina Fabian, *Boom in der Krise. Boom, Tourismus und Individualverkehr in der Bundesrepublik Deutschland und Großbritannien (1970-1990)* (Göttingen, 2016), 160.

Ulrike Wolff-Thomsen

THE SEA

Artistic Positions since 1800

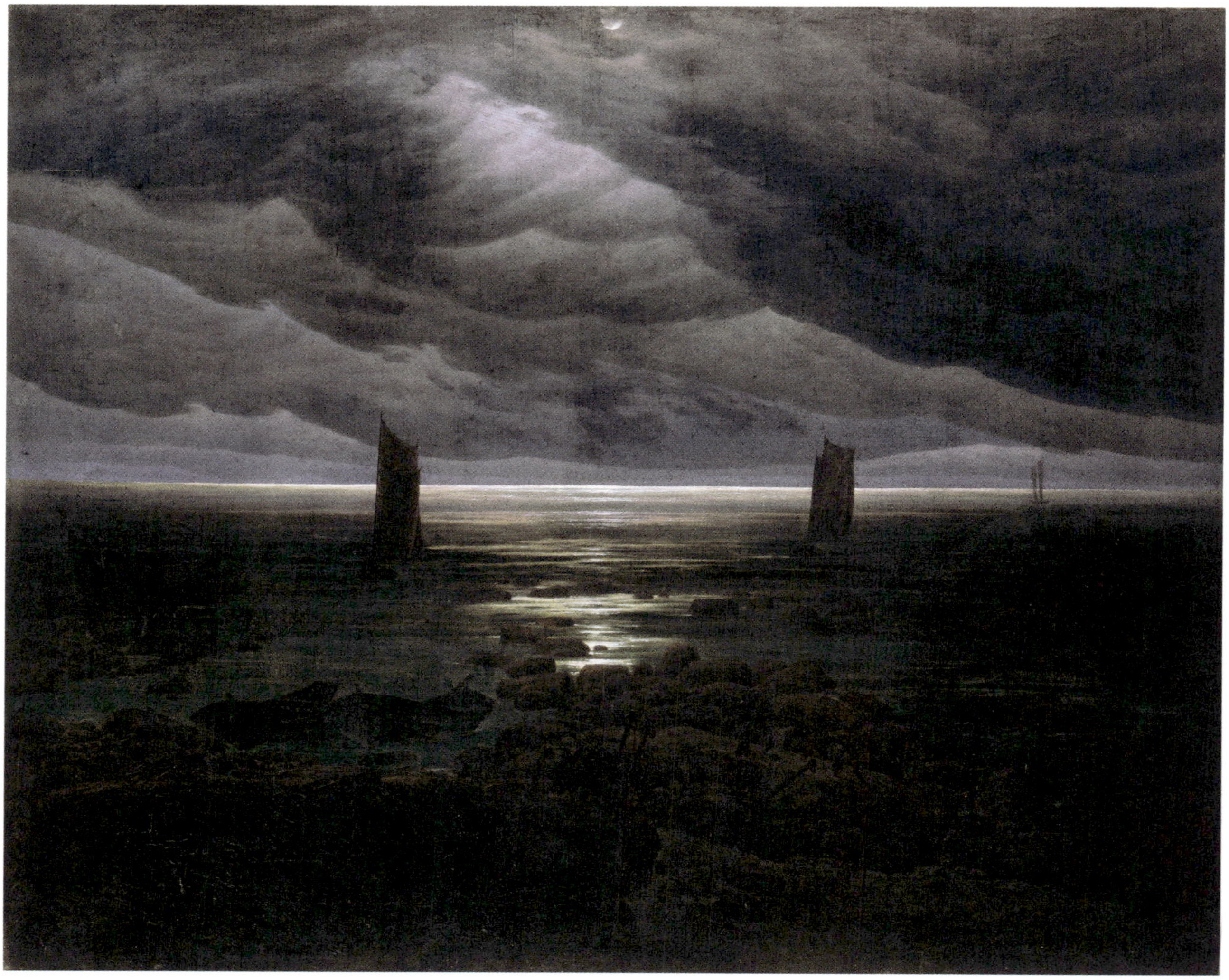

The ideas that people have had about the sea are broad and diverse. In physical terms, the sea has dimensions that, thanks to the invention of sonar and other technical achievements in the twentieth century, have been determined to have a volume of about 1,338 billion cubic metres. Yet this calculation tends to confirm received ideas about the ocean's infinite breadth and depth; such dimensions simply overwhelm our capacity for imagination. When we look at the sea, almost all of us respond emotionally and assume a stance towards it. Artists in particular have felt called upon for centuries to "capture" what they experience and observe, to engage with a subject that is inherently in eternal motion, in constant and irregular movement, that has a broad variety of colour and consistency. The sea enchants the eye with its calm, flat, mirroring surfaces that occasionally "boil" and spray, or in waves that are crowned with white foam.

In the history of European painting, landscape painting, including seascapes, was reassessed around 1800 due to the scientific advances of the eighteenth century and an attitude towards nature informed by the Enlightenment. Along with Jean Jacques Rousseau (1712–1778), who wrote about the terms "nature" and "natural" in a way that bestowed an emotionally emphatic colouring, the Irish-British writer and philosopher Edmund Burke (1729–1797) played a major role in this development.[1] In his *Philosophical Inquiry into the Origin of our Ideas of the Sublime and the Beautiful*, he described the ocean as an "object of no small terror", a place that touches the soul and exercises an overwhelming effect on the observer.[2] This sensibility led towards the rediscovery of regions that stood for wildness and primitiveness.

The valorisation of landscape as a subject, which had long languished at the academies of art as the lowest form of art, found obvious expression in the offer of a reward by the trendsetting Parisian Academy in its Prix de Rome, awarded for the first time in 1817. In the age of Romanticism, various artistic interpretations increasingly began to take form. Caspar David Friedrich (1774–1840), who was the first German artist to discover the maritime landscape as a subject, viewed the sea as a metaphor for life, as a mirror of the individual confrontation with being itself and as a symbol of a metaphysical world order that encompassed man and nature, thereby leading to Friedrich's expression of a visionary experience of landscape. The Norwegian artist Johan Christian Dahl (1788–1857), however, pursued compositions that were more firmly anchored in worldly reality.[3] Dahl, during his time from 1811 to 1818 at the Copenhagen Academy, engaged in an intensive study of the Dutch Baroque painter Allaert van Everdingen (1621–1675), whose paintings were held in Copenhagen collections. Everdingen's works mirrored motifs from his Norwegian travels. Moving from this work, Dahl arrived at a new conception of nature; in particular, he assigned artistic dignity to "wild nature". It seems curious that Dahl, who had been away from his homeland for decades and lived in Dresden, together in a household with Friedrich, would go on to shape the imagination of "Norway" like no other in landscape painting and become the "father" of modern Norwegian landscape painting. He was the first Norwegian painter to attain international fame, and did so with motifs from his homeland.

Caspar David Friedrich,
Sea Shore in Moonlight, 1836

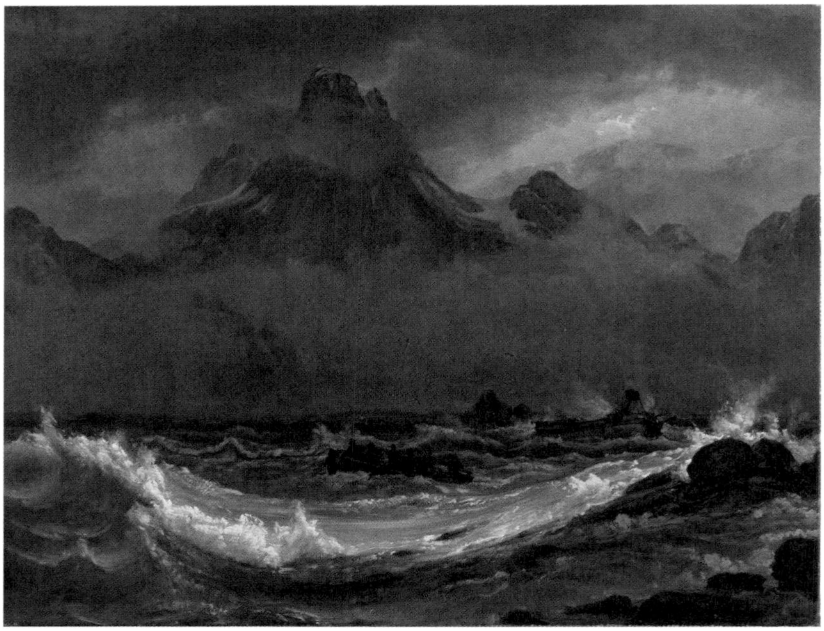

Johan Christian Dahl, *Shipwreck on the Coast of Finnmark*, 1847

The 1847 painting, *Schiffswrack an der Küste Finnmarks* (*Shipwreck on the Coast of Finnmark*) is exemplary in this regard. During his Norwegian travels in 1826, 1834, 1844 and 1850, Dahl may have studied the landscape, but he did not journey to Finnmark in the extreme north of Norway. He wrote to a friend and colleague that he had been inspired by an unspecified oil sketch by his fellow Norwegian and student of the Dresden School, Peder Balke (1804–1887), who undertook a journey to the northern reaches, including the Finnmark region.[4] Dahl's painting depicts the dramatic situation of a ship that has run aground on the craggy, rocky reef of a fjord. The observer, whose location cannot be determined, assumes the role of a direct observer. Against the towering, imposing backdrop of mountains shrouded in deep tendrils of fog, a small boat in which several people have managed to rescue themselves becomes visible in the seething sea. It is almost impossible to tell whether the danger is past because the powerful storm darkens the entire natural space. The North Sea at the edge of this nearly uninhabited, inhospitable region is too agitated, and the coast too rough, to assume that the men in the small lifeboat will survive. Nevertheless, Dahl eschews heroic pathos and symbolic attributions that still shaped maritime landscape paintings from previous centuries. Consequently, he visualises, from his atelier in Dresden, a landscape oriented toward reality, one that he can only have perceived through the imaginative lens of Balke's work.

The fathoming of the relationship between man and nature was a major theme of the age and is represented here in exemplary fashion by a shipwreck with an unresolved conclusion. This painting exerted great fascination on art audiences of the time as a symbol of the powerlessness and subjection of man before the unpredictable natural violence of the "sea". It was only over the course of the age of industrialisation, and after the invention and development of the steamship and the use of iron and steel in ship construction, that people began to feel safer from the kinds of disasters portrayed by Dahl – although this contradicted reality. The discrepancy between hubris, longing for primitiveness and recognition of the uncontrollability of the forces of nature became increasingly palpable for bourgeois society in the nineteenth century.

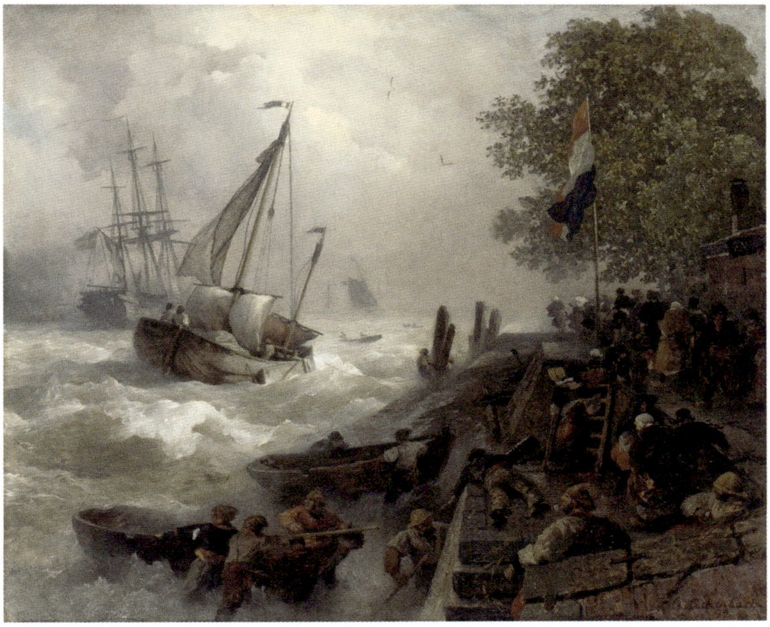

Andreas Achenbach, *Returning to port in rough seas*, 1893

Andreas Achenbach (1815–1910), a significant representative of the Düsseldorf School of painting who was regarded by contemporaries as the "master over land and sea", exhibited a different nuance in his images.[5] Shifting the scene from the open ocean to the coast, in this case a pier in a Dutch port, occasions a shift in emphasis. In the painting *Rückkehr in den Hafen bei rauer See* (*Returning to port in rough seas*) – which is illustrative of a number of similar works created since the 1850s – the relationship between man and nature is plumbed anew. A diagonal line divides two areas, one with the sky and the churning sea, the other with a fixed coastline. This creates an impression that the struggle against the vicissitudes of the sea might be mastered. Even if the sea is turbulent and the ships' crews – including a three-master already in the roads and a flat bottom boat, a *Bomschuit*, with its sails taken down – have not landed, the people on water and on land seem to have everything "in hand". Nothing seems loud or excited. The men in the foreground pull the small boats on land in a systematic fashion, with great exertion of strength; many people, among them women in traditional dress, watch from the quay, their bodies tense as they watch what is happening on the sea. The viewer is given the signal, so to speak, that there will be no losses and that the Dutch – a flag on the quay was not taken down, despite the wind – with their centuries of experience with such situations, can defy the dangers and live in harmony with the forces of nature. Achenbach's staging is masterful. The light and dark shadings, the elaboration of atmospheric qualities, the nuanced tones of colour and the warm colouration call forth a harmonious tone that conveys a calming, positive mood to the viewer, despite the composition's dynamism.

The painters of the artists' colony of Skagen in North Jutland held another notion of the "sea". Their focus was seldom directed directly at the element itself. The word "Skagen" conjured up a vision of a special atmosphere called forth by the convergence of sunlight, salty air, the sea and a beach of light dunes and sand. Scandinavian and German artists discovered the northern tip of Jutland, where the Skagerrak and the Kattegat, the North Sea and the Baltic Sea, come together, around

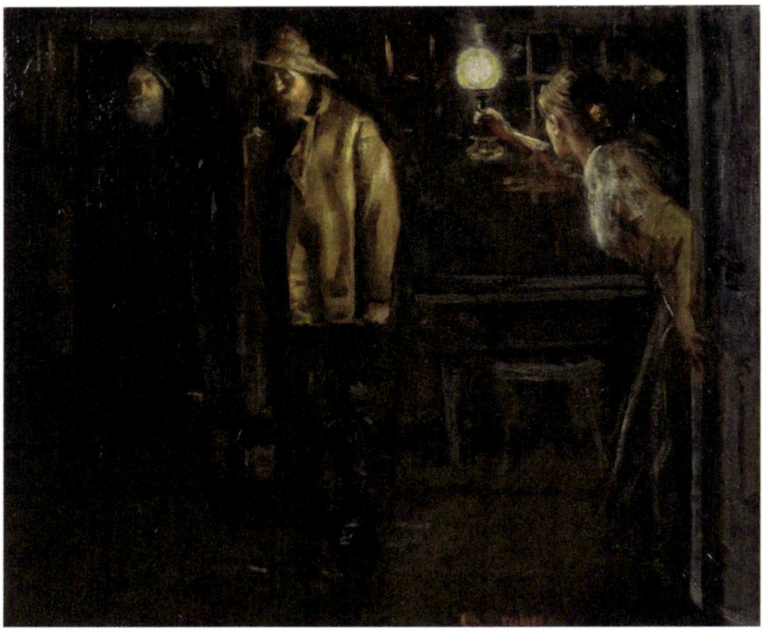

Christian Krohg, *Eyewitnesses*, c. 1895

1870, and they saw it as a pristine region where most of the population lived from fishing. Painters who had worked previously in Paris and came into contact there with the rise of French Realism and Impressionism developed their own independent visual idiom under the impression of the northern lights.

We can discern two broad topical fields within this body of work. On one hand, artists focused on the fishermen and their everyday life. Even if the sea itself is not at the centre of these works, its presence is implied in many compositions. This is evident in the painting *Augenzeugen* (*Eyewitnesses*) by the Norwegian painter Christian Krohg (1852–1925). In the 1890s, he picked up on a story that met with such resonance that he produced more than thirty versions of it by 1918/19. The viewer becomes witness to a moment in which two fishermen, dressed in black and yellow oilskins, enter a fisherwoman's home. A woman runs to them from an adjacent room at the right. She holds an oil lamp with outstretched arm so that she can see the faces of the men. Their facial expressions are petrified; they gaze at the floor and remain silent. Their postures, however, have a great deal to say; the fishermen have been charged with the difficult task of informing the fisherwoman that her husband or son is dead. Her hunched body – her face is not visible – conveys her dismay about the message that she has intuitively sensed beforehand, and which is now confirmed by the men's eyes. The scene is easy to understand, like a still from a film. Every viewer, even those who have never seen the sea, unconsciously calls up images of the sea and its potential dangers from their storehouse of memories. On the other hand, many of Christian Krohg's painter friends turned their attentions to the sunny side of Skagen. In the small, broad-format oil painting, *Fischer am Strand von Skagen. Milder Sommerabend* (*Fishermen on Skagen Beach. A mild summer evening*), the Norwegian-Danish plein air painter Peder Severin Krøyer (1851–1909) captures a landscape panorama that appears to have dreamlike qualities. While the sky and its loose formations of clouds define the upper third of the painting, a sea reaching to the horizon, smooth as glass, shares the lower part with a broad, flat beach. This is what is called the blue hour, that short space of time in which, after sunset in high summer, the sky and the water are submerged in a unique, nuanced blue and seem to flow into one another. A group of fishermen, lying on the edge of a dune, enjoy the warm evening air after a day of work. The man standing with his back to us becomes a figure of projection: how much we would like to take his place, to gaze out at the ocean and feel the last warm rays of the sun on our skin. Although this natural phenomenon only lasts for a short moment, Krøyer grants it a sense of timelessness, thereby evoking a place on the sea to which the viewer wants to return again and again, a place of memory. Thus was the myth of Skagen born. Today, thousands of holidaymakers come to Skagen, and not just in summer, to experience precisely these imaginative moments.

Around 1900, under the aegis of changing social conditions and rising prosperity, the seashore and the coast increasingly came to be perceived as places for rest, recovery and leisure. This shift can be traced particularly well in the work of Max Liebermann (1847–1935), who spent time on the Dutch coast every summer from 1872 to 1914. He turned away from the thematic complex of working people in nature or in specific communities and towards motifs related to the upper class and its glamorous leisure activities on the coast. The painting *Der Muschelfischer – Graue See* (*Mussel Fisherman – Grey Sea*) illustrates this shift in emphasis. Liebermann is no longer portraying the hard work of mussel fishermen on the North Sea coast; he is not telling the story of the men and women who work shoulder-to-shoulder, casting their nets on to the flat sea floor, often for several hours, until the water comes almost to their chests.[6] Now he is describing the sea as a space for leisure, with a free flow: standing in the flat water, bathed in softly approaching waves, a boy, dressed in a blue shirt and grey trousers, pushes the handle of a mussel scoop through the water. This ascribes a new function to the sea, reinterpreting it as a place for idleness. At the upper edge of the painting, another motif appears, one to which Liebermann has also granted autonomy within the image. Beginning in 1894/95, he was interested in the motif of *Badende Knaben* (*Bathing boys*), a genre that granted him –

Peder Severin Krøyer, *Fishermen on Skagen Beach. A mild summer evening*, 1883

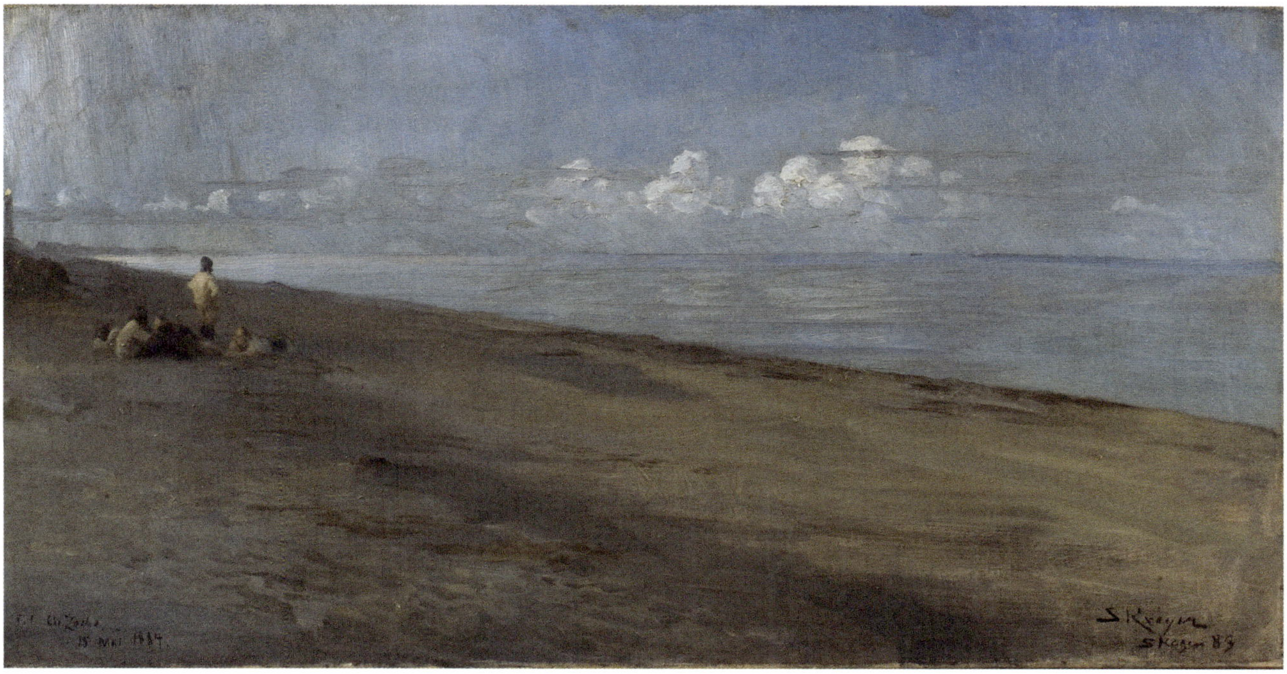

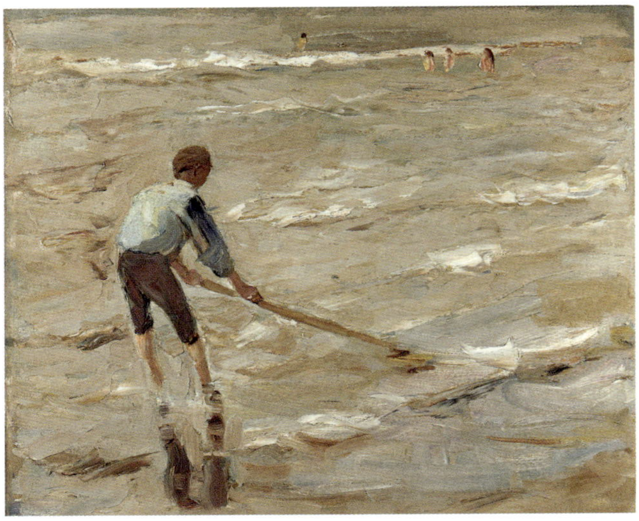

Max Liebermann, *Mussel Fisherman – Grey Sea*, 1908

quite incidentally – the opportunity to study human beings in motion in the outdoors. The boys do not care about the social conventions governing swimming, which at the time mandated bathing machines, a structure that enabled people to change out of their clothes and into swimwear in privacy, and bathing areas separated by gender. The harmony between man and nature, the refreshing pleasure of being in the water, comes front and centre in this visual depiction. The painting itself, which was crafted in Liebermann's atelier in Berlin, consequently mirrors the sea as a place of memory, and maintains the idea of a beautiful summer day on the coast. Nevertheless, Liebermann, a German Impressionist, focused less on the content components than the free artistic recording of light, air and atmosphere, a transcript of something once observed, so to speak.

In early Expressionism, the artistic emphasis shifted away from the sea towards a strongly subjective bent. Many painters sought to express their emotional states, such as Max Beckmann (1884–1950), who described his connection to the sea as follows: "And then to the sea, my old girlfriend; I had not been with her for far too long. You whirling infinity with your sharp-sown dress. [...] And this loneliness. [...] Everything alive was outside. Beyond. If I were the emperor of the earth, I would ask, as my highest right, to be a month alone on the coast."[7] In these words and his painterly works, such as the painting *Strandlandschaft bei beginnender Flut* (*Coastal landscape as the tide comes in*), he postulates a claim to possession of something universal and timeless, along with an awareness that the sea could mirror his existential sensitivities. Emil Nolde (1867–1956) and Erich Heckel (1883–1970) pursued comparable intentions.

As we turn to more contemporary positions, new political and social implications surface. The British-Nigerian artist Yinka Shonibare (born in 1962) refers to Théodore Géricault's (1791–1824) famous monumental work, *Das Floß der Medusa* (*The raft of the Medusa*), and formulates a critique of the old colonial powers. Géricault's painting works through a historical event that had shaken French society at the time. After the disaster of the frigate Medusa in July 1816, about 250 passengers and relatives of crew members had scrambled aboard the lifeboats. The 150 sailors and soldiers, however, for whom there was no more space in the boats, were forced under threat of violence on to a raft that had been hastily assembled and was com-

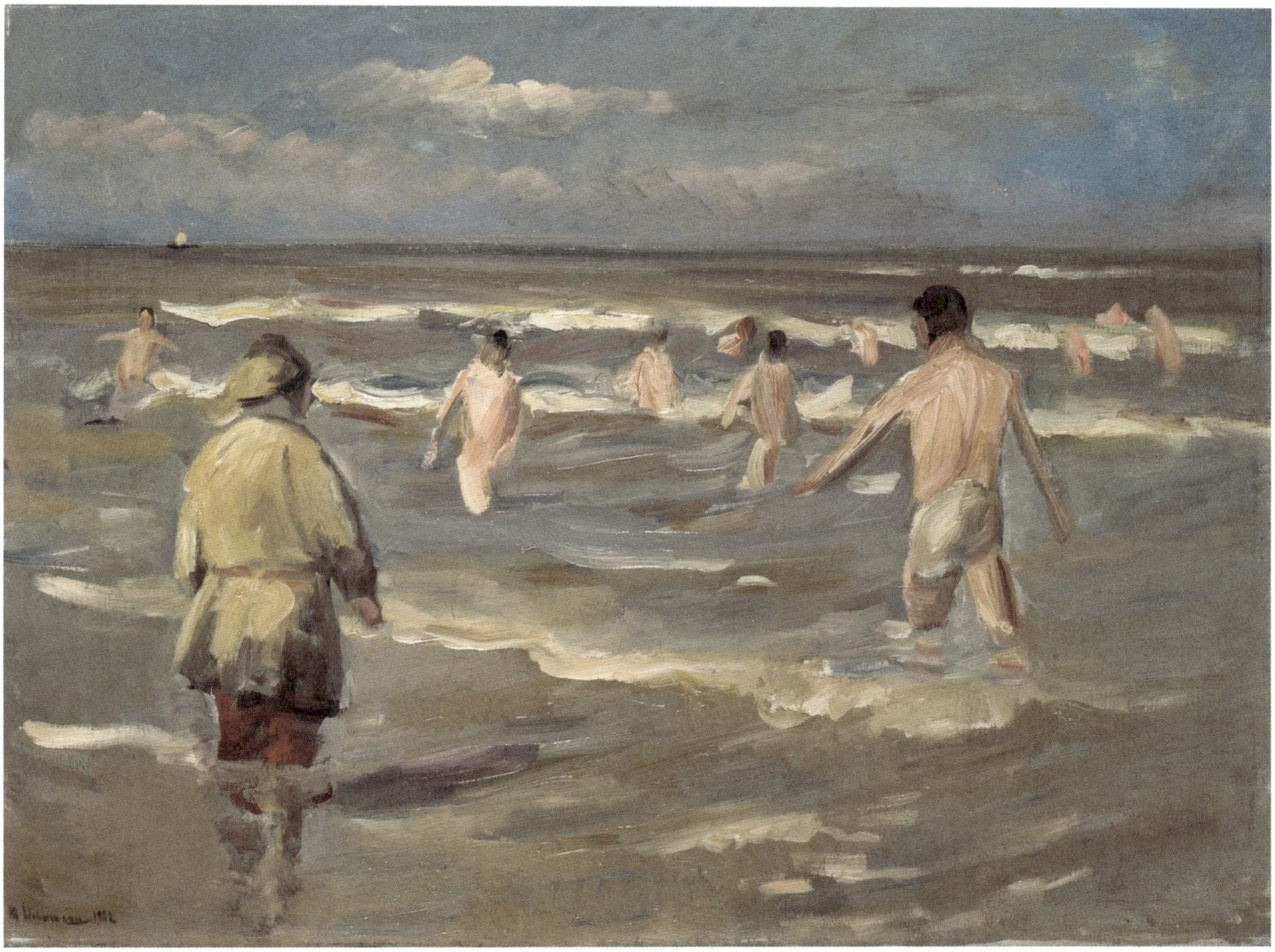

13/6
Max Liebermann, *Bathing boys*, 1902

Max Beckmann, *Coastal landscape as the tide comes in*, 1904

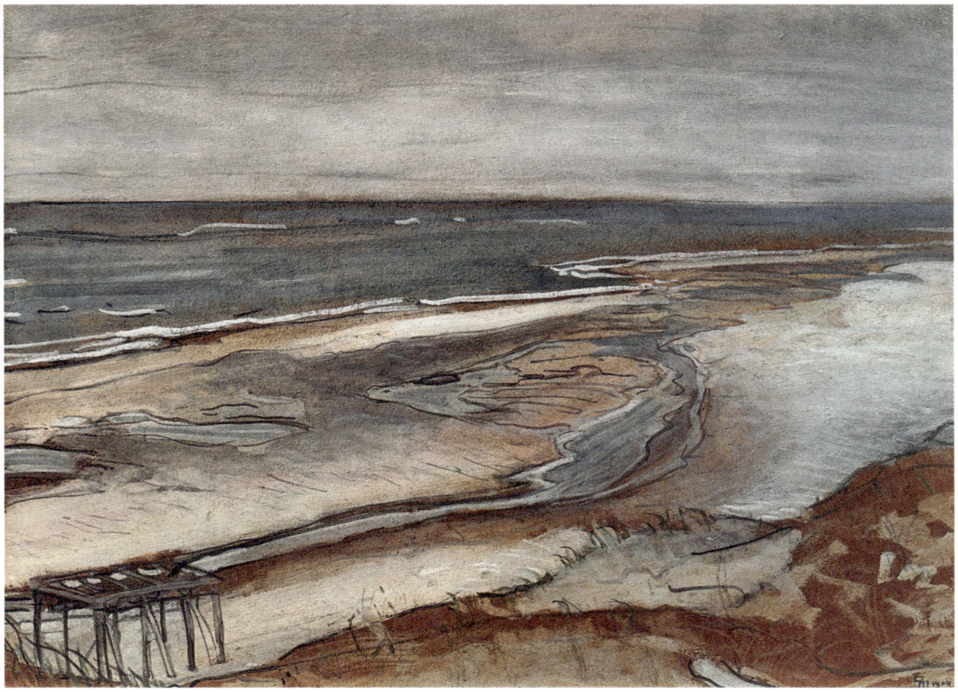

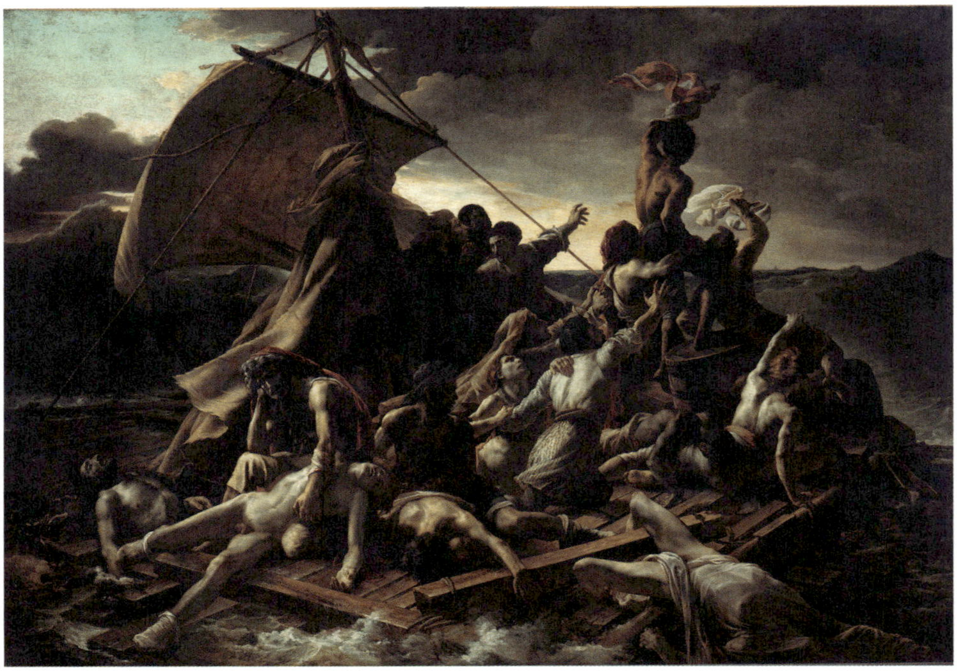

Théodore Géricault, *The Raft of the Medusa*, 1818/1819

Yinka Shonibare, *La Méduse*, 2008

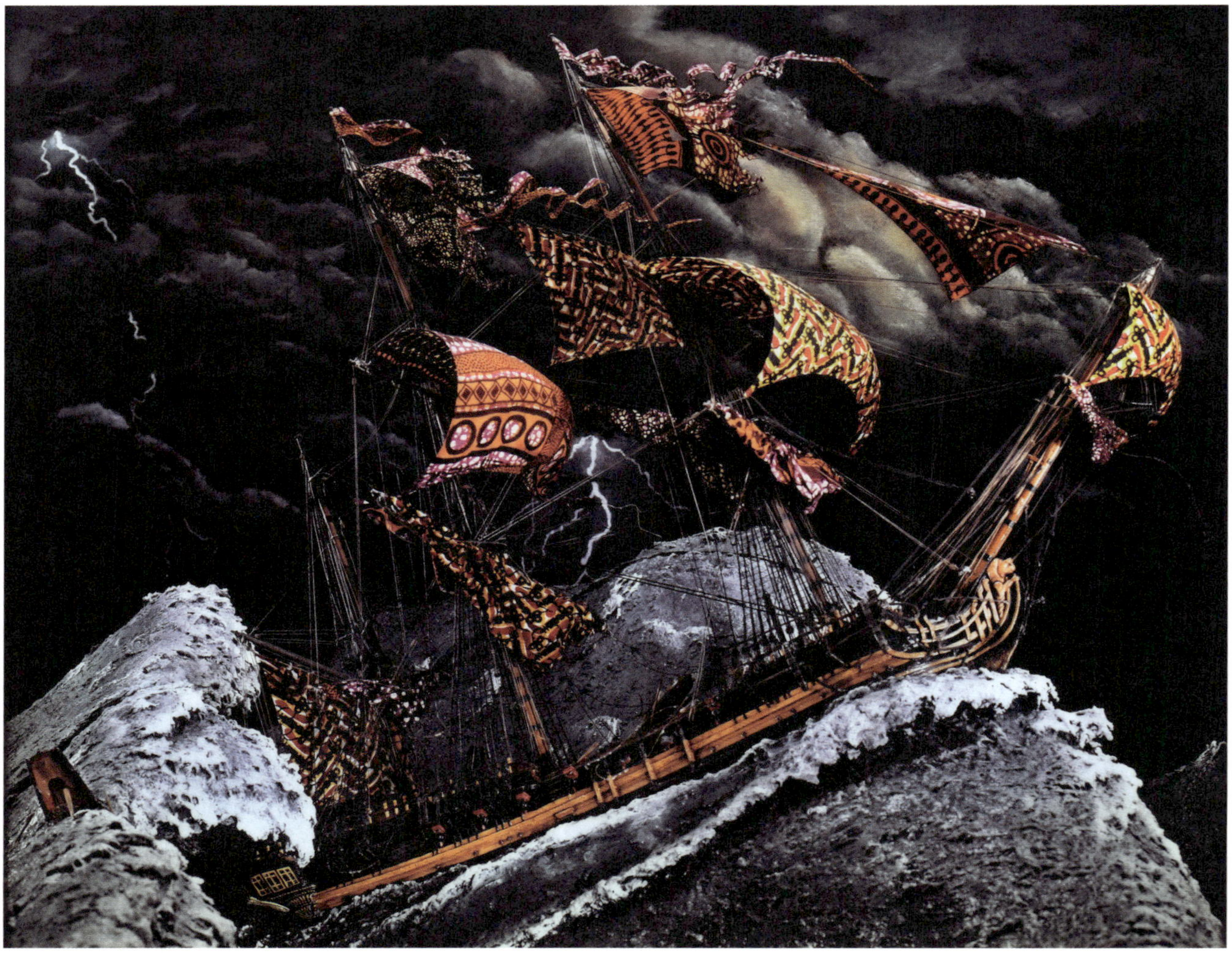

pletely unseaworthy, and then were left to their fate before the West African coast. Only fifteen men survived the twelve-day ordeal. Shonibare restages the story in his 2008 photographic work, *La Méduse*: The men fighting for their lives are no longer represented; instead, a large sailing vessel climbs over a giant wave. A second wave, spewing foam, threatens to overwhelm the stern. A black sea of clouds, streaked with lightning, darkens the atmosphere. Colourful patterned batik fabric serves as sails, which are today viewed as quintessentially African, yet were produced in Polynesia and only came to Africa via colonial trade routes. Even if Shonibare's intentions are more complex, one reading can interpret the sea as a place of remembrance, as an oceanic space in which colonial domination was, and is, exercised.

The Hamburg painter Jochen Hein (born in 1960) demonstrates that the motif of the sea remains universal and can lay claim to timelessness.[8] His monumental triptych *Nordsee* (*North Sea*) seems at a distance to be photorealistic and allows the viewer to pretend that he or she is floating like a bird above a turbulent, seemingly unending ocean surface allowing the gaze to roam again and again. Yet upon closer examination, this illusion gained by distance is destroyed, and this vexatious puzzle dissolves into abstraction. This representation of the "sea" again offers no reference to a place for people or human activity; it makes no interpretive claims and is therefore open to anything that the viewer associates with the ocean. The viewer therefore becomes aware that the closer he or she comes, their ideas are merely a projection. The viewer no longer sees the sea; instead, there are layers and surfaces of colour. The "sea" is always what we associate with it.

1 See Torsten Gunnarsson, "Johan Christian Dahl und die Freilichtmalerei. Seine Ölstudien im europäischen Kontext", in *Wolken. Wogen. Wehmut. Johan Christian Dahl 1788–1857. Der Freund Caspar David Friedrichs*, ed. Herwig Guratzsch, Exhibition Catalogue (Cologne, 2002) 37.

2 Edmund Burke, *Philosophical Enquiry into the Origin of our Ideas of the Sublime and the Beautiful* (London: Thomas McLean, Haymarket, 1823), 75.

3 Regarding Friedrich, see also Martin Faass und Felix Krämer, "Seestücke – eine Einführung", in *Seestücke. Von Caspar David Friedrich bis Emil Nolde*, ed. Martin Faass and Felix Krämer, Exhibition Catalogue (Munich 2005), 14.

4 Marie Lødrup Bang, *Johan Christian Dahl 1788–1857. Life and Works*, Vol. 2 (Oslo, 1987), 314f.

5 Wolfgang Müller von Königswinter (1854), in *Das A und O der Landschaft*, ed. Andreas and Oswald Achenbach ,Exhibition Catalogue (Cologne, 1997), 57.

6 "Die Wattfischerei", in *Föhr und Umgebung in Wort und Bild*, ed. C. J. Christiansen and W. Segeberg (Wyk, 1899), 24.

7 Max Beckmann. *Briefe*, ed. Klaus Gallwitz et al, Volume 1: 1899–1925 (Munich and Zürich, 1993), 108, no. 102.

8 For more on Jochen Hein, see Ulrike Wolff-Thomsen, "Über die Tiefe", in *Jochen Hein. Über die Tiefe*, ed. Ulrike Wolff-Thomsen and Nicole Nix-Hauck, Exhibition Catalogue (Heide, 2016).

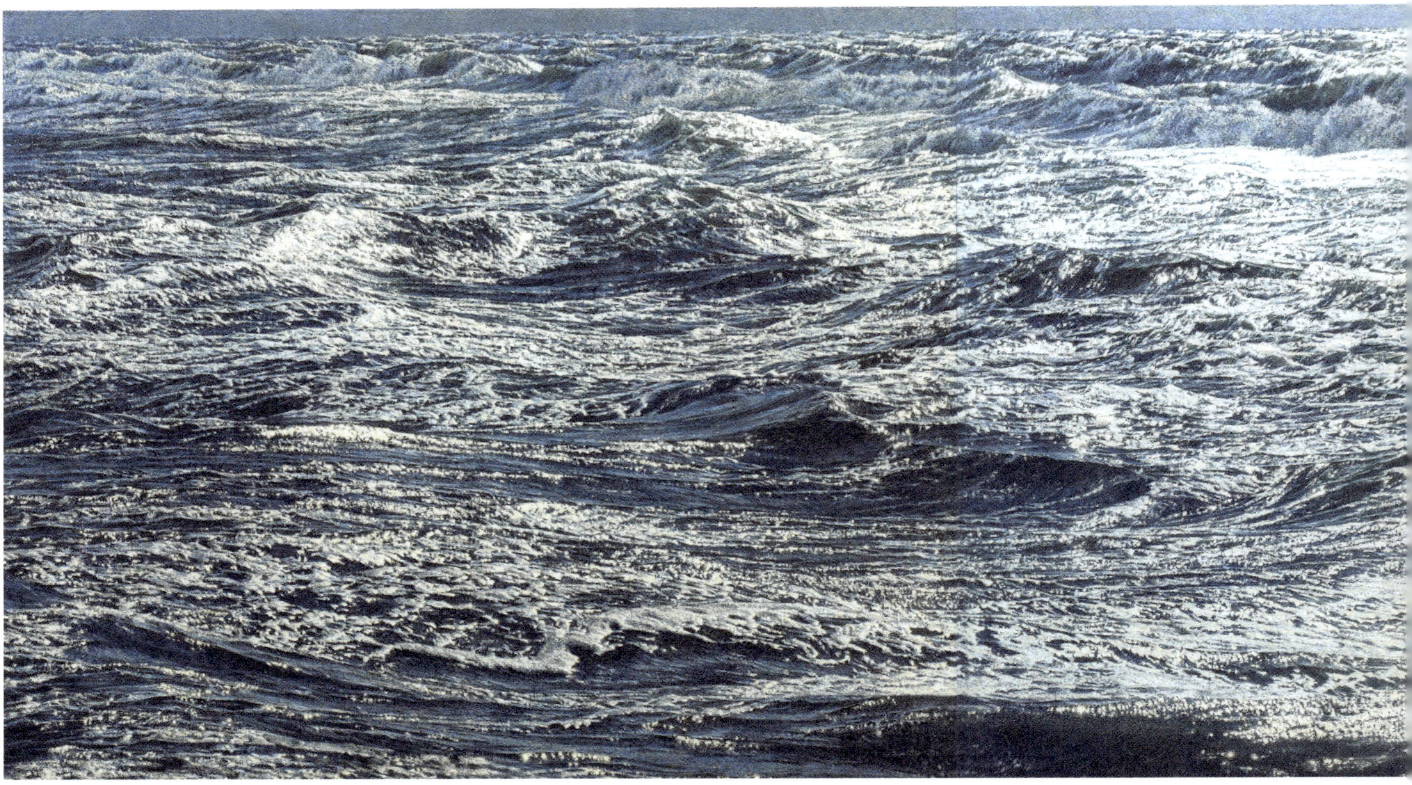

13/11
Jochen Hein, *North Sea*
(triptych), 2003

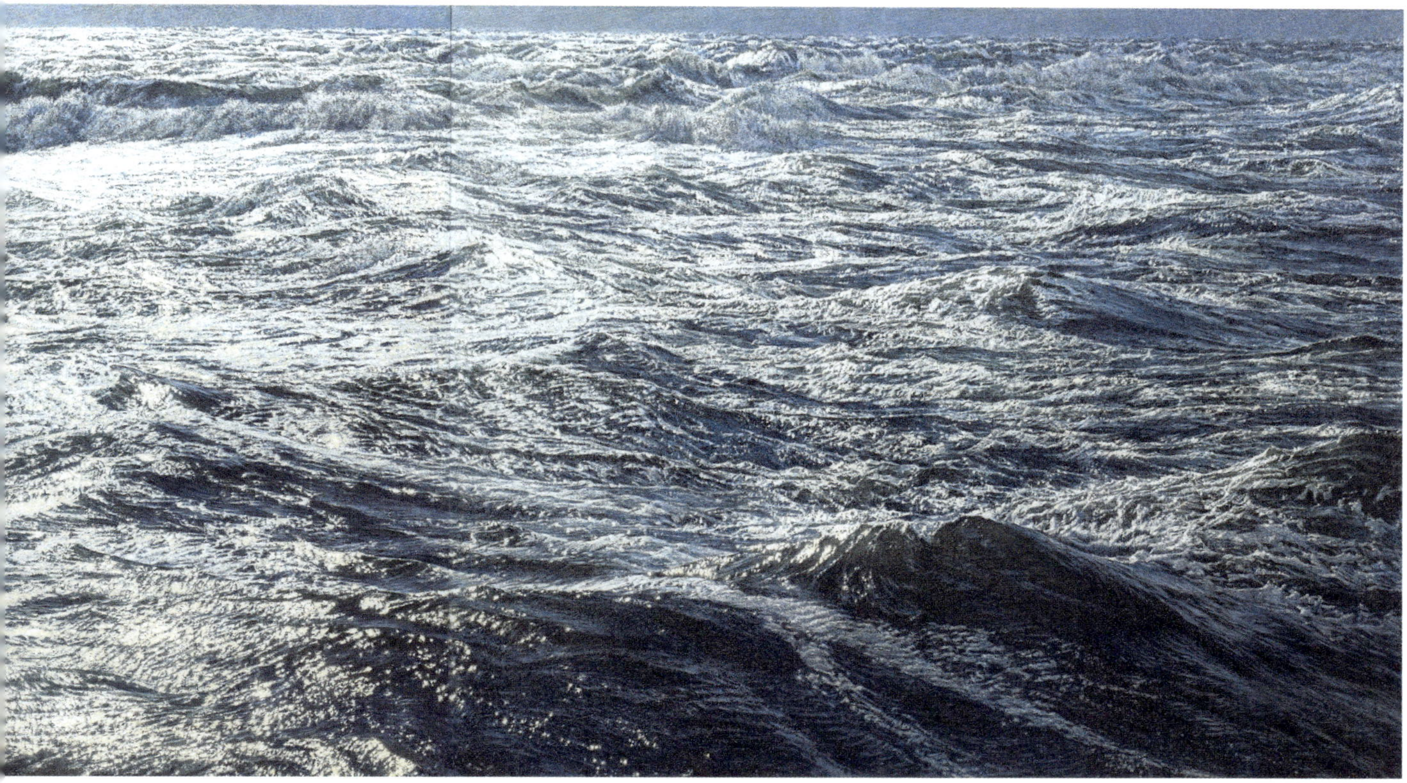

Dieter Richter

WAVES AND WORDS

Literature and the Sea

The mythical ocean

The ocean, Earth's oldest landscape, is also one of literature's most ancient themes. The myth of the beginning is connected with the sea as the element of all creation, everything fixed, living, trusted: "And the earth was without form, and void; and darkness was upon the face of the deep. And the Spirit of God moved upon the face of the waters" (Genesis 1:2). Other accounts of the creation, such as the Babylonian and Egyptian narratives, tell of primordial waters that existed before time. This primeval body of water is omnipresent in mythology as a mortal threat to the cosmos: Oceanus, the salt waters encircling the fruitful earth, the boundary of all living things. Ancient oriental tales of the "Great Flood" – the best-known version of which is the Biblical flood – focused on this theme, seeking at the same time to banish the fear that this could reoccur at any time, that terra firma could sink once again beneath the primordial chaos of the waves. God, in his covenant with Noah, imposed eternal boundaries on the ocean (Genesis 9). In his *West-Eastern Divan* (1819), Goethe wrote, "The sea swells ever / The land restrains it never," thereby getting to the heart of the matter (although its optimism threatens to collapse today).

The mythological ocean therefore plays two roles as the site of creation: it is the element from which life emerges (the *arché*, the "origin" in the natural philosophy of Thales of Miletus in the sixth century B.C.), and it is the element in which all life ends. Ancient literature knew the sea, the "barren" (Homer), above all as an image of death – already in the *Epic of Gilgamesh* (3,000 B.C.), we have a hero to whom the human riddle of death is revealed after a journey across the sea. This ocean of death lies in the outermost reaches of the west, beyond the "pillars of Hercules," the Strait of Gibraltar; Odysseus descends into the realm of the dead through "deep-flowing Oceanus, that bounds the Earth" (*The Odyssey* XI:13).

The idea that the journey into the afterlife goes through water, whether an ocean or a river, became a fixed image in European literature that was popularized in the English-speaking world by John Bunyan's *Pilgrim's Progress* (1678). In the texts of Christian mystics from Meister Eckhart to Gerhard Tersteegen, the ocean presents an image of eternity and the unfathomable nature of the divine. The experience of death is also mirrored in secular literary contexts in images of the sea or of water;

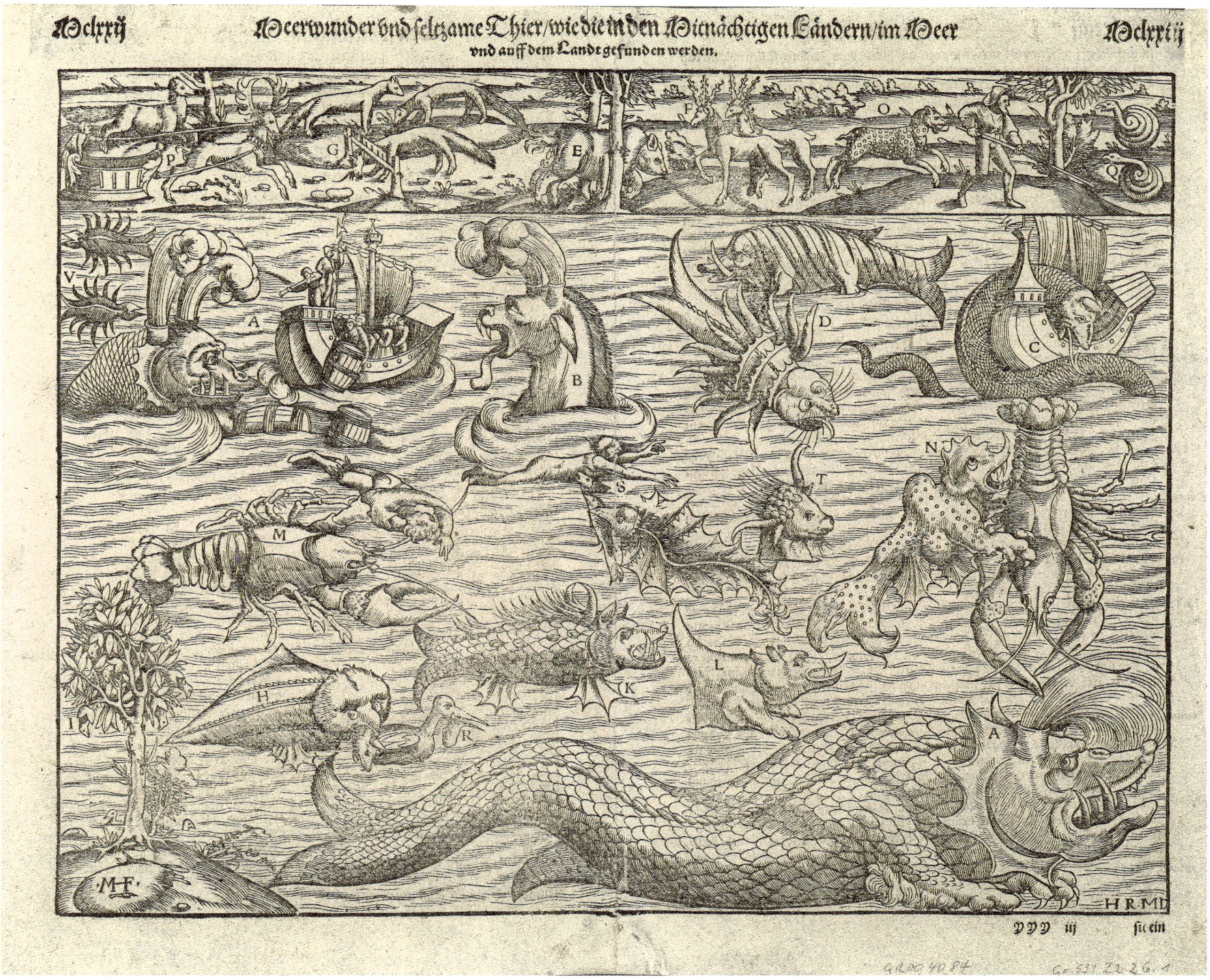

Sebastian Münster, *Wonders of the sea and curious beasts*, 1559/1588

the ocean conveys the existential primordial experience of being without time or place (for example, in the chapter "A Stroll by the Shore" in Thomas Mann's 1924 novel, *The Magic Mountain* (VII, 1).

The ocean of adventure

The real ocean, the elemental contrast to terra firma, has long appeared as hostile to mankind. The colours that observers attributed to the waters were dark in tone; Homer described the waves as "gray", "black", "dark brown" or "wine-coloured"; the ocean only became "blue" in the eighteenth century. The deeps were the home of uncanny creatures, the Leviathan and other marine monsters, from giant fish that could swallow a Jonah, to the terrifying squids that terrorise the crew of the NAUTILUS in Jules Verne's novel, *Twenty-thousand Leagues under the Sea* (1869/70). Oceanographers remain occupied to this day with the question of whether or not these submarine behemoths actually exist. Other legendary threats include the viscous "sluggish sea" (in which ships become stuck), the "magnetic mountain" (that pulls nails out of planks) or the insatiable "maelstrom" (as described in great detail by

Edgar Allan Poe in his 1841 tale, *A Descent into the Maelstrom*). In medieval literature, these stories were called *Wazzermaere* (water fables), yet who could really know whether these "fables" from the water really were "fairy tales"?

These fantastical dangers also had their real counterparts: storms, doldrums, shipwreck, stranding. Sea storms and shipwrecks became major themes in world literature, initially as adventure narratives and then later as allegories. There are innumerable variations on this primordial existential theme: the struggle of man against nature. The ocean becomes the stage upon which humanity (or even better, masculinity) proves itself in its struggle for life. It was in this context that Sophocles, in his famous chorus in *Antigone* (442 B.C.), which praises the greatness of mankind (and warns of its arrogance), places seafaring as the beginning of all of civilization's accomplishments: "Wonders are many, and none is more wonderful than man. This power spans the sea, even when it surges white before the gales of the south-wind" (verses 332–336). The struggle against the ocean appears as the prototypical form of the struggle against nature.

The credo of older seafaring narratives is that although this fight claims many victims, it still ends in victory. The classic text in this regard is the dramatic "storm at sea" episode in *The Odyssey* (V: 291ff.), in which friendly or hostile deities intervene "from above", yet Odysseus's courage and resolve are equally decisive for the positive outcome. This also applies to the Greek legend of the Argonauts, although it is a seafaring collective in this case that has to overcome dangers mythical and real in their quest for the Golden Fleece. Other older literatures include seafaring stories about individual or collective heroes, such as the Irish *Brendan* legend (sixth century), the Persian stories of *Sinbad the Sailor* (ninth/tenth century), or the Middle High German *Kudrun* epic (ca. 1230), just to name a few.

The Age of Discovery brought new wind into the sails of marine themes in literature, allowing narratives to more closely approximate reality without however doing away with the old fantastical elements. This applies to the Portuguese national epic, the *Os Lusíadas* by Luis de Camões (1572), which celebrates an entire nation as a seafaring people. Authors who had maritime experience themselves wrote seafaring novels in English that were highly "realistic", from James Fenimore Cooper (*The Pilot*, 1824) to Robert Louis Stevenson (*Treasure Island*, 1883 or *Kidnapped*, 1886) to Joseph Conrad (*The Nigger of the 'Narcissus'*, 1897). German adventure literature, by contrast, kept its distance from the ocean. One exception is the writings of Friedrich Gerstäcker (for example, *Die Flußpiraten des Mississippi*, or *The River Pirates of the Mississippi*, 1848), who was popular in his time as an author of books for young people. There was also Ret Marut, alias B. Traven, with his socially critical novel, *The Death Ship* (1926), which put to rest nineteenth-century "seafaring Romanticism" by means of the murderous conditions of the capitalist economy; at the end of the story, the hero wanders lost upon the sea.

The most complex of all of the "sea novels", one which consistently plumbs the philosophical limits of mankind, is Herman Melville's *Moby-Dick; or: The Whale* (1851). Unlike the long tradition of the old sea adventure, in which the hero's struggle ends in victory, *Moby-Dick* ends in destruction. The old symbolism of triumph over nature and its subjection seems to have come to an end. In Theodor Storm's novella, *The Rider on the White Horse* (1888), the ocean also prevails in the struggle against human arrogance. And in Hemingway's short novel *The Old Man and the Sea* (1952), the fight between man and the ocean remains undecided. Hemingway artic-

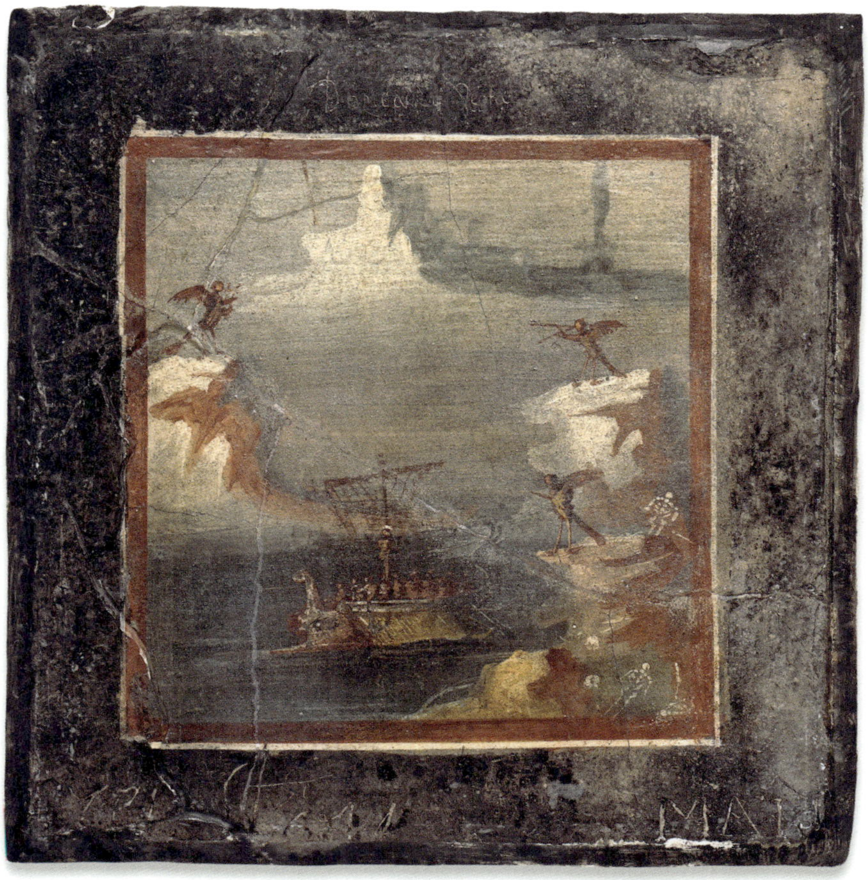

Mural from Pompeii showing Odysseus and the Sirens, 50–75 B.C.

ulates the fundamental scepticism about the reckless optimism of being able to "subjugate" the ocean, to render it "subservient". The sea is demonised once again. It was likely the fact that the catastrophe of the TITANIC (1912) was the subject of many literary treatments that firmly anchored the awareness of this event in the collective consciousness.

It is therefore not surprising that contemporary science fiction literature presents the ocean as a dangerous enemy for mankind. In Stanisław Lem's novel *Solaris* (1961), it was an ocean on a distant planet; in Frank Schätzing's *The Swarm* (2004), it is the Earth's ocean itself that acts as an intelligent collective being against mankind, wreaking its revenge. The struggle of man against the sea has become a defensive battle.

The experience of the sea

The question of how people who have individual biographical experience of the ocean have spoken of it takes us in another direction, and into other literary genres. Even if the literary first-person narrator often tended to be a topos in older times, there are still impressive testaments to patterns of perception that were typical for the time.

In his *Tristia* (*Lamentations*), the Roman poet Ovid wrote for the first time of being forced to embark upon a sea voyage against one's will. In the year 8 A.D., Emperor Augustus banished Ovid, after a life of luxury and fame, from the metropolis of Rome to Tomis, a small city on the Black Sea (now in Romania). During the journey into exile, Ovid's ship met with a powerful storm in the eastern Mediterranean: "Wretched me! what vast mountains of water heave themselves aloft! [...] / The waters overwhelm my face. The billows will crush this life of mine, and with lips that pray in vain I shall drink in the destroying water" (Tristia I, II, 13-26). The fear of physical destruction joins the fear of the civil death, the loss of homeland and honour. This is an experience that innumerable people have had since: they have been forced to leave their homes and travel over sea to a new land.

A southern German poet named Tannhäuser, who had no experience with the sea, embarked on a sea journey without his full consent in the thirteenth century. He took part in a crusade (possible the one proclaimed by Kaiser Friedrich II in 1228/29) that involved a journey from Apulia to the Holy Land via the Adriatic Sea. The poem that he left behind ("Happy is he who can now embark with his falcon upon the hunt...") portrays the contradictions of the journey in a dramatic and detailed way: a nocturnal shipwreck at Crete, a six-day-long storm, bad food, mouldy wine, the stench onboard. ("I sway upon the sea"): This was a cry for help from a desperate person who longed to return to land.

The Tyrolean poet Oswald von Wolkenstein had a similar experience. In one of his songs, he reports ("When I was ten years old, the following came to pass ...", around 1416) on his awful experiences at sea, of storms, high waves and a shipwreck in the Black Sea, which he only survived by clambering atop a barrel. The Old English poem *The Seafarer* (tenth century) presents a fearful man horrified by travelling on the sea (the Arctic Ocean); fear and terror long remained dominant themes in texts in which a biographical narrator encounters the ocean. A chorus of the terrified and despairing offer a counterpoint to the proud epic songs about the "conquest" of the seas, to the theatrical fanfare of *Navigare necesse est*, "to sail is necessary." This is because the fear of the ocean is one of the primal fears of mankind,[1] and a Neapolitan saying of the baroque period captures, better than any theory, the distrust with which people regard the ocean: *Loda il mare e resta a terra* ("Praise the sea, but remain on land").[2]

The first German author to complete a long, dangerous sea journey with enjoyment and in high spirits was Johann Gottfried Herder. For Herder, the ocean offered an occasion for a major revelation of a new life of freedom. Born in a small city in East Prussia, Herder studied with Kant in Königsberg, became a teacher, and embarked in 1769 at the age of twenty-five on an "educational journey". He set out at Riga, sailed over the Baltic to Helsingör, from there through the Skagerrak, to the North Sea and the canal to the western coast of France; this was a sea journey lasting a total of six weeks, on a particularly "raw" northern route. In his *Journal of my journey in the year 1769*, Herder expressed his excitement: "[...] what a wide scope for thought a ship, suspended between sky and sea, provides! Everything here adds wings to one's thoughts, gives them motion and an ample sphere! [...] On land one is chained to a fixed point and restricted to the narrow limits of a situation. Often this point is a student's chair in a musty study, a place at a monotonous boarding-house table, a pulpit, a lecture-desk. [...]. [...] But let a man suddenly retire from this scene – or rather be thrown out, without books, writing, occupation or homogeneous society – what a different prospect!"[3]

The themes of the Sturm und Drang movement signalled a general shift in attitudes towards the ocean that broke fresh ground in the second half of the eigh-

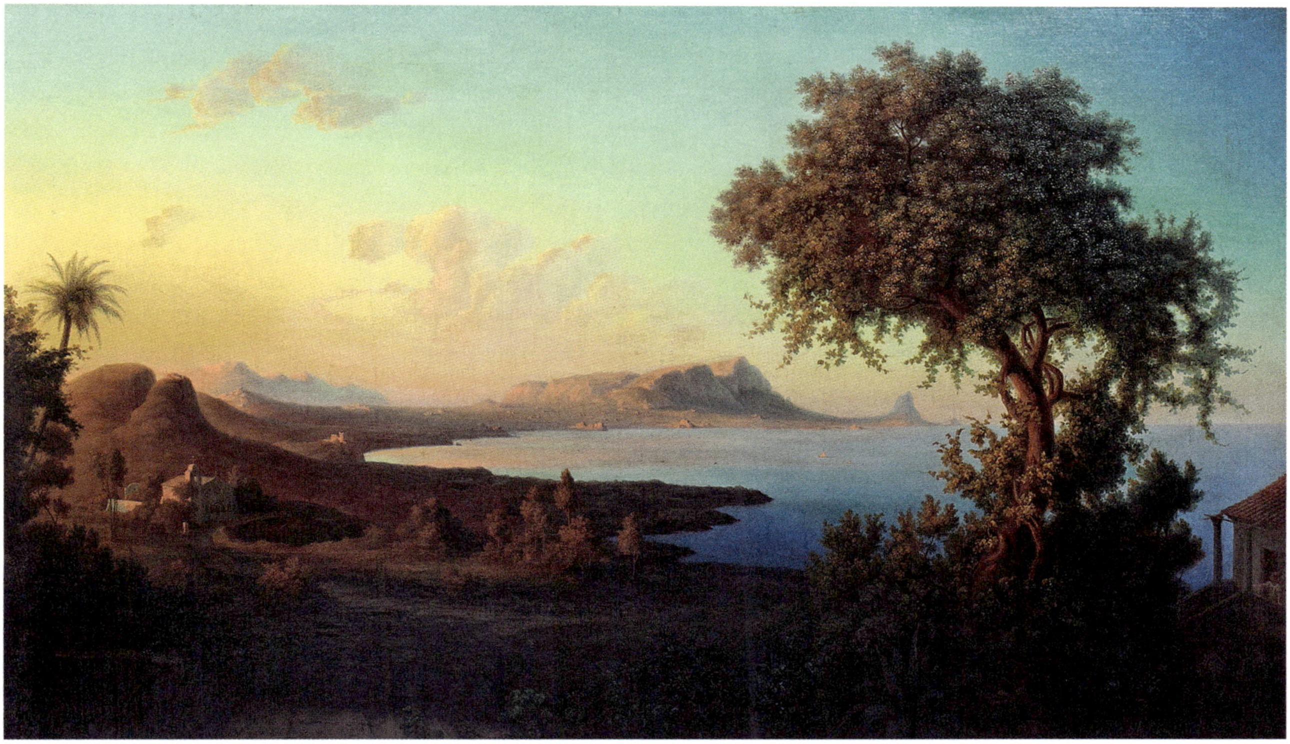

13/3
August Kopisch, *Cape Zaffarano in Sicily*, 1840

teenth century. The ocean becomes beautiful, a space in which to experience human autonomy. The philosopher Edmund Burke, who hailed from Ireland, opened up a new aesthetic of the landscape in his juxtaposition of the "sublime" with the "beautiful" (*A philosophical enquiry into the origin of our ideas of the sublime and beautiful*, 1757). In Burke's estimation, it was precisely wild, shapeless, destructive nature that becomes the subject of appreciation, including the high mountains, volcanoes, and last but not least, the ocean. Friedrich Schiller, in his essay *On the sublime* (1801), picked up this thread, arguing that such natural phenomena allow man to become aware of his own greatness for the first time: "The sight of unlimited distances, and heights lost to view, the vast ocean at his feet and the vaster ocean above him, pluck his spirit out of the narrow sphere of the actual and out of the oppressive bondage of physical life."[4]

For writers and artists from German-speaking countries, such impressive accounts of seafaring experiences occurred less in the domestic Baltic and North Seas (as in the case of Herder) than in the Mediterranean. Hardly anyone expressed more excitement about the sea than the brilliant Wilhelm Heinse from the small Thuringian town of Langewiesen, who wrote about his six-day crossing from Marseille to Genoa in October 1780. A powerful storm caught the ship at sea, but the author enjoyed it nonetheless, floating "with delight on this glorious element".[5]

During his Italian journeys, Goethe also encountered a severe storm during the four-day crossing from Naples to Palermo in March 1787. On the return journey from Messina, the ship was almost smashed to smithereens on the rocky coast of Capri due to calm seas (the poem *Quiet Sea*, published in 1796, recalls the incident). Goethe was also fascinated with the experience of the open seas, as he noted with the philosophical observation: "He who has never seen himself surrounded on all sides by the sea, can never possess an idea of the world and his relation to it."[6] He meant to say that it is only from the sea that we first become aware of the world and our selves. In the scene "Rocky Coves in the Aegean Sea" in the second act of *Faust II* (1832), Goethe portrays the ocean, especially the Mediterranean, laden with mythology, as the origin of beauty and life itself: "By beauty and truth my whole being's imbued .../ In water all that there is has its source, / By water all that there is is renewed, / Ocean, your dominion forever enforce!"[7]

The Grand Tour, the educational journey to Italy, became the most important medium for maritime experiences. Many travellers from the North (the Germans often came from small farming towns) saw the sea for the first time on these journeys, whether in Venice (from August von Platen's *Sonnets from Venice*, 1825, to Thomas Mann's *Death in Venice*, 1913; Venice became a major site of German-language maritime literature), Genoa or Trieste. Today, in the age of medial worlds of experience, we can scarcely conceive of how overwhelming these "first sights" must have been. "I have seen the sea," wrote Adalbert Stifter in Trieste; "All of the things that I have seen of this Earth – the Alps, forests, plains, glaciers, etc. – descend to the level of trivialities in the face of the ocean's sublimity".[8] And Felix Mendelssohn-Bartholdy wrote from Naples (another main site where Northerners experienced the sea): "The ocean is, and remains, the most beautiful thing in nature".[9]

This is the expression of a radical change in the perception of the ocean – and it has shaped the foundations of our (Western!) ideas to the present day.[10] Looking out upon the sea, experiencing it firsthand, and the sea journey itself became aesthetic revelations of a "more beautiful", not commonplace life, often combined with archaic experiences opposed to civilisation. "It's a delightful, disturbing emotion, plunging over the water into this emptiness of the night, far from everywhere. You feel as if you're taking yourself out of this world, that you're never going to arrive anywhere again, that there'll never be another daylight." Thus wrote Guy de Maupassant in his 1876 novella, *Afloat*, about a crossing with a sailboat along the Mediterranean coast of France.[11]

The landscape of the soul

The new aesthetic of nature that emerged in the eighteenth century combined a new kind of subjective experience that became typical of modernity. The sea, a landscape without boundaries, becomes, in the language of images, one of the major anthropological metaphors. While medieval mysticism had conceived of the sea as a mirror of the infinitude of God, the Romantics interpreted it as a mirror of the boundless, autonomous subject. "I love the sea as my own soul. I am often overcome by the feeling that the sea is actually my soul itself", wrote Heinrich Heine in *The North Sea*[12] (1827). He compared the dreamlike view from the boat into the depths of the ocean with the gaze into the abysses of one's own soul, from which the vestiges of memory ("day residues," as Sigmund Freud called them in his *Interpretation of Dreams* (1899)) climb from the subconscious to the surface.

The sea appears as a landscape of the soul, becomes an image for strong emotions, whether it be (as in Heine) in the form of regression into the quiet depths of the subconscious, or in the parallelism of the raging sea with the agitated human passions, as Charles Baudelaire conjures up in his poem, *Man and the Sea* (*L'Homme et la mer*, 1857): "Free man, you'll always love the sea – for this, / That it's a mirror,

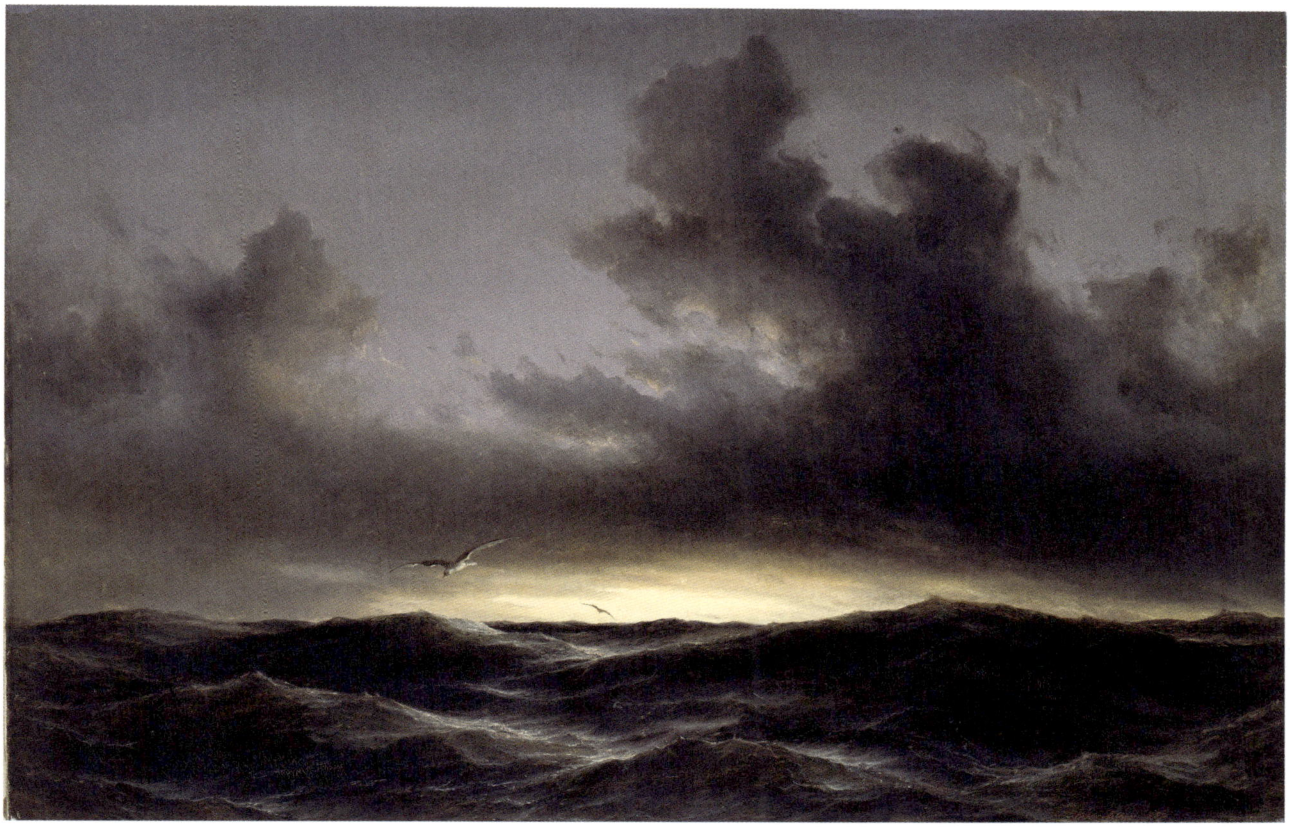

13/2
Daniel Hermann Anton Melbye, *Sea Solitude*, 1852

where you see your soul / In its eternal waves that chafe and roll; / Nor is your soul less bitter an abyss."[13] The metaphor of freedom, of setting out for new shores, of free thinking (as in Nietzsche), was combined with the sea. Thus have these ideas become ubiquitous in our language, and thereby in our present-day consciousness, where the geography of broad distance lies, as one of the major images of mankind itself.

The island mythology

Part of the literary fascination with the sea also focuses on islands. Islands are land, yet are not mainland; they can disappear from view and appear again, much like the "floating islands" of fairy tales and myths. Islands are places situated far from the world, locations of loneliness, of penance, as in the medieval poem *Gregorius* by Hartmann von Aue (ca. 1190), which Thomas Mann incorporated into his novel, *The Holy Sinner* (1951). Yet islands can also be the secluded scene of a life marked by more freedom and more beauty, as we see in the motifs of the "isle of paradise," "the island of love," or the "blessed isles." In contrast to the mainland and to normality, the island can also become a popular field of experimentation for alternative forms of living. In Daniel Defoe's novel *Robinson Crusoe* (1719), the eponymous hero is stranded on a lonely island where he constructs an ideal bourgeois model of order. The novel inspired a wealth of imitations called "Robinsonades," including *Swiss Family Robinson* by Johann David Wyss (1812), in which entire groups of people had to survive on distant islands.

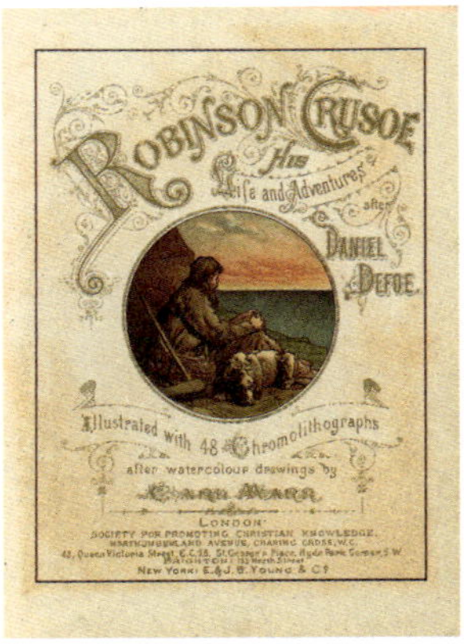

Daniel Defoe, illustrated edition of *Robinson Crusoe*, c. 1890

The explicitly political utopia of the island was destined for even greater influence, founded by the English humanist and statesman Thomas More in his work, *Utopia* (1516). The remote island becomes a model for an improved social and political order for the world. Popular utopias such as the land of milk and honey were transported to equally distant islands, and the myth of the island lives on today in the field of tourism.

The island utopia however was completely ambivalent, enabling the genesis of both paradisiacal and infernal systems in a space outside of civilization. In William Golding's novel, *Lord of the Flies* (1954), a group of children rescued from nuclear war is sent to an island where they descend into barbarism and atavism. In Ingeborg Bachmann's radio play *The Cicadas* (1955), the island is a place where the lost and the meditative congregate. And in H. G. Wells' fantastical novel, *The Island of Dr. Moreau* (1896), a traveller meets a scientist on a remote island who wants to find the "true" nature of man in the beast by means of vivisection.

D. H. Lawrence's story, *The Man who loved Islands* (1927), brings the ambivalence of the insular most forcefully into view by portraying the gathering twilight of a hero who, after an initial rush of happiness, has become lonely, in the undertow of an indifferent natural world. The islands only exist in a permanent, tense relationship with the mainland – this is one reading – only in the ocean's eternal opposition to the mainland.

1 Jean Delumeau, *Angst im Abendland. Die Geschichte der kollektiven Ängste im Europa des 14. bis 18. Jahrhunderts*, Vol. 1 (Reinbek: 1985), 49.
2 Giambattista Basile, *Lo cunto de li cunti, a cura di Michele Rak* (Milano: 1986), 87.
3 Johann Gottfried Herder, *J. G. Herder on Social and Political Culture*, trans. and ed. F. M. Barnard (Cambridge: Cambridge UP, 1969), 65-66.
4 Friedrich von Schiller, *Naïve and Sentimental Poetry and On the Sublime*, trans. Julius A. Elias (New York: Frederick Ungar Publishing Co., 1966), 204.
5 Letter to Friedrich Jacoby, Venice, 26 January 1781, in Wilhelm Heinse, *Schriften*, Vol. 9 (Leipzig, 1838), S. 98.
6 Johann Wolfgang von Goethe, *Goethe's Travels in Italy: Together with his Second Residence in Rome and Fragments on Italy* (London: George Bell and Sons, 1885), 220.
7 Johann Wolfgang von Goethe, *Faust: A Tragedy, Parts One and Two, Fully Revised*, trans. Martin Greenberg (New Haven: Yale UP, 2014), 306.
8 Letter to Gustav Heckenast, 20 July 1857, in Adalbert Stifter, *Sämtliche Werke*, Vol. 19 (Reichenberg, 1929), 36.
9 Letter to his family, 13 April 1831, in Felix Mendelssohn-Bartholdy, *Reisebriefe aus den Jahren 1830–1832* (Potsdam, 1861), 134.
10 The attitude of the Japanese and other East Asian societies toward the ocean is radically different, marked far more by respect and fear.
11 Guy de Maupassant, *Afloat*, trans. Douglas Parmée (New York: NYRB Classics, 2008), 35.
12 Heinrich Heine, *Sämtliche Schriften*, Vol. 2 (Munich, 1976), 224.
13 Roy Campbell, *Poems of Baudelaire* (New York: Pantheon Books, 1952), 20.

Boris Belge

THE PORT CITY OF ODESSA

A Site of Longing

Odessa is a stunning place, today as in the past. In the nineteenth century, many visitors to the port city on the Black Sea took up pen and paper to record their impressions and experiences. Innumerable travel reports, prose pieces and poems portray the city's exposed location on the terrace-like hills between the steppes and the sea, its grandiose architecture, its prosperity, the diversity of people found there, and its social dynamism. Mark Twain (1835–1910), after a long journey through the steppes in the 1860s, believed himself to be "in America"; a German traveller, upon seeing the port, was impressed by the "constant comings and goings, waves and crowds of thousands of people and cartloads of never-ending streams of goods".[1] Profits were made in Odessa, where speculators placed bets on the future in the form of commodities investments. The "gangster king" Benya Krik in Isaak Babel's (1894–1940) *The Odessa Tales* – which first appeared in 1931 – may have been more than just a fictional figure; he was a prototypical resident of a city where, according to the *Tales*, shrewdness, cunning and relentless assertiveness assured one's own advancement.

Whoever wanted to do so could enjoy the bright side of life: the pleasant seaside climate, the world of theatre and opera, the excitements of city life and Odessa's many different cultural influences. Another contemporary recalled how he heard "a Babylonian chaos of languages": "Italian, English, German, Greek, Turkish, Persian, Tatar, Serbian, Polish and Russian, with every possible dialect".[2] Odessa also witnessed terrible violence, such as pandemics, epidemics, pogroms and the devastating consequences of both World Wars. Since the founding of Odessa, there has been a broad range of interpretations, myths and re-interpretations of the city and its history. Several Odessas arose in the imagination, blurring the boundary between fiction and reality. Nostalgic memories of Odessa were often an important source of stability for residents, visitors and emigrants during turbulent times.

Myth and utopia: Odessa as a project of the future

Odessa remains to this day a symbol for nostalgic retrospection. References to a mythical past shaped the city's political framework as early as its founding. The

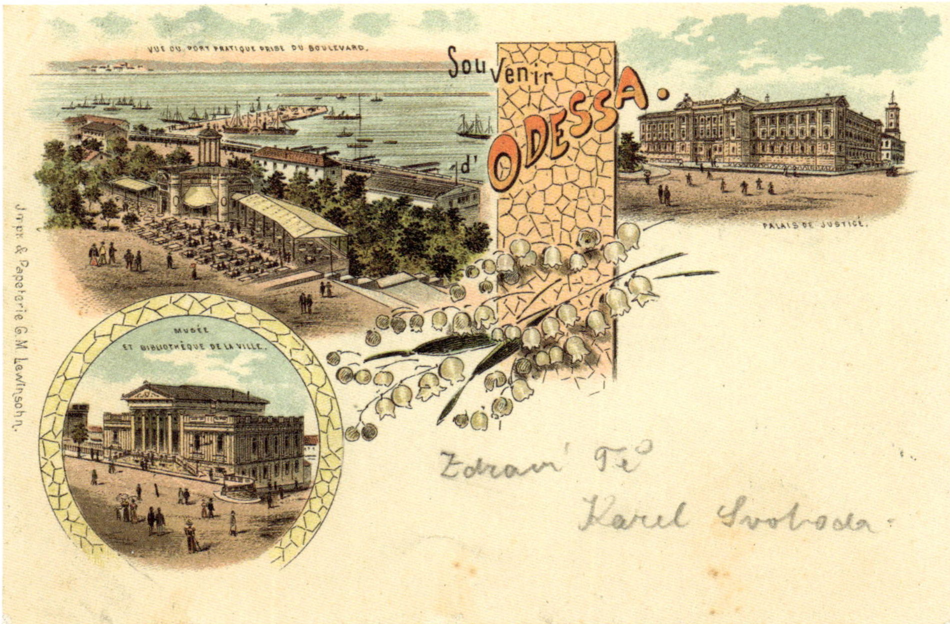

Picture postcard, "Souvenir d'Odessa", 1900

"New Russia" project, which sought to fill the power vacuum left behind by the Ottoman Empire, engaged in targeted settlement of the steppes in southern Ukrainian territory, which became a new imperial governorate. The city's name recalls the ancient Greek history of the area and negates the Ottoman past. Odessa is the female form of Odessos, a Greek colony that was supposed to have existed at this site. However, the city was planned as a futurist utopian project when Catherine II (1729–1796) initiated efforts to transform the former Tatar village of Khadjibey into a modern European city by the name of Odessa. Josep de Ribas y Boyons (1749–1800), a Neapolitan military officer in Catherine's service, had conquered the Tatar village without a fight as a secondary battlefield in the Russo-Turkish War (1787–1792), at which point he recommended to the empress that she found a metropolis at the site, located favourably as it was between the steppes and the sea.

In 1794 – Washington, D.C. had been under construction for two years at this time – development began on a city with a layout similar to that of a chessboard. Odessa was meant to be a beacon of civilisation and trade in an ambitious empire that was ascending on to the European and global stage. In the decades leading up to the Crimean War (1853–1856), Odessa developed into a prosperous hub of global trade flows and to one of the world's most important grain ports. Under the governor general of New Russia, Armand du Plessis, Duc de Richelieu (1766–1822) and his successor, Mikhail Vorontsov (1782–1856), Odessa created networks throughout the world. Thanks to Odessa's excellent connection to international sea routes, people could reach Odessa faster from London than they could from St. Petersburg.

Wherever prosperity beckoned with short routes and seemingly inexhaustible opportunities, people came from all over to settle within just a few years. A Swiss traveller remarked in 1845: "In Odessa, Russians encounter Turks, Germans Greeks, British Armenians, French Arabs, Italians Bulgarians or Wallachs, Poles Circassians, Hungarians Persians or Bukharans. Everything rolls and tumbles

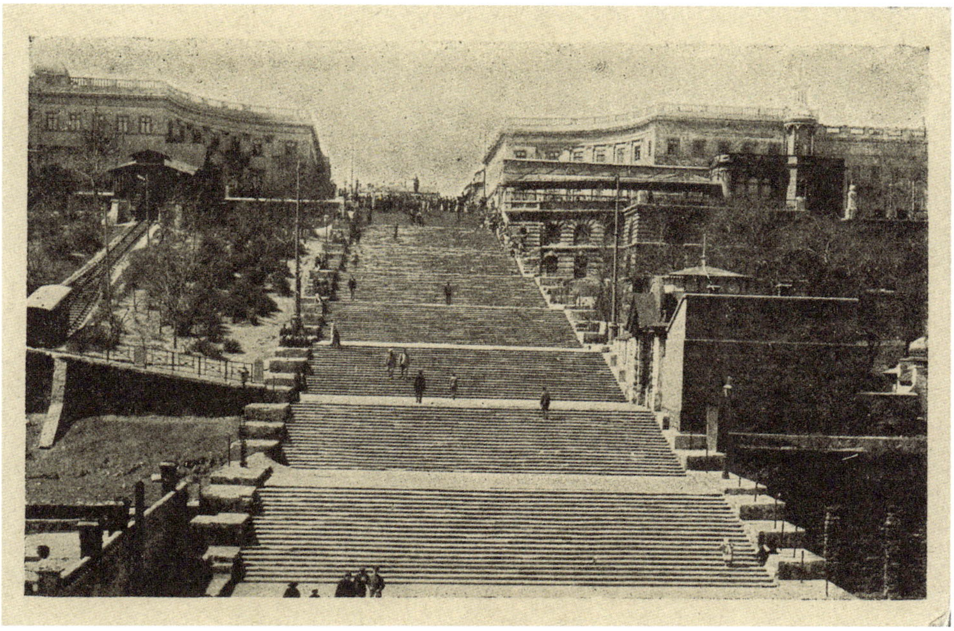

Picture postcard of Odessa showing the harbour stairway, 1918

together, the swallow-tailed coat of the western European with the caftans and robes of the Orientals; the modern hat of a Frenchman peeks out of the colourful masses, along with the towering cap of a Persian, the turban of an Anatolian, the fez of a Moreot […]".[3] In the south of the Russian Empire, a cultural melting pot had formed that brought together many people of different origins; wealthy merchants from the Mediterranean were just as well represented there as newly settled German farmers and Jews. Odessa was located within what was called the "Pale of Settlement", an area in the western Russian Empire in which the residential and labour rights of the Jewish population had been restricted since the end of the eighteenth century. This is why Odessa became a central place for Jews in particular; they were the middlemen who ensured that grain was brought from the hinterlands to the ships, and they established a rich cultural life.

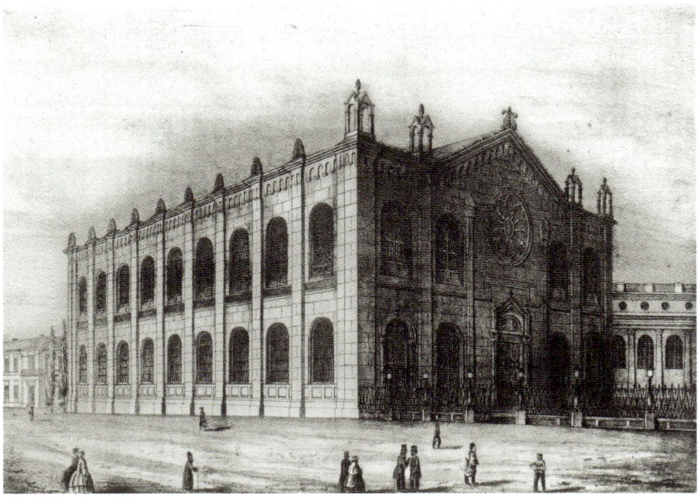

View of the main synagogue in Odessa, 1860

The limits of openness: Violence and pogroms

Tolerance and openness formed the foundation for Odessa's emergence as a boomtown. The population's extreme diversity, however, presented both the opportunity, as well as fertile ground in times of danger, for anti-cosmopolitanism and radicalism. Wars, economic depressions and the rise of Russian nationalism provided occasions for pogroms, acts of violence motivated by various causes, and revolutionary uprisings. These phenomena could only attain such dimensions in Odessa because latent conflicts broke out openly, and the Enlightenment project of founding a port and trade city upon rational ideals turned upon itself.

Russia's defeat in the Crimean War brought two incisive changes to Odessa: the Great Powers no longer relied on the "bread basket" of Europe in the Black Earth Region; instead, they sought alternative suppliers of wheat, rye and oats. They found what they were looking for on the American continent. Argentina and the USA became two dangerous competitors for the Russian Empire and its trading centre in Odessa in the increasingly global world market for grain. Furthermore, Odessa lost its status as a duty-free port in 1857, thereby stripping it of all the privileges that had made it an outstanding site for trade. The darkening economic situation in Odessa found expression in the form of growing poverty, criminality and political radicalisation, which caused the Jews in particular to suffer.

There had already been violent eruptions against Jews in the early nineteenth century. The major pogroms of 1871, and especially of 1881, were however a new phenomenon in terms of their quality. Those who had not profited from the "great reforms" of Alexander II now took advantage of ubiquitous virulent anti-Semitism as an outlet. After the deadly attack on Tsar Alexander II in 1881, which was attended by rumours that a Jewish woman was involved, what John Klier has called the Russian "mal-ordered police state" was scarcely able to curb the ensuing pogroms. In order to prevent future pogroms, Minister of the Interior Nikolay Pavlovich Ignatyev (1832–1908) proposed a renewed prohibition against Jewish settlements outside the city, in the Pale of Settlement. Although this plan was never implemented, it nevertheless illustrated the one-sided efforts that some of the political elite sought to apply as a solution to the problem. In the final analysis, they victimised the Jews once again after the pogroms by restricting their freedoms.

The sorrowful climax of the history of Jewish pogroms in Odessa was reached in 1905. The Russian Empire had just suffered defeat in the Russo-Japanese War, meaning that Odessa lost the Far East as one of its major trading partners. Grain exports fell by half, resulting in bankruptcies and unemployment. The political mood, which was already agitated, exploded into the worst pogrom against the Jews that the city had ever seen. Dozens of people were murdered and the mob plundered hundreds of Jewish businesses. What many had believed to be an exemplar of peaceful coexistence of cultures and religions turned out to be nothing more than a thin veneer of civilisation.

Given the Jews' experience of violence and hopelessness, it is not surprising that Odessa became a hotbed of the Zionist movement in the early twentieth century. The idea of boarding a ship to go establish a Jewish state in the British territory of Palestine found an ideal breeding ground in a port city defined by mobility. Vladimir Ze'ev Jabotinsky (1880–1940), the intellectual forefather of the Israeli state, wrote for various newspapers in Odessa up to 1908 under the pseudonym Altalena.[4]

Odessa was not significant only for the Zionist movement; it also served as the point of departure for several different political, artistic and scientific movements. The literary work of such writers as Isaac Babel and Sholem Aleichem (1859–1916) was shaped by Odessa's ethnic and social complexity; Élie Metchnikoff (1845–1916), who later received the Nobel Prize in Physiology or Medicine, benefitted from the expansion of the city's educational system when he accepted a teaching position in Odessa in 1867. Leon Trotsky (1879–1940) was born in the village of Yanovka in the territory of Odessa, and he completed his schooling at the German Lutheran secondary school at St. Paul's in Odessa. Various revolutionary circles made Odessa a refuge for radical liberalism; indeed, Czar Nicholas I (1796–1855) had already referred to the city pejoratively as a "nest of conspirators".

Despite all of the violence, Odessa remained a place of hope up to the end of the nineteenth century. In the 1890s, for example, Sholem Aleichem had his fictional hero Menachem Mendel claim that gold lay upon the streets of Odessa. Opportunity and threat, cosmopolitanism and radical nationalism, peaceful coexistence and violent conflicts – it was impossible to know in advance which way the pendulum would swing. Many contemporaries retrospectively constructed a well-ordered image of "their" Odessa, which they held up as a bulwark against the confusing present day. The feeling of nostalgia, namely that Odessa's best days were behind it, had already become the dominant mood by the mid-nineteenth century. The catastrophes visited upon the city in the twentieth century only amplified this perception.

Birthplace of revolution and city of heroes: The reinvention of Odessa in the 1920s and 1950s

The first half of the twentieth century was a terrible time for Odessa: dissolving statehood, changing occupiers, civil war, terror, starvation, the Holocaust. When the Bolsheviks conquered the city in 1920, tens of thousands of residents had already emigrated by sea or fled. Thousands of houses stood empty, and the movement of supplies had come to a halt. Yet reconstruction proceeded quickly; the population grew from just over 300,000 in 1920 to almost 600,000 by the beginning of the "Great Patriotic War". A new identity accompanied reconstruction: the empire's former cosmopolitan city was elevated to the birthplace of the Bolshevik movement, thanks to an icon of Soviet film history. Sergei Eisenstein (1898–1948) invented nothing less than a new Odessa in his silent film, *Battleship Potemkin*, which placed the city in an impressive context. His film, produced on the occasion of the twentieth anniversary of the 1905 Revolution, became famous throughout the world. The montage technique that Eisenstein used was not intended to communicate a consistent plot; instead, it sought to elicit strong emotions in the audience. The film's impact stemmed in large part from Eisenstein's staging of Odessa's topography. In the film's most famous Odessa Steps scene, soldiers march down the giant Potemkin Stairs and fire into the fleeing masses. This scene portrays, in a particularly drastic way, downward-marching soldiers, monumental architecture and the movement of helpless people trying to escape. Eisenstein turned Odessa into a "storm bell that heralded the outbreak of the Revolution", the "true birthplace of the Soviet Union".

This mythical glorification, however, did not protect the city from the fatal consequences of starvation in the early 1930s. The city fell under Romanian-German occupation in the Second World War. Whoever was able to do so left the city in the late 1930s and during the Siege of Odessa in the summer of 1941. During this period, thousands made their way to the port, taking "their" Odessa with them as mental luggage into the cities of the Soviet Union, Western Europe and the American continent. Odessa once again became a site associated with longing for a golden past. The final doom of Old Odessa came shortly after to the shores of the Black Sea. After a bomb attack by partisans on the headquarters of the Romanian occupiers on 22 October 1941, the dictator Ion Antonescu (1882–1946) ordered a campaign of revenge in which tens of thousands of Jews were murdered. This was only the beginning of the Holocaust in the Odessa territory, which killed a majority of the remaining Jewish population before the Red Army reclaimed the city in 1944.

"Odessa Mama": The port city as a site of longing

At the end of the Second World War, Odessa had very little in common with the city remembered by numerous emigrants in Tel Aviv, Brighton Beach (New York) and Berlin. The disappearance of the Jews meant the loss of one of the city's major ethnic groups; bombardments and battles had destroyed buildings and infrastructure; and a majority of the surviving population had fled to nearby villages. The

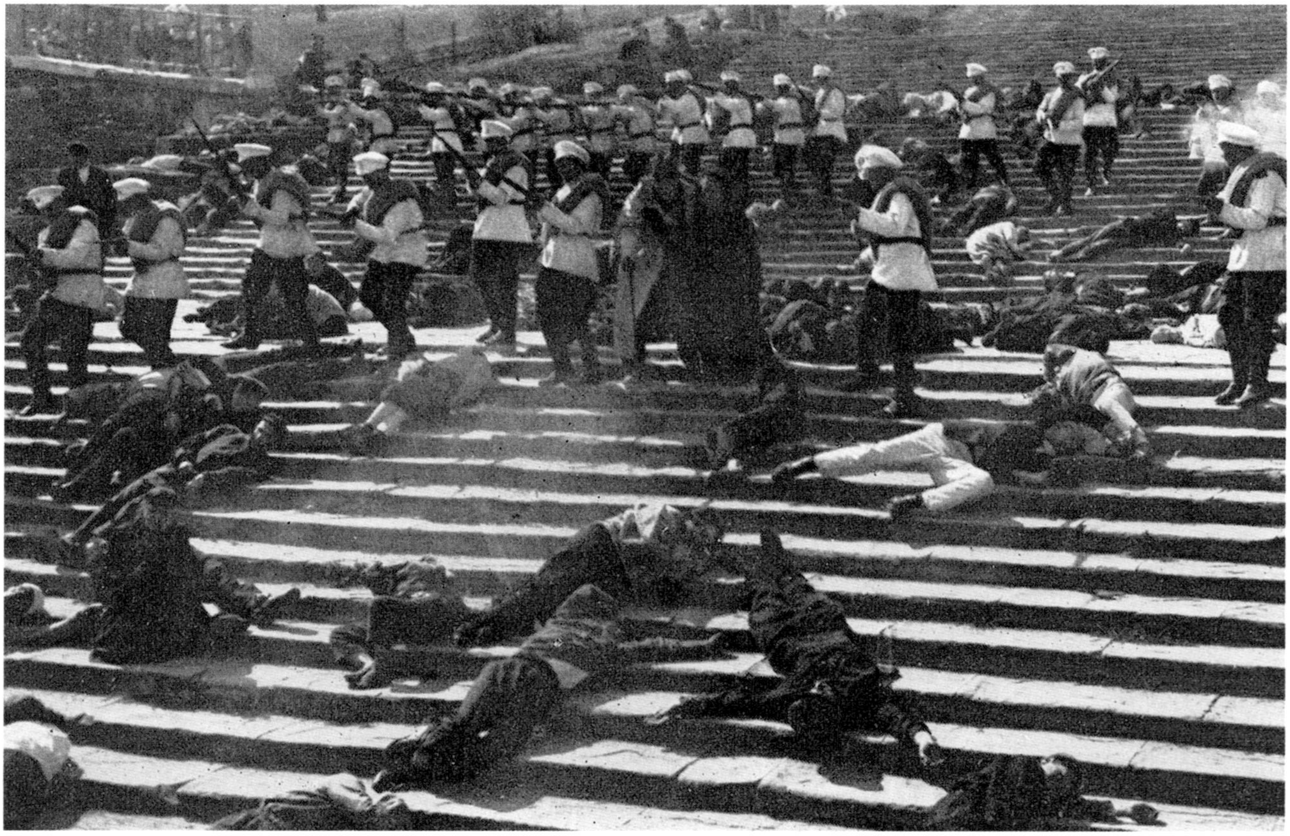

Still frame from the film *Battleship Potemkin* showing the suppression of the sailors' mutiny in 1905, 1926

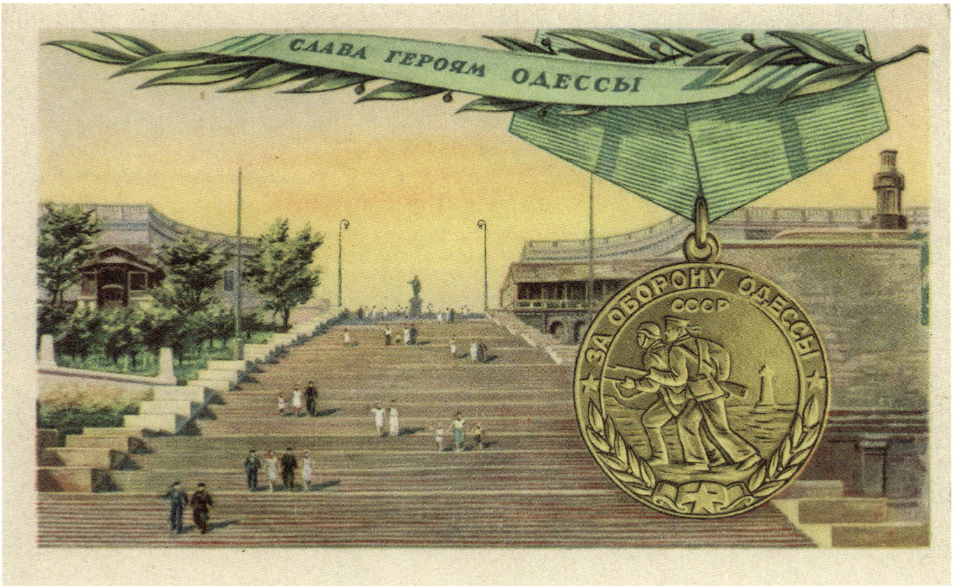

View of the stairway in Odessa with Soviet medal, c. 1950

port and its loading stations lay in ruins; maritime trade had ground to a halt. It therefore seemed all the more important to the Soviet rulers to support the city's reconstruction in a dignified way and to construct new images and ideas about the port city. On 1 May 1945, Odessa was declared to be one of four "cities of heroes" in the Soviet Union; the city was allowed from then on to fly its municipal flag with the additional decorations of the Order of Lenin and the "Great Star" medal. Odessites now saw the name of their city on commemorative coins and on a plaque on the wall of the Kremlin in Moscow. The city had become an integral component of the official commemoration of the "Great Patriotic War", which, up to the end of the Soviet Union, was the most important point of reference for national historiography and affirmation.

Alongside official honours, there was also a feature film that sought to make "Odessa" the prototype of all things Soviet: *Dva boica* ("Two Soldiers"), already filmed in 1943, told the story of two befriended soldiers in besieged Leningrad. Mark Bernes (1911–1969) played the character Arkady Dzubin, a courageous young man from Odessa who is incited by the fascist occupation of his home city to fight heroically in Leningrad. In the post-war period, the fictional Dzubin became one of Odessa's most famous residents and a representative of Stalin's "last generation," those who maintained a sense for entertainment and amusement despite their self-sacrificing service to the Soviet Union.

Odessa again became the Soviet Union's largest port in the 1960s and 1970s. The city grew enormously and was confronted once again with a major population exchange. Some of the Russian-speaking elite emigrated to Moscow and Leningrad so that they could continue their ascent among the powerful. Ukrainians from the nearby area moved into the region's centre. Skilled workers from all over the Soviet Union were recruited with the intention of ensuring the functional capacity of the port's complex infrastructure and of surrounding industry. It was in this way that Odessa developed into a "normal" Soviet metropolis, with over one million inhabitants by 1974.

At the same time, however, another Odessa arose that completely dispensed with "normal" characteristics. The longing of many Soviet citizens and emigrants for amusement in exciting, different worlds manifested particularly strongly in the nostalgic transfiguration of the port city on the Black Sea. In the age of mass media and modern tourism, Odessa became a sort of Mississippi Delta of the Russian Empire. Leonid Utyosov (1895–1982), the famous jazz musician born in Odessa, established the myth of "Old Odessa" with his disreputable pubs, gangs of criminals and klezmer bands; his music was the nucleus of jazz in the Russian Empire and the Soviet Union. The autobiography of the writer Konstantin Paustovsky (1892–1968), in which the passages about his childhood and youth in Odessa disseminated the image of an exotic city, became a bestseller in late socialist Russia. It is no wonder that many Soviet citizens set out for Odessa themselves to add the spice of new experiences to their uniform everyday lives. It was because of the travel restrictions imposed on citizens from Warsaw Pact states that the city developed in the 1960s and 1970s into a popular travel destination and a centre of Soviet tourism. Swimming in the sea, strolling along Deribasivska Street, enjoying fresh fruit and vegetables from the countryside, attending concerts and the opera – all of this meant relaxation and holiday. In their imaginations, these tourists were probably less in the contemporary Soviet city than they were in the fictional construct of late-nineteenth-century Odessa, as is demonstrated by a wealth of available memorabilia. Illustrated books, postcard collections and the ubiquitous writings of local historians forged a connection over the large span of time separating the late Soviet present and the late imperial past. However, this nostalgic retrospection and its distortions turned a blind eye to the dark side of the city's history. Pogroms, expulsions and occupation simply did not exist in this narrow view of "Mama Odessa", as the city was lovingly called.

An uncertain future: Odessa as part of the Ukraine

The collapse and voluntary liquidation of the Soviet Union was a turning point for Odessa. A city that had hardly considered itself Ukrainian, and whose ethnic composition certainly did not fit such a narrow ascription, now found itself suddenly in a new state. In the 1990s, the political self-definition of the now sovereign Ukraine national state remained marked by the contradiction of striving towards the European Union while also seeking to maintain close political and economic ties to Moscow. For an international seaport such as Odessa, the decisions made in the Ukrainian capital of Kiev were of critical importance.

During the course of the "Orange Revolution" of 2004, a majority of the city's population leaned towards the pro-Russia camp. Several thousand demonstrators assembled to protest the pro-Western presidential candidate Viktor Yushchenko (born 1954). They called for regional independence if he was voted into office. Ten years later, Odessa was a site in the Ukraine conflict. On 2 May 2014, the participants of a "march for Ukrainian unity" collided with several hundred pro-Russian activists. The following violent conflicts between both sides, and also within each side, resulted in the burning of the Trade Union Building, and at least forty-two pro-Russian activists died as the consequence of the late arrival of fire-fighters to the scene. The 200 dead and injured alarmed the international community. Events became explosive when Moscow began offering argumentative support. As late as

August 2014, Vladimir Putin, speaking in a television interview about the southern part of the Ukraine, which includes Odessa and the neighbouring city of Mykolaiv, invoked the term "New Russia", thereby creating a rhetorical link to the era of Catherine the Great, from which the port city had issued. When one year later the "New Russia" project was completely off the table and the separatist uprising withdrew to the new "people's republics" in Donetsk and Lugansk in the east, violence in the city came to a halt. This did not, however, spell the end of debates about Odessa as a historical site. The city's image testifies even now to its multi-layered past and contentious present. Whoever walks through the city can admire the memorial honouring Catherine II, reinstalled in 2007, and sense an echo of old imperial grandeur. The main synagogue, property of the Jewish community since 1996, tells of the Jewish past at this city on the Black Sea, and the Odessa Steps remain a central hub of urban life. The port city remains a site of longing for people from both the West and the East.

1 Karl Schlögel, *Entscheidung in Kiew. Ukrainische Lektionen* (Munich, 2015), 128.
2 Schlögel 129.
3 Daniel Wegelin, *Erinnerungen aus Russland und dem Orient*, ed. Heinrich Leemann, Vol. 1 (Zürich, 1843–1845), 177.
4 Vladimir Ze'ev Jabotinsky, *The Iron Wall (1923)*, Jewish Virtual Library, accessed 5 January 2018, http://www.jewishvirtuallibrary.org/quot-the-iron-wall-quot.

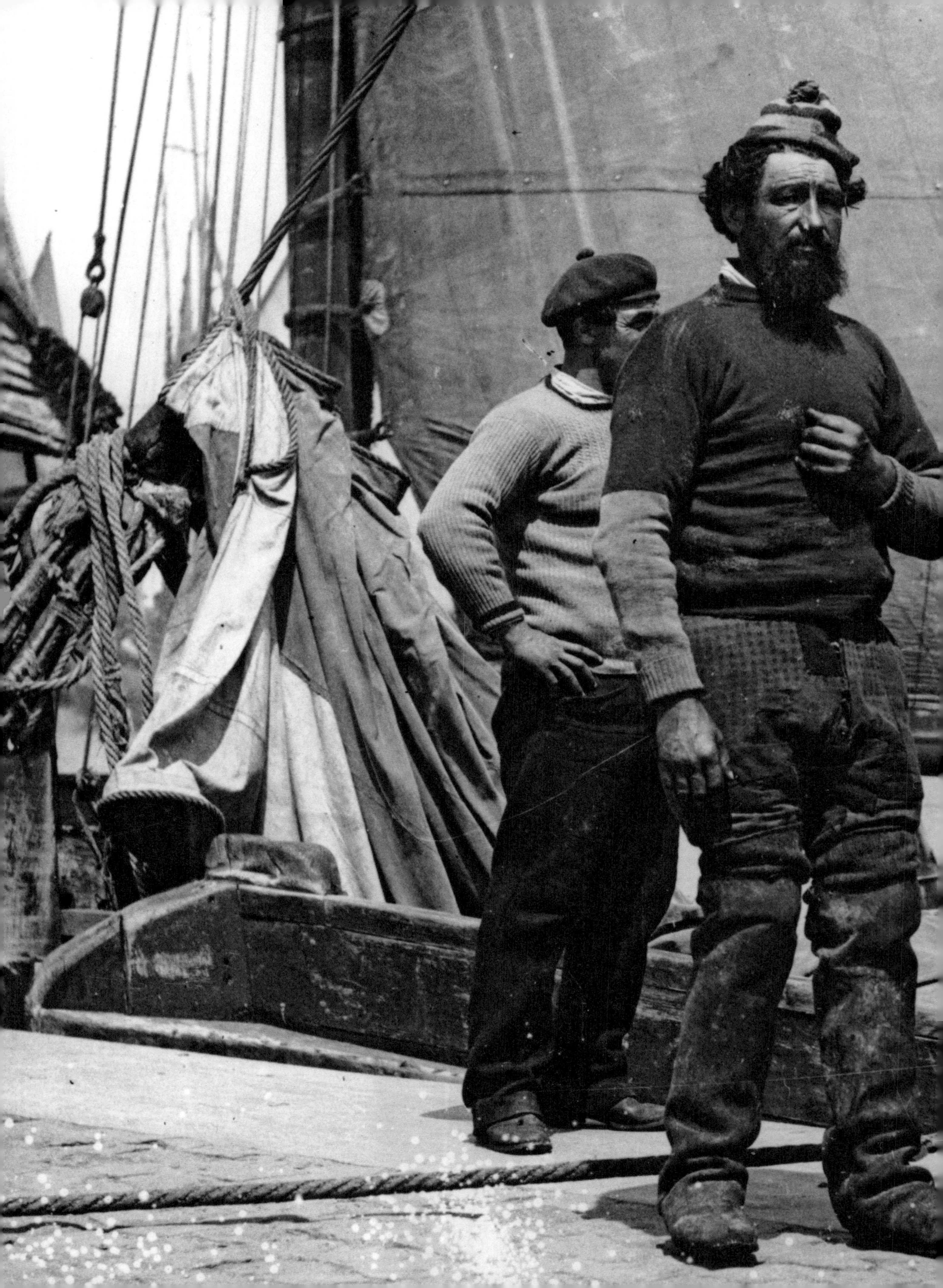

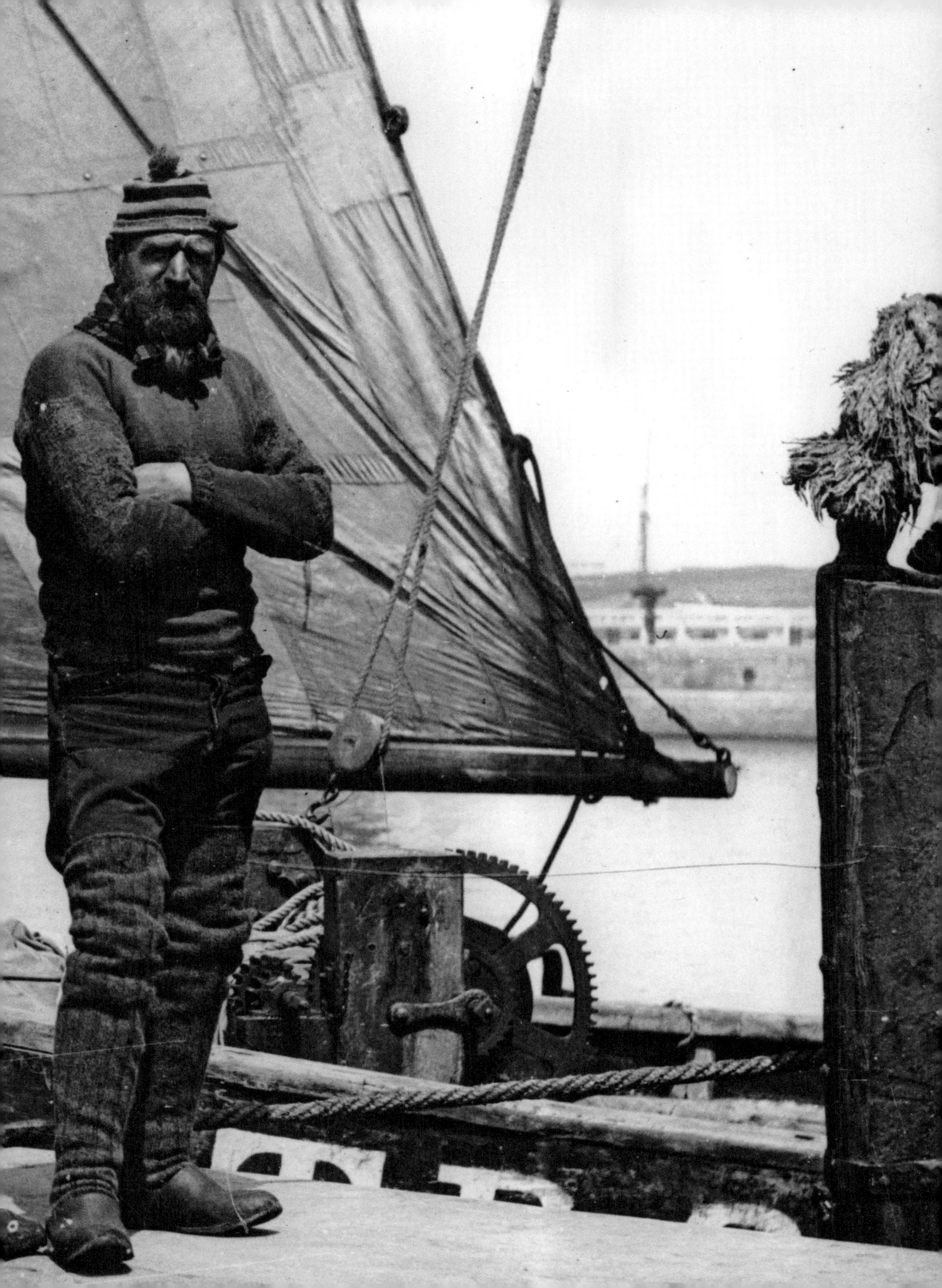

Prologue

Europe is a maritime continent. The exhibition *Europe and the Sea* reveals the importance of the sea to the development of European civilization, identifying four primary roles that it has played over many centuries up to the present day. The sea has been an arena for conducting trade and competing for territory, a bridge and barrier between people and continents, a resource for food and raw materials, and a focus of yearning and imagination. These broad themes are elaborated over the course of thirteen chapters, arranged in chronological order. Each is introduced by a European port that exemplifies the phenomena associated with that chapter's particular topic. Port cities are more than interfaces between the land and the sea; they are hubs for the movement of goods, people and information. This has transformed many of them into major centres of power, each which has left its own mark on the history of Europe and the world.

The largest section of the exhibition looks at how Europeans have used the sea to expand their commercial and political territories. For hundreds of years, command of the sea was an essential part of European efforts to establish hegemony. European powers used the sea for travel and transport, building up empires all around the world. Commercial interests and territorial ambitions almost always went hand in hand. The chapters in this section examine the gradual appropriation of the sea in Antiquity, Venetian naval supremacy in the Middle Ages, European expansionism in the fifteenth and sixteenth centuries with Portugal and Spain as its protagonists, the rise of the Netherlands as a shipbuilding nation in the seventeenth century, the slave trade, and lastly British dominance during the long nineteenth century, which is illustrated in the chapter on the global economy. Europe's exploration of the world, accompanied by processes of exchange, have fundamentally shaped European history and culture. The consequences for people on other continents have been no less profound: for many, the arrival of the Europeans meant violence, oppression, exploitation and extermination.

Oceans are bridges and barriers alike. The Migration section, placed at the centre of the exhibition, follows Europe's transition from a continent of emigration in the nineteenth century to one of immigration in the twentieth and twenty-first. It is largely devoted to the historical dimension of the subject, using the port of Bremerhaven to illustrate the main waves of emigration from Europe in the nineteenth century. Rather than looking into their causes or how the emigrants fared in their host societies, it focuses on the passage by ship, the actual act of emigrating across the sea. A similar approach is taken in the second part of the section, which begins with the evolution of Europe into a continent of net immigration from 1945 onwards and ends with present-day migration across the Mediterranean.

The third section of the exhibition deals with the importance of the sea as a resource and an area of research, which is especially relevant today. A survey of the millennia-old tradition of fishing leads into the scientific study of the sea and more recent issues of use and over-use. These apply not only to the extraction of oil and natural gas, but increasingly to mineral resources such as manganese nodules, cobalt-rich ferromanganese crusts and methane hydrate. Their discovery is entirely due to deep-sea research, which has been gathering pace for several decades. This section also addresses the risks and rewards of resource utilisation and exploration, and highlights issues that are crucial to the future of the environment and the world's climate.

In the two final chapters, Tourism and Painting, the exhibition turns to cultural perspectives on the sea as a catalyst of yearning and imagination. It shows how the emergence of a new, 'sensitive' perception of nature led to a change in mentality that elevated the sea to the epitome of beauty and revitalisation. In the middle of the eighteenth century, scientists discovered its therapeutic qualities, and soon the first seaside resorts were established, first in England and then on the continental coasts of the North Sea and the Baltic Sea. At around the same time, painters began to treat the sea and coastal landscapes as subjects of art in their own right.

With each chapter starting from a different European port, the exhibition takes visitors on a series of imaginary voyages that reveal the enduring importance of the sea to Europe. Even Europa, the continent's mythical namesake, came here across the sea. As the story goes, she was a Phoenician princess whom Zeus, in the shape of a bull, carried off across the eastern Mediterranean to the island of Crete. In the beginning, there was violence and love, a migrant who gave her name to a continent and – as ever – the sea.

Dorlis Blume, Christiana Brennecke, Ursula Breymayer, Thomas Eisentraut

Further Reading

David Abulafia, *Das Mittelmeer. Eine Biographie*, Frankfurt a. M. 2013

Die Verführung der Europa, revised by Barbara Mundt, exhib. cat., Berlin 1988

Jürgen Elvert et al (eds.), *Das maritime Europa. Werte – Wissen – Wirtschaft*, Stuttgart 2016

Konrad Heldmann, *Europa und der Stier oder der Brautraub des Zeus. Die Entführung der Europa in den Darstellungen der griechischen und römischen Antike*, Göttingen 2016

Idee Europa. Entwürfe zum »Ewigen Frieden«, ed. by Marie-Louise von Plessen, exhib. cat., Berlin 2003

Michel Mollat du Jourdin, *Europa und das Meer*, Munich 1993

Michael North, *Zwischen Hafen und Horizont. Weltgeschichte der Meere*, Munich 2016

Dieter Richter, *Das Meer. Geschichte der ältesten Landschaft*, Berlin 2014

Philip de Souza, *Die Beherrschung der Meere. Wie die Seefahrt die Menschheitsgeschichte prägte*, Munich 2006

Simon Winchester, *Der Atlantik. Biographie eines Ozeans*, Munich 2010

Eva Zahn, *Europa und der Stier*, Würzburg 1983

0/1 **Europa on the Bull**
Greece, 500–475 B.C.
Clay; 16.2 x 17 x 6.3 cm
Berlin, Staatliche Museen zu Berlin, Antikensammlung: TC 8493

This terracotta sculpture shows the mythical abduction of Europa. The Phoenician princess aroused the desire of Zeus, the chief of the gods on Mount Olympus. He turned himself into a bull and carried Europa off across the sea to Crete, where she ultimately bore him three sons. In Greece, the myth came to symbolise the bride being led to her wedding. For this reason, its imagery is often found on vessels used in the rite of marriage. Terracotta statuettes such as the one shown here would be laid in the graves of children and unmarried girls as a substitute for the wedding that they had not lived to experience. This piece was probably made in the Greek region of Boeotia. It still bears traces of ancient paint, especially red, on the shoes, the hem of the robe, and the shawl-like cape. AS

In ancient times, the tale of Europa was not seen as a founding myth that supplied an identity for this part of the world. It was not until the Renaissance that artists began to depict Europa on the bull, in works whose symbolism alluded to the continent's mythical birth "over the sea". This idea remains current today. The Greek 2 Euro coin bears a representation of Europa on the bull, which has been adapted from a mosaic found in Sparta, dating from the third century. DB

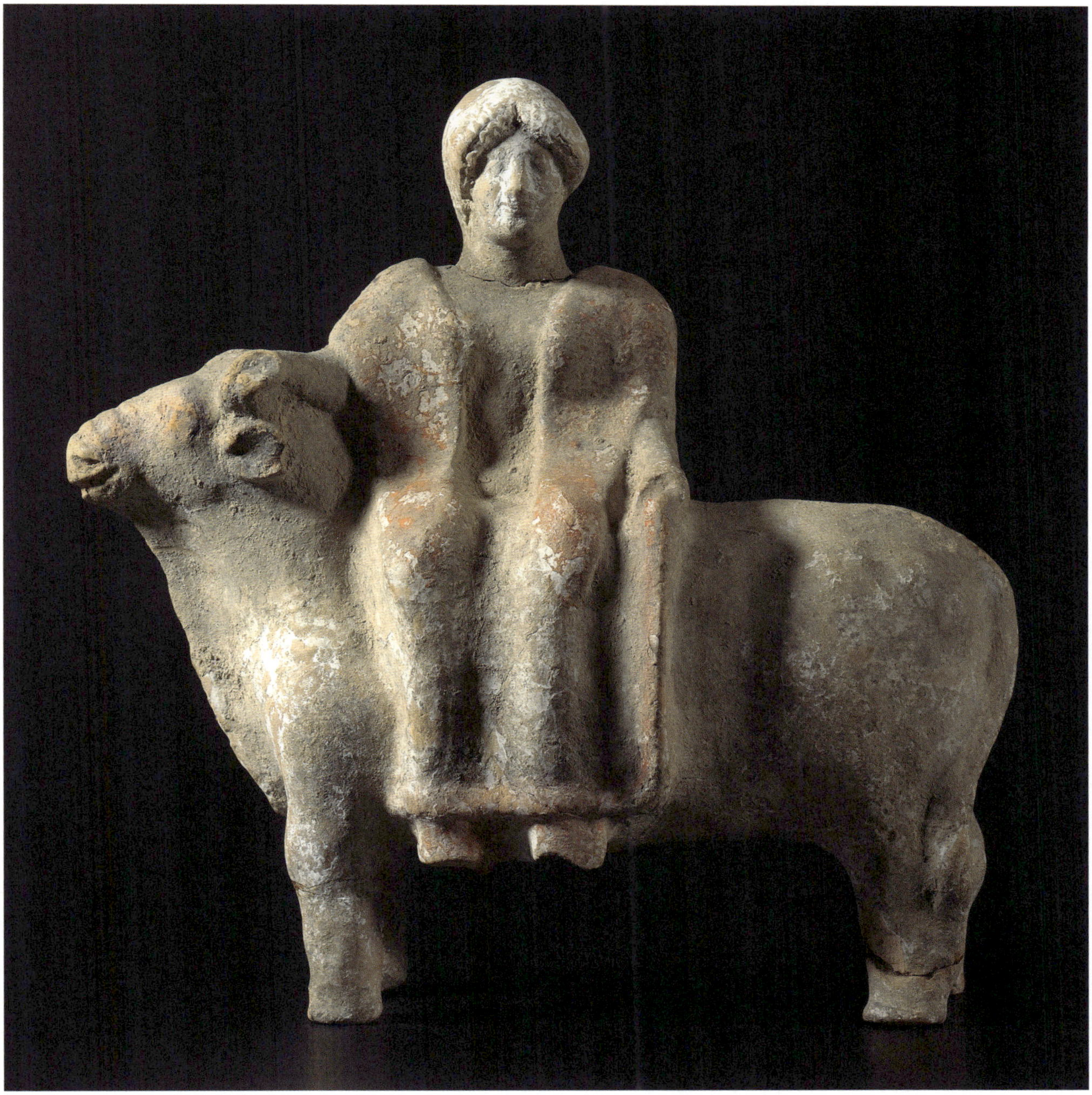

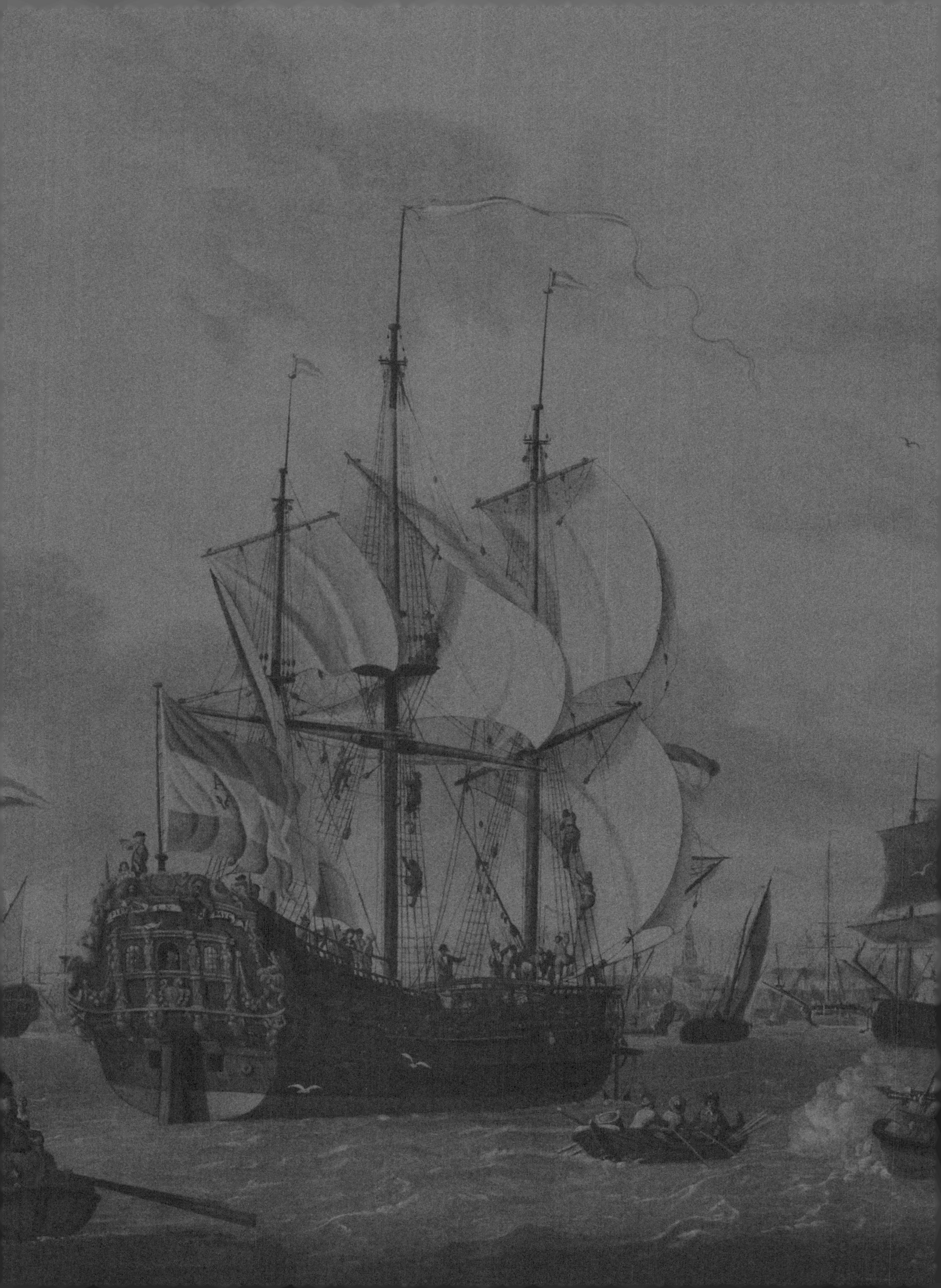

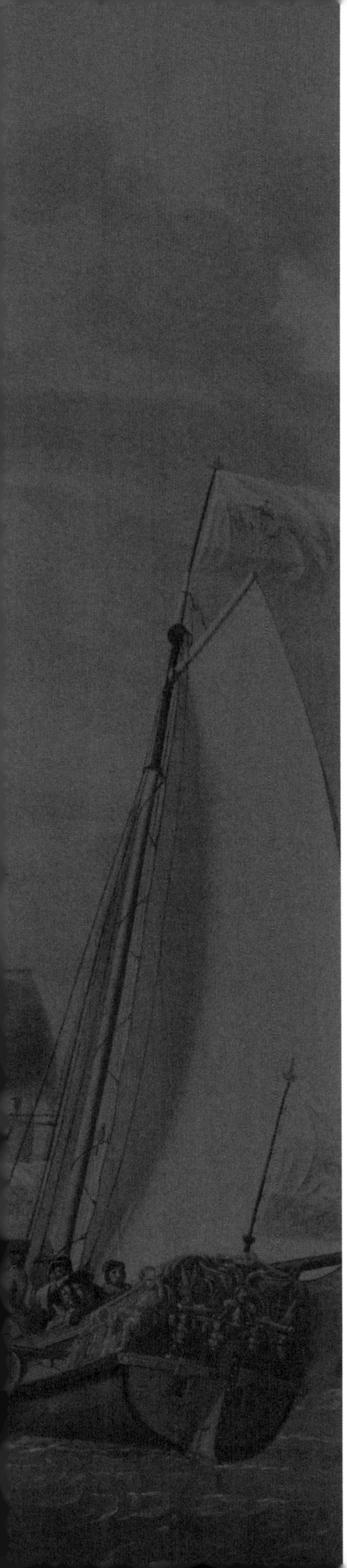

I
TERRITORY AND TRADE

1 Ancient Foundations The Port of Piraeus

The people of Greece and Western Asia Minor had a rather distanced relationship to the sea during the Archaic period. The poet Homer (presumed 850/750 B.C.) conveys this powerfully in the *Odyssey*, which contains the earliest written accounts of seafaring in Antiquity. Homer tells of the Greeks sailing mostly near to the coast with longships that could be pulled up onto sandy beaches sheltered from the wind (Homer, *Odyssey*, 2, 389; 6, 263 seq.). They preferred to eat meat from land animals; fish and seafood were largely rejected as unsuitable for eating and were consumed only as a last resort. In the *Odyssey*, the sea is portrayed as the haunt of gods, Cyclopes, demons and sorceresses – a realm that only true heroes dare to cross. One such hero was Odysseus, who experienced many dangerous adventures with his companions on the way back from Troy to his home island of Ithaca in Greece. In the end, he was the only one of them to survive, arriving home only after wandering the seas for ten years. A passage describing the encounter between Odysseus and the Phaeacian princess Nausicaa is the earliest to list features that qualify as typical of a port. The land and the sea meet in the form of a harbour, which has berths for mooring boats and a walled basin to provide shelter from storms, strong currents and enemies. Nearby there are adequate storage facilities for merchandise, a market place for selling perishable goods, and a lighthouse marking the location of the harbour by night.

From the eighth century B.C. onwards, the sea was gradually appropriated and lost its mythical character. This went hand in hand with the Greeks' development of a new form of settlement, which Homer calls the *polis*. The bare fields of the mountainous regions of Greece and Asia Minor were no longer sufficient to feed growing populations, so people left the hill villages, which until then had been the traditional form of settlement, and began to farm areas of fertile alluvial land on the coast, usually at the mouth of a river. The *poleis* were the starting points for the colonisation of the entire Mediterranean and Black Sea regions, leading in turn to the emergence of trading posts and the development of the area as a whole with the help of relatively accurate maps.

The most important *polis* was Athens with its port, Piraeus. The foundation of the Delian League in 478/477 B.C. allowed Athens to become the leading power in the Mediterranean. The allied *poleis* adopted Athenian currency and the Athenian system of weights and measures as the league's trade passed more and more through the port of Athens. The naval power of Athens was thus based on a network of colonised coastal areas throughout the Mediterranean.

The Romans, who were not a seafaring people to begin with, followed the Greek model in building up their navy and ultimately achieved what no country before them had managed: the sole command of the Mediterranean. They kept it for nearly three hundred years, from the 2nd century B.C. to the 2nd century A.D. This found expression in the commonly used term *mare nostrum* (our sea). The Roman military leader and ruler of Sicily, Sextus Pompeius (76/66?–35 B.C.) went so far as to claim the sea personally. On the coins that he issued, he portrayed Neptune and the sea monster Scylla in a manner that implied that the sea itself fought on his side. This may be the first overt expression of the idea that a ruler could have command of the sea. *Dorlis Blume*

Further Reading

Bernard Andreae (ed.), *Odysseus. Mythos und Erinnerung* (exhib. cat. Haus der Kunst München), Mainz 1999

Ernst Baltrusch u. a. (eds.), *Seemacht, Seeherrschaft und die Antike*, Stuttgart 2016

Karl Christ, *Pompeius*, Munich 2004

Eva Hofstetter, *Sirenen im archaischen und klassischen Griechenland*, Würzburg 1990

Interactive catalogue of the Numismatic Collection, with literature under the item number of each object: http://ikmk.smb.museum/

Peter Knoblauch, *Studien zur archaisch-griechischen Tonbildnerei in Kreta, Rhodos, Athen und Böotien*, Halle 1937

Peter F. Mittag, *Alte Köpfe in neuen Händen*, Bonn 1999

Kurt Regling, *Die antike Münze als Kunstwerk*, Berlin 1924

Agnes Schwarzmaier, *Griechische Klappspiegel. Untersuchungen zu Typologie und Stil*, Mitteilungen des Deutschen Archäologischen Instituts, Athenische Abteilung, 18. Beiheft, Berlin 1997

Raimund Schulz, *Die Antike und das Meer*, Darmstadt 2005

Elke Stein-Hölkeskamp, *Das archaische Griechenland. Die Stadt und das Meer*, Munich 2015

Elena Walter-Karydi, *Skylla*, Jahrbuch des Deutschen Archäologischen Instituts 112, 1997, p. 167–189

Christina Wawrzinek, *Tore zur Welt. Häfen in der Antike*, Darmstadt 2016.

Kathryn Welch, *Magnus Pius. Sextus Pompeius and the Transformation of the Roman Republic*, Swansea 2012

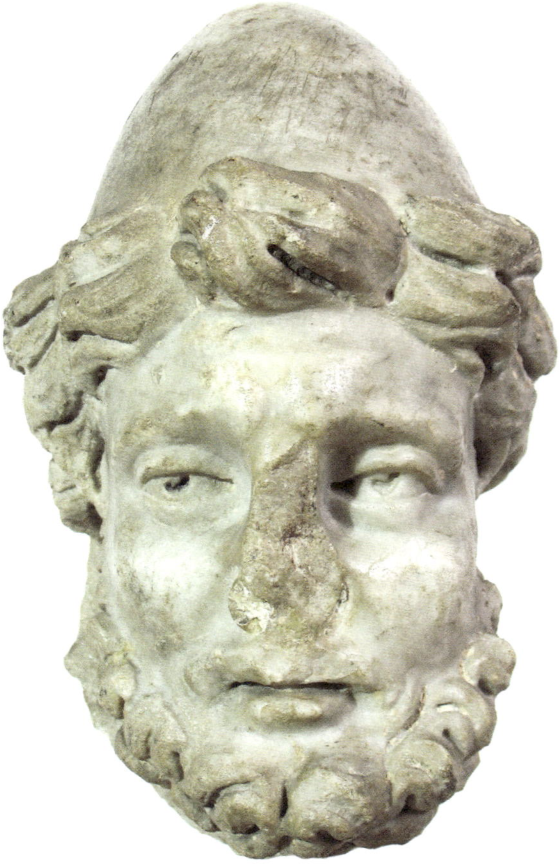

1/1

Ancient Myths: Homer's Odyssey

1/1 **Head of Odysseus**
Copy of a Hellenistic original
c. 250 A.D.
Marble, 30 x 20 cm
Monschau, Kunst- und Kulturzentrum (KuK) der StädteRegion Aachen: 99

Odysseus is a legendary Greek king and the eponymous hero of the *Odyssey*, an epic poem thought to have been written by Homer in the eighth century B.C. It deals with the homeward voyage of Odysseus (Ulysses in Latin) and his companions to Ithaca after the victory of the Greeks in the Trojan War. After Odysseus angers the god of the sea, Poseidon (Neptune in Latin), their return is hindered by countless perils, such as the song of the Sirens, or the passage between the sea monsters Scylla and Charybdis. After ten years of wandering the sea, Odysseus, the sole survivor, returns to his wife and son. In almost every depiction of him, Odysseus wears a *pilos*, the cap traditionally worn by fishermen, sailors and craftsmen. This head of Odysseus was found during excavations in Nettersheim, near the western border of Germany. DB

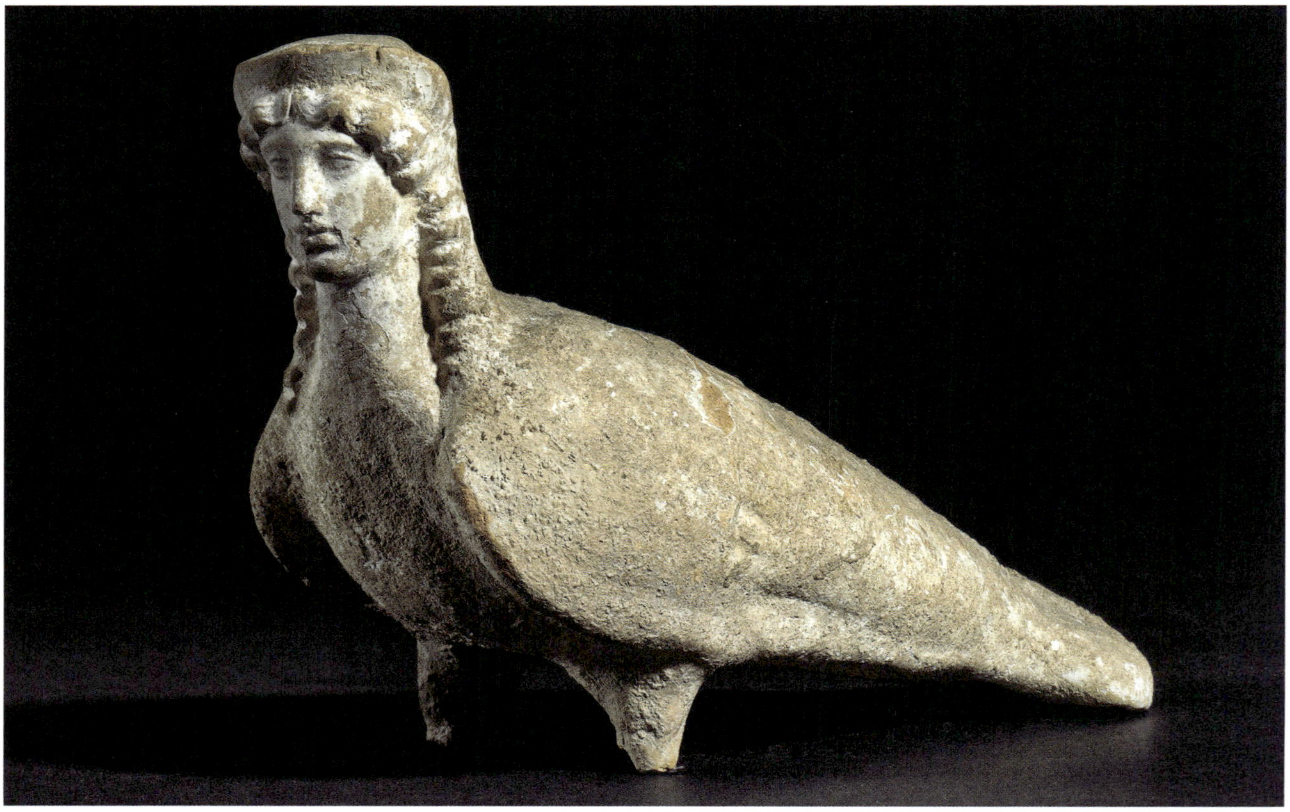

1/2

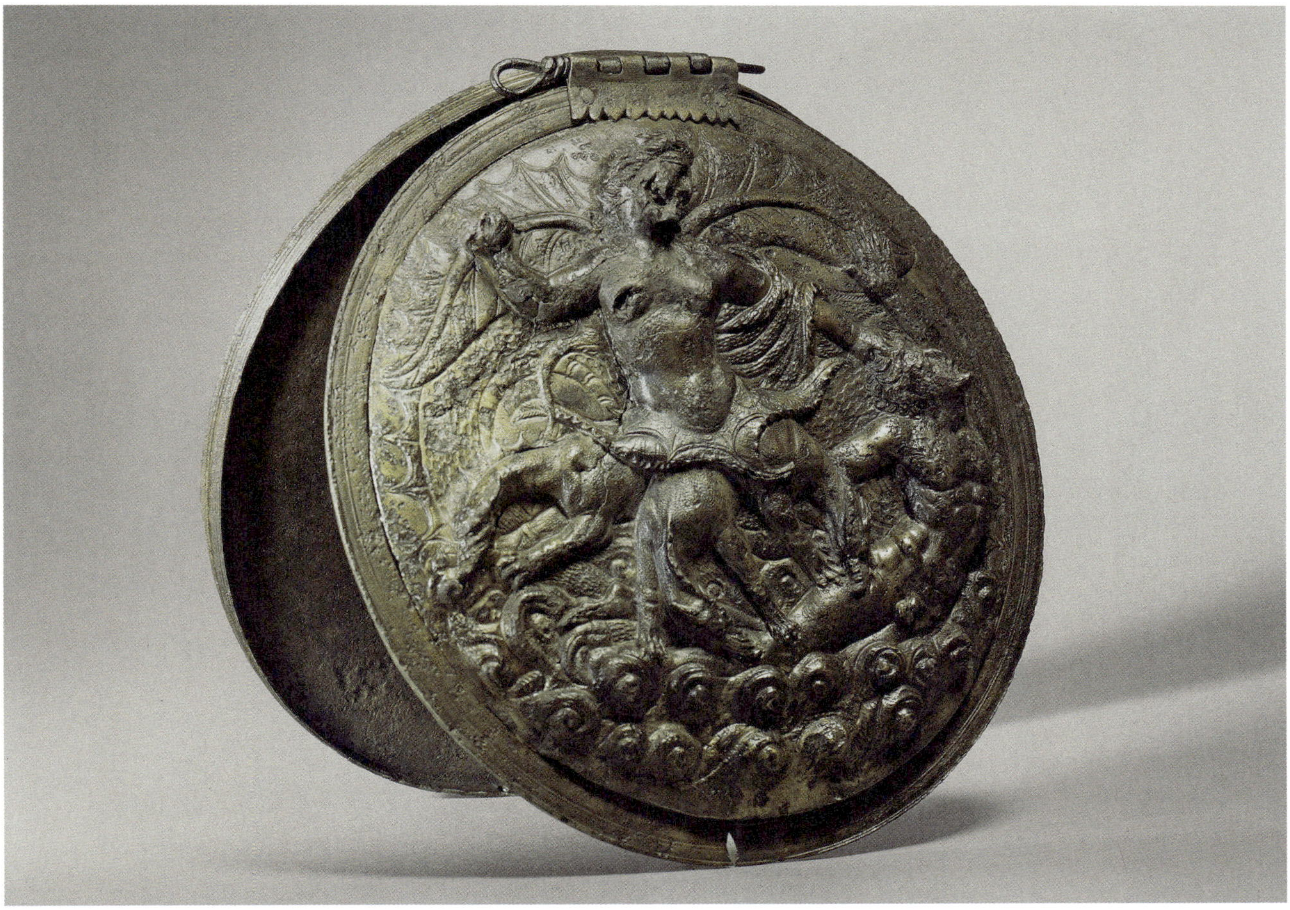

1/3

1/2 **Siren**
Terracotta statuette
Eretria, c. 450–440 B.C.
Clay, 11.5 x 20 x 7 cm
Berlin, Staatliche Museen zu Berlin, Antikensammlung: TC 8478

In the twelfth book of the *Odyssey*, Homer relates how Odysseus gets his ship safely past the rocky island of the Sirens. The Sirens – mythical creatures with the body of a bird and the head of a beautiful girl – were said to enchant men with their song and thus lure them to their deaths. The sorceress Circe advised Odysseus to plug the ears of his companions with wax, but bid them to bind him fast to the ship's mast so that he could listen to the Sirens without jumping overboard to join them. Because their song was said to arouse the longing for love, the Sirens also served as a symbol for girls who wished to enchant a bridegroom. That is why this earthenware figure of a Siren has the head of a girl with a bridal crown, of the kind that is also found on Athenian female figures. It may have been placed in the grave of an a unmarried girl. AS

1/3 **Folding mirror with a depiction of Scylla**
Eretria, c. 320 B.C.
Bronze, diam. 21.7 cm
Berlin, Staatliche Museen zu Berlin, Antikensammlung: Misc. 8391

Scylla was a mythical sea monster with the naked torso and head of a beautiful girl, sometimes with wings. The forequarters of several dogs sprouted from her waist, which ended below in multiple tentacles or fish tails. Homer tells of how Odysseus, towards the end of his long voyage, had to guide his ship along a narrow channel of water between two monsters, Scylla and Charybdis. Charybdis created whirlpools that smashed ships against the rocks, while Scylla snatched sailors from the deck and devoured them. Odysseus decided that it was better to lose some of his companions than the ship with the entire crew. Tradition locates the monsters in the Strait of Messina between Sicily and southern Italy. The relief adorns the cover of a hinged mirror, which had the reflecting surface on the inside of the lower disc. It is not yet known why a figure of this kind was used for a woman's cosmetic accessory. AS

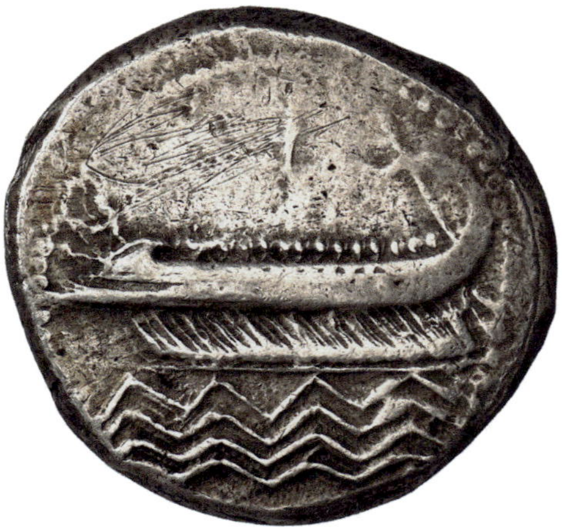

1/5

1/4 **Odysseus and Scylla**
Contorniate medallion
Rome (mint), c. 355–395/423
Bronze, diam. 3.8 cm
Berlin, Staatliche Museen zu Berlin, Münzkabinett: 18206978

People still believed in the existence of sea monsters in the Christian era, and the Roman upper classes continued to cultivate ancient pagan traditions. Pictorial evidence of this is given by medallions struck in the official mint of Rome, which refer to elements of the pre-Christian past. Homer's works, in particular the *Odyssey* and the *Iliad*, were still considered essential reading for a good education. This heavily worn medallion shows the encounter between Odysseus and Scylla as his ship is passing through the strait. She has grabbed one of his companions, who is about to be dragged overboard. Other members of the crew are already in the water, being attacked by the dog-heads that form part of the mythical creature's body. The medal-makers knew what she should look like, because Scylla's iconography follows a tradition that reaches back to the fifth century B.C. (Fig. p. 14) BW

The first description of a European port is found in a passage spoken by Nausicaa, daughter of the king of Phaeacia:
Presently, however, we shall come to the city,
which has a high wall running all round it,
a good harbour on either side and a narrow entrance,
and the curved ships are pulled ashore along the road,
for each has a place where his own ship can lie.
There, too, is the meeting place around the fair temple of Poseidon,
paved with large stones bedded deep in the earth.
Here the men are busy with the tackle of their black ships,
with cables and sails, and here they form the thin oar blades,
for the Phaeacians care not for bows and quivers,
but for masts and oars and graceful ships,
and delight in sailing them far over the grey sea.
(Homer, *Odyssey* 6, 262–272, trans. Samuel Butler, 1900; rev. Richard Toovey)

The poet Aristophanes, writing in the fifth century B.C., described the typical characteristics of a port:
You'd doubtless have three hundred ships at sea straight off,
the city filled with warlike clamour all at once,
talking of nought but armour for the trireme ships,
of salaries, Palladian statues gilded,
of warehouses well stocked, provisions measured out,
of waterskins and oar thongs, purchasing the casks
of garlic and olives, nets filled with onions,
of chaplets, sprats, and piper girls – and black eyes too –
and timber being shaped to oars in the dockyards,
pegs hammered into place and oars attached with straps,
a din of whistles, bagpipes, trumpeted commands.
(Aristophanes, *The Acharnians*, 425 B.C., verses 512–522, trans. C. A. Wheelwright, 1837; rev. Richard Toovey)

Appropriation of the Sea

1/5 **Sidon as a Naval Base**
Double shekel of ʻAbdʻAshtart III, King of Sidon
Sidon (mint), 342/341 B.C.
Silver, diam. 2.9 cm
Berlin, Staatliche Museen zu Berlin, Münzkabinett: 18200164

One of the most important ports in the eastern Mediterranean was Sidon, located in what was then Phoenicia and is now Lebanon. One face of this large silver coin shows King Artaxerxes III Ochus of Persia (c. 390–338 B.C.), who was the overlord of the city in the year of minting. He is standing on a chariot. Marching behind it is the issuer of this coin, the King of Sidon, who carries a sceptre and a cult vase. The obverse, depicting a war galley and a fourfold wave motif, alludes not only to the coastal location of the city and its two harbours, but above all to its importance as a naval base of the Achaemenid (First Persian) Empire. Spreading out from their main cities of Sidon, Tyros and Byblos, the Phoenicians had begun to establish trading posts and colonies in the central and western Mediterranean long before this, in the twelfth century B.C. BW

1/6 **The Thracian port of Apollonia Pontika**
Drachma
Apollonia Pontika (mint), c. 420–390 B.C.
Silver, diam. 1.4 cm
Berlin, Staatliche Museen zu Berlin, Münzkabinett: 18235353

Towns that began as Greek colonies line the west coast of the Black Sea like a string of pearls. Apollonia was founded in the sixth century B.C. by the Milesians. Its name alludes to Apollon Delphinios of the city of Miletus. Apollonia Pontika – today's Sozopol in Bulgaria – is one of the ports that opened up trade in the inland regions of Thrace and northwards to the Crimea and the great river deltas. The finds of coins are concentrated in the Thracian hinterland and indicate the direction of trade relations. The anchor became the symbol (*parasema*) of Apollonia Pontika. It was used for centuries – not only for coins, but also for municipal standard weights and for amphora stamps. (Fig. p. 17) BW

1/7 **The Harbour of Ostia**
Sestertius of the Roman Emperor Nero (37–68 A.D.)
Rome (mint), c. 64 A.D.
Bronze, diam. 3.5 cm
Berlin, Staatliche Museen zu Berlin, Münzkabinett: 18204503

Nero issued this magnificent coin to celebrate the expansion of the port of Ostia. The old harbour had silted up and Claudius (10 B.C. – 54 A.D.) had begun the excavation of a new hexagonal harbour basin. The coin was minted to celebrate its completion. The harbour is lined with covered colonnades (porticos). At the top, a statue of Neptune guards the entrance. In the harbour basin are seven ships of different designs and sizes: cargo ships and a war galley can be seen. Reclining at the bottom is the god of the River Tiber. Ships from overseas docked in Ostia to unload their goods, which were transferred to barges and taken up the Tiber to Rome. Further expansion of the harbour, which continued into the reign of Trajan (53–117), helped Ostia and Rome to flourish. BW

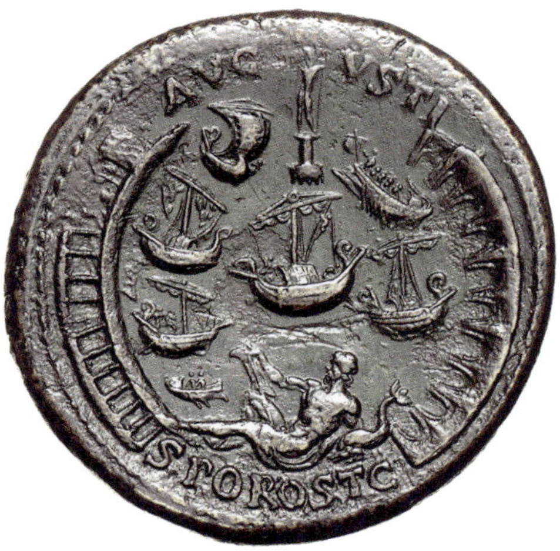

1/7

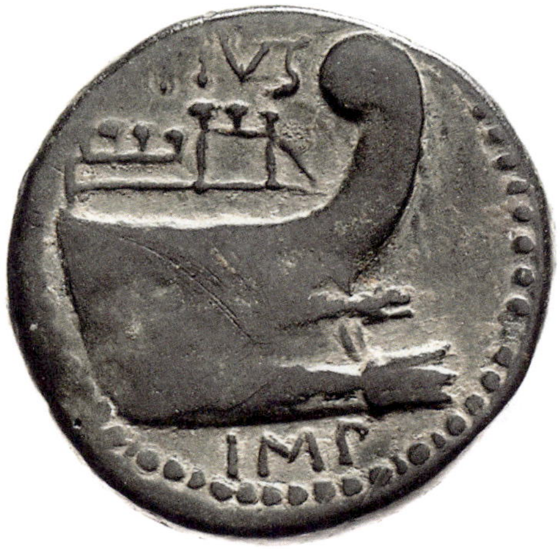

1/8

1/8 **Prow of a ship**
As from the coin programme of Sextus Pompeius (76/66?–35 B.C.)
Sicily, after 45 B.C.
Bronze, diam. 3 cm
Berlin, Staatliche Museen zu Berlin, Münzkabinett: 18202193

The reverse face of this coin shows a ship's prow – a traditional republican motif that Sextus' elder brother, Gnaeus Pompeius Magnus the Younger (c. 80/76–45 B.C.) had previously used on coins he minted on the Iberian Peninsula. The brothers were defeated by Gaius Julius Caesar (100–44 B.C.) at the Battle of Munda (17 March 45 B.C.) and Gnaeus was killed shortly afterwards. Sextus escaped and subsequently adopted the prow motif on his own coins. DB

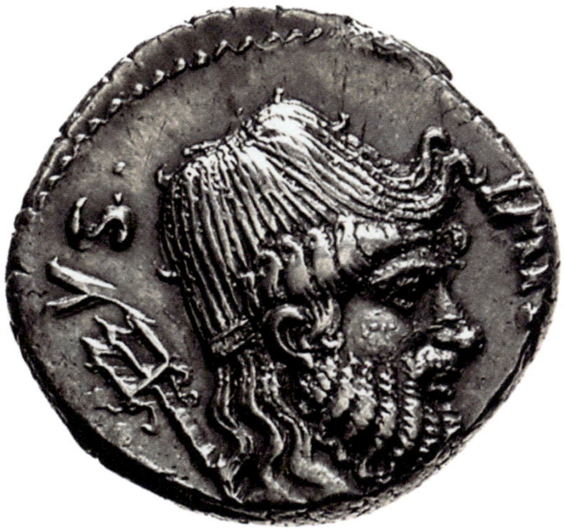

1/11

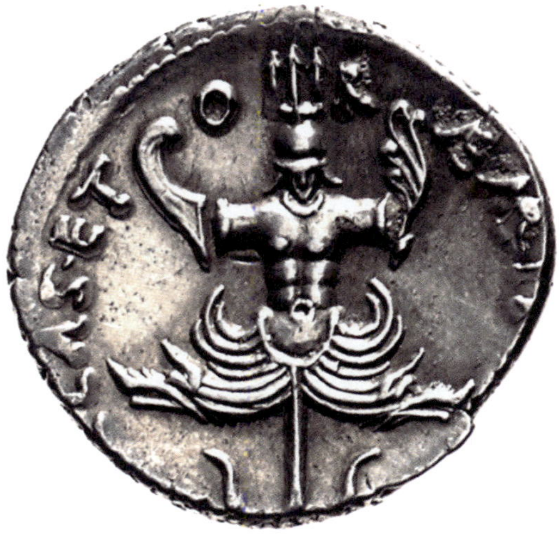

1/12

1/9 **Gnaeus Pompeius Magnus with the attributes of Neptune, god of the sea**
Denarius of the Roman Republic
Sicily, 44–43 B.C.
Silver, diam. 2.1 cm
Berlin, Staatliche Museen zu Berlin, Münzkabinett: 18202201
(Fig. p. 201)

1/10 **Galley**
Denarius of the Roman Republic
Sicily, 44–43 B.C.
Silver, diam. 2.1 cm
Berlin, Staatliche Museen zu Berlin, Münzkabinett: 18202202

These coins show the obverse and reverse of a Roman denarius. One face bears the head of the Roman politician and general Gnaeus Pompeius Magnus (106–48 B.C.) with a trident (on one side) and dolphin (below). These are the attributes of Neptune, the god of the sea, who is named in the inscription. A rowing galley under sail graces the other face, with a star above it. This star might imply that Sextus' fleet is watched over by his father, who had been killed only a few years before this coin was minted. By associating his father with Neptune's attributes of the trident and dolphin – and thus with the sea god himself – Sextus lays claim to a genealogical connection with the divine ruler of the seas. These coins name Quintus Nasidius, an adherent of the Pompey family, who was responsible for minting this coinage. (Fig. p. 201) DB

1/11 **Neptune, god of the sea**
Denarius from the coin programme of Sextus Pompeius (76/66?–35 B.C.)
Sicily, 42–40 B.C.
Silver, diam. 1.7 cm
Berlin, Staatliche Museen zu Berlin, Münzkabinett: 18202204

1/12 **Maritime *tropaeum***
Denarius from the coin programme of Sextus Pompeius (76/66?–35 B.C.)
Sicily, 42–40 B.C.
Silver, diam. 1.8 cm
Berlin, Staatliche Museen zu Berlin, Münzkabinett: 18202203

Sextus Pompeius ruled Sicily from 43/42 B.C. The obverse of this coin shows a head of Neptune with a trident over his shoulder. It has been suggested that the features are those of Sextus. On the reverse is a symbol of victory called a *tropaeum* – the origin of our word "trophy". It combines maritime attributes (anchor, ship's ornament and prow) with pieces of armour (helmet, breastplate and trident) and the dog-heads of the sea monster Scylla. The coin thus makes a connection between one of Sextus' naval victories and the intervention of Neptune in his favour. The inscription around the *tropaeum* states the title conferred on him by the Roman Senate, "praefectus classis et orae maritimae" (prefect of the fleet and the sea coasts). Its purpose is to legitimise his position of power. DB

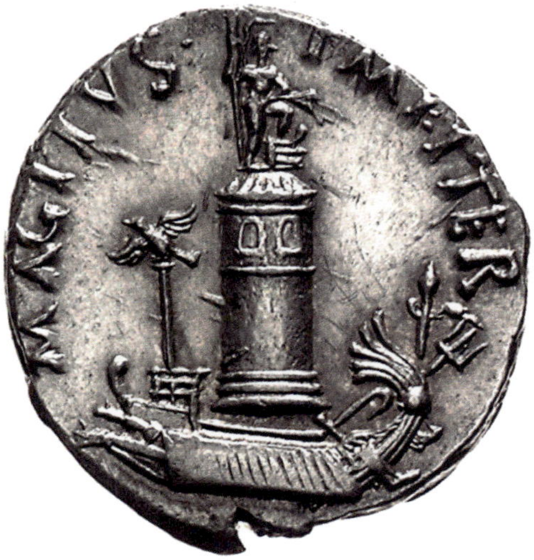

1/13

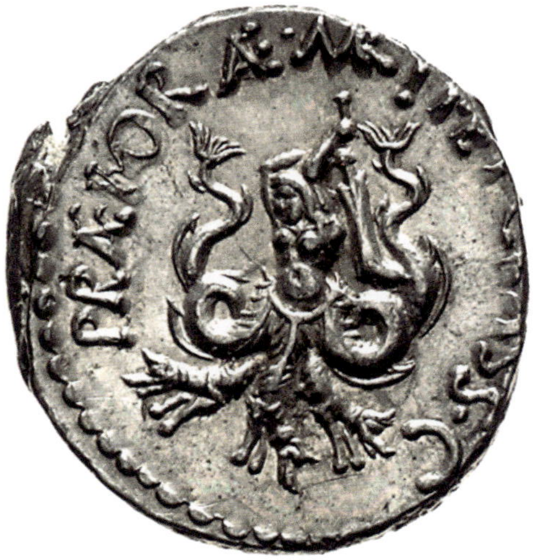

1/14

1/13 **Lighthouse and warship**
Denarius from the coin programme of Sextus Pompeius (76/66?–35 B.C.)
Sicily, 42–40 B.C.
Silver, diam. 1.9 cm
Berlin, Staatliche Museen zu Berlin, Münzkabinett: 18202271

1/14 **Depiction of Scylla, about to strike a blow with a ship's oar**
Denarius from the coin programme of Sextus Pompeius (76/66?–35 B.C.)
Sicily, 42–40 B.C.
Silver, diam. 1.9 cm
Berlin, Staatliche Museen zu Berlin, Münzkabinett: 18208560

The obverse shows a lighthouse crowned with a helmeted statue as well as maritime objects (trident, oar, ship's prow). In front of it is a galley. On the reverse is Scylla, depicted with a female torso rising from lower parts consisting of fish tails and dog's forequarters. She is swinging back a ship's oar to strike. The coin alludes to the war between Sextus Pompeius and Octavian (63 B.C. – 14 A.D.), who later became the first Emperor of Rome, Augustus. In 42 B.C. and again in 38 B.C., Octavian's fleet suffered disastrous defeats in the Strait of Messina when his ships were driven onto the rocks in a storm, while Sextus' fleet managed to gain the safety of a harbour despite the heavy seas. The violence of the sea is personified here by Scylla, who was believed to lurk in the Strait of Messina. This imagery can be interpreted as meaning that the sea monster – and thus the sea itself – fights against Octavian on the side of Sextus. DB

Laura Kersten

Discourse: The Sea King

The Maritime Image of Sextus Pompeius

Sextus Pompeius (c. 76/66–35 B.C.) was referred to as *Neptunius dux*[1] in ancient times and apostrophised as "sea king" again and again in later literature.[2] Often called Sextus Pompey by English authors, he was the youngest son of Pompey the Great (106–48 B.C.). After Julius Caesar's death in 44 B.C., he became one of the leading figures in the bloody civil wars that flared up again between various Roman factions. In the course of these conflicts, he created an image that was meant to express his supremacy in the Mediterranean Sea. It is known to us in particular from his coinage and from historiographical works of the subsequent Imperial era.

Up until 45 B.C., Sextus Pompeius stood in the shadow of his brother Gnaeus Pompeius (c. 80/76–45 B.C.) and even more so of his father, who had been awarded the epithet "the Great" for good reason and was said to have achieved unprecedented glory during his lifetime. The military successes of Pompey the Great had been celebrated as outstanding achievements. They included the campaign against pirates in the Mediterranean, who he had suppressed within a very short time, having been granted *imperium* (military power of command) over the sea and coastal territory.

After his father was assassinated, Sextus fled to the Iberian peninsula, where his brother led a large force of his father's followers in opposition to Julius Caesar. Gnaeus Pompeius was killed soon after losing the battle of Munda in 45 B.C., but Sextus escaped. He soon regrouped the forces loyal to his father and brother, and eventually became the new leader of resistance to Julius Caesar on the Iberian peninsula. After Caesar's assassination, relations between Sextus Pompeius and Rome's political elite improved to the extent that he considered returning to the city. It is in this context that the title of a *praefectus classis et orae maritimae* (Prefect of the Fleet and the Coasts) was awarded to him by the Senate. It is not clear exactly what role and powers this conferred, but it was surely intended to recall Sextus' father and the *imperium* granted to him for the purpose of suppressing piracy.

However, when the Second Triumvirate (Mark Antony, Octavian, and Lepidus) seized power in Rome and issued proscription lists, Sextus was included as one of those to be killed and have their property confiscated. This ended his hopes of rehabilitation in Rome. Instead, he went with some of his forces to Sicily, which he quickly brought under military control in 43/42 B.C. There he gave refuge to other proscribed citizens and sympathisers, even taking measures to rescue them. A growing number of escaped slaves also swelled the ranks of his army and fleet. Raids and the blockade of the Italian peninsula by Sextus and his adherents severely disrupted the shipment of food supplies to Rome. This forced the triumvir Octavian (later Emperor Augustus, 63 B.C.–14 A.D.) to begin military operations against Sextus at sea (*bellum Siculum*). This led to several naval battles in the waters around Sicily, especially in the Strait of Messina, between 42 and 36 B.C. The hostilities between Octavian and Sextus were interrupted only temporarily in 39 B.C. by the Pact of Misenum, in which the three members of the Second Triumvirate formally recognised Sextus' authority in the Mediterranean Sea and on certain islands. Until the final battles of Mylae and Naulochos in 36 B.C., after which Sextus fled and was ultimately executed in 35 B.C., he emerged from every naval engagement as the winner. In 42 B.C., for instance, Octavian's fleet suffered a defeat in the Strait of Messina when one of his generals tried to invade Sicily. A similar scenario was repeated in 38 B.C. in the very same place. These outcomes were not due to naval warfare alone, however, but also to stormy weather and heavy seas, which had an even stronger effect in the narrow waters of the strait. When storms approached, Sextus' fleet was able to seek shelter in a harbour such as that of Messana [sic] while Octavian's fleet stayed out at sea in the strait. Thus exposed, his ships were swept against each other and capsized, or were wrecked on the rocky coast. At times, the situation became so dangerous that Octavian had to send a signal that he had survived the storm.[3] The fact that natural phenomena of this kind had coincided with military engagements was perceived as particularly unusual, because they took place in the summertime.[4] Octavian's run of bad luck with the weather – albeit not in the Strait this time – continued when he resumed the Sicilian campaign with the help of his general Marcus Agrippa (64/3–12 B.C.), who made elaborate logistical preparations and built up a fleet of better equipped ships. It was with these that Octavian set sail for Sicily in 36 B.C. He was still moving south along the coast of the mainland when another storm damaged his ships in the bay of Elea.

In connection with these events, historiographers of the Imperial era relate that Sextus had command of the surrounding seas and styled himself the son of Neptune "since his father had once ruled the whole sea"[5]. This kind of self-portrayal included the re-enactment of a sea battle (using prisoners), which Sextus staged at the original location, where it could be seen by his defeated enemies on the mainland.[6] Some accounts even claim that Sextus was truly convinced that he was the son of Neptune, and had yielded to this idea to such an extent that he wrapped himself in a blue cloak and believed that divine power was acting in his favour.[7] Projecting this kind of image actually worked very well for Sextus, because it appealed to his contemporaries and became widely known. For example, a statue of the sea god was borne aloft at games in the circus, and this was cheered by the Romans, who understood it as a reference to Sextus.[8]

In the Roman Republic – especially during its late phase – it was nothing new for people to adopt a divine or mythical genealogy as part of their image as members of the nobility, even if their true ancestry was well known. To this extent, the mere assertion of descent from Neptune neither constituted a particularly surprising narrative, nor does it seem to have met with repudiation from contemporaries. In retrospect, however, the historiographers of the Imperial era judged Sextus' confidence in his divine father and his stylisation as the god's son to be excessive presumption or even a sign of hubris.

From today's perspective, the remarkable thing about the maritime image projected by Sextus is therefore not that he claimed a deity as his ancestor, but that he combined a divine genealogy with natural maritime phenomena. Such a connection not only implied that Sextus – and his fleet – fared well in storms thanks to Neptune, but also aimed to make his opponents believe that it would be almost impossible to defeat him at sea. The coins issued by Sextus make this clear by using the mythical sea monster Scylla, standing for the elements of the sea as a whole, to help explain his naval victories. This made Scylla, who struck terror into the heart of any sailor navigating the Strait of Messina, into a fighter on the side of Sextus.

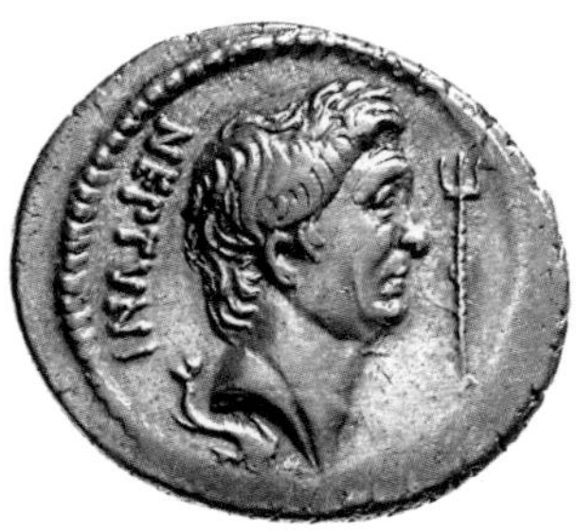

1/9

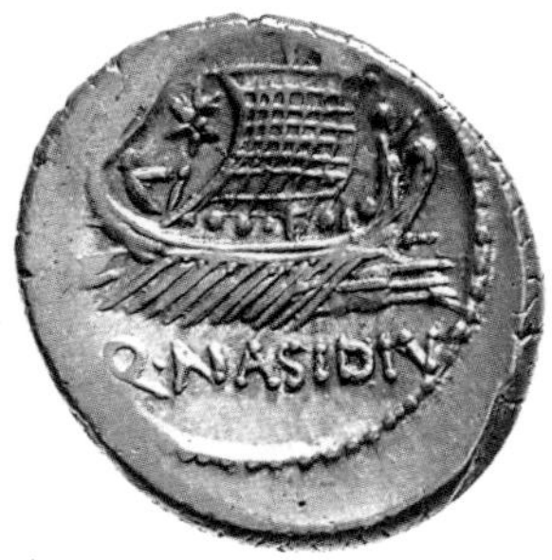

1/10

Furthermore, the image created by Sextus implied that only he was entitled to such a connection with the sea. According to the logic of this construct, the *gens Pompeia* was linked to Neptune through his father and Sextus was the only rightful heir. Such monopolisation of access to the sea and of the elements as his allies ultimately went hand in hand with his appropriation of the sea as a domain by virtue of genealogically conferred, divine empowerment. Florus, a historiographer of the later, Imperial era, testified to this when he wrote that Sextus offered sacrifice to Neptune "in order to induce the ruler of the sea to allow him to reign in his domain"[9].

So the figure of Sextus and especially his visual representation show that the sea was stylised as an object that he could control. In this case, the sea is not merely part of a territory composed of various separate areas of land – rather, Sextus' representation implies dominion over the sea as such. The vastly different nature of this claim becomes evident if one considers the dread with which the sea was often associated in ancient times[10] and the contrast offered by Sextus. The formulation of such a claim also gave rise to an idea that had consequences of its own, because in the course of the *bellum Siculum* it would be adopted by Octavian and later become part of the Roman emperor's concept of dominion, whereby his empire did not end at the coast, but included the sea.

1 Horace, *Epodes* 9, 7 seq.
2 Alfred von Domaszewski, *Geschichte der römischen Kaiser* (History of the Roman emperors), Leipzig 1909, 2 vols., vol. 1, pp. 94, 118, 121, 126, 132; Ute Schall, *Herodes. König der Juden, Freund der Griechen, Verbündeter Roms. Eine Biographie* (Herod. King of the Jews, friend of the Greeks, ally of Rome. A biography), Hamburg 2011, p. 130; Peter Schreiner Frandsen, *M. Vipsanius Agrippa. Eine historische Untersuchung* über *dessen Leben und Wirken* (M. Vipsanius Agrippa, A historical examination of his life and deeds), Altona 1836, p. 103.
3 Appian, *The Civil Wars* 5, 87.
4 Suetonius, Augustus 16, 1 in: *The Twelve Caesars*; Appian, op. cit. 5, 100.
5 Cassius Dio, *Roman History* 48, 19, 2, English translation by Earnest Cary.
6 Baltrusch 2016, p. 296 seq.
7 Appian, op.cit. 5, 100.
8 Cassius Dio, op. cit. 48, 31, 5.
9 Florus, *Epitome of Roman History* 2, 18, 3, English translation by Edward Seymour Forster.
10 See Ernst Baltrusch's article in this exhibition catalog.

2 Command of the Sea
The Port of Venice

Dominion over the sea and through the sea is an ever-present theme in European power politics. As ships ventured farther across the seas and oceans, the waters lost their mythological status and gained importance as transport and transit routes. This, in turn, offered coastal states and cities new opportunities for trade and expansion – opportunities that steadily grew with advances in shipbuilding and navigation. Europe used the seas to conduct trade and acquire territory, and command of the sea became key in the struggle for dominance among major European powers.

The prototype of the modern maritime power was the Republic of Venice, which flourished from the thirteenth to the fifteenth century. As a "city in the sea" or "sea state" (*Stato da mar*), Venice had a unique connection to the sea, and maritime trade quickly became its most profitable source of income. To expand and protect its mercantile activities, which made Venice a key hub of trade between the Holy Roman Empire and the Orient as well as the wealthiest city in Europe, the *Serenissima Repubblica di San Marco* founded an empire that extended across the Mediterranean and the Black Sea, far into the Orient. The only way to reach these territories, and therefore the only way to defend them, was via the sea. Venice consequently established a standing navy to protect its merchant ships, along with a system of bases from which to control the sea routes – an approach that was copied later by all the large maritime powers.

Venice's first rivals for dominance in the Mediterranean region were Genoa and then, beginning in the fourteenth century, the rapidly expanding Ottoman Empire. In addition to the constant threat of pirate attacks, Venice was also kept on edge by numerous maritime wars, which largely determined the character of everyday life in the "lagoon city". The financing and organisation of defensive wars and wars of aggression, were, like trade, the responsibility of the Venetian people as a whole. Victories and defeats affected the maritime city-state more directly than they did large states on the mainland. The success of Venice was rooted in its citizens' strong sense of identification with the state. Like no other power, the merchant republic grasped the importance of sharing its success with the population at large, publicly celebrating its status as a maritime power and keeping faith in the *Serenissima* alive through extravagant festivals.

Whether and to what degree territorial claims might extend to the sea became a topic of heated debate in the early seventeenth century. The rise of European maritime nations and their competing claims to power posed a challenge to countries that had acquired territory during the Age of Discovery and led to the concept of the "freedom of the seas". The pamphlets *Mare Liberum*, published by Dutch jurist Hugo Grotius (1583–1645) in 1609, and *Mare Clausum*, published by English jurist John Selden (1584–1654) in 1635, laid the foundations for maritime law, which is now regulated by the United Nations Convention on the Law of the Sea, adopted in 1982. Even if countries today would not presume to want to rule the seas, the world's oceans still possess great strategic importance in those countries' struggle for power. Free trade and unimpeded transit passage, as well as the use of marine resources, are still at the top of foreign-policy and political agendas. *Christiana Brennecke*

Further Reading

Charles Beddington (ed.), *Canaletto in Venedig. Der Meister und seine Rivalen*, exhib. cat., Stuttgart 2010

Kornelia von Berswordt-Wallrabe (ed.), *Von Venedig bis Neapel. Renaissance und Barock in Italien*, exhib. cat., Berlin 1999

Roger Crowley, *Venedig erobert die Welt. Die Dogen-Republik zwischen Macht und Intrige*, Stuttgart 2011

Roger Crowley, *Entscheidung im Mittelmeer. Europas Seekrieg gegen das Osmanische Reich 1521–1580*, Stuttgart 2009.

Peter Feldbauer et al, *Venedig 800–1600. Die Serenissima als Weltmacht*, Vienna 2010

Stefan Hanß, *Lepanto als Ereignis. Dezentrierende Geschichte(n) der Seeschlacht von Lepanto (1571)*, Göttingen 2017

Arne Karsten, *Geschichte Venedigs*, Munich 2012

Helmut Pemsel, *Seeherrschaft. Eine maritime Weltgeschichte von den Anfängen bis 1850*, vol. 1, Augsburg 1995

VENEDIG. Seemacht, Kunst und Karneval, ed. by Schallaburg Kulturbetriebs ges.m.b.H. in cooperation with Kunsthistorisches Museum Wien, Vienna 2011

VENEZIA! Kunst aus venezianischen Palästen. Sammlungsgeschichte Venedigs vom 13. bis 19. Jahrhundert, ed. by Kunst- und Ausstellungshalle der Bundesrepublik Deutschland GmbH, Bonn 2002

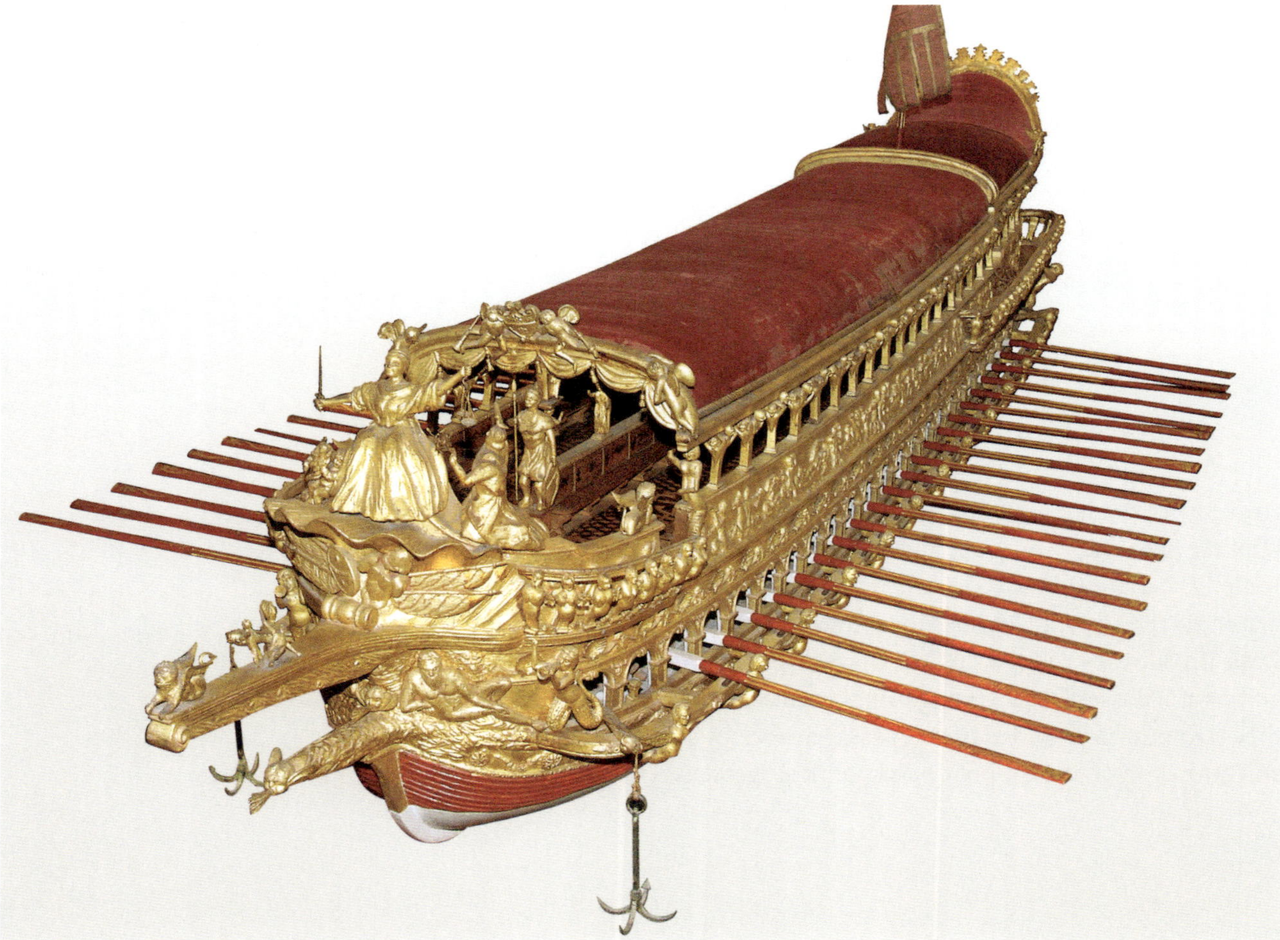

2/1

Venice – A Maritime Power

2/1 **Model of the last bucentaur**
Aldo Baradel (1907–1985)
1972–1976
Wood, gold leaf; 46 x 86 x 175 cm
Venice, Aldo Baradel Collection

The wealth and splendour of Venice – as well as its presentation of itself as master of the seas – can be seen in this model of the city's last 'bucentaur'. Starting in the fourteenth century, the bucentaur, a magnificently ornamented barge belonging to the doges of Venice, was launched to celebrate the glory of the city-state. It was made famous by the "Marriage of Venice with the Sea", a ceremony performed on Ascension Day for many hundreds of years. The doge, at the head of a large procession of ships, would be rowed out to the open sea, where he would cast a golden ring into the waters with the words "we wed thee, sea, as a sign of our true and everlasting dominion", thus symbolically reaffirming Venetian command of the Adriatic. The entire leadership of the city-state of Venice took part in the procession, and foreign diplomats were often invited as well so they could experience this demonstration of the city's power. The model was created according to the original drawings of the last bucentaur (built in 1728), which are preserved in the *Archivio di Stato di Venezia*. CB

2/2 ***The Piazzetta and the Doge's Palace in Venice***
Gaspar van Wittel (1652–1736)
Between 1695 and 1736
Oil on canvas; 65.5 x 98 cm
Dresden, Gemäldegalerie Alte Meister, Staatliche Kunstsammlungen Dresden: Gal.-Nr. 640

Views of the city of Venice have been tremendously popular for centuries. Gaspar van Wittel was a Dutch painter who lived in Rome from about 1674 to his death in 1736. Working under the Italianised name of Gaspare Vanvitelli, he gained a reputation as the first painter to specialise in cityscapes, called *vedute* in Italian. His *vedute* of Rome and Venice were

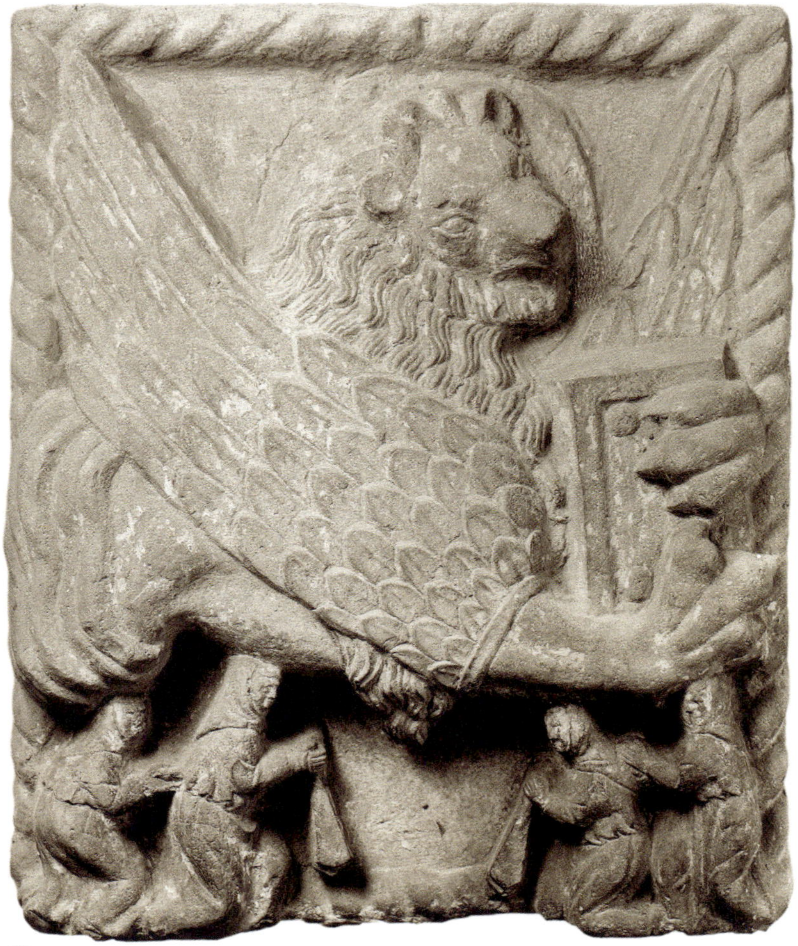

2/3

in high demand internationally among noblemen who travelled to Italy on the Grand Tour. Van Wittel probably stayed in Venice in 1695, completing large-format drawings of the city's most striking scenes, which in subsequent years he transferred to oil paintings. This painting shows a very familiar view of Venice, featuring the Piazzetta and the Doge's Palace as seen from the *Bacino*, or San Marco Basin. The busy waters and bustling pier (where the bucentaur can be seen) are depicted in lively detail. Following the introduction of the genre by van Wittel, *vedute* by painters such as Giovanni Antonio Canal (1697–1768) and his nephew Bernardo Bellotto (1721/22–1780), both known under the name Canaletto, became internationally famous. (Fig. p. 24) KK

2/3 **Stone relief with the Lion of St. Mark**
First half of the fourteenth century
Stone relief; 89 x 68 x 12 cm
Venice, Fondazione Musei Civici di Venezia, Museo Correr: CL. XXV n. 990

Venice's transformation from a provincial Byzantine town to the mighty *Serenissima Repubblica di San Marco* was closely linked to the emergence and growth of the cult of St. Mark. The legendary relocation of St. Mark's relics from Alexandria to Venice in 828 meant that the Venetians now had a new patron saint. They used it to establish a new ecclesiastical and political legitimacy, which quickly developed into a state cult. The Evangelist, usually in the figure of the Lion of Saint Mark, came to symbolise Venetian identity, and soon appeared on coins, flags and seals as well as in the architecture and ceremonial life of the maritime republic, or, as it called itself, the *Stato da mar*. The most common forms are the standing lion and the lion *in moleca*. The lion *in moleca* shown here is the oldest and, in a sense, the typical 'Venetian' form. Its round body and curved wings are reminiscent of small crabs (*moléca* in Venetian), which used to be found quite commonly in the city's canals. CB

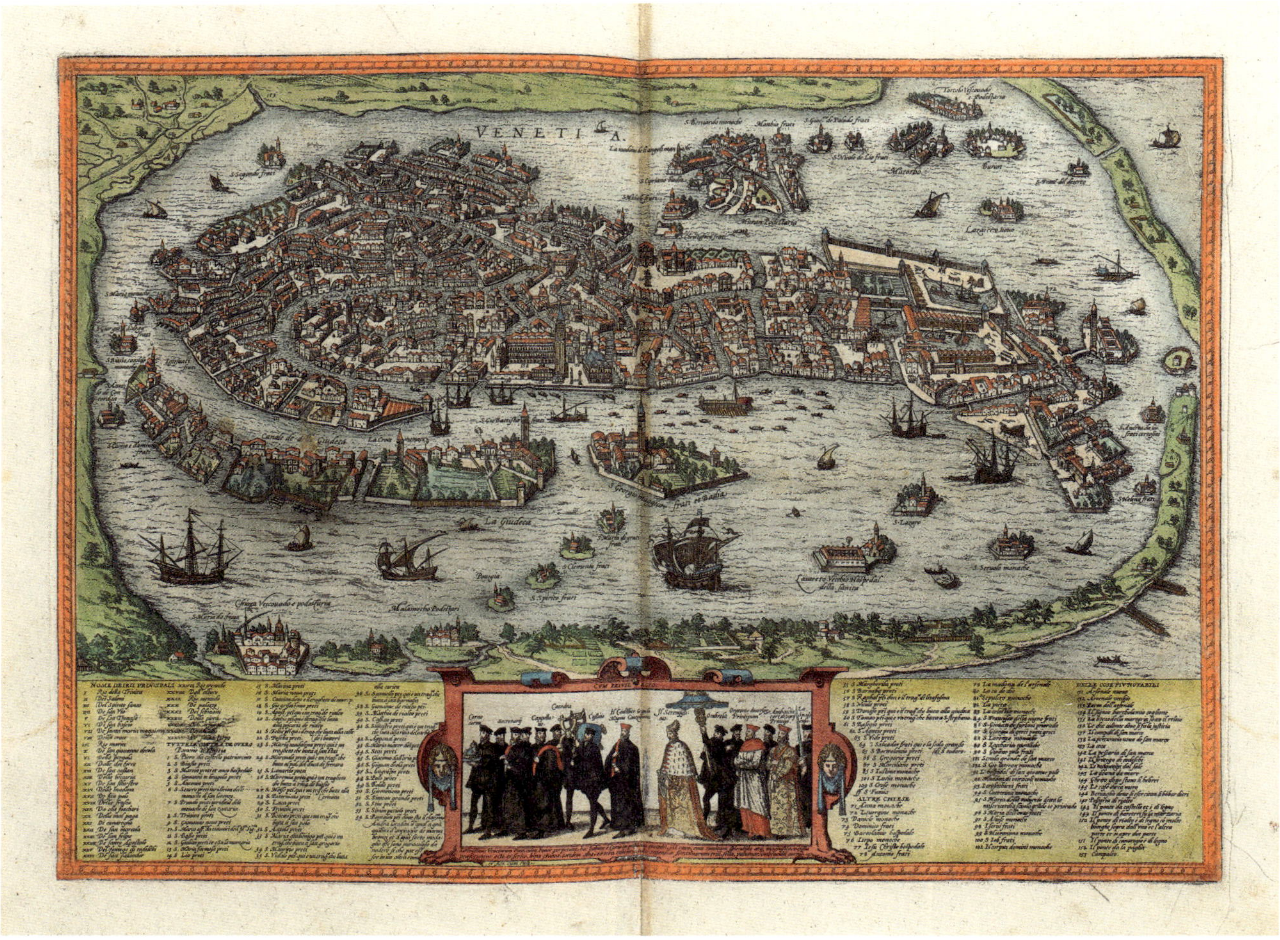

2/4

2/4 **View of Venice, from *Civitates orbis terrarum* (Cities of the World), vol. 2**
Artist: Georg Braun (1542–1622)
Engraver: Franz Hogenberg (1538–1590)
Cologne, 1599
Paper, coloured copper engraving; binding: cardboard, leather and silk; 42 x 29 cm
Berlin, Deutsches Historisches Museum: RB 53/2979-1

As a city in the sea, Venice has always exerted a special fascination. Its location – in a lagoon, spread out over multiple islands off the mainland – and its attendant affinity for all things maritime led Venice (probably founded in the sixth century) to become a major sea power in the Middle Ages. Within just a few centuries, the Venetians were prospering greatly from maritime trade, which made the city, situated on the northern coast of the Adriatic Sea, one of the main links between the Holy Roman Empire and the Orient. This view of Venice by Georg Braun and Franz Hogenberg shows the city, grown wealthy from trade, in the second half of the sixteenth century. Large numbers of warships and cargo ships are crossing the lagoon. An additional illustration presents the dignitaries of the merchant republic, with the doge in the middle. CB

2/5 ***Il Milione* (*The Travels of Marco Polo*)**
Das Buch des edlen Ritters Marco Polo
Marco Polo (1254–1324)
Published by Friedrich Creussner (d. 1496)
Nuremberg, 1477
Print; 30 x 21 cm
Berlin, Staatsbibliothek zu Berlin – Preußischer Kulturbesitz, Handschriftenabteilung: Inkunabelsammlung, 4° Inc 1801

The two main factors behind Venice's success were its advantageous geographical location and its trade activities. All the institutions of the republic were geared toward maritime trade, with its domestic as well as its foreign policies shaped by the interests of merchants and seafarers. This was due not least to Venice's unusually high degree of civic engagement. At first, it was the *fraterne*, or family clans, that confronted the dangers and uncertainties of maritime trade. The most famous example is the Polo family, whose travels show that even in the thirteenth century the arm of Venice reached extraordinarily far. Later, private trading companies assumed the risks of long-distance trade. To protect its cargo ships, Venice developed a tightly organised convoy system, called the *mude*. Five to ten merchant galleys would set out together, escorted by state warships for protection against enemy attacks. (Fig. p. 208/209) CB

2/6 **View of the Arsenal of Venice**
Giovanni Maria Maffioletti (1740–1803)
Venice, 1798
Drawing; 71 x 100 cm
Trieste, Biblioteca Civica "A. Hortis":
St4118_02 / Inv. PRG 118935

To protect trade and safeguard transport routes, Venice maintained a navy, which, insofar as it was a permanent institution, was very modern. The Venetian Arsenal, a complex of state-owned shipyards established in 1104, was the largest ship-building facility of its time and one of the key factors in Venice's success as a maritime power. Up to 3,000 craftsmen worked there, making the city's famous galleys. They were able to turn out an entire battle fleet in very short order. Thanks to excellent logistics and the Arsenal's practice of stockpiling material and components, the *arsenalotti* could construct and equip up to 100 ships in three months – a feat that was unparalleled in all of Europe. As a result, the fleet was always in readiness and Venice could respond quickly to crises and threats of war. This detailed architectural drawing shows the Arsenal operating at full capacity and conveys the impressive scale of the facility. CB

2/7 ***Dante's Divine Comedy***
Dantes Göttliche Komödie
Dante Alighieri (1265–1321)
Translated by Karl Streckfuß (1778–1844)
Published by J. G. Cotta'sche Buchhandlung
Nachfolger, Stuttgart
Stuttgart/Berlin, 1893
Paper, cardboard; 18.1 x 12.3 cm
Berlin, Deutsches Historisches Museum: R 67/2495

Like most of his contemporaries, Dante was fascinated by the productivity of the Venetian Arsenal. In the *Divine Comedy*, he describes the Venetians' exemplary division of labour in about 1320, when, long before the Industrial Age, they had transformed their shipyards into a perfectly organised factory. In Canto 21 of the Inferno, he writes:

"As in the arsenal of the Venetians,
all winter long a stew of sticky pitch
boils up to patch their sick and tattered ships
that cannot sail (instead of voyaging,
some build new keels, some tow and tar the ribs
of hulls worn out by too much journeying;
some hammer at the prow, some at the stern,
and some make oars, and some braid ropes and cords;
one mends the jib, another, the mainsail);"

(The Divine Comedy. Allen Mandelbaum, trans. New York: Bantam Books, 1980) CB

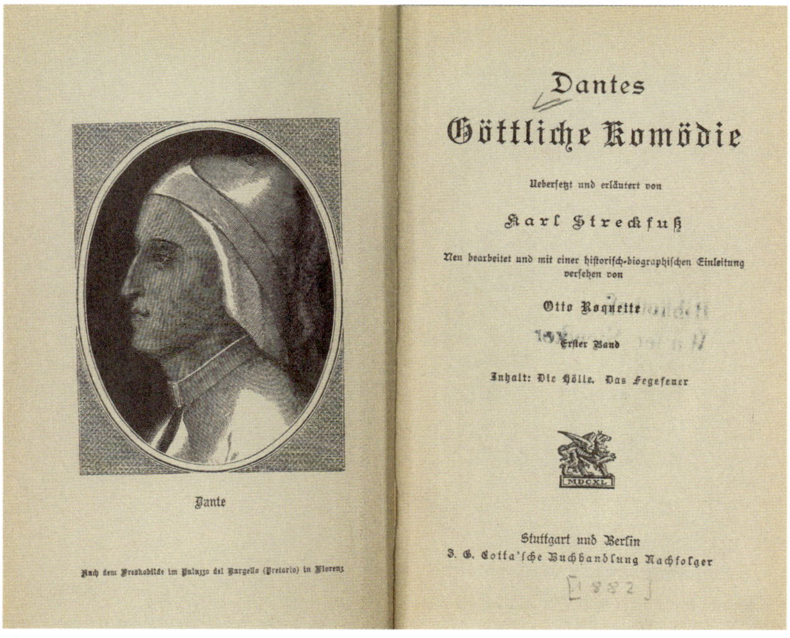

2/7

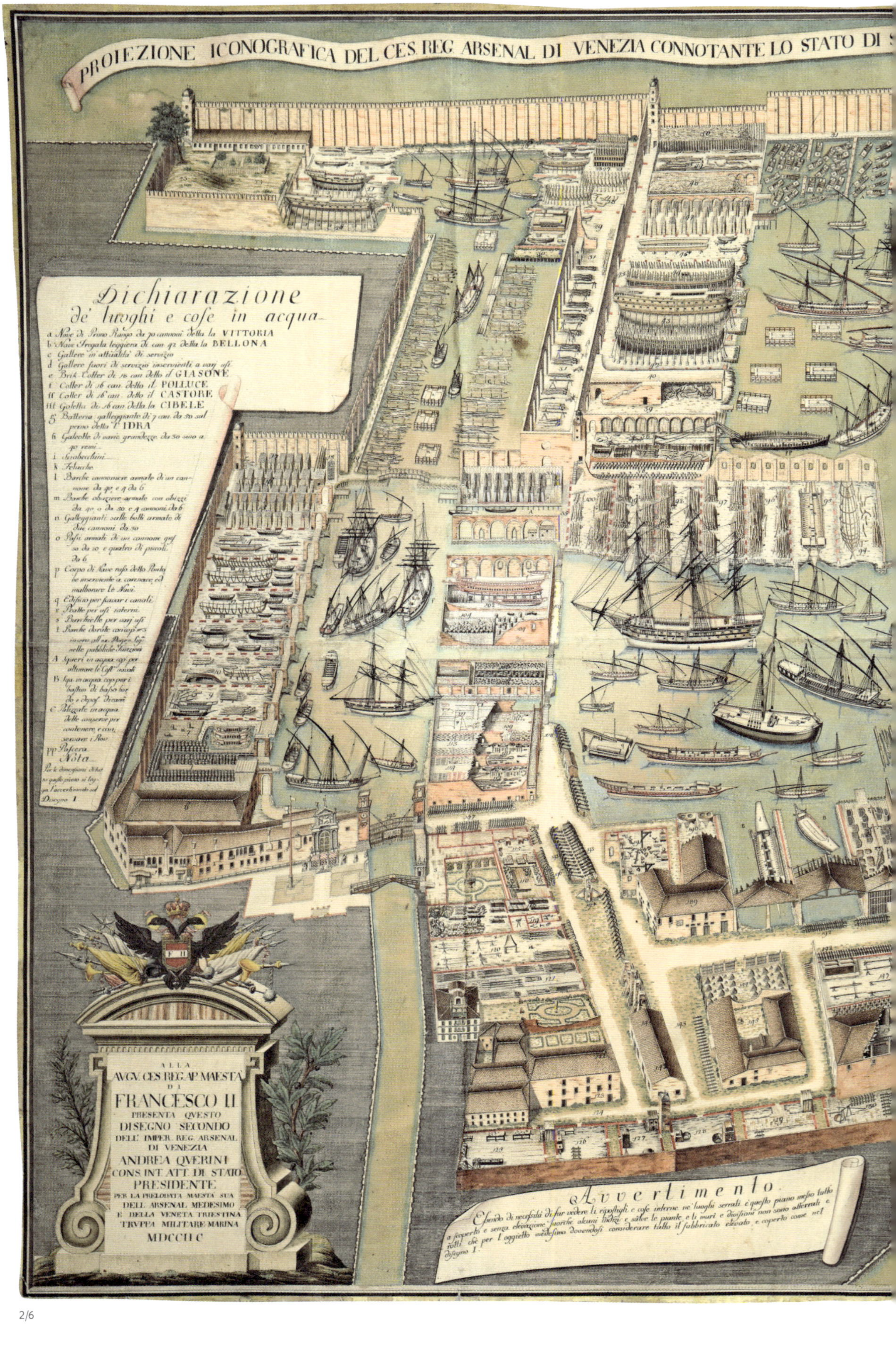
PROIEZIONE ICONOGRAFICA DEL CES. REG. ARSENAL DI VENEZIA CONNOTANTE LO STATO DI S
Dichiarazione
de' luoghi e cose in acqua
a Nave di Primo Rango da 70 cannoni detta la VITTORIA
b Nave Fregata leggiera di can. 42 detta la BELLONA
c Gallere in attualità di servizio
d Gallere fuori di servizio inservienti a varj usi
e Brik-Cotter di 16 can. detto il GIASONE
f Cotter di 16 can. detto il POLLUCE
ff Cotter di 16 can. detto il CASTORE
fff Goletta di 16 can. detta la CIBELE
g Batteria galleggiante di 7 can. da 50 sul ... detta l'IDRA
h Galeotte di varie grandezze da 30 sino a 40 remi
i Sciabecchini
k Feluche
l Barche cannoniere armate di un cannone da 40 e 4 da 6
m Barche obiziere armate con obizzi da 40 o da 30 e 4 cannoni da 6
n Galleggianti sulle botti armate di due cannoni da 30
o Passi armati di un cannone grosso da 20 e quattro di piccoli da 6
p Corpo di Nave raso detto Pontone inserviente a carenare ed alberare le Navi
q Edifizio per scavar i canali
r Peatte per usi interni
s Barchette per varj usi
pp Pascera
Nota
Per le dimensioni di tutto questo piano si legga l'avvertimento nel Disegno I
ALLA
AVGV. CES. REG. AP. MAESTA
DI
FRANCESCO II
PRESENTA QVESTO
DISEGNO SECONDO
DELL' IMPER. REG. ARSENAL
DI VENEZIA
ANDREA QVERINI
CONS. INT. ATT. DI STATO
PRESIDENTE
PER LA PRELODATA MAESTA SUA
DELL' ARSENAL MEDESIMO
E DELLA VENETA TRIESTINA
TRVPPA MILITARE MARINA
MDCCIIC
Avvertimento
Essendo di necessità di far vedere li ripostigli e cose interne ne' luoghi serrati è questo piano messo tutto a scoperto e senza elevazione fuorchè alcuni indizi e salve le piante, e li muri e divisioni non sono alterati e tolti che per l'oggetto medesimo dovendosi considerare tutto il fabbricato elevato e coperto come nel disegno I.

2/6

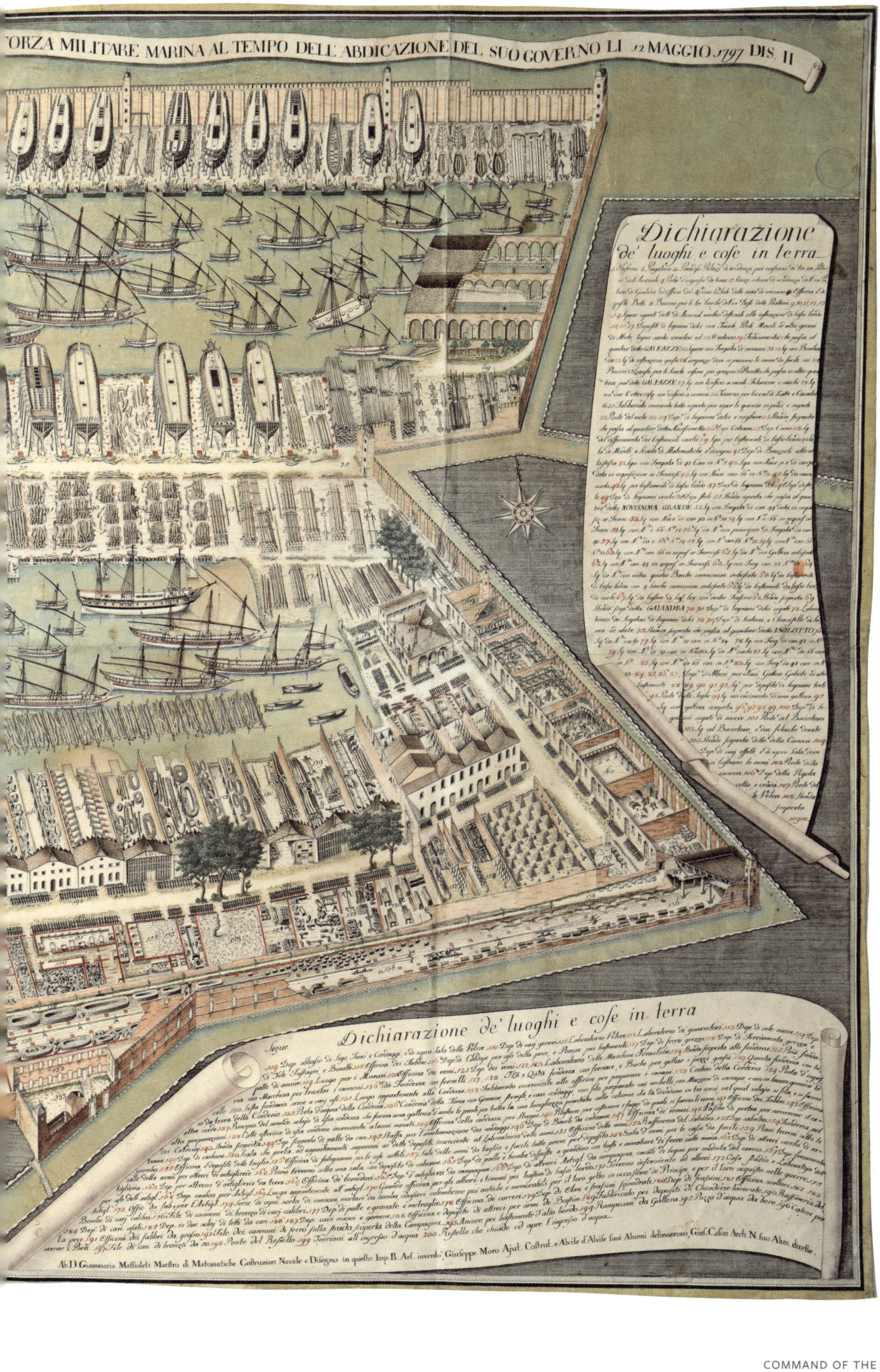
FORZA MILITARE MARINA AL TEMPO DELL' ABDICAZIONE DEL SUO GOVERNO LI 12 MAGGIO 1797 DIS. II
Dichiarazione de' luoghi e cose in terra
Dichiarazione de' luoghi e cose in terra

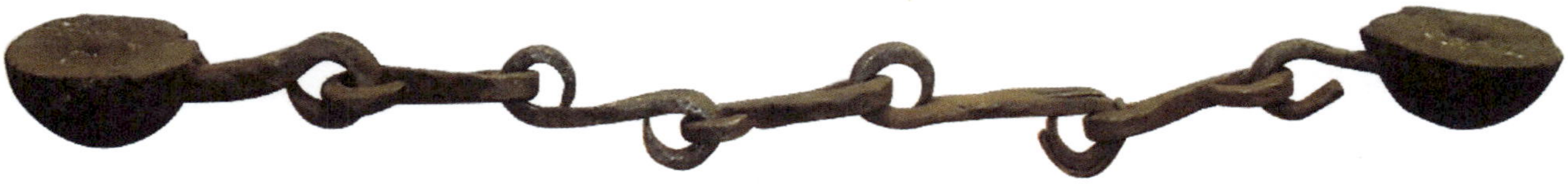

2/8

2/8 **Chain-shot**
Venice, 16th cent.
Iron; 7 x 12 x 99 cm
Venice, Museo Storico Navale della Marina Militare Italiana: 1005

The Arsenal's large depots and storehouses held everything needed for the building and arming of warships. Over time, more and more suppliers moved their businesses to the steadily expanding shipyards, and began making the requisite ropes, sailcloth, oars and weapons on site. Once finished, these would then be very carefully put into storage. Weapons included cannons, cannon balls and small arms, as well as iron chain-shot, which would be fired on enemy ships. The chain between the half-balls would fully extend and rotate in the air, developing a unique trajectory and impact. Chain-shot was used primarily to destroy an opponent's masts and rigging. CB

2/9 **The craft of the Arsenal caulkers**
Venetian artisans
Venice, 1513–1518
Oil on wood; 66 x 107.5 x 3 cm
Venice, Fondazione Musei Civici di Venezia, Galleria dell'Accademia, in deposito presso il Museo Correr: Cl. I n. 2108

Because the Arsenal state shipyards were vital to the success of the maritime republic, artisans working there were held in high esteem. While ship's carpenters, oar-makers, cannon casters and sailcloth-makers all had their place, caulkers were particularly important. They used oakum, cotton, tar or pitch to seal the seams between the wooden planks of the ships, which were not watertight until this work was done. Like other *arsenalotti*, caulkers enjoyed a number of privileges, such as fixed wages, tax reductions and a lifelong pension. They were also provided with small flats close to the Arsenal. In return, they were sworn to secrecy and only allowed to leave Venice with the permission of the state. In

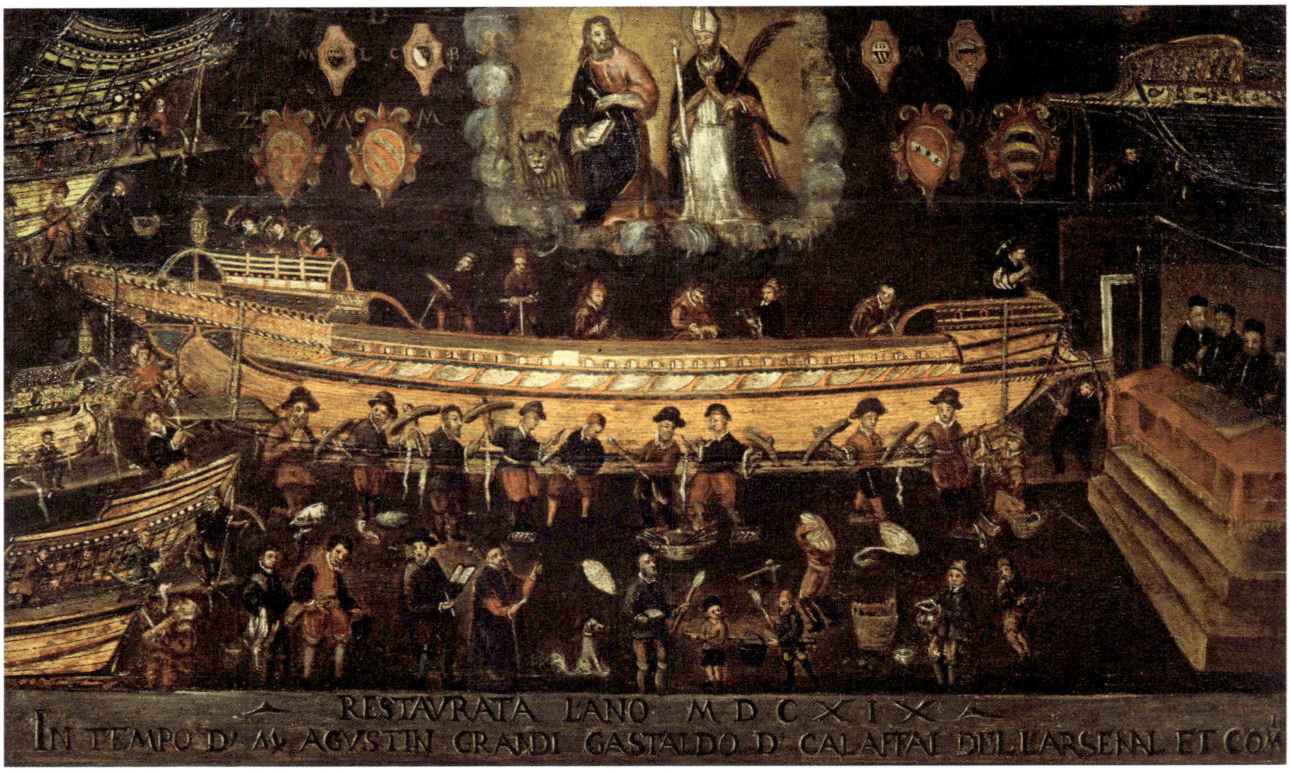

2/9

addition to their work in the shipyards, the *arsenalotti* also served as honour guards at the Doge's Palace and as firefighters – a position they held until the early eighteenth century. CB

2/10 **Cover of the statutes of the confraternity of Arsenal caulkers**
Venice, 1577
Brass, silver-plated; 32 x 21.9 x 7 cm
Venice, Fondazione Musei Civici di Venezia, Museo Correr: Cl.IV 214

The caulkers, like their fellow artisans working outside the shipyards, were organised in a confraternity, which in Venice was called a *scuola*. The *scuole* supported widows, the poor, and the sick, thus playing a crucial role in the city's social services. The *scuole* of various trades saw to it that practitioners followed the trade statutes (*mariegole*). These statues were passed on orally at first, but were documented in written form from the thirteenth century onwards. This magnificently decorated binding for the Arsenal caulkers' statutes speaks to the self-assurance of the confraternity, while the Lion of St. Mark displayed on the front cover attests to its strong identification with the Republic of Venice. CB

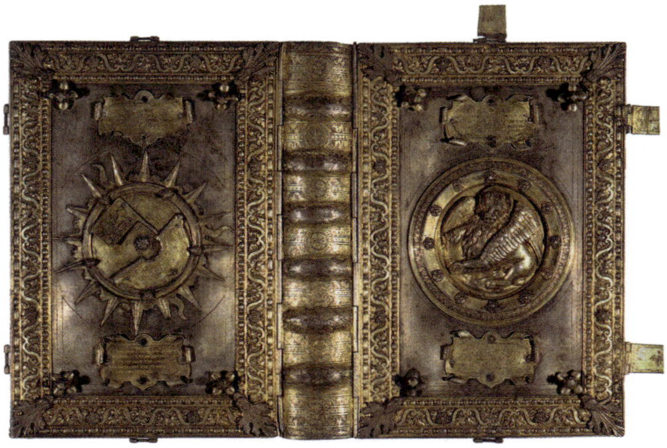

2/10

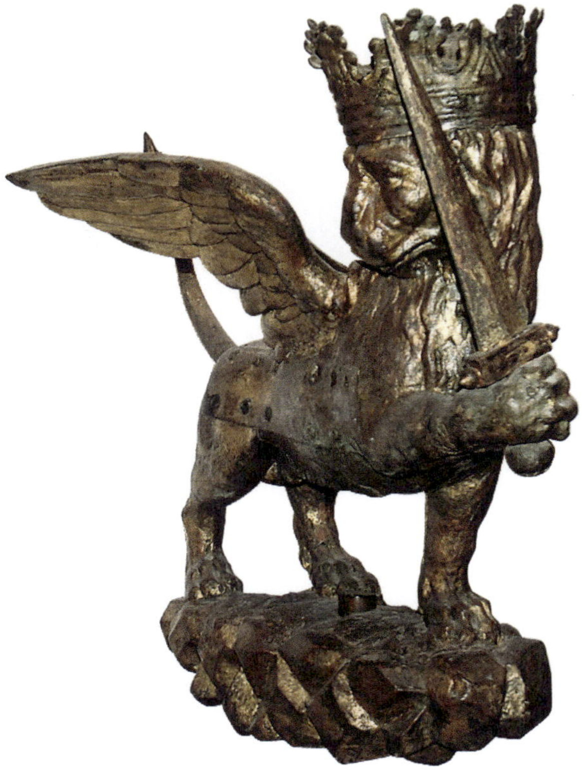

2/11

Command of the Sea

2/11 **Lion of St. Mark with sword and crown**
Venice, 17th cent.
Wood, gilded; 47 x 53 x 34 cm
Venice, Museo Storico Navale della Marina Militare Italiana: 1103

Venice's navy, which could be mobilised at virtually a moment's notice, and its strategic military bases in the Mediterranean region were key to its ability to protect and defend its trade routes. Skilled diplomacy, coupled with a distinct lack of scruples and a readiness to use violence, allowed Venice to acquire key islands and ports in the Adriatic, the Aegean and the Levant over a period from the eleventh to the sixteenth century. When at war, the Republic of Venice adopted the symbol of the Lion of St. Mark holding a sword. In peaceful contexts, the standing lion was typically depicted with a book displaying the message "Pax tibi marce evangelista meus", or "Peace be with you, O Mark, my Evangelist". This version could be found throughout the city, integrated into its art and architecture. On flags of war and warships, the lion was frequently shown with a sword, or the book was closed so that the message could not be read. This Lion of St. Mark, with a crown and sword, adorned a seventeenth-century Venetian ship. CB

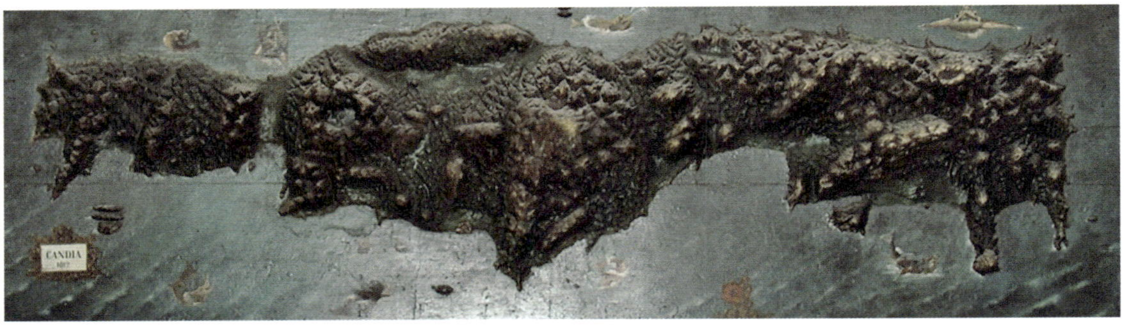

2/12

2/12 **Model of the island of Crete (1612)**
17th cent.
Wood, plaster, painted; 120 x 362 x 20 cm
Venice, Museo Storico Navale della Marina Militare Italiana: 1024

The most important base held by Venice in the Aegean was the island of Crete, which came into Venetian hands following the division of spoils from the inglorious Fourth Crusade (1202–1204). From Crete, the Venetians controlled sea routes between Constantinople and northern Africa and between Venice and the Levant. The fertile island also ensured that Venice would be supplied with wheat. This model is one of a collection of seventeen, each representing a different Venetian base in the eastern Mediterranean. The collection is held in the *Museo Storico Navale* in Venice. These unique artworks from the sixteenth and seventeenth centuries show entire islands and important fortifications, and were used by the military leaders of Venice as tools for planning military strategies. In view of the great distances between the city-state's foreign possessions and its centre of power at the Doge's Palace, they were often the only way to convey special topographical features of the bases. CB

2/13 **Model of fortifications at Famagusta on Cyprus**
16th/ 17th cent.
Wood, plaster, painted; 87 x 122 x 15 cm
Venice, Museo Storico Navale della Marina Militare Italiana: 1120

The island of Cyprus came under Venetian control in 1489. For centuries, Venice and its arch-rival Genoa fought bitterly for control of trade in the Mediterranean, with each seeking to establish a base on Cyprus, the third-largest island in the Mediterranean. Venice was able to prevail, thanks not only to its mighty navy but also to the fact that Genoa was increasingly weakened by internal political conflicts. Cyprus

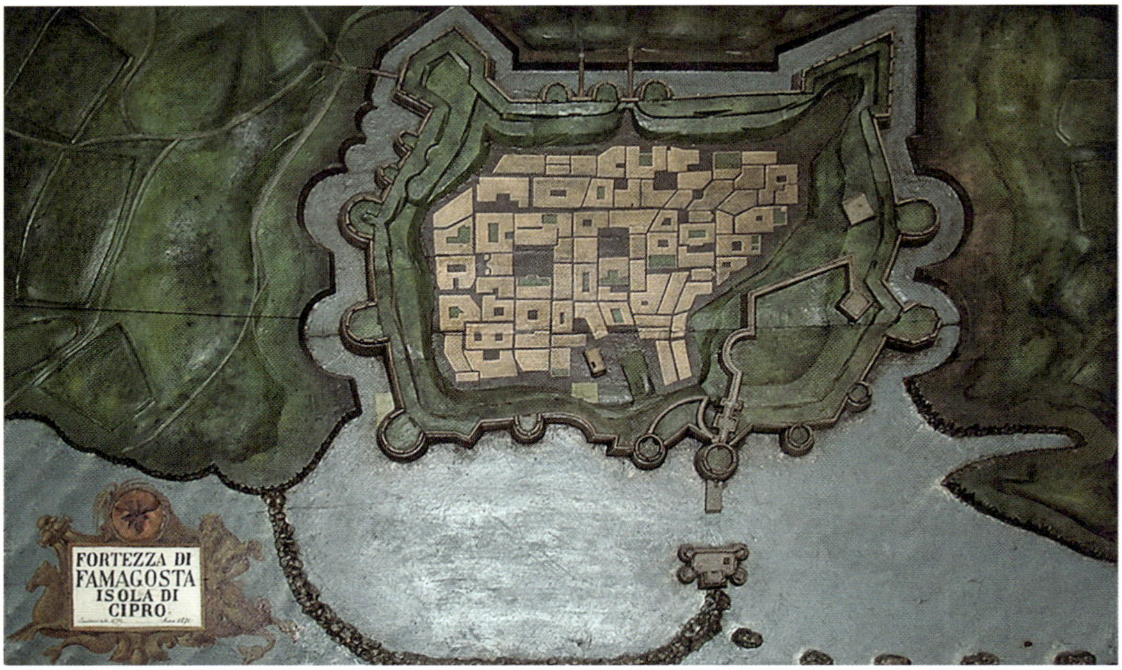

2/13

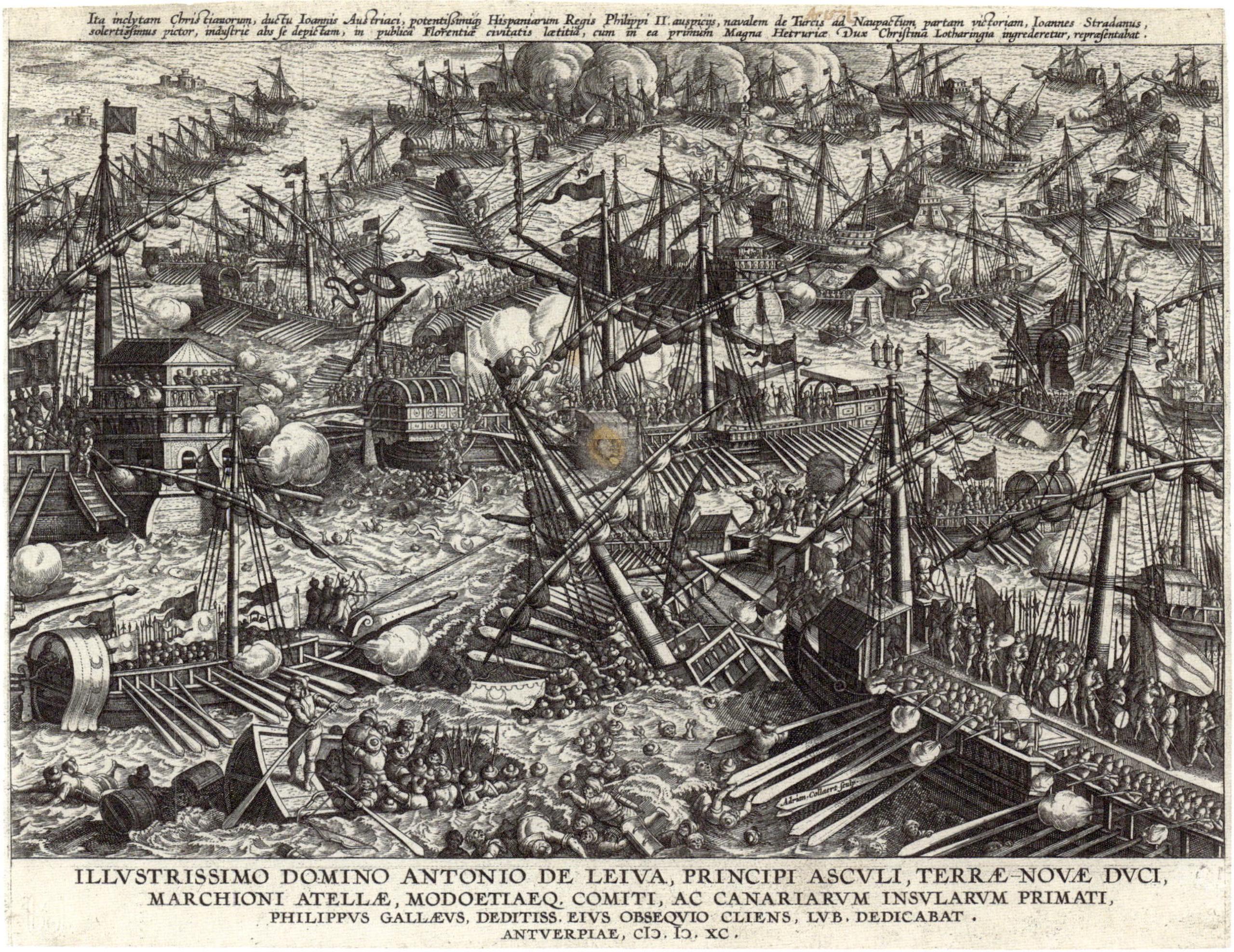

2/14

did not remain in Venetian hands for long, however, despite great efforts by Venice to strengthen fortifications at key locations such as Famagusta. As the Ottoman Empire expanded in the fourteenth century, Venice saw itself confronted with a dangerous new rival that would challenge its ascendancy in the eastern Mediterranean. In January 1570, Sultan Selim II (1524–1574) demanded that the Republic of Venice cede Cyprus. On 1 July 1570, Ottoman troops invaded the island, precipitating what would become one of the bloodiest naval engagements in the history of the world. CB

2/14 **The Battle of Lepanto on 7 October 1571**
Original artist: Jan van der Straet (1523–1605)
Engraver: Adrian Collaert (c. 1560–1618)
Antwerpen, 1590
Copper engraving on paper; 24 x 31.3 cm
Berlin, Deutsches Historisches Museum: Gr 53/2222

2/15 **Battle formation of the Christian and Ottoman fleets on 7 October 1571**
Balthasar Jenichen (16th cent.)
Nuremberg, after 1571
Etching on paper; 28.2 x 40.3 cm
Berlin, Deutsches Historisches Museum: Gr 53/2280

No other naval engagement has resonated more strongly in European art and literature than the Battle of Lepanto (7 October 1571). The battle between the fleet of the Ottoman Empire and a "Holy League" made up of Venice, Spain and the Holy See was depicted as a clash between East and West and as the defence of Christianity against encroaching Islam. Venice had not been able to assemble a fleet of its own large

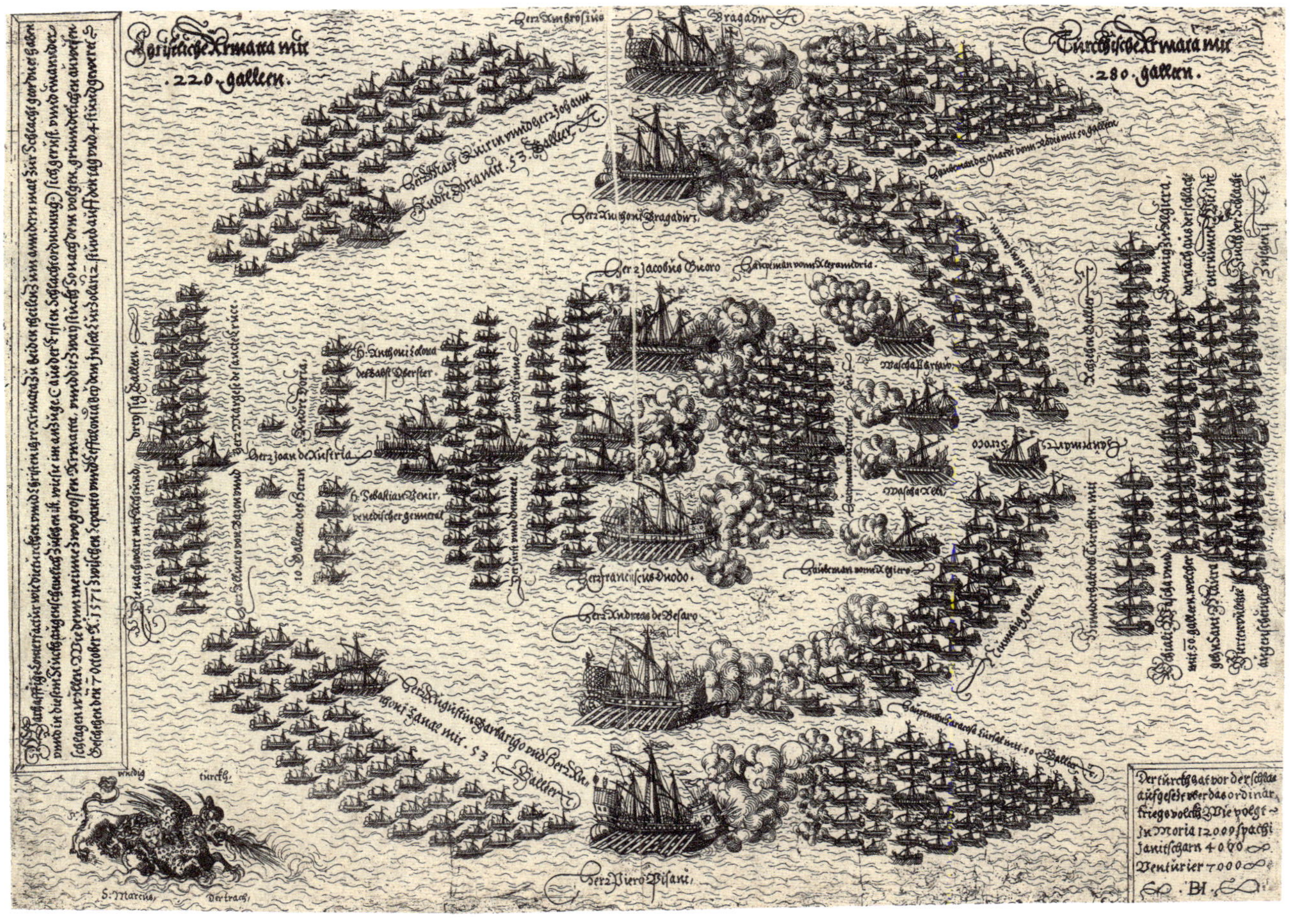

2/15

enough to respond to Ottoman aggression against Cyprus. After protracted and difficult diplomatic negotiations, it therefore formed an alliance with Spain and the Vatican. Their combined fleet, commanded by Don Juan de Austria (of the House of Hapsburg, 1547–1578), possessed 207 galleys and 6 galleasses. By the end of the battle, approximately 20,000 Ottoman soldiers and more than 8,000 combatants on the Christian side had lost their lives; the Ottoman forces were overwhelmingly defeated. News of the victory spread through Europe like wildfire. Countless prints – elaborate compositions portraying the "victory of Christianity" – were inspired by the accounts of men who had fought in the battle, and commissions were given in Venice, Rome and Madrid for lavish paintings to celebrate their triumph. The political pay-off for Venice, however, was negligible. In a separate peace settlement signed in 1573, the Republic of St. Mark ceded Cyprus to the Ottomans in exchange for trade advantages. CB

2/16 **Portrait of Sebastiano Venier**
Workshop of Jacopo Tintoretto (1518–1594)
Between 1571 and 1577
Oil on canvas; 118 x 100 cm
Schwerin, Staatliche Schlösser, Gärten und Kunstsammlungen Mecklenburg-Vorpommern: G 1692

The Venetian contingent of the "Holy League" was commanded by Sebastiano Venier (c. 1496–1578), portrayed here as a victor of the Battle of Lepanto. The painting was completed in the workshop of Jacopo Tintoretto, which, in addition to monumental altarpieces and history paintings for Venice's churches and palaces, produced portraits for the *Serenissima*, like this one depicting the victory celebrated across Europe. The bottom of the painting was presumably cut off at a later date. It shows the admiral in three-quarter figure, dressed in armour and a dark-red cape. He is perhaps recalling the battle scene in the background, where warships are partially obscured by the smoke of gunfire. In 1577, Venier was appointed Doge at the age of 81. In this portrait, his face is depicted with realistic detail, wearing an expression that commands respect. The dark overall colour scheme focuses attention on Venier's brightly lit face and magnificent, gleaming armour. KK

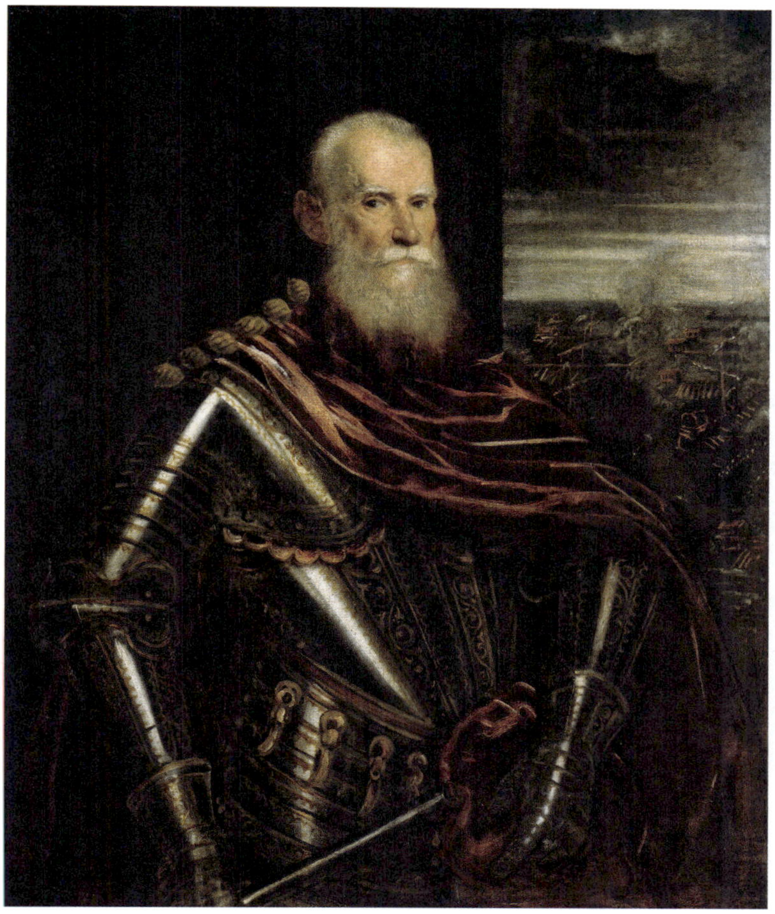

2/16

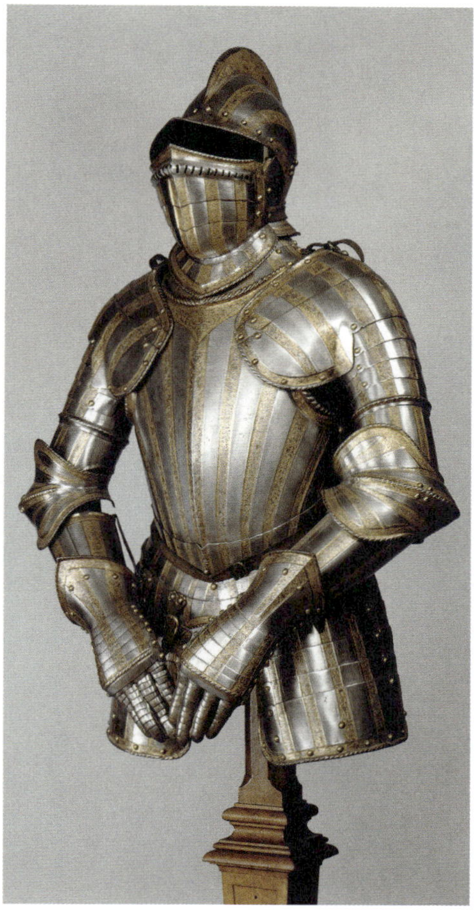

2/17

2/17 Armour belonging to Sebastiano Venier
Brescia, c. 1540
Polished iron, etched, gilded; 105 x 68 x 44 cm
Vienna, KHM-Museumsverband: HJRK A 984

Hostilities between the Ottoman Empire and the Christian countries of Europe lasted for many centuries, with battles fought on land and sea. Both sides had magnificently worked armour and weapons designed both to protect the body and to advertise the owner's wealth and status. This impressive armour belonged to Sebastiano Venier, a member of an old Venetian family who held several high-ranking state offices and distinguished himself in various capacities in the war against the Ottomans. He can be seen wearing the armour in a painting probably completed in Florence in about 1575. It depicts the victors of the Battle of Lepanto and shows Venier as the commander-in-chief of the Venetian fleet (in the rank of admiral). Both the painting and the armour later found their way into the collection of "arts and curiosities" kept by Archduke Ferdinand II (1529–1595) at Ambras Castle. Today, the armour can be seen in the Imperial Armoury section of the Kunsthistorisches Museum in Vienna. CB

2/18 Ottoman Turban helmet
Ottoman Empire, 16th cent.
Iron, chased, damascened with gold and silver;
32 x 24 cm
Berlin, Deutsches Historisches Museum: W4695

Ottoman expansion in the fourteenth century relied on a well-organised military and an abundance of well-armed soldiers. Turban helmets, with their unique shape, originated in Iran. They were common among the Turkmens of Central Asia in the fifteenth century and made their way from there into the army of the Ottoman Empire, where they were worn in large numbers in the sixteenth century. At first, they were made of steel or iron. Some later ones were made of copper. The lower band, vertical flutes and knob finial all provided space for cartouche inscriptions and inlays of precious metal. The helmet was not padded, and was worn over a turban or quilted cap. On the front side, this helmet bears the mark of the Ottoman arsenal, located in the former Hagia Irene church inside the palace complex in Istanbul. This means that it came from the sultan's armoury. SL

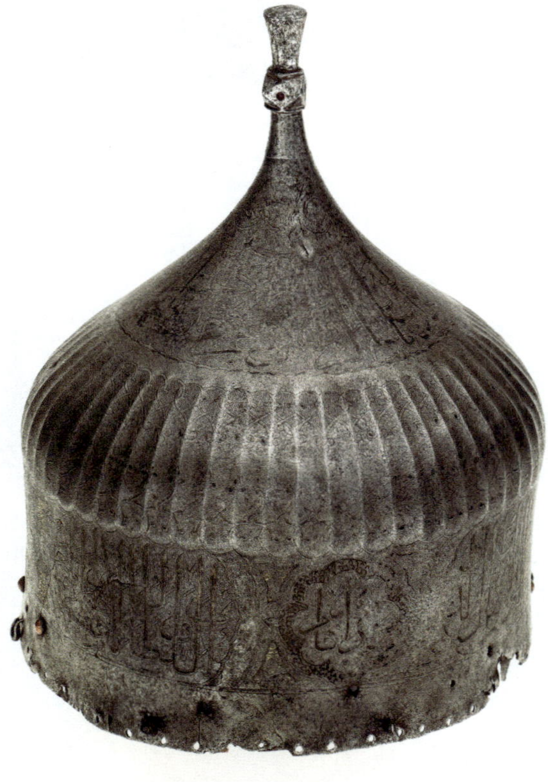

2/18

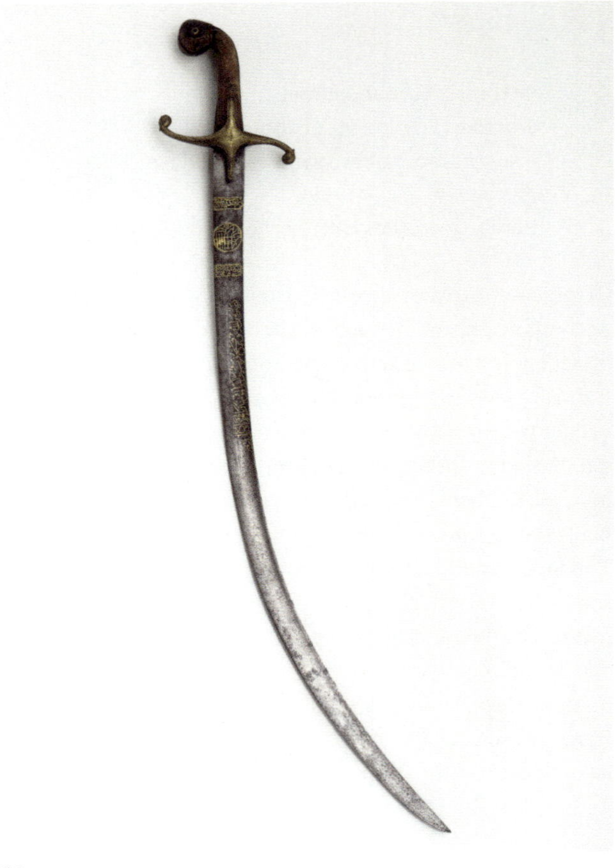

2/19

2/19 **Ottoman sabre**
Ottoman Empire, blade 16th cent., hilt including cross-guard 19th cent.
Damascus steel, horn grip plates, damascened with gold; 9 x 3.2 x 87 cm; blade L 74 cm
Berlin, Deutsches Historisches Museum: W 4170

Exceptionally high-quality, richly ornamented weapons were made in the fifteenth and sixteenth centuries of the Ottoman Empire, in particular under Suleiman the Magnificent (reign 1520–1566). Curved sabres were light weapons typically used by the cavalry. They originated in the Indo-Persian region and held special meaning for the Ottomans. The single-edged blade of this flexible sabre, made of Damascus steel, is decorated with many Koran verses in gold inlay; one cartouche names the bladesmith as Hajji Murad bin Khosh Qadam. Other richly decorated blades by the same artisan have survived and are currently located in Cairo and in Topkapı Palace in Istanbul. SL

2/20 **Hand grenade of Murano glass**
Venetian, 1648–1669
Glass, cast iron; diam. 8–10 cm
Venice, Museo Storico Navale della Marina Militare Italiana: 1033/1034

The war for Crete fought by Venice and the Ottoman Empire in the seventeenth century was the longest siege in recorded history. From 1644 to 1669, the Ottomans attempted to capture Crete and its largest town, Candia (today Heraklion). They faced bitter opposition from Venice, which was not prepared to relinquish its last big base. While the fortress of Candia was besieged on land, the Venetians continually supplied it from the sea with fresh troops, food and weapons, including hand grenades made of Murano glass, which were filled with gun powder and ignited using a wooden plug. The loss of Crete marked the final blow for Venice as a maritime power, following some 200 years of accelerating decline. With the discovery of the 'New World' to the west and new trade routes to Asia, Portugal assumed the role of Europe's leading maritime power. CB

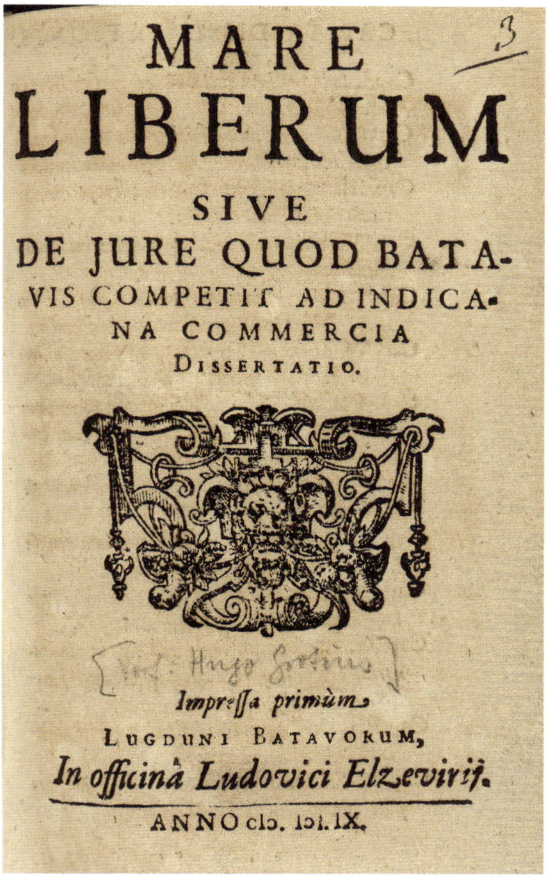

MARE
LIBERUM
SIVE
DE JURE QUOD BATA-
VIS COMPETIT AD INDICA-
NA COMMERCIA
DISSERTATIO.

Impreſſa primùm
LUGDUNI BATAVORUM,
In officinâ Ludovici Elzevirij.
ANNO cIↄ. Iↄc. IX.

2/21

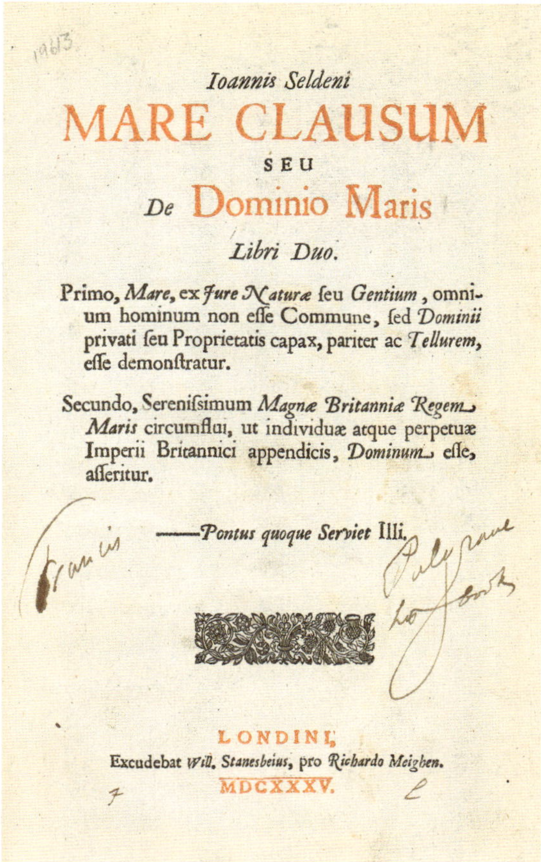

Ioannis Seldeni
MARE CLAUSUM
SEU
De Dominio Maris
Libri Duo.

Primo, Mare, ex Jure Naturæ ſeu Gentium, omnium hominum non eſſe Commune, ſed Dominii privati ſeu Proprietatis capax, pariter ac Tellurem, eſſe demonſtratur.

Secundo, Sereniſsimum Magnæ Britanniæ Regem Maris circumflui, ut individuæ atque perpetuæ Imperii Britannici appendicis, Dominum eſſe, aſſeritur.

——Pontus quoque Serviet Illi.

LONDINI,
Excudebat Will. Stanesbeius, pro Richardo Meighen.
MDCXXXV.

2/22

2/21 ***Mare Liberum* (The Freedom of the Sea)**
Hugo Grotius (1583–1645)
Leiden, 1609
Print; 15.4 x 11 cm
Berlin, Staatsbibliothek zu Berlin – Preußischer Kulturbesitz, Abteilung Historische Drucke: 3 in: Bibl. Diez oct. 1883

As Europe's maritime powers rose, and the world was divided up in the wake of Iberian expansion in the fifteenth and sixteenth centuries, the question of whether territorial claims could be extended to the sea grew ever more critical. *Mare Liberum*, published anonymously by Dutch jurist Hugo Grotius in 1609, challenged the claim articulated by Portugal and argued for the freedom of the seas, which Grotius asserted should be seen as international territory. The pamphlet had been commissioned by the Dutch East India Company in defence of its seizure of the Portuguese merchant ship, SANTA CATARINA. Beginning in the seventeenth century, the Netherlands and England began to vehemently challenge and contest Iberian dominance on land and on sea. TE

2/22 ***Mare Clausum* (Closed sea)**
John Selden (1584–1654)
London, 1635
Print, leather binding; 28.2 x 19.5 cm
Berlin, Staatsbibliothek zu Berlin – Preußischer Kulturbesitz, Abteilung Historische Drucke: 50 MB 2633

Nine years after *Mare Liberum* was published, the Englishman John Selden composed a rebuttal which was published under the title *Mare Clausum* in 1635. Selden's work was not a direct response to Grotius. Its primary purpose, rather, was to argue for England's sovereignty over the waters around the British Isle and, at the same time, to push back against Dutch influence. In this respect, it mirrored the English view of the time that a country could have sovereignty over the sea just as it did over land. Both works, *Mare Liberum* and *Mare Clausum*, laid the foundation for the emergence of maritime law in the seventeenth century, and significantly shaped later developments in international law. Debate on whether the seas (and, by extension, travel on the seas), were "free" or "closed" continued until 1982, when the United Nations Convention on the Law of the Sea was adopted. TE

3 Coastal Trade
The Port of Gdańsk

The Baltic Sea area was a major centre of trade in the Middle Ages, with key trade routes connecting Russia and the Baltic region with central and western European markets. Maritime trade was an important economic driver on the North Sea and Baltic Sea coasts, propelling some port towns to regional prominence. Among these towns was Danzig (now Gdańsk), which not only had a prime spot on the south Baltic Sea but also profited from its advantageous position on the crossing of two major waterways (the Motława and Vistula rivers). First mentioned in writing in 997, the city took on a leading economic and political role in Pomerelia in the mid-fourteenth century and joined the Hanseatic League in 1361. The next two centuries saw Danzig prosper as never before.

Starting in the mid-twelfth century, many of the Low German merchants operating in the region's trading towns formed a loose confederation, which later founded the Hanseatic League. Initially a network of merchants and then of whole towns, it soon encompassed the entire North Sea and Baltic Sea coasts as well as areas further inland. A number of benefits, including common laws, better protection of transport routes, and expanded trade rights, made the concept so attractive that at the turn of the fourteenth century approximately 200 towns belonged to the association. Despite being relatively loosely organised – there was no formally certified act of establishment – the Hanseatic League dominated the region's economic life and trade for almost 300 years. Major decisions were made by representatives of the Hanseatic towns at gatherings called the 'Hanseatic Days'. Within the broader Hanseatic network, four cities in particular played a prominent role: Bruges in Flanders, Bergen in Norway, London in England, and Novgorod in Russia. It was in these cities that the *Kontore* were located. A *Kontor* was the permanent commercial and residential headquarters of the Hanseatic League within a specific country or region, and it possessed unique rights and privileges.

The most common type of Hanseatic trading ship was the 'cog', which could carry between 80 and 200 tonnes of cargo. Because of its distinctive shape, it was often used as an emblem on seals, such as the city seal of Danzig. Later, cargo ships called 'hulks' were used – they were similar in design to cogs but could carry more freight. In 1975/76, divers in the Bay of Gdańsk found the remains of one of these wooden ships, which was dated to the early fifteenth century. Because its hold was filled largely with copper plates, it was dubbed the Copper Ship. Merchandise shipped from western to eastern Europe in the late medieval and early modern periods also included luxury goods such as spices, salt, textiles and wine. For the voyage back, traders loaded the ships with beer, grain, wood and fur pelts, all to be sold in western European markets.

Over the course of the sixteenth century, Dutch merchants increased their trading activities in the Baltic, initially as competitors of the Hanseatic League and later as their direct successors. The Danish Sound Dues Register, kept from 1497 to 1857, provides a record of those changes through the centuries. The Dutch led the transition from European coastal trade to overseas trade. In the sixteenth century, Dutch architects redesigned the houses of wealthy merchants along western lines, and as a result the influence of Dutch trading contacts in Danzig was even reflected in the city's architecture. *Thomas Eisentraut*

Further Reading

Ole Degn, *Tolden i Sundet. Toldopkrævning, politik og skibsfart i Øresund 1429–1857*, Told-og Skattehistorisk Selskab, Copenhagen 2010

Philippe Dollinger, *Die Hanse*, Stuttgart 1998

Frank Fischer, *Danzig. Die zerbrochene Stadt*, Berlin 2006

Iwan A. Iwanov, *Die Hanse im Zeichen der Krise. Handlungsspielräume der politischen Kommunikation im Wandel (1550–1620)*, Vienna/Cologne/Weimar 2016

Jerzy Litwin, *Maritimer Reiseführer Danzig*, Hamburg 1997

Peter Oliver Loew, *Danzig. Biographie einer Stadt*, Munich 2011

Olaf Mörke, *Die Geschwistermeere. Eine Geschichte des Nord- und Ostseeraumes*, Stuttgart 2015

Waldemar Ossowski (ed.), *The Copper Ship. A medieval Shipwreck and its cargo / Miedziowiec. Wrak średniowiecznego statku i jego ładunek*, Gdańsk 2014

Ferdinand Seibt et al, *Transit Brügge - Novgorod. Eine Straße durch die europäische Geschichte*, Bottrop/Essen 1997

Heinz Stoob, *Die Hanse*, Graz/Vienna/Cologne 1995

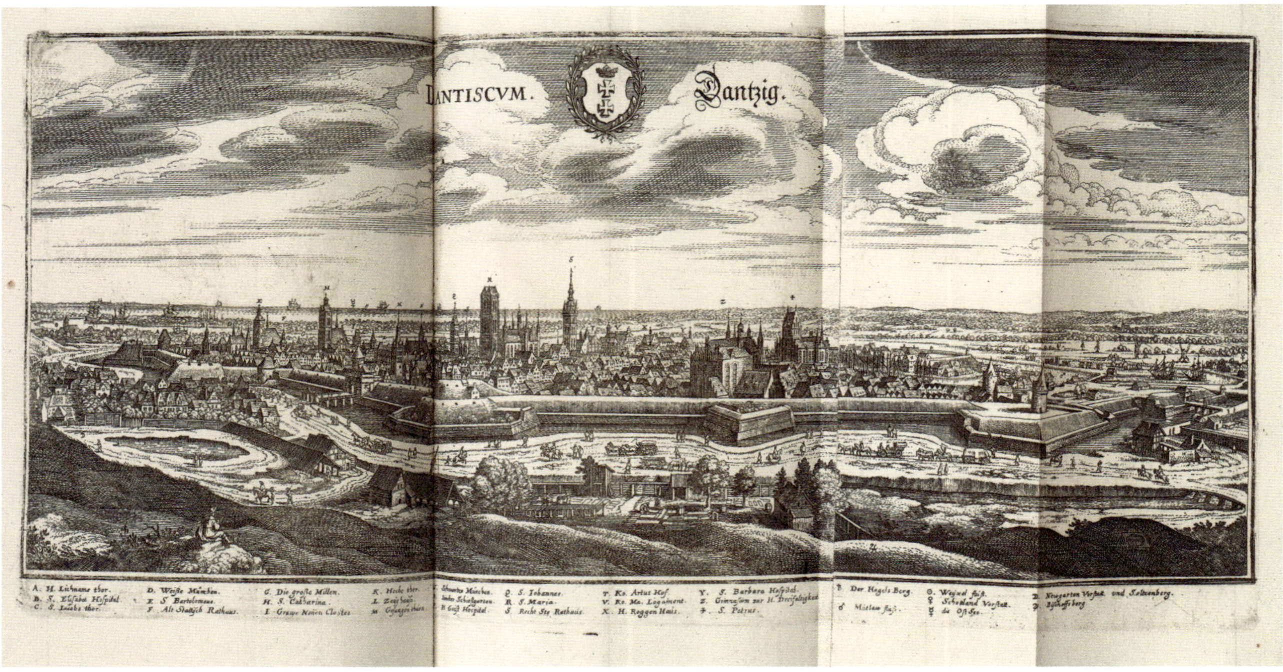

3/1

Danzig and the Hanseatic League

3/1 **View of Danzig, from Werdenhagen's history of Hanseatic towns**
De Rebus publicis Hanseaticis [...], vol. 1
Johann Angelus von Werdenhagen (1581–1652)
Printed by Matthäus Merian (1593–1650)
Frankfurt a. M., 1641
Print, copper engraving; 35 x 23 cm
Berlin, Deutsches Historisches Museum: RA 68/413

Danzig (now Gdańsk) and its environs were settled as far back as Roman times and it is thought that the amber trade, which extended as far as the Mediterranean, started here. Its sheltered position at the mouth of the Motława River, near the Vistula River and boasting direct access to the Baltic Sea, was conducive to trade. The town joined the Hanseatic League in 1361, at which time it was already a major hub of Baltic Sea trade. Brick churches and merchant houses were long a common feature of Hanseatic architecture, which had its origins in Lübeck. They can still be found all along the North Sea and Baltic Sea coasts. One outstanding example is St. Mary's Church in Danzig, built between 1343 and 1502. It was the largest brick church in the world and could hold up to 25,000 people. Later, Dutch influence played a major part in the city's architecture. TE

3/2 **Large city seal of Danzig, c. 1400**
Reproduction by Hermann Eitzen, after 1945
Plaster; H 1.5 cm, diam. 8.5 cm
Berlin, Deutsches Historisches Museum: SW 2009/9

The seal features a cog flying the Danzig coat of arms from its mast. The Latin inscription reads *Sigillum Burgensium In Dantzike* (seal of the burghers of Danzig). In the late thirteenth century, most Hanseatic towns possessed their own seals, which were used to certify contracts and purchases as well as diplomatic agreements. These seals demonstrate that cities and not just travelling merchants had begun to act as contractual partners by this time. As such, they illustrate the league's transition from a merchants' association to a confederation of trading towns. The seals were changed at irregular intervals in order to make counterfeiting more difficult. TE

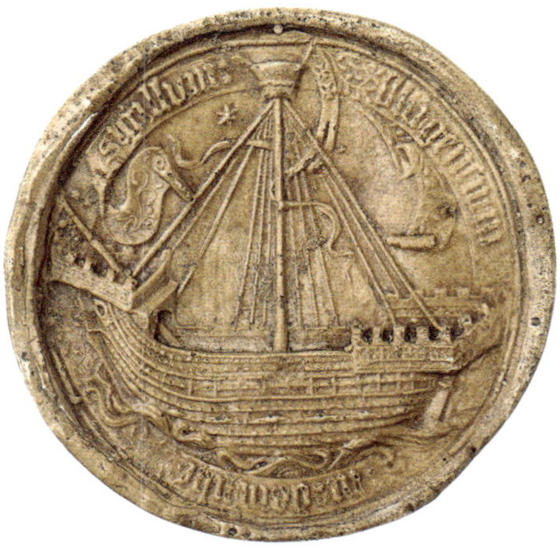

3/2

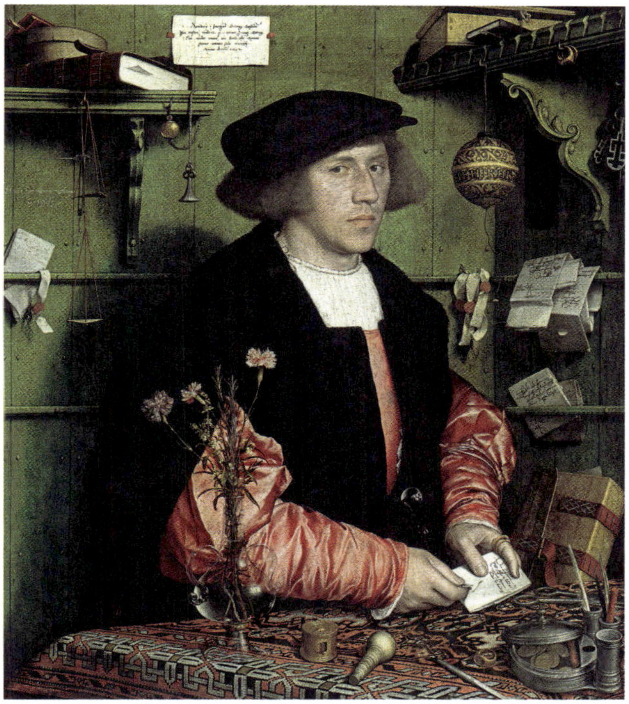

3/3

3/3 **The merchant Georg Giese (1497–1562)**
Hans Holbein the Younger (1497/98–1543), 1532
Reproduction
Berlin, bpk-Gemäldegalerie: 00012218

Danzig-born merchant Georg Giese is one of the better-known Hanseatic merchants. In recognition of his financial acumen, he was elevated to the nobility by Sigismund I of Poland in 1519. Giese lived in the London *Kontor*, dubbed the Steelyard, from 1522 to 1533. In 1533, he held the office of deputy alderman there. This portrait was painted during his time in London. The typical accoutrements of a merchant – letters, coins, account books, scales, seal and writing materials – as well as some wares he may have traded in, including an Oriental carpet and a glass vase (presumably from Murano), can be seen distributed about the room. While traditionally it had been primarily the nobility and the clergy that had their portraits painted, starting in the early sixteenth century the rising class of burghers had the financial means to commission paintings. Thus, portraits such as these also reflect a change in confidence on the part of the burghers. TE

The Copper Ship – A Medieval Shipwreck and Its Cargo

3/4 **Five iron bars**
Salvage from the Copper Ship
Modern-day Slovakia, or Sweden, 15th cent.
Iron; L 50–60 cm
Gdańsk, National Maritime Museum in Gdańsk:
CMM/HŻ/987/12, 20, 30, 52, 55

In 1975/76, the remains of a medieval ship were raised from the Bay of Gdańsk. The ship had sunk in the early fifteenth century when it caught fire shortly after leaving the port of Gdańsk. The tar it had been carrying preserved other cargo on board, large parts of which were salvaged. The first really striking objects to be identified at the underwater archaeological site were oval copper plates, and the ship was accordingly dubbed the Copper Ship. (Its official designation in scientific papers was W5). In terms of design, it was a type of ship called a 'hulk'. Its sides were clinker-built, meaning they were constructed with overlapping planks. The cargo hold was filled with goods typical of late medieval trade between western European countries and the Baltic region, including forestry and mining products. Various types of iron bars were found on board the Copper Ship, some of which had been bundled together for shipping. Shorter bars were tied together with two strips of bast fibre. The longer bars, which

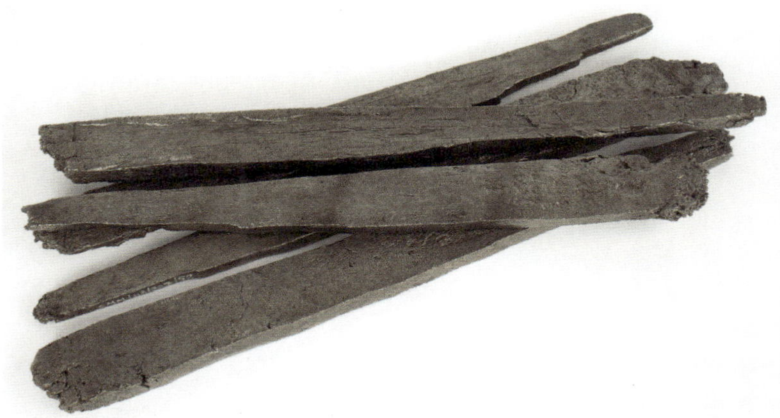

3/4

were thinner and flatter, were girded with iron bands. A total of 63 loose iron bars were also found, some in the lower and middle sections of the stern and others amidships. These bars are rectangular and wedged at one end. They are well-preserved and weigh between 1.6 and 1.9 kg (after conservation work). Like the copper, the iron may have been imported via Kraków from the region that is today Slovakia. On the other hand, it could be processed raw material originally imported from Sweden. The bars were very likely semi-finished goods that would have been used to manufacture weapons or tools. EW

3/5 **Three wooden barrels**
Salvage from the Copper Ship
Gdańsk and the greater Gdańsk region, 15th cent.
Wood; H 67–70, diam. 31.5–34 cm
Gdańsk, National Maritime Museum in Gdańsk:
CMM/HŻ/2559, CMM/HŻ/2610, CMM/HŻ/3765

A large part of the cargo aboard the Copper Ship was transported in barrels. In the Late Middle Ages, barrels were the best containers for shipping since they were robust, watertight, and could be moved simply by rolling them. Generally built of oak, barrels were resistant to rot and sturdy enough not to be damaged if they happened to knock into other objects when the ship listed. Barrels were well suited to storing and shipping finished products as well as foodstuffs, metalware, and wood products. The barrels on board the Copper Ship were carrying three kinds of products: iron, wood tar, and potash. They were cylindrical in form, and relatively high and narrow. The barrels found on and salvaged from the Copper Ship bore a number of seals from different merchants. EW

3/6 **Two copper plates**
Salvage from the Copper Ship
Modern-day Slovakia, 15th cent.
Copper; 56 x 50 cm; 41.3 x 47.8 cm
Gdańsk, National Maritime Museum in Gdańsk:
CMM/HŻ/1973, CMM/HŻ/3175/3

Excavation records indicate that the copper plates were stored on board the wreck in stacks of about 10 pieces each, placed between barrels and other goods. This type of storage indicates that the cargo contained shipments belonging to a number of different owners. Salvage efforts recovered a total of 226 plates, with considerable variation in size and weight. They varied in length from 21.5 to 61 cm, in width from 13.8 to 51 cm, and in weight from 1.65 to 17.6 kg. Earlier finds of similar plates point toward a trade route being taken from mines in present-day Slovakia to Gdańsk, with stops in Kraków and Toruń. EW

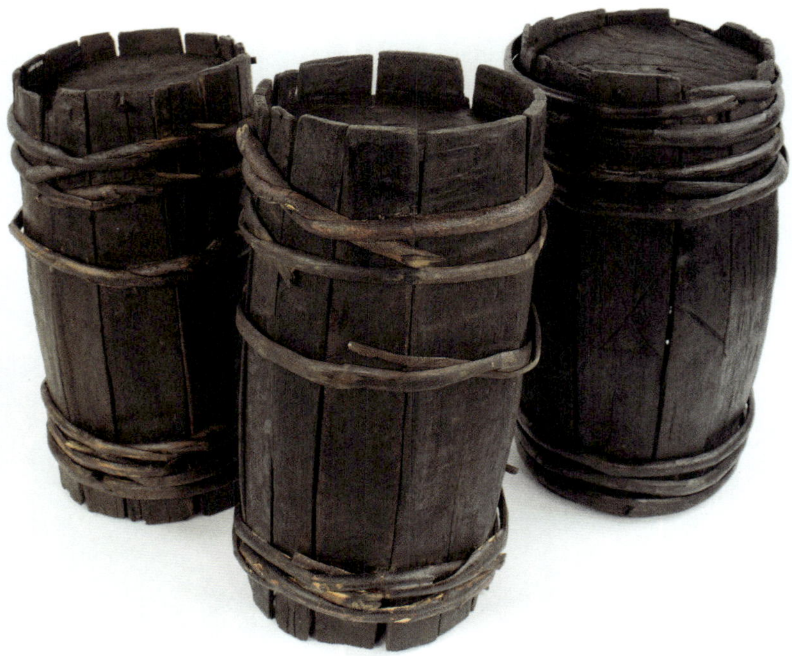

3/5

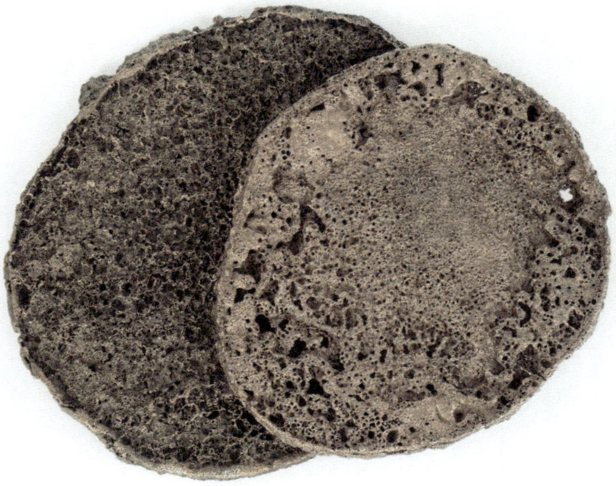

3/6

3/7 **25 Wooden staves**
Salvage from the Copper Ship
Pomerelia/Pomerania, 15th cent.
Wood; L 54–85.7 cm, W 7–17.3 cm, T 1.3–3 cm
Gdańsk, National Maritime Museum in Gdańsk:
CMM/HŻ/973/1, CMM/HŻ/974/1, CMM/HŻ/975/3, CMM/HŻ/980, CMM /HŻ/982/1, CMM/HŻ/982/6, CMM/HŻ/982/7, CMM/HŻ/982/8, CMM/HŻ/984, CMM/HŻ/2292/6, CMM/HŻ/2736/1, CMM/HŻ/2736/3, CMM/HŻ/2750/5, CMM/HŻ/2759/2, CMM/HŻ/2759/3, CMM/HŻ/3206/1, CMM/HŻ/3206/2, CMM/HŻ/3206/3, CMM/HŻ/3206/4, CMM/HŻ/3206/15, CMM/HŻ/3206/16, CMM/HŻ/3206/18, CMM/HŻ/3211, CMM/HŻ/3214, CMM/HŻ/3299

The Copper Ship was carrying two kinds of oak wood products, among them staves that varied in size from 54 to 85.7 cm long, 7 to 17.3 cm wide, and 1.3 to 3 cm thick. Staves are lengths of wood used primarily for making barrels. A total of 243 of them were salvaged. They were stored amidships in the hull, towards the stern, and lay directly next to some long planks (the other wood product found on board). They were cut from trees that grew in Eastern Pomerania. Split radially from the trunk, they have a layer of sapwood but not of heartwood. Their size suggests that they were raw material for manufacturing barrel staves. Tree-ring analysis of the 46 staves on board found that most had come from trees felled in 1406 or 1407, and a few from trees cut in 1404. The Copper Ship is the only vessel discovered in the North Sea / Baltic Sea region to have such a large and well-preserved range of cargo. The parts of the hull that were found are the best-preserved remains of any medieval ship salvaged in Polish waters. The study of the shipwreck is the largest underwater archaeology and maritime conservation research project yet conducted in Poland. EW

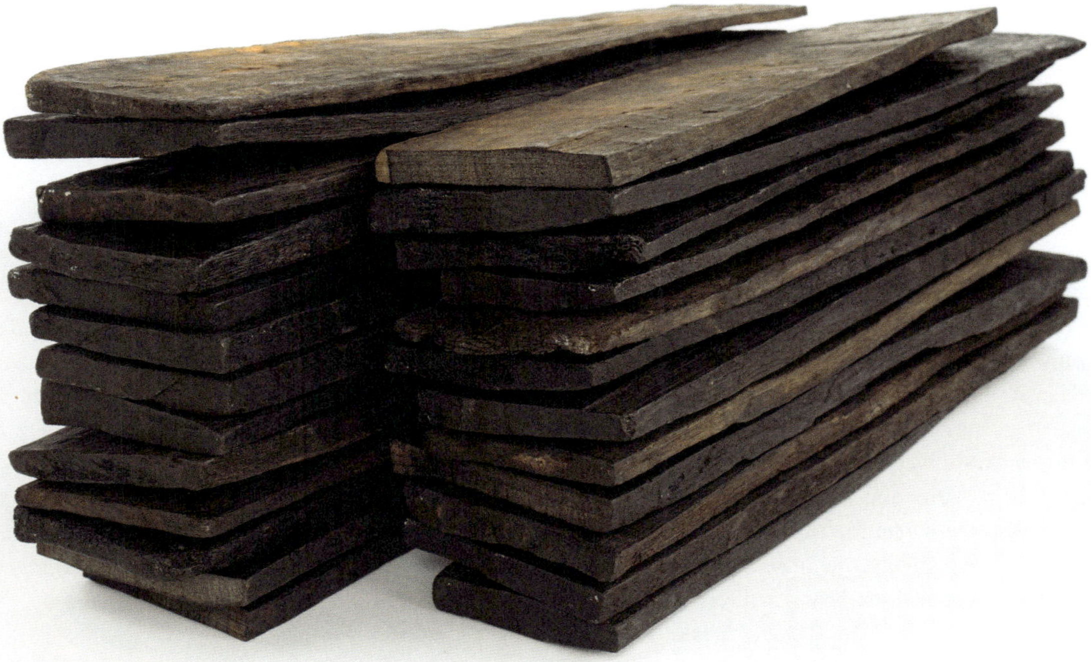

3/7

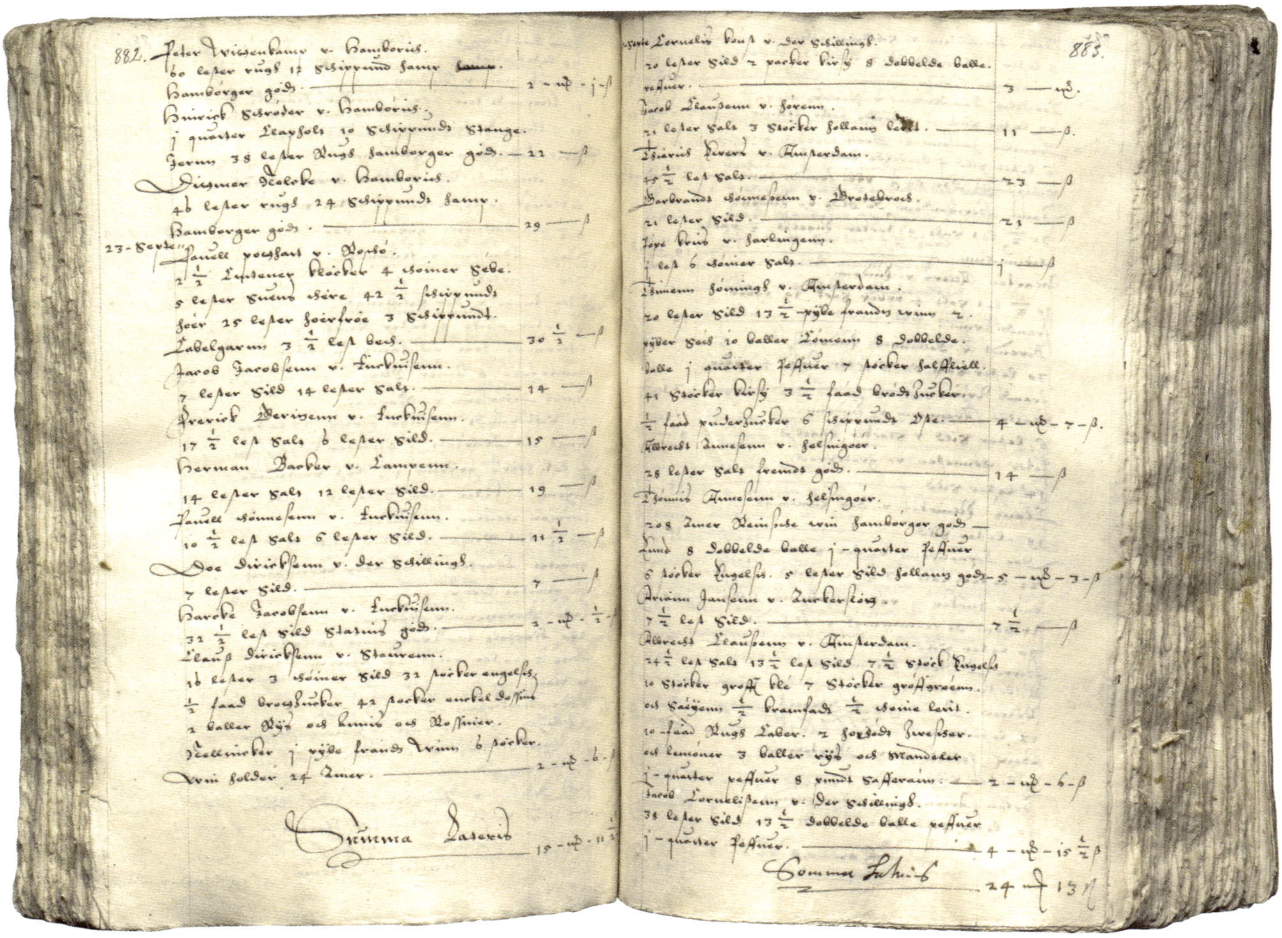

3/8

The Øresund and Its Importance for European Costal Trade

3/8 **Sound Dues Register, with lists of ships of various nationalities**
Elsinore, 1600
Paper, handwritten; 36 x 27 cm
Copenhagen, Rigsarkivet Danmark: Øresundstoldregnskaber 1600

There are only three straights connecting the North Sea to the Baltic Sea: the Little Belt, the Great Belt and the Øresund. The safest and easiest passage is through the Øresund, one of the busiest waterways in Europe. From the Middle Ages to the early modern era, the Øresund and the two shores on either side were firmly in the hands of the Danish. Kronborg Castle played a major role in securing payment of the dues. It was equipped with heavy artillery to prevent unauthorised passage through the straight. Desire for free access to the Baltic Sea and to the lucrative trading that it afforded was a constant source of tension, resulting again and again in armed conflict. The Sound Dues (or Sound Toll) Registers meticulously recorded the passage of every ship through the Øresund Straight from 1497 to 1857. A total of approximately 1.7 million passages are listed in the registers. The Sound Dues were introduced by a decree of Erik VII, King of Denmark (c. 1382–1439). Starting in 1429, every ship that passed through the Øresund had to pay a toll to the Danish crown. The first toll was set at one to two Rose Nobles (English gold coins) per ship. The amount varied over the centuries; initially it was based on the size of the ship and later on its cargo. The toll was paid directly at Kronborg Castle. The Sound Dues were abolished in 1857 owing to international pressure, but not before the naval powers had agreed to compensate Denmark with a one-off payment of 30 million Danish rigsdaler.
The Sound Dues Registers – 700 volumes in total – were accepted for inclusion on the Memory of the UNESCO World Register in 2007. The University of Groningen started digitizing them in 2009. TE

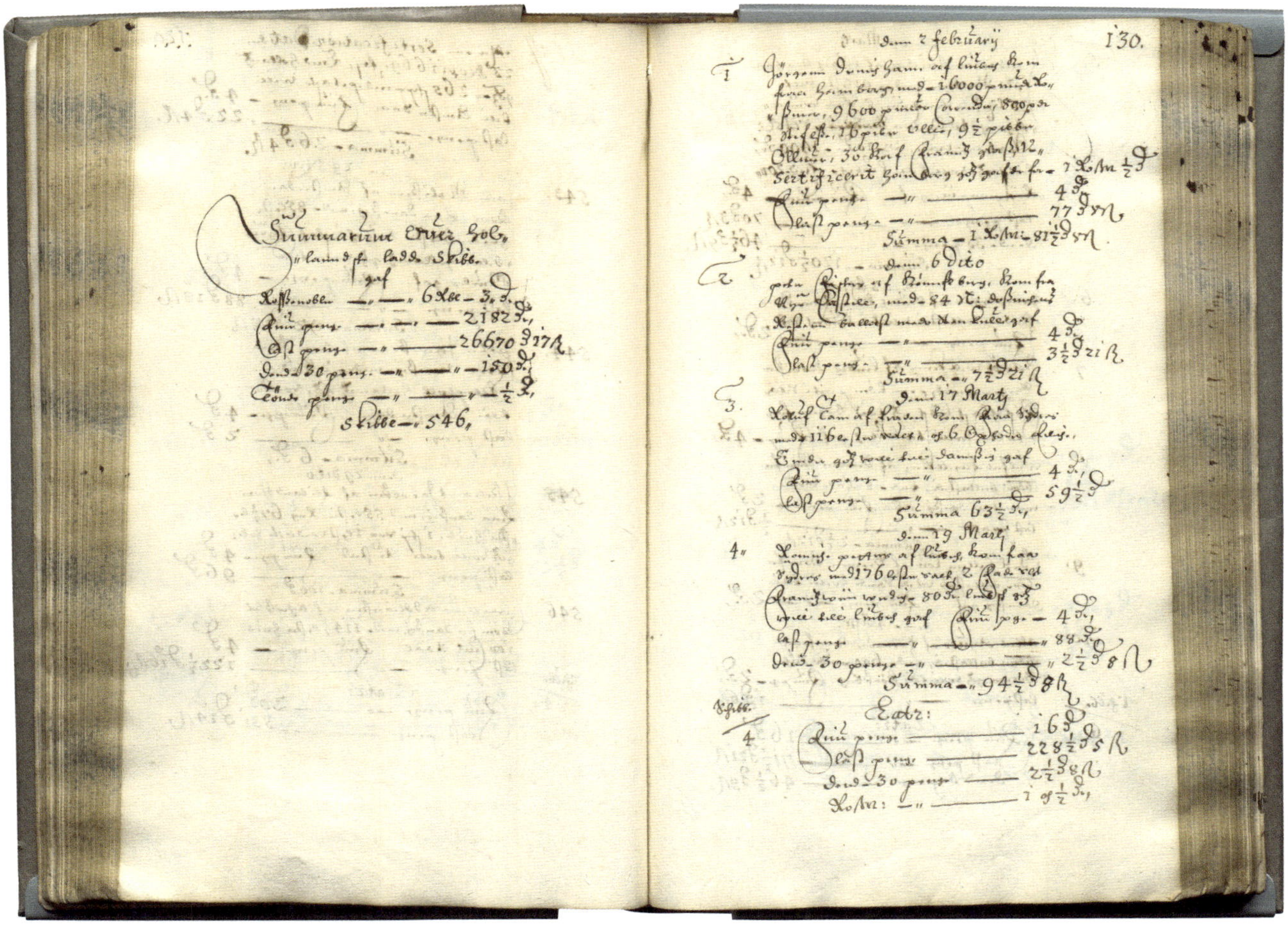

3/9

3/9 **Sound Dues Register listing the passages of Dutch ships**
Elsinore, 1669
Paper, handwritten; 33.5 x 21.5 cm
Copenhagen, Rigsarkivet Danmark: Øresundstoldregnskaber 1669

Some of the Sound Dues Registers grouped ships' passages according to the ships' port of departure. A list of this kind was kept for the year 1669. It recorded the passage of every ship through the Øresund (with each passage accorded a separate entry) for a total of 1,957 ships passing through the straight that year. The ports of departure were as follows: 441 Swedish ships, 167 Danish and Wendish ships; 140 ships from Bremen, Danzig and Lübeck; 118 English, French and Scottish ships; and 1,091 Dutch ships, which were divided into ships carrying ballast (545) and those carrying merchandise (546). Ships from the Netherlands constituted 55.7 per cent of the total, while vessels from Lübeck, Danzig and Bremen made up only 7.2 per cent. Throughout the seventeenth century, Dutch ships accounted for well over 50 per cent of all ships passing through the Øresund. For each passage, additional information was recorded. The name of the captain was noted, as well as the ports of departure and destination, and the ship's cargo. TE

4 Expansion
The Port of Seville

The discovery and conquest of 'new worlds' on the other side of the Atlantic marked the beginning of a new era for Europe. This phase of expansion in the fifteenth and sixteenth centuries provided European nations with new room to manoeuvre, both economically and politically. What is more, the expeditions they undertook fundamentally changed their understanding of the world and of themselves.

The main actors in this process were the states of the Iberian Peninsula, which by virtue of their geographic position were destined to explore and cross the Atlantic. Looking for new trade routes to Asia that would allow them to partake in the lucrative spice trade, mariners – initially in the service of the Portuguese crown – explored waters to the west and south, and established trading posts on the African coasts. As the Spanish kingdoms made progress in recapturing the Iberian Peninsula from the Moors (*Reconquista*), they too ventured further and further beyond the borders of the known world. While seafarers on expeditions for Portugal and Spain charted the oceans, their sponsors confidently claimed the 'newly found' lands for themselves. The Treaty of Tordesillas (1494), with its division of the world into Portuguese and Spanish territories, ushered in the first phase of European colonialism.

The first stage of Spanish expansion was the conquest of the Canary Islands (1402–1496), which had been rediscovered in 1312. In many ways, it was a forerunner and testing ground for Spain's later conquest of the Americas. Here, Spanish conquerors encountered an unknown, indigenous population for the first time and found themselves confronted with the practical challenges of appropriation, Christianisation and economic exploitation. The inhabitants' Neolithic way of life prompted early debates on the way 'savages' should be treated – debates that intensified after the conquest of the Americas. Navigational and organisational considerations were another reason the Canary Islands were so important for voyages to the Americas. Wind conditions on the Atlantic made it essential to head for the Canaries before sailing westward across the ocean. Also, the islands afforded the opportunity to stock up on provisions for the long voyage ahead. For decades after Columbus made for the Canaries in the late summer of 1492 before heading westward in search of a route to India, every Spanish ship on its way to the 'new world' stopped at the islands. The Canaries were Spain's springboard to the oceans.

For many decades, Europe's gateway to the 'new world' was the port of Seville. Already the largest and economically most powerful city in southern Spain, Seville was chosen as the headquarters of the *Casa de la Contratación* (House of Trade) in 1503. From then on, it had the monopoly on all movement of ships and goods between the old world and the 'new' one now under Spanish control. Alongside the key role it played in the economy, Seville became a seat of learning and a centre for the spread and exchange of information in the Age of Discovery. One of the main functions of the *Casa de la Contratación* – aside from protecting its trade monopoly – was the collection and analysis of the steadily growing pool of knowledge that accrued as Spain expanded.

It was not just Europe that felt the profound consequences of overseas expansion. For the inhabitants of the 'discovered' lands, the arrival of the Europeans mainly meant violence, oppression, exploitation and death. Even among contemporaries, the conquerors' atrocities provoked criticism and debate on the legitimacy of European expansion. The centuries of European colonialism that followed left an impact that can still be felt today, and many countries have not undertaken a critical reappraisal of this period until recently. *Christiana Brennecke*

Further Reading

David Abulafia, *The Discovery of Mankind. Atlantic Encounters in the Age of Columbus*, New Haven/London 2008

Amerika 1492–1992. Neue Welten – Neue Wirklichkeiten. Geschichte, Gegenwart, Perspektiven, ed. by Dietrich Briesemeister et al, Ibero-Amerikanisches Institut Berlin, Braunschweig 1992

Paulino Castañeda Delgado (ed.), *Fray Bartolomé de Las Casas. Obras completas*, 14 vols., Seville 1989–1999

España y América. Un oceano de negocios. Quinto centenario de la Casa de la Contratación 1503–2003, ed. by Guiomar de Carlos Boutet, Sociedad Estatal de Conmemoraciones Culturales, Seville 2003

David González Cruz (ed.), *Descubridores de América. Colón, los marinos y los puertos*, Madrid 2012

Novos Mundos – Neue Welten. Portugal und das Zeitalter der Entdeckungen, ed. by Michael Kraus and Hans Ottomeyer, Deutsches Historisches Museum, Berlin 2007

Wolfgang Reinhard, *Die Unterwerfung der Welt. Globalgeschichte der europäischen Expansion 1415–2015*, Munich 2016

Stefan Rinke, *Kolumbus und der Tag von Guanahani. 1492: Ein Wendepunkt der Geschichte*, Stuttgart 2013

Jürgen Sarnowsky, *Die Erkundung der Welt. Die großen Entdeckungsreisen von Marco Polo bis Humboldt*, Munich 2015

Bruno Schmidt, *Die Ureinwohner der Kanarischen Inseln. Ihre Geschichte, Herkunft und Hinterlassenschaft*, Münster 1996

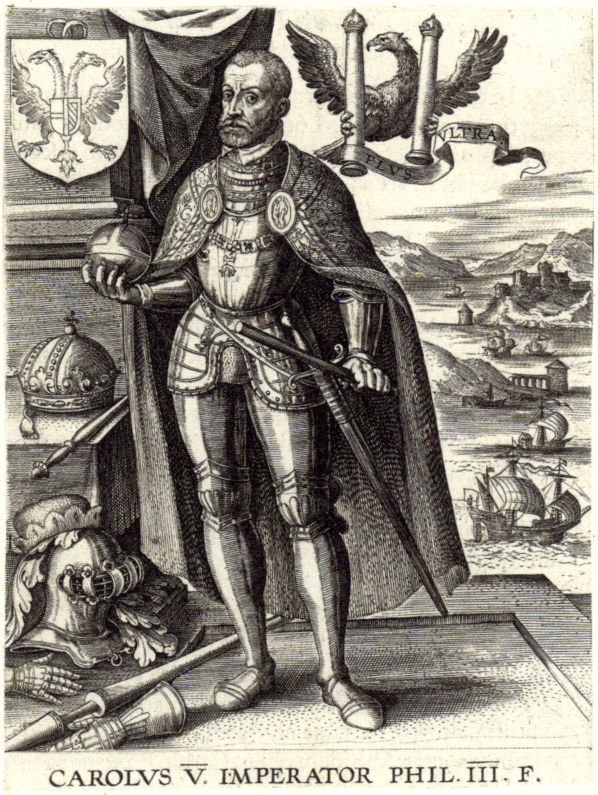

4/1

Plus Ultra: The Discovery and Conquest of "New Worlds"

4/1 **Portrait of Charles V, Holy Roman Emperor**
1601/1750
Etching, paper; 19.2 x 14.7 cm (folio)
Berlin, Staatsbibliothek zu Berlin – Preußischer Kulturbesitz, Handschriftenabteilung: Portr. Slg / Slg Hansen / Lothringen, Niederlande / 2° / vol. 1 / no. 128

The Pillars of Hercules flanking the Strait of Gibraltar had been considered the edge of the habitable world since ancient times. According to Greek mythology, the demigod Hercules inscribed on them the warning *non plus ultra* (Latin for 'not further beyond') to mark the end of the world. In the Age of Discovery, a variation of this phrase – *plus ultra* (further beyond) – was adopted by the Spanish kings as their motto and came to stand for Spanish expansion. The Pillars of Hercules and a banner reading "Plus Ultra" have adorned the Spanish coat of arms since Charles V (1500–1558, styled Charles I after he became King of Castile and Aragon in 1516). In this portrait of Charles V, the pillars and banner are carried by the Eagle of St John, which served as the supporter of the Spanish coat of arms under the Catholic Monarchs (the joint title for Queen Isabella I of Castile and King Ferdinand II of Aragon). Charles himself later replaced this eagle with the *Reichsadler*, the double-headed eagle of the Holy Roman Empire. CB

4/2 ***Conquête et les Conquérants des Iles Canaries*, chronicle**
(The conquest and the conquerors of the Canary Islands)
Pierre Bontier, Jean le Verrier (both 13th/14th cent.)
France, c. 1405
Parchment codex; 26.5 x 18 cm
London, The British Library Board: Egerton 2709

In May 1402, two French knights named Jean de Béthencourt (1362–1425) and Gadifer de la Salle (1340–1415) set sail from La Rochelle to conquer the Canary Islands. This account of their expedition, which was sanctioned by Henry III (1379–1406), is the first chronicle of conquest ever recorded. In the magnificently illustrated parchment codex, the two authors (priests who accompanied the campaign), describe what the Europeans saw in the Canaries. They also reveal what motivated the knights to set off on their voyage. Even if repeated references are made to their missionary zeal, it is clear that this European venture was driven by greed and the pursuit of profit. By 1405, they had succeeded in conquering the islands now known as Lanzarote, Fuerteventura and El Hierro. Attempts to seize Gran Canaria and Tenerife, on the other hand, failed in the face of indigenous resistance. CB

4/3 **Portulan chart showing the Canary Islands, rediscovered in 1312**
(Carte marine de la mer Baltique, de la mer du Nord, de l'océan Atlantique Est, de la mer Méditerranée, de la mer Noire et de la mer Rouge / Hoc opus fecit angelino dulcert/ ano M CCC XXX VIIII de mense augusti/ [in civitate] maioricharum)
Angelino Dulcert (13th/14th cent.)
Palma de Mallorca, 1339
Vellum, tinted; 75 x 102 cm
Paris, Bibliothèque nationale de France: CPL GE B-696 (RES)

The ancient world knew of the Canary Islands, but that knowledge (contained in Ptolemy and Pliny) was lost in the Middle Ages. It was not until the fourteenth century that Genoese mariner Lanzarotto Malocello (1270–1336) rediscovered the islands off the African coast. The first written mention of them since their rediscovery was on this portulan chart, drawn by Catalan cartographer Angelino Dulcert in 1339. It shows two large islands and a smaller island

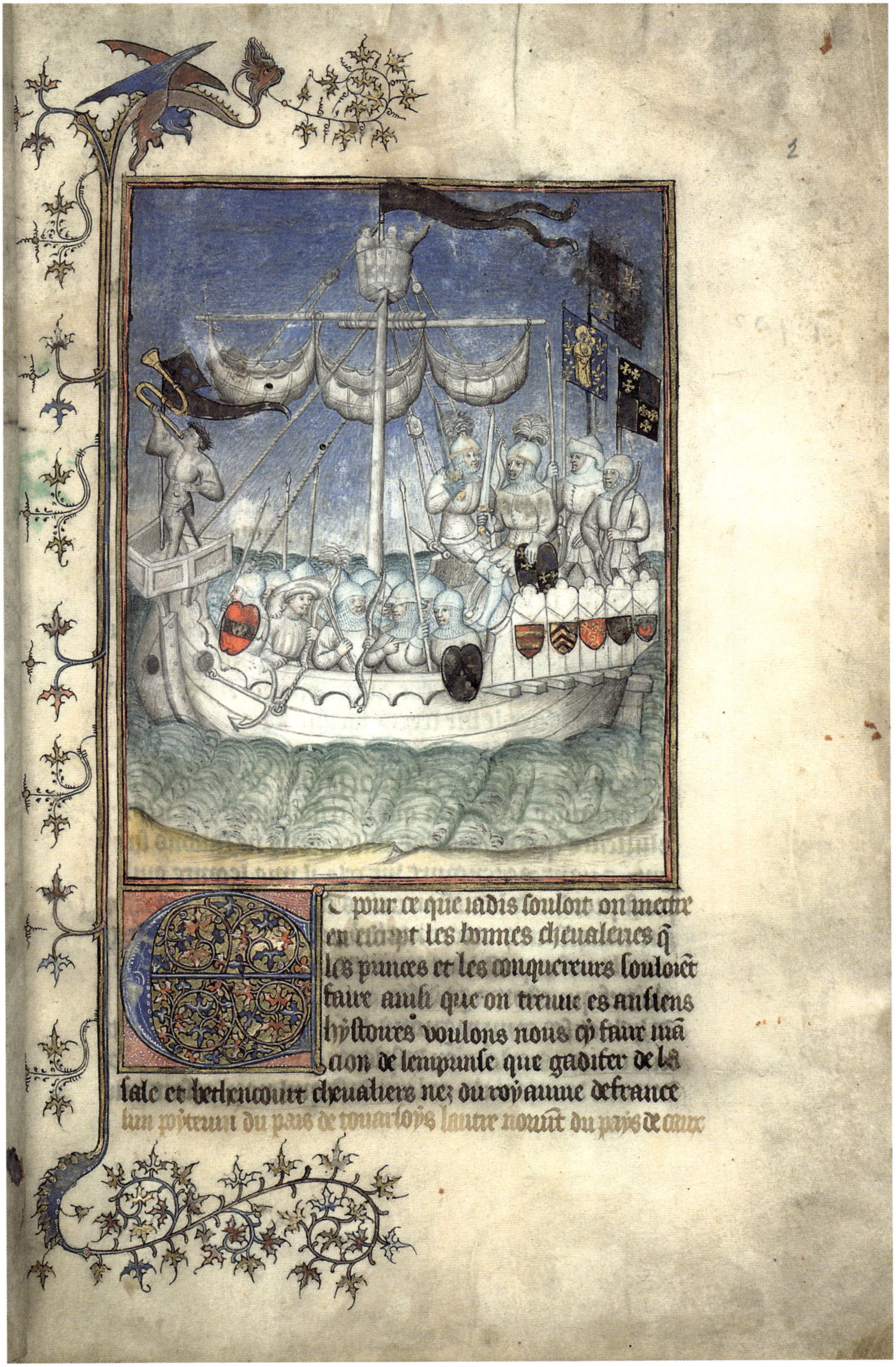

4/2

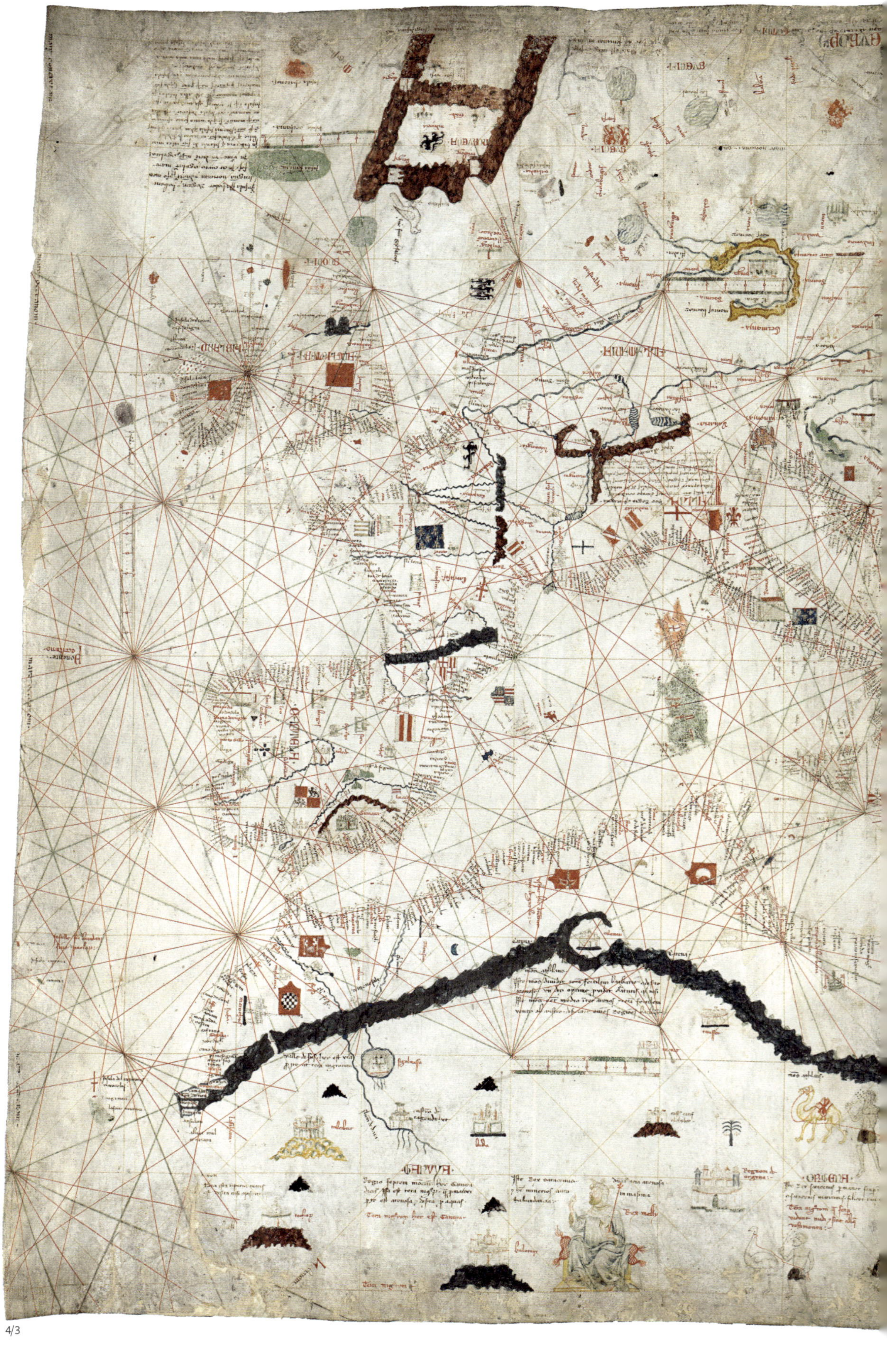

4/3

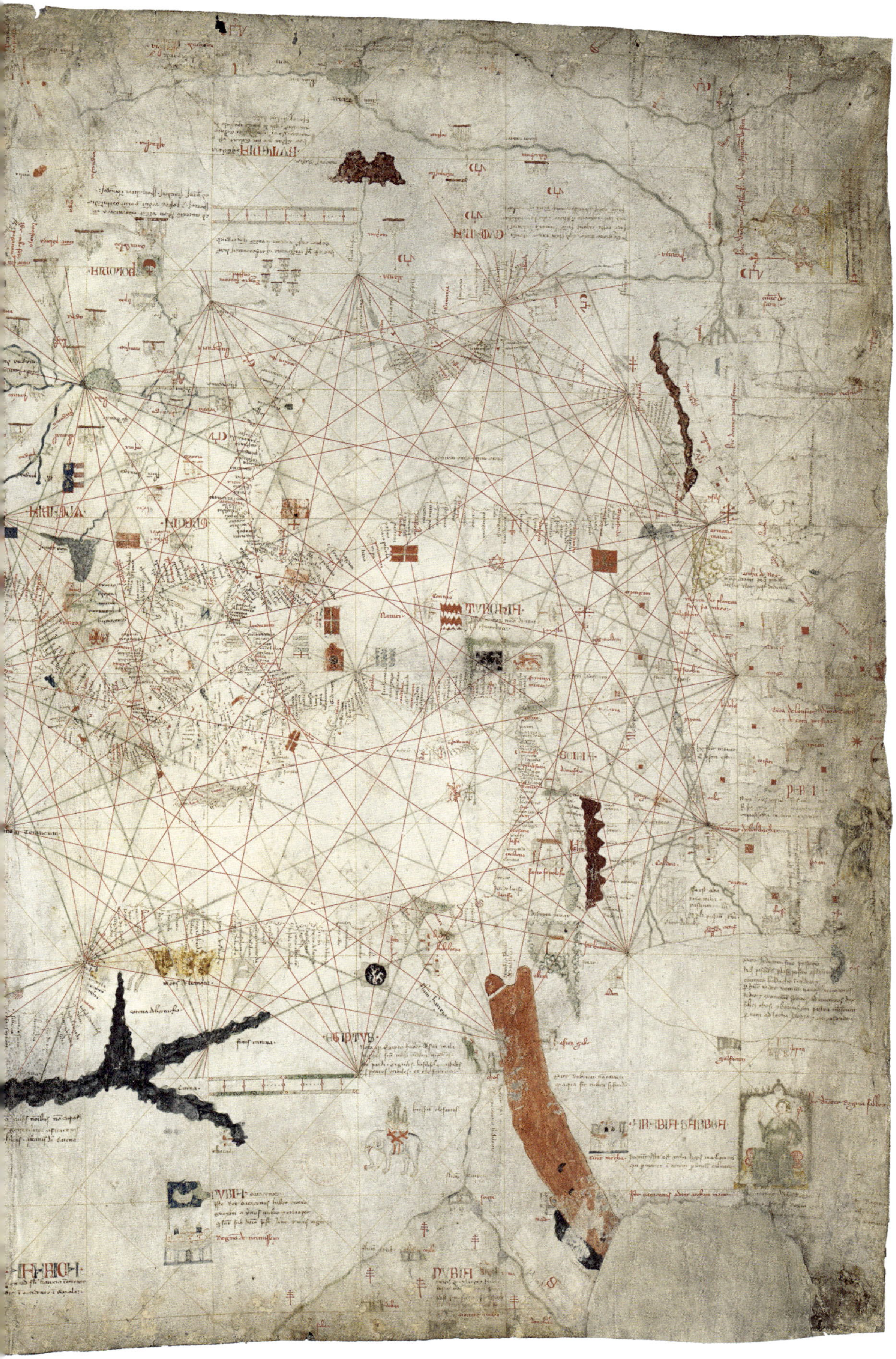

labelled Lanzarotus Marocelus (Lanzarote), Forte Ventura (Fuerteventura) and Vesci Marina (Lobos). The Genoese coat of arms can be seen next to the islands. The first portulan charts, drawn on parchment or vellum, were mostly maps of the Mediterranean extending as far eastwards as the Black Sea. They contained precise descriptions of the coastlines and a great deal of practical information that facilitated navigation. CB

4/4 **Hauberk (chain mail shirt)**
Spain, 15th cent.
Iron, leather; 84 x 50 x 1.1 cm
Excmo. Ayuntamiento de Santa Cruz de Tenerife.
Museo de Bellas Artes, depositado en el Museo Militar Regional: MTCN-229

Spain did not succeed in conquering the two large Canary islands of Gran Canaria and Tenerife until the Catholic Monarchs declared that the state would organise the campaign. Castilian crown troops took the islands by force over a period lasting from 1478 to 1496. At the same time, Crown of Castile secured its territorial claims in several treaties with Portugal. An important factor in the conquistadors' campaign against the indigenous population – one that also proved crucial later in the Americas – was their technical superiority. European chain mail shirts, for example, were made of thousands of interconnected iron rings. This body armour provided effective protection against the stones and spears of the native population, which were made of animal bone, stone and leather. CB

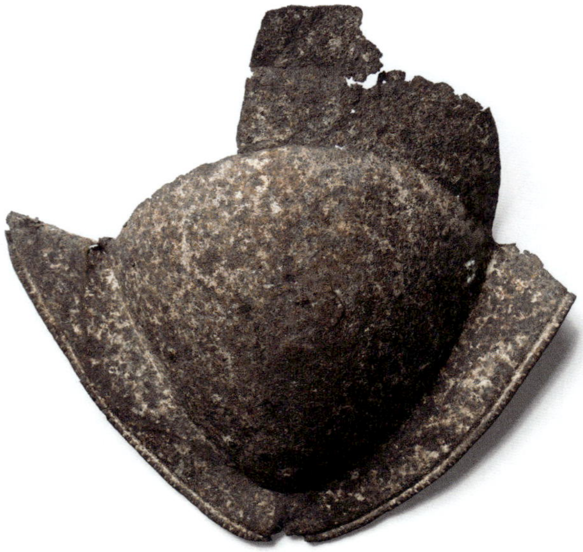
4/5

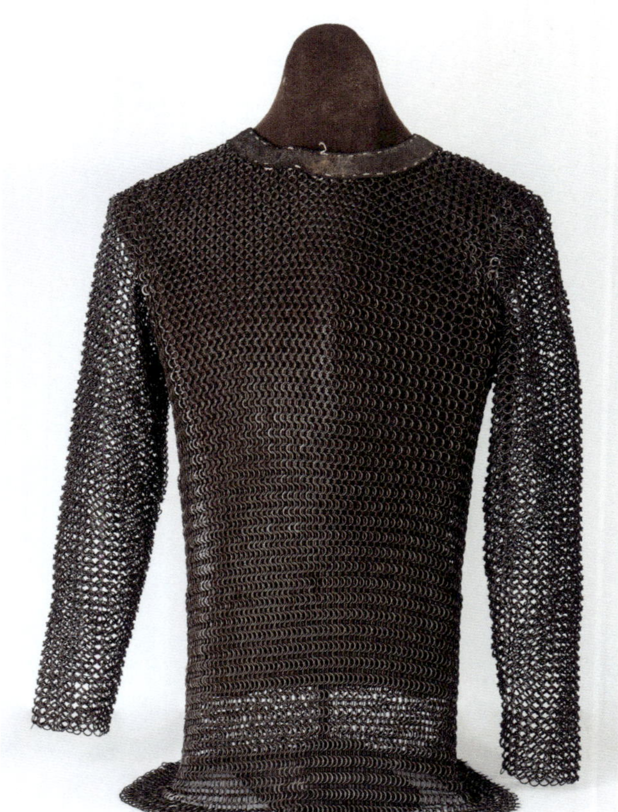
4/4

4/5 **Remains of an iron helmet**
Spain, 16th cent.
Iron; 32 x 38 x 2 cm
Excmo. Ayuntamiento de Santa Cruz de Tenerife.
Museo de Bellas Artes, depositado en el Museo Militar Regional: MTCN-222

4/6 **Sword (rapier)**
Spain, 16th cent.
Iron; blade L: 74 cm, B: 2.8 cm
Excmo. Ayuntamiento de Santa Cruz de Tenerife.
Museo de Bellas Artes, depositado en el Museo Militar Regional: MTCN-219

These are the remains of armour and weapons used in the conquest of Tenerife. They were found in the valley of Acentejo, where the Spanish suffered their greatest defeat by the indigenous Guanches, and where just two years later their victory (facilitated by epidemics in the native population) paved the way for the conquest of the island. Even today, the Tenerife towns of *La Matanza* (The Slaughter) and *La Victoria de Acentejo* (The Victory of Acentejo) recall these two major battles. The helmet fragments display the iconic shape of the *morrión*, which, although it was used in many

European countries in the sixteenth and seventeenth centuries, has become popularly associated with the Spanish conquistadors. This type of helmet is distinguished by its conical form, wide brim, and comb. The rapier, a double-edged sword, was a typical weapon of the conquistadors and was used above all for fighting on horseback. The sword shown here is clearly damaged. It is missing both its pommel and the tip of its blade. The hilt is made of wood and copper. CB

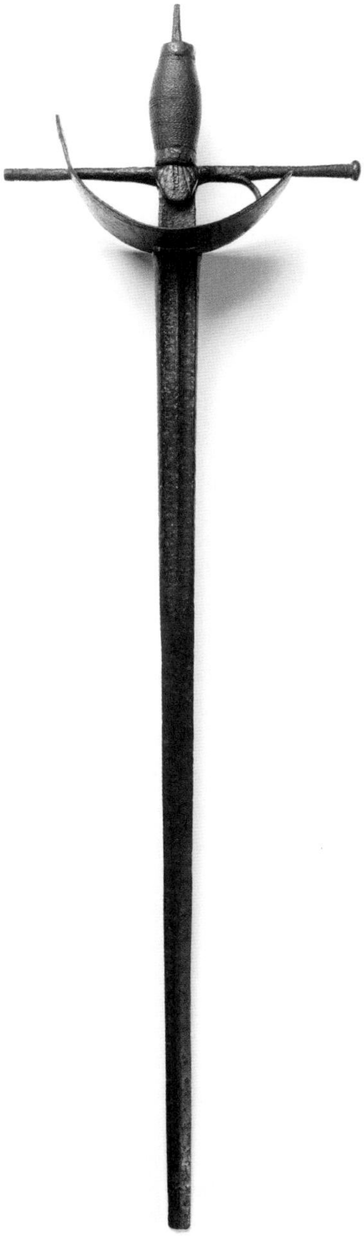

4/6

4/7 **Arquebus**
Spain, 15th cent.
Wood, iron; 14.5 x 138.5 cm
Excmo. Ayuntamiento de Santa Cruz de Tenerife. Museo de Bellas Artes, depositado en el Museo Militar Regional: MTCN-93

The use of firearms contributed to the conquerors' success, even if the arquebuses used in the *Conquista* were not terribly accurate. Targets more than 50 metres away were difficult to hit. The noise, flashes of fire, and smell of gunpowder caused terror in the indigenous populations of the Canaries and later in the Americas. What is more, native populations did not have any body armour to protect them from the Europeans' unfamiliar weapons. The firing mechanism employed by the gun shown here is called a 'matchlock'. It is one of the oldest firearm triggering mechanisms and was used from the fifteenth to the seventeenth century. CB

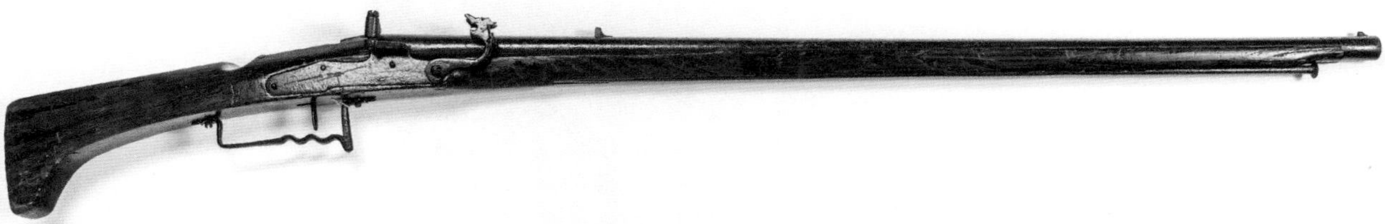

4/7

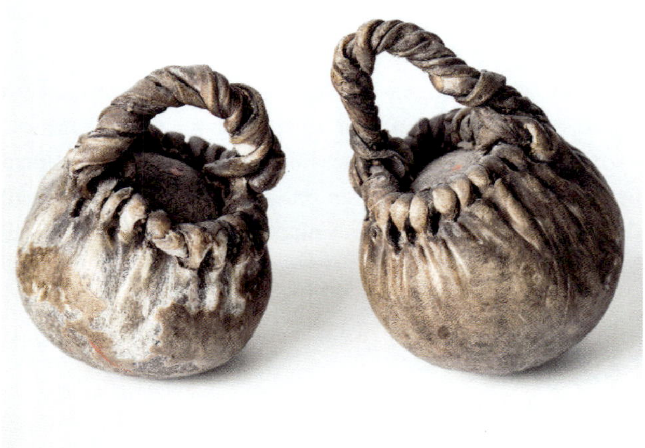

4/8

4/8 **Projectile stones**
Tenerife, 15th cent.
Stone, leather; 7.3 x 5.6 x 7.3 cm, 8.5 x 6 x 8.5 cm
Excmo. Ayuntamiento de Santa Cruz de Tenerife.
Museo de Bellas Artes, depositado en el Museo Militar Regional: MTCN-211, MTCN-212

Iron was unknown to the Guanches, the indigenous people of the Canary Islands. They fashioned their weapons from stone, volcanic glass (obsidian), wood and animal materials. Shields made of dragon tree bark were used for self-defence. They wore a cape made of animal hide called a *tamarco*, which they wound around their left arm for protection when under attack. The classic weapons of the native Canary Islanders were stones, clubs, obsidian knives, and spears made of wood with tips hardened by fire or made of goat horn. They were unfamiliar with weapons such as bows and arrows or spear-throwers. Stones like those displayed here were used as projectiles, and tied with leather cords to a person's wrist or the tip of a stick. They were spherical in shape and sewn into a covering made of animal skin. The braided handle is also made of leather. CB

4/9 **Idol**
Gran Canaria, pre-Hispanic
Clay, red earth; 26.1 x 23.7 cm
Las Palmas de Gran Canaria, El Museo Canario: 2899

4/10 **Pintaderas (stamps)**
Gran Canaria, pre-Hispanic
Clay; 6.2 x 7.9 cm, diam. 4.7 cm, 4.2 x 9.2 x 4 cm
Las Palmas de Gran Canaria, El Museo Canario: 3.032, 3.060, 3.162

The Europeans who landed on the Canary Islands in the fourteenth and fifteenth centuries considered the indigenous people to be 'savage' heathens, their inferiors in every way. Even the earliest observers noticed differences among the islands with respect to their level of development. Current theory suggests that they were settled in several migratory waves from North Africa. The culture of the inhabitants of Gran Canaria was the most developed, as evidenced by the many archaeological finds that have been recovered. The diverse forms of agriculture, the construction of houses and cave dwellings, and a perfectly organised system for storing provisions all point to a highly civilised way of life. A number of artefacts found on Gran Canaria, including the island's well-known idols and *pintaderas*, have not been recorded on the other islands.
Pre-Hispanic Canarian idols, made of ceramic or clay, are thought to have had cultic and religious significance. They are

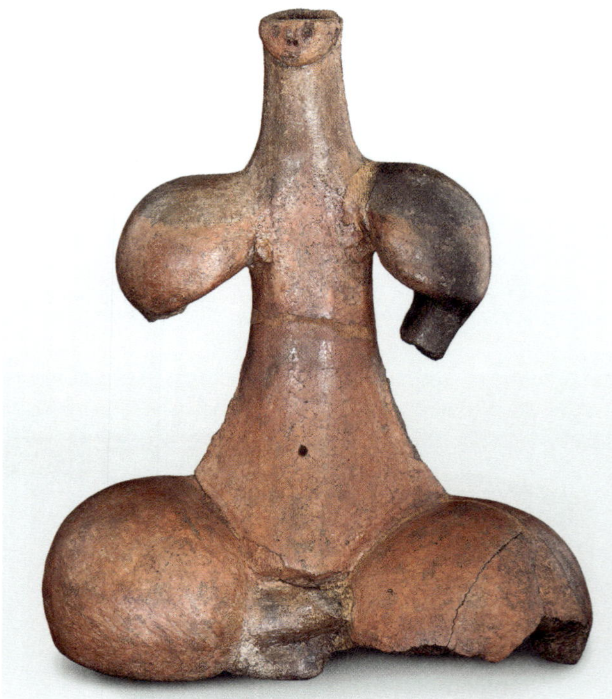

4/9

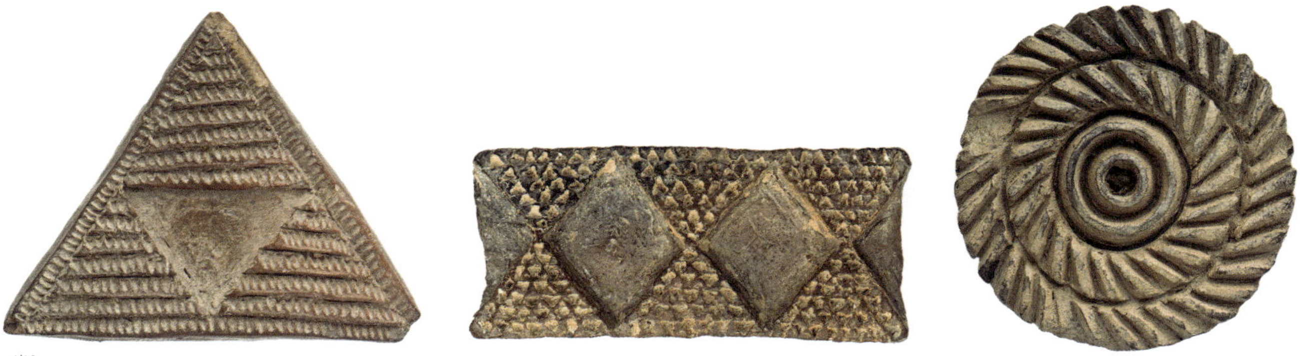

4/10

frequently in the form of a human or animal. Many of them feature exaggerated gender-specific characteristics, mostly female ones, and for that reason are thought to be connected with fertility rites. The figurine shown here is probably the most well-known of the pre-Hispanic Canarian finds and is celebrated as the "Idol of Tara". The name refers to an archaeological site in the Telde region. There is no scientific evidence corroborating that it was actually found there, however. *Pintaderas* are small, clay stamps whose function is still unclear. Large numbers of them have survived. They were made in a great variety of geometric forms, and were decorated using different engraving techniques. It is believed that they were used for labelling materials and for body decoration. Some new research is looking at the possibility that they could have been used as a form of visual communication. CB

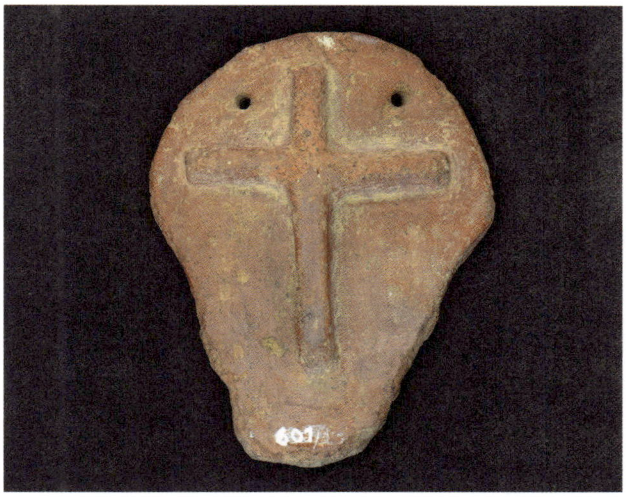

4/11

4/11 **Cross made of fired clay**
Fuerteventura, 15th cent
Clay; 10.5 x 8 cm
MUSEOS DE TENERIFE. Cabildo Insular de Tenerife.
Museo Arqueológico de Tenerife, expuesto en el Museo de Historia y Antropología de Tenerife: 12.1995.18

4/12 **Rosary**
Fuerteventura, 15th cent
Wood; L 23 cm
MUSEOS DE TENERIFE. Cabildo Insular de Tenerife.
Museo Arqueológico de Tenerife, expuesto en el Museo de Historia y Antropología de Tenerife: 12.1995.16

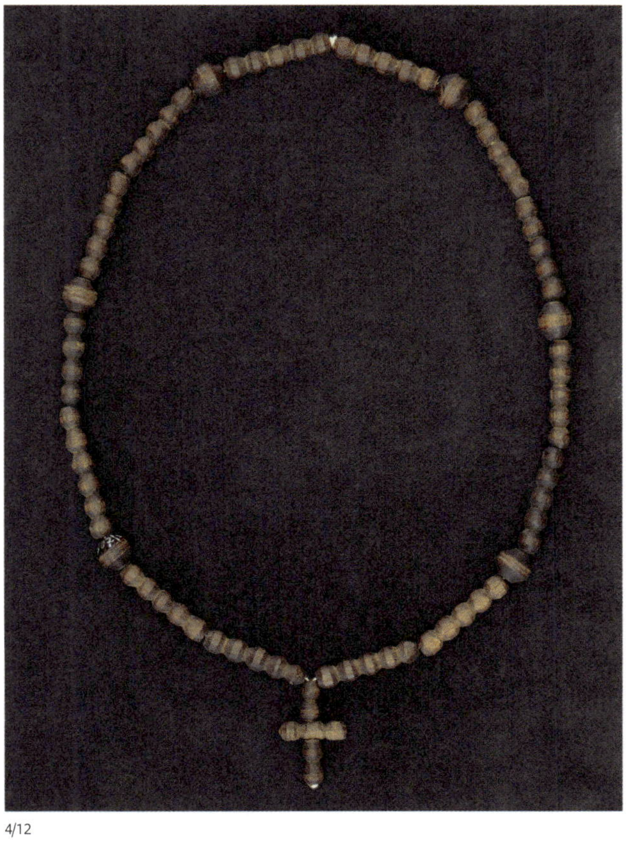

4/12

Unlike what later happened on the American continent, the process of converting the Canary Islanders to Christianity began before they were conquered and was relatively peaceful. Directly after the first exploratory expeditions of the fourteenth century, Majorcan monks settled on Gran Canaria for missionary purposes. At the same time, the Curia ordered the Christianisation of the rediscovered islands in a series of papal bulls. Chroniclers of the conquest later reported that the native people were open to Christianity because religious beliefs on the islands were largely monotheistic. There is no record of physical violence being used to force the islanders to convert. This cross and rosary were both found on the island of Fuerteventura, near the town Santa María de Betancuria. This location suggests that they stem from the time of the first colonialisation and were used by indigenous people preparing for baptism. Because the islanders accepted Christianity, Pope Eugene IV (1383–1447) issued a bull in 1434 forbidding their enslavement and the waging of war against them. CB

4/13 **Pilot guide for western seas and lands**
Itinerario de navegación de los mares y tierras occidentales. Carta de navegar para la derrota desde la Barra de Sanlúcar hasta las Islas Canarias
Juan Escalante de Mendoza (c. 1530–1596)
Seville, 1575
Paper, handwritten and tinted; 32 x 24 x 6 cm
Madrid, España. Ministerio de Defensa. Archivo del Museo Naval: Ms. 2519

Following several voyages to the 'new world', mariner Juan Escalante de Mendoza wrote a pilot guide which ranks among the most important and detailed descriptions of navigation from the sixteenth century. Divided into three books and written in the form of a dialogue, it presents contemporary knowledge on the subjects of shipbuilding, maritime warfare, and navigation. It also describes routes to the 'new world' at great length. The first two books give detailed information about the route from Seville to the Canary Islands and from there to the Americas. These descriptions are illustrated by the navigational chart shown here. The guide thus underlines the importance of the Canaries as a stop-off point on the voyage to the 'new world'. The Spanish authorities classified the work as confidential, barring its publication and thereby its dissemination. Several handwritten copies of it were made, however, and reserved for the exclusive use of the Spanish. CB

4/14 **Letter written by Christopher Columbus from the 'new world'**
Epistola … de Insulis Indię supra Gangem nuper inuentis
Printed by Stephan Plannck
Rome, after 29 April 1493
Paper, cardboard/parchment (modern); 22 x 16 x 0.5 cm
Berlin, Deutsches Historisches Museum: R 53/2894

Columbus's 1493 letter is considered to be the first piece of Americana. During the return voyage, Christopher Colum-

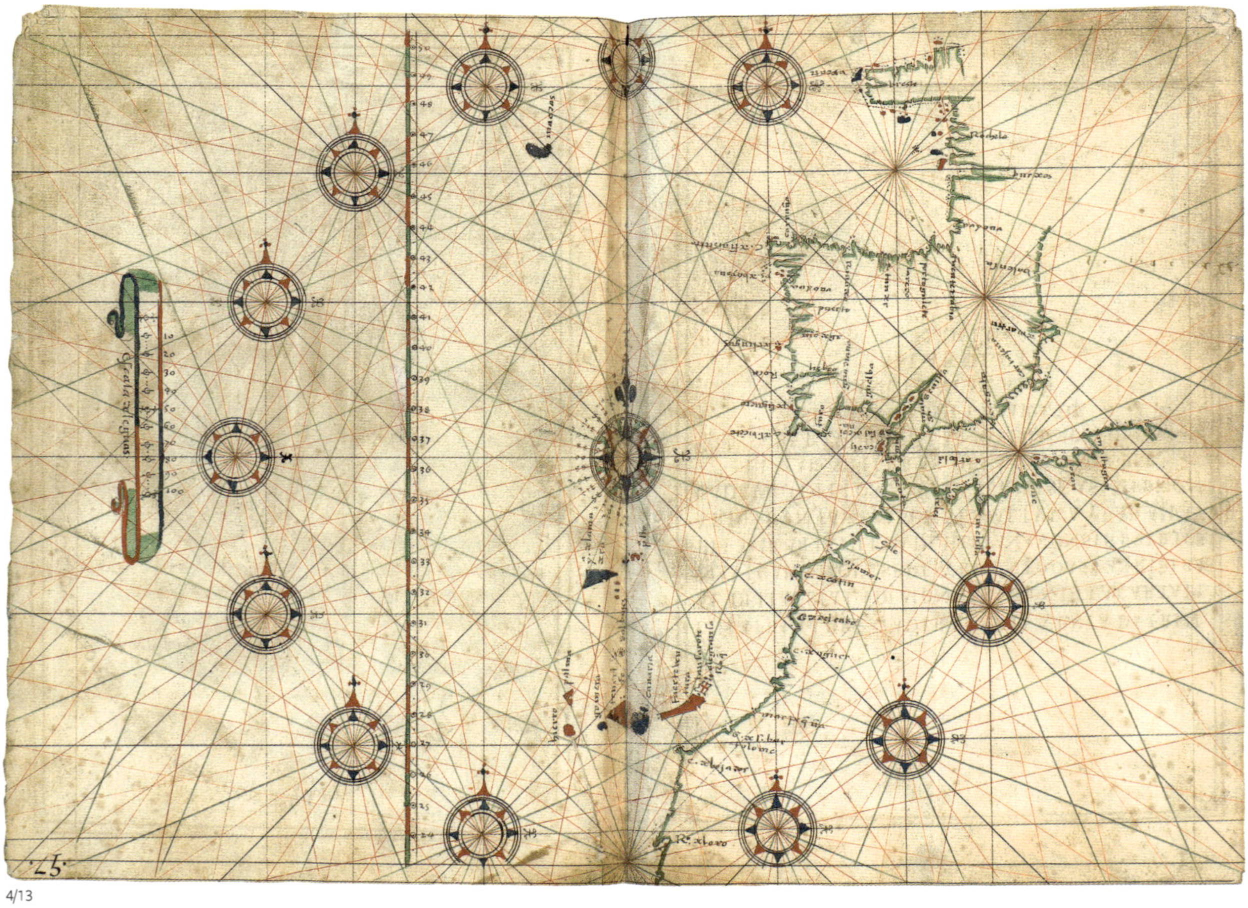

4/13

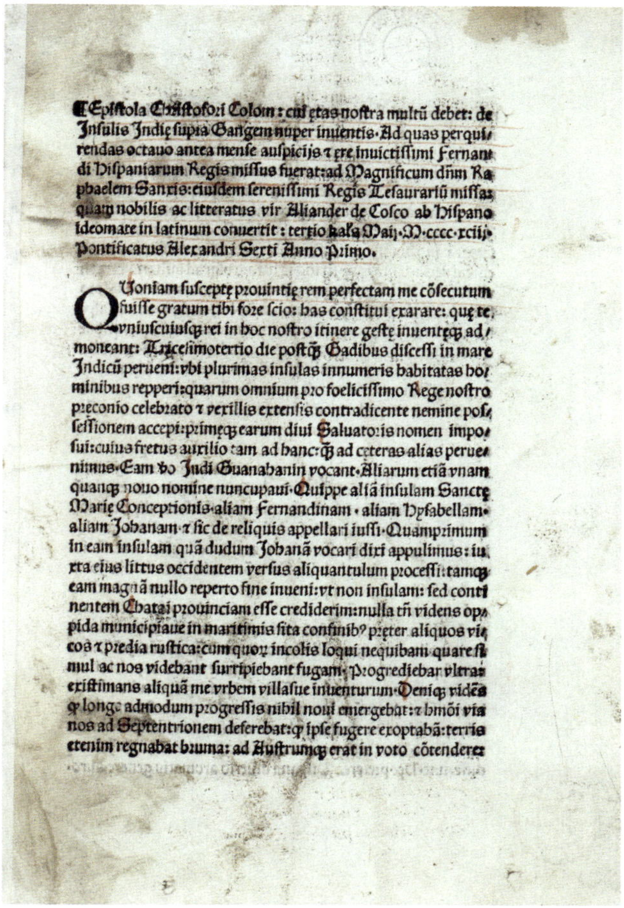

Epistola Christofori Colom: cui ętas nostra multū debet: de Insulis Indię supra Gangem nuper inuentis. Ad quas perqui-
rendas octauo antea mense auspicijs et ere inuictissimi Fernan-
di Hispaniarum Regis missus fuerat: ad Magnificum dn̄m Ra-
phaelem Sanxis: eiusdem serenissimi Regis Tesaurariū missas
quam nobilis ac litteratus vir Aliander de Cosco ab Hispano
ideomate in latinum conuertit: tertio kal̄s Maij. M.cccc.xciij.
Pontificatus Alexandri Sexti Anno primo.

Quoniam suscepte prouintię rem perfectam me cōsecutum
fuisse gratum tibi fore scio: has constitui exarare: que te
vniuscuiusqȝ rei in hoc nostro itinere gestę inuentęqȝ ad-
moneant: Tricesimotertio die postq̄ȝ Gadibus discessi in mare
Indicū perueni: vbi plurimas insulas innumeris habitatas ho-
minibus repperi: quarum omnium pro foelicissimo Rege nostro
preconio celebrato et vexillis extensis contradicente nemine pos-
sessionem accepi: primeqȝ earum diui Saluatoris nomen impo-
sui: cuius fretus auxilio tam ad hanc: q̄ȝ ad ceteras alias perue-
nimus. Eam vo Indi Guanahanin vocant. Aliarum etiā vnam
quanqȝ nouo nomine nuncupaui. Quippe aliā insulam Sanctę
Marię Conceptionis. aliam Fernandinam. aliam Hysabellam.
aliam Iohanam. et sic de reliquis appellari iussi. Quamprimum
in eam insulam quā dudum Iohanā vocari dixi appulimus: iu-
xta eius littus occidentem versus aliquantulum processi: tamqȝ
eam magnā nullo reperto fine inueni: vt non insulam: sed conti-
nentem Chatai prouinciam esse crediderim: nulla tn̄ videns op-
pida municipiaue in maritimis sita confinibus preter aliquos vi-
cos et predia rustica: cum quorum incolis loqui nequibam quare si-
mul ac nos videbant surripiebant fugam. Progrediebar vltra:
existimans aliquā me vrbem villasue inuenturum. Deniqȝ vidēs
q longe admodum progressis nihil noui emergebat: et hmōi via
nos ad Septentrionem deferebat: q ipse fugere exoptabā: terris
etenim regnabat bruma: ad Austrumqȝ erat in voto cōtendere:

4/14

bus (c. 1451– 1506) wrote an account of his discoveries to his patrons, emphasising that he had taken possession of the new-found islands for the Castilian crown. Spanish copies of the letter were printed in Barcelona and Valladolid in 1493 and a Latin translation was produced a short time later. While the Spanish version truthfully reports that Columbus set sail from the Canary Islands in the direction of India, the Latin version translated by Leandro de Cosco (15th/16th cent.) omits any mention of the islands in the Atlantic and identifies the start of the voyage as "Gadibus" (Cádiz). Columbus's letter conveys matter-of-fact, contemporary images of unfamiliar worlds. It met with a muted response, in contrast to the *Mundus Novus* letter by Amerigo Vespucci (c. 1454–1512), which was read as a scientific travelogue and translated into many vernacular languages. In his 1507 world map, Martin Waldseemüller (1475–1518/21) therefore labelled the newly discovered continent "America". MM

4/15 **Account of Spain's violent conquest of South America**
Umbständige warhafftige Beschreibung der Indianischen Ländern, so vor diesem von den Spaniern eingenomen und verwüstet worden …
Bartolomé de Las Casas (1484–1566)
Printed by Johann Christian Walter
Heidelberg, 1665
Paper, edge coloring, cardboard and parchment binding; 20 x 16.5 cm
Berlin, Deutsches Historisches Museum: R 55/4087.2

The violent conquest and seizure of non-European territories by Spain and Portugal took on completely new dimensions following the discovery of the 'new world', even prompting some contemporaries to voice their disapproval. One of the first to challenge the legitimacy of Spain's expansion was Dominican friar Bartolomé de Las Casas. Having previously been an official in the Spanish colonial system, he was ordained to the priesthood in 1514. Soon afterwards, he began to draw attention to the intolerable conditions in the overseas territories and to call for a change in treatment of indigenous people. His best-known work, *A Short Account of the Destruction of the Indies*, written in 1542 and first published in 1552 in Seville, pilloried Spain for its behaviour as a colonial power. The publication displayed here (bearing a somewhat different title from the original) is based on a Latin version from 1598, which was the first edition to contain the famous copper engravings by Theodor de Bry (1528–1598). (Fig. p. 238) CB

4/16 **Letter from Bartolomé de las Casas to His Majesty on the right of the 'Yndios' to freedom**
Bartolomé de Las Casas (1484–1566)
1549
Manuscript, paper; 30.8 x 21.7 cm
Seville, Archivo General de Indias: Patronato, 252, R.9

Questions regarding the rights of the inhabitants of the 'discovered' and conquered territories dogged European expansionism from the very beginning. Europeans saw indigenous peoples as 'heathens' and 'savages', and did not accept them as equals. Local populations were either enslaved outright or forced into a similar state of dependence. A policy called *encomienda* (meaning "entrustment") was introduced in the Spanish territories in 1503. As a reward for services to the crown, it granted the conquistadors a piece of land and a certain number of indigenous people, whom they were free to put to work as they chose. In return, they were responsible for providing instruction in the Christian faith. The outcome of this policy was the unchecked exploitation of the indigenous population under inhumane conditions that

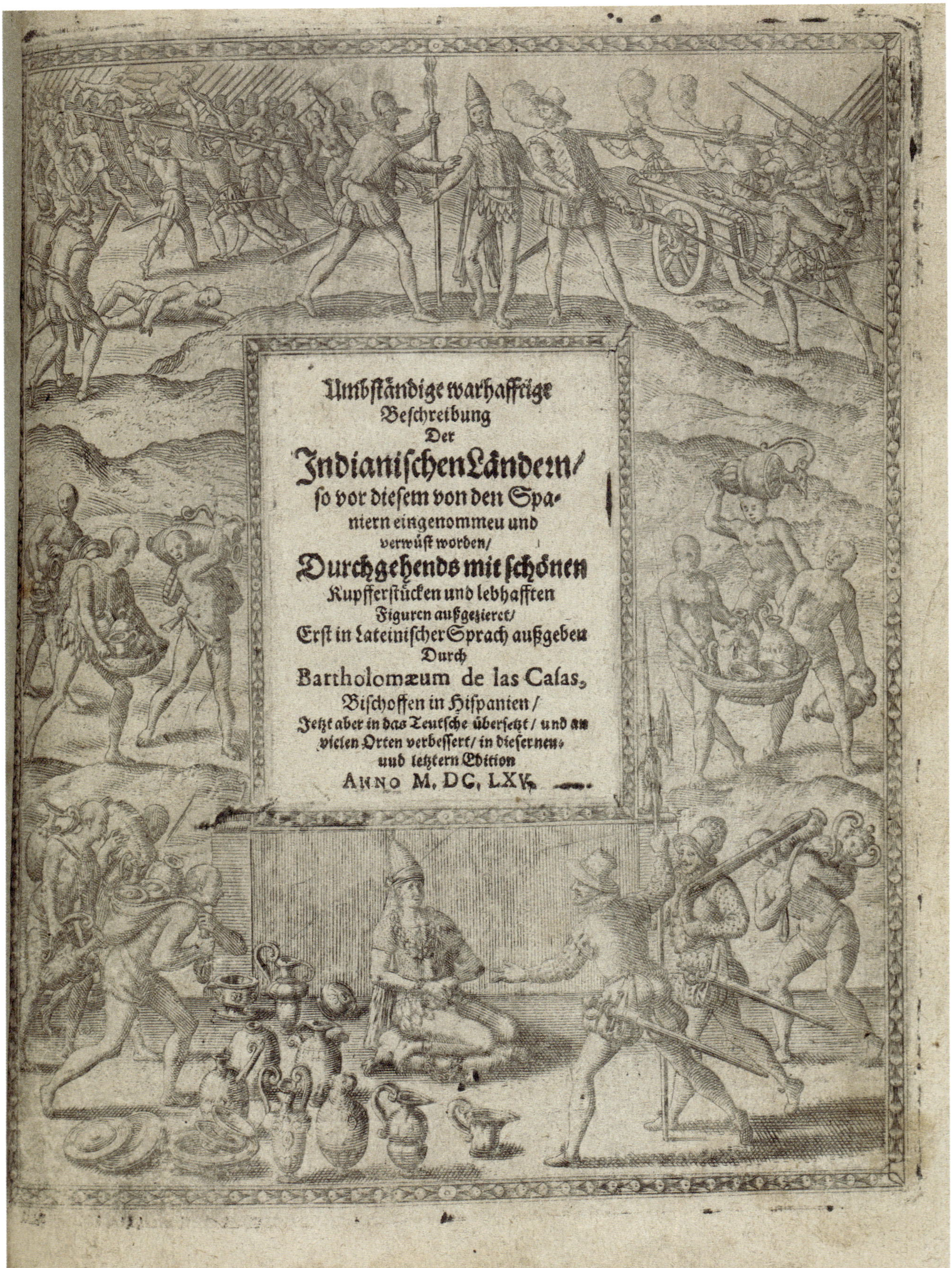

Umbständige warhafftige
Beschreibung
Der
Indianischen Ländern/
so vor diesem von den Spa-
niern eingenommeu und
verwüst worden/
Durchgehends mit schönen
Kupfferstücken und lebhafften
Figuren außgezieret/
Erst in Lateinischer Sprach außgeben
Durch
Bartholomæum de las Casas,
Bischoffen in Hispanien/
Jetzt aber in das Teutsche übersetzt/ und an
vielen Orten verbessert/ in dieser neu-
uud letztern Edition
ANNO M. DC. LXV.

4/15

4/16

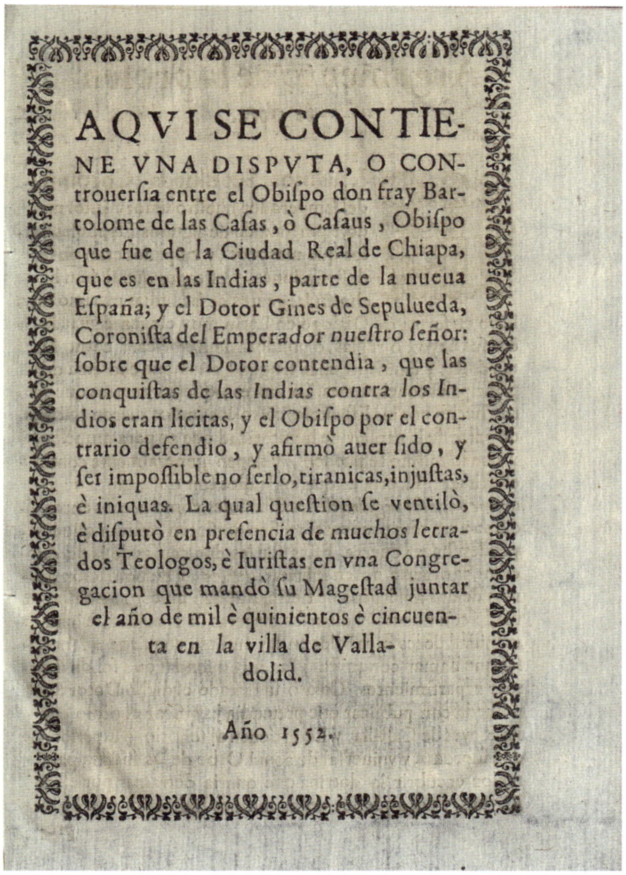

AQVI SE CONTIENE VNA DISPVTA, O CONTrouerſia entre el Obiſpo don fray Bartolome de las Caſas, ò Caſaus, Obiſpo que fue de la Ciudad Real de Chiapa, que es en las Indias, parte de la nueua Eſpaña; y el Dotor Gines de Sepulueda, Coroniſta del Emperador nueſtro ſeñor: ſobre que el Dotor contendia, que las conquiſtas de las Indias contra los Indios eran licitas, y el Obiſpo por el contrario defendio, y afirmò auer ſido, y ſer impoſſible no ſerlo, tiranicas, injuſtas, è iniquas. La qual queſtion ſe ventilò, è diſputò en preſencia de muchos letrados Teologos, è Iuriſtas en vna Congregacion que mandò ſu Mageſtad juntar el año de mil è quinientos è cincuenta en la villa de Valladolid.

Año 1552.

4/17

frequently resulted in death. Bartolomé de Las Casas dedicated much of his life to the abolition of the *encomienda*. It was not least because of his persistent criticism that the Spanish crown issued the *Nuevas Leyes* (New Laws) in 1542, protecting the indigenous population. They were partially overturned in 1545, however, in response to vociferous protests by affected landowners. In this letter, Las Casas uses the occasion of the protests to once again vehemently defend the right of the 'Yndios' to freedom. CB

4/17 **Pamphlet by Bartolomé de Las Casas on the Valladolid debate**

Aqui se contiene vna disputa, o controuersia: entre el Obispo don fray Bartholome de Las Casas ... y el doctor Gines de Sepulueda ...

Bartolomé de Las Casas (1484–1566)

Published by Trugillo

Seville, 1552

Print; 20 x 15 x 4 cm

Berlin, Staatsbibliothek zu Berlin – Preußischer Kulturbesitz, Abteilung Historische Drucke: in: Ux 108

The Debate of Valladolid (1551/52) was the first debate on indigenous rights to be conducted publicly. Its proceedings were later made accessible to a wider community of scholars. In Valladolid, before a panel of distinguished scholars, Bartolomé de Las Casas took on the court chronicler and leading ideologue of the *Conquista*, Juan Ginés de Sepúlveda (1490–1573). While Sepúlveda represented the interests of the *encomenderos*, characterising indigenous people as inferior and pronouncing slavery to be legitimate, Las Casas defended the rights of the native Americans, whom he considered to be freeborn men. Las Casas refuted Sepúlvedas' argument that the *Conquista* was a just war and pleaded for a peaceful process of conversion to Christianity in the conquered territories. Even though neither side was declared the winner and there were no concrete political consequences, the debate strengthened Bartolomé de Las Casas' reputation as a co-initiator of the first major human-rights debate in European history. CB

Seville – Spain's Gateway to the New World

4/18 **View of Seville**
Unknown Spanish artist
Spain, c. 1600
Oil on canvas; 193 x 334 cm
Madrid, Museo Nacional del Prado: 2005/010.0001

Seville was an important centre of trade even in ancient times and the Middle Ages. In the Age of Discovery, it grew to become one of Europe's largest cities and soon served as a hub of travel between Europe and the 'new world'. Thanks to its location on the navigable Guadalquivir River, 80 kilometres from the open ocean, the harbour of Seville was sheltered and had room to expand. Both of these features were essential for its task of organising and overseeing the lucrative trade with 'newly discovered' territories across the ocean. This painting shows bustling activity in the port of Seville. The shipyards as well as prominent city landmarks such as the Giralda bell tower can be seen in the background. This contemporary copy was painted after a work ascribed to Alonso Sánchez Coello (1531/32–1588), who served as court painter to Philip II (1527–1598) from 1560 to 1588. (Fig. p. 10/11) CB

4/19 **Act of foundation for *the Casa de la Contratación* in Seville**
Alcalá de Henares, 22 January 1503
Manuscript, paper; 30.5 x 21 cm
Seville, Archivo General de Indias: Patronato, 251, R.1, F.1r-4v

The act of foundation for the *Casa de la Contratación*, signed by the Catholic Monarchs, consists of 20 articles defining the responsibilities of the new institution. While its Portuguese counterpart, the *Casa da India* (also a royal institution), managed and even initiated trade with Africa and Asia, the *Casa de la Contratación* was conceived primarily as a supervisory body. Its key mission was to safeguard and oversee trade with the 'new world'. This included supervising trade with the Canary Islands and managing agricultural production on the islands. As the Spanish empire expanded and maritime traffic steadily grew, the responsibilities of the *Casa* gradually increased and were formalised in the royal decrees of 1510, 1539 and 1552. (Exhibit not shown) CB

4/20

4/20 **Petition of Miguel de Cervantes for a civil service position in the 'new world'**
Miguel de Cervantes Saavedra (1547–1616)
Madrid, 21 May 1590
Manuscript, paper; 21 x 30.5 cm
Seville, Archivo General de Indias: Patronato, 253, R.1

In addition to overseeing trade, one of the chief functions of the *Casa de la Contratación* was to manage emigration. Anyone who wanted to leave Seville for the islands of the West Indies or the Americas had to register with the *Casa*. There were even stricter rules for those who wanted a civil service position in the 'new world'. They had to present the *Casa de la Contratación* with proof of royal consent as well as documents demonstrating their social status, lack of a criminal record and purity of blood. With this petition to the Council of the Indies, Miguel de Cervantes applied for a position in the 'new world'. His application, in which he cited his service in the Battle of Lepanto, was rejected, however. Cervantes stayed in Spain and, a few years later, started work on his acclaimed novel *Don Quijote*. CB

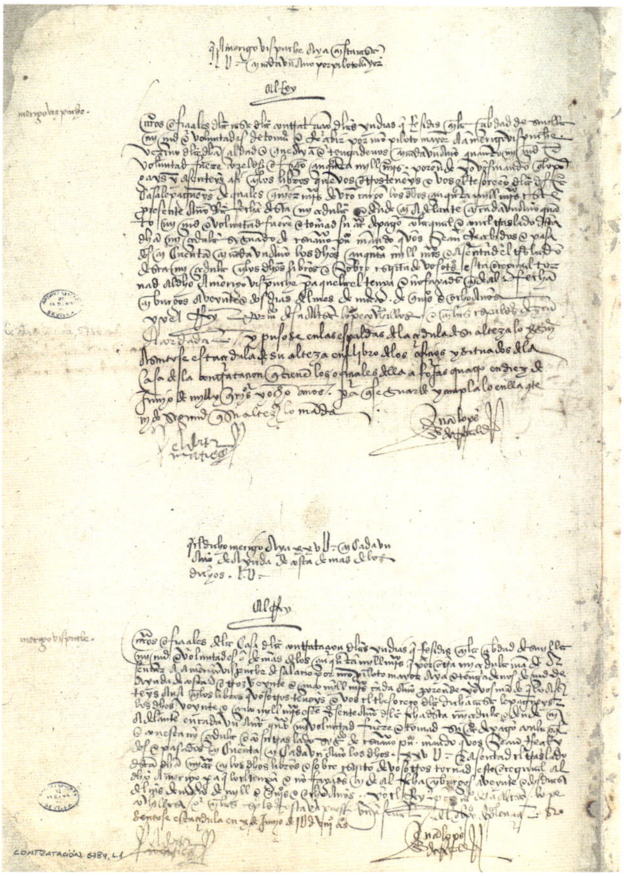

4/21

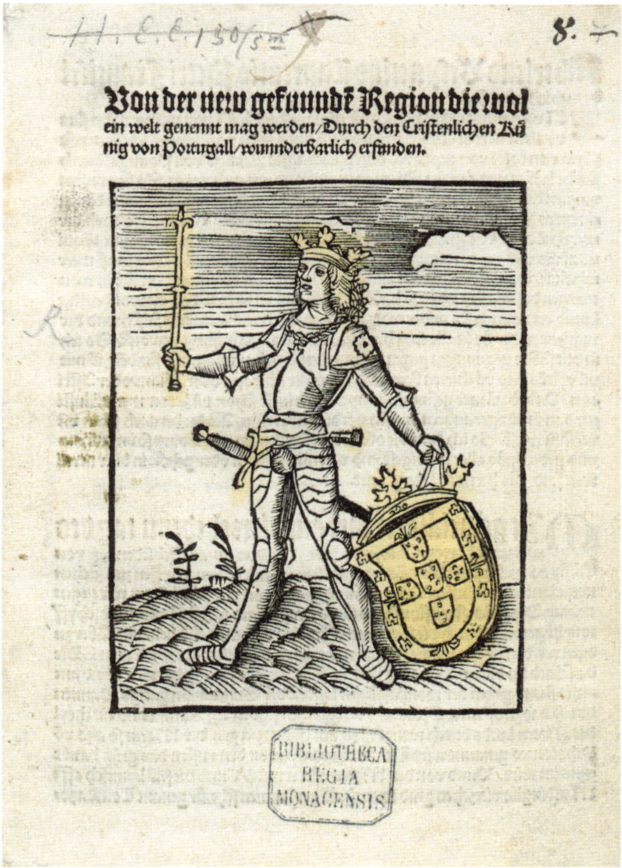

Von der new gefunndē Region die wol ein welt genennt mag werden/Durch den Cristenlichen Kü nig von Portugall/wunnderbarlich erfunden.

4/22

4/21 **Letter appointing Amerigo Vespucci *piloto mayor* at the *Casa de la Contratación***
Burgos, 22 March 1508
Facsimile, 39.8 x 27.9 cm
Seville, Archivo General de Indias: Contratación, 5784, L.1, F.4V

European understanding of geography and navigation grew steadily in the wake of Spanish and Portuguese expeditions. In 1508, the *Casa de la Contratación* created the office of *Piloto Mayor* (chief navigator and cartographer), whose job was to collate and analyse new information and plan new expeditions. Other responsibilities associated with this prestigious position included training pilots for routes to the 'West Indies' and preparing the official maps that every ship in the service of the Castilian crown were required to carry. The first *piloto mayor* was Amerigo Vespucci (1451–1512). This royal letter of appointment indicates that he was paid 50,000 maravedis per year, as well as 25,000 maravedis for additional expenses. CB

4/22 **Pamphlet with Amerigo Vespucci's account of the 'new world'**
Von der neuw gefunden Region die wol ain welt genent mag werden / durch den Cristenlichen künig von portugal / wunderbarlich erfunden
Amerigo Vespucci (1451 –1512)
Nuremberg, 1505
Woodcut, binding of marbled paper with parchment spine; 20 x 15 cm
Munich, Bayerische Staatsbibliothek: Rar. 5k

While Christopher Columbus believed until his death in 1506 that he had discovered the western sea route to India as well as islands off the coast of Asia, the idea of a 'new world' was first put forward by Amerigo Vespucci (in late 1502 / early 1503). In a letter to Lorenzo di Pierfrancesco de' Medici (1463–1503), Vespucci described his impressions of a Portuguese expedition to the Brazilian coast, referring to the area that it explored as a new continent. This letter was printed in numerous editions and disseminated quickly throughout Europe as the *Mundus Novus* letter. In the title of this German-language pamphlet (printed in Nuremberg in 1505) and again in an illustration it contains, the king of Portugal is given credit for having found a 'new world'. CB

Europe's Changing View of the World

4/23 ***Oikumene*. Map of the known world in a facsimile edition of the Vatican copy of Ptolemy's *Cosmographia***
Claudius Ptolemy (83–161)
2nd cent. A.D. (original) / Zurich, 1983
Facsimile; 61.5 x 45 x 4.5 cm
Berlin, Deutsches Historisches Museum: RB 98/1673

In his description of the world, which has survived in Greek manuscripts, astronomer and geographer Claudius Ptolemy of Alexandria gives the location of about 8,000 places that he knew of around the globe, noting for each its latitude and longitude. Among the places he mentions are the Canary Islands off the west coast of Africa, known in antiquity as the *Insulae Fortunatae* (Fortunate Isles). Ptolemy was rediscovered in the late Middle Ages after printing was invented. Until the modern era, European understanding of world geography was significantly shaped by the eight books of his *Cosmographia*. World maps continued to be produced based on the information they contained until the late sixteenth century. This meticulous facsimile of *Cosmographia* is based on a magnificent edition completed in 1472/73 with the support of Florentine bookseller Vespasiano da Bisticci (1421–1498). That version contains 34 regional maps and 10 city maps, and is kept in the Vatican's Biblioteca Apostolica. (Fig. p. 47) DB

4/24 **Copy of the Behaim Globe**
Martin Behaim (1459–1507)
c. 1892 (original made in Nuremberg, 1492)
Metal (sphere), iron (frame), brass, painted varnished wood; H 133, diam. 63 cm
Berlin, Deutsches Historisches Museum: AK 2010/202

The Behaim Globe reflects the picture that Europeans had of the world before the discovery of the Americas by Christopher Columbus (c. 1451–1506). Made in 1492, it is the oldest surviving representation of the Earth in spherical form. It provides a detailed record of the cartographic knowledge of the time, which derived mainly from Ptolemy's writings, travelogues written by Marco Polo (c. 1254–1324) and Jean de Mandeville (d. 1372), and medieval portulan charts. Because it is missing the continents of the Americas, a voyage across the Atlantic would go directly to Zipangu (Japan). The representations of western and southern Africa, on the other hand, show that Martin Behaim was aware of the latest information gained from Iberian expeditions. Islands in the Atlantic were also marked on the globe. In addition to Iceland, Madeira, and the Azores ("hawk islands"), the Canary Islands are represented in their entirety and labelled *Canarie* and "islands of the wild Guanches". (Fig. p. 44) CB

4/25 **World map**
Carta Vniversal En Qve Se Contiene Todo Lo Qve Del Mvndo Se A Descubi[erto] Fasta Aora Hizola Vn Cosmographo De Sv Magestad Anno M.D.XX.VII. En Sevilla
Diogo Ribeiro (c. 1490–1532)
Seville, 1527
Hand drawing on parchment; 86 x 213 cm
Weimar, Klassik Stiftung Weimar, Herzogin Anna Amalia Bibliothek: Kt 020 - 57 S

Diogo Ribeiro's map of the world is among the most important cartographic artefacts of the first third of the sixteenth century. It is one of the first maps to incorporate information gained from the circumnavigation of the globe undertaken by Ferdinand Magellan (1480–1521) and Juan Sebastián Elcano (1476–1526). Drawn on parchment in 1527, when Ribeiro was the royal cosmographer at the *Casa de la Contratación*, it is probably a scaled-down copy of the *padrón real* – the large map of the world that it was the job first of the *piloto mayor* and later of the cosmographer to create. It was based on the latest geographical and navigational information, and was provided to every ship in the service of the Spanish crown. The map already shows the entire Atlantic coast of the Americas, from the Strait of Magellan in the south to Labrador in the north. The names of areas which were known or expected to have gold deposits were lettered in gold. (Fig. p. 244/245) CB

4/26 **Globe of the Earth showing routes taken by geographic explorers**
Daniel Friedrich Sotzmann (1754–1840)
Manufacturer: Johann Georg Franz (1775–1836)
Nuremberg, 1808
Wood, brass, paper; sphere probably of papier mâché with a plaster base; 129 x 75 x 46 cm
Berlin, Museumsstiftung Post und Telekommunikation: 3.2007.1204

Exploratory expeditions undertaken in the eighteenth century completed Europe's picture of the world. After Dutch forays into the Pacific region resulted in major discoveries in the seventeenth century, it was mainly the British and French who charted the Pacific ocean in the eighteenth century, claiming for themselves the lands they 'discovered' in the course of their many voyages. This 1808 globe, drawn by Daniel Sotzmann, shows the routes of 36 major eighteenth-century expeditions, including the voyages of James Cook

(1728–1779), George Vancouver (1757–1798) and Louis Antoine de Bougainville (1729–1811). Sotzmann was a geographer at the Royal Prussian Academy of Sciences in Berlin and one of the most distinguished German cartographers of his time. His globe of the Earth is one of the greatest achievements of German globe making. CB

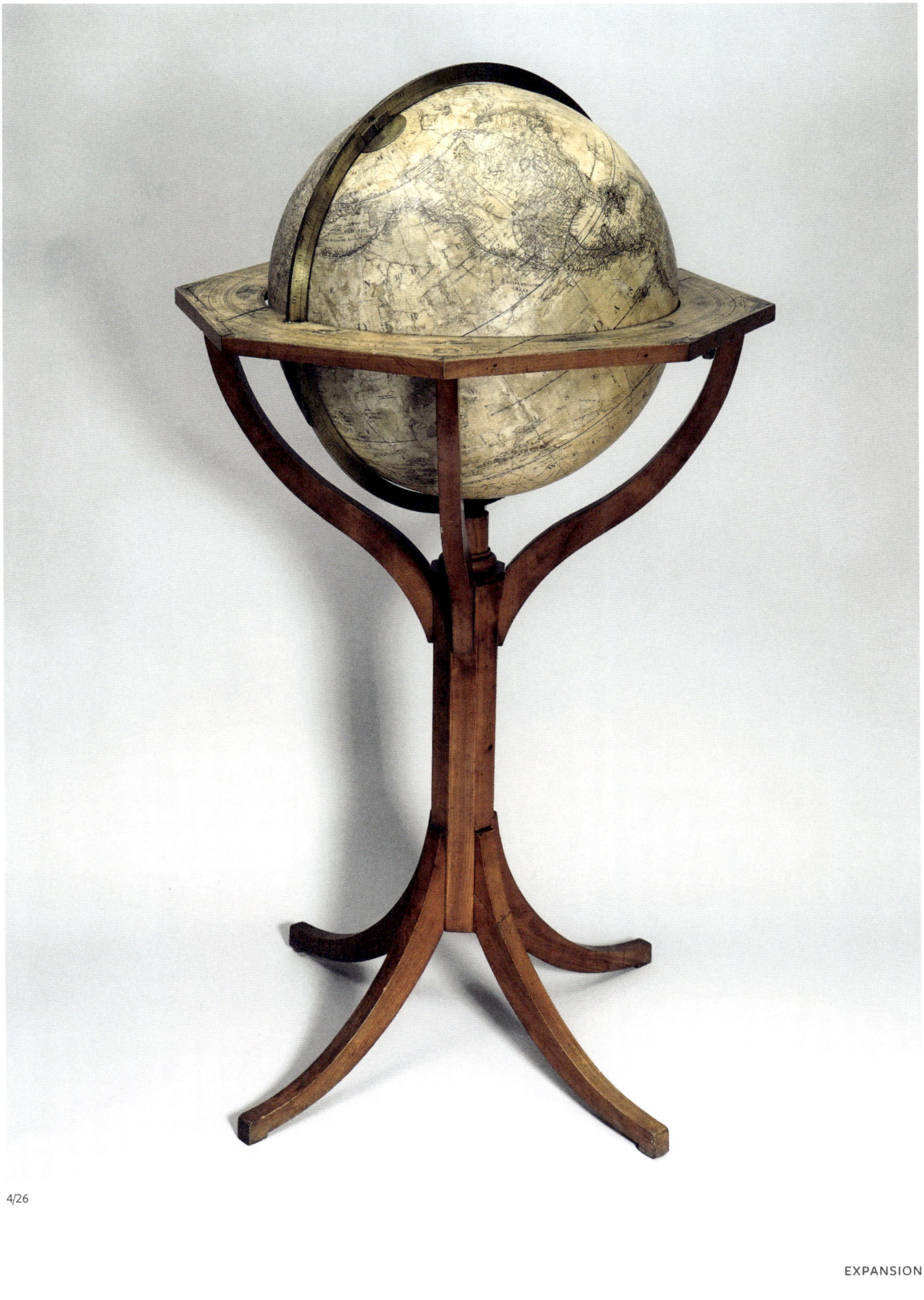

4/26

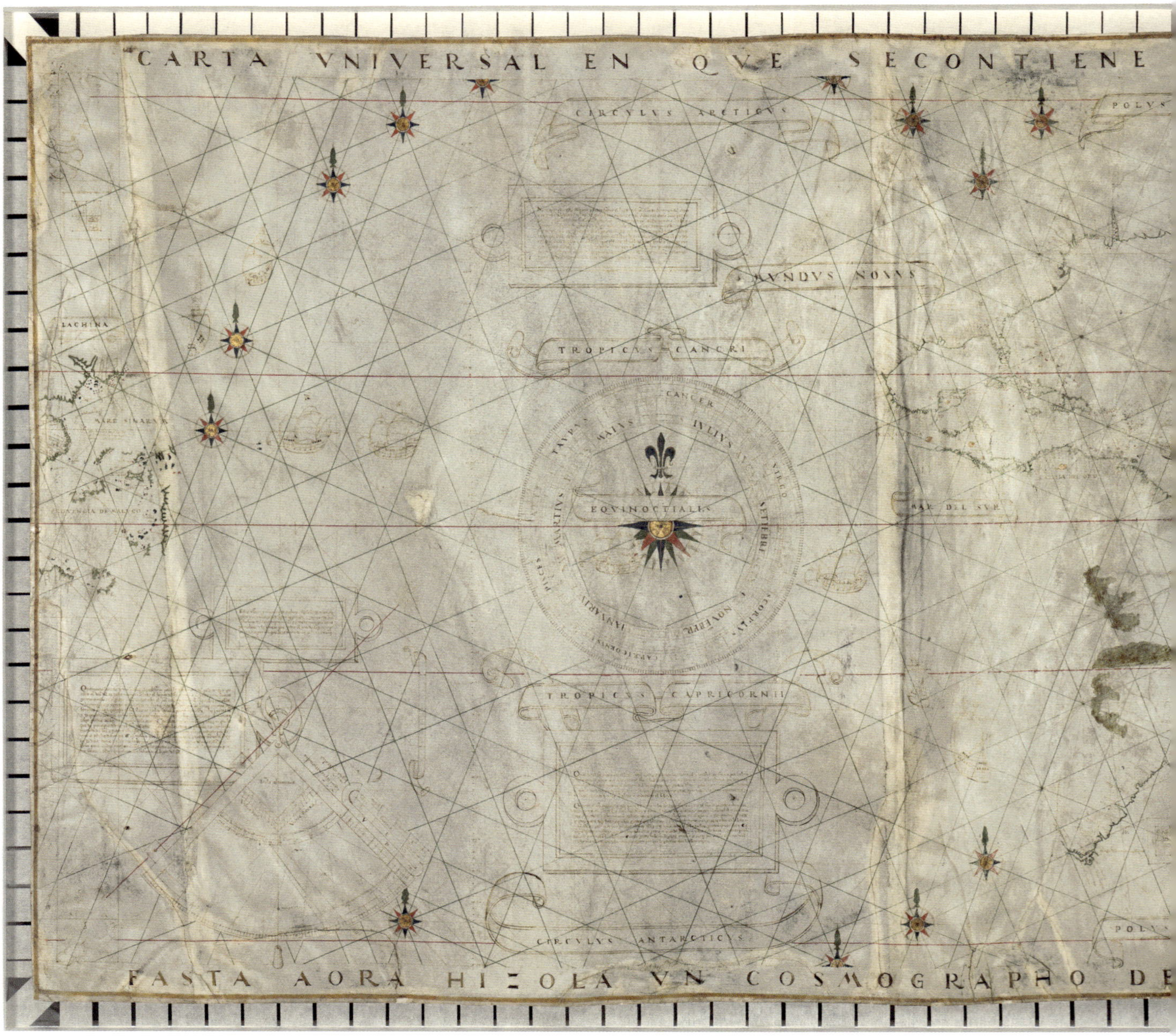
CARTA VNIVERSAL EN QVE SECONTIENE
CIRCVLVS ARCTICVS
MVNDVS NOVVS
TROPICVS CANCRI
EQVINOCTIALIS
TROPICVS CAPRICORNII
CIRCVLVS ANTARCTICVS
FASTA AORA HIZOLA VN COSMOGRAPHO DE

4/25

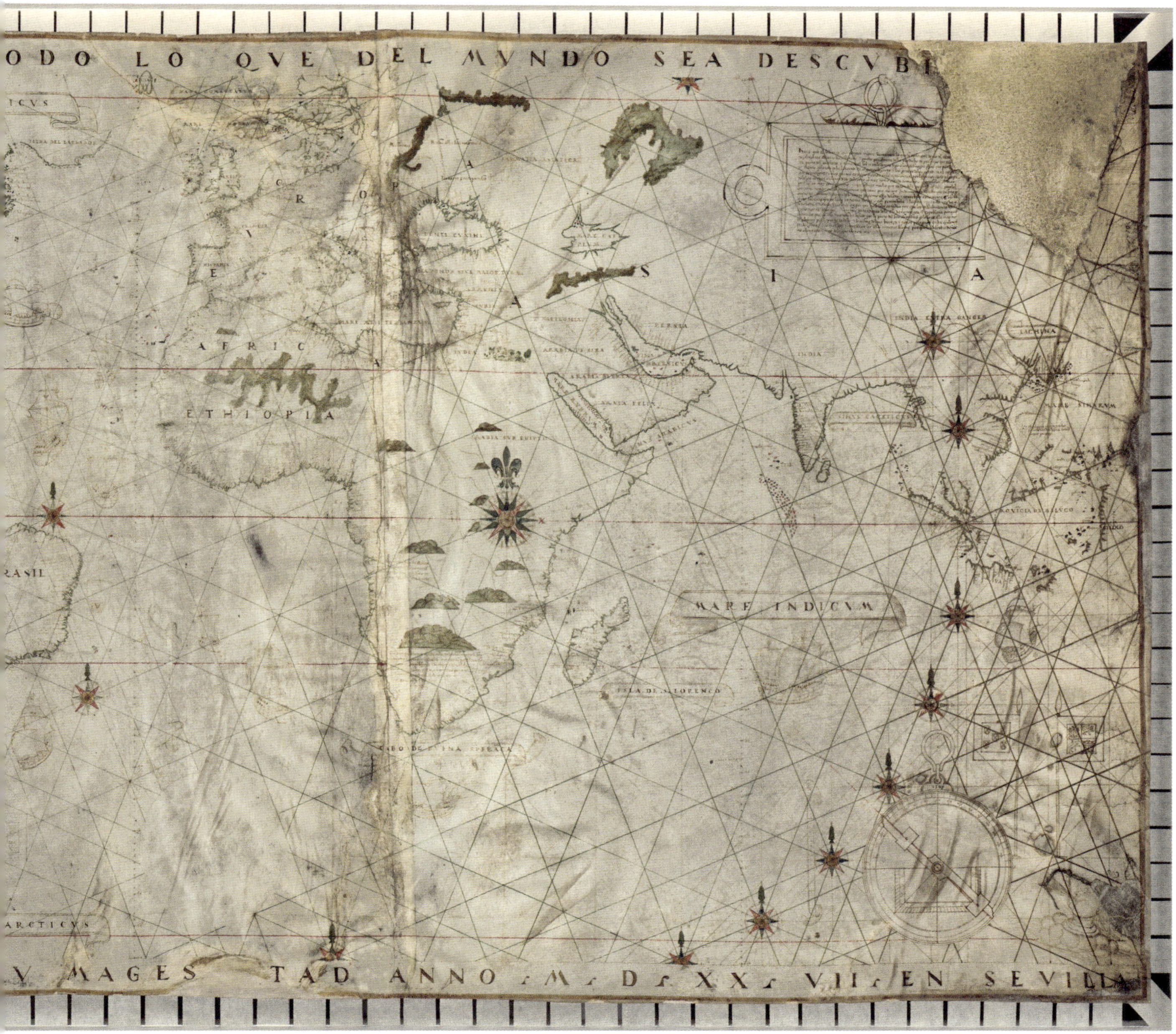
ODO LO QVE DEL MVNDO SEA DESCVBI
ETHIOPIA
MARE INDICVM
Y MAGES TAD ANNO M D XX VII EN SEVILLA

5 Missionary Activity and Cultural Exchange in East Asia The Port of Lisbon

Cultural exchange was an unintended but significant consequence of Europeans' military and trading expeditions. Not only did the adventurers change the worlds that they encountered and subjugated, but they also changed Europe itself by bringing back foodstuffs and consumer goods as well as introducing foreign practices. The phenomenon of cultural exchange is nicely illustrated by the Jesuit order's missionary activity in East Asia. It clearly demonstrates the kinds of interaction that were typical of overseas cultural contact.

Building on the success of its seafaring expeditions to the east, Portugal established a colonial empire in the course of the sixteenth century, which in its heyday was known as *Estado Português da Índia* (Portuguese State of India). The *Estado da Índia* ranged from East Africa to Japan, encompassing various territories in India and South-east Asia. These formed a network of strategically important trading and military posts around the Indian Ocean, enabling Portugal to maintain its control of the sea routes used for trade and missionary activity in the region for more than a hundred years. The capital and religious centre of the *Estado da Índia* was Goa, on the west coast of India, which was modelled on Lisbon in terms of its civic administration and privileges. The Portuguese Crown was represented there by a governor-general, who usually bore the title of Viceroy and was appointed by the king for a three-year term. Lisbon, the Portuguese capital, served as an economic and cultural hub between Asia and Europe.

When the first Portuguese fleet, under the command of Vasco da Gama (c. 1469–1524), reached the west coast of India in 1498, the purpose of its voyage was summed up in the words: "We come in search of Christians and spices." In addition to trade, such ventures were expected to spread the Christian faith, which lent them moral legitimacy at the time. Missionary work in the overseas territories was mainly undertaken by religious orders such as the Franciscans, the Dominicans and increasingly, after their founding in 1539, the Society of Jesus. The Jesuits' approach set them apart from their rivals because their representatives were more willing to engage with the languages, customs and thought of Asian cultures. They did so in order to communicate directly with the countries' educated elites, whose influence they hoped to turn to advantage. The Jesuits' strategy of accommodating elements of local culture proved to be successful. In particular, Jesuit missionaries acquired great influence at the imperial court of China, where they were commissioned to reform the Chinese calendar and were placed in charge of the imperial astronomical observatory – a position that Jesuits held for the next two hundred years. Their willingness to embrace Chinese culture led to serious accusations in Europe, however, and in response, the Jesuits began publishing informative literature about the country. This stimulated an interest in China ('chinoiserie') whose influence in Europe lasted into the eighteenth century. It is well known that the Europeans learned about tea, gunpowder and porcelain from China, but few people today are aware that paper money, toilet paper, noodles and ice cream also originated there. Conversely, the Jesuits introduced the Chinese to European methods of predicting lunar and solar eclipses, technology for making scientific instruments, clockwork, the telescope, algebra, and the use of latitude and longitude in cartography. Such encounters with an initially unfamiliar foreign culture inspired the inhabitants of Europe and Asia alike to explore new directions in art and design. *Dorlis Blume*

Further Reading

Marcel van den Broecke, *Ortelius Atlas Maps. An illustrated Guide*, Westrenen 1996

Europa und die Kaiser von China (1240–1816), ed. by Berliner Festspiele GmbH, exhib. cat., Frankfurt a. M. 1985

Johann Adam Schall von Bell SJ, 1592–1666. Ein Kölner Astronom am chinesischen Hof, ed. by Diözesan- und Dombibliothek Köln, exhib. cat., Cologne 1992

Novos Mundos – Neue Welten. Portugal und das Zeitalter der Entdeckungen, ed. by Michael Kraus and Hans Ottomeyer, exhib. cat., Berlin 2007

Michael North (ed.), *Artistic and Cultural Exchanges between Europe and Asia, 1400–1900: Rethinking Markets, Workshops and Collections*, Farnham 2010

Michael North, *Zwischen Hafen und Horizont. Weltgeschichte der Meere*, Munich 2016

Jürgen Osterhammel, *Die Entzauberung Asiens. Europa und die asiatischen Reiche im 18. Jahrhundert*, Munich 1998

Wolfgang Reinhard, *Geschichte der Welt. Weltreiche und Weltmeere, 1350–1750*, Munich 2014

Wolfgang Reinhard, *Die Unterwerfung der Welt. Globalgeschichte der europäischen Expansion 1415–2015*, Munich 2016

Hartmut Walravens (ed.), *China illustrata. Das europäische Chinaverständnis im Spiegel des 16. bis 18. Jahrhunderts*, Wolfenbüttel 1987

Lucas Heinrich Wüthrich, *Matthaeus Merian d.Ä., Eine Biographie*, Hamburg 2007

5/1 **Statuette of a European, Qing Dynasty**
China, 17/18th century
Bronze, gilt, enamel cloisonné, champlevé; H 36.5 cm
Vienna, MAK – Österreichisches Museum für angewandte Kunst / Gegenwartskunst: EM 127

This Chinese bronze statuette is of a man raising his hands as if to greet someone. It is thought to represent an envoy from a European country. The physiognomy, especially the big round eyes, the bushy eyebrows and oversized ears, reveals how Europeans looked to the Chinese. The same applies to his expansive gesticulation, animated facial expression and open mouth, as well as his clothes, which are cut according the fashion of the day in Europe. His cloak is decorated, however, with Chinese floral motifs. The cloak, hat and collar are worked using the cloisonné and champlevé techniques: two kinds of enamelling that, like the deep blue colour of the cape, had become a feature of Chinese art in particular. Here, the European and Asian motifs exist in symbiosis. DB

5/2 **Statuette of a Chinese man, model 369, "Japanese"**
Designed by Friedrich Elias Meyer (1723–1785)
Königliche Porzellanmanufaktur Berlin
Berlin, 1768
Porcelain, white body, polychrome painting, gilding; 40.5 x 19 cm
Berlin, Stiftung Stadtmuseum Berlin: II 60/408 B

This statuette of a Chinese man, curiously titled "Japanese", reflects the fashion for Chinese culture (chinoiserie) in eighteenth-century Europe. It is made of porcelain, a material that Europeans had got to know from imported Chinese goods, and as the detailed costume indicates, it is clearly meant as a realistic portrayal of an Asian lifestyle and culture. In the face, however, European features seem to be showing through. As with the Chinese figure of a European, this statuette exhibits respect for foreign qualities as well as a mixture of Asian and European elements. On the other hand, the fact that a single figure could conflate Japanese with Chinese, while the hand-held cymbals are typical of a Turkish janissary, shows how little people's ideas of other nationalities corresponded to reality. DB

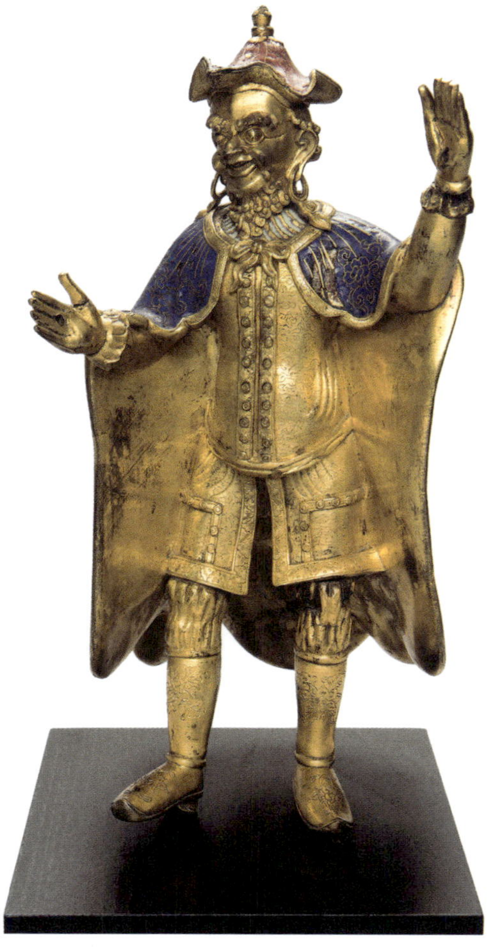

5/1

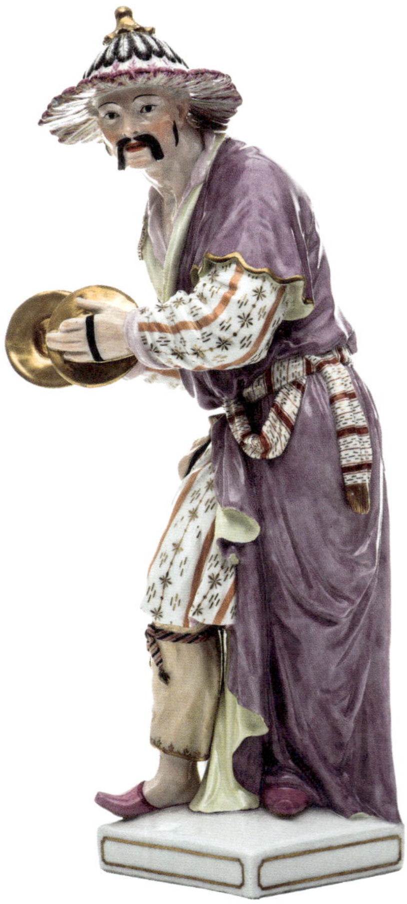

5/2

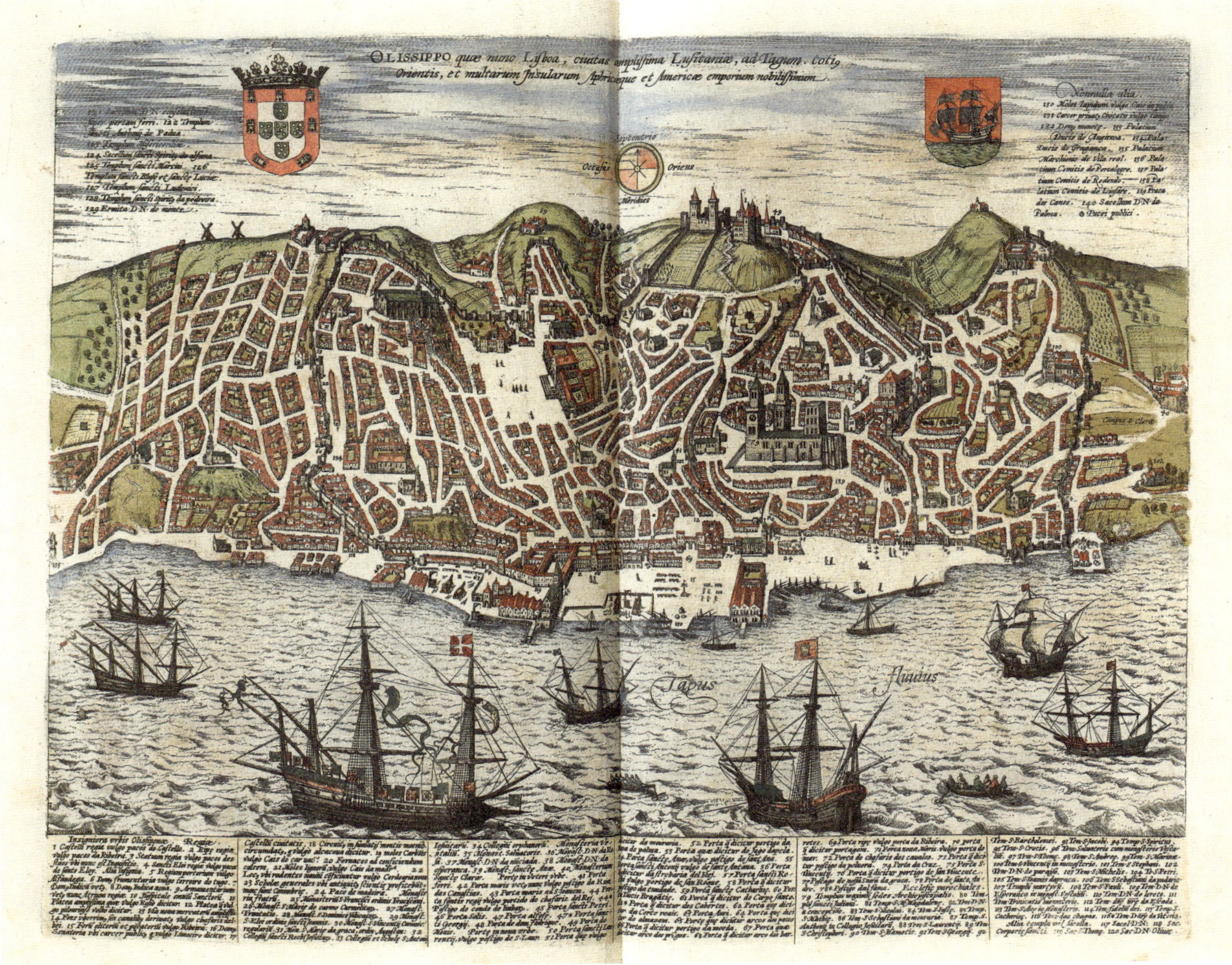

5/3

The *Estado da Índia*

5/3 ***Olissipo quae nunc Lisboa* (Olissipo which [is] now Lisbon), in *Urbium praecipuarum mundi theatrum quintum***
Author: Georg Braun (1542–1622)
Engraved by Franz Hogenberg (1540–1590)
Cologne, c. 1599
Copper engraving, coloured; cover: cardboard, leather, silk; 42 x 29 cm
Berlin, Deutsches Historisches Museum: RB 53/2979 -5

This map, which is not to scale, shows the Portuguese capital, Lisbon. The city lies on the northern bank of the Tagus River, which forms an estuary at this point before flowing into the Atlantic. The history of the settlement goes back to prehistoric times. The hilltop castle, marked "I" on the drawing, had been the residence of the kings of Portugal since the city was recaptured from the Moors in 1147. During the sixteenth century, Lisbon developed into an international metropolis. The harbour area expanded enormously, while the city became a hub for the exchange of nautical and geographical knowledge. Many legends grew up about the city's name, one of which claims that it derives (via "Olissipo" in this map's title) from Ulysses – the Latin name of the ancient Greek hero Odysseus. DB

5/4 **Map of South-east Asia, in *Theatrum orbis terrarum***
Abraham Ortelius (1527–1598)
Antwerp, 1579
Print; 41.5 x 29.5 cm
Berlin, Staatsbibliothek zu Berlin – Preußischer Kulturbesitz, Kartensammlung: 2° Kart. B 130

Belonging to an atlas produced by Abraham Ortelius, a Flemish scholar and geographer, this map shows Portuguese India, which relied on a network of bases along the coasts of India and (not shown here) East Africa. Goa and Cochin in India, and Malacca on the Malay Peninsula, were of particu-

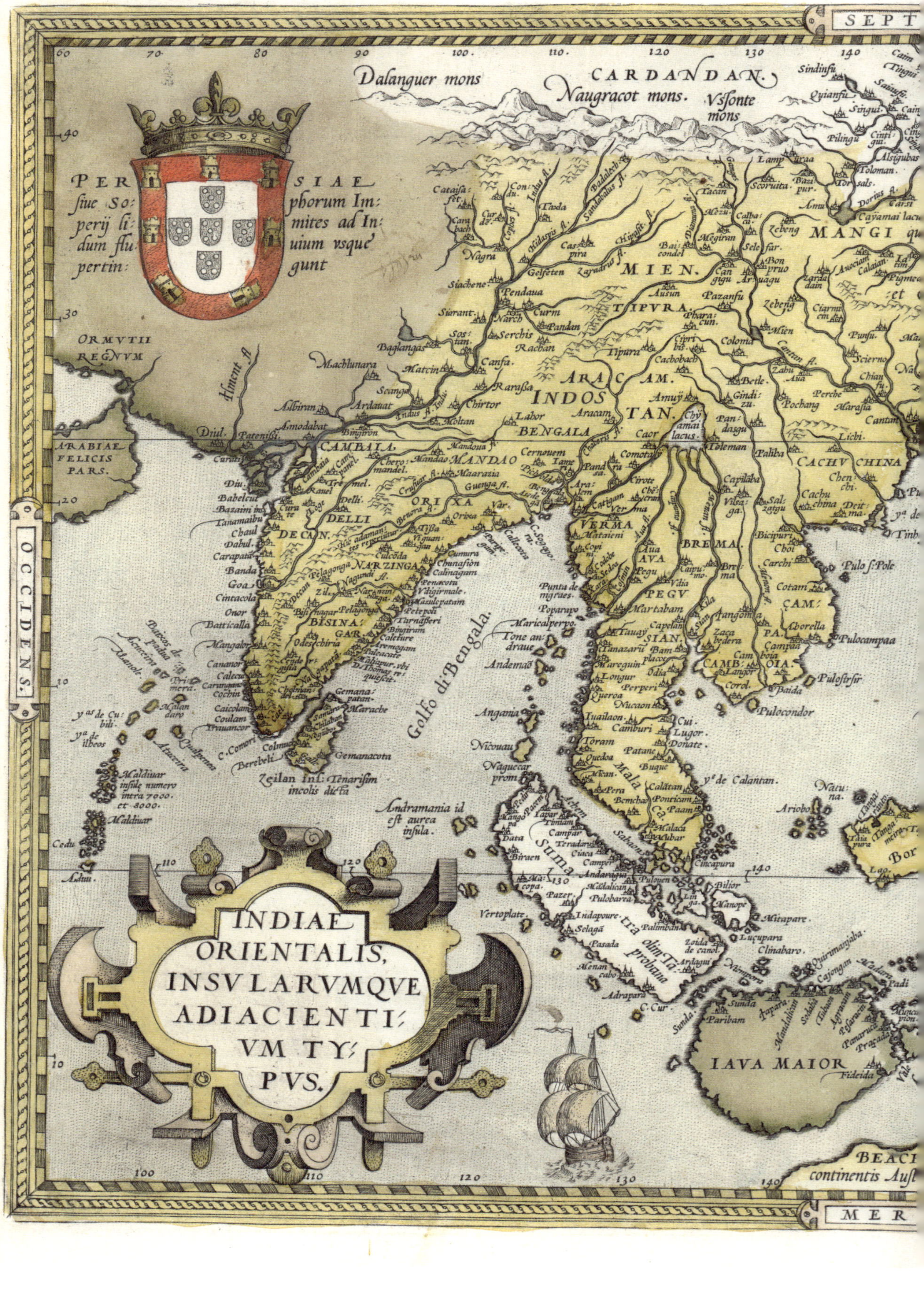
SEPT
OCCIDENS.
MER
PERSIAE sive Sophorum Imperij limites ad Indum fluvium vsque pertingunt
ORMVTII REGNVM
ARABIAE FELICIS PARS.
CARDANDAN.
Dalanguer mons
Naugracot mons.
Vsfonte mons
MANGI
MIEN.
TIPVRA.
ARACAM.
INDOSTAN.
BENGALA
CAMBAIA.
MANDAO
ORIXA
DELLI
DECAN.
NARZINGA
BISINAGAR
VERMA
BREMA.
PEGV
SIAN.
CAMBOIA.
CAMPA.
CACHV CHINA
Golfo di Bengala.
Zeilan Insl: Tenarisim incolis dicta
Sumatra olim Taprobana
IAVA MAIOR
BEACH continentis Aust
INDIAE ORIENTALIS, INSVLARVMQVE ADIACIENTIVM TYPVS.

5/4

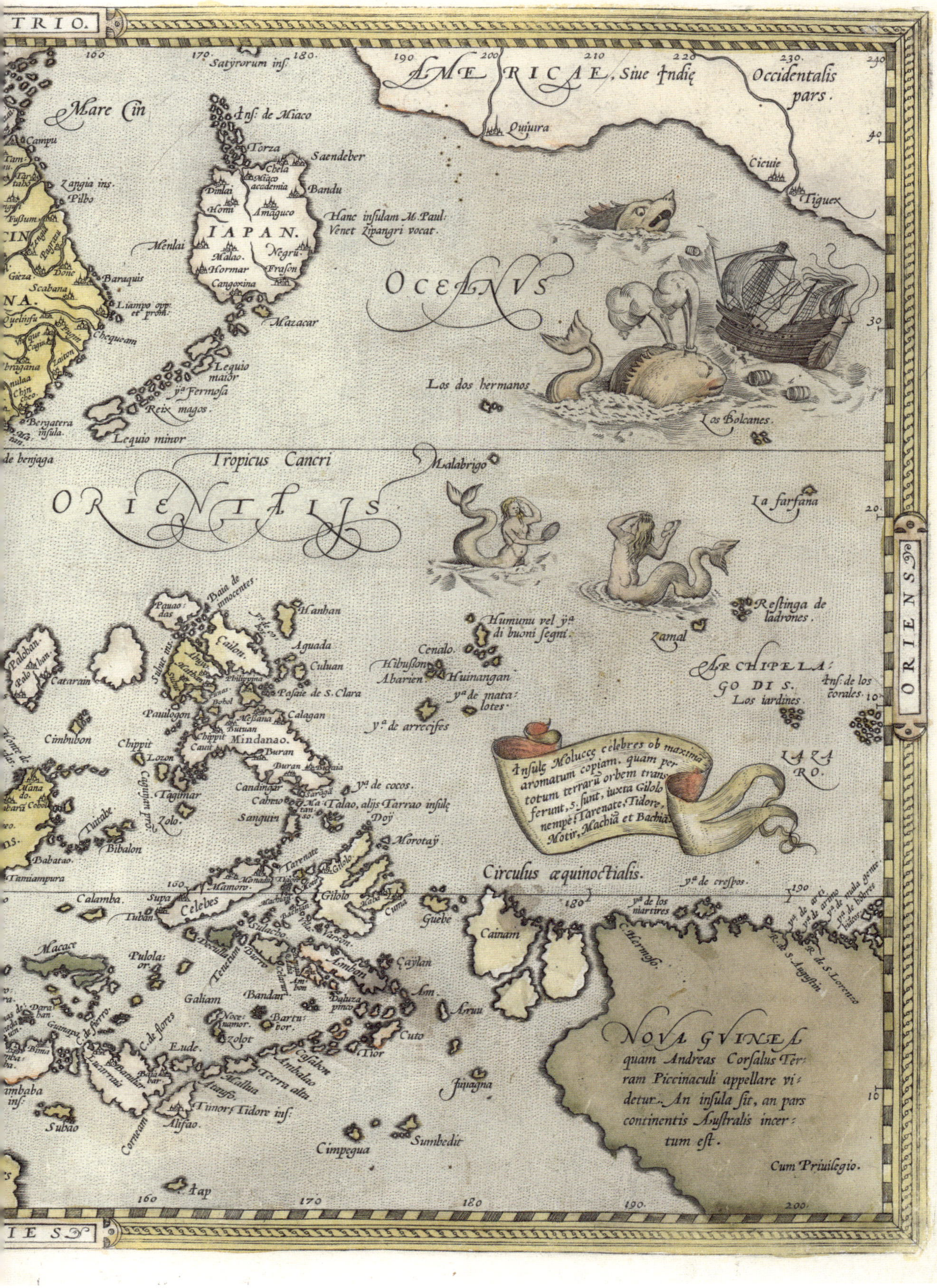
TRIO.
Satyrorum ins.
AMERICAE, Siue Indie Occidentalis pars.
Quiura
Cicuie
Tiguex
Mare Cin
Ins. de Miaco
Torza
Saendeber
Bandu
Amaguco
IAPAN.
Hanc insulam M. Paul. Venet Zipangri vocat.
Menlai
Malao.
Hormar
Cangoxina
Negru.
Frason
Baraquis
Mazacar
OCEANVS
Chequeam
Lequio maior
ya Fermosa
Reix magos
Lequio minor
Los dos hermanos
Los Bolcanes.
Tropicus Cancri
ORIENTALIS
Malabrigo
La farfana
ORIENS
Restinga de ladrones.
Zamal
Humunu vel ya di buoni segni
Cenalo.
Huinangan
Abarien
ya de mata lotes
ya de arrecifes
ARCHIPELAGO DI S. Los iardines.
Ins. de los corales.
Aguada
Culuan
Calagan
Mindanao.
Paulogon
Cimbubon
Catarain
Chippit
Tagimar
Zolo
Bibalon
Sanguin
ya de cocos.
Talao, alijs Tarrao insule
Insule Molucce celebres ob maximam aromatum copiam, quam per totum terraru orbem transferunt, 5. sunt, iuxta Gilolo nempe Tarenate, Tidore, Motir, Machia et Bachia.
LAZARO.
Morotay
Circulus æquinoctialis.
ya de crespos.
Calamba.
Celebes
Gilolo
Gueb
Cainam
C. Hermoso.
Macaca
Pulola
Galiam
Bandan
Amboina
Aruu
Cuto
Tior
Jujagna
Cimpegua
Sumbedit
Eude.
C. de flores
Timor, Tidore ins.
Alifao.
Subao
NOVA GVINEA quam Andreas Corsalus Terram Piccinaculi appellare videtur. An insula sit, an pars continentis Australis incertum est.
Cum Priuilegio.
IES

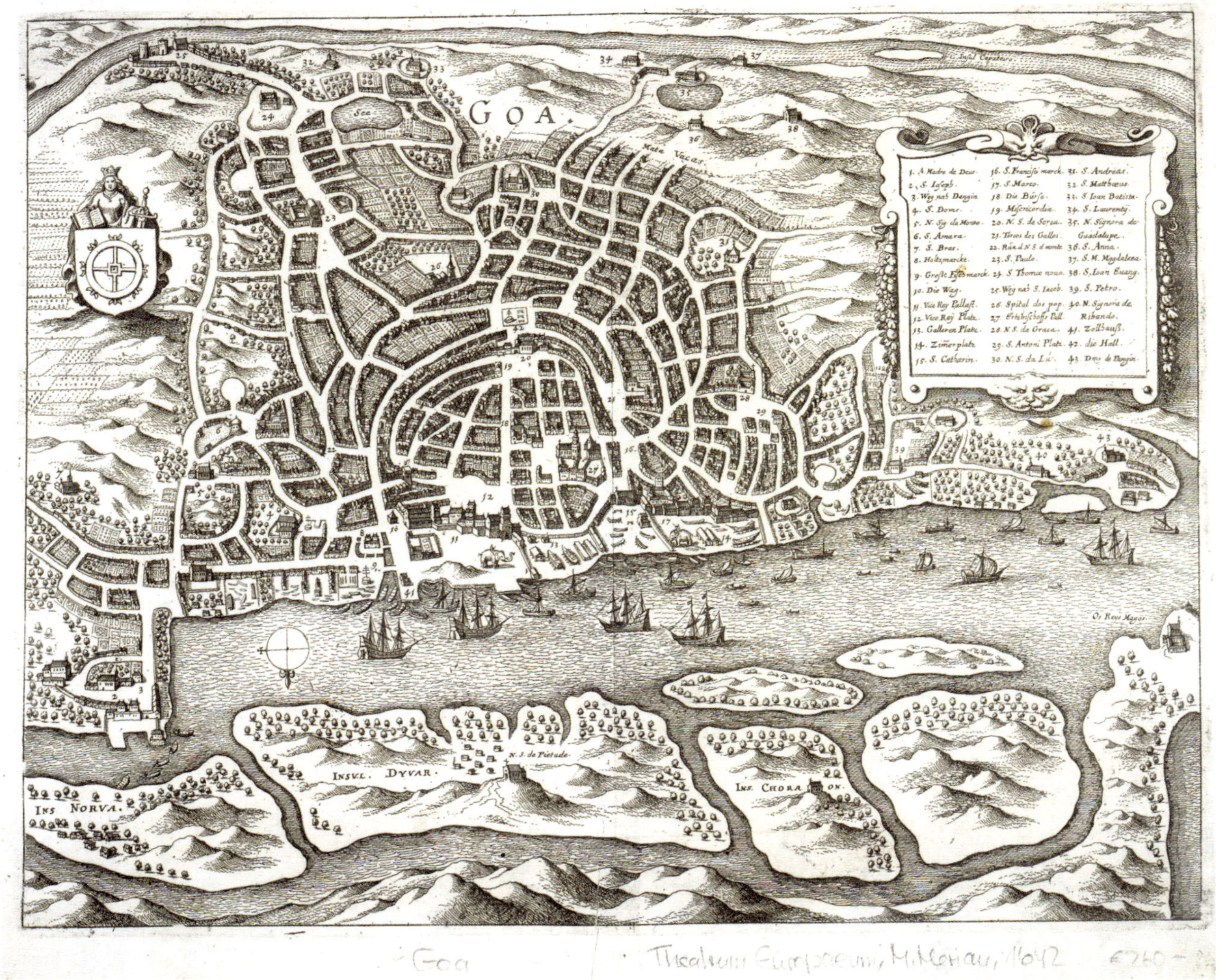

5/5

lar strategic value, enabling Portugal to establish and maintain control over shipping and trade in the Indian Ocean. As an expression of this dominance, Ortelius has even emblazoned the map with Portugal's coat of arms, which was otherwise only customary for kingdoms and principalities in Europe. A banner near the Moluccan archipelago mentions the wealth of spices found there, reflecting the role of the spice trade in motivating Portuguese expansion. Ortelius' *Theatrum orbis terrarum* comprised a series of maps on loose sheets accompanied by a text bound in book form. It was the most widely used atlas of its time, with some 7,500 copies printed in 31 editions between 1570 and 1612. (Fig. p. 250/251)
DB

5/5 **City map of Goa**
Engraved by Matthäus Merian the Elder (1593–1650)
Frankfurt a. M., c. 1642
Copperplate engraving on paper; 31.5 x 37 cm
Berlin, Deutsches Historisches Museum: Do 2007/1

This 'south-up' map of Goa shows the capital of the *Estado da Índia* in its heyday near the end of the sixteenth century. Goa's coat of arms, at the top left, is held by St. Catherine, the patron saint of the city. In the centre is the main shopping street, Rua Direita, where the main public buildings are also located. It starts at Terreiro do Paço with the Viceroy's palace and fortress near the northern gate, which connects the city centre with the wharves on the banks of the Mandovi River. In the south, the street ends at a gate that marks the boundary of the pre-colonial city. Beyond it are suburbs that have sprung up in the meantime, containing the settlements of many religious orders. This city map from *Theatrum Europaeum* was not drawn from Merian's personal experience or knowledge, but copied from earlier documents dating from the sixteenth century. The galleons shown in the foreground, however, are typical vessels of the early seventeenth century. DB

Jesuit Missions to East Asia

5/6 **Treatise on China, *China illustrata***
Athanasius Kircher (1602–1680)
Published by Joannes Janssonius à Waesberge and Elizeum Weyerstraet
Amsterdam, 1667
Paper, printed; cover: cardboard, parchment; 39 x 25.5 cm
Berlin, Deutsches Historisches Museum: RB 68/421

China illustrata brought together all that was known in the West about contemporary China in the seventeenth century. It explained the language and the culture and was richly illustrated. Originally published in Latin, the book sold in large numbers and was translated into several languages, including Dutch (1668), English (1669) and French (1670). It is still seen as marking the beginning of Sinology in the West. Its author, Athanasius Kircher, was a Jesuit, but he never travelled to China himself. His treatise was based on accounts given by other members of his order.
The frontispiece of *China illustrata* portrays the four Jesuits who were central to the mission. At the top, above the clouds, are the founder of the order, Ignatius Loyola (1491–1556), and the first missionary to work in India and China, Franz Xaver (1506–1552). Standing below them are Johann Adam Schall von Bell (1592–1666), the director of the imperial observatory in Beijing, and Matteo Ricci (1552–1610), the founding father of the mission in China. They hold a cloth on which the outline of China is drawn. (Fig. p. 56) DB

5/7 ***The Jesuits in China*, in *A Description of the Empire of China and Chinese-Tartary*, vol. 3**
Ausführliche Beschreibung des Chinesischen Reichs und der grossen Tartarey
Author: Jean-Baptiste du Halde (1674–1743)
Published by Johann Christian Koppe
Rostock, 1749
Print; 24.5 x 52.5 cm
Berlin, Staatsbibliothek zu Berlin – Preußischer Kulturbesitz, Abteilung Historische Drucke: 4°Un 2052a-3

Du Halde's four-volume descriptive work was compiled from reports made by his fellow Jesuits. It summarised all that was known about China in eighteenth-century Europe. Its purpose was not only to make the Jesuits' first-hand knowledge of China available to a wide readership, but also to gain support in Europe for their missionary activity in China. This engraving shows three of the most important missionaries in China with their scientific instruments: Matteo Ricci (1552–1610), an Italian, had established the mission to China in the sixteenth century; Johann Adam Schall von Bell (1592–1666), a German, had reformed the Chinese calendar as director of the astronomical observatory and had served as an advisor to the Shunzhi Emperor (1638–1661); Ferdinand Verbiest (1623–1688), a Belgian, had been appointed director as Bell's successor. DB

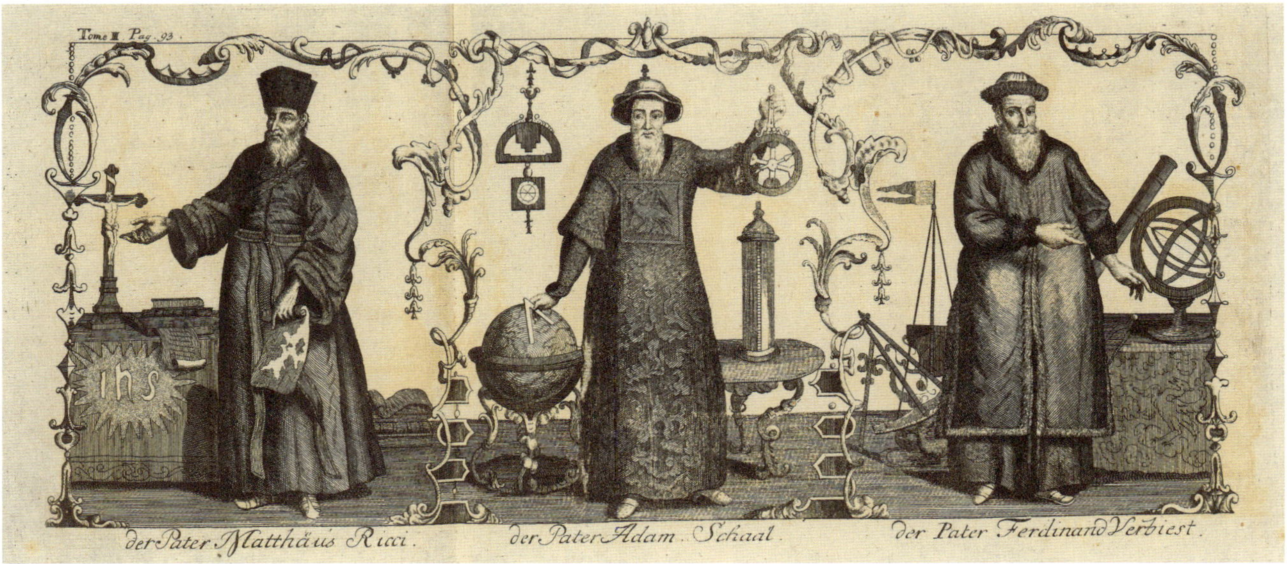

5/7

5/8 **Map of China with scenes of the Christian mission to Japan**
Jodocus Hondius (1536–1612)
Amsterdam, c. 1606
Copper engraving, coloured, on paper; letterpress print; 42 x 56.5 cm
Berlin, Deutsches Historisches Museum: Do 94/123

This map comes from a German-language edition of the Mercator/Hondius atlas. It is illustrated with scenes from the history of the Christian mission to Japan. One clearly alludes to the landing of three Portuguese traders from a Chinese junk in the south of the island of Kyushu. They were followed in 1549 by the Jesuit Franz Xaver (1506–1552), who had great success in making converts. In 1587, however, the practice of Christianity in Japan was banned and the priests had to leave the country. In 1597, Spanish, Portuguese and Japanese Christians were even crucified in Nagasaki. Since the Jesuits had built up a good reputation in China, the Christian mission there was largely tolerated, whereas the missionaries in Japan were expelled. A few Japanese Christians continued to practise their religion in secret. DB

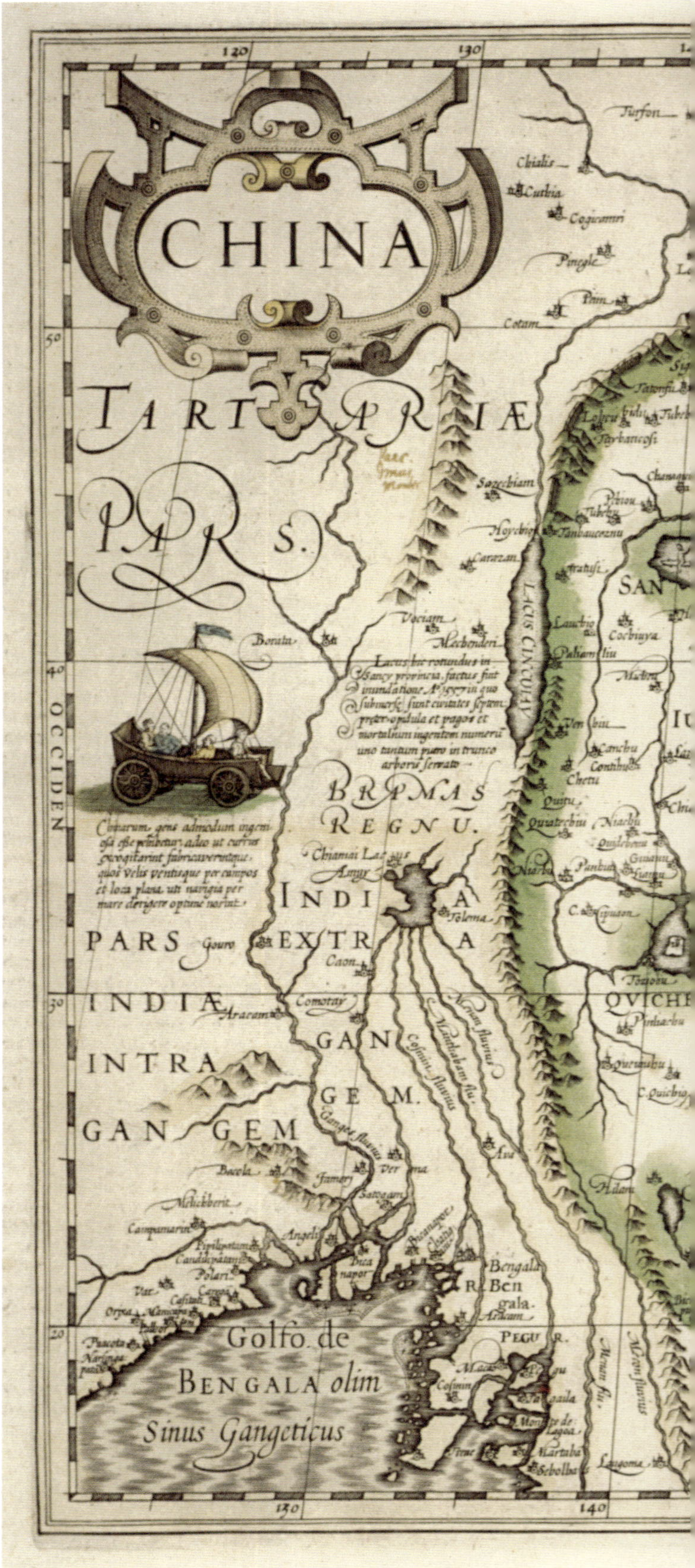

5/8

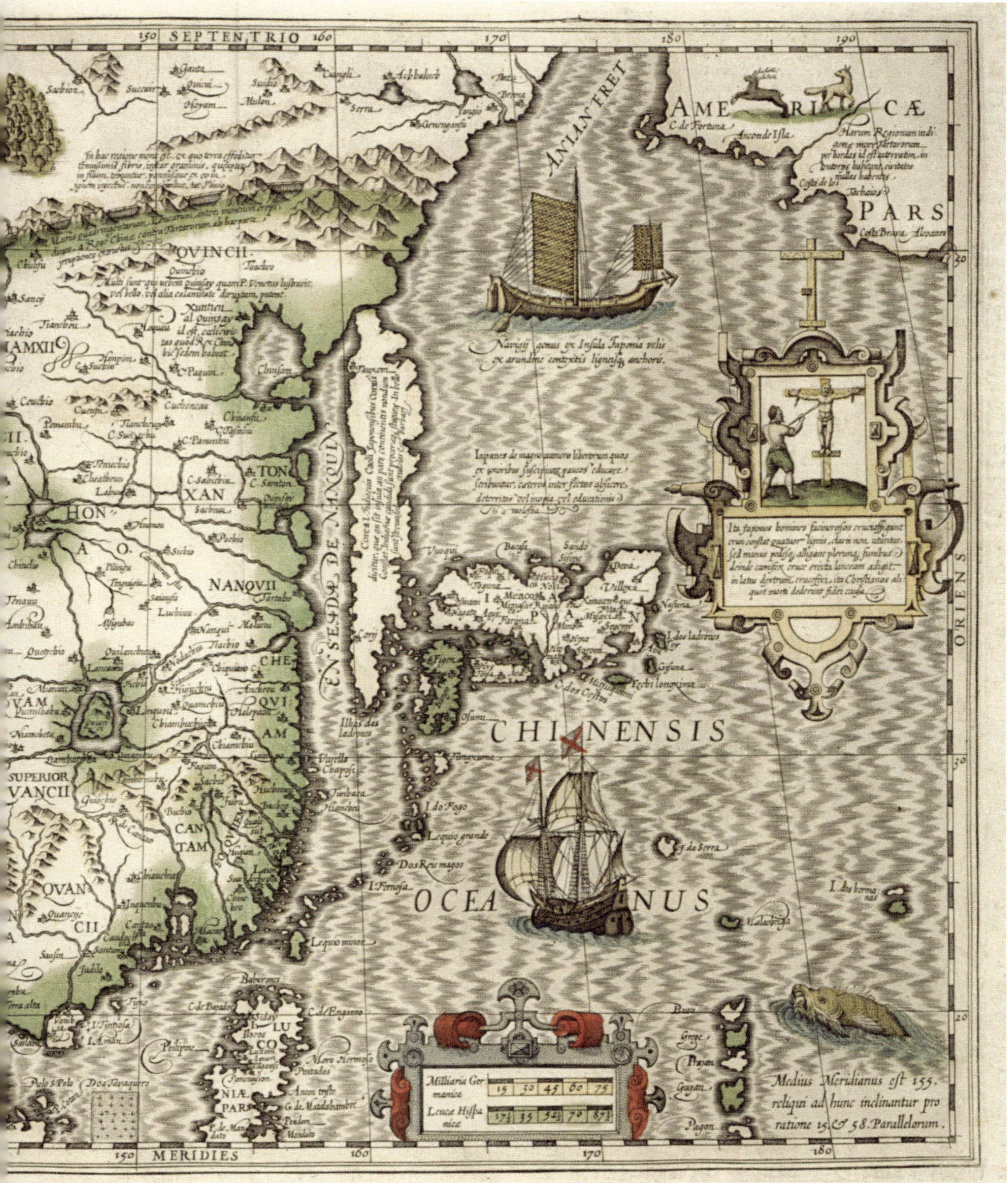
SEPTENTRIO
AMERICÆ PARS
ANIAN FRET
QVINCII
TON
XAN
HON
NANOVII
CHE
QUI
AM
SUPERIOR VANCII
CAN TAM
QVAN
CII
ENSEADA DE NANQUIN
IAPAN
CHINENSIS OCEANUS
I. do Fogo
Lequio grande
Dos Reis magos
I. Fermosa
Lequio minor
LUCONIÆ PARS
Navigii genus ex Insula Japonia velis ex arundine contextis ligneisq anchoris.
Milliaria Germanica | 15 | 30 | 45 | 60 | 75
Leucæ Hispanicæ | 17½ | 35 | 52½ | 70 | 87½
Medius Meridianus est 155. reliqui ad hunc inclinantur pro ratione 15 & 58. Parallelorum.
MERIDIES
ORIENS

6 Shipbuilding and Seafaring
The Port of Amsterdam

For almost two hundred years, the Dutch were a major force in the European shipbuilding and shipping industries, as well as in European arts and culture generally. Their lucrative trade with lands in Asia meant they needed a commercial fleet that could be readied at short notice. To guarantee this over the long term, the Netherlands continually expanded and modernised their shipyards. Shipbuilding skills were the preserve of highly trained experts whose knowledge was closely guarded and, until the mid to late seventeenth century, almost always passed on orally. Over the course of the 1670s, this expert knowledge became a science, as a well-known book on shipbuilding by Nicolaas Witsen (1641–1707) clearly illustrates. Dutch shipbuilders had to import much of their building materials. Wood, pitch, tar and flax were shipped from the Baltic region to Amsterdam, where the largest shipyards were located.

Amsterdam was the economic, political and maritime centre of the Netherlands. The Dutch East India Company (*Vereenigde Oostindische Compagnie, VOC*), which conducted trade with the East Indies, was founded here in 1602. Amsterdam was also the financial centre of the Western world and its main hub for news and exchange. As in Venice, another port city, the houses of Amsterdam were built on timber pile foundations to stabilise the ground. Man-made waterways – the canals or *grachten* – made it possible for people and goods to be transported directly into the centre of town, while large cargo ships berthed in extensive anchorage grounds off the coast. The shipyards, located a little outside Amsterdam, produced technologically sophisticated vessels, initially only for Dutch merchants but later for customers from throughout Europe.

The fluyt, a type of ship developed in the Netherlands in the late sixteenth century, featured a unique design that revolutionised commercial shipping. It combined increased cargo capacity with a reduction in crew size. Rulers from foreign lands, including Tsar Peter I of Russia (1672–1725), visited the Netherlands to expand their nation's expertise. Peter did not stop at purchasing books and hiring nautically skilled personnel. It is said that he personally took instruction in shipbuilding theory and practice, as well as seamanship in general.

The Dutch also established a reputation as superb seafarers. Dutch sailors charted the seas and coastal areas, recording their results in early instructional guides and maritime atlases, which were published in large numbers. The long sea routes to the East Indies provided optimal conditions for testing and improving navigational instruments. Sea travel was always very international, with ships' crews coming from a wide variety of countries. Our understanding of life aboard ship stems from diaries of the time, while the many archaeological finds salvaged from wreck sites also provide a record of daily life. Even today, visitors to Amsterdam will immediately recognise the city's maritime features. Its canals and countless ships, but also its paintings with themes of the sea, tell of the Dutch Golden Age and are vivid reminders of the era. *Thomas Eisentraut*

Further Reading

Robert Bohn, *Geschichte der Seefahrt*, Munich 2011

Jan de Vries and Ad van der Woude, *The First Modern Economy: Success, failure, and Perseverance of the Dutch Economy, 1500–1815*, Cambridge 1997

Georg-Michael Fleischer, *Schiffschirurgen von Kolumbus bis Nelson. Vergessene Helden der Seefahrtsgeschichte*, Heidelberg 2017

Joeron Giltaij and Jan Kelch, *Herren der Meere – Meister der Kunst. Das holländische Seebild im 17. Jahrhundert*, Ghent 1996

Wolfgang Griep and Frauke Krahé, *Peter der Große in Westeuropa. Die große Gesandtschaft 1697–1698*, exhib. cat., Bremen 1991

Donald S. Johnson and Juha Nurminen, *Die große Geschichte der Seefahrt. 3000 Jahre Expeditionen, Handel und Navigation*, Hamburg 2008

Brian Lavery, *Ship: The Epic Story of Maritime Adventure*, New York 2004

Eberhard Schmitt (ed.), *Indienfahrer 2. Seeleute und Leben an Bord im Ersten Kolonialzeitalter (15. bis 18. Jahrhundert)*, Dokumente zur Geschichte der europäischen Expansion, vol. 7, Wiesbaden 2008

Eberhard Schmitt et al (eds.), *Kaufleute als Kolonialherren: Die Handelswelt der Niederländer vom Kap der Guten Hoffnung bis Nagasaki 1600–1800*, Schriften der Universitätsbibliothek Bamberg, ed. by Dieter Karasek, vol. 6., Bamberg 1988

Richard W. Unger, *Dutch shipbuilding before 1800: ships and guilds*, Assen 1978

Roelof van Gelder, *Das ostindische Abenteuer: Deutsche in Diensten der Ostindischen Kompanie der Niederlande (VOC), 1600–1800*, Hamburg 2004

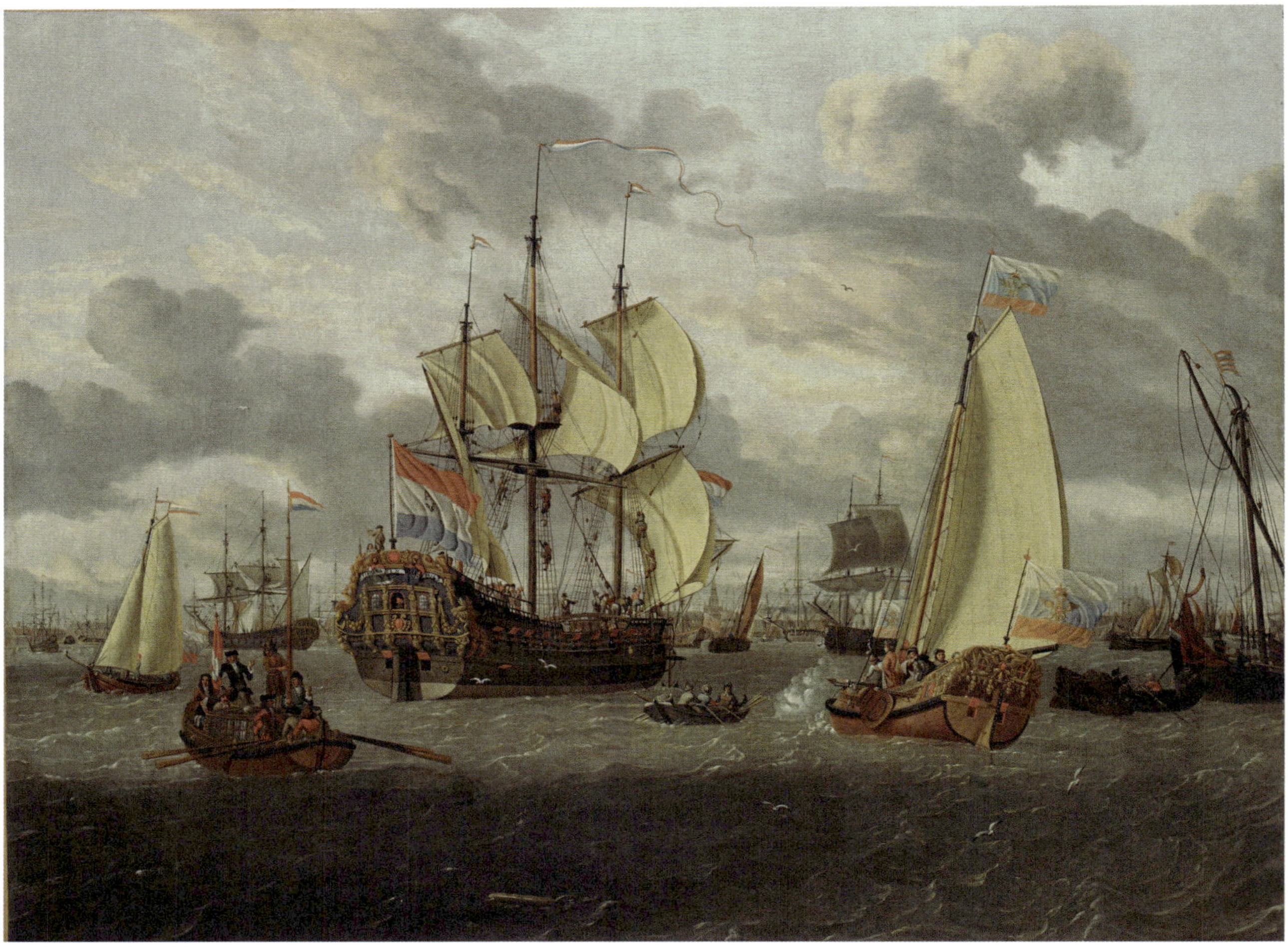

6/1

Amsterdam's Shipyards and Dutch Shipbuilding in the Seventeenth and Eighteenth Centuries

6/1 **Tsar Peter the Great on board his yacht, heading toward the frigate Pieter en Paul**
Czaar Peter de Grote aan boord van zijn jacht op weg naar de Pieter en Paul
Abraham Storck (1644–1708)
Amsterdam, c. 1698
Oil on canvas; 72 x 96 cm
Amsterdam, Amsterdam Museum: SA 8251

This painting shows Tsar Peter I of Russia (in a red military jacket) on board a small sailing boat flying a Russian flag. The Dutch frigate Pieter en Paul (construction of which began during the tsar's visit) can be seen in the middle of the picture. Peter I undertook a tour of Europe from 1697 to 1698, and stopped for a time in Amsterdam. Nicolaas Witsen (1641–1717), a Dutch politician, diplomat and author of scholarly publications, arranged for him to receive some basic instruction in the theory and practice of shipbuilding while he was in the city. It is said that Peter I worked incognito as a ship's carpenter in the shipyard of the Dutch East India Company. While in Europe, he acquired a large collection of tools and equipment and, what is more, hired expert craftsmen who he hoped would accelerate technological development in Russia. The scene portrayed in this picture is an imaginary one, as the tsar left before the frigate was finished and never saw it in full sail. TE

6/2 **Bird's eye view of Amsterdam**
Pieter Bast (c. 1550–1605)
Amsterdam, 1597
Hand-coloured engraving; 93 x 82 cm
Amsterdam, Het Scheepvaartmuseum: S.4328

Seen from above, Amsterdam is clearly a city shaped by shipping and trade. This map shows Amsterdam from the north. Its expansive harbour was large enough to offer anchorage to the many cargo ships which, from 1602 onwards, sailed under the flag of the Dutch East India Company (*Vereenigde Oostindische Compagnie, VOC*). The shipyards, where ships were built and repaired, are located in the east of the city (on the left-hand side of the picture).

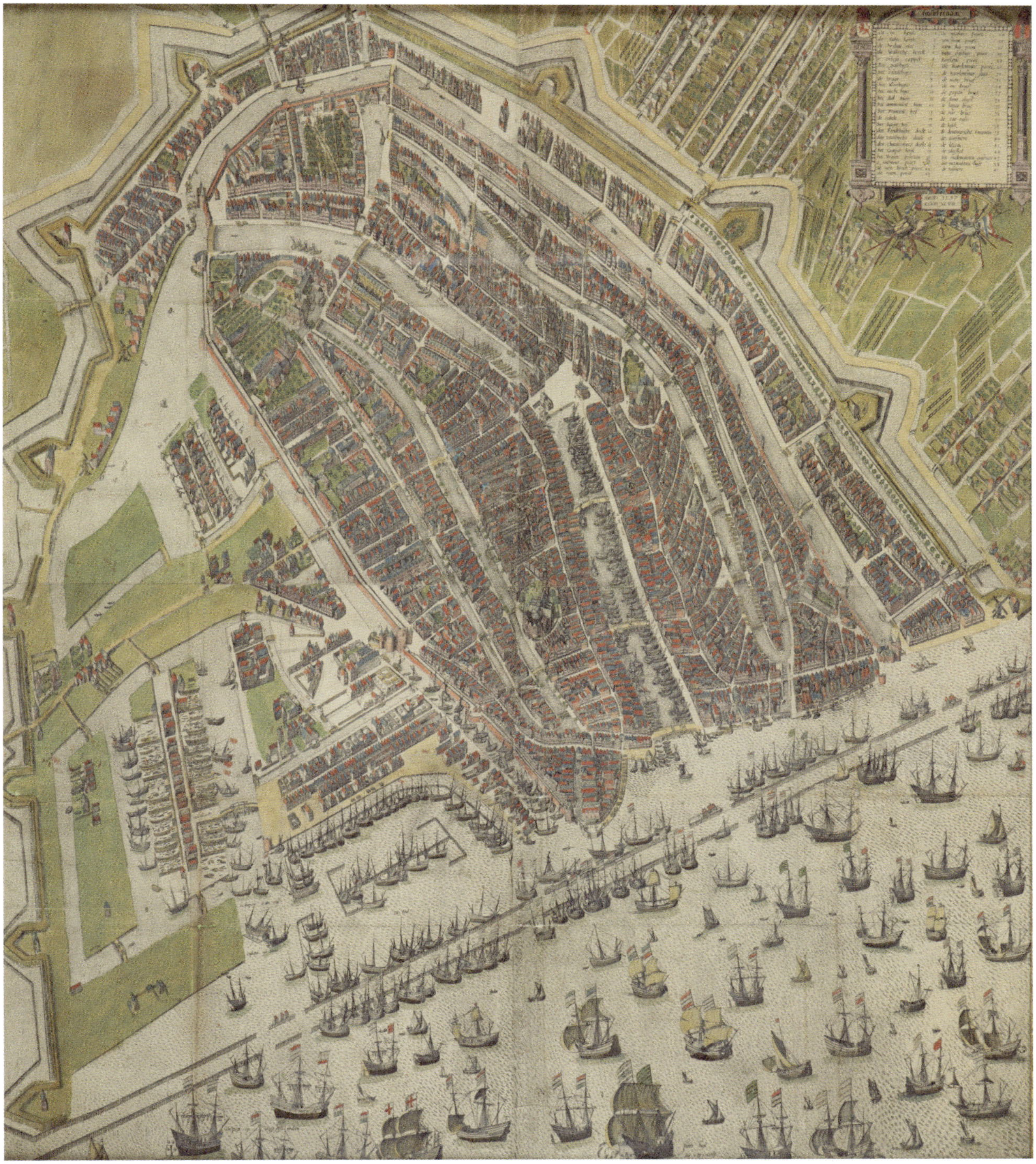

6/2

A number of artificial waterways (the canals, or *grachten*) run through the city, allowing smaller ships to sail straight into the centre of town. Houses were built on strong foundations for the most part, with thousands of tree trunks rammed into the ground to ensure their stability. This map of Amsterdam by Pieter Bast was the first to be made since 1544, meaning that for the first time in over 50 years, there was an accurate map of the city. TE

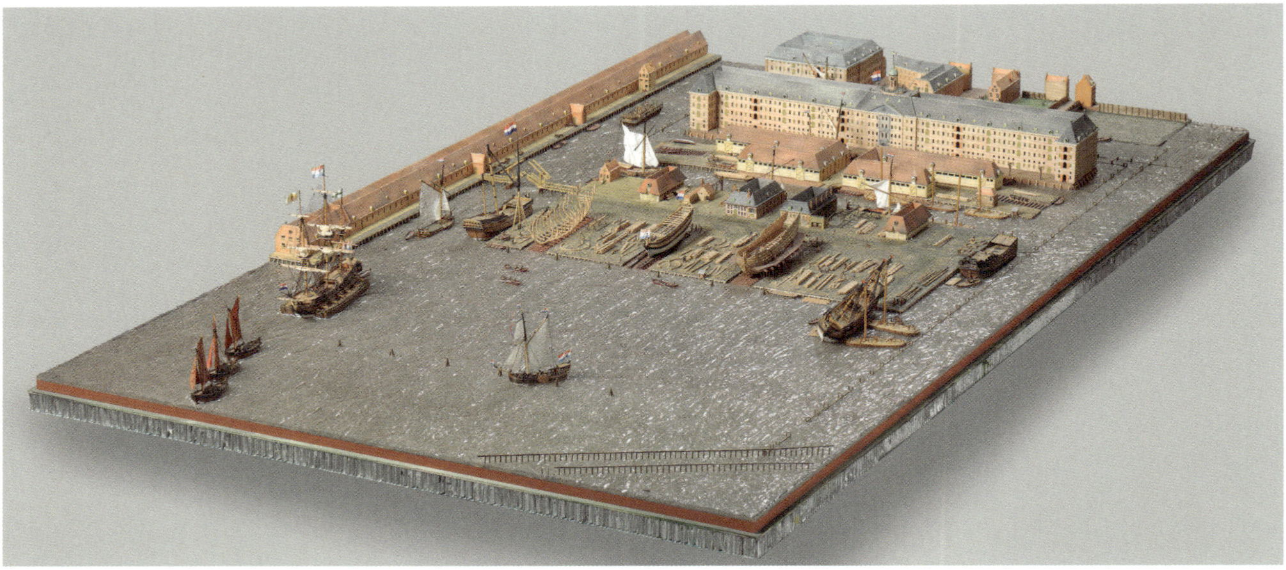

6/3

6/3 **Model of the Dutch East India Company shipyard in Amsterdam in the seventeenth century**
Built by Hans Bonke, Ab J. Hoving
Amsterdam, 1988–89
Wood, coloured; 26.5 x 112.5 x 202.5 cm
Amsterdam, Rijksmuseum: NG-2001-20

The shipyard of the Dutch East India Company (*Vereenigde Oostindische Compagnie*) was the leader in seventeenth-century European shipbuilding. The ropeyard – the long, narrow building along the edge of the model – made the ships' rigging, which amounted to kilometres of rope per ship. The other buildings, including the central storehouse in the middle, held various shipbuilding materials. The ships were built on land, on a slight slope (the 'slipway') that made it easier to launch the ship. This model shows three ships at various stages of construction and one ship sliding into the water. Another ship is being towed out of the shipyard by three sailing ships. *Scheepskameelen* (floats attached to the sides) are used to prevent it from lying too deep in the water. The model is based on a view of the shipyard seen in drawings such as the 1726 copper engraving *T Oost Indische Magazijn en Scheeps-Timmerwerf* by Joseph Mulder (1658–1742). TE

6/4 **Wooden box containing tools used at the Westhof shipyard**
Zoeterwoude, 1790–1994
Wood, iron; 31 x 60 x 30 cm
Amsterdam, Het Scheepvaartmuseum: 2012.0966, 2012.0921-3, 2012.0922-1, 2012.0923, 2012.0932, 2012.0939, 2012.0954, 2012.956, 2012.0961, 2012.0963, 2012.1077, 2012.1080, 2012.1227, 2012.1244, 2012.1251

A great variety of woodworking tools were needed in shipbuilding, and even if their names have changed over the centuries, their form and function have remained essentially the same. Until the nineteenth century, ships were made primarily of wood. It was not until the Industrial Revolution that shipbuilders – initially in the UK, and spreading out from there – began to experiment more with iron and steel. This solid wooden box contains the following tools, which were in use through the late twentieth century and show corresponding signs of wear: caulking mallet, brace, iron drill, branding iron (for branding the wood), knife, marking gauge, rebate plane, a pair of compasses, forging tongs, planking gauge, sliding T bevel, and a chisel. The tools came from the Westhof shipyard in the province of South Holland, and are an impressive record of how ship carpentry tools have evolved over the centuries. TE

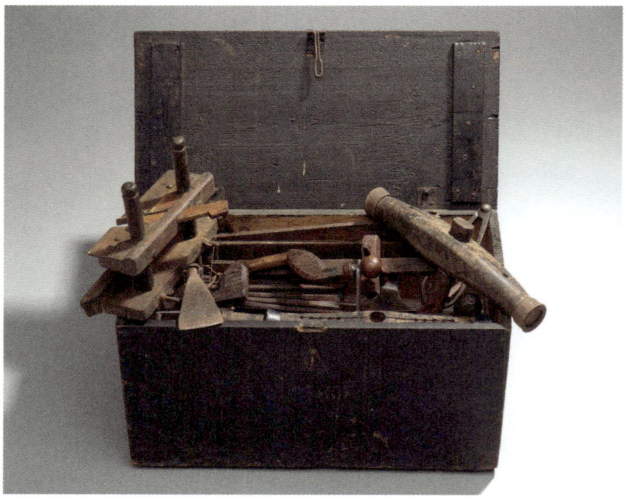

6/4

6/5 **De Eendragt, model of an East Indiaman Ship**
The Netherlands (?), 1775–1800
Wood, textile; c. 100 x 47 x95 cm
Nuremberg, Germanisches Nationalmuseum: HM1016

This model of an East Indiaman ship symbolises the Dutch Golden Age. The term 'East Indiaman' did not refer to a particular type of ship, but was used for ships of any variety that regularly travelled between Europe and the Asian colonies. This model of an East Indiaman was probably made in the Netherlands. It has three slightly overlong masts and 44 guns; its hull is made of a single block of wood. Unlike the hull, the rigging and masts were modelled with great precision. The figurehead adorning the hull is a crowned lion. Lettered in gold on the stern are the year 1756 and the ship's name. This name, De Eeendragt (meaning concord), was often used for Dutch ships. East Indiamen were primarily merchant ships. They had guns on board and sailed in convoy to defend themselves against attacks by pirates or privateers. In times of war, it was possible to equip the ships with additional arms, and they could also be used to transport troops. (Fig. p. 71) TE

6/6 **Milestones in the history of European shipbuilding**
Multimedia kiosk
Berlin, Deutsches Historisches Museum

People have built ships for thousands of years, adapting them to specific purposes and regions. Every sea has its own unique properties that will affect the construction of the ships that sail it. One major innovation in shipbuilding was the 'fluyt', a cargo ship developed by the Dutch in 1595. Somewhat longer than usual, it combined a large cargo capacity with a shallow draught (i.e., it didn't lie low in the water) and could be sailed by a small crew – all factors that helped maximise profits. This multimedia kiosk describes and explains pioneering developments in shipbuilding, from prehistoric dugouts (canoes) to modern container ships. Special attention is paid to the wooden sailing ships which shaped European seafaring traditions for many hundreds of years. (Exhibit not shown) TE

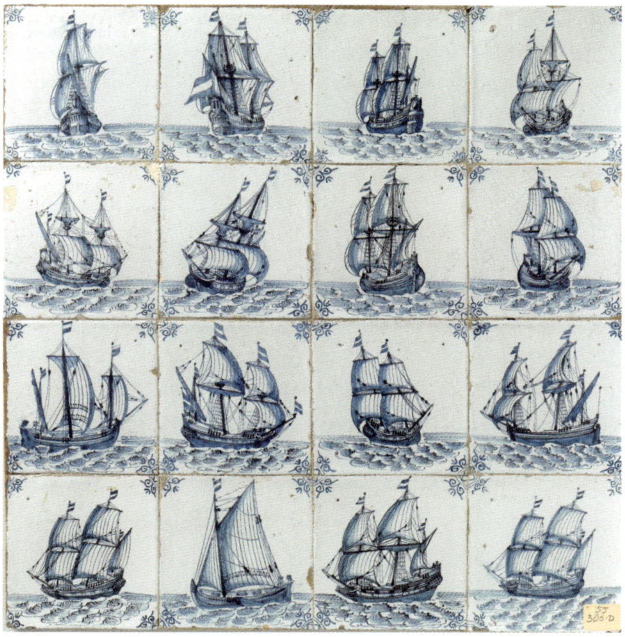

6/7

6/7 **Wall tiles with various ship motifs**
The Netherlands, c. 1650–1680
Tin-glazed ceramic, majolica; 52.5 x 52.5 cm
Amsterdam, Rijksmuseum: BK-1955-306-D

These wall tiles feature 16 different ship motifs. The ships are styled in blue and purple, and each tile is tin-glazed. Because the tiles were hand-painted, no one picture is the same as any other. In this respect, tile-making was similar to shipbuilding; since they were made of material that grew unevenly, wooden ships were also all unique. No two ships were alike, even if the design of their exterior was intended to convey uniformity. Maritime themes – pictures of ships, in particular – were very popular across Europe, especially thanks to the high quality of Dutch wall tiles. A distinctive feature of these tiles was the corner decoration – in the case of those on display here, it is an ox head, indicating that they were made in or around Delft. TE

6/8 **_Architectura Navalis_, a monograph on shipbuilding**
Joseph Furttenbach (1591–1667)
Printed by Jonas Saur
Ulm, 1629
Cardboard, parchment, print on paper; 30.5 x 20.7 cm
Berlin, Deutsches Historisches Museum: RA 62/87

Joseph Furttenbach, a scholar from southern Germany, published a series of monographs from 1628 to 1641, summarising the current state of knowledge in various fields. His 1629 *Architectura Navalis* described major ship types, such as galleys, galleasses, frigates etc. Similar in form to an encyclopaedia aimed at the layperson, it focused on written explanations and provided selected illustrations. The decision to include a shipbuilding monograph in the series shows the high regard in which seamanship and shipbuilding were held in Europe. In addition to detailed information on ship design and equipment, it contains a long passage about the naval battle of Lepanto (1571), which is illustrated by several copperplate engravings. While this book on shipbuilding does provide basic information, it cannot hide the fact that the author was neither a sailor nor a shipwright. (Exhibit not shown) TE

6/9 **Book on shipbuilding including old traditions and modern methods**
Aeloude en Hedendaegsche Scheeps-bouw en Bestier [...]
Nicolaas Witsen (1641–1717)
Amsterdam, 1671
Print on paper; 32 x 21.5 cm
Amsterdam, Het Scheepvaartmuseum: S.0525(26)

In a pioneering textbook on shipbuilding, Dutch statesman Nicolaas Witsen examined the evolution of European shipbuilding from ancient times to his own day. His descriptions of contemporary shipbuilding in the Netherlands provide a detailed record of what was then the state of the art. In many engravings and drawings, Witsen even labels the tools used by the ship's carpenters and names all the parts of the ship. The publication of this sort of specialist literature marked a clear turning point in how shipbuilding was taught. Shipbuilding skills had previously been acquired through experience and passed on from person to person, but that changed completely when they were written down. For the first time, it was possible to reach a wider swathe of people, without their always having to be physically present. A second, revised edition of the work was published in 1690. Only four copies of it are known to still exist. TE

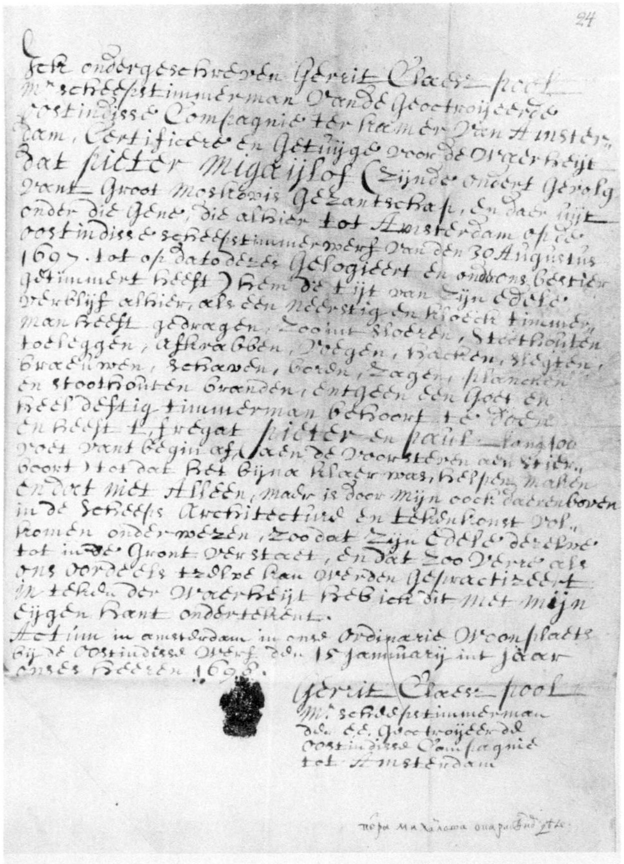

6/10

6/10 **Copy of an apprenticeship certificate, issued by Gerrit Claesz Pool for Pieter Migaijlof (pseudonym of Tsar Peter I), dated 15 January 1698**
Reproduction
Amsterdam, Het Scheepvaartmuseum: NII (volgenr. 03508)

This apprenticeship certificate, issued in the name of an alias used by Tsar Peter I of Russia, illustrates just how leading a role the Netherlands played in European shipbuilding. The document, which survives only in the form of a modern copy, lists the theoretical knowledge and practical skills that a budding shipwright would have to have mastered in the late seventeenth century. It was issued on 15 January 1698 by Gerrit Glaesz Pool (1651–1710), a master shipwright whose reputation extended beyond his native Amsterdam. The tsar met him while touring Europe and stayed with him for a time. There is some debate about whether Peter actually acquired this knowledge.
His presence in the Amsterdam shipyard is recorded in other documents than the certificate, however, and later inspired the opera by Albert Lortzing (1801–1851), *Zar und Zimmermann* (Tsar and carpenter), which premiered in the Leipzig Stadttheater (city theatre) on 22 December 1837. TE

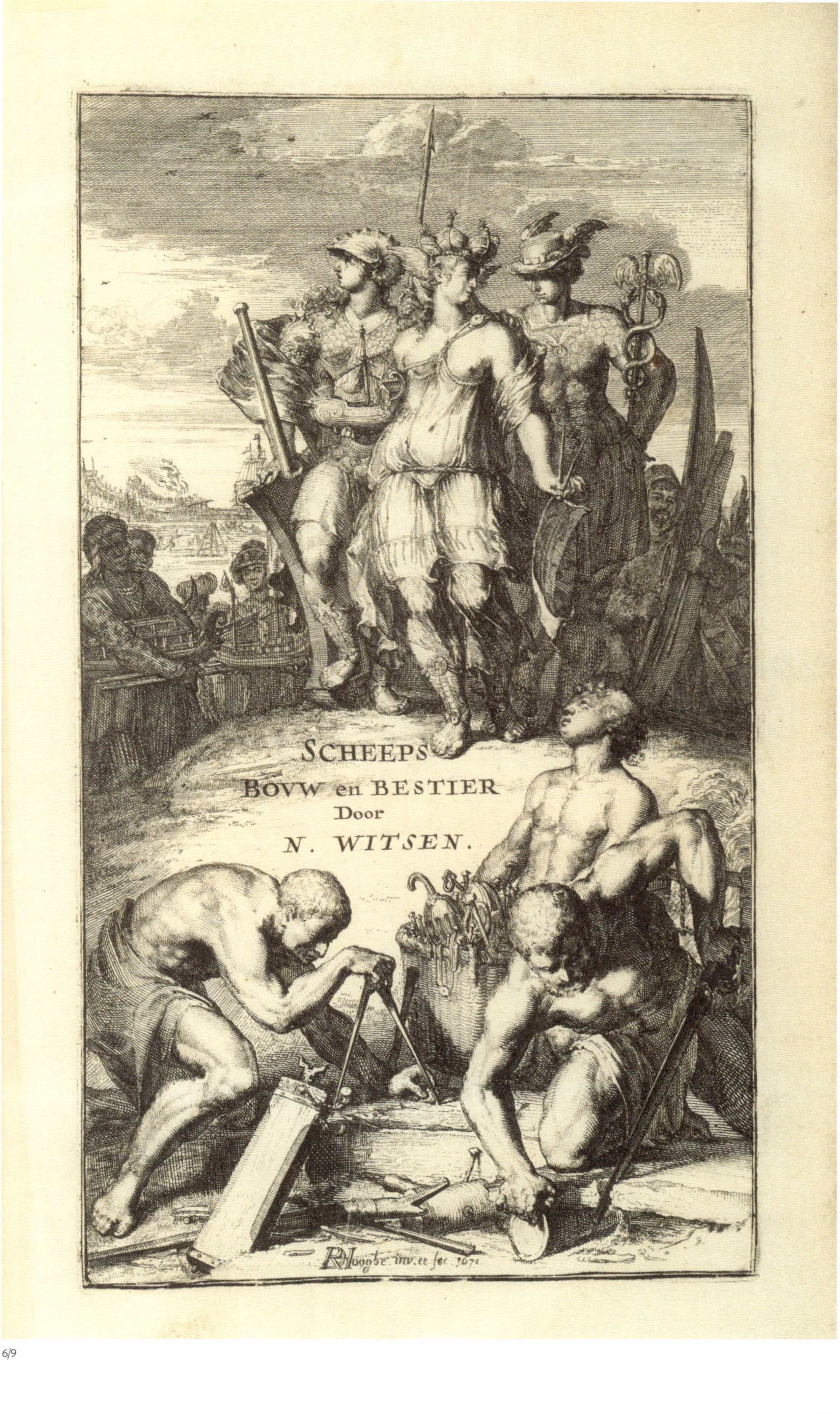
SCHEEPS
BOUW en BESTIER
Door
N. WITSEN.
RDHooghe. inv. et fec. 1671

6/9

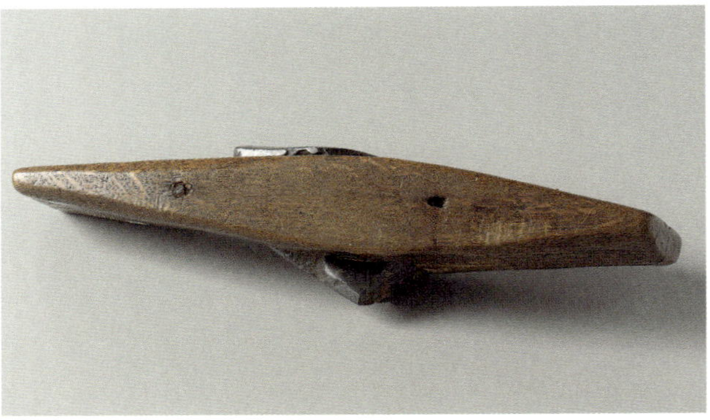

6/11

6/11 **Lodestone (magnetite)**
The Netherlands, c. 1697
Wood, iron; magnetite: 10 x 4.5 x 7.7 cm, mount: 32 x 7.4 x 4.2 cm
Amsterdam, Rijksmuseum: NG-NM-12786-A

A 'lodestone' is a piece of naturally magnetised mineral, or magnetite. Regularly found in large iron ore deposits, particularly in Norway and Sweden, magnetite was prized in the early modern period for its unusually good magnetic properties. Lodestones were used to magnetise new compass needles or remagnetise them when they became less effective. Any compass needle on a ship would become weaker due to natural meteorological effects such as oxidation. Through direct contact with a lodestone, the compass needle could be remagnetised. The lodestone shown here is said to have been used by Tsar Peter I during his stay in Zaandam, roughly six kilometres northwest of Amsterdam. TE

6/12 **Wooden box for storing documents and a lodestone belonging to Tsar Peter I**
The Netherlands, c. 1697
Wood, copper, iron wool, sealing wax; 8.2 x 35.6 x 24.2 cm
Amsterdam, Rijksmuseum: NG-NM-12786-B

This Dutch-made wooden box is elaborately worked and features brass fittings with floral motifs and two copper handles. A lock prevents it from being opened by unauthorised persons. Its small size ensures that it can be transported easily. The box is among the items said to have belonged to Tsar Peter I. The tsar presumably stored important documents in it while he was staying incognito in Zaandam, located not far from Amsterdam. It is said that the lodestone was also kept in the box. (Exhibit not shown) TE

Marine Navigation

6/13 **Interactive navigational instruments**
Multimedia kiosk
Software development: Kiss the Frog (Delft)
Amsterdam, Het Scheepvaartmuseum

Navigational instruments played an increasingly important role for Europeans from the end of the Middle Ages onwards. There were two main problems facing seafarers of the time: firstly, how to calculate one's own position at sea with precision, and, secondly, how to find places discovered previously. Especially when on the high seas, the lack of permanent landmarks (distinctive coastlines, church towers, mountain peaks, etc.) made it almost impossible to fix one's exact position without the aid of tools. Celestial positioning was also very imprecise, as the rolling of the ship made it difficult to measure angles on deck. Navigators not only needed to know how to handle these sensitive instruments but also had to acquire certain skills in maths and astronomy before they could use the readings to calculate their position correctly. The multimedia kiosk explains how five common navigational instruments worked. These instruments are the compass, astrolabe, Jacob's staff, Davis quadrant, and sextant. (Exhibit not shown) TE

6/14 ***Spieghel der Zeevaerdt*, an atlas of sea charts and a pilot guide**
Lucas Janszoon Waghenaer (1533/34–1605/06)
Printed by Christoffel Plantijn (c. 1520–1589)
The Netherlands, 1584/85
Coloured copper engraving; 41 x 30 cm
Amsterdam, Het Scheepvaartmuseum: A.0145(103)

Spieghel der Zeevaerdt (The Mariner's Mirrour [sic]) is the earliest collection of sea charts and navigational instructions to be compiled in a comprehensive maritime atlas. Published by Lucas Janszoon Waghenaer (1533/34–1605/06), a Dutch steersman from the town of Enkhuizen, it features double-spread illustrations and is divided into two parts. The first part focuses on the western seas (the Atlantic coast from Portugal to Norway), while the second part is dedicated to the North Sea and the Baltic Sea. In a first for its time, the charts include easily understandable comments with detailed information on anchorage grounds, fairways, water depths, shallows, and prominent seamarks. In subsequent centuries, the publisher's name became synonymous with maritime atlases and sea charts of comparable quality, which were often called 'waggoners' (a corruption of his surname, Waghenaer). TE

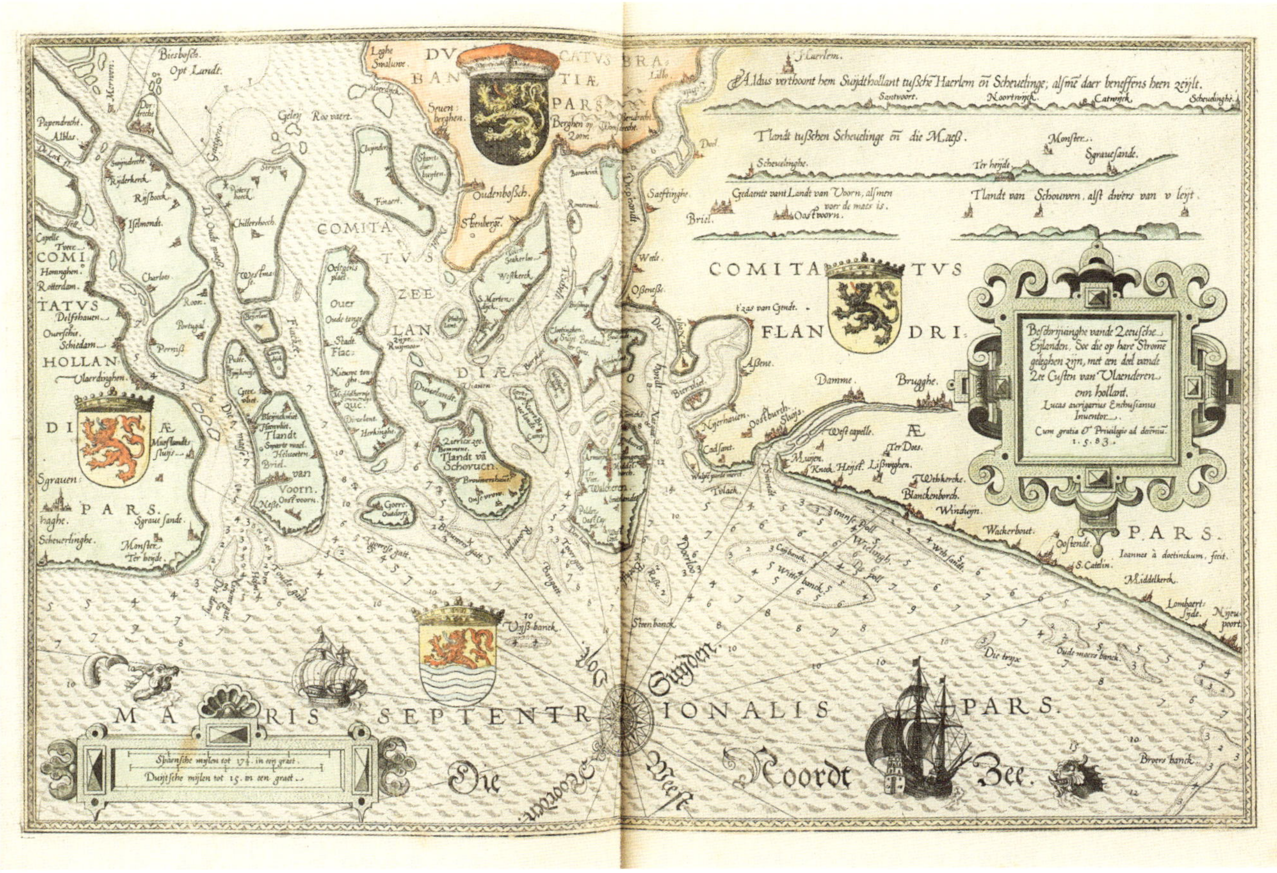

6/14

6/15 **Navigational divider**
The Netherlands, c. 1590–1596
Brass; 7.9 x 3.3 cm
Amsterdam, Rijksmuseum: NG-NM-7750

A navigational divider is one of the most important tools a seaman can possess. Together with a sea chart, it is used to measure distances on a map and transfer them to other maps. Later maps had a measuring scale along their edges. Dividers also made it possible to take bearings and plot positions with greater ease and precision. TE

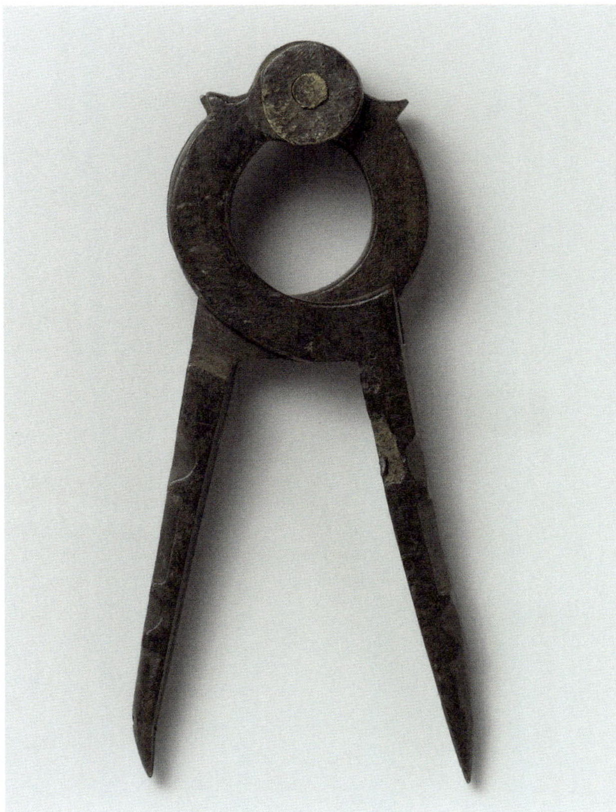

6/15

6/16 **Hand lead**
The Netherlands, c. 1743
Lead; 55 x 7 x 5 cm
Amsterdam, Het Scheepvaartmuseum: S.4715(22)

There is evidence that 'hand leads' were used in northern European waters as early as the eleventh century. A hand lead was an elongated piece of lead attached to a very long rope (called a 'lead line' or 'sounding line'). To measure (or 'plumb') the depth of the water, the lead was cast overboard and the length of rope that had unwound was recorded. To make the process easier, the lead line had coloured markings

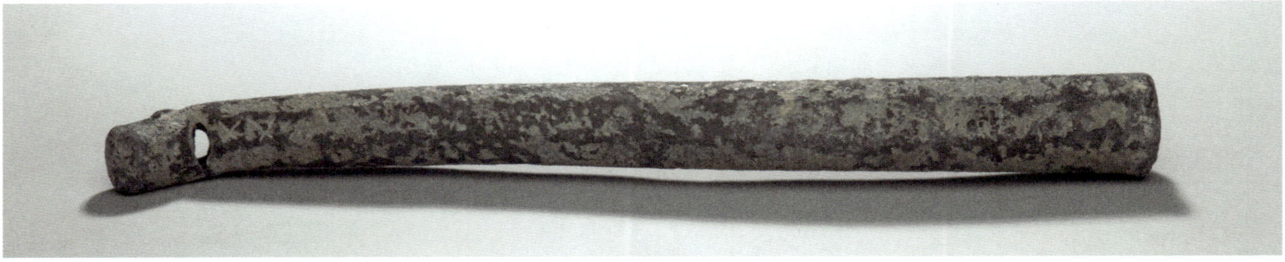

6/16

at set intervals, measured in units called fathoms (1 fathom = 6 feet or 1.828 m). The bottom of the lead often had a little cavity that could be smeared with tallow. As soon as the lead touched the seabed, a bit of sediment would stick to the tallow, providing useful information for anchoring. When sailing along unfamiliar coastlines, sounding the depth and determining the composition of the seabed was essential both for preventing the ship from running aground and for finding a good place to anchor. TE

6/17 **Dutchman's log (chip log, log reel and log glass)**
The Netherlands, 1850–1900
Wood, iron, flax, glass; chip log: 2 x 19 x 19 cm, log reel: 24 x 68 x 26 cm
Amsterdam, Het Scheepvaartmuseum: A.0097, A.0105

The Dutchman's log, invented in the Netherlands in the sixteenth century, was a device for measuring a ship's speed. It consisted of a piece of wood (called a chip log) attached to a line wound on a reel. The sailor taking the measurement would drop the chip log overboard, release the line until the sand in the log glass had run out, and then measure the length of line that had been 'paid out'. Speed was calculated as the ratio of line length over time, and was measured in 'knots'. This term, which we still use today, comes from the practice of tying knots in the line at regular intervals, making it easier to handle. For a long time, people thought that a ship's speed also said something about the distance it had travelled. In fact, however, a ship's speed is always relative to the surrounding water. Factors such as sea currents and leeway (the drift of a ship caused by winds blowing it off course) affect the distance the ship has to travel, but do not change its speed. TE

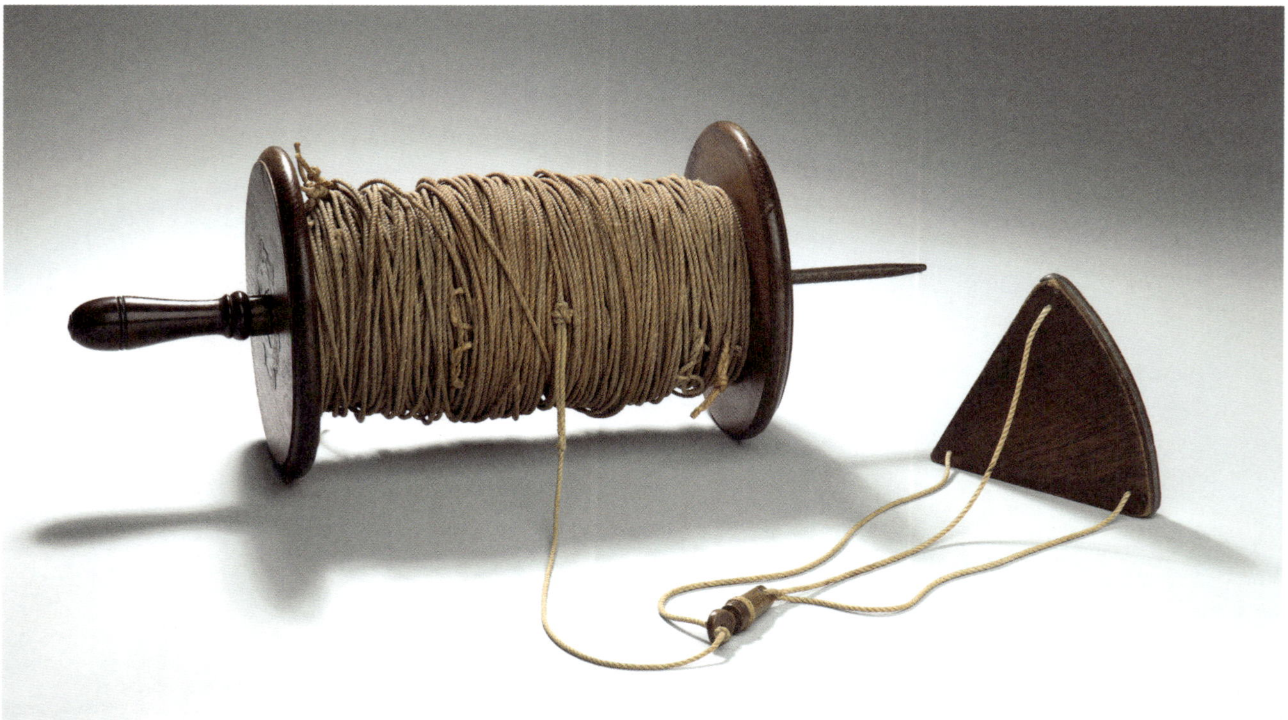

6/17

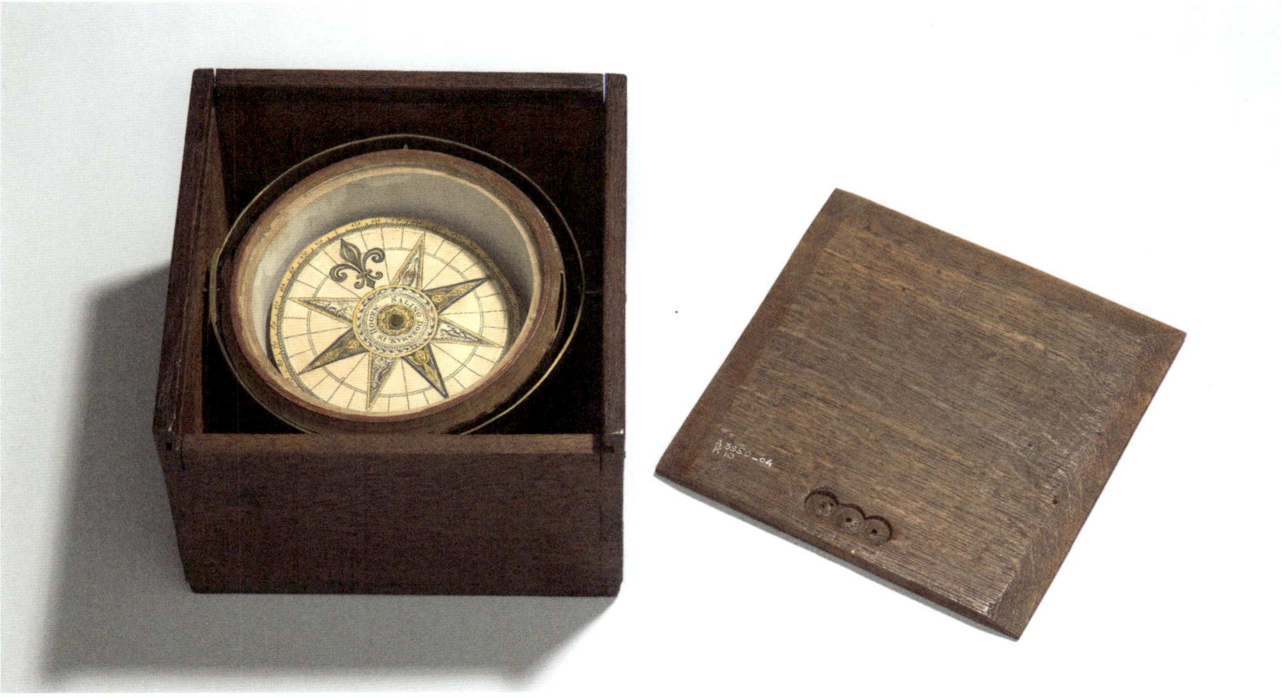

6/18

6/18 **Mariner's compass**
Saling Dorsman (c. 1750–1824)
Hoorn, the Netherlands, 1775–1825
Brass, wood, paper, glass; 14 x 20.5 x 20.5 cm
Amsterdam, Het Scheepvaartmuseum: A.3950(4)

The first compass was a 'wet compass', consisting of a magnetic sliver of iron attached to a piece of wood that floated in the water. It was used to identify the directions of the north and the south. Chinese sailors are known to have taken bearings using this method as far back as the eleventh century. The 'dry compass', on the other hand, was invented or refined in the Mediterranean region sometime in the thirteenth century. Its inventor is traditionally held to be Flavio Gioia, an Italian mariner who laid a card called a 'compass rose' under the needle, making it easier to read directions. The cardinal points (four main points) of the compass were originally named after the corresponding Mediterranean winds. Compasses were being used aboard European ships by the early fifteenth century at the latest. They were the primary navigational instrument from that point on, and got steadily better as improvements were made to the suspension of the compass needle. TE

6/19 **Hanging compass**
Anthonij Krighout, Ignatius Lega
Rotterdam, 1715/1720–1799
Brass, glass, paper; 10 x 28 x 28 cm
Amsterdam, Het Scheepvaartmuseum: A.3950(15)

A hanging compass was a special kind of ship's compass. The markings for east and west are reversed on the compass card used with this type of compass. This is because the compass hangs from the ceiling and is read from below. With a hanging compass mounted over his bed, the captain could even read the ship's bearings while lying down. This meant the captain could check the ship's course at any time and, if necessary, give instructions to correct it without having to go to the afterdeck and consult the compass installed near the rudder. (Exhibit not shown) TE

6/20 **Astrolabe (for celestial navigation)**
Muhammad Ibn as-Saffar (d. 1035)
Toledo, 1029/30
Cast brass, engraved and punched; diam. 13.5 cm
Berlin, Staatsbibliothek zu Berlin – Preußischer Kulturbesitz, Orientabteilung: Sprenger 2050

Arab influence on the development and spread of early navigational instruments was substantial. The astrolabe is a prime example of a navigational instrument whose development was driven in large part by research conducted by Arab scholars. The one on display here was made in the town of Toledo (in the Muslim-controlled part of the Iberian Peninsula) by Muhammad Ibn as-Saffar, an astronomer whose name was celebrated even in his own time. It has one main disk and nine flat plates that could be inserted into the disk and rotated. It is engraved in Arabic and Hebrew. Given clear skies, people with the requisite mathematical and astronomical skills could use an astrolabe to measure the angle between a celestial body and the horizon, thus fixing their position. Astrolabes were employed for a variety of purposes, two primary ones being to measure distance and determine one's location. From the fifteenth to the seventeenth century in particular, modified variants of the astrolabe were used aboard ships. Eventually they were replaced by sextants. TE

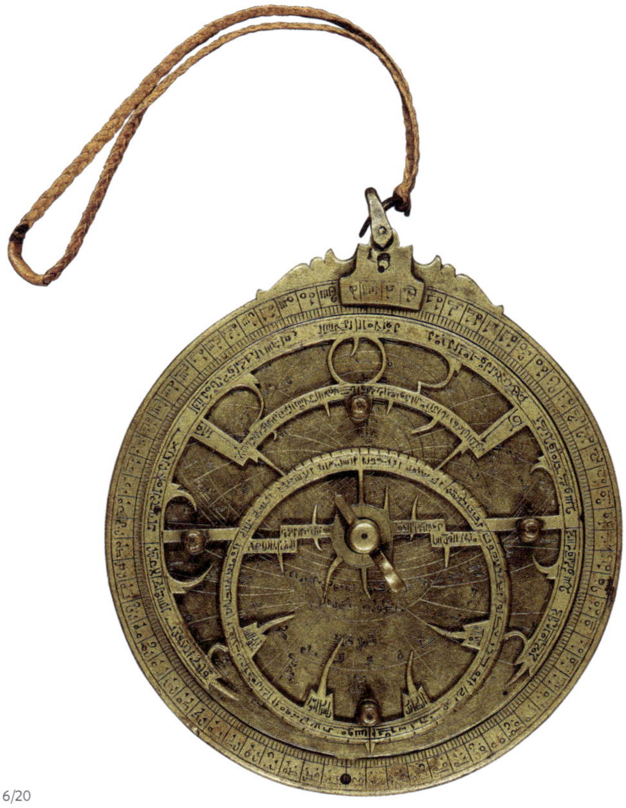

6/20

6/21 **Jacob's staff (cross-staff)**
The Netherlands, c. 1780
Wood, bone; 6 x 79 x 52.5 cm
Amsterdam, Het Scheepvaartmuseum: B.0025(4)

One of the most basic problems in seamanship was determining location and direction. As long as the ship was close to shore, the crew always knew where they were. This changed as soon as they lost sight of the coast. For a long time, the standard way to fix position was celestial navigation, which involved measuring the altitude of a celestial body (as the angle between the celestial body and the hori-

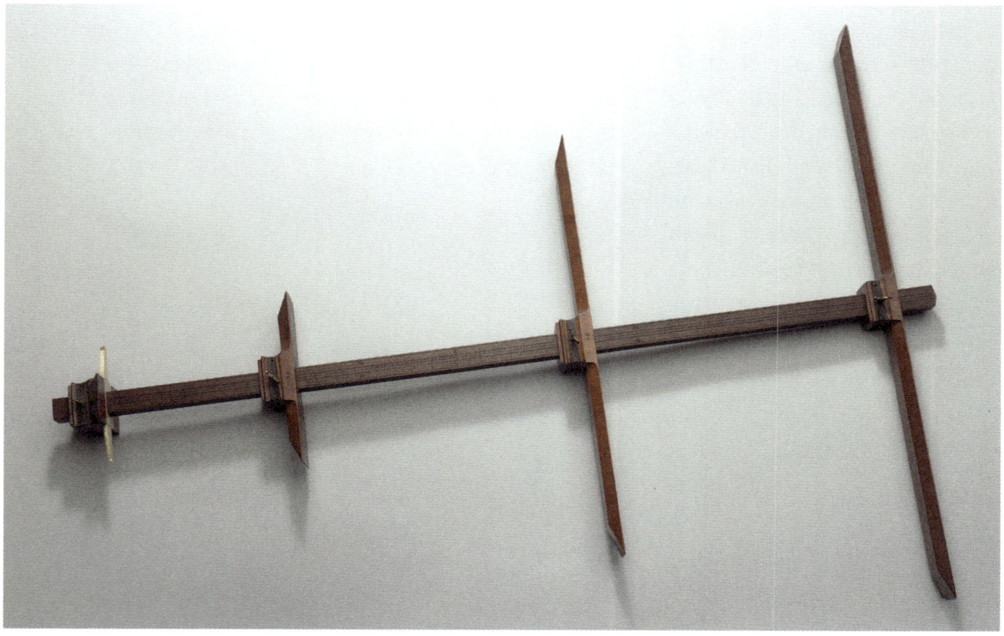

6/21

zon). Jacob's staffs were used for this purpose, as were quadrants and astrolabes. There is evidence that the Jacob's staff was being used in Europe by the fourteenth century at the latest. The navigator placed one end of the main staff below his eye and pointed it at a fixed star (the sun or a pole star). He would then adjust one of the four crossarms (a longer one if the star were higher in the sky, and a shorter one if it were lower) until the top end covered the star and the bottom end the horizon. Using conversion tables, he could then calculate the ship's latitude. Because it is built in the form of a cross, the Jacob's staff is also known as a cross-staff. It could only be used to determine latitude, and so the navigator only knew how far north or south of the equator the ship was located. By the late sixteenth century at the latest, the Jacob's staff was gradually being replaced by the Davis quadrant. TE

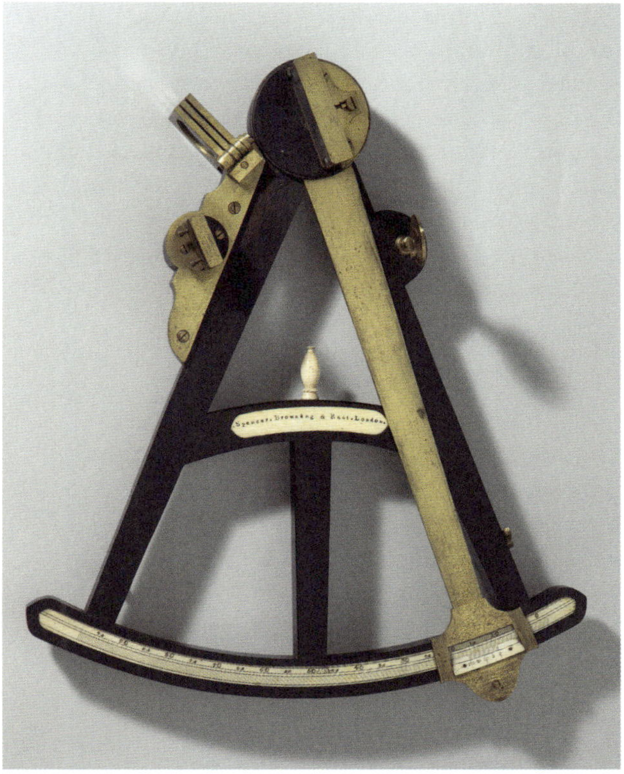

6/22

6/22 **Octant**
Manufacturer: Spencer, Browning & Rust
London, 1784–1839
Ebony, brass, bone; 8 x 32 x 25 cm
Amsterdam, Het Scheepvaartmuseum: S.3055(1)

The octant was invented in the eighteenth century. In 1714, the British government established the 'longitude rewards' as an inducement to develop improved methods and tools for fixing a ship's position at sea. In 1731 British mathematician and astronomer John Hadley (1682–1744) presented the programme's administrative board with just such a device and was rewarded part of the prize money for his invention. The octant made it possible for a ship to fix its position even in rough seas. In a first for instruments of its kind, it used small mirrors and a measurement arc that spanned 45 degrees, or one-eighth of a circle, which is where it gets the name 'octant'. The devices were initially made of wood. Because it was not always possible to prevent weather damage or to keep the wood from losing its shape, octants soon began to be manufactured in brass instead. The London firm of Spencer, Browning & Rust produced high-quality navigational instruments from 1784 to 1840. TE

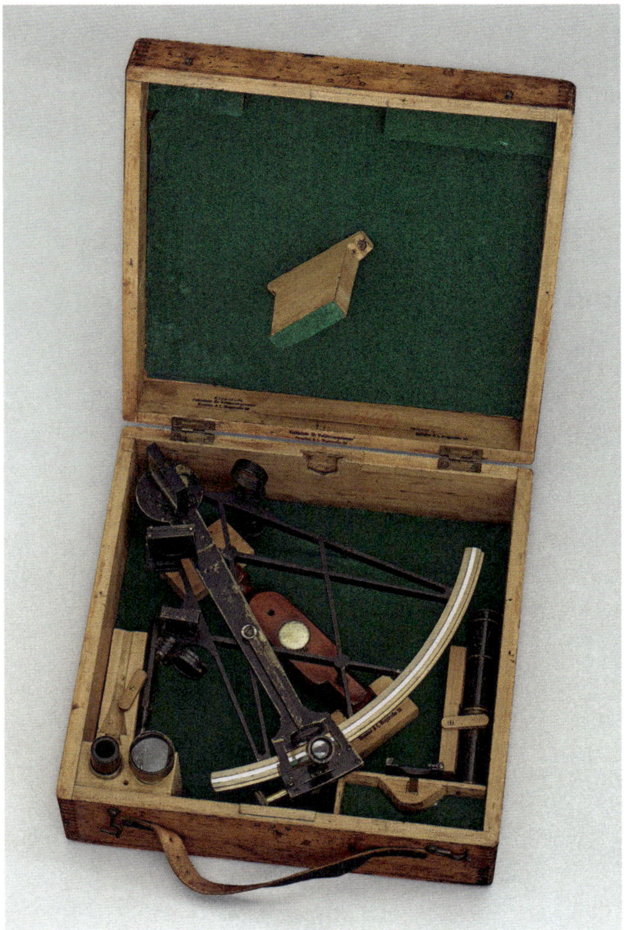

6/23

6/23 **Sextant (in its original box with accessories)**
Manufacturer: H. Haecke (Berlin)
Berlin, 1901/1915
Brass, steel, glass, mirror, fabric, wood; sextant:
25.5 x 30 x 10 cm, box: 12.8 x 31.5 x 31.5 cm
Berlin, Deutsches Historisches Museum: Pro 63/154

Navigational instruments were very costly when they first became available, as they were rare and expensive to produce. To protect these sensitive devices, manufacturers built padded carrying cases which were also used to store accessories (a lens, eyepiece, screwdriver and mount). A navigator using the sextant would sight the horizon and a star (the sun or a polar star), and read the angle from the arc scale on the side. It is quite a precise instrument, with measurements accurate to within one arc minute, which converts to one sea mile. Sextants can be used to measure not only latitude, but also longitude. This is done via the lunar distances method. Sextants are still used for navigation today, even though there are many modern methods for fixing a ship's position. TE

Life Aboard Ship: Sailors in the Eighteenth Century

6/24 **Greybeard jug**
Salvaged from the wreck of the Swedish warship
PRINSESSAN HEDVIG SOFIA
Frechen (near Cologne), before 1715
Ceramic; H 19.1 cm, diam. 23 cm
Schleswig, Museum für Archäologie Schloss Gottorf, Landesmuseen Schleswig-Holstein: SH2008-67.116

Certain striking ceramic jugs are regularly salvaged from shipwrecks found in the North Sea / Baltic Sea region. These jugs have a figure resembling the face of a bearded man fired into their neck, and for this reason, they are known as 'Greybeards' (or 'Bellarmines', after Cardinal Robert Bellarmine). They were used to transport drinks of all kinds, mainly alcoholic ones. They were manufactured throughout Europe, with leading production centres in Frechen and Cologne (both in Germany). The jugs were exported from the Rhineland to the entire North Sea / Baltic Sea region, where they were common household items. This Greybeard was discovered on the wreck of the Swedish warship (or 'ship of the line', to use the historical term) PRINSESSAN HEDVIG SOFIA, which sank at the entrance to the Kiel Fjord in April 1715. Her crew included sailors from the Netherlands. Dutch sailors were known to be experienced seamen and enjoyed an excellent reputation in all European fleets. TE

6/25 **Ship's biscuit**
Great Britain, 13 April 1784
Wheat; H 1 cm, diam. 9.5 cm
Greenwich, London, National Maritime Museum: AAB0003

Non-perishable foods were an absolute necessity aboard ship, particularly during long voyages. Ship's biscuits, sometimes called 'hard tack', were twice-baked wheat biscuits. Because of their low water content, ship's biscuits are fairly resistant to spoilage. Being easy to store and transport, they were considered the ideal food for a sea voyage. Before it was eaten, the biscuit would be softened in liquid of some kind. This particular biscuit was given as a gift in 1784 and bears the following inscription: "This biscuit was given – Miss Blacket at Berwick on Tuesday 13 April 1784, Berwick". The place name is not entirely legible, and may refer to the village of Berwick in Sussex (located not far from Portsmouth, the base of the British fleet) or to HMS BERWICK, a British 74-gun ship launched in 1775. TE

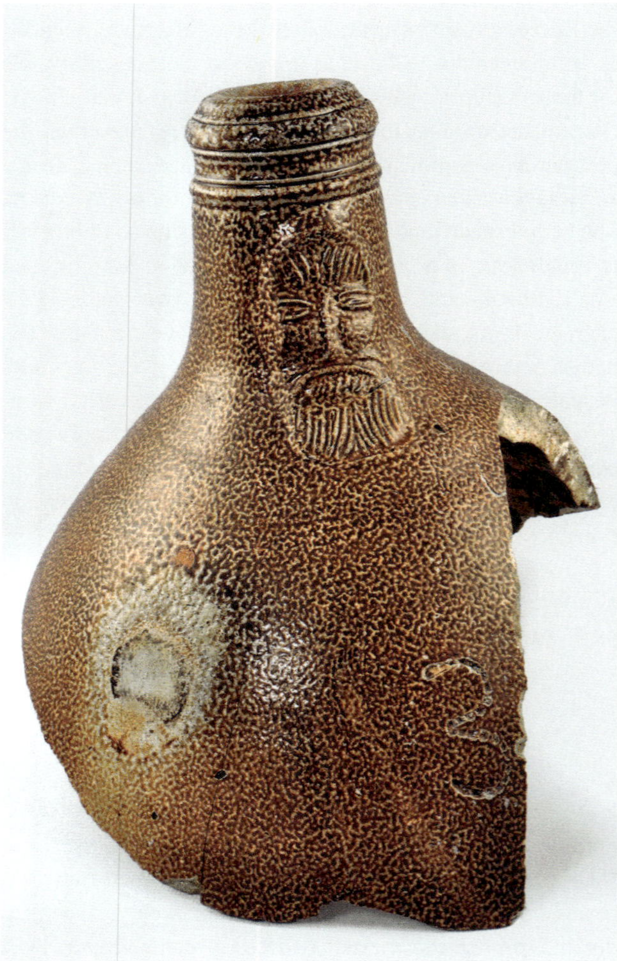

6/24

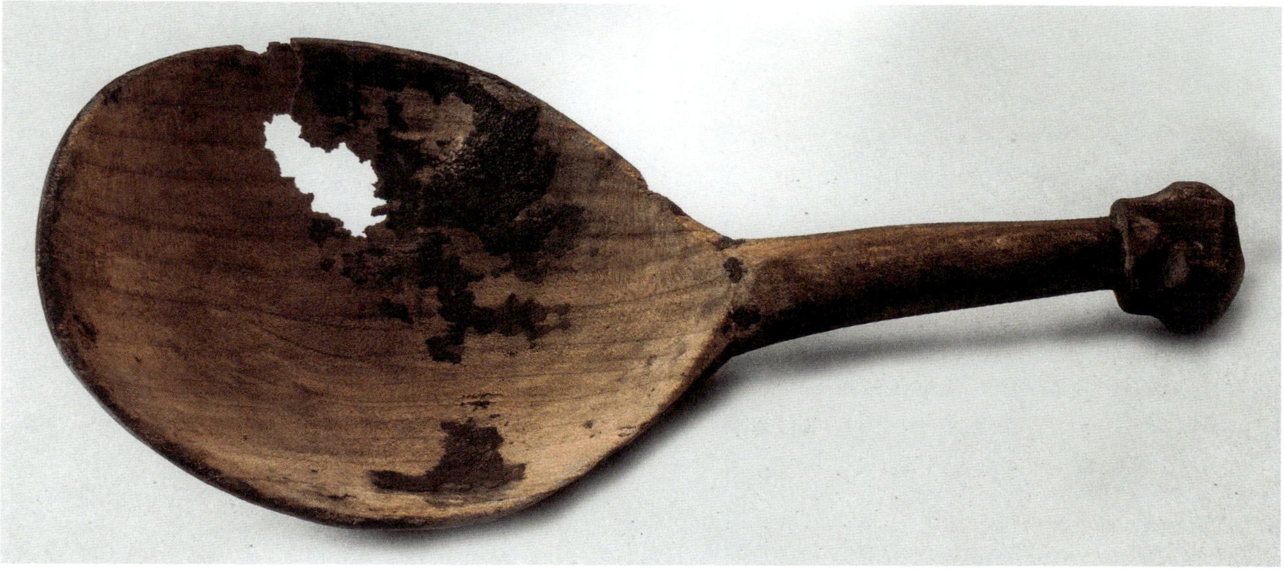

6/26

6/26 **Wooden spoon**
Salvaged from the wreck of the Swedish warship
Prinsessan Hedvig Sofia
Sweden, before 1715
Wood; L 15 cm
Schleswig, Museum für Archäologie Schloss Gottorf,
Landesmuseum Schleswig-Holstein: SH2011-866.92

Spoons made of various materials have been salvaged from many of the shipwrecks in the Baltic Sea region. So far, divers have recovered wood, pewter and even gold spoons dating from the seventeenth and eighteenth centuries. A lot of porridge, groats and stews were eaten aboard ship, making spoons an essential piece of cutlery. All sailors had their own spoons – often ones they had made themselves – and they always carried them with them. The German phrase *den Löffel abgeben* (to hand over or give up one's spoon, slang for dying) has its origins in this custom. When a sailor died, he literally gave up his spoon. Nor could sailors necessarily expect to get warm meals. Every time the hearth was fired up, the ship – being made of wood – was at greater risk of catching fire. The ship's kitchen, or 'galley', was therefore often lined in brick. In heavy seas or shortly before a battle, the kitchen – and the food – stayed cold. TE

6/27 **Repaired clay pipe with a leather sleeve**
Salvaged from the wreck of the Swedish warship
Prinsessan Hedvig Sofia
Sweden, before 1715
Clay, leather; L 14.7 cm
Schleswig, Museum für Archäologie Schloss Gottorf,
Landesmuseum Schleswig-Holstein: SH2011-866.93

This clay pipe had broken in two and been repaired by a creative sailor who fashioned a leather sleeve for it. Burn marks on the bowl indicate that the pipe was used for some time after it was repaired. For a long time, clay pipes were manufactured primarily in Great Britain and the Netherlands. Manufacturer's stamps provide clues as to when they were made. Tobacco was completely unknown in Europe until the late fifteenth century. It was not until expeditions to the Americas that returning sailors introduced tobacco-smoking to Europe, ushering in new cultural customs and consumer behaviours. (Fig. p. 79) TE

6/28 **Knife handle**
Salvaged from the wreck of the Swedish warship
Prinsessan Hedvig Sofia
Sweden, before 1715
Horn; W 2 cm, L 7.1 cm
Schleswig, Museum für Archäologie Schloss Gottorf,
Landesmuseum Schleswig-Holstein: SH2011-866.48

One of the most important work tools aboard ship was the handy knife. Knives and spikes were used to detach rotten or frayed rigging and reconnect the ends. The proper nautical term for this sort of repair was 'rope splicing'. Knife handles

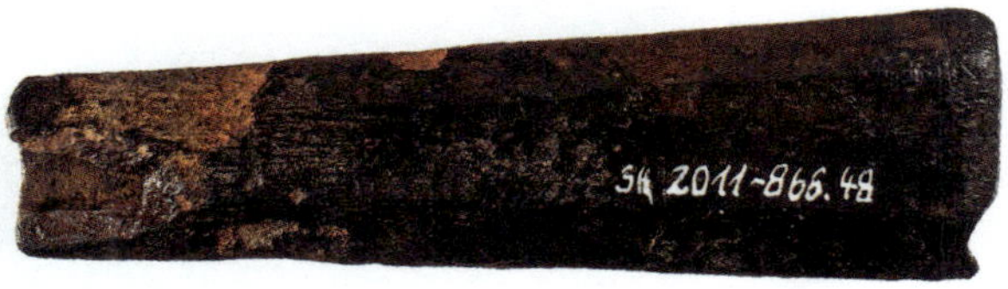

6/28

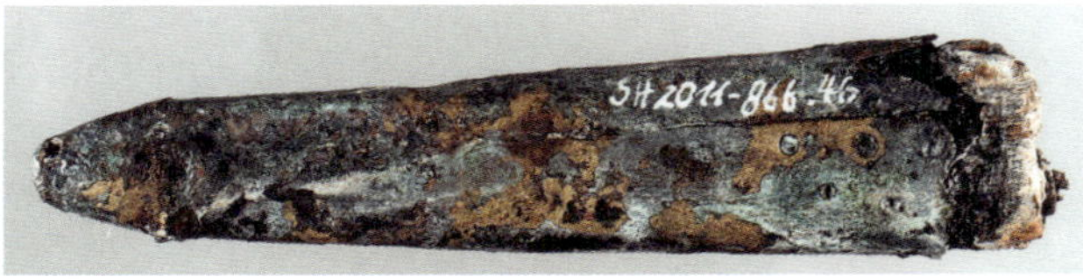

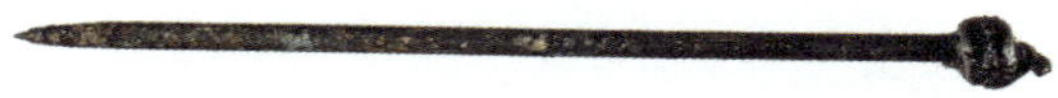

6/29

varied greatly according to the preferences of their owners. For the most part, they were made of wood, bone or horn, which was easy to work. Occasionally, small metal rivets were set in the handle to give it a firmer grip. Not many of these rivets have survived. Because they were made of iron, like the blades, they rusted away as they lay underwater. TE

6/29 **Needle case with needle**
Salvaged from the wreck of the Swedish warship
Prinsessan Hedvig Sofia
Sweden, before 1715
Velvet, iron; W 1.5 cm, L 7 cm; needle: L 2.2 cm
Schleswig, Museum für Archäologie Schloss Gottorf,
Landesmuseum Schleswig-Holstein: SH2008-67.100, SH2011-866.46

Sewing needles were stored in needle cases. This ensured that the needles were out of harm's way and yet easy to access. This case was covered in metal on the outside to protect it from knocks and bumps and was lined with red velvet. Needles could be stuck into the velvet lining easily. While at sea, ships had to be self-supporting for long periods, so it was essential that the crew made all the materials and tools on board last as long as possible. They did their utmost not to lose anything, as it was not easy to get new supplies. This applied not only to wood-working tools, but to sewing equipment, too. TE

6/30 **Leather shoe**
Salvaged from the wreck of the Swedish warship
Prinsessan Hedvig Sofia
Sweden, before 1715
Cowhide, birch bark, birch tar; 13 x 28 x 11.5 cm
Schleswig, Museum für Archäologie Schloss Gottorf,
Landesmuseum Schleswig-Holstein: SH2011-866.91

Sailors' footwear varied according to their rank and responsibilities on board. While the captain and officers mostly wore boots, ordinary seamen had simpler leather shoes with wooden soles. Different types of soles were used, depending on where in the ship the sailor was stationed. Sailors who worked on deck and in the rigging preferred shoes with small heels. These provided a better foothold on the ratlines (rope ladders), making climbing less dangerous. Powder masters, on the other hand, wore 'list slippers' while they worked. The soles of these shoes were not nailed and therefore

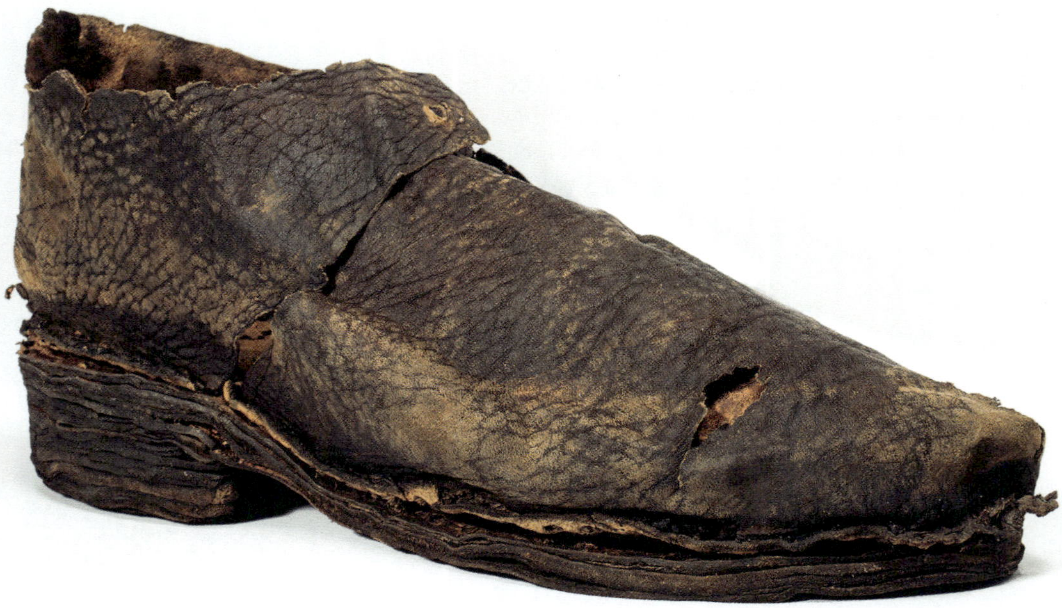

6/30

lacked any metal that might have sparked when they hit the floor, causing the powder to explode. TE

6/31 **Game piece**
Salvaged from the wreck of the Swedish warship
PRINSESSAN HEDVIG SOFIA
Sweden, before 1715
Wood; diam. 1.9 cm
Schleswig, Museum für Archäologie Schloss Gottorf, Landesmuseum Schleswig-Holstein: SH2008-67.122, SH2011-866.94

Board games such as draughts (aka checkers), Nine Men's Morris, and chess were played aboard ship as far back as the eighteenth century. A seaman's chest was often used as a game board, with the playing field carved into the lid with a knife. Because sailors lived on the steerage deck, which tended to be gloomy – every light had the potential to spread fire, after all – it was essential to have game pieces that could be easily distinguished by touch (rather than colour). These pieces, being made of wood, could be easily replaced if they were lost. Games were a popular form of entertainment on board. Sailors, who did not travel with many articles of value, usually played either for money, drink rations, or food rations. Gambling wasn't actually allowed on board, as it tended to undermine morality and discipline, in some cases even leading to fights. Nevertheless, most of the officers permitted gambling or least looked the other way. TE

6/32 **Comb**
Salvaged from the wreck of the Swedish warship
PRINSESSAN HEDVIG SOFIA
Sweden, before 1715
Bone; 6.5 x 1.9 cm
Schleswig, Museum für Archäologie Schloss Gottorf, Landesmuseum Schleswig-Holstein: SH2011-866.58

For the sake of simplicity and probably also tradition, sailors had long hair which they often plaited together into pigtails. Hair was frequently tarred and greased. Sailors consequently used combs to manage their hair and beards. These combs were two-sided, with more widely spaced teeth used to get rid of dirt and tangles, and finer teeth to remove lice and other parasites. Some sailors made their own combs, using materials that were available on board and that could be easily worked with knives. Bone and wood were the most common materials. The size and shape of the combs varied greatly. TE

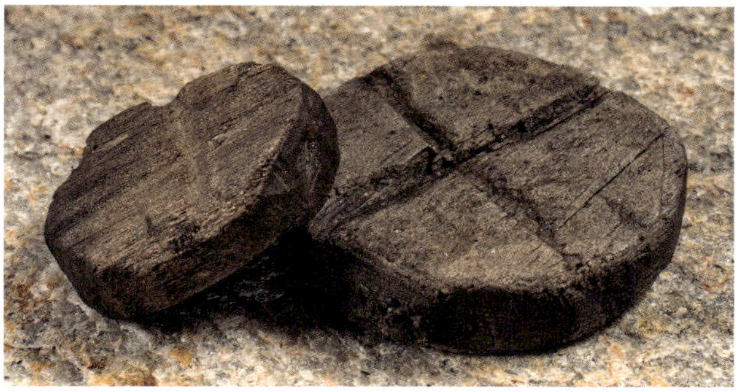
6/31

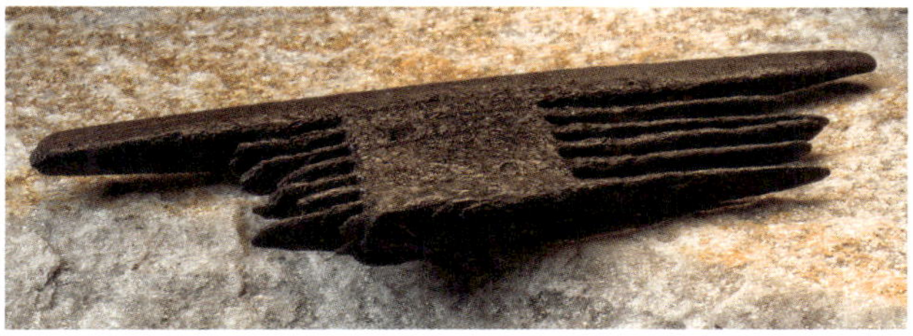
6/32

6/33 **British ship's apothecary**
Kent/England, second half of 19th century
Iron, horn, textile, cardboard, glass; 21.5 x 22.5 x 17.2 cm
Bremerhaven, Deutsches Schiffahrtsmuseum – Leibniz-Institut für deutsche Schifffahrtsgeschichte: I/878/74

Options for medical treatment aboard ship were limited. Sailors consistently suffered from lockjaw (tetanus) and scurvy (vitamin C deficiency) until the mid to late eighteenth century, when lengthy scientific expeditions provided some insight into these diseases, leading to improved medical care aboard ship. The earliest surviving lists of medication date back to 1800 and contain up to 54 different medicines. At this time, ship's apothecaries carried a large number of medicinal herbs and spices. Ginger, for example, has stomach-soothing properties that mitigate seasickness. A mortar and pestle would be used to crush or grind the substances and produce effective blends. The apothecary used wound clamps made of metal as well as other surgical instruments such as tweezers, forceps, and scalpels. The main standby of any ship's doctor, however, remained the bone saw. (Fig. p. 77) TE

7 Slave Trade
The Port of Nantes

The French port of Nantes, located on the estuary of the Loire, profited greatly from its position as a hub of the transatlantic slave trade. Over the entire period of this trade, which extended from the sixteenth to the nineteenth century, about 400,000 ships transported over 13 million people from the coasts of Africa to colonies in the Americas. Approximately 20 per cent of the slave trade was conducted from France, and up to 80 per cent of the French trade used ships whose home port was Nantes. Sugar, a product of slave labour, accounted for around 60 per cent of imports to Nantes. For a time, anyone in Nantes who worked in maritime trade would have been involved directly or indirectly in the slave trade. By the start of the nineteenth century, an estimated 495,000 African men, women and children had been taken across the ocean on slave ships from Nantes.

The legal basis for the French slave trade was the *Code Noir*, drafted under the direction of Jean-Baptiste Colbert and promulgated by King Louis XIV in March 1685. According to the code, slaves were both "creatures of God" and *meubles*, that is, movable goods. Because the actual practice of slavery was banned in France, slaves were only rarely seen in Nantes, despite the fact that in the eighteenth century the entire city lived from the trade. The transatlantic slave trade was a complex operation with three primary routes forming a triangle that spanned the ocean. Ships leaving Europe were loaded with merchandise such as guns, gunpowder, brandy and printed cotton fabrics imported from India. Their first ports of call were trading posts on the coast of West Africa. There, traders exchanged their wares for slaves, who had been brought to the coast from the continent's interior by tribal chieftains and indigenous traders. The slaves were then transported to the Caribbean, where they laboured on plantations under the most dire conditions and without any legal rights, producing sugar, rum, tobacco and cotton. These crops were mainly sold in European towns and cities, completing the last leg of the triangle. Most slave ships began their journey across the Atlantic with 350 to 450 enslaved men, women and children on board. For two months (the length of an average crossing), they were held in steerage, between the enclosed cargo hold and the upper deck. Only rarely were they allowed up on deck to get a breath of fresh air and recover somewhat. These brief periods of relief, termed 'refreshment', were almost entirely done away with following revolts, but were increasingly permitted as the date of sale approached.

The world's only successful slave uprising took place on the French colony of Saint-Domingue in 1791–92. Slavery was consequently banned there, but it was not until the colony prevailed against French forces in 1803 that it gained independence.

There had been efforts in Europe to abolish slavery since the end of the eighteenth century. The abolitionist movement quickly spread from the UK to other European countries, paving the way for the end of slavery and the slave trade. In 1817, trading in slaves was banned in the French colonies. Nevertheless, the merchants of Nantes continued the lucrative business until 1848, when France abolished slavery itself in the colonies. During this period of illegal slave trade, another 193,000 enslaved Africans were taken on French ships to the colonies. Of those ships, 70 per cent came from Nantes. Today, Nantes is actively engaging with this painful part of its past. The city's history museum features exhibits on the topic. There is also a memorial to the abolition of slavery, and information panels and plaques can be found throughout the city. *Dorlis Blume*

Further Reading

David Eltis et al, *The Atlantic Slave Trade; A Database on CD ROM*, Cambridge 1999

Claus Füllberg-Stolberg, *Transatlantischer Sklavenhandel und Sklaverei in den Amerikas*, in: Ulrike Schmieder and Hans-Heinrich Nolte (eds.): *Atlantik. Sozial- und Kulturgeschichte in der Neuzeit*, Vienna 2010, pp. 86–115

Bertrand Guillet, *La Marie-Séraphique. Navire Négrier*, Nantes 2009

Robert Harms, *Das Sklavenschiff. Eine Reise in die Welt des Sklavenhandels*, Kempten 2004

Lawrence Jennings, *French Anti-Slavery. The Movement for the Abolition of Slavery in France. 1802–1848*, Ottawa 2006

Christopher L. Miller, *The French Atlantic Triangle. Literature and Culture of the Slave Trade*, London 2008

Jean-François Niort, *Le Code Noir. Idées reçues sur un texte symbolique*, Paris 2015

Olivier Pétré-Grenouilleau, *Nantes au temps de la traite des Noirs*, Paris 2016

Frédéric Récent et al (eds.), *Libres et sans Fers. Paroles d'esclaves français*, Paris 2016

Dominique Rogers (ed.), *Voix d'esclaves. Antilles, Guyane et Louisiane françaises, XVIIIe–XIXe siècle*, Paris 2016

Michael Zeuske, *Sklaven und Sklaverei in den Welten des Atlantiks 1400–1940. Umrisse, Anfänge, Akteure, Vergleichsfelder und Biographie*, Münster 2006

Michael Zeuske, *Handbuch der Geschichte der Sklaverei. Eine Globalgeschichte von den Anfängen bis zur Gegenwart*, Berlin/Boston 2013

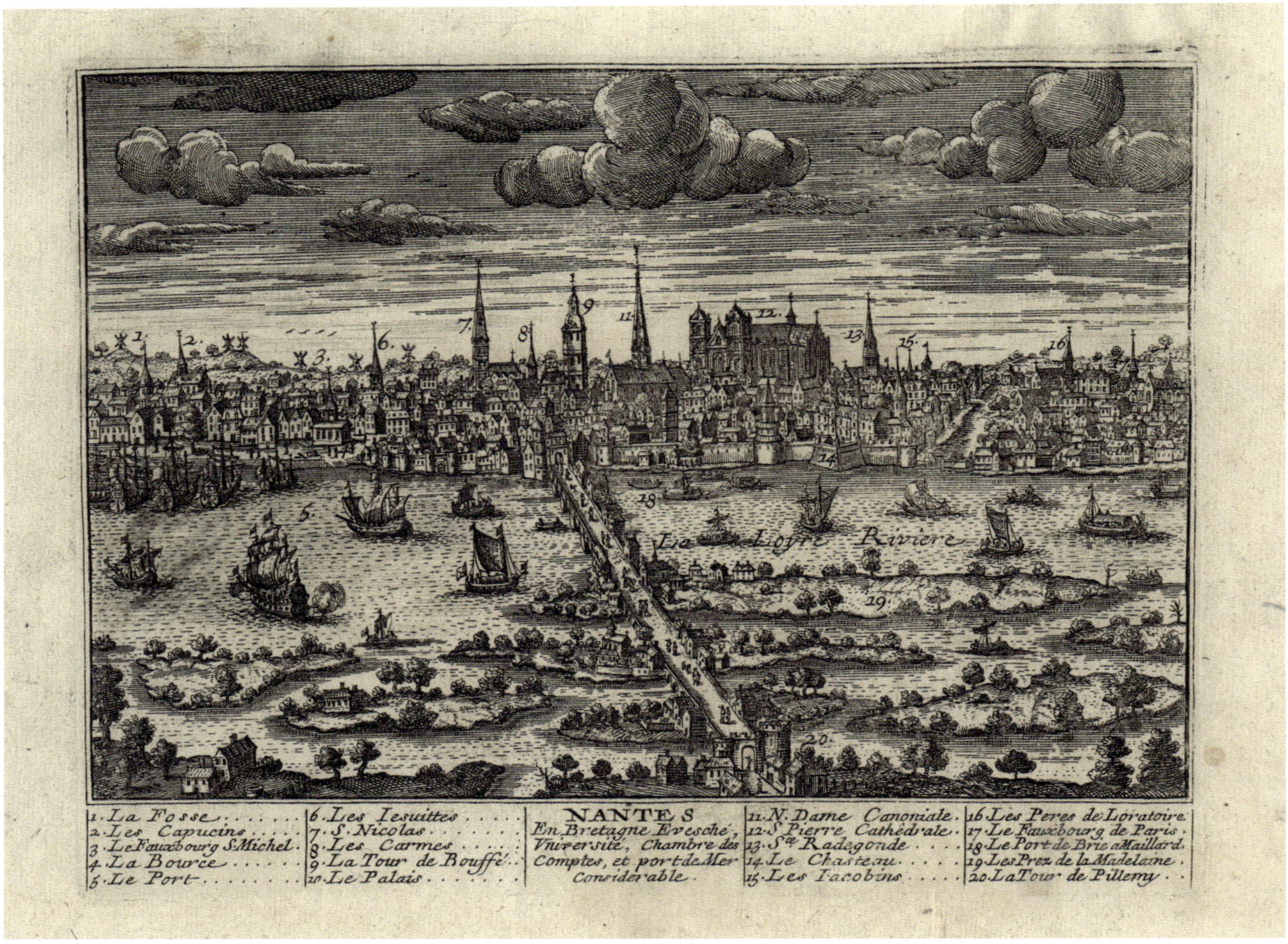

7/1

Nantes – Capital City of the French Slave Trade

7/1 **View of Nantes, seen from the southern bank of the Loire**
Pierre Aveline (1675–1725)
France, c. 1700
Copper engraving; 19.4 x 30.3 cm
Nantes, Château des ducs de Bretagne.
Musée d'histoire de Nantes: 2002.35.2

Even in Gallo-Roman times, Nantes was a city with a flourishing port. It lies on the Loire River, which flows into the Atlantic approximately 30 kilometres to the west. Its heyday as the capital of the Duchy of Brittany lasted from the tenth to the sixteenth century, and ended when Brittany was united through marriage with the Kingdom of France in 1532. Its entry into the slave trade led to an economic boom, which by the eighteenth century had made Nantes France's leading port in the transatlantic slave trade. This copper engraving shows Nantes and its sea port, with the offshore islands of Saulzaie, Gloriette and Madeleine. DB

7/2 **Perspective view of the city of Nantes, as seen from Quai Brancas**
Antoine Hénon (1713–1789)
Nantes, 1767–1771
Nantes, Château des ducs de Bretagne.
Musée d'histoire de Nantes: 939.18.1

The port of Nantes gained new life and prosperity from the royal sanction permitting it to participate directly in the slave trade. Antoine Hénon, an architect in Nantes, sketched the city's transformation in the mid to late eighteenth century. New bridges were built and medieval buildings were torn down to make room for new properties on the pier, where wealthy traders and merchants settled. The Memorial to the Abolition of Slavery, located at Quai de la Fosse and dedicated on 25 March 2012, is quite close to the site shown here. (Fig. p. 82) DB

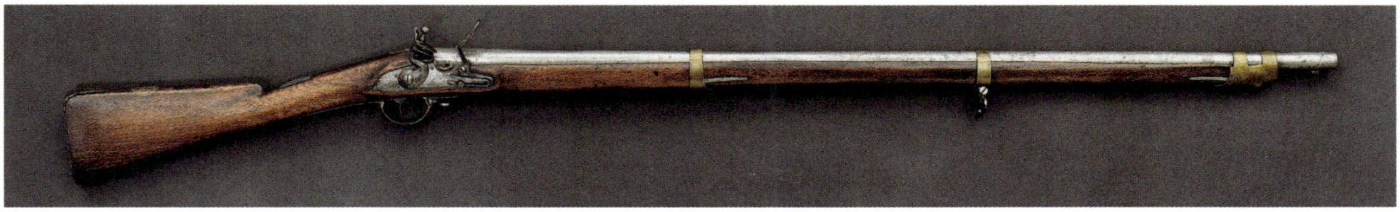

7/5

Transatlantic Slave Trade

7/3 **The *Code Noir* (Black Code) decree**
Jean-Baptiste Colbert (1619–1683), among others
Printed by Prault Père
Paris, 1742
Print; 13.3 x 8cm
Berlin, Staatsbibliothek zu Berlin – Preußischer Kulturbesitz, Benutzungsabteilung: Hs 8741

The *Code Noir*, promulgated in 1685, regulated the treatment of slaves and their legal status in the French colonies. Its main author was Jean-Baptiste Colbert, the chief minister of state under King Louis XIV. After his death, others continued his work. Given the economic importance of slavery and the slave trade, the Code regulated new conditions that arose from considering people as property. It was intended, above all, to clarify practical issues: Who owns the children of slaves belonging to different masters? May slaveholders free children that result from 'concubinage' with their female slaves? May slaveholders mutilate their slaves? Do slaves have to be baptised? The Code remained in force until 1848, when France banned slavery. (Fig. p. 82) DB

7/4 **List of equipment for the slave ship Maréchal de Levis**
France, 6 February 1788
Paper, handwritten; 38.0 x 23.5 cm
Nantes, Château des ducs de Bretagne.
Musée d'histoire de Nantes: 972.1.210

Slaving expeditions required extensive preparations and massive financial investments. Shipowners often formed partnerships with multiple investors, who co-founded the construction, refitting or repair of the ship and helped to purchase cargo for the first leg. The Maréchal de Levis was a Nantes-based ship used for the transatlantic slave trade and fitted out for it by the Michel family, prominent shipowners from Nantes. A third of the cost of the equipment itemised here was borne by the "Widow Michel". The ship carried over one hundred different kinds of merchandise, including calico from Nantes, fabric from the Netherlands and cotton textiles from India. (Exhibit not shown) DB

7/5 **Flintlock muskets**
1750–1800
Steel, iron, brass, wood; each approx.
17.5 x 6.7 x 139.1 cm
Berlin, Deutsches Historisches Museum: W 59/4359, W 59/1344, W 59/1376, W 59/4141, W 59/1291

Flintlock muskets use a flint-striking mechanism to generate a spark, which in turn ignites the gunpowder. This simple technique works fairly reliably in dry weather. All European armies were equipped with these guns from the late seventeenth to the early nineteenth century. Flintlocks were manufactured in craft production throughout most of Europe in large numbers and at low cost. They were also in high demand among slave-trading African rulers, who used them as hunting or war weapons and prized them as status symbols. Popular trading items, they were often found in the cargo of slave ships. Records from 1789 show that in the port of Luango, on the coast of Angola, up to eight muskets were paid for a grown man, and two for a boy. SL

7/6 **Cowrie (*Cypraea moneta*)**
Indian Ocean, probably 18th cent.
Aragonite; diam. c. 1.5 cm each
Berlin, Museum für Naturkunde: ZMB/Moll 240115

Slaving expeditions to Africa took place in several stages, as the ships had to sail to multiple locations before they could fill their holds. Once they had arrived at the slave market, the captain would make contact with local traders and negotiate

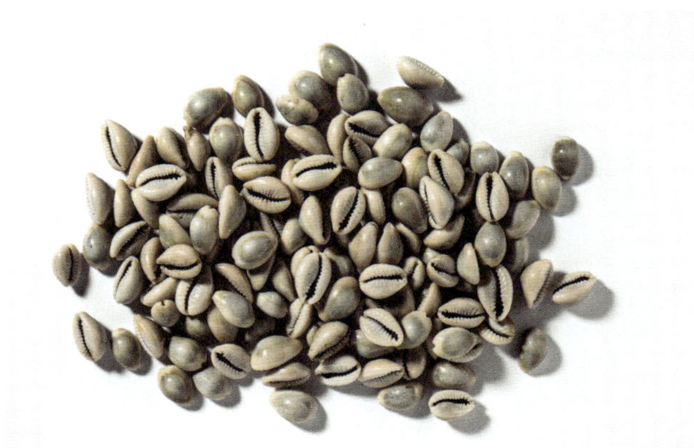

7/6

7/7

prices. In the mid to late eighteenth century, a slave cost between 100 and 300 livres, depending on age and sex. Frequently, however, payment took the form of the equivalent value in goods. For example, cowrie shells (from sea snails) were used as a form of currency and were often traded alongside goods such as fabrics. These shells, well-known for their smooth, porcelain-like surface, had been used as currency in China, India and Africa since approximately 2000 B.C. and were imported by Europeans for trade in Africa. JR

7/7 **Printed cloth**
Probably manufactured by Manufacture Gorgerat
France, 1790
Cotton, printed; 110 x 170 cm
Nantes, Château des ducs de Bretagne.
Musée d'histoire de Nantes: 978.26.3

It was forbidden to trade in or manufacture printed cotton cloth (for example, calico or chintz) in France between 1686 und 1757. Slave ship outfitters, however, found suppliers in the Netherlands, England and Switzerland. After 1758, a number of cotton textile manufacturers (including Langevin, Gorgerat, Favre Petitpierre, Davies, Forestier and Dubern) established factories in Nantes, on the islands of Petite and Grande Biesse in the Loire River. Around 1,200 people worked there, producing about 112,000 cloths per year. A variety of different patterns were printed – some for the European market and some for the African market. Printed cotton cloth made up 60 to 80 per cent of the total cargo value on the outgoing leg of slave ship voyages. DB

7/8 **Map of West Africa, with slave market locations**
Nicolas de Fer (1646–1720)
France, 1700/1725
Print; 53.3 x 73 cm
Nantes, Château des ducs de Bretagne.
Musée d'histoire de Nantes: 972.20.4 (92)

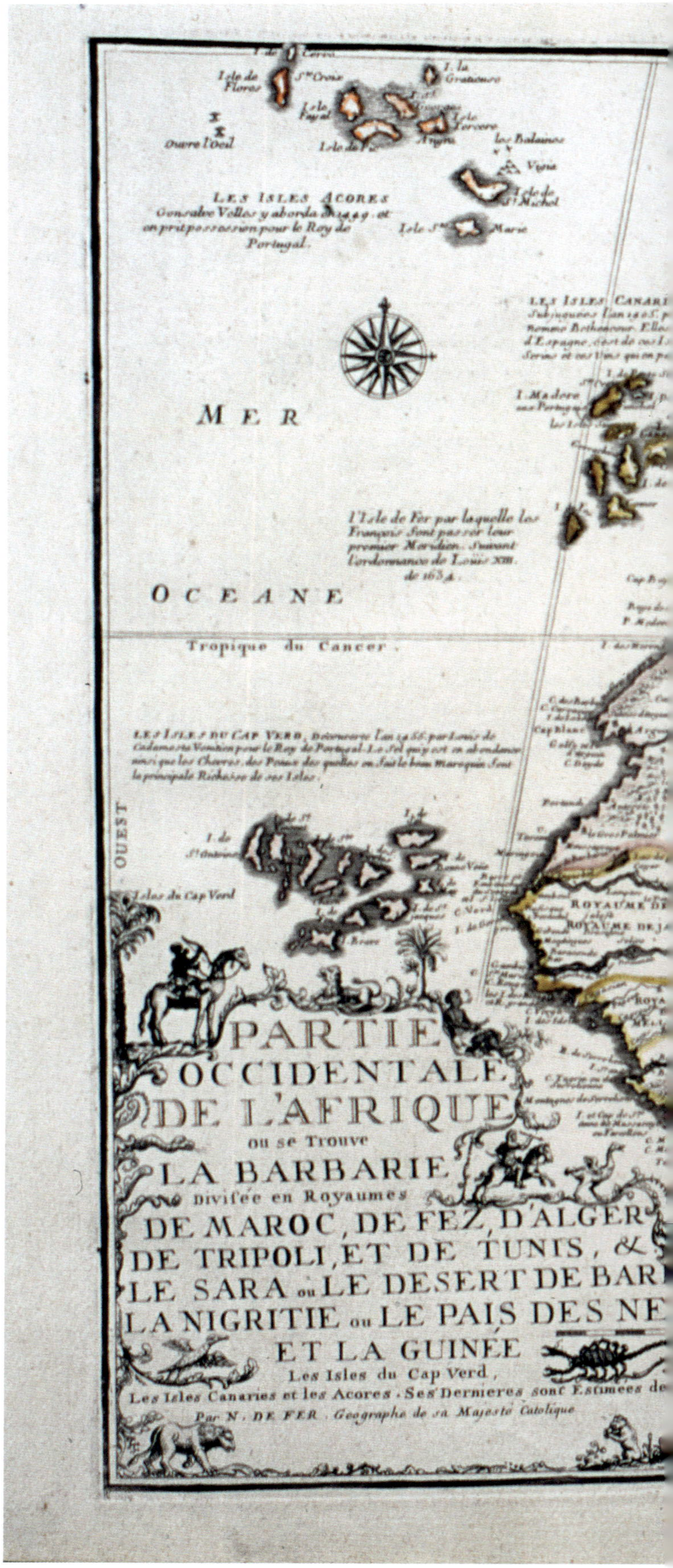

7/8

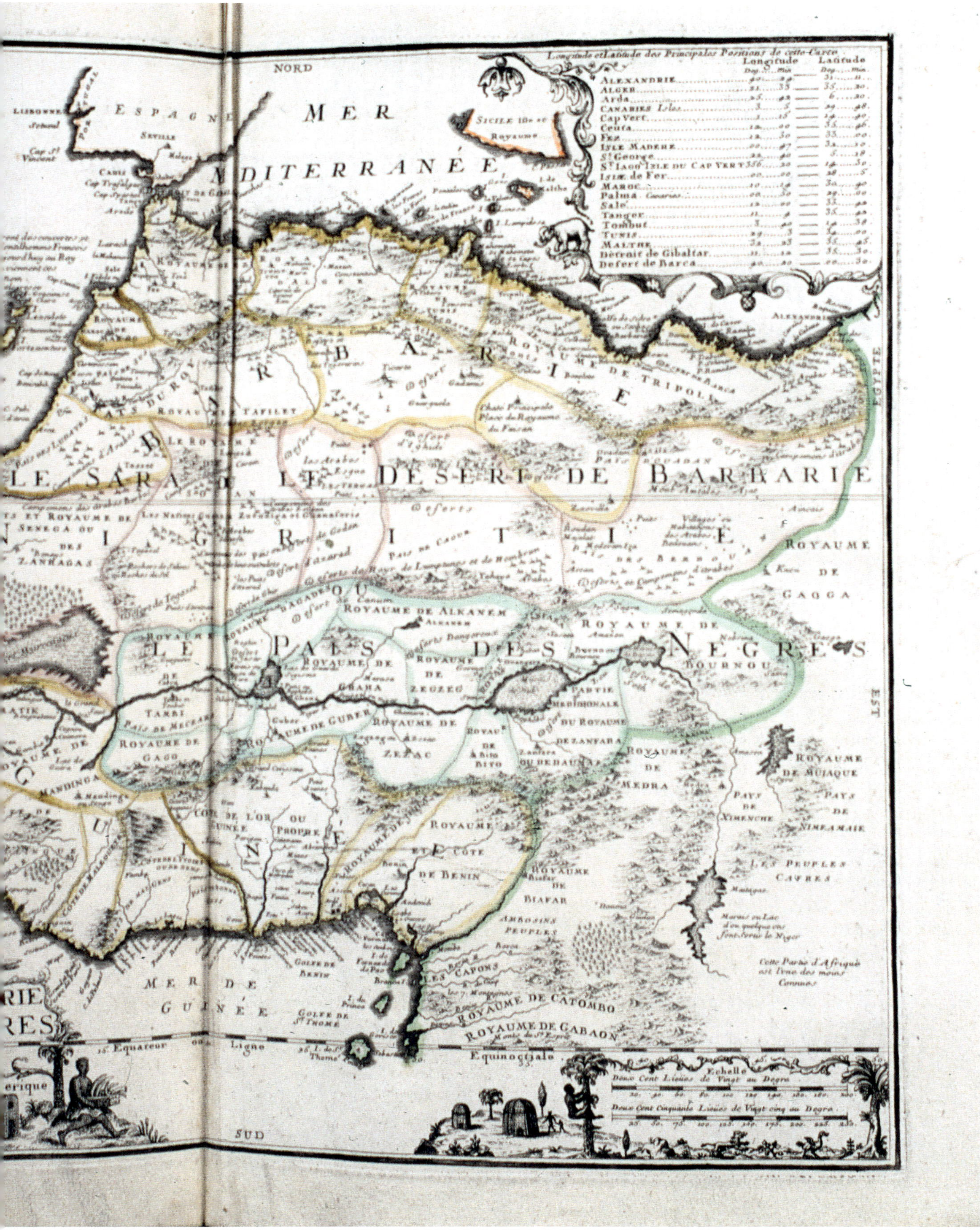
NORD
MER
MEDITERRANÉE
ESPAGNE
SICILE Isle et Royaume
Longitude et Latitude des Principales Positions de cette Carte
Longitude
Latitude
Alexandrie
Alger
Arda
Canaries Isles
Cap Vert
Ceuta
Fez
Isle Madere
St George
St Iago Isle du Cap Vert
Isle de Fer
Maroc
Palma Canaries
Sale
Tanger
Tombut
Tunis
Malthe
Détroit de Gibaltar
Desert de Barca
BARBARIE
ROYAUME DE TRIPOLI
LE SARA OU LE DESERT DE BARBARIE
NIGRITIE
ROYAUME DE GAOGA
ROYAUME DE ALKANEM
LE PAIS DES NEGRES
BOURNOU
ROYAUME DE GUBER
ROYAUME DE GAGO
ROYAUME DE ZEGZEG
ROYAUME DE ZANFARA
ROYAUME DE MEDRA
ROYAUME DE MUJAQUE
PAYS DE XIMENCHE
PAYS DE NIMEAMAIE
LES PEUPLES CAFRES
GUINEE
COTE DE L'OR OU GUINEE PROPRE
ROYAUME ET COTE DE BENIN
ROYAUME DE BIAFAR
AMBOSINS PEUPLES
GOLFE DE BENIN
MER DE GUINEE
GOLFE DE St THOME
ROYAUME DE CATOMBO
ROYAUME DE GABAON
Equateur
Ligne
Equinoctiale
Echelle
Deux Cent Lieües de Vingt au Degré
Deux Cent Cinquante Lieües de Vingt cinq au Degré
Cette Partie d'Afrique est l'une des moins Connues
EST
SUD

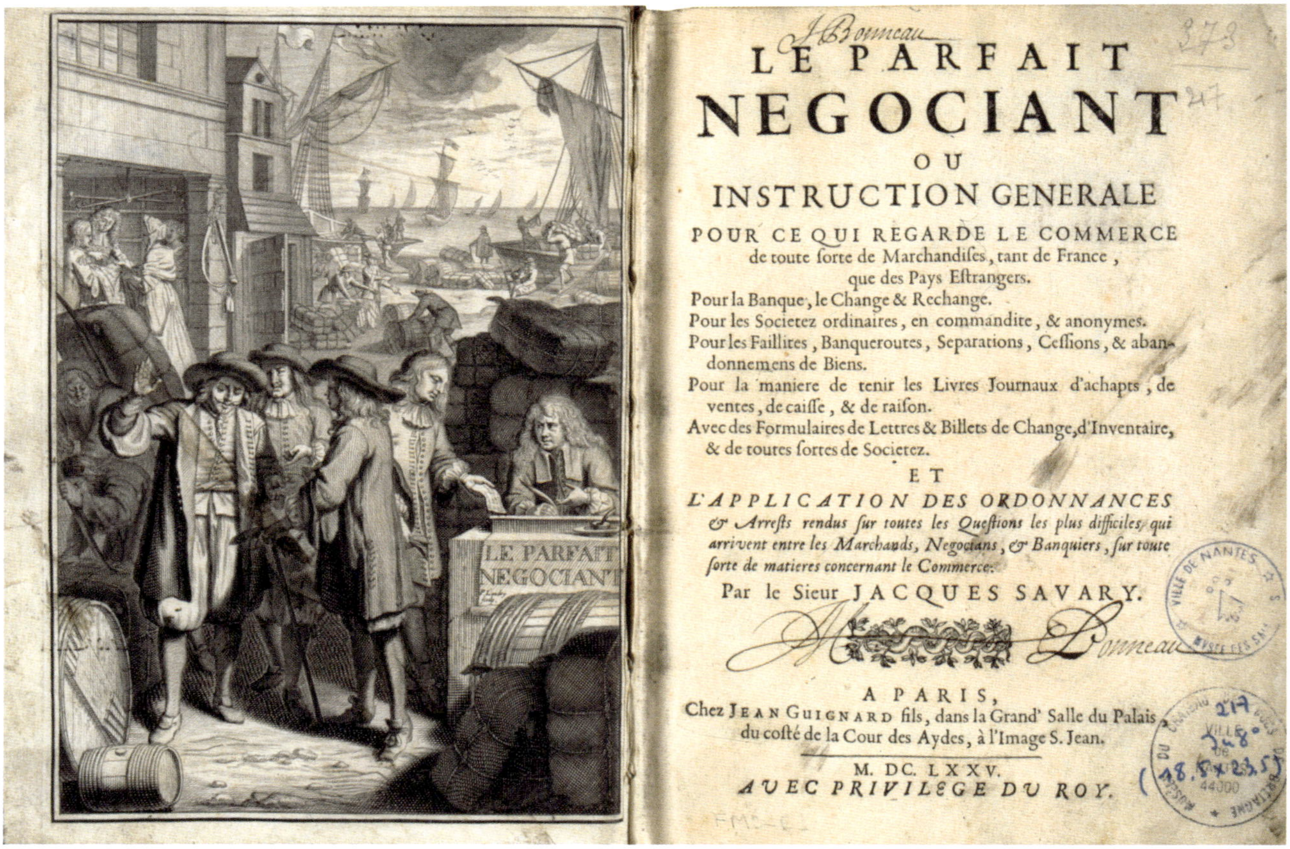
LE PARFAIT NEGOCIANT

LE PARFAIT
NEGOCIANT
OU
INSTRUCTION GENERALE
POUR CE QUI REGARDE LE COMMERCE
de toute sorte de Marchandises, tant de France, que des Pays Estrangers.
Pour la Banque, le Change & Rechange.
Pour les Societez ordinaires, en commandite, & anonymes.
Pour les Faillites, Banqueroutes, Separations, Cessions, & abandonnemens de Biens.
Pour la maniere de tenir les Livres Journaux d'achapts, de ventes, de caisse, & de raison.
Avec des Formulaires de Lettres & Billets de Change, d'Inventaire, & de toutes sortes de Societez.
ET
L'APPLICATION DES ORDONNANCES
& Arrests rendus sur toutes les Questions les plus difficiles qui arrivent entre les Marchands, Negocians, & Banquiers, sur toute sorte de matieres concernant le Commerce.
Par le Sieur JACQUES SAVARY.
A PARIS,
Chez JEAN GUIGNARD fils, dans la Grand' Salle du Palais du costé de la Cour des Aydes, à l'Image S. Jean.
M. DC. LXXV.
AVEC PRIVILEGE DU ROY.

7/9

By the end of the eighteenth century, the entire coast of Africa was lined with slave-trading centres – over 400 in total. These forts and 'factories' (establishments for conducting business in foreign lands) were not a sign of European rule over African lands, but rather were fortified trading posts. This map of the west coast of Africa also shows the locations where French traders preferred to buy slaves: Whydah on the Bay of Benin and Dahomey on the Gulf of Guinea. Starting in the late eighteenth century, their ships made for the more southerly Luango instead, located on the coast of Angola. The map is decorated with idealized depictions of the lives of indigenous people and of exotic animals including tigers, lions, crocodiles, ostriches and scorpions. DB

7/9 ***Le parfait négociant* (The perfect merchant), a manual on trade**
Jacques Savary (1622–1690)
Published by Jean Guignard fils
Paris, 1675
Print; 24.5 x 19.5 cm
Nantes, Château des ducs de Bretagne.
Musée d'histoire de Nantes: FMS.B1.G1

French merchant and civil servant Jacques Savary started out as an administrator in the crown lands and subsequently became a member of the Committee for the Reform of Mercantile Law, convened by chief minister of state Jean-Baptiste Colbert. France's commercial code, the *Code Savary*, published in 1673, was named after him. Savary's manual for merchants and traders, published in 1675, summarised the most important trade laws, rules and regulations, and also provided sales and accounting advice. Because slaves were seen as commodities, the manual was indispensable for slave traders as well. Twenty editions and multiple translations were published, the first German one in 1676. The vignette on the cover depicts a typical scene at the port: while cargo is being unloaded in the background, traders have already begun to sell their wares. DB

7/10 ***Le grand Roy de Monomotapa* (The great king of Monomotapa)**
François Gérard Jollain (1641–1704)
France, 1675/1699
Copper engraving; 38 x 23.3 cm
Nantes, Château des ducs de Bretagne.
Musée d'histoire de Nantes: 2007.7.1

The empire of Mutapa, located in present-day Zimbabwe and Mozambique on the east coast of Africa, acquired its wealth from the tenth century onwards through gold mining

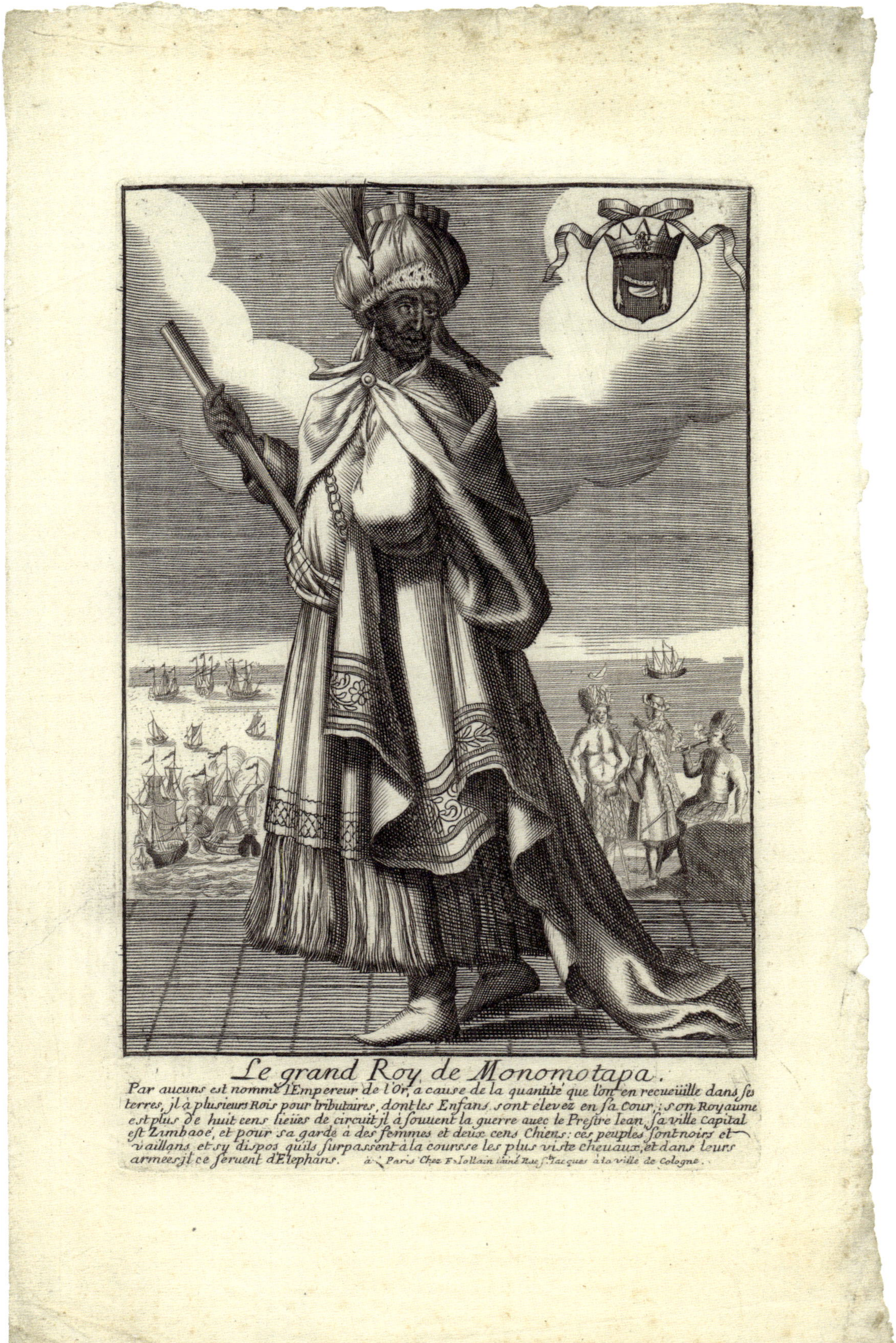
Le grand Roy de Monomotapa.
Par aucuns est nommé l'Empereur de l'Or, à cause de la quantité que l'on en recueüille dans ses
terres, jl à plusieurs Rois pour tributaires, dont les Enfans sont élevez en sa Cour; son Royaume
est plus de huit cens lieües de circuit jl à souuent la guerre auec le Prestre Iean, sa ville Capital
est Zimbaoé, et pour sa garde à des femmes et deux cens Chiens: ces peuples sont noirs et
vaillans et sy dispos quils surpassent à la coursse les plus viste cheuaux, et dans leurs
armees jl ce seruent d'Elephans.
à Paris Chez F. Jollain l'ainé Rue S.t Jacques à la ville de Cologne.

7/10

and trade with India and the Arab world. The King of Mutapa (or Monomotapa) portrayed here is accordingly referred to as the *Empereur de l'Or* (emperor of gold) in the description under the title. Portugal was the first European country to establish trading posts on this coast. In the eighteenth century, traders from Nantes moved their operations here when markets on the West African coast were not able to supply enough men, women and children. This is evident from the western ships in the background of the picture and from the trader speaking with local people. DB

7/11 **Balance sheet for the slave ship Marquis de Bouillé**
14 October 1789 to 15 February 1790
Paper, handwritten; 32.7 x 20.8 cm
Nantes, Château des ducs de Bretagne.
Musée d'histoire de Nantes: 972.1.230

The purchase of slaves on the African coast was a protracted process, with ships usually stopping at several locations along the coast for a total of three to six months until their holds were full. Opening negotiations was an important step in that process and it required meticulous record-keeping, as every slave was bought not in cash, but in commodities whose total value was equivalent to the negotiated price. Tobacco, liquor, guns, silk fabrics and handkerchiefs were among the chief goods in these barters. Since slave ships from Nantes were funded by multiple traders, the balance sheet for the Marquis de Bouillé contained 38 pages listing, for every slave purchased, who the trader was and what goods were exchanged. The page displayed here, for example, shows that an adult, male slave was traded for 2 bundles of tobacco, 8 guns, 4 ounces of liquor, 4 pieces of Indian cloth (called 'siamoises') and 8 handkerchiefs. (Fig. p. 84) DB

7/12 **Design, profile and layout of the slave ship Marie-Séraphique**
Jean-René Lhermitte (1745–1785)
Nantes, c. 1770
Ink and watercolour; 75 x 53 cm
Nantes, Château des ducs de Bretagne.
Musée d'histoire de Nantes: 2005.3.1

The Marie-Séraphique, owned by Jacques-Barthélémy Gruel (c. 1731–1787), a resident of Nantes who originally came from French colony of Saint-Domingue, was first used for the slave trade in 1769. When it moored off Cap Français (Saint-Domingue), it had 307 men, women and children on board, all of whom were to be sold. This drawing, commissioned by the owner of the ship, which he had named after his late wife, provides a realistic picture of the inside of a slave ship. Drinking water and food fill every available space. On the steerage deck, the captives are packed closely together, like goods in a cargo hold, men on one side and women and children on the other. The middle picture shows the ship sailing away from the African coast. The bottom section contains a detailed list of the goods they had brought with them to purchase the slaves, the number of slaves they had been able to acquire, and the prices at which the slaves had been sold. DB

7/13 **Hand shackle**
Probably 18th cent.
Iron; 15.5 x 13.5 x 3.8 cm
Nantes, Château des ducs de Bretagne.
Musée d'histoire de Nantes: 932.13.31

Hand shackles, leg irons, and chains were used by slave traders to keep their 'human commodities' under control. They were used largely on the march from the African interior to forts on the coast, while transporting the captives onto ships, and during negotiations at the point of sale in the Caribbean. Once aboard, chains were only used at the beginning of the journey in order to prevent escape (by jumping overboard). The risk of injuries and infections from the iron shackles was high, and so apart from these times, the captives were put in chains solely as a disciplinary measure after revolts. As a rule, women and children were not chained. (Fig. p. 85) DB

7/14 **Scene depicting the sale of slaves on board the Marie-Séraphique, moored off Cap Français in Saint-Domingue**
France, 1775/1800
Watercolour; 57.9 x 45.2 cm
Nantes, Château des ducs de Bretagne.
Musée d'histoire de Nantes: 950.4.3

Here we see the Marie-Séraphique on its third voyage in the transatlantic slave trade. The upper part depicts the sale of slaves on board the ship. They were presented on the main deck for inspection by buyers. Cap Français was one of Saint-Domingue's most important ports. Slaves were regularly sold here to the owners or managers of sugar, coffee and indigo plantations. The longitudinal section shows the three typical levels of a slave ship: the upper deck for the crew, the steerage deck for the slaves, and below it the hold, where water and food were stored for the crossing. The bottom part of the drawing contains a complete record of the goods brought from Nantes to barter for slaves, the purchases made on the African coast, and the proceeds from the sale in Cap Français. (Fig. p. 87) DB

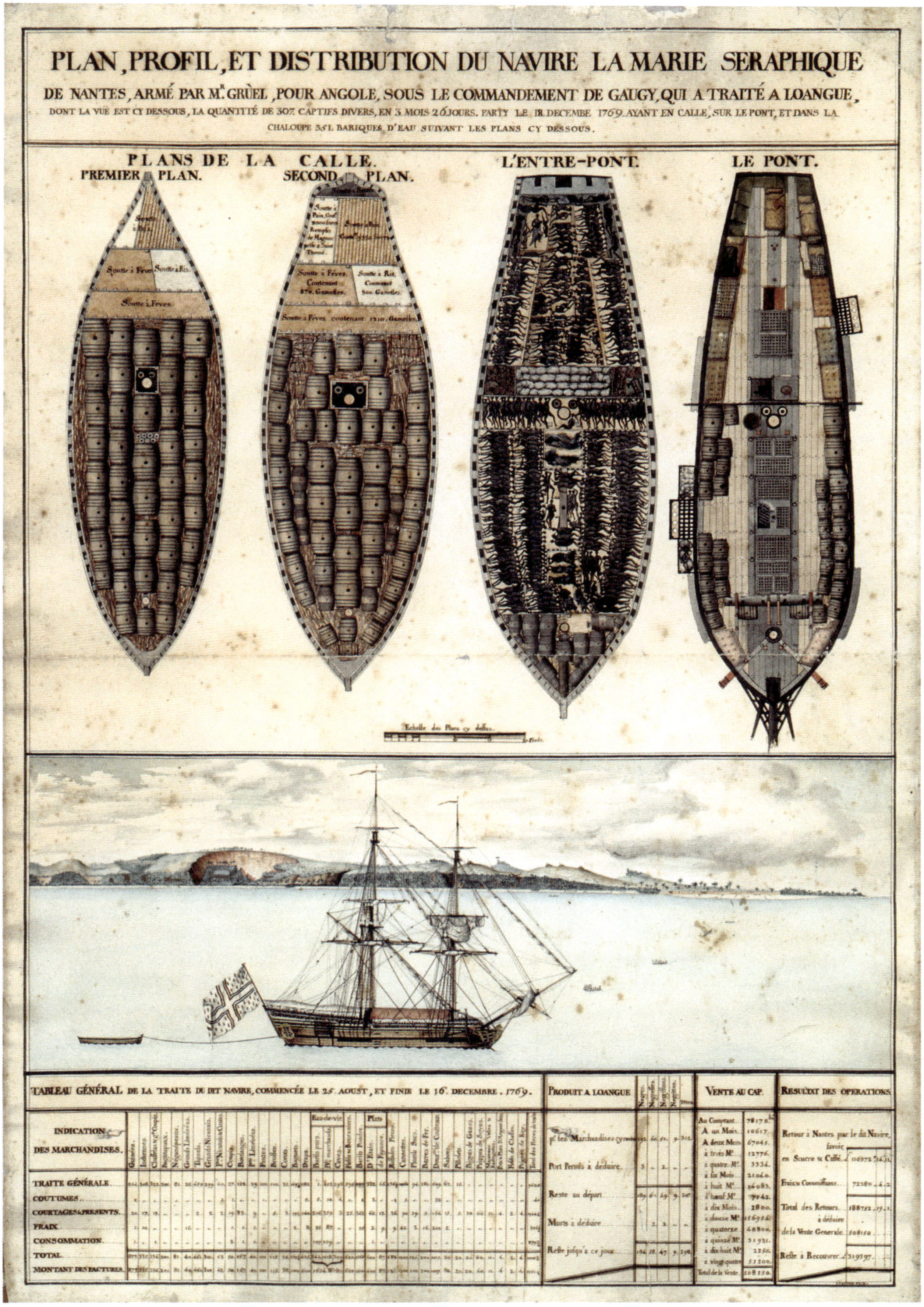
PLAN, PROFIL, ET DISTRIBUTION DU NAVIRE LA MARIE SERAPHIQUE
DE NANTES, ARMÉ PAR Mr. GRÜEL, POUR ANGOLE, SOUS LE COMMANDEMENT DE GAUGY, QUI A TRAITÉ A LOANGUE,
DONT LA VUE EST CY DESSOUS, LA QUANTITÉ DE 307 CAPTIFS DIVERS, EN 3 MOIS 26 JOURS. PARTY LE 18 DECEMBE 1769 AYANT EN CALLE, SUR LE PONT, ET DANS LA CHALOUPE 351 BARIQUES D'EAU SUIVANT LES PLANS CY DESSOUS.
PLANS DE LA CALLE.
PREMIER PLAN.
SECOND PLAN.
L'ENTRE-PONT.
LE PONT.
Soutte à Fèves
Soutte à Ris
Soutte à Fèves contenant 1210 Gamelles
TABLEAU GÉNÉRAL DE LA TRAITE DU DIT NAVIRE, COMMENCÉE LE 25 AOUST, ET FINIE LE 16 DECEMBRE. 1769.
PRODUIT A LOANGUE
VENTE AU CAP.
RESULTAT DES OPERATIONS.
INDICATION DES MARCHANDISES.
TRAITTE GÉNÉRALE
COUTUMES
COURTAGES & PRESENTS
FRAIX
CONSOMMATION
TOTAL
MONTANT DES FACTURES
Port Permis à deduire
Reste au départ
Morts à deduire
Reste jusqu'à ce jour
Retour à Nantes par le dit Navire, savoir
Fraix & Commissions
Total des Retours à deduire
de la Vente Generale
Reste à Recouvrer

7/12

7/15 **Record of sale for 587 men, women and children transported from Angola to Port-au-Prince on the slave ship Père de Famille**
Port-au-Prince, 10 November 1788
Paper, handwritten; 73.5 x 51.7 cm
Nantes, Château des ducs de Bretagne.
Musée d'histoire de Nantes: 944.19.6 (12)

The Père de Famille had a considerable cargo capacity and was able to transport a large number of slaves. This record lists the names of all the purchasers involved in the sale of the 587 people. It also notes how much they paid for each slave and when payment was due. Nine of the slaves are labelled *pacotille*. This term, which has Spanish roots and means package, referred to the share that came to the officers at the end of a slaving expedition. Specifically, the *pacotille* consisted of slaves for the captain, the navigator, the ship's doctor, and the shipowner himself. They selected the youngest and strongest of the men for themselves. (Exhibit not shown) DB

7/16 **Receipt for the purchase of a slave, made out to the captain of the slave ship Sainte-Anne**
Saint Marc, 18 June 1787
Paper, handwritten; 23.9 x 18.7 cm
Nantes, Château des ducs de Bretagne.
Musée d'histoire de Nantes: 992.13.2

As noted on the receipt, a price of 2,600 livres was paid for an adult, male slave from the Nantes ship Sainte-Anne at an auction in Saint-Domingue in 1787. This was not an unusual price in the late eighteenth century for men who appeared to be strong enough for plantation work. Receipts like these testify to the high prices that slaves fetched on the Antilles islands and to the large profits that could be made – slaves purchased on the West African coast cost just 100 to 300 livres. The annual income of an unskilled worker of the time was 300 livres. It often took plantation owners several years to made good the costs they incurred from purchasing slaves. (Exhibit not shown) DB

Abolition of Slavery

7/17 ***Vue des 40 jours d'incendie des habitations de la plaine du Cap Français. Arrivée le 23 Aout 1791.* (View of the 40-day fire that burned down plantations on the plains of Cap Français. Broke out on 23 August 1791)**
Jean Baptiste Chapuy (1760–1802)
France, 1795
Copper engraving, coloured; 52.2 x 72.5 cm
Nantes, Château des ducs de Bretagne.
Musée d'histoire de Nantes: 2007.1.2

The slave uprising on the French colony of Saint-Domingue started on 23 August 1791 and continued until June 1792. Fires and devastation were widespread. Peace was restored in the summer of 1792, when the French revolutionary government recognized the political equality of whites and free blacks. Under pressure from new representatives, France's National Convention abolished slavery in Saint-Domingue in 1793 and extended the ban to France's other colonies in 1794 – a decision that was reversed in 1802 by Napoleon Bonaparte (1769–1821) in his capacity as First Consul. In 1804, Saint-Domingue declared independence under its new name of Haiti. Engravings like the one shown here were made to satisfy the appetite of Europeans for illustrations of significant events. Chapuy embellished the image with dramatic and aesthetic elements aimed at increasing its sales value. Some of the stylistic devices seen here, such as the night view and the blazing flames in the foreground, had been used to great effect in his earlier drawing of the eruption of Mount Vesuvius in 1779. DB

7/18 ***Traite des Nègres* (The slave trade)**
After George Morland (1763–1804)
Paris, 1791/99
Copper engraving; 41.8 x 49.2 cm
Nantes, Château des ducs de Bretagne.
Musée d'histoire de Nantes: 989.11.2

This engraving is a somewhat modified and simplified copy of the painting *The Slave Trade* by the English painter George Morland. Also known by the title *Execrable Human Traffic*, it shows a black man being captured by European sailors. The scene was intended to depict the inhumanity of the slave trade and to strengthen support for the abolitionist movement (that is, the movement to abolish, or ban, the slave trade). The image was circulated widely throughout Europe, and in France a statement against the slave trade was added to the engraving: "Quel Contrat infâme, L'un Marchande Ce qui n'appartient à Personne. L'autre Vend la Propriété De la Nature" (What an

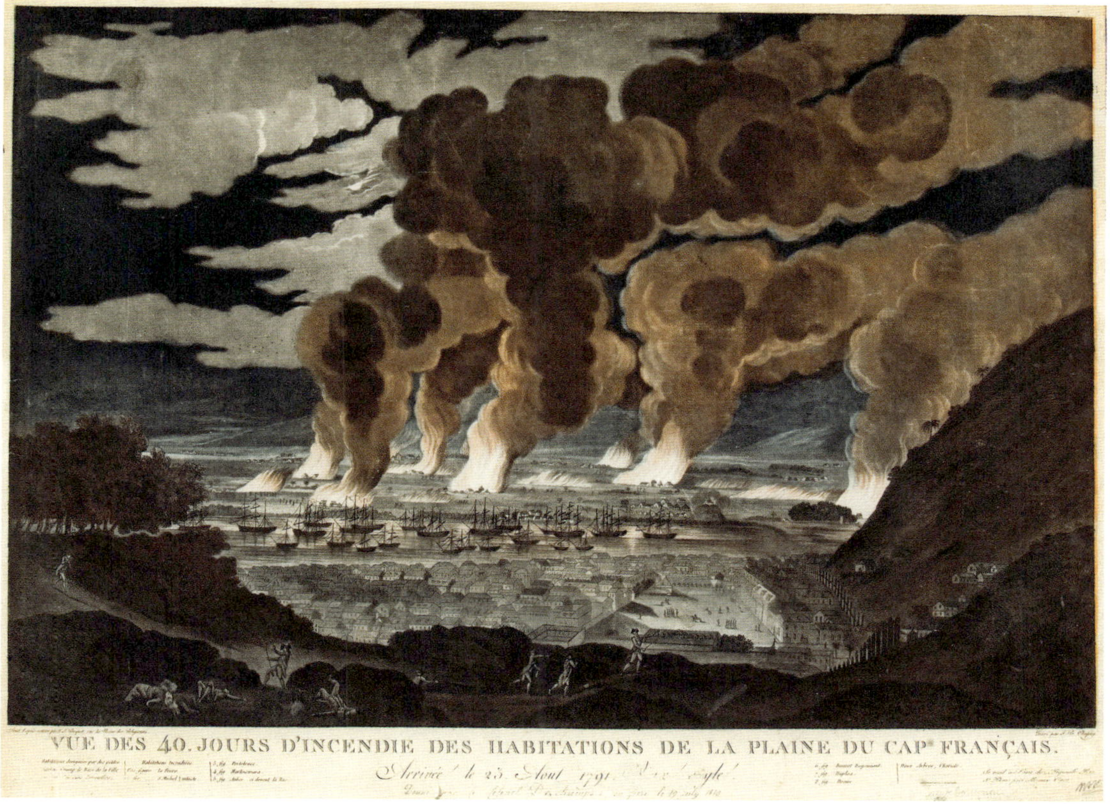
VUE DES 40. JOURS D'INCENDIE DES HABITATIONS DE LA PLAINE DU CAP^e FRANÇAIS.

7/17

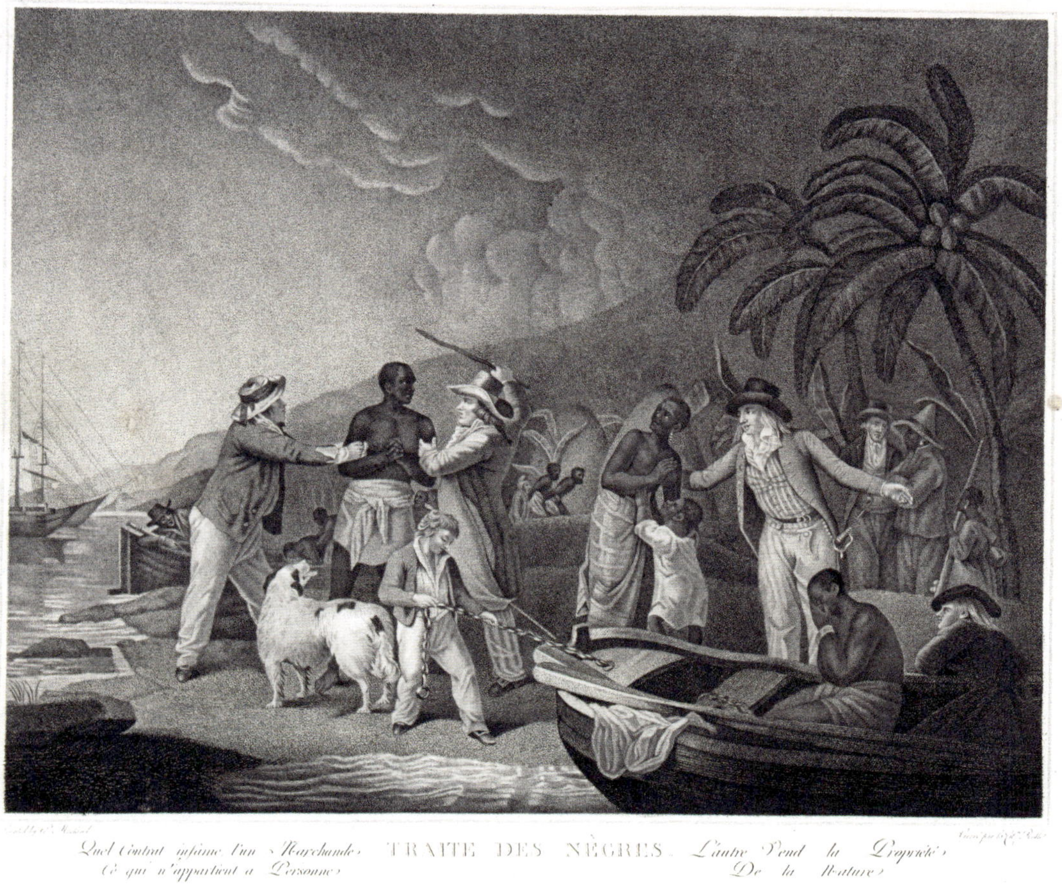
Quel Contrat infâme l'un Marchande
Ce qui n'appartient a Personne
TRAITE DES NÈGRES
L'autre Vend la Propriété
De la Nature

7/18

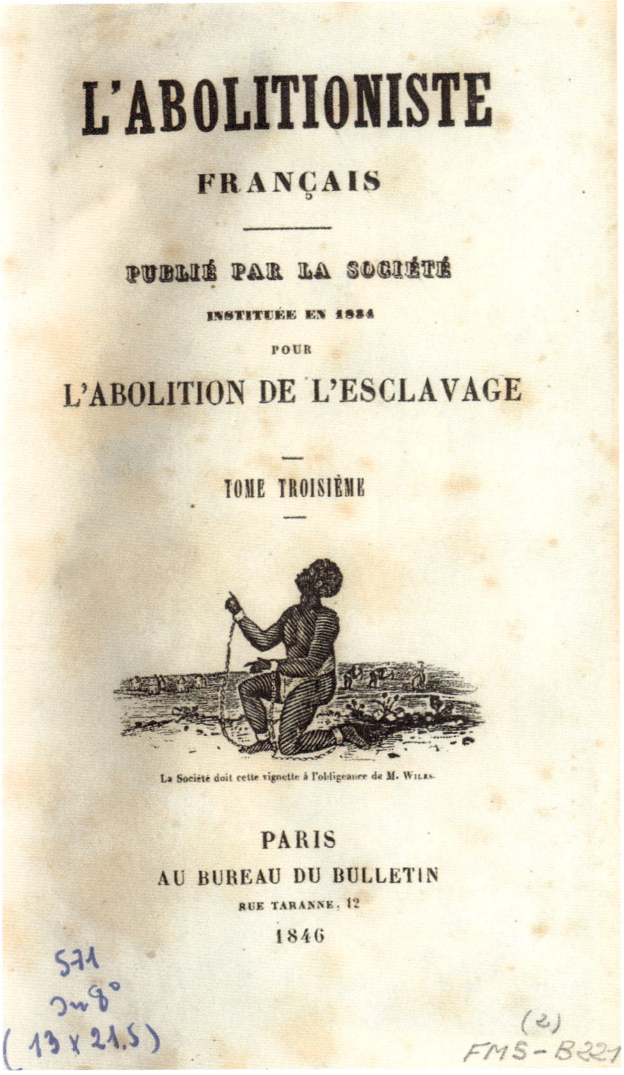

L'ABOLITIONISTE
FRANÇAIS

PUBLIÉ PAR LA SOCIÉTÉ
INSTITUÉE EN 1834
POUR
L'ABOLITION DE L'ESCLAVAGE

TOME TROISIÈME

La Société doit cette vignette à l'obligeance de M. Wilks.

PARIS
AU BUREAU DU BULLETIN
RUE TARANNE, 12
1846

7/19

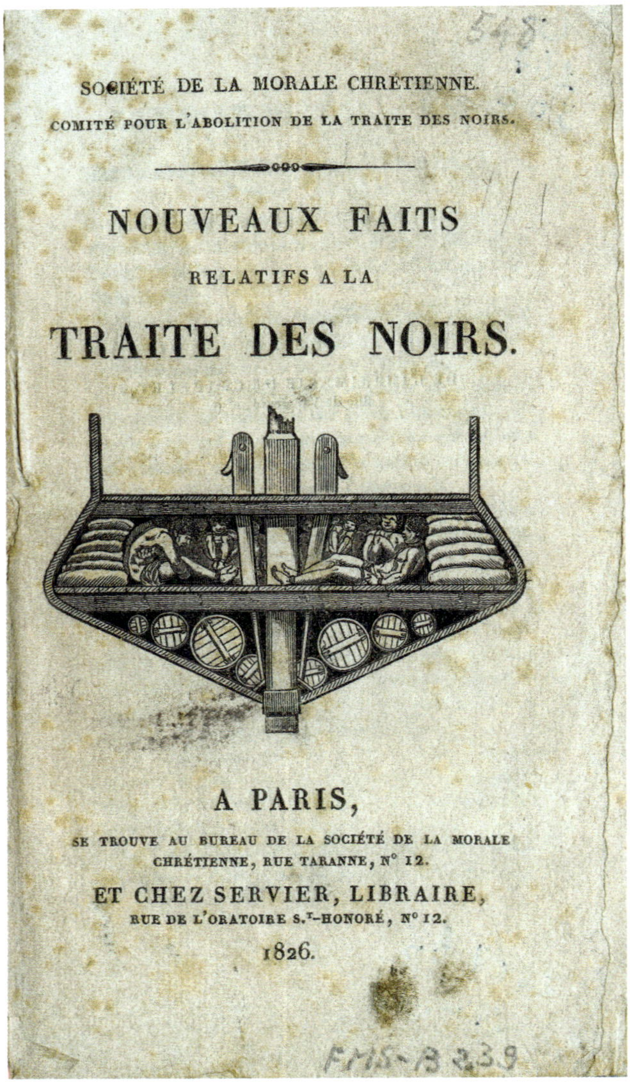

SOCIÉTÉ DE LA MORALE CHRÉTIENNE.
COMITÉ POUR L'ABOLITION DE LA TRAITE DES NOIRS.

NOUVEAUX FAITS
RELATIFS A LA
TRAITE DES NOIRS.

A PARIS,
SE TROUVE AU BUREAU DE LA SOCIÉTÉ DE LA MORALE CHRÉTIENNE, RUE TARANNE, N° 12.
ET CHEZ SERVIER, LIBRAIRE,
RUE DE L'ORATOIRE S.T-HONORÉ, N° 12.
1826.

7/20

abominable contract, one person haggles for that which belongs to no-one. The other sells the property of nature). DB

7/19 ***L'Abolitioniste Français* (The French abolitionist)**
Cover page of the magazine published by the French Society for the Abolition of Slavery
Cover vignette: Mark Wilks (1759–1831)
Printed by E. Duverger
Paris, 1846
Print; 20.7 x 12.3 cm
Nantes, Château des ducs de Bretagne.
Musée d'histoire de Nantes: FMS.B221.V2.T3.G7

The Société française pour l'abolition de l'esclavage (French Society for the Abolition of Slavery) was founded in December 1834. Victor Schœlcher (1804–1893), a fierce advocate of abolitionism, was an active member, alongside other intellectuals and politicians such as Alexis de Tocqueville (1805–1859), Alphonse de Lamartine (1790–1869), Victor de Broglie (1785–1870) and Alexandre Ledru-Rollin (1807–1874). The society's seal, showing a supplicant slave in chains, was similar to that of the English abolitionist society but without their motto, "Am I Not a Man and a Brother?" DB

7/20 **Pamphlet produced by the slave trade abolition committee of the "Société de la morale chrétienne": *Nouveaux faits relatifs à la traite des Noirs* (New facts regarding the slave trade)**
Printed by Servier
Paris, 1826
Print; 20.8 x 13.9 cm
Nantes, Château des ducs de Bretagne.
Musée d'histoire de Nantes: FMS.B239.G1

The *Société de la morale chrétienne*, founded by Protestants in 1821, supported the efforts of the abolitionists, who had been

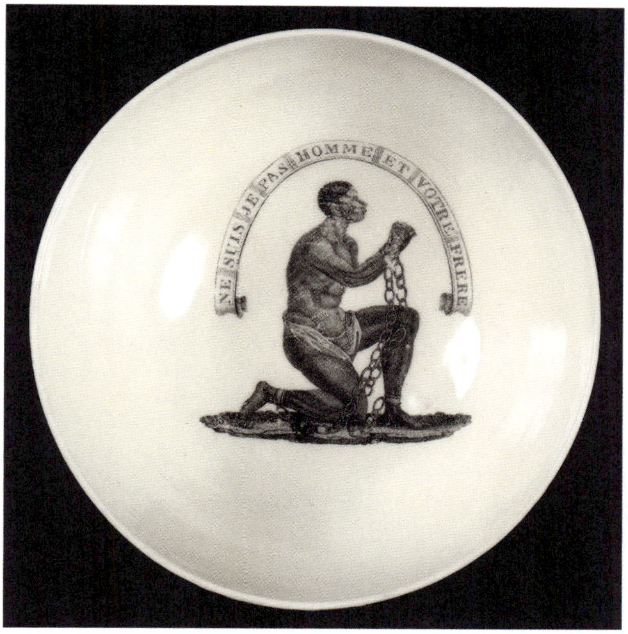

7/21

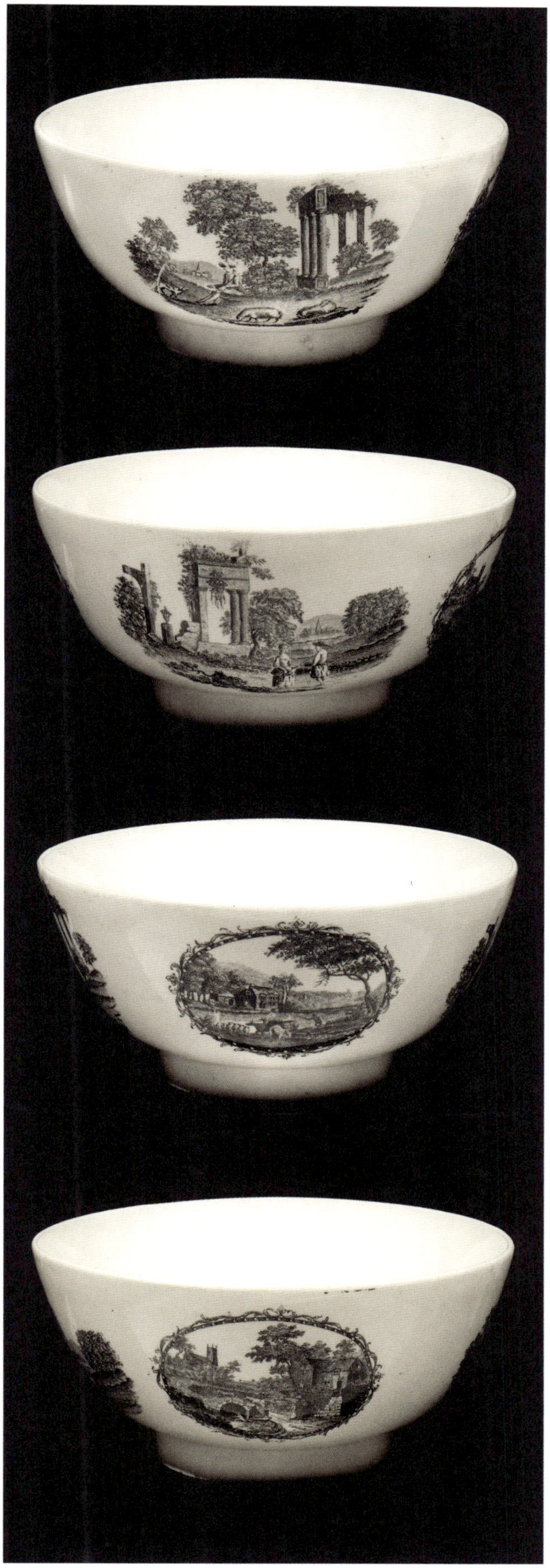

working to ban slavery and slave trade around the world since the late eighteenth century. The group published numerous pamphlets on the slave trade, among them translations of works by the Englishman Thomas Clarkson (1760–1846). In 1787, together with Granville Sharp (1735–1813), he had founded the Society for Effecting the Abolition of the Slave Trade, a pioneering organization in the abolitionist movement. This engraving, accompanied by a description of the transatlantic crossing, is a copy of an illustration of the English slave ship Brookes which appeared in one of Clarkson's books in 1788. DB

7/21 **Bowl promoting the French abolitionist movement**
Manufacture de Creil
Creil, 1808/1818
Fayence; 8.5 x 18 cm
Nantes, Château des ducs de Bretagne.
Musée d'histoire de Nantes: 2008.35.1

The centre of this bowl features the main symbol of the abolitionist movement. The movement aimed to ban, or abolish, the slave trade, and was spearheaded in England by the Society for Effecting the Abolition of the Slave Trade, formed in 1787. A French offshoot of the society was launched in 1788. The inscription ("Ne suis-je pas homme et votre frère") echoes the English society's slogan, "Am I Not a Man and a Brother?" Abolitionists frequently had this motto and figure printed on their pamphlets, and the English entrepreneur Josiah Wedgwood (1730–1795) produced large numbers of medallions with the same figure. Porcelain bowls and plates were also popular and sold by adherents of abolitionism in many countries and languages. DB

8 Global Economy
The Port of London

Great Britain was the driving force in the development of ever more modern trading systems and of global interconnection in the long nineteenth century. Through its widespread network of maritime bases, the "seaborne empire" was in an optimal position to dominate global trade routes. London had been an important port even in Roman times, with easy access to the sea through the Thames estuary, which ultimately allowed it to grow into a world metropolis. By 1900, it was home to more than six million people.

European countries began importing goods from overseas around the end of the fifteenth century. They had no scruples about exploiting the lands that they later colonised and the people who already lived or were taken there. The products referred to as "colonial goods" were initially classed as luxury items, but over time they became cheaper as the quantity of imports increased. Coffee, tea, chocolate, tobacco and cotton permanently changed Europeans' drinking and eating habits and their clothing fashions. Things that were foreign at first soon became part of their own culture. The raw materials were brought by ship. Since the merchandise arrived in large quantities, not all of which could be resold immediately, temporary storage facilities were needed. In London, this led to the creation of the Docklands: vast areas of docks and warehouses, which were built and extended between 1800 and 1828. This phase began with the West India Docks and the East India Docks, named after the origins of the goods that were stored there. In Germany, the North Sea port of Hamburg on the River Elbe later acquired similar importance. As Germany's largest port, it was enlarged between 1883 and 1927 with the construction of the Speicherstadt, a duty-free zone with warehouses, which henceforth played a key role in the transit of merchandise destined for the interior.

The Industrial Revolution that began in the Great Britain around the turn of the nineteenth century created new technological opportunities and changed Europe's economic orientation in the world. The invention of the steam engine caused commodity prices to fall and improved the quality of products. It became increasingly feasible and profitable to import raw materials, mostly for processing in European factories. The finished products were sold all over the world. As Europe developed ever greater capacity to reduce manufacturing costs, it also began exporting technical equipment overseas.

In the course of the nineteenth century, sailing ships were gradually superseded by steam ships. The use of iron and steel in the new ships changed their size and appearance. Visionary maritime construction projects such as the Great East-

ERN, the largest ship in the world at the time, also required huge investments, so companies were formed to raise funds from shareholders. For the first time, it became possible to undertake long sea voyages according to a calculated timetable, because steam power allowed ships to progress independently of the wind. Schedules were printed with fixed departure and arrival times, while new sea routes were created by digging canals. Opened in 1869, the Suez Canal shortened the journey between Asia and Europe by up to 3,400 nautical miles – a third of the previous distance. This increased the importance of the Mediterranean Sea as an international waterway.

New maritime postal services and the need for ever faster communication led to the enlargement of the telegraph network, beginning with the United Kingdom. The transatlantic cable laid undersea in 1858 physically connected two continents for the first time. Submarine cables have now become central to modern communications and they carry around 95 per cent of global Internet traffic. Shipping continues to play a crucial role in the economic integration of the world. Internationally recognised norms and standards, universal time, and standardised transportation units such as the shipping container – we owe them all to the global maritime economy. *Thomas Eisentraut*

Further Reading

Sven Beckert, *King Cotton. Eine Geschichte des globalen Kapitalismus*, Munich 2014

Jonathan Betts, *Harrison*, London 2007

Eberhard Petzold and Sebastian Meißner, *Güterströme der Welt. The Global Cargo Flow*, Hamburg 2017

Alexander Klose, *Das Container-Prinzip. Wie eine Box unser Denken verändert*, Hamburg 2009

Olaf Preuß, *Eine Kiste erobert die Welt. Der Siegeszug einer einfachen Erfindung*, Freiburg 2010

Steven Brindle, *Brunel: The Man Who Built the World*, London 2005

Olaf Matthes (ed.), *Stadt Bild Wandel. Hamburg in Fotografien 1870–1914/2014*, Hamburg 2015

Jürgen Osterhammel, *Die Verwandlung der Welt. Eine Geschichte des 19. Jahrhunderts*, Munich 2009

Peter Wende, *Das Britische Empire. Geschichte eines Weltreichs*, Munich 2008

Reinhard Wendt, *Vom Kolonialismus zur Globalisierung. Europa und die Welt seit 1500*, Paderborn 2016

British Dominance

8/1 **Red Ensign, national flag of British naval and merchant ships at sea**
Great Britain, 2017
Polyester fabric, hand-sewn; 137 x 274 cm
Berlin, Deutsches Historisches Museum

No other national symbol evokes the dominance of Great Britain in the nineteenth century as potently as the flag then flown by its merchant ships at sea, the Red Ensign. In 1674, an earlier version was officially confirmed as the flag of English merchant ships by King Charles II (1630–1685). Over the centuries, the design changed several times. It was also one of three flags used by the Royal Navy until 1864 and thus became a visible expression of the close connection between economic and military interests. The sea routes were the real lifelines of the British Empire. The British colonies and protectorates scattered around the globe mainly bordered on the sea and were therefore easily accessible by ship. Every British ship flew the Red Ensign as the recognised signal of its nationality. During the long nineteenth century, European expansionism fuelled a race for overseas colonies. The long-term negative consequences of this unilateral exploitation of other countries are still evident today. (Exhibit not shown) TE

8/2 **Slaves in a sugar factory**
Curieuse aenmerckingen der bysonderste Oost- en West-Indische verwonderens-waerdige dingen: nevens die van China, Africa, en andere gewesten des werelds, vol. 1
Simon de Vries (1624–1708)
Original artist: Romeyn de Hooghe (1645–1708)
Utrecht, 1682
Etching; 22 x 27.5 cm
Berlin, Staatsbibliothek zu Berlin – Preußischer Kulturbesitz, Abteilung Historische Drucke: Uz 20924

This etching shows sugar cane being harvested and processed on a Brazilian plantation. Sugar cane originally grew in South and Southeast Asia. From India it was brought along the early trade routes to the Orient and thence to Europe. In the course of European expansion, it was taken on ships to overseas colonies. It is thought that Christopher Columbus (1451–1506) brought the first sugar cane seedlings to the Caribbean islands. The climate there proved highly conducive to the growth of the plants, as the Europeans quickly recognised. Soon they were creating large plantations on which sugar cane was grown along with some other crops. From the late sixteenth century onwards, the workforce consisted mainly of African slaves. In an environmental context, this transfer and spread of plants and animals by Europeans is known as the Colombian Exchange. Not only did they bring food plants such as potatoes, maize and tomatoes back to Europe, they also introduced animals such as horses, goats and pigs to the Americas. (Fig. p. 81) TE

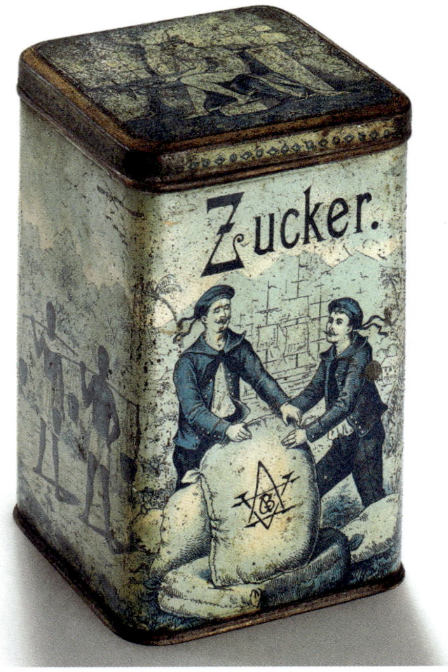

8/3

8/3 **Metal box for storing sugar**
Germany, 1900/1930
Iron; 13.7 x 8.8 x 8.8 cm
Berlin, Deutsches Historisches Museum: AK 94/516.5281

Sugar was exclusively an imported commodity until the end of the eighteenth century. It was shipped to Europe mainly from the West Indies. The sugar was brought on board in sacks and crates. In the "colonial good shops" of Europe, it was sold in smaller quantities by weight. Often it was prepacked in metal boxes because they could be tightly closed, kept moisture out, and did not break. Cane sugar had been known to Europeans since Antiquity. In the Roman Empire, it was imported as a luxury product from the Orient. Sugar cane was cultivated in the tropics, where it grew naturally. The prevailing climate in Europe did not allow large-scale cultivation, so the Europeans were always on the lookout for alternative locations. They found suitable growing conditions in their overseas territories, and soon had viable plantations. Even the production of sugar on a large scale, beginning around 1500, barely caused any fall in the price, because the demand kept growing in step with the supply. Its relative scarcity made sugar into a status symbol among the Euro-

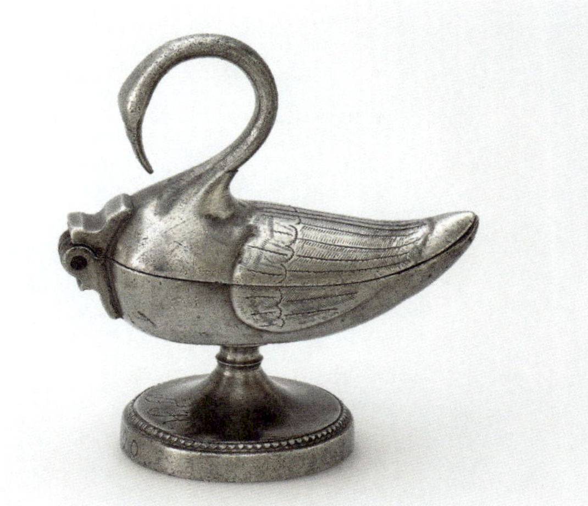

8/4

pean nobility during the sixteenth century. It was used in particular as a sweetener for coffee, tea and drinking chocolate. TE

8/4 **Sugar bowl in the shape of a swan**
1820
Pewter; 10.5 x 10 x 5.5 cm
Berlin, Deutsches Historisches Museum: MK 61/17

Sugar was a valuable commodity well into the nineteenth century, so it was almost always kept in finely crafted bowls of porcelain and silver. In the late eighteenth century, pewter containers were made in growing numbers, mostly as imitations of the silver designs. From 1797 onwards, apprentice pewterers in the duchy of Brandenburg were usually required to make a sugar bowl as their masterpiece. Many of these containers could be closed, and in large households they were often locked away to prevent servants from pilfering the contents. This bowl with a hinged lid in the shape of a swan, and a pedestal engraved with the date "1820" above a beaded rim, corresponds in every respect to the taste of the Biedermeier period around 1820/1830. LK

8/5 **Title vignette *Traitéz nouveaux & curieux du cafe, du thé, et du chocolate***
A Turk, a Chinese and a native American represent coffee, tea and chocolate
Philippe Sylvestre Dufour (1622–1687)
Den Haag, 1685
Print; 14 x 8.7 cm
Berlin, Staatsbibliothek zu Berlin – Preußischer Kulturbesitz, Abteilung Historische Drucke: Jp 2025

The three men gathered around a table represent three parts of the world: the Orient, East Asia and America. They symbolise the drinks that come from their respective continents: coffee, tea and chocolate. The import of these goods changed Europeans' drinking and eating habits. They now combined warm drinks with cold dishes, whereas in the fifteenth century only the reverse had been customary. The first European account of tea-drinking in China comes from a travelogue by an Italian geographer, Giovan Giambattista Ramusio (1485–1557), which was published posthumously in 1559. The first cargo of tea was brought to Europe by Dutch ships around 1610. The tea plant was cultivated almost exclusively in China until the nineteenth century, and even afterwards its dried leaves remained an imported commodity. Especially fast sailing vessels, called clippers, vied to be first in the annual 'tea race' to bring the fresh crop from China to Europe. TE

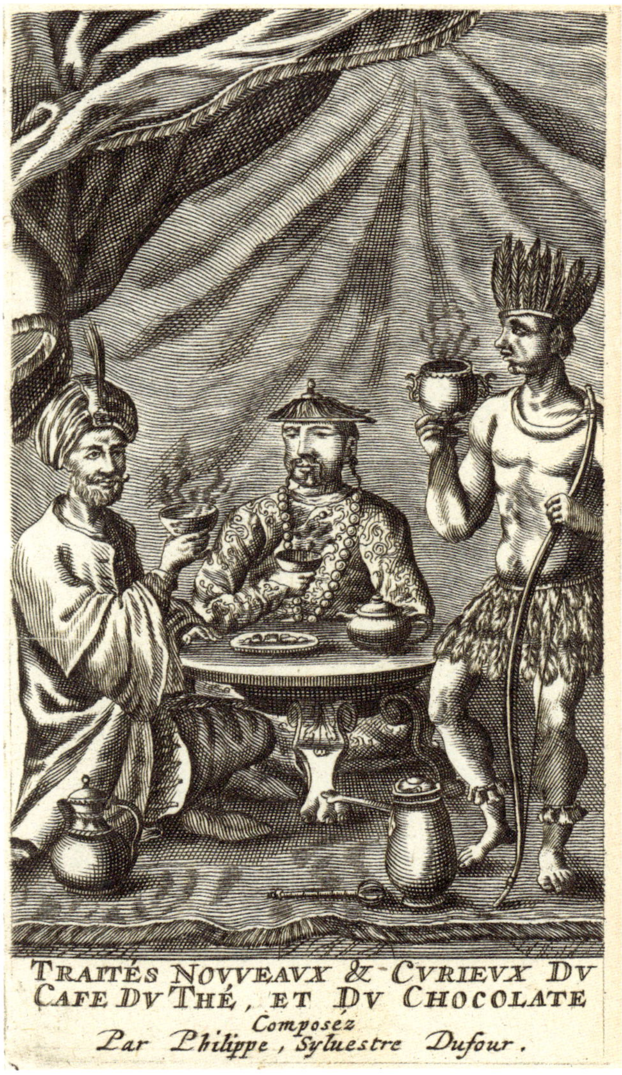

8/5

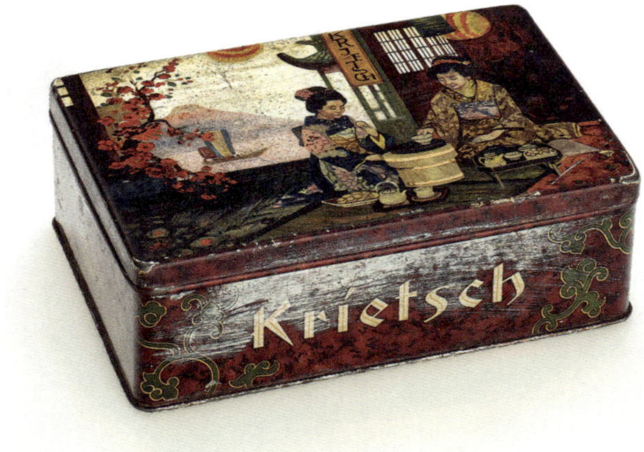

8/6

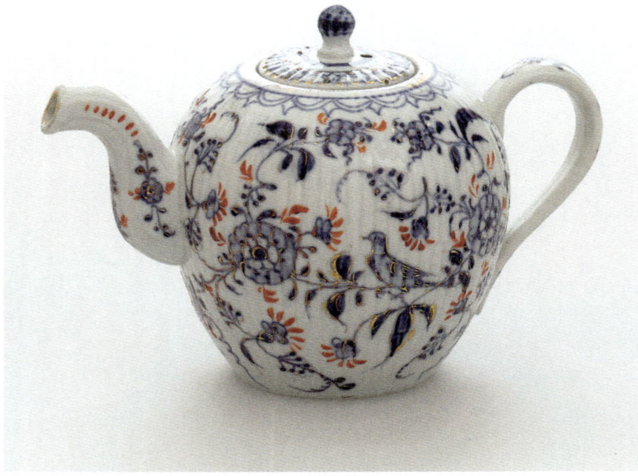

8/7

8/6 **Metal box with depiction of a Chinese tea ceremony**
Germany, 1900/1930
Iron, tinplate; 5.7 x 16.4 x 10.9 cm
Berlin, Deutsches Historisches Museum: AK 94/516.4367

The illustration shows two women of Chinese appearance performing a tea ceremony. The roots of Chinese tea culture go back many centuries. The consumption of hot drinks and their effects on the human body were fiercely debated in seventeenth-century Europe. In the case of tea, its advocates finally carried the day and established the notion that tea promotes a long life. Among them was a Dutch physician, Cornelius Bontekoe (1647–1685), who as the personal physician to Elector Friedrich Wilhelm I of Brandenburg (1620–1688) played a significant role in the introduction of coffee, tea and drinking chocolate to the court in Berlin. TE

8/7 **Teapot from an eight-part service with bird decor**
Porcelain manufactory Friedrich Christian Greiner und Söhne
Rauenstein, after 1860
Porcelain (painted), wood; 12 x 18 cm, max. diam. 11 cm (body)
Berlin, Deutsches Historisches Museum: MK 61/193.2

Tea first became popular in German-speaking countries over the course of the eighteenth century. Porcelain manufactories in Meissen and Berlin borrowed the shape of their teapots from the smaller porcelain teapots imported from China. The painted decor with motifs of birds and flower tendrils was likewise based on the Chinese patterns. As tea drinking became more widespread, the demand for tea services grew. Many small porcelain manufactories were founded in Thuringia at the end of the eighteenth century, such as the one in Rauenstein. This specialised in the production of simple tableware, mainly tea and coffee services in the Meissen style. The pieces were often made of thicker porcelain than the Meissen originals. LK

8/8 **Coffee bean tasting and coffee trading via the port of Mocha**
Voyage de l'Arabie heureuse, [...] *La Relation particulière d'un Voyage du Port de Moka à la Cour du Roy d'Yemen, dans la seconde Expedition des années 1711, 1712 & 1713.*
Jean de La Roque (1661–1745)
Published by Steenhouwer & Uytwerf
Amsterdam, 1716
Print; 16 x 11 cm
Berlin, Staatsbibliothek zu Berlin – Preußischer Kulturbesitz, Benutzungsabteilung: Um 1506

The engraving shows traders in European dress tasting coffee beans and bidding for them at auction. The scene is set not far from the Yemeni port of Mocha, which was the main marketplace for coffee beans in the seventeenth century. The mocha coffee bean has a faint flavour of chocolate, which is why, in the English-speaking world, 'mocha' came to mean a milky coffee mixed with cocoa. The coffee plant originated in the upland plateaus of Ethiopia in Africa. Arab merchants exported the dried seeds via Mecca (beginning in 1551), Constantinople (1554), Venice (1645/47) and even Marseille (1659). The Arabs held a monopoly on coffee trade. This was not really broken until 1680, when the Dutch succeeded in smuggling out some plants and cultivating them in their colonies in Java and Ceylon. Nowadays, coffee is grown in over seventy countries. It is the world's second most important trading commodity after oil. The market is dominated by the beans of two different species: 'arabica', with a

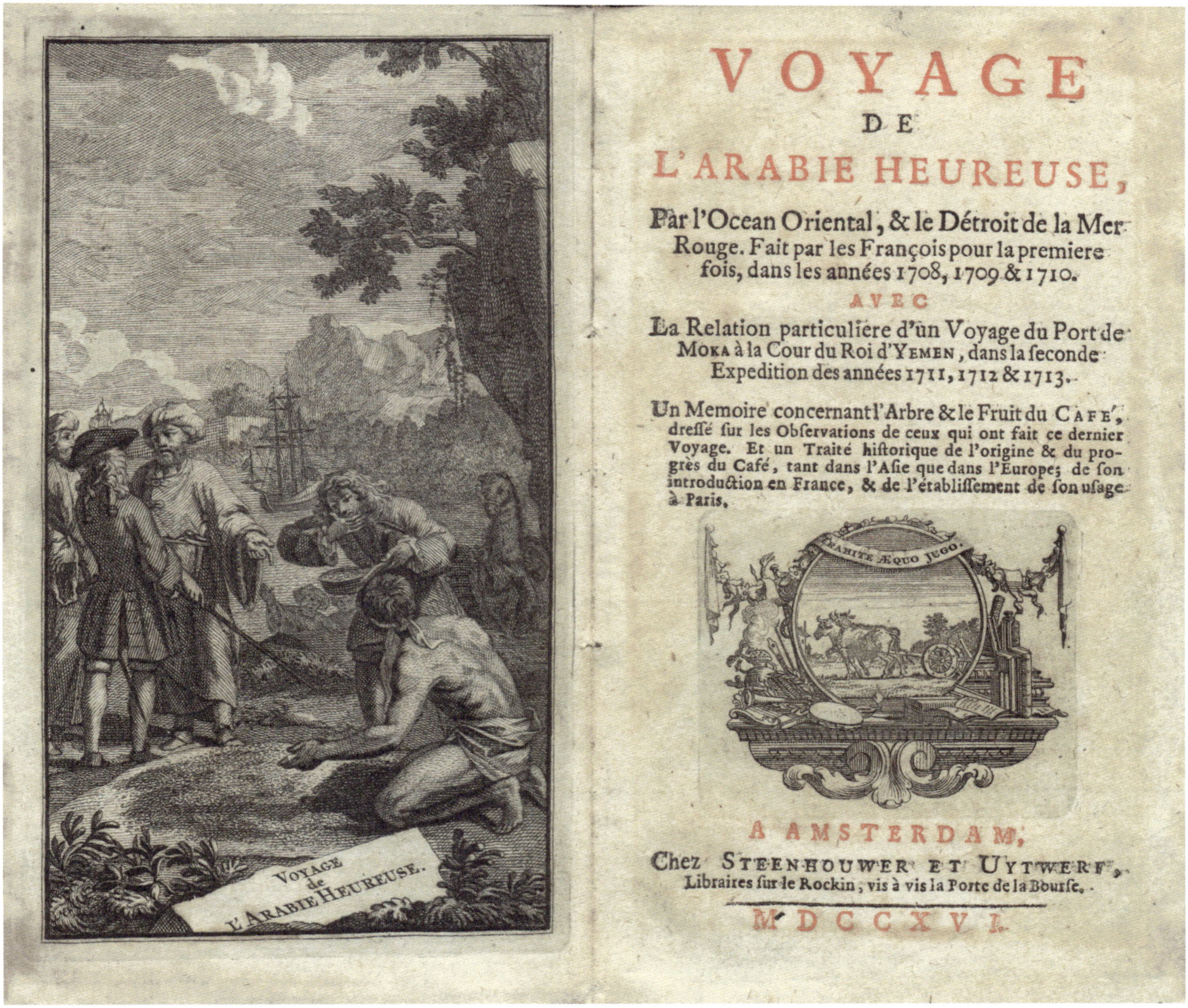

VOYAGE
DE
L'ARABIE HEUREUSE,
Par l'Ocean Oriental, & le Détroit de la Mer Rouge. Fait par les François pour la premiere fois, dans les années 1708, 1709 & 1710.
AVEC
La Relation particuliére d'un Voyage du Port de Moka à la Cour du Roi d'Yemen, dans la seconde Expedition des années 1711, 1712 & 1713.
Un Memoire concernant l'Arbre & le Fruit du Cafe', dressé sur les Observations de ceux qui ont fait ce dernier Voyage. Et un Traité historique de l'origine & du progrès du Café, tant dans l'Asie que dans l'Europe; de son introduction en France, & de l'établissement de son usage à Paris.

ÆQUO JUGO.

A AMSTERDAM,
Chez Steenhouwer et Uytwerf, Libraires sur le Rockin, vis à vis la Porte de la Bourse.
MDCCXVI.

8/8

market share of about 70–75 per cent, and 'robusta' with about 25–30 per cent. TE

8/9 **Coffee grinder**
c. 1800
Wood, iron; 24 x 16 x 15.5 cm
Berlin, Deutsches Historisches Museum: K 59/497

Three steps are needed to release the flavour and aroma of coffee beans: first they are roasted, then ground using a burr mill or a mortar and pestle, and finally brewed. The refinement of milling technology for coffee began in sixteenth-century Syria and continued until the coffee grinder became a machine in its own right. Coffee absorbs odours easily, so the mill hopper and the grinding burrs or blades must be made of odourless materials. The thirst for coffee among the wealthy middle classes led to the establishment of countless coffee houses, which soon became important meeting

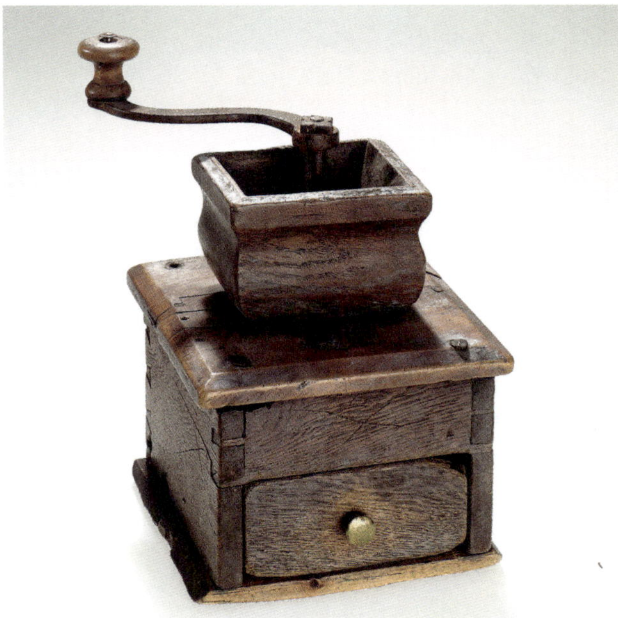

8/9

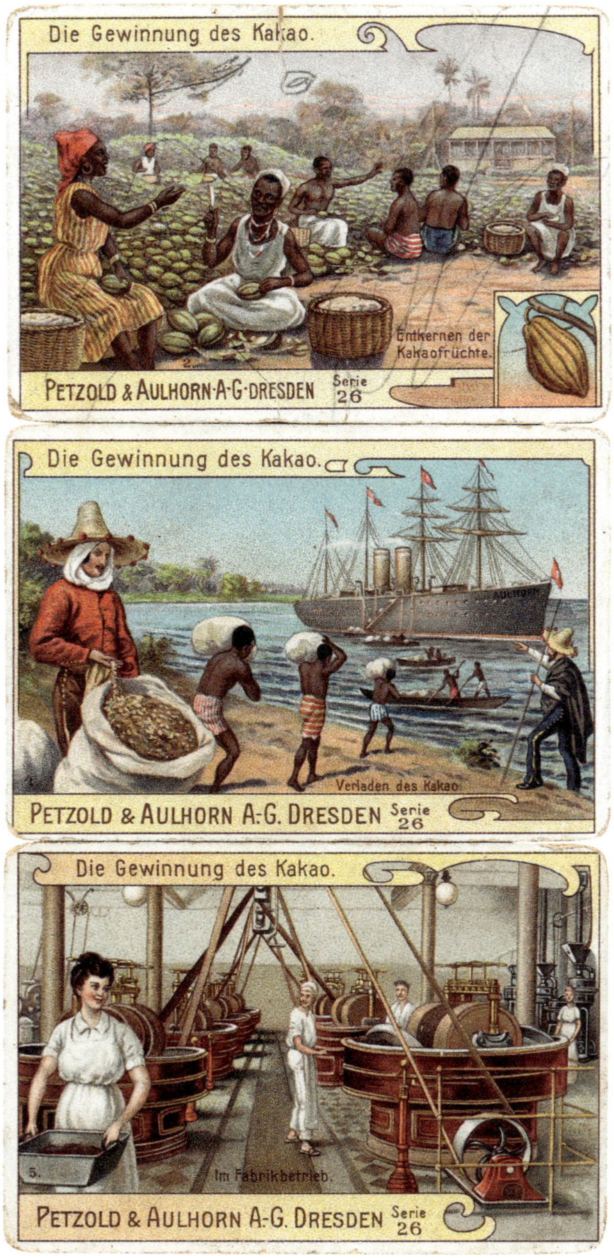

8/11

places. The first coffee house in Europe was opened not in Vienna (1685), as many people think, but in Venice (1647). They were soon followed by establishments in Oxford (1650), London (1652), Paris (1672), Bremen (1673) and Hamburg (1677). The desire for suitable cups was one reason why the Europeans sought to discover the secret of making porcelain. TE

8/10 **Coffee pot for a silver wedding anniversary**
Germany, c. 1900
Porcelain (painted); 23 x 18.9 cm
Berlin, Deutsches Historisches Museum: 1988/1115.1-2

Around 1900, porcelain manufacturers often sold decorative coffee services to mark special occasions such as a wedding or an anniversary. The decor was certainly lavish, but not necessarily ambitious from an artistic point of view. This coffee pot with an inscription meaning "For your silver wedding anniversary" is not personalised with a name or a date, nor does it bear a maker's mark, which would identify it as coming from a certain factory. As a silver wedding anniversary gift, it may have suggested that the recipients had achieved a certain social status and were now the kind of people who could afford to serve coffee in porcelain tableware. (Exhibit not shown) LK

8/11 **Collectors cards showing "The production of cocoa", series no. 26**
Petzold und Aulhorn AG
Dresden, c. 1900
Lithograph on cardboard; 7 x 10.8 cm each
Berlin, Deutsches Historisches Museum: Do 2005/75.a-c

These collectors' cards advertise a cocoa and chocolate factory in Dresden. The story behind the products is told in three scenes: harvesting cocoa pods, transporting them by ship, and processing them in a factory. It is noticeable that the heavy physical work is being done by black labourers. Designed around 1900, the cards give some idea of working conditions at the time. Whereas the raw commodity – in this case cocoa beans – was extracted from the pods by hand in the colonies, it was shipped to Europe on modern steamships. In the factories of Europe, it was processed using machines. Because the commodity prices were low and the refined products fetched high prices in Europe, companies and individuals could make huge profits from exploiting the colonies. TE

8/12 **Chocolate pot painted with hunting scenes**
Königliche Porcellain Fabrique / Ferner-Werkstatt (decor)
Meissen, 1745/1750
Porcelain (painted), bronze, wood; 16 x 22 x 15 cm
Berlin, Deutsches Historisches Museum: KG 2002/11

Cocoa beans were first imported commercially from Mexico to Spain in the late sixteenth century. In the course of the seventeenth century, they became popular throughout Europe. Prepared as a hot drink, chocolate was believed to

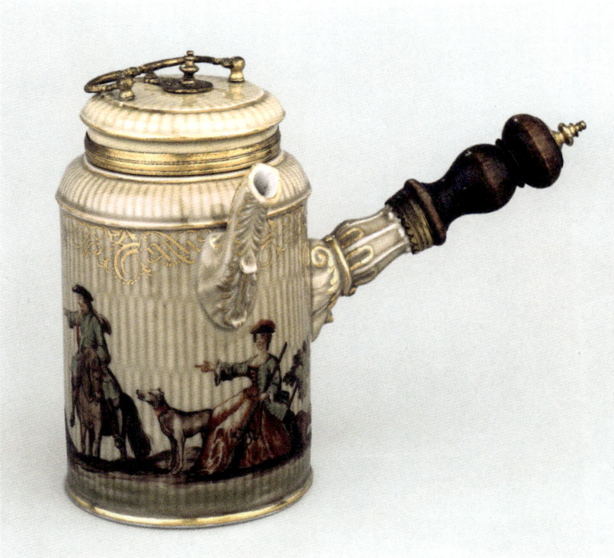

8/12

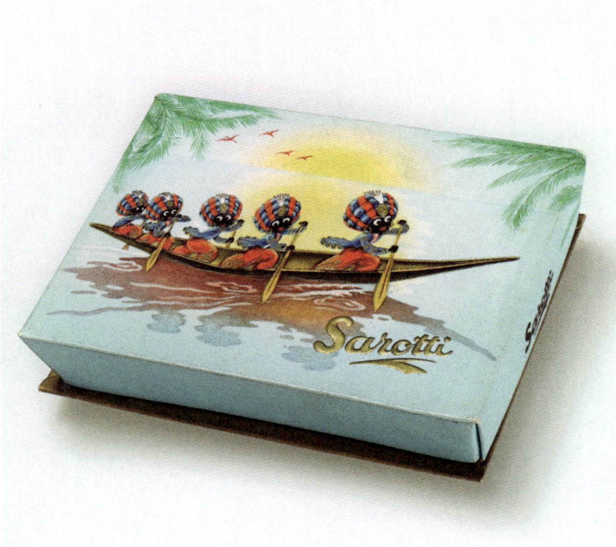

8/14

be an aphrodisiac. Even in the eighteenth century, it was still considered to be a luxury item. Drinking chocolate was prepared and served in a special pot whose form differed from those used for coffee and tea. It was cylindrical, with a handle of turned wood mounted at 90 degrees to a tubular spout. This pot is painted with hunting scenes, which indicates that it was used by members of the nobility, because hunting was the exclusive preserve of the aristocracy in the Baroque period. LK

8/13 **Chocolate pot with heart decor**
Traugott Friedrich Pilz (1756–1824)
Freiberg, c. 1800
Pewter, wood; 18.5 x 22.5 cm
Berlin, Deutsches Historisches Museum: MK 88/42

The chocolate pots created by porcelain manufacturers in the eighteenth century had a cylindrical shape, which was then adopted by silversmiths and pewterers. The town of Freiberg in Saxony, some 40 km south of Meissen, was a major centre of the pewterer's art from the fifteenth to the nineteenth century. The first chocolate pots of pewter were made there in the late eighteenth century. By the end of the nineteenth century, chocolate had become affordable for many middle-class households and consumers had a choice of pots made of porcelain, silver, pewter, copper, or enamelled tinplate. (Exhibit not shown) LK

8/14 **Box for Sarotti confectionery**
Sarotti AG
Germany, 1920/1960
Cardboard, glued; 3 x 15 x 11 cm
Berlin, Deutsches Historisches Museum: AK 94/516.4448

The company owned by confectioner Hugo Hoffmann (1844–1911) in Berlin made chocolates and sweets, which were sold from 1872 under the Sarotti brand name. In 1918, the 'Sarotti Moor' was adopted as a trademark. This stereotypical portrayal of the black serving man, adapted for use as an exotic 'brand ambassador', reveals the assumption of superiority among Europeans that was typical of the colonial era. In 1828, Coenraad Johannes van Houten (1801–1887) patented a method of separating the fat from cocoa beans with a hydraulic press to produce a mass that could be pulverised into cocoa powder. This and a chemical treatment that he invented made it possible to mass produce chocolate for both drinking and eating. TE

8/15 **View of a cotton or hemp factory in East Africa**
East Africa, c. 1900
Stereo photograph (new print from a glass negative)
Berlin, Deutsches Historisches Museum:
71/2710/024/013/024

In many overseas territories, cotton plantations were created as a means of exploiting a region's agricultural potential and gaining a sought-after raw material that could be processed at a considerable profit. In German East Africa (a colony that existed from 1878 to 1918) there were also cotton production facilities, which partly made use of forced labour. There were health risks associated with harvesting cotton

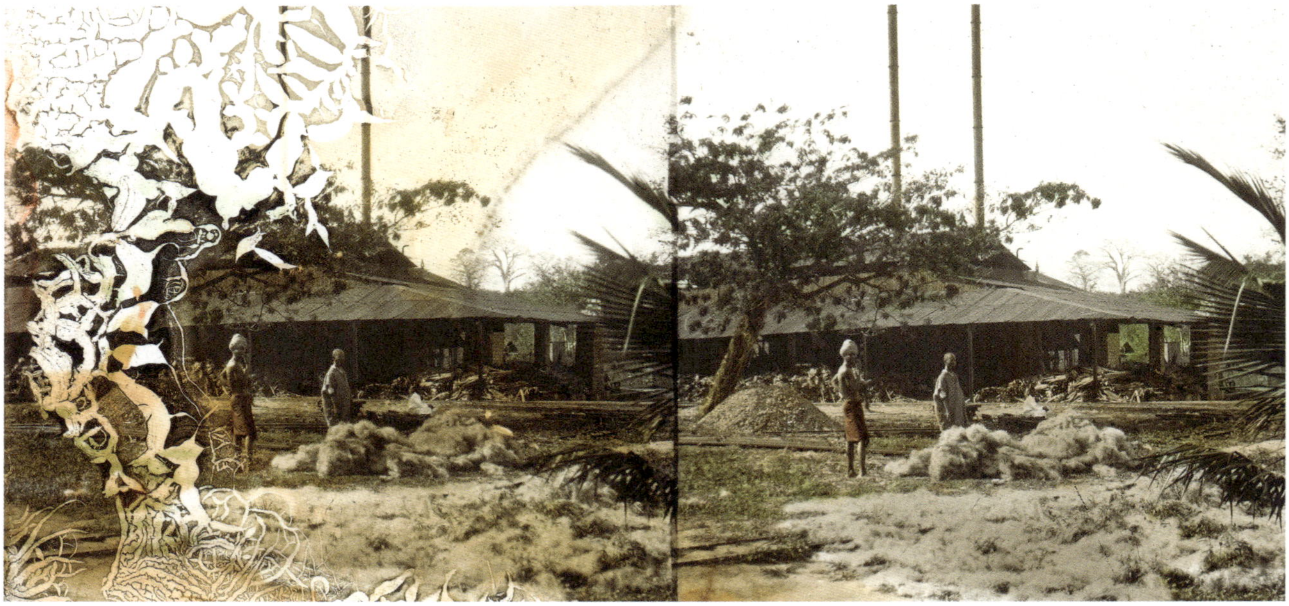

8/15

plants, which are toxic to humans, especially the seeds. The shrub is native to tropical and subtropical regions of Africa, America and Asia, where it has been cultivated for millennia. Cotton fabric first came to Europe along the Oriental trade routes. TE

8/16 **Sample of fabric for cotton towels**
Germany, 1880/1920
Cotton damask; 38 x 600 cm
Berlin, Deutsches Historisches Museum: KTe 85/45

It is hard to imagine what life would be like today without cotton products. Yet they remained luxury goods well into the seventeenth century, and Europeans were willing to pay high prices to import them. Untreated cotton cloth has a greyish white colour. Over time, manufacturers produced clothing and towels in different colours and designs. In order to present the full range of patterns, they sent fabric samples to retailers for customers to choose from. The strength of demand for cotton is shown by the figures for its global consumption, which doubled from 1860 to 1890. Until the middle of the eighteenth century, the highest quality cotton products in the world were manufactured in India; they were brought to Europe by sea. Between 1750 and 1769, these exports increased more than tenfold. The booming trade in cotton products from India was a major economic factor in the rise of the British East India Company. (Exhibit not shown) TE

8/17 **Fabric patterns: Marga, Selma, Wera and Wilma**
Germany, 1920/1929
Cotton, linen, cotton damask, linen/cotton blend, damask; 15 x 23.5 cm each
Berlin, Deutsches Historisches Museum: KTe 85/108.1, 3, 5, 6

The abundance of different colours and patterns meant that more and more fabric samples were needed to help the customer to choose between them. The Europeans developed systems of standardisation and designation early on. Each of the patterns was uniquely identified by a number or a name. The fabric samples shown here were given familiar women's names. They are taken from a twenty-piece series of mattress covers from the 1920s. The fabrics had repeating patterns that included floral motifs, geometric shapes and stylised representations of animals. Pattern books have also survived from earlier centuries. They contained a huge range of materials, allowing customers to compare not just their appearance but also their feel. TE

8/18 **Advertisement for cotton gins**
Fr. Haake Maschinenfabrik und Mühlenbau-Anstalt
Berlin, before 1912
Relief print; 29 x 22.3 cm
Berlin, Deutsches Historisches Museum: Fs 85/3357.1

The Industrial Revolution, spreading from Great Britain, fundamentally changed textile manufacturing. The improvement of the steam engine by Scottish inventor James Watt (1736–1819) made it possible to use steam-powered mechanised looms and spinning wheels. For the first time, British

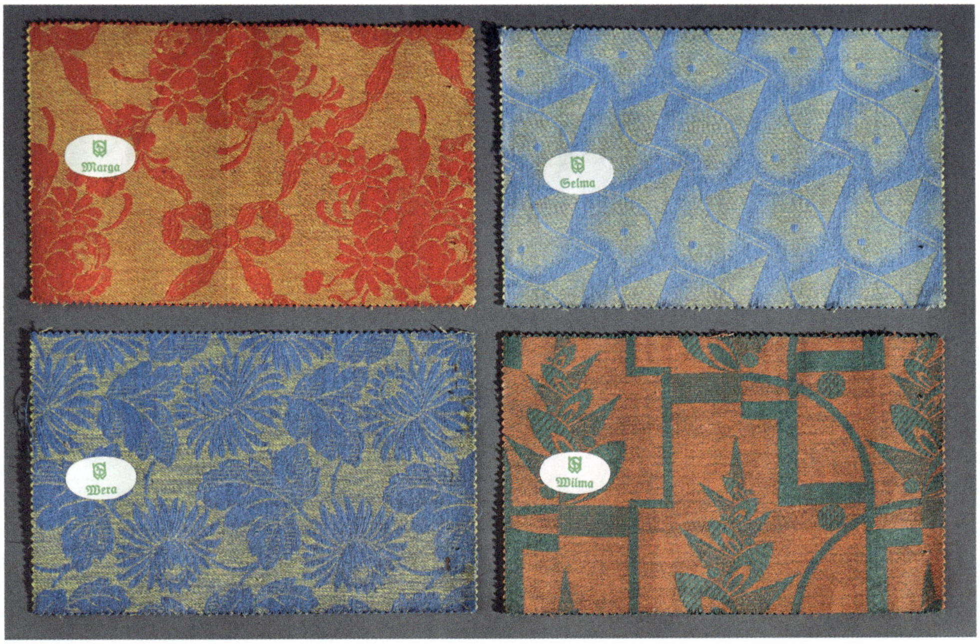

8/17

factories were able to produce textiles more cheaply and quickly than their competitors outside Europe. Soon, German companies joined the ranks of leading machinery manufacturers. Cotton gins – machines to separate fibres from seeds in the cotton pods or 'bolls' – performed this laborious task much more quickly than people could, thus greatly reducing the cost of processing. Some manufacturers printed pamphlets to advertise the advantages of their machines. The brochure lists prices with and without seaworthy packaging. This indicates that the machinery was intended for processing raw material in overseas territories. (Exhibit not shown) TE

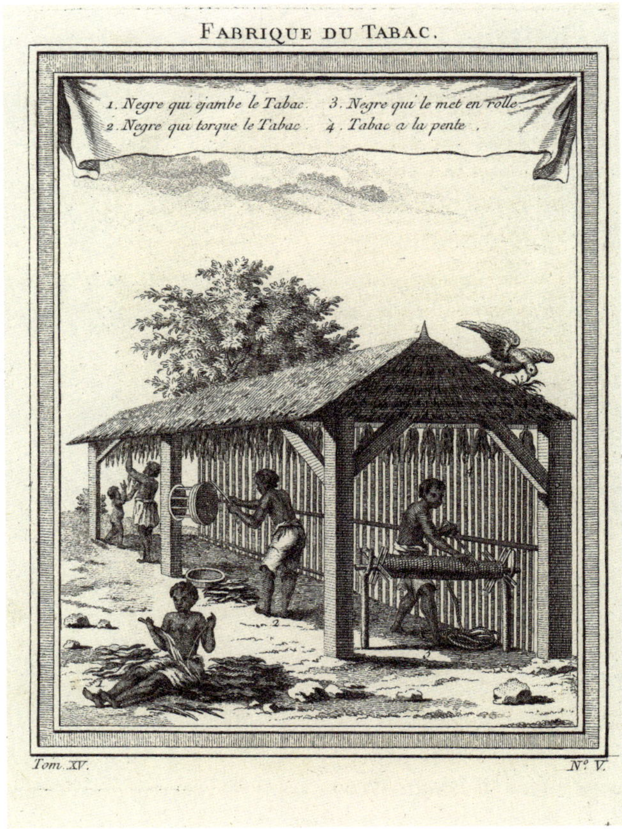

8/19

8/19 **_Fabrique du Tabac_ (Tobacco production)**
Jacques-Philibert Rousselot de Surgy (1737–?)
Engraved by Antoine François Prévost (1697–1763)
Paris, 1759
Copperplate engraving; 25.5 x 18 cm
Berlin, Thomas Eisentraut

This engraving shows various stages of tobacco production such as separating, curing and sorting the leaves. Tobacco was consumed in three main ways: pipe tobacco, which was smoked in a variety of pipes; snuff, which was inhaled directly through the nose; and chewing tobacco. During the sixteenth and seventeenth centuries, London became the main centre of the tobacco trade. In turn, the booming consumption of tobacco in Great Britain led to an exponential increase in prices as demand exceeded the quantity imported. King James I (1566–1625) was a fierce opponent of tobacco consumption and therefore authorised the intro-

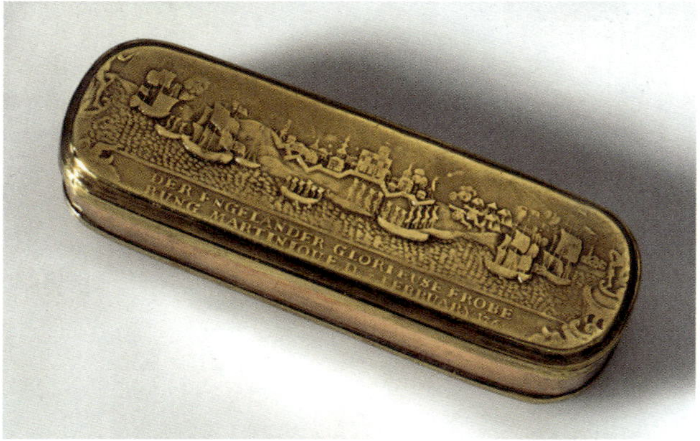

8/20

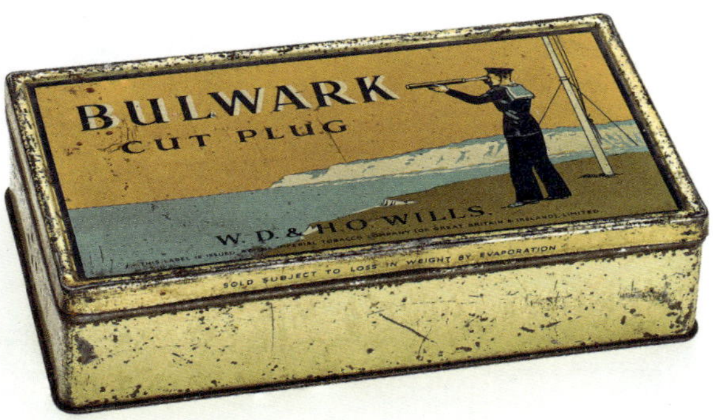

8/22

duction of punitive customs duties on tobacco imports. This led to a rise in smuggling and illegal imports without any possibility of control, so after a short time the tariffs had to be lowered. TE

8/20 **Tobacco tin commemorating the conquest of Martinique**
Probably Iserlohn, 1762
Copper, brass; 3.3 x 13.5 x 4.5 cm
Berlin, Deutsches Historisches Museum: K 57/292

This tobacco tin celebrates a victory of English over French forces during the Seven Years' War, with the inscription: DER ENGELANDER GLORIEUSE EROBERUNG MARTINIQUE D 4 FEBRUARY 1762. Above it is a harbour scene with ships and cannons. The Caribbean island of Martinique was very important to overseas trade. British troops had attempted to take it from the French once before, in January 1758, but failed. After February 1762, it only stayed in British hands for about a year. In the 1763 Treaty of Paris, which concluded the Seven Years War, Great Britain returned the islands it had captured from France in the Antilles, in exchange for all of the French colonies in Canada. Tobacco had been cultivated on the islands of Guadeloupe and Martinique as far back as the seventeenth century. This tobacco was mainly shipped to the Baltic Sea region via France. Tobacco was used as an unofficial currency in the colonies until it was superseded by raw sugar around 1670. LK

8/21 **Carter's pipe**
Germany, 1731
Wood, horn, metal; 30.5 x 3.5 x 11 cm
Berlin, Deutsches Historisches Museum: K 57/100

In Europe, the fashion for consuming tobacco spread inland along transport routes from the ports. This carter's pipe made of briar wood with a bowl in the form of a fish illustrates this development. Tobacco had been unknown in Europe until the end of the fifteenth century. The habit of consuming it was introduced by sailors returning from voyages to the Americas, where they had seen the locals chewing or smoking the leaves and, noticing the beneficial effects, had imitated their unfamiliar behaviour. While the pipes used on board ship were mainly cheap clay ones made in Great Britain and the Netherlands, the Europeans used a wide variety of designs at home. Their form and ornamentation varied according to the materials used, but also the price. As an object that could display its owner's purchasing power and taste, the pipe quickly became a status symbol. (Exhibit not shown) TE

8/22 **Tin for Bulwark Cut Plug tobacco**
Manufacturer: W.D. & H.O. Wills
Bristol/London, 1900/1930
Iron, tinplate; 3.9 x 17 x 9.8 cm
Berlin, Deutsches Historisches Museum: AK 94/516.3356

Tins allowed people to carry their tobacco ready for use, without any risk of it drying out or spilling. They would buy the tin ready filled with a particular blend of tobacco. Heated and pressed into a tin, such blends were notable for a particularly long shelf life. The Bulwark Cut Plug blend contained several kinds of tobacco in separate layers. The consumer could combine these different kinds as desired, be it the same favourite mixture or a new variation. Sailors found the lightweight tins especially suitable for storing their tobacco – and since sailors were a major group of customers for tobacco manufacturers, maritime motifs were often printed on the lids. This one shows a sailor standing on the shore and looking out to sea through a telescope. TE

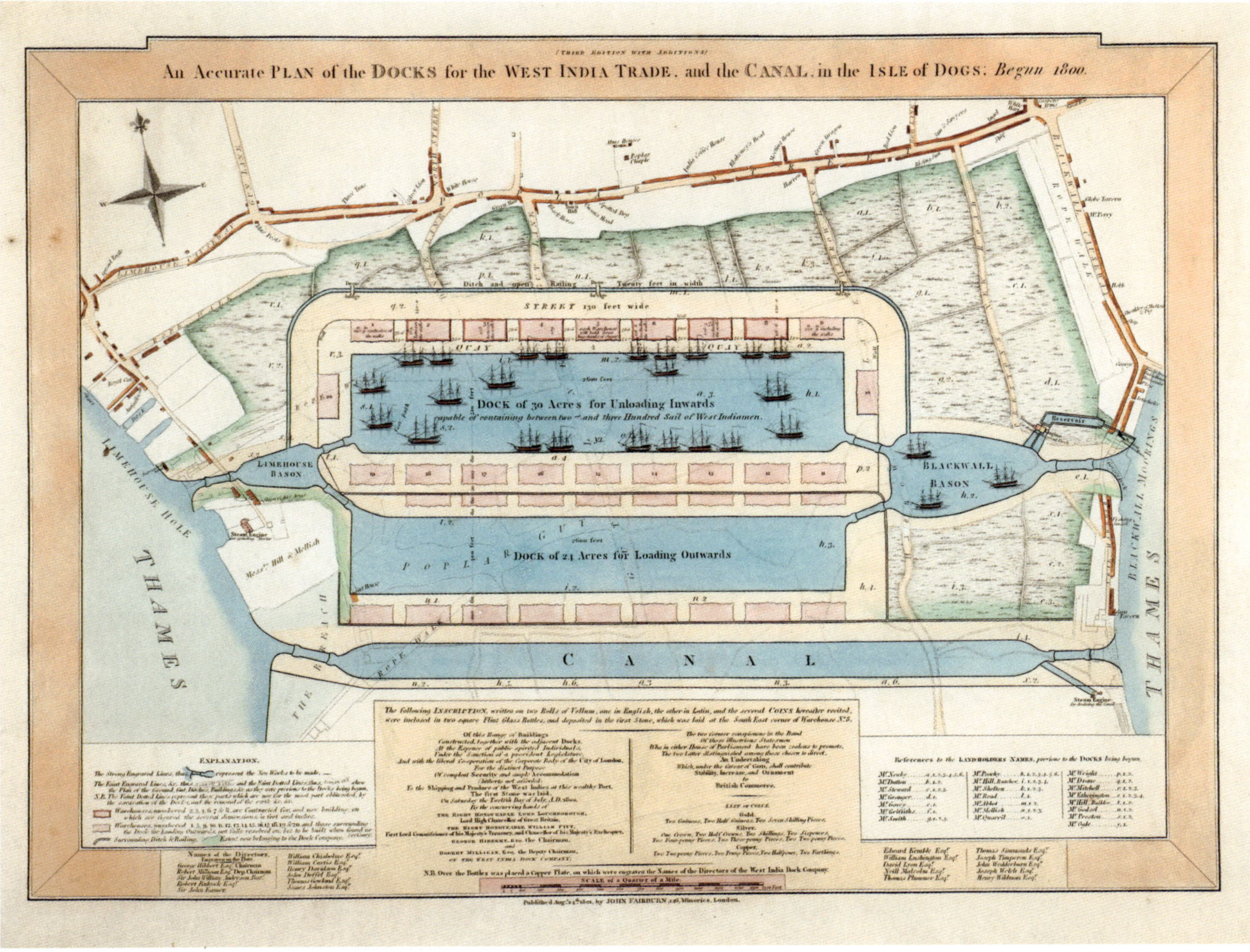

8/23

The Construction of the London Docklands (1799–1828)

8/23 ***Plan of the West India Docks and Canal in the Isle of Dogs; Begun 1800***
John Fairburn (c. 1789–1840)
London, 24 August 1801
Hand-coloured engraving; 54.6 x 70.5 cm
London, Museum of London: 58.22/4

The role and importance of maritime trade for Great Britain is illustrated very clearly by the example of the London Docklands. By the end of the eighteenth century, the existing warehouse capacity in London had become insufficient for the ever-growing volume of merchandise passing through. This plan shows the West India Docks, which were under construction at the time. In fact, not all of the warehouses planned were built. Planned since 1799 and begun in 1800, the West India Docks initially consisted of two (later three) docks designed for large sailing ships. Ships could thus unload in the northern Import Dock and proceed to reload in the southern Export Dock. Locks at the eastern entrance and the western exit prevented incoming and outgoing ships from getting in each other's way. The West India Docks were created largely on the initiative of Robert Milligan (1786–1862), a Scottish merchant who had amassed great wealth through the West Indies trade. To reduce the high rate of loss from theft, he and his associates lobbied for permission to build a properly secured dock and warehouse complex. The warehouses were subsequently surrounded by a high wall that rose to 6.10 metres in places. TE

8/24 ***A View of the East India Docks***
William Daniell (1769–1837)
London, 1 October 1808
Aquatint, hand-coloured; 66.1 x 95.6 cm
Greenwich, London, National Maritime Museum: PAJ2438

The East India Docks were begun in 1803, following the opening of the West India Docks, and were laid out on a smaller scale. The warehouses were used to store goods in

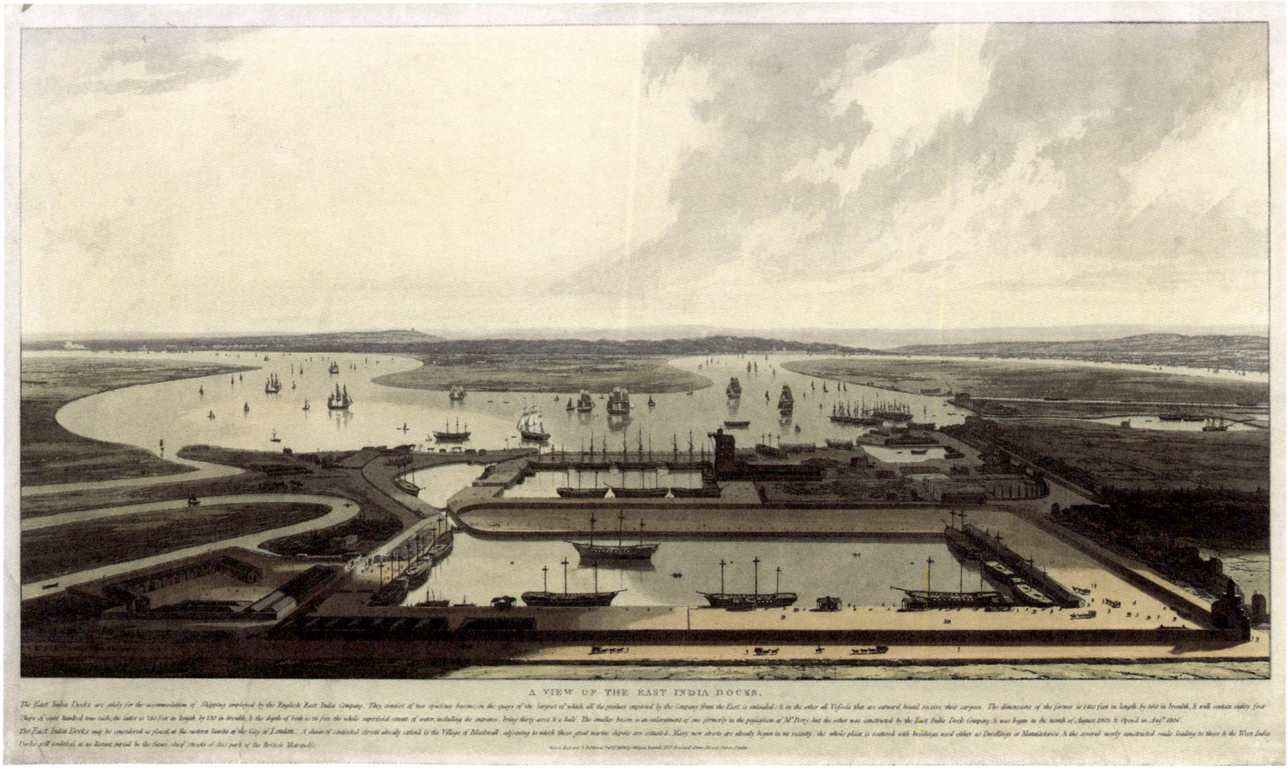

8/24

transit from the territories in eastern India, in particular tea, spices, indigo and textiles. In 1838, the East India Dock Company and the West India Dock Company merged in order to function more profitably. The docks consisted of large water basins that could accommodate up to a hundred ships of average size. Modern port logistics made it possible to unload and load them more quickly than before. In addition, the transport routes were more efficient, as the warehouses stood on the quayside, next to the ships' berths. While in the docks, the ships could also be refitted and loaded for the next voyage. The East India Docks gradually declined in importance with the advent of the steamship, as the new vessels were larger and therefore unable to enter the docks. TE

8/25 ***Docklands in London***
London, c. 1813
Paper, etching, coloured; 18 x 21.8 cm
Berlin, Deutsches Historisches Museum: Gr 53/2395

Between 1799 and 1815, new port facilities called the London Docks were created in London's Wapping district. This aerial perspective view shows the docks from the west. The quayside warehouses were mainly used to store luxury goods in transit, such as spices, coffee, ivory and wine. These were highly valuable commodities, so measures were taken to ensure their security. The grounds were surrounded by a high wall to discourage thieves, and access was strictly controlled. In 1864, the London Docks were merged with the St. Katharine Docks. The capital's favourable location on the navigable, tidal River Thames resulted in the port area of London extending for many kilometres. New warehouses were built further and further to the east, towards the Thames estuary. This was mainly because merchant ships were growing ever larger, with a deeper draught, and were therefore no longer able to come upstream as far as the City of London. (Fig. p. 94) TE

8/26 ***Opening of the St. Katharine Docks, on Saturday the 25th of October 1828***
Edward Duncan (1803–1882)
London, 1 January 1829
Aquatint, hand-coloured; 38.3 x 56.3 cm
Greenwich, London, National Maritime Museum: PAH9912

In the nineteenth century, London was the commercial centre of the world. Its population increased from 2.6 million (1850) to 4 million (1870) and then to 6.5 million (1900). Housing was not only thing in short supply. The boom in trade made new warehouses and other storage facilities necessary. There was not enough vacant land near the city centre for the construction of a new dock complex, so in 1827 the authorities decided to demolish the medieval St. Katha-

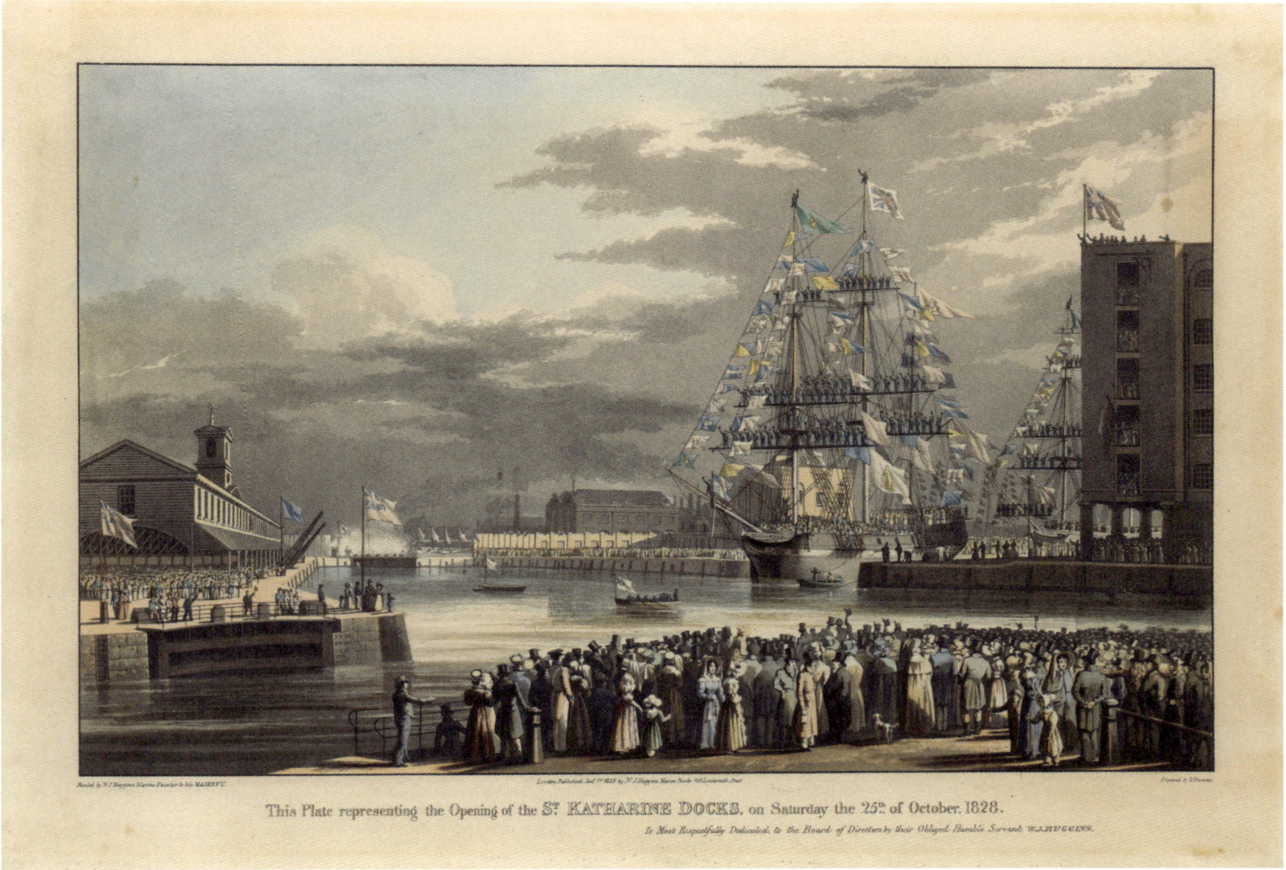

8/26

rine's hospital and many surrounding houses. More than a thousand buildings were demolished and over 11,000 residents – mainly dock workers of modest means – lost their homes. The opening of the St. Katharine Docks was staged as a public relations event. In total, the new docks had over one million square metres of storage space. From a commercial point of view, they were not a lasting success, because the areas of water had been planned too small for large ships to manoeuvre in them. In 1864, the St. Katharine Docks were amalgamated with the London Docks. The warehouses in particular were severely damaged in the Second World War and were not fully rebuilt. The entire facility was closed in 1968. TE

The Construction of the Speicherstadt in Hamburg (1883–1927)

8/27 **Photograph, Rear of buildings on the Mührenfleet**
Georg Koppmann (1842–1909) & Co.
Hamburg, c. 1881
Reproduction
Hamburg, Stiftung Historische Museen Hamburg, Museum für Hamburgische Geschichte: EB 1939, 154

The north German city of Hamburg grew in importance over the course of the nineteenth century. It was a port of entry for imports and a major marketplace for overseas products and merchandise. The quantity of goods kept increasing, almost exhausting the capacity of the warehouses in the city by the middle of the nineteenth century. After the German wars of unification, Hamburg joined the North German Confederation, from which it hoped to gain trading and customs advantages. Although it became part of the German Reich when it was constituted in 1871, Hamburg remained outside the customs border and thus enjoyed privileged trading and commercial conditions. When Hamburg finally acceded to the German Customs Union in 1888, it obtained an exception that preserved the free port status for a part of the harbour

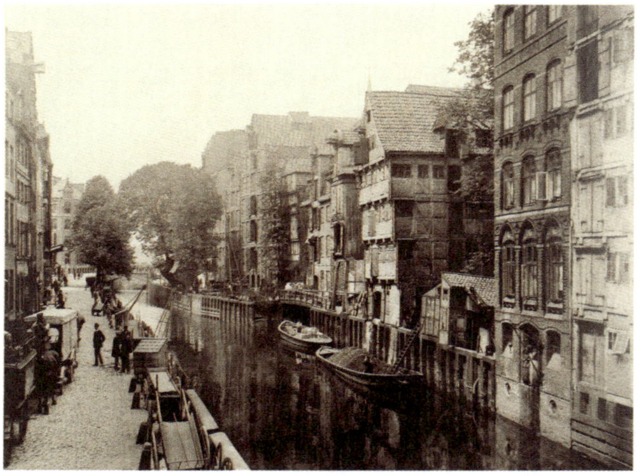

8/28

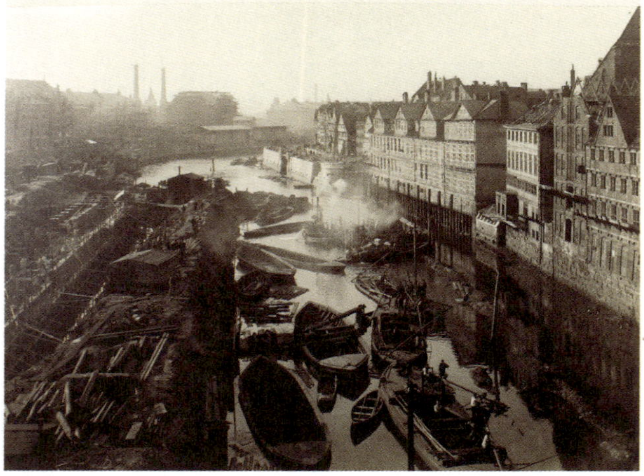

8/29

area, which became the Speicherstadt. The photograph shows the Mührenfleet, which was later widened and became part of the new customs canal. A *Fleet* was a natural channel through the marshes along the River Elbe, navigable by shallow boats transporting goods. (Exhibit not shown) TE

8/28 **Photograph, view of the *Fleet* at Holländischer Brook**
Georg Koppmann (1842–1909) & Co.
Hamburg, c. 1881
Reproduction
Hamburg, Stiftung Historische Museen Hamburg, Museum für Hamburgische Geschichte: EB 1964, 236

Hamburg, like all port cities, was a multicultural place. In the seventeenth century, Dutch Protestants fled to Hamburg to escape religious persecution. They shaped the architecture of entire streets such Holländischer Brook (*Brook* means 'marsh' or 'swamp'). The Dutch influence was especially noticeable in the covered winches high on the houses' front gables. These pulley systems made it possible to lift heavy loads from ships or wagons and bring them directly to the upper floors, especially the attic where goods were stored. Since Hamburg had many small canals, merchandise could be transported economically by water. Special shallow barges with a flat bottom (lighters) were used. They were pushed along and steered using a long wooden oar. TE

8/29 **Photograph, excavation of the customs canal between Kannengiesser bridge and Kornhaus bridge**
Georg Koppmann (1842–1909) & Co.
Hamburg, 4 November 1887
Reproduction
Hamburg, Stiftung Historische Museen Hamburg, Museum für Hamburgische Geschichte: 2015-29-1

The agreement of 15 June 1881 on Hamburg's accession to the German Customs Union provided, in return, for the creation of the Speicherstadt. This self-contained duty-free zone would ensure that Hamburg could continue to function as a free port. Large warehouses were the major component of the new complex, which was constructed on the islands of Wandrahm and Kehrwieder in the River Elbe between 1883 and 1888. To make way for it, the existing residential buildings were demolished. Similarly to the St. Katharine Docks in London, the inhabitants were forced to relocate. This affected more than 20,000 people, mostly dock workers and craftsmen. Altogether, 17 new warehouse complexes were planned, arranged in consecutively numbered blocks to aid identification. The construction work continued until 1927. TE

8/30 **Photograph, excavations between Kannengiesser bridge and Kornhaus bridge for the construction of the free port**
Georg Koppmann (1842–1909) & Co.
Hamburg, 20 July 1887
Reproduction
Hamburg, Stiftung Historische Museen Hamburg, Museum für Hamburgische Geschichte: 2010-3231

The progress of construction on the Speicherstadt in Hamburg is well documented, mainly in a great many photographs taken by Georg Koppmann for the municipal building department. They were published in a portfolio titled "Views of the neighbourhood to be knocked down". After the houses had been demolished, wooden piles up to 12 metres long were driven into the ground by steam-powered rams. These increased the bearing capacity of the soil so that the new foundations would be able to support the weight of multi-storey warehouses. In this photograph from 1887, piles made from tree trunks are clearly visible in the excavated

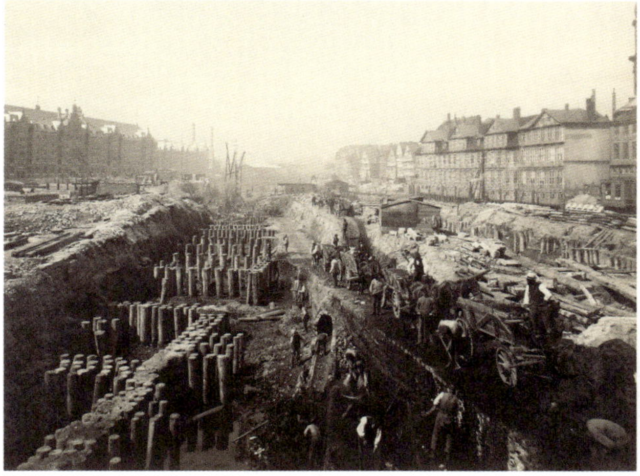

8/30

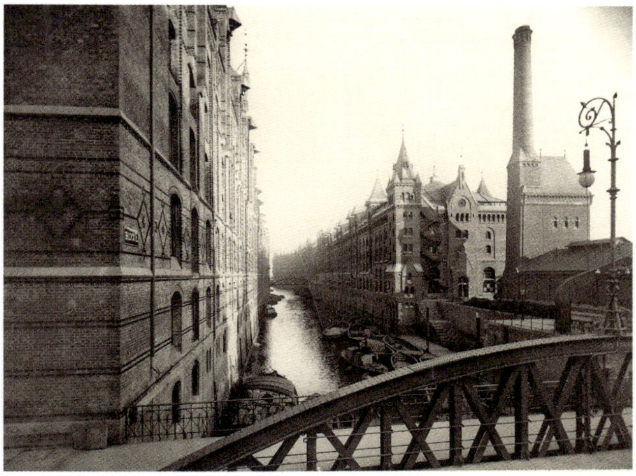

8/31

pit. The man in charge of construction work on this vast project was the city's chief engineer, Franz Andreas Meyer (1837–1901). As the developer's chief adviser, he decisively influenced the appearance of the Speicherstadt. TE

8/31 **Photograph, freeport warehouses at Kehrwiederfleth, block E and central substation**
Georg Koppmann (1842–1909) & Co.
Hamburg, November 1888
Reproduction
Hamburg, Stiftung Historische Museen Hamburg, Museum für Hamburgische Geschichte: 2015-784

Once complete, the warehouses were fitted with the latest technical equipment. Machine-operated winches and cranes increasingly dispensed with the need for manual labour. A boiler house supplied the Speicherstadt with energy which was distributed by the central substation on Sandtorkai. Steam engines produced both hydraulic and electrical power, which was used to operate lifts, cranes, and other heavy machinery. The boilers consumed large quantities of coal, which was brought in on lighter barges. From 1879 onwards, the electricity they produced also powered electric lighting systems, which made it possible to load and unload ships at night while reducing the risk of injury to dock workers. TE

8/32 **Photograph, main customs office on Alter Wandrahm with Kornhaus bridge**
Georg Koppmann (1842–1909) & Co.
Hamburg, 9 August 1901
Reproduction
Hamburg, Stiftung Historische Museen Hamburg, Museum für Hamburgische Geschichte: 2009-4972

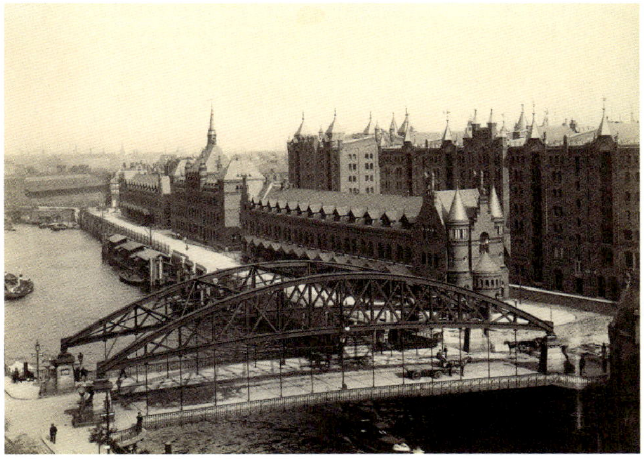

8/32

The construction of the Speicherstadt was divided into several phases. It began with the work on blocks A to O, built between 1885 and 1888. Kaiser Wilhelm II (1859–1941) attended the celebrations held to mark the completion of the first phase and the accession of the City of Hamburg to the German Customs Union on 29 October 1888. Blocks P, Q and R were built in the second phase from 1891 to 1896, followed by blocks S to X between 1899 and 1927. Altogether, 24 warehouse blocks were built, containing some 300,000 m² of storage space. The photo shows the main customs office, built in 1899 and 1900. In the summer of 1943, about half of Hamburg's Speicherstadt was destroyed in Allied air raids. After the end of the Second World War, the Speicherstadt was partly rebuilt, but this work ceased in 1967. On 5 July 2015, the Speicherstadt, together with the adjacent Kontorhaus district and the Chilehaus office building, was listed as a UNESCO World Heritage Site. TE

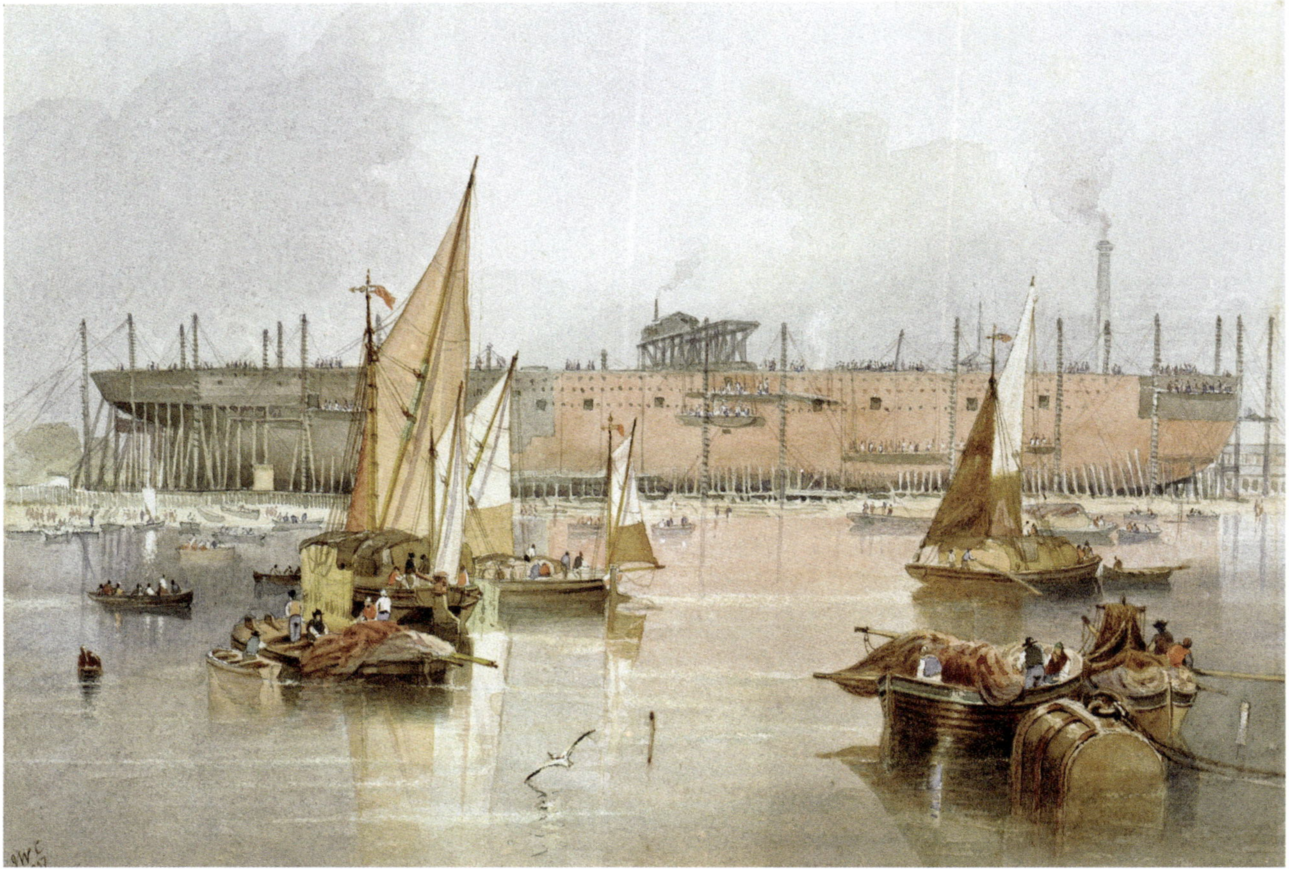

8/33

Industrialisation and Maritime Construction Projects in the Nineteenth Century

8/33 ***The Building of the Great Eastern***
John Wilson Carmichael (1800–1868)
England, 1857
Watercolour; 21.7 x 32 cm
Greenwich, London, National Maritime Museum: PAF6224

British dominance of the seas was reflected in global trade and in large-scale maritime construction projects – above all in the construction of gigantic ships. New technical processes made it possible to build much larger ships of iron and steel, which were capable of carrying both freight and passengers across the oceans. The largest ship of the nineteenth century was built in the Millwall district of London between 1854 and 1858. Initially christened Leviathan and shortly afterwards renamed Great Eastern, the ship was 211 metres long. It was not only a technical masterpiece of its time, but also twice as large as any ship hitherto built. There was no dock large enough to build it in, so its designer, the celebrated engineer Isambard Kingdom Brunel (1806–1859), chose a shipyard on the banks of the Thames, where it could be launched sideways. The Great Eastern carried up to 4,000 passengers and could do the England-Australia run without stopping to refuel. It was propelled by a combination of systems – twin paddle wheels and a single screw – which were powered by separate steam engines. In addition, there were auxiliary sails, fitted to six masts. TE

8/34 **Photograph of Isambard Kingdom Brunel**
Robert Howlett (1831–1858)
London, November 1857
Reproduction
London, National Portrait Gallery: NPG P112

In 2002, Isambard Kingdom Brunel (1806–1859) was ranked the second greatest Briton after Winston Churchill (1874–1965) in a BBC television poll that attracted 447,423 votes. He was in fact the son of a French immigrant, Sir Marc Isambard Brunel (1769–1849), who was himself a successful engineer. He assisted his father as a lead engineer on various projects, notably the first tunnel under the River Thames. The younger

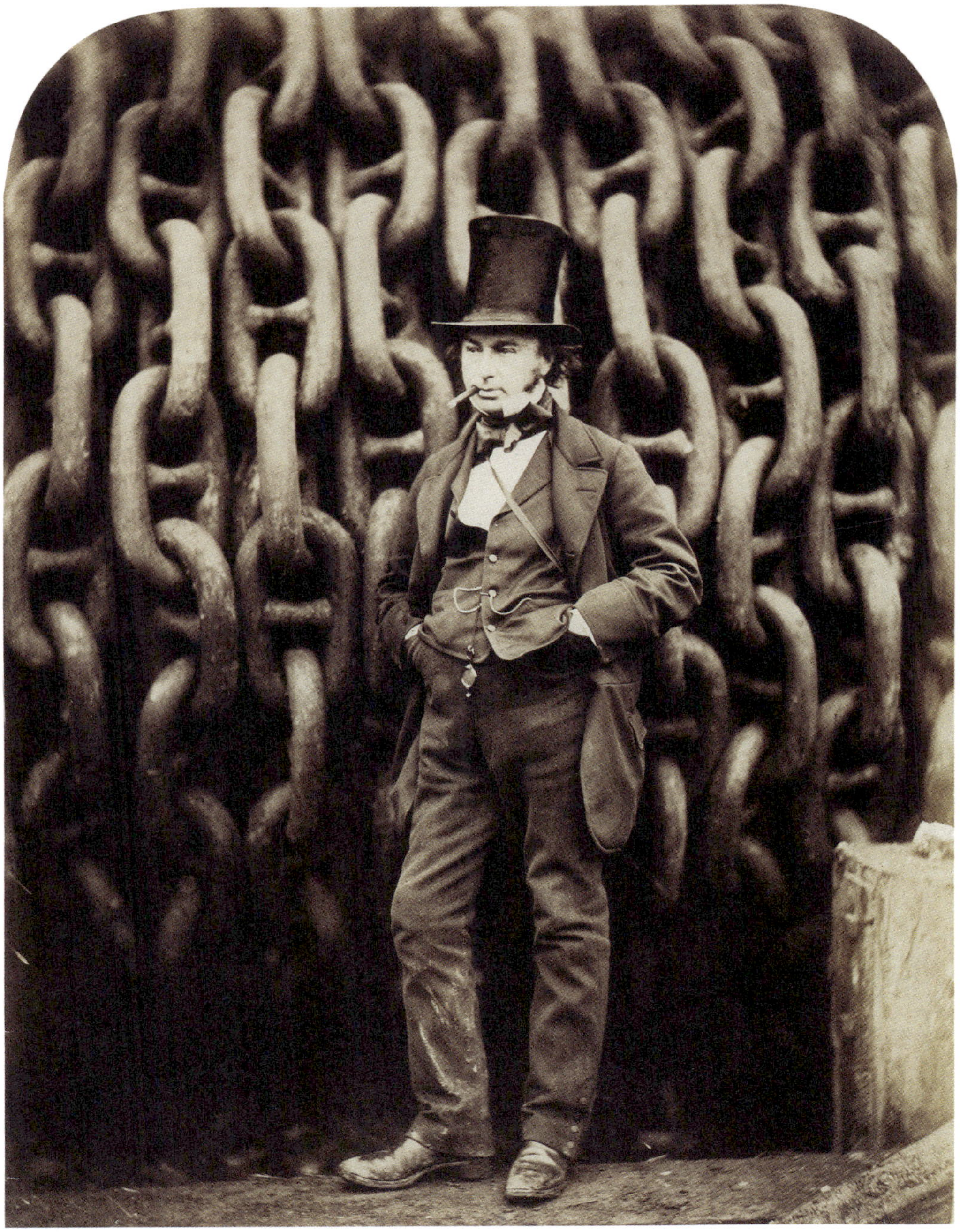

8/34

Brunel designed and built tunnels, suspension bridges, harbour complexes and railway lines in Great Britain, India, Italy and Australia. At the peak of his fame, he designed the largest ship of his time, the GREAT EASTERN. Brunel was photographed in November 1857 in front of its launching chains. He always wore a large top hat to compensate for his short stature – just under 160 cm. He saw the ship launched, but not completed. On 15 September 1859 he died from a stroke he had suffered ten days earlier, one day before the maiden voyage. TE

8/35 **Medal commemorating the GREAT EASTERN**
Medallist: John Moore
England, 1859
Bronze; diam. 3.6 cm
Greenwich, London, National Maritime Museum: MEC1584

A commemorative medal was struck at the end of 1859 to mark the maiden voyage of the GREAT EASTERN. The front portrays its designer, the engineer Isambard Kingdom Brunel. On the reverse is the GREAT EASTERN itself, shown steaming ahead with sails set. The inscription mentions the

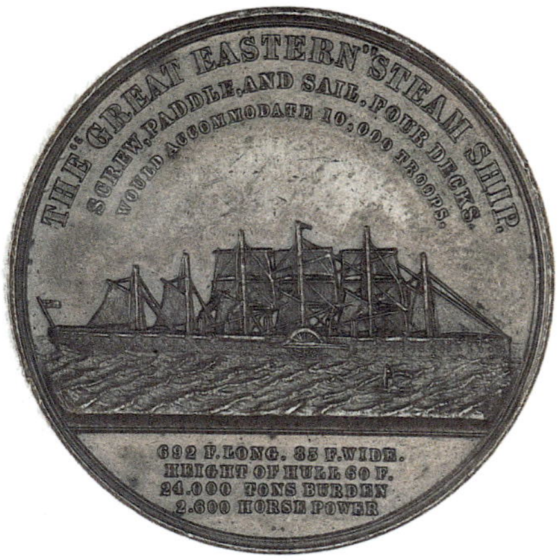

8/35

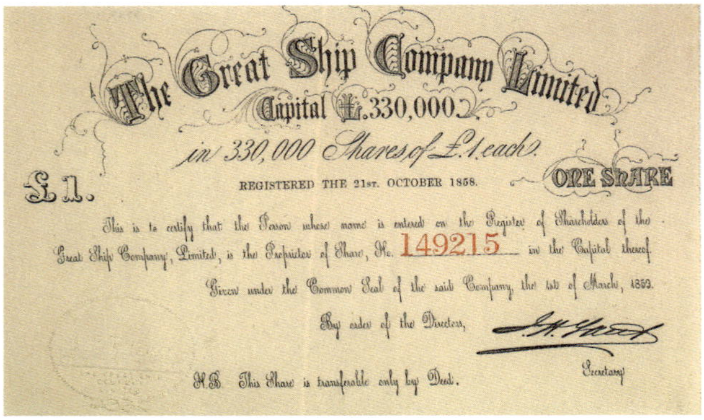
The Great Ship Company Limited
Capital £330,000
in 330,000 Shares of £1 each
£1. REGISTERED THE 21st. OCTOBER 1858. ONE SHARE
This is to certify that the Person whose name is entered on the Register of Shareholders of the Great Ship Company, Limited, is the Proprietor of Share, No. 149215 in the Capital thereof
Given under the Common Seal of the said Company the 1st of March, 1859.
By order of the Directors,
Secretary
N.B. This Share is transferable only by Deed.

8/37

ship's unusual combination of propulsion systems: screw, paddle (meaning the paddle wheels) and sail. Although fitted out as a passenger liner, it was designed to be easily convertible and could thus be chartered to transport troops to the British colonies. In wartime it could theoretically carry 10,000 soldiers. The ship added to British prestige, but it was never a financial success. Only 35 paying passengers travelled on the maiden voyage across the Atlantic. In 1865, the Great Eastern was converted for laying submarine telegraph cables, beginning with the first transatlantic cable to function for a significant length of time. TE

8/36 **Shell of a turban snail engraved with technical data of the Great Eastern**
England, after 1856
Mollusc shell; 9 x 14 x 13 cm
Greenwich, London, National Maritime Museum: OBJ0475

Well-publicised, ambitious undertakings such as the Great Eastern attracted engineering enthusiasts and casual onlookers alike, even during the construction period. To make a little money from this interest, souvenirs were made and sold. This shell of a green turban shell is inscribed with technical details of the steamship Leviathan, which was later renamed Great Eastern. With a length of 690 feet (211 m), a draft of 60 feet (18.3 m), tonnage of 24,000 tons and engine power of 2,600 hp, the vessel was the largest to be built in the nineteenth century. Isambard Kingdom Brunel is named as the engineer, with John Scott Russell (1808–1882) as the ship's builder. The first launch failed because the ship was simply too heavy and could only be moved a few metres. It was finally launched on 31 January 1858. During its service, the ship was involved in more than the average number of accidents. Its unprofitability in a changing market led to the Great Eastern being scrapped in 1889. (Exhibit not shown) TE

8/37 **Share certificate, nominal value £ 1, issued by the Great Ship Company Limited**
London, 1 March 1859
Lithograph; 12.5 x 21 cm
London, Museum of London: 85.69/1

The construction of the Great Eastern was not just a technical challenge. Financial difficulties arose repeatedly over the course of the project. The immense cost of the ship brought the Eastern Steam Navigation Company to the brink of bankruptcy. The failure of the first launch attempt made it necessary to raise additional funds. The costs of the re-launch alone were estimated at £ 170,000, while about £ 160,000 was still needed to complete the fitting out of the ship. In order to raise equity for the completion of the project, a new company was founded on 21 October 1858: the Great Ship Company. Its stock capital consisted of 330,000 shares of one pound each. This low nominal value suggests that they were meant to attract investment from members of the British public. Large construction projects with good prospects of success promised a high yield at a low risk and were therefore generally in high demand. On 6 September 1859, after further delays, the Great Eastern was finally ready to set out on its maiden voyage. TE

8/38 **Subscriber's share in a company for building a Dover-Calais railway tunnel under the English Channel**
London, 19 May 1892
Lithograph; 26.1 x 32 cm
Berlin, Deutsches Historisches Museum: Do 94/153

French and English railway companies were already promoting the project of a tunnel between England and France in the nineteenth century. An Anglo-French channel tunnel company was founded in 1872, and ten years later the first pilot tunnels were drilled by machine in the chalk strata on both sides of the water. The British authorities put a stop to the project in 1882, not least because of military concerns. At

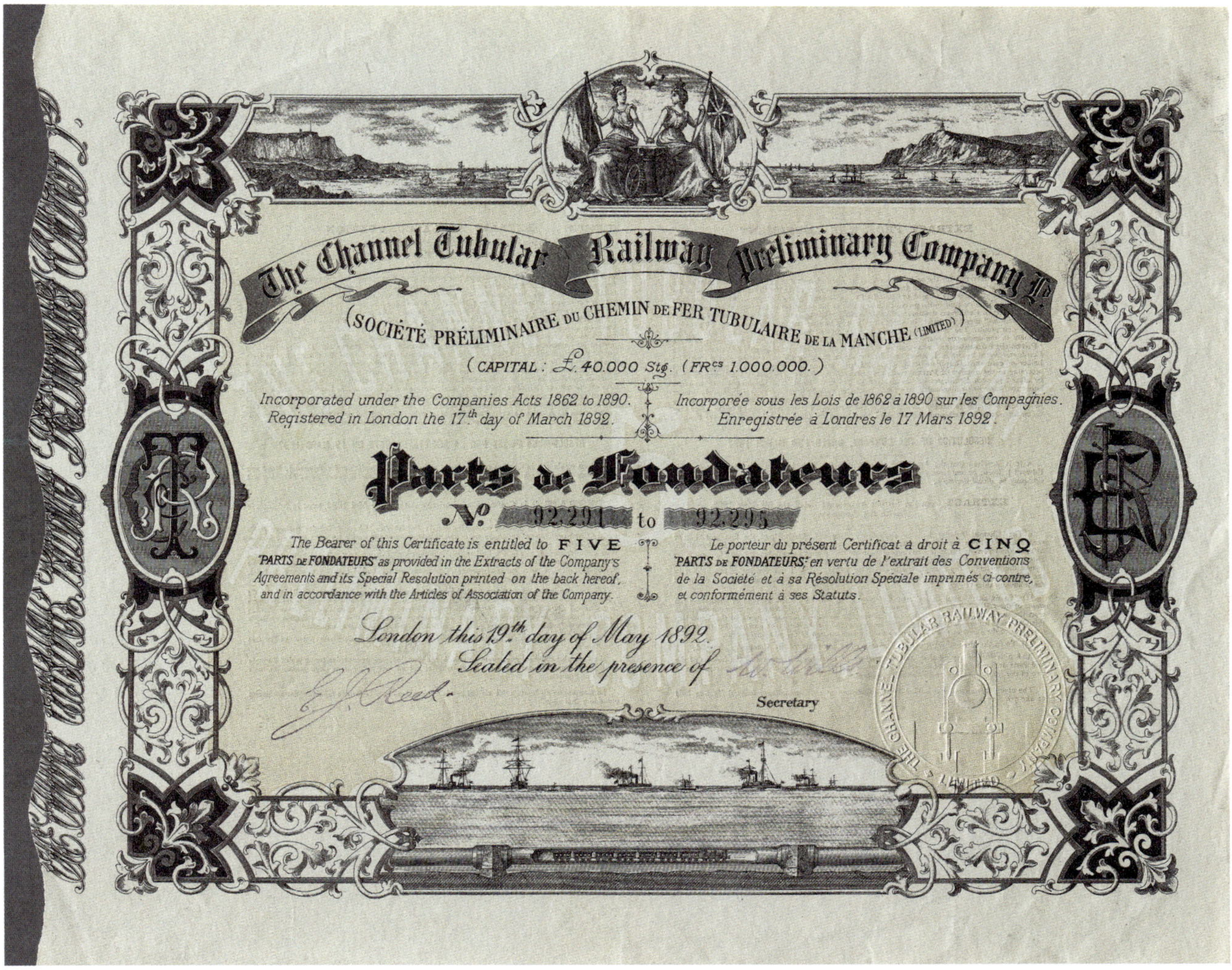

8/38

the suggestion of Sir Edward James Reed (1830–1906), an engineer and politician, a new corporation was set up in 1892, which promised to pay out 20 per cent of the future annual net profit to investors. This too failed. A hundred years went by until the Channel Tunnel was finally built. England and France have been connected by a twin railway line since 1994. MK

8/39 **Share certificate, nominal value 300 Reichsmarks, Allgemeine Deutsche Schiffszimmerer Genossenschaft zu Hamburg**
Printed by Drexel & Adler
Hamburg, 20 February 1930
Lithograph; 23.5 x 30.2 cm
Berlin, Stiftung Historische Wertpapiere Martius am Deutschen Historischen Museum: M 111-03740

The City of Hamburg dissolved the guild of shipwrights in 1838 and deregulated the profession in 1865. In the face of increasing hardship, seven hundred ship's carpenters held strikes and formed unofficial trade unions. In 1875, they founded a cooperative for the "purchase and operation or rental of shipyards". Two shipyards in Memel and Kiel were acquired and run at a profit. Shipbuilding was turning increasingly to iron construction, however, so in 1890 the cooperative began to shift the focus of its activities to social housing in Hamburg. Members of the cooperative bought shares valued at 300 marks each, which entitled them to rent a flat at an affordable price. Today, the shipwrights cooperative manages almost 9,000 residential units. (Fig. p. 308) MK

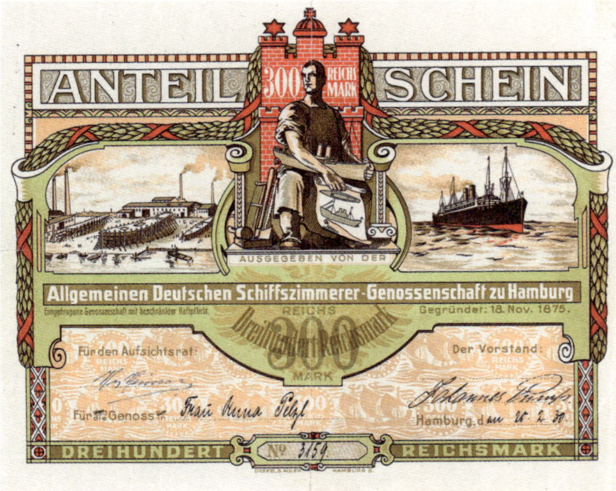

ANTEIL 300 REICHSMARK SCHEIN

AUSGEGEBEN VON DER

Allgemeinen Deutschen Schiffszimmerer-Genossenschaft zu Hamburg

Gegründet: 18. Nov. 1875.

Dreihundert Reichsmark

Für den Aufsichtsrat:

Der Vorstand:

Hamburg, den

DREIHUNDERT № 3159 REICHSMARK

8/39

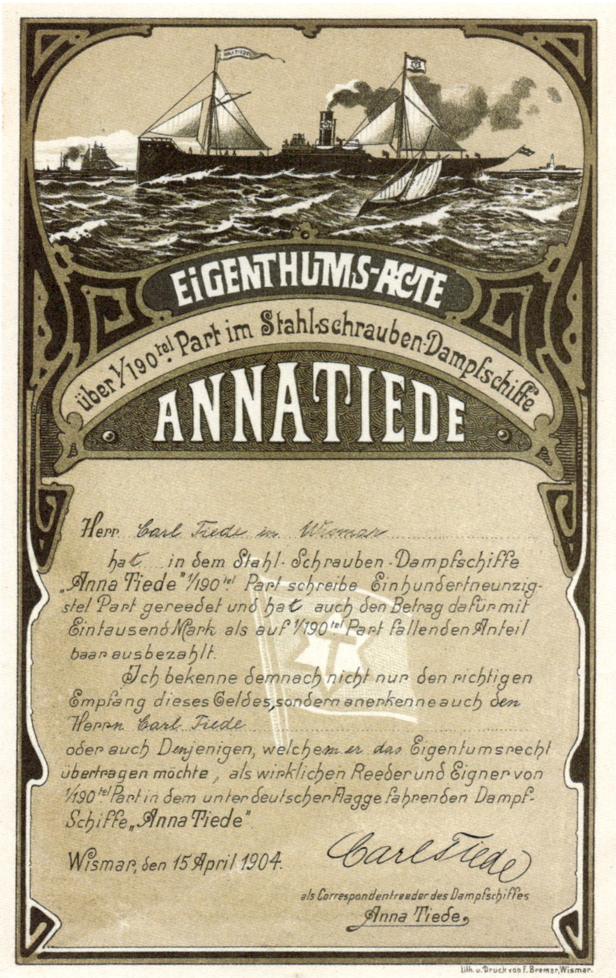

EIGENTHUMS-ACTE

über 1/190tel Part im Stahl-schrauben-Dampfschiffe

ANNA TIEDE

Herr Carl Tiede in Wismar

hat in dem Stahl-Schrauben-Dampfschiffe „Anna Tiede" 1/190tel Part schreibe Einhundertneunzigstel Part gereedet und hat auch den Betrag dafür mit Eintausend Mark als auf 1/190tel Part fallenden Anteil baar ausbezahlt.

Ich bekenne demnach nicht nur den richtigen Empfang dieses Geldes, sondern anerkenne auch den Herrn Carl Tiede oder auch Denjenigen, welchem er das Eigentumsrecht übertragen möchte, als wirklichen Reeder und Eigner von 1/190tel Part in dem unter deutscher Flagge fahrenden Dampf-Schiffe „Anna Tiede".

Wismar, den 15 April 1904.

Carl Tiede

als Correspondentreeder des Dampfschiffes Anna Tiede

Lith. u. Druck von F. Bremer, Wismar.

8/40

8/40 **Ownership share for a 1/190th part of the Anna Tiede**
Printed by F. Bremer
Wismar, 15 April 1904
Lithograph; 33 x 21 cm
Berlin, Stiftung Historische Wertpapiere Martius am Deutschen Historischen Museum: M 111-08001

The Anna Tiede was launched at the Henry Koch shipyard in Lübeck on 26 March 1904. It was the third steel screw cargo steamer owned by Johann Carl Martin Tiede (1858–1930) from Wismar. As was usual for small shipping firms, its construction was financed by issuing part ownership shares with a nominal value of 1,000 marks each. Such transferable shares offered small investors a way of achieving high returns, as long as the vessel remained seaworthy and competitive. The Anna Tiede went to sea under Wismar's own flag for five years until Carl Tiede retired from the shipping industry after thirty years in the customs brokerage and freight forwarding business. His ships were sold and registered under other flags. In 1942, the Anna Tiede ended up in the service of the Italian Navy. It was sunk off the coast of Africa by a British submarine. MK

8/41 **Chart of the World on Mercator's Projection, 6th edition**
Published by Justus Perthes
Hermann Berghaus (1828–1890)
Gotha, 1871
Paper on linen backing, lithograph; 97 x 154.5 cm, scale 1:28,000,000
Berlin, Museumsstiftung Post und Telekommunikation: 3.2014.365

The number of maritime transport routes and telegraph cables increased sharply in the second half of the nineteenth century. To see where they ran, people would consult a large, high-quality chart of the world such as those published by Justus Perthes of Gotha in central Germany. This one appeared in a total of sixteen editions between 1863 and 1924. Such wall charts hung mainly in trading company offices and ministries, to be used as a reference or for planning transactions and travel. The world was now being shown in terms of the oceans, and Europe was no longer at its centre. The graphics are dominated by the global routes of steamship companies and the lines of telegraph cables. Information about ocean currents and ocean floor profiles was also relevant to navigation, making it possible to plan an efficient route and decide on good anchorage grounds. Published in 1871, this chart shows the Suez Canal, completed in 1869, which would rapidly become the world's most important waterway. (Fig. p. 90) TE

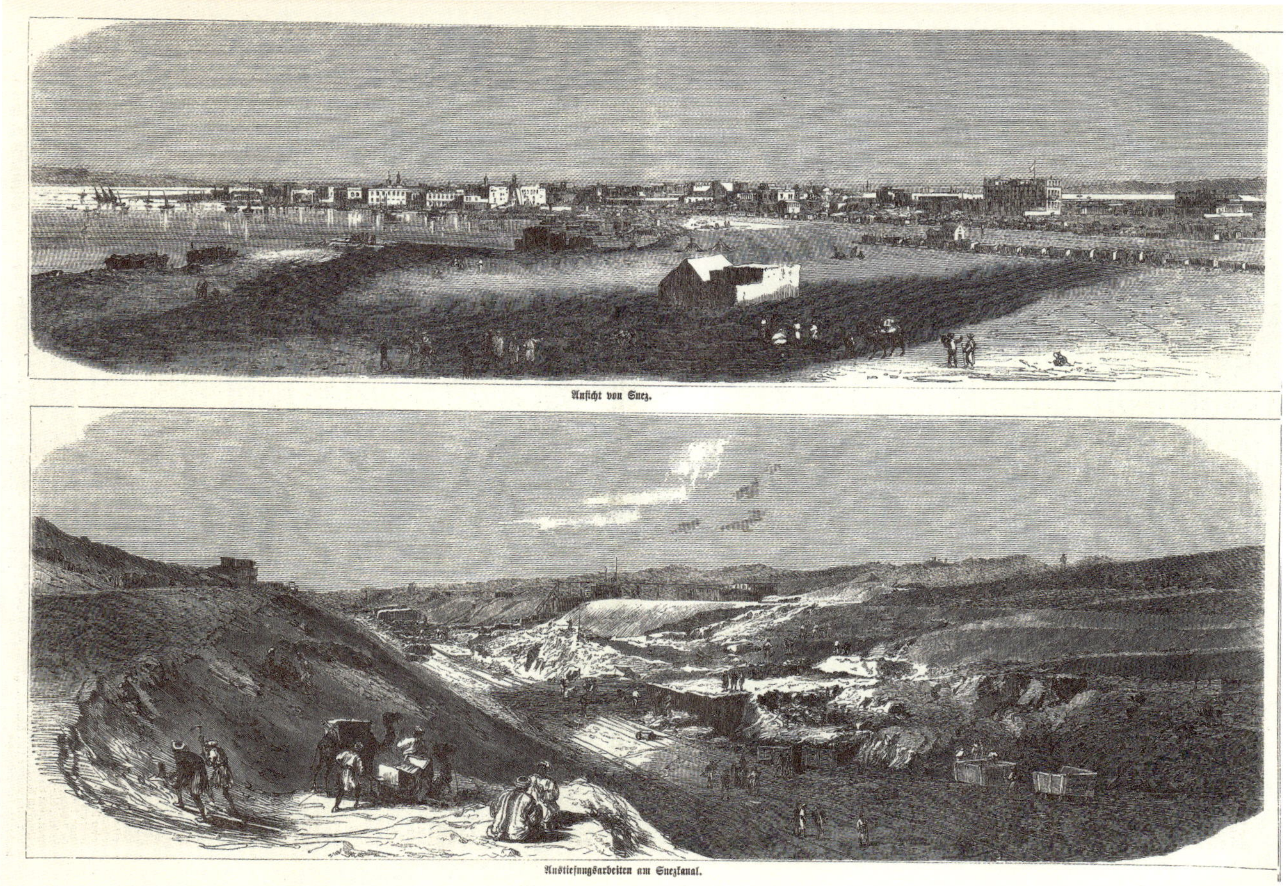

8/42

8/42 **Page from the *Illustrirte Zeitung* with views of the Suez Canal under construction**
Published by Johann Jacob Weber (1803–1880)
Leipzig, 6 November 1869
Print, wood engravings; 39.5 x 28.5 cm
Berlin, Deutsches Historisches Museum: ZB 20-53.1869 (Juli-Dez.)

After ten years of construction work, the Suez Canal was ceremonially opened on 17 November 1869. It covered 164 kilometres between the Egyptian ports of Suez, on the Red Sea, and Port Said, on the Mediterranean Sea. This visionary project was initiated by a French diplomat, Ferdinand de Lesseps (1805–1894). To raise funds, he formed the *Compagnie universelle du canal maritime de Suez* (Suez Canal Company). The idea of such a canal had been around for centuries, but it was not feasible until heavy machinery became available in the nineteenth century. Nevertheless, it was dug by hand at first and the spoil was taken away on camels. High completion costs and unexpectedly low revenues in the early years of operation swelled Egypt's already huge national debt to a critical level. In 1875, Egypt's large stake in the company was sold to Great Britain in a deal that paved the way for the British to take control of the world's most important waterway. The Suez Canal shortened the shipping route and the journey time between Western Europe and Asia by more than a third. This greatly facilitated the transport of perishable goods in particular. TE

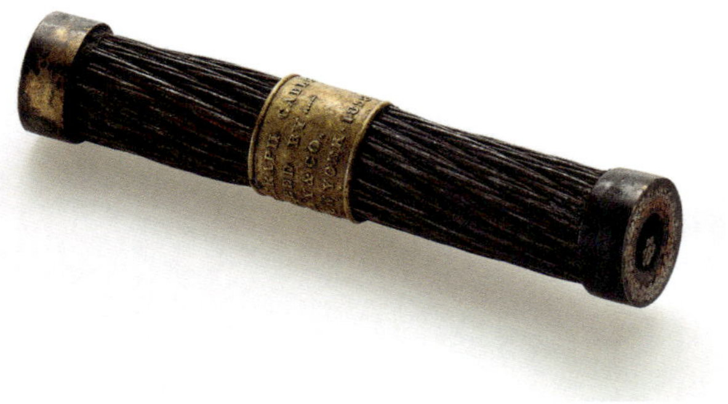

8/43

The Connection of the World by Telegraph

8/43 **Presentation piece of the first transatlantic cable**
Glass, Elliott & Co., Tiffany & Co.
London/New York, 1858
Steel, copper, brass, gutta-percha: L 10.2 cm, diam. 1.3 cm
Berlin, Deutsches Historisches Museum: AK 2017/93

The laying of the first transatlantic telegraph cable between Ireland and Newfoundland was a pioneering technological achievement. Essential to its success was the preparatory survey of the seabed by an American naval officer, Matthew F. Maury (1806–1873). The British government gave considerable support to the project. The cable was around 4,630 kilometres long and weighed some 2,500 tons. Although the work had not been without setbacks, the first telegraphic connection between Europe and America was completed on 5 August 1858. The first official telegram was a message of congratulations from Queen Victoria (1819–1901) of the United Kingdom to the President of the United States, James Buchanan (1791–1868). Technical problems soon arose, however, and the connection only worked for a few weeks. Excessive electrical voltage had been applied which, together with deteriorating insulation, rendered the copper cable unserviceable. Previously, upon completion of the laying work, the New York jeweller Tiffany & Co. had acquired surplus lengths of the cable. They were cut into pieces, set, and sold as souvenirs with a certificate. TE

8/44 **NSW MINISUB SA 144-1, presentation sample of a submarine telecommunications cable**
Norddeutsche Seekabelwerke GmbH
Nordenham, 2007/2008
Fibreglass, plastic, copper; L 24 cm, diam. 2.9 cm
Kiel, GEOMAR Helmholtz-Zentrum für Ozeanforschung Kiel: 2017-2010

The importance of submarine cables is illustrated by the fact that today about 95 percent of the world's Internet traffic passes along submarine cables. As the backbone of digital communication, they are irreplaceable. Submarine cables like this one connect the French port of Marseille and the islands of Sicily and Crete with Alexandria in Egypt. They have a combined length of about 4,300 kilometres and lie at depths of as much as 2,500 metres. The composition of such cables varies, depending on where they are to be laid. The deep sea cable shown here has a lightweight metal sheath with thin insulation. The submarine cables laid in shallower waters are considerably thicker. That is because they also need to be protected from damage caused by ships' anchors and shark bites. The cable itself is therefore wrapped in metal sheathing. Newly developed materials and improved manufacturing processes have greatly increased data transmission rates and physical durability. In the 1980s, the first experiments were made with fibre-optic cables, which are now standard. The copper cables used previously, which were primarily suited to telegraphic purposes, are no longer adequate for Internet traffic. Submarine cables are used not only for telecommunications, but also, in a different design, for distributing electrical power. GHW/TE

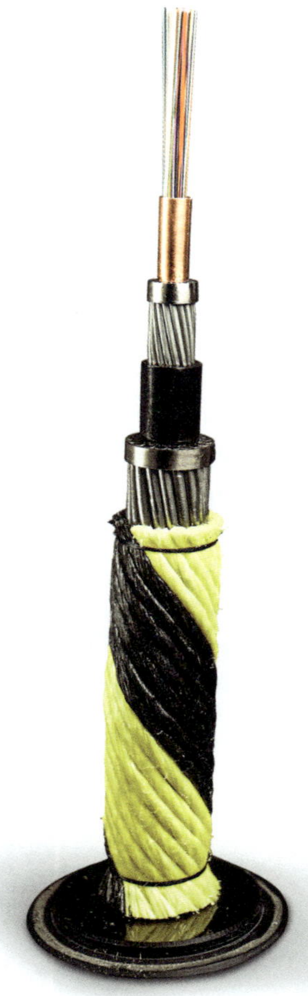

8/44

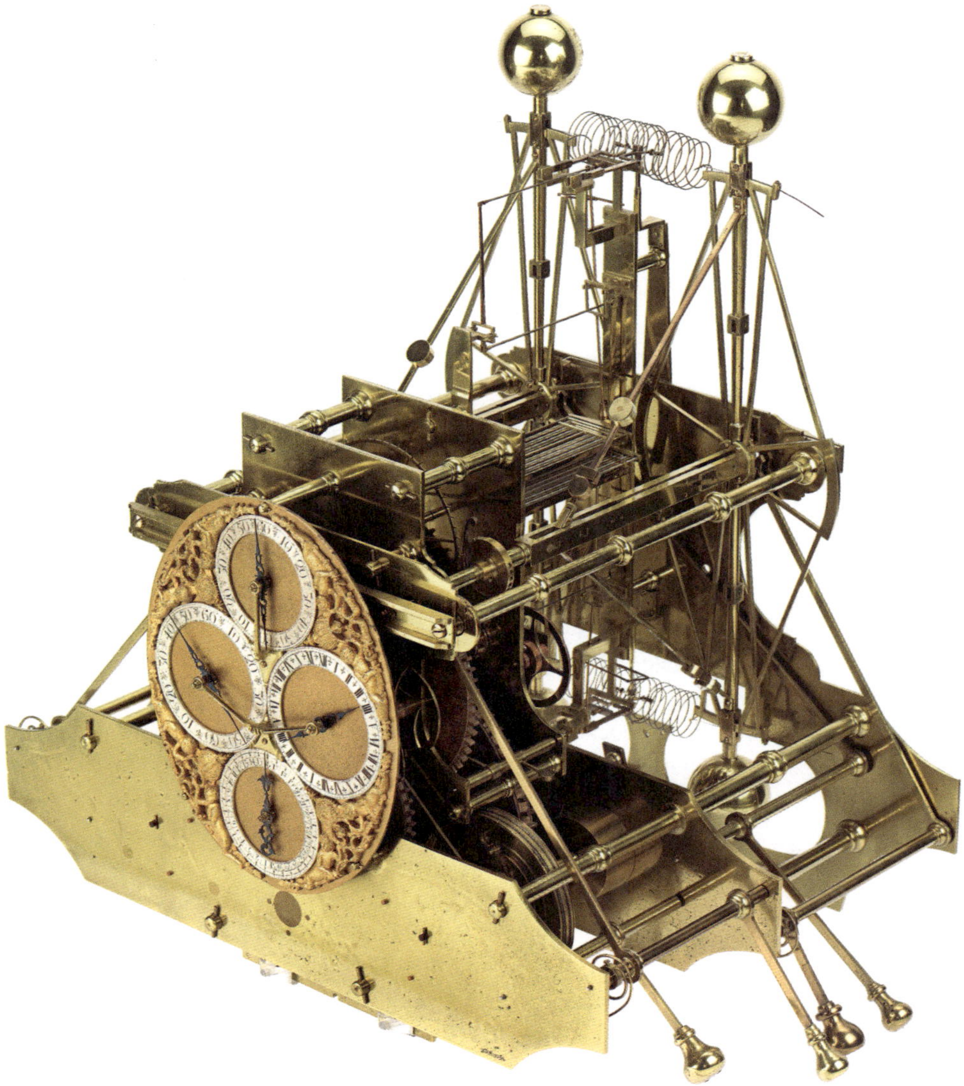

8/45

The Synchronisation and Standardisation of the World

8/45 **Replica of John Harrison's first marine chronometer, H1**
Leonard Salzer (1922–1990)
London, 1970
Brass, bronze, steel, oak, guayacan wood (lignum vitae); 63.5 x 76.2 x 65 cm
Greenwich, London, National Maritime Museum: ZAA0276

A problem that emerged for seafarers in the eighteenth century evolved into a global concern during the nineteenth: the accurate measurement of time. In 1714, several warships of a British fleet were wrecked on the Isles of Scilly after inaccurately determining their positions. This disaster led the British Admiralty to announce generous cash awards for any technical instrument or method that would improve the calculation of longitude on a ship at sea. One possible approach was to compare the local time with the time at a known point of reference, but this required a reliable, accurate timepiece. The clock would need to keep time consistently for a long period without being affected by the salt air, the motion of the sea, and changing climatic conditions. The awards of up to £20,000 – an astronomical sum at the time – led many people to submit devices, lunar tables and other solutions. The most successful applicant was a British clockmaker, John Harrison (1693–1776), who first presented his concept for a precision chronometer in 1728. By 1735, Harrison was ready to demonstrate his first portable "sea clock", H1, to the authorities. Over the next few decades, he made the mechanism more accurate and the design more compact, culminating in his "sea watch", H4. James Cook (1728–1779) took a copy of H4 on his second circumnavigation of the world in 1775, proving that Harrison's marine chronometer kept time accurately enough to calculate the degree of longitude. TE

8/46 **Marine chronometer No. 16**
John Arnold (1736–1799)
London, c. 1783
Casing: mahogany, domed glass; dial: cream-coloured enamel, blued steel hands; movement: bimetal, gold, diamond cap jewel; 10 x 14 x 14 cm
Furtwangen, Deutsches Uhrenmuseum: 2012-031

The manufacture of highly accurate marine chronometers in the second half of the eighteenth century demonstrates the great craftsmanship and technical knowledge of contemporary watchmakers. To begin with, the instruments were both time-consuming and costly to make, as many different materials of high quality were needed. A London watchmaker, John Arnold, refined Harrison's design principles to create more efficient chronometers. Technical advances enabled him to simplify the construction and finally made it possible to produce identical copies in large numbers. Important innovations were the spring detent escapement and the temperature-compensated balance, which Arnold developed in 1782. Each chronometer made by Arnold has its own serial number. This example, bearing the number 16, is one of the first to incorporate his technical innovations. (Exhibit not shown) TE

8/47 **Pocket watch with world-time dial**
Léopold J. Béguelin
Tramelan (Switzerland), c. 1885
Gold, brass; diam. 6 cm
Furtwangen, Deutsches Uhrenmuseum: 2000-092

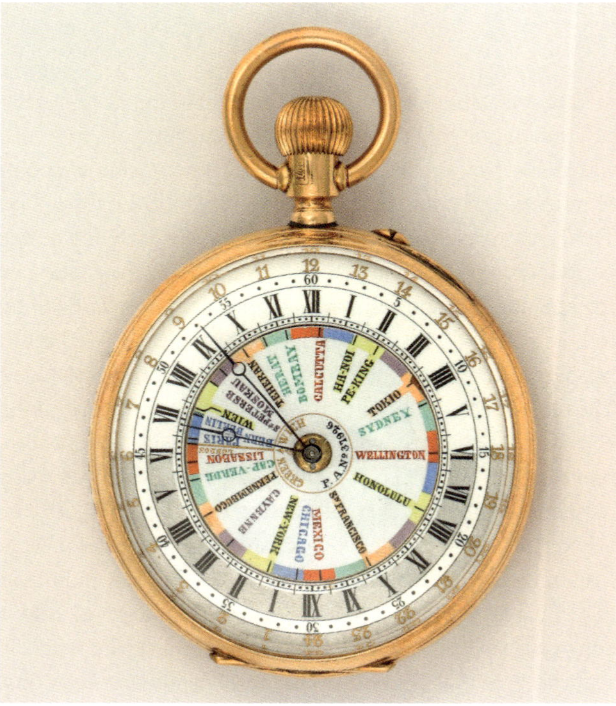

8/47

This world-time pocket watch illustrates the increasing importance of timekeeping and universal timetables. Place names are printed in different positions around the dial. This allows the local time in any of these cities to be told at a glance. Before 1884, the concept of time zones was unfamiliar to most people. Until well into the nineteenth century, each city or region set its own time. It was not until the world became increasingly interconnected by steamer routes and railway lines, together with postal and telegraph services, that it became necessary to agree on a standard basis for universal time. Experts had been considering the division of the globe into 24 time zones, each with 15 degrees of longitude, since 1876, but it was not until 1884 that the International Meridian Conference in Washington agreed on a binding location for zero longitude. This meridian runs through the Royal Observatory at Greenwich, near London. Beside its leading economic role, Great Britain thus became the centre for the worldwide synchronisation of time. TE

8/48 **Door of a 20-foot shipping container**
China, 2015
Cor-Ten steel; 260 x 120 x 0.6 cm
Berlin, Containermanufaktur, Gesellschaft für modulare Seecontainerbauten mbH

Colourful 20-foot and 40-foot containers are used all around the world. Both models are based on standard dimensions: 2.59 m high and 2.44 m wide, with a length of 6.06 m and 12.19 m respectively. The smaller container is known as a TEU (Twenty-foot Equivalent Unit) and the larger one as an FEU (Forty-foot Equivalent Unit). The introduction of the container to shipping as an efficient means of transporting goods in bulk goes back to the 1950s. An American businessman, Malcom McLean (1913-2001), is credited with making the idea a practical reality. Attempts had previously been made in Europe to simplify transportation by using standardised containers. This avoided the problems caused by having to handle and store many different transport containers based on different systems. On 26 April 1956, the IDEAL X, a wartime oil tanker converted into a freighter, left the New Jersey harbour and headed for the Port of Houston in Texas. On board were 58 containers, which could be transported on trucks as well as on ships. For many, this voyage marks the start of modern container shipping. The first container ship to call at a European port was the FAIRLAND. It berthed in Bremen on 6 May 1966. With clear practical and financial advantages, the system was soon in use everywhere. There are now over 20 million shipping containers in circulation, accounting for about 70 per cent of general cargo worldwide. TE

8/49 **Container ships in the Port of Hamburg**
Hamburg, c. 2016
Photograph (reproduction)
Hamburg, Bildarchiv Hamburg: 8942

The dominance of the shipping container as a universal transport container has transformed the appearance not only of ships, but also of ports. Most port facilities are now automated and make relatively little use of manpower, handling much higher volumes of freight than before. They are served by dedicated road and rail links for the direct transport of goods. The Port of Hamburg's container terminal at Burchardkai (CTB) began handling container ships as early as 1968. Long quays with 30 gantry cranes allow numerous vessels to be loaded and unloaded at in parallel. Today, the world's largest container ports are in China. In Europe, the ports with the highest throughput in 2015 were Rotterdam (12.2 million TEU), Antwerp (9.6 million TEU) and Hamburg (8.8 million TEU). (Fig. p. 97) TE

8/50 ***shipmap.org*, interactive map of worldwide shipping movements in 2012**
Created by Kiln Enterprises Ltd, UCL EI, exactEarth, Clarksons
London, 2014
London, Kiln Enterprises Ltd

Today, up to 90 percent of global freight is transported by sea. Over the last few centuries, the ship has lost none of its importance as the main means of transport for international trade. This map shows that while new sea routes have come into being, the old established ones continue to be well used. It reproduces the movement of ships around the world in 2012, and is based on 250 million data records. In our digital age, large vessels are fitted with transponders that identify them and track their position in real time. Europe's coastal areas are still busy sea routes, although traffic is now concentrated in narrow stretches of water such as the Øresund, the English Channel and the Strait of Gibraltar. The Suez Canal, opened in 1869 to connect the Mediterranean Sea with the Indian Ocean, is still used to shorten the journey between East Asia and Europe, strengthening the regions' maritime connection. At present, 26 per cent of the world's container freight comes from China. TE

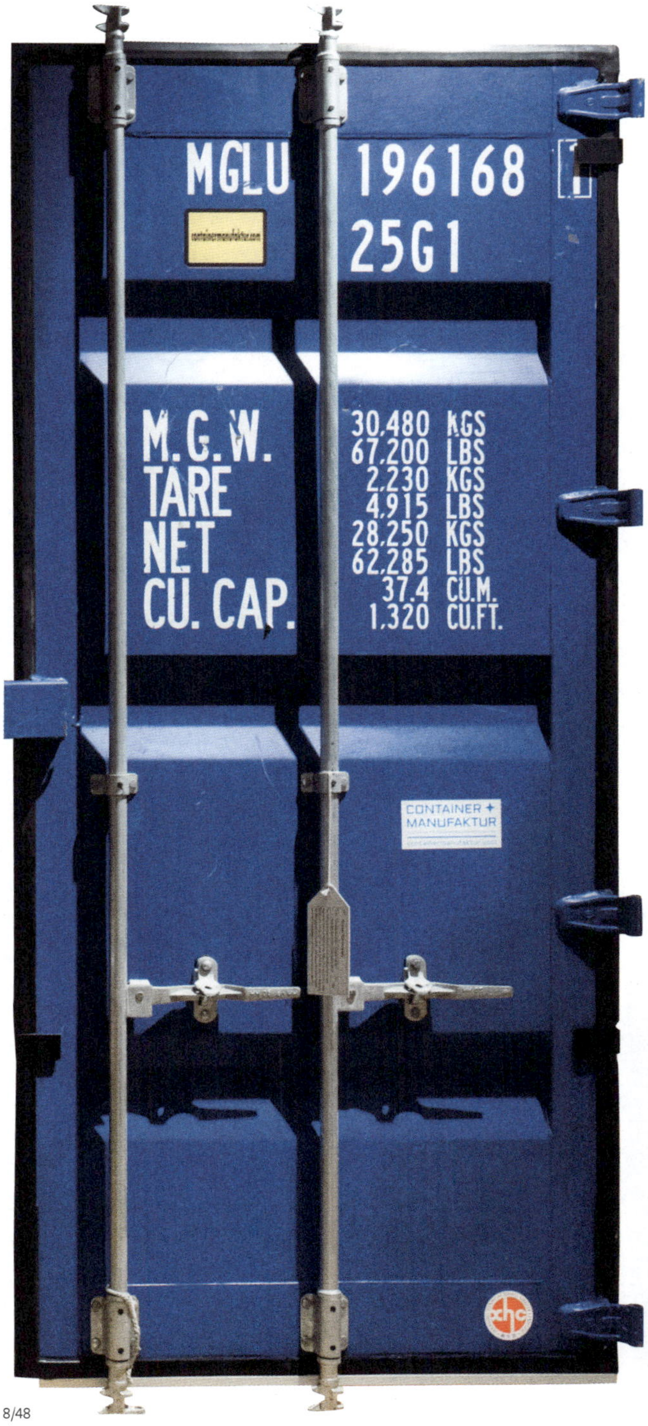

8/48

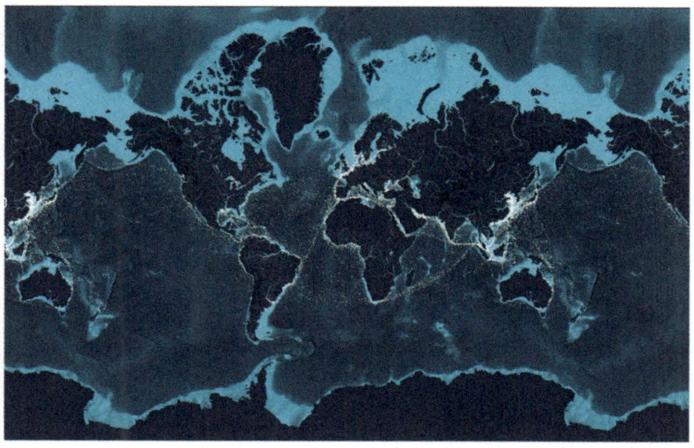

8/50

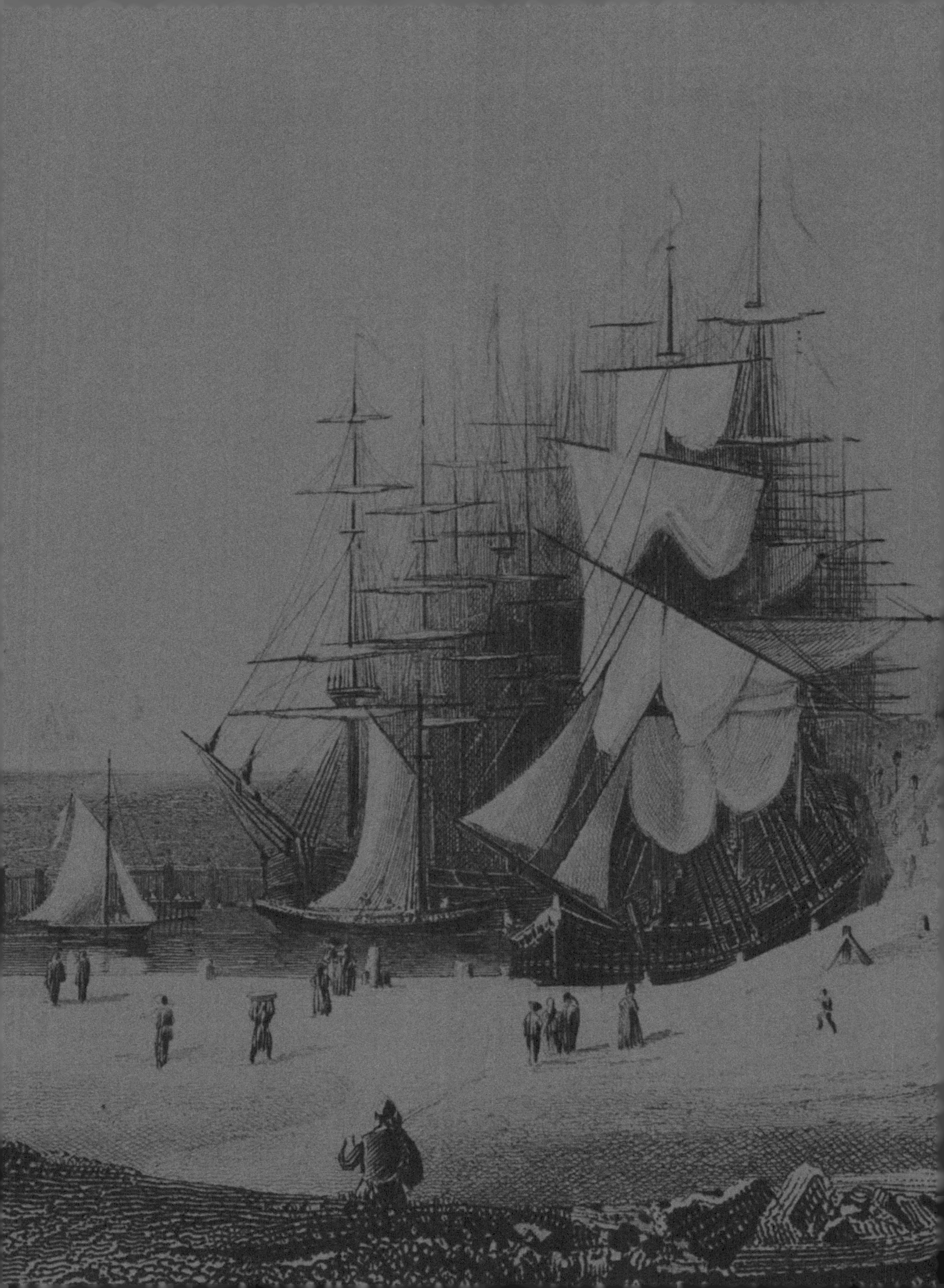

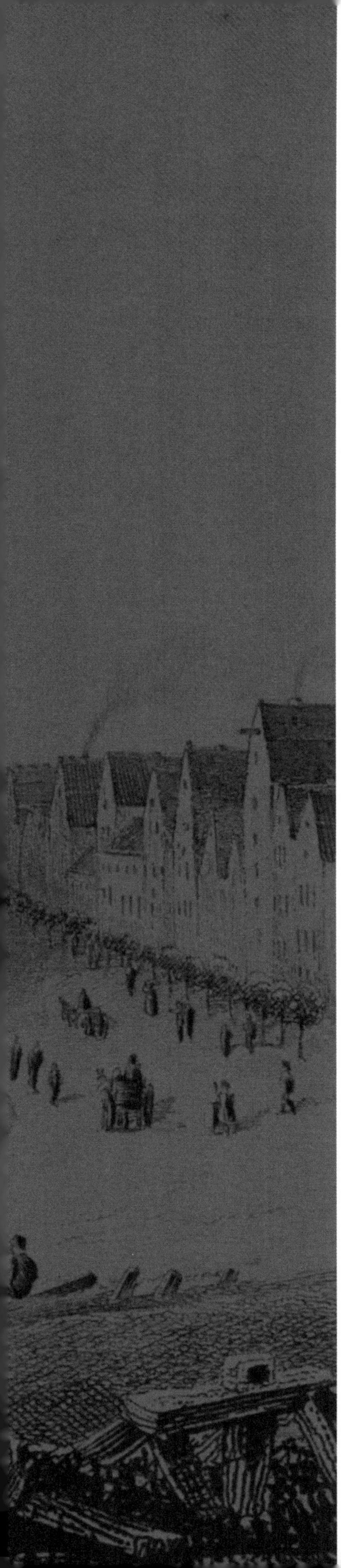

II
BRIDGE AND BARRIER

9 Migration
The Port of Bremerhaven

Migration is one of the defining elements of human history. It was never an anomaly, but rather a historical normality – and that remains true today. At first, the oceans formed virtually impassable barriers for people who wanted or had to leave their homes. But as technology advanced over the course of the nineteenth century, they also came to serve as bridges between the continents. Maritime migration brought the world closer together.

In the 1840s, for the first time in history, transatlantic migration became a mass phenomenon. By 1880, approximately 15 million Europeans had emigrated to North America. One of the reasons was unemployment, which in turn was mainly due to an enormous increase in population. Between 1800 and 1850, Europe's population grew from about 187 million to over 266 million. The port city of Bremerhaven provides a useful case study for the history of transatlantic migration. Founded in 1827, it evolved into the main hub of European emigration by the late nineteenth century. Bremerhaven shows how emigration became an industry in its own right, with increasingly professional services provided by specialised organisations and institutions. These included shipping lines such as the Bremen-based Norddeutsche Lloyd (est. 1857), municipal and state agencies, and religious and privately funded charities.

Countless guides, newspaper and magazine articles, travelogues and novels explained more or less truthfully everything a potential emigrant needed to know, including the risks and rewards of emigration. Letters from people who had emigrated previously were the primary means of communication and a crucial source of information for people still in their home countries. For most emigrants, the crossing was a traumatic experience, both physically and emotionally. Rough seas and storms made people seasick and even afraid for their lives; their quarters in steerage were cramped and unhygienic; and there was not enough food. The advent of steamships significantly improved travel conditions and reduced prices. Ocean liners, now operating on regular schedules, shortened the voyage from Europe to the United States from an average of 44 days to just two weeks.

The mid-1880s saw another large rise in the number of people emigrating overseas, this time to about 800,000 per year. From the turn of the century to the First World War, an average of 1.3 million Europeans left their homes every year for a new life across the sea. The majority of them were no longer coming from western and northern Europe, but instead from southern, south-eastern and eastern Europe, and in particular from the multi-ethnic empires of Austria-Hungary and Russia. This wave of migration was called "new immigration" in the United States and *Durchwanderung* (transit migration) in Germany, which served as a transit country for people from eastern and southern Europe. Stricter controls were put in place at European borders and ports of departure in response to increasingly restrictive policies on the part of American immigration authorities.

In the twentieth century, Europe evolved from a continent of emigrants to one of immigrants. Following struggles for independence in French, Dutch, Belgian and British colonies after the Second World War, the numbers of people emigrating from former colonies to their erstwhile 'mother countries' increased greatly. This gave rise to what German historian Jochen Oltmer calls a "paradox in the history of European expansion" – that is, the colonial empires of Europe were more present on the mainland, in the form of immigrants, during and after the dissolution of its colonies than they ever had been before. The classic example of this phenomenon is the UK's "Windrush generation", who represent postcolonial immigration and the evolution of Great Britain into a multi-ethnic society.

Europe continues to be a continent of immigration in the twenty-first century, a dream destination for people seeking to escape bitter poverty or fleeing war and terror. In the last few years, the Mediterranean in particular has seen millions of people migrating from countries in Africa and the Middle East. For the most part, their passage across the sea is a much more make-shift and dangerous affair than it was in the nineteenth century. Stories of refugees that come to a happy ending cannot disguise the fact that thousands of people drown during the crossing. As Europe increasingly closes its doors to immigrants, the sea forfeits its role as a bridge and again becomes a massive barrier. *Ursula Breymayer*

Further Reading

Klaus Bade et al (eds.), *Enzyklopädie Migration in Europa. Vom 17. Jahrhundert bis zur Gegenwart*, Munich 2007

Anja Benscheidt and Alfred Kube, *Brücke nach Übersee. Auswanderung über Bremerhaven 1830-1974*, Bremerhaven 2006

Tobias Brinkmann, *Migration und Transnationalität*, Paderborn 2012

Sebastian Conrad, *Dekolonisierung in den Metropolen*, in: Geschichte und Gesellschaft 37, 2011, pp. 135-156

Birgit Gelberg, *Auswanderung nach Übersee. Soziale Probleme der Auswandererbeförderung in Hamburg und Bremen von der Mitte des 19. Jahrhunderts bis zum Ersten Weltkrieg*, Hamburg 1973

Rolf Engelsing, *Bremen als Auswandererhafen 1683-1880*, Bremen 1961 (Veröffentlichungen aus dem Staatsarchiv der Freien Hansestadt Bremen Heft 29)

Michael Just, *Ost- und südosteuropäische Amerikawanderung 1881-1914.Transitprobleme in Deutschland und Aufnahme in den Vereinigten Staaten*, Stuttgart 1988

Leo Lucassen, *The Immigrant Threat. The Integration of Old and New Migrants in Western Europa since 1850*, Urbana/Chigago 2005

Jochen Oltmer, *Migration: Geschichte und Zukunft der Gegenwart*, Darmstadt 2017

Jochen Oltmer, *Globale Migration: Geschichte und Gegenwart*, Munich 2016, (2nd, revised and extended edition)

Jochen Oltmer, *Migration vom 19. bis zum 21. Jahrhundert*, Berlin 2016 (3rd, revised and extended edition)

Europe in the Long Nineteenth Century – A Continent of Emigrants

9/1 **Steamer trunk**
c. 1880
Wood covered with jute, iron fittings, iron lock;
92 x 55 x 63 cm
Bremerhaven, Historisches Museum Bremerhaven:
01/837

Until the twentieth century, emigrants typically travelled with steamer trunks, which looked more like furniture than luggage. Sturdy wood bodies (usually oak) and iron fittings ensured that they could stand up to the stresses of the voyage. They were initially crafted by carpenters and metal-workers, and fitted with wheels on the bottom (as can be seen on the trunk shown here). The hand-painted initials "M.B." are those of the former owner, and the number "3" indicates that the trunk is one of several pieces of luggage. Trunk lids, which were initially arched, became flat to facilitate stacking in cargo holds and baggage cars. (Exhibit not shown) UB

9/2 **Steamer trunk**
c. 1890
Wood covered with jute; 95 x 58 x 57 cm
Bremerhaven, Historisches Museum Bremerhaven:
97/293

Though it looks like an old-fashioned chest, this trunk was not actually crafted by hand. Luggage began to be mass-produced in the mid-nineteenth century, partially in response to demand from growing numbers of emigrants. Starting in the 1870s, a number of luggage manufacturers started up businesses in Europe and the United States. Wood was used as the primary material for a long time. (Exhibit not shown) UB

9/3 **Steamer trunk**
c. 1900
Wood covered with jute, leather handle, fabric lining;
85 x 50 x 42 cm
Bremerhaven, Historisches Museum Bremerhaven: 97/7
(Exhibit not shown)

9/4 **Steamer trunk**
c. 1910
Vulcanised fibre, wooden reinforcing strips, metal fittings and locks, leather handle, cotton straps on the inside; 75.5 x 45.4 x 22.5 cm
Bremerhaven, Historisches Museum Bremerhaven:
00/1325

By the mid-nineteenth century, luggage manufacturers had moved away from wood in favour of a jute or cellulose-based synthetic substance called vulcanised fibre. The corners were reinforced with metal fittings, and straps provided additional stability. This new type of luggage was very similar in design to the suitcases we use today. The decorative pattern of black lines recalls the old trunks, however, which were typically painted in a similar fashion. (Exhibit not shown) UB

9/5 **Hand luggage**
c. 1900
Wicker, leather; 61 x 40 x 15.5 cm
Bremerhaven, Historisches Museum Bremerhaven:
99/290

Luggage made of wicker, a relatively delicate material, was not typically used by emigrants. The owner of this small suitcase, a woman who emigrated to the United States in the 1920s, probably travelled in a single cabin and had the luxury of storing her luggage there. (Exhibit not shown) UB

9/6 ***Emigrants' farewell***
Antonie Volkmar (1827–1903)
Berlin, 1860
Oil on canvas; 112.4 x 190.5 cm
Berlin, Deutsches Historisches Museum: 1991/3264

This painting is a symbolic representation of emigration and does not portray a historically documented event. It shows men, women and children of different social classes and ages sitting in a rowing boat. They are on their way out to a sailing ship flying an American flag. Most of them appear worried and apprehensive as they contemplate the future and their impending voyage. The work was probably inspired by *Crossing at Schreckenstein*, painted in 1837 by Ludwig Richter (1803–1884). The two paintings show a remarkable similarity in their grouping of figures on the boat and in the landscape featuring a castle in the background. There is also very little difference in their use of metaphor. The ship, tossing in the waves, evokes the uncertainties and vicissitudes of life. UB

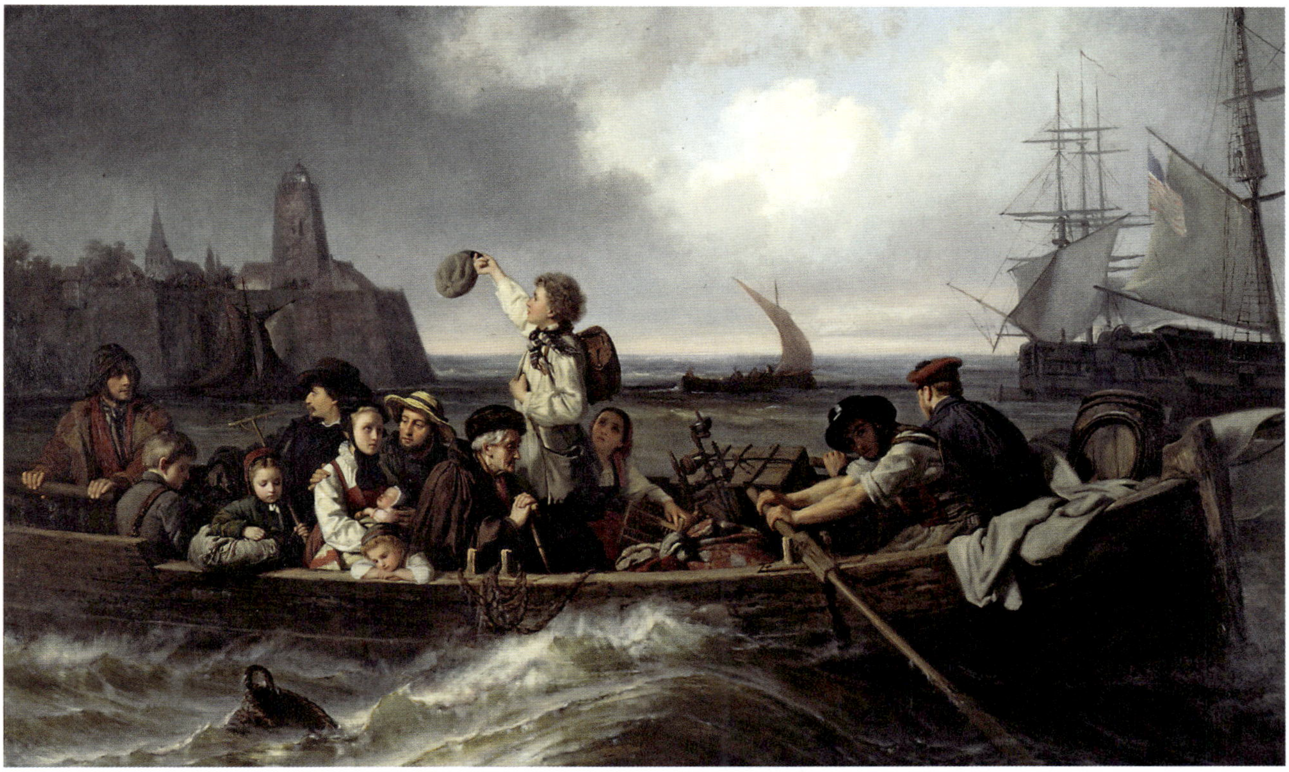

9/6

Forms of Communication

9/7 **Letter written by emigrant Otto Guden to his sister Agnes**
New York, 22 September 1865
Paper with printed graphic, handwritten; 19.5 x25 cm
Bremerhaven, Historisches Museum Bremerhaven: 97/636.01-08

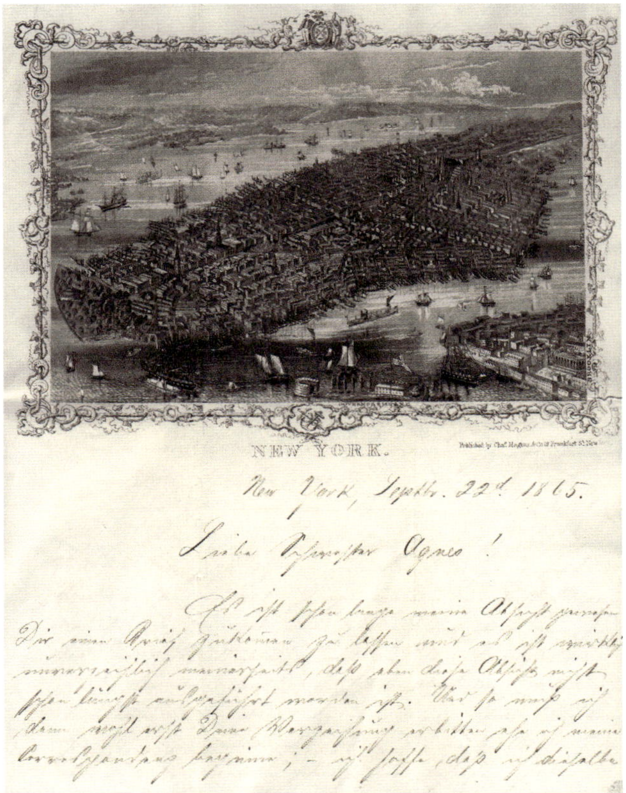
NEW YORK.

New York, Septbr. 22d 1865.

Liebe Schwester Agnes!

9/7

Until about the mid-nineteenth century, anyone who emigrated across the Atlantic was essentially leaving Europe forever. Preparations for the journey consequently took some time. People obtained information from earlier immigrants to America about the best ports and most affordable passages, good places to settle, and the risks and rewards of emigration generally. Letters played a key role here – between 1820 and 1914, at least 100 million private letters are thought to have been sent from immigrants in the United States back to Germany. The sender of the letter shown here, Otto Guden, emigrated to the United States in about 1863 with his brothers. They came from the little town of Dransfeld, near Göttingen, in southern Lower Saxony. The letterhead has been printed with an aerial view of the Manhattan peninsula. Starting in 1855, all immigrants arriving in New York were processed at Castle Garden, a former military fort that had been repurposed as an "emigrant landing depot". UB

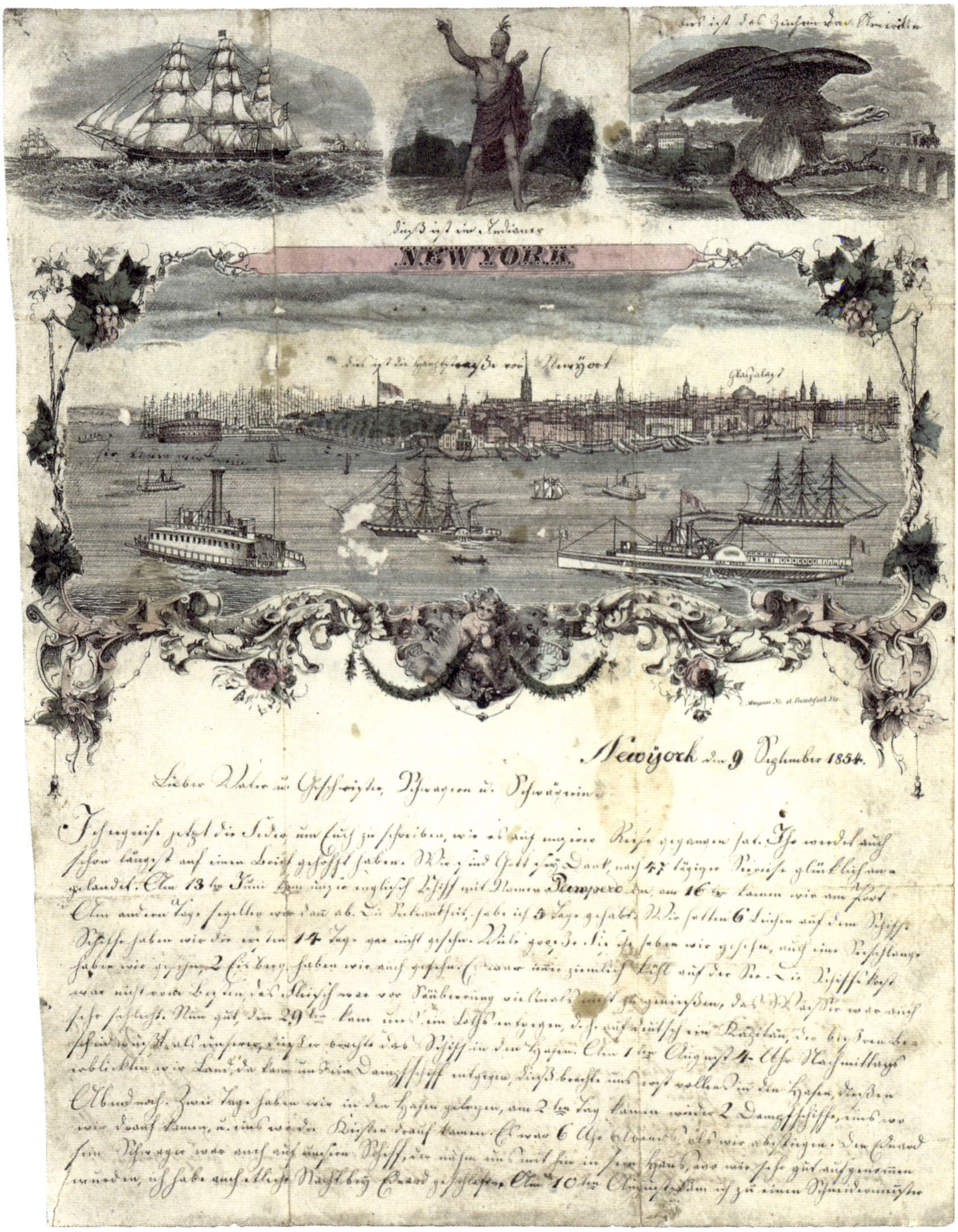

9/8

9/8 **Letter written by emigrant Sebastian Fritz to his family**
New York, 9 September 1854
Paper, printed and coloured, handwritten; 28 x 21 cm
Deutsches Historisches Museum: Do 97/17.1-2

When Sebastian Fritz wrote to his family from New York in September 1854, he had recently completed a difficult voyage across the Atlantic. After 47 days at sea – during which time he had contended with seasickness, bad food and foul drinking water, but had also been exhilarated to see whales, sea snakes and icebergs for the first time – Fritz had made it to the United States, the number one destination of emigrants at the time. It is not known what drove him to leave his home (probably in Hesse). Whatever the reasons were, they were serious enough for him to make the dangerous crossing. As he had reason to know, it could have cost him his life. In his letter, he wrote “we had six dead bodies on the ship”. TJ

9/9 **Good advice for immigrants to the United States of America**
Guter Rath an Einwanderer in die Vereinigten Staaten von Nordamerika
J. P. Dewis
Edited by W. K. Riedlen
Published by J. J. Christen
Aarau, 1834
Paper, cardboard, calfskin, marbled paper; 17 x 12 cm
Berlin, Deutsches Historisches Museum: R 96/1666

Information about emigration could be had from a variety of sources, including guides and advice books, more or less autobiographical novels and travelogues, and countless newspaper and magazine articles. (Exhibit not shown)

9/10 **Traugott Bromme's handbook and travel guide for emigrants and travellers to North, Central and South America**
Traugott Bromme's Hand- und Reisebuch für Auswanderer und Reisende nach Nord-, Mittel- und Süd-Amerika
Traugott Bromme (1802–1866)
Edited by Gustav Struve (1805–1870)
Published by Verlag der Buchner'schen Buchhandlung
Bamberg, 1866
Paper; 19.1 x 13 cm
Berlin, Staatsbibliothek zu Berlin – Preußischer Kulturbesitz, Benutzungsabteilung: Ut 3348

Traugott Bromme's handbook, originally published in 1840 and already in its eighth edition by 1866, was the best-known German-language 'emigration guide'. The title page features a steel engraving of the Washington Capitol, and a map of North America can be found inside. Bromme, a native of Leipzig, had emigrated to the United States in 1821 but returned just a few years later. (Exhibit not shown) UB

9/11 **The German emigrant**
Der deutsche Auswanderer. Zeitschrift zur Kenntnis des deutschen Elements in allen Ländern der Erde, no. 8, vol. 4
Published by the Nationalverein für Deutsche Auswanderung und Ansiedlung
Frankfurt a. M., 23 February 1850
Paper, printed; 28 x 22.5 cm
Berlin, Deutsches Historisches Museum: RZA 6892 -4.1850

Heinrich Wilhelm August Freiherr von Gagern (1799–1880), who later became chairman of the Frankfurt National Assembly (Germany's first freely elected parliament), founded the National Society for German Emigration and Settlement in 1847. The society printed a newsletter called *Der deutsche Auswanderer* (The German emigrant), which was targeted at potential emigrants and contained information on the practicalities, risks and rewards of emigration. It focused on the United States, which was seen as a suitable location for German settlements. The group emerged in a time of growing German nationalism, and was intended in no small part to preserve, defend and spread "German culture" abroad through the establishment of self-contained German settlements. (Exhibit not shown) UB

9/12 **Emigrant's map and guide to North America**
Auswanderer-Karte und Wegweiser nach Nordamerika
Gotthelf Zimmermann
Published by J. B Metzler'schen Verlagsbuchhandlung
Stuttgart, 1852
Lithograph; 50.5 x 67 cm, scale approx. 1 : 51,000,000
Stuttgart, Württembergische Landesbibliothek: 51Cg/576

The lengthy subtitle in the margin names the subject matter, target group and purpose of this widely used emigrant's map "in which European ports of departure, routes taken by ships across the ocean, ports of arrival in North America, land routes and waterways from the ports of arrival to the American interior, distances between major American cities and towns in German hours, and fares for the main routes in Rhenish guilders and thalers are explained in easily understandable language for everyone, and in particular for emigrating tradesmen and farmers." The area on the map to the west of the Mississippi is relatively bare, but that would change with the westward expansion of white settlers. (Fig. p. 322/323) UB

Bremerhaven – A Hub for Transatlantic Migration out of Europe

9/13 **View of the Old Port of Bremerhaven**
Albert Henry Payne (1812–1902), after Johann Heinrich Sander (1810–1865)
Englische Kunst Anstalt
Leipzig, 1841
Steel engraving; 10.3 x 15.9 cm
Bremerhaven, Historisches Museum Bremerhaven: 90/858

Bremerhaven grew to be one of Europe's key ports of departure for emigrants in the nineteenth century, thanks largely

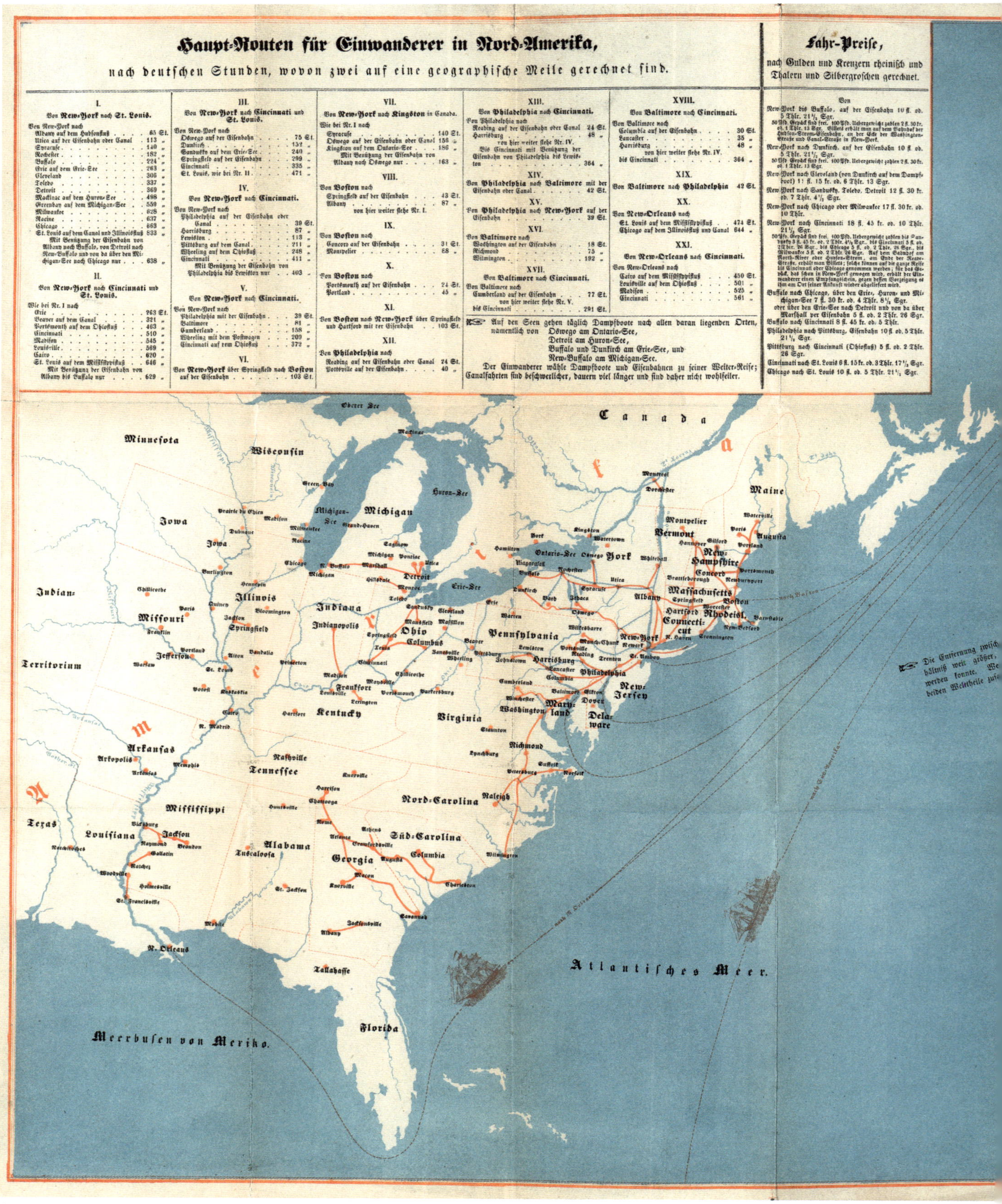
Haupt-Routen für Einwanderer in Nord-Amerika,
nach deutschen Stunden, wovon zwei auf eine geographische Meile gerechnet sind.
Fahr-Preise,
nach Gulden und Kreuzern rheinisch und Thalern und Silbergroschen gerechnet.
Canada
Minnesota
Wisconsin
Michigan
Huron-See
Iowa
Illinois
Indiana
Ohio
Missouri
Indian-
Territorium
Pennsylvania
New-York
Vermont
New-Hampshire
Maine
Massachusetts
Connecticut
Rhodeisl.
New-Jersey
Maryland
Delaware
Virginia
Kentucky
Tennessee
Nord-Carolina
Süd-Carolina
Georgia
Alabama
Mississippi
Louisiana
Arkansas
Texas
Florida
Atlantisches Meer.
Meerbusen von Meriko.

9/12

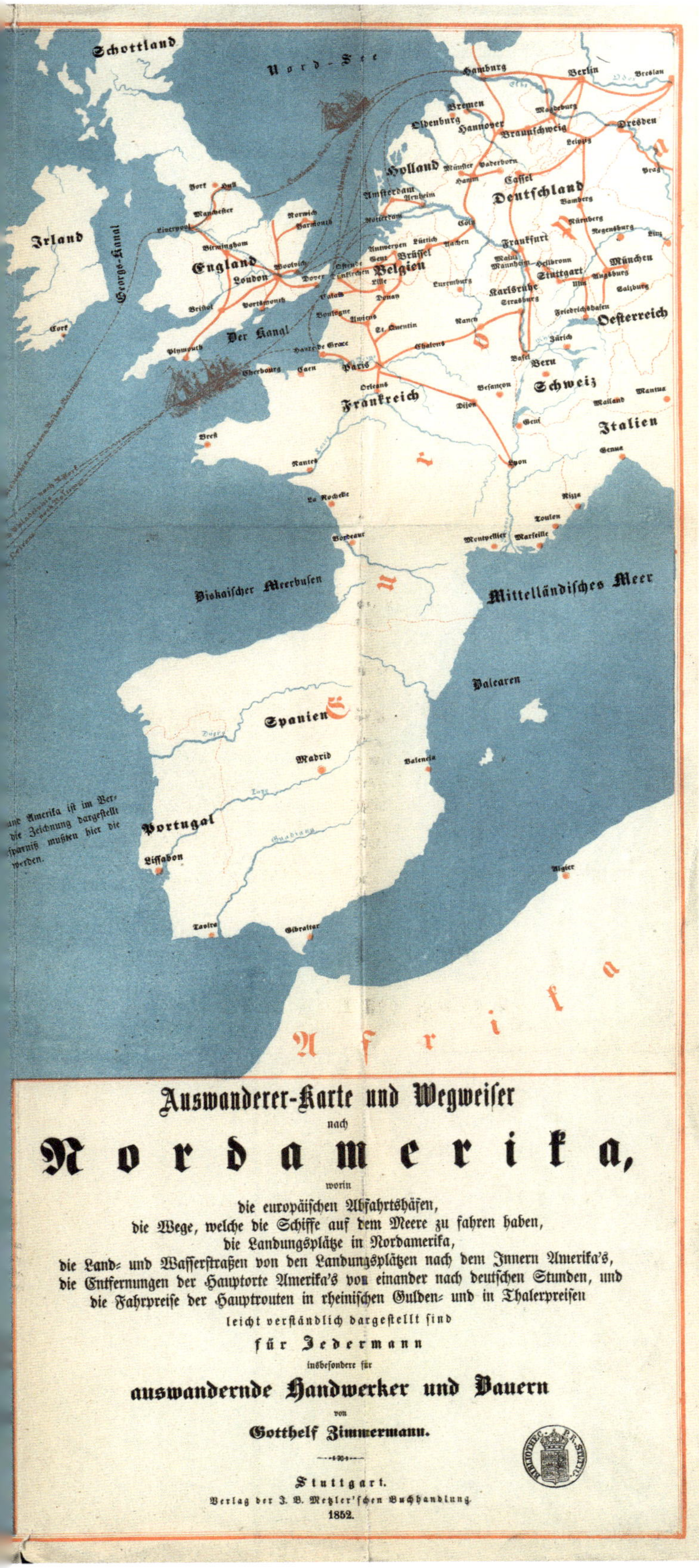

to its close political and economic ties to the Hanseatic City of Bremen. As a transshipment port for merchandise and a departure port for transatlantic emigrants, Bremen faced two distinct disadvantages: it was only connected to the sea by the Weser River, and that river was increasingly silting up. To remain competitive, the city founded Bremerhaven (meaning "Bremen harbour") on the mouth of the Weser River in 1827. The Old Port shown in this engraving was planned by Dutch harbour builders. As can be seen by the bustling activity and large number of sailing ships, the port was doing good business because of the emigration industry, which had been thriving since the 1830s. (Fig. p. 105) UB

9/14 **Cross-sectional model of an emigration ship, c. 1850**
Bremerhaven, 2007
Wood, Paper, textiles; 20 x 20 x 19.5 cm
Bremerhaven, Deutsches Schiffahrtsmuseum – Leibniz-Institut für deutsche Schifffahrtsgeschichte: I/10134/07

Bremen's merchants mainly imported goods such as tobacco, rice, cotton, coffee, sugar and rum from the New World. To utilize the ships' space effectively on the voyage out, they built steerage decks in the holds and transported emigrants as paying 'cargo' across the Atlantic. The steerage deck can be seen on one side of the model, furnished with bunks, tables and benches. Passengers stayed in these rooms throughout the voyage, sleeping, eating and spending their days there. The rear side of the model gives an idea of what the ship looked like on the return voyage. The furnishings have been removed to make space for merchandise. (Exhibit not shown) UB

9/15 **Double-page spread from the *Illustrirte Zeitung*, with views of the docks and the emigrant hostel in Bremerhaven, c. 1851**
Published by Johann Jacob Weber (1803–1880)
Leipzig, 11 January 1851
Print, wood engravings; 40 x 28.5 cm
Berlin, Deutsches Historisches Museum: ZB 20 -16.1851<a> (Jan-Juni)

In 1832, Bremerhaven became the first German city to enact legislation aimed at protecting emigrants. These laws compelled shipowners, agents, innkeepers and others who profited from business with emigrants to maintain certain minimum standards. This gave Bremerhaven a competitive edge over rival ports in northern Europe. In 1849, an emigrant

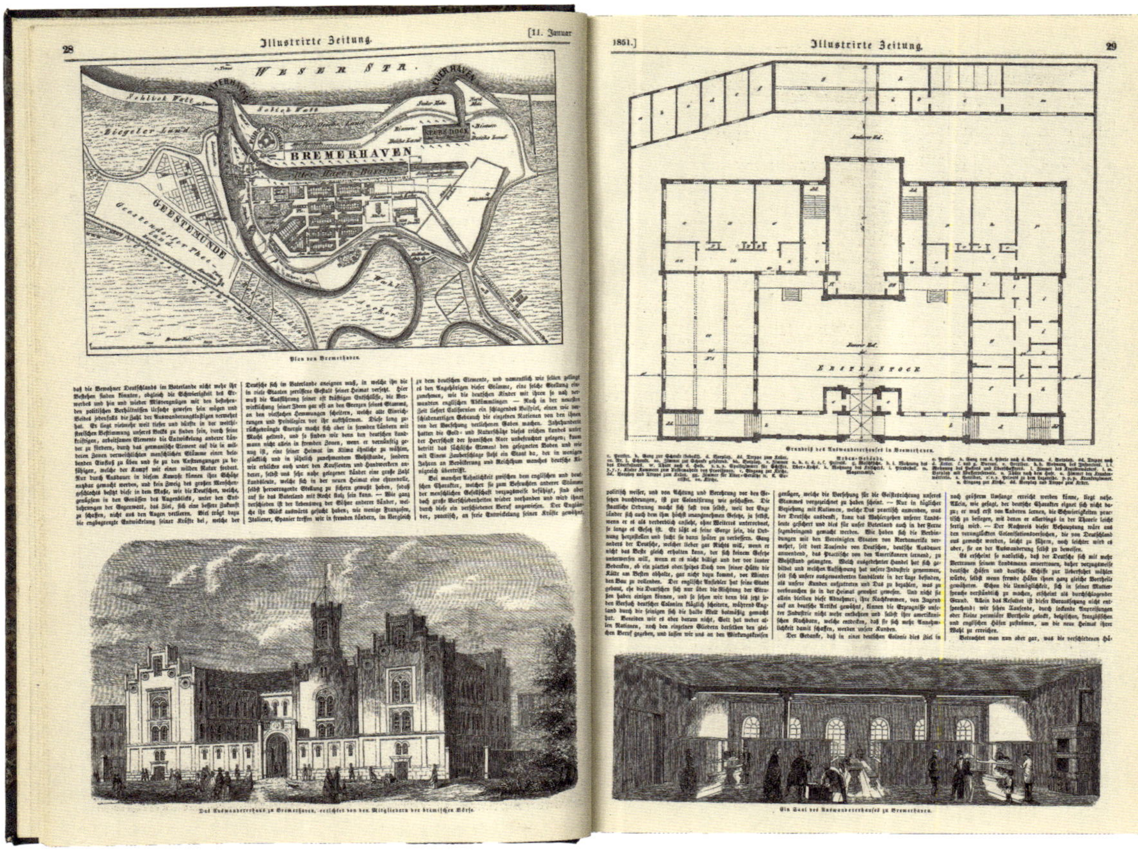
28 Illustrirte Zeitung. [11. Januar

1851.] Illustrirte Zeitung. 29

9/15

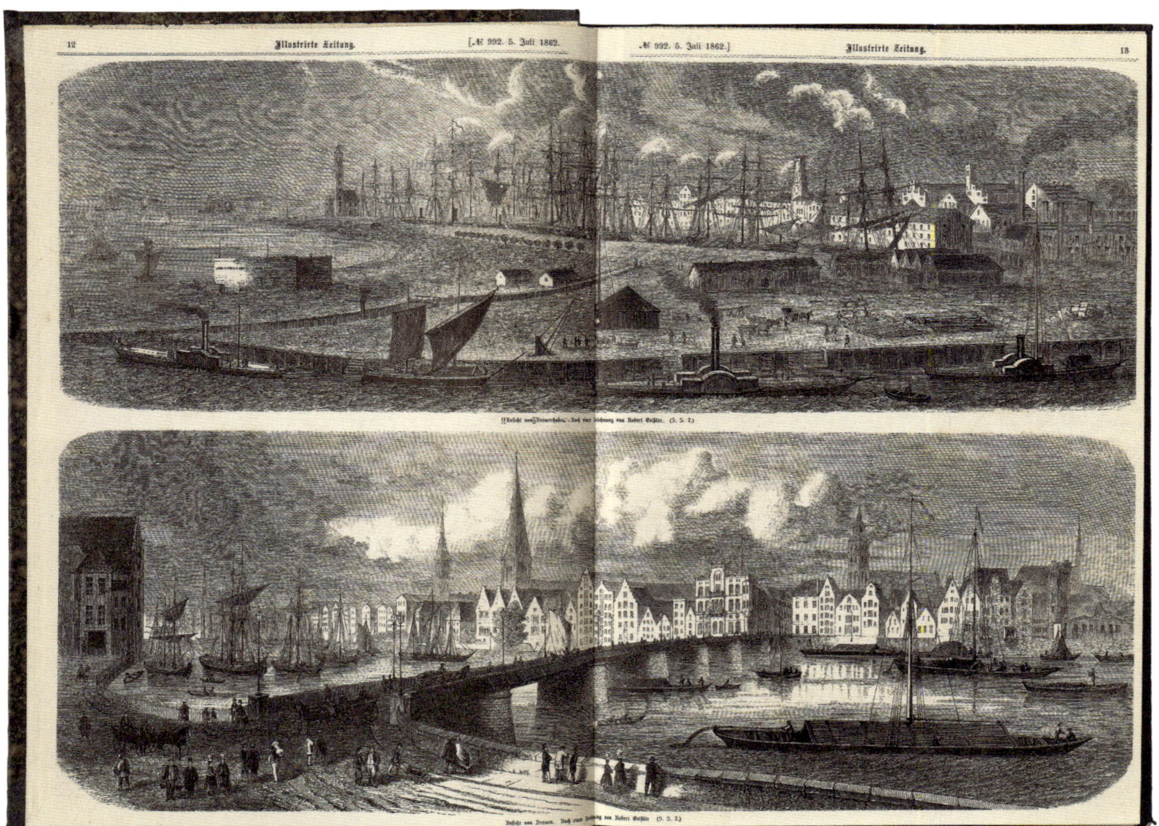
12 Illustrirte Zeitung. [№ 992. 5. Juli 1862.]

№ 992. 5. Juli 1862.] Illustrirte Zeitung. 13

9/16

hostel was built in Bremerhaven. Emigrants received accommodation and food there, and there was even an infirmary with 35 beds. There was no facility like this in any other European port at the time. In 1854, Bremen created the Behörde für das Auswandererwesen, a government emigration agency. It reported to the Bremen Senate and was in charge of overseeing all matters related to emigration. The rival port of Hamburg created a similar authority in 1855, called the Deputation für das Auswandererwesen. UB

9/16 **Double-page spread from the *Illustrirte Zeitung* magazine, with views of the New Port in Bremerhaven, c. 1862**
Wood engraving by Robert Geißler (1819–1893)
Published by Johann Jacob Weber (1803–1880)
Leipzig, 5 July 1862
Print, wood engravings; 40 x 28.5 cm
Berlin, Deutsches Historisches Museum:
ZB 20 -39.1862<a> (Juli–Dez.)

Bremerhaven continued to build new docks, completing its New Port in 1852. The Bremerhaven bank of the Geeste River can be seen in the upper section of this engraving, in the foreground. The paddle steamers and flat-bottomed boats that took emigrants from Bremen to their port of departure in Bremerhaven anchored here. The new port was not the only development Bremerhaven was celebrating in 1862: the city was also connected to the railway line. Special trains now took emigrants from Bremen to Bremerhaven shortly before their ships departed. The *Illustrirte Zeitung*, founded in 1843, frequently featured picture-essays on the subject of emigration. UB

9/17 **Double-page spread from the *Illustrirte Zeitung*, with a view of the Norddeutscher Lloyd waiting hall in Bremerhaven, c. 1871**
Graphic by Carl Justus Fedeler (1837–1897)
Published by Johann Jacob Weber (1803–1880)
Leipzig, 24 June 1871
Print, wood engravings; 40 x 28.7 cm
Berlin, Deutsches Historisches Museum: ZB 20 -56.1871

The waiting hall of the Norddeutscher Lloyd (NDL) shipping line was also located in the New Port. It was completed in 1871, the year in which the German Empire was founded. Passengers were processed here (each class separately) before their departure. The artist, Carl Justus Fedeler, has made the hall appear much larger than it actually was. He shows the NDL flag flying from the masts of all of the ships, presumably to underscore its status as the leading shipping line. Trains from Bremen can be seen stopping directly between the waiting hall and the steamships. While Fedeler renders the technological innovations of the day in some detail, he portrays the emigrants as an anonymous mass. (Fig. p. 106)

9/18 **Advertising poster for the Norddeutscher Lloyd shipping line**
Themistokles von Eckenbrecher (1842–1921)
Bremen, c. 1907
Lithograph; 109 x 75 cm
Bremerhaven, Historisches Museum Bremerhaven:
96/705

One of the driving forces in the emigration business was Norddeutscher Lloyd (NDL), a shipping line founded in 1857 and headquartered in Bremen. It was due to NDL that Bremen and Bremerhaven expanded their roles as principal ports of departure. In 1858, the Lloyd steamer Bremen was the first to make a direct crossing from Bremerhaven to New York. By 1859, regular fortnightly crossings facilitated emigrants' planning considerably. Not long afterwards, in the 1860s and 1870s, NDL branched out to include regular service to Baltimore, New Orleans and South America. Passenger services were now a key source of income for Bremen businesses, second only to tobacco. This poster, based on a work by well-known landscape and marine painter Themistokles von Eckenbrecher, presents NDL's global liner service. Each of the corners proudly shows one of the company's four-funnel liners: Kaiser Wilhelm der Grosse, Kaiser Wilhelm II, Kronprinz Wilhelm and Kronprinzessin Cäcilie. (Fig. p. 326) UB

9/19 **Advertising poster, "Norddeutscher Lloyd express steamer Bremen"**
Bremen/Zurich, 1907
Lithograph; 115 x 60 cm
Bremerhaven, Historisches Museum Bremerhaven:
99/247

By the late 1870s, 85 per cent of the ships serving the Bremerhaven – New York – Bremerhaven route were steamers, not sailing ships. In 1883, NDL introduced a weekly express steamer on this route. Steamers could carry up to 880 emigrants in steerage. A Europe-wide network of agencies sold tickets for passages on NDL ships. The poster shown here hung in an agency in Zurich. It advertises voyages to New York for the most part, but mentions South America, eastern Asia and Australia as well. In naming their ships (listed on the right), NDL paid patriotic homage to contemporary and earlier Hohenzollern monarchs. (Fig. p. 109) UB

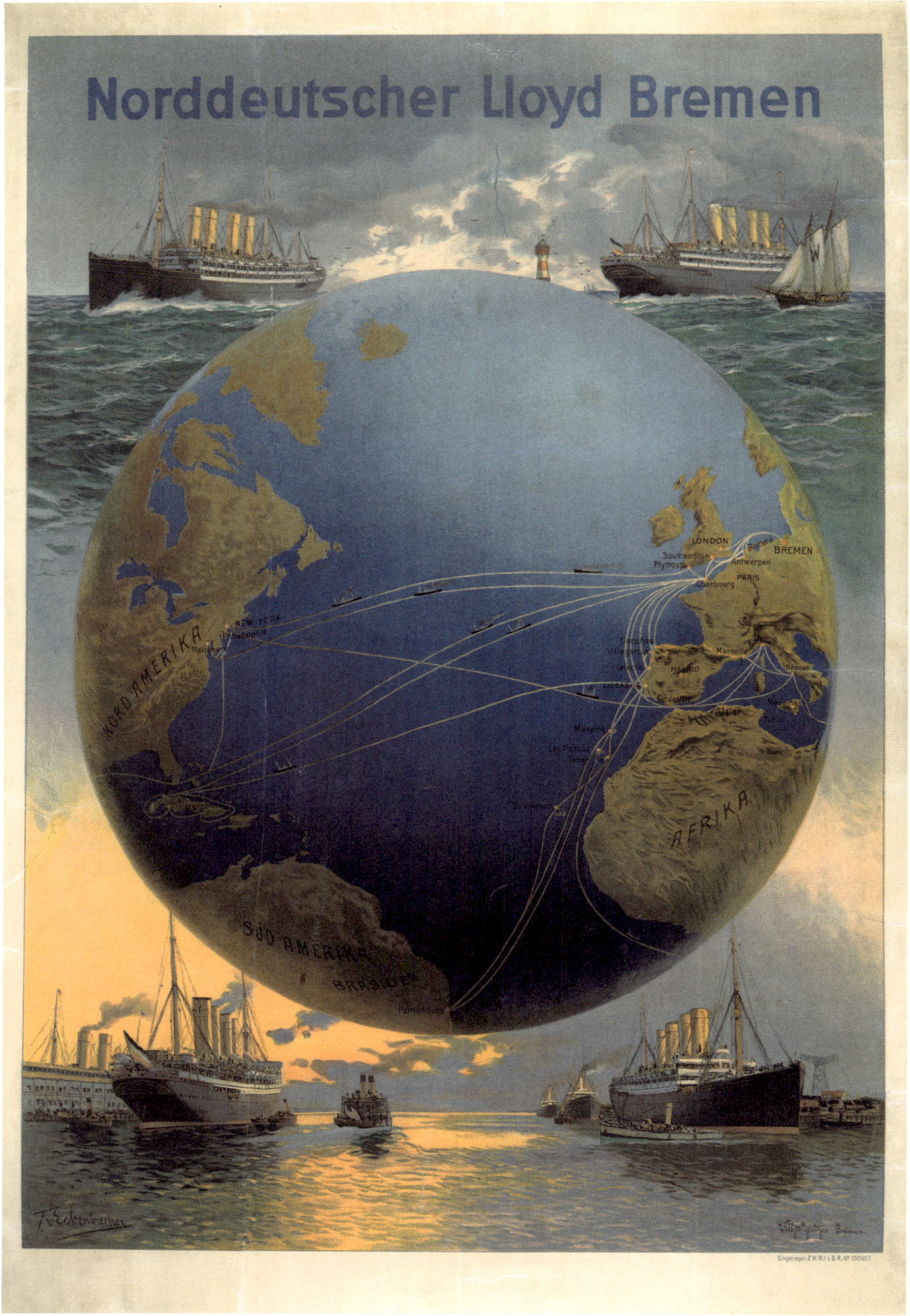
Norddeutscher Lloyd Bremen
LONDON
BREMEN
Southampton
Plymouth
Antwerpen
PARIS
Cherbourg
NEW YORK
NORD AMERIKA
AFRIKA
SÜD AMERIKA

9/18

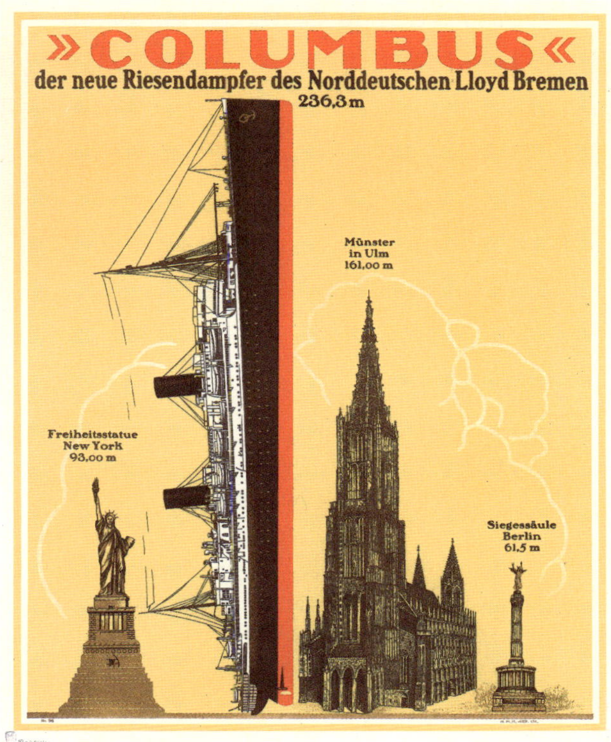

9/20

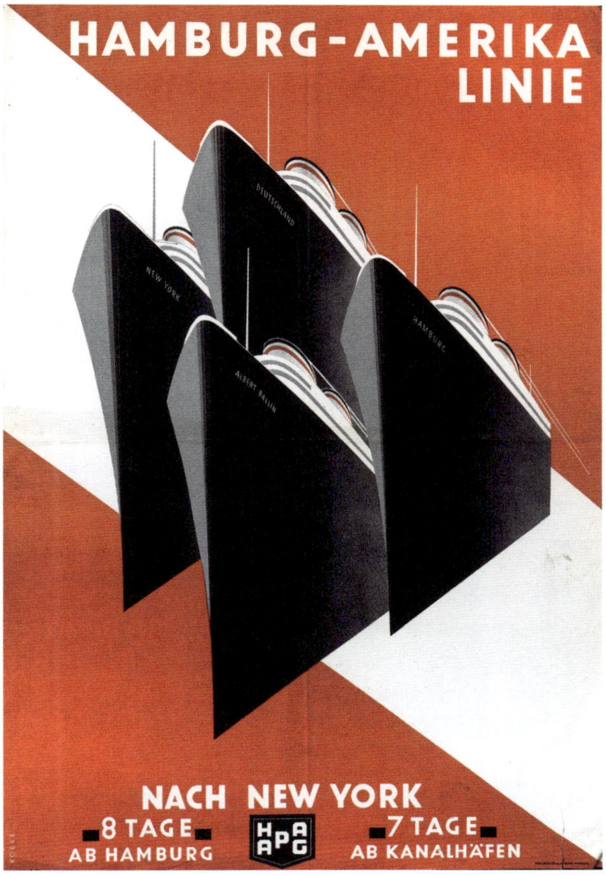

9/21

9/20 **Advertising poster, "Columbus – The colossal new steamship of Norddeutscher Lloyd"**
Bremen, 1924/1925
Lithograph; 59.8 x 50.2 cm
Berlin, Deutsches Historisches Museum: P 57/945

At the turn of the century, thousands of emigrants were still making for new homes across the ocean, but as economic conditions improved before the First World War, fewer and fewer people made the long journey. Shipping lines tried to compensate for shrinking emigration numbers by developing the tourism side of the business. The luxury steamship Columbus, which was not completed until after the war, was designed with this trend in mind. The steerage deck, which in earlier ships had held large numbers of emigrants in cramped quarters, now contained accommodations for third-class passengers. While they were considerably less comfortable than first and second-class quarters, now at least there were cabins with bunks, a dining saloon with servers, a ladies saloon, a smoking saloon, and a lounge. With all these amenities, the weeks at sea were quite tolerable. AvH

9/21 **Advertising poster, "Hamburg-America line – to New York"**
Henning Koeke (1909–1998)
Printed by Mühlmeister und Johler
Hamburg, c. 1930
Offset print; 120.8 x 84 cm
Berlin, Deutsches Historisches Museum: P 74/4132

The Hapag shipping line (Hamburg-Amerikanische Packetfahrt-Actien-Gesellschaft) was founded in Hamburg in 1847. It was not until Albert Ballin (1857–1918) joined the company, however, that it became a serious competitor to Norddeutscher Lloyd. Ballin was made head of passenger services in 1886 and advanced to become Hapag's general director in 1899. This poster uses the motif of a stylised ship's bow – a popular image in the 1920s. The emphasis on diagonal lines suggests power, dynamism and progress. Somewhat contrary to the abstract nature of the design, the names of the ships are lettered on their hulls: Albert Ballin, Deutschland, Hamburg and New York. All four ships were built in the Hamburg shipyard of Blohm & Voss in the 1920s and entered service in the North Atlantic between 1923 and 1927. In 1935, the Ballin was renamed Hansa on orders of the Reich Ministry of Public Enlightenment and Propaganda, because Ballin was Jewish. UB

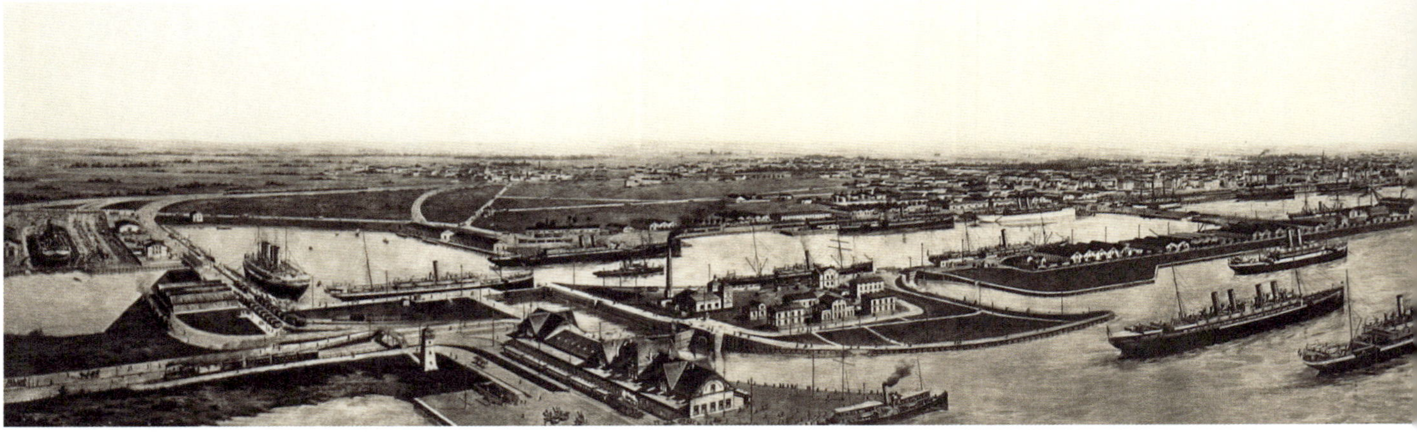

9/22

9/22 **View of the new docks in Bremerhaven**
Jakob Weeser-Krell (1841–1903)
Published by Weeser-Krell
Upper Austria, 1899
Lithograph; 60.1 x 140.4 cm
Bremerhaven, Historisches Museum Bremerhaven: 06/40

Norddeutscher Lloyd (NDL) commissioned Jakob Weeser-Krell (known for his paintings of industrial scenes) to create a panoramic view of their new dock, called the Kaiserhafen, when it opened just outside Bremerhaven in 1897. The NDL's new waiting hall doubled as a train station, and can be seen on the left-hand side of the picture in the foreground, directly at the water's edge. The artist included a total of 24 NDL passenger liners in his lithograph, which he completed in 1899. The names of the ships are listed beneath the picture. UB

9/23 **Protective sleeve for travel documents, imprinted with "F.-Missler Bremen"**
Bremen, c. 1910
Cotton, piping; 17.1 x 21.2 cm
Bremerhaven, Historisches Museum Bremerhaven: 99/481

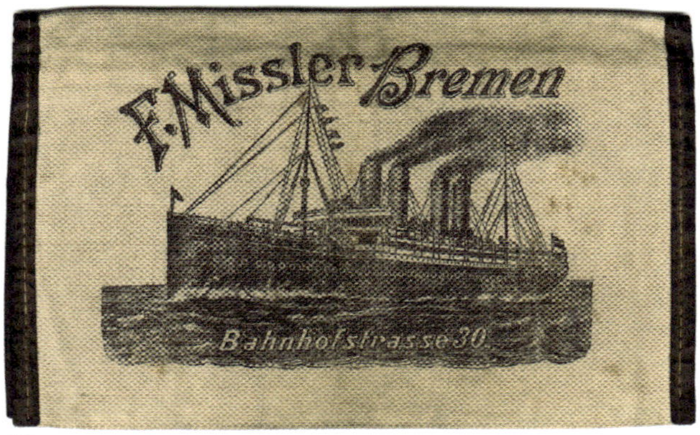

9/23

Friedrich Missler (1858–1922), whose travel agency was Norddeutscher Lloyd's main ticket broker, founded a company to build and operate emigrant hostels in 1906. By 1911, there were eleven buildings – commonly called "Missler halls" – offering accommodation for a total of about 3,400 emigrants in the Bremen city district of Findorff. Missler even had protective sleeves made in which emigrants could keep their travel documents safe. The NDL express steamer KAISER WILHELM DER GROSSE can be seen on the front. UB

9/24 **English textbook for emigrants, imprinted with "Norddeutscher Lloyd Bremen"**
E. F. Stahlschmidt
Braunschweig, c. 1900
Print; 11 x 16 cm
Bremerhaven, Historisches Museum Bremerhaven: 93/272

Anyone emigrating to America would have needed to learn English. The Norddeutscher Lloyd shipping line had their own English textbooks and dictionaries. UB

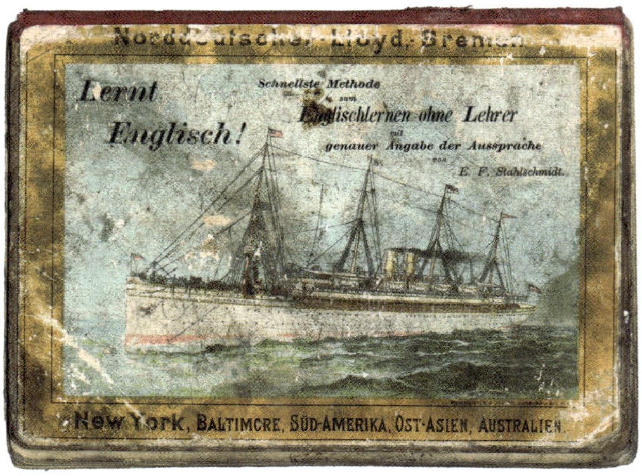

9/24

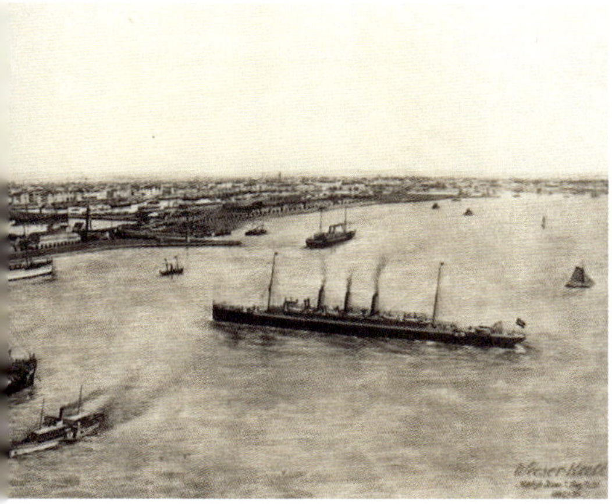

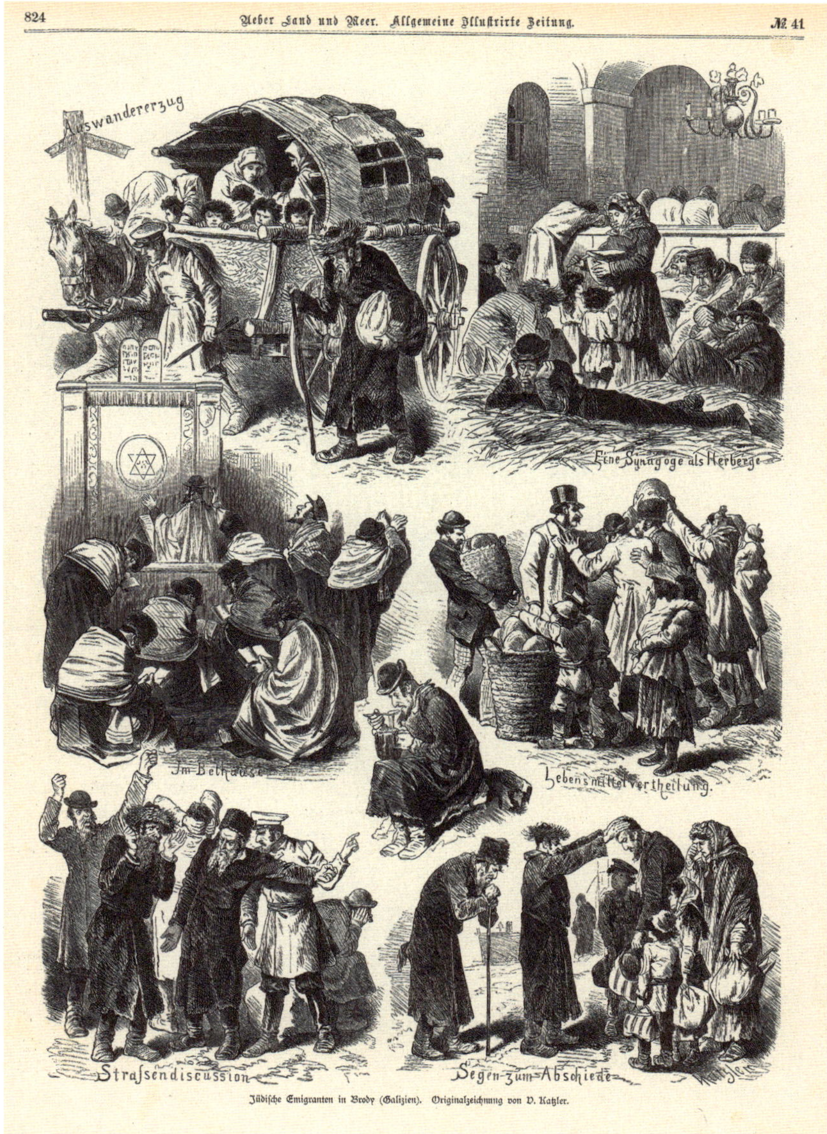

9/25

Transatlantic Emigration from 1880: Transit Migration

9/25 **Jewish emigrants in Brody (Galicia)**
Original artist: Vinzenz Katzler (1823–1882)
Published by Deutsche Verlagsanstalt
Stuttgart, 1882
Wood engraving; 37 x 27.5 cm
Berlin, Deutsches Historisches Museum: Gr 93/67.4

Millions of eastern and south-eastern European Jews emigrated overseas during the second large wave of migration from Europe to start in the last third of the nineteenth century. They came mainly from Polish-speaking Galicia, the most populous and at the same time least industrialised of the Habsburg Monarchy's crown lands. UB

9/26 **Escaping Jewish persecution in Russia: A train to the west**
Gustaf Broling (1831–1905)
c. 1882
Wood engraving; 23 x 22.1 cm
Berlin, Deutsches Historisches Museum: Gr 93/67.3

Bitter poverty and organized massacres (pogroms) led many Jews in the Russian Empire to emigrate westwards, particularly after the Odessa pogrom of 1871. The assassination of Tsar Alexander II (1818–1881) was also followed by the imposition of discriminatory regulations and a succession of violent pogroms against the Jewish population. (Exhibit not shown) UB

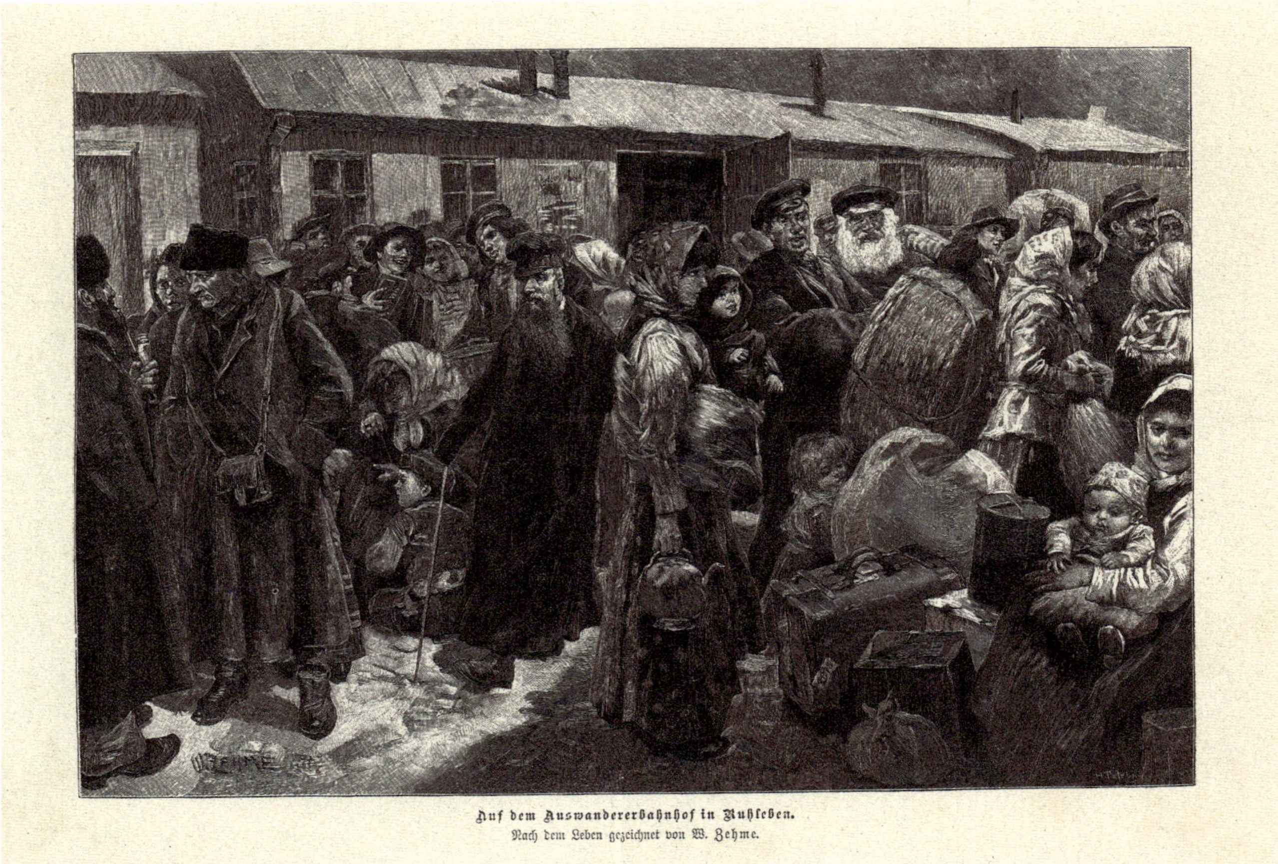

9/27

9/27 **Magazine article, "At the emigration train station in Ruhleben"**
"Auf dem Auswandererbahnhof in Ruhleben.",
Die Gartenlaube. Illustrirtes Familienblatt, no. 9
Drawn by Werner Zehme (1859–1916)
Engraved by Hermann Tafel (1861–1914)
Published by Ernst Keil's Nachfolger
Leipzig, 1895
Wood engraving; 21.1 x 31.1 cm
Berlin, Deutsches Historisches Museum: Gr 2005/44

After Hamburg suffered a devastating epidemic of cholera allegedly introduced by Russian emigrants in 1892, a new approach was taken to 'transit migration'. In 1893, American authorities started demanding that all Russian immigrants be disinfected and held in quarantine for several days at their port of departure in Europe. The German shipping lines NDL and Hapag managed to convince the Prussian government to give them complete responsibility for eastern border controls (which had been intermittent up to then), medical supervision, and all transport to the emigrants' ports of departure, thus privatizing these services. They profited from Germany's central location within Europe and the fact that eastern Europeans had to pass through the country on their way to the North Sea ports. Hapag and NDL opened control stations at major railway crossings between Russia and Prussia. All transit migrants had to undergo a physical examination and disinfection procedure, in accordance with American immigration regulations. These stations more or less adopted the system used by the emigration train station in Ruhleben, near Berlin, which had been in operation since 1891. Anyone who failed to pass the medical check was sent back. UB

9/28 **Photo spread, "Hapag's new emigrant city on Veddel Island, Hamburg"**
Johann Hamann (1859–1935), Heinrich Hamann (1883–1975)
Printed by Sascha Mintkiewicz
Hamburg, c. 1909
New prints 2000/2001; each approx. 41 x 54 cm
Hamburg, Staatsarchiv Hamburg: Photograph: Hamann family, 720-1/343-1/no. 12 H 300 1156, no. 7 H 300 1120, no. 5 H 300 1113, no. 12 H 300 1132, no.26 H 300 1153

At the initiative of Albert Ballin, who had been appointed general director of Hapag in 1899, a large fenced-in area on the island of Veddel (in the Elbe River, southeast of down-

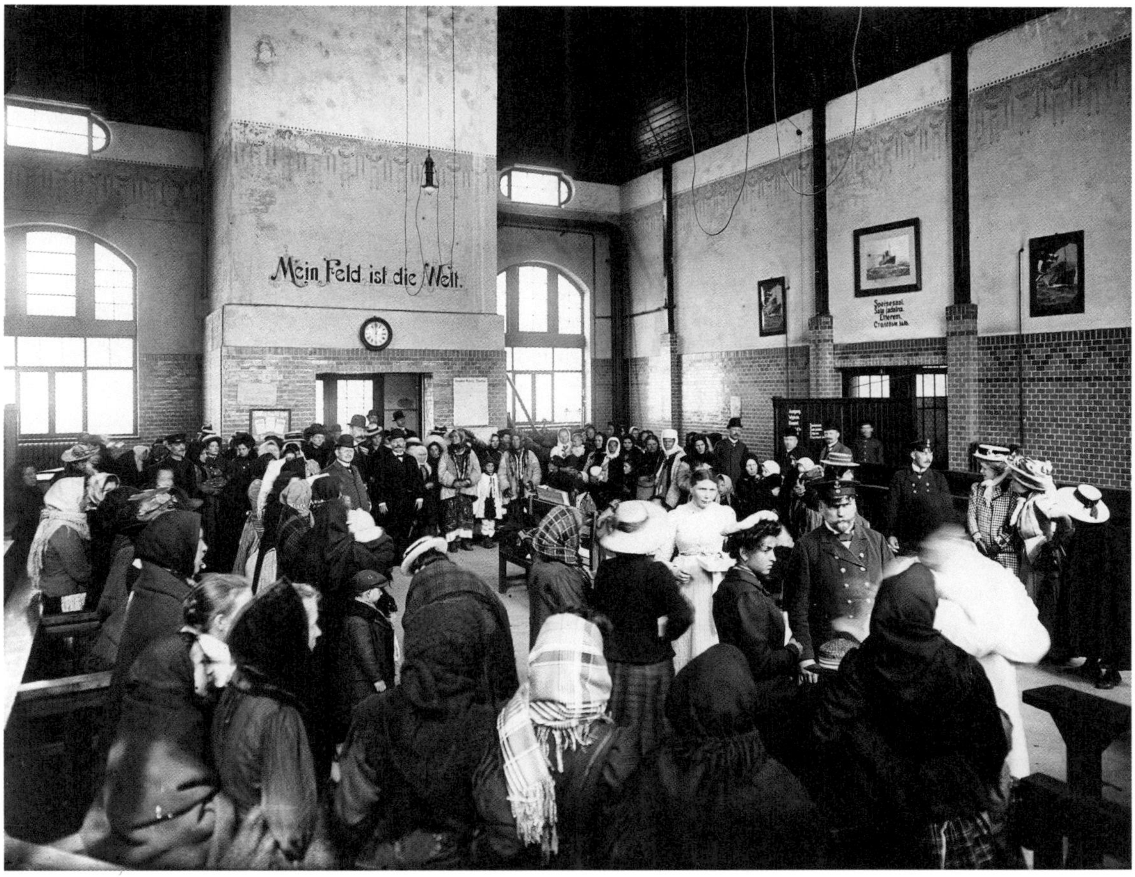

9/28 e

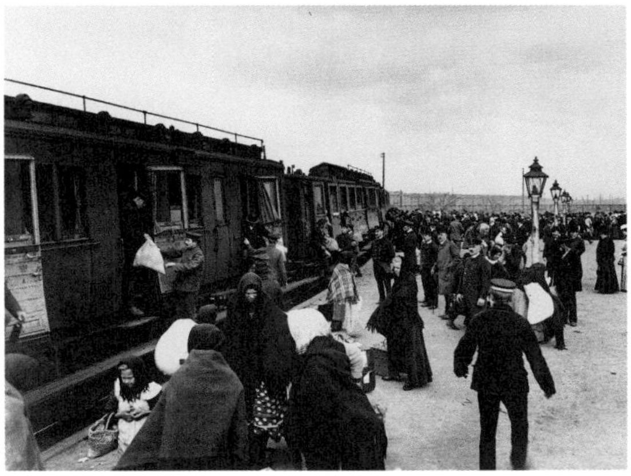

9/28 a

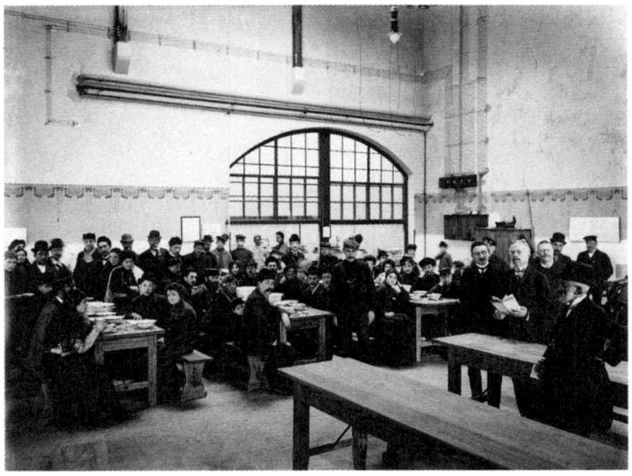

9/28 b

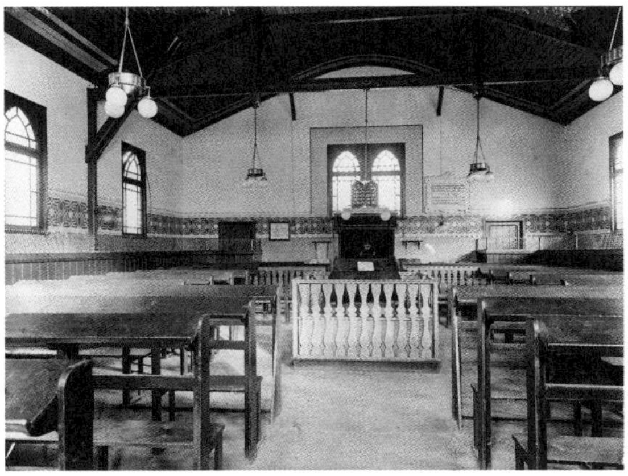

9/28 c

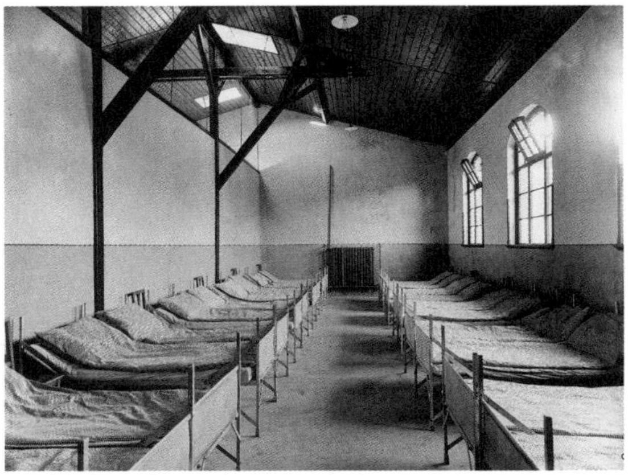

9/28 d

town Hamburg) was established for emigrants in 1901. When it was completed in 1907, the facilities were able to accommodate up to 5,000 people at a time. About 180 Hapag employees, among them interpreters and medical personnel, were responsible for providing medical supervision, as well as food and other services. There were 30 pavilions, each containing dormitories for 22 people in addition to toilets and day rooms. Catholics, Protestants and Jews all had their own prayer areas. There were also separate kosher kitchens and dining halls. Hapag agents offered emigrants a 'package deal' covering both their passage by ship and their train journey from the border control station to the port city, and guaranteeing them the right to accommodation and food in an emigrant hostel. This efficient, 'end-to-end' approach was not only profitable and good for the image of the shipping line, but it also enabled greater control and monitoring of the migrants. In 1909, as part of a construction project it was promoting, Hapag commissioned a series of photographs which today provide a valuable historical record. UB

9/28a **A train brings eastern European emigrants to the Hamburg emigrant centre**

9/28b **Dining hall for Jewish emigrants in the Hamburg emigrant centre**

9/28c **Interior view of the synagogue in the Hamburg emigrant centre**

9/28d **Dormitory in the Hamburg emigrant centre**

9/28e **Dining hall in the Hamburg emigrant centre, with Albert Ballin's motto, *Mein Feld ist die Welt* (My field is the world)**

9/29 **Paper identification tag for German emigrants, produced by the Protestant emigrant mission**
Bremen, 1880s
Print; 10.4 x 14.5 cm
Berlin, Deutsches Historisches Museum: Do 2015/123

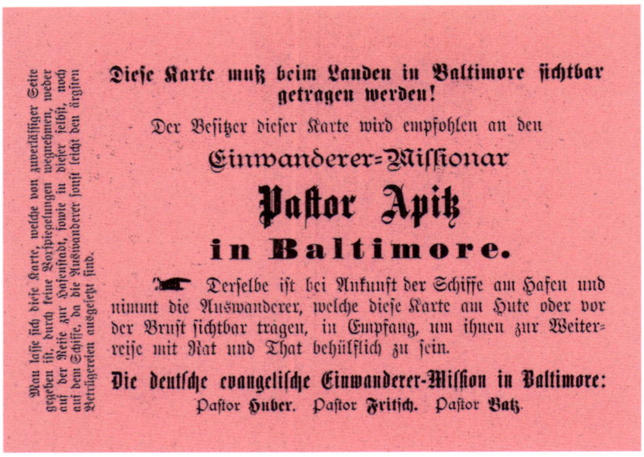

Man lasse sich diese Karte, welche von zuverlässiger Seite gegeben ist, durch keine Vorspiegelungen wegnehmen, weder auf der Reise zur Hafenstadt, sowie in dieser selbst, noch auf dem Schiffe, da die Auswanderer sonst leicht den ärgsten Betrügereien ausgesetzt sind.

Diese Karte muß beim Landen in Baltimore sichtbar getragen werden!

Der Besitzer dieser Karte wird empfohlen an den

Einwanderer=Missionar

Pastor Apitz

in Baltimore.

Derselbe ist bei Ankunft der Schiffe am Hafen und nimmt die Auswanderer, welche diese Karte am Hute oder vor der Brust sichtbar tragen, in Empfang, um ihnen zur Weiterreise mit Rat und That behülflich zu sein.

Die deutsche evangelische Einwanderer-Mission in Baltimore:
Pastor **Huber**. Pastor **Fritsch**. Pastor **Batz**.

9/29

In addition to the shipping lines, which were largely profit-oriented, religious organisations also provided support to emigrants. All faiths and denominations maintained their own societies or facilities in the departure ports. Protestant emigrant missions were established in Hamburg in 1873 and in Bremen in 1881. They offered pastoral counselling and assistance with matters ranging from bureaucratic procedures to money transfers. They also helped emigrants to find accommodation and get safely from port to port. St. Raphaels-Verein was particularly active on behalf of Catholics. It opened a branch in Hamburg in 1872 and another one in Bremen in 1873. The colourful tags shown here were intended to be pinned to clothing. Emigrants wearing them would be seen and tended to immediately at the port of arrival by members of the respective organisation. UB

9/30 **Paper identification tag for German emigrants, produced by the Protestant emigrant mission**
Bremen, 1880s
Print; 9.2 x 14.2 cm
Berlin, Deutsches Historisches Museum: Do 2015/122
(Exhibit not shown)

9/31 **Pamphlet, "Jewish emigration"**
"Jüdische Auswanderung", *Korrespondenzblatt für Auswanderungs- und Siedlungsfragen*
Published by Hilfsverein der Juden in Deutschland
Printed by Schmoller und Gordon
Berlin, 1938
Print; 31.2 x 23.2 cm
Deutsches Historisches Museum, Do2 91/194

The Hilfsverein für deutsche Juden (Benevolent Society for German Jews) was a religiously neutral organisation founded in 1901. It was headquartered in Berlin and had branches in Hamburg and Bremen. Initially, it provided aid to eastern European Jewish emigrants, in particular those from Russia and Galicia, accompanying them as they passed through Germany. After the National Socialists assumed power in 1933, the society focused on German Jews, who were being driven out of the country and forced to emigrate. They fled the country in three main waves: after the first organised anti-Semitic attacks in 1933, after the Nuremberg Laws were passed in 1935, and after the November pogrom of 1938. Emigrants often travelled within Europe before moving on to Palestine, the United States or South America. The society, forced by the Nazis to change its name to Hilfsverein für Juden in Deutschland (Benevolent Society for Jews in Germany), supplied information on life in various countries; helped with bureaucratic matters, passport-related issues and vocational training; and provided financial assistance. TJ

9/32 **Government notice directed at potential emigrants**
Printed by Hollerbaum & Schmidt
Berlin, c. 1920
Paper; 47.6 x 70.4 cm
Deutsches Historisches Museum, Do2 87/176.22

This poster, issued by the Imperial Migration Agency, promotes counselling for potential emigrants. The agency was founded on 7 May 1919 and remained Germany's main body for controlling migration until 1924. After the First World War, many Germans – struggling to cope with massive inflation, among other things – sought to go abroad, preferably overseas. They had to attend a counselling session before they left, however. This was aimed at either changing their minds (thus preventing the loss of employable workers) or steering them to German-speaking areas. Emigration declined as the economy recovered, and the agency was dissolved. A total of 600,000 people left Germany for countries overseas during the Weimar Republic (1919–1933). (Exhibit not shown) TJ

9/33 **Public warning issued by the Imperial Migration Agency: "Emigrants!"**
Kurt Heiligenstaedt (1890–1964)
Berlin, 1919
Lithograph, printed sticker; 71.5 x 48 cm
Berlin, Deutsches Historisches Museum: 1987/176.1

Unemployment, hunger and housing shortages were rampant in Germany after the First World War, causing many people to seek a better life overseas. The country had suffered catastrophic losses, however, and could not afford to lose any more of its workforce. This poster, issued by the Reichswanderungsamt (Imperial Migration Agency), warns of disreputable emigration agents and the consequences of a hasty decision to emigrate, showing at the same time, with smoking chimney stacks and apartment buildings in the background, that life will improve for families in need. AvH

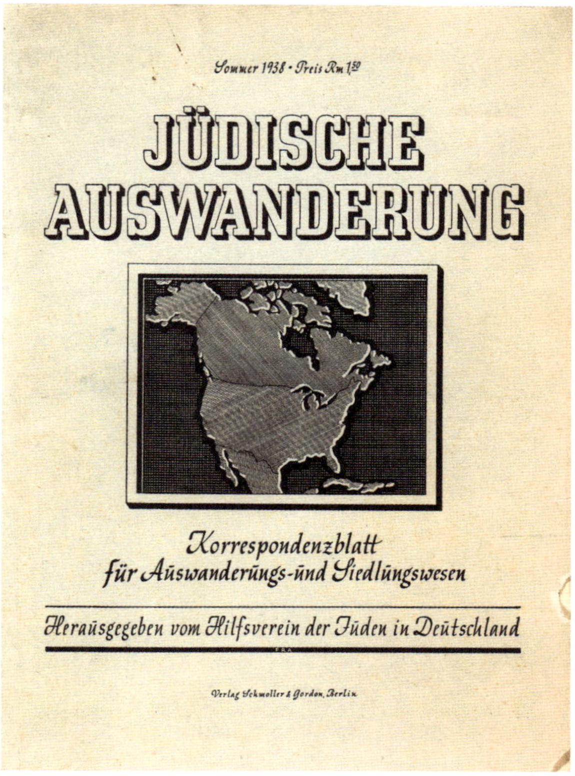

9/31

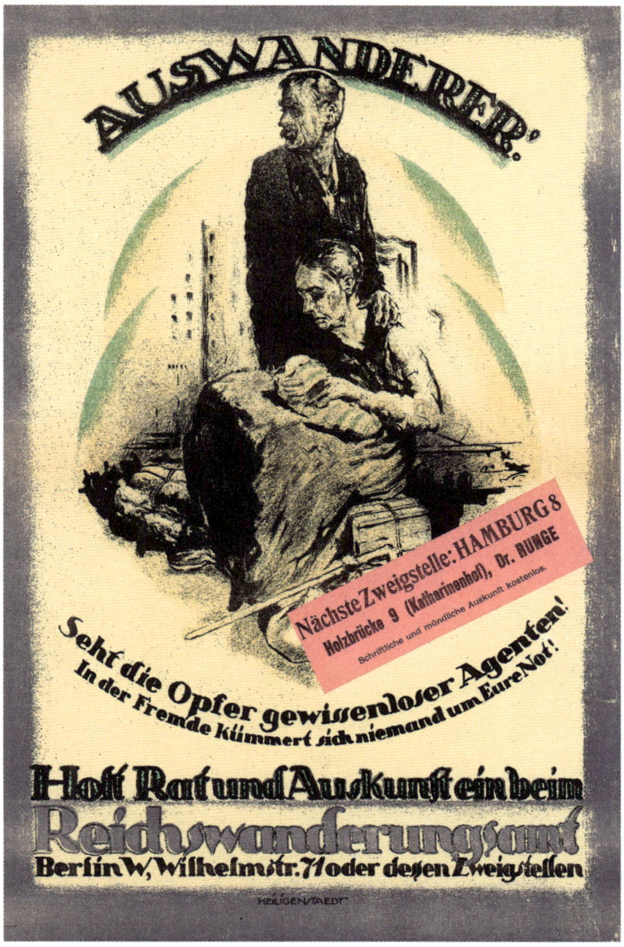

9/33

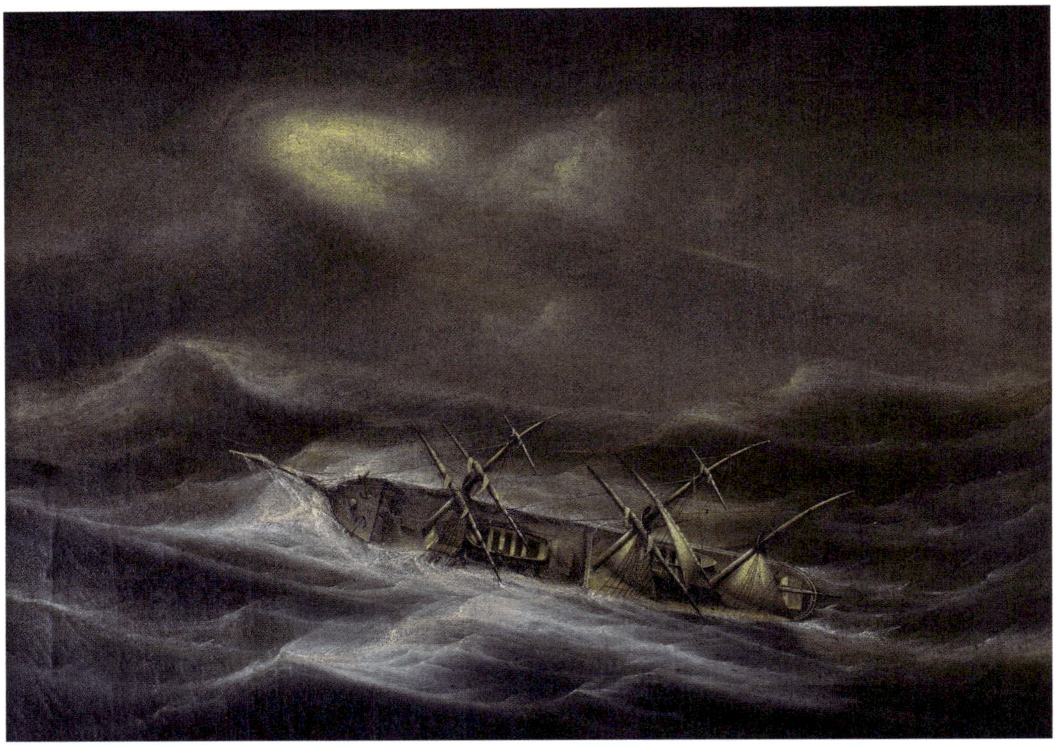

9/34

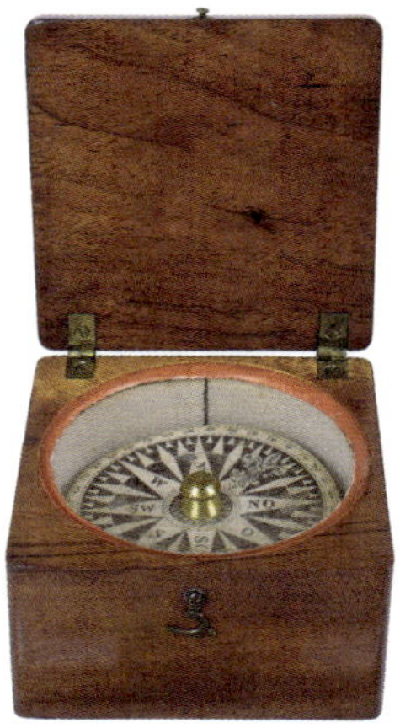

9/35

At Sea: Life Aboard an Emigration Ship

9/34 ***Helvetia in a Storm***
Carl Justus Fedeler (1837–1897)
Bremen, 1862
Oil on canvas; 60 x 82 cm
Bremerhaven, Deutsches Schiffahrtsmuseum – Leibniz-Institut für deutsche Schifffahrtsgeschichte: I/04772/89

The barque Helvetia was built at Bremen's Tecklenborg shipyard in 1858 and served the Bremerhaven – New York route for many years, carrying emigrants. Franz Brandorff commanded the ship until 1862, when he commissioned the well-known marine painter Carl Justus Fedeler to produce this painting as a memento of his captaincy. It shows the Helvetia on stormy seas. The date "26. Febr. 1862" and the coordinates N.B. 39°49' W.L. 62°23' suggest that the painting depicts a real event and that the vessel had been caught in a severe storm about 1,000 kilometres away from its destination port of New York. The captain is the only person on deck; steadfast in the face of the gales, he holds the heavily listing ship on course. EMB

9/35 **Compass belonging to the Helvetia**
TR Barckhahn
Bremerhaven, c. 1860
Wood, metal, glass, paper; 5 x 7.8 x 7.8 cm
Bremerhaven, Deutsches Schiffahrtsmuseum – Leibniz-Institut für deutsche Schifffahrtsgeschichte: I/04775/89

This compass, with its fine mahogany case, was produced for Captain Franz Brandorff in Bremerhaven in 1860. It still works flawlessly today. In the 1860s, Brandorff commanded the newly built barque Helvetia, an emigration ship that ran a regular route between Bremerhaven and New York. At the time, this sort of compass would have been the only type of directional instrument aboard. EMB

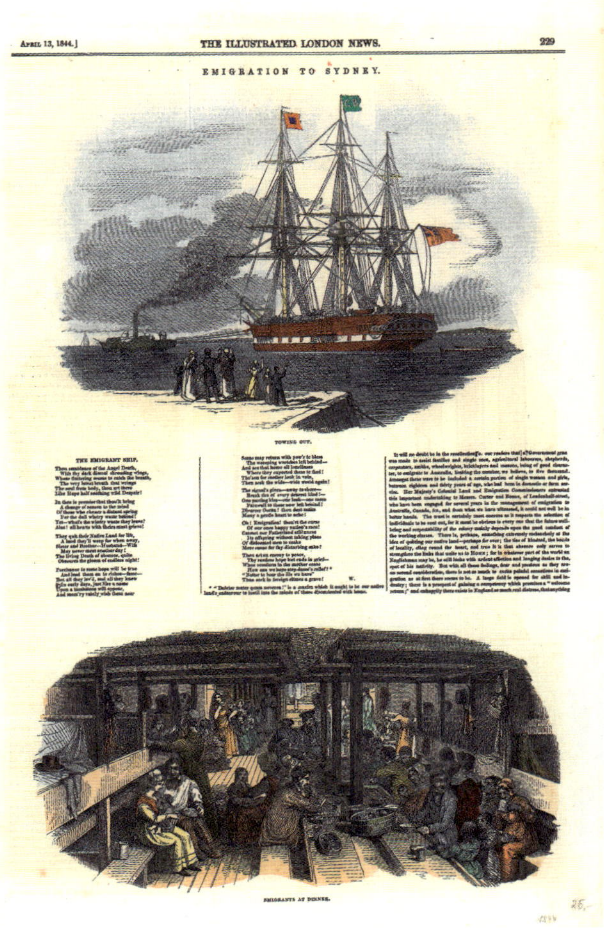

April 13, 1844.] THE ILLUSTRATED LONDON NEWS. 229

EMIGRATION TO SYDNEY.

TOWING OUT.

EMIGRANTS AT DINNER.

9/36

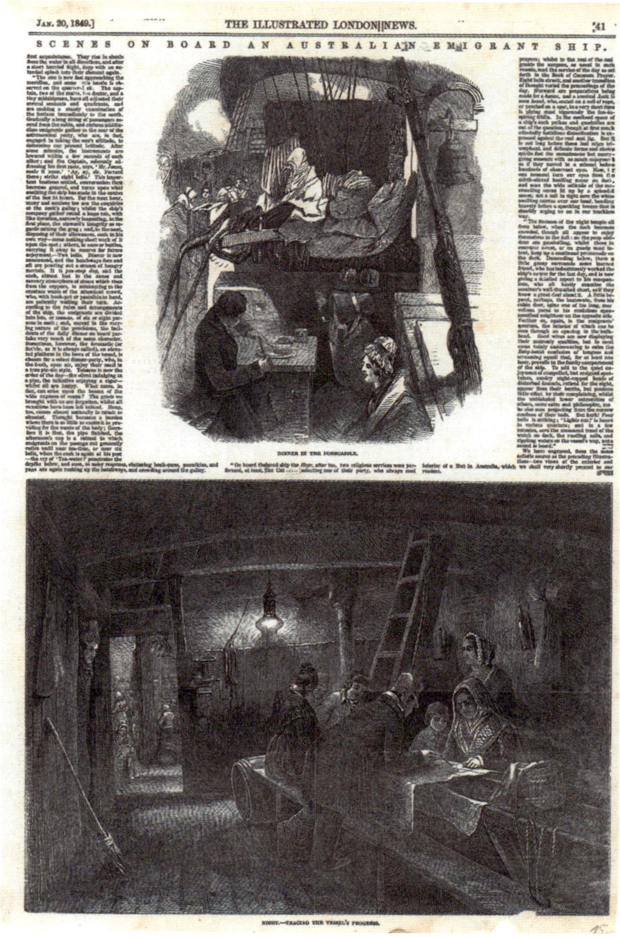

Jan. 20, 1849.] THE ILLUSTRATED LONDON NEWS. 41

SCENES ON BOARD AN AUSTRALIAN EMIGRANT SHIP.

DINNER IN THE FORECASTLE.

NIGHT.—TRACING THE VESSEL'S PROGRESS.

9/37

9/36 **Page from *The Illustrated London News*, with a picture-essay on emigration to Sydney**
London, 13 April 1844
Lithographs; 54.8 x 20.3 cm
Bremerhaven, Historisches Museum Bremerhaven: 13/1254.01-04

Around 1850, passengers travelling in steerage were each allotted a space the size of a very narrow, short bed. Only by stacking the beds was it possible to gain any open floor space on the steerage deck. Up to the 1880s, emigrants had to bring their own pillows, blankets and bed linens, as well as tables, chairs and dishes. Hunger and thirst were an inevitable part of a passage in steerage, and if the voyage took longer than planned, the daily rations got smaller and smaller. What is more, after a few weeks passed, food and water supplies often spoiled. UB

9/37 **Page from *The Illustrated London News*, with a picture-essay on life aboard an emigration ship bound for Australia**
London, 20 January 1849
Lithographs; 52.8 x 20.3 cm
Bremerhaven, Historisches Museum Bremerhaven: 13/1283.01-05

The Illustrated London News, which had been in print since 14 May 1842, was the inspiration behind Leipzig's *Illustrirte Zeitschrift* and other illustrated magazines. This essay, unlike many contemporary newspaper and magazine articles, gave a relatively realistic picture of life aboard an emigration ship. UB

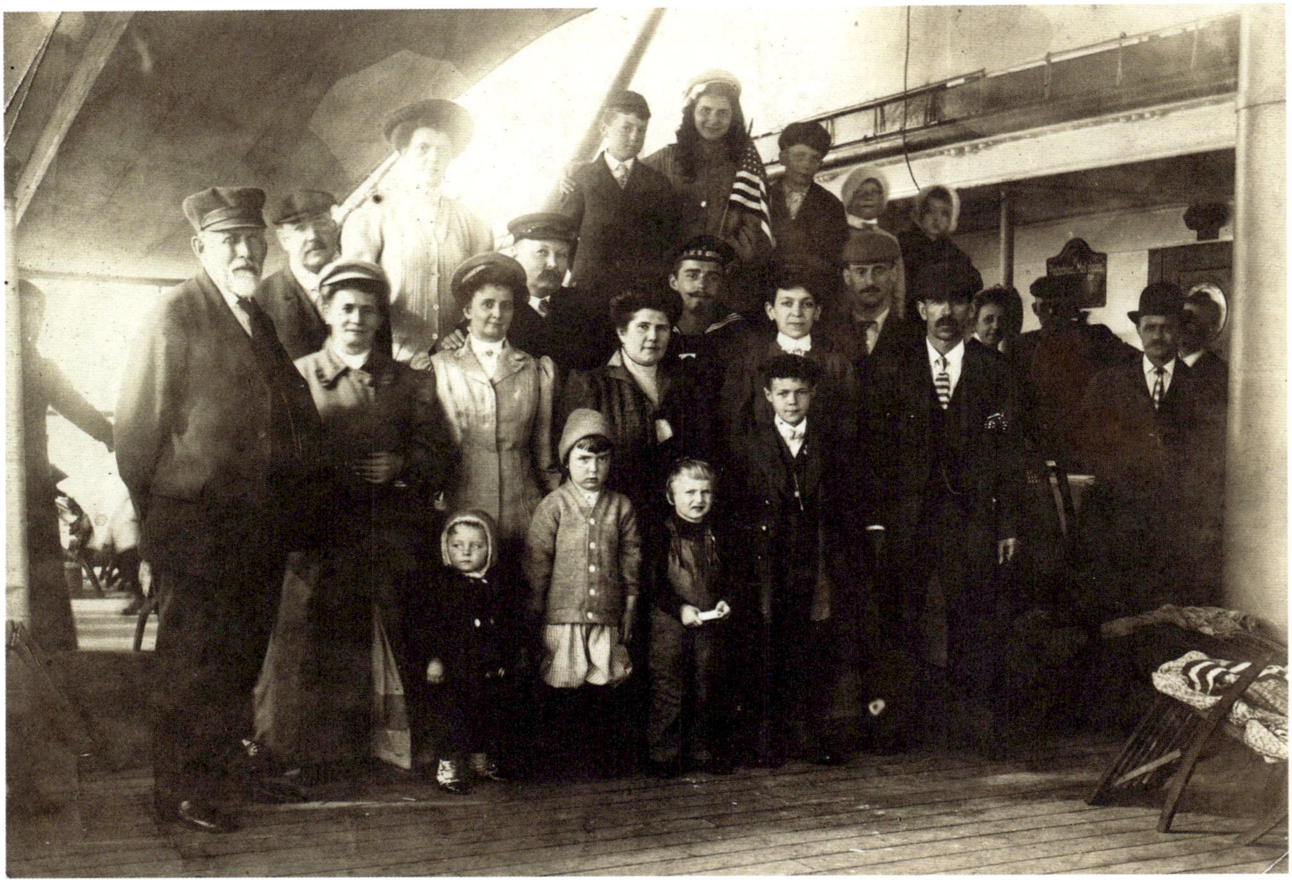

9/38

9/38 **Emigrant aboard the ocean liner BREMEN II**
Richard Fleischhut (1881–1951)
1909
Gelatin silver paper, old print; 11.7 x 16.7 cm
Berlin, Deutsches Historisches Museum: PH 2011/496.626

At least aboard ships of the Norddeutscher Lloyd shipping line, emigrants were permitted to go on deck and get some fresh air during the day (unless there was a storm).
Richard Fleischhut was a photographer with NDL from 1905 to 1939. He travelled on almost all of their larger passenger steamers, documenting over 150 transatlantic crossings and cruises with his camera. UB

9/39 **Crew and emigrants on the deck of the ocean liner BREMEN II**
Richard Fleischhut (1881–1951)
1909
Gelatin silver paper, old print; 11.8 x 16.9 cm
Berlin, Deutsches Historisches Museum: PH 2011/496.630
(Exhibit not shown)

9/40 **Chamber pot from a ship in the Norddeutscher Lloyd fleet**
Bauscher
Weiden (Upper Palatinate), c. 1925
Porcelain; 14.2 x 19 x 23 cm
Bremerhaven, Historisches Museum Bremerhaven: 04/381

This chamber pot, featuring the NDL emblem, probably belonged to a third-class cabin. These cabins replaced steerage dormitories and were available to emigrants from the 1920s onwards. NDL ships began using Bauscher porcelain in the 1890s. (Exhibit not shown) UB

9/41 **Cutaway model of the express steamer KAISER WILHELM DER GROSSE, which entered service in 1897**
Built by Detlef John, Cuxhaven
Paper, cardboard, wood; 75 x 32 x 77 cm
Bremerhaven, Historisches Museum Bremerhaven: 01/94

A flagship of Norddeutscher Lloyd, the four-funnel liner KAISER WILHELM DER GROSSE was a combination of emigration ship and luxury steamer for rich tourists. At its launch on 4 May 1897, it was the largest ship in the world, measuring 197.7 metres in length and a good 20 metres in width. It could accommodate 1,074 passengers in steerage, up to 340 people in first class, and up to 346 in second class. Almost all of the first and second-class cabins were on the upper deck. Steerage passengers now slept in dormitories, where bunks (1.80 m long, approx. 0.5 m wide) were arranged in pairs, one above the other. Their meals were served in dining saloons. A passage in steerage from Bremerhaven to North America cost from 120 to 160 marks. A first-class ticket, depending on the season, cost between 490 and 8.000 marks. (Exhibit not shown) UB

9/42 **Menu from the express steamer Kaiser Wilhelm der Grosse**
Bremen, 3 November 1897
Print; 19.2 x 13.5 cm
Bremerhaven, Historisches Museum Bremerhaven: 04/537 .62

First and second-class passengers, most of them wealthy tourists and business travellers, enjoyed dining and accommodation on a par with that of a luxury hotel. There were multi-course meals from breakfast to dinner, and concerts for entertainment. Upper-deck passengers had no contact with people travelling in third class. The Kaiser Wilhelm der Grosse was named after the first German Kaiser, Wilhelm I (1797–1888), whose portrait (in the style of a Roman emperor, complete with laurel wreath) adorns the cover page of this menu. His grandson, Wilhelm II (1859–1941), was frequently seen at ships' christenings and on special excursions, living proof of the close relationship between Norddeutscher Lloyd and the crown that was suggested by the names of its ships. UB

9/43 **Armchair from the first-class smoking saloon on the express steamer Kaiser Wilhelm der Grosse**
c. 1897
Mahogany, leather-covered seat cushion; 77 x 53 x 64 cm
Bremerhaven, Historisches Museum Bremerhaven: 99/295 .01-02

Large ocean liners provided luxurious saloons for first and second-class passengers, including elegant smoking saloons for the men. The armchair shown here was removed from a smoking saloon on the Kaiser Wilhelm der Grosse in 1913, when the ship was redesigned to carry emigrants only (in steerage and third class). It was at this time that emigration numbers in Bremerhaven reached their last peak. 239,564

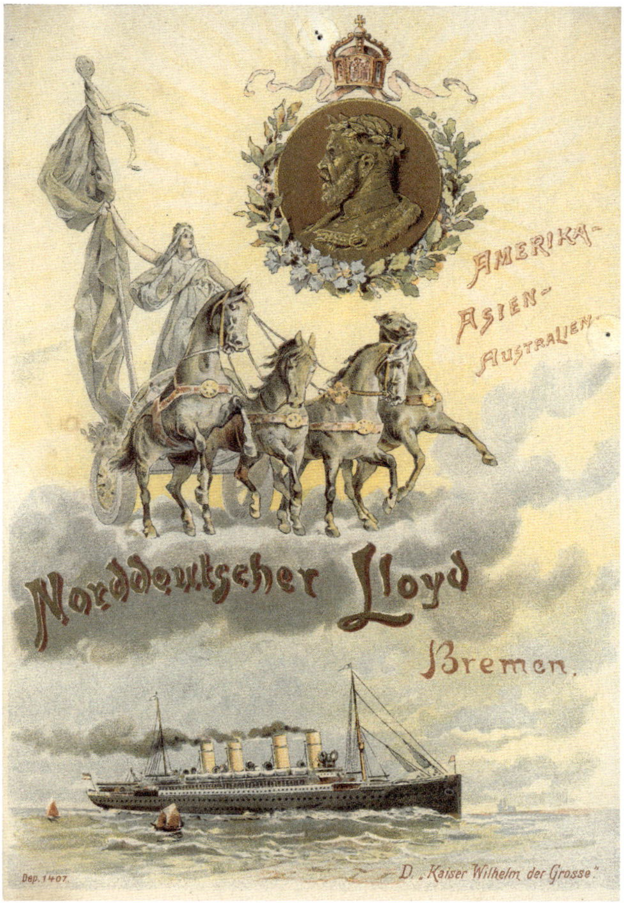

9/42

emigrants boarded ship in 1913, more than ever before. Transatlantic passages were discontinued when the First World War began, and the emigration business ground to a halt. The Kaiser Wilhelm der Grosse entered war service as an auxiliary cruiser and was scuppered (deliberately sunk) just weeks later. (Exhibit not shown) UB

Arrival in the 'New World'

9/44 ***The Columbus on its maiden voyage to New York***
Claus Bergen (1885–1964)
Germany, 1924
Tempera on paper; 95 x 120 cm
Bremerhaven, Deutsches Schiffahrtsmuseum – Leibniz-Insitut für deutsche Schifffahrtsgeschichte: I/02573/83

Passenger service on transatlantic routes was interrupted during the First World War. When it resumed, the express steamer Columbus was the largest and most technologically advanced of the German ships making the crossing. Passen-

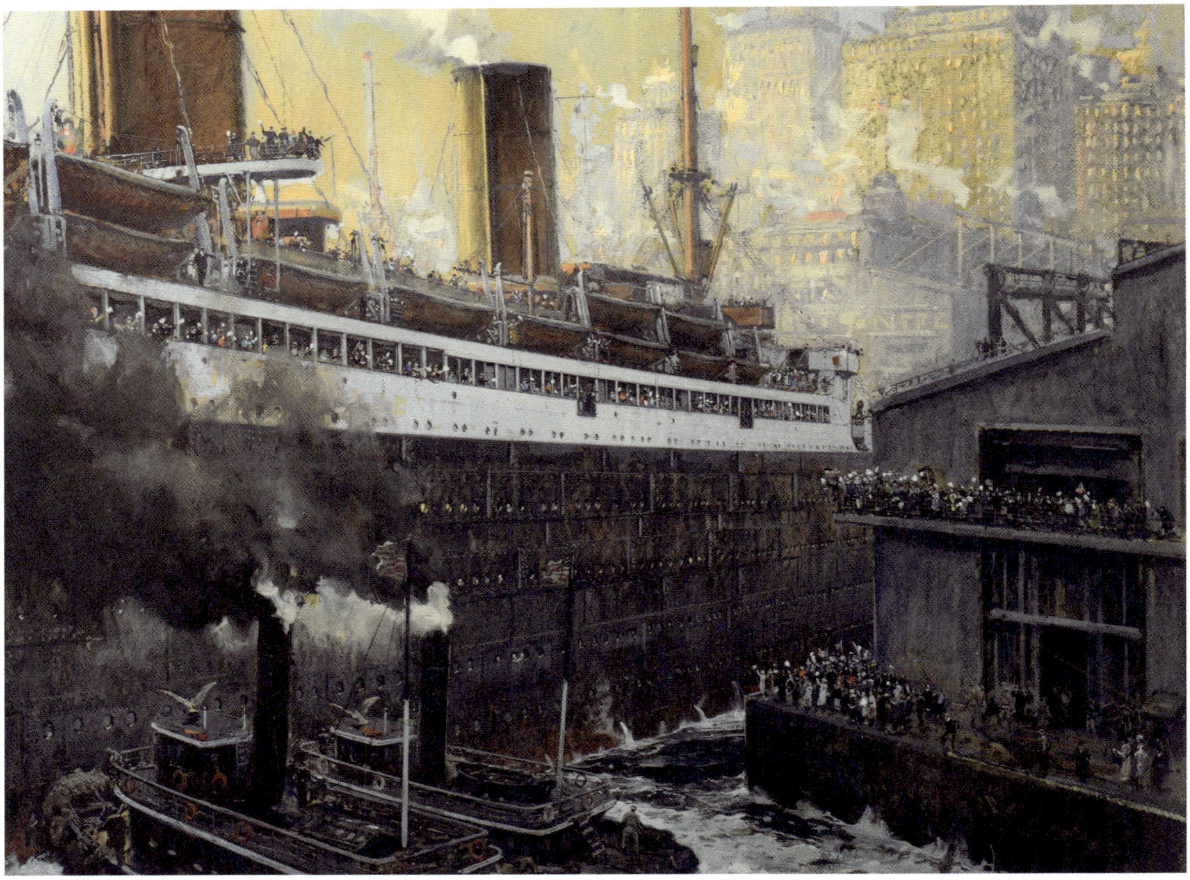

9/44

ger accommodations were divided into three classes. Emigrants travelled in the third class, in quarters that were clearly superior to those offered before the war. The COLUMBUS set off from Bremerhaven on its maiden voyage to New York on 22 April 1924. The marine painter Claus Bergen was on board as an honoured guest of Norddeutscher Lloyd. Here, he depicts the arrival of the COLUMBUS in the port of New York as a triumphant event. The towering ship is proceeding into the harbour, cheered on by exuberant, flag-waving crowds, while in the background the New York skyline with its soaring skyscrapers is bathed in a golden light. This imagery alludes to the vision of America as a 'golden land'. EMB

9/45 **View of Ellis Island and the port of Manhattan**
New York / New Jersey, 1930
Photograph (reproduction); 24 x 30 cm
Berlin, ullstein bild – Süddeutsche Zeitung Photo / Scherl: # 6901529367

Ellis Island, situated in the Upper New York Bay, was the main gateway into the New World for over half a century. Between 1892 (when it opened) and 1954, about 12 million immigrants were processed there. In the 1890s, U.S. immigration inspections and regulations were tightened and a new immigrant station was established on Ellis Island, where people could be isolated and would not be able to make it to the mainland unnoticed. In 1921, the country introduced immigration quotas, which were intended mainly to reduce the numbers of southern and eastern European immigrants. The US instituted further severe restrictions on immigration with the Immigration Act of 1924. UB

9/46 **Immigrants arriving on Ellis Island**
ullstein bild – Granger, NYC
New York / New Jersey, 1895
Photograph (reproduction); 24 x 30 cm
Berlin, ullstein bild – Granger, NYC: # 30012358

The main building on Ellis Island was completed in 1900. Immigrants called Ellis Island the "Island of Tears" because the decision would sometimes be made, after questioning and a medical exam, to send someone back on the next ship. The cost of the return journey would generally be borne by the shipping line, and it was consequently in their interest to discover any serious illnesses or other potential obstacles to immigration before the ship left Europe. The control stations operated by the NDL and Hapag and the exams performed in emigrant hostels served this purpose. (Exhibit not shown) UB

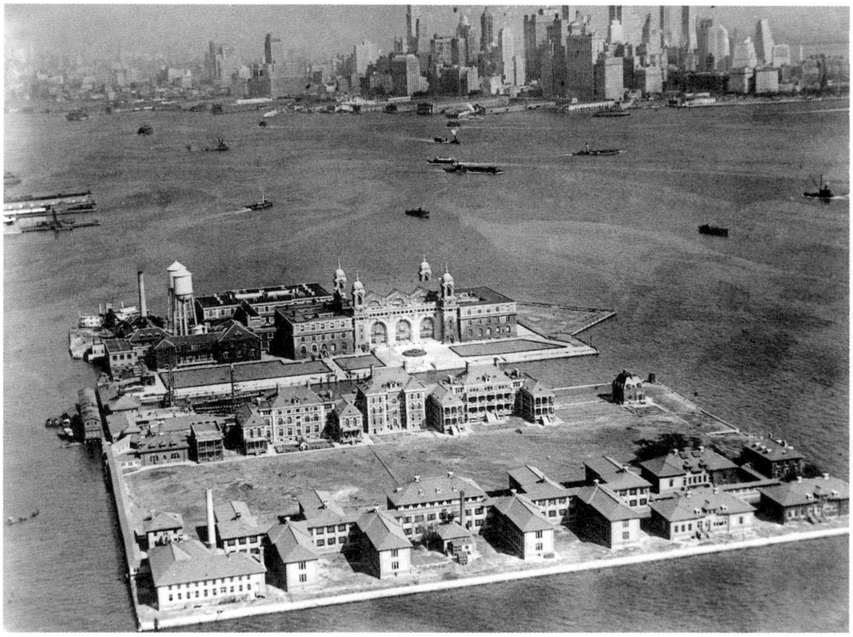

9/45

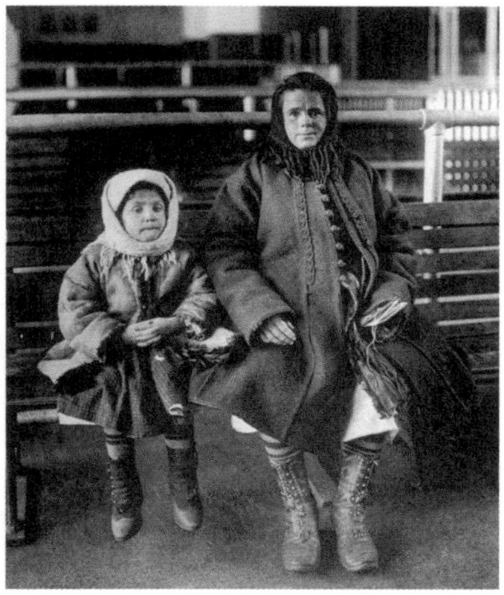

9/48

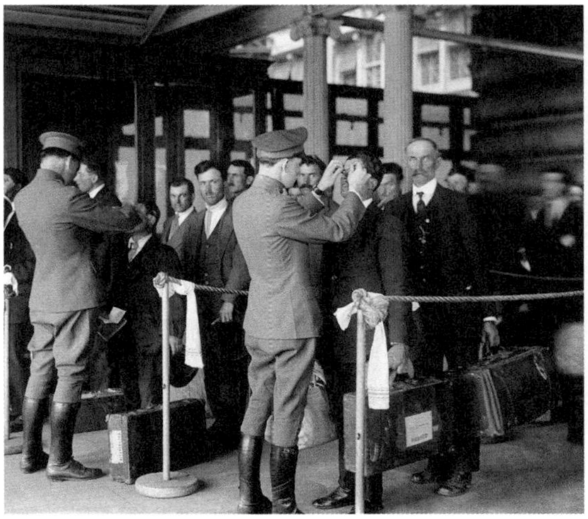

9/47

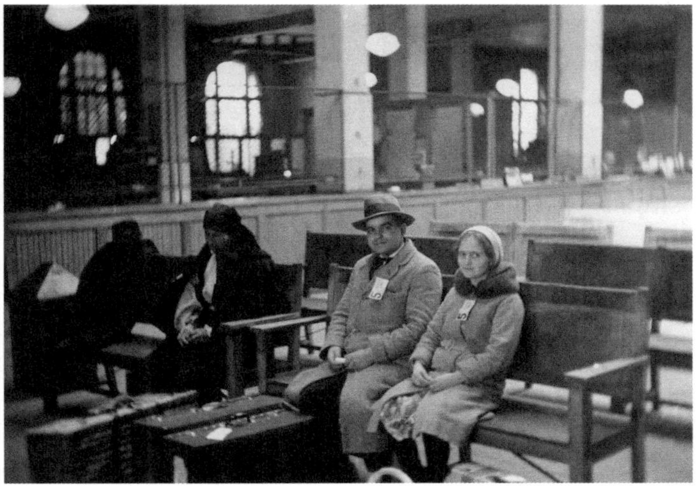

9/49

9/47 **Medical examinations on Ellis Island**
ullstein bild – United Archives, World History Archive
New York / New Jersey, 1920
Photograph (reproduction); 24 x 30 cm
Berlin, ullstein bild – United Archives / World History Archive: # 1313505290

The immigration authorities paid particular attention to the immigrants' state of health. Through questioning and physical exams, they attempted to uncover any contagious diseases, heart trouble, eye diseases, addictive disorders, or psychological problems. Ellis Island was at its busiest from 1900 to 1924, when it processed between 5,000 and 7,000 immigrants every day. UB

9/48 **Emigrant with her daughter on Ellis Island**
ullstein bild – JT Vintage, Glasshouse Images
New York / New Jersey, c. 1902
Photograph (reproduction); 24 x 30 cm
Berlin, ullstein bild – JT Vintage / Glasshouse Images: # 1009148286

9/49 **Couple waiting on Ellis Island**
ullstein bild – Erich Salomon (1886–1944)
New York / New Jersey, 1931
Photograph (reproduction); 24 x 30 cm
Berlin, ullstein bild – Erich Salomon: # 00205132

The couple in the photograph have successfully passed the inspection and are waiting for a train that will take them to

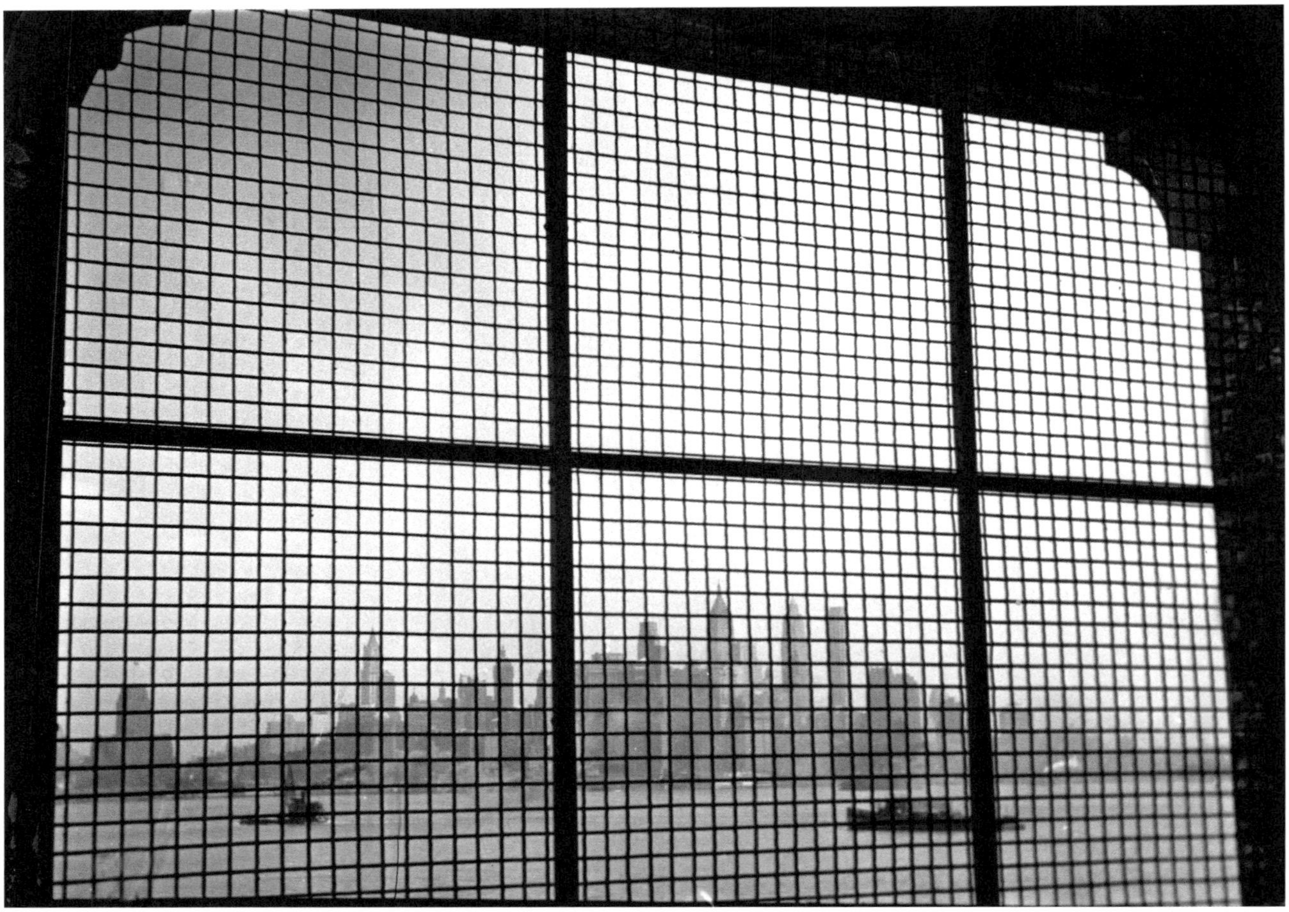

9/50

their future home. The Berlin-born photojournalist Erich Salomon took a series of photographs on Ellis Island in 1931. UB

9/50 **View of the Manhattan skyline through a barred window on Ellis Island**
ullstein bild – Erich Salomon (1886–1944)
New York / New Jersey, 1931
Photograph (reproduction); 24 x 30 cm
Berlin, ullstein bild – Erich Salomon: # 00167951

This photograph of a barred window, taken by Erich Salomon, suggests the dream of successful emigration, which for many people remained unfulfilled. Salomon, who was Jewish, went into exile in the Netherlands in 1933 and lived underground until 1942/43. In 1944, he was deported with his wife and one of his sons, and was murdered in Auschwitz. UB

A Continent of Immigration: Postcolonial Migration to Europe. The Windrush Generation in Great Britain

9/51 ***Caribbean Family in Trafalgar Square***
Harold Dearden (1888–1962)
London, 1950–1962
Oil on canvas; 76.5 x 73.6 x 1.8 cm
London, Museum of London: 99.115/1

The United Kingdom, once one of the world's leading colonial powers, found itself diminished politically and economically following the two world wars and decolonisation. In 1948, in an effort to address dramatic manpower shortages, it passed the British Nationality Act, which granted all nationals of British colonies and Commonwealth member states the right to British citizenship, allowing them to immigrate and work in the UK. This resulted in a wave of migration that began in the Caribbean islands; by 1960, about 170,000 people from the West Indies had come to Great Britain. Harold Dearden was one of very few painters who took on the subject. This scene, painted in light colours, shows an African-Caribbean family feeding pigeons; a white family can be seen doing the same thing in the background. Set at the heart of London in Trafalgar Square, with its famous fountains, it suggests that Caribbean immigrants were becoming part of mainstream British society. UB

9/52 **The Empire Windrush arriving from Jamaica**
Tilbury/Essex, 21 June 1948
Photograph (reproduction)
Berlin, ullstein bild – NMSI/Science Museum / Daily Herald Archive/NMeM: 80249020

The turbulent past of the Empire Windrush is a reflection of European maritime history. The ship was launched under the name Monte Rosa by the Hamburg shipyard of Blohm & Voss in December 1930. It served as a passenger liner and cruise ship for the Hamburg-Süd shipping line before being used by the Nazi leisure organization Kraft durch Freude (Strength Through Joy). It was then deployed as a troopship from the start of the Second World War until late 1941, when it started transporting prisoners of the Nazi regime, many of them Jews, to concentration camps and death camps. In early 1945, though severely damaged, it evacuated over 5,000 people – some wounded and most fleeing the Red Army – to Copenhagen. Back in German waters in Kiel, it was captured by British forces and later put to use as a troop carrier under the name Empire Windrush. It entered into history in June 1948, when it brought the first 492 Caribbean immigrants from Jamaica to Great Britain. After a serious accident when returning to England from Japan in March, 1954, the Empire Windrush sank off the coast of Algeria. UB

9/53 **Passengers on the Empire Windrush**
Tilbury/Essex, 21 June 1948
Photograph (reproduction)
Berlin, ullstein bild – NMSI/Science Museum / Daily Herald Archive/NMeM1: 80247483

The arrival of the Empire Windrush on 21 June 1948 at the port of Tilbury (London's newest docks) marks the beginning of post-war, post-colonial immigration from the islands of the West Indies to Great Britain. There were 492 passengers aboard the ship, most of them men from Jamaica, Trinidad, Tobago and other Caribbean islands. The voyage from Jamaica to Europe took almost a month. Many of the men had fought on the side of the British forces during the war and were now being recruited as labourers. As members of the Commonwealth, they had the right to British citizenship and could enter the country unimpeded. Most of the immigrants worked in the construction and textile industries or in the public transport and health services. The first generation of immigrants, who were comparatively successful at integrating into British society, entered British history as the "Windrush generation". They have continued to shape the way both West Indian communities and British society as a whole see themselves. (Exhibit not shown) UB

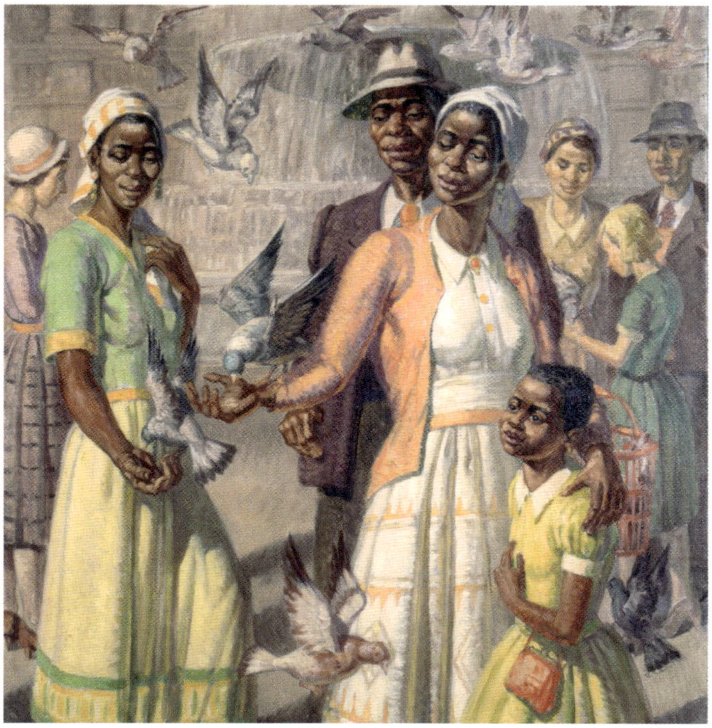

9/51

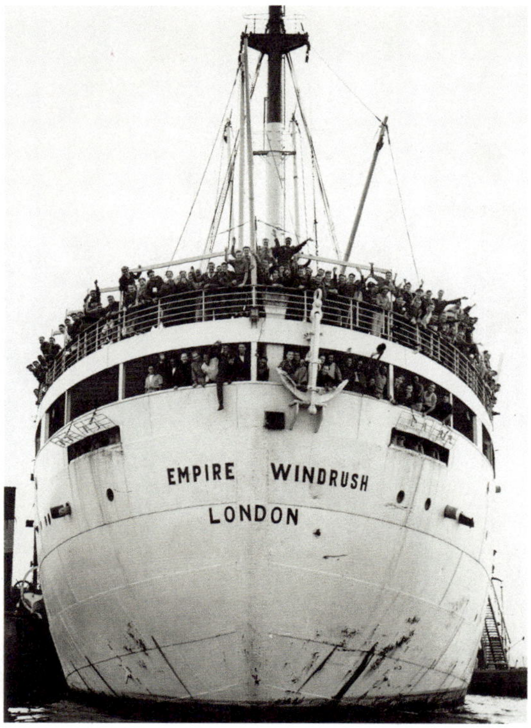

9/52

9/54 **Group photo with Caribbean immigrants on the EMPIRE WINDRUSH**
Tilbury/Essex, 21 June 1948
Photograph (reproduction)
Berlin, ullstein bild – TopFoto: 80047507

Shortly before the EMPIRE WINDRUSH's Caribbean passengers disembarked to begin their new lives, they gathered one last time for a group photo. Great Britain initially welcomed its new citizens, which is perhaps not surprising, considering that they had been educated in British colonial schools. This amicable disposition toward them and other non-white immigrants did not last long, however. In the wake of a recession in the late 1950s, in particular, there were attacks against immigrants and the London district of Notting Hill was rocked by major riots. Immigration regulations became more restrictive in 1962 with the passage of the Commonwealth Immigrants Act (introduced by the Conservative Party). Ever since, the issue of immigration in Britain (as in the rest of Europe) has had great potential for conflict. UB

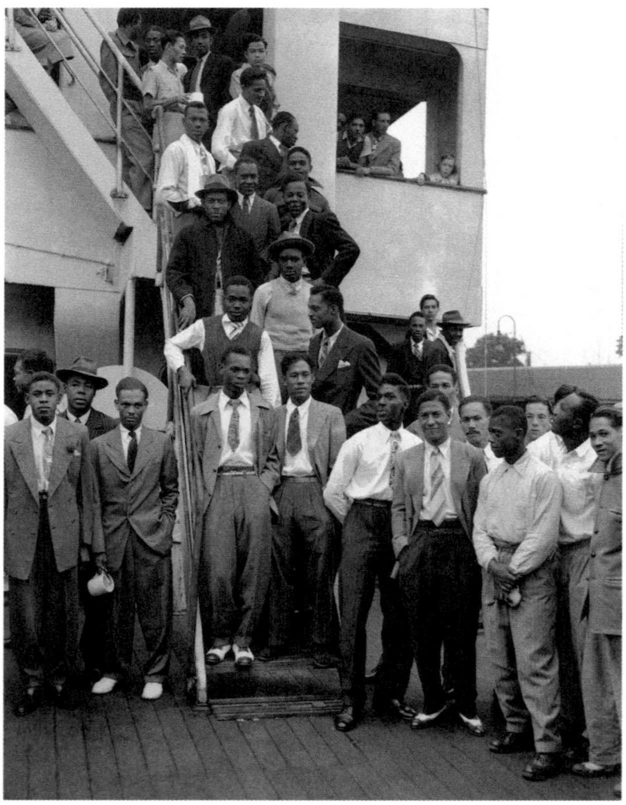

9/54

A Continent of Immigration: Fleeing to Europe across the Mediterranean

9/55 **Video interview with Najlaa Malik (35) from Damascus, Syria**
Berlin, 2017
Produced by Anna Reschop, Berlin
Video by Mirko Kubein
Berlin, Deutsches Historisches Museum

After Najlaa Malik spoke out publicly against the Assad regime in her home country of Syria, there were two attempts to abduct her. She left Syria in 2013. First she emigrated to Lebanon. In 2015, she decided that it was not safe there and made her way to Marmaris in Turkey – a stopover on her way to Greece. Malik began her journey on a badly overloaded ten-metre yacht carrying 150 people. The boat developed a leak along the way. Malik could not swim but, like many people who set out for Europe across the Mediterranean, she had to make the crossing without a life jacket. After nine hours, the boat reached the shores of Greece. Here, Malik says, she felt safe again for the first time. Today she is living in Berlin, learning German and taking part in community projects. (Exhibit not shown) SB

9/56 **Neck pouch belonging to Najlaa Malik**
c. 2015
Nylon; 20 x 34 cm
Berlin, Najlaa Malik

This small pink neck pouch was made to hold valuables for joggers; similar ones can be found in sports equipment stores in Germany. Najlaa Malik had this pouch with her when she fled from Damascus (Syria) via Marmaris (Turkey) and Kos (Greece) to Berlin. She wore it around her neck underneath her clothes, where it protected her most valuable possessions: her money and her passport. SB

9/57 **Video interview with Paul Nkamani (35) from Douala, Cameroon**
Berlin, 2017
Produced by Anna Reschop, Berlin
Video by Mirko Kubein
Berlin, Deutsches Historisches Museum

Paul Nkamani's journey began in Douala in 2011 and ended in Berlin in 2015. The young Cameroonian studied politics and law in his home country. He was active in the fight against corruption and other abuses, and consequently was not permitted to complete his education. He left his home after his father died in 2011, a victim of the poor health care

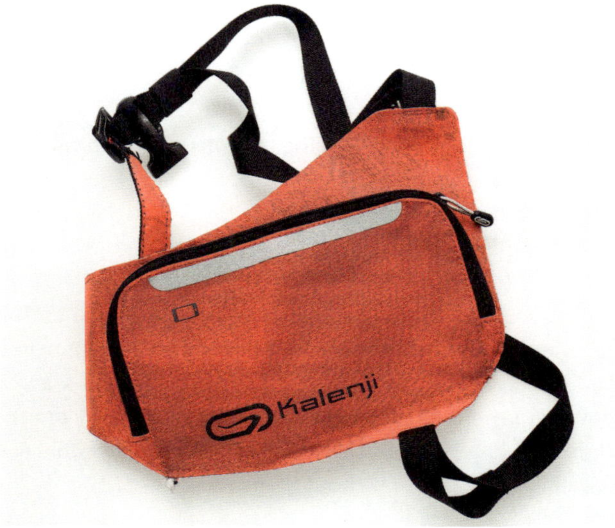

9/56

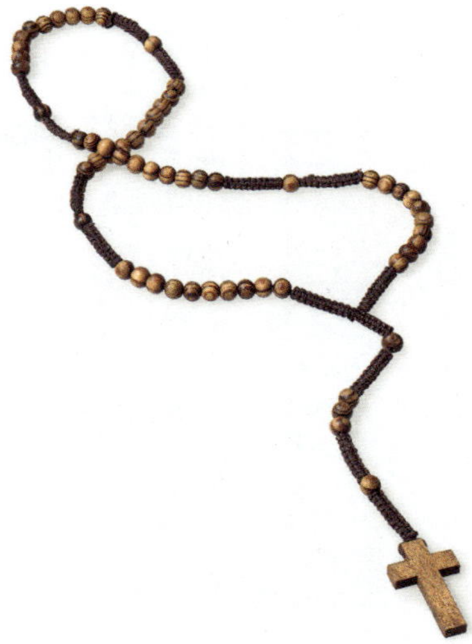

9/58

system. Nkamani travelled through Nigeria, Niger, Libya and Algeria, camping outside the small Spanish territory of Melilla until he could afford a smuggler. Many African refugees try to get to Europe via Melilla in an attempt to avoid the dangerous sea route. Nkamani finally risked the sea crossing, which he describes as a catastrophe. Because of strong currents and bad weather conditions, the boat veered off course and got into difficulties. Half of the passengers died before the Spanish coast guard found them. With the help of a friend who was a documentary film maker, Nkamani ended up coming to Berlin. As of 2017, he was trying to get a residence permit and was working as a medical orderly. His brother and mother are both still living in Cameroon. (Exhibit not shown) SB

9/58 **Rosary belonging to Paul Nkamani**
c. 2011
Wood, cotton thread; L 50 cm
Berlin, Paul Nkamani

Paul Nkamani carried this rosary with him during his flight from Nigeria, which took him through Niger, Algeria and Morocco, and then on to Spain and Germany. Everything else was taken away from him by the police when he arrived on the Spanish coast. Nkamani felt protected by the rosary. SB

9/59 **Video interview with Mehdi Sawari (31) from Ahwaz, Iran**
Berlin, 2017
Produced by Anna Reschop, Berlin
Video by Mirko Kubein
Berlin, Deutsches Historisches Museum

Mehdi Sawari lived a sheltered life as a child and young adult. The young Arab man passed his school leaving exams, trained as a plumber, and wanted to study IT. His family are Sunni Muslims, a minority in Iran. He experienced discrimination even as a child. In 2015, when his university application was rejected again, presumably because of his religious background, he decided to leave the country. His travels took him first across the Turkish border and then to İzmir. He paid a smuggler to take him over the sea to Mytellini in Greece. The crossing was traumatic. Unable to swim, he found himself aboard an inflatable dinghy with 50 people and not a single piece of life-saving equipment. Still, Sawari reached Greece in 2016 and then made his way to Germany. He began studying at the Technische Universität Berlin in the winter semester of 2017/18. (Exhibit not shown) SB

9/60 **Backpack belonging to Mehdi Sawari**
c. 2015
Nylon; 70 x 50 cm
Berlin, Mehdi Sawari

Mehdi Sawari took this black and red knapsack with him when he fled Ahwaz (Iran), carrying it through Izmir (Turkey) and Mytellini (Greece), and then ultimately on to Berlin. It held the few items that Sawari was able to take with him from home and, what is more, it represented the life he left behind. Refugees often start from home with a number

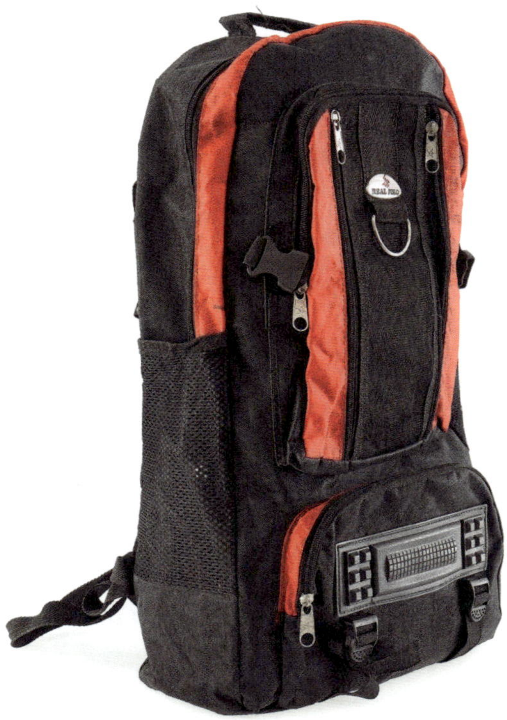

9/60

of things that they don't want to leave behind, but in the end, all they have left is their passport. Sawari's backpack therefore means a lot to him – it holds many memories. He has bought a new backpack for his new life in Berlin. SB

9/61 **Video interview with Mohammed Ebrahimi (28) from Daykundi, Afghanistan, and Sakineh Karimi (23) from Tehran, Iran**
Berlin, 2017
Produced by Anna Reschop, Berlin
Video by Mirko Kubein
Berlin, Deutsches Historisches Museum

Mohammed Ebrahimi grew up in a relatively affluent family in Afghanistan. The Taliban was a constant threat, however, prompting Ebrahimi to go to university in Iran in 2014. He worked part-time in a mobile-phone shop, where he met Sakineh Karimi. They fell in love and wanted to marry, but the young woman's father had already arranged a marriage for her. He threatened to kill his daughter if she did not follow his wishes. The couple fled to Izmir in Turkey. At the same time, Ebrahimi's family had left their home and were waiting in northern Turkey for an opportunity to get to Europe. While there, his father organised a smuggler for the two young people. They left for Samos with 40 others on an inflatable dinghy much too small for that number. The passengers had been forced to throw away all their possessions to make room for more people. The boat made it to the island and the couple came to Berlin. Today they are happily married. (Exhibit not shown) SB

9/62 **Mobile phone belonging to Mohammed Ebrahimi**
c. 2014
Plastic, glass i.a.; 13 x 6.5 cm
Berlin, Mohammed Ebrahimi

Mohammed Ebrahimi's smartphone, which he used during his travels, was not kept in a protective case. The screen was badly damaged as a result. Ebrahimi has not thrown it away, however – it means too much to him. It was the only connection to his family during that arduous time, and he would not have been able to flee without them. SB

9/63 **Mobile phone belonging to Sakineh Karimi**
c. 2014
Plastic, glass i.a.; 10 x 5.5 x 1 cm
Berlin, Sakineh Karimi

Sakineh Karimi's smartphone, which she brought with her from Iran to Germany, has a small crack in the lower right corner of the screen. Like her husband's phone, it no longer works. The phone holds different memories for Karimi than her husband's phone does for him. On the one hand, it was through the phone that she met him and it represents the beginning of their love; on the other hand, it reminds her of the horror of their escape and journey – the part of her life that she wants to leave behind. At first, she didn't want to keep it at all. SB

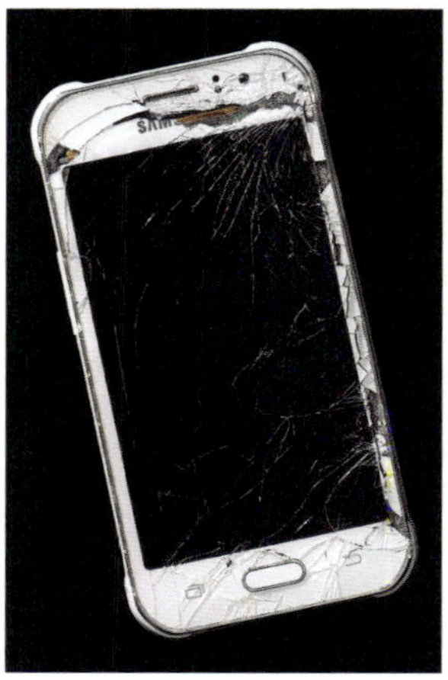

9/62

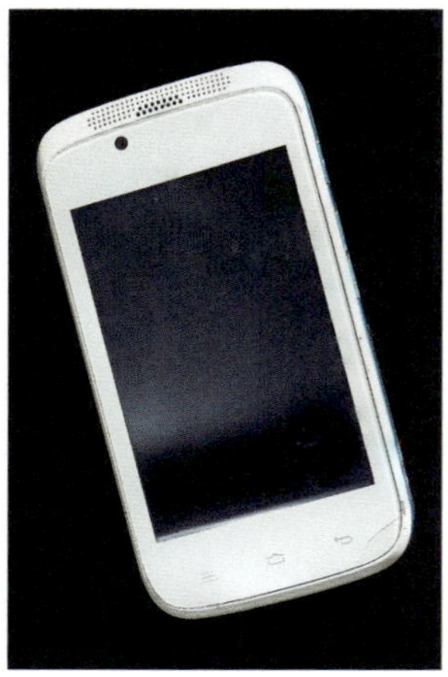

9/63

Ahmad Mustafa

Discourse: Smartphones

When you go to a refugee reception center, or when you meet a refugee in the street, the first thing which attracts your sight is this fancy smartphone. Why do refugees hold smartphones? And do they really need it?

It's a question that we hear often from the migrants haters, or even from the supporters. As a refugee from Syria, I will try to clarify this issue.

This small plastic device that you have in your pocket is a big need for a person who is risking his life on the way through the sea and through a strange land that he never saw before.

The first use of the cellphone might be when you ride the "dinghy", crossing the sea between Turkey and Greece. A lot of boats lose their way, or the motor stops stupidly in the middle of two darks: the sea and the black night. Then you should try to call the coastguards to inform them that you are in danger by locating your position and asking for an urgent help. In that moment, your life becomes meaningless compared to the lives of the crying women and the scream of the children. You simply have a moral obligation to what is happening, and the cellphone might be a turning point between death and life.

What is as important as the cellphone is the tool that keeps it alive. Your second friend that charges the phone for several times in the critical moments (because there is no electricity in the empty fields and along the railways that the groups of people follow through Macedonia). Nevertheless, the first thing that a migrant does when he finds a hotel or a resting place is to charge the phone and the power bank, and to buy a sim card of the new country that he reached to be able to stay connected to the internet.

Also, there is a point not less important than the previous ones, which is to stay in touch with the family back home which is getting further and further away day after a day. To open the "Gallery " and to take a look at the last photos back home, the face of your mother or the neighborhood where you grew up and that you never excepted to leave one day. But here you are.

Coming back to reality, tomorrow a very hard day is coming. You have to take a rest, but not before studying this geographical spot of the map that you have to cross the next day and to download it as an off-line map because there might be no signal there. As soon as you will reach this unfriendly border (I mean Hungary), you might also need to put your phone on the air plane mode because you don't want to take the risk to be located because of the signal of your phone. Our footsteps are heavy where we are now, because the footsteps of the outsiders are always heavy on every strange land.

Your phone gives you the access to text friends and family members who did this long journey before, so that they can guide you and give you valuable information: to know where to go, to avoid dangerous places and what you should do exactly at the next step.

Once you reach your final destination, this photo of yourself that you take in front of a monument and that you share on the social media: the sign that a hard chapter of your life is now behind you and that a new one is going to be written.

The job of the smartphone doesn't end with the end of the journey but a new use comes up: to stay up-to-date with the situation of your homeland through the social media (Facebook, Twitter... etc.), because most of the time there is no TV in the place where you are living and to keep the contact with your loved ones.

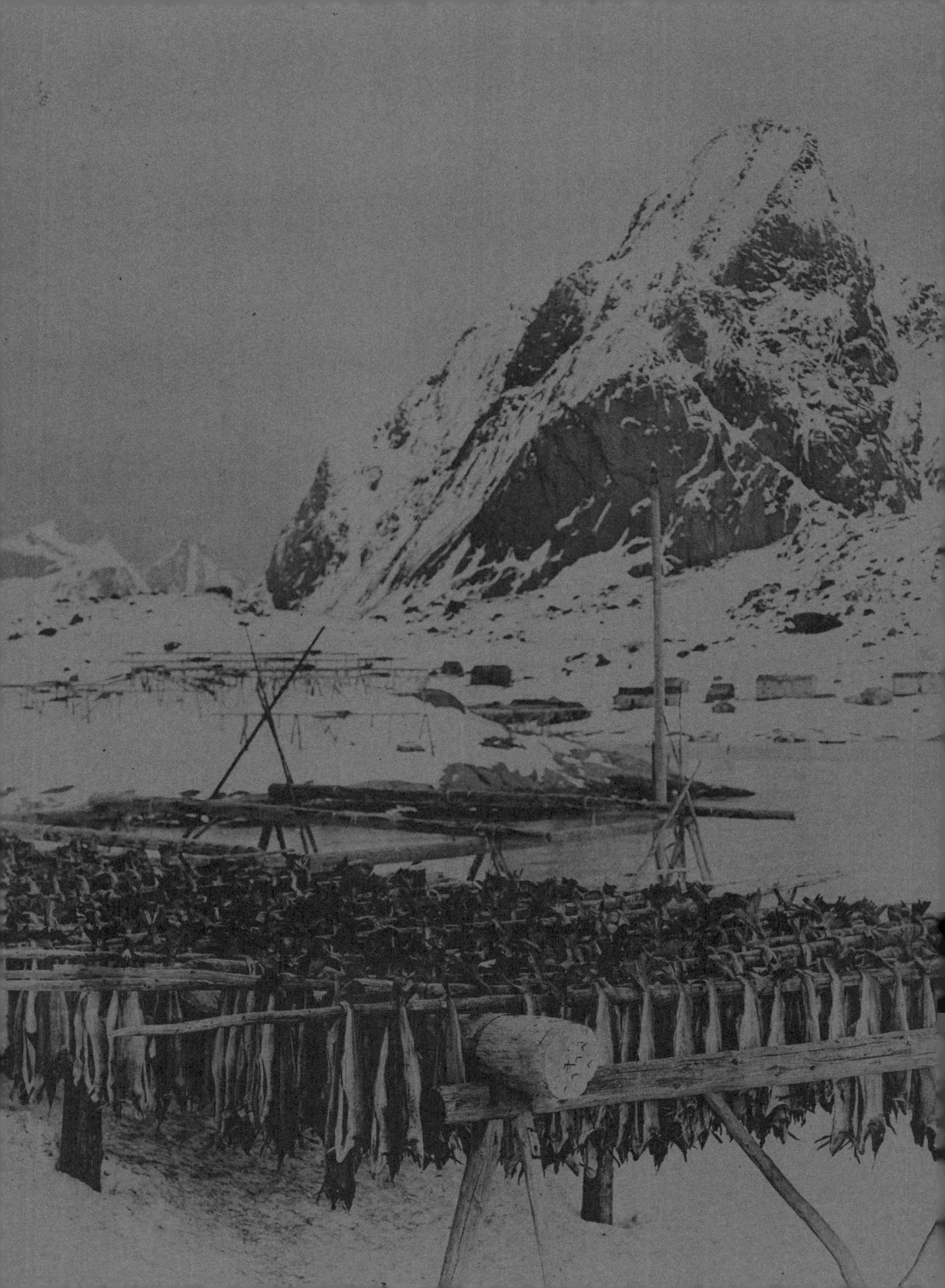

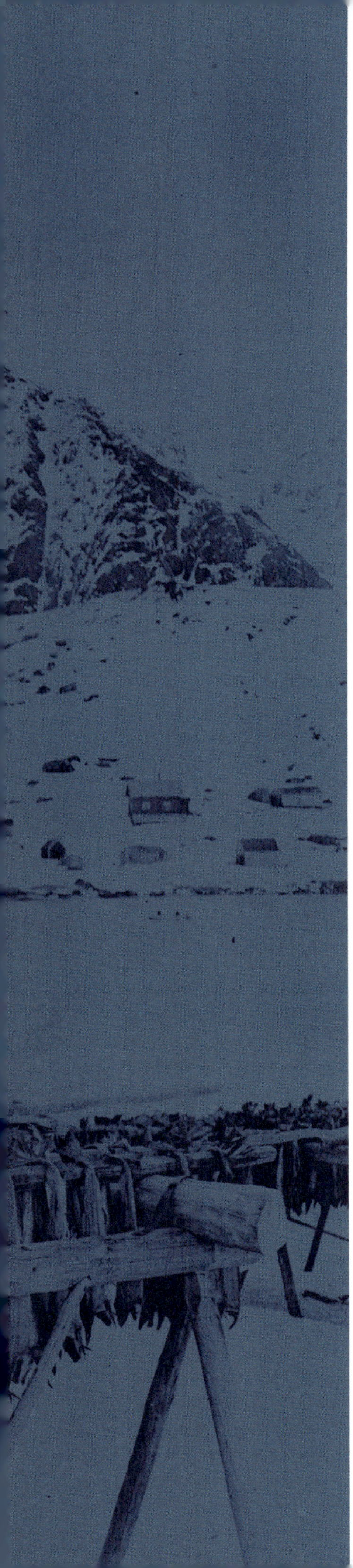

III
RESOURCES

10 Use and Overuse
The Port of Bergen

The sea holds a rich variety of resources, and Europe has a long tradition of using them. Over the centuries, fish, more than any other food from the sea, has played a defining role in people's daily lives. Since the Middle Ages at least, northern European waters have been known for their productive fishing grounds. Stockfish (air-dried fish) was produced in Lofoten, Norway, and shipped from the port of Bergen to locations throughout Europe. Bergen prospered thanks to the lucrative fish trade, and in 1365 the Hanseatic League established a *Kontor* there called *Tyske Bryggen* (Norwegian for "German quay"). A *Kontor* was the permanent commercial and residential headquarters of the Hanseatic League in a specific country or region. Hanseatic merchants from towns all across northern Germany sailed to Bergen to buy stockfish. They came in such large numbers that there was a term for them: *Bergenfahrer*, or "Bergen-goers".

In the Middle Ages, Europeans fished for cod, pollack, haddock, and herring. The latter was known as the 'silver of the sea'. Without non-perishable food aboard, early voyages across the ocean would have been unthinkable. The great demand for fish in southern Europe was due partly to the important role it played for Catholics as an alternative to meat on fast days. High yields and low processing costs made fish affordable for all social classes.

Mariners stayed close to the coast at first, but as demand for processed fish and fish products rose, they expanded their fishing grounds into the high seas. As voyages across the Atlantic grew more common, people became better at dealing with the dangers of the marginal seas in the far north. They also came to realise how large the ocean's whale stocks were. Starting in the seventeenth century, first the English and then the Dutch began to specialise in whaling. Products that could be manufactured from whale parts included soap, leather, pitch, rope and whale oil. Until the late nineteenth century, the most commonly used lamp fuel in European households was whale oil. A horn-like substance on the jaws of some whales, called baleen or (more commonly) whalebone, was used for picture frames, knife handles, parasol ribs, and corset stays. A combination of overfishing and the discovery of new resources led to a reduction in whaling expeditions.

In the nineteenth century, fossil fuels such as petroleum and natural gas began to be used more commonly. Oil and gas reservoirs were sought in Europe, as in other places, and discovered in the North Sea. A major find was made in the waters of Norway on 24 December 1969. The Ekofisk oil field contained reservoirs of oil and gas that turned Norway into one of the richest countries in the world overnight. The seas continue to be scoured for resources today. Manganese nodules, cobalt-rich ferromanganese crusts, and black smokers contain valuable minerals and ore that are of great interest to industry. Methane hydrate, first discovered during drilling in the Black Sea in 1971, is known to be buried underneath rock in large parts of the world's oceans and is considered the fuel of the future. For a long time, it was unclear who these reserves belong to, but that debate ended with the establishment of the International Seabed Authority in 1994. The mining and refining of maritime mineral resources will not be commercially viable until some time in the future, as the associated costs and risks are currently quite high.

Plastic debris likewise poses a threat to the seas and the organisms that live there. The world's oceans now hold 100 to 150 million tonnes of plastic waste, and several million tonnes are added to that every year. Because plastic takes several hundred years to decompose, the oceans now contain huge islands of garbage, with currents causing them to grow ever larger and denser. Researchers estimate that by 2050 there will be more plastic in the ocean than fish. *Thomas Eisentraut*

Further Reading

Elena Balzamo and Reinhard Kaiser, *Olaus Magnus. Die Wunder des Nordens*, Frankfurt a.M. 2006

Peter-René Becker and Ulf Beichle, *»Mensch, Fisch!«*, Oldenburg 2012

Espen Bowitz Andersson, *Bryggen. Das Hanseatische Kontor in Bergen*, Bergen 1982

Kristin Øye Gjerde (ed.), *Crossing Boundaries. Frigg Industrial Heritage*, Stavanger 2010

Torbjørn Kindingstad and Fredrik Hagemann (eds.), *Norwegian Oil history*, Stavanger 2002

Rasso Knoller, *Norwegen. Ein Länderporträt*, Bonn 2013

Hans Joachim Kürtz, *I hanseatenes tider. Handel og vandel på hansakontorene i Bergen – Brügge – London og Novgorod*, Lübeck 1983

Joachim Münzing, *Der historische Walfang in Bildern*, Herford 1987

Corinna Roeder (ed.), *Große, fette Wale. Die Geschichte des Walfangs in Drucken des 15.–21. Jahrhunderts*, Oldenburg 2006

Marco Trebbi and Jiri Havran, *Bryggen. The Heart of Bergen*, Oslo 2007

Andres von Brandt, *Das große Buch vom Fischfang – international. Zur Geschichte der fischereilichen Fangtechnik*, Innsbruck 1975, pp. 119–132, 146–171

World Ocean Review No. 3, *Rohstoffe aus dem Meer – Chancen und Risiken*, Hamburg 2014

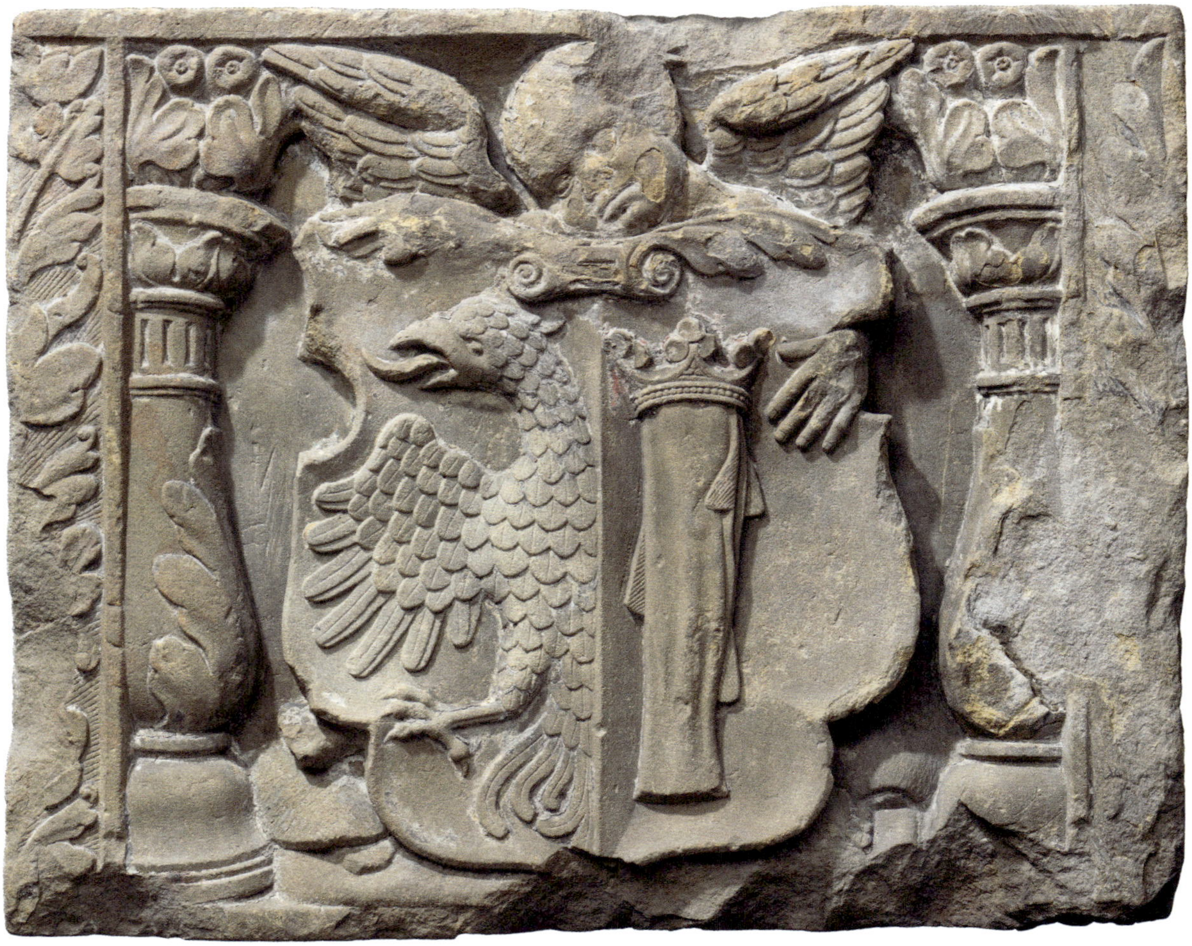

10/2

Stockfish and Northern European Fishing

10/1 **View of the city of Bergen, in *Civitates orbis terrarum* (Cities of the World), vol. 4**
Written by Georg Braun (1542–1622)
Engraved by Franz Hogenberg (1538–1590)
Cologne, after 1588
Paper, coloured copper engraving; 41.5 x 61 cm
Berlin, Deutsches Historisches Museum: RB 53/2979-4

The Norwegian port of Bergen, founded in 1070, was a major centre of trade in processed fish. The dual advantages of being a transshipment centre for stockfish and possessing a trade monopoly from the Norwegian crown allowed the town to expand rapidly. Two pieces of sacred architecture – the cathedral and St. Mary's Church – dominated its skyline. The church, built of stone in the twelfth century, was commissioned by German merchants. The port was in the centre of the town, next to the commercial district of *Tyske Bryggen* (meaning "German quay"). Its rows of wooden trading houses were used in part to store valuable goods, chief among them stockfish and fish oil, until they were reshipped to locations further south. Bergenhus Fortress dates back to the thirteenth century, when it was the Norwegian royal residence. For a time, Bergen was the largest city in Norway and the fourth-largest transshipment centre in the Hanseatic League, which established a permanent headquarters (or *Kontor*) there. The city suffered great damage from fires in 1702, 1855, 1916, and 1955. (Fig. p. 123) TE

10/2 **Coat of arms of the Bremen *Bergenfahrer***
Bremen, mid-16th cent.
Sandstone relief; 52 x 65 cm
Bremen, Focke-Museum – Bremer Landesmuseum für Kunst und Kulturgeschichte: H.118

Northern Europe's major export in the Middle Ages and early modern period was stockfish. The port of Bergen had a monopoly on trade in stockfish, which was produced on the Lofoten Islands and brought from there to Bergen on small boats. It was resold to the European mainland through the Hanseatic League. Stockfish is still known in many European countries under a variety of names (*stoccafisso, baccalà, bacalhau*). Just how important the stockfish trade was for the

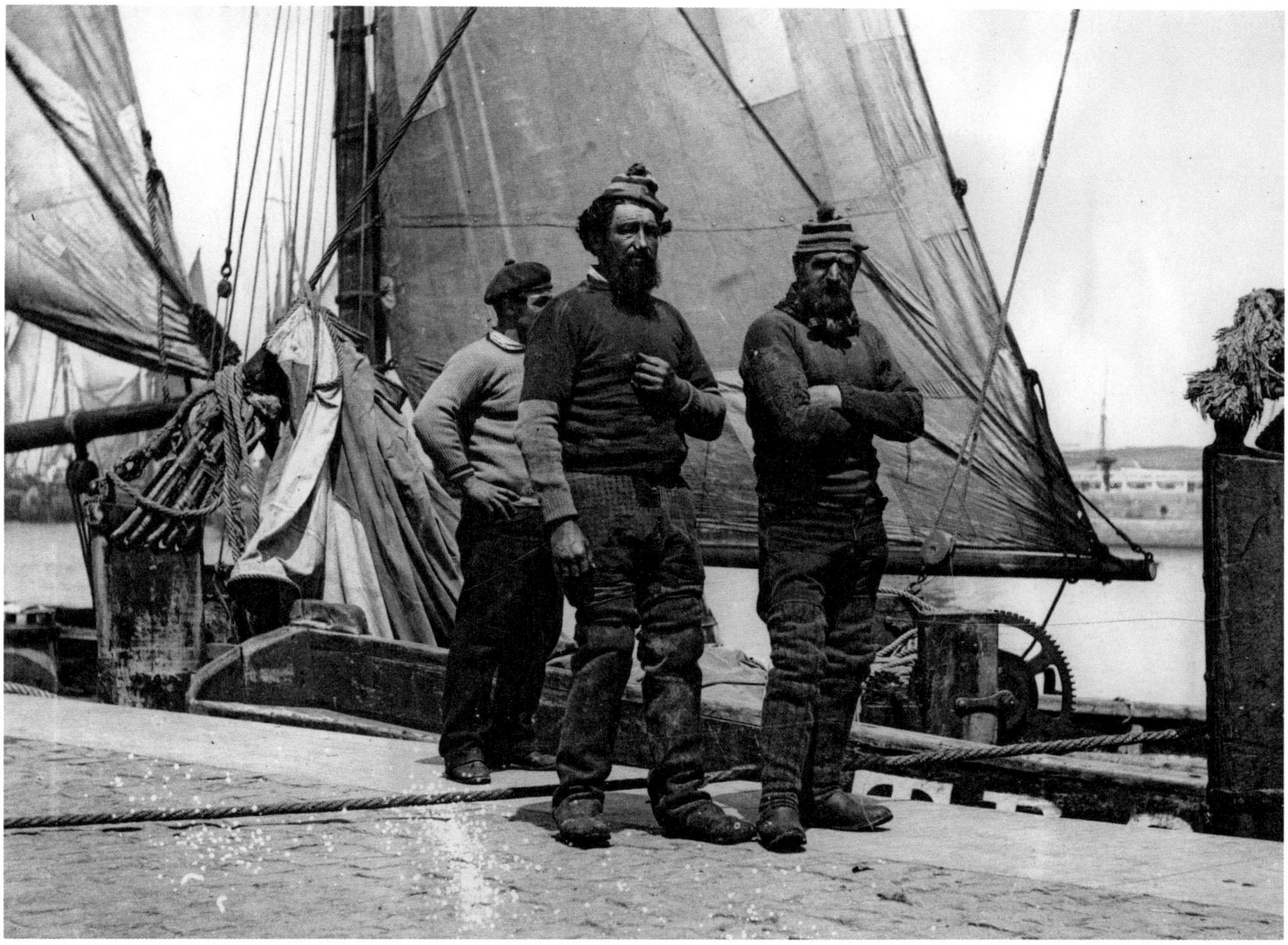

10/3

Hanseatic League can be seen in this coat of arms for the Bremen *Bergenfahrer* (meaning "those who sail to Bergen" or "Bergen-goers"). It features an upright, crowned stockfish symbolising the Norwegian town of Bergen. The league's German merchants were subjects of the Holy Roman Empire, represented by the half double-eagle. TE

10/3 **Seamen on a dock in front of a sailing boat**
North Sea, c. 1900
Photograph (new print)
Berlin, Deutsches Historisches Museum: BA 97/7690

Over the centuries, sailing and fishing in the North Sea have been of central importance to the Norwegian population. Good fishing grounds in the North Sea guaranteed profitable revenues and also led to the establishment of many seaports along the Norwegian Atlantic coast. Norway is still one of the biggest fishing countries in the world. Fish products are Norway's fourth-largest export after fossil fuels (petroleum and natural gas) and metals. This turn-of-the-century photograph shows bearded seamen in machine-knit pullovers. The man in the middle is wearing a kind of pullover featuring multi-coloured sleeves that was made in England and originally produced for the Dutch market. The hats could be of Scottish design. It is not clear whether the seamen in the photograph come from Norway, the Netherlands, England or Scotland. TE

10/4 **Cod, being dried to make stockfish**
Reine (Lofoten, Norway), 1924
Photograph (new print)
Bergen, The Norwegian Fisheries Museum

Stockfish was a catchall phrase for processed fish (cod, haddock, pollack or ling) that had been caught in the Atlantic or Arctic Ocean. Pairs of fish would be tied together by the tail fin and hung from a wooden frame (*stokk*). The head and guts were removed beforehand. Even in the age of the Vikings, in the late eighth century, northern Europeans preserved fish by drying it in the open air. The climate in Lofoten was excellently suited for this method, as the weather was stable, with adequate sunshine, wind and steady temperatures. After several weeks, the fish were well-preserved and would keep for four to five years. Stockfish could be

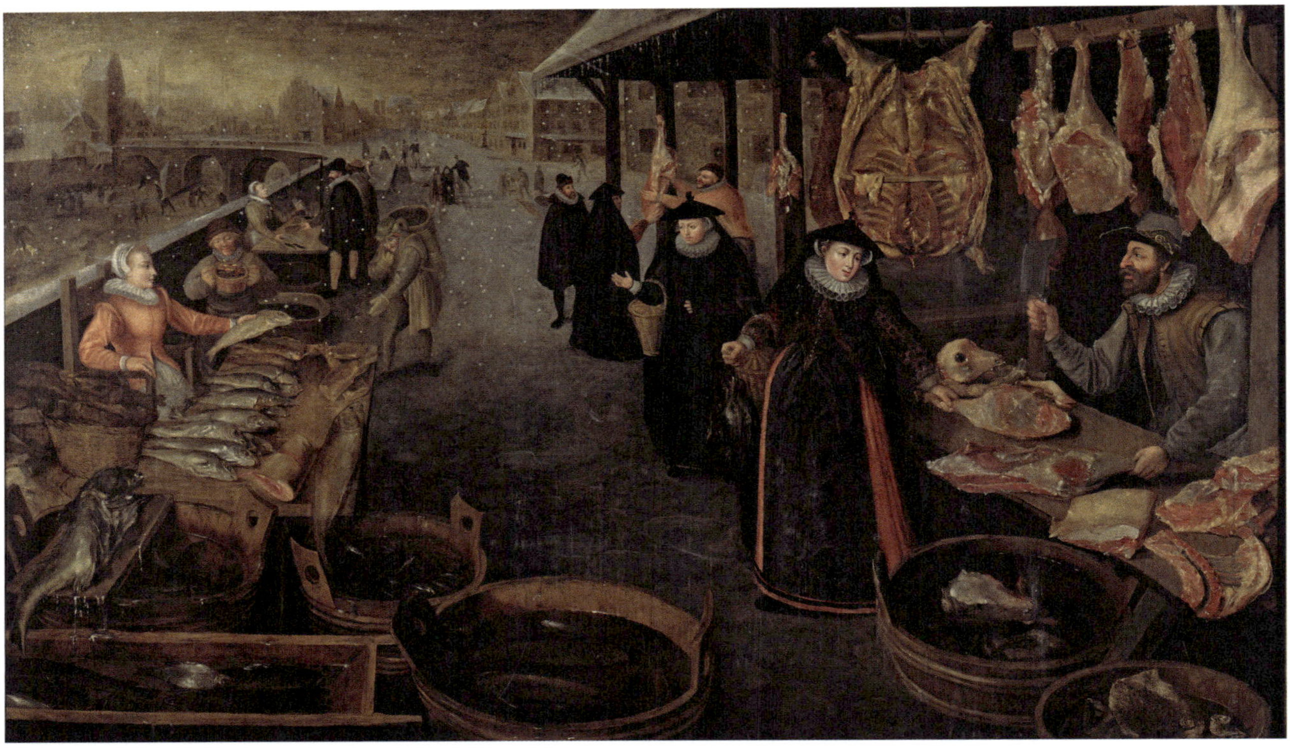

10/5

stacked and were therefore inexpensive to transport. The fact that they could be carried on long ship voyages without spoiling was another key factor in their widespread consumption in the Mediterranean region. (Fig. p. 124) TE

10/5 ***Meat and Fish Market (Winter)***
Lucas van Valckenborch (1535–1597)
Frankfurt a. M., 1595
Oil on canvas; 106 x 182 cm
Berlin, Deutsches Historisches Museum: 1989/1980

This painting shows a winter market scene in a Dutch town. The market is clearly separated into fish stands and meat stands. While a wealthy patrician woman turns her attention to a meat vendor, a poor-looking man in the background approaches the fish stand with a basket on his back. The painting shows food consumption plainly divided on lines of social class. Because fish stocks in the North Sea and Baltic Sea were large and yields were high, fish was very affordable compared to meat. During a period of sustained population growth in the sixteenth century, fish remained a guaranteed source of food for the poor. Religious customs were another major factor in food consumption patterns across Europe. In Catholic regions, for example, eating meat was forbidden on 180 to 200 days per year. Fish was considered a legitimate alternative and consequently played a key role in the region's economy. TE

10/6 **Wood engraving, *Of dangerous fishing in the Norwegian Sea***
(De piscatura periculosa in Noruegiano Oceano)
Olaus Magnus (1490–1557)
Rome, 1555
Reproduction
Oslo, Nasjonalbiblioteket: Lib. rar. 393

Most contemporary knowledge of the Scandinavian regions and their particular customs and cultures can be found on a large map drafted by Olaus Magnus (1490–1557), a Swedish bishop and polymath, in 1539. He had left Sweden fifteen years earlier, in 1524, to escape the Reformation. As an exile in Rome, he dedicated himself to publishing scholarly works, with the aim of making knowledge of northern Europe available to a wider public. This knowledge was based on travels that he had undertaken himself. One of his maps is known today throughout the world as the *Carta Marina* (Marine map and Description of the Northern Lands). In addition to the map, Olaus Magnus wrote *Historia de Gentibus Septentrionalibus (A Description of the Northern Peoples)*, which was illustrated with woodcuts and published in Rome in 1555. It was so popular that it was translated into other languages, including German (1567), French (1560), Italian (1561), Dutch (1562) and English (1658). The work also goes into great detail on the subject of northern European fish, their distinctive features and the methods used to catch them. (Fig. p. 126) TE

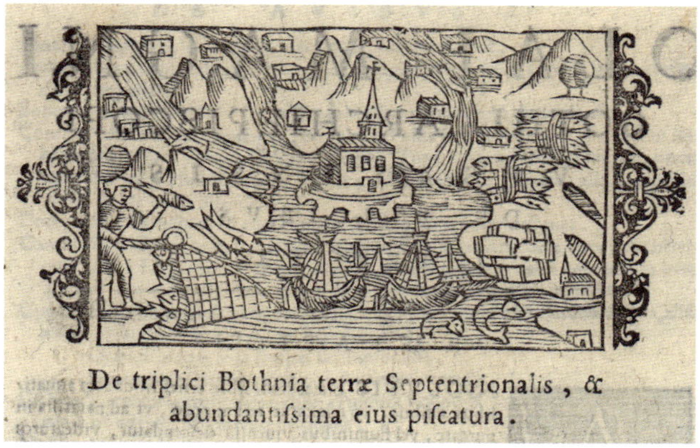

10/7

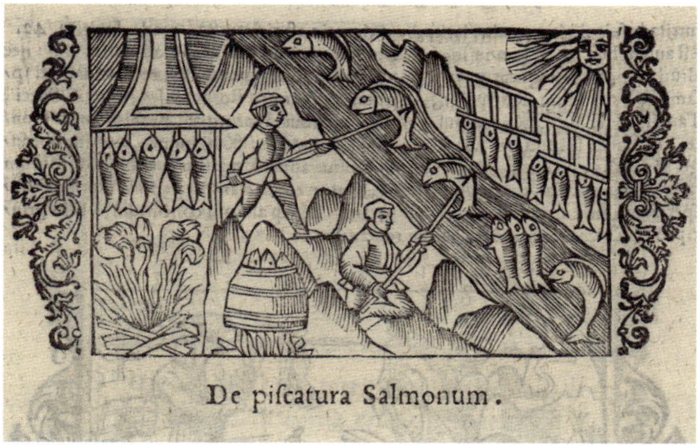

10/8

10/7 **Wood engraving, *Of the three Bothnia in the far north and the rich fishing grounds there***
(De triplici Bothnia terræ Septentrionalis, & abundantissima eius piscatura)
Olaus Magnus (1490–1557)
Rome, 1555
Reproduction
Oslo, Nasjonalbiblioteket: Lib. rar. 393

Olaus Magnus describes the Gulf of Bothnia, the northern arm of the Baltic Sea, as being unusually rich in fish. The excellent quality of that fish made it a highly sought-after European commodity. Merchants from Spain and Portugal brought salt, wine and textiles to trade for it. Fishing techniques varied greatly in the Baltic Sea region, and in some cases, the fish would be processed according to the preferences of the area that it was sold to. Once preserved, the fish could be transported easily to southern regions. In addition to air-drying, fish were commonly preserved with salt. Salted herring was transported in wooden barrels. Because the salinity of the Baltic Sea was low, salt could not be harvested profitably and always had to be imported. TE

10/8 **Wood engraving, *How to fish for salmon***
(De piscatura Salmonum)
Olaus Magnus (1490–1557)
Rome, 1555
Reproduction
Oslo, Nasjonalbiblioteket: Lib. rar. 393

By the sixteenth century, if not earlier, people had noticed that salmon were an unusual fish. Every year in the summer, they migrated inland from saltwater to freshwater, leaping high in the air to pass any obstacles in their way. They do this by flexing their tail toward their lower body, then releasing their tensed tail muscles to propel themselves upward. After spawning, they swim back to salty waters. Salmon grew unusually large in Scandinavia's nutrient-rich waters. They were mostly caught in rivers, using spears or harpoons. Olaus Magnus gave an account not only of the distribution and methods of catching salmon, but also of their taste. He described the meat as having a reddish colour and a sweet and pleasant taste. The preferred method of preserving salmon was to cure it with smoke. TE

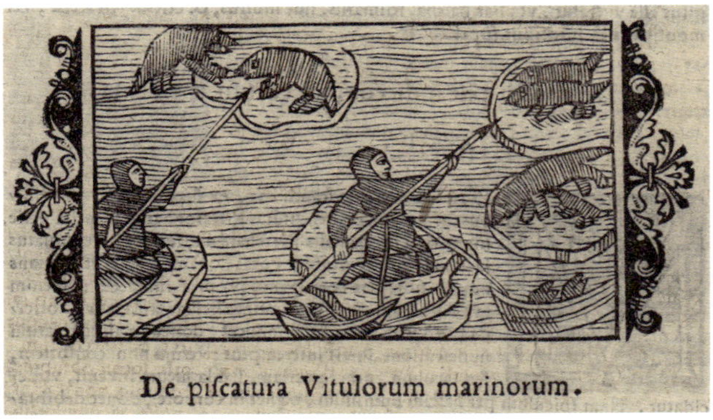

10/9

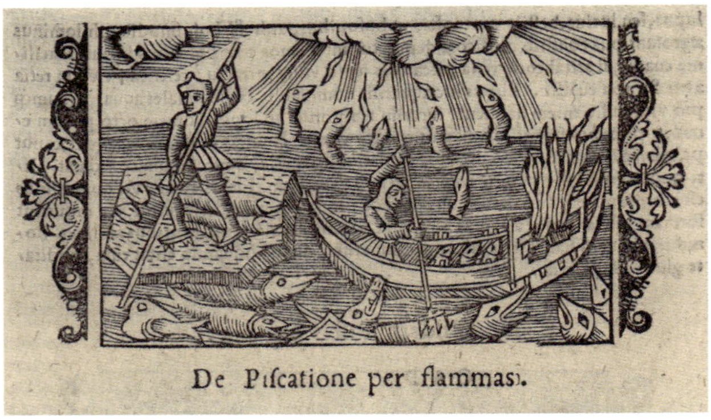

10/10

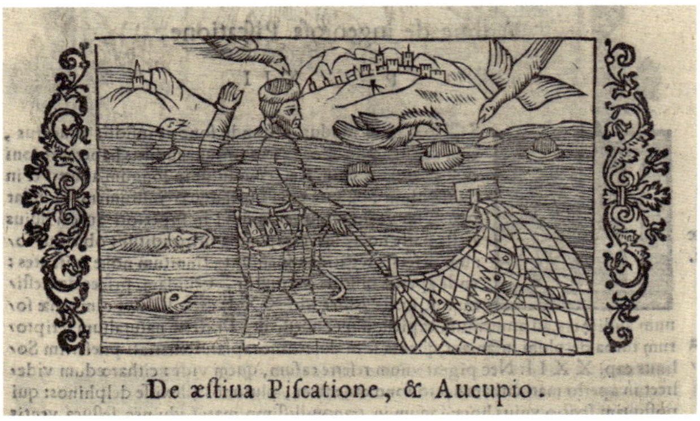

10/11

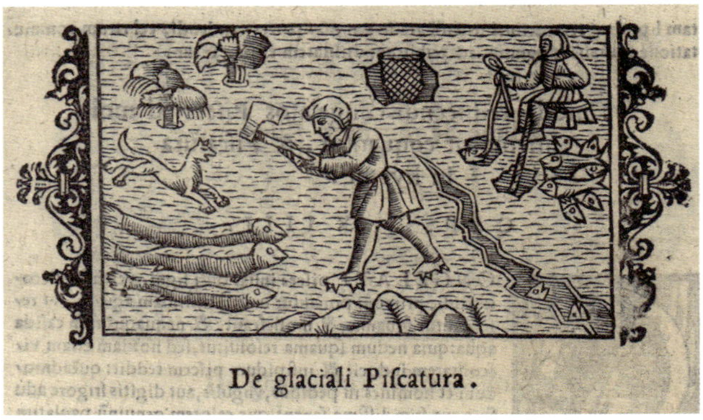

10/12

10/9 **Wood engraving, *Of sea calves***
(*De piscatura Vitulorum marinorum*)
Olaus Magnus (1490–1557)
Rome, 1555
Reproduction
Oslo, Nasjonalbiblioteket: Lib. rar. 393

In the sixteenth century, people did not yet distinguish between fish and mammals. Any animal that lived in the sea was considered fish, and that included 'sea calves', as seals were then known. The question of whether seals were fish had some practical relevance, as Catholics needed to know whether they could be eaten on fast days. The matter was discussed at a church consistory, but no clear ruling resulted. A guideline was suggested, however: if they jumped into the water when hunted, they were to be considered fish. If they ran away on land, they were to be considered land animals and therefore could not be eaten on fast days. In *A Description of the Northern Peoples*, seals were described as having firm and flesh-like bodies. They could not be killed quickly and the death-blow had to be struck on the temple. Their voice was said to be like that of a bull; they had four legs, but no ears as they dwelt and fed in the water. Seals were found in large numbers in the North Sea and the Baltic Sea in the sixteenth century. It was not until the nineteenth and twentieth centuries that they were hunted on a large scale, bringing them to the brink of extinction. TE

10/10 **Wood engraving, *How to fish with fire***
(*De Piscatione per flammas*)
Olaus Magnus (1490–1557)
Rome, 1555
Reproduction
Oslo, Nasjonalbiblioteket: Lib. rar. 393

Some of the fishing methods described by Olaus Magnus seem curious to us today. In a passage of *A Description of the Northern Peoples* describing the practice of fishing with the aid of fire, Magnus wrote that when people wanted fish, they used small boats made from a single piece of wood. At the front of the boat, they lit torches made of fir which would cause pike and eels, fascinated by the light, to draw closer in great numbers. The fishermen would then stab them with hooked forks and pull them into the boat. Magnus also described ice-fishing. For southern Europeans, luring fish by means of light or fire was a rather unusual method. They could only explain it by the fact that in winter the days in northern Europe were shorter and the nights correspondingly longer. As a result, they concluded, the fish reacted more strongly to light. TE

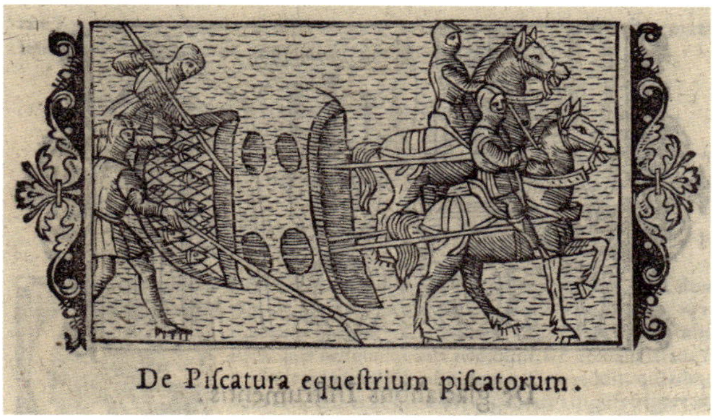

10/13

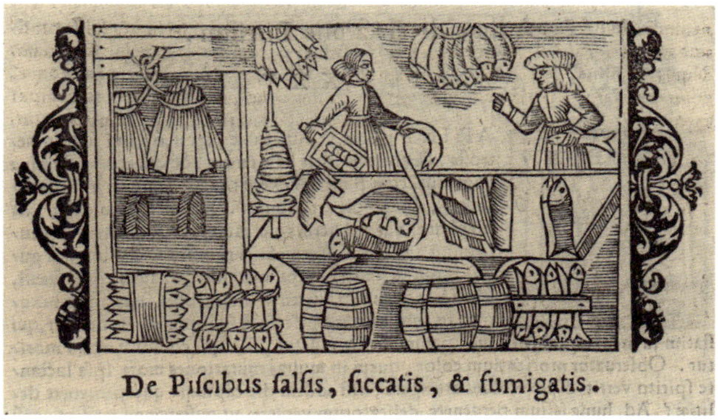

10/14

10/11 **Wood engraving, *Of summer fishing and hunting***
(*De æstiua Piscatione, & Aucupio*)
Olaus Magnus (1490–1557)
Rome, 1555
Reproduction
Oslo, Nasjonalbiblioteket: Lib. rar. 393

One traditional way of catching fish was to use nets and traps, either from the shore or from aboard ship. Applying a combination of different methods at the same time promised the best results. For example, a fisherman might walk into the water with a cast net, agitating the seabed as he walked so the fish could not see through the murk. He might also carry a fishing rod and a string and hook, trying to catch even more fish using these additional approaches. The best time of day for fishing was the early morning, shorty before sunrise, when the fish were still "blind", as Olaus Magnus put it. It was also important to move quietly, so as not to startle the fish. TE

10/12 **Wood engraving, *Of winter fishing***
(*De glaciali Piscatura*)
Olaus Magnus (1490–1557)
Rome, 1555
Reproduction
Oslo, Nasjonalbiblioteket: Lib. rar. 393

Among the fishing methods described by Olaus Magnus is ice fishing, which is still practiced today, if only for sport. As the northern seas and lakes generally froze in the winter months, a variety of techniques were developed so that people could continue to fish. They used a drill or axe to bore or chop a hole through the ice. Then they lowered a fishing rod, or a string with a hook attached to it, through the hole to catch the fish. The angler sat on a stool or piece of wood so as not to catch a chill. TE

10/13 **Wood engraving, *How to fish on horseback***
(*De Piscatura equestrium piscatorum*)
Olaus Magnus (1490–1557)
Rome, 1555
Reproduction
Oslo, Nasjonalbiblioteket: Lib. rar. 393

One of the illustrations shows a special form of ice fishing. After several large holes had been broken through the ice, a trawl net would be lowered into the water. Then, using horses, the net would be pulled through the water beneath the ice. Men standing at the sides would push the net down with poles so it did not catch on the sharp undersides of the ice. The fish trapped beneath the ice swam directly into the net. This technique is still practiced in some parts of Scandinavia and Russia. Today, however, horses have been replaced by power winches (lifting devices consisting of rope wound on a drum turned by a motor). TE

10/14 **Wood engraving, *Of salted, dried and smoked fish***
(*De Piscibus salsis, siccatis, & fumigates*)
Olaus Magnus (1490–1557)
Rome, 1555
Reproduction
Oslo, Nasjonalbiblioteket: Lib. rar. 393

This picture shows a fishmonger selling fresh fish and different kinds of preserved fish. Smoked and dried fish was often salted in order to preserve its natural flavour. Preserved fish remained edible for a long time, which was an advantage on long sea voyages and during sieges in wartime. Public inspections and penalties were instituted to ensure that no-one traded in spoiled fish. Bad fish was burned at the market or thrown into the water, although the latter measure was taken only very rarely because it posed a risk to healthy fish stocks. The German phrase *dem Fass den Boden ausschlagen* (literally "to beat the bottom out of the barrel", meaning to "take the biscuit" or "be the last straw") derives from a similar procedure. If the fish inspector found people trying to sell inferior or spoiled food,

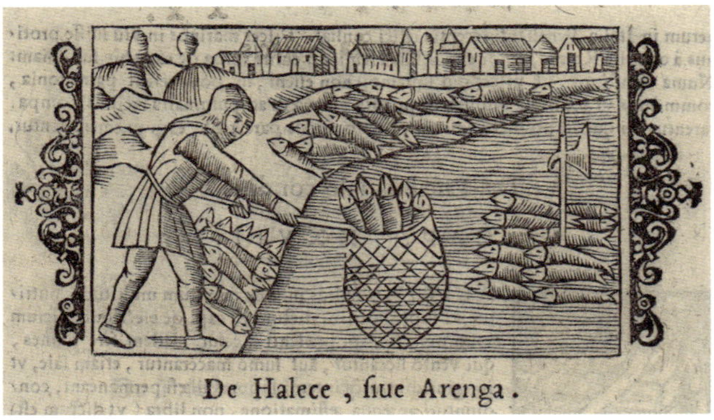

10/15

their wares would be destroyed. The barrels they were stored in would have the bottom beaten out of them, rendering the contents unsellable and the barrels unusable. TE

10/15 **Wood engraving, *Of herring or kipper***
(*De Halece, siue Arenga*)
Olaus Magnus (1490–1557)
Rome, 1555
Reproduction
Oslo, Nasjonalbiblioteket: Lib. rar. 393

In the Middle Ages, herring was one of the key foodstuffs of the Baltic region's rapidly growing population and, what is more, a valuable commodity for Hanseatic merchants. It was sold at the Skåne (or Scania) Market, which had been held since the early thirteenth century on the Skanör-Falsterbo peninsula at the southern mouth of the Öresund strait (between present-day Denmark and Sweden). Merchants came from all parts of Europe to trade fish and other products. In the Middle Ages, there were still large stocks of herring making their annual late-summer run from the North Sea into the western Baltic Sea to spawn. The herring would be caught in the autumn, cured with salt and exported across all of Europe, where they were eaten in great quantities on fast days. Large catches kept prices relatively low. This illustration alludes to the legend that herring were so thick in the water that a halberd could be stood upright among them without falling over. TE

10/16 **Wood engraving, *Of pike***
(*De Lupis, siue Luciis*)
Olaus Magnus (1490–1557)
Rome, 1555
Reproduction
Oslo, Nasjonalbiblioteket: Lib. rar. 393

Pike, which live in both fresh and brackish waters, were caught in lakes and on the open sea, using traditional cast

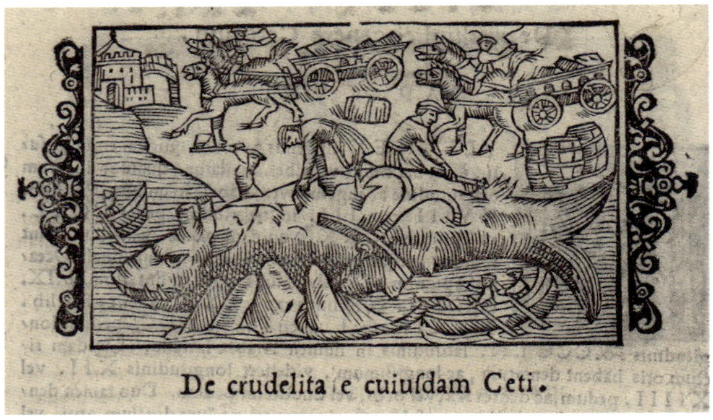

10/17

nets. Olaus Magnus described them as being very aggressive, with sharp teeth and wide mouths, and wrote that they attacked and ate other fish. Today, pike are found primarily in large, enclosed bodies of water, but also in the Baltic Sea. Because pike stocks in the lands of the far north were considered more than large enough for local consumption and the fish (typically salt-cured) were popular abroad, they were an important export item, with Germany constituting the largest market. (Exhibit not shown) TE

10/17 **Wood engraving, *How to catch whales***
(*De crudelitate cuiusdam Ceti*)
Olaus Magnus (1490–1557)
Rome, 1555
Reproduction
Oslo, Nasjonalbiblioteket: Lib. rar. 393

There are several recorded cases of whales being washed ashore, particularly after heavy storms. The stranded whale was then cut up on the spot. This work required powerful axes and hatchets. One of the products obtained from sperm whales was ambergris. It was considered to have medicinal properties and was used to treat heart disorders and epilepsy. It was also used in perfume manufacture. Olaus Magnus thought that ambergris was whale sperm. Today, we know that ambergris originates as a secretion in the whale's intestine and is used to coat undigested food, which is frequently regurgitated. The illustrations of whales and sea monsters found on the *Carta Marina* and in *A Description of the Northern Peoples* may have been put there to deter intruders. According to this theory, they were intended to discourage fishermen and sailors from the south from sailing to the rich fishing grounds of the north. TE

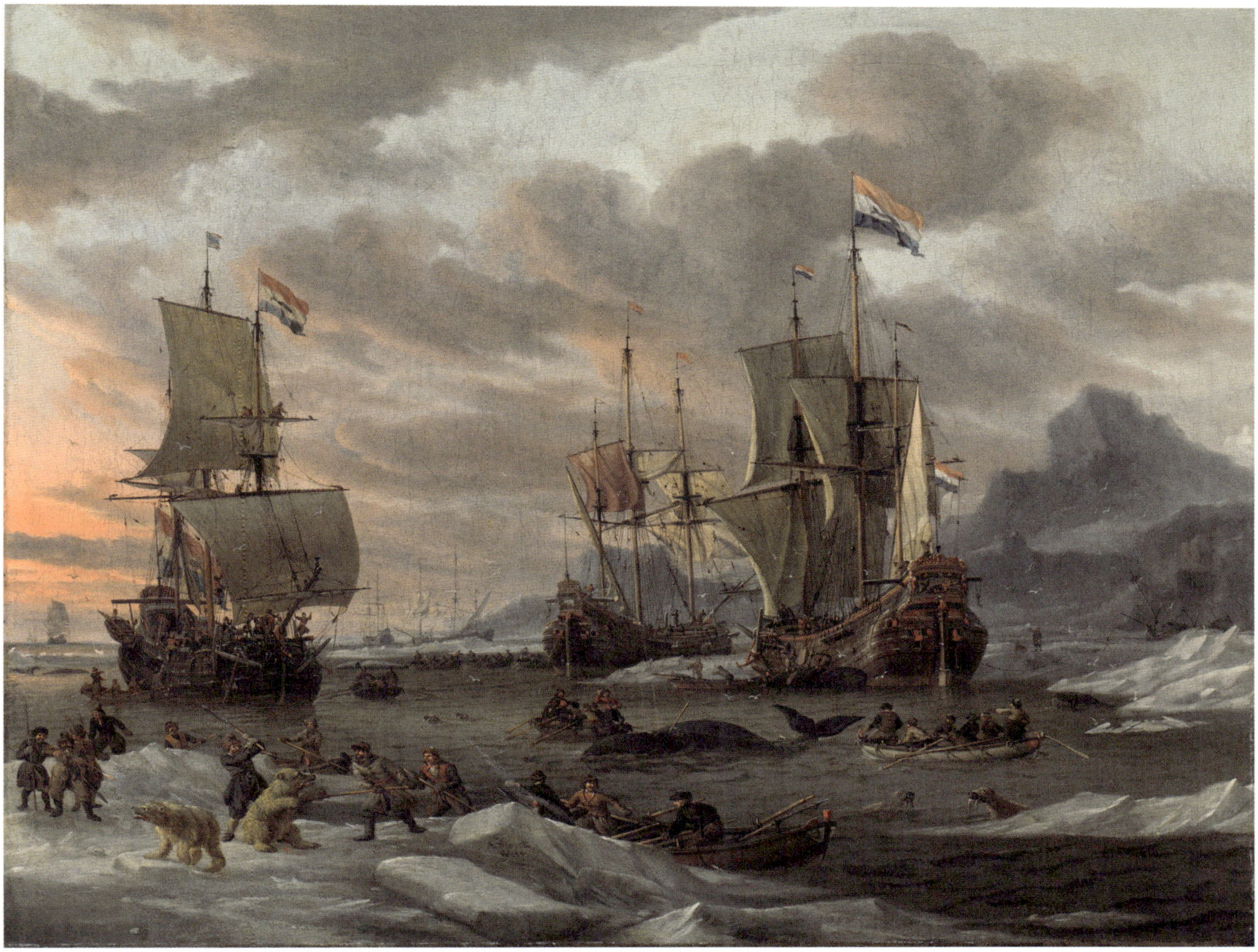

10/18

10/18 **Whaling Grounds in the Arctic Ocean**
Walvisvangst in de Poolzee
Abraham Storck, before 1708
Amsterdam, 1654–1708
Oil on canvas; 50.5 x 66.5 cm
Amsterdam, Rijksmuseum: SK-A-4102

Commercial whaling started in England and the Netherlands and expanded over the course of the eighteenth century. Specially equipped ships, like the whaler De Jonas shown here, were used on voyages in the iceberg-filled waters of the north. Once the whales were caught, they would be cut up aboard ship and partially processed. Whalers also had small facilities on land, among other things for boiling blubber, which was dangerous to do aboard ship. Almost the entire animal was utilised, its parts going into a variety of products such as soap and leather goods. Whale oil sold particularly well and fetched high prices. Whales were not the only animals of commercial interest in the far north – polar bears and walruses were hunted, too. Growing awareness of large whale stocks in northern waters and an increase in the range of whale products ultimately led to large-scale, professional whaling. Between 1675 and 1721, a total of 32,097 whales were killed by 5,886 Dutch whalers alone. This mercenary greed brought some whale populations to the edge of extinction. TE

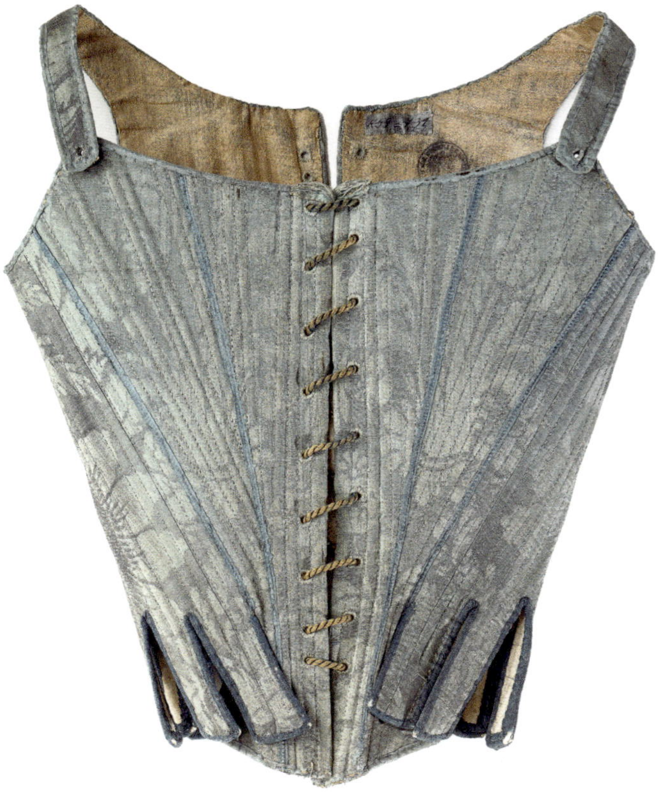

10/19

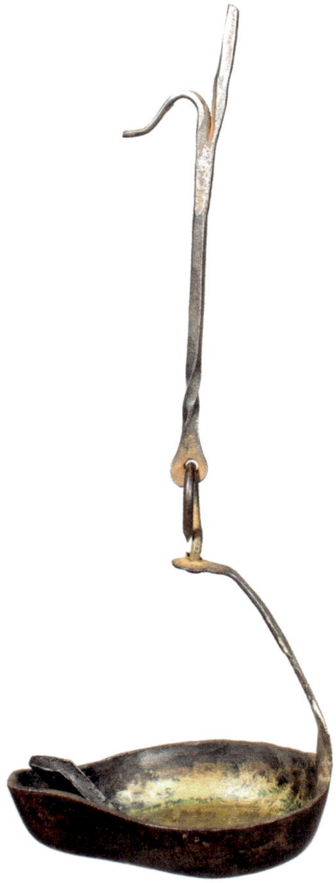

10/20

10/19 **Corset**
Berlin, c. 1770
Silk damask, linen, leather, whalebone; 80 x 52 cm
Berlin, Deutsches Historisches Museum: KTe 62/2

Baleen whales such as the blue whale or fin whale have no teeth. Instead, they have bristly plates of 'baleen', which they use to filter plankton. This material, rather than actual bone, is the source of what we call 'whalebone'. After the baleen was cleaned, it was heated and then torn into fine strips. This process produced irregular strips which were ideally suited for corset stays, being strong and flexible in equal measure. Demand for whalebone remained steady from the seventeenth to the twentieth century, a period during which corsets were an indispensable part of women's fashion. Whalebone was also used in making umbrellas and fans. Baleen whales in particular were hunted to satisfy the demands of the fashion industry. It was not until the Industrial Revolution that modern materials capable of replacing whalebone were developed. TE

10/20 **Whale oil lamp**
Northern Germany (?), first half 19th cent.
Wrought iron; 23 x 6 x 9 cm
Brake, Schiffahrtsmuseum Unterweser: 2000/0016

The most important product derived from whales – and one for which there was constant demand in Europe – was whale oil. For centuries, it was used as fuel, both in private households and in street lanterns (introduced in the late seventeenth century). While whale oil lamps varied widely in terms of design and materials, they all worked on the same principle. The oil travelled up the wick and burned there, generating light in the process. Whale oil was made from whale fat, or 'blubber'. The blubber was heated in a large cauldron (or 'try-pot'), boiled, filtered, and poured into barrels. This was generally done in whale oil refineries ('try-works') on land, but to some extent aboard ship as well. Whaling declined over a period of about 150 years. A number of factors contributed to its demise. For one thing, whale stocks became so depleted in the nineteenth century that hunting slowly ceased to be profitable. For another, the discovery of petroleum and the advent of electricity meant that whale oil was no longer needed for lamp fuel. TE

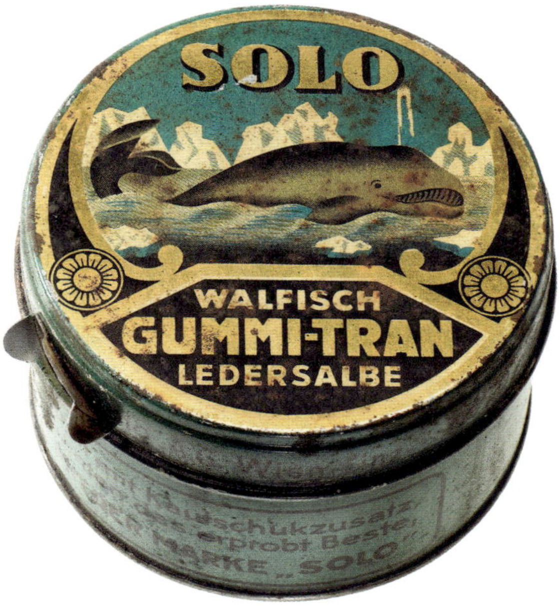

10/21

10/21 **Tins of water-proofing leather polish containing whale oil, "Solo" brand, no. 70**
Solo Zündwaren- und Chemische Fabriken AG
Vienna/Linz, 1920/1939
Pressed, riveted and printed tinplate; 6.6 x 12.3 cm
Berlin, Deutsches Historisches Museum: 1990/66.26.1-5

Whale oil was used as an additive in shoe polish, as it provided effective and long-lasting waterproofing. This manufacturer even used a picture of a 'waterproof' whale to market the high quality of its product. The company was founded in 1903 through the consolidation of a number of matchstick manufacturers, and this background is reflected in its original name, *Solo – Zündwaren- und Wichse-Fabriken Actien Gesellschaft* (Solo Matchsticks and Polish Factories). Later, when it expanded to produce a wider range of chemical products containing whale oil, it was renamed *Solo Zündwaren- und Chemische Fabriken AG* (Solo Matchsticks and Chemical Factories). These products included candles and lubricants, which continued to be made with whale oil well into the twentieth century. It was not until petroleum products became more advanced that lubricants were made with synthetic oils instead. TE

Energy Production and Modern Mineral Resources from the Sea

10/22 **North Sea at night, satellite image featuring oil and gas platforms**
North Sea, 2012
NASA Earth Observatory/Science Photo Library
Reproduction
London, Science Photo Library Ltd.: C015/1922

Petroleum and natural gas, both fossil fuels, play a major role in Europeans' daily lives. They are used primarily to power vehicles, machinery, and heating systems. In Europe, as elsewhere, the seabed was explored in search of fossil fuel reserves. This view of the North Sea by night shows clearly where extraction and processing platforms are located. Europe's most productive offshore fields are concentrated between Great Britain and Norway. The lights in the image come from the controlled burning of associated gas, a form of natural gas found with deposits of petroleum. When this gas is burned off on-site rather than being processed for use as a fuel, it is called 'flare gas' and the burning of it is called 'flaring'. Processing associated gas is very costly and only rarely profitable. In Norway, flaring is now permitted only in exceptional circumstances. (Exhibit not shown) TE

10/23 **Aerial view of the Frigg offshore gas field, with drilling and extraction platforms**
North Sea, after 1978
Photograph (new print)
Stavanger, Norwegian Petroleum Museum: NOMF-02741.087

In 1971, a natural gas field was discovered in the North Sea that surpassed anything found in the area before. The field, located 100 metres below sea level and extending to depths up to 1,800 metres, was named after the Norse goddess Frigg. In geographic terms, the reserves were at about the same latitude as the Norwegian port city of Bergen. The field was unique in that it crossed national borders, with Norway and the UK each owning a share of the gas (40 per cent for Norway and 60 per cent for the UK). This split was in accordance with the equidistance principle, by which the North Sea had been divided in 1964. The discovery of petroleum and natural gas in the North Sea propelled Norway into the ranks of oil-exporting nations in the 1970s. Norway has invested its 'black gold' revenues as security against a time when its wells are no longer productive. The Norwegian *Statens pensjonsfond* (Government Pension Fund), valued at over 865 billion euros, is the largest sovereign wealth fund in the world. (Fig. p. 360) TE

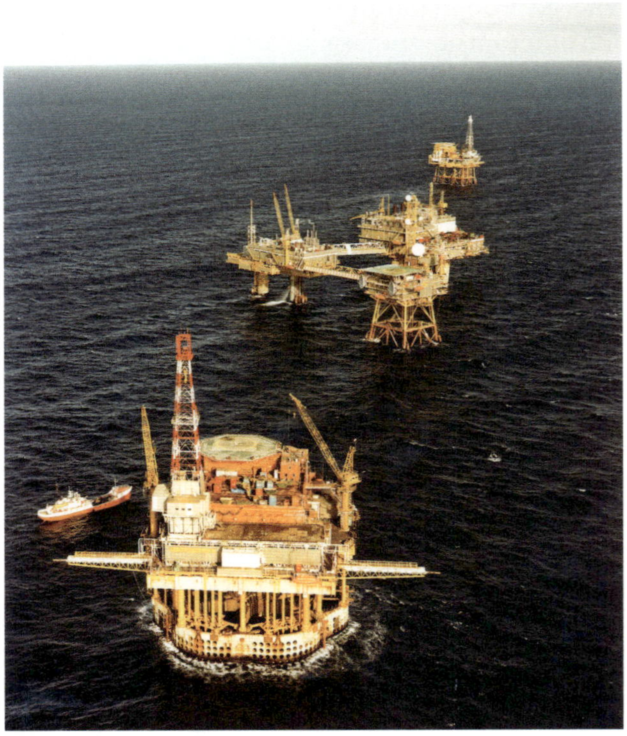

10/23

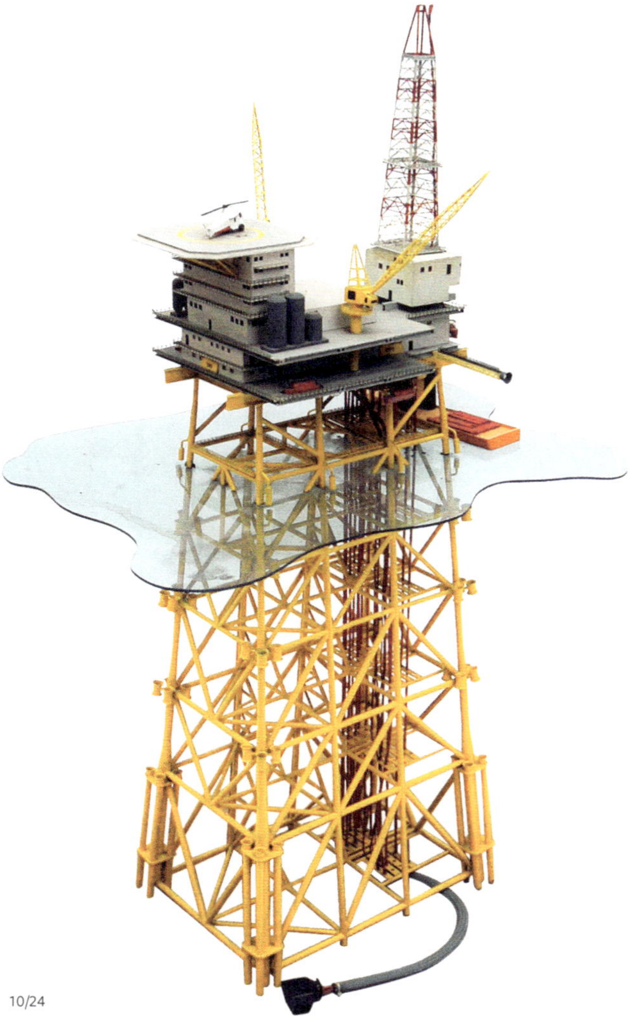

10/24

10/24 **Model of the DP2 drilling platform**
Paris, before 2005
Plastic; 100 x 62 x 48 cm
Stavanger, Norwegian Petroleum Museum: NOMG-01767

Initially, Norway awarded licences for offshore gas and oil production to foreign companies. Its DP2 drilling platform was built by France's *Union Industrielle et d'Entreprise* (UIE, based in Cherbourg) between May 1976 and July 1977 and was operated by French oil company Elf Aquitaine. Extraction began on 8 May 1978 and continued until 26 October 2004, when the reserves were depleted to the extent that extraction was no longer economical. In addition to traditional eight-legged steel structures, other platform designs have been created and tested. Norwegian engineers have developed new platforms that rely more on concrete than steel. Today's 'Condeep' (concrete deep water structure) platforms have proven effective in the North Sea and have been the standard in Norway since 1973. They are easily recognisable, having three to four concrete columns, each up to 300 metres high. TE

10/25 **Sign marking the British-Norwegian border between platforms TP1 and TCP2**
Norway, c. 1978
Iron, steel; 20 x 81 x 0.5 cm
Stavanger, Norwegian Petroleum Museum: NOMG-01701

Because oil and gas reserves are not always located within a single nation's borders, there are often disagreements about who owns them and who has the right to exploit and profit from them. Long-term international solutions are especially important in the case of offshore reserves. The Frigg gas field was located within the exclusive economic zones (200 sea miles) of both the UK and Norway. Gas was extracted from platforms on either side of the border. The British treatment platform TP1 was permanently connected to the Norwegian treatment compression platform TCP2 by a metal structure that functioned as a pedestrian bridge. Offshore personnel could use it to 'shuttle' between the UK and Norway. Above the bridge was a sign stating "YOU ARE NOW – LEAVING THE BRITISH SECTOR – ENTERING THE NORWEGIAN SECTOR" (and vice versa on the other side). TE

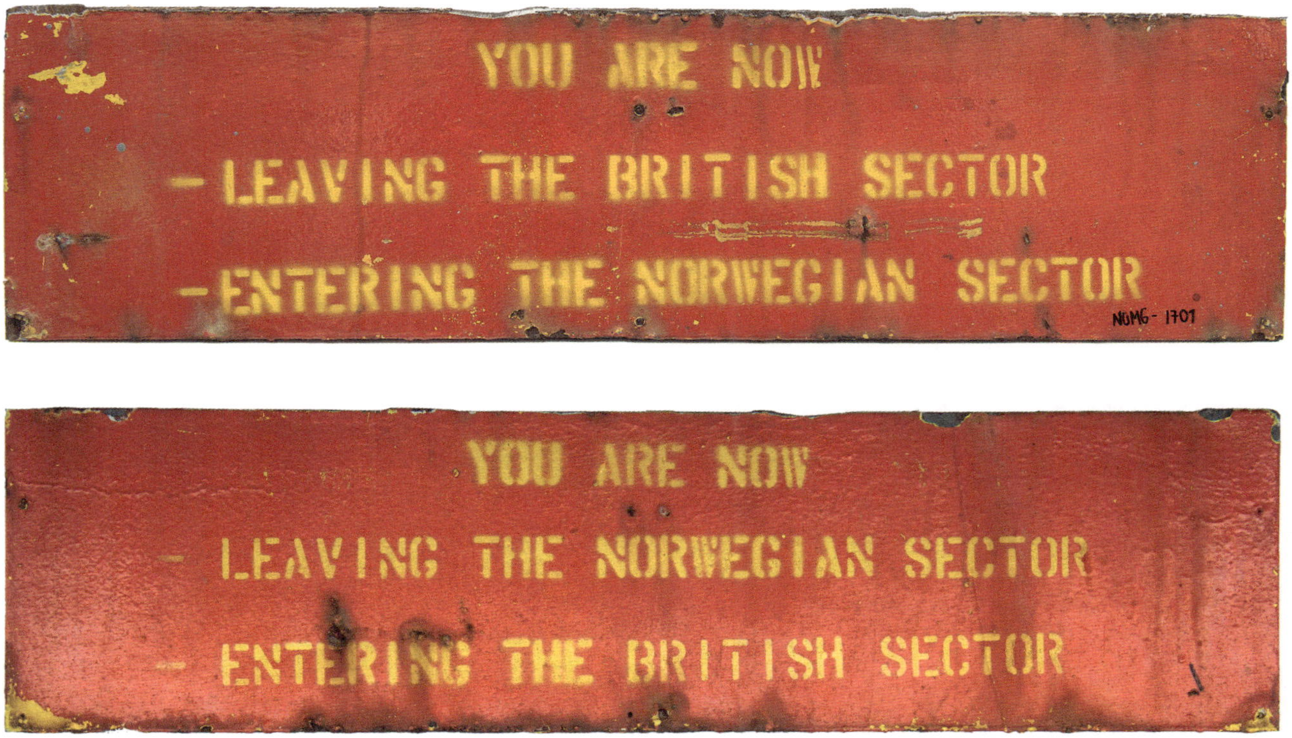

10/25

10/26 **Drill bit with 8 ½-inch thread**
Norway, 1987
Steel with diamond teeth; diam. 40 cm
Stavanger, Norwegian Petroleum Museum:
NOMG-00459

Oil and gas prospectors use deep drilling and seismic surveying to discover new reserves. Offshore drilling is done either from ships or floating platforms and is especially risky. It employs a variety of specialised drill bits. Drill bits with diamond teeth have proven particularly well-suited to work in the North Sea and have been the most commonly used drill bit there since the 1970s. To maintain the bit's performance over the long term, a chemical drilling fluid is used during the drilling process to keep the bit optimally lubricated and prevent overheating. Drill bits are made in various sizes and shapes, each of them suited to a particular job and rock type. With oil and gas extraction now a transnational business, drill bit sizes are quoted in inches, in accordance with international standards. TE

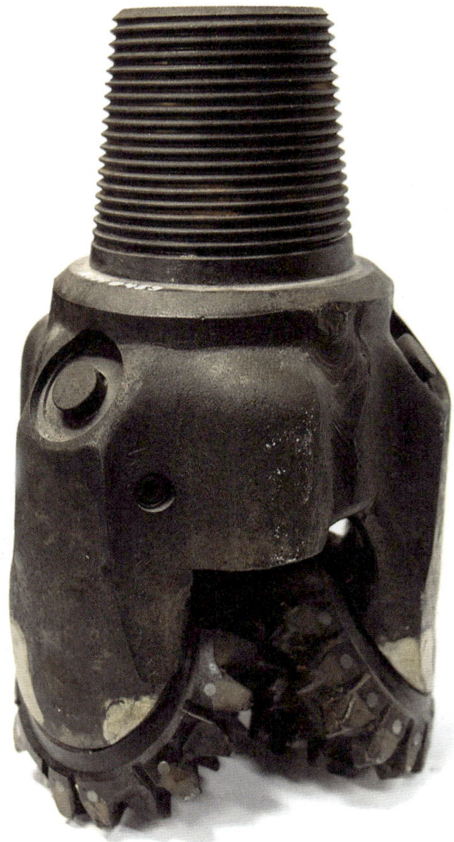

10/26

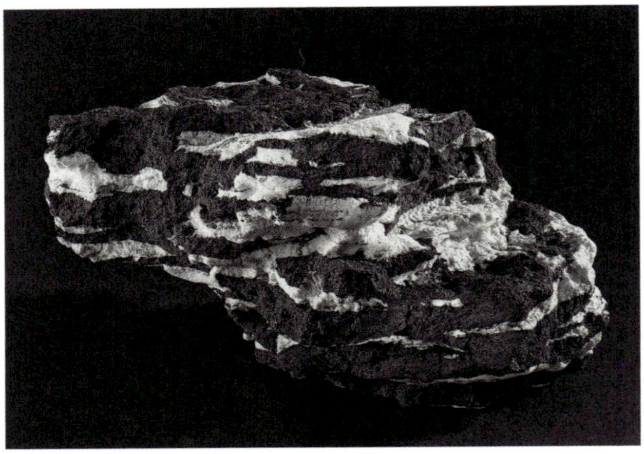

10/27

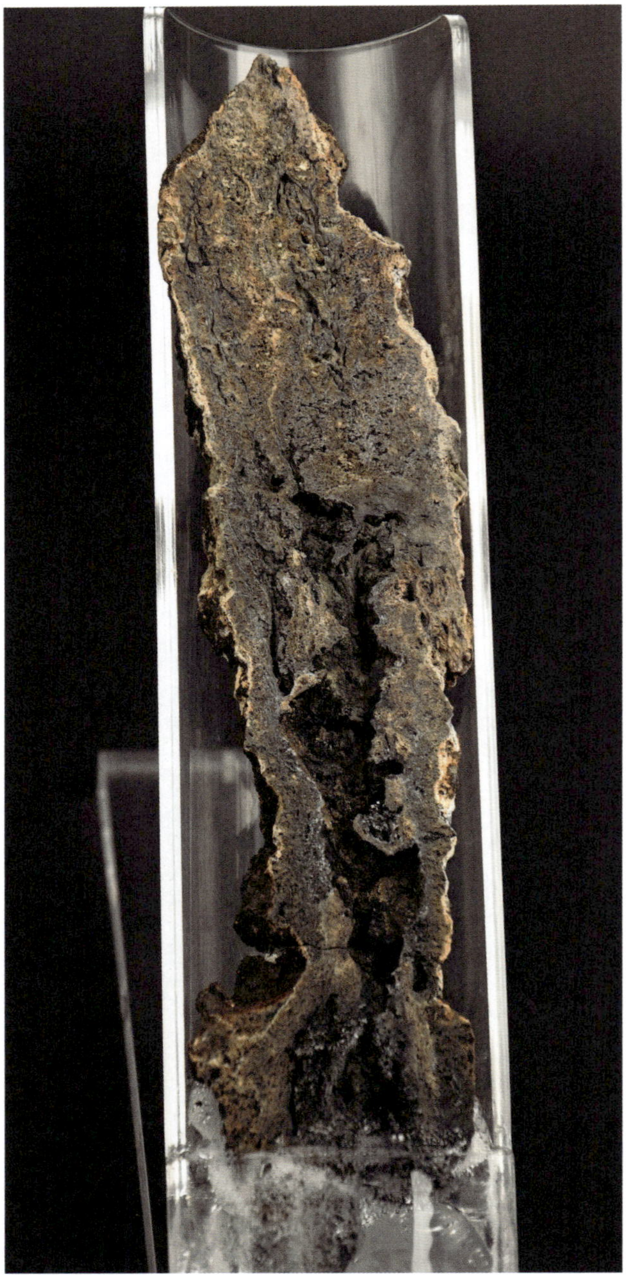

10/28

10/27 **Methane hydrate (model)**
Built by Hendrik Lörper
Kiel, 2018
Artificial stone, acrylic compound, pigment;
12.5 x 25 x 21 cm
Berlin, Deutsches Historisches Museum: w/o inv. no.

In the mid to late twentieth century, scientific exploration of the deep seas resulted in the discovery of valuable minerals and exploitable resources. Until just a few years ago, methane hydrate was not something many people had heard of. It is the term for methane gas which has been trapped in frozen water. Methane hydrate is stable only at low temperatures and under high pressure – conditions that prevail in the seas. Methane hydrate is seen as the fuel of the future, even if its extraction is not yet profitable and, what is more, is associated with incalculable risks to the Earth's climate. The continued discovery of new offshore gas and oil reserves, as well as other mineral resources, led to ever greater disagreements among nations. To bring an end to these conflicts, the International Seabed Authority was created in 1994 and charged with managing the world's deep-sea mineral resources. Its headquarters are in Jamaica. TE

10/28 **Vertical section through a sample of a black smoker**
Deep sea off Tonga (Pacific), recovered from a depth of 1,160 m
Metals, rare earths; 28 x 6 x 3.5 cm
Kiel, GEOMAR Helmholtz-Zentrum für Ozeanforschung Kiel: 2017-208

Ocean seabeds are known to contain metal deposits that form at hydrothermal vents and in manganese nodules at depths of 1,100 to 5,500 metres. These deposits are currently being discussed as potential resources. The most common metals are nickel, cobalt and copper. There are also rare metals such as gallium, germanium, indium, selenium and terbium , which have unique properties needed in the computer, electronics and solar industries. These and other 'industries of the future' therefore look on these deposits with great interest. Studies of the marine geology and biology of resources located in international waters are coordinated through the International Seabed Authority. Germany is a member of this organisation, along with 150 other countries. The mining of deep-sea resources is subject to strict environmental regulations. Germany has been awarded contracts to explore areas containing black smokers in the Indian Ocean and manganese nodules in the Pacific Ocean. Its application was submitted by the German Federal Ministry for Economic Affairs and Energy. GHW

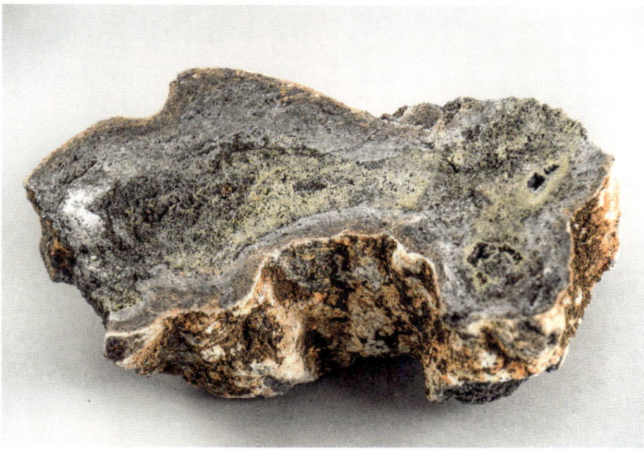

10/29

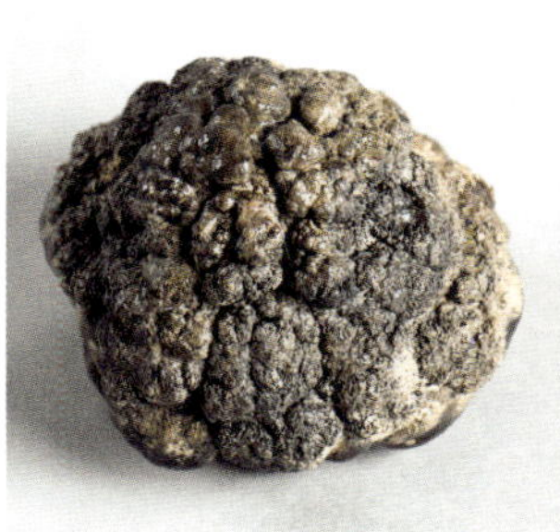

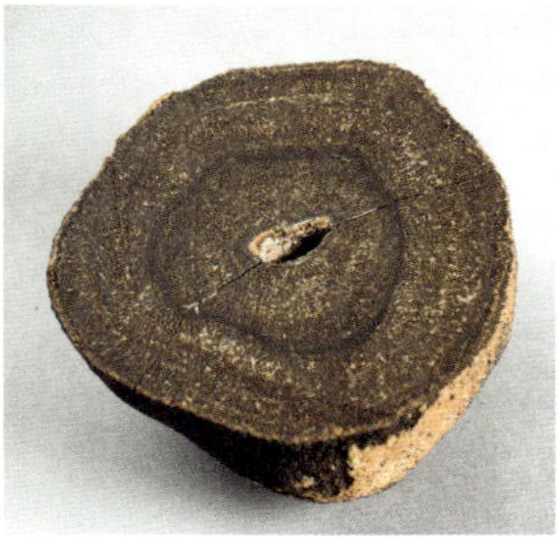

10/30

10/29 **Horizontal section through a sample of a black smoker**
Deep sea off Tonga (Pacific), recovered from a depth of 1,160 m
Metals, rare earths; 13 x 22 x 8 cm
Kiel, GEOMAR Helmholtz-Zentrum für Ozeanforschung Kiel: 2017-207

About 275 active black smokers are known to exist. They are found for the most part near the Ocean Ridge, which measures approximately 70,000 kilometres in length and has the largest surface area of any mountain range on earth. At these sites, hydrothermal solutions issue from the seabed at temperatures up to 450 °C. When they make contact with the cold water of the ocean (only 2 to 3 °C), dissolved minerals such as copper, zinc, iron, manganese, tin, silver and gold precipitate out to form chimney-like structures up to 50 metres high. These seemingly hostile environments host a unique community of organisms, with the kind and number of species varying from one black smoker to another. Evolutionary biologists think that these organisms may have been the origin of life on our planet. This horizontal section shows the structure of a smoker. The countless pores through which the mineral-rich fluid emerges can be seen in cross-section. As metal deposits build up over time, these pores gradually clog up. When all the channels are blocked, the main channel looks for a new release; a new smoker is formed, and the old one turns into a 'fossil' chimney. GHW

10/30 **Manganese nodules**
Peru Basin (Pacific), recovered in 1991
Manganese, iron, copper, cobalt, nickel, zinc; diam. 5–20 cm
Kiel, GEOMAR Helmholtz-Zentrum für Ozeanforschung Kiel: 2017-206

Manganese nodules, like hydrothermal vents, are a marine geological resource whose metal content makes them of commercial interest. They are found in the deep sea, far away from land, where the sedimentation rate is extremely low (that is, where there is very little sediment build-up). Manganese nodules are created when free metal compounds in the water combine over time to form concentric layers around an organic core (a piece of shell, for example). The nodes are composed primarily of manganese and iron, but their economic significance stems from the copper, nickel and zinc that they contain. These coveted metals, however, only make up about 2.5 to 3 per cent of a given nodule's total weight. The nodules grow extremely slowly – a fist-sized nodule would be about three million years old. Manganese nodules are typically found at depths ranging from 3,000 to 5,500 metres. GHW

Exploiting the Seas: Rewards and Risks

10/31 ***Das Drama der Meere* (The Drama of the Oceans)**
Elisabeth Mann Borgese (1918–2002)
Frankfurt a. M., 1977
Print; 28.6 x 24.5 cm
Berlin, Thomas Eisentraut

Elisabeth Mann Borgese saw the oceans as the 'shared heritage of humanity'. More than any of her previous work, her 1976 book *The Drama of the Oceans* opened the eyes of the world to that vision. The book focuses on the importance of the oceans to humanity and on the role they play for the future of the planet. She argues that the fate of the oceans, which cover about 70 per cent of the Earth's surface, will be determined largely by people and the way they deal with natural resources. An early advocate of sustainable ocean management, she was the initiator and organiser of the internationally respected Pacem in Maribus conferences. Held from 1970 to 2013, they explored global maritime challenges and conflicts. As the founder of the International Ocean Institute (1972) and a delegate at the United Nations Conference on the Law of the Sea (1974), Mann Borgese turned a spotlight on activities that endangered the sea, including the constant threats of whaling, tanker spills, illegal dumping and even armaments. (Exhibit not shown) TE

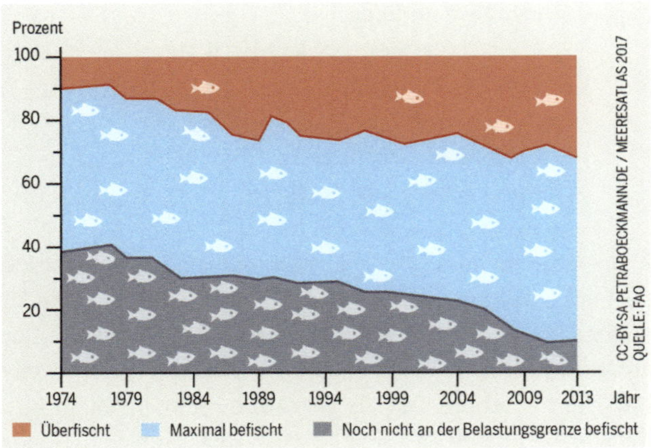

10/32

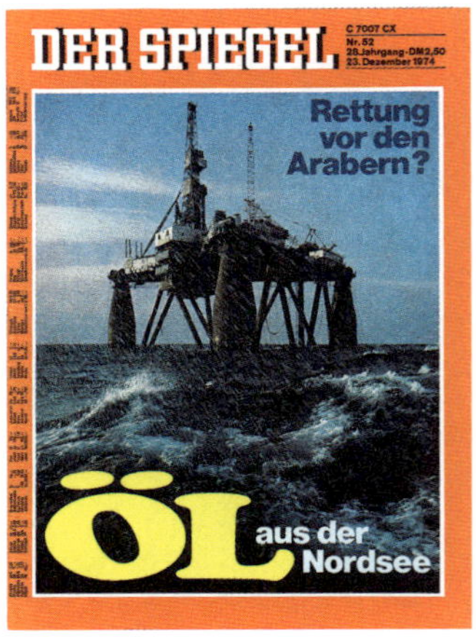

10/33

10/32 **Global trends in the state of world marine fish stocks since 1974, in *Meeresatlas 2017***
Paderborn, 2017
Berlin, Heinrich-Böll-Stiftung

Today it is theoretically possible to catch all of the world's fish stocks. New fishing methods that use modern sonar technology in combination with huge trawl nets and bottom trawl nets make it possible to systematically detect schools of fish. European trawler fleets have been fishing beyond coastal areas for quite a long time now. The state of the world's marine fish stocks in 2013 was described as follows: 31 per cent of the stocks were "overfished" and 58 per cent were "fully fished", leaving only 10 per cent that were not yet being fished beyond sustainable limits. One way to combat overfishing may be aquaculture, essentially a type of farming in which fish are raised in enormous enclosures. Farming, however, has wide-reaching impacts on the ecological stability of the oceans. The use of medication (in the form of antibiotics) as well as large amounts of fish excrement are testing the waters to their limits. TE

10/32 **"Saved from the Arabs? Oil from the North Sea", magazine article**
"Rettung vor den Arabern? – Öl aus der Nordsee",
Der Spiegel, 52/1974
Hamburg, 23 December 1974
Rotogravure; 28 x 21.4 cm
Berlin, Thomas Eisentraut

The oil crisis of 1973 hit European markets hard. As the price of fossil fuels rose, so did Europe's interest in its own offshore reserves. It had been known as far back as 1959 that the North Sea had fossil fuel reserves. In the 1970s the search for these reserves was intensified and expanded, because any nation that could extract gas and oil within its own borders would be less dependent on Arab oil-exporting countries. By 1974, about 65 per cent of the North Sea seabed had already been licenced to international exploration companies. The reserves were expected to total between three and six billion tonnes of oil. The UK and Norway ultimately came away the winners, as international law (specifically, the equidistance principle) awarded them the majority of the seabed. The building of offshore oil platforms in the North Sea posed a great challenge to European construction companies. Difficult weather conditions, including storm-force winds and waves up to 30 metres high, demanded extremely stable structures capable of resisting great stresses. It was not long before these platforms had been designed and built. TE

10/34 **"Who owns the ocean – Standing up to Shell", magazine article**
"Wem gehört der Ozean? – Aufstand gegen Shell",
Der Spiegel, 25/1995
Hamburg, 19 June 1995
Rotogravure; 28 x 21.1 cm
Berlin, Thomas Eisentraut

It wasn't just tanker spills, like the Amoco Cadiz running aground off the coast of Brittany in March 1978, that were making headlines in European papers. In 1995, the Shell oil corporation announced plans to sink an unused oil platform called the BRENT SPAR into the Atlantic, and an international crisis ensued. As the company felt dismantling it on land would be too expensive (£ 46 million), it decided to dispose of it in the sea (£ 11.8 million). After receiving approval from the British government, Shell started making the necessary preparations. On 30 April 1995, however, Greenpeace activists occupied the BRENT SPAR, driven by concerns that the sinking of the structure could set a precedent. They were afraid that large amounts of radioactive salts and oil residues, as well as highly toxic PCBs (polychlorinated biphenyl), would end up in the sea if the platform were sunk. In response to Shell's attempt at offshore disposal, there were boycotts against the company throughout Europe. They had a significant impact in Germany, where in some large cities petrol sales at Shell stations fell briefly by up to 50 per cent. Discussions at an international level led to a formal ban on offshore disposal. Most of the platform was later dismantled on land in Norway. (Exhibit not shown) TE

10/35 ***The Sea – A Rubbish Dump***
Berlin, 2018
Plastic; 200 x 50 cm
Berlin, Deutsches Historisches Museum / NABU – Naturschutzbund Deutschland e.V.

Every day, large amounts of waste end up in the seas. Every year, more than 20,000 tonnes of plastic rubbish find their way into the North Sea. For seas and oceans across the world, that figure is 8 million tonnes. Plastic constitutes 75 per cent – the large majority – of this waste. Because it decomposes slowly, plastic remains in the seas for many years. A PET bottle, for example, takes 450 years to decompose. About 70 per cent of plastic waste sinks down to the seabed, where humans cannot see it but it causes considerable damage to wildlife and marine ecosystems. Microplastics in particular are becoming a serious issue. When fleece jackets are washed, for example, they shed plastic fibres that leave the machine with the waste water. These and many other kinds of plastic particles make their way into the animal food chain and ultimately end up in the human food chain. Many marine creatures confuse plastic waste with food and die as a result. Plastic, which has only been in existence since the 1940s, is not the only big problem facing the seas and oceans, however. Abandoned 'ghost nets', biological and chemical waste, and even slowly rusting munitions from the world wars are causing irreversible damage to sea and ocean habitats. (Exhibit not shown) TE

10/36 **Friendly Floatees – Bathtub toys and global ocean currents**
Manufacturer: The First Years Inc.
Hongkong, 1992
Plastic; max. 5.5 x 7.5 x 12 cm
Sitka/Alaska, Dean Orbison

In January 1992, the Ever Laurel container ship (under the Greek flag) was on its way from Hong Kong to Tacoma in the US. During a storm in the middle of the Pacific, three 40-foot containers with a total of about 29,000 plastic animals were swept overboard. Yellow ducks, green frogs, red beavers and blue turtles started to swim the seas. Eight months later, the first of them were discovered 3,200 kilometres away on the west coast of Alaska. This prompted American oceanographer Curtis Charles Ebbesmeyer (b. 1943) to track their progress. Some of the toy animals, traveling in pack ice via the Bering Strait and the Northwest Passage, made it all the way to the North Atlantic. In 2003, one of the frogs was found on the Hebrides off the west coast of Scotland. From July to December 2003, the manufacturer offered a 100-dollar finder's fee to anyone who recovered and reported a Friendly Floatee. Research on the routes taken by the bath toys has provided new insight into the network of global ocean currents. TE

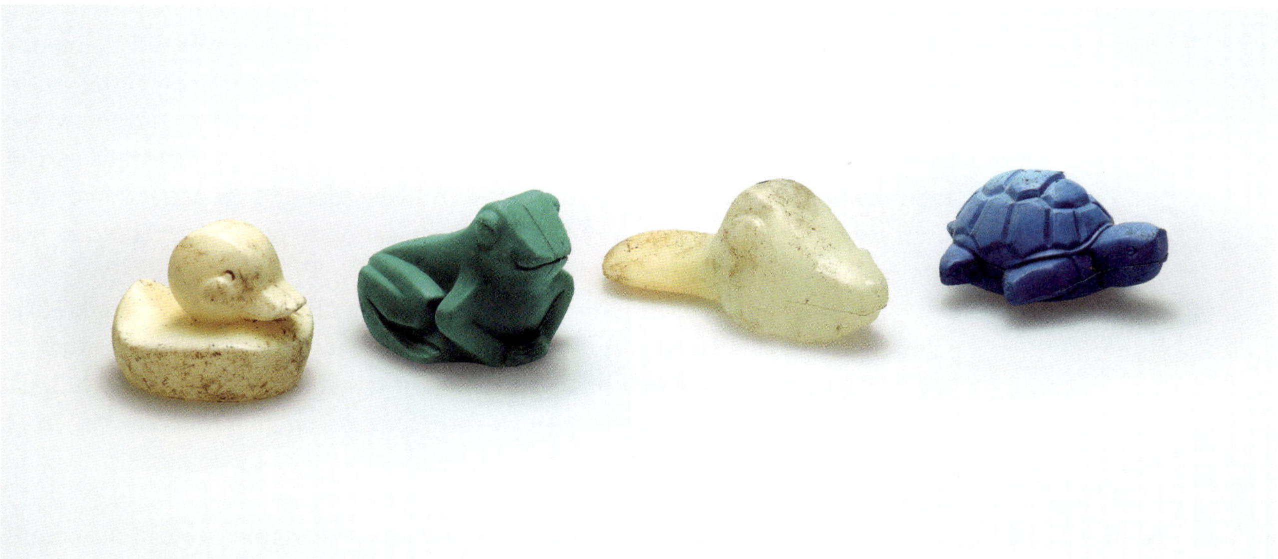

10/36

11 Marine Research The Port of Kiel

The oceans cover more than 70 per cent of the Earth's surface. With an average depth of 3,800 metres, they form one of the world's largest continuous habitats. Interest in the oceans as such, and in their economic potential, took an organised form in the eighteenth century, as can be seen from the early scientific research trips that were taken at the time. The sea floor was surveyed, for example, making it possible to identify secure anchorage grounds and to reduce the risk of shipwreck by detecting reefs and shoals in advance. The first investigations took place near the coast, where soundings were taken to measure the water's depth and specimens of marine organisms were collected for examination and classification. The first great advances in modern ichthyology (the study of fish) were made in the late eighteenth century, due in no small part to the work of Marcus Élieser Bloch (1723–1799). Multi-volume printed works gave information about the fish known at the time and their habitats.

In the nineteenth century, large-scale expeditions enabled researchers to penetrate the 'deep sea' – the lowest layer of the ocean waters. Among the better known ones are the Challenger Expedition (1872–1876), the Pola Expedition (1890–1898), and the Valdivia Expedition (1898–1899). Each of these research voyages was planned around a clearly defined objective with the additional aim of publishing detailed scientific findings afterwards. Of particular interest in the twentieth century was the Meteor Expedition (1925–1927), better known today as the German Atlantic Expedition. Although the expedition was politically motivated, with the aim of improving Germany's international reputation after the First World War, important scientific research was conducted. This included a systematic study of the southern Atlantic, an exact survey of the seabed, and the charting of ocean currents in the Atlantic. The search for modern mineral resources was also an important part of their mission, so the scientists were tasked with investigating the extraction of gold from sea water, which in view of Germany's obligation to pay war reparations, was potentially of national importance.

The port and university city of Kiel has a long tradition of marine research. The Christian Albrechts University of Kiel is internationally renowned for its study of maritime subjects. It is also home to leading international research institutions, such as the GEOMAR Helmholtz Centre for Ocean Research in Kiel. The city has a natural deepwater port, which can accommodate large research vessels. Now as then, Kiel is the port of departure for many research voyages.

Today's marine research focuses on questions related to the role of the oceans in climate change and to the effect of human activity on marine ecosystems. It is also making significant contributions to the search for biological, mineral, and energy resources in the sea. These include evaluating options for environmentally responsible mining and the sustainable use of resources from the oceans. Deep-sea research is comparable to space exploration in terms of its technical and financial requirements. Today, the oceans' part in the mechanisms of climate change is widely recognised, even if the consequences cannot be fully predicted. A better understanding of the oceans' importance can be gained from probes capable of taking continuous measurements, including more than 3,500 'deep drifters'. In the future, observatories installed in the deep sea will acquire a major role, especially in taking measurements over long periods. *Thomas Eisentraut*

Further Reading

Carl Chun, *Aus den Tiefen des Weltmeeres*, Jena 1900

Gotthilf Hempel et al, *Faszination Meeresforschung: Ein ökologisches Lesebuch*, Berlin/Heidelberg 2016

Reinhard Hoheisel-Huxmann, *Die Deutsche Atlantische Expedition 1925–1927*, Hamburg 2007

Gerd Hoffmann-Wieck, *Das GEOMAR Helmholtz-Zentrum für Ozeanforschung Kiel und die Geschichte der Kieler Meereskunde*, in: Oliver Auge (ed.), *Christian-Albrechts-Universität zu Kiel. 350 Jahre Wirken in Stadt, Land und Welt*, Kiel 2015, pp. 699–723

Uwe Jenisch and Boris Culik, *Kiel Maritim II – mit Jules Verne und Albert Einstein in die Zukunft*, Bonn 2013

Mojib Latif, *Das Ende der Ozeane. Warum wir ohne die Meere nicht überleben werden*, Freiburg 2014

Elisabeth Mann Borgese, *Das Drama der Meere*, Frankfurt a. M. 1977

Fritz Spieß, *Die Meteor-Fahrt. Forschungen und Erlebnisse der Deutschen Atlantischen Expedition 1925–1927*, Berlin 1928

World Ocean Review No. 1, Mit den Meeren leben, Hamburg 2010

Solvin Zankl and Lars Abromeit, *Ozeane. Expedition in unerforschte Tiefen*, Munich 2013

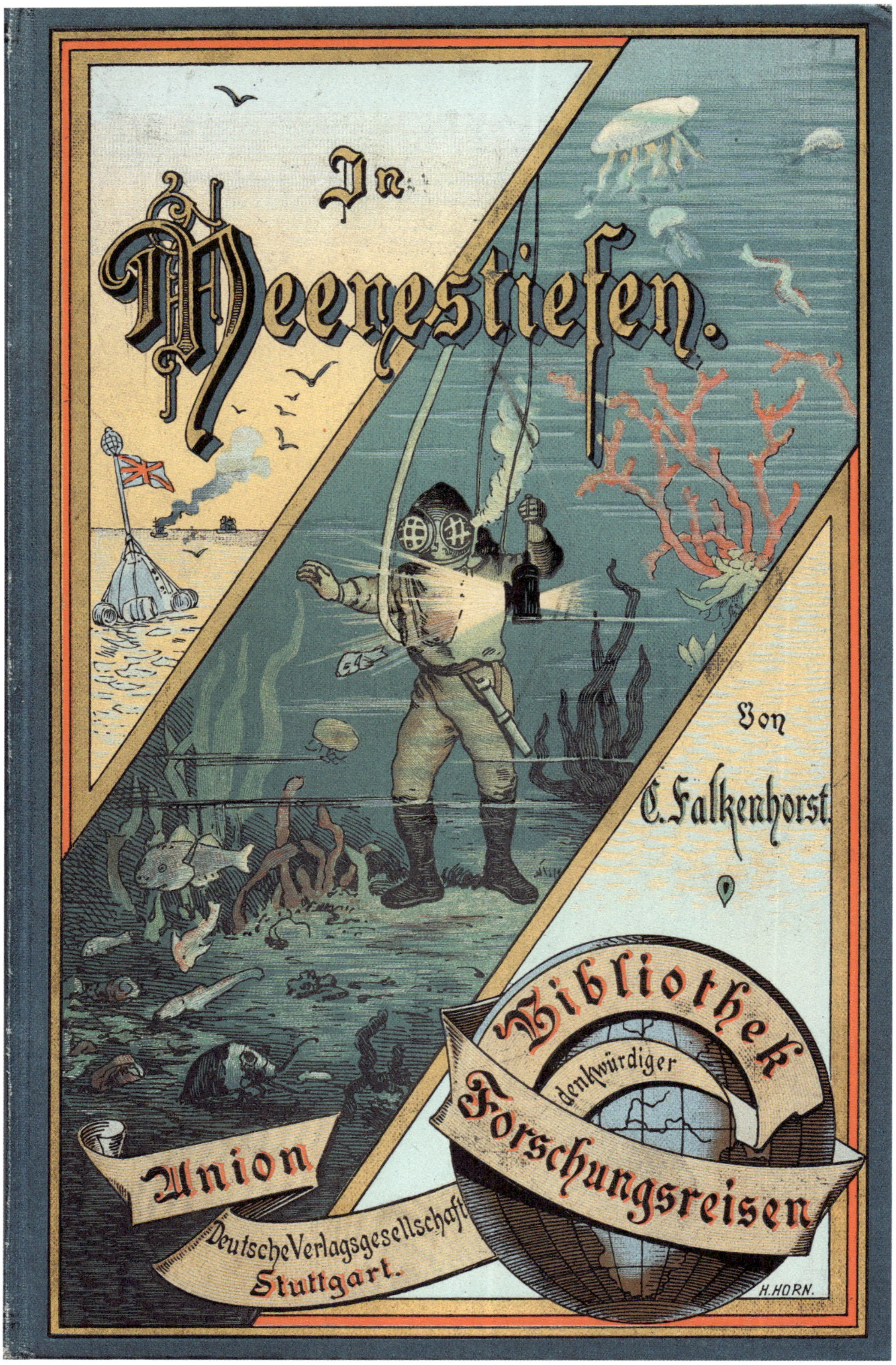
In
Meerestiefen.
Von
C. Falkenhorst.
Bibliothek
denkwürdiger
Forschungsreisen
Union
Deutsche Verlagsgesellschaft
Stuttgart.
H. HORN.

11/1

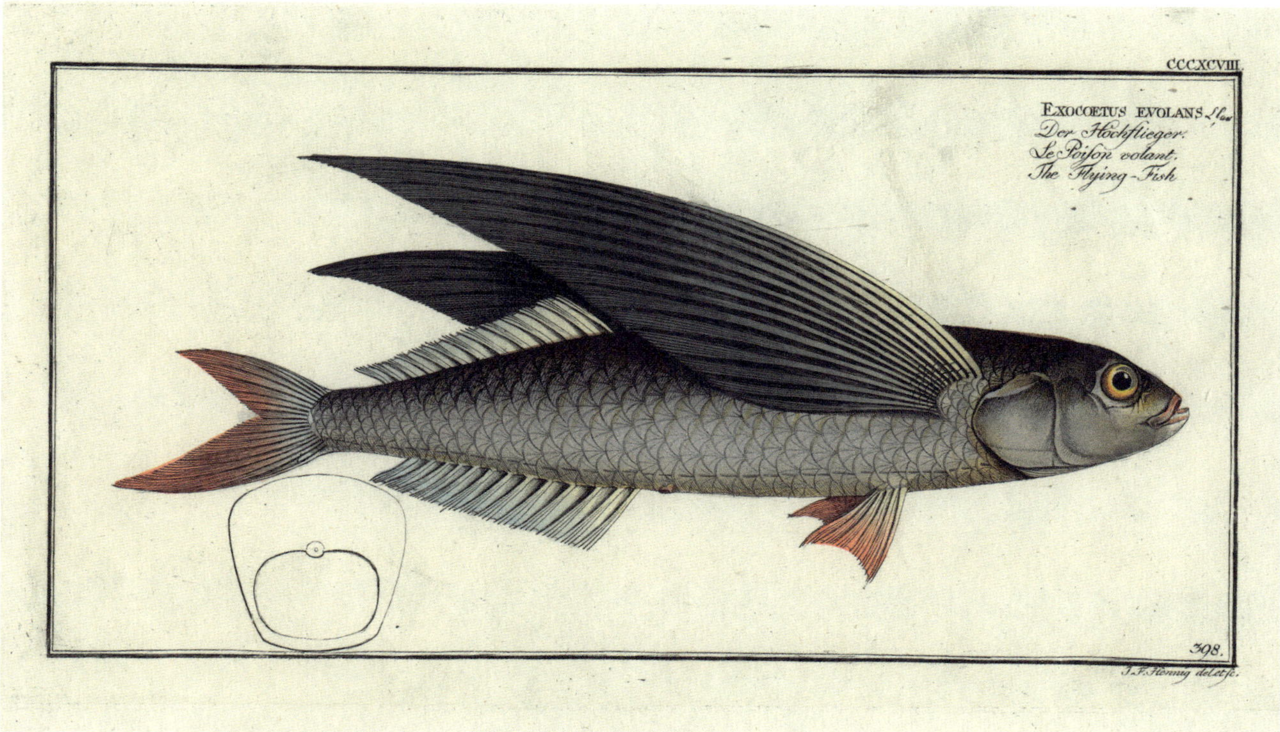

11/2

Ichthyology and the Beginnings of Marine Research

11/1 ***In Meerestiefen. Geschichte der Erforschung und Eroberung der Meere* (In the Sea Depths. A History of the Exploration and Conquest of the Seas)**
Bibliothek denkwürdiger Forschungsreisen (Library of Remarkable Research Expeditions), vol. VII
Carl Falkenhorst (1853–1913)
Published by Union Deutsche Verlagsgesellschaft Stuttgart
Berlin/Stuttgart, 1891
Letterpress print; 20.5 x 14 cm
Berlin, Deutsches Historisches Museum:
R 96/1311-7

Carl Falkenhorst realised that although many people found research trips and discoveries fascinating, the specialists' presentations of their new findings were barely – if at all – intelligible to the lay public. With his twelve-volume series on key scientific expeditions of the nineteenth century, published in 1890–1891, Falkenhorst became the 'father' of the non-fiction book. The seventh volume concentrates on the depths of the sea and their scientific study. Aiming for a book that would be easy to read, Falkenhorst conveyed historic knowledge and the latest findings in a vivid and entertaining way. Besides illustrations of deep-sea fish, the book contains articles on subjects such as laying deep-sea cables and attempts to construct submersible boats. TE

11/2 **Plate 398, "Exocoetus evolans – The Flying Fish", from *Naturgeschichte der ausländischen Fische* (A natural history of foreign fish), vol. 9**
Published by Marcus Élieser Bloch (1723–1799)
Drawn and engraved by J. F. Hennig
Berlin, 1795
Hand-coloured copperplate print; 25.3 x 42 cm
Berlin, Museum für Naturkunde Berlin:
HBSB, ZM, B IX/1670

Between 1782 and 1795, Marcus Élieser Bloch, a physician and naturalist, published the twelve volumes of his encyclopaedic work *Allgemeine Naturgeschichte der Fische* (A general natural history of fish). The first three volumes appeared under the title *Ökonomische Naturgeschichte der Fische Deutschlands* (An economic natural history of the fish of Germany). The subsequent nine volumes, *Naturgeschichte der ausländischen Fische*, deal with the natural history of "foreign fish". Bloch describes the appearance and the specific characteristics of countless species, illustrated with 432 hand-coloured copperplate prints like that of the flying fish here. He gathered his knowledge from prepared specimens, which middlemen sent him from every corner of the world. His private collection contained around 1,500 wet and dry specimens of fish. In 1810, the collection passed into the hands of the Berlin Zoological Museum. Today, about 800 of the specimens are in the care of its successor, the Museum of Natural History in Berlin. Bloch is regarded as one of the main founders of systematic ichthyology in the late eighteenth century. TE

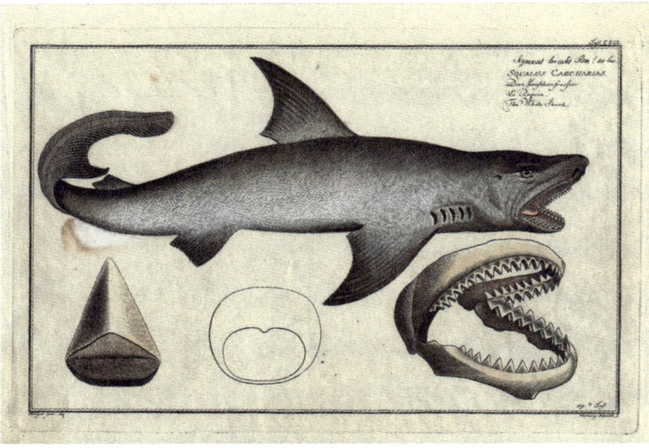

11/3

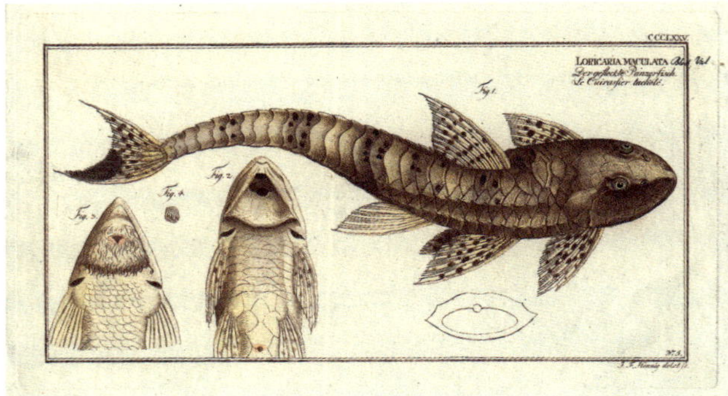

11/4

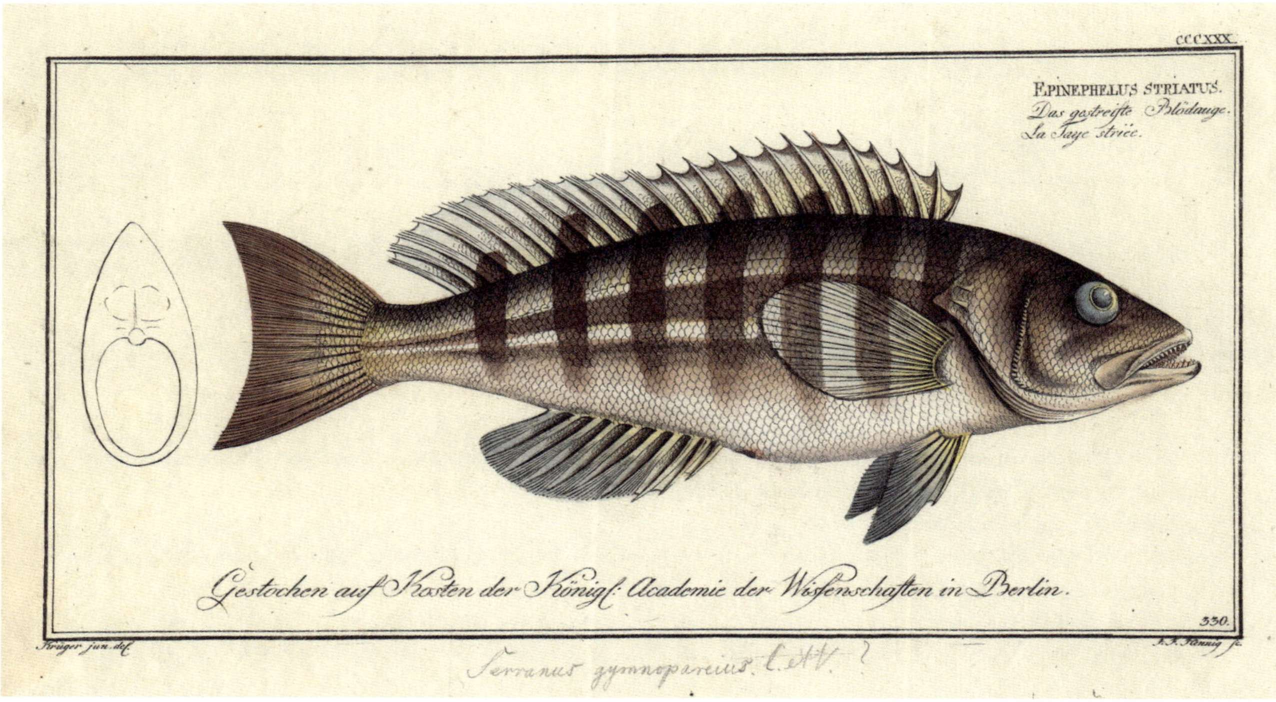

11/5

11/3 **Plate 119, "Squalus carcharias – The White Shark", from *Naturgeschichte der ausländischen Fische* (A natural history of foreign fish), vol. 1**
Author: Marcus Élieser Bloch (1723–1799)
Drawn by Krüger jun.
Engraved by Ludewig Schmidt
Berlin, 1785
Hand-coloured copperplate print; 25.5 x 42.5 cm
Berlin, Museum für Naturkunde Berlin:
HBSB, ZM, B IX/1462

Bloch was not able to obtain all of his information solely by examining prepared specimens – they did not reveal anything about the behaviour of certain species, for example. The great white shark is one such case. Bloch names it as a shark species and records its most striking feature: the serrated triangular teeth and their special arrangement. This characteristic is so significant that the illustration includes a detail showing the jaw with multiple rows of teeth. He complements this with information, gleaned from anecdotal accounts, on the great white's habitat (the Mediterranean Sea) and its aggressive behaviour, which extends to attacking other shark species. Initially classified as *Squalus carcharias*, it was first scientifically described in 1758 by a Swedish naturalist, Carl von Linné, better known as Linnaeus (1707–1778). Still known to many people as the 'man-eater' of the illustration's German caption (*Menschenfresser*), the great white has since been reclassified among the mackerel sharks. TE

11/4 **Plate 373, "Loricaria maculata – The Armoured Catfish", from *Naturgeschichte der ausländischen Fische* (A natural history of foreign fish), vol. 8**
Published by Marcus Élieser Bloch (1723–1799)
Drawn and engraved by J. F. Hennig
Berlin, 1794
Hand-coloured copperplate print; 25.2 x 42 cm
Berlin, Museum für Naturkunde Berlin:
HBSB, ZM, B IX/1631

During the eighteenth century and the Age of Enlightenment in Europe, natural science gained hugely in importance. The systematic study of wildlife was undertaken by amateur naturalists like Marcus Élieser Bloch, who worked in their spare time and with their own resources. The increasing availability of reference objects in the form of wet or dry specimens, as well as drawings, made it possible to draw new conclusions about the evolutionary history of animal species and, consequently, about the formation of the Earth. This interest always had an economic aspect. Information about kinds of fish, their habitats, and their distribution was of great value to the fishing industry. These copperplate prints usually depict the fish from the right-hand side. They sometimes use a different point of view to illustrate significant characteristics. This is the case with the species of armoured catfish shown here. Bloch considered the triangular shape of its head to be a conspicuous external identifying feature, so he had it illustrated in separate details. TE

11/5 **Plate 330, "Epinephelus striatus – The Nassau Grouper", from *Naturgeschichte der ausländischen Fische* (A natural history of foreign fish), vol. 7**
Published by Marcus Élieser Bloch (1723–1799)
Drawn by Krüger jun.
Engraved by J. F. Hennig
Berlin, 1793
Hand-coloured copperplate print; 25.2 x 42 cm
Berlin, Museum für Naturkunde Berlin:
HBSB, ZM, B IX/1626

Bloch paid for the publication of the early volumes of his *General Natural History of Fish* out of his own money. His savings were soon used up, however, so he had to find ways of getting third-party funding. Some of the illustrations bear the names of sponsors, which included private individuals as well as institutions. For example, copperplate no. 330, depicting the Nassau grouper, was "engraved at the expense of the Royal Academy of Sciences in Berlin", according to the note at the bottom of the frame. Financial support also came from members of the nobility and from the vast network of naturalists that Bloch knew personally. TE

11/6 **Plate 17, "Siphonophorae", from *Kunstformen der Natur* (Art Forms in Nature)**
Ernst Haeckel (1834–1919)
Leipzig/Vienna, 1904
Lithograph; 36.3 x 27.3 cm
Berlin, Ursula Breymayer

Marine research and a new aesthetic perception of the marine world enter into an impressive symbiosis in the work of Ernst Haeckel, a zoologist and evolutionary biologist from Jena. Microscope technology made it possible not only to image the fine structures of familiar sea creatures such as jellyfish, molluscs, and corals, but also to discover previously unknown marine micro-organisms. Haeckel applied the microscope to the study of the sea's fauna and flora, making exquisite drawings of what it revealed. These he published as large-format lithographs, some of them coloured, initially in ten separate volumes. In 1904, a complete edition with 100 plates appeared with the title *Kunstformen der Natur* (Art Forms in Nature). Haeckel's work transformed the "lower forms of life" into fascinating entities of peculiar beauty. (Exhibit not shown) UB

11/7 **Plate 26, "Trachomedusae", from *Kunstformen der Natur* (Art Forms in Nature)**
Ernst Haeckel (1834–1919)
Leipzig/Vienna, 1904
Lithograph; 36.3 x 27.3 cm
Berlin, Ursula Breymayer

Haeckel, who had originally wanted to become a landscape painter, considered nature to be superior to art. In nature, beauty was evident even in the smallest things. In particular, the tiny marine organisms hidden in the depths of the ocean allowed the sea to demonstrate its skill as an artist. In *Art Forms in Nature*, Haeckel constantly emphasises the ornamental and symmetrical aspects of a species' appearance. For all the realistic accuracy and scientific integrity that characterise his depictions, he nevertheless arranged the illustrations symmetrically on his plates in order to express the analogy between nature and art. Haeckel was a scientist and an artist at the same time. (Exhibit not shown) UB

Haeckel, Kunstformen der Natur. Tafel 31 — *Calocyclas.*

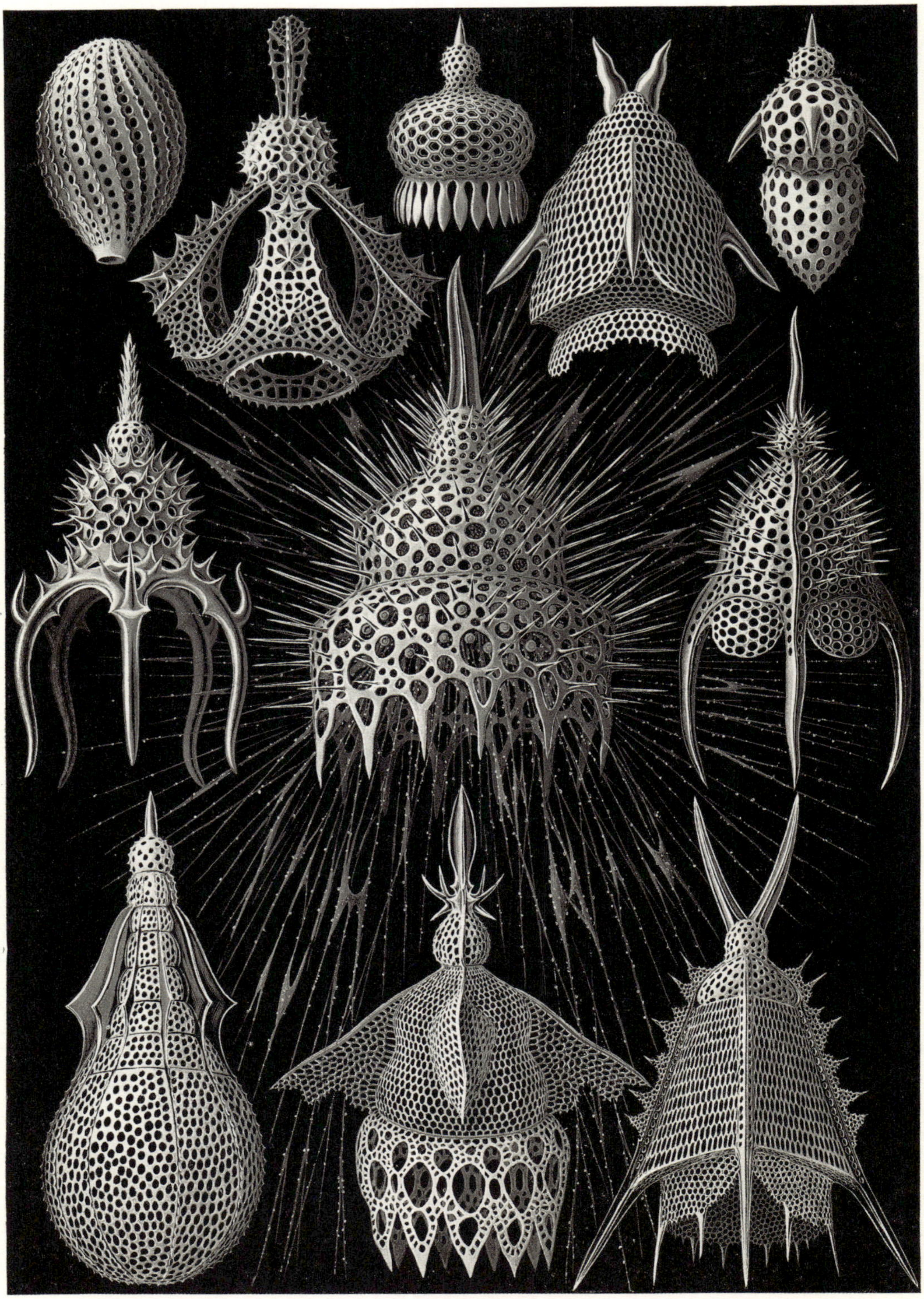

Cyrtoidea. — Flaschenstrahlinge.

11/8

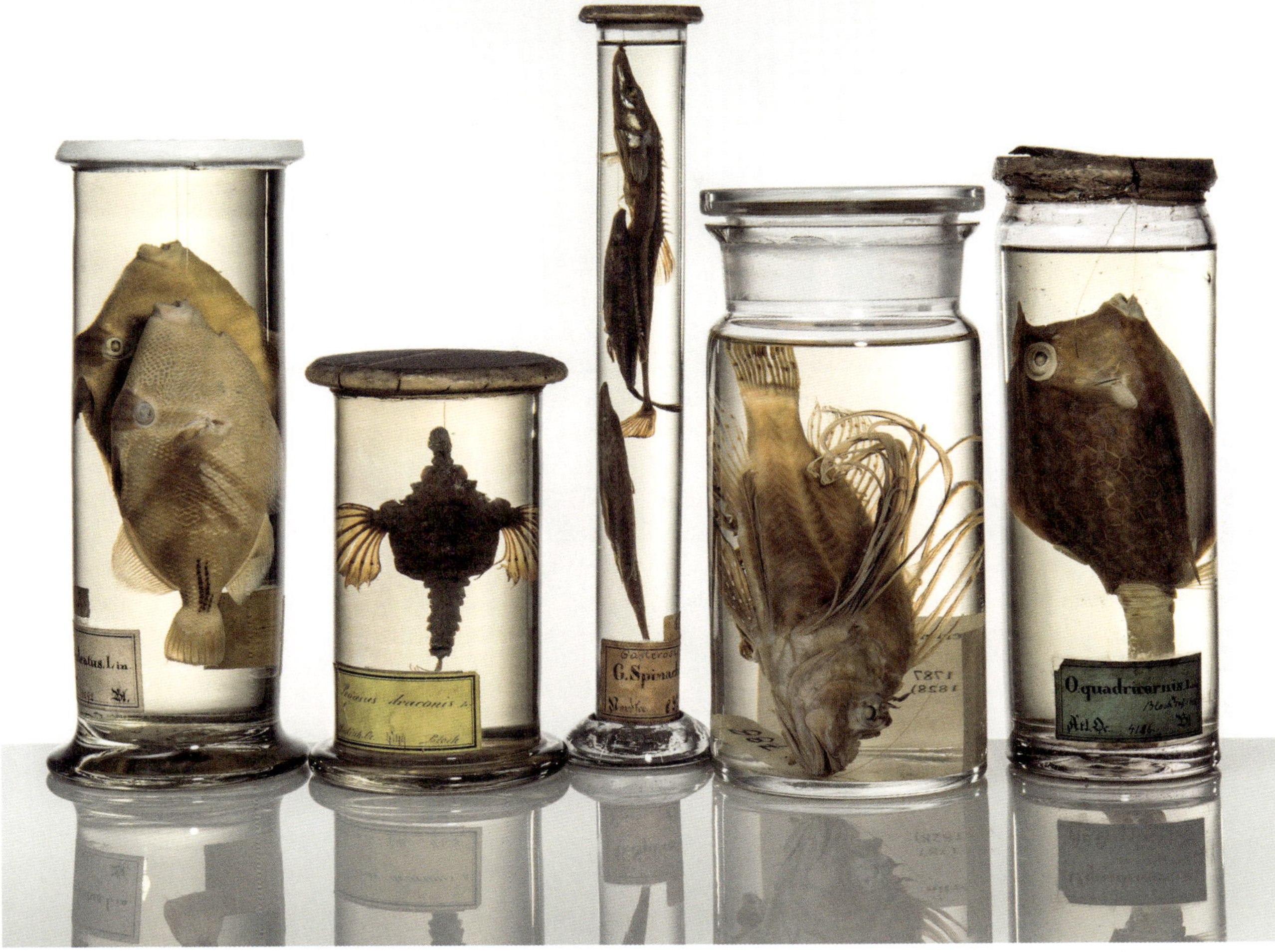

11/11 11/13 11/10 11/9 11/12

11/8 **Plate 31, "Cyrtoidea", from *Kunstformen der Natur* (Art Forms in Nature)**
Ernst Haeckel (1834–1919)
Leipzig/Vienna, 1904
Lithograph; 36.3 x 27.3 cm
Berlin, Ursula Breymayer

The impact of Haeckel's *Art Forms in Nature* was most obvious at the entrance to the Paris World Fair of 1900. The architect René Binet (1866–1911) clearly used jellyfish of the kind shown in plate 31 as decorative motifs for the large entrance gate, *La Porte Monumentale*. Haeckel had published his first monograph, on radiolarians, back in 1862, since when he had meticulously studied these single-celled organisms and published works about them. The influence of his illustrations on contemporary architecture can be seen in numerous Art Nouveau buildings, such as those by Austrian architect Josef Maria Olbrich (1867–1908) or Berlin-based August Endell (1871–1918). Haeckel's ornamental forms also inspired many works of decorative art. UB

11/9 **Wet specimen, "Pterois miles – Common Lionfish"**
From the collection of Marcus Élieser Bloch
East coast of India, before 1799
Specimen preserved in alcohol, glass jar; H 18.5 cm, diam. 9.5 cm
Berlin, Museum für Naturkunde Berlin: ZMB_Pisces 788

As well as a variety of dry specimens, Marcus Élieser Bloch possessed a large number of wet specimens. These are dead animals that have been placed in a glass container filled with alcohol. The alcohol slows down the process of biological decay. Preparing fish as wet specimens preserved them in a state that retained as much of their anatomical structure as possible and kept them available for scientific examination for a long time. The lionfish has spines alongside the dorsal fin that secrete a powerful venom. As more and more species of fish were discovered, scientists realised the need to introduce clear conventions for naming them, which in turn required a universal system of classification. The names of the majority of fish species were assigned by Carl von Linné (1707–1778) in Sweden, Marcus Élieser Bloch (1723–1799) in

Germany, and Edward Turner Bennett (1797–1836) in Britain. TE

11/10 **Wet specimen, "Spinachia spinachia – Sea Stickleback"**
From the collection of Marcus Élieser Bloch
North Sea, before 1799
Specimen preserved in alcohol, glass jar; H 24.5 cm, diam. 5.3 cm
Berlin, Museum für Naturkunde Berlin: ZMB_Pisces 837

Bloch's fish collection mainly contained species that lived in coastal habitats. The sea stickleback, for example, inhabits shallow waters along the entire west coast of Europe. It is found today in both the Atlantic Ocean and the North Sea. In the Baltic Sea, this saltwater fish is limited to the western areas, where the water has an adequately high salt content. Adult specimens can grow to 20 centimetres in length. Also known as the fifteen-spined stickleback, it is characterised by small spines, which it can raise and lower, in front of the dorsal fin. TE

11/11 **Wet specimen, "Rhinecanthus aculeatus – Lagoon Triggerfish"**
From the collection of Marcus Élieser Bloch
Indian Ocean, before 1799
Specimen preserved in alcohol, glass jar; H 20 cm, diam. 8.5 cm
Berlin, Museum für Naturkunde Berlin: ZMB_Pisces 4092

The lagoon triggerfish is mainly found in the Indo-Pacific region and the Red Sea. This fish defends its territory and offspring aggressively and is known to attack divers on this account. Lagoon triggerfish can produce clearly audible noises if they feel threatened. Triggerfish get their name from the anterior dorsal fin, which recalls the trigger mechanisms of the guns commonly used in earlier time. Its secret lies in the unusual configuration of the fin's front two spines. When the foremost, larger spine is raised, the second spine folds forward to lock it in place. The stiff main spine cannot then be pushed down by external force. This mechanism enables the fish to wedge itself into the crevices of coral reefs so that predators cannot pull it out. The species shown here is also known as the Picasso triggerfish – a name it acquired in the twentieth century because its features and bright colours reminded people of portraits by Pablo Picasso (1881–1973). TE

11/12 **Wet specimen, "Acanthostracion quadricornis – Scrawled Cowfish"**
From the collection of Marcus Élieser Bloch
Atlantic Ocean, before 1799
Specimen preserved in alcohol, glass jar; H 19.2 cm, diam. 7 cm
Berlin, Museum für Naturkunde Berlin: ZMB_Pisces 4186

The scrawled cowfish got its name partly from the shape of its head, including a pair of spines above its eyes that suggest the horns of a cow, and partly from its irregular, colourful markings. Its upper parts are protected by a rigid carapace consisting of polygonal plates that have fused together. Adult specimens can grow up to 55 centimetres in length. They mainly inhabit the warmer waters of the Atlantic and Indo-Pacific, to a depth of about 80 metres. The cowfish are distant relatives of the highly poisonous puffer fish family, and may be poisonous themselves to some predators. Many people consider them an excellent food fish, however, and they are often shown in public aquaria. TE

11/13 **Wet specimen, "Eurypegasus draconis – Short Dragonfish"**
From the collection of Marcus Élieser Bloch
Indian Ocean, before 1799
Specimen preserved in alcohol, glass jar; H 12.7 cm, diam. 9 cm
Berlin, Museum für Naturkunde Berlin: ZMB_Pisces 4749

The short dragonfish lives at depths down to 93 metres, preferably in sandy areas and coral reefs. It is a member of the seamoth family, which is widespread in the Indo-Pacific as well as off the east and south coasts of Africa. Their characteristic features are an elongated snout and fan-like pectoral fins. They are often caught by fishermen incidentally ('bycatch') and are then used to make traditional medicines or are sold as aquarium fish. In 2013, the dragonfish was included on the Red List of the International Union for the Conservation of Nature. The fact that Bloch's collection also contains specimens from regions outside Europe increases its international importance. At the time, this broader scope made his works and research findings even more interesting to European readers, as it lent them an air of exotic glamour. TE

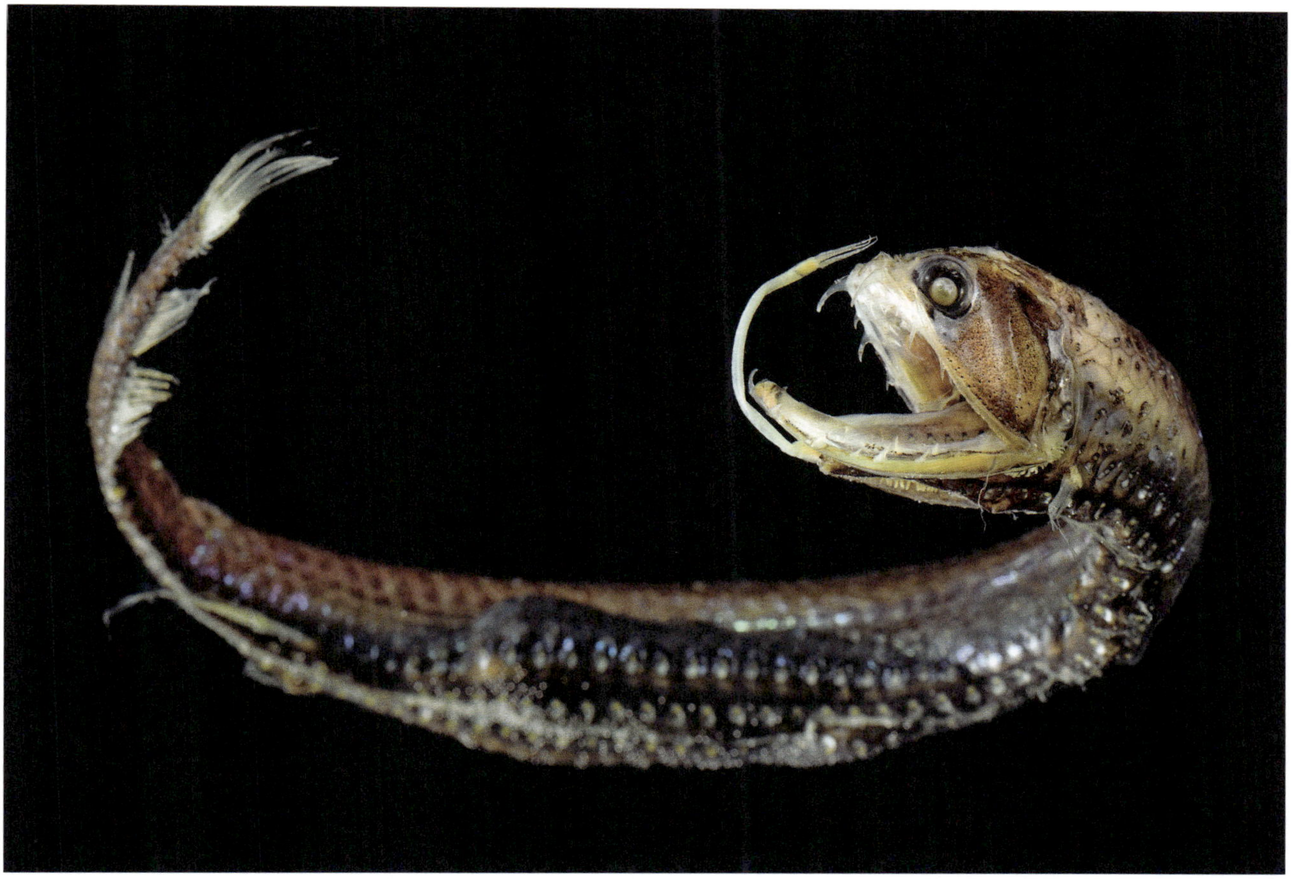

11/14

11/14 **Wet specimen, "Stomias boa boa – Scaly Dragonfish"**
From the collection of Dr. Johannes Kinzer
Western Mediterranean, 14 May 1991
Specimen preserved in alcohol, glass jar; H 20.3 cm, diam. 15.7 cm
Kiel, GEOMAR Helmholtz-Zentrum für Ozeanforschung
Kiel: 2017/11

The scaly dragonfish has sharp fangs and huge jaws, which it can open extremely wide to devour much larger fish. It lures prey by means of a luminous organ on the end of a long, flexible stalk, which is attached to the lower jaw. Once the victim is close enough, the dragonfish lunges forward with its mouth wide open and swallows it, digesting the body whole. The low availability of nutrients in the deep sea has led many organisms to evolve features that allow them to specialise. These include extremely long, sharp teeth and a variety of light-producing organs, which they use to attract sexual partners or prey. Since the Census of Marine Life was completed in 2010, the number of classified organisms in the sea, excluding microbes, stands at around 250,000. Taking statistical factors into account, marine biologists estimate the total number to be one million, which would mean that the vast majority of marine life has not yet been identified. GHW

11/15 **Wet specimen, "Argyropelecus olfersii – Silver Hatchetfish"**
From the collection of Dr. Johannes Kinzer
Atlantic, 29 June 1985
Specimen preserved in alcohol, glass jar; H 20.3 cm, diam. 15.7 cm
Kiel, GEOMAR Helmholtz-Zentrum für Ozeanforschung
Kiel: 2017-204

Hatchetfish are resident throughout the Atlantic and Pacific Oceans, living at depths between 100 and 800 metres. They migrate vertically over the course of the day, using the darkness to their advantage. During the night, they rise into the euphotic or 'sunlight' zone, where enough light still penetrates for them exploit the relative abundance of food there. Their most striking features are large eyes and luminous blue spots. Hatchetfish are remarkable for one particular adaptation, which they use during their nocturnal ascent into the euphotic zone. In order to remain unseen by predators approaching from below, they activate countless bioluminescent organs. These they adjust continuously to match the intensity of light from above, which makes their opaque silhouette virtually disappear. (Exhibit not shown) GHW

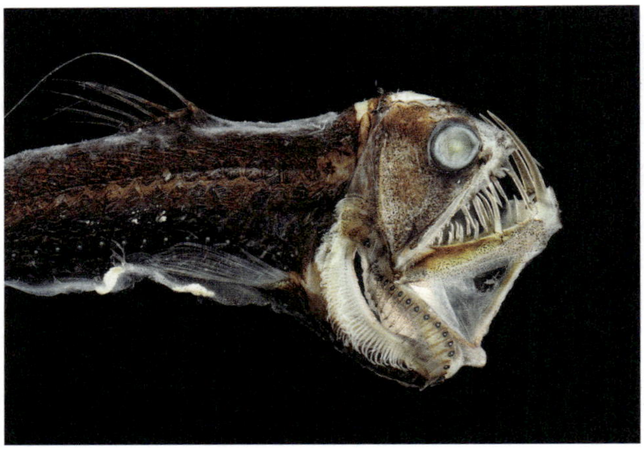

11/17

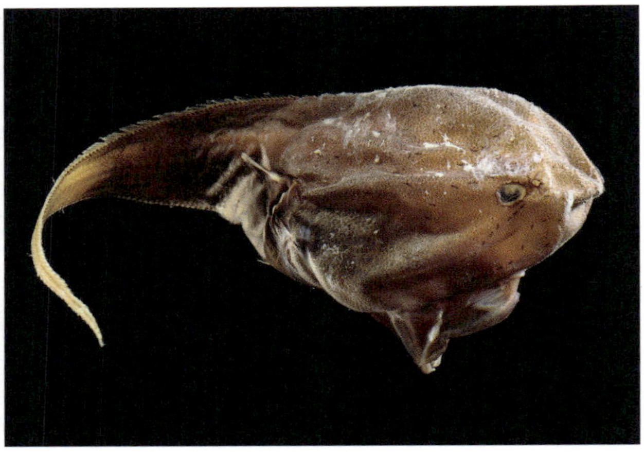

11/18

11/16 **Wet specimen, "Anoplogaster cornuta – Common Fangtooth"**
From the collection of Dr. Johannes Kinzer
Atlantic, 7 May 1991
Specimen preserved in alcohol, glass jar; H 20.3 cm, diam. 15.7 cm
Kiel, GEOMAR Helmholtz-Zentrum für Ozeanforschung
Kiel: 2017-203

The fearsome facial appearance of the common fangtooth is reinforced by its prominent skeleton. The serrated ridges separate translucent cavities, which are in fact sensitive sensory organs. They enable the fish to perceive the slightest movement in its surroundings. Measuring about 15 centimetres long when fully grown, the fangtooth is able to devour prey almost as large as itself. It is found at depths from 200 to 5,000 metres. (Fig. p. 139) GHW

11/17 **Wet specimen, "Chauliodus sloani – Sloane's Viperfish"**
From the collection of Dr. Johannes Kinzer
Atlantic, 30 April 1991
Specimen preserved in alcohol, glass jar; H 20.3 cm, diam. 15.7 cm
Kiel, GEOMAR Helmholtz-Zentrum für Ozeanforschung
Kiel: 2017-202

Adapting to a specialised way of life in the deep sea does not only bring advantages. The viperfish has sharp, interlocking fangs, which few prey escape from. They are so long, however, that when it closes its mouth, they stick out and come dangerously close to its eyes. Moreover, if a viperfish misjudges the size of its prey and bites into a fish or crustacean that is too large, it can neither swallow nor release it and is thus doomed to die together with its last catch. Viperfish live at depths of up to 4,400 metres. GHW

11/18 **Wet specimen, "Macrouridae – Grenadier fish"**
From the collection of Dr. Johannes Kinzer
Atlantic, 13 May 1979
Specimen preserved in alcohol, glass jar; H 20.3 cm, diam. 15.7 cm
Kiel, GEOMAR Helmholtz-Zentrum für Ozeanforschung
Kiel: 2017-201

Grenadier fish have a stocky body tapering into a long tail without a caudal fin, from which they get their other name: rattail. The head and eyes are relatively large. The first radial of the dorsal fin may be formed as a spine. The lateral line (the organ of balance) is well developed. Some species also have light-producing organs. Others can make sounds by using the swim bladder (the gas-filled organ that helps keep fish buoyant) as a resonating chamber. Members of the grenadier family are found at great depths in every ocean, especially near black smokers (a kind of hydrothermal vent in the seabed). Grenadier fish can grow to about 80 centimetres long. They make up an estimated 15 per cent of deep-sea fish numbers. GHW

Surveying the Oceans: The German Atlantic Expedition (1925–1927)

11/19 **Ocean relief globe**
Manufacturer: geo-institut Columbus GmbH
Porta Westfalica, 2017
Plastic; H 120 cm, diam. 70 cm, scale 1:20,000,000
Berlin, Deutsches Historisches Museum: w/o inv. no.

This globe shows the terrestrial and submarine areas of the earth in relief. To date, only about seven per cent of the seabed has been surveyed with echo sounders and thus recorded in detail, but seabed depths have been charted in general with the help of satellites. The latter process does not, however, pick up features that are smaller than ten square kilometres, which is about twice the size of the island of Heligoland. The Atlantic was one of the first marine areas to be systematically explored and surveyed. The first depth chart of the Atlantic ocean floor was published in 1885, using data compiled by the British CHALLENGER Expedition (1872–1876). Later research trips such as the German VALDIVIA Expedition (1898–1899) improved the precision of the existing charts. Further surveys were undertaken in the 1920s. The METEOR Expedition (1925–1927), for example, took more than 67,000 depth soundings to create what, at the time, was the most detailed picture of the South Atlantic seabed. (Exhibit not shown) GHW/TE

11/20 **"The METEOR Voyage", advertisement for the publication of Fritz Spieß's account of the German Atlantic Expedition on the research vessel METEOR**
Fritz Ahlers (1890–1973)
Plakatkunstdruck Eckert
Berlin, 1928
Lithograph; 66.9 x 43.4 cm
Berlin, Deutsches Historisches Museum: P 90/9804

The METEOR, a German naval gunboat that had been refitted for research and surveying work, sailed from Wilhelmshaven with a crew of 130 men in April 1925. They spent the next two years criss-crossing the Atlantic between South America and Africa. The main task of the oceanographic expedition, funded by the *Notgemeinschaft der deutschen Wissenschaft* (Emergency Community of German Science), was to chart the circulation of water in the Atlantic Ocean. Fritz Spieß (1881–1959), the commander of the METEOR, published an account in popular-science style, based on his logbook entries. He describes the expedition's planning and organisation, the instruments and their installation on board the ship, all of the research work, and time spent ashore in former German colonies, among other places. The importance of this ambitious undertaking lay primarily in its scientific findings. Only a few years after the First World War, the Atlantic expedition was also regarded as a political success for the nation, as it helped Germany – or at least German science – to rebuild its international reputation. (Fig. p. 134) AvH

11/21 **View of the research vessel METEOR**
Atlantic, 1925–1927
Reproduction from glass negative
Kiel, GEOMAR Helmholtz-Zentrum für Ozeanforschung
Kiel: w/o inv. no.

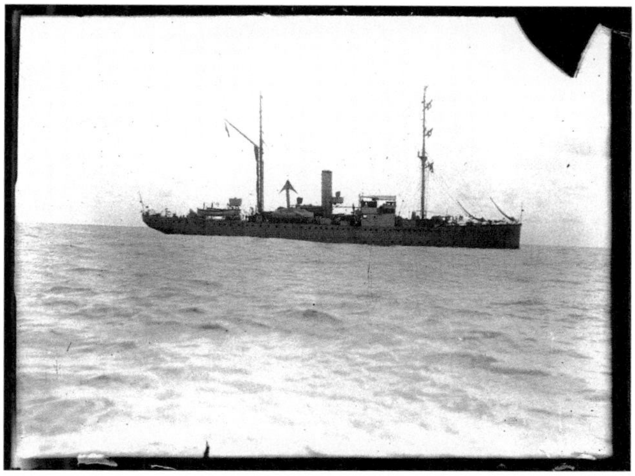

11/21

In February 1914, the Imperial Shipyard in Danzig began constructing a sea-going gunboat for service in the coastal waters of the German colonies and at foreign bases. Since its mission in those areas was meant to include surveying and scientific work, it was fitted with a sounding machine and a kite winch. The ship was 71 metres long and 10.90 metres wide. After the start of the war, it was provisionally launched and christened METEOR , but not completed. The hull was relocated to Kiel in 1919, when the Treaty of Versailles stipulated that Danzig be made a Free City and cease to be German territory. In October 1920, the Allied Naval Control Commission approved the refitting of the METEOR as a research vessel. The refit was carried out in the Imperial Naval Shipyard in Wilhelmshaven. In 1921, Professor Alfred Merz (1880–1925) of the Berlin Institute of Oceanography planned the research programme of the German Atlantic Expedition, which took place from 1925 to 1927. GHW

11/22 **Photographs from the German Atlantic Expedition**
Atlantic, 1925–1927
Reproductions from glass negatives
Kiel, GEOMAR Helmholtz-Zentrum für Ozeanforschung
Kiel: w/o inv. no.

The officers and crew of the METEOR were responsible not only for navigation and the technical operation of the ship, but also for many different research tasks. These included taking regular depth soundings using both a lead and an echo sounder, helping to take samples of seabed sediment using a drop grab, and sending up weather balloons or kites for meteorological studies. The geological and biological samples were prepared and packaged in the ship's laboratory. Each was recorded in the laboratory book. The plankton samples were processed by the ship's doctor. The conditions on board were cramped and the voyage lasted over two years – much longer than the four to eight weeks that are

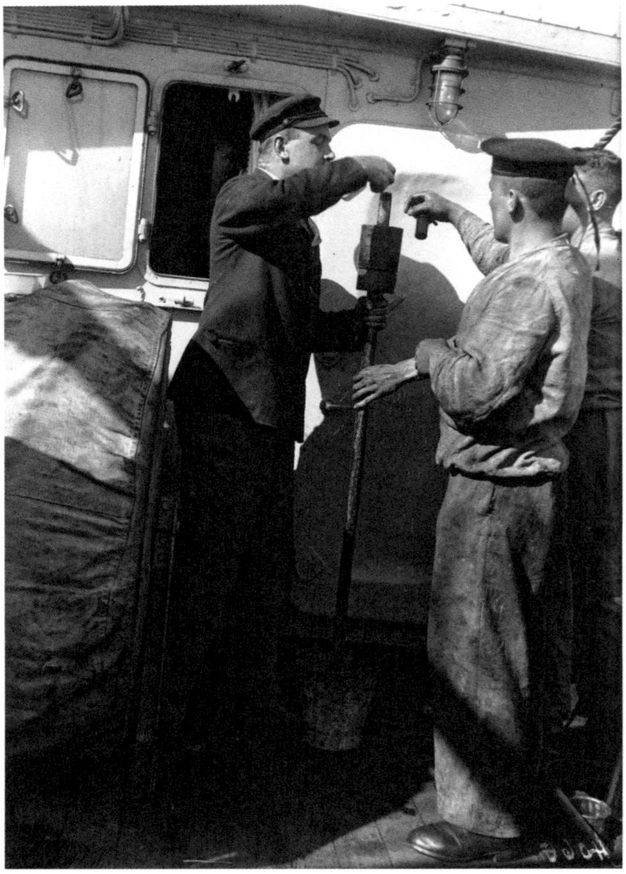

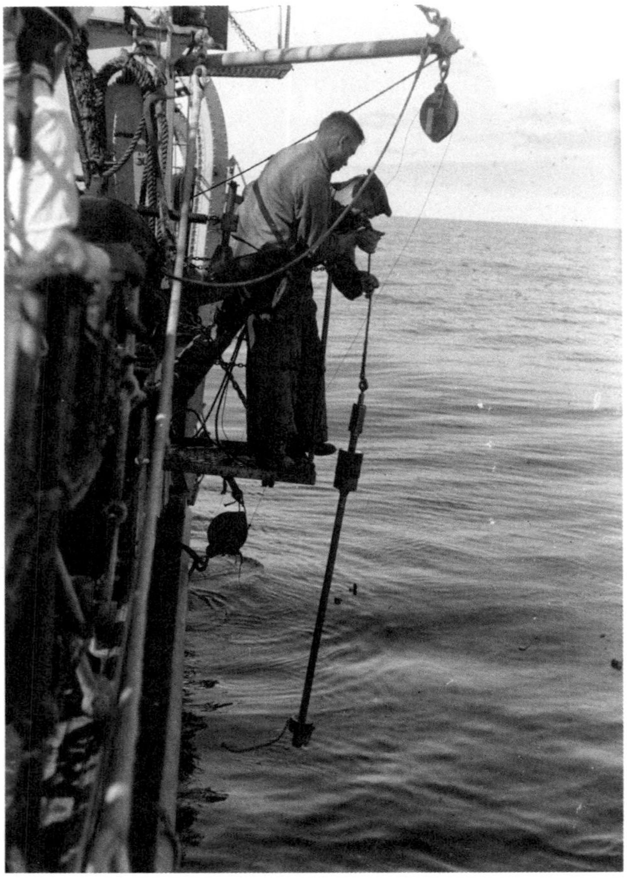

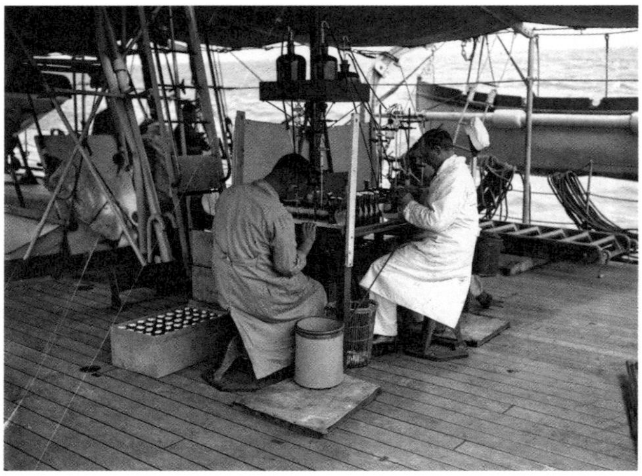

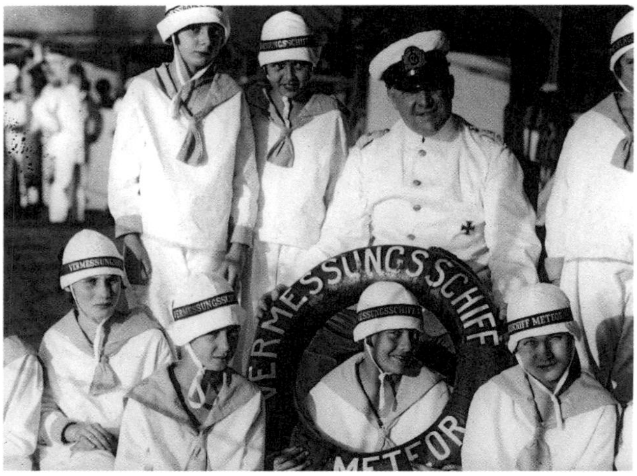

11/22

normal for large German research vessels today. Leisure activities were therefore important. There were talks on geographical, historical, or scientific subjects, and parties to mark various occasions. The 'equatorial baptism' was given to anybody on board who could not show that he had been 'baptised' on a previous crossing. Line-crossing ceremonies involving all kinds of initiation rites are still performed today, mostly for the amusement of the older crew members. The men hunted sharks, turtles, and albatrosses, but also held tortoise races and played with the ship's dog (and later a monkey). The photograph featuring Professor Alfred Merz (1880–1925), the leader of the expedition, was probably taken soon before the METEOR set sail from Wilhelmshaven. GHW

11/23 **"The Atlantic Voyage of the Survey Vessel METEOR"**
Film footage from the German Atlantic Expedition (1925–1927)
Atlantic, 1928
b/w silent film; running time: 80 min.
Berlin, Bundesarchiv – Filmarchiv: 17649

The historical importance of the German Atlantic Expedition was recognised from the start, so it was documented using 3.5 mm movie film. The film shows the daily routine of research work and operating the ship, as well as some of the social life on board. It even features the 'baptism' at the equator and a tortoise race. The footage ends with graphics presenting the scientific findings. The outstanding achievement of the German Atlantic Expedition is still considered to be its creation of detailed profiles of the South Atlantic ocean floor. The ship, the METEOR, gave its name to both the shallowest and the deepest places yet measured in the South Atlantic: the Meteor Bank at 560 metres and the Meteor Deep at 8,264 metres below the surface. (Exhibit not shown) TE

11/24 **Deep-sea thermometer**
Manufacturer: Gohla
Kiel, c. 1900
Glass, mercury, wood; L 40 cm, diam. 4 cm
Kiel, GEOMAR Helmholtz-Zentrum für Ozeanforschung
Kiel: 2017-123

Ocean currents can be distinguished by their salt content and temperature. By measuring the temperature and salinity at many depths in one place (a notional 'water column') and repeating this in various parts of the ocean, separate ocean currents can be identified at different depths. In the nineteenth century, it was generally assumed that the water temperature decreases as one descends. Scientists soon realised

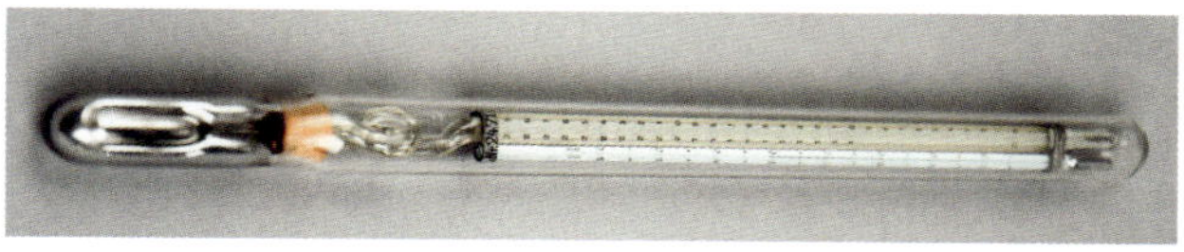

11/24

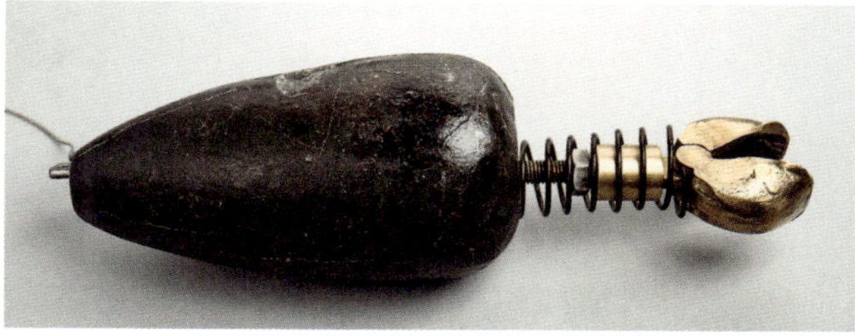

11/25

that in the polar regions, however, currents of cold, fresh water from melting ice can be found above warmer, but denser, salt water. They needed a thermometer with an internal cut-off that would preserve the reading from a particular depth and not change as it was pulled up through warmer layers of water near the surface. This was the 'reversing thermometer', which remained in use until about 1995. Its leading manufacturers in Germany were Richter & Wiese, in Berlin, and Gohla, in Kiel. It has since been superseded by electronic probes, which likewise guarantee the required accuracy of 0.002 degrees and are less time-consuming to use. GHW

11/25 **Bucket grab for taking geological samples from the seabed**
Kiel, c. 1900
Lead, iron, copper, steel; 48 x 37 x 37 cm
Kiel, GEOMAR Helmholtz-Zentrum für Ozeanforschung
Kiel: 2017-124

In shallow waters, sinkers with weights of up to 30 pounds were used to drive the sampler into the seabed. In deeper water, heavier weights were used, in the form of plates which were then detached on the ocean floor. The buckets of the grab remained open until they had penetrated the ground. Then a spring closed them together, thus scooping up a soil sample. There were grabs of various sizes for use in gravelly soils. In relatively shallow waters, the entire apparatus would be recovered, while in deeper waters, a larger version with a detachable weight was used. GHW

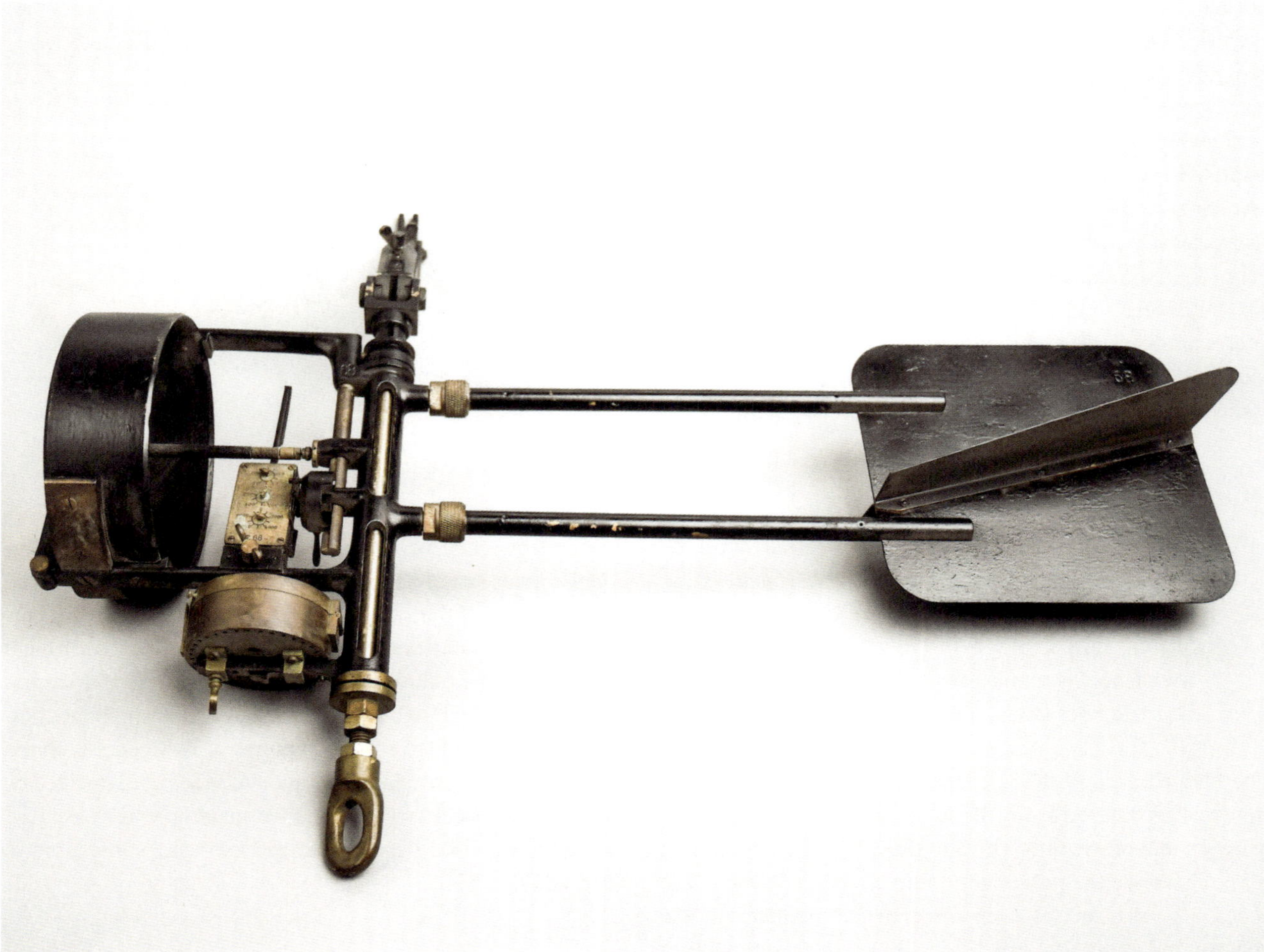

11/26

11/26 **Ekman-Merz current meter**
Kiel, after 1905
Brass, lead, bronze; 60 x 77 x 18 cm
Kiel, GEOMAR Helmholtz-Zentrum für Ozeanforschung Kiel: 2017-031A

This complicated device was not only able to measure currents, but also to save the data it obtained until they could be analysed. A further innovation was that it allowed the direction of flow and the lateral deviation to be determined precisely. As soon as the propeller was set in motion by the ocean current, the device began to register the direction it was pointing in. After every fifty revolutions of the propeller, a piece of lead shot dropped from a hopper onto the grooved surface of the compass needle, from where it rolled into one of the 36 compartments of the compass box. By examining which compartments the shot had fallen into, the direction of flow could be determined with an accuracy of 10 degrees. In 1906, the device was refined by replacing the lead shot with numbered bronze balls. The hopper and the feed mechanism were redesigned so that the balls fell into the compass box every 100 revolutions. This made it possible to track the characteristic movements of a given body of water at any phase of the tide or at different times of year. GHW

11/27 **Behm echo sounder**
Alexander Behm (1880–1952)
Kiel, after 1912
Iron, glass, plastic; 56 x 38 x 20 cm
Kiel, Kieler Stadt- und Schifffahrtsmuseum: 47/1970

Water has long been known to be a good conductor of sound; the phenomenon was even studied by Leonardo da Vinci (1452–1519). The speed of sound in water was first determined in 1826 by two Swiss mathematicians: Jean-Daniel Colladon (1802–1892) and Charles François Sturm (1803–1855). From this speed (1,450 metres per second) and the measured interval of time, the observer can calculate the distance that a pulse has covered to the seabed and back, and thus the depth. In response to the sinking of the TITANIC, physicist Alexander Behm in Kiel created the world's first echo-sounding device, patented on 22 July 1913. By 1921, he had made sufficient progress to found the *Behm-Echolot-Ge-*

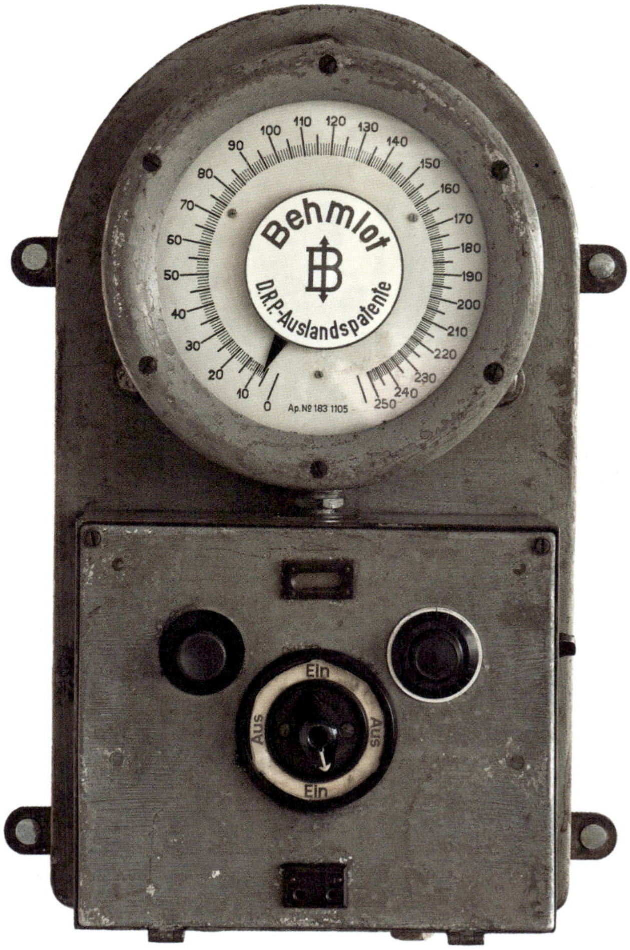

11/27

sellschaft (Behm Echo Sounding Company) in Kiel. After the measuring technology had been refined, Behm's echo sounder was successfully tested on the German Atlantic Expedition. On board the METEOR, depth soundings were also taken by hand to check the measurements obtained by the echo sounder. These control measurements proved the reliability of the acoustic method so clearly that subsequent expeditions no longer took a sounding machine. GHW

Current Marine and Ocean Research

11/28 **GEOMAR Report 31: RV POSEIDON Cruise Report**
Kiel, November 2016
Print on paper, hardback; 29.5 x 20.5 cm
Kiel, GEOMAR Helmholtz-Zentrum für Ozeanforschung
Kiel: 2017-301

The reports of completed expeditions are published in the GEOMAR Reports series. The teams are generally scientists based at research institutions in Germany and other countries. Each report is published by the expedition leader, shortly after the end of the research trip. They therefore appear at irregular intervals, but in the last few years, they have mostly been available in digital form, which makes them more accessible from other parts of the world. The cruise reports describe the research objectives, the scientific equipment used, and the details of the expedition itself. The cover of GEOMAR Report 31 shows Germany's only manned research submersible, JAGO, in operation during an expedition to the Canary Islands. JAGO has two seats, one for the pilot and one for an observer, and is capable of diving to a depth of 400 metres. (Exhibit not shown) GHW

11/29 **GEOMAR Report 23: RV SONNE Cruise Report**
Kiel, March 2015
Print on paper, hardback; 29.5 x 20.5 cm
Kiel, GEOMAR Helmholtz-Zentrum für Ozeanforschung
Kiel: 2017-300

On its maiden voyage from 14 December 2014 to 26 January 2015, the newly built research vessel SONNE took scientists to study the Puerto Rico Trench in the Atlantic. Running along the border with the Caribbean, the trench is much deeper than the surrounding seabed. Samples were taken to see whether the organisms living in the trench differ from those in the neighbouring areas of the Atlantic. This was the first complete, high-resolution survey to be undertaken along a fracture zone. Its objective was to provide insights into life on the ocean floor and how it functions in this vast habitat. In the Atlantic, the shape of the ocean floor is characterised above all by transform faults and fracture zones. On this voyage, scientists investigated one of the largest fracture zones in the Atlantic, the Vema Fracture Zone. They used an autonomous underwater vehicle (AUV) named ABYSS, which carried out photographic mapping to record the deep sea fauna in detail. (Exhibit not shown) GHW

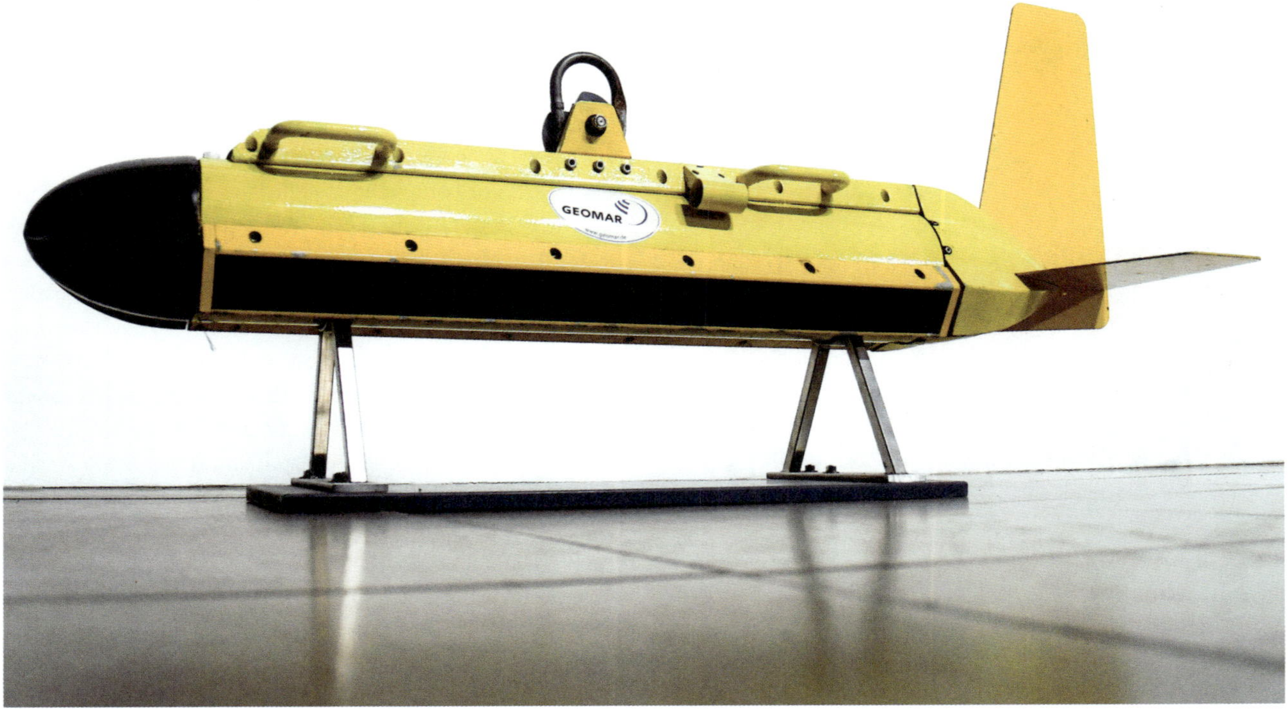

11/30

11/30 **Deep-sea side-scan sonar for use at depths down to 6,000 m**
Kiel, after 1980
Iron, steel, glass; 45 x 164 x 63 cm
Kiel, GEOMAR Helmholtz-Zentrum für Ozeanforschung
Kiel: 2017-104

Deep-sea side-scan sonar is often used to image large areas of the sea floor and their geological features at high resolution. The data obtained are used to draw conclusions about the marine ecosystem in the deep sea, tectonic disturbances, and anthropogenic intervention. Acoustic pulses in the form of sound waves are emitted on both sides of the scanner vehicle, which is towed behind the research vessel on a cable near the ocean floor. When the pulses hit the seabed, they are reflected, picked up by sensors on the vehicle and transmitted to the ship at the surface, where they are displayed on a screen. The intensity of the reflection or 'backscattering' depends on the inclination of a seabed feature relative to the beam. This makes it possible to chart different deposits such as silt, sand, or gravel as well as bedrock. Even quite small objects can be distinguished using the device. GHW

The Future of Marine Research

11/31 **Cold-water coral – *Lophelia pertusa***
Trondheim fjord, retrieved from a depth of 175 m
Calcium carbonate; 25 x 24 x 34 cm
Kiel, GEOMAR Helmholtz-Zentrum für Ozeanforschung
Kiel: 2017-200

In addition to ocean warming, the associated rise of sea level, and the loss of oxygen, the most significant consequence of climate change resulting from human activity is an increase in the acidity of ocean water. Carbon dioxide from the atmosphere dissolves in seawater and reacts to form carbonic acid. This makes it harder for a great many marine organisms to build shells or skeletons, which they do by extracting calcium carbonate from the water. In this context, scientists have examined the effects of acidification on cold-water corals. These corals, which also occur in the deep sea layer, differ considerably from the tropical corals, which occur only in the upper, sunlight zone of the sea. Cold water corals do not photosynthesise, but feed on microscopic algae and other plankton drifting past. The reefs formed by cold-water corals are now also threatened by bottom trawling, a fishing method that has already destroyed half of the

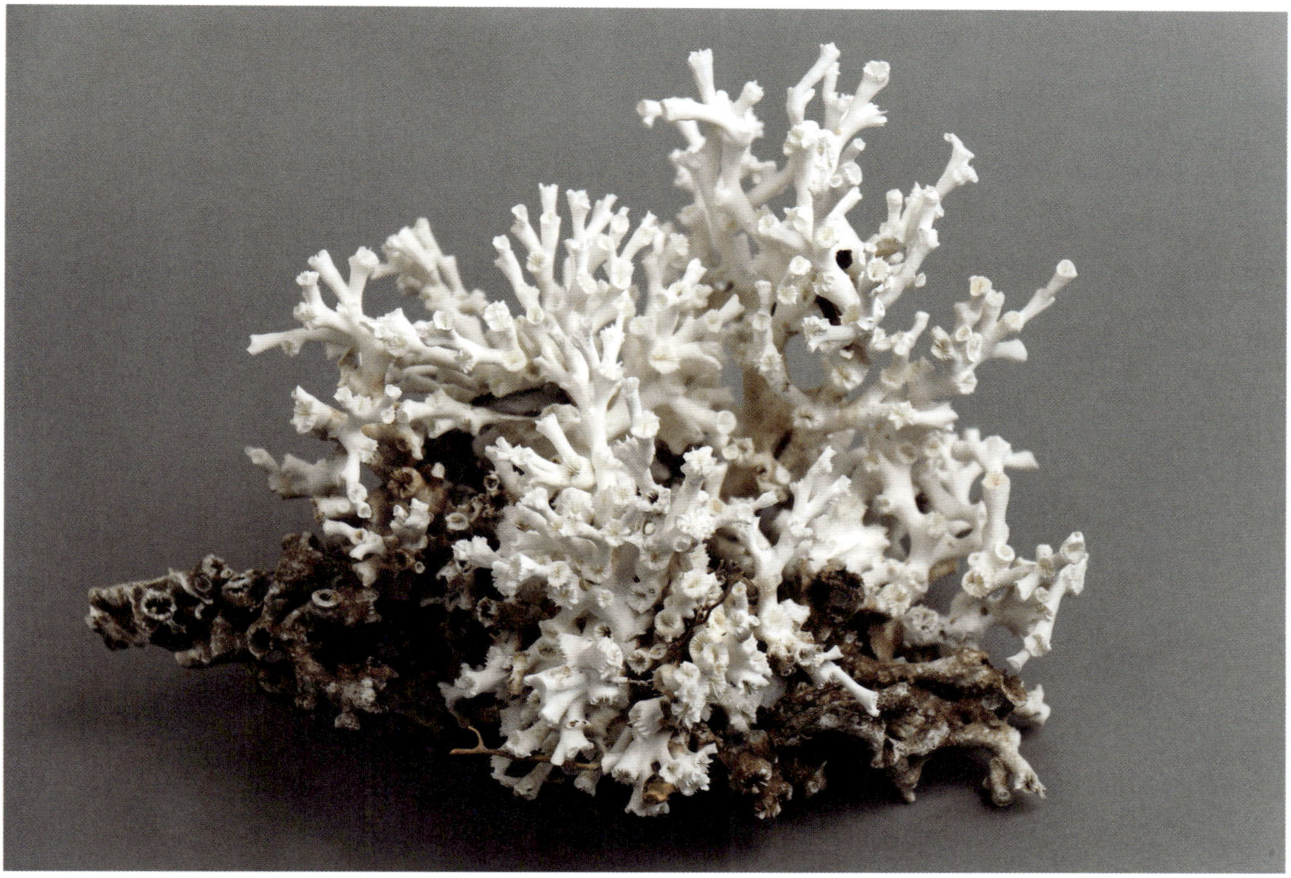

11/31

reefs in some regions. Acidification affects not just cold water corals and zooplankton such as the larvae of sea snails, but the entire ecosystem of the seabed. GHW

11/30 **Model of the Deep Sea Observatory in the Fram Strait**
Concept and development:
Dr. Gerd Hoffmann-Wieck, GEOMAR, with
Horst Reschenberg, Schönkirchen (model-maker)
Berlin/Brussels, 2011
Iron, brass, plastic; 96.5 x 180 x 107 cm
Berlin, Konsortium Deutsche Meeresforschung

In deep-sea research, as in space travel, it is essential to develop and apply new technology. Research vessels – essentially platforms for marine research – have become indispensible, as have mobile robotic systems such as remote operated vehicles (ROV) and autonomous underwater vehicles (AUV). In the future, long-term measurements in the deep sea zone will be needed in key regions of the world's oceans. They will require a variety of devices performing complementary tasks for different disciplines. The equipment may be housed in deep-sea observatories like the one shown here as a model, some parts of which have already been built. It will be sited in the Fram Strait between eastern Greenland and the Norwegian arctic island of Spitsbergen. The observatory will monitor the long-term consequences of sea ice decline and climate change, as well as changes in the Arctic Ocean's ecosystem and biodiversity. Progress in deep-sea research greatly depends on continuing to apply new technology in the future. (Exhibit not shown) GHW

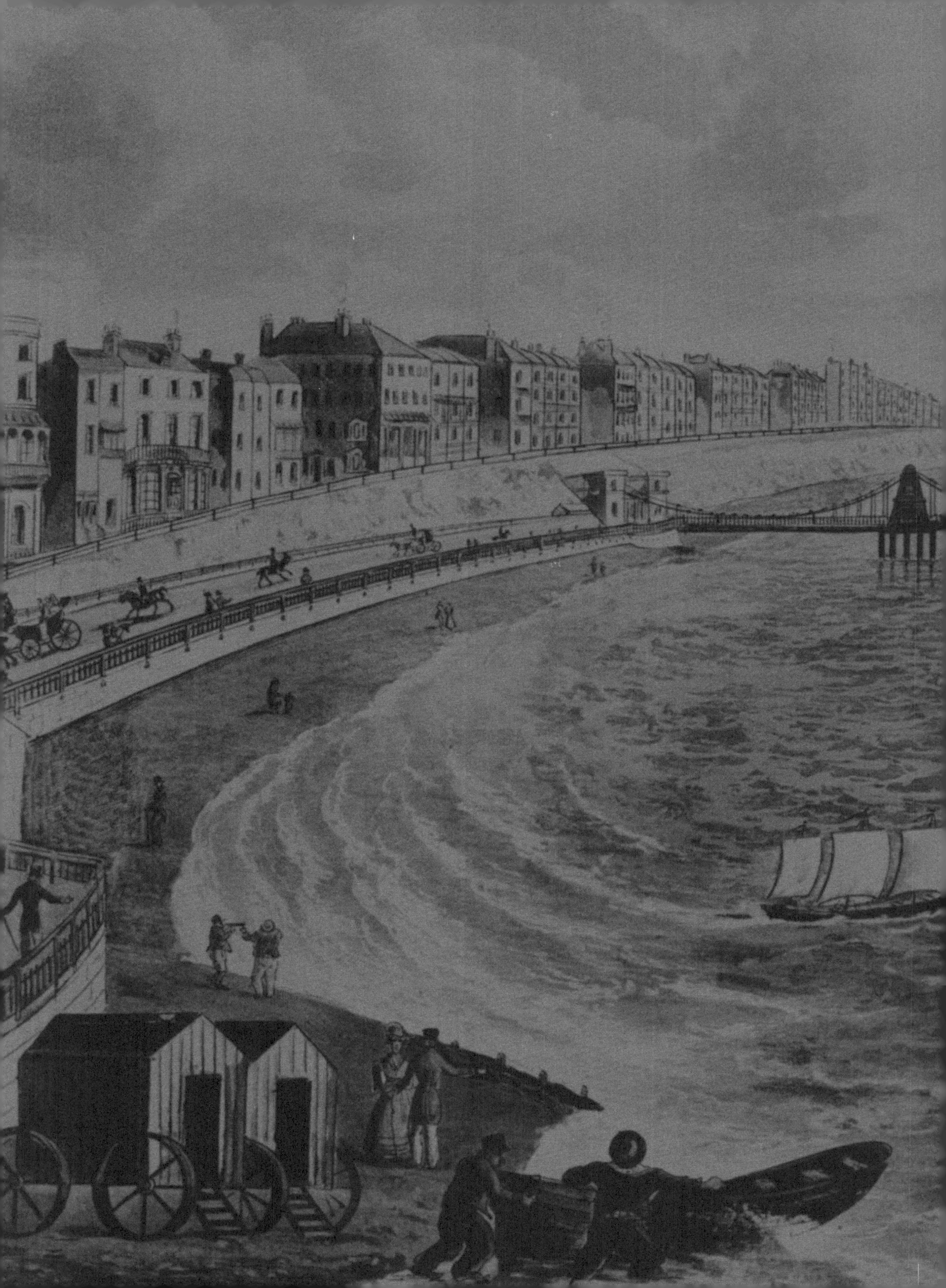

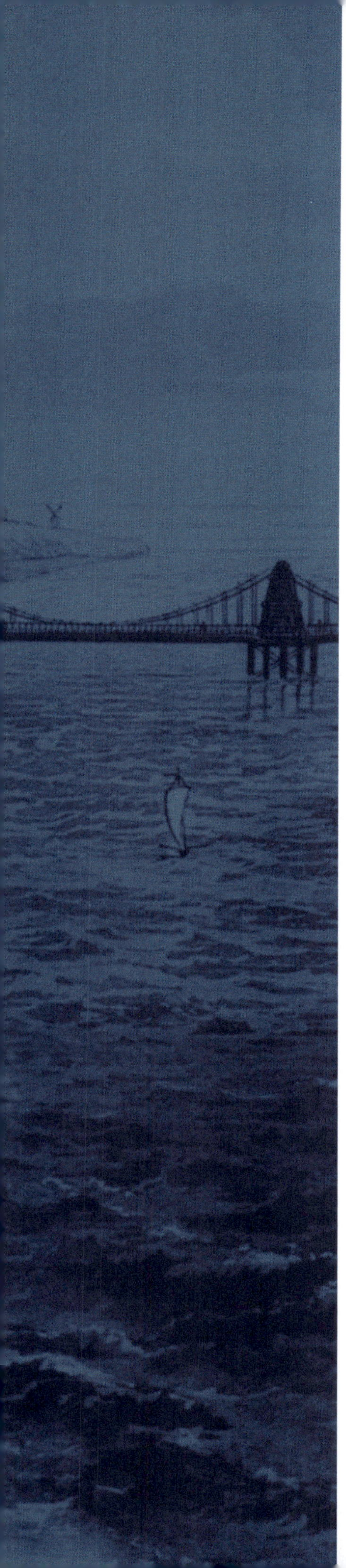

IV
FOCUS OF IMAGINATION AND YEARNING

12 Tourism
The Port of Brighton

The seaside holiday – bathing in the sea – is a European invention that followed the reappraisal of the sea from a philosophical and medical point of view during the Enlightenment era of the eighteenth century. Great Britain, as a seafaring nation, was at the forefront of this development. As the aesthetic perception of nature developed, the sea came to epitomise 'the Sublime', which, according to the Irish-British political philosopher Edmund Burke (1729–1797), goes far beyond 'the Beautiful'. At the same time, scientists had been discovering the therapeutic qualities of the sea. Its medical properties were first described by Richard Russell (1687–1759) in his 1750 dissertation on the use of seawater to treat "diseases of the glands".

Russell practiced as a doctor in Brighton on the south coast of England. The town became established as a seaside resort in the second half of the eighteenth century, visited at first by aristocrats and wealthy pillars of society. With its pier and its seafront promenade lined with hotels, spa facilities and entertainment venues, Brighton served as a model for the bathing and health resorts that soon sprang up in rapid succession along the coasts of the North Sea and the Baltic Sea. From these breezy northern shores, the fashion for sea bathing spread throughout Europe during the nineteenth century, and later around the world. Over time, the medical aspect faded into the background, and the beach became a place for relaxed socialising in loose clothing, seemingly free of the constraints of civilization. New spheres of "intimate anonymity" emerged.

Railways and steamships helped to open up spa culture to a broader section of society. By the early twentieth century, the upper-middle class had taken over the beaches – not least as a way of demonstrating their closeness to their social betters. In the meantime, the steamship had opened up a new area of marine tourism exclusively for the elite: the cruise. Kaiser Wilhelm II of Germany undertook annual voyages to the far north while large shipping companies competed for the favour of their wealthy clientele by fitting out luxury cruise ships.

The golden age of European seaside resorts, up until the First World War, coincided with the heyday of the picture postcard – not only as a means of personal communication, but also as an increasingly important marketing tool. The main advertising medium used by the big shipping companies from 1870 onwards, however, was the illustrated poster. The early ones used depictions of ships by well-known naval painters. After 1900 – especially during the cruise holiday boom of the 1920s – the designs became more evocative, with images that suggested faraway, exotic destinations. On posters issued by local and national tourist boards, golden beaches and deep blue seas awakened the desire for a perfect holiday paradise.

The history of beach tourism does not, however, show a constant process of liberation and social inclusion. Long before 1933, radical anti-Semitism was rife in many German resorts on the North Sea and the Baltic Sea. The National Socialist leisure organisation, "Kraft durch Freude" (Strength through Joy), planned mass holiday complexes such as the "Sea Baths of the Twenty Thousand" in Prora on the island of Rügen, which were only partially completed. These were for the exclusive use of the 'Aryan master race' propagated by the Nazi state. They can also be seen as prototypes of the standardised beach holiday: an organisational prerequisite for mass tourism and the high-rise hotels of the post-war decades.

Seaside holidays did not really become affordable for most of society until the 1960s. Today, the tourism industry is one of the world's most important growth sectors. In the meantime, it has opened up coastal regions all over the world, creating virtually indistinguishable holiday developments with few local roots.

Ursula Breymayer

Further Reading

Frank Bajohr, *»Unser Hotel ist judenfrei«. Bäder-Antisemitismus im 19. und 20. Jahrhundert*, Frankfurt a. M. 2003

Alain Corbin, *Meereslust. Das Abendland und die Entdeckung der Küste*, Berlin 1990

Alexa Geisthövel, *Der Strand*, in: Alexa Geisthövel and Habbo Knoch (eds.), *Orte der Moderne. Erfahrungswelten des 19. und 20. Jahrhunderts*, Frankfurt a. M./New York 2005, pp. 121–130

Fred Gray, *Designing the Seaside. Architecture, Society and Nature*, London 2006

Rüdiger Hachtmann, *Tourismus-Geschichte*, Göttingen 2007

Sonja Kinzler and Dorlis Tillmann (eds.), *Nordlandreise. Die Geschichte einer touristischen Entdeckung* (exhib. cat. Kieler Stadt- und Schifffahrtsmuseum), Berlin n. d. [2010]

Dieter Richter, *Das Meer. Geschichte der ältesten Landschaft*, Berlin 2014

Hasso Spode, *Ein Seebad für zwanzigtausend Volksgenossen. Zur Grammatik und Geschichte des fordistischen Urlaubs*, in: Peter J. Brenner (eds.), *Reisekultur in Deutschland. Von der Weimarer Republik zum »Dritten Reich«*, Tübingen 1997

Hasso Spode, *Wie die Deutschen »Reiseweltmeister« wurden. Eine Einführung in die Tourismusgeschichte*, Erfurt 2003

Hasso Spode and Christiane Klemm, *Zur Geschichte der Ferienarchitektur*, in: Felizitas Romeiß-Stracke (ed.), *Tourismusarchitektur. Baukultur als Erfolgsfaktor*, Berlin 2008, pp. 95–109

Albrecht Steinecke, *Internationaler Tourismus*, Stuttgart 2014

Michael Wildt, *»Der muß hinaus! Der muß hinaus!« Antisemitismus in deutschen Nord- und Ostseebädern 1920–1935*, in: Mittelweg 36. Zeitschrift des Hamburger Instituts für Sozialforschung, 4/2001, pp. 3–25

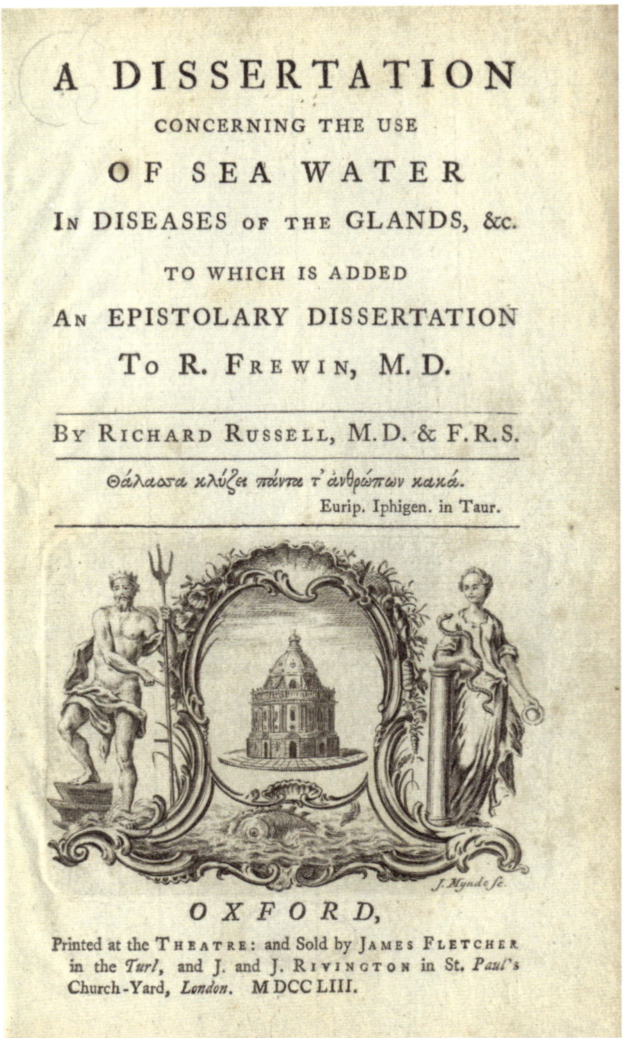

A DISSERTATION
CONCERNING THE USE
OF SEA WATER
IN DISEASES OF THE GLANDS, &c.
TO WHICH IS ADDED
AN EPISTOLARY DISSERTATION
TO R. FREWIN, M. D.

BY RICHARD RUSSELL, M. D. & F. R. S.

Θάλασσα κλύζει πάντα τ' ἀνθρώπων κακά.
Eurip. Iphigen. in Taur.

OXFORD,
Printed at the THEATRE: and Sold by JAMES FLETCHER in the Turl, and J. and J. RIVINGTON in St. Paul's Church-Yard, London. MDCCLIII.

12/1

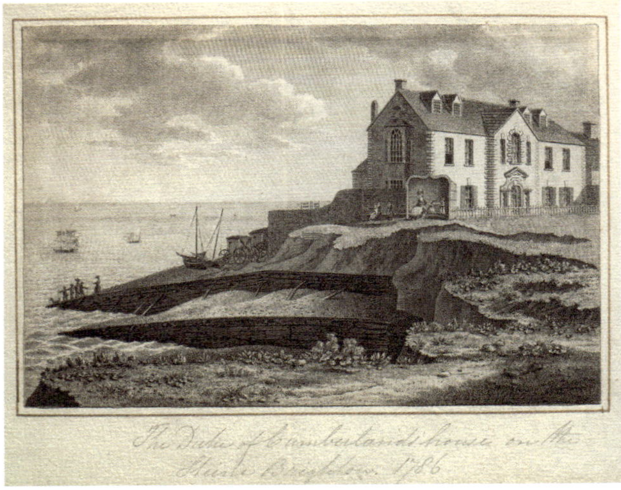

12/2

The Roots of Beach Tourism in the Eighteenth Century: Brighton as a Model

12/1 **Richard Russell's dissertation on the use of seawater in treating glandular diseases**
(A Dissertation Concerning The Use Of Sea Water In Diseases Of The Glands)
Richard Russell (1687–1759)
Published by James Fletcher, J. Rivington
Oxford/London, 1753
Print; 20.3 x 13.6 cm
Berlin, Staatsbibliothek zu Berlin – Preußischer Kulturbesitz, Benutzungsabteilung: 50 MA 8635

Richard Russell first published his dissertation in Latin, in 1750. The English translation came out three years later. Russell's propositions can be summarised as follows: sea water cleanses the body and the mind of any "decay"; therefore people should bathe in the sea, drink sea water and eat food that comes from the sea. The figures illustrated on the title page, together with a quotation written in Ancient Greek characters, allude to the ancient origins of sea water therapy: On the left is a depiction of Poseidon, the god of the sea in Greek mythology. The female figure on the right portrays a mythical character, Iphigenia. The Greek poet Euripides (480–406 BC) made her the heroine of his drama *Iphigenia in Tauris*, from which the verse quoted here is taken: "The sea washes away all men's evils". UB

12/2 **View of Richard Russell's former property in Brighton**
(The Duke of Cumberland's House on the Steine, Brighton)
William Watts (1752–1871), after James Luttrell (1751–1788)
England, 1786
Reproduction
Brighton, Royal Pavilion Museums, Brighton & Hove: FA202132

Russell's therapeutic methods aroused great interest. In 1753, he had a handsome building erected in the town of Brighthelmstone, later shortened to Brighton. Besides being his home, it was also where he received and treated his patients. They soon came in ever greater numbers, contributing to an upturn in the fortunes of the run-down fishing port. After Russell's death in 1759, his house was rented to well-heeled spa guests, most of whom were aristocrats, such as the Duke of Cumberland. By 1780, Brighton had become the best-known and most fashionable seaside resort in the United Kingdom. Russell's house was demolished in 1826 to make way for a hotel. Sea bathing establishments also sprang up in other places on the coasts of England and Wales from the middle of the eighteenth century onwards, notably at Margate, Ramsgate and Blackpool. UB

12/3 **Illustration of a 'dipper' at work in Brighton**
("Amphibious", from: *Fashionable Handbook for Visitors to Brighton*)
Alfred Crowquill (1804–1872), Charles J. Basebi (1818–1880)
Published by W. H. Mason, Brighton, 1848
Reproduction
Brighton, Royal Pavilion Museums, Brighton & Hove: FA205673

The medical part of spa treatment usually went as follows: the men or women were taken separately into shallow water in a covered horse-drawn cart, like a changing room on wheels. Then they went down a few steps into the cold sea and immersed themselves completely for a short time, as a kind of shock treatment for the body. Doctors drew up detailed rules on how long and how often their patients should bathe, and at what times of day. The owners of the 'bathing machines', as the carts were called, hired fishermen and their wives as 'dippers' to help the bathers undress and assist them while in the water. (Fig. p. 144) UB

12/4 **View of Brighton with the Prom and the Pier**
(*Brighton Suspension Chain Pier*)
John Bruce
England, c. 1825
Reproduction
Brighton, Royal Pavilion Museums, Brighton & Hove: FA207546

Benefiting from its proximity to London, Brighton grew to be one of Britain's most elegant bathing resorts. From the 1820s onwards, the town's appearance was characterised by seafront terraces and promenades lined with splendid buildings, which formed a suitable backdrop against which the privileged classes could see and be seen. The illustration shows the *Marine Parade* in Brighton with the *Chain Pier* in the background. Elegantly dressed people are strolling along it, or riding in horse-drawn carriages. A steamship is leaving the bay. Starting in 1824, a regular cross-Channel boat service ran between Brighton and Dieppe, a similarly exclusive seaside resort on the coast of Normandy. UB

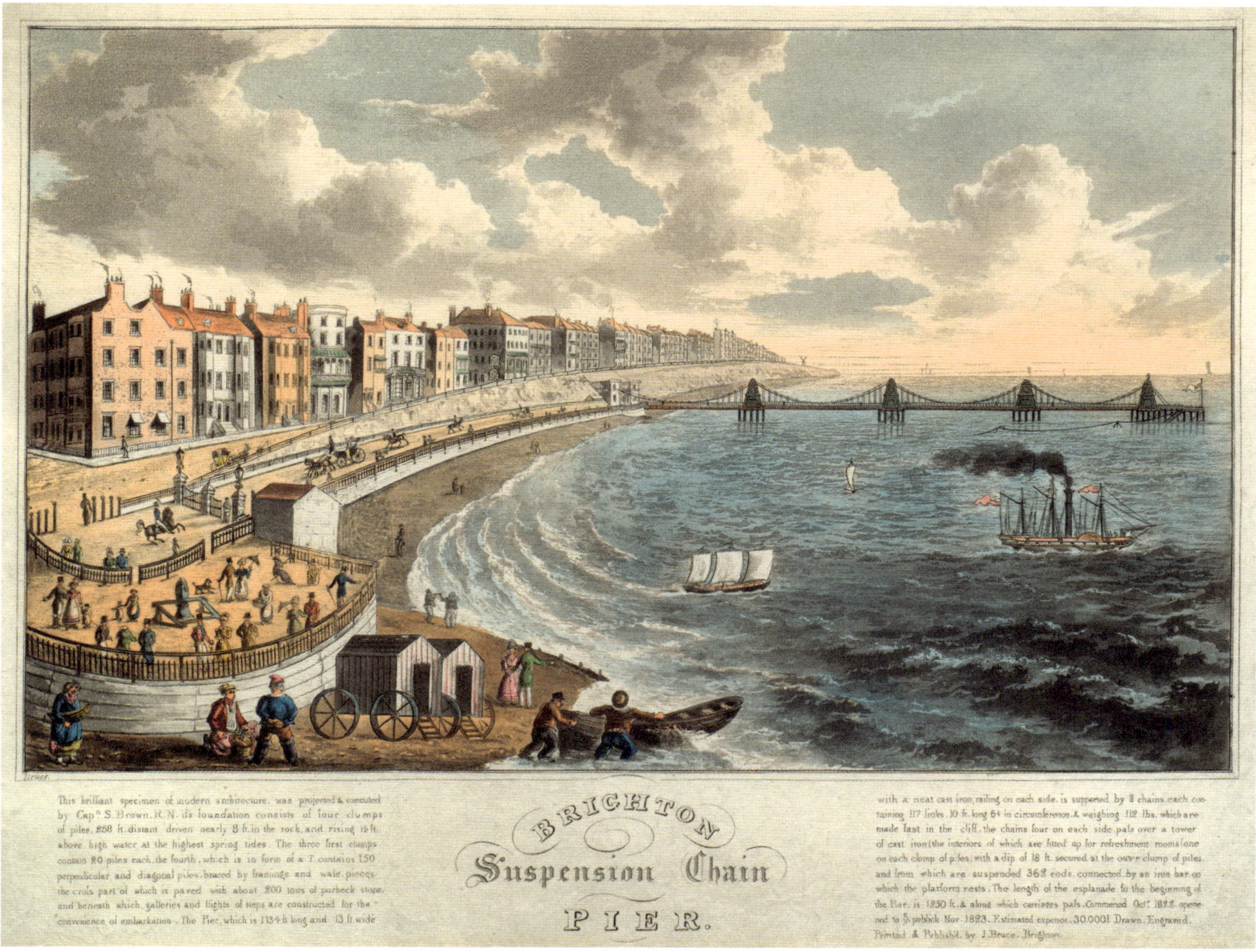

12/4

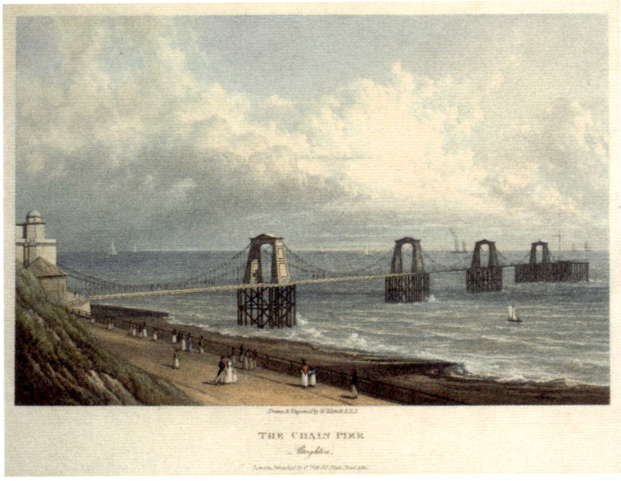

12/5

12/5 **View of the pier in Brighton**
(The Chain Pier, Brighton)
William Westall (1781–1850)
Published by C. Tilt
London, 1830
Reproduction
Brighton, Royal Pavilion Museums, Brighton & Hove: FA202783

Opened in 1823, the *Chain Pier* was around 345 metres long and 4 metres wide, making it a memorable landmark in Brighton. It fulfilled both practical needs and leisure purposes: in places without any harbour or wharf, like Brighton, a sea pier served as a landing stage for ships, allowing passengers to board and disembark as conveniently as possible. Additionally, people could walk out to sea along it, filling their lungs with the salty air. The *Chain Pier* was designed by Captain Samuel Brown (1776–1852), a pioneer of chain design and early suspension bridges. The deck was suspended on cast-iron chains from four pyramidal cast-iron frames. The foundations consisted of massive oak piles. A carved stone staircase connected the pier to the waterfront promenade. The entrance kiosks housed a lounge, a library and a reading room for the use of visitors. This was also where they paid the entrance fee. Placards offered information on the weather, the day's news and the entertainment programme. UB

12/6 **View of Brighton, seen from the far end of the pier**
(Brighton and the Chain Pier from the Pier Head)
Caleb William Wing (1801–1875)
Published by W. M. Tuppen, Royal Marine Library
Brighton, c. 1830
Reproduction
Brighton, Royal Pavilion Museums, Brighton & Hove: FA207896

The pier head – that is, the far end of the pier that stood in the sea – broadened out into a rectangular platform, which was used for social gatherings and for concert performances by the town orchestra. The supporting pylons were clad and ornamented in a classical style, as the illustration shows. All four of them contained small booths for selling souvenirs. UB

12/7 **View of the new pier in Brighton**
(The New Pier. Brighton. No 1.)
Printed and published by J. S. & Co.
England, c. 1866
Reproduction
Brighton, Royal Pavilion Museums, Brighton & Hove: R3969_45

The opening of a railway to London in 1841 led Brighton's population to multiply many times over, earning it a new nickname: London-by-Sea. The number of visitors was even greater, estimated at around 250,000 a year by 1848. In 1866, a second pier was built: the *West Pier*, which stood at the western end of the seafront promenade. It was a cast-iron frame structure, with a length of 340 metres and a pier head of 94 metres in width. A third pier was opened in 1899. The *Palace Pier* was built to replace the *Chain Pier*, whose remains were destroyed by a heavy storm in 1896. UB

12/8 **View of the Chain Pier and the Aquarium in Brighton**
Printed and published by J. Newman & Co
Southwark, London, 1870s
Reproduction
Brighton, Royal Pavilion Museums, Brighton & Hove: FATMP000251

As a fashionable seaside resort, Brighton offered a variety of leisure activities designed to satisfy the high expectations of its visitors. There were ballrooms, assembly rooms, gambling salons, lending libraries, theatres, concert halls and horse-racing courses. One attraction was the marine aquarium, opened in 1872. Its architect, Eugenius Birch (1818–1884), had also designed Brighton's *West Pier* and other major piers in England and Wales. Large private and public

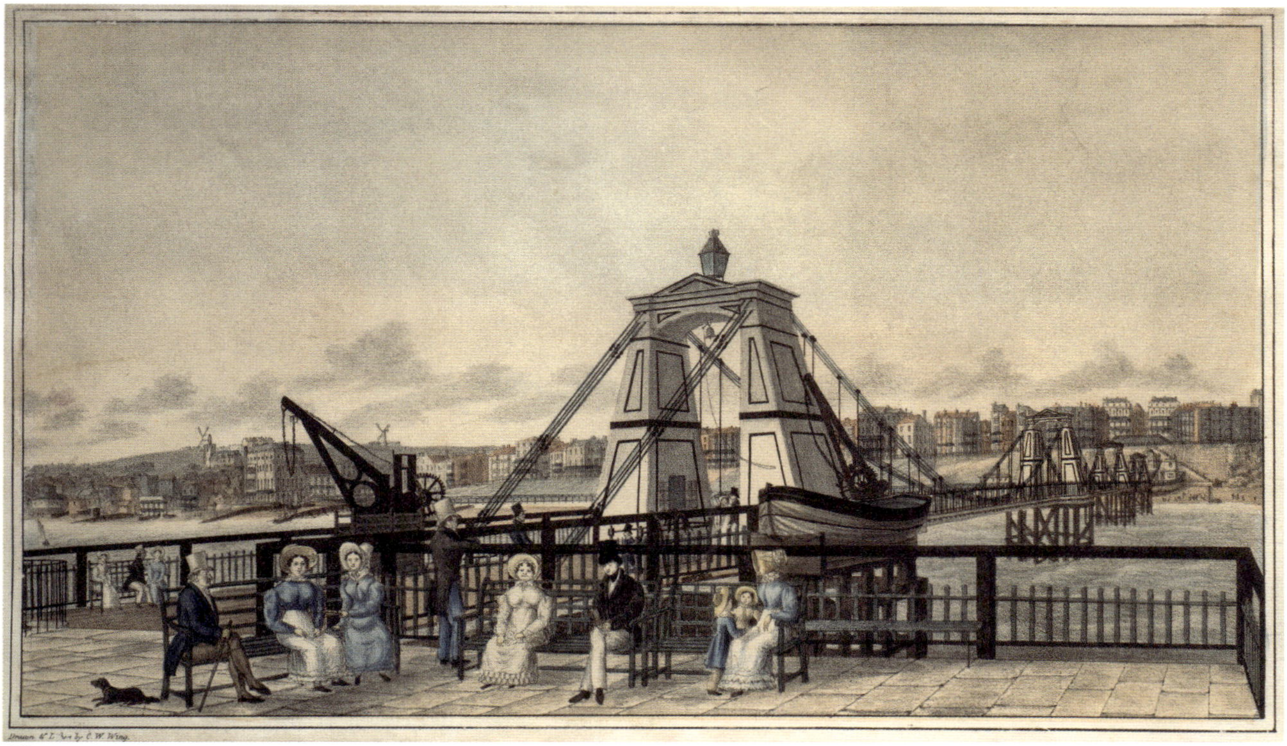

12/6

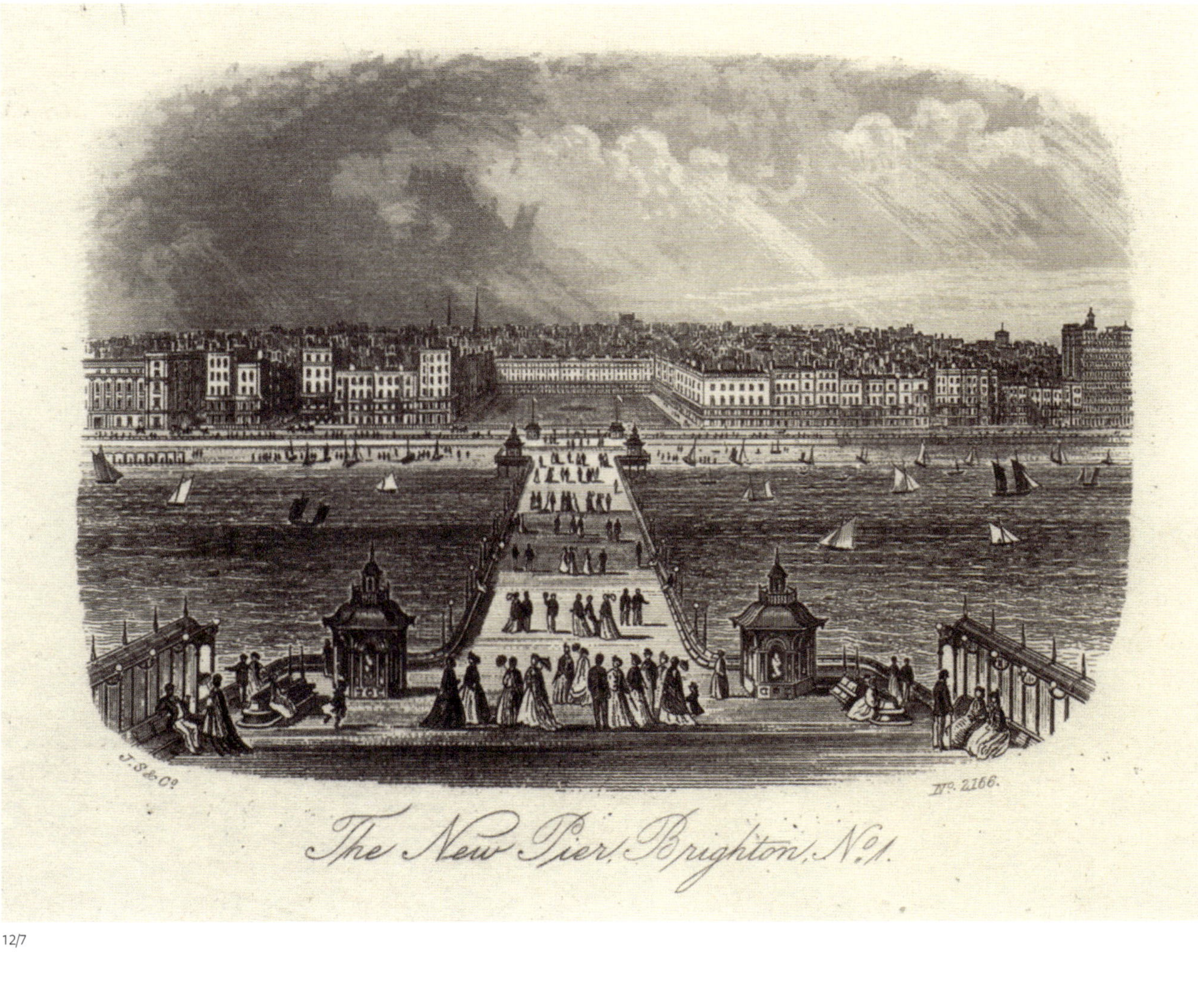

12/7

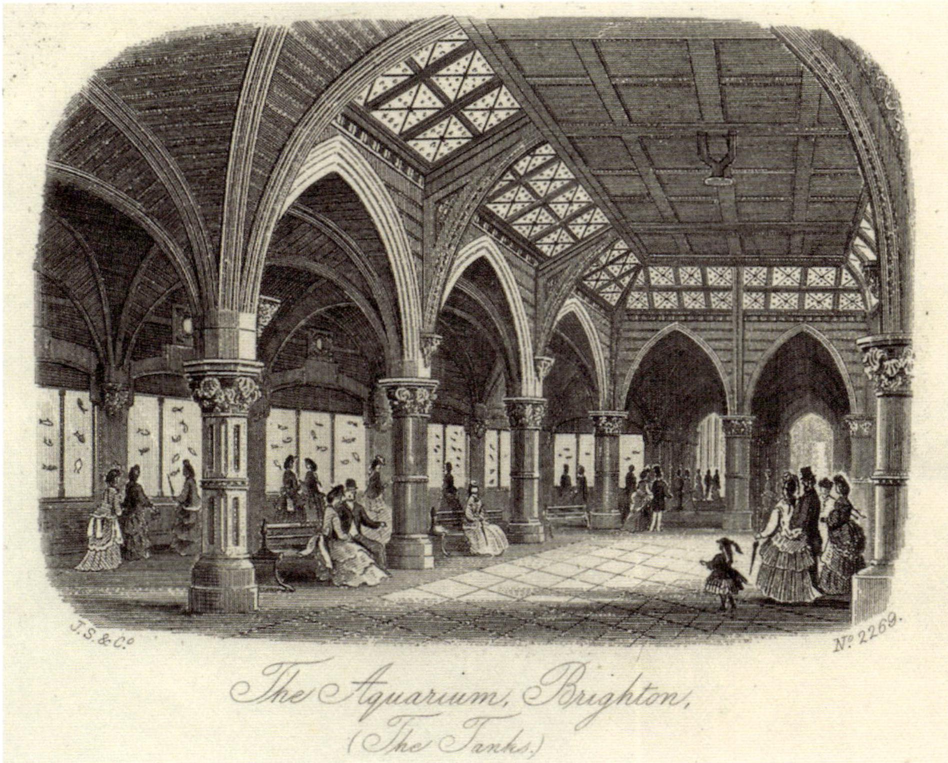

12/9

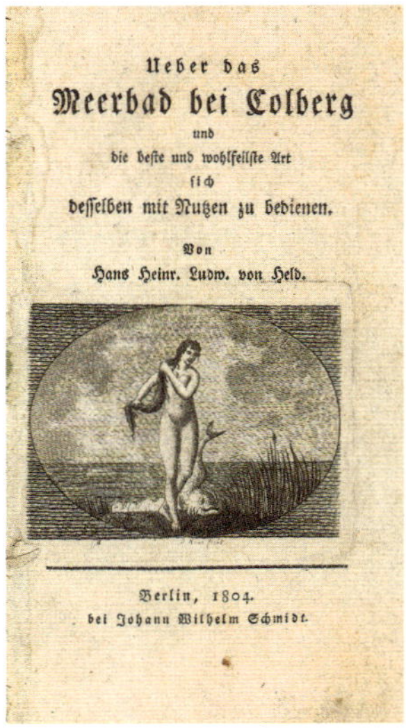
Ueber das
Meerbad bei Colberg
und
die beste und wohlfeilste Art
sich
desselben mit Nutzen zu bedienen.
Von
Hans Heinr. Ludw. von Held.

Berlin, 1804.
bei Johann Wilhelm Schmidt.

12/10

marine aquaria are among the innovations that became possible during the nineteenth century. The term was coined by Philip Henry Gosse (1810–1888), whose book *The Aquarium: An Unveiling of the Wonders of the Deep Sea* was published in 1854. The first public aquaria went into operation at around the same time – and here too, the British led the way, with the opening, in 1853, of the *Fish House* in London's *Regent's Park*, which Gosse had created and stocked. (Exhibit not shown) UB

12/9 **Interior view of the marine aquarium in Brighton**
(*The Aquarium, Brighton,* (*The Tanks*))
Printed by J. S. & Co.
England, c. 1875
Reproduction
Brighton, Royal Pavilion Museums, Brighton & Hove: FATMP000440

The Brighton Aquarium contained not only large tanks displaying sea creatures, but also a restaurant, a reading room and a conservatory. The imposing interior, with its eclectic mixture of styles and elaborately carved stonework, soon became a popular place for spa visitors to go for a stroll and socialise. UB

12/10 **Title page of the essay *Ueber das Meerbad bei Colberg und die beste und wohlfeilste Art sich desselben mit Nutzen zu bedienen* (On the sea bath near Colberg and the best and cheapest way of making good use of it)**
Hans Heinrich Ludwig von Held (1764–1842)
Published by Johann Wilhelm Schmidt
Berlin, 1804
Print; 17.5 x 10.5 cm
Berlin, Deutsches Historisches Museum: R 16/166

Brighton's "sea architecture" (Alain Corbin) served as a model for other seaside resorts in Britain and on the continent. At the time, countless essays were published by authors who considered the beneficial effects of seawater on the health, drew up detailed rules for bathing, or recommended certain bathing resorts. According to contemporary scientific opinion, spa treatment should help to cure a variety of diseases affecting adults or children, including rashes, rickets, gout, rheumatism, liver and kidney diseases, growth disorders, thyroid ailments and even impotence or sterility, as well as hypochondria, hysteria, sleepwalking and other nervous afflictions. The publication shown here is typical of this more or less scientific literature and is one of the earliest German essays in the genre. Its author, a Prussian official named Hans von Held, sings the praises of the sea baths established in 1802 near Kolberg in West Pomerania (today Kołobrzeg in Poland). UB

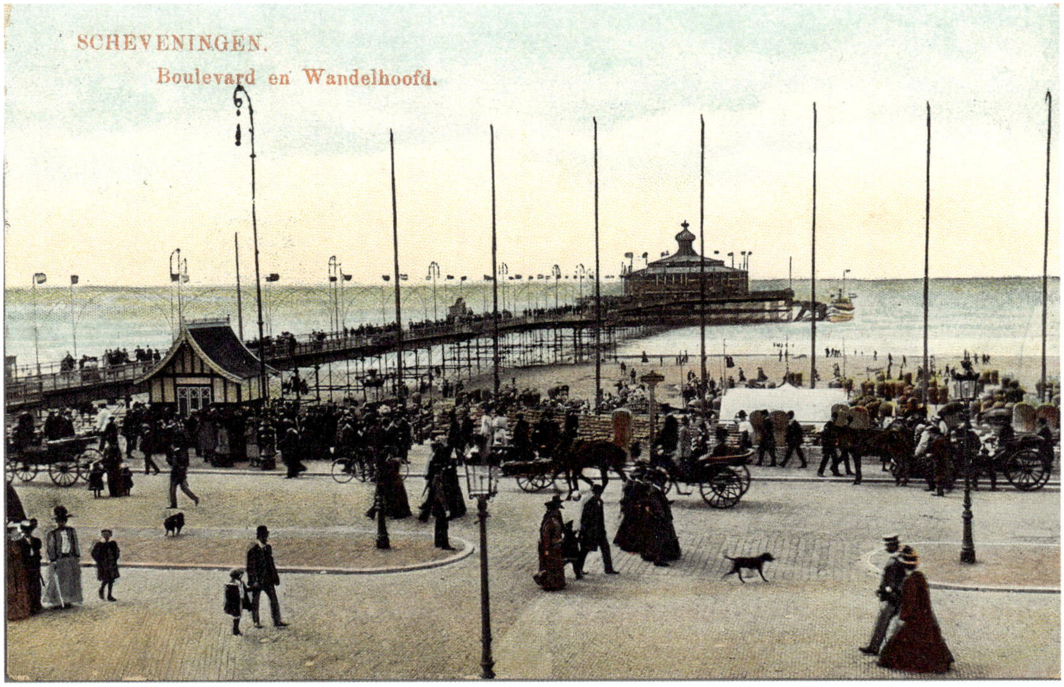

12/12 b

12/11 ***Zweites Verzeichniß der Badegäste und Fremden, welche auf der Insel Norderney angekommen sind* (Second directory of spa guests and visitors who have arrived on the island of Norderney)**
Hannover, 1822
Print; 22.5 x 19.1 cm
Berlin, Deutsches Historisches Museum: Do 2003/962

Germany's first North Sea resort was established on the island of Norderney in 1797, on the advice of Medical Councillor Friedrich Wilhelm von Halem (1762–1835) and with the permission of King Friedrich Wilhelm II of Prussia (1744–1797). In 1815 it was awarded, along with the rest of East Frisia, to the Kingdom of Hanover. Expanded spa facilities, including the Spa House built in 1822, soon made Norderney popular with the nobility, especially from 1836 onwards, when the Crown Prince of Hanover, later King Georg V (1819–1878), chose it as his summer residence. The names and occupations in this guest list from 1822 show that a spa holiday was the exclusive preserve of the privileged classes, which included military men and landowners of noble birth, county commissioners and mayors, doctors and wealthy merchants. (Exhibit not shown) UB

The Evolution of the Beach Holiday in the Nineteenth and Early Twentieth Centuries

12/12 **Four picture postcards from European seaside resorts**
Chromolithographs, photochroms; each approx. 9 x 14 cm
Berlin, Deutsches Historisches Museum:
w/o inv. no., w/o inv. no., PK 2008/411.36, PK 2008/411.35

Sea bathing establishments based on the British model also emerged in growing numbers on the European mainland, initially in the north. They included the French spa at Dieppe, on the coast of Normandy, which began its evolution into a luxurious seaside resort during the 1820s. The spa at Scheveningen on the Dutch coast was established around 1818, making it one of the oldest. Ostend in Belgium, on the other hand, grew from modest beginnings, developing from the 1830s onwards into a particularly elegant spa town, which was also popular with German guests. Towards the end of the century, this trend was followed by countless new establishments, leading up to the heyday of the North European seaside resort in the early twentieth century. In England and Wales alone, there were 145 official seaside resorts in 1911; seaside tourism had become a major economic force. The situation was similar on the continent. UB

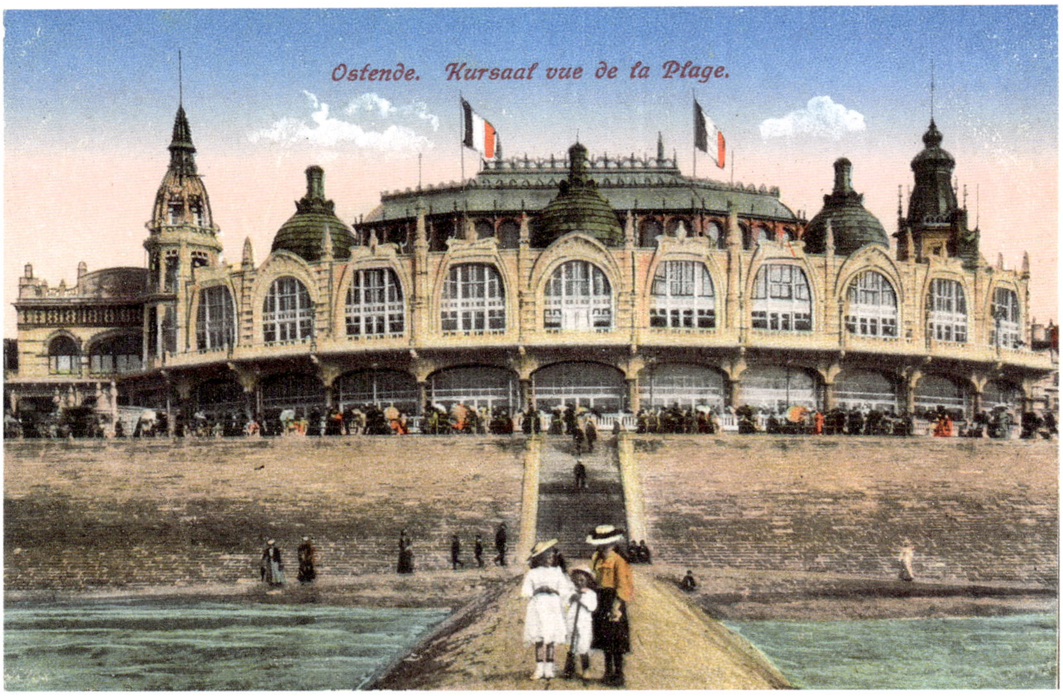

12/12 c

12/12a **"Dieppe – Le Casino et la Plage"**
1903 (postmark) (Exhibit not shown)
12/12b **"Scheveningen Boulevard en Wandelhoofd"**
1912 (postmark)
12/12c **"Ostende. Kursaal vue de la Plage"**
1916 (postmark)
12/12d **"Ostende. Les Hotels de la Digue Quest"**
1916 (postmark) (Exhibit not shown)

12/13 **Eleven picture postcards of Baltic resorts**
Chromolithographs, photochroms, photographs; each approx. 9 x 14 cm
Berlin, Deutsches Historisches Museum: w/o inv. no., PK 95/147, w/o inv. no., w/o inv. no., w/o inv. no., PK 95/176, PK 95/149, PK 99/365, PK 92/17.604, w/o inv. no., PK 2011/813

The first German seaside resort (and probably the first on the European mainland) was founded on the Baltic Sea in 1793/94. Acting on the advice of his physician, Samuel Gottlieb Vogel (1750–1837), the Duke of Mecklenburg, Friedrich Franz I (1756–1837) had a bathing establishment built at Heiligen Damm, not far from his summer residence in Doberan. Travemünde, near Lübeck, and Kolberg in West Pomerania followed around 1802, Putbus on the island of Rügen in 1816, Zoppot on the then Bay of Danzig in 1821, Kiel in 1822 and Warnemünde around 1824. The island of Usedom offered sea bathing facilities in Swinemünde (1824) and Heringsdorf (1825), followed soon after by Ahlbeck and, in 1897, Bansin, which was purpose-built as a seaside resort.

As their number grew, the sea baths opened up socially, in particular to the middle classes. Before long, a resort had to be accessible by railway if it was to prosper. Well-to-do city dwellers made a habit of staying by the sea at least once a year. Soon a differentiation by social class emerged, as in the neighbouring resorts on Usedom: military families went to Swinemünde, the middle class to Ahlbeck, factory owners and businessmen to Heringsdorf, and artists to Bansin. The number of visitors to the fifty or so official seaside resorts in Germany rose to an annual total of around 700,000 in the years before the First World War.

The places shown on the postcards differ only slightly: there are splendid seafront promenades, spa houses, and piers reaching out to sea. Well-dressed people of all ages are out for a stroll or having fun on the beach. In addition to the 'bathing machines', hooded beach chairs made of wickerwork were standard equipment at many seaside resorts from the 1880s onwards. They are thought to have been invented in the Baltic port of Rostock by Wilhelm Bartelmann (1845–

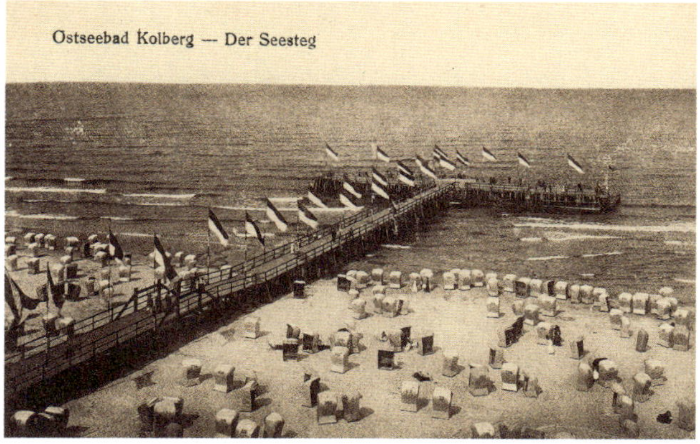

12/13c

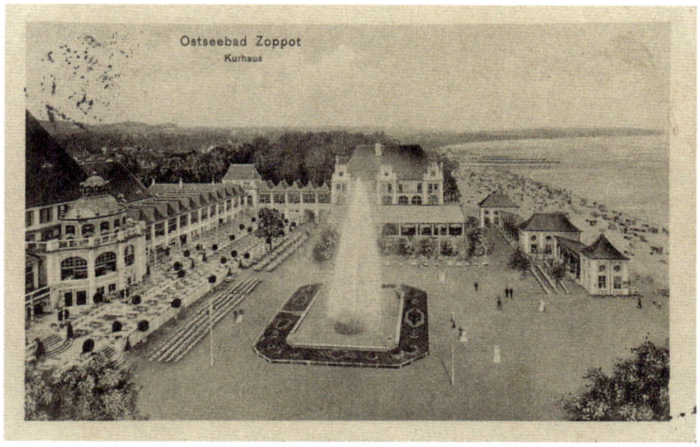

12/13e

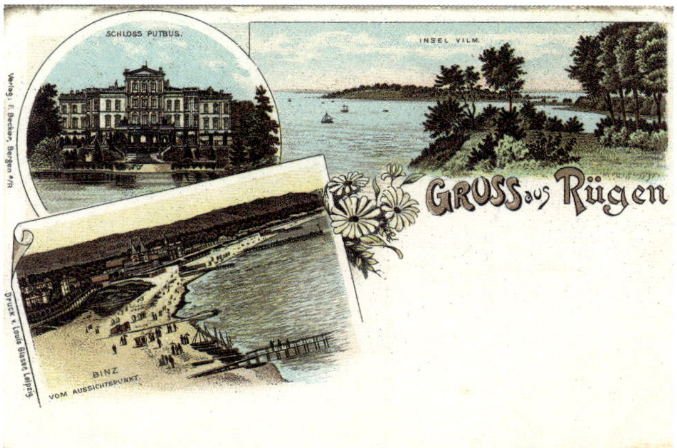

12/13d

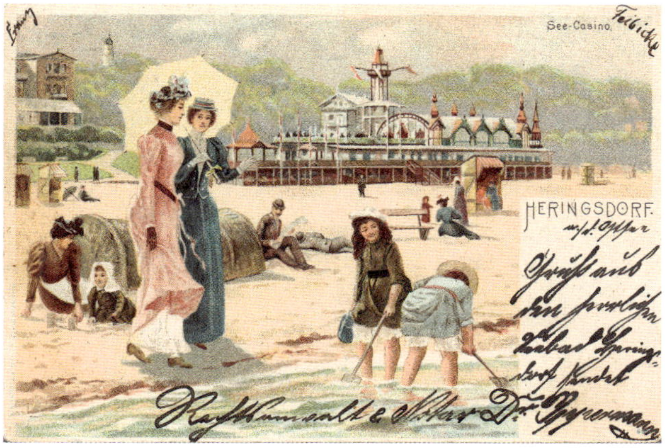

12/13i

1930), basket-maker to the Grand Duke of Mecklenburg-Schwerin. Around 1880, this practical accessory also began to appear on the North Sea coasts of Germany, Holland and Belgium. It provided not only shelter from wind and sunshine, but also privacy. UB

12/13a **"Heiligendamm Baltic Sea Baths. View of the beach promenade"**
c. 1910 (Exhibit not shown)

12/13b **"Travemünde beach life"**
1912 (postmark) (Exhibit not shown)

12/13c **"Kolberg Baltic Sea Baths – the pier"**
c. 1910

12/13d **"Greetings from Rügen" with vignettes of Putbus Palace, Vilm Island and Binz**
c. 1900

12/13e **"Zoppot Baltic Sea Baths – Pier"**
c. 1910

12/13f **"Kiel. Sea bathing establishment. Beach promenade with a view of the war harbour"**
1915 (postmark) (Exhibit not shown)

12/13g **"Warnemünde. On the beach"**
1912 (postmark) (Exhibit not shown)

12/13h **"Swinemünde Baltic Sea Baths – Beach with Spa House"**
1911 (postmark) (Exhibit not shown)

12/13i **"Sea Casino. Heringsdorf"**
1901 (postmark)

12/13j **"Ahlbeck. Beach life"**
1906 (postmark) (Exhibit not shown)

12/13k **"Bansin Baltic Sea Baths. Langenberg with a view of the pier"**
c. 1930 (Exhibit not shown)

12/14 **Four picture postcards of North Sea resorts**
Chromolithographs, photochroms, photographs; each approx. 9 x 14 cm
Berlin, Deutsches Historisches Museum: 1989/1302.65, w/o inv. no., w/o inv. no., w/o inv. no.

The next seaside resort to be established on the North Sea after Norderney in 1797 was on the island of Wangerooge in 1804. Sea bathing establishments were set up in Cuxhaven on the mainland in 1816 and in Wyk on the island of Föhr in 1819. Other German North Sea islands followed suit, with Helgoland (1826), Langeoog (1830), Juist (1840), Borkum (1850), Westerland on Sylt (1855) and Baltrum (1876), to name but a few. (Fig. p. 396) UB

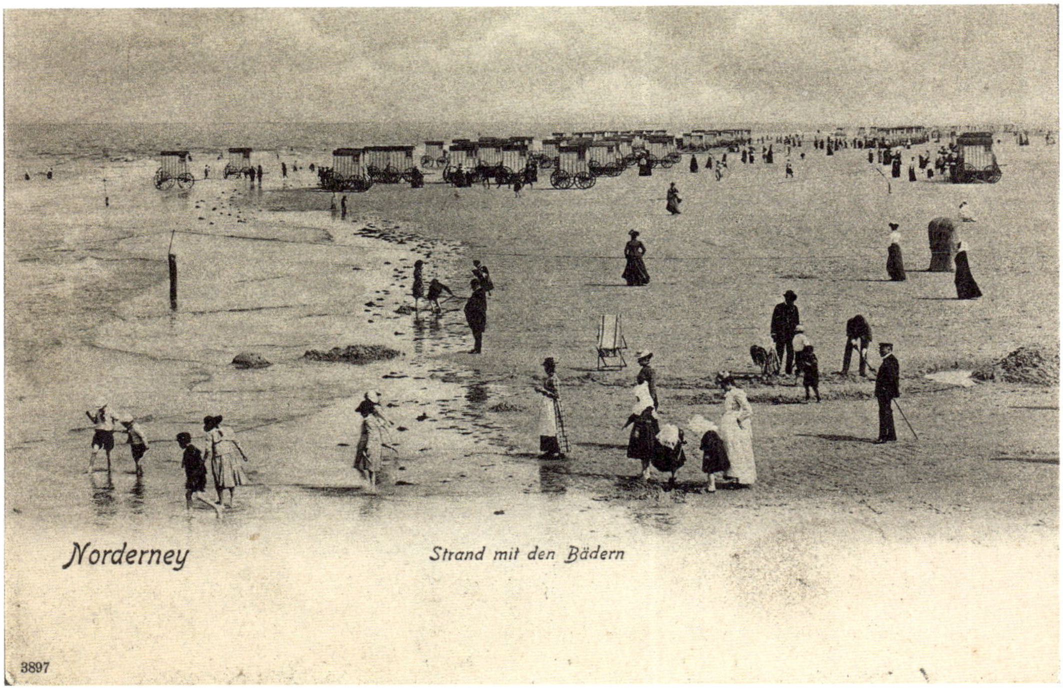

12/14a

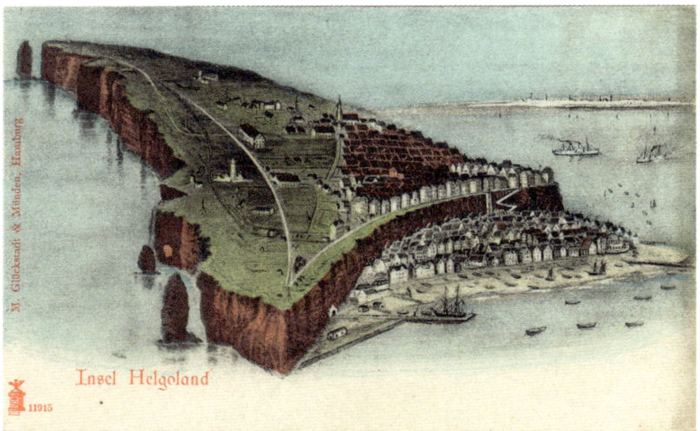

12/14c

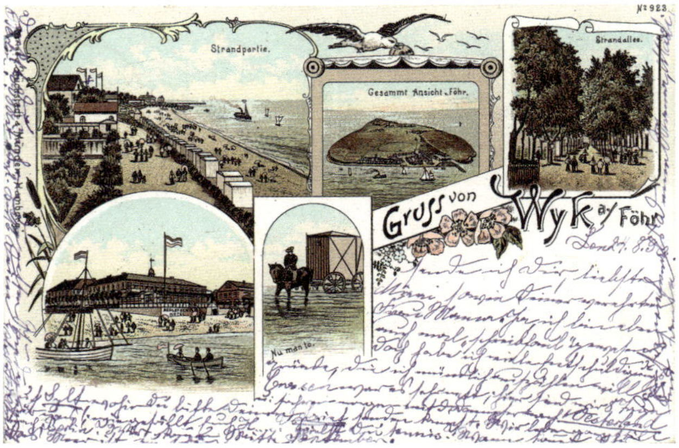

12/14b

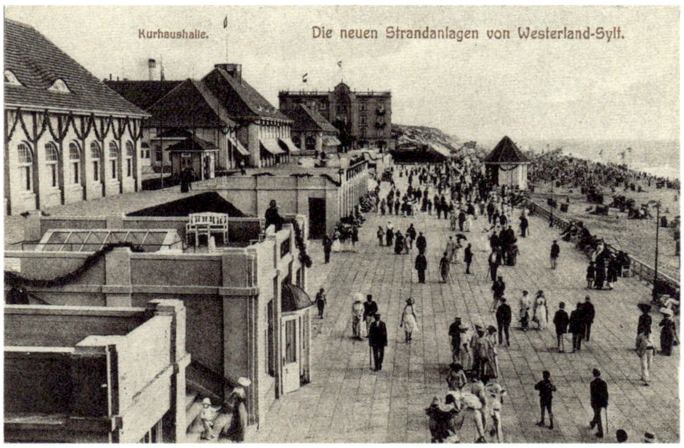

12/14d

12/14a **"Norderney. Beach with the baths"**
1870s

12/14b **"Greetings from Wyk on Föhr"**
1896 (postmark)

12/14c **"Island of Helgoland"**
c. 1870

12/14d **"Spa House Avenue. The new beach facilities in Westerland-Sylt"**
c. 1900

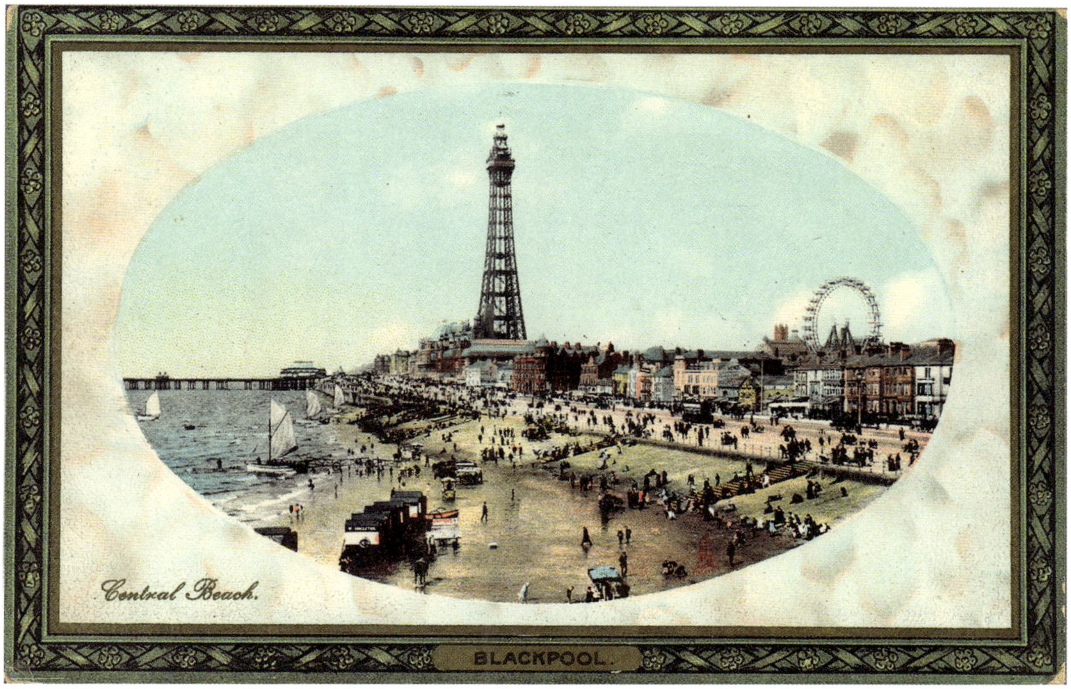

12/15

12/15 **Picture postcard of Blackpool, "Central Beach"**
c. 1895 (postmark)
Photochrom; 9 x 14 cm
Berlin, Deutsches Historisches Museum: w/o inv. no.

By the mid-nineteenth century, some seaside resorts had begun to focus on day trippers and guests on a tight budget. Here too, England led the way, especially Blackpool in the county of Lancashire. Sea baths had existed there since the late eighteenth century, and their character had initially been exclusive. The opening of a railway line to the town in 1840 turned it into a popular destination for Sunday trips and excursions organised by workers' associations. The railway company encouraged mass tourism by offering Sunday and group discounts. In the 1870s, visitor numbers increased sharply; several piers and a variety of attractions such as dance halls and the Ferris wheel kept them entertained. On 14 May 1894, the city acquired a new landmark, visible on the postcard. At 158 metres high, the steel truss tower was the tallest structure in Britain at the time. UB

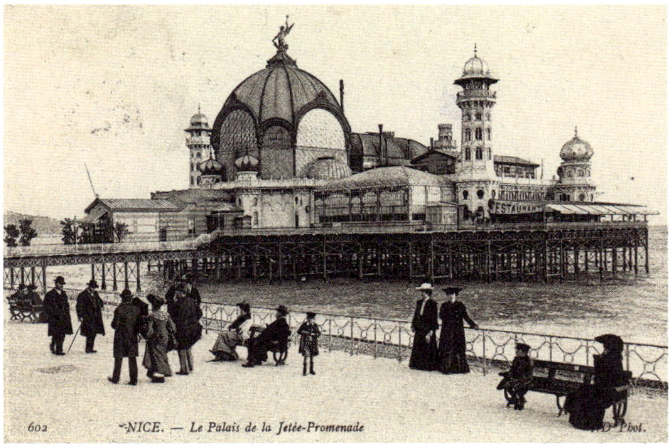

12/16a

12/16 **Two picture postcards of the Côte d'Azur**
Photograph, lithograph; each approx. 9 x 14 cm
Berlin, Deutsches Historisches Museum:
PK 90/955, PK 90/738

Meanwhile, the members of the upper crust were looking for new destinations where they could be among themselves once again. France and Italy, in particular the Côte d'Azur and the Italian Riviera, offered the right kind of place, where the well-off and the well-bred could build villas with a sea view or take up quarters in palatial hotels. Here, too, the

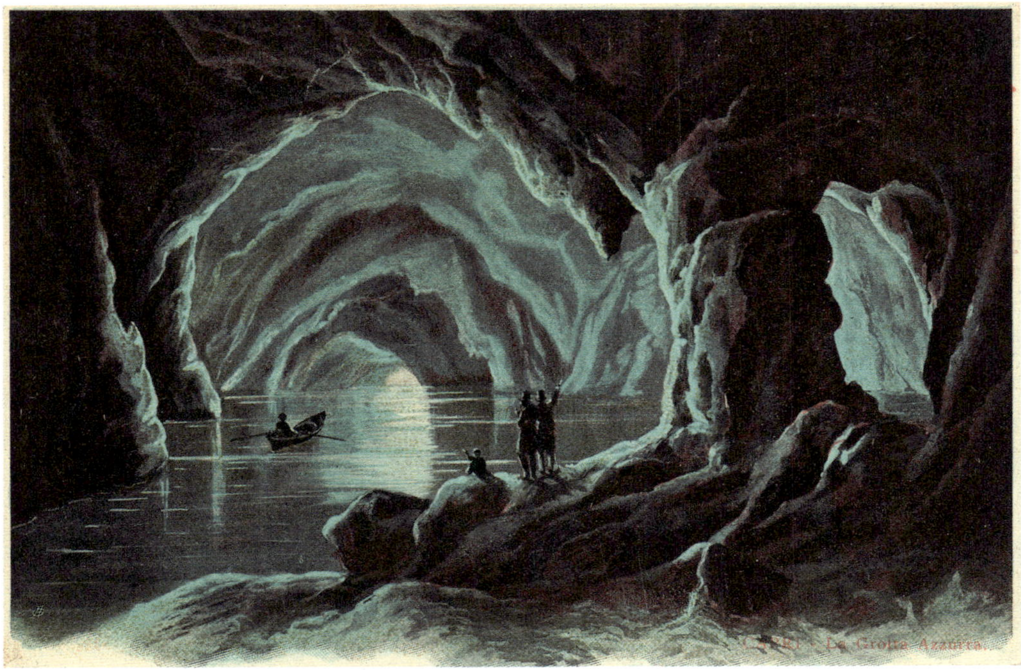

12/18

first guests were noblemen from England – a fact that is recalled today by street names such as the Promenade des Anglais in Nice. UB

12/16a **"Nice – Le Palais de la Jetée-Promenade"**
1908 (postmark) (Fig. p. 397)
12/16b **"Souvenir de Cannes. Boulevard de la Croisette"**
c. 1910 (Exhibit not shown)

12/17 **Picture postcard of Naples**
1906 (postmark)
Photochrom; 9.2 x 14.2 cm
Berlin, Deutsches Historisches Museum: Do 2013/105

The educational and artistic 'Grand Tours' of the late eighteenth century led to the discovery of southern Italy, Naples, the Gulf of Sorrento and the Amalfi Coast as outstanding tourist attractions. For the Germans in particular, this region, steeped in history and myth, came to epitomise Mediterranean culture and nature. After Theodor Fontane (1819–1898) had crossed to Norderney by ferry in the summer of 1880, he wrote in a letter, "The voyage [...] was very nice and took two hours. But it cannot compare with that from Capri to Sorrento". (Exhibit not shown) UB

12/18 **Artist's postcard, "Capri. La Grotta Azzurra"**
c. 1914
Lithograph; 9 x 14 cm
Berlin, Deutsches Historisches Museum: w/o inv. no.

After the writer and history painter August Kopisch (1799–1853) and the landscape painter Ernst Fries (1801–1833) 'rediscovered' and wrote about the Blue Grotto on Capri in 1826, the island became one of the most popular havens for German artists. The grotto, with its unusual natural illumination, has since been depicted in countless paintings and graphic works. The postcard shown here is based on an original work by an unknown artist. At the turn of the twentieth century, a German colony grew up on Capri after many prominent Germans had settled there – a sort of Italian forerunner of the Spanish Balearic island of Majorca, which some seventy years later was jokingly dubbed a 'German island'. The steamer that brought tourists from Naples to the island operated under the flag of Norddeutscher Lloyd and there was a German church, a German bookshop, and even German beer. UB

12/19 **Picture postcard, "Abbazia. Slàtina Bucht"**
c. 1910
Photochrom; 9 x 14 cm
Berlin, Deutsches Historisches Museum: PK 94/123

Beginning in the second half of the nineteenth century, Abbazia (today Opatija in Croatia) and Grado (today in Italy) on the Adriatic Sea were popular destinations for well-heeled visitors from Vienna, Prague, or Budapest. These were the rivieras patronised by the elites of the Austro-Hungarian Empire, easily accessible from their political centres. Before long, the middle class followed in their wake, taking advantage of railway lines that offered convenient direct connections from the big cities. In the 1880s, accommodation inspired by English railway hotels began to appear. In Abbazia, for example, visitors could stay in luxury establishments run by the Südbahn, a Viennese railway company which operated between the capital and the Adriatic coast. (Exhibit not shown) UB

12/20 **Picture postcard of Grado**
("Grado, Il movimento sulla spiaggia. L'ammassamento delle capanne")
1930 (postmark)
Photochrom; 9 x 14 cm
Berlin, Deutsches Historisches Museum: w/o inv. no.

Grado lies at the eastern end of the Gulf of Venice on the northern Adriatic; it belonged to Austria-Hungary from 1815 to 1919. The first bathing cabins appeared there in the middle of the nineteenth century and sea baths were set up in 1868. In 1892, the Grado Spa and Bathing Establishment was founded by a decree of Emperor Franz Josef I (1830–1916), thus completing the transformation of a fishing village into an imperial seaside resort. After the First World War, Grado was returned to Italy, but it remained very popular through the 1920s and '30s. The postcard shows a typical feature of Italian beaches to the present day: *stabilimenti balneari* or *bagni*. These are sections of beach that are fenced off and run commercially. Only if you pay an admission fee may you go onto the beach and use the facilities such as changing huts and showers. UB

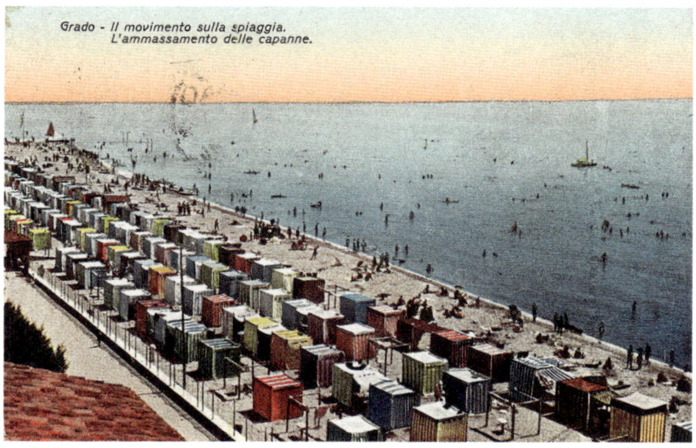

12/20

Anti-Semitism at German Resorts on the North and Baltic Seas

12/21 **Anti-Semitic picture postcard, "Greetings from Borkum"**
1905 (postmark)
Colour print; 9 x 14 cm
Berlin, Deutsches Historisches Museum: PK 2014/3365

Seaside resorts mirror social developments and conflicts. Given that anti-Semitic sentiment in German society increased enormously during the Wilhelmine period, it is hardly surprising that shows of resentment, acts of discrimination and physical attacks on Jews also occurred at holiday locations and beaches. At first, anti-Jewish measures in German seaside towns were instigated by guests with far-right political convictions, who then encouraged spa administrators and hotel operators to exclude Jews. This process was evident, in particular, at the resorts of Borkum in the North Sea and Zinnowitz on the Baltic island of Usedom, which became strongholds of anti-Jewish agitation at an early date. Countless postcards bore captions denigrating Jews as outlandish and as upstarts. (Fig. p. 149) UB

12/22 **Anti-Semitic picture postcard, "Greetings from Borkum. 'He's got to go!'"**
Published by Wolffram und Comp., Borkum/Bremen
Printed by Louis Glaser, Leipzig
c. 1900
Print; 9 x 14 cm
Berlin, Deutsches Historisches Museum: PK 96/407

The words of the "Borkum Song", sung to the tune of the popular "Kaiser March", unequivocally demanded the expulsion and exclusion of Jewish holiday guests. Decades before the National Socialists seized power in 1933, radical anti-Semitism was already being expressed publicly in ways like this, with the aim of making places "Jew-free", regardless of the rule of law. The wide variety of postcards with anti-Semitic texts and images shows that they were obviously in demand and were sent in large numbers by holidaymakers. (Exhibit not shown) UB

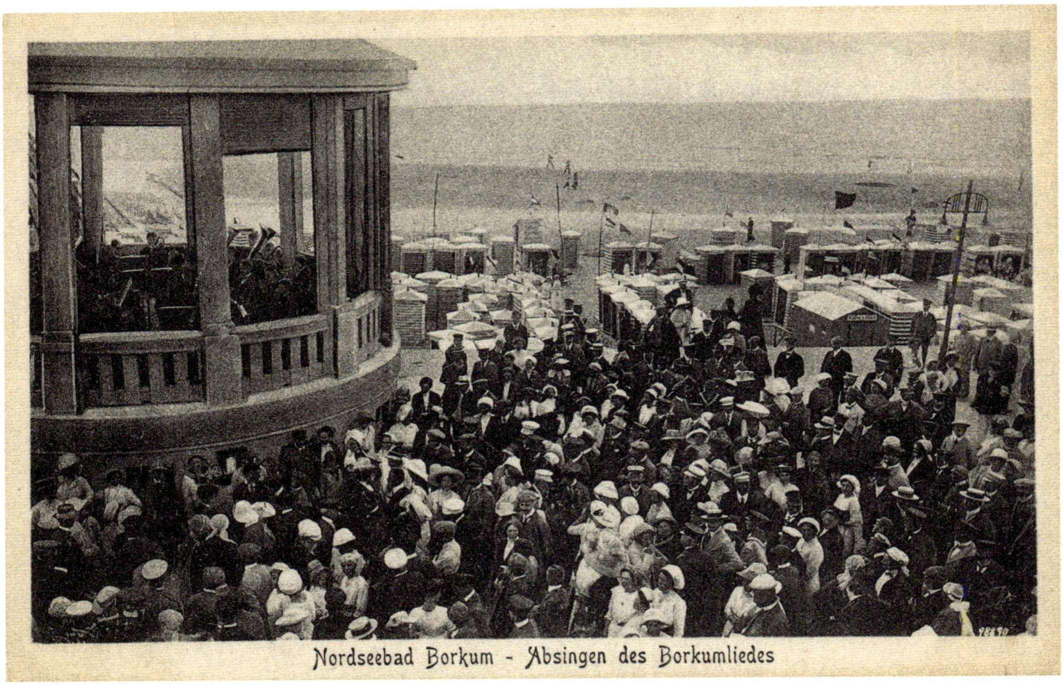

12/23

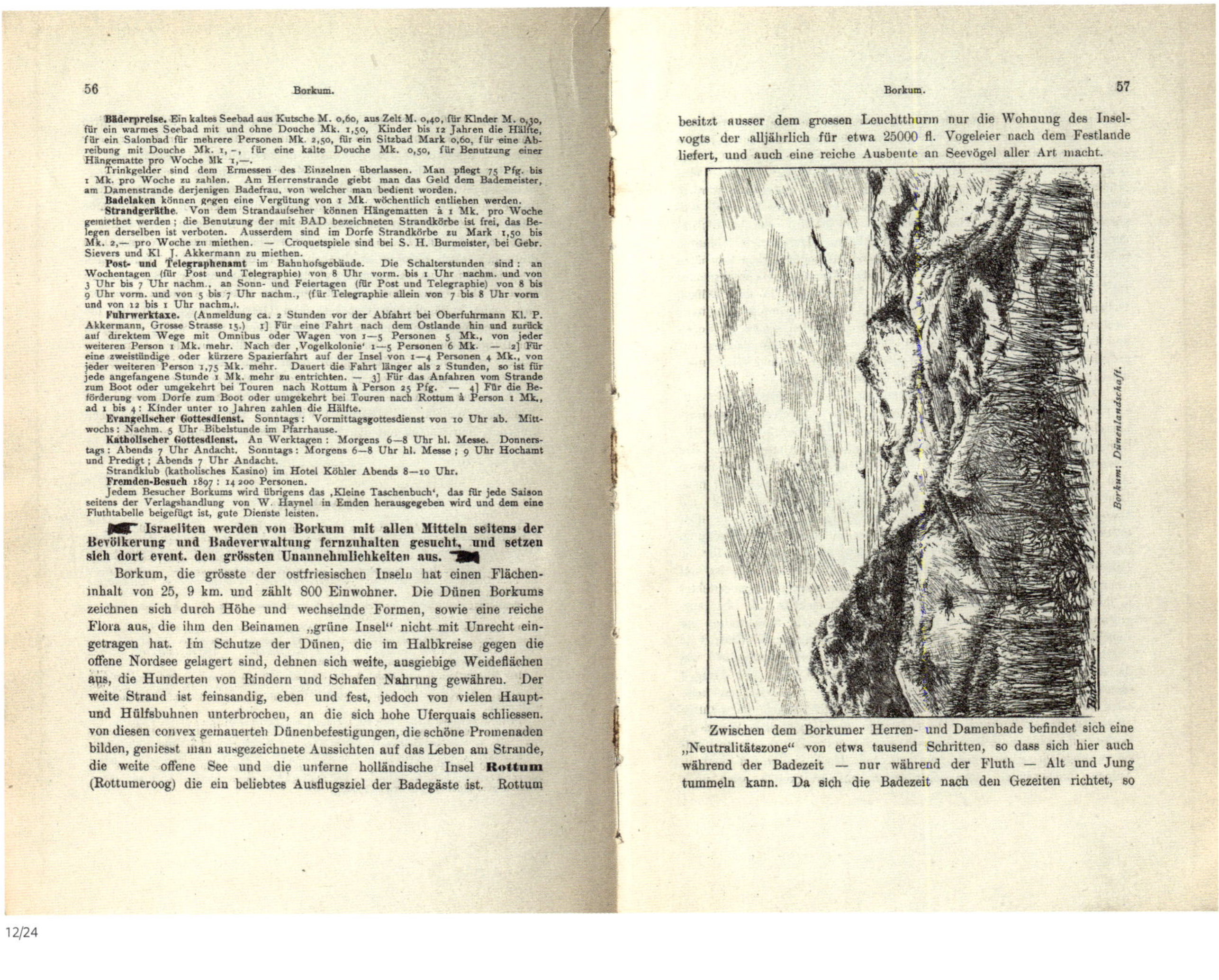

56 Borkum.

Bäderpreise. Ein kaltes Seebad aus Kutsche M. 0,60, aus Zelt M. 0,40, für Kinder M. 0,30, für ein warmes Seebad mit und ohne Douche Mk. 1,50, Kinder bis 12 Jahren die Hälfte, für ein Salonbad für mehrere Personen Mk. 2,50, für ein Sitzbad Mark 0,60, für eine Abreibung mit Douche Mk. 1,–, für eine kalte Douche Mk. 0,50, für Benutzung einer Hängematte pro Woche Mk 1,—.

Trinkgelder sind dem Ermessen des Einzelnen überlassen. Man pflegt 75 Pfg. bis 1 Mk. pro Woche zu zahlen. Am Herrenstrande giebt man das Geld dem Bademeister, am Damenstrande derjenigen Badefrau, von welcher man bedient worden.

Badelaken können gegen eine Vergütung von 1 Mk. wöchentlich entliehen werden.

Strandgeräthe. Von dem Strandaufseher können Hängematten à 1 Mk. pro Woche gemiethet werden; die Benutzung der mit BAD bezeichneten Strandkörbe ist frei, das Belegen derselben ist verboten. Ausserdem sind im Dorfe Strandkörbe zu Mark 1,50 bis Mk. 2,— pro Woche zu miethen. — Croquetspiele sind bei S. H. Burmeister, bei Gebr. Sievers und Kl. J. Akkermann zu miethen.

Post- und Telegraphenamt im Bahnhofsgebäude. Die Schalterstunden sind: an Wochentagen (für Post und Telegraphie) von 8 Uhr vorm. bis 1 Uhr nachm. und von 3 Uhr bis 7 Uhr nachm., an Sonn- und Feiertagen (für Post und Telegraphie) von 8 bis 9 Uhr vorm. und von 5 bis 7 Uhr nachm., (für Telegraphie allein von 7 bis 8 Uhr vorm und von 12 bis 1 Uhr nachm.).

Fuhrwerktaxe. (Anmeldung ca. 2 Stunden vor der Abfahrt bei Oberfuhrmann Kl. P. Akkermann, Grosse Strasse 15.) 1] Für eine Fahrt nach dem Ostlande hin und zurück auf direktem Wege mit Omnibus oder Wagen von 1—5 Personen 5 Mk., von jeder weiteren Person 1 Mk. mehr. Nach der ‚Vogelkolonie' 1—5 Personen 6 Mk. — 2] Für eine zweistündige oder kürzere Spazierfahrt auf der Insel von 1—4 Personen 4 Mk., von jeder weiteren Person 1,75 Mk. mehr. Dauert die Fahrt länger als 2 Stunden, so ist für jede angefangene Stunde 1 Mk. mehr zu entrichten. — 3] Für das Anfahren vom Strande zum Boot oder umgekehrt bei Touren nach Rottum à Person 25 Pfg. — 4] Für die Beförderung vom Dorfe zum Boot oder umgekehrt bei Touren nach Rottum à Person 1 Mk., ad 1 bis 4: Kinder unter 10 Jahren zahlen die Hälfte.

Evangelischer Gottesdienst. Sonntags: Vormittagsgottesdienst von 10 Uhr ab. Mittwochs: Nachm. 5 Uhr Bibelstunde im Pfarrhause.

Katholischer Gottesdienst. An Werktagen: Morgens 6—8 Uhr hl. Messe. Donnerstags: Abends 7 Uhr Andacht. Sonntags: Morgens 6—8 Uhr hl. Messe; 9 Uhr Hochamt und Predigt; Abends 7 Uhr Andacht.

Strandklub (katholisches Kasino) im Hotel Köhler Abends 8—10 Uhr.

Fremden-Besuch 1897: 14 200 Personen.

Jedem Besucher Borkums wird übrigens das ‚Kleine Taschenbuch', das für jede Saison seitens der Verlagshandlung von W. Haynel in Emden herausgegeben wird und dem eine Fluthtabelle beigefügt ist, gute Dienste leisten.

☛ **Israeliten werden von Borkum mit allen Mitteln seitens der Bevölkerung und Badeverwaltung fernzuhalten gesucht, und setzen sich dort event. den grössten Unannehmlichkeiten aus.** ☚

Borkum, die grösste der ostfriesischen Inseln hat einen Flächeninhalt von 25, 9 km. und zählt 800 Einwohner. Die Dünen Borkums zeichnen sich durch Höhe und wechselnde Formen, sowie eine reiche Flora aus, die ihm den Beinamen „grüne Insel" nicht mit Unrecht eingetragen hat. Im Schutze der Dünen, die im Halbkreise gegen die offene Nordsee gelagert sind, dehnen sich weite, ausgiebige Weideflächen aus, die Hunderten von Rindern und Schafen Nahrung gewähren. Der weite Strand ist feinsandig, eben und fest, jedoch von vielen Haupt- und Hülfsbuhnen unterbrochen, an die sich hohe Uferquais schliessen, von diesen convex gemauerten Dünenbefestigungen, die schöne Promenaden bilden, geniesst man ausgezeichnete Aussichten auf das Leben am Strande, die weite offene See und die unferne holländische Insel **Rottum** (Rottumeroog) die ein beliebtes Ausflugziel der Badegäste ist. Rottum

Borkum. 57

besitzt ausser dem grossen Leuchtthurm nur die Wohnung des Inselvogts der alljährlich für etwa 25000 fl. Vogeleier nach dem Festlande liefert, und auch eine reiche Ausbeute an Seevögel aller Art macht.

Borkum: Dünenlandschaft.

Zwischen dem Borkumer Herren- und Damenbade befindet sich eine „Neutralitätszone" von etwa tausend Schritten, so dass sich hier auch während der Badezeit — nur während der Fluth — Alt und Jung tummeln kann. Da sich die Badezeit nach den Gezeiten richtet, so

12/24

12/23 **Anti-Semitic picture postcard, "Borkum North Sea Baths – Singing the Borkum Song"**
Published by Paul Scharphuis, Borkum
c. 1910
Print; 9 x 14 cm
Berlin, Deutsches Historisches Museum: PK 2011/678

The "Borkum Song" was played regularly by the Borkum spa band. In 1908, the prussian Minister of the Interior, Friedrich von Moltke (1852-1927), described the singing of this song as a "gross insult", but at the same time he stated that no legal action could be taken against it. UB

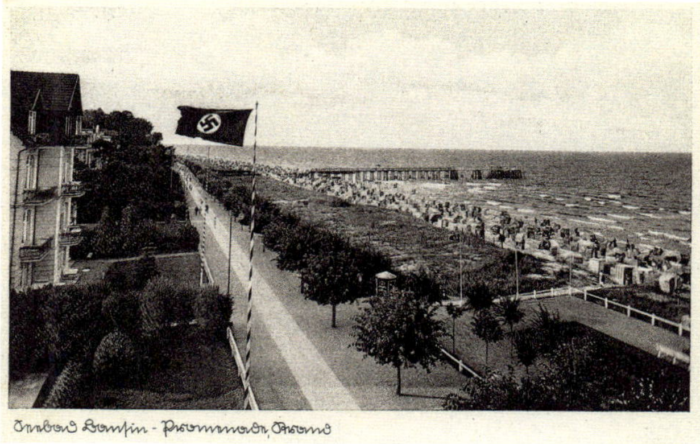

12/27

12/24 ***Deutschland's Seebäder. VII. Die Nordseebäder von der Weser bis Borkum. Illustrirter Reiseführer für Freunde des Seestrandes* (Germany's seaside resorts. VII. The North Sea resorts from the Weser to Borkum. Illustrated travel guide for friends of the sea beach)**
Erwin Volckmann
Published by C. J. E. Volckmann, Rostock 1897
Print; 20 x 13.5 cm
Berlin, Deutsches Historisches Museum: 12/710

Being characterised as "Jew-free" was apparently especially important for the resorts established at a later date. They also emphasised their closeness to nature and supposedly unspoiled character. This, they claimed, was in contrast to the metropolitan luxury of the traditional resorts, which allegedly attracted mainly Jewish holidaymakers. In this travel guide, published in 1897, the information on Borkum contains the following sentence, set in an extra-large, bold font: "Israelites are kept away from Borkum by the population and the spa administration using every means available, and are likely to experience great unpleasantness there." In the section on the North Sea island of Juist, it says "Israelites should stay away from Juist, as they are subject to a surcharge of at least 50 per cent". UB

12/25 **Picture postcard, "Borkum North Sea Baths. Adolf Hitler Beach Promenade"**
1934 (postmark)
Photograph; 9 x 14 cm
Berlin, Deutsches Historisches Museum: w/o inv. no.

Some guests who supported the democratic ideals of the Weimar Republic did lodge protests against anti-Jewish agitation and a few took legal action in the hope of stopping it, but after the Nazis' electoral successes in 1929/30, the situation progressively worsened. Seaside resorts were used with increasing frequency for marches and events run by local branches of the National Socialist party or by Nazi organisations. After the Nazis seized power in 1933, spa administrators and local businessmen demonstrated their support for the new regime by renaming streets and squares and by raising the swastika flag above public institutions and hotels. Legal and administrative restrictions were increasingly placed on Jewish guests – at first in the form of local regulations, and finally in the mandatory exclusion of Jews from bathing and health resorts throughout the country by decree in 1937 and 1938. (Exhibit not shown) UB

12/26 **Picture postcard, "Zinnowitz Baltic Sea Baths. Pier"**
1936 (postmark)
Published by Schöning & Co, Lübeck
Photograph; 9 x 14 cm
Berlin, Deutsches Historisches Museum: w/o inv. no.

In the early days of the Weimar Republic, the anti-Semitic "Borkum Song" spawned many imitations in other resorts on Germany's North and Baltic sea coasts, including a "Zinnowitz Song" with similar content. In 1920, regular guests founded the "Association for Maintaining Zinnowitz Bathing Resort for the Exclusive Use of Spa Guests of German Blood". In 1926, the resort management produced a brochure advertising the "German Baltic Sea Baths of Zinnowitz", in which it declared that "the guests who regularly return to our lovely resort have always made efforts to keep the baths free of Semitic spa guests." Both spa administrators and hotel operators deliberately exploited anti-Semitic attitudes in their advertising with the aim of attracting a certain clientele and setting themselves apart from their competitors. (Exhibit not shown) UB

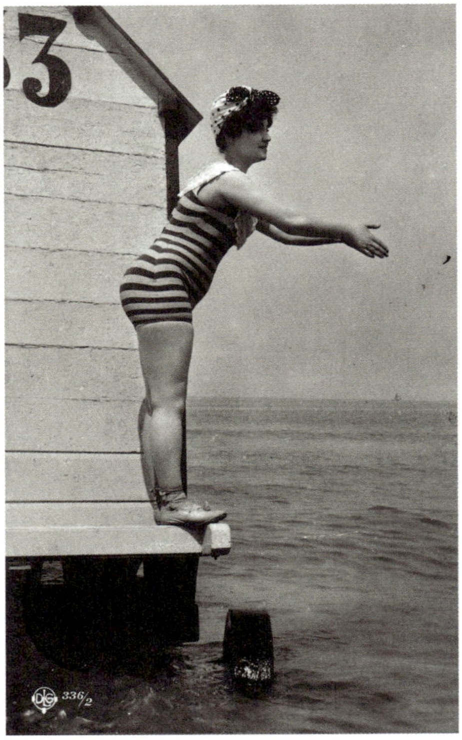

12/28a

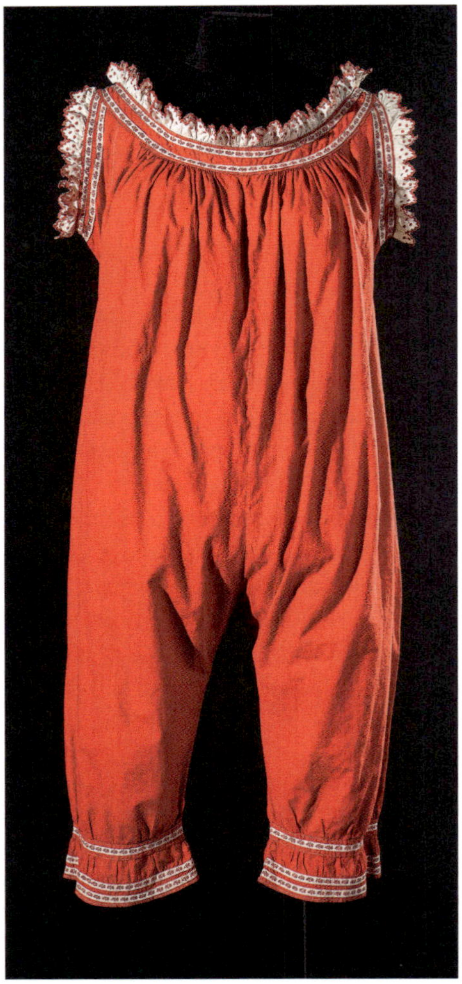

12/29

12/27 **Picture postcard, "Bansin Sea Baths. Promenade, beach life on the pier"**
1939 (postmark)
Published by Schöning & Co, Lübeck
Photograph; 9 x 14 cm
Berlin, Deutsches Historisches Museum: w/o inv. no.

Bansin Baltic Sea Baths was categorised as anti-Semitic in 1914 by the Central Association of German Citizens of the Jewish Faith. In 1939, displaying swastika flags in the way shown on the postcard was part of daily life. Anti-Semitism at seaside resorts was not, however, solely a German phenomenon; it also occurred in other places such as Austria and the countries of Eastern Europe. In the United States, anti-Semitism had also become established among hotel owners from about 1870 onwards – the same period as in Germany. This discrimination was mainly aimed at Jewish immigrants from Germany. (Fig. p. 401) UB

From Cure to Pleasure Principle: The Beach as a New Experience and Leisure Space

12/28 **Three greetings cards with women in swimwear**
Photographs; each approx. 13 x 9 cm
Berlin, Deutsches Historisches Museum: PK 92/25.61, PK 92/17.897, PK 92/17.893

Over the course of time, the original purpose of bathing in the sea – to cure illnesses – faded into the background. People went there rather to socialise and relax in a pleasant environment. While at the beach, bathers could rid themselves of the restrictive and unwieldy clothing of the time and enjoy tantalising glimpses of more or less scantily clothed members of the opposite sex outside the limits of their own four walls. The beach became a place for erotically charged communication. This too left its mark in the media of the day, specifically the picture postcard. Countless postcard series from the late nineteenth and early twentieth centuries feature young ladies posing in swimwear, clad as skimpily as the current fashion allowed – the forerunners of the pin-up girl. UB

12/28a **Woman on a bathing machine**
1908 (postmark)

12/28b **Three women on a bathing machine, "Nos Baigneuses"**
Brussels, c. 1920 (Exhibit not shown)

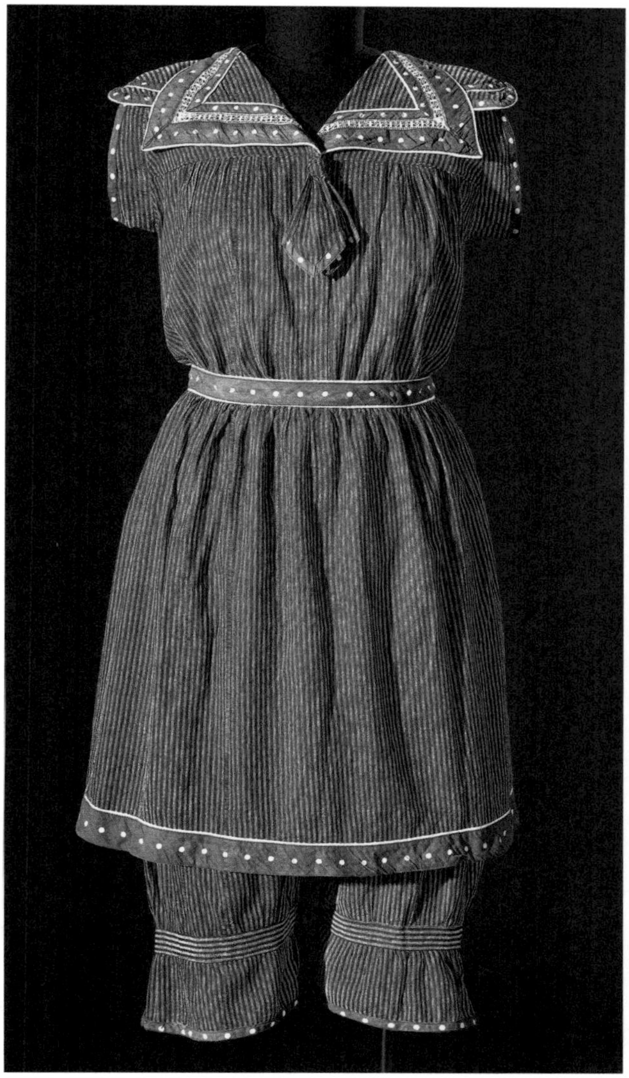

12/30

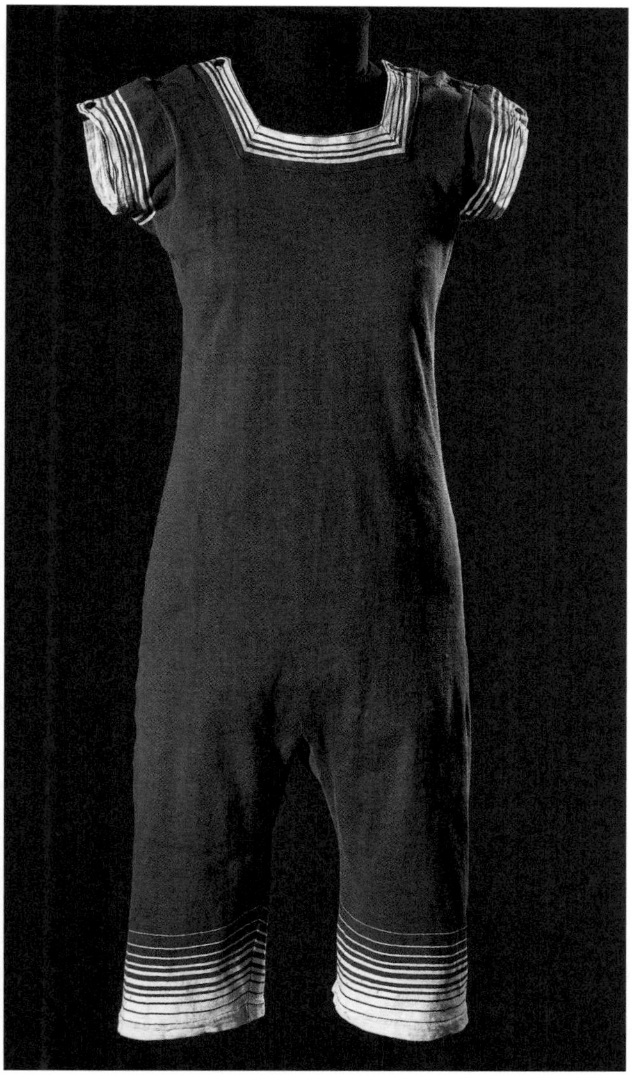

12/31

12/28c **Woman in a bathing suit, "Nos Baigneuses"**
Brussels, c. 1920 (Exhibit not shown)

12/29 **Bathing costume for women**
c. 1900
Cotton, plain weave, machine-made lace; L 106 cm
Berlin, Deutsches Historisches Museum: 1991/399

Purpose-made swimwear and beachwear did not emerge until the middle of the nineteenth century. Whereas the beach dress, which a lady would wear when strolling along the promenade or the beach, reflected the current fashion, her actual bathing costume needed to have a more functional character, so it was based on the underwear worn at the time. For going into the water, women put on leggings that went down over their calves or knees, overlapped by a short-sleeved top with lace trimming, with or without a collar. The most common colours were red and blue. Imitations of sailor uniforms were especially popular, in particular for children's swimwear. UB

12/30 **Two-piece swimsuit for women (bodysuit and skirt)**
1907
Cotton, plain and twill weave, cutwork lace, mother-of-pearl buttons; suit, L 118 cm; skirt, L 55 cm
Berlin, Deutsches Historisches Museum: KTe 80/64

Although swimwear initially covered much of the body, wearing such a thing in public was a whole new experience for its owners, male and female. In order to maintain the "order and morality" required by the authorities, women and men bathed on strictly separated sections of the beach. In addition, bathing machines and beach chairs screened them from prying eyes. This gender segregation continued for some years into the twentieth century. In Prussia, the state government legalised the establishment of mixed-sex family baths in 1902; the first of these was opened in Westerland on Sylt. UB

12/31 **Bathing suit for women**
1917/1920
Cotton, machine knitwear; L 110 cm
Berlin, Deutsches Historisches Museum: KTe 74/261

Tight-fitting tricot fabrics did not make their breakthrough as material for bathing suits until the 1920s; they were long considered improper as they revealed the body's contours. The demand for more functional swimwear came mostly from men and women involved in competitive swimming. Yet on 28 September 1932, the Prussian Ministry of the Interior introduced specifications for bathing suits in its much-ridiculed 'gusset decree'. After that, women were allowed to bathe in public only if they wore a bathing suit that completely covered the chest and torso at the front and continued some way down the legs with a gusset. The back was not to be cut deeper than the lower end of the shoulder blades. Nude bathing in public was forbidden entirely. (Fig. p. 403) UB

12/32 **Swimsuit for men**
c. 1920
Cotton, machine knitwear; L 135 cm
Berlin, Deutsches Historisches Museum: 1990/1911

One-piece swimsuits for men came in around 1900. For the most part, they were striped and made of tricot fabric, which was apparently not considered improper for men. However, these fabrics became very heavy when wet and took a long time to dry. Men did not generally wear short bathing trunks in public bathing establishments until the 1920s. (Exhibit not shown) UB

12/33 **Bikini top and bottom**
c. 1949
Wool, machine knitwear, embroidered, elastic band; 14 x 40 cm and 46 x 30 cm
Berlin, Deutsches Historisches Museum: KT 2000/46.1–2

Two-piece swimwear for women was already being worn by some naturists at the turn of the century, but it did not appear on public beaches until the mid-1920s in the United States (where it was called the Palm Beach Combination) and the 1930s in Germany. As people became used to showing more of their bodies, sunbathing grew in popularity. A healthy tan replaced a pale, refined complexion as the traditional ideal of beauty. Bathing suits were being cut out ever more generously at the front and back, with shorter legs. The bikini is said to have been invented by a Frenchman, Louis Réard (1897–1984), who on 5 July 1946, presented to the Parisian public a revealing two-piece, with a striptease dancer as the model. Réard was well aware of the explosive effect of this garment on notions of public decency, so he named it after the Pacific atoll of Bikini, where atomic bomb tests had been carried out a few days earlier. (Exhibit not shown) UB

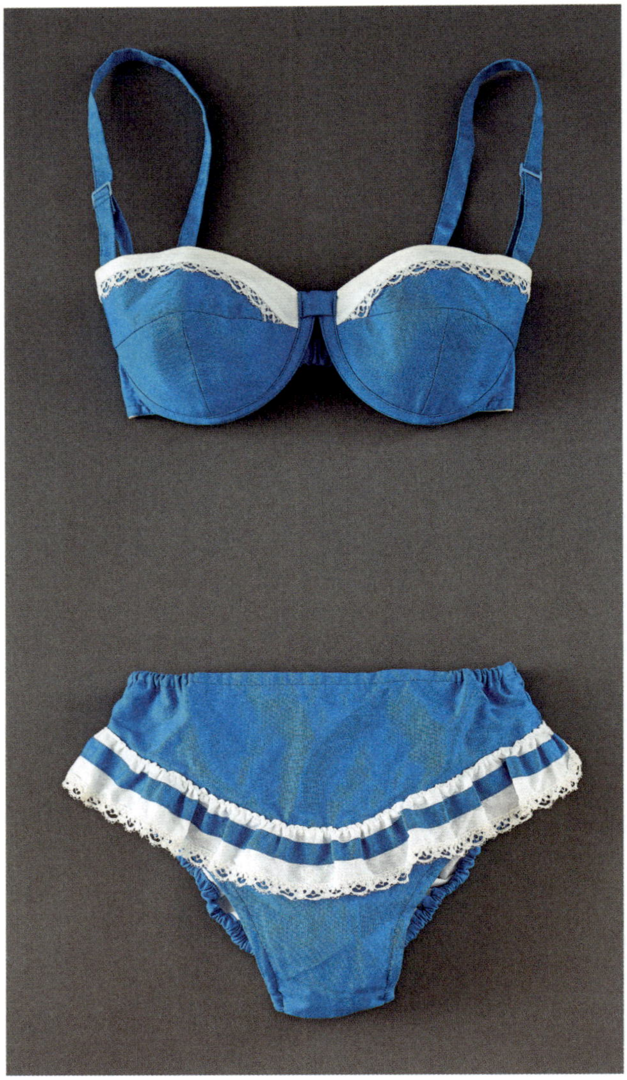

12/34

12/34 **Bikini of the "felina" brand**
1970s
Cotton fabric, plain weave, machine-made lace, elastic band; 40 x 47 cm
Berlin, Deutsches Historisches Museum:
KT 2005/136.1–2

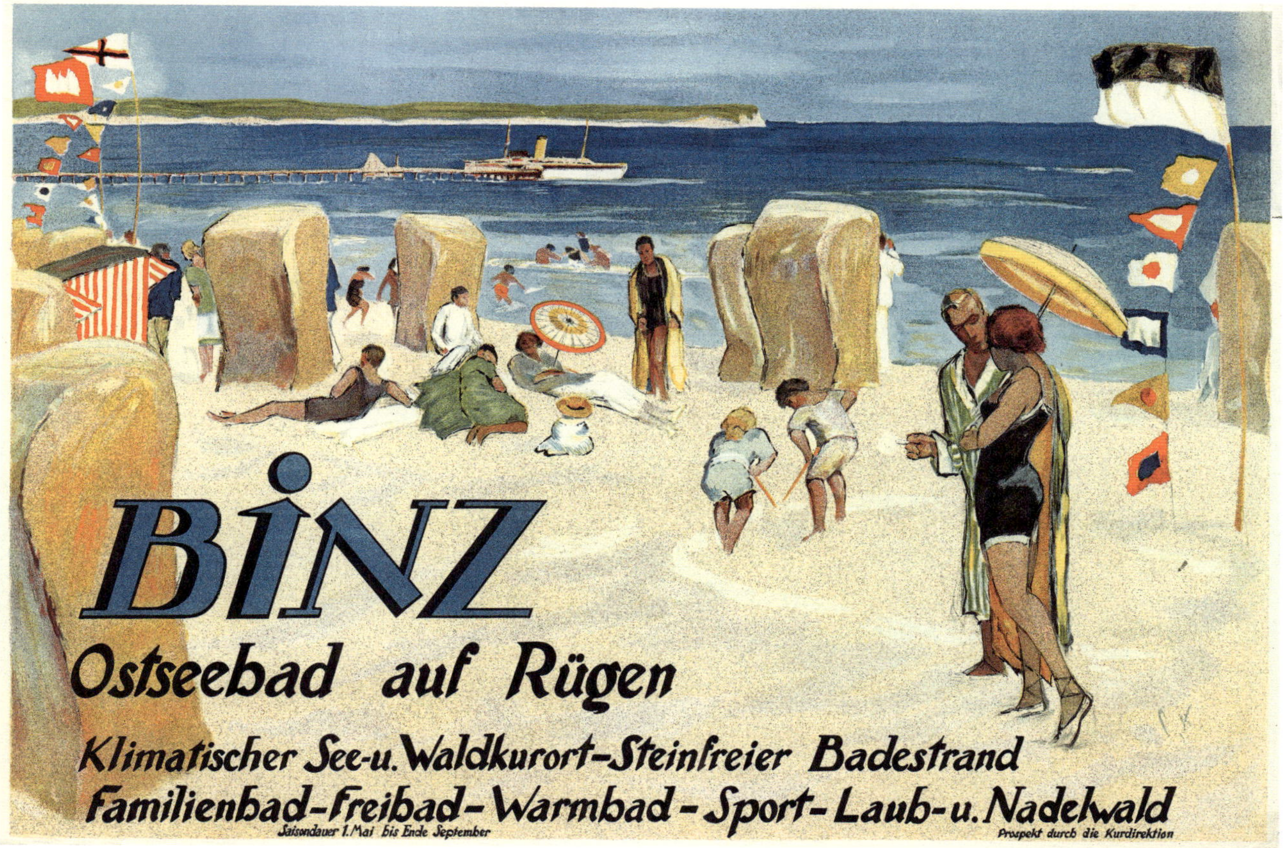

12/35

The production of swimwear soon became an important branch of business for the traditional corsetry industry. The brand name "felina" on the textile label of this bikini harks back to that of a novel brassiere introduced in 1915 by Herbst, a German bodice and corset-manufacturer based in Mannheim. Later on, "felina" was adopted as the company's name, continuing as such up to today. The turquoise-coloured bikini has underwire support and shaped cups. It also features removable straps, which was a strong selling point with sunbathers who wanted to avoid getting tan lines. UB

12/35 **Advertising poster, "Binz – Baltic Sea Baths on Rügen"**
1927/28
Lithograph; 60 x 90.2 cm
Berlin, Deutsches Historisches Museum: P 90/10403

The one-time village of Binz on the Baltic island of Rügen was officially recognised as a seaside resort in 1884. Sea bathing facilities and the first hotel buildings had appeared in the decades before that. From 1895 onwards, Binz also had a beach promenade and was served by a narrow-gauge railway. In 1900, the Spa House was opened, followed two years later by a pier almost 600 metres long. Men and women bathed on different sections of the beach with separate facilities. Around 1925, the spa administrators demolished the bathing establishments and lifted the sea bathing restrictions, as most places were doing at the time. This brightly coloured poster dates from this time. With the pier of Binz in the background, holidaymakers of all ages and both sexes mingle on the beach, bathing, relaxing and playing in the sand. UB

12/36 **Advertising poster, "Zingst – Baltic Sea Baths on the Darss"**
Design: Haberg
Printed by Hollerbaum und Schmidt
Berlin, 1927/28
Lithograph; 67.2 x 45 cm
Berlin, Deutsches Historisches Museum: P 74/2065

In 1881, an innkeeper and a ship's captain founded the first "baths committee" for promoting tourism in the seamen's and fishermen's village of Zingst on the Baltic Sea. In the same year, separate bathing facilities for men and women were installed on the spacious beach. After a railway line opened, allowing Zingst to be reached from Berlin in around five hours, the number of visitors grew rapidly. As in Binz, the segregated bathing establishments were demolished in

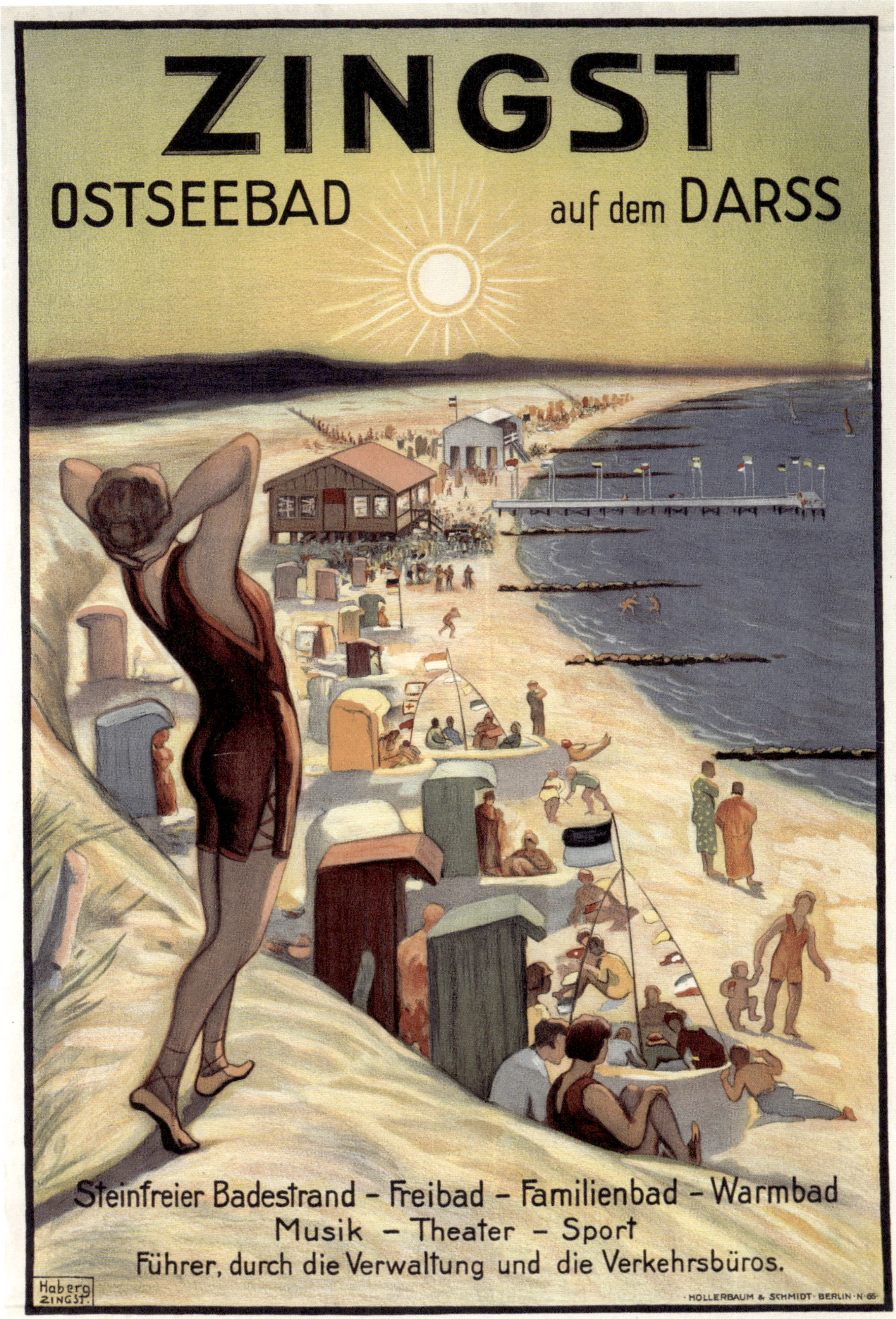
ZINGST
OSTSEEBAD auf dem DARSS
Steinfreier Badestrand - Freibad - Familienbad - Warmbad
Musik - Theater - Sport
Führer, durch die Verwaltung und die Verkehrsbüros.
Haberg ZINGST
HOLLERBAUM & SCHMIDT · BERLIN · N · 65

12/36

the mid-1920s to make way for mixed bathing. The woman standing in the foreground of the poster, stretching to soak up the sunshine, is reminiscent of figures by the painter known as Fidus (Hugo Höppener, 1868–1948), whose work strongly influenced the imagery of a new cult of the body and various 'back to nature' movements. (Fig. p. 406) UB

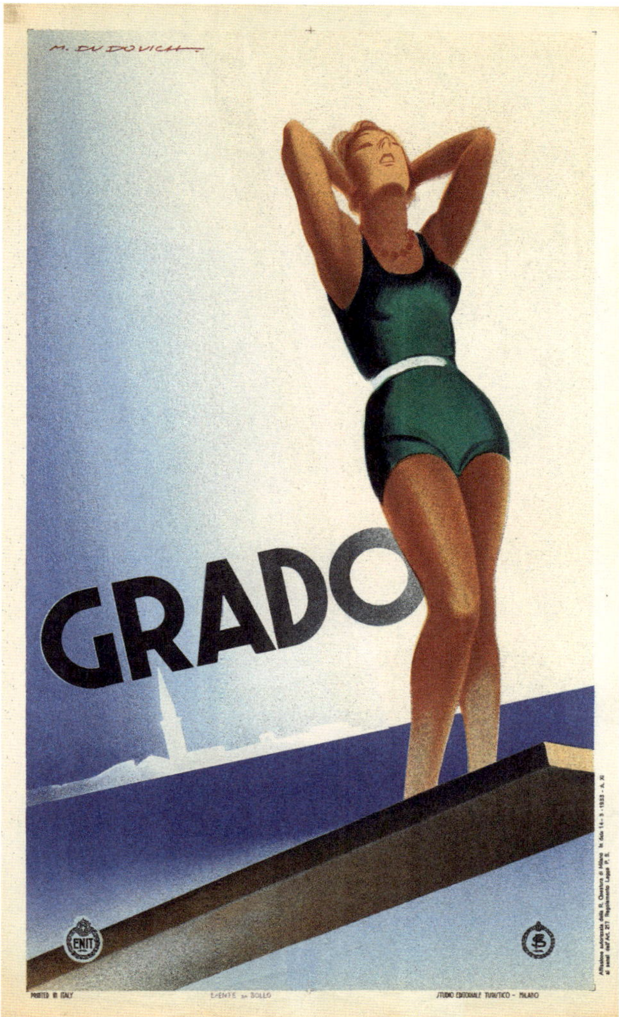

12/37

12/37 **Advertising poster for the Italian seaside resort of Grado**
Design: Marcello Dudovich (1878–1962)
Published by ENIT (Italian National Agency for Tourism)
Printed by Studio Editoriale Turistico
Milan, 1933
Lithograph; 100 x 62 cm
Berlin, Deutsches Historisches Museum: P 90/10122

Spa administrators often commisioned posters from well-known commercial illustrators and artists, as did the tourism boards that were then being created at a regional – and later a national – level. Marcello Dudovich, a native of Trieste, was one of Italy's best-known illustrators. As well as work for magazines such as the German satirical weekly *Simplicissimus*, he created over 600 posters. Many of them featured high society and a luxurious lifestyle. He was often commissioned to produce posters advertising fashionable resorts. The attractions of Grado on the Adriatic Sea are evoked here by a woman in the pose of a pin-up model. At first, Dudovich was influenced by the gentle, ornamental forms of Art Nouveau, but he later drew inspiration from Expressionism, which is evident here in the sharp contours and asymmetrical composition. UB

Holidays at Sea: The Cruise

12/38 **Advertising poster for "Hapag Mediterranean and Oriental Voyages ..." on the steamers Oceana and Reliance**
Design: Lohmann
Printed by Gustav Petermann
Hamburg, 1927
Rotogravure print; 84.5 x 60.2 cm
Berlin, Deutsches Historisches Museum: P 73/3785

From the 1840s onwards, sailing ships were replaced gradually by steam-powered ships and, later, motor ships. The liners on the transatlantic crossing now ran to fixed timetables. Competition between the shipping companies grew more intense; the ships became faster and their interior furnishings more comfortable. As the number of emigrants booking

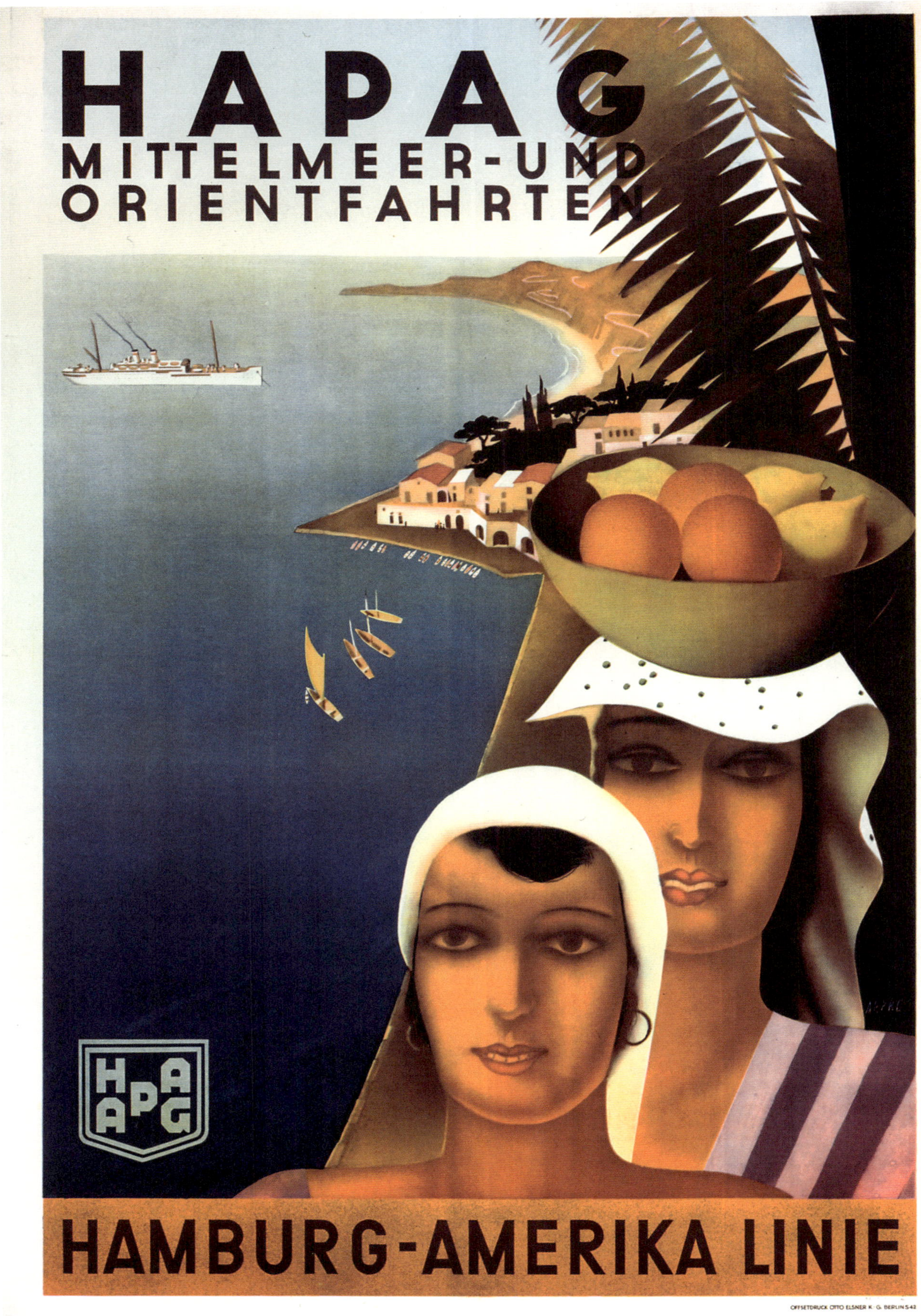
HAPAG
MITTELMEER-UND
ORIENTFAHRTEN
HAPAG
HAMBURG-AMERIKA LINIE
OFFSETDRUCK OTTO ELSNER K.-G. BERLIN S42

12/39

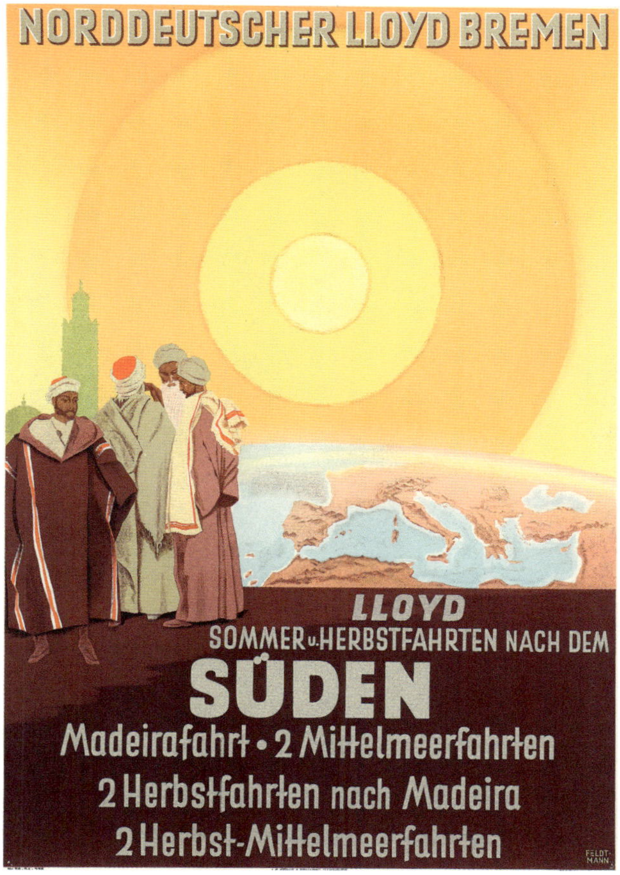

12/40

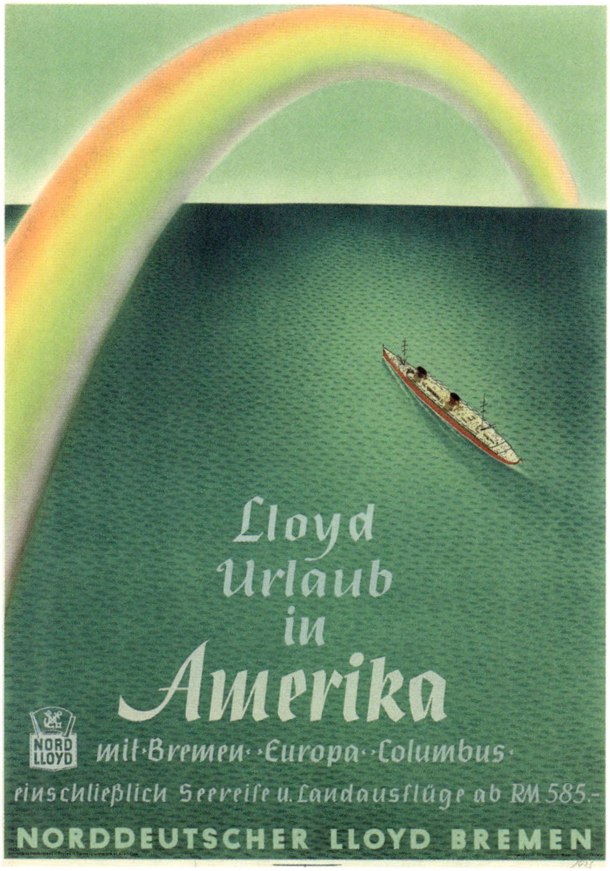

12/41

passages usually dropped sharply in the autumn and winter months, the ships needed to be utilised in other ways. Albert Ballin (1857–1918), the general director of Hamburg-American Packetfahrt-Actien-Gesellschaft (Hapag / Hamburg America Line), founded in 1847, had the idea of offering long boat trips and marketing them as pleasure cruises. The Hapag poster shown here uses a collage of easily recognised motifs from the countries on the itinerary: Greek columns dominate the left half of the picture – presumably the Acropolis – while smoke rises from Vesuvius in the background. (Exhibit not shown) UB

12/39 **Advertising poster for "Hapag Mediterranean and Oriental Voyages ..."**
Design: Otto Arpke (1886–1943)
Printed by Otto Elsner
Berlin, 1933
Offset print; 120 x 84 cm
Berlin, Deutsches Historisches Museum: P 73/3785

The first cruise to begin at a German port departed from Cuxhaven in 1891. With 255 passengers on board, the Augusta Victoria steamed via Southampton and Gibraltar into the Mediterranean as far as Alexandria, and from there to Constantinople. Billed as an "Oriental journey", the success of this innovation led to cruises in the Mediterranean – and later in the North Sea and the Caribbean – being offered every winter by the two main shipping companies: Hapag and its main competitor, Norddeutscher Lloyd (NDL), founded in 1858. Another Hapag poster likewise aims to arouse yearnings for faraway, exotic lands: the portrayal of women, fruit and foliage against a deep blue sea fading into the horizon seems to promise a paradise on earth. UB

12/40 **Advertising poster for "Lloyd Summer/Autumn Trips to the South ..."**
Design: Hugo Feldtmann (1900–1990)
Printed by J. C. König und Eberhardt
Hannover, 1936
Lithograph; 83.7 x 59.8 cm
Berlin, Deutsches Historisches Museum: P 74/2196

In the 1920s and 1930s, Norddeutscher Lloyd (North German Lloyd) took steps to make its advertising campaigns more professional, although they were still far from using standard imagery in the sense of a corporate identity. They were run by a so-called "propaganda department" with a permanent staff of graphic artists, including Hugo Feldt-

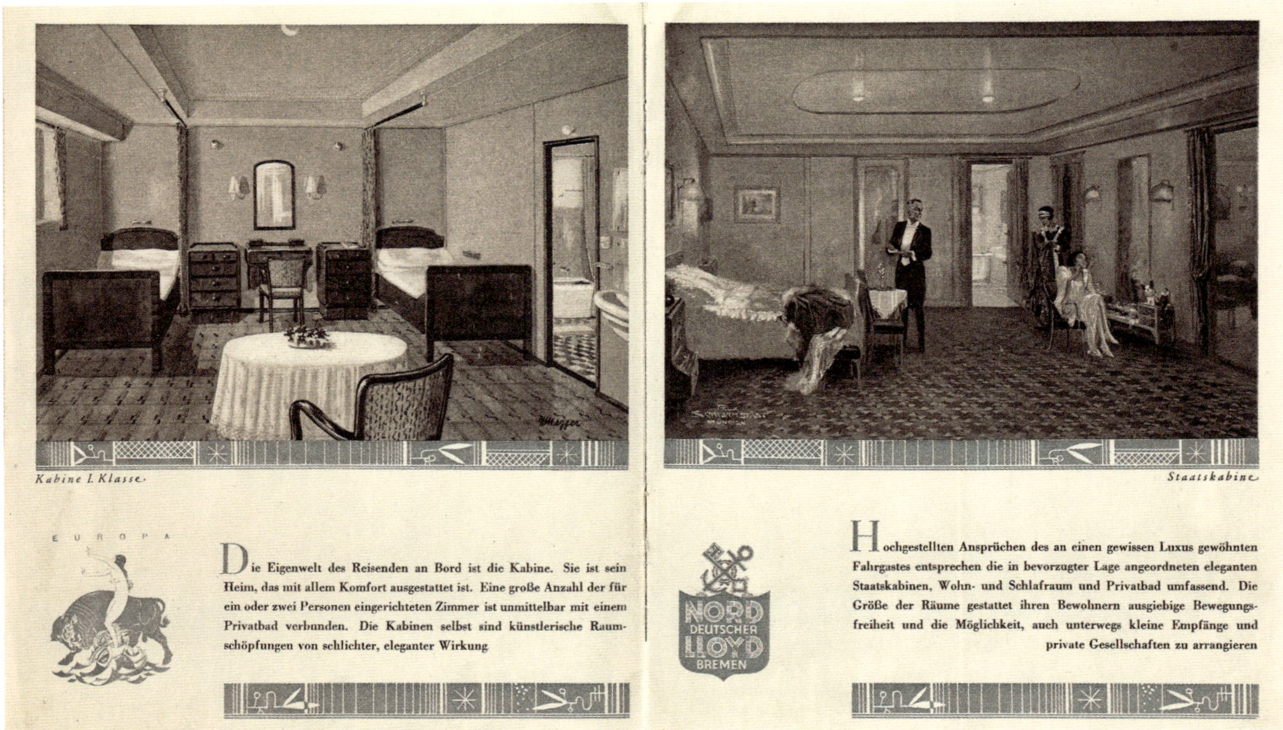

12/42

mann. His poster design is dominated by the concentric circles of a huge sun occupying the upper half of the picture. In the middle is a map of the Mediterranean Sea and the countries that border on it, flanked on the left by four men whose clothing and skin colour are stereotypically North African. The warm tones and the emphasis placed on the word *Süden* (south) announce that this is less about a particular destination than about a region associated with exciting novelty and a pleasant, if hot, climate. UB

12/41 **Advertising poster for "Lloyd holiday in America ..."**
Printed by Aktiengesellschaft für Kunstdruck
Niedersedlitz bei Dresden, 1936
Offset print; 86.3 x 59.7 cm
Berlin, Deutsches Historisches Museum: P 74/2194

This poster for Norddeutscher Lloyd advertises its three transatlantic steamers: BREMEN, EUROPA and COLUMBUS. However, the ship heading towards the horizon is not really given prime of place. Instead, the predominant element is the seemingly endless expanse of the ocean. Here, it is no longer threatening but calm, even tamed. The surface of the water is as smooth as a mirror, glowing in harmonious shades of green; the sea and the sky are spanned from here to the horizon by a rainbow, the Christian symbol of the reconciliation of heaven and earth and a sign of hope. (Fig. p. 409) UB

12/42 **Travel brochure for the express steamer EUROPA**
Published by Norddeutscher Lloyd, Bremen
Printed by Schünemann Tiefdruck
Bremen, 1928
Paper, cardboard, print; 23.6 x 20.1 cm
Berlin, Deutsches Historisches Museum: 09/869

The EUROPA was the flagship of NDL in the early 1930s, together with the BREMEN. With luxurious furnishings for the first class passengers, it was one of the preferred vessels for making the transatlantic crossing, especially among wealthy Americans. Like her sister ship the BREMEN, the EUROPA was rarely used for cruises after 1936. The usual destinations of these voyages were the Caribbean Sea, the islands of the West Indies, and Bermuda. When serving on

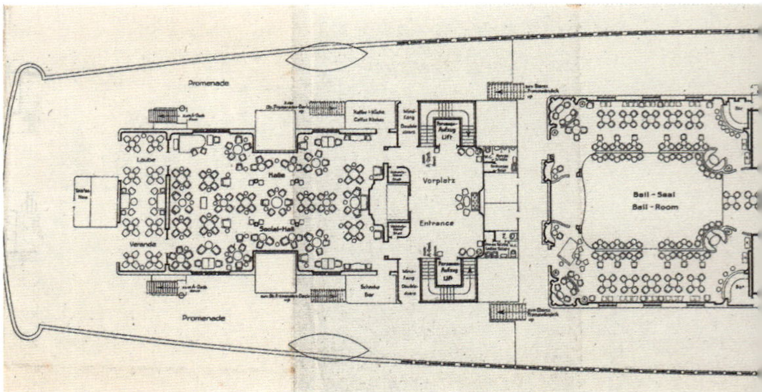

12/44

the transatlantic route, the ship could carry a good 2,000 passengers in 870 cabins. These were divided into four classes with very different standards of furnishing. On cruises to the tropics, it took only 600 passengers, who were accommodated in the outer cabins, which greatly increased the level of comfort, but also the prices. MM

12/43 **Brochure advertising the steamer Columbus**
Published by Norddeutscher Lloyd, Bremen
Bremen, 1924
Paper, cardboard, linen; 25.6 x 21 cm
Berlin, Sammlung Miller

The Columbus served on the North Atlantic route from 1924 until 1927, when she set out on her first four-week cruise trip, from New York to the West Indies. After NDL commissioned two new express steamers, Bremen and Europe, the Columbus was used for many cruises in different parts of the world. Her last cruise was ended early in Havana on 26 August 1939, in preparation for war. The luxuriously equipped ship offered its 419 first-class passengers a multitude of magnificent lounges, whose architecture and furnishings resembled those of the saloons and halls of grand hotels. They were created as a cooperative venture by the architect Paul Ludwig Troost (1878–1934) and the Deutscher Werkbund. (Exhibit not shown) MM

12/44 **"Kajütenplan / Cabin Plan" by Norddeutscher Lloyd of "Vierschrauben-Turb. Schnelldampfer / Quadr. Screw Turb. Express Steamer Bremen"**
Published by Norddeutscher Lloyd, Bremen
Bremen, after 5 July 1929
Paper, cardboard; 27 x 15 (unfolded, up to 143)
Berlin, Sammlung Miller

Delivered to NDL in 1929, the Bremen represents the modernisation of German passenger ships in several ways. On her maiden voyage, she beat the record set twenty years earlier by the Mauretania for the fastest crossing of the Atlantic and thus held the Blue Riband. With two relatively short chimneys and sophisticated interiors, she also became an icon of Modernist design. Moving the position of the boilers' smoke flues towards the sides of the ship made it possible for the interior designer, Fritz August Breuhaus de Groot (1883–1960), to create a 160-metre-long suite of luxurious lounges on the main promenade deck. Because of her high speed, the Bremen was operated almost exclusively in scheduled liner service. Her only major cruise, in 1939, took her from New York around South America, in the course of which she became the largest ship to pass through the Panama Canal up to that time. MM

12/45 **Advertising poster of the Hamburg-Südamerikanische Dampfschifffahrts-Gesellschaft (Hamburg-South American Steamship Company) for "exceptionally inexpensive Nordic voyages in summer 1928"**
Printed by Gerhard Stalling AG, Oldenburg
Hamburg, 1928
Offset print; 72.3 x 49.8 cm
Berlin, Deutsches Historisches Museum: P 57/1073

Kaiser Wilhelm II (1859–1941) of Germany blazed a trail for cruises to the Norwegian Sea. From 1889 up to the First World War in 1914, he went on 26 voyages to this part of the Arctic Ocean on his yacht Hohenzollern. The inaccessible fjord landscapes, rising steeply from the sea, had already been discovered as a tourist attraction by the English around 1830. Wilhelm II saw the lands of the north as the "cradle of the Teutons". Despite his conservative attitudes, the emperor was interested in research on his trips to the Norwegian Sea, taking with him not only marine painters, but also oceanographers and meteorologists. After the First World War, the Nordic cruise business continued to expand, with the lion's share in the hands of three companies: NDL,

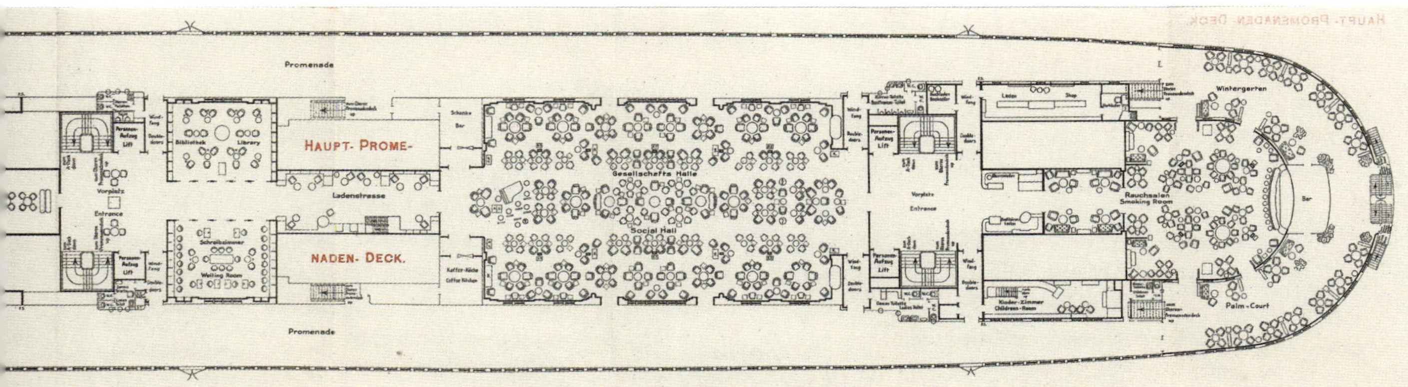

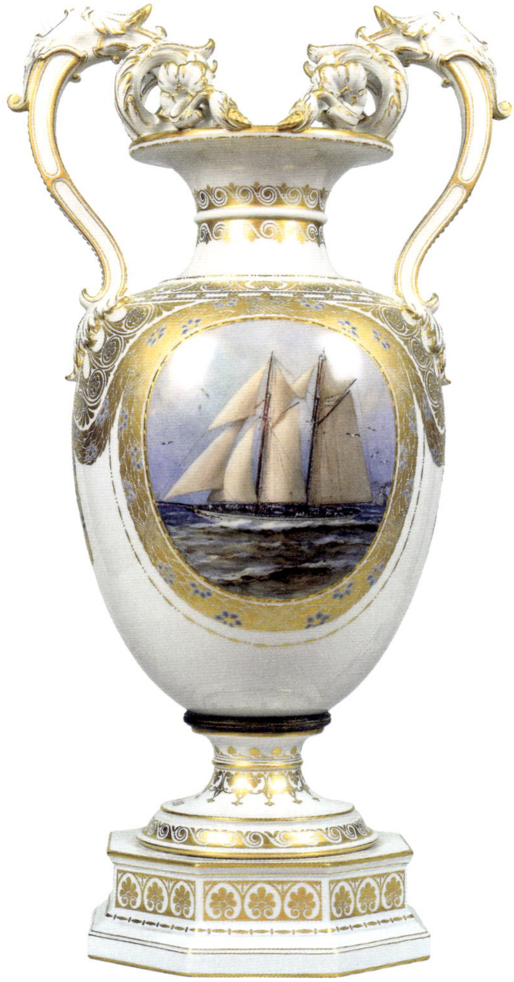

12/46

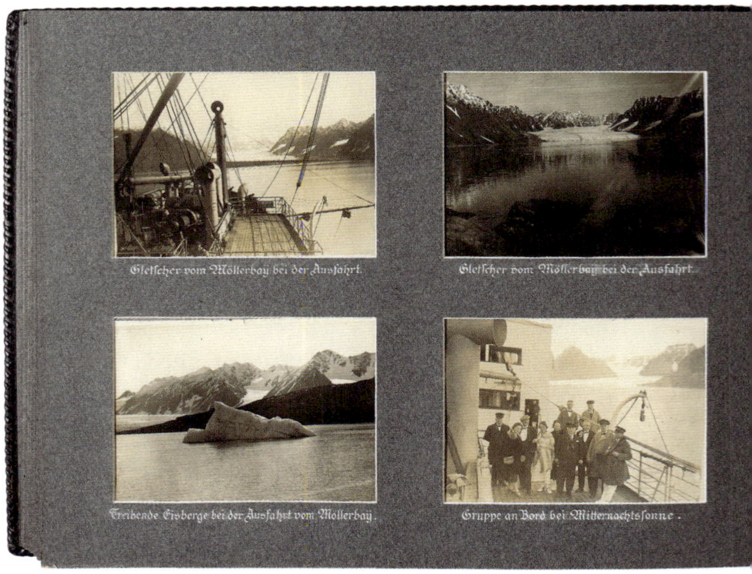

12/47

Hamburg-Süd and Hapag. For the National Socialists, Norway symbolised the "Nordic-Germanic" character. This made it an ideologically valuable destination, so it was included in the travel programme of the Nazi leisure organisation, "Kraft durch Freude". (Fig. p. 147) UB

12/46 **Amphora vase as a prize for Cowes Week**
Königliche Porzellan-Manufaktur (KPM)
Berlin, 1914
Porcelain, white body, polychrome painting, gold decor; inscribed on pedestal: COWES 1914; H 61 cm, diam. 23 cm
Bremerhaven, Deutsches Schiffahrtsmuseum – Leibniz-Institut für deutsche Schifffahrtsgeschichte: I/01495/77

Shown on the vase are the Kaiser's own yachts: on one side is the Hohenzollern, with which Wilhelm II (1859–1941) went on his Nordic voyages, and on the other side is his racing yacht, Meteor IV. He commissioned the vase in 1914 as a prize to be presented at Cowes Week, an annual sailing regatta based on the Isle of Wight in southern England. The vase was never awarded, however. The regatta had to be cancelled because the First World War had just begun. UB

12/47 **Photo album, "Polar cruise in 1925 on the steamer München from 17 July to 12 August"**
Richard Fleischhut (1881–1959)
1928
Leather cover with gold embossing, photographs glued to cardboard; 35 x 48 cm
Berlin, Deutsches Historisches Museum: Ph 2012/141

Richard Fleischhut worked as a ship's photographer for Norddeutscher Lloyd. In the summer of 1914, shortly before the First World War, he got his first cruise assignment, to the North Cape. Not until 1925 was he sent to the Arctic again, this time on the NDL steamer Munich . In this album, he has recorded every stage of the voyage, offering glimpses of life aboard a cruise ship. On-board photographers were part of the service. They took pictures of the sea, the ship and the destinations. They would also take professional portraits and group pictures of the cruise passengers. The prints were

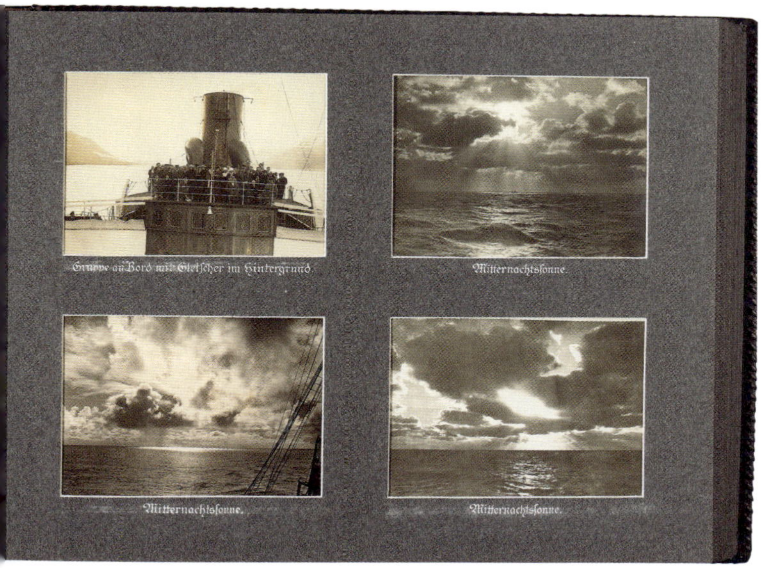

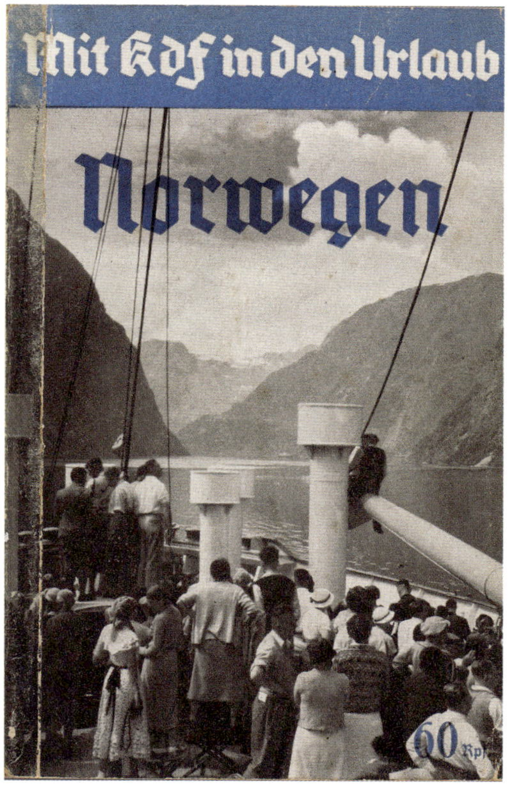

12/49

offered for sale to the customers, while the shipping company could use the images for advertising. UB

"Volk zu Schiff" and "Seebad der Zwanzigtausend" – Holidays under National Socialism

12/48 **Menu from the 58th "Kraft durch Freude" tour to Norway on the Monte Olivia, dated 13 June 1937**
Cover illustration: Adolf Bock (1890–1968)
Print; 18.8 x 13.6 cm
Berlin, Deutsches Historisches Museum: Do2 91/1795.6

The National Socialists used the exclusive image of the cruise as propaganda for "Kraft durch Freude" (Strength through Joy), a sub-division of the Deutsche Arbeitsfront (German Labour Front). They made it the centrepiece of the organisation's leisure programme. "Cruises for all" was the deliberately sensational slogan devised to impress not only the population of Germany, but also international public opinion. The aim was to add substance to the ideology of the *Volksgemeinschaft*, a racially homogeneous national community which the Nazis claimed would eliminate class distinctions and make class privileges irrelevant. To this end, ships were chartered, purchased and, finally, built. The Monte Olivia was a motor ship belonging to the Hamburg Südamerikanische Dampfschifffahrts-Gesellschaft, which had been launched in 1924 and which the shipping company used for cruises to the far north, among other places. In 1934 it was chartered for the first time by the KdF for a trip to Norway. (Exhibit not shown) UB

12/49 **Travel guide, "On holiday with KdF. Norway", issue no. 1**
Herbert Leisegang, Fritz-Otto Busch (1890–1971)
Wehrverlag Joseph Bercker
Berlin, 1937
Paper, cardboard; 17.2 x 11.5 cm
Berlin, Deutsches Historisches Museum: G 1939

The small travel guide for KdF trips to Norway provides useful advice for the voyage, but it is permeated by National

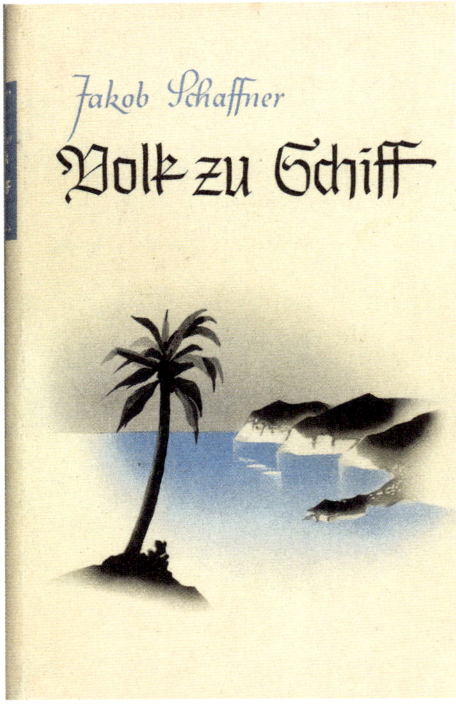

12/50

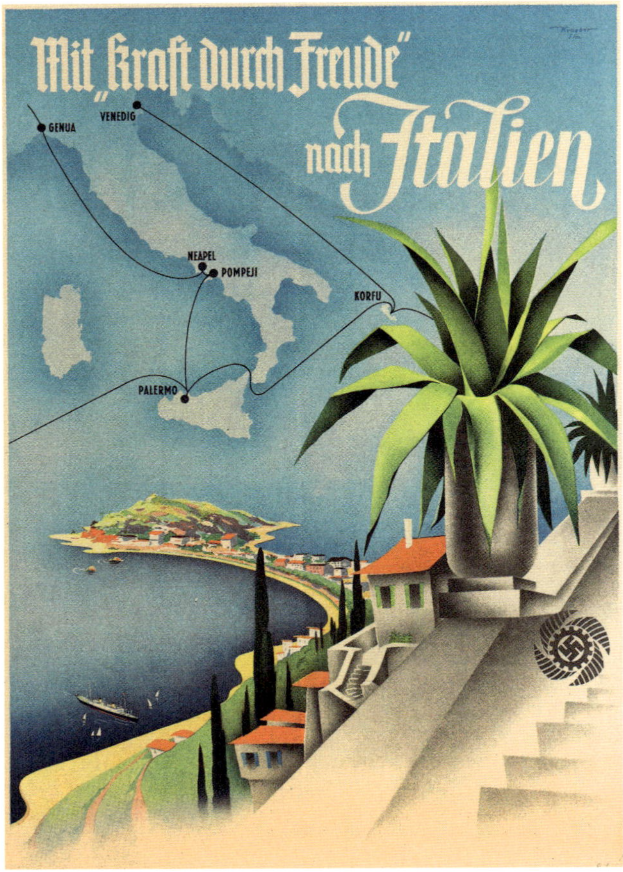

12/51

Socialist doctrine. For instance, as well tips on dealing with seasickness and choosing the right clothing to wear on board, it describes the course of the naval battle of Jutland in 1916 and depicts the silhouettes of German warships that passengers might see practising military manoeuvres during the course of the trip. It also provides the music and lyrics of the "Song of the Norway Voyagers", which Heinz Friedrich Hartig (1907–1969) had composed on board a KdF ship in 1936. The Norway cruises were mostly five or six days long, but the passengers did not go ashore anywhere. It is thought that this was due to a wish to save time and to limit the outflow of currency from Germany. (Fig. p. 413) MM

12/50 **Travelogue, "Volk zu Schiff. Zwei Seefahrten mit der KdF-Hochseeflotte" (Nation Aboard. Two sea voyages with the KdF High Seas Fleet)**
Jakob Schaffner (1875–1944)
Hanseatische Verlagsanstalt
Hamburg, 1936
Paper, cardboard, linen; 19.7 x 13.2 cm
Berlin, Deutsches Historisches Museum: G 2583

Swiss writer Jakob Schaffner went on two leisure cruises aboard KdF ships in 1935 and 1936: the first to Norway on the steamer Der Deutsche, which had gone into service for Norddeutscher Lloyd in 1923 as the Sierra Morena, and the second to Madeira on the St. Louis, built for Hapag in 1928. Schaffner was strongly attracted to National Socialist ideology, and his account of the voyage to Madeira, which had few scenic highlights and consisted mainly of days at sea, focuses on the sense of togetherness conferred by the *Volksgemeinschaft*, as a racially homogeneous community. It was this that the holidays run by "Kraft durch Freude", a Nazi organisation, were meant to reinforce. Schaffer was one of about 120,000 people who went on a KdF trip in 1936. MM

12/51 **Advertising poster "Mit 'Kraft durch Freude' nach Italien" (With "Strength through Joy" to Italy)**
Kroeber, Frankfurt a. M.
Printed by Verlag der Deutschen Arbeitsfront GmbH
Berlin, c. 1938
Offset print; 59.8 x 42.2 cm
Berlin, Deutsches Historisches Museum: 1989/1722.3

Passengers paid around 150 Reichsmarks for a ten to twelve-day cruise around Italy on a ship of the "KdF Peace Fleet", including the transfer on special trains. The days on board were tightly organised, starting with an early morning bugle

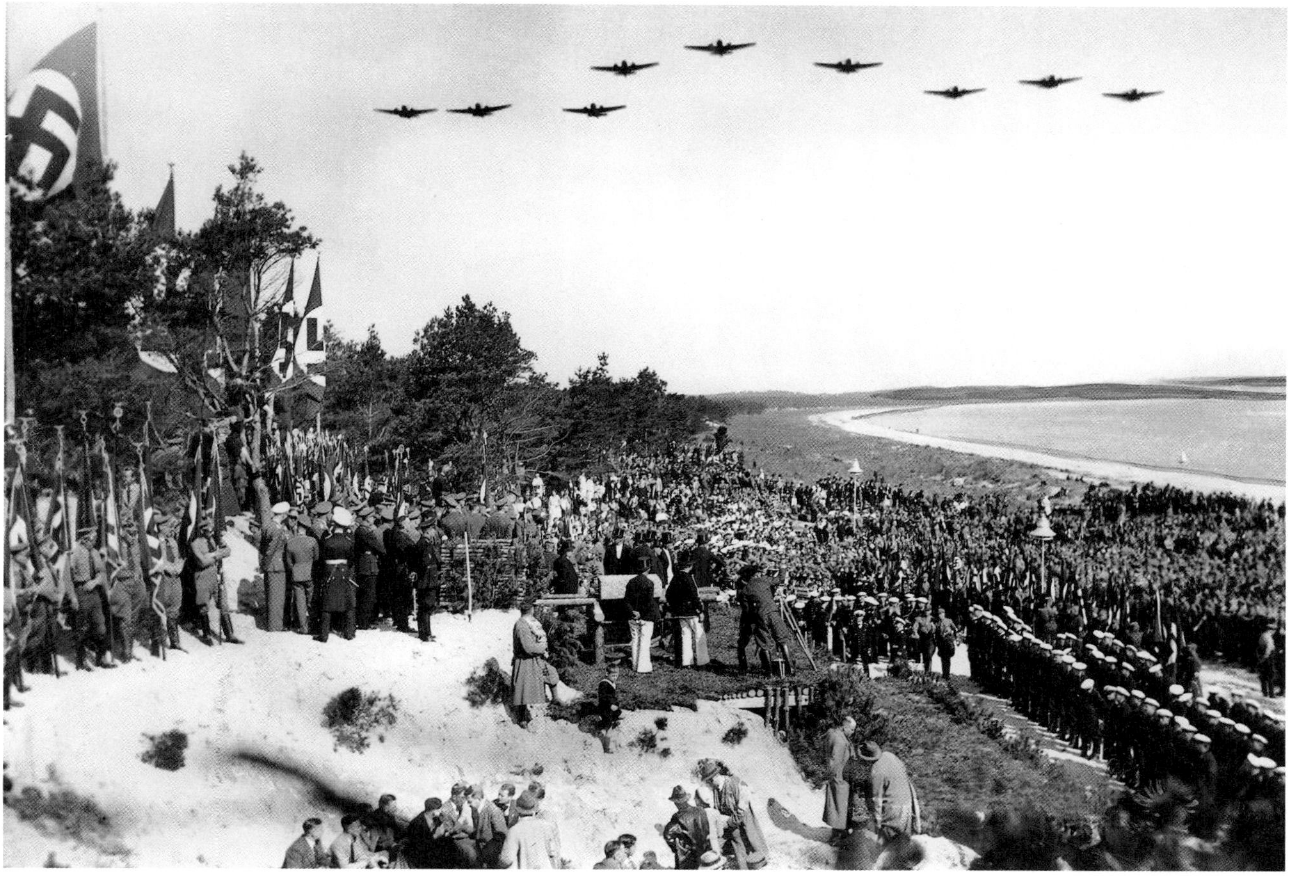

12/52

call followed by physical exercise. Then, with breaks for five to six meals of several courses each, came a succession of activities: a 100-kilometre 'march' on the sports deck, slide shows in preparation for excursions on land, documentaries and concerts on the radio, parties and evening dances on board. The passengers were not forced to take part in these events, but anyone who conspicuously avoided communal activities risked arousing suspicion. Informers disguised as holidaymakers observed their fellow travellers, paying special attention to their ideological soundness. KdF trips like these were meant less for the personal benefit of the participants than to strengthen the National Socialist community. AvH

12/52 **Laying the cornerstone of the KdF seaside resort of Prora on Rügen, 2 May 1936**
Scherl, Berlin
Reproduction
Munich, Süddeutsche Zeitung Photo: 00073145

The Nazi organisation "Kraft durch Freude" (Strength through Joy) grew to be the largest tour operator in Germany and – in terms of volume – the world. Five mass resorts were planned on the Baltic Sea coast as "holiday communities" for the National Socialist *Volksgemeinschaft*. By the start of the war in 1939, only one of them had been built: the "Sea Baths of the Twenty Thousand" at Prora on Rügen. Designed as a complex of buildings extending for five kilometres along a curved sandy bay, it had to be left partially completed. The cornerstone was laid on 2 May 1936 in the presence of Robert Ley (1890–1945), the head of the Deutsche Arbeitsfront (German Labour Front). Luftwaffe aircraft flew over the building site as part of the ceremony. UB

12/53 **Construction work on the KdF seaside resort of Prora on Rügen, 19 August 1938**
Heinrich Hoffmann (1885–1975)
Reproduction
Berlin, bpk | Bayerische Staatsbibliothek: 50050597

The KdF seaside resort, which was only completed in parts, was designed by Clemens Klotz (1886–1969), whom Robert Ley (1890–1945) had appointed in 1933 as the "architect commissioned by the Reichsleitung for the construction of training buildings for the NSDAP and the DAF". In 1938, he was also designated "trusted architect of the DAF". Klotz also designed an *Ordensburg* (training centre for Nazi party cadre) at Vogelsang and another at Crössinsee. This photo

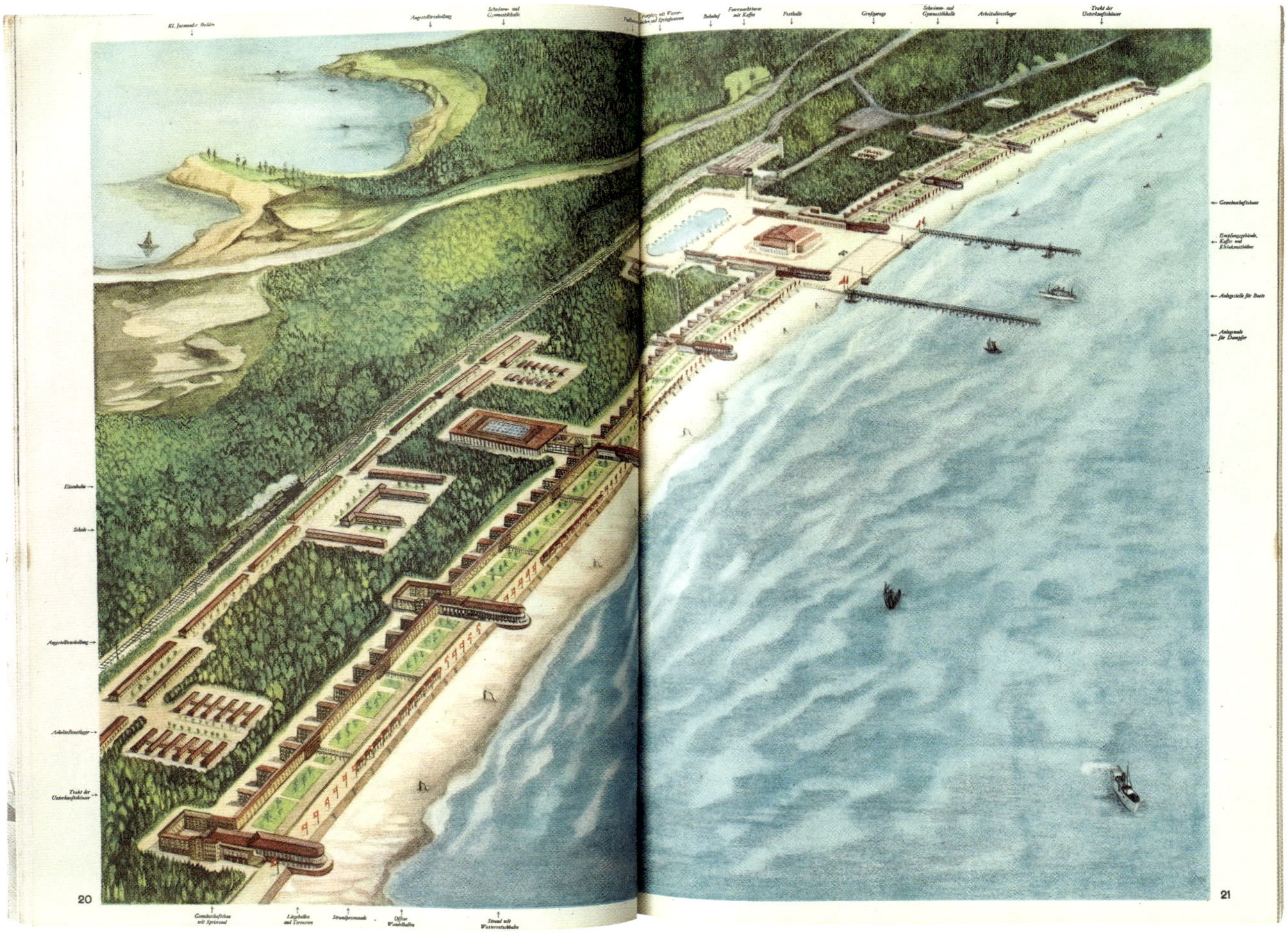

12/54

shows the buildings of Prora under construction, with the brick walls of the accommodation blocks and the rear staircases half built. In terms of its architectural style and layout, this was a thoroughly modern holiday 'factory', at least as far as accommodation and services were concerned. The site layout and circulation were designed to influence the guests' thinking and behaviour, both in the buildings and on the beach. In this sense, the KdF Sea Baths of Prora is a forerunner of the holiday resorts that emerged along beaches all over Europe after 1945 and made the package holiday possible for millions. (Fig. p. 149) UB

12/54 **Double-page spread from the June 1938 issue of *die neue linie* magazine, with a view of the KdF Sea Baths of Prora on Rügen**
Vol. 9 1937/38, issue no. 10
Illustration: Gerda Rotermund (1902–1982), Berlin
Verlag Otto Beyer, Leipzig
Print; 36.8 x 27 cm
Berlin, Deutsches Historisches Museum:
RZB 1182 -9.1937/38,10

The resort, comprised of a series of standard units, adopted the Modernist architectural style of the New Objectivity school. All of the rooms had a sea view and were arranged along a corridor with a service core at the rear, which contained the staircase and sanitary facilities. At the centre of the development was a huge square with a "community hall", two piers, an observation tower and a pond. Meals were served in ten separate dining halls along the coastline. Prora also had its own branch railway line. The Nazis were not alone in standardising beach holidays. At about the same time in Great Britain, entrepreneur Bill Butlin (1899–1980) was opening the first holiday camps, whose architecture is likewise in a restrained Modernist style. In Italy, at Marina di Massa, the car-maker Fiat built two modern holiday complexes in cooperation with the fascist leisure organisation, Dopolavoro. UB

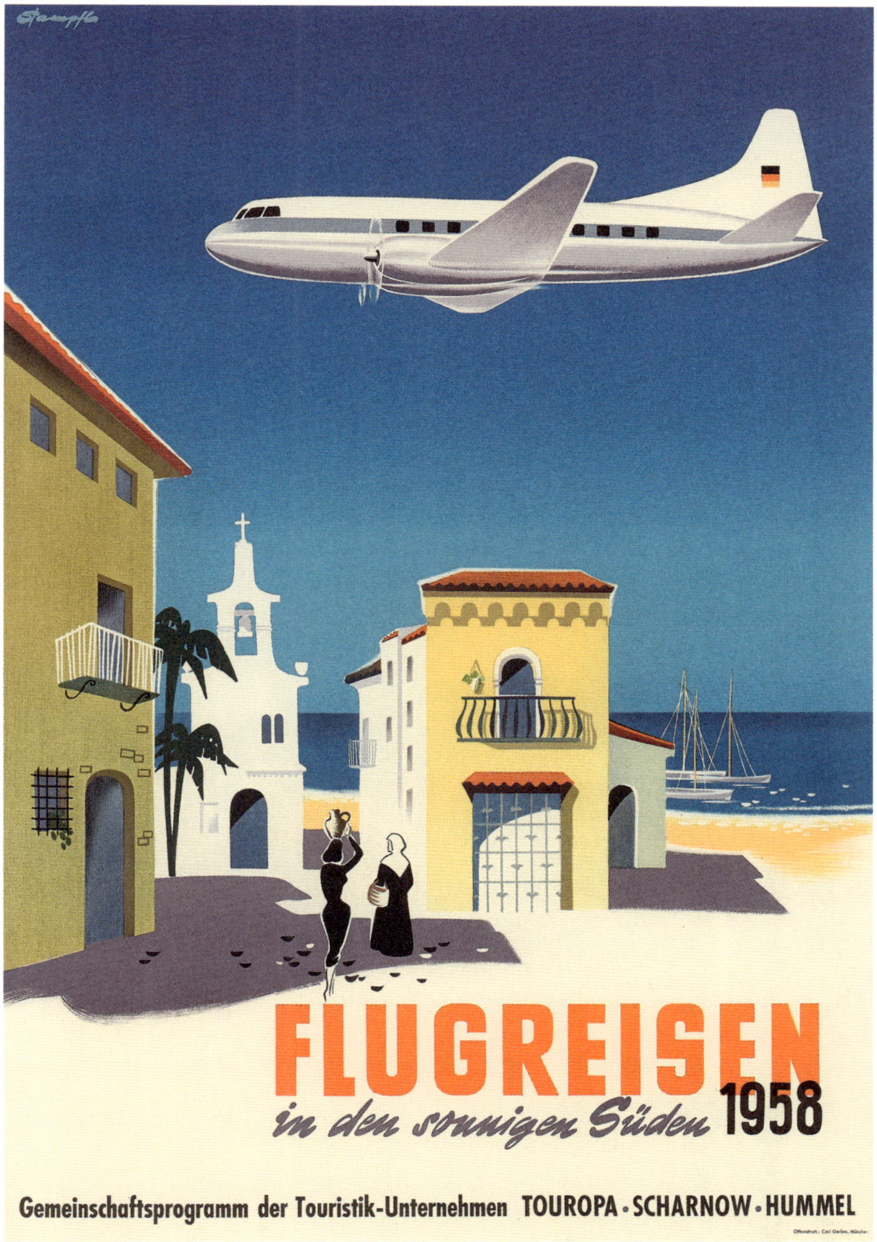

12/55

Seaside Holidays Since 1945: Flights, Package Deals and Last-Minute Booking

12/55 **Advertising poster "Air travel to the sunny south in 1958" for the tour operators Touropa, Scharnow and Hummel**
Printed by Carl Gerber
Munich, 1958
Offset print; 83.9 x 59.2 cm
Berlin, Deutsches Historisches Museum: P 90/10360

So-called mass tourism, which broke the virtual monopoly of the wealthy on foreign travel, really began to develop after 1945, focusing initially on the beaches of the Mediterranean. As demonstrable evidence of a beach holiday, the sun tan became a symbol of prosperity, which gave a competitive advantage to regions that could guarantee sunshine. From the 1960s onwards, the growing availability of air travel brought the countries of Europe – and later of the whole world – ever closer together. The introduction of cheap charter flights made Spain the most popular holiday destination for Germans, especially the Balearic island of Majorca and the Canary Islands. In 1968, several companies – Scharnow, Touropa, Dr. Tigges and Hummel – merged to form Touristik Union International (TUI). Ever since then, the market has been dominated by large corporations offering package holidays. UB

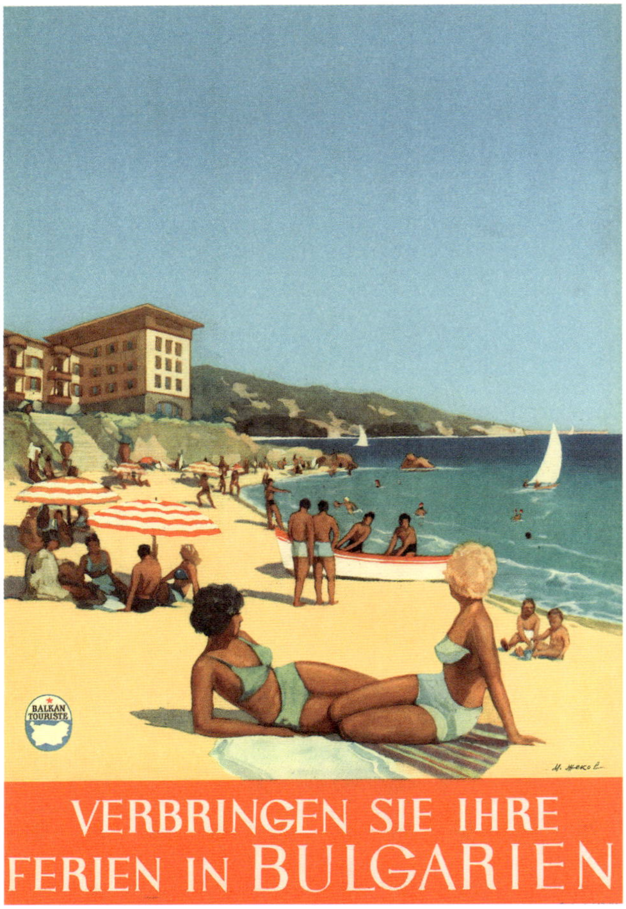

12/56

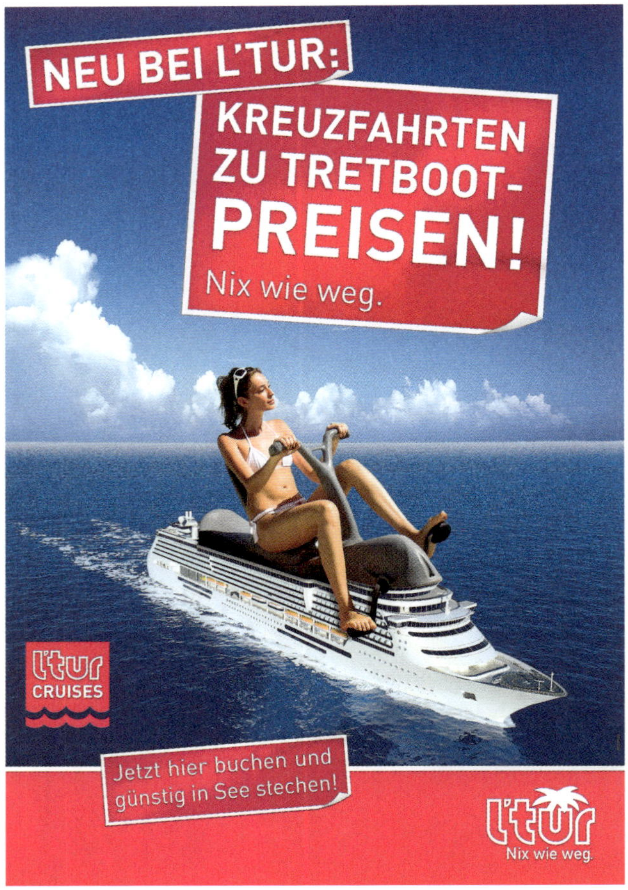

12/57

12/56 **Advertising poster, "Spend your holidays in Bulgaria"**
Published by Reisegesellschaft Balkantourist für Badeurlaub in Bulgarien
M. Shekov
Printed by Lito Balkan
Bulgaria, 1954
Offset print; 98.9 x 66.9 cm
Berlin, Deutsches Historisches Museum: P 90/10224

From the mid-1950s onwards, the Bulgarian government promoted the development of international tourism as an important means of boosting the economy and earning foreign currency. In order to match the standards of competing destinations in the Mediterranean and Adriatic regions, the state-owned tour operator Balkantourist invested in the construction of modern hotel complexes along the Black Sea. Each had several hundred beds, with specialty and folklore restaurants, cafés, parks and bars. Holiday homes and bungalows were also built. Its advertisements highlighted the picturesque coastal landscape, the warm, dry climate, the fine, golden sand, the dark-blue sea, and the variety of local cuisine as special attractions of Bulgarian seaside resorts. Holidays in Bulgaria were especially popular with East Germans from the 1960s onwards, as it was the only permissible foreign destination that possessed similar qualities to the Mediterranean coast. AvH

12/57 **Advertising poster for the tour operator l'tur "New from l'tur: Cruises at pedalo prices! Off and away"**
2012/2013
Offset print; 84.3 x 59.6 cm
Berlin, Deutsches Historisches Museum: P 2013/12

This poster is advertising last-minute holidays. These are deals where the date of arrival is within the next 14 days. In the 1980s, airlines began offering seats left vacant by cancellations and over capacity at discounted rates, purchasable directly at the airports. This met with such success that the concept was applied to other products, such as package holidays, and ended up being offered by specialised middlemen as well as traditional tour operators. There are even last minute offers for cruises, which now come in all price categories. The text and photo collage on the poster give an ironic slant to the once exclusive image of the cruise. In 2016, nearly two million Germans went on a cruise. It is becoming increasingly apparent, however, that cruise ships inflict immense damage on the ecology of the oceans and the coasts. UB

12/58 **Advertising poster for the tour operator I'tur, "Today a couch potato. Tomorrow a fried potato"**
2012/2013
Offset print; 84.2 x 59 cm
Berlin, Deutsches Historisches Museum: P 2013/13

Europeans, in particular, seem to love the beach as much as they ever did: around two-thirds of all European tourists go on summer holidays by the sea. The desire to visit a particular place continues to be less of a factor in their choice than a combination of sea, beach and sunshine as well as a beachside hotel with a pool, all-inclusive catering and a variety of entertainment on offer. Tourist destinations and their infrastructure have become more and more similar, be they in Spain, Turkey, or the Dominican Republic. (Exhibit not shown) UB

12/59 **Photograph, "GB. England. Cornwall. St Ives. 2017"**
Martin Parr (b. 1952)
Gelatin silver print; 60 x 87 cm
Paris, Magnum Photos: NN11521829 (PAM2017046G00643)

British photographer Martin Parr began capturing seaside holiday scenes in his home country in the 1970s. In the meantime, he has taken photographs on beaches all over the world. In the foreword to his photo reportage *Life's a Beach*, from 2012, he writes:
"In the United Kingdom, one is never more than seventy-five miles away from the coast. With this much shoreline, it's not surprising that there is a strong British tradition of photography by the seaside. American photographers may have given birth to Street photography; but in the UK, we have the beach. [...] Here people can relax, be themselves, and show off all those traces of mildly eccentric British behavior. [...] You can read a lot about a country by looking at its beaches: across cultures, the beach is that rare public space in which all absurdities and quirky national behaviors can be found." UB

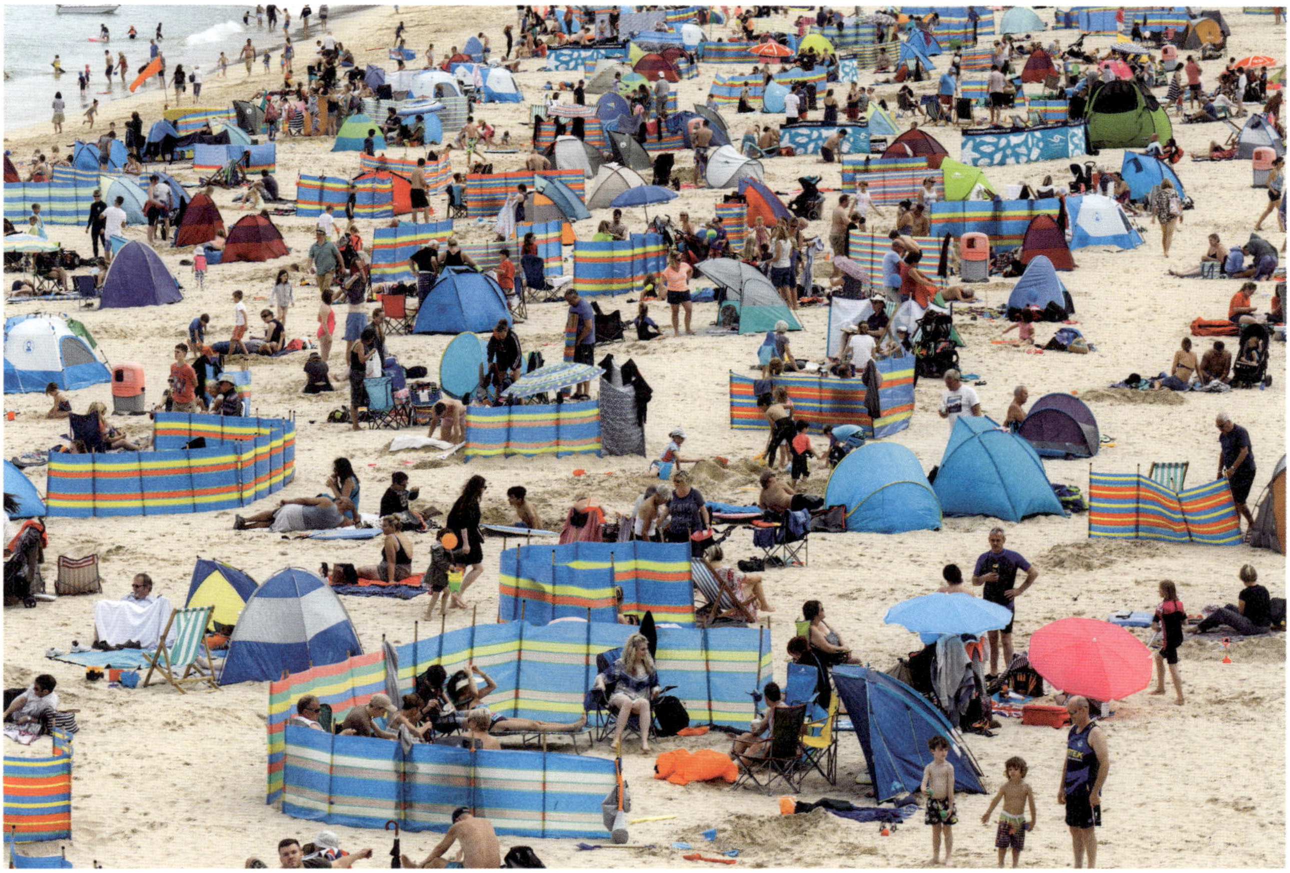

12//59

13 Changes in Mentality
The Sea and the Beach as Subjects of Painting

"Nothing can give someone who has never set foot on the seashore any idea of this magnificent scene. [...] be it calm or turbulent; in every shade of colour from dark brown to the deepest sea green; whether the sun is apparently floating like a glowing metal ball on the pearly grey rim of the water, or the waves are glowing with a pale blue, phosphorescent light on a dark night, the sea is always sublime and grand [...]."

These euphoric lines about the beauty of the sea do not come from the pen of an artist, but from a guide to the "sea baths of Ostend .. for spa guests", written by a Belgian spa doctor by the name of Hartwig and published in 1845. The newly emerging aesthetic perception of the sea was a phenomenon closely related to the meanwhile established belief in the healing properties of the sea. The revaluation of nature since the eighteenth century and the fact that the sea was now capable of arousing powerful emotional responses not only gave rise to bathing tourism, but also fundamentally transformed landscape painting.

Maritime subjects had been an important part of European art for centuries. Naval battles, ship portraits, and views of ports reached a peak of popularity in Dutch painting of the seventeenth century, during the country's Golden Age. Storms at sea, shipwrecks, and religious or allegorical scenes related to the sea likewise found their way onto many canvases, especially as ships and shipwrecks were generally understandable metaphors for earthly life, its risks and its failures. In many paintings, however, the sea remained merely a stage or an atmospheric backdrop for the actual subject. This changed at the start of the nineteenth century, when the 'empty' sea – and even a single wave – became worthy of depiction in themselves. The artist's interest now centred primarily on the experience of nature itself: the immense breadth and depth of the sea and its elemental power, demonstrated in extreme weather such as storms or thunderstorms, or revealed in calm waters on a clear evening or a moonlit night. The lowly genre of pure landscape painting grew in importance, and the range of symbolic interpretations of the sea expanded.

The raising of the sea and the coastal landscape to the status of subjects in their own right is closely linked to the advent of open-air painting at the beginning of the nineteenth century. In terms of the accurate observation of nature, its forerunners were the English landscape painters, notably John Constable (1776–1837), who strove to reproduce the nuances of natural colours, and his contemporary William Turner (1775–1851), who sought above all to capture atmospheric qualities. By the middle of the nineteenth century, open-air painting had spread throughout Europe and become a broad artistic movement. At a time of increasing urbanisation and industrialisation, numerous painters settled in rural areas close to nature and established artists' colonies. One of the earliest of these, which began in Barbizon in France during the 1830s, is considered to have paved the way for Impressionism. In their quest for unspoiled nature, artists came across humble villages such as Nidden (on the Curonian spit by the Baltic), Worpswede (near Bremen) and Skagen (on the northern coast of Jutland in Denmark), to name just a few places where artists established colonies in the last third of the nineteenth century. The beaches, mudflats and barren heaths that characterise the coastal regions of northern Europe became part of the established catalogue of subjects for painting. The 'discovery' of a region by the art world often attracted visitors and led to the development of a corresponding infrastructure, demonstrating the close link between art and tourism. As the popularity of coastal resorts boomed at the end of the nineteenth century, the spa guests themselves became the focus of artists' attention. They appeared in bathing and beach scenes, strolling along seafront promenades or piers, and enjoying various holiday pastimes. *Ursula Breymayer*

Further Reading

Anja Dauschek, Regine Gerhardt, Vanessa Hirsch (eds.), *Melbye. Maler des Meeres* (exhib. cat. Stiftung Historische Museen Hamburg, Altonaer Museum), Munich 2017

Roger Diederen, María López Fernández, Blanca Pons-Sorolla (eds.), *Joaquín Sorolla. Spaniens Meister des Lichts* (exhib. cat. Kunsthalle der Hypo-Kulturstiftung München, Musée des impressionnismes Giverny, Museo Sorolla Madrid), Munich 2016

Martin Faass, Felix Krämer, Uwe M. Schneede (eds.), *Seestücke. Von Caspar David Friedrich bis Emil Nolde* (exhib. cat. Hamburger Kunsthalle), Munich 2005

Udo Kittelmann, Birgit Verwiebe (eds.), *August Kopisch: Maler, Dichter, Entdecker, Erfinder* (exhib. cat. Alte Nationalgalerie Berlin), Berlin 2016

Petra Kuhlmann-Hodick, Gerd Spitzer, Bernhard Maaz (eds.), *Carl Gustav Carus. Natur und Idee* (exhib. cat. Staatliche Kunstsammlungen Dresden, Staatliche Museen zu Berlin), Munich 2009

Katrin Maibaum, Katharina Gräber (eds.), *Wenzel Hablik – Expressionistische Utopien, Malerei Zeichnung, Architektur* (exhib. cat. Martin-Gropius-Bau Berlin), Munich 2017

Mieke Mels, Philip Van den Bossche, *Das Meer. The Sea. La Mer. De Zee* (exhib. cat. De Zee Oostende), Ostfildern 2015

Magdalena M. Moeller, Ulrich Schulte-Wülwer, *Erich Heckel an der Ostsee*, (exhib. cat. Brücke-Museum Berlin, Städtische Galerie Bietigheim-Bissingen, Museumsberg Flensburg), Munich 2006

Ulrich Pohlmann, Ortrud Westheider (eds.), *Über Wasser. Malerei und Photographie von William Turner bis Olafur Eliasson* (exhib. cat. Bucerius Kunst Forum Hamburg), Munich 2015

Dieter Richter, *Das Meer. Geschichte der ältesten Landschaft*, Berlin 2014

Thorsten Sadowsky (eds.), *Kunst und Küste. Ausgewählte Werke der Sammlung Kunst der Westküste*, Alkersum/Föhr 2013

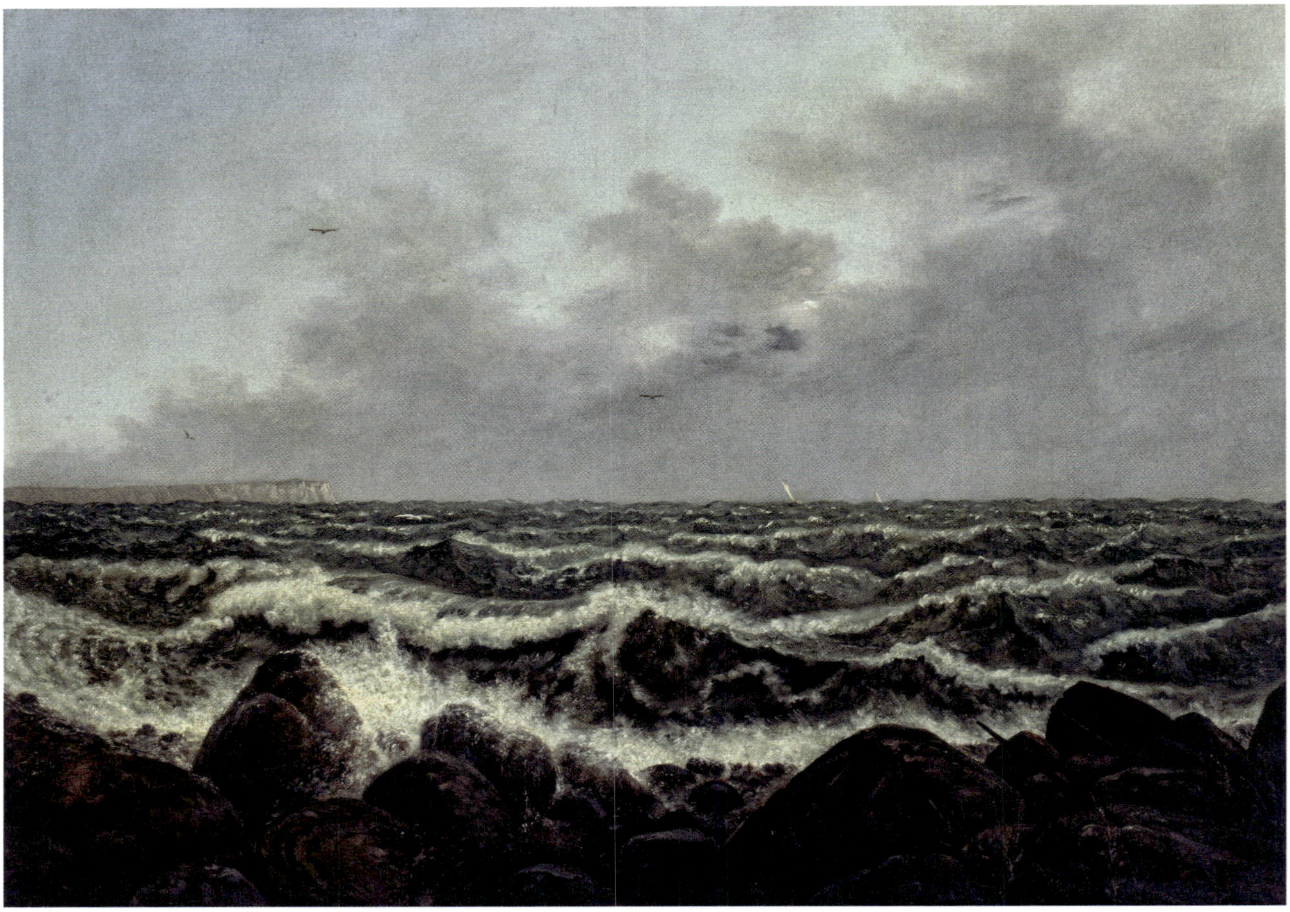

13/1

13/1 **Breaking Waves on Rügen**
Carl Gustav Carus (1789–1869)
1819
Oil on canvas; 64.5 x 93.5 cm
Dresden, Albertinum, Staatliche Kunstsammlungen Dresden: Gal.-No. 2215 H

Powerful waves roll into the shore and break on the rocks, throwing up white spray. Just discernible on the horizon are the chalk cliffs of Rügen and the white sails of two ships. This scene was painted by Carl Gustav Carus, a physician by profession, who observed the sea with a scientist's objectivity and an artist's enthusiasm for the motion of the waves. Here, he confronts the Baltic Sea head on. In doing so, he follows the example set by Caspar David Friedrich (1774–1840), whose seascape The Monk by the Sea, painted between 1808 and 1810, was widely appreciated for its stark simplicity. In a similar way, the image shown here seems to extend beyond the bounds of the canvas, evoking the incomprehensible extent of the sea, which is highlighted by the uniform horizontal line of the coast. Carus had got to know Friedrich in Dresden in 1818 or earlier. In 1819, inspired by the latter's paintings of his native region, Carus went on a trip to the Baltic island of Rügen. In his works, the broad expanse of the sea expresses, among other things, the yearning for freedom. Together with paintings of megalithic tombs on Rügen, this motif came to symbolise a nostalgic utopia projected onto the distant Nordic past, in deliberate contrast to the narrow, reactionary mindset of the Bourbon Restoration period. Carus painted this scene in his studio, immediately after returning from one such trip. The "elementary salty flood, constantly churning and surging within itself", as he described it, was a subject that occupied him for many years. HB

13/2 **Sea Solitude**
Daniel Hermann Anton Melbye (1818–1875)
1852
Oil on canvas; 68.7 x 107.5 cm
Hamburg, Hamburger Kunsthalle: 1252

Anton Melbye gained fame throughout Europe in the nineteenth century as the "painter of the sea". After studying at the Royal Danish Academy of Fine Arts in his native Copenhagen, he went to Paris, where he developed a style characterised by heightened, finely differentiated colours. Beginning in 1849, he stayed frequently in Hamburg and from 1860

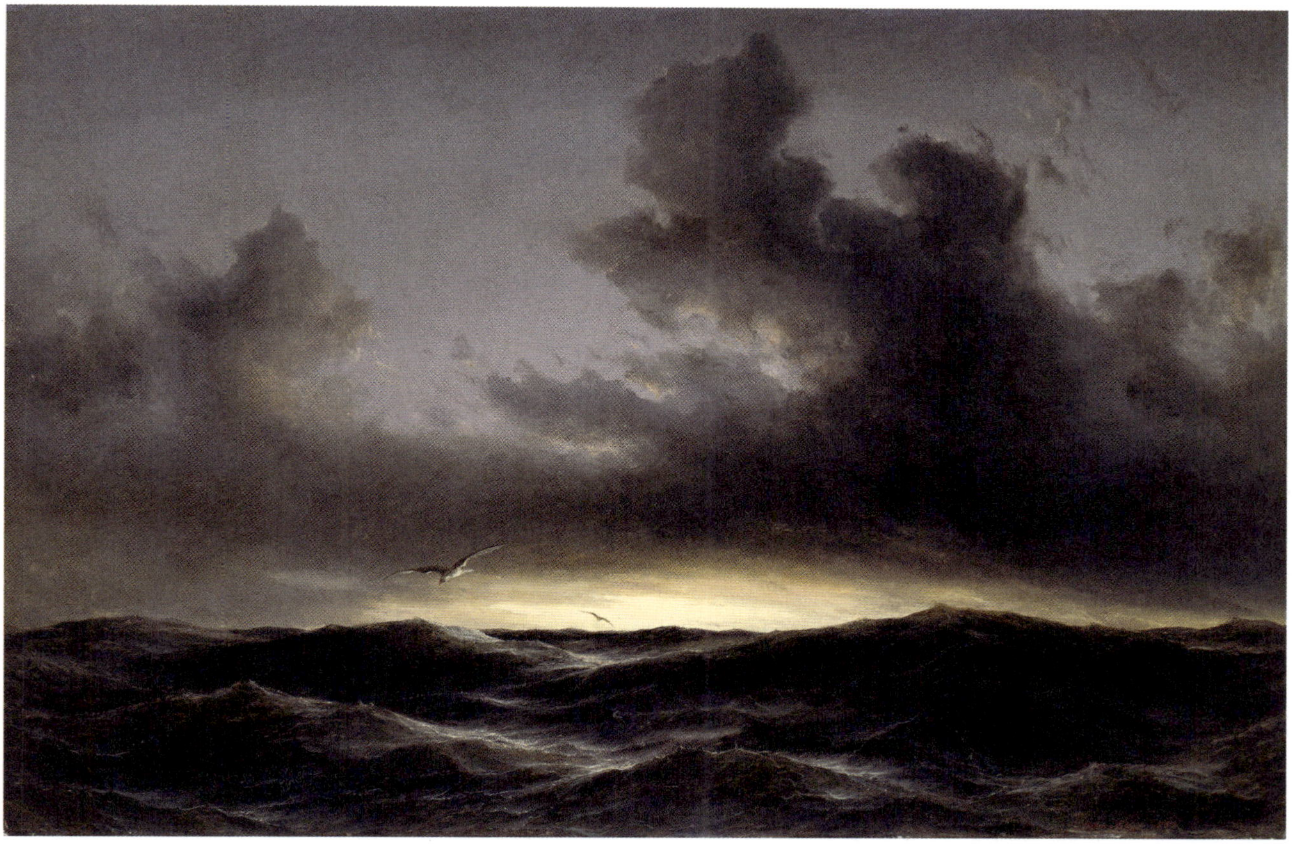

13/2

to 1871 he maintained a residence on the Inner Alster lake. Many of his paintings were bought by wealthy Hamburg merchants, ship-owners, and shipbuilders. His maritime themes ranged from classic set-piece compositions, such as ship portraits and naval battles, to harbour panoramas and pure landscape paintings. Melbye also followed the example of the open-air painters and went to the coast of Normandy. His paintings of lonely coasts or rough seas are symbolically charged, as the title of this painting, *Sea Solitude*, indicates. The viewpoint is set almost level with the crests of the waves, exposing the viewer directly to the eternal, primal force of the sea. With its restrained palette of sombre blues and greys, this composition conveys a feeling of powerlessness and forebodings of ineluctable death. UB

13/3 **Cape Zaffarano in Sicily**
August Kopisch (1799–1853)
1840
Oil on canvas; 62 x 110 cm
Bad Homburg, Verwaltung der Staatlichen Schlösser und Gärten Hessen: 1.1.271

August Kopisch's colourful paintings are unique among the German landscape paintings of his time. After stays in Vienna and Dresden, he went to Italy in 1824, settling in 1826 in Naples, where he lived for the next three and a half years. Like Sicily, where he stayed for several months in 1827, the region was rich in picturesque scenery and historical sights. It provided Kopisch (who was both an artist and a writer) with ideal subjects for his paintings and for his study of Italian folk culture. His interest in spectacular phenomena of light and colour was due not least to the Blue Grotto on the island of Capri, which he and the Romantic painter Ernst Fries (1801–1833) from Heidelberg 'rediscovered' in 1826 and subsequently made famous. Kopisch's preferred subjects were sunrises and sunsets, scenes in the moonlight, and volcanic eruptions. His painting of Cape Zaffarano in Sicily shows the coast east of Palermo at sunset. The extraordinary, almost neon-bright coloration of the sky and the intensely glowing blues of the sea lend the coastal landscape a magical effect, elevating it to the very essence of Mediterranean beauty. King Friedrich Wilhelm IV of Prussia (1795–1861), a lover of Italy, purchased the painting and had it exhibited at the Berlin Academy Exhibition of 1844. (Fig. p. 171) UB

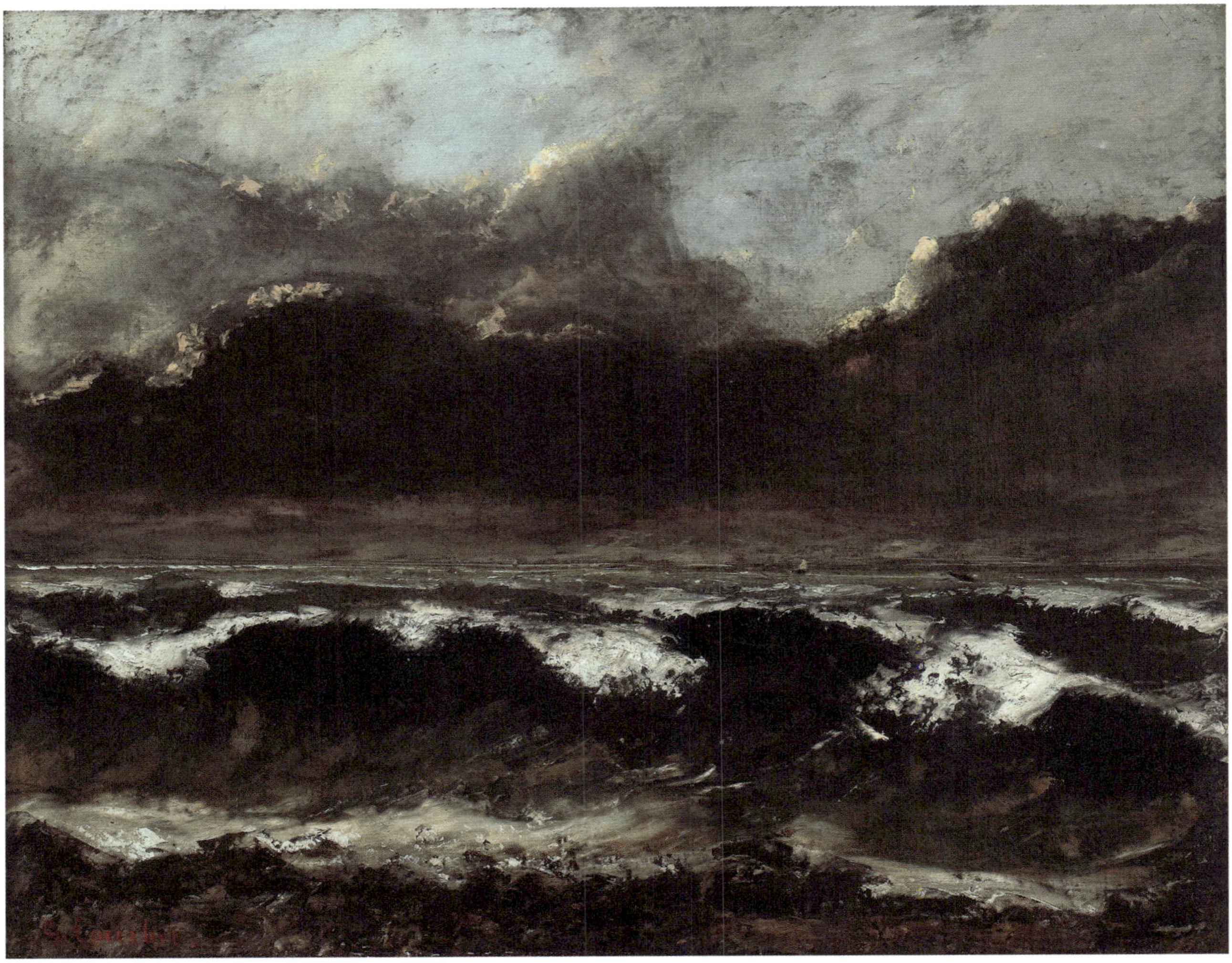

13/4

13/4 **Breaking Waves with Three Sailing Ships**
Gustave Courbet (1819–1877)
c. 1870
Oil on canvas; 51 x 66 cm
Private Collection

Gustave Courbet, the foremost proponent of Realism in France, spent the summer of 1869 in the coastal town of Étretat, known for its steep cliffs. Working in a studio situated directly on the coast, he painted a series of pictures that focus exclusively on waves. These are strong waves, breaking on a narrow stretch of shore with foaming crests and surf. The horizon line is clearly drawn across the canvas, sharply separating the darkening sky from the sea and the coast in a radical shift from the traditional viewpoint. Courbet thus confronts the viewer with the high breakers head on. He emphasises the mass and force of the waves by applying the paint thickly with a palette knife, which makes the water appear peculiarly solid. It seems as though he has frozen the action just as the waves are breaking. Courbet captured this brief moment, which recurs in endless variations along the shoreline, not just in one painting, but in a series, thus expressing both the fleeting and the perpetual aspects. KK

13/5 **View from Skagen Beach in the Early Evening**
Michael Ancher (1849–1927)
1892
Oil on canvas; 40 x 52 cm
Alkersum (Föhr), Museum Kunst der Westküste:
2 ANC 04

Michael Ancher founded the Danish artists' colony in Skagen. This was a small fishing village in north Jutland, far from the bustle of Copenhagen. From the 1870s onwards, it was popular among a group of artists who rejected the Academic concept of art and preferred to paint in the open air, inspired by the Realist painters in France as well as by the Impressionists. Their subjects were drawn mainly from the traditional way of life of the local fishermen and crofters as well as the unspoiled nature surrounding them: barren heathland, rolling dunes, and seascapes. In the summer,

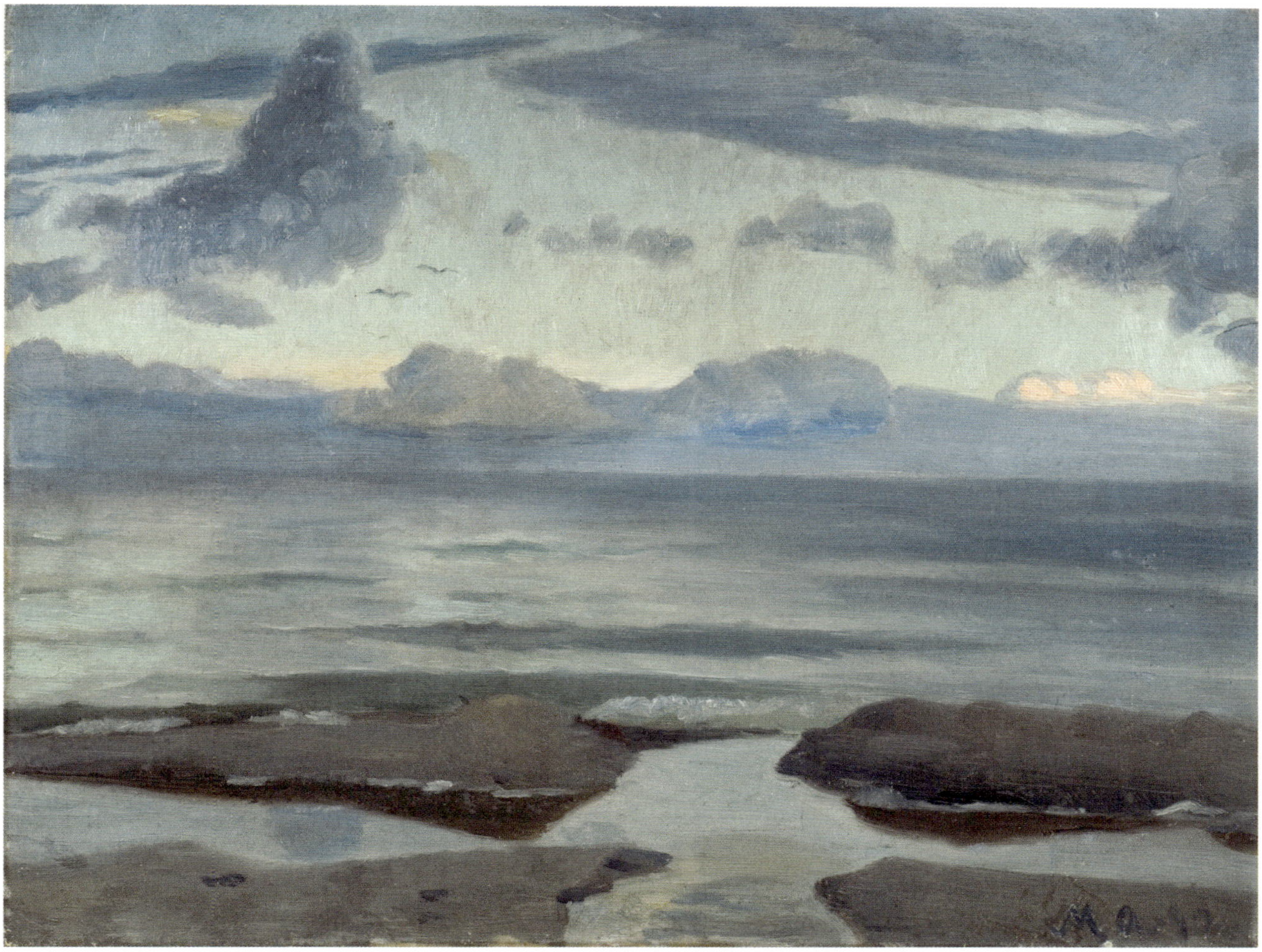

13/5

these scenes were enhanced by unusual lighting conditions that resulted from Skagen's remote location at the head of a promontory between two bodies of water, the Skagerrak and the Kattegat. Ancher's painting shows a landscape of sea and sky at the 'blue hour' of early evening. The finely graduated shades of blue and the clouds shimmering orange with the light of the passing day evoke the mildly melancholic mood of the time just after sunset and seem to encourage motionless contemplation. UB

13/6 **Boys Bathing**
Max Liebermann (1847–1935)
1902
Oil on canvas, relined; 65 x 88.5 cm
Alkersum (Föhr), Museum Kunst der Westküste:
2 LIE 01

Summer holidays at a seaside resort have been popular with the middle classes since the second half of the nineteenth century. The Berlin-based painter Max Liebermann often stayed in the fashionable Dutch coastal towns of Scheveningen and Noordwijk. He produced sketches and paintings of beach scenes in which people are bathing, going for walks or rides, and playing with children. Inspired by the French Impressionists, who sought to portray coastal scenery and its bright, intense light as vividly as possible, Liebermann began using a light brushstroke for his beach subjects from about 1894/95 onwards. This painting, *Boys Bathing*, shows the sea on a summer's day with young men wading into the water under the gaze of a beach warden. Liebermann was one of the first German painters to take bathing on the beach as the subject of a painting. He conveys the changeable nature of the light in the colours of the sea, which range from deep blue to ochre shades, even pinks and reds. (Fig. p. 161) KK

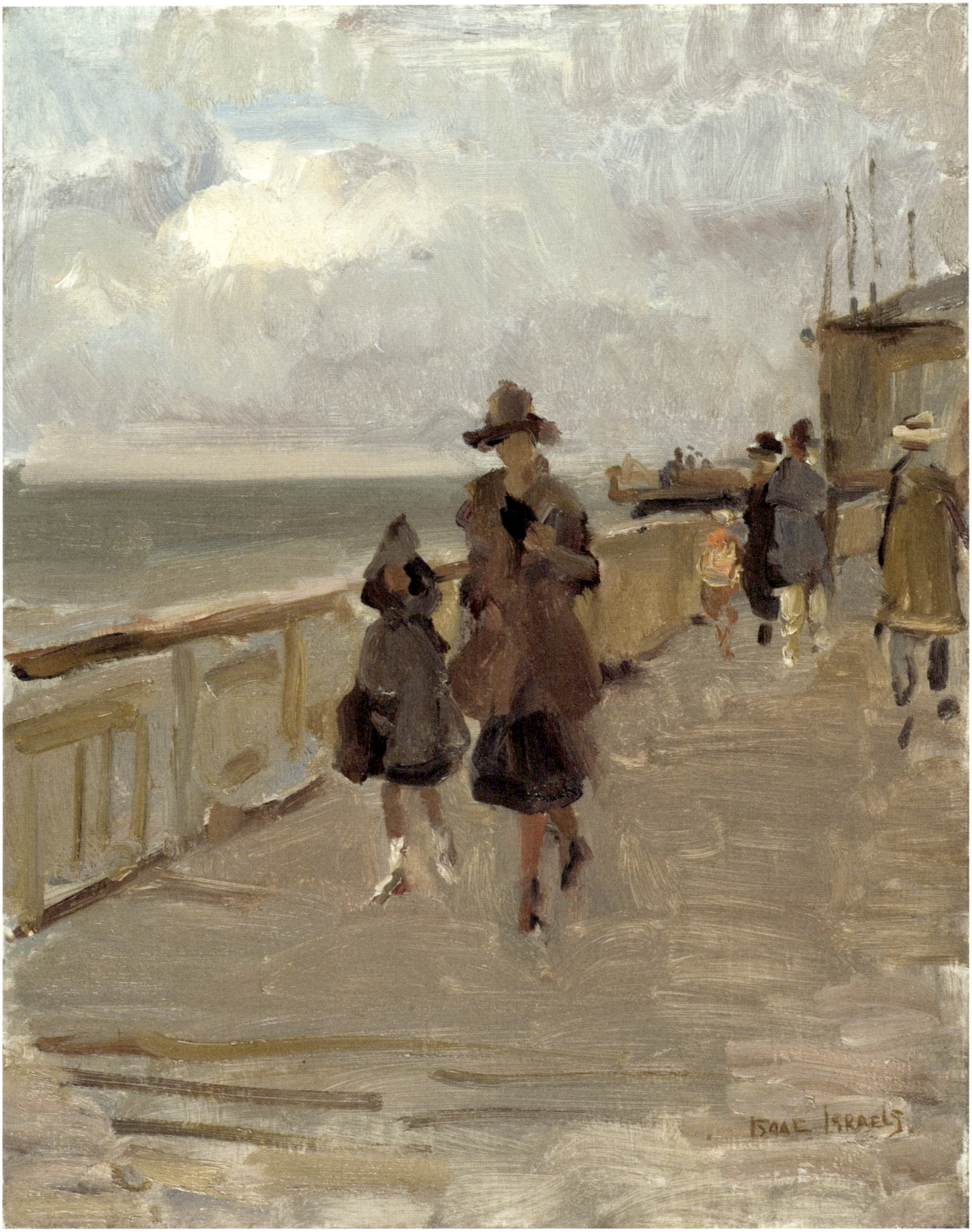

13/7

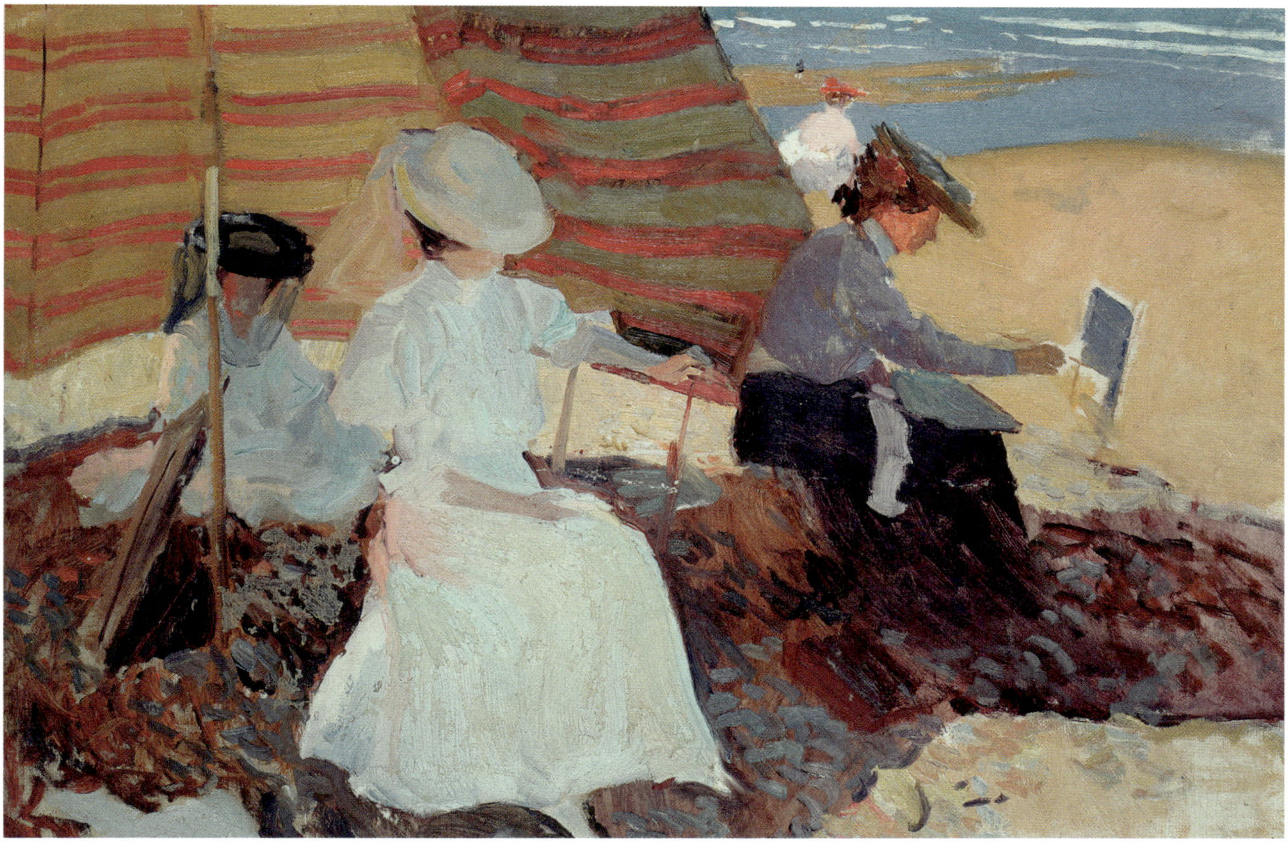

13/8

13/7 **Fresh, Early Springtime on the Pier at Scheveningen**
Isaac Israëls (1865–1934)
Undated
Oil on canvas; 50.5 x 40 cm
Alkersum (Föhr), Museum Kunst der Westküste: 1 ISI 01

Isaac Israëls, one of the great Dutch Impressionists, was also a devotee of open-air painting. He was a friend of Max Liebermann (1847–1935), who went with him to the fashionable seaside resort of Scheveningen, near The Hague, several times in the early twentieth century. This painting, which bears no date, shows the pier at Scheveningen, which was opened in 1901. The pier's railing runs diagonally right across the canvas, linking the foreground with the horizon. It leads the eye to the pavilion at the pier head – a movement picked up by the distant figures walking out to sea. Approaching the viewer at the centre of the picture are a woman dressed elegantly in the fashion of the 1920s, and a girl. Shades of ochre, brown and grey predominate. Israëls uses sketchy brushstrokes to conjure up the atmosphere of a cool, cloudy day, typical of springtime by the North Sea. Despite the dull weather, the spa guests are still passing the time in the conventional manner: taking a relaxed stroll along the seafront, seeing and being seen. UB

13/8 **Bajo el toldo, Biarritz**
Joaquín Sorolla y Bastida (1863–1923)
1906
Oil on canvas; 62 x 93 cm
Madrid, Museo Sorolla: 00770

This work reveals how open-air painting had grown in popularity in the previous half century. It shows two middle-class women in elegant summer clothing, sitting in the shade of a red-and-yellow striped awning while a third woman paints a small picture. In the background, the sand and the pale blue sea glow brightly. Joaquín Sorolla y Bastida, the most important Spanish artist at the turn of the century, became known for sun-drenched beach scenes. He intensified the Impressionists' palette of colours and enhanced their luminosity by introducing the play of sunlight. This makes his pictures seem like snapshots of the Mediterranean way of life. In his native Valencia, on the Mediterranean coast of Spain, Sorolla's fishing and beach scenes were bathed in shimmering sunlight, but in 1906, he began spending the summers in Biarritz, in south-west France. In this period, his wife and daughters usually served as his models. Instead of pure white, the artist used tints of pale blue and violet to reproduce the cooler light of the Atlantic. KK

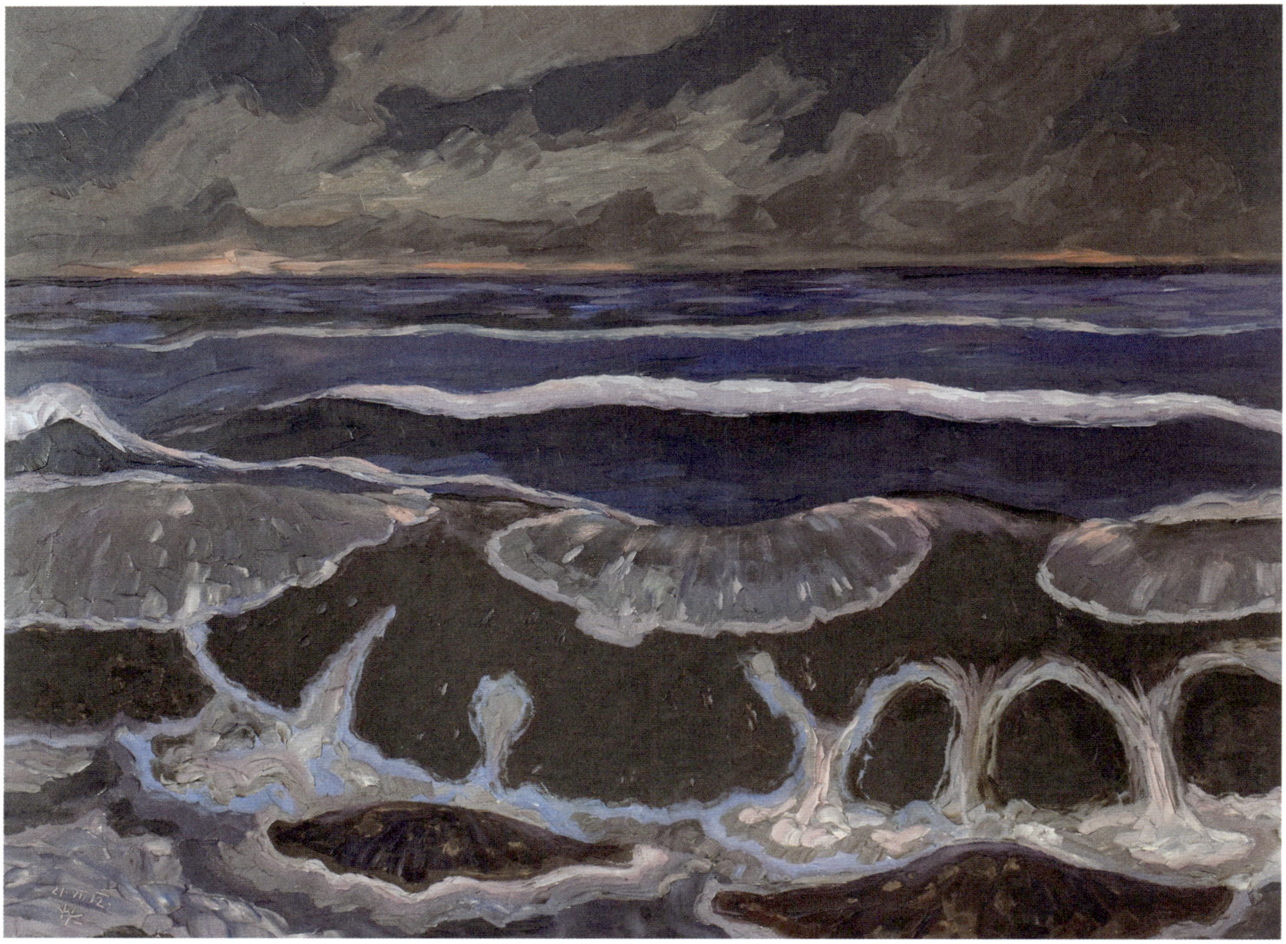

13/9

13/9 **Breakers After a Heavy Storm on Sylt**
Wenzel Hablik (1881–1934)
1912
Oil on canvas; 95 x 130 cm
Itzehoe, Wenzel-Hablik-Stiftung: 1969-170

Extreme weather, unusual light, and expressive cloud formations fascinated Wenzel Hablik, who settled in Holstein. These waves crashing ashore under a lowering sky with torn storm clouds were doubtless experienced at first-hand on the island of Sylt, which the artist and designer visited frequently from 1907 onwards, seeking artistic inspiration in nature. His pictures were not begun outdoors, however; he painted them from memory in the studio, without making preliminary studies. Hablik moulded the power of nature into new forms with an expressive, impasto application of paint, and here the ornamental patterns of the surf hint at his artistic roots in Art Nouveau. He revered nature as the supreme creative force, drawing inspiration from the imposing presence of the mountains and the elemental power of the sea. With an oeuvre that brought together art, architecture, craft and interior design, Hablik made important contributions to the avant-garde of modernism. KK

13/10 **Bathers at the Fjord**
Erich Heckel (1883–1970)
1913
Oil on canvas; 97 x 119 cm
Bochum, Kunstmuseum: MB 393

In 1905, Erich Heckel co-founded *Die Brücke* (The Bridge), an artists' group whose other leading members included Ernst Ludwig Kirchner (1880–1938), Karl Schmidt-Rottluff (1884–1976), Otto Mueller (1874–1930) and Max Pechstein (1881–1955). Inspired by notions of an idyllic existence in the South Seas, they sought to unify art and life through an alternative lifestyle. Far from social constraints and urban civilisation, they found ideal surroundings for artistic experimentation on trips to the countryside and the coast. The Expressionists

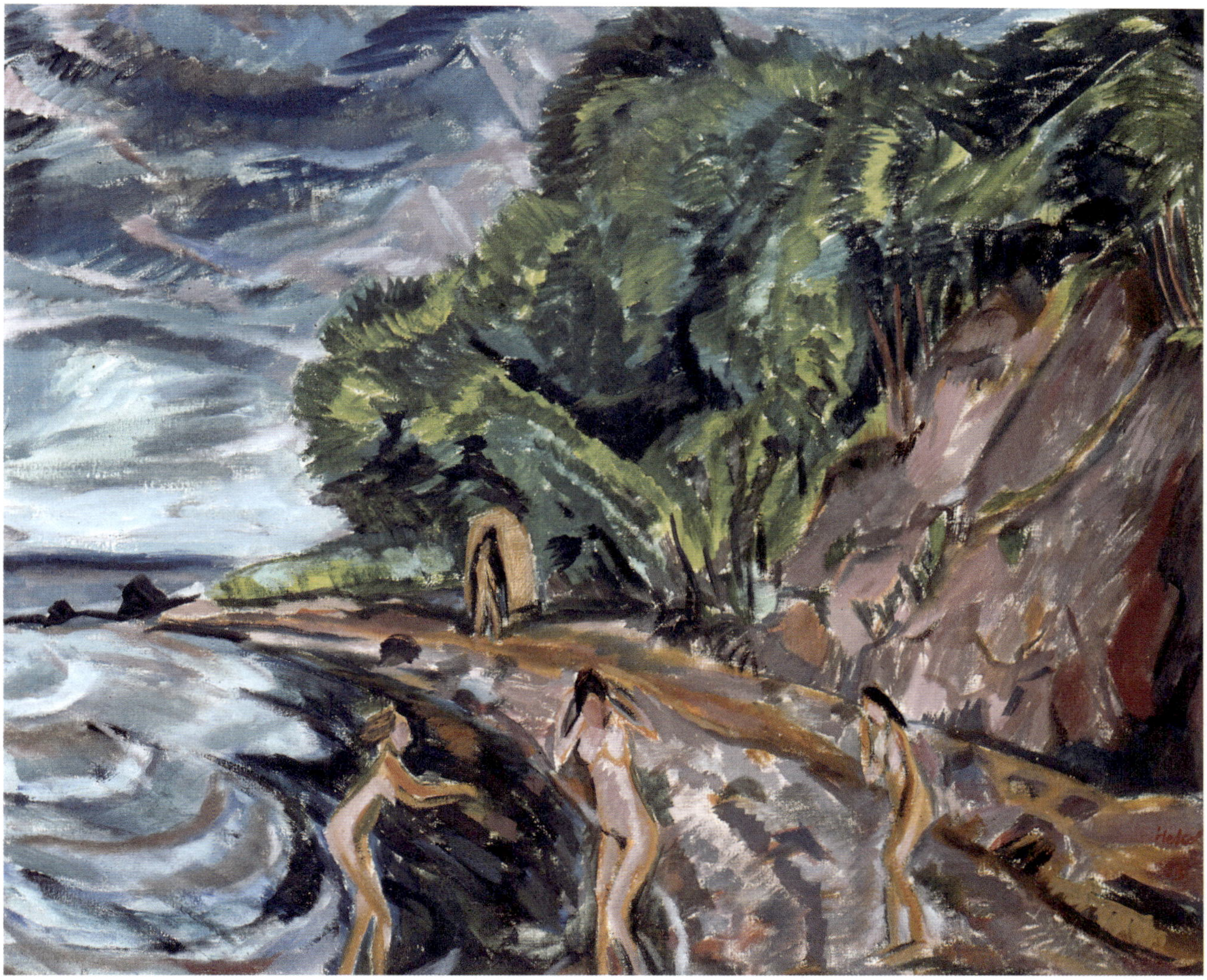

13/10

often returned to the subject of bathers – by then an established motif – and associated it with their vision of an unspoiled paradise. In 1913, after *Die Brücke* was dissolved, Heckel discovered the coast of the Flensburg Firth both as a home and as a subject for his art. This scene of naked bathers below a cliff is painted with restless, overlaid feathery brushstrokes, using black to offset the colours. The bathers are depicted in harmony with nature; even the figures' skin tones have taken on the coloration of their surroundings. KK

13/11 **North Sea (triptych)**
Jochen Hein (b. 1960)
2003
Acrylic on jute; 145 x 540 cm
Alkersum (Föhr), Museum Kunst der Westküste: 4 HEJ01

The painter Jochen Hein, who was born in Husum and lives in Hamburg, explores nature in his own way. Seen from a distance, his images of the sea appear incredibly realistic, but as one comes closer they break down into abstract forms and blocks of colour. We see something that is familiar to begin with, but which turns out to be merely the material surface of a reality. Hein has developed special techniques to achieve this effect. First, he primes the surface for painting. Over this he pours, as he puts it, "skins of paint". Next, he rubs off the paint in some places and applies more paint. Speaking in an interview, Hein described his relationship to the sea as follows: "For me, the beach is not so much the horizon as a border to the Hereafter. Contrary to what many people think, I don't love the water. I'm rather afraid of it; I'm in awe of it. For me, it's an expression of a primordial state of matter, from which we come, but will ultimately find ourselves in again". (Interviewed by Nicole Büsing and Heiko Klaas, 2015) (Fig. p. 164/165) UB

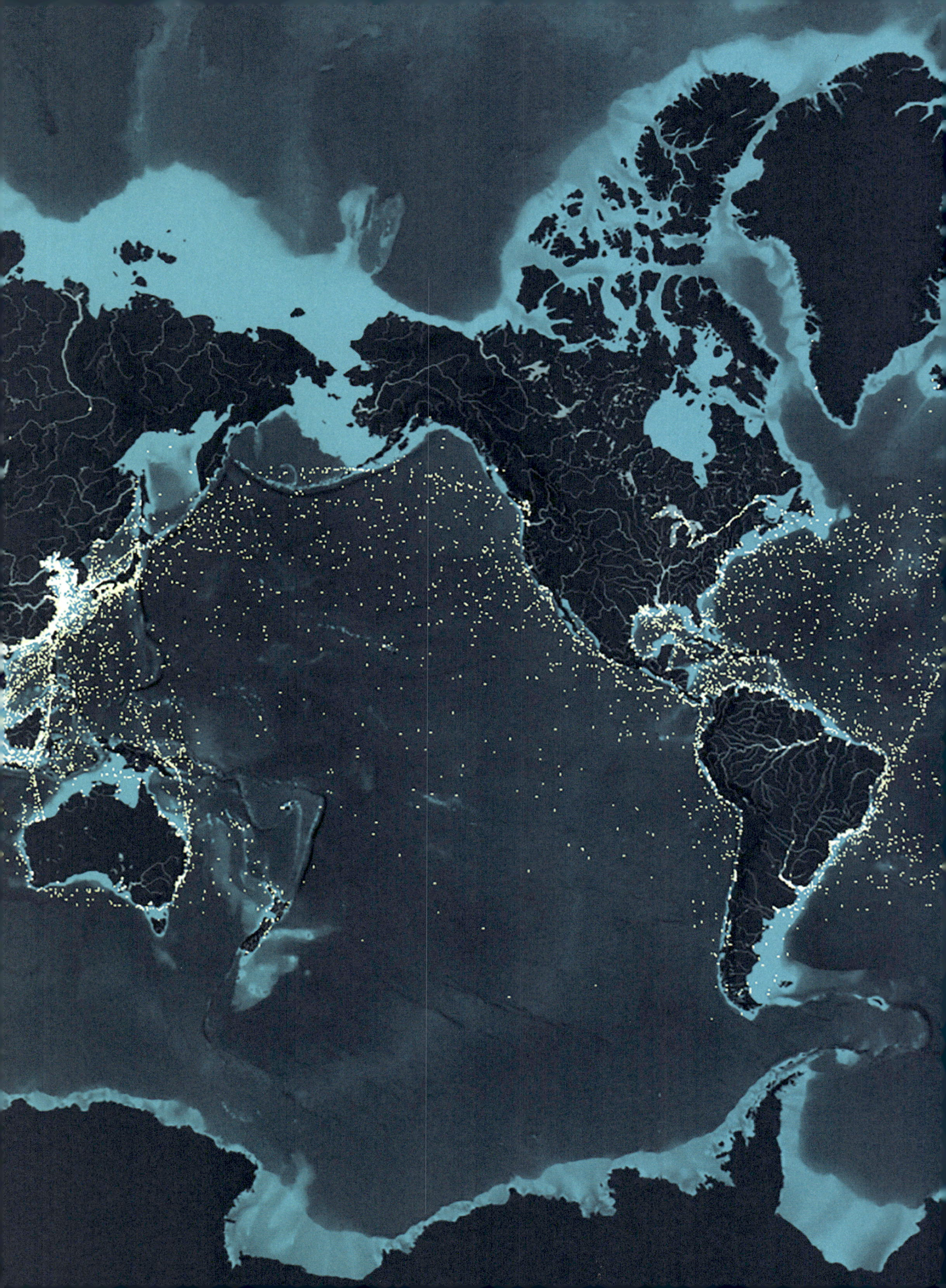

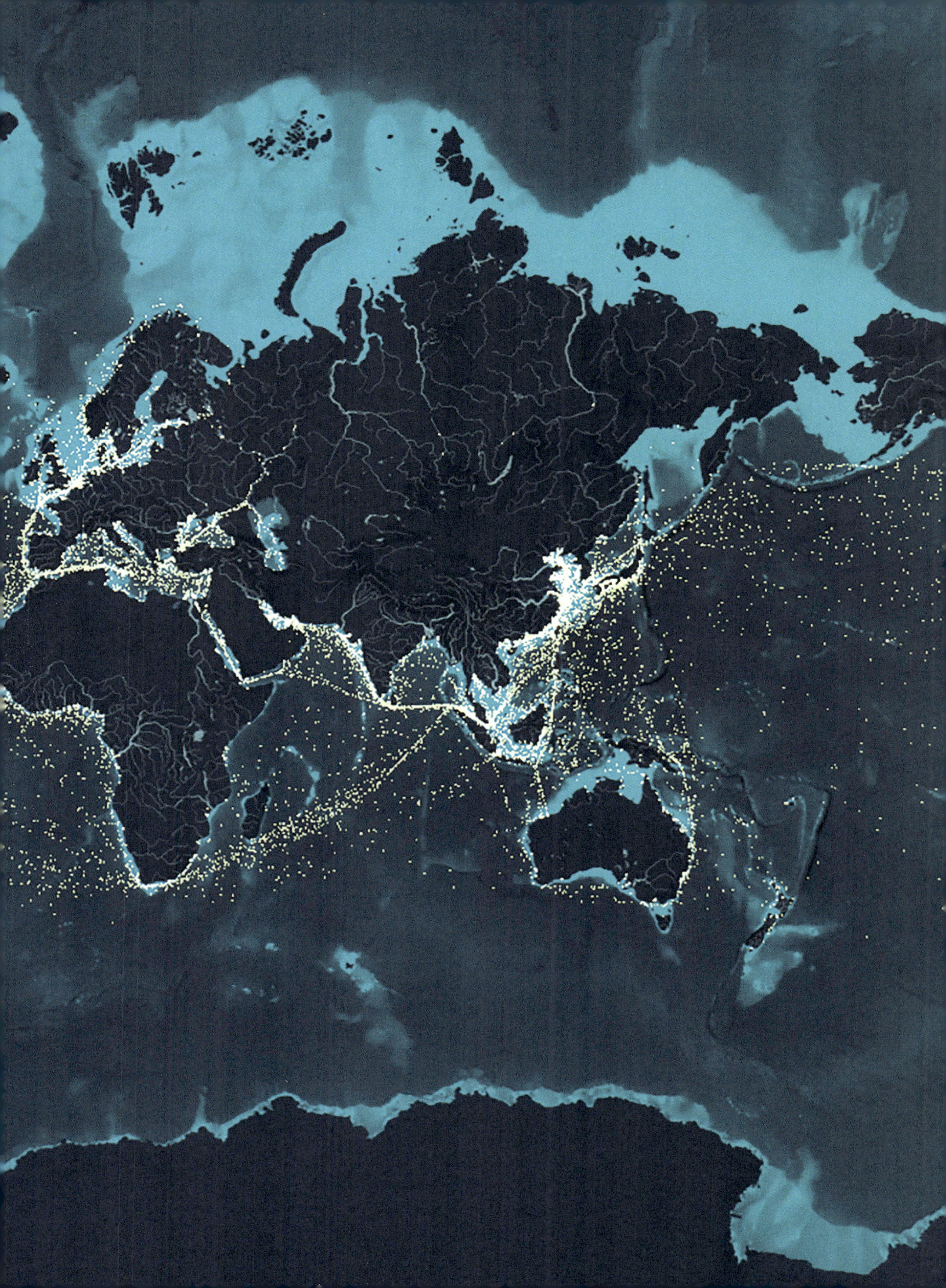

Lenders and Acknowledgements

We would like to express our gratitude to all the museums and private collections which have provided loans for this exhibition

Denmark
Copenhagen
Rigsarkivet

Germany
Alkersum/Föhr
Museum Kunst der Westküste

Bad Homburg
Verwaltung der Staatlichen Schlösser und Gärten Hessen

Berlin
bpk – Bildagentur
Ursula Breymayer
Containermanufaktur, Gesellschaft für modulare Seecontainerbauten mbH
Mohammed Ebrahimi
Thomas Eisentraut
Heinrich-Böll-Stiftung
Sakineh Karimi
Konsortium Deutsche Meeresforschung
Museum für Naturkunde Berlin
Museumsstiftung Post und Telekommunikation
Najlaa Malik
Sammlung Miller
Paul Nkamani
Mehdi Sawari
Staatliche Museen zu Berlin, Antikensammlung
Staatliche Museen zu Berlin, Münzkabinett
Staatsbibliothek zu Berlin – Preußischer Kulturbesitz, Benutzungsabteilung
Staatsbibliothek zu Berlin – Preußischer Kulturbesitz, Handschriftenabteilung
Staatsbibliothek zu Berlin – Preußischer Kulturbesitz, Abteilung Historische Drucke
Staatsbibliothek zu Berlin – Preußischer Kulturbesitz, Kartenabteilung
Staatsbibliothek zu Berlin – Preußischer Kulturbesitz, Orientabteilung
Stiftung Stadtmuseum Berlin
ullstein bild

Bochum
Kunstmuseum Bochum

Brake
Schiffahrtsmuseum Unterweser

Bremen
Focke-Museum, Bremer Landesmuseum für Kunst und Kulturgeschichte

Bremerhaven
Deutsches Schiffahrtsmuseum – Leibniz-Institut für deutsche Schifffahrtsgeschichte
Historisches Museum Bremerhaven

Dresden
Albertinum, Staatliche Kunstsammlungen Dresden
Gemäldegalerie Alte Meister, Staatliche Kunstsammlungen Dresden

Furtwangen
Deutsches Uhrenmuseum Furtwangen

Hamburg
Bildarchiv Hamburg
Hamburger Kunsthalle
Staatsarchiv
Stiftung Historische Museen Hamburg, Museum für Hamburgische Geschichte

Itzehoe
Wenzel-Hablik-Stiftung

Kiel
GEOMAR Helmholtz-Zentrum für Ozeanforschung Kiel
Kieler Stadt- und Schifffahrtsmuseum

Monschau
Kunst- und Kulturzentrum (KuK) der StädteRegion Aachen

Munich
Bayerische Staatsbibliothek
Süddeutsche Zeitung Photo

Nuremberg
Germanisches Nationalmuseum

Schleswig
Museum für Archäologie Schloss Gottorf, Landesmuseen Schleswig-Holstein

Schwerin
Staatliche Schlösser, Gärten und Kunstsammlungen Mecklenburg-Vorpommern

Stuttgart
Württembergische Landesbibliothek

Weimar
Klassik Stiftung Weimar, Herzogin Anna Amalia Bibliothek

France
Nantes
Château des ducs de Bretagne. Musée d'histoire de Nantes

Paris
Bibliothèque nationale de France
Martin Parr/Magnum Photos

United Kingdom
Brighton
Royal Pavilion & Museums, Brighton & Hove

Greenwich, London
National Maritime Museum

London
Kiln Enterprises Ltd
Museum of London
National Portrait Gallery
Science Photo Library Ltd.
The British Library Board

Italy
Trieste
Biblioteca Civica "A. Hortis"

Venice
Aldo Baradel Collection
Fondazione Musei Civici di Venezia, Museo Correr
Museo Storico Navale della Marina Militare Italiana

Netherlands
Amsterdam
Amsterdam Museum
Het Scheepvaartmuseum
Rijksmuseum

Norway
Bergen
The Norwegian Fisheries Museum

Oslo
Nasjonalbiblioteket

Stavanger
Norwegian Petroleum Museum

Austria
Vienna
KHM-Museumsverband
MAK – Österreichisches Museum für angewandte Kunst / Gegenwartskunst, Wien

Poland
Gdańsk
National Maritime Museum in Gdańsk

Spain
Las Palmas de Gran Canaria
El Museo Canario

Madrid
Museo Nacional del Prado
Ministerio de Defensa. Archivo del Museo Naval
Museo Sorolla

Santa Cruz de Tenerife
Excmo. Ayuntamiento de Santa Cruz de Tenerife. Museo de Bellas Artes, Museo Militar Regional
MUSEOS DE TENERIFE, Cabildo insular de Tenerife. Museo Arqueológico de Tenerife, Museo de Historia y Antropología de Tenerife

Seville
Archivo General de Indias

United States
Sitka/Alaska
Dean Orbison

and to private lenders who wish to remain anonymous.

We would like to thank the following individuals for their advice and assistance:

Peter Bartsch, Berlin
Andrea Bellieni, Venice
Anja Benscheidt, Bremerhaven
Holger Birkholz, Dresden
Robert Blyth, London
Eva-Maria Bongardt, Bremerhaven
Gaëlle Corbin-Blorec, Nantes
Maria del Carmen Cruz de Mercadal, Las Palmas de Gran Canaria
Aurélie de Decker, Nantes
Jesús Roberto Duque Arimany, San Cristóbal de La Laguna
Ulrich Fellmeth, Stuttgart
Thomas Förster, Stralsund
Claus Füllberg-Stolberg, Hannover
Karine Garcia-Lebailly, Nantes
Krystel Gualdé, Nantes
Bertrand Guillet, Nantes
Sabine Hackethal, Berlin
Jochen Hein, Hamburg
Monika Jankiewicz-Brzostowska, Gdańsk
Arne Karsten, Wuppertal
Christine Keitsch, Brake
Hans Kopp, Berlin
Finn E. Krogh, Stavanger
Alfred Kube, Bremerhaven
Évelyne Le Magadure, Nantes
Jerzy Litwin, Gdańsk
Peggy Marx, Bremerhaven
Ahmad Mustafa, Berlin
Jürgen Oltmer, Osnabrück
Wolfgang Reinhard, Freiburg
Anna Reschop, Berlin
Joaquín Reyes García, Santa Cruz de Tenerife
Alvise Rossi, Venice
Jens Ruppenthal, Bremerhaven
Ruth Schilling, Bremerhaven
Hasso Spode, Berlin
Svein Terje Pisani Førland, Stavanger
Juliane Tetzlaff, Berlin
Jeroen van der Vliet, Amsterdam
Jan Werquet, Bremen
Finbarr Whooley, London
Ulla Marie Wig, Copenhagen
Diederick Wildemar, Amsterdam
Ulrike Wolff-Thomsen, Alkersum
Elżbieta Wróblewska, Gdańsk
Michael Zeuske, Cologne

We would also like to thank all our colleagues from the Deutsches Historisches Museum.

Index of Persons

Further Reading

David Abulafia, *The Discovery of Mankind. Atlantic Encounters in the Age of Columbus*, New Haven/London 2008
David Abulafia, *Das Mittelmeer. Eine Biographie*, Frankfurt a. M. 2013
Edward A. Alpers, *The Indian Ocean in World History*, Oxford 2014
Amerika 1492–1992. Neue Welten – Neue Wirklichkeiten. Geschichte, Gegenwart, Perspektiven, ed. by Dietrich Briesemeister et al, Ibero-Amerikanisches Institut Berlin, Braunschweig 1992
Bernard Andreae (ed.), *Odysseus. Mythos und Erinnerung* (exhib. cat. Haus der Kunst München), Mainz 1999
Andreas Achenbach und Oswald Achenbach. Das A und O der Landschaft, exhib. cat., Cologne 1997
Arno Armgort, *Bremen–Bremerhaven–New York. Geschichte der europäischen Auswanderung über die Bremischen Häfen*, Bremen 1991
Klaus J. Bade, *Europa in Bewegung. Migration vom späten 18. Jahrhundert bis zur Gegenwart*, Munich 2000
Frank Bajohr, *"Unser Hotel ist judenfrei". Bäder-Antisemitismus im 19. und 20. Jahrhundert*, Frankfurt a. M. 2003
Ernst Baltrusch et al (eds.), *Seemacht, Seeherrschaft und die Antike*, Stuttgart 2016
Elena Balzamo and Reinhard Kaiser, *Olaus Magnus. Die Wunder des Nordens*, Frankfurt a. M. 2006
Peter-René Becker and Ulf Beichle, *"Mensch, Fisch!"*, Oldenburg 2012
Sven Beckert, *King Cotton. Eine Globalgeschichte des Kapitalismus*, Munich 2014
Charles Beddington (ed.), *Canaletto in Venedig. Der Meister und seine Rivalen*, exhib. cat., Stuttgart 2010
Giovanni Maria Bellu, *I fantasmi di Portopalo. Natale 1996: la morte di 300 clandestini e il silenzio dell'Italia*, Segrate 2004
Anja Benscheidt and Alfred Kube, *Brücke nach Übersee. Auswanderung über Bremerhaven 1830-1974*, Bremerhaven 2006
Anne Berlan-Baiard, *Les spectacles aquatiques romains*, Rome 2006
Kornelia von Berswordt-Wallrabe (ed.), *Von Venedig bis Neapel. Renaissance und Barock in Italien*, exhib. cat., Berlin 1999
Volkmar Billig, *Inseln. Geschichte einer Faszination*, Berlin 2010
Hans Blumenberg, *Schiffbruch mit Zuschauer*, Frankfurt a. M. 1997
Leonard Blussé, *Visible Cities. Canton, Nagasaki, and Batavia and the Coming of the Americans*, Cambridge, MA/London 2008
Espen Bowitz Andersson, *Bryggen. Das Hanseatische Kontor in Bergen*, Bergen 1982
Andres von Brandt, *Das große Buch vom Fischfang – international. Zur Geschichte der fischereilichen Fangtechnik*, Innsbruck 1975, pp. 119–132, 146–171
Fernand Braudel, *Das Mittelmeer und die mediterrane Welt in der Epoche Philipps II.*, vols. 1–3, Frankfurt a. M. 1998
Steven Brindle, *Brunel: The Man Who Built the World*, London 2005
Robert Bohn, *Geschichte der Seefahrt*, Munich 2011
Tobias Brinkmann, *Migration und Transnationalität*, Paderborn 2012
Marcel van den Broecke, *Ortelius Atlas Maps. An illustrated Guide*, Westrenen 1996
Christian Buchet (ed.), *The Sea in History/La Mer dans l'Histoire*, 4 vols., Woodbridge 2017
Edmund Burke, *Philosophische Untersuchung über den Ursprung unserer Ideen vom Erhabenen und Schönen*, translated by Friedrich Bassenge, Hamburg 1989
Paulino Castañeda Delgado (ed.), *Fray Bartolomé de Las Casas. Obras completas*, 14 vols., Seville 1989–1999
Karl Christ, *Pompeius*, Munich 2004
Carl Chun, *Aus den Tiefen des Weltmeeres*, Jena 1900
Carlo M. Cipolla, *Segel und Kanonen. Die europäische Expansion zu See*, Berlin 1999
Carlo M. Cipolla, *Guns, Sails and Empires: Technological Innovation and the Early Phases of European Expansion 1400–1700*, New York 1965
Alain Corbin, *Meereslust. Das Abendland und die Entdeckung der Küste*, Frankfurt a. M. 1994
Roger Crowley, *Die Eroberer. Portugals Kampf um ein Weltreich*, Darmstadt 2016
Roger Crowley, *Venedig erobert die Welt. Die Dogen-Republik zwischen Macht und Intrige*, Stuttgart 2011
Roger Crowley, *Entscheidung im Mittelmeer. Europas Seekrieg gegen das Osmanische Reich 1521–1580*, Stuttgart 2009
Thomas DaCosta Kaufmann and Michael North (eds.), *Mediating Netherlandish Art and Material Culture in Asia*, Amsterdam 2014
Anja Dauschek, Regine Gerhardt, Vanessa Hirsch (eds.), *Melbye. Maler des Meeres* (exhib. cat. Stiftung Historische Museen Hamburg, Altonaer Museum), Munich 2017
Ole Degn, *Tolden i Sundet. Toldopkrævning, politik og skibsfart i Øresund 1429–1857*, Told- og Skattehistorisk Selskab, Copenhagen 2010
Roger Diederen, María López Fernández, Blanca Pons-Sorolla (eds.), *Joaquín Sorolla. Spaniens Meister des Lichts* (exhib. cat. Kunsthalle der Hypo-Kulturstiftung München, Musée des impressionnismes Giverny, Museo Sorolla Madrid), Munich 2016
Kenneth Onwuka Dike, *Trade and Politics in the Niger Delta, 1830–1885. An Introduction to the Economic and Political History of Nigeria*, Oxford 1966 (1956)
Philippe Dollinger, *Die Hanse*, Stuttgart 1998
Alfred von Domaszewski, *Geschichte der römischen Kaiser*, 2 vols., vol. 1, Leipzig 1909
Thomas Eisentraut, *Das Tagebuch von Nils Trosner, 1710–1714*, in: *Staat – Militär–Gesellschaft. Festschrift für Jens E. Olesen zum 65. Geburtstag* (Publikationen des Lehrstuhls für Nordische Geschichte, vol. 20), ed. by Robert Oldach and Thomas Wegener Friis, Greifswald 2015, pp. 163–195
David Eltis et al, *The Atlantic Slave Trade; A Database on CD ROM*, Cambridge 1999
David Eltis and David Richardson, *Atlas of the Transatlantic Slave Trade*, New Haven/London 2010
Jürgen Elvert, *Europa, das Meer und die Welt. Eine maritime Geschichte der Neuzeit*, Munich 2018
Jürgen Elvert et al (eds.), *Das maritime Europa. Werte – Wissen – Wirtschaft*, Stuttgart 2016
Rolf Engelsing, *Bremen als Auswanderhafen 1683–1880*, (Veröffentlichungen aus dem Staatsarchiv der Freien Hansestadt Bremen, vol. 29), Bremen 1961
España y América. Un oceano de negocios. Quinto centenario de la Casa de la Contratación 1503–2003, ed. by Guiomar de Carlos Boutet, Sociedad Estatal de Conmemoraciones Culturales, Seville 2003

Europa und die Kaiser von China (1240–1816), ed. by Berliner Festspiele GmbH, exhib. cat., Frankfurt a. M. 1985
Peter Feldbauer et al, *Venedig 800–1600. Die Serenissima als Weltmacht*, Vienna 2010
Frank Fischer, *Danzig. Die zerbrochene Stadt*, Berlin 2006
Georg-Michael Fleischer, *Schiffschirurgen von Kolumbus bis Nelson. Vergessene Helden der Seefahrtgeschichte*, Heidelberg 2017
Markus Friedrich, *Die Jesuiten. Aufstieg, Niedergang, Neubeginn*, Munich/Berlin 2016
Claus Füllberg-Stolberg, *Transatlantischer Sklavenhandel und Sklaverei in den Amerikas*, in: Ulrike Schmieder and Hans-Heinrich Nolte (eds.), *Atlantik. Sozial- und Kulturgeschichte in der Neuzeit*, Vienna 2010, pp. 86–115
Alexa Geisthövel, *Der Strand*, in: Alexa Geisthövel and Habbo Knoch (eds.), *Orte der Moderne. Erfahrungswelten des 19. und 20. Jahrhunderts*, Frankfurt a. M./New York 2005, pp. 121–130
Roelof van Gelder, *Das ostindische Abenteuer. Deutsche in Diensten der Ostindischen Kompanie der Niederlande (VOC), 1600–1800*, Hamburg 2004
Joeron Giltaij and Jan Kelch, *Herren der Meere – Meister der Kunst. Das holländische Seebild im 17. Jahrhundert*, Ghent 1996
Kristin Øye Gjerde (ed.), *Crossing Boundaries. Frigg Industrial Heritage*, Stavanger 2010
Christopher Görlich, *Urlaub vom Staat. Zur Geschichte des Tourismus in der DDR*, Cologne et al 2012
David González Cruz (ed.), *Descubridores de América. Colón, los marinos y los puertos*, Madrid 2012
Gabriele del Grande, *Mamadous Fahrt in den Tod. Die Tragödie der irregulären Migranten im Mittelmeer*, Karlsruhe 2008
Fred Gray, *Designing the Seaside. Architecture, Society and Nature*, London 2006
Wolfgang Griep and Frauke Krahé, *Peter der Große in Westeuropa. Die große Gesandtschaft 1697–1698*, exhib. cat., Bremen 1991
Michael Grüttner, *Brandstifter und Biedermänner. Deutschland 1933–1939*, Bonn 2015
Markus Günther, *Auf dem Weg in die Neue Welt. Die Atlantiküberquerung im Zeitalter der Massenauswanderung 1818–1914*, Augsburg 2005
Bertrand Guillet, *La Marie-Séraphique. Navire Négrier*, Nantes 2009
Torsten Gunnarsson, *Johan Christian Dahl und die Freilichtmalerei. Seine Ölstudien im europäischen Kontext*, in: *Wolken. Wogen. Wehmut. Johan Christian Dahl 1788–1857. Der Freund Caspar David Friedrichs*, ed. by Herwig Guratzsch, exhib. cat., Cologne 2002, pp. 35–46
Rüdiger Hachtmann, *Das Wirtschaftsimperium der Deutschen Arbeitsfront*, Göttingen 2012
Rüdiger Hachtmann, *Tourismus-Geschichte*, Göttingen 2007
Rolf Hammel-Kiesow, *Die Hanse*, 4th ed., Munich 2008
Robert Harms, *Das Sklavenschiff. Eine Reise in die Welt des Sklavenhandels*, Kempten 2004
Stefan Hanß, *Lepanto als Ereignis. Dezentrierende Geschichte(n) der Seeschlacht von Lepanto (1571)*, Göttingen 2017
John B. Hattendorf (ed.), *The Oxford Encyclopedia of Maritime History*, 4 vols., New York 2007
Lasse Heerten, *Ankerpunkte der Verflechtung. Hafenstädte in der neueren Globalgeschichtsschreibung*, in: Geschichte und Gesellschaft 43 (2017), no. 1, pp. 146–175
Konrad Heldmann, *Europa und der Stier oder der Brautraub des Zeus. Die Entführung der Europa in den Darstellungen der griechischen und römischen Antike*, Göttingen 2016
Gotthilf Hempel et al, *Faszination Meeresforschung: Ein ökologisches Lesebuch*, Berlin/Heidelberg 2016
Dirk Hoerder, *Geschichte der deutschen Migration. Vom Mittelalter bis heute*, Munich 2010
Dirk Hoerder, *The Traffic of Emigration via Bremen/Bremerhaven. Merchants' Interest, Protective Legislation, and Migrants' Experiences*, in: *Journal of American Ethnic History* 13 (1993), pp. 68–101
Gerd Hoffmann-Wieck, *Das GEOMAR Helmholtz-Zentrum für Ozeanforschung Kiel und die Geschichte der Kieler Meereskunde*, in: Oliver Auge (ed.), *Christian-Albrechts-Universität zu Kiel. 350 Jahre Wirken in Stadt, Land und Welt*, Kiel 2015, pp. 699–723
Eva Hofstetter, *Sirenen im archaischen und klassischen Griechenland*, Würzburg 1990
Reinhard Hoheisel-Huxmann, *Die Deutsche Atlantische Expedition 1925–1927. Planung und Verlauf*, ed. by Deutschen Schiffahrtsmuseum, Hamburg 2007
Valeska Huber, *Channelling Mobilities. Migration and Globalisation in the Suez Canal Region and Beyond, 1869–1914*, Cambridge 2013
Idee Europa. Entwürfe zum "Ewigen Frieden", ed. by Marie-Louise von Plessen, exhib. cat., Berlin 2003
Iwan A. Iwanov, *Die Hanse im Zeichen der Krise. Handlungsspielräume der politischen Kommunikation im Wandel (1550–1620)*, Vienna/Cologne/Weimar 2016
Anna Jackson and Amin Jaffer (eds.), *Encounters. The Meeting of Asia and Europe 1500–1800*, London 2004
Uwe Jenisch and Boris Culik, *Kiel Maritim II – mit Jules Verne und Albert Einstein in die Zukunft*, Bonn 2013
Lawrence Jennings, *French Anti-Slavery. The Movement for the Abolition of Slavery in France. 1802–1848*, Ottawa 2006
Johann Adam Schall von Bell SJ, 1592–1666. Ein Kölner Astronom am chinesischen Hof, ed. by Diözesan- und Dombibliothek Köln, exhib. cat., Cologne 1992
Donald S. Johnson and Juha Nurminen, *Die große Geschichte der Seefahrt. 3000 Jahre Expeditionen, Handel und Navigation*, Hamburg 2008
Michael Just, *Ost- und südosteuropäische Amerikawanderung 1881–1914. Transitprobleme in Deutschland und Aufnahme in den Vereinigten Staaten*, Stuttgart 1988
Arne Karsten, *Geschichte Venedigs*, Munich 2012
Torbjørn Kindingstad and Fredrik Hagemann (eds.), *Norwegian Oil history*, Stavanger 2002
Charles King, *Odessa. Genius and Death in a City of Dreams*, New York and London 2011
Sonja Kinzler and Doris Tillmann (eds.), *Nordlandreise. Die Geschichte einer touristischen Entdeckung* (exhib. cat. Kieler Stadt- und Schifffahrtsmuseum), Berlin n.d. [2010]
Udo Kittelmann and Birgit Verwiebe (eds.), *August Kopisch: Maler, Dichter, Entdecker, Erfinder* (exhib. cat. Alte Nationalgalerie Berlin), Berlin 2016
Alexander Klose, *Das Container-Prinzip. Wie eine Box unser Denken verändert*, Hamburg 2009
Rasso Knoller, *Norwegen. Ein Länderporträt*, Bonn 2013
Hans Kopp, *Das Meer als Versprechen. Bedeutung und Funktion von Seeherrschaft bei Thukydides*, Göttingen 2017
Hans Joachim Kürtz, *I hanseatenes tider. Handel og vandel på hansakontorene i Bergen – Brügge – London og Novgorod*, Lübeck 1983

Petra Kuhlmann-Hodick, Gerd Spitzer, Bernhard Maaz (eds.), *Carl Gustav Carus. Natur und Idee* (exhib. cat. Staatliche Kunstsammlungen Dresden, Staatliche Museen zu Berlin), Munich 2009

Mojib Latif, *Das Ende der Ozeane. Warum wir ohne die Meere nicht überleben werden*, Freiburg 2014

Brian Lavery, *Ship: The Epic Story of Maritime Adventure*, New York 2004

Brian Lavery (ed.), *Shipboard life and organisation, 1731–1815*, Singapore/Sydney 1998

Archibald R. Lewis and Timothy J. Runyan, *European Naval and Maritime History 300–1500*, Bloomington 1990

J. Thomas Lindblad, *Louis de Geer (1587–1652). Dutch Entrepreneur and the Father of the Swedish Industry*, in: Clé Lesger and Leo Noordegraaf (eds.), *Entrepreneurs and Entrepreneurship in Early Modern Times. Merchants and Industrialists within the Orbit of the Dutch Staple Market*, Den Haag 1995, pp. 77–84

Jerzy Litwin, *Maritimer Reiseführer Danzig*, Hamburg 1997

Kurt Löcher, *Der Londoner Stahlhof und Hans Holbein*, in: Cord Meckseper (ed.), *Stadt im Wandel. Kunst und Kultur des Bürgertums in Norddeutschland 1150–1650*, 4 vols., vol. 3, exhib. cat., Stuttgart-Bad Cannstatt 1985, pp. 667–686

Marie Lødrup Bang, *Johan Christian Dahl 1788–1857. Life and Works*, 3 vols., Oslo 1987

Peter Oliver Loew, *Danzig. Biographie einer Stadt*, Munich 2011

Leo Lucassen, *The Immigrant Threat. The Integration of Old and New Migrants in Western Europa since 1850*, Urbana/Chicago 2005

Katrin Maibaum, Katharina Gräber (eds.), *Wenzel Hablik – Expressionistische Utopien, Malerei Zeichnung, Architektur* (exhib. cat. Martin-Gropius-Bau Berlin), Munich 2017

Elisabeth Mann Borgese, *Das Drama der Meere*, Frankfurt a. M. 1977

Olaf Matthes (ed.), *Stadt Bild Wandel. Hamburg in Fotografien 1870–1914/2014*, Hamburg 2015

Mieke Mels and Philip Van den Bossche, *Das Meer. The Sea. La Mer. De Zee* (exhib. cat. De Zee Oostende), Ostfildern 2015

Christopher L. Miller, *The French Atlantic Triangle. Literature and Culture of the Slave Trade*, London 2008

Maren Möhring, *Fremdes Essen. Die Geschichte der ausländischen Gastronomie in der Bundesrepublik Deutschland*, Munich 2012

Magdalena M. Moeller and Ulrich Schulte-Wülwer, *Erich Heckel an der Ostsee*, (exhib. cat. Brücke-Museum Berlin, Städtische Galerie Bietigheim-Bissingen, Museumsberg Flensburg), Munich 2006

Olaf Mörke, *Die Geschwistermeere. Eine Geschichte des Nord- und Ostseeraumes*, Stuttgart 2015

Michel Mollat du Jourdin, *Europa und das Meer*, Munich 1993

Peter Moraw, *Von offener Verfassung zu gestalteter Verdichtung. Das Reich im späten Mittelalter 1250 bis 1490*, Frankfurt a. M. 1985

Joachim Münzing, *Der historische Walfang in Bildern*, Herford 1987

Rupert and Christel Neudeck, *Was man nie vergessen kann. Erinnerungen vietnamesischer Bootsflüchtlinge*, Wuppertal 2017

Jean-François Niort, *Le Code Noir. Idées reçues sur un texte symbolique*, Paris 2015

Michael North, *Zwischen Hafen und Horizont. Weltgeschichte der Meere*, Munich 2016

Michael North, *Geschichte der Ostsee. Handel und Kulturen*, Munich 2011

Michael North (ed.), *Artistic and Cultural Exchanges between Europe and Asia, 1400–1900: Rethinking Markets, Workshops and Collections*, Farnham 2010

Michael North, *Die Niederlandisierung des Ostseeraumes*, in: Jörg Hackmann and Robert Schweitzer (eds.), *Nordosteuropa als Geschichtsregion*, Helsinki/Lübeck 2006, pp. 368–377

Novos Mundos – Neue Welten. Portugal und das Zeitalter der Entdeckungen, ed. by Michael Kraus and Hans Ottomeyer, exhib. cat., Berlin 2007

Jochen Oltmer, *Migration: Geschichte und Zukunft der Gegenwart*, Darmstadt 2017

Jochen Oltmer, *Globale Migration. Geschichte und Gegenwart*, Munich 2016 (2nd, revised and updated edition)

Jochen Oltmer, *Migration vom 19. bis zum 21. Jahrhundert*, Berlin 2016 (3rd, revised and extended edition)

Waldemar Ossowski (ed.), *The Copper Ship. A medieval Shipwreck and its cargo/ Miedziowiec. Wrak średniowiecznego statku i jego ładunek*, Gdańsk 2014

Jürgen Osterhammel, *Die Verwandlung der Welt. Eine Geschichte des 19. Jahrhunderts*, Munich 2009

Jürgen Osterhammel, *Die Entzauberung Asiens. Europa und die asiatischen Reiche im 18. Jahrhundert*, Munich 1998

Helmut Pemsel, *Seeherrschaft. Eine maritime Weltgeschichte von den Anfängen bis 1850*, 2 vols., Augsburg 1995

Olivier Pétré-Grenouilleau, *Nantes au temps de la traite des Noirs*, Paris 2016

Eberhard Petzold and Sebastian Meißner, *Güterströme der Welt. The Global Cargo Flow*, Hamburg 2017

Ulrich Pohlmann and Ortrud Westheider (eds.), Über Wasser. Malerei und Photographie von William Turner bis *Olafur Eliasson* (exhib. cat. Bucerius Kunst Forum Hamburg), Munich 2015

Olaf Preuß, *Eine Kiste erobert die Welt. Der Siegeszug einer einfachen Erfindung*, Freiburg 2010

Michael Rathmann, *Tabula Peutingeriana. Die einzige Weltkarte aus der Antike. Eingeleitet und kommentiert von Michael Rathmann*. Darmstadt 2016

Ernst Georg Ravenstein (ed.), *A Journal of the First Voyage of Vasco da Gama 1497–1499*, London 1898

Gordon Read, *Transithafen Liverpool. Die europäische Auswanderung über England nach New York, 1870–1913*, in: Karin Schulz (ed.), *Hoffnung Amerika. Europäische Auswanderung in die Neue Welt*, Bremerhaven 1994, pp. 151–162

Frédéric Récent et al (eds.), *Libres et sans Fers. Paroles d'esclaves français*, Paris 2016

Karl-Heinz Reger, *"Dann sprang er über Bord". Alltagspsychologie und psychische Erkrankung an Bord britischer Schiffe im 19. Jahrhundert*, Göttingen 2014

Wolfgang Reinhard, *Die Unterwerfung der Welt. Globalgeschichte der europäischen Expansion 1415–2015*, Munich 2016

Wolfgang Reinhard, *Geschichte der Welt. Weltreiche und Weltmeere, 1350–1750*, Munich 2014

Dieter Richter, *Das Meer. Geschichte der ältesten Landschaft*, Berlin 2014

Stefan Rinke, *Kolumbus und der Tag von Guanahani. 1492: Ein Wendepunkt der Geschichte*, Stuttgart 2013

Corinna Roeder (ed.), *Große, fette Wale. Die Geschichte des Walfangs in Drucken des 15.–21. Jahrhunderts*, Oldenburg 2006

Dominique Rogers (ed.), *Voix d'esclaves. Antilles, Guyane et Louisiane françaises, XVIIIe–XIXe siècle*, Paris 2016

Georg Eberhard Rumphius, *D'Amboinsche Rariteitkamer*, Amsterdam 1705

Thorsten Sadowsky (ed.), *Kunst und Küste. Ausgewählte Werke der Sammlung Kunst der Westküste*, Alkersum/Föhr 2013

Jürgen Sarnowsky, *Die Erkundung der Welt. Die großen Entdeckungsreisen von Marco Polo bis Humboldt*, Munich 2015

Bruno Schmidt, *Die Ureinwohner der Kanarischen Inseln. Ihre Geschichte, Herkunft und Hinterlassenschaft*, Münster 1996

Carl Schmitt, *Land und Meer. Eine weltgeschichtliche Betrachtung*, Leipzig 1942

Eberhard Schmitt (ed.), *Indienfahrer 2. Seeleute und Leben an Bord im Ersten Kolonialzeitalter (15. bis 18. Jahrhundert)*, (Dokumente zur Geschichte der europäischen Expansion, vol. 7), Wiesbaden 2008

Karl Schlögel, *Entscheidung in Kiew. Ukrainische Lektionen*, Munich 2015

Jonathan Schneer, *London 1900. The Imperial Metropolis*, New Haven 1999

Raimund Schulz, *Die Antike und das Meer*, Darmstadt 2005

Raimund Schulz, *Die Antike und das Meer*, in: Ilse Fischer and Johannes Hahn (eds.), *Die andere(n) Seite(n) des Meeres*, Salzburg 2016, pp. 25–31

Raimund Schulz, *Europa und das Meer in der Antike*, in: Michael Gehler et al (eds.), *Europa-Räume. Von der Antike bis zur Gegenwart*, Hildesheim et al 2016, pp. 59–72

Mary Sears and Daniel Merriman, *Oceanography: The Past*, New York et al 1980

Seestücke. Von Caspar David Friedrich bis Emil Nolde, ed. by Martin Faass and Felix Krämer, exhib. cat., Munich 2005

Ferdinand Seibt et al, *Transit Brügge - Novgorod. Eine Straße durch die europäische Geschichte*, Bottrop/Essen 1997

Philip de Souza, *Die Beherrschung der Meere. Wie die Seefahrt die Menschheitsgeschichte prägte*, revised and extended by Christian Weller, Munich 2006

Philip de Souza, *Seafaring and Civilization: Maritime Perspectives on World History*, London 2001

Fritz Spieß, *Die Meteor-Fahrt. Forschungen und Erlebnisse der Deutschen Atlantischen Expedition 1925–1927*, Berlin 1928

Hasso Spode and Christiane Klemm, *Zur Geschichte der Ferienarchitektur*, in: Felizitas Romeiß-Stracke (ed.), *Tourismusarchitektur. Baukultur als Erfolgsfaktor*, Berlin 2008, pp. 95–109

Hasso Spode, *Wie die Deutschen "Reiseweltmeister" wurden*, Erfurt 2003

Hasso Spode, *Ein Seebad für zwanzigtausend Volksgenossen. Zur Grammatik und Geschichte des fordistischen Urlaubs*, in: Peter J. Brenner (ed.), *Reisekultur in Deutschland. Von der Weimarer Republik zum "Dritten Reich"*, Tübingen 1997

Elke Stein-Hölkeskamp, *Das archaische Griechenland. Die Stadt und das Meer*, Munich 2015

Albrecht Steinecke, *Internationaler Tourismus*, Stuttgart 2014

Heinz Stoob, *Die Hanse*, Graz/Vienna/Cologne 1995

Sandra Trudgen Dawson, *Holiday Camps in Twentieth Century Britain. Packaging Pleasure*, Manchester 2011

Richard W. Unger, *Dutch Shipbuilding before 1800: Ships and Guilds*, Assen 1978

Barbara Watson Andaya and Leonard Y. Andaya, *A History of Early Modern Southeast Asia, 1400–1830*, Cambridge 2015

François Valentyn, *Oud en Nieuw Oost-Indiën*, Dordrecht 1724–1726

VENEDIG. Seemacht, Kunst und Karneval, ed. by Schallaburg Kulturbetriebsges.m.b.H. in cooperation with Kunsthistorisches Museum Wien, Vienna 2011

VENEZIA! Kunst aus venezianischen Palästen. Sammlungsgeschichte Venedigs vom 13. bis 19. Jahrhundert, ed. by Kunst- und Ausstellungshalle der Bundesrepublik Deutschland GmbH, Bonn 2002

Die Verführung der Europa, revised by Barbara Mundt, exhib. cat., Berlin 1988

Wolfgang Graf Vitzthum, *Der Staat der Staatengemeinschaft* (Schönburger Gespräche zu Recht und Staat, vol. 6), Paderborn et al 2006

Klaus Volbehr, *Kleine Geschichte der Hygiene und Arzneimittelversorgung auf Schiffen*, Hamburg 1987

Jan de Vries and Ad van der Woude, *The First Modern Economy: Success, failure, and Perseverance of the Dutch Economy, 1500–1815*, Cambridge 1997

Hartmut Walravens (ed.), *China illustrata. Das europäische Chinaverständnis im Spiegel des 16. bis 18. Jahrhunderts*, Wolfenbüttel 1987

Christina Wawrzinek, *Tore zur Welt. Häfen in der Antike*, Darmstadt 2016

Kathryn Welch, *Magnus Pius. Sextus Pompeius and the Transformation of the Roman Republic*, Swansea 2012

Peter Wende, *Das Britische Empire. Geschichte eines Weltreichs*, Munich 2008

Reinhard Wendt, *Vom Kolonialismus zur Globalisierung. Europa und die Welt seit 1500*, Paderborn 2016

Christian Wendt, *Poseidons Söhne – Seeherrschaft als Legitimation des Prinzipats*, in: *Der Erste. Augustus und der Beginn einer neuen Epoche*, ed. by Ernst Baltrusch and Christian Wendt, Darmstadt 2016, pp. 86–99

Michael Wildt, "Der *muß hinaus! Der muß hinaus!" Antisemitismus in deutschen Nord- und Ostseebädern 1920–1935*, in: *Mittelweg 36*. Zeitschrift des Hamburger Instituts für Sozialforschung, 4/2001, pp. 3–25

Simon Winchester, *Der Atlantik. Biographie eines Ozeans*, Munich 2010

Ulrike Wolff-Thomsen, *Über die Tiefe*, in: *Jochen Hein. Über die Tiefe*, ed. by Ulrike Wolff-Thomsen and Nicole Nix-Hauck, exhib. cat., Heide 2016

Eva Zahn, *Europa und der Stier*, Würzburg 1983

Kees Zandvliet, *De Nederlandse ontmoeting met Azië 1600–1950. [Tentoonstelling De Nederlandse ontmoeting met Azië, 1600–1950 in het Rijksmuseum te Amsterdam, van 10 oktober 2002 tot en met 9 februari 2003]*, Amsterdam/Zwolle 2002

Michael Zeuske, *Sklaven und Sklaverei in den Welten des Atlantiks 1400–1940. Umrisse, Anfänge, Akteure, Vergleichsfelder und Biographie*, Münster 2006

Michael Zeuske, *Handbuch Geschichte der Sklaverei. Eine Globalgeschichte von den Anfängen bis zur Gegenwart*, Berlin/Boston 2013

Michael Zeuske, *Sklavenhändler, Negreros und Atlantikkreolen. Eine Weltgeschichte des Sklavenhandels im atlantischen Raum.* Berlin/Boston 2015

Authors

Prof. Dr. Ernst Baltrusch
Professor of Ancient History at the Freie Universität Berlin

Dr. Boris Belge
Historian, Research Associate, Universität Basel

PD Dr. Holger Birkholz
Curator, Albertinum, Staatliche Kunstsammlungen Dresden

Dorlis Blume, M.A.
Head of Special Exhibitions and Projects, Deutsches Historisches Museum, Berlin; Head of Project and Curator *Europe and the Sea*

Dr. Christiana Brennecke
Historian, Berlin; Curator *Europe and the Sea*

Ursula Breymayer, M.A.
Free Curator of Exhibitions, Cultural Historian, Berlin; Curator *Europe and the Sea*

Dr. Eva-Maria Bongardt
Art Historian, Research Associate at the Deutsches Schiffahrtsmuseum – Leibniz Institut für deutsche Schifffahrtsgeschichte

Svenja Budziak, B.A.
Student of Islamic Sciences and History, Christian-Albrechts-Universität zu Kiel

Roger Crowley
Author, Gloucestershire

Prof. Dr. Philip de Souza
Apl. Professor, University College Dublin

Thomas Eisentraut, M.A.
Historian, Berlin; Curator *Europe and the Sea*

Dr. Gunnar Ellingsen
Historian, Leader of the Norwegian Fisheries Museum and of The Hanseatic Museum, Bergen

Krystel Gualdé
Scientific Director at the Musée d'Histoire de Nantes

Anders Haaland
Historian, Senior Researcher at the Norwegian Fisheries Museum, Bergen

Prof. Dr. Rüdiger Hachtmann
Research Associate at the Centre for Contemporary History, Potsdam

Dr. Lasse Heerten
Research Associate and Head of Research Area "Imperial Gateway. Hamburg, Imperial Germany and the Making of a Global Port", Freie Universität Berlin

Andrea von Hegel, M.A.
Head of Poster Collection, Deutsches Historisches Museum, Berlin

Dr. Gerd Hoffmann-Wieck
Communication and Media, Research Associate at the GEOMAR Helmholtz Centre for Ocean Research Kiel

Thomas Jander, M.A.
Head of Document and Numismatic Collection, Deutsches Historisches Museum, Berlin

Kerstin Kemner, M.A.
Art Historian, Berlin; Project Assistance *Europe and the Sea*

Laura Kersten, M.A.
Research Associate and Ph.D. Student at the Friedrich-Meinecke-Institute, Freie Universität Berlin

Dr. Leonore Koschnick
Head of Arts and Crafts & Graphics Collection, Deutsches Historisches Museum, Berlin

Dr. Alfred Kube
Director of the Historisches Museum Bremerhaven

Dr. Michael Kunzel
Curator of Numismatic Collection, Deutsches Historisches Museum, Berlin

Dr. Sven Lüken
Head of Military Collection, Deutsches Historisches Museum, Berlin

Dr. Matthias Miller
Head of the Library and of manuscripts collection of old and rare books, Deutsches Historisches Museum, Berlin

Prof. Dr. Olaf Mörke
Director of the Chair of Medieval and Modern History, Christian-Albrechts-Universität zu Kiel

Ahmad Mustafa
Former Student of English Literature, University of Aleppo/Syrien, since 2015 living in Berlin

Prof. Dr. Dr. h.c. Michael North
Professor of the General History of the Modern Period, Universität Greifswald

Dr. Cord Pagenstecher
Historian, Freie Universität Berlin

Prof. Dr. Dieter Richter
Cultural Historian and Writer, Universität Bremen

Johanna Riedel, B. A.
Student of the Department of History, Humboldt-Universität zu Berlin

Prof. Dr. Stefan Rinke
Professor History of Latin America and Chairperson of the Latin American Institute at the Freie Universität Berlin

Dagmar Röhrlich, M.A.
Geologist, Freelance Science Writer, Cologne

PD Dr. Agnes Schwarzmaier
Research Associate, Antikensammlung, Staatliche Museen zu Berlin

Prof. Dr. Bernhard Weisser
Director Münzkabinett, Staatliche Museen zu Berlin

Prof. Dr. Ulrike Wolff-Thomsen
Art Historian, Director of the Museum Kunst der Westküste, Alkersum/Föhr and apl. Professor at the Institute for Art History, Christian-Albrechts-Universität zu Kiel

Dr. Elżbieta Wróblewska
Ph.D, Head of History of Shipping and Trade Department, Senior Curator, National Maritime Museum in Gdańsk

Picture credits

Denmark

Copenhagen
Rigsarkivet, p. 224, 225

Germany

Alkersum / Föhr
Museum Kunst der Westküste, p. 156, 157, 158, 159, 160, 161 top, 161 bottom (© VG Bild-Kunst, Bonn 2018), 162 bottom (© VG Bild-Kunst, Bonn 2018), 164/165 (© Jochen Hein, Hamburg), 425, 426

Bad Homburg
Verwaltung der Staatlichen Schlösser und Gärten Hessen, photo: Renate J. Deckers-Matzko, p. 171

Berlin
Gregor Baron, p. 115

bpk, Antikensammlung, SMB, photo: Johannes Laurentius, p. 15, 189, 194 bottom, 195

bpk, Bayerische Staatsbibliothek, photo: Heinrich Hoffmann, p. 149

bpk, Gemäldegalerie, SMB, photo: Jörg P. Anders, p. 221

bpk, Hamburger Kunsthalle, photos: Elke Walford, p. 155, 173, 423

bpk, Münzkabinett, SMB, p. 14, 17 (photos: Reinhard Saczewski), 196 (photo: Lutz-Jürgen Lübke), 197 top, 198 left, 198 right, 199 left, 199 right, 201 left, 201 right (photos: Dirk Sonnenwald), 197 bottom

bpk, RMN - Grand Palais, photo: Michel Urtado, p. 162 top

bpk, Staatliche Kunstsammlungen Dresden, photo: Elke Estel / Hans-Peter Klut, p. 24

bpk, Albertinum, Staatliche Kunstsammlungen Dresden, photo: Elke Estel, p. 422

bpk, Staatliche Schlösser, Gärten und Kunstsammlungen Mecklenburg-Vorpommern, photo: Elke Walford, p. 215

bpk, Staatsbibliothek zu Berlin – Preußischer Kulturbesitz, Abteilung Historische Drucke, p. 52, 81, 217 left, 217 right, 239 right, 253, 291 right

bpk, Staatsbibliothek zu Berlin – Preußischer Kulturbesitz, Benutzungsabteilung, p. 16, 82 top, 293 top, 388 left

bpk, Staatsbibliothek zu Berlin – Preußischer Kulturbesitz, Handschriftenabteilung, p. 46, 228

bpk, Staatsbibliothek zu Berlin – Preußischer Kulturbesitz, Kartenabteilung, p. 250/251

bpk, Staatsbibliothek zu Berlin – Preußischer Kulturbesitz, Orientabteilung, photo: Dietmar Katz, p. 268 top

bpk, The Trustees of the British Museum, p. 169

Ursula Breymayer, photo: DHM (Sebastian Ahlers, Indra Desnica), p. 372

Narciso Contreras / SOS MEDITERRANEE, p. 111

Deutsches Historisches Museum, photos: Sebastian Ahlers, Indra Desnica, p. 28, 33, 35, 36, 37, 44, 47, 49, 54, 55, 56, 91, 94, 112 top, 112 bottom, 113 (© VG Bild-Kunst, Bonn 2018), 123, 134, 146 left (© VG Bild-Kunst, Bonn 2018), 146 right, 147, 149, 150, 152, 167, 174, 176, 177 top, 180, 181, 184/185, 351, 206, 207, 213, 213, 216 top, 216 bottom, 220 top, 237, 238, 249, 252, 254/255, 269 bottom, 277 top, 290, 291 left, 292 left, 292 right, 293 bottom, 294, 295 left, 295 right, 296, 297 top, 298 top, 298 bottom, 307, 309, 310 top, 319 top, 319 bottom, 320, 324 top, 324 bottom, 327 left, 327 right, 329, 330, 332, 333 top, 333 bottom (© VG Bild-Kunst, Bonn 2018), 336, 352, 358 left, 359, 362 top, 368, 392 right, 393, 394, 395, 396, 397 top, 397 bottom, 398, 399, 400 top, 400 bottom, 401, 402 top, 402 bottom, 403 left, 403 right, 404, 405, 406, 407 (© VG Bild-Kunst, Bonn 2018), 408, 409 left, 409 right, 410, 412/413, 413 left, 414 left, 414 right, 416, 417, 418 link, 418 right

Mohammed Ebrahimi, photo: DHM (Sebastian Ahlers, Indra Desnica), p. 344 bottom left

Thomas Eisentraut, photos: DHM (Sebastian Ahlers, Indra Desnica), p. 297 bottom, 364 right

Heinrich-Böll-Stiftung, illustration: petraboeckmann.de, p. 364 left

Sakineh Karimi, photo: DHM (Sebastian Ahlers, Indra Desnica), p. 344 bottom right

Najlaa Malik, photo: DHM (Sebastian Ahlers, Indra Desnica), p. 343 left

Kevin McElvaney / SOS MEDITERRANEE, p. 116

Museum für Naturkunde Berlin, p. 369, 370 left top, 370 right top, 370 bottom, photos: Carola Radke, Museum für Naturkunde Berlin: p. 277 bottom, 373

Museumsstiftung Post und Telekommunikation, p. 32, 243 (photos: Peter Boesang), 313 left (photo: Kay Herschelmann), 90, 95

Paul Nkamani, photo: DHM (Sebastian Ahlers, Indra Desnica), p. 343 right

Sammlung Miller, photo: DHM (Sebastian Ahlers, Indra Desnica), p. 410/411

Mehdi Sawari, photo: DHM (Sebastian Ahlers, Indra Desnica), p. 344 top

Stiftung Historische Wertpapiere Martius am Deutschen Historischen Museum, photos: DHM (Sebastian Ahlers, Indra Desnica), p. 308 top, 308 bottom

Stiftung Stadtmuseum Berlin, Reproduktion: Oliver Ziebe, Berlin, p. 248 right

ullstein bild, p. 399 top left (photo: Süddeutsche Zeitung Photo / Scherl), 339 top right (photo: JT Vintage / Glasshouse Images), 339 bottom left (photo: United Archives / World History Archive), 339 bottom right, 340 (photos: Erich Salomon), 341 right (photo: NMSI/Science Museum/ Daily Herald Archive/NMeM), 342 (photo: TopFoto)

Berlin/Münster
BOK + Gärtner GmbH, p. 21, 26, 38

Bochum
Kunstmuseum Bochum, photo: Archiv Kunstmuseum Bochum (© Nachlass Erich Heckel, Hemmenhofen), p. 429

Brake
Schiffahrtsmuseum Unterweser, photo: Linda Thorlton, p. 358

Bremen
Focke-Museum, Bremer Landesmuseum für Kunst und Kulturgeschichte, photo: Martin Luther, p. 350

Bremerhaven
Deutsches Schiffahrtsmuseum - Leibniz-Institut für deutsche Schifffahrtsgeschichte, p. 77, 135, 334 top, 334 bottom, 338 (© VG Bild-Kunst, Bonn 2018), 412 left

Historisches Museum Bremerhaven, p. 98/99, 101, 102, 103, 105, 106, 107, 109, 314/315, 326, 328/329 top, 328 bottom left, 328 bottom right, 335 left, 335 right, 337

Frankfurt am Main
Universitätsbibliothek Frankfurt am Main, Digitale Sammlungen Judaica, p. 177 bottom

Furtwangen
Deutsches Uhrenmuseum Furtwangen, p. 312

Hamburg
Bildarchiv Hamburg, photo: fotograf-hamburg.de, p. 97

Staatsarchiv Hamburg, photo: Familie Hamann, p. 331

Stiftung Historische Museen Hamburg, Museum für Hamburgische Geschichte, p. 93, 303 top left, 302 left, 302 right, 303 top right, 303 bottom

Itzehoe
Wenzel-Hablik-Stiftung, photo: SHMH-Altonaer Museum, Michaela Hegenbarth, p. 428

Kiel
GEOMAR Helmholtz-Zentrum für Ozean-forschung Kiel, p. 310, 362 bottom, 363 top, 363 bottom, 379 top, 379 bottom, 380, 382, 383 (photos: Lina Plagmann), 375, 376 left, 376 right (photos: Solvin Zankl), 138, 140, 377, 378

Kieler Stadt- und Schifffahrtsmuseum, p. 381

Solvin Zankl, p. 139

Monschau
Kunst- und Kulturzentrum (KuK) der StädteRegion Aachen, p. 194 top

Munich
Bayrische Staatsbibliothek, p. 241

Süddeutsche Zeitung Photo, photo: Scherl, p. 415

Nuremberg
Germanisches Nationalmuseum, p. 71

Schleswig
Museum für Archäologie Schloss Gottorf, Landesmuseen Schleswig-Holstein, p. 79, 270, 271 top, 271 bottom, 272 top, 272 bottom, 273 top, 273 bottom

Stuttgart
Württembergische Landesbibliothek, p. 322/323

Weimar
Klassik Stiftung Weimar, Herzogin Anna Amalia Bibliothek, Foto: PhaseOne A/S Kulturerbe (C. Wieser, H. Papst), p. 244/245

France

Nantes
Château des ducs de Bretagne. Musée d'histoire de Nantes, p. 82 bottom, 84, 85, 87, 88, 276, 278 top, 278/279, 280, 281, 283, 285 top, 285 bottom, 286 left, 286 right, 287

Paris
Bibliothèque nationale de France, p. 230/231

Martin Parr / Magnum Photos, p. 419

United Kingdom

Brighton
Royal Pavilion & Museums, Brighton & Hove, p. 142/143, 389, 144, 384/385, 388, 389, 390, 391 top, 391 bottom, 392 left

Greenwich, London
National Maritime Museum, Greenwich, p. 76, 300, 301, 304, 306 left, 311

London
Kiln Enterprises Ltd, © Kiln.digital, with data from UCL and ExactEarth, p. 313, 430/431

Museum of London, p. 299, 306 right, 341 left (© Harold Dearden)

National Portrait Gallery, p. 305

The British Library Board, Egerton 2709, f.2., p. 45, 229

Italy

Trieste
Biblioteca Civica "A. Hortis", p. 208/209

Venice
Aldo Baradel Collection, photo: Gianfranco Munerotto, p. 204

Fondazione Musei Civici di Venezia, Museo Correr, photos: 2018 © Photo Archive – Fondazione Musei Civici di Venezia, p. 205, 210 bottom, 211 bottom

Museo Storico Navale della Marina Militare Italiana, p. 210 top, 211 top, 212 top, 212 bottom

Netherlands

Amsterdam
Amsterdam Museum, p. 12/13, 190/191, 258

Het Scheepvaartmuseum, p. 259, 260 bottom, 262, 263, 265 top, 266 top, 266 bottom, 267 top, 268 bottom, 269 top

Rijksmuseum, p. 19, 29, 58, 66, 72, 74, 260 top, 261, 264, 265 bottom, 357

The Hague
RKD - Netherlands Institute für Art History, p. 59

Zeist
Van de Poll-Wolters-Quina Stichting, photo: RKD - Netherlands Institute für Art History, Den Haag, p. 61

Norway

Bergen
The Norwegian Fisheries Museum, p. 121/122, 124, 346/347 (photos: Anders B. Wilse, Norwegian Fisheries Museum, Museum Vest); 125 (The Hanseatic Museum in Bergen, photo: Marco Trebbi), 127 (photo: Fjellanger Widerøe AS), 128 (illustration: The Norwegian Government/Sigurd Kristiansen), 129 (photo: Paul Olai-Olssen), 131 (source: Statoil)

Oslo
The National Archives of Norway, p. 75

Nasjonalbiblioteket, p. 126, 353 left, 353 right, 354 top left, 354 top right, 354 bottom left, 354 bottom right, 355 left, 355 right, 356 left, 356 right

Stavanger
Norwegian Petroleum Museum, p. 360 top (photo: Bob Fleumer), 360 bottom, 361 top (photo: Jan A. Tjemsland), 361 (photo: Shadé Barka Martins)

Austria

Vienna
KHM-Museumsverband, p. 215

Karl Klaus Körner, p. 30/31

MAK – Österreichisches Museum für angewandte Kunst / Gegenwartskunst, photo: © MAK/Nathan Murrell, p. 248 left

Poland

Gdańsk
National Maritime Museum in Gdańsk, p. 221, 222, 223 top, 223 bottom

Spain

Las Palmas de Gran Canaria
El Museo Canario, p. 234 bottom, 235 top

Madrid
Ministerio de Defensa. Archivo del Museo Naval, p. 236

Museo Nacional del Prado, p. 9/10

Museo Sorolla, p. 427

Santa Cruz de Tenerife
Excmo. Ayuntamiento de Santa Cruz de Tenerife. Museo de Bellas Artes, Museo Militar Regional, photos: MLaura Benavente Sovieri, p. 232 bottom, 232 top, 233 top, 233 bottom, 234 top

MUSEOS DE TENERIFE. Cabildo insular de Tenerife. Museo Arqueológico de Tenerife, Museo de Historia y Antropología de Tenerife, p. 235 center, 235 bottom

Seville
Archivo General de Indias, p. 239 left, 240, 241

Sweden

Uppsala
Uppsala University Library, p. 40/41

USA

Sitka / Alaska
Dean Orbison, photo: DHM (photos: Sebastian Ahlers, Indra Desnica), p. 365

Other picture sources
Private collection, photography: Günter Maniewski, Frankfurt am Main, p. 424
Anonymous, p. 118

Pictures published in:

P. 16 in: Report on the Scientific Results of the Voyage of H.M.S. Challenger during the Years 1873-76... / Prep. under C. Wyville Thomson and John Murray: A summary of the scientific results, London 1895, vol. 1, Plate 1

P. 52 in: Bartolomé de Las Casas, “Wahrhafftiger und gründlicher Bericht (...)”, Oppenheim 1613, p. 54 f.

P. 174 in: Daniel Defoe, Robinson Crusoe. His Life and Adventures, London/New York c. 1890, cover

P. 177 bottom in: Allgemeine illustrirte Judenzeitung, Pest: 21 (1860), p. 165, http://sammlungen.ub.uni-frankfurt.de/cm/periodical/pageview/4884329

P. 180 in: F. Slang, Panzerkreuzer Potemkin, der Matrosenaufstand vor Odessa 1905, Berlin 1926, p. 44

Credits

Europe and the Sea
An exhibition of the
Deutsches Historisches Museum
13 June 2018 to 6 January 2019

DEUTSCHES
HISTORISCHES
MUSEUM

in cooperation with:

Universität zu Köln

Programm für lebenslanges Lernen

funded by:

Die Beauftragte der Bundesregierung für Kultur und Medien

kindly supported by:

Königreich der Niederlande

EXHIBITION

President
Raphael Gross

Head of Exhibitions
Ulrike Kretzschmar

Idea
Jürgen Elvert

Head of Project
Dorlis Blume

Curators
Dorlis Blume, Christiana Brennecke, Ursula Breymayer, Thomas Eisentraut

Scientific Advisor
Werner Konitzer

Project Assistance
Kerstin Kemner

Expert Advisory Board
Jürgen Elvert, Sunhild Kleingärtner, Lisa Kosok, Michael North, Rudolf Schieffer, Günther Heydemann, Michael Kraus

Research Advisory Council
Markus A. Denzel, Jürgen Elvert, Martina Elvert, Ulrich Fellmeth, Gerd Hoffmann-Wieck, Michael Jeismann, Jochen Oltmer, Wolfgang Reinhard, Jens Ruppenthal, Christoph Schäfer, Wolfgang Schmale, Hasso Spode, Heinrich Walle, Reinhard Wendt, Michael Zeuske

Exhibition Design
Nadine Rasche, Werner Schulte

Registrar
Nicole Schmidt

Assistant Students
Marcel Flach, Flora Fuchs, Christian Stielow

Interns
Svenja Budziak, Freya Elvert, Till Goßmann, Anna Retzer, Johanna Riedel, Ariane Tavernier

Assistance in Research
Torsten dos Santos Arnold, Frankfurt a. O., Ingrid Damerow, Berlin

Exhibition Graphics
BOK + Gärtner GmbH, Berlin/Münster

Media Design and Media Technology
Mirko Kubein

Film Series
Stephan Ahrens

Picture Archive
Sarah Kindermann, Anne-Dorte Krause, Claudia Küchler

Photography
Sebastian Ahlers, Indra Desnica

Graphics Production
Digidax, Potsdam

Editing
Frauke Berchtig, Berlin

Translations
Andreas Förster, Valentine Meunier, Patricia Newman, Richard Toovey

Conservation
Martina Homolka (Head of Department), Michaela Brand, Sabine-Josefine Brand, Vendulka Cejchan, Kay Draber, Julia Garve, Kerstin Häussermann, Ulrike Hügle, Elke Kiffe, Barbara Korbel, Andrea Lang, Mathias Lang, Antje Liebers, Matthes Nützmann

Framing
Malte Spohr, Katharina Siedler, Berlin

Exhibition Construction and Workshops
Nicholas Kaloplastos (Head of Department), Jens Albert, Sven Brosig, Christin Elle, Anette Forkert, Susanne Hennig, Torsten Ketteniß, Katrin Kunze, Holger Lehmann, Jörg Petzold, Thomas Strehl, Ralf Schulze, Stefan Thimm, Gunnar Wilhelm

Painters
Malermeister Antosch, Berlin

Carpenters
Restaurierungswerkstätten Berlin GmbH

Object Installation
Abrell & van den Berg - Ausstellungsservice GbR, Berlin

Collections
Fritz Backhaus (Director of Department), Willi Beier, Saskia Bendrich, Ingeborg Bojahr, Bernd Dürrwald, Manuela Ehses, Regine Falkenberg, Andrea von Hegel, Thomas Jander, Carola Jüllig, Leonore Koschnick, Michael Kunzel, Sven Lüken, Andreas Michaelis, Matthias Miller, Stefan Negelmann, Brigitte Reineke, Dorothé Rößling, Jörg Rudolph, Ronny Stefanowski, Thomas Vetter, Thomas Weißbrich, Rainer Wiehagen

Communications
Barbara Wolf (Director of Department), Julia Black, Ina Frodermann, Jenny Jakubik, Daniela Lange, Ilka Linz, Jana Nawrot, Nicola Schnell, Peter Schützhold, Oliver Schweinoch, Anna-Julia Senchyshyn, Nike Thurn, Sonja Trautmann, Anne Vitten, Johanna Zehe, Julia Ziemann

IT
Gerhard Schmitt (Head of Department), Björn Eichberg, Jan Dirk Kluge, Uwe Naujack, Magnus Wagner

Controlling
Nathalie Scholz, Ramona Selchow

Education and Communication
Stefan Bresky, Brigitte Vogel-Janotta (Heads of Department), Veronika Hager, Patrick Helber, Helene Henze, Matthias Holliger, Nathanael Kuck, Christin Noll, Friedrun Portele-Anyangbe, Maike Schimanowski, Martin Steinbrück, Tobias Wissinger
Andrea Schenk, Mareike Teichmann (Booking Service)

Inclusion and Accessibility
Allgemeiner Blinden- und Sehbehindertenverein Berlin gegr. 1874 e.V.
AWO Büro Leichte Sprache, Berlin
Deutsche Zentralbücherei für Blinde zu Leipzig (DZB), Leipzig (Tactile Media)
Sign Support, Berlin (DGS-Interpreter)
Yomma Schäfer & Sequeira Gerardo GbR, Berlin

Audio Guide
Katja Hauser, Florian Wieler, Berlin
K13, Kinomischung und Tonstudio, Berlin
soundgarden audioguidance, Munich

Exhibition Poster
Stan Hema GmbH, Berlin

CATALOGUE

Europe and the Sea

Published by
Dorlis Blume, Christiana Brennecke, Ursula Breymayer, Thomas Eisentraut for the Deutsches Historisches Museum

Concept and Editing
Ursula Breymayer

Assistance in Concept and Editing
Bernd Ulrich, Berlin

Photo Editing
Kerstin Kemner

Authors of the Object Texts
Holger Birkholz (HB), Dorlis Blume (DB), Eva-Maria Bongardt (EMB), Christiana Brennecke (CB), Ursula Breymayer (UB), Svenja Budziak (SB), Thomas Eisentraut (TE), Andrea von Hegel (AvH), Gerd Hoffmann-Wieck (GHW), Thomas Jander (TJ), Kerstin Kemner (KK), Leonore Koschnick (LK), Michael Kunzel (MK), Sven Lüken (SL), Matthias Miller (MM), Johanna Riedel (JR), Agnes Schwarzmaier (AS), Bernhard Weisser (BW), Elżbieta Wróblewska (EW)

Copy Editor
Katja Widmann, Berlin

Translations
Adam Blauhut, Andreas Förster, Ina Goertz, Lee Holt, Patricia Newman, Richard Toovey

Photography
Sebastian Ahlers, Indra Desnica

Coordination and Production Management
Ilka Linz

Project Supervision Hirmer
Kerstin Ludolph

Project Management Hirmer
Karen Angne, Sabine Frohmader

Production Hirmer
Sabine Frohmader

Design
Peter Nils Dorén, Berlin

Reprography
Reproline mediateam GmbH, Munich

Printing and Binding
Printer Trento S.r.l., Trento

Printed in Italy

ISBN 978-3-86102-210-7
(German museum edition)
ISBN 978-3-7774-3014-0
(German trade edition)
ISBN 978-3-86102-211-4
(English museum edition)
ISBN 978-3-7774-3016-4
(English trade edition)

www.dhm.de
www.hirmerpublishers.com

We would like to thank all persons and institutions for their permission for publication. We have endeavoured to locate all copyright holders and request permission for publication. If we have not cited a source, or have not cited a source completely, please refer the matter to Stiftung Deutsches Historisches Museum, Berlin.

Cover Illustration
Antonie Volkmar, Emigrants' farewell, 1860
© Deutsches Historisches Museum, Berlin